Contents

4 Rounding up   979

Something special for you...

David and Ursula Burr

Unique Hotels offer top luxury resorts and small romantic

Young Island

hideaways to suit the most discerning client. Rediscover the art of travel with the personal approach of directors David and Ursula Burr.

They 'tailor-make' your hotel stays using their extensive and personal knowledge of the Caribbean; having lived and worked in the islands for many years. And working closely with two of the local carriers, Air St Kitts and Nevis and Mustique Airways, ensures that whatever the final destination, they will get you there in style. Whether you want to laze in the sun, learn to scuba dive or island hop, Unique Hotels is waiting to help.

Unique Hotels
The Old Warehouse
Old Market, Nailsworth
Glos. gl6 0DU England
Tel: (0-1453) 835801
Fax: (0-1453) 835525
Email: res@uniqueuk.telme.com

One Continent. 36 destinations. 1,000's of surprises.

MEXICO CITY (Mexico)
CANCUN (Mexico)
HAVANA (Cuba)
PUNTA CANA (Dominican Republic)
GUATEMALA CITY (Guatemala)
SANTO DOMINGO (Dominican Republic)
SAN PEDRO SULA (Honduras)
ST. MARTIN
SAN SALVADOR (El Salvador)
SAN JUAN (Puerto Rico)
MANAGUA (Nicaragua)
ARUBA
CARACAS (Venezuela)
PORLAMAR (Venezuela)
SAN JOSE (Costa Rica)
CARTAGENA (Colombia)
PANAMA CITY (Panama)
BOGOTA (Colombia)
QUITO (Ecuador)
MANAUS (Brazil)
LIMA (Peru)
LA PAZ (Bolivia)
SANTA CRUZ (Bolivia)
RIO DE JANEIRO (Brazil)
SAO PAULO (Brazil)
ASUNCION (Paraguay)
IGUAZU (Argentina)
PORTO ALEGRE (Brazil)
SANTIAGO (Chile)
BUENOS AIRES (Argentina)
PUNTA DEL ESTE (Uruguay)
MONTEVIDEO (Uruguay)

Latin America. A land full of surprises simply waiting to be discovered.

From the exotic islands of Cuba, Margarita and Aruba to the culture of the ancient Mayan and Inca civilisations, Latin America has enough to fulfil everyone's desire for adventure.

But what won't surprise you is that the best way to fly to this spectacular continent is with Iberia and its sister companies – Viasa, the international airline of Venezuela and Aerolineas Argentinas.

Iberia was the first airline to connect Europe and Latin America – over 50 years ago. And today the Iberia Group continues to lead the way. No one takes you to more Latin American destinations. And no one looks after you more.

Thanks to our unmatched Latin American network, you can now fly from London Heathrow or Manchester (via Madrid) to a total of 36 destinations.

Whether you choose the exceptional value of our special 'Circular Fares' or our unbeatable return fares, you'll be surprisingly better off flying with Iberia, Viasa or Aerolineas Argentinas.

So book now on 0171-830 0011 or see your travel agent. We can't wait to surprise you!

VIASA   IBERIA

Leading the way to Latin America.

Caribbean Islands
Handbook

Sarah Cameron
with Ben Box

Footprint Handbooks

A tourist comes to see what he wants to see. A visitor comes to see what is there.

G K Chesterton

Footprint Handbooks

6 Riverside Court, Lower Bristol Road
Bath BA2 3DZ England
T 01225 469141 F 01225 469461
E mail handbooks@footprint.compulink.co.uk

ISBN 0 900751 75 4 ISSN 0967-4748
CIP DATA: A catalogue record for this book is
available from the British Library

In North America, published by

PASSPORT BOOKS
a division of *NTC Publishing Group*

4255 West Touhy Avenue, Lincolnwood
(Chicago), Illinois 60646-1975, USA
T 847 679 5500 F 847 679 24941
E mail NTCPUB2@AOL.COM

ISBN 0-8442-4907-6
Library of Congress Catalog Card
Number 96-69593
Passport Books and colophon are registered
trademarks of NTC Publishing group

©Footprint Handbooks Limited
8th Edition
September 1996

First published in 1989 by Trade & Travel
Publications Ltd

Cover design by Newell and Sorrell;
photography by Tony Stone Images and Dave
Saunders

Production: Design by Mytton Williams;
Secretarial assistance from Jane Battell and
Sara Smith; Typesetting by Jo Morgan, Ann
Griffiths and Melanie Mason-Fayon; Maps by
Sebastian Ballard, Alasdair Dawson and Kevin
Feeney; Proofread by Pam Cobb and Tim
Heybourne.

Printed and bound in Great Britain by
Clays Ltd., Bungay, Suffolk

The Editor

Sarah Cameron

Sarah Cameron's interest in Latin America and the Caribbean began with a degree in Iberian and Latin American Studies, during which time she spent a year in Colombia. Following a spell with the British Council she joined Lloyds Bank International in 1977 rising through the ranks to become Lloyds Bank Economic Advisor on Latin America and the Caribbean. During this time she also worked as a sub-editor on the **South American Handbook** and contributed articles and chapters to many publications on the region. In 1990 Sarah decided to part company with the world of finance and debt rescheduling to devote more time to the **Handbooks**. Together with Ben Box she wrote the **Caribbean Islands Handbook**, which she now edits annually, she is associate editor of the **Mexico & Central American Handbook** and occasional sub-editor of the **South American Handbook**, while keeping an eye on the economic data in all three. Her travels both for the bank and the **Handbooks** have been extensive and enjoyable; she also appreciates her life in rural Suffolk, where she takes the role of mother and groom to two daughters, their horses and many other animals.

Acknowledgements
Much additional help has been received during the preparation of this edition. All contributions have been tremendously helpful and are acknowledged on page 979.

Editorial team

Associate editor: Ben Box turned his attention to contemporary Iberian and Latin American affairs in 1980, beginning a career as a freelance writer at that time. During his frequent visits to the region he travelled extensively in the Caribbean when researching and editing with Sarah the first edition of Caribbean Islands Handbook. He also edits the **Mexico & Central America** and **South American Handbooks**.

Specialist contributors Mark Wilson for Miami, Caribbean Geology and walking; Mark Eckstein of David Bellamy Associates, UK for responsible tourism and fauna and flora; Erich Hoyt for whale and dolphin watching; Alyce M McDaniel also for Miami; Dr David Snashall for health; Rosie Mauro for watersports; Kathy Irwin for sailing; Martha Watkins Gilkes for scuba diving; Nicolette Clifford, for windsurfing.

Correspondents We are most grateful to all our regular and not so regular correspondents in the Caribbean region, who are thanked at the end of the relevant chapters. Thanks also go to John Alton (Strand Cruise and Travel Centre, London), Frank Bellamy and the staff of Transatlantic Wings (London), Rod Prince (*Caribbean Insight*, London) and the many Tourist Offices in Europe and the Caribbean who provided much information and answered our queries.

Preface

I T ALWAYS SEEMS TO happen that as soon as we go to print, a natural disaster makes a nonsense of at least one of our chapters. In 1995 a spate of hurricanes and tropical storms cut a swathe through a group of islands in the NE Caribbean, while a volcano on Montserrat has kept everyone on their toes for at least a year (so far). Hurricane season has come early in 1996 and Bertha is ploughing her way through Puerto Rico, the Virgin Islands and the Bahamas as we write. Nevertheless, a year after Iris, Luis and Marilyn, there is little evidence of their passing and only a handful of resorts remain closed as we go to print for the 1997 edition. There is little doubt that by Christmas, when high season starts, it will be business as usual, regardless of what this hurricane season brings.

This year we carry a guest article by David Howard, of Jesus College, Oxford, who won the John Brooks Memorial Travel Award in 1994. The late John Brooks was a long serving editor of the *South American Handbook*, in whose name a fund was set up, administered by the Institute of Latin American Studies in London, partly to finance postgraduate student travel to Latin America and the Caribbean. It was agreed that if the recipient of the travel grant wrote a short essay after his/her travels, we would endeavour to publish it in the relevant *Handbook*. David Howard has written for us about the Dominican Republic, Haiti and Cuba, which are the subject of his studies on race.

Sarah Cameron paid a particularly rewarding research visit to Trinidad and Tobago for this edition. She is most grateful to all the staff at TIDCO for their assistance; the trip would not have gone so smoothly without their cheerful teamwork. Highlights were scuba diving off Little Tobago and kayaking in the Nariva Swamp, but the diversity of the islands and their people made every day an experience to remember.

We note that interest in Cuba continues to rise despite the tightening of the US noose around the island in 1996, a US election year. We have received many letters this year from travellers to Cuba and hope to receive many more. Keep them coming! The chapter for this edition has benefited from new information provided by Tom Clough (a former Bolivia correspondent for the *South American Handbook*), who spent several months in Cuba in 1996, as well as from our readers.

The Editor

Will you help us?

Our authors explore and research tirelessly to bring you the most complete and up-to-date package of information possible. Yet the contributions we receive from our readers are also **vital** to the success of our Handbooks. There are many thousands of you out there making delightful (and sometimes alarming!) discoveries every day.

So important is this resource that we make a special offer to every reader who contacts us with information on places, experiences, people, hotels, restaurants, well-informed warnings or any other features which could enhance the enjoyment of our travellers everywhere. When writing to us, please give the edition and page number of the Handbook you are using.

So please take a few minutes to get in touch with us - we can benefit, you can benefit and all our other readers can benefit too!

Please write to us at:

Footprint Handbooks,
6 Riverside Court, Lower Bristol Road, Bath BA2 3DZ England
Fax: +44 (0)1225 469461 E Mail handbooks@footprint.compulink.co.uk

Responsible tourism

Much has been written about the adverse impacts of tourism on the environment and local communities. It is usually assumed that this only applies to the more excessive end of the travel industry such as the Spanish Costas and Bali. However travellers can have an impact at almost any density and this is especially true in areas 'off the beaten track' where local people may not be used to western conventions and lifestyles, and natural environments may be very sensitive.

Of course, tourism can have a beneficial impact and this is something to which every traveller can contribute. Many National Parks are part funded by receipts from people who travel to see exotic plants and animals, El Yunque (Puerto Rico) and the Asa Wright Centre (Trinidad) are good examples of such sites. Similarly, travellers can promote patronage and protection of valuable archaeological sites and heritages through their interest and entrance fees.

However, where visitor pressure is high and/or poorly regulated, damage can occur. This is especially so in parts of the Caribbean where some tour operators are expanding their activities with scant regard for the environment or local communities. It is also unfortunately true that many of the most popular destinations are in ecologically sensitive areas easily disturbed by extra human pressures. Eventually the very features that tourists travel so far to see may become degraded and so we seek out new sites, discarding the old, and

leaving someone else to deal with the plight of local communities and the damaged environment. Fortunately, there are signs of a new awareness of the responsibilities that the travel industry and its clients need to endorse. For example, some tour operators fund local conservation projects and travellers are now more aware of the impact they may have on host cultures and environments. We can all contribute to the success of what is variously described as responsible, green or alternative tourism. All that is required is a little forethought and consideration. It would be impossible to identify all the potential impacts that might need to be addressed by travellers, but it is worthwhile noting the major areas in which we can all take a more responsible attitude in the countries we visit. These include changes to natural ecosystems (air, water, land, ecology and wildlife), cultural values (beliefs and behaviour) and the built environment (sites of antiquity and archaeological significance).

At an individual level, travellers can reduce their impact if greater consideration is given to their activities. For example in most Caribbean countries dress codes are fairly strictly adhered to; shorts and T shirts are OK on the beach but less so when shopping or cashing cheques. Avoid topless or nude bathing except where it is expressly allowed. Do not take photographs of people without permission. Recognition of these cultural cues goes a long way towards reducing the friction that can develop between host and visitor. Collecting or purchasing wildlife curios might have an effect on local ecosystems and may well be illegal under either local or international legislation (see below). Similarly, some tourist establishments have protected wildlife (especially turtle) on the menu, don't add to the problem by buying it. Some environmental impacts are caused by factors beyond the direct control of travellers, such as the management and operation of a hotel chain. However, even here it is possible to voice concern about damaging activities and an increasing number of hotels and travel operators are taking 'green concerns' seriously, even if it is only to protect their share of the market.

Environmental Legislation

Legislation may have been enacted to control damage to the environment, and in some cases this can have a bearing on travellers. The establishment of National Parks may involve rules and guidelines for visitors and these should always be followed. In addition there may be local or national laws controlling behaviour and use of natural resources (especially wildlife) that are being increasingly enforced. If in doubt, ask. Finally, international legislation, principally the Convention on International Trade in Endangered Species of Wild Fauna and Flora (CITES), may affect travellers.

CITES aims to control the trade in live specimens of endangered plants and animals and also 'recognizable parts or derivatives' of protected species. Sale of black coral, some hard corals, turtle shells, rare orchids and other protected wildlife is strictly controlled by signatories of the convention. The full list of protected wildlife varies, so if you feel the need to purchase souvenirs and trinkets derived from wildlife, it would be prudent to check whether they are protected. CITES parties in the Caribbean include: Dominican Republic, Trinidad

and Tobago, St Lucia, St Vincent, the Bahamas, Guyana and Cuba. Puerto Rico and the US Virgin Islands are included in the US ratification of CITES. The UK dependencies (Anguilla, British Virgin Islands, Cayman and Turks and Caicos Islands) all look to the UK government for advice and support in the implementation of international wildlife legislation and in particular CITES regulation as the UK is a party to the convention. In addition, most European countries, the USA and Canada are all signatories. Importation of CITES protected species into these countries can lead to heavy fines, confiscation of goods and even imprisonment. Information on the status of legislation and protective measures can be obtained from Traffic International (T UK 01223 277427; e-mail traffic@wcmc.org.uk).

Green travel companies and information

The increasing awareness of the environmental impact of travel and tourism has led to a range of advice and information services as well as spawning specialist travel companies who claim to provide 'responsible travel' for clients. This is an expanding field and the veracity of claims needs to be substantiated in some cases. The following organizations and publications can provide useful information for those with an interest in pursuing responsible travel opportunities.

International organizations

Green Flag International aims to work with travel industry and conservation bodies to improve environments at travel destinations and also to promote conservation programmes at resort destinations; provides a travellers' guide for 'green' tourism as well as advice on destinations, T UK 01223 890250.

Tourism Concern aims to promote a greater understanding of the impact of tourism on host communities and environments, T UK 0181-944-0464; e-mail tourconcern@gn.apc.org.

Centre for Responsible Tourism (CRT) co-ordinates a North American network and advises on North American sources of information on responsible tourism: CRT, PO Box 827, San Anselmo, California 94979, USA.

Centre for the Advancement of Responsive Travel (CART) has a range of publications available as well as information on alternative holiday destinations, T UK 01732 352757.

Caribbean conservation organizations

The conservation organizations described below may also be able to provide advice on sites of historical or wildlife interest and possibly provide guides. The use of local experts as guides can of course provide an important source of income for small conservation bodies. In addition, they are often far more sensitive to the cultural taboos and ecological constraints of sites whose long term survival they can help to ensure. (**NB** Visitors should not be disappointed when a guide uses the local, rather than the technical name for wildlife; few local people know the names of animal and plant life.)

Anguilla Archeological and Historical Society, PO Box 252, The Valley, Anguilla.

Antigua Archeological and Historical Society, PO Box 103, English Harbour, Antigua.

Bahamas National Trust, PO Box N 4105, Nassau, Bahamas.

Barbados National Trust, 10th Avenue, Belleville, St Michael, Barbados.

British Virgin Islands National Parks Trust, c/o Ministry of Natural Resources, Road Town, Tortola, BVI.

Caribbean Conservation Association, Savannah Lodge, The Garrison, St Michael, Barbados.

Dominican Republic National Parks office (Dirección Nacional de Parques), Av Independencia 539 esq Cervantes, Santo Domingo (Apartado Postal 2487). **Ecoturisa**, Santiago 203, B, Santo Domingo.

Dominica Conservation Association, PO Box 71, Roseau, Dominica.

Grenada Historical Society, St George's, Grenada.

Jamaica Conservation and Development Trust, PO Box 1225, Kingston 8, Jamaica.

Montserrat National Trust, PO Box 54, Plymouth, Montserrat.

Natural History Society of Puerto Rico Inc.

Netherlands Antilles National Parks Foundation (STINAPA), PO Box 2090, Curaçao.

Nevis Historical and Conservation Society, c/o Mr S Byron, PO Box 476, Charlestown, Nevis.

Pointe à Pierre Wildfowl Trust (Trinidad), 18 Grove Road, Valsayn Park North, Trinidad.

St Lucia National Trust, PO Box 525, Castries, St Lucia.

St Lucia Naturalists Society, PO Box 783, Castries.

Trinidad and Tobago Field Naturalists Club, 1 Errol Park Road, St Ann's, Port of Spain.

Turks and Caicos National Trust, Box 261, Grand Turk, Turks and Caicos Islands.

Union Régionale des Associations du Patrimoine et de l'Environment de Guadeloupe, BP82L, Pointe-à-Pitre, Leder 97112, Guadeloupe.

Union Régionale des Associations du Patrimoine et de l'Environment de Martinique, Centre du PNRM, Caserne Bouille, Rue Redoute de Matouba, Fort de France 97200, Martinique.

Virgin Islands Conservation Society, PO Box 12379, St Thomas, US Virgin Islands 00801 USA. **Environmental Association**, PO Box 3839, Christiansted, St Croix, US Virgin Islands 00822.

In **Guyana** there are various private organizations, see that chapter; similarly **Suriname**.

Publications

The Good Tourist by Katie Wood and Syd House (1991: Mandarin Paperbacks), addresses issues surrounding environmental impacts of tourism, suggests ways in which damage can be minimized, suggests a range of environmentally sensitive holidays and projects.

Introduction and hints

GETTING THERE

AIR

All the main airlines flying to each island are given in the Information for Visitors sections. In addition to the scheduled flights listed, there are a great many charter flights from Europe and North America. For details on both types of service, you are advised to consult a good travel agent. An agent will also be able to tell you if you qualify for any student or senior citizen discount on offer.

Baggage allowance

Airlines will only allow a certain weight of luggage without a surcharge; this is normally 30 kg for first class and 20 kg for business and economy classes, but these limits may not be strictly enforced if the plane is not going to be full. On the other hand, weight limits for inter-island flights are often lower; it is best to enquire beforehand.

Specialist operators

In Switzerland, Globetrotter Travel Service, Rennweg, 8001 Zürich, has been recommended for arranging cheap flights to the region. At certain times of the year, Air France and Aéromaritime have flights at very advantageous prices from several southern French cities and Paris to Guadeloupe and Martinique; travellers from France, Switzerland and southern Germany should be able to use them. Air France flights can also be combined with Liat air passes. From the USA, Puerto Rico and Antigua are the only islands to which student fares are available; it is worth checking these out since it may be cheaper to take a student flight then continue to your destination rather than flying direct to the island of your choice (contact CIEE in the USA). For those over 65, Delta Airlines has a Senior Citizen Young at Heart programme, which offers a 10% discount on published fares on Delta between any US cities (except in Alaska or Hawaii) including San Juan, Puerto Rico, and the US Virgin Islands. You can carry on from there on another airline. If buying tickets routed through the USA, check that US taxes are included in the price.

SEA

The most popular way of visiting the Caribbean by ship is on a cruise liner, as the figures given in the Economy sections below attest. There are also sailing cruisers (eg the Windjammer and Star Clipper fleets) which allow flexible itineraries for cruising between

the islands; very spectacular when under sail. A travel agent will advise on these modes of transport. Windjammer Barefoot Cruises, which operates 5 tall-masted ships, can be contacted direct at PO Box 120, Miami Beach, Florida 33119, USA, T 800-327 2601, (305) 534 7447, 1 week cruises from US$650.

For **cargo ships** which carry passengers, it is best to enquire in your own country. In general it is very difficult to secure a passage on a cargo ship from Europe to the Caribbean without making full arrangements in advance. Full details on this type of travel are available from The Strand Cruise and Travel Centre, Charing Cross Shopping Concourse, The Strand, London WC2N 4HZ, T 0171-836-6363, F 0171-497 0078. In the USA, contact Freighter World Cruises, 180 South Lake Ave, Pasadena, CA 91101, T (818) 449-3106, or Travltips Cruise and Freighter Association, 163-07 Depot Road, PO Box 188, Flushing, NY 11358, T (800) 872-8584.

The Strand Cruise and Travel Centre can also advise on the Compagnie Générale Maritime's 3 sailings a month from Dunkerque or Le Havre to Fort-de-France and Pointe-à-Pitre, 23 days voyage (£800-890 one way with wine at dinner and lunch, good cuisine, greater availability of one-way tickets). The Horn Line has regular sailings on the following route: Dover, Antwerp, Hamburg, Felixstowe, Le Havre, Ponta Delgada (Azores), Pointe-à- Pitre, Fort-de-France, Moín (Costa Rica), Dover. On some voyages the ship calls at Bridgetown and Castries. The round trip fare is £2,300-2,500; the voyage's duration is 35 days. From Felixstowe, Projex Line's *EWL Venezuela* sails to Paramaribo, Georgetown, Port of Spain, La Guaira and Puerto Cabello (Venezuela), Willemstad, Oranjestad, Cartagena and Santa Marta (Venezuela), Bremen, Rotterdam to Felixstowe, 44-day round trip, £2,600 pp. Fyffes banana boats carry passengers

from Portsmouth and Flushing direct to Paramaribo, Suriname, and occasionally to Georgetown. The fare for the 35-38 day round trip is £1,980 pp. German sailings from Livorno (Italy) to Colombia and Ecuador call at San Juan, Puerto Rico.

From the USA, Ivaran Lines' container ship, *Americana*, carries 80 passengers in luxury accommodation: New Orleans, Houston, Puerto Cabello, La Guaira, Rio de Janeiro, Santos, Buenos Aires, Montevideo, Rio Grande do Sul, Itajaí, Santos, Rio, Salvador, Fortaleza, Bridgetown, San Juan, Veracruz, Tampico, New Orleans; fare £6,645-11,340, depending on cabin and month of departure, for the 54-day round trip, one way N or S possible. The *Sven Oltmann* makes a 2-week round trip Fort Lauderdale, Oranjestad, Willemstad, Puerto Cabello, La Guaira, Fort Lauderdale, £1,300 pp. The supply ship, MV *Amazing Grace*, sails every month from West Palm Beach, picking up southbound passengers in Freeport, Bahamas and visiting lots of islands before turning round in Trinidad after 2 weeks and stopping at different ports from the southbound trip, from US$950 for 2 weeks.

Yacht crewing

For those with 1,000 miles offshore sailing experience, a cheap way to get to the Caribbean is crewing on a yacht being delivered from Europe or the USA to the region.

MIAMI

Journeys to (and between) the Caribbean Islands often involve a change of planes in Miami. A 5-hr transfer in the middle of a tiring journey may seem like a daunting prospect, but Miami airport is surprisingly user-friendly and there is quite a lot to do in the city if you have a longer stopover.

The airport is rather like a big, horseshoe-shaped suburban shopping mall.

The upper level has shops and airline check-in counters; the lower level has other services like car rentals and baggage claim. The airport is divided into a series of concourses labelled B to H.

On arrival

Immigration queues are long, and can take 30-50 mins. Heavy hand luggage is more of a nuisance than at most airports, both in the queues and because of the long walk up and down the fingers which lead to the planes. Customs is crowded, but the queue moves faster.

Passengers arriving from the Bahamas pre-clear in Nassau, which saves time. Pre-clearance is also possible in Aruba. From London, through bookings of baggage is now available; ask for a suitable label.

US Customs

The United States Department of Agriculture informs travellers: "The US Department of Agriculture places restrictions on agricultural items brought to the United States from foreign countries as well as those brought to the mainland from Hawaii, Puerto Rico, and the US Virgin Islands. Prohibited items can harbor foreign animal and plant pests and diseases that could seriously damage America's crops, livestock, pets, and the environment."

Travellers are required to list on the Custom's declaration form any meats, fruits, vegetables, plants, animals, and plant and animal products they are bringing into the country. The declaration must list all agricultural items carried in baggage, hand luggage and in vehicles coming across the border.

USDA inspectors will confiscate illegal items for destruction. Travellers who fail to declare items can be fined up to US$100 on the spot, and their exit from the airport will be delayed. Some items are permitted. Call 301-436-5908 for a copy of the helpful pamphlet, *Travelers Tips*. The best advice is to check before purchasing an agricultural item and trying to bring it back to the United States.

Baggage There are baggage carts in customs, but these must be left behind when you have been cleared. From this point on there are *skycaps* (tip around US$1-2 per large bag). Skycaps can also be called from the *paging phones* which are thick on the ground in the concourses and entrances.

There are luggage lockers at all entrances to the airport and at various other points. They cost US$1 in quarters (25 cents – look for change machines, or ask information counters). After 24 hrs, bags are taken to a storage facility next to the *lost and found* office in concourse E. The charge for storage here is US$2 per day.

For very large items there is a left luggage office (baggage service office) on the lower level of concourse G and on the second level of concourse B. Charges are US$2-6 per day, depending on the size of the item.

Filling in time

The concourses are chocabloc with snackbars, duty free shops, and gift shops selling overpriced junk. Once through Customs and into the duty free area there is one newsagent selling a limited amount of confectionery and newspapers, magazines, etc, and one poorly-stocked, overpriced Duty Free shop. Some items, such as cosmetics and perfumes, are better value in town. Drinking fountains only become plentiful once you get near the bus stops. **NB** A 6½% sales tax is added to the marked price. Watch out if you are fine-tuning your US currency before departure. The best place to pass the time and relax is probably the *Hotel MIA*, in the middle of the horseshoe on concourse E. The Lobby Lounge, open 1000-0100, is on the same floor as flight check in. The upper floors have a sundeck (free), an open air swimming pool, gym and sauna area (US$5 per day), racquetball courts (US$8 per hour), snackbar, lounge bar (the happy hour, 1700-1900, has drinks on special and complimentary snacks). There is also the *Top of The Port* restaurant, with pleasant surroundings and much better food than on the concourses (open 0700-2300; full breakfast US$7.75, lunch specials from US$8, dinner specials from US$15). The hotel has special day rates between 0800 and 1800.

Information There are very helpful information counters in concourse E and just outside customs. They can also be contacted from any paging phone. (Counters open 0630-2230; paging phone service 24 hrs.) They will advise on ground transport, airport services, and the Miami area generally. They also have information on the full calendar of events in the city throughout the year.

Nursery Mainly for changing or feeding babies, on concourse E. If locked, the information office in this concourse has a key.

Banking Barnett Bank on concourse C, Monday to Friday 0900-1600, Saturday 0900-1200. Visa and Mastercard cash advances (US$25 minimum, US$2,000 maximum) on production of passport and one other piece of identification. 24-hr cashpoint on concourse outside the bank. Several foreign exchange counters, including a 24-hr one on concourse E.

Service Centre between concourses B and C has stamp machines, credit card phones, TDD phone for deaf or mute passengers, and another cashpoint.

Post Office Leave the building at the lower level of concourse B and walk a couple of metres along the airport road. Open Monday to Friday 0830-2100 and 0930-1330 on Saturday. Also sells bubble packing, padded envelopes, mailing tubes for posters etc. Express mail service in the post office is open 24 hrs.

Leaving the Airport

If you want to venture into the real world, you can use:

Rental cars This works out at around US$30 per day for a small car. Many companies have offices on the lower level concourses. It can take an hour or more to book a car, take the company bus to its main office, fill out all the forms, and pick up a car. Leaving the car can take just as long. The information counters have a full list of companies. Some car hire firms may offer lower rates to passengers booking in advance through a Caribbean travel agent, or flying with certain airlines. Check in advance.

Drive away Look for agencies, under D in the phone book, who handle cars belonging to people who have flown to their destination, but need their car driven there by someone else. It can be a quick, uncomplicated way to leave Miami if you have your passport and an international driving licence; sometimes accommodation and fuel are included.

Buses Miami has a good bus service. Fare is US$1.25, with US$0.25 for a transfer to another route. Buses stop outside concourse E. Route 37 runs N-S every 30 mins in the day, every hour late evenings and weekends; Route 42 also runs N-S, every hour. Route J runs every 20-30 mins or every hour on Sundays to Miami Beach; Route 7 runs every 20-40 mins. Eastbound buses go downtown, westbound buses go to the Mall of the Americas and the International Mall, two big shopping complexes.

Routes J and 42 connect with the *Greyhound* bus terminal at Coral Gables.

Metrorail All of the airport bus routes connect with stations on the Metrorail line. This gives a quick service every 15 mins from 0600 to 2400 between downtown Miami and many suburban areas.

Metromover Metrorail tickets give a free connection to Metromover, a 1.9 mile (3 km) elevated track which whizzes round downtown Miami. The connection is at Government Center station.

Tri-Rail is another rail system which connects Miami and points N. The full journey to West Palm Beach takes 1 hr 52 mins. Connecting buses leave from outside concourse E; it is an 18-min ride to the station. Departures between 0430 and 2220 on weekdays, fewer at weekends, T 1-800-TRI-RAIL/1-800-874-7245.

Super Shuttle is a minibus running to and from the airport. You can book ahead to be picked up from a hotel or private house. The Super Shuttle at the airport can be found at several locations on the lower concourse, look for the 'Van Service' signs. The attendant will ask you where you are going, using the Zip Code as a reference. Zip Codes are classified into zones which will determine which van can take you to your destination as well as fix cost (T 305-871-2000). The fare is US$8-12 for downtown, US$10-20 for S Miami Beach, US$20 to Fort Lauderdale airport.

Taxis are more expensive. A flat rate taxi service operates from the airport, with fares fixed according to zone, eg US$22 to South Miami Beach.

Hotels Rooms at the *Miami International Airport Hotel (MIA)* in the airport start at **L2** plus 12.5% tax for a double, **L3** corporate rate. Rooms quite small but double glazing keeps out aircraft noise, very impersonal, T 1-800-327-1276 from within the USA, or 305-871-4100 from elsewhere. F 305-871-0800. Quick access from airport: **L2** *Sheraton River House*, 3900 NW 21st St, T 305-871-3800, travel industry and senior discount available. Information has a good listing of downtown hotels, starting from the cheapest (*Bayman International*, Flagler Street, T 266-5098 and *Miami Springs Hotel*, 661 E Drive, T 888-8421) and ending with the most expensive (*Miami Airport Hilton*, 5101 Blue Lagoon Drive, T 262-1000, and *Marriott Hotel*, 1202 NW LeJeune Road, T 649-5000). 1 min from the terminal is **A1** *Ramada Hotel Miami International Airport*, 3941 NW 22nd St, T 871-1700, F 871-4830, courtesy van from airport, shuttle buses to various points in the city. **B** *Miami Airways Motel*, T 883-4700, F 888-8072, free airport shuttle, pool, breakfast, good value.

Information also has a separate listing of Miami Beach hotels (alphabetical, not by price). Best value in Miami Beach are: *Miami Beach International Hostel*, 236 9th St, Miami Beach, T 305-534-0268, F 305-534-5862, **D** hostel accommodation, **B** for private room; take bus J from airport to 41st Street and Indian Creek Rd, transfer to bus C to 9th and Washington. *Clay Hotel*, 1438 Washington Avenue, which has a youth hostel attached is reached by the same buses, but get off bus C at 14th and Washington. Single rooms are **C**, hostel accommodation is **D** (cheaper with ISIC or IYHA card), T 305-534-2988, F 305-673-0346. *Clay Hotel* has young and friendly staff and caters for many young European tourists; it has a kitchen, but no utensils. *The Tropics*, 1550 Collins Ave, Miami Beach, FL 33139, T 305-531-0361, F 305-531-8676, **D** in a 4-bedded room, swimming pool, rec. There are direct free phone lines to several hotels next to the baggage check in on lower level concourse F.

There are also reservations services which will make reservations for you. Try CRS (Toll free 1-800-683-3311), Express Reservation (Toll free 1-800-627-1356), or Room with a View (305- 433- 4343).

Shopping For bargains, try Flagler Street in downtown Miami, it's crowded and full of action. Bayside Market Place Shopping Center, 401 Biscayne Blvd, is easily reached from the airport by bus or Super Shuttle. Here you can catch the Old Town Trolley Bus (see below). The suburban malls are more expensive and more relaxed: Mall of the Americas and International Mall are easiest to reach by bus.

Things to see in Miami

This guide is not the place for a full listing. Two 90-min tours are offered by the Old Town Trolley Bus: Miami Magic City Tour and Miami Beach Tour. Both allow you to stay on board or to disembark at any stop to sightsee, shop or eat. You can reboard free and make as many stops as you like. No reservations necessary. Miami Beach Tour (US$14 adults, US$5 children 3-12) stops at Ocean Drive, 11th Street in the wonderful Art Deco district, the Holocaust Memorial (very powerful and interesting), Collins Avenue and 46th Street and Lincoln Road Mall. It runs every 2 hrs 1045-1645 (last at 1645). Miami Magic City Tour includes stops at the Seaquarium, Coconut Grove, Coral Gables, including the Venetian Pool on Desoto Boulevard (historic landmark with lagoon-style pool, caves, bridges all carved out of coral rock and a sandy beach; small café, admission US$4 adults, US$3.50 13-17 year-olds, US$1.50 under 12s; Monday-Friday 1100 1930, weekends 1000-1630). The airport information office has a useful booklet, *Destination Miami*, which gives details of a wide range of cultural events.

Miami is about the nearest that the continental USA gets to a tropical environment. Many attractions are designed for visitors from the N. The Monkey Jungle, Parrot Jungle, etc may not be that exciting if you have just seen the real thing. With half a day to spare, however, you should be able to visit any of these, or the Metrozoo, or the Seaquarium. Museums include Vizcaya, a Renaissance-style villa with formal gardens, and the Spanish Monastery in North Miami Beach, brought to America in pieces by William Randolph Hearst from Segovia in Spain, where it was first built in 1141.

Miami Beach is probably the best place for a short stay. There are plenty of interesting Art Deco buildings, with restaurants and cafes along the sea front. Shops, hotels, nightclubs, etc are all within walking distance. Moreover, you can walk around at night without getting mugged. It also has the Bass Museum, with a good collection of European paintings. North of the Haulover channel is a section of beach where nude bathing is tolerated.

If you have a full day in Miami, there would be time to rent a car and drive to the *Everglades National Park*, a huge freshwater swamp with interesting wildlife and an excellent network of interpretative centres and nature trails (50 mins-1 hr in heavy traffic from the airport). The nearer Florida Keys would be an alternative, but are probably not so exciting if you have just been in the Caribbean.

ON ARRIVAL

TRAVEL IN THE EASTERN CARIBBEAN

Certain conditions are common to the former British colonies, or still British dependencies, in the Leewards and Windwards, including Barbados. At immigration on arrival, say you want to stay longer than planned because getting an extension is time-consuming and difficult. If asked where you are staying and you have not booked in advance, say any hotel (they do not usually check), but do not say you are going to camp and do not say that you are going to arrange accommodation later. Do not imagine that you can go to the Eastern Caribbean to work. Make sure that you have a ticket home: in Barbados, Trinidad, St Lucia and Dominica, the immigration laws state that visitors will not be allowed to enter without a ticket back to the home country shown on the passport. Tickets to other countries will not suffice. This becomes a problem if you are not going home for 12 months since airline tickets become void after a year. Some airlines sell tickets on the 6-12 month extended payment plan; these can be credited when you have left the islands with restrictive entry requirements.

In this part of the Caribbean, including the French islands, it is difficult to buy single tickets between islands because of the entry requirements mentioned above. This is a problem if you enter the region on a one-way ticket, intending to continue to South America and fly home from there, buying the tickets en route. You may be required to buy at once all the tickets up to the point of departure for home. This would be more expensive than buying all flight tickets at home so, even if you propose to take some boat trips between islands, we recommend that you purchase flights in advance and refund those that have not been used later.

The International Student Identity Card (ISIC)

If you are in full-time education you will be entitled to an ISIC, which is distributed by student travel offices and travel agencies in 77 countries. The ISIC gives you special prices on all forms of transport (air, sea, rail, etc), and access to a variety of other concessions and services. If you need to find the location of your nearest ISIC office contact: The ISIC Association, Box 9048, 1000 Copenhagen, Denmark T (+45) 33 93 93 03.

DOCUMENTS

Individual island entry requirements are given in the relevant chapters under Information for Visitors. North Americans, British and Commonwealth citizens in some cases need only show proof of identity. If intending to visit Puerto Rico or the US Virgin Islands, or making connections through Miami or another US gateway, a visa for the United States will not be necessary if your home country and the airline on which you are travelling are part of the US Visa Waiver Program. A US consulate will supply all relevant details. An onward ticket is a common prerequisite for entry. Australians and New Zealanders should note that many islands impose strict entry laws on holders of the above passports. Satisfying visa and other requirements, if not done at home, can take at least a day, usually involve expense, and passport photographs will be needed: be prepared.

On all forms, refer to yourself as a 'visitor' rather than a 'tourist'.

Many islands insist that visitors have an air ticket to their home country before being allowed to enter (not just the Eastern Caribbean, see below); for non-US citizens travelling to the Caribbean from the USA, this means a ticket from the USA to their home country, not a ticket back to the USA.

You should always carry your passport in a safe place about your person, or if not going far, leave it in the hotel safe (see below under **Currency**). If staying in a place for several weeks, it is worth while registering at your Embassy or Consulate. Then, if your passport is stolen or lost, the process of replacing it is quicker. Keeping photocopies of essential documents, and some additional passport-sized photographs, is recommended.

MONEY

COST OF LIVING

The Caribbean is not a cheap area to visit. Transport is expensive (unless you are staying in one place and using only buses), but if you book your flights in advance, taking advantage of whatever air pass or stopovers are suitable, that expenditure at least will be out of the way.

Accommodation is generally expensive, too, even at the lower end of the market. There is no shortage of luxury resorts and beach hotels throughout the price range. In a number of instances you can book all-inclusive packages which are often good value and let you know in advance almost exactly what your expenditure will be. However, you will not see much of your chosen island outside your enclave. To find cheaper accommodation you need mobility, probably a hired car. One option is renting a self-catering apartment, villa or house, the range of which is also vast, and here the advantage is that a group of people can share the cost (this is not an economical prospect for single travellers).

Since, on a number of islands, resort-type hotels form the majority, turning up at a cheaper place may not always yield a room because competition is great. The term guest house is usually applied to places at the lower end of the market; they tend, but by no means in all cases, to be basic. Note also that, if booking ahead, tourist office lists may not include the cheapest establishments, so you may have to reserve a dearer room, then look around. This is probably what you will have to do in any event, time permitting, to find the best value. In the main, tourist offices publish accurate, up-to-date lists of accommodation, which are a great help for making preliminary bookings. Remember that the Dominican Republic has the most hotel rooms in the Caribbean, so there is no real problem in finding a space there; see each island section for details. Some islands, such as the French Antilles, have well-organized camp sites, but on many camping is actually prohibited, eg Antigua.

The following tips on economizing were sent by Steve Wilson and Debra Holton of San Francisco: even if not travelling with a tent, take a cooking stove and prepare your own food; much cheaper than eating in restaurants. Look out bunk rentals on boats (see above).

Exchange rates (12 July 1996)			
COUNTRY	CURRENCY	ABBREVIATION	EXCHANGE RATE/US$
Anguilla	East Caribbean dollar	EC$	2.70
Antigua & Barbuda	East Caribbean dollar	EC$	2.70
Aruba	Aruban florin	Afl	1.77
Bahamas	Bahamian dollar	B$	1.00
Barbados	Barbados dollar	B$	2.00
Bonaire	Guilder	Naf	1.79
British Virgin Islands	US dollar	US$	1.00
Cayman Islands	Cayman dollar	CI$	0.80
Cuba	Cuban peso		1.00
		(Black market 20 pesos = US$1)	
Curaçao	Guilder	Naf	1.79
Dominica	East Caribbean dollar	EC$	2.70
Dominican Rep	Dominican peso	RD$	14.06
Grenada	East Caribbean dollar	EC$	2.70
Guadeloupe	French franc	F	5.15
Guyana	Guyanese dollar	G$	138.90
Guyane	French franc	F	5.15
Haiti	Gourde		16.18
Jamaica	Jamaican dollar	J$	32.75
Martinique	French franc	F	5.15
Montserrat	East Caribbean dollar	EC$	2.70
Puerto Rico	US dollar	US$	1.00
Saba	Guilder	Naf	1.79
St Barthélémy	French franc	F	5.15
St Kitts & Nevis	East Caribbean dollar	EC$	2.70
St Lucia	East Caribbean dollar	EC$	2.70
St Martin	French franc	F	5.15
St Vincent & the Grenadines	East Caribbean dollar	EC$	2.70
Sint Eustatius	Guilder	Naf	1.79
Sint Maarten	Guilder	Naf	1.79
Suriname	Suriname guilder	Sf	419.00
Trinidad & Tobago	Trinidad dollar	TT$	5.74
Turks & Caicos	US dollar	US$	1.00
US Virgin Islands	US dollar	US$	1.00
Venezuela	Bolívar	Bs	470.25

Happy Hours in bars often have free food, couples sharing costs can often take advantage of Ladies' Night in a bar or nightclub, which either permits free entry or cheap drinks. If you stay in guest houses and don't eat in restaurants, the minimum you should budget for is an average of US$50 a day, not including transport between islands.

CURRENCY

In general, the US dollar is the best currency to take, in cash or travellers' cheques. The latter are the most convenient and, if you follow the issuer's instructions, can be replaced if lost or stolen. On the most frequently-visited holiday islands, eurocurrencies can be exchanged without difficulty but at a poor rate and US dollars are preferred. In some places, the US dollar is accepted alongside local currency (but make sure in which currency prices are being quoted). In others, only the local currency is accepted. On the French islands dollars are accepted, but the franc is the preferred currency. Credit cards are widely used. Remember to keep your money, credit cards, etc, safely on your person, or in a hotel safe. If your guest house has no safe in which to store money, passport, tickets, etc, try local banks (eg Royal Bank, Scarborough, Tobago, TT$70 for 2 weeks).

A list of currencies and exchange rates is provided, see page 22.

TELEPHONES

Many airport lounges and phone companies in the region have AT&T's USA Direct phones by which the USA and Canada may be called using a charge card (which bills your home phone account), or by calling collect. The service is not available to Europe. Public card phones have been introduced by Cable and Wireless on those islands where it operates. This company offers discounts on evening rates for IDD calls from card-phones 1800-2300 15%, 2300-0500 40%. Discounts do not apply to credit card calls (1-800-877-8000). Phone cards usually come in several denominations, with a tax added on, and can be useful for local and international calls, particularly as you then avoid the extra charges made by hotels on phone calls. Communicating by fax is a convenient way of sending messages home. Places with public fax machines may receive messages as well as send.

LANGUAGE

In the majority of cases, English is widely spoken and understood (although non-native speakers of English may have difficulty understanding some of the local dialects). In the French Antilles and Haiti, French is the main language. However, in these last, and on English islands which at one time belonged to France, Créole is spoken. The population is bilingual, so on English islands the English-speaking traveller will have no problems with communication and on the French islands, knowledge of French is of great benefit. The Netherlands Antilles speak Dutch, English and Papiamento. English and Spanish are both spoken on Puerto Rico. The principal language in the Dominican Republic, Cuba and Venezuelan islands is Spanish. If visiting non-English islands, a basic knowledge of the main language is a great advantage.

SPORT

Information on sport is given under each island, but for those visiting the former British colonies, British dependencies and even the US Virgin Islands, an understanding of cricket is an advantage. It is more than a national game, having become a symbol of achievement and a unifying factor (baseball and basketball serve much the same function in Puerto Rico). Spectating at a match is entertaining both for the cricket itself and for the conversation that arises.

WHERE TO STAY

HIGH AND LOW SEASON

High season in the Caribbean is usually called 'winter'; in other words it comes in the Northern Hemisphere's colder months. Dates vary a little but the season is roughly from mid-Dec to mid-April. At this time air fares, room rates and other costs rise. In addition, air fares are also increased at European and US holiday times, ie July, Aug and Sept if flying from the UK, July and Aug from the USA, etc. Flights to the Caribbean from the UK are at a premium in the pre-Christmas period.

PRICES

Prices are either given in US dollars, or the local currency, whichever is appropriate. Hotel prices are indicated according to the following code and are for a double room in high season:

L1 – over US$200	L2 – US$151-$200
L3 – US$101-$150	A1 – US$81-$100
A2 – US$61-$80	A3 – US$46-$60
B – US$31-$45	C – US$21-$30
D – US$12-$20	E – US$7-$11
F – US$4-$6	G – up to US$3

Rates are subject to change without notice and therefore those given in this book should only be taken as representative. High season is normally referred to as 'winter', running from roughly mid-Dec to mid-April. 'Summer' is low season, the remainder of the year.

Certain abbreviations are used in relation to hotel prices. These are:

EP – European Plan, room only

CP – Continental Plan, room and breakfast

MAP – Modified American Plan, room, breakfast and dinner

AP – American Plan, room with three daily meals

FAP – Full American Plan, room and all meals (including afternoon tea, etc).

Other abbreviations used in the text are: pp = per person; d = double; s = single; a/c = air conditioned; T = telephone; F = fax; TCs = travellers' cheques; rec = recommended; inc = including; N = north; S = south; E = east; W = west.

GETTING AROUND

AIR

The most extensive links between islands are by air, either with the scheduled flights on the regional and international carriers (again given in the text), or by chartered plane. If you are in a group, or family, the latter option may not cost very much more than a scheduled flight. It often has the advantage of linking the charter direct to your incoming or homeward flight.

AIR PASSES

Travellers from the UK should note that it is best to go to Transatlantic Wings, 70 Pembroke Road, London W8 6NX, T 0171-602 4021, F 0171-603 6101, who have experience in arranging flights within the Caribbean as well as trans-Atlantic (see below Air Passes). They will also book accommodation for independent travellers through The Caribbean Experience, specializing in the Eastern Caribbean.

The regional carriers with most routes in the Caribbean are Liat (with its headquarters in Antigua, co-owned by 11 Caribbean states, but being prepared for privatization in 1996), BWIA (based in Trinidad, privatized in 1995) and ALM (of the Netherlands Antilles). All three offer air passes.

Liat

Liat's air passes are called *Explorer tickets*: the *Liat Explorer* costs US$199, valid for 21 days, maximum 3 stops between San Juan, Puerto Rico and Trinidad; the *Liat Super Explorer* costs US$367 for a 30-day ticket, allowing unlimited stop overs in 25 destinations between San Juan and Caracas and Georgetown as well (do not overload your itinerary, a lot of time can be spent waiting at airports for flights). The Super Explorer, which must be booked in advance, should be bought in the West Indies, but Transatlantic Wings (see below) are permitted to sell it. Note that a Super Explorer bought in the West Indies will be liable to local taxes. Liat operates an airpass in which each flight costs US$60 midweek (Monday-Thursday), US$70 at weekends, valid for 21 days; minimum 3 stop overs, maximum 6. These tickets may only be purchased in conjunction with an international flight to a Caribbean gateway, the itinerary must be settled in advance, with no changes permitted, and the fares must be paid for in Europe (including the UK and Eire). Travellers from the UK should note that it is best to go to Transatlantic Wings,

70 Pembroke Road, London W8 6NX, T 0171-602 4021, F 0171-603 6101, who have experience in arranging Liat flights. Liat has no representation in Europe outside the UK, so here again Transatlantic Wings in London should be contacted for details.

In the USA, contact a specialist travel agent. Liat's telephone number on Antigua is (809) 462 0700, or 462 2682 for Fax.

For those who fly regularly within the Caribbean, Liat runs a frequent flyer club, organized in Antigua. Try to book Liat flights as far in advance as possible; planes are not large and fill up quickly. A golden rule when flying with Liat: just because you are *not* booked on a flight it does not mean you will not get on (be patient and sweet-talking); just because you *are* booked on a flight it does not mean you will get on (never be last in the queue).

BWIA

BWIA's intra-Caribbean unlimited mileage fare is US$356; no destination may be visited more than once, except for making a connection and the entire journey must be fixed at the time of payment (changes are subject to a US$20 surcharge); dates may be left open. This airpass is valid for 30 days, no refunds are given for unused sectors.

ALM

ALM has an airpass costing US$695, permitting 8 trips to 8 different ALM destinations, maximum stay 30 days. Its Island Pass, for Aruba, Bonaire and Curaçao, minimum 7 days, maximum 21, costs US$135 if journeys start and end at Aruba or Curaçao, US$249 out of Sint Maarten and US$305 out of the Dominican Republic.

SEA

Island-hopping by boats with scheduled services is fairly limited. Boat services are more common between dependent islands, eg St Vincent and the Grenadines, Trinidad and Tobago, Belize City and Caye Caulker. Again, full details are given in the relevant sections below. Windward Lines Limited run a weekly passenger and cargo ferry service: St Lucia- Barbados- St Vincent- Trinidad- Güiria or Isla Margarita-Trinidad- St Vincent-Barbados-St Lucia. For information and tickets contact Global Steamship Agencies Ltd, Mariner's Club, Wrightson Road, PO Box 966, Port of Spain, Trinidad, T (809) 624-2279/ 625-2547, F (809) 627-5091.

Irregular passenger services on cargo boats (with basic accommodation, usually a hammock on deck, no meals supplied), schooners, crewing or hitching on yachts can only be discovered by asking around when you are in port. Crewing on yachts is not difficult in winter (in the hurricane season yachtsmen stay away). If you are looking for a job on a yacht, or trying to hitch a ride, it will be easier to make contact if you are living at the yacht harbour. Boat owners often advertise bunks for rent, which is a very cheap form of accommodation (US$10-30); ask around, or look on the bulletin boards. If arriving by sea, make sure you are aware of the island's entry requirements before setting out.

DEPARTURE TAX

Departure tax is payable on leaving every island; make sure you know what this is in advance so you do not get caught out.

TRAVEL ON LAND

Buses are cheap, but services tend not to be very convenient, in the sense that they often involve a night away from the point of departure, even on small islands. This is because buses start in outlying towns in the early morning and return from the capital in the afternoon. Another limiting factor to public transport is a shortage of funds for spare parts, so buses may be scarce and crowded. Many smaller islands do not even have a bus service.

Taxis are plentiful, but generally not cheap. Some islands, eg Trinidad, have route taxis, which are inexpensive and travel only on set routes. On many islands, taxi fares are set by the tourist office or government.

Renting a car gives the greatest flexibility, but is also hardest on the pocket. You can expect to pay more than in the USA or Europe. A number of islands require drivers to take out a temporary, or visitor driver's licence (these are mentioned in the text), but some places will not issue a licence to those over 70 years of age without a medical certificate. In small places, to rent a motorcycle, scooter or bicycle is a good idea.

FURTHER READING

A number of books are suggested for further reading, these will be found in the Culture, Tourist Information and other sections. Similarly, maps that may be consulted are indicated; see also in **Walking** page 61.

By no means all the writers of history, fiction, poetry and other topics will be found below. There is no room to talk of the many authors who have been inspired by aspects of the Caribbean for their fiction, eg Robert Louis Stevenson, Graham Greene, Ernest Hemingway, Gabriel García Márquez. Nor have the travellers been mentioned: Patrick Leigh Fermor, *The Traveller's Tree*, Quentin Crewe, *Touch the Happy Isles*, Trollope, *Travels in the West Indies and the Spanish Main*, Alec Waugh, *The Sugar Isles*, James Pope-Hennessy, among others. Of the histories of the region, *A Short History of The West Indies*, by J H Parry, P M Sherlock and Anthony Maingot (Macmillan, 1987) is very accessible; also *From Columbus to Castro: The History of the Caribbean 1492-1969*, Eric Williams (Harper and Row, 1970). For an introduction to the geography of the

Caribbean, Mark Wilson's *The Caribbean Environment* (Oxford University Press, 1989), prepared for the Caribbean Examinations Council, is a fascinating text book. Another introductory book is *Far from Paradise, An Introduction to Caribbean Development*, by James Ferguson (Latin American Bureau, 1990). An economic study is *The Poor and the Powerless, Economic Policy and Change in the Caribbean*, by Clive Y Thomas (Latin American Bureau, 1988). A recent study of tourism in the Caribbean and its impact on the economies and people is Polly Pattullo's *Last Resort, The Cost of Tourism in the Caribbean* (Cassell and Latin American Bureau, 1996).

The work of a great many English-speaking poets is collected in *The Penguin Book of Caribbean Verse in English*, edited by Paula Burnett (1986); see also *Hinterland: Caribbean Poetry From the West Indies and Britain*, edited by E A Markham (Bloodaxe, 1990), and *West Indian Poetry*, edited by Kenneth Ramchand and Cecil Gray (Longman Caribbean, 1989). For a French verse anthology, see *La Poésie Antillaise*, collected by Maryse Condé (Fernand Nathan, 1977). There are a number of prose anthologies of stories in English, eg *Stories from the Caribbean*, introduced by Andrew Salkey (Paul Elek, 1972), or *West Indian Narrative: an Introductory Anthology*, by Kenneth Ramchand (Nelson, 1966). Heinemann's Caribbean Writers series publishes works of fiction by well-established and new writers. *The Story of English*, by Robert McCrumb, William Cran and Robert MacNeil (Faber and Faber/BBC, 1986) has an interesting section on the development of the English language in the Caribbean. The Commonwealth Institute in London publishes useful checklists on Caribbean writing: No 4 on literature, 1986; No 6 on general topics, 1987, both compiled by Roger Hughes.

FT Caribbean publishes *The Caribbean Handbook*, a business and reference guide, with a useful bibliography on all Caribbean topics, and the inflight magazine of Liat *(Liat Islander)*. FT Caribbean Head Office, PO Box 1037, St John's, Antigua, or PO Box 675, St George's Grenada, or Suite 53, The Omnibus Business Centre, 39-41 North Road, London N7 9DP. A rival to *The Caribbean Handbook* is *The Caribbean Business Directory* and *Caribbean Yellow Pages Telephone Directory* (Antigua: Caribbean Publishing Co, 2 vols), a good source of current information on telephone and fax numbers, key companies, economic statistics, business and government information. The *Business Directory* contains a section on each island in the Caribbean, plus Florida, North America and selected South American countries; the *Yellow Pages* volume is a listing of telephone and fax numbers for companies. BWIA's inflight magazine, *BWIA Caribbean Beat*, is published quarterly by MEP, 6 Prospect Avenue, Maraval, Port of Spain, Trinidad, T (809) 622-3821, F 628-0639. *Caribbean Insight*, published monthly in London by the West India Committee in association with Caribbean Publishing Company (T 0171 976 1493, F 0171 976 1541) is an informative newsletter covering the entire region.

Finally, a generally excellent series of Caribbean books is published by Macmillan Caribbean; this includes island guides, natural histories, books on food and drink, sports and pirates, and wall maps (for a full catalogue, write to Macmillan Caribbean, Houndmills, Basingstoke, Hampshire, RG21 2XS, England).

This list is not exhaustive, concentrating mainly on books in English, published (or readily available) in the UK. For any favourites omitted, we apologize.

Health

WITH THE FOLLOWING advice and precautions, you should keep as healthy as you do at home. In the Caribbean the health risks are different from those encountered in Europe or the USA, especially in the tropical regions, but at the same time the region's medical practitioners have particular experience in dealing with locally-occurring diseases. Most of the islands have a tropical climate but this does not mean that tropical diseases as such are an enormous problem or even the main problem for visitors.

Medical care

The problems of infectious disease still predominate in most of the islands, but vary in severity between town and rural areas and from island to island depending on the state of economic development and the attention paid to public health. Thus there are few hard and fast rules. You will often have to make your own judgements on the healthiness or otherwise of your surroundings.

Language is not on the whole a problem and throughout the islands there are well-qualified doctors who speak good English. Medical practises vary from those you may be used to, but there is likely to be better experience at dealing with locally occurring disease.

Medicines

A certain amount of self medication may be necessary and you will find that many of the drugs available have familiar names. However, always check the date stamping and buy from reputable pharmacies because the shelf life of some items, especially vaccines and antibiotics, is markedly reduced in tropical conditions.

With the following precautions and advice you should keep as healthy as usual. Make local enquiries about health risks if you are apprehensive and take the general advice of European and North American families who have lived or are living in the country.

BEFORE YOU GO

Take out medical insurance. You should have a dental check-up, obtain a spare glasses prescription and if you suffer from a chronic disease such as diabetes, high blood pressure, cardio-pulmonary disease, or a nervous disorder, arrange for a check-up with your doctor who can at the same time provide you with a letter explaining details of your disability. Check the current practice for malaria prophylaxis (prevention) if you are going to the Guianas, Dominican Republic or Haiti.

Vaccination and immunisation

Smallpox vaccination is no longer required. Neither is yellow fever vaccination unless you are going to or are coming from South America. As of mid-1995 the cholera epidemic in South and Central America had not spread to any of the Caribbean islands but they were all on the alert for the possibility. Although cholera vaccination is largely ineffective, immigration officers may ask for proof of such vaccination if coming from a country where the epidemic has occurred.

The following vaccinations are recommended:

Typhoid (monovalent): one dose, followed by a booster in 1 month's time (an oral preparation has been developed and a newer, more expensive vaccination against Typhoid, Typhim Vi, which is less likely to cause post-injection symptoms). Immunity from this course lasts 2 to 3 years.

Poliomyelitis: this is a live vaccine generally given orally and a full course consists of three doses with a booster in tropical regions, every 3 to 5 years.

Tetanus: one dose should be given with a booster at 6 weeks and another at 6 months and 10 yearly boosters thereafter are recommended.

Children should in addition be properly protected against diphtheria, against whooping cough, mumps, measles and HIB. Teenage girls, if they have not had the disease, should be given Rubella (german measles) vaccination. Consult your doctor for advice on tuberculosis inoculation; the disease is still present in the British Virgin Islands, Grenada, Guadeloupe, Haiti, and Martinique.

Infectious Hepatitis (Jaundice) is of some concern throughout the Caribbean, more so in Cuba, Dominica, Haiti, and Montserrat. It seems to be frequently caught by travellers. The main symptoms are pains in the stomach, lack of appetite, lassitude, and the typical yellow colour of the eyes and skin. Medically speaking there are two different types: the less serious, but more common, is Hepatitis A for which the best protection is the careful preparation of food, the avoidance of contaminated drinking water and scrupulous attention to toilet hygiene. Human normal immunoglobulin (gamma- globulin) confers considerable protection against the disease and is particularly useful in epidemics. It should be obtained from a reputable source and is certainly recommended for travellers who intend to live rough. The injection should be given as close as possible to your departure and, as the dose depends on the likely time you are to spend in infected areas, the manufacturer's instructions should be taken as to dose. At last vaccination against Hepatitis A has been developed and is generally available. Three shots over 6 months would seem to give excellent protection lasting up to 10 years. Havrix monodose is now available, and Junior Havrix.

The other, more serious, version is Hepatitis B, which is acquired usually from injections with unclean needles, blood transfusion, as a sexually transmitted disease and possibly by insect bites. You may have had jaundice before, or you may have had hepatitis of either type before without becoming jaundiced in which case you may be immune to either Hepatitis A or B. This can be tested for before you travel. If you are not immune to Hepatitis B a vaccine is available (three shots over 6 months) and if you are not immune to Hepatitis A, then you should consider having gamma-globulin.

AIDS

Aids in the Caribbean is increasing in its prevalence, as in most countries, but is not wholly confined to the well known high risk sections of the population, ie homosexual men, intravenous drug abusers, prostitutes and children of infected mothers. Heterosexual transmission is now the dominant mode and so the main risk to travellers is from casual sex. The same precautions should be taken as when encountering any sexually transmitted disease. The AIDS virus (HIV) can be passed via unsterile needles which have been previously used to inject an HIV positive patient but the risk of this is very small indeed. It would however be sensible to check that needles have been properly sterilized or disposable needles used. If you take your own disposable needles, be prepared to explain what they are for. The risk of receiving a blood transfusion with blood infected with the HIV virus is greater than from dirty needles because of the amount of fluid exchanged. Supplies of blood for transfusion should now be screened for HIV in all reputable hospitals so again the risk must be very small indeed. Catching the AIDS virus does not usually produce an illness in itself; the only way to be sure if you feel you have been put at risk is to have a blood test for HIV antibodies on your return to a place where there are reliable laboratory facilities. The test does not become positive for many weeks. Presently the higher risks are probably in Haiti, Dominican Republic, Trinidad and Bahamas.

MALARIA

In the West Indies, malaria is confined to the island of Hispaniola, being more prevalent in Haiti than the Dominican Republic. It also exists in parts of the Guianas (seek up-to-date advice on the type in the location to be visited). It remains a serious disease and you are advised to protect yourself against mosquito bites as above, and to take prophylactic (preventive) drugs. Start taking the tablets a few days before exposure and continue to take 6 weeks after leaving the malaria zone. Remember to give drugs to babies and children also. The subject of malaria prevention is becoming more complex as the malaria parasite becomes immune to some of the older drugs. However, at the present time Proguanil (Paludrine), 100 mgs two tablets a day, should give sufficient protection. You can catch malaria even when taking these drugs, though it is unlikely. If you do develop symptoms (high fever, shivering, headaches), seek medical advice immediately.

If this is not possible and the likelihood of malaria is high the treatment is Chloroquine a single dose of 4 tablets (600 mgs) followed by two tablets (300 mgs) in 6 hrs and 300 mgs each day following. Pregnant women are particularly prone to malaria and should stick to Proguanil for prophylaxis. Chloroquine can also be used to prevent malaria on a weekly basis. The risk of malaria is obviously greater the further you move from cities and into rural areas with primitive facilities and standing water.

OTHER COMMON PROBLEMS

HEAT AND COLD

Full acclimatization to high temperatures takes about 2 weeks and during this period it is normal to feel relatively apathetic, especially if the relative humidity is high. Drink plenty of water (up to 15 litres a day are required when working physically hard in the tropics), use salt on your food and avoid extreme exertion. Tepid showers are more cooling than hot or cold ones. Large hats do not cool you down, but prevent sunburn. Remember that, especially in the mountains, there can be a large and sudden drop in temperature between sun and shade and between night and day, so dress accordingly. Loose fitting cotton clothes are still the best for hot weather.

INSECTS

These can be a great nuisance and some of course are carriers of serious diseases such as malaria, dengue fever, filariasis and various worm infections. The best way of keeping mosquitos away at night is to sleep off the ground with a mosquito net and to burn mosquito coils containing Pyrethrum. Aerosol sprays or a 'flit' gun may be effective as are insecticidal tablets which are heated on a mat which is plugged into the wall socket (if taking your own, check the voltage of the area you are visiting so that you can take an appliance that will work; similarly check that your electrical adaptor is suitable for the repellent's plug-Ed) The best repellents contain a high concentration of di-ethyl-toluamide. Clothes impregnated with the insecticide Permethrin or Deltamethrin are now becoming available, as are wide-meshed mosquito nets impregnated with the same substance. They are lighter to carry and less claustrophobic to sleep in.

Liquid is best for arms and face (care around eyes and make sure they don't dissolve the plastic of your spectacles or watch glass), aerosol spray on clothes and ankles deter mites and ticks. Liquid DET suspended in water can be used to impregnate cotton clothes and mosquito nets. If you are bitten, itching may be relieved by baking soda baths, anti-histamine tablets (care with alcohol or driving), corticosteroid creams (great care – never use if any hint of sepsis) or by judicious scratching. Calamine lotion and cream have limited effectiveness and anti-histamine creams (Anthisan) have a tendency to cause skin allergies and are therefore not generally recommended. Bites which become infected (commonly in the tropics) should be treated with a local antiseptic or antibiotic cream such as Cetrimide (Savlon), as should infected

scratches. Skin infestation with body lice, crabs and scabies are unfortunately easy to pick up. Use gamma benzene hexachloride for lice, and benzyl benzoate for scabies. Crotamiton cream (Eurax CIBA) alleviates itching and also kills a number of skin parasites. Malathion lotion 5% (Prioderm) is good for lice but avoid the highly toxic full strength Malathion.

INTESTINAL UPSETS

Most of the time these are due to the insanitary preparation of food so do not eat uncooked fish or vegetables or meat (especially pork), fruit with the skin off (always peel your fruit yourself) or food that is exposed to flies (especially salads.)

Drinking water

Tap water may be unsafe outside the major resort areas, especially in the rainy season. Filtered or bottled water is usually available and safe. If unsure how ice has been made, ask for a cold bottle.

Pasteurized or heat-treated milk is now widely available as is ice cream and yoghurt. Unpasteurized milk products including cheese are sources of Tuberculosis, Brucellosis, Listeria and food poisoning germs. You can render fresh milk safe by heating it to 62 degrees centigrade for 30 mins followed by rapid cooling, or by boiling it. Matured or processed cheeses are safer than fresh varieties.

At certain times of the year, some fish and shellfish concentrate non-infectious toxins from their environment and cause a kind of food poisoning. If the local authorities notify the public not to eat these foods, do not ignore the warning.

Diarrhoea

Diarrhoea is usually caused by eating food which is contaminated by food poisoning germs. Drinking water is rarely the culprit. Seawater or river water is more likely to be contaminated by sewage and so swimming in such dilute effluent can also be a cause. Infection with various organisms can give rise to diarrhoea, eg viruses, bacteria (eg Escherichia coli, probably the most common cause), protozoa (amoeba), salmonella and cholera. The diarrhoea may come on suddenly or rather slowly. It may or may nor be accompanied by vomiting or by severe abdominal pain and the passage of blood or mucus when it is called dysentery. How do you know which type you have and how to treat it?

If you can time the onset of the diarrhoea to the minute (acute) then it is probably due to a virus or a bacterium and/or the onset of dysentery. The treatment, in addition to rehydration is Ciprofloxacin 500 mgs every 12 hrs. The drug is now widely available as are various similar ones.

If the diarrhoea comes on slowly or intermittently (sub-acute) then it is more likely to be protozoal ie caused by an amoeba or giardia and antibiotics will have little effect. These cases are best treated by a doctor, as is any outbreak of diarrhoea continuing for more than 3 days. Sometimes blood is passed in sub-acute amoebic dysentery and for this you should certainly seek medical help. If this is not available then the best treatment is probably Tinidazole (Fasigyn) 1 tablet 4 times a day for 3 days. If there are severe stomach cramps, the following drugs may help but are not very useful in the management of acute diarrhoea: Loperamide (Imodium, Arret) and Diphenoxylate with Atropine (Lomotil). They should not be given to children.

Any kind of diarrhoea whether or not accompanied by vomiting responds well to the replacement of water and salts taken as frequent small sips of some kind of rehydration solution. There are preparatory preparations consisting of sachets of powder which you dissolve in boiled water, or you can make your own by adding half a teaspoonful of salt (3.5 grams) and 4 tablespoonfuls of sugar (40 grams) to a litre of boiled water.

Thus the lynchpins of treatment for diarrhoea are rest, fluid and salt replacement, antibiotics such as Ciprofloxacin for the bacterial types and special diagnostic tests and medical treatment for the amoeba and giardia infections. Salmonella infections and cholera can be devastating diseases and it would be wise to get to a hospital as soon as possible if these were suspected. Fasting, peculiar diets and the consumption of large quantities of yoghurt have not been found useful in calming travellers' diarrhoea or in rehabilitating inflamed bowels. Oral rehydration has on the other hand, especially in children, been a lifesaving technique and it should always be practised whatever other treatment you use. As there is some evidence that alcohol and milk might prolong diarrhoea they should probably be avoided during and immediately after an attack. Diarrhoea occurring day after day for long periods of time (chronic diarrhoea) is notoriously resistant to amateur attempts at treatment and again warrants proper diagnostic tests. There are ways of preventing travellers' diarrhoea for short periods of time by taking antibiotics, but this is not a foolproof technique and should not be used other than in exceptional circumstances. Doxycycline is possibly the best drug. Some preventatives such as Enterovioform can have serious side effects if taken for long periods.

SUNBURN

The burning power of the tropical sun is phenomenal. Always wear a wide brimmed hat and use some form of sun cream lotion on untanned skin. Normal temperate zone suntan lotions (protection factor up to 7) are not much good. You need to use the type designed specifically for the tropics or for mountaineers or skiers, with the highest protection factor. Lotions with a factor of 25 or 30 can be found on some islands. They are waterproof and well worth using for sailing or golf. Glare from the sun can cause conjunctivitis so wear sunglasses especially on tropical beaches.

SNAKE AND OTHER BITES

If you are unlucky enough to be bitten by a venomous snake, spider, scorpion, centipede or sea creature, try (within limits) to catch the animal for identification. The reactions to be expected are: fright, swelling, pain and bruising around the bite, soreness of the regional lymph glands, nausea, vomiting and fever. If any of the following symptoms supervene get the victim to a doctor without delay: numbness, tingling of the face, muscular spasms, convulsions, shortness of breath and haemorrhage. Commercial snake bite or scorpion sting kits are available, but are only useful for the specific type of snake or scorpion for which they are designed. The serum has to be given intravenously so is not much good unless you have had some practice in making injections into veins. If the bite is on a limb, immobilize the limb and apply a tight bandage between the bite and the body, releasing it for 90 seconds every 15 mins. Reassurance of the bitten person is very important because death from snake bite is in fact very rare. Do not slash the bite area and try to suck out the poison because this sort of heroism does more harm than good. Hospitals usually hold stocks of snakebite serum. Best precaution: do not walk in snake territory with bare feet, sandals, or shorts; in Guyana's interior, look out for snakes in the trees as well as on the ground. If swimming in an area where there are poisonous fish, such as stone or scorpion fish (also called by a variety of local names) or sea urchins on rocky coasts, tread carefully or wear plimsoles. The sting of such fish is intensely painful and this can be helped by immersing the stung part in water as hot as you can bear for as long as it remains painful. This is not always very practical and you must take care not to scald yourself, but it does work. Avoid spiders and scorpions by keeping your bed away from the wall, look under lavatory seats and inside your shoes in the morning. In the rare event of being bitten, consult a doctor.

THINGS TO WATCH OUT FOR

Remember that **rabies** is endemic in some countries including Trinidad and Tobago, Puerto Rico, Haiti, Grenada, and possibly more so in the Dominican Republic and Cuba. Avoid dogs that are behaving strangely and cover your toes at night to foil the vampire bats which also carry the disease. If you are bitten by a domestic or wild animal, don't leave things to chance. Scrub the wound with soap and water and/or disinfectant, try to have the animal captured (within limits) or at least determine its ownership where possible and seek medical assistance at once. The course of treatment depends on whether you have already been satisfactorily vaccinated against rabies. If you have (and this is worthwhile if you are spending lengths of time in developing countries) then some further doses of vaccine are all that is required. Human diploid cell vaccine is the best, but expensive: other, older kinds of vaccine such as the derived from duck embryos may be the only types available. These are effective, much cheaper and interchangeable generally with the human derived types. If not already vaccinated then anti- rabies serum (immunoglobulin) may be required in addition. It is wise to finish the course of treatment whether the animal survives or not.

Dengue fever is increasing worldwide, including throughout the Carribean. The more severe haemorrhagic dengue is much more of a problem for local people who have been exposed to the disease more than once. The treatment for simple dengue is painkillers and rest. For haemorrhagic dengue hospital treatment is necessary. There is no vaccine against the Aedes mosquito that carries the virus: you must just avoid mosquito bites.

Intestinal worms are common and the more serious ones such as **hookworm** can be contracted from walking bare foot on infested earth or beaches.

Schistosomiasis (Bilharzia) is caused by a parasite which lurks in lakes and slow-moving rivers infested with snails and can have serious consequences later. The main problem is in St Lucia.

Leptospirosis Various forms of leptospirosis occur in most of the Caribbean islands, transmitted by a bacterium which is excreted in rodent urine. Fresh water and moist soil harbour the organisms which enter the body through cuts and scratches. If you suffer from any form of prolonged fever, consult a doctor.

Prickly heat, a very common, intensely itchy rash, is avoided by frequent washing and by wearing loose clothing. It is helped by the use of talcum powder to allow the skin to dry thoroughly after washing. **Athletes Foot** and other fungal skin infections are best treated with sunshine and a proprietory preparation such as Tinaderm or Canestan.

WHEN YOU RETURN HOME

Remember to take your anti-malarial tablets for 6 weeks. If you have had attacks of diarrhoea, it is worth having a stool specimen tested in case you have picked up amoebic dysentery. If you have been living rough, a blood test may be worthwhile to detect worms and other parasites. If you have been exposed to bilharzia by swimming in lakes, etc, check by means of a blood test when you get home, but leave it for 6 weeks because the test is slow to become positive. Report any untoward symptoms to your doctor and tell the doctor exactly where you have been and, if you know, what is the likelihood of diseases to which you were exposed.

BASIC SUPPLIES

The following items you may find useful to take with you from home: sunglasses (if you use clip-on sunglasses, take a spare pair – Ed), ear plugs, suntan cream, insect repellent, flea powder, mosquito net, coils or tablets, tampons, condoms, contraceptives, water sterilizing tablets, anti-malaria tablets, anti-infective ointment, dusting powder for feet, travel sickness pills, antacids tablets, anti-diarrhoea tablets, sachets of rehydration salts and a first aid kit.

FURTHER INFORMATION

Further information on health risks abroad, vaccinations, etc, may be available from a local travel clinic. If you wish to take specific drugs with you such as antibiotics, these are best prescribed by your own doctor. Beware, however, that not all doctors can be experts on the health problems of tropical countries. More detailed or more up-to-date information than local doctors can provide are available from various sources.

In the UK there are hospital departments specializing in tropical diseases in London, Liverpool, Birmingham and Glasgow and the Malaria Reference Laboratory at the London School of Hygiene and Tropical Medicine provides free advice about malaria, T 0891-600350. In the USA the local public health services can give such information and information is available centrally from the Centres for Disease Control in Atlanta, T (404) 332 4559.

There are in addition computerized databases which can be accessed for a specific destination, up to the minute information. In the UK there is MASTA (Medical Advisory Service to Travellers Abroad), T 0171-631 4408, Tx 895 3474, F 0171-436 5389 and Travax (Glasgow, T 0141-946 7120, extension 247).

Further information on medical problems overseas can be obtained from the book by Richard Dawood (Editor) – *Travellers Health, How to Stay Healthy Abroad*, Oxford University Press, 1992, £7.99. We strongly recommend this revised and updated edition, especially to the intrepid traveller heading for the more out of the way places. General advice is also available in the UK in *Health Advice for Travellers* published jointly by the Department of Health and the Central Office of Information available free from your UK Travel Agent.

The above information has been compiled for us by Dr David Snashall, who is presently Senior Lecturer in Occupational Health at the United Medical Schools of Guys and St Thomas' Hospitals in London and Chief Medical Advisor of the British Foreign and Commonwealth Office. He has travelled extensively in Central and South America, worked in Peru and in East Africa and keeps in close touch with developments in preventative and tropical medicine.

Horizons
The land and the sea

PRE-COLUMBIAN CIVILIZATIONS

The recorded history of the Caribbean islands begins with the arrival of Christopher Columbus' fleet in 1492. Our knowledge of the native peoples who inhabited the islands before and at the time of his arrival is largely derived from the accounts of contemporary Spanish writers and from archaeological examinations as there is no evidence of indigenous written records.

The Amerindians encountered by Columbus in the Greater Antilles had no overall tribal name but organized themselves in a series of villages or local chief-doms, each of which had its own tribal name. The name now used, Arawak, was not in use then. The term Arawak was used by the Indians of the Guianas, a group of whom had spread into Trinidad, but their territory was not explored until nearly another century later. The use of the generic term, Arawak, to describe the Indians Columbus encountered, arose because of linguistic similarities with the Arawaks of the mainland. It is therefore surmised that migration took place many centuries before Columbus' arrival, but the two groups were not in contact at that time. The time of the latest migration from the mainland, and consequently the existence of the island Arawaks, is in dispute, with some academics tracing it to about the time of Christ (the arrival of the Saladoids) and others to AD 1000 (the Ostionoids).

The inhabitants of the Bahamas were generally referred to as Lucayans, and those of the Greater Antilles as Tainos, but there were many sub-groupings. The inhabitants of the Lesser Antilles were, however, referred to as Carib and were described to Columbus as an aggressive tribe which sacrificed and sometimes ate the prisoners they captured in battle. It was from them that the Caribbean gets its name and from which the word cannibal is derived.

The earliest known inhabitants of the region, the Siboneys, migrated from Florida (some say Mexico) and spread throughout the Bahamas and the major islands. Most archaeological evidence of their settlements has been found near the shore, along bays or streams, where they lived in small groups. The largest discovered settlement has been one of 100 inhabitants in Cuba. They were hunters and gatherers, living on fish and other seafood, small rodents, iguanas, snakes and birds. They gathered roots and wild fruits, such as guava, guanabana and mamey, but did not cultivate plants. They worked with primitive tools made out of stone, shell, bone or wood, for hammering, chipping or scraping, but had no knowledge of pottery. The Siboneys were eventually absorbed by the advance of the Arawaks migrating from the S, who had made more technological advances in agriculture, arts and crafts.

The people now known as Arawaks migrated from the Guianas to Trinidad and on through the island arc to Cuba. Their population expanded because of the natural fertility of the islands and the abundance of fruit and seafood, helped by their agricultural skills in cultivating and improving wild plants and their excellent boatbuilding and fishing techniques. They were healthy, tall, good looking and lived to a ripe old age. It is estimated that up to 8 million may have lived on the island of Hispaniola alone, but there was always plenty of food for all.

Their society was essentially communal and organized around families. The smaller islands were particularly egalitarian, but in the larger ones, where village communities of extended families numbered up to 500 people, there was an incipient class structure. Typically, each village had a headman, called a *cacique*, whose duty it was to represent the village when dealing with other tribes, to settle family disputes and organize defence. However, he had no powers of coercion and was often little more than a nominal head. The position was largely hereditary, with the eldest son of the eldest sister having rights of succession, but women could and did become *caciques*. In the larger communities, there was some delegation of responsibility to the senior men, but economic activities were usually organized along family lines, and their power was limited.

The division of labour was usually based on age and sex. The men would clear and prepare the land for agriculture and be responsible for defence of the village, while women cultivated the crops and were the major food producers, also making items such as mats, baskets, bowls and fishing nets. Women were in charge of raising the children, especially the girls, while the men taught the boys traditional customs, skills and rites.

The Tainos hunted for some of their food, but fishing was more important and most of their settlements were close to the sea. Fish and shellfish were their main sources of protein and they had many different ways of catching them, from hands, baskets or nets to poisoning, shooting or line fishing. Cassava was a staple food, which they had successfully learned to leach of its poisonous juice. They also grew yams, maize, cotton, arrowroot, peanuts, beans, cocoa and spices, rotating their crops to prevent soil erosion. It is documented that in Jamaica they had three harvests of maize annually, using maize and cassava to make breads, cakes and beer.

Cotton was used to make clothing and hammocks (never before seen by Europeans), while the calabash tree was used to make ropes and cords, baskets and roofing. Plants were used for medicinal and spiritual purposes, and cosmetics such as face and body paint. Also important, both to the Arawaks and later to the Europeans, was the cultivation of tobacco, as a drug and as a means of exchange.

They had no writing, no beasts of burden, no wheeled vehicles and no hard metals, although they did have some alluvial gold for personal ornament. The abundance of food allowed them time to develop their arts and crafts and they were skilled in woodwork and pottery. They had polished stone tools, but also carved shell implements for manioc preparation or as fishhooks. Coral manioc graters have also been found. Their boatbuilding techniques were noted by Columbus, who marvelled at their canoes of up to 75 ft in length, carrying up to 50 people, made of a single tree trunk in one piece. It took 2 months to fell a tree by gradually burning and chipping it down, and many more to make the canoe.

The Arawaks had three main deities, evidence of which have been found in stone and conch carvings in many of the Lesser Antilles as well as the well populated Greater Antilles, although their relative importance varied according to the island. The principal male god was Yocahú, *yoca* being the word for cassava and *hú* meaning 'giver of'. It is believed that the Indians associated this deity's power to provide cassava with the mystery of the volcanoes, for all the carvings, the earliest out of shells and the later ones of stone, are conical. The Yocahú cult was wiped out in the Lesser Antilles by the invading Caribs, and in the Greater Antilles by the Spaniards, but it is thought to have existed from about 200 AD.

The main female diety was a fertility goddess, often referred to as Atabeyra, but she is thought to have had several names relating to her other roles as goddess of the moon, mother of the sea, the tides and the springs, and the goddess of childbirth. In carvings she is usually depicted as a squatting figure with her hands up to her chin, sometimes in the act of giving birth.

A third deity is a dog god, named Opiyel-Guaobiran, meaning 'the dog deity who takes care of the souls of the immediately deceased and is the son of the spirit of darkness'. Again, carvings of a dog's head or whole body have been found of shell or stone, which were often used to induce narcotic trances. Many of the carvings have holes and Y-shaped passages which would have been put to the nose to snuff narcotics and induce a religious trance in the shaman or priest, who could then ascertain the status of a departed soul for a recently bereaved relative.

One custom which aroused interest in the Spaniards was the ball game, not only for the sport and its ceremonial features, but because the ball was made of rubber and bounced, a phenomenon which had not previously been seen in Europe. Catholicism soon eradicated the game, but archaeological remains have been found in several islands, notably in Puerto Rico, but also in Hispaniola. Excavations in the Greater Antilles have revealed earth embankments and rows of elongated upright stones surrounding plazas or courts, pavements and stone balls. These are called *bateyes, juegos de indios, juegos de bola, cercados* or *corrales de indios. Batey* was the aboriginal name for the ball game, the rubber ball itself and also the court where it was played. The word is still used to designate the cleared area in front of houses in the country.

The ball game had religious and ceremonial significance but it was a sport and bets and wagers were important. It was played by two teams of up to 20 or 30 players, who had to keep the ball in the air by means of their hips, shoulders, heads, elbows and other parts of their body, but never with their hands. The aim was to bounce the ball in this manner to the opposing team until it hit the ground. Men and women played, but not usually in mixed sex games. Great athleticism was required and it is clear that the players practised hard to perfect their skill, several, smaller practice courts having been built in larger settlements. The game was sometimes played before the village made an important decision, and the prize could be a sacrificial victim, usually a prisoner, granted to the victor.

In 1492 Arawaks inhabited all the greater islands of the Caribbean, but in Puerto Rico they were being invaded by the Caribs who had pushed N through the Lesser Antilles, stealing their women and enslaving or killing the men. The Caribs had also originated in South America, from around the Orinoco delta. In their migration N through the Caribbean islands they proved to be fierce warriors and their raids on the Arawak settlements were feared. Many of their women were captured Arawaks, and it was they who cultivated the land and performed the domestic chores. Polygamy was common, encouraged by the surplus of women resulting from the raids, and the Arawak female influence on Carib culture was strong.

Despite rumours of cannibalism reported to Columbus by frightened Arawaks, there appears to be no direct evidence of the practice, although the Spaniards took it seriously enough to use it as an excuse to justify taking slaves. After some unfortunate encounters, colonizers left the Caribs alone for many years. The Arawaks, on the other hand, were soon wiped out by disease, cruelty and murder. The Spanish invaders exacted tribute and forced labour while allowing their herds of cattle and pigs to destroy the Indians' unfenced fields and clearings. Transportation to the mines resulted in shifts in the native population which could not be fed from the surrounding areas and starvation became common. Lack of labour in the Greater Antilles led to slave raids on the Lucayans in the Bahamas, but they also died or committed collective suicide. They felt that their gods had deserted them and there was nowhere for them to retreat or escape. Today there are no full-blooded Arawaks and only some 2,000 Caribs are left on Dominica (there has been no continuity of Carib language or religious belief on Dominica). The 500 years since Columbus' arrival have served to obliterate practically all the evidence of the indigenous civilization.

THE CONTEMPORARY CARIBBEAN

The decisive date in the shaping of the modern Caribbean was 1492, when Christopher Columbus successfully crossed the Atlantic to make landfall in the Antilles. Although Spain did not exert its influence here to the same degree as on the American mainland, the way was open for Europeans to follow Columbus, take possession of, fight over and exploit the islands for profit. Over the following 5 centuries, the population of the region has been imported and almost all traces of the precolumbian past have been removed. Similarly, the majority of food and cash crops grown have been transplanted from elsewhere.

At one stage, the islands were some of the most valuable colonies ever known, but little of the wealth they generated stayed in the region. Being for the most part small, the territories still depend on the outside world for their prosperity (commodity exports, tourism), but with limited regional organization and economic imbalances there is great inequality of reward. Politically the region is disunited. Its own major events, like the Haitian and Cuban Revolutions, the movement towards black consciousness, have had tremendous, lasting impact outside their immediate realm, but at the same time have been engulfed in wider, global concerns.

The culture that the immigrants brought with them is now confronted by influences of global media systems. Ease of travel has also brought cultural pressures, not solely from the incoming tourist, but also from the large number of emigrants who, having sought work abroad, bring home the culture of their adopted countries. Conversely, emigration, the result of the unemployment which followed the decline of labour intensive agriculture, takes Caribbean culture to Europe and North America. At the same time, though, it causes a social structure which is heavily biased towards female heads of families when the men go elsewhere to work.

Yet for all the new cultural clashes, which build up on top of older ones (French spoken on 'English' islands, islands divided between nations), the struggle for a Caribbean identity continues, particularly in the work of writers and artists. Different colours and faiths coexist; the African and European mix to make some of the most vibrant music; the goal of the Jamaican national motto applies to all: "Out of many, one people".

CARIBBEAN GEOLOGY

The Caribbean Sea is geologically separate from the North and South American continents. Together with Central America, it forms a tectonic plate which is moving W at about 4 cm a year. At the same time, the North American and South American plates, which lie under the continents and the eastern half of the Atlantic Ocean, are moving W.

Most of the Caribbean islands are close to the boundaries of the Caribbean plate. Plate boundaries are geologically active; this is why most parts of the Caribbean experience earthquakes from time to time, and why there are a number of active volcanoes in the region.

The Windward islands, along the eastern boundary of the plate, are the most volcanically active area. This is because they lie over a subduction zone, where the Caribbean plate is being pushed E, over the edge of the Atlantic portions of the North American and South American plates. Sediments from the ocean floor are drawn down below the surface. They melt, and move up towards the surface as magma. Where a plume of magma reaches the surface, a volcanic island is formed.

There are active volcanoes on Montserrat (where the local population had to be evacuated from the S to the N several times in 1995-96 because of eruptions). St Vincent and Guadeloupe (both called the Soufrière, because of the strong smell of sulphur); and Martinique, of course, has Mont Pelée, which wiped out the city of St Pierre on 8 May 1902. There is also a submarine volcano with the picturesque name of Kick 'Em Jenny, to the N of Grenada.

All the Windwards, and most of the Leeward Islands, have clear signs of geologically recent volcanic activity, and could become active again in the future. There are recognisable volcanic craters, hot springs, solfataras (of which St Lucia's famous 'drive-in-volcano', also called Soufrière, is one example), and the famous 'boiling lake' on Dominica.

Barbados is not a volcanic island. It lies more directly on the plate boundary, and is formed by a wedge of sediments which are being pushed upwards as the plates move together. The surface rocks in most of Barbados are the remains of old coral reefs which grew as the water over this wedge of sediments became shallow. The eastern part of Guadeloupe, Grande Terre, and the small island of Marie Galante were formed in much the same way.

The oldest rocks in the Greater Antilles: Jamaica, Hispaniola, and Puerto Rico, were formed about 70 million years ago, when the Caribbean plate was moving N, and there was a line of volcanic islands along the plate boundary. There are no active volcanoes in this part of the Caribbean now, because the plate is no longer moving N. But there is intense faulting and fracturing of the crust as the Caribbean plate moves E, past the southern boundary of the North American plate. This faulting has thrust these three large islands up above sea level. The rocks in the Greater Antilles have also been folded by earth movements. The combination of folding and faulting has produced a hilly and sometimes mountainous landscape.

Large areas of Puerto Rico and Jamaica are also covered by limestone, which was formed about 30 million years ago when this part of the earth's crust was below sea level. The island of Jamaica is now being gradually tilted to the S – the N coast is being pushed up above sea level, and the S drowned. Off the coast of southern Jamaica, there are large areas of relatively shallow sea which were land when sea levels were about 30m lower than they now are, during the ice ages of the past million years.

Cuba and the Bahamas are part of the North American plate. Southern Cuba is mountainous, and strongly affected by the plate boundary. But the rest of Cuba and the Bahamas are geologically quite stable, and are formed mainly of limestone.

The Bahamas are on a section of crust which has been stretched and weakened over the past 120 million years as the North American plate moved away from the African plate and the Atlantic Ocean became wider. For the whole of this period, the Bahamas has formed a shallow tropical sea. Evaporation from the warm sea surface causes the concentration of calcium carbonate on the water to become very high, so tiny grains of this mineral, ooliths, form and collect on the sea bed. These grains form a rock known as oolite. The Bahama Banks are a platform of oolite several kilometres thick. During the glacial periods, sea level fell, and the Banks became enormous islands. Sand dunes which formed in the ice ages solidified, and remained above sea level when the ice melted and the sea rose again, to form the present-day Bahama islands.

To the S, Trinidad and Tobago were joined to the South American mainland when sea levels were low in the ice ages, hence the richness and variety of their plant and animal life. The boundary between the South American and Caribbean plate actually runs through N Trinidad, so these islands are another earthquake zone. There are also signs of early volcanic activity on Tobago, though not from a geologically recent period.

Many Caribbean coastlines are being pushed upwards by earth movements: Barbados, the N coast of Jamaica, NW Haiti for example. Along many of these emergent coastlines, the land rises in a series of steps, each one marking an old coastline and a fossil coral reef. Where the land is being slowly submerged, as along the S coast of Jamaica, in the Bahamas, Antigua, and many of the Windwards, there is an indented coast with many offshore islands. Some shallow bays in these areas are being filled in by mud and other sediments; this makes interesting wetland wildlife.

The Guianas on the South American mainland are by contrast geologically very stable, and are formed of ancient rocks several thousands of millions of years old. Guyana's gold and diamonds are derived from these ancient rocks. In the coastal belt of the Guianas, however, there is a layer of geologically more recent river-borne and marine sediments over the ancient rocks. This includes fertile silt, disastrously infertile white silica sands, and, below the surface in some areas, valuable bauxite deposits.

The above information has been compiled for us by Mark Wilson, teacher of geography and journalist, currently based in Trinidad.

FLORA AND FAUNA

For many travellers, a trip to the Caribbean offers a first glimpse of the tropics, complete with luxurian vegetation and exotic wildlife. Images of untouched beaches and rainforest form a major selling point of many travel brochures. In fact there is very little 'untouched' wilderness left and what visitors see is an environment that has been affected by the activities of man (this is not the case in the interior of the Guianas, where much forest is untouched). Forestry, agriculture, fisheries and increasingly tourism have all helped to mould the modern landscape and natural heritage of the Caribbean. However, there is still much of interest to see, and it is true to say that small islands can combine a variety of habitats within a limited area. On many islands, it is possible to move between the coastal reefs and beaches through thorn scrub and plantation into rainforest within a matter of miles. Increasingly, the complexity and fragility of island ecosystems is being appreciated and fortunately most countries have recognized the value of balancing development and the protection of the natural environment and have begun to develop national parks and protected areas programmes. Many islands also have active conservation societies or national wildlife trusts (see page 11 below).

Wildlife

Over long periods of time, islands tend to develop their own unique flora and fauna. These endemic species add to the interest of wildlife and natural history tours. The St Lucia parrot and Dominica's sisserou have become a regular part of the tour circuit of these islands, and have undoubtedly benefited from the interest that tourists have shown in their plight. Details of National Parks and wildlife are included under the specific island chapter headings (Fauna and Flora). This section provides a broad overview of the range of animals, plants and habitats that are to be found in the region.

Mammals

Mammals are not particularly good colonizers of small islands and this has resulted in a general scarcity of species in the Caribbean. Many of the more commonly seen species (mongoose, agouti, opossum, and some of the monkeys) were introduced by man. Bats are the one exception to this rule and most islands have several native species. Again, in the forested interior of the Guianas there are many mammals associated with rain forest habitats. There are also the animals of the S savannas and mountains.

Mongoose were introduced to many islands to control snakes, they have also preyed on many birds, reptiles and other animals and have had a devastating effect on native fauna.

Of the monkeys, the green monkeys of Barbados, Grenada and St Kitts and Nevis were introduced from West Africa in the 17th century. Similarly, rhesus monkeys have been introduced to Desecheo Island off Puerto Rico. The red howler monkeys on Trinidad are native to the island as are several other mammals including the brocket deer,

squirrel and armadillo. These species have managed to colonize from nearby Venezuela.

There are endemic mammals on some islands for example the pygmy racoon, a species of coati and 'jabli' in Cozumel and possibly the Guadeloupe racoon.

Sailors may encounter marine mammals including dolphin, porpoise and whales. Between Nov and Dec hump back whales migrate through the Turks and Caicos Passage on their way to the Silver Banks breeding grounds off the Dominican Republic. The ungainly manatee, or sea cow, can still be seen in some coastal areas in the Greater Antilles (especially Jamaica, Cuba – Zapata Peninsula – and Puerto Rico) although it is becoming increasingly uncommon.

Birds

It is the birds perhaps more than any other group of animals that excite the most interest from visitors to the region. Many islands have their own endemic species such as the Grenada dove, yellow-billed parrot and 24 other species in Jamaica and Guadeloupe woodpecker. The islands also act as important stepping stones in the migration of many birds through the Americas. As a result, the region is highly regarded by ornithologists and there are several internationally important nature reserves.

Trinidad and Tobago demonstrate the influence of the nearby South American mainland. While they have no endemic species they still support at least 433 species and the Asa Wright Centre is regarded as one of the premier bird watching sites in the World. At the other end of the Caribbean, Inagua (Bahamas) is the site of the world's largest flamingo colony at Lake Windsor. There is also an important flamingo colony on Bonaire in the S Caribbean.

Many of the endemic species have become rare as a result of man's activities. Habitat destruction, introduction of new species (especially the mongoose) and hunting for food and the international pet trade have all had an effect. Parrots in particular have suffered as a result of these activities. Fortunately, measures are now being undertaken to protect the birds and their habitats on many islands (eg Bahamas, Jamaica, Dominica, Puerto Rico and St Lucia).

Reptiles

Lizards and geckos are common on virtually all the islands in the region and may even be seen on very small offshore islets. There are also a number of species of snakes, iguanas and turtles scattered throughout the region. Many are restricted to one island and Jamaica has at least 27 island endemics including several species of galliwasp. The vast majority of reptiles found in the region are completely harmless to man although there are strong superstitions about the geckos (*mabouya*) and of course the snakes. For example, the skin and fat of boa constrictors (*tête chien*) are used for bush remedies on some of the Windward Islands.

The fer de lance snake (St Lucia, Martinique and also South America), deserves to be treated with extreme caution; although the bite is not usually lethal, hospitalization is required. It is found in isolated areas of dry scrubland and river valley. The best protection is to wear long trousers and stout boots and to avoid walking in these areas at night. Local advice should be sought if in doubt.

Iguanas are still found on many islands although they have declined as a result of hunting throughout the region. Although of fearsome appearance, they are herbivorous and spend much of their time in trees and low scrub feeding on leaves and trying to avoid man.

Marine turtles including the loggerhead, leatherback, hawksbill and green turtles are found throughout Caribbean waters and on the coasts of the Guianas and they may occasionally be seen by divers and snorkellers. Females come ashore on isolated sandy beaches between the months of May and Aug to lay eggs. There may be opportunities for assisting natural history and wildlife societies (St Lucia Naturalists Society, Fish and Wildlife Dept in the US Virgin Islands) in their turtle watches, to record numbers and locations of nests and to protect the turtles from poachers. There is a large commercial breeding programme for green turtles in the Cayman Islands. Freshwater turtles are also found on some islands including Jamaica and Cat Island (Bahamas). Caiman have been introduced to Puerto Rico and are also found on Cuba and the Dominican Republic.

Many species of reptile are now protected in the region (especially the marine turtles and iguana) and reserves have been specifically established to protect them. For example, the Maria Islands Nature Reserve on St Lucia is home to the St Lucia ground lizard and grass snake. The latter is possibly the rarest snake in the world with an estimated population of 150 individuals.

Amphibians

Frogs and toads are common in a variety of shapes and colours. There are generally more species on the larger islands (Greater Antilles and Trinidad; there are also many in the Guianas). The Cuban pygmy frog is described as the world's smallest frog, while at the other end of the scale, the mountain chicken of Dominica and Montserrat is probably the largest frog in the region. Its name relates to its supposed flavour. The call of the piping frogs (*eleutherodactylus spp*) is often mistaken for a bird and these small animals are common throughout the Lesser Antilles, becoming especially vocal at night and after rain. The largest and most visible amphibian is probably the marine toad which has been introduced to islands throughout the region in an attempt to control insects and other invertebrate pests. The male toads use flat exposed areas from which to display, often roads. Unfortunately, they have not evolved to deal with the car yet and as a result many are killed.

Invertebrates

This group includes the insects, molluscs, spiders and a host of other animals that have no backbones. For first time travellers to the tropics, the huge range of invertebrates can seem daunting and it is estimated that there are at least 290 species of butterfly in the Caribbean. No one knows how many species of beetles, bugs or mollusc there are.

Of the butterflies, the swallowtails are perhaps the most spectacular, with several species being found in the Greater Antilles (especially Cuba). However the other islands also have large colourful butterflies including the monarch and flambeau which are present throughout the region. Another insect of note is the hercules beetle, reportedly the world's largest beetle which may reach a length of 12cm and is occasionally found in rainforest in the Lesser Antilles.

Land and freshwater crabs inhabit a range of environments from the rainforest (eg bromeliad crab from Jamaica) to the dry coastal areas (many species of hermit crab). Tarantula spiders are also fairly common, although they are nocturnal and rarely seen. Their bite is painful but, in most of the species found in the region, no worse than a bee sting. Of far more concern are the large centipedes (up to 15 cm long) that can inflict a nasty and painful bite with their pincers. They are mostly restricted to the dry coastal areas and are most active at night. Black widow spiders are also present on some of the islands in the Greater Antilles. Fortunately they are rarely encountered by the traveller.

Marine Environments (Beaches, Coral Reef, Sea Cliffs)

A diving or snorkelling trip over a tropical reef allows a first hand experience of this habitat's diversity of wildlife. There are a number of good field guides to reef fish and animals (see book list) and some are even printed on waterproof paper. Alternatively, glass bottomed boats sail over some sites (Buccoo Reef, Tobago), and there are underwater trails which identify types of corals and marine habitats (eg Buck Island and US Virgin Islands).

Amongst the commonest fish are the grunts, butterfly, soldier, squirrel and angel fish. Tiny damsel fish are very territorial and may even attempt to nip swimmers who venture too close to their territories (more surprising than painful).

There are over fifty species of hard coral (the form that builds reefs) with a variety of sizes and colours. Amongst the most dramatic are the stagshorn and elkhorn corals which are found on the more exposed outer reefs. Brain coral forms massive round structures up to 2m high and Pillar coral forms columns that may also reach 2m in height. Soft corals, which include black corals, sea fans and gorgonians, colonize the surface of the hard coral adding colour and variety. Associated with these structures is a host of animals and plants. Spiny lobsters may be seen lurking in holes and crevices along with other crustaceans and reef fish. The patches of sand between outcrops of coral provide suitable habitat for conch and other shellfish. Some islands now restrict the collection and sale of corals (especially black corals) and there are also legal restrictions on the sale of black corals under CITES. Overfishing is affecting conch and lobster in some parts and there are reports of them being taken from the sea too small.

The delights of swimming on a coral reef need to be tempered by a few words of caution. Many people assume the water will be seething with sharks, however these animals are fairly uncommon in nearshore waters and the species most likely to be encountered is the nurse shark, which is harmless unless provoked or cornered. Other fish to keep an eye open for include the scorpion fish with its poisonous dorsal spines; it frequently lies stationary on coral reefs onto which the incautious can blunder. Finally moray eels may be encountered, a fearsome looking fish, but harmless unless provoked at which point they can inflict serious bites. Of far more concern should be the variety of stinging invertebrates that are found on coral reefs. The most obvious is fire coral which comes in a range of shapes and sizes but is recognizable by the white tips to its branches. In addition, many corals have sharp edges and branches that can graze and cut. Another common group of stinging invertebrates are the fire worms which have white bristles along the sides of their bodies. As with the fire coral, these can inflict a painful sting if handled or brushed against. Large black sea urchins are also common on some reefs and their spines can penetrate unprotected skin very easily. The best advice when observing coral reefs and their wildlife is to look, but don't touch.

Other coastal habitats that may have interesting wildlife include beaches and sea cliffs. Some islands, especially those in the southern part of the Caribbean, have spectacular cliffs and offshore islets. These are home to large flocks of sea birds including the piratical frigate bird which chases smaller birds, forcing them to disgorge their catch; another notable species is the tropic bird with its streamer like tail feathers. The cliffs may also provide dry sandy soils for the large range of Caribbean cacti, including prickly pear (opuntia sp) and the Turks head cactus.

Wetlands (Rivers, Swamps, Mangroves)

Wetlands include a wide range of fresh and brackish water habitats such as rivers, marsh and mangroves. They are important for many species of bird, as well

as fish. Unfortunately they are also home to an array of biting insects, including mosquitos which can be unpleasant though only a serious problem in Hispaniola where malaria is still present.

Important coastal wetlands include the Baie de Fort de France (Martinique), the Cabrits Swamp (Dominica), Caroni (Trinidad), Negril and Black Morass (Jamaica). These sites all support large flocks of migratory and resident birds including waders, herons, egrets and ducks. In addition, some of the mangroves in the Greater Antilles also provide habitats for manatee, and the Negril and Black Morass has a population of American crocodiles. Large freshwater lakes are less common although Grenada, Dominica and St Vincent all have volcanic crater lakes and these are used by migratory waders and ducks as well as kingfishers.

Woodland and Forest (Thorn Scrub, Plantations, Rainforest)

There is little if any primary rainforest left in the Caribbean Islands, although there may be small patches in Guadeloupe. Nevertheless, many of the islands still have large areas of good secondary forest which has only suffered from a limited amount of selective felling for commercially valuable wood (eg gommier, balata and blue mahoe). This does not apply to the Guianas on mainland South America. The widest selection of woods can be found in Guyana.

Martinique has some of the largest tracts of forest left in the Caribbean (eg rainforest at Piton du Carbet, cloud forest on Mt Pelée, dry woodland in the S). Many other islands also have accessible forest, although you should always use a local guide if venturing off the beaten track.

The Caribbean rainforests are not as diverse as those on the South and Central American mainland, however they still support a very large number of plant species many of which are endemic (Jamaica has over 3,000 species of which 800 are endemic). The orchids and bromeliads are particularly impressive in many forests and it is not unusual to see trees festooned with both these groups. The wildlife of the rainforest includes both native and introduced species, although they are often difficult to see in the rather shady conditions. Agouti, boa constrictor, monkeys and opossum may be seen, but it is the bird life that is most evident. Hummingbirds, vireos, thrashers, todies and others are all found along with parrots, which are perhaps the group most associated with this habitat. Early morning and evening provide the best times for birdwatching.

Plantations of commercial timber (blue mahoe, Caribbean pine, teak, mahogany and others) have been established in many places. These reduce pressure on natural forest and help to protect watersheds and soil. They are also valuable for wildlife and some species have adapted to them with alacrity (cg hummingbirds in blue mahoe plantation).

Closer to the coasts, dry scrub woodland often predominates. The trees may lose their leaves during the dry season. One of the most recognizable of the trees in this woodland is the turpentine tree, also known as the tourist tree because of its red peeling bark!

Bush medicines and herbal remedies are still used in the countryside although less so than previously. Leaves and bark can be seen for sale in markets.

Books: Field Guides

There are not many good books on Caribbean wildlife. The following are worth looking for: *Tropical Wild Flowers*, V E Graham (Hulton Educational Publications); *Caribbean Wild Plants and their Uses*, P Honeychurch (Macmillan); *Birds of the West Indies*, J Bond (Collins); *A Guide to the Birds of Trinidad and Tobago*, Richard ffrench (Horowood); *Flora and Fauna of the Caribbean*, P Bacon (Key Caribbean Publications, PO Box 21, Port of Spain, Trinidad); *Fishwatchers Guide to West Atlantic Coral Reefs*, C C Chaplin (Horowood Books

– some printed on plastic paper for use underwater); *Guide to Corals and Fishes of Florida, the Bahamas and the Caribbean*, I Greenberg (Seahawk Press).

Macmillan also produce short field guides on *The Flowers of the Caribbean, The Fishes of the Caribbean, Fishes of the Caribbean Reefs, Marine Life of the Caribbean, Butterflies and Other Insects of the Caribbean*; and the *Ephemeral Isles, a Natural History of the Bahamas*.

In Search of Flowers of the Amazon Forest, by Margaret Mee (Nonesuch Expeditions Ltd, 48 Station Rd, Woodbridge, Suffolk, UK). *A Guide to the Birds of Venezuela*, by R Meyer de Schauensee and W H Phelps Jr (Princeton).

Specialist reading

For the more serious naturalist, there are several detailed reviews of the natural history and conservation of wildlife in the Caribbean. Among the best and most widely available are the *Floristic Inventory of Tropical Countries* (World Wide Fund for Nature) which contains a short report on the Caribbean; *Biodiversity and Conservation in the Caribbean*, Profiles of selected islands (includes Cozumel, Dominica, Grenada, Guadeloupe, Jamaica, Martinique, Montserrat, Puerto Rico, St Lucia, St Vincent, San Andrés) published by the International Council for Bird Preservation, ISBN 0 946888 14 0; *Fragments of Paradise* which covers conservation issues in the UK dependencies (Pisces Publications, ISBN 0 9508245 5 0). *A Field Guide to the Coral Reefs of the Caribbean and Florida including Bermuda and the Bahamas*, Peterson Field Guides Series no 27 (Houghton Mifflin Company). *Coral Reefs of the World* – Volume I, S Wells et al (IUCN)

The Natural History Book Service (T UK 01803 865913) holds a very large stock of wildlife and conservation books on the Caribbean.

The above information has been compiled for us by Mark Eckstein of David Bellamy Associates, Durham, UK, with additional information from Mark Wilson.

WHALE AND DOLPHIN WATCHING

Whale and dolphin watching, long popular around North America, is starting to take off in the Caribbean, too. There are three main attractions: the **humpback whales**, the acrobatic whale-watchers' favourite, come to the Caribbean during the winter to mate, raise their calves and sing; the **sperm whales** are resident in various spots around the Caribbean but are easiest to see along the W coast of Dominica and Martinique; **spotted** and other **dolphin** species travel in large herds and are resident around many of the reefs, mangrove forests and offshore fishing banks. It is possible to see whales and dolphins from land and on some regular ferries, and even on air flights between the islands, but the best way to encounter them close-up is on boat tours. Some of these are general marine nature or even birding tours that include whales and dolphins. Others are specialized tours offered by diving, sportfishing or new eco-tourism ventures. Following is a guide to the best of whale and dolphin watching in the waters covered by this *Handbook*.

In the **Bahamas**, tours to meet and sometimes swim with Atlantic spotted dolphins are offered May to September. The tours leave either from E Florida ports or from West End, on Grand Bahama Island. Cost is about US$1,500 for a week on the 62 ft catamaran *Stenella* and various other boats.

Two of the best tour operators are Wild Dolphin Project, PO Box 8436, Jupiter, FL 33468 USA, T 407-575-5660 or Oceanic Society Expeditions, Fort Mason Center, Building E, San Francisco, CA 94123 USA, T 415-441-1106. Others include: Bottomtime Adventures, PO Box 11919, Fort Lauderdale, FL 33339 USA, T 800-234-8464; Jennifer Marie, Royal Palm Yacht Club, 629 NE 3rd, Dania, FL 33339 USA, T 305-922-2351; Dream Team, PO Box 3271, Indialantic, FL 32903 USA, T 407-723-9312; Sea Fever, PO Box 39-8276, Miami Beach, FL 33139 USA, T 305-531-3483; Gulfstream Eagle, 278 Sussex Circle, Jupiter FL 33458 USA, T 407-575-9800; Crown Cruise Lines, Box 3000, Boca Raton, FL 33431 USA, T 407-394-7450; Coral Star, 17 Fort Royal Isle, Fort Lauderdale, FL 33308 USA, T 305-563-1711; Innerspace Visions, 6800 SW 40th St, Suite 499, Miami, FL 33155 USA, T 305-669-0118; Shearwater Excursions, 113 Timber Run E, West Palm Beach, FL 33407 USA, T 407-842-4744.

Extended whale-watching trips with researchers and a chance to help on whale surveys to determine the abundance and distribution of large whales in the Bahamas are offered by Earthwatch out of Hope Town, Elbow Cay. Earthwatch, 680 Mount Auburn St, PO Box 403, Watertown, MA 02272 USA, T 617-926-8200.

From the **Turks & Caicos Islands**, humpbacks can be found offshore with bottlenose and other dolphins which are also seen close to shore. Boats can be chartered from Leeward Marina on Providenciales, but there are no organized tours.

In **Puerto Rico**, humpback whales and dolphins can be seen from land and occasional tours, particularly off the W coast of the island. Best lookouts are Aguadilla and from an old lighthouse near Punta Higuera, outside Rincón.

The **Dominican Republic** has the most popular and well-established whale watching in the Caribbean. The industry is centred on humpback whales, but pilot whales and spotted dolphins can also be seen in Samaná Bay, and bottlenose, spinner, and spotted dolphins, Bryde's and other whales on Silver Bank. The season for both locales is Jan through Mar. In 1994, 15,200 people went whale watching, most of them to Samaná Bay where the trips last 2 to 4 hrs. The trips to Silver Bank are more educational and take a full day. In Samaná Bay, Whale Samaná is the oldest tour operator in the region and highly rated. Boats leave from the port of Samaná and cost US$50.

Contact: Kim Beddall, Whale Samaná, *Hotel Gran Bahía*, Samaná, Dominican Republic, T 538-2588. Other boats available in Samaná Bay to see humpbacks include 2 boats available for charter at the Victoria Marina in Samaná. As well, Miguel Bezi, another operator, has 6 boats over 100 ft long. Contact: Transporte Marítimo Miraniel, Samaná Bay, Dominican Republic, T 538-2556. For tours to see humpbacks on Silver Bank, some 50 miles (33 kms) N of Puerto Plata, contact: Coral Bay Cruises, 17 Fort Royal Isle, Fort Lauderdale, FL 33308 USA, T 305-563-1711, or Animal Watch, Granville House, London Road, Sevenoaks, Kent TN13 1DL, UK, T 01732-741612. It is also possible to book through travel agencies in Puerto Plata, such as Turinter, Dorado Travel or Go Caribic.

For whale watching from land from Jan to Mar, but especially in Feb, try Cabo Francés Viejo, E along the coast from Puerto Plata, near Cabrera, as well as Punta Balandra light and Cabo Samaná (near Samaná).

The **US Virgin Islands** and **British Virgin Islands** also have periodic trips to see the 60-100 humpback whales that winter N of the islands. There are also spinner and other dolphins to be seen. Season is Oct through Feb and a little later in the BVIs. On St Thomas, the 100 ft trimaran yacht *Wild Thing*, which operates out of Ramada Yacht Haven Marina, is used for the tours. Cost: US$45 for half a day.

Contact: Wild Thing, Suite 5, Long Bay, St Thomas, VI 08002 USA, T 774-8277. Arrangements can also be made through *Frenchman's Reef Hotel*. On Tortola in the BVIs, air tours are offered by Fly BVI, Beef Island Airport, British Virgin Islands.

On **Guadeloupe**, from Nov to April, there are tours to see humpback, sperm and pilot whales and dolphins offered through a fishermen's cooperative at Le Moule, a small, friendly, artisanal fishing town on the Atlantic coast. The boats are open, high-side, 21 to 25 ft 'yoles' with twin outboards, which are normally used for fishing. US$50 for a day trip includes a visit to an offshore island for a swim and French/creole lunch.

Contact: Mme Mireille Prompt, La Poterie, Le Moule, 97160 Guadeloupe, T 590-23-5136.

On **Dominica**, 8-12 resident sperm whales delight visitors almost year-round. You can also see spinner and spotted dolphins, pilot whales, false killer whales, and pygmy sperm whales. Occasional sightings are made of bottlenose, Risso's and Fraser's dolphins, orcas, dwarf sperm whales and melon-headed whales. The tours are run by naturalist-diver-photographer Fitzroy Armour, his wife Sharon, and brother Andrew out of the *Anchorage Hotel*. Hydrophones are used to find and listen to the whales. The tours are US$80 for 3-4 hrs. Dominica Tours, PO Box 34, Roseau, Dominica, T 448-2638.

Whale-watching tours are also offered by a well-equipped diving operator, Derek Perryman, at the *Castle Comfort Guest House* near Roseau. Dive Dominica Ltd, PO Box 63, Roseau, Dominica, T 448-2188.

For land-based whale watching of sperm whales and others, Scotts Head, at the SW tip of Dominica, overlooking Martinique Passage, is good most of the year.

On **Martinique**, sperm and the other whales and dolphins found off Dominica can also be seen off the W side. At St Pierre, whale- and dolphin-watching tours are part of the varied activities of a large diving club. Using Boston Whalers and other motor boats, they see spinner and spotted dolphins year-round and sperm whales and humpbacks mainly in the winter high season.

Contact: Carib Scuba Club, Villa Populo Bel Event, Morne Verte, Carbet, Martinique 97221, T 596-55-5944.

Off the W coast of **St Vincent**, large herds of spinner and spotted dolphins are seen regularly. Sometimes bottlenose dolphins and pilot whales are also found and, sporadically, humpback whales. Tours go aboard the 36 ft sloop, *Sea Breeze*, or on a 21 ft power boat. Snorkelling and a trip to Baleine Falls are also included. Almost year-round but avoid windy weather months of mid-Dec to mid-Feb. Best April to Sept when there is an 80% success rate. Trips depart from Calliaqua Lagoon on Indian Bay, SE of Kingstown and Arnos Vale Airport. Cost for tours is US$30.

Contact: Hal Daize, Arnos Vale Post Office, St Vincent, T 458-4969.

Other attractions include the island of **Petit Nevis**, off Bequia, 9 miles (15 kms) S of St Vincent, which is the site of the old whaling station once the hub of Caribbean whaling in this century. Access will require making arrangements locally as Petit Nevis is currently for sale.

From St George's Marina on **Grenada**, Mosden Cumberbach offers whale watching from his reliable 44 ft sloop or 34 ft power boat. He takes people off the S coast and to the Grenada Bank where humpbacks are often sighted from Jan through Mar, as well as up the coast to meet various dolphins and sometimes pilot whales. US$50 includes lunch and snorkelling.

Contact: Starwind Enterprise, PO Box 183, St George's, Grenada, T 440-3678.

From **Carriacou**, 23 miles (37 kms) NE of Grenada, humpbacks are often seen between Dec and April, as well as various dolphins and pilot whales year-round. Tours are offered aboard two catamarans by researchers working in wildlife conservation. Trips include touring bird sanctuaries, pristine coral reefs and Ile de Ronde, the submarine volcano N of Grenada. US$50 per person per day.

The catamarans, *Hokule A* and *Kido IV*, are docked in N Hillsborough Bay. Contact: Dario Sandrini, Kido Project, Carriacou, T 443-7936.

In eastern **Venezuela**, tucuxi and other tropical dolphins, can be seen close to shore on educational field trips. Oceanic Society Expeditions leads dolphin expeditions to work with researchers. Various whales are also sometimes seen.

For more information, contact Oceanic Society Expeditions, Fort Mason Center, Building E, San Francisco, CA 94123 USA, T 415-441-1106.

By watching whales and dolphins in the Caribbean, you can actually contribute to saving them. Many dolphins are killed mainly by fishermen, for food or fish bait. As well, pilot whales and even rare beaked whales are commonly harpooned, particularly in the eastern Caribbean. Whale and dolphin watching provides local people with another way to look at these intriguing animals – as well as a potentially more sustainable source of income.

Your support of whale watching may have the biggest impact in countries of the eastern Caribbean: Dominica, Grenada, St Lucia, and St Vincent and the Grenadines. Over the past few years, Japan has contributed to the development of these nations, by helping to build airports and adding fish docks and piers. In exchange, Japan has counted on the support of these four governments, all members of the International Whaling Commission (IWC), in its attempt to re-open commercial whaling. At the May 1994 IWC meeting in Mexico, however, these countries refrained from voting on the establishment of a southern ocean sanctuary for the whales, effectively allowing this important conservation measure to pass. The credit was partly given to a tourism boycott of the four countries organized earlier in the year by a US conservation group (since lifted), and partly to local people and conservation groups who are trying to encourage responsible ecotourism, including whale and dolphin watching. You can help conservation here by simply saying you enjoy seeing whales and dolphins in local waters. However, when referring to dolphins, use the word 'porpoises'. In most parts of the Caribbean, the word 'dolphin' means the dolphin fish. Best to specify that it is the mammal and not the fish that you want to see. And, in any case, if you see whales and dolphins being killed at sea, express your views to local and national tourism outlets of the country concerned.

For more information about whale watching in the Caribbean and how to help whales and dolphins, contact the Whale and Dolphin Conservation Society, Alexander House, James Street West, Bath, BA1 2BT, UK.

The above information has been compiled for us by Erich Hoyt, consultant for the Whale and Dolphin Conservation Society, marine ecologist and author of 6 books on whales and dolphins including The Whale Watcher's Handbook *and* Seasons of the Whale.

Watersports and walking

THE CRYSTAL CLEAR waters of the sunny Caribbean combined with the constant NE trade winds make the islands a paradise for watersports enthusiasts. The great increase in tourism in the area has brought a corresponding development in watersports and every conceivable watersport is now available. For a full range of watersports with all arrangements, if not at hotel reception at only a short walk down the beach, some of the best islands to head for are Barbados, Jamaica, Antigua, Martinique, the Bahamas, Cayman Islands, Puerto Rico and the Virgin Islands.

On these islands you can find hobie-cats and sunfishes for rent, windsurfers, water skiing, glass-bottomed boats plying the reefs, charter yachts and booze cruises, scuba diving, snorkelling and deep sea fishing. Prices for such watersports vary from island to island and often increase by about 30% in the peak tourist season (Dec to April). It is worth knowing that prices can often be reduced for regular or long term rentals and that bargaining with individual beach operators is definitely worth trying.

SWIMMING

If all you want is sea and sand, these abound on nearly every island. The coral islands have the white postcard-perfect beaches and some of the islands of the Grenadines are nothing more than this. Swimming is safe on almost all Caribbean coasts, but do be careful on the exposed Atlantic coasts where waves are big at times and currents rip. Swimming in the Atlantic can be dangerous and in some places it is actually forbidden.

WATER SKIING

This is almost always available in developed resort areas and beginners are looked after well. If you are a serious water skier it may be worth bringing your own slalom ski as many boats only cater for beginners.

SURFING

Good breaks for surfing and boogey-boarding can be found on the N shores of Puerto Rico, the Dominican Republic, Tobago and in Barbados. In both Puerto Rico and Barbados, custom-made surfboards can be bought and several competitions are organized every year. There are several good surf spots in Puerto Rico and the most consistent break in Barbados is at Bathsheba. In the Dominican Republic and Tobago, the sport is less developed. Waves tend to be bigger and more consistent in winter.

FISHING

Sportfishing is excellent in many of the islands of the N Caribbean. Almost every variety of deep-sea game fish: marlin, swordfish, tuna, mackerel and dorado abound in the waters. Over 50 world record catches have been made off the Bahamas alone. In the reefs and shallows there are big barracuda, tarpon and bonefish. There are areas for all methods of fishing: surf fishing, bottom fishing or trolling. Spearfishing, however, is banned in many islands. Although most fish seem to run between Nov and Mar, there is really no off-season in most islands and a good local captain will always know where to find the best fishing grounds. Note, fishermen should beware of eating large predators (eg grand barracuda) and other fish which accumulate the ciguatera toxin by eating coral-browsing smaller fish.

Fishing is very well organized in such islands as the Bahamas where Bimini, lying close to the Gulf Stream, is devoted entirely to game fishing. Exciting game fishing is also available very close to the shore off Puerto Rico, especially in the area which has become known to the enthusiasts as Blue Marlin Alley. Fishing is also very good off the Cayman Islands, Jamaica and the US Virgin Islands. In many islands there are annual fishing tournaments open to all, such as the Million Dollar Month Fishing Tournament held in June in the Caymans. Deep-sea fishing boats can be chartered for a half or full day and some are available on a weekly basis. Anglers can also pay individually on split charters. When arranging a charter, be careful to clarify all details in advance.

The above information has been compiled for us by Rosie Mauro, Barbados.

SAILING

Exploring the Caribbean by boat has never been easier. New marinas and local communities near popular anchorages are catering to the increasing number of yachts which have made the Caribbean their home. The Caribbean islanders have coined the name 'yachties' to refer to those people who live and travel on their own boats as contrasted with those who visit the islands on their vacations on chartered boats, cruise ships or landbased resorts. While this information is directed toward the yachties, bareboat charterers will also find the information useful.

From Europe to the Caribbean For boats crossing the Atlantic along the trade wind route, Barbados is the first landfall. Boats have the option of going on to Venezuela and Central America or through the Windward Islands of Grenada, St Vincent and the Grenadines. The Atlantic Rally for Cruisers offers support and entertainment for any sailors contemplating an Atlantic crossing. Departure is from Gran Canaria at the end of Nov and the yachts arrive in St Lucia to a warm welcome for Christmas.

From the USA to the Caribbean The two routes from the USA to the Caribbean are (a) from New England or Norfolk directly to the US Virgin Islands with the possibility of a stop in Bermuda or (b) island-hopping from Florida through the Bahamas across the 'Thornless Path' to windward described by Bruce Van Sant in his book *Passages South*. The Caribbean 1500 Rally organizes cruisers wishing to travel in a group to the Caribbean and depart from Newport, Rhode Island or Norfolk, Virginia, in late Oct arriving in St Thomas in the US Virgin Islands.

Ports of Entry Arrive during weekday working hours to avoid overtime fees. Have the sun at your back to navigate through reefs, sand bars or other water hazards even if it means a midnight or late afternoon departure and an over-night sail. When making windward pas-sages, overnight trips often mean lighter winds and seas.

Customs and Immigration Yachties cross many countries and have to deal with more officials and procedures than tourists aboard cruise ships or travelling to resorts. No matter how many guide-books are available, there will be at least one country with a change in procedures. Be careful to clear immigration on arrival as there are heavy fines for failing to do so. Plan to pay fees and to fill out paper-work in all countries. Occasionally, there are no fees; however, most countries have airport departure taxes and most have realized that these fees are another source of income. Different fees are often charged for charter boats and cruisers on their own boats who may wish to stay for a longer period of time.

Q Flag and Courtesy Flags Fly your 'Q' or quarantine flag until paperwork is completed. The captain should take ship's papers, passports and a list of the places you wish to stop and visit as in some countries you must be given spe-cific clearance to stop and anchor. All crew should remain aboard until they have received clearance from the port authorities. Even though many of the islands are still a part of the British Commonwealth, they prefer to see their country's courtesy flag flown. (And by all means, fly the flag right side up!)

Liveaboard Community Anchorages are found with a good, well protected anchorage, provisions, water, laundry available in Marsh Harbour in the Aba-cos, Georgetown in the Exumas, Lu-perón, Samaná and Puerto Plato in the Dominican Republic, Boquerón in Puerto Rico, Phillipsburg in Sint Maarten, Bequia in the Grenadines, Se-cret Harbour in Grenada, and in Chaguaramas in Trinidad.

Yacht Charters Charter fleets operate from the US and British Virgin Islands,

in the Abacos in the Bahamas, Antigua, St Martin, Martinique, Guadeloupe, St Lucia, St Vincent and Grenada. One way charters can often be arranged for an additional fee. Yachts can be chartered on a daily or term basis, either bareboat or with skipper and crew. Skippered day charters are now found in almost any area where there are landbased tourists.

Marinas Dry dock facilities for long term boat storage are found in the Turks and Caicos, Puerto Rico, the Virgin Islands, St Martin, St Lucia, Antigua and the newest major dry dock facilities are found in Trinidad. Most marinas will hold mail addressed to yachts for pickup.

Hitching Rides Hitching and working on yachts is another way to see the islands for the adventurous person with time on his/her hands. Many yachts charter in the Caribbean in winter and go N to the USA or Mediterranean for the charter season there. Other yachts are cruisers passing on their way around the world. Yachties are friendly people and if you ask in the right places, frequent the yachtie bars and put up a few notices, crew positions can often be found. Bulletin boards are found in Georgetown (Bahamas), Turtle Cove Marina (Turks and Caicos), Great Bay and Marina in the Lagoon (Sint Maarten), Fort-de-France, Trois-Ilets and Le Marin (Martinique), Rodney Bay and Marigot Bay (St Lucia), English Harbour (An-tigua), Admiralty Bay (Bequia) and An-chorage (Union Island) in the Grenadines, Secret Harbour (Grenada), and any marina or yacht club in Chaguaramas in Trinidad. If you want to crew, check you have all necessary visas and documentation and confirm with the skipper that your paperwork is in order. Puerto Rico and the US Virgin Islands require visas for boat travellers as though you were travelling to the USA.

Weather Information SSB: US weather broadcasts, US Ham net (E coast of USA & Bahamas), in the Caribbean, David on SV *Mystine* is on SSB kHz 6224 at

0800, with weather summaries covering the Dominican Republic, Puerto Rico, Virgin Islands, Leewards and Windwards, Trinidad and Tobago, northern Venezuela, central Caribbean basin, Colombia and Honduras. In case of marine advisory, he will come up on 6224 at 1815 with updates. Cruisers are invited to call in their location and current information. Weather information is critical before making long passages or during hurricane season (June-November). This is also the rainy season as tropical waves cross over the Caribbean bringing rain and squalls.

VHF Nets In those areas where there are a substantial number of liveaboard sailors, VHF nets seem to spring up with volunteers taking turns providing weather information, arrivals and departures, information about services and announcements about local activities, sharing taxis or tours; guests returning home often offer to take mail back to the USA or Europe.

Fishing Permits, Park Rules The Caribbean islands are becoming more eco-conscious. They are interested in preserving their natural resources and beauty and have established parks, marine preserves or national trust foundations. Some have mooring buoys, no-anchoring or anchoring limitations. Most prohibit taking of coral or live creatures in shells; many prohibit taking of shells. Don't anchor in areas where coral may be growing. Don't dispose of rubbish in enclosed anchorages.

Rubbish This is a problem on many of the smaller islands; don't give rubbish to boat boys as they often just take the money and throw the waste into the water. Try to dispose of edible waste at sea while travelling between islands in deep water; take paper, cans and bottles ashore to the town dump or a marina where they have waste disposal facilities.

Scuba Diving Saba and Dominica require special permits and St Eustatius requires divers to go with a local dive group. Do not assume you can dive wherever you like even if you have all your own tanks and equipment.

Weapons Some countries want weapons and ammunition checked in ashore until you are ready to depart. Others will let you keep them locked on board and others don't really ask questions. Make sure clearance papers have the correct serial numbers and ammunition counts to avoid confusion when it comes time to pick up the weapons that were checked ashore.

Regattas or Special Activities Sailboat races of all types are held throughout the Caribbean during the entire year. Spectator boats may go out to watch the races, there may be crew-sign-up lists for those who would like to sail and best of all, there are usually parties and activities on shore. Most regattas have various different types of classes, even including liveaboard classes.

Guidebooks cover most areas of the Caribbean and are updated periodically. Julius Wilensky's guides have good sketch charts that are still useful even if not updated. *Yachtsman's Guide to the Bahamas and Turks and Caicos*, *Cruising Guide to Abaco*, Steve Dodge; *Cruising Guide to the Abacos* (2nd edition) Julias Wilensky; *Yachtsman's Guide to the Virgin Islands*, *Southern Waterway Guide* (covers Bahamas and Turks & Caicos), *Passages South*, Bruce Van Sant; *Guide to the Leeward Islands*, Chris Doyle; *VIP Cruising Guide* (Sint Maarten area), *Guide to the Windward Islands*, Chris Doyle; *Guide to Venezuela, Trinidad & Tobago*, Chris Doyle; *Donald Street's Guides to the Caribbean* (Volumes I, II, III, IV).

NB see individual chapters for more detailed information on ports of entry, customs and immigration fees and procedures, courtesy flag, marinas, bareboat charter fleets.

The above information has been compiled for us by Kathy Irwin, an experienced sailor from Heath, Texas.

SCUBA DIVING

Scuba diving has become the 'in sport' with the numbers of divers having increased dramatically in recent years. The epitome of a scuba dive is in clear, tropical waters on a colourful reef abounding with life. The Caribbean is a scuba diver's paradise, for there is a conglomeration of islands surrounded by living reefs providing different types of diving to suit everyone's dreams. Unfortunately, some of the islands have turned into a 'diving circus', as in some of the more developed northern Caribbean islands where 30 or 40 divers are herded onto large dive boats and dropped on somewhat packaged dive sites where 'tame' fish come for handouts. Other islands in the region are still virginal in the diving sense, which can lead to an exciting undersea adventure. Nevertheless, this can also be frustrating on a diving holiday as on the more remote islands facilities are not often available and diving can be more difficult and basic.

The **Cayman Islands** are among the most developed for scuba diving and there is a fine organization of over 20 dive operations, including liveaboard boats. There is also a well-run decompression facility on Grand Cayman, which is an added safety factor. The Caymans are very conservation minded and it is a criminal offence to take ANY form of marine life while scuba diving. In fact, it is illegal on Cayman Brac, the smaller sister island, even to wear gloves while scuba diving. This helps ensure that divers will not hold or damage the delicate coral formations and other marine life.

The **British Virgin Islands**, with some 50 coral islands, are well worth a mention as the diving is exciting and varied. Both liveaboard and land-based operations are available with well-developed facilities for divers. Popular diving sites include the wreck of the *HMS Rhone*, a 310 ft British mail ship sunk in 1867 in a hurricane. She was the site for the Hollywood movie *The Deep*, which is what really made her famous. Other interesting sites include Turtle Cave in Brewers Bay which offers a spiral arch divers can swim through beginning at a depth of 45 ft and winding up to 15 ft. Many sites lie in the string of islands to the S between Tortola and the island of Virgin Gorda. To the N lies Mosquito Island, the site of The Cousteau Society's Project Ocean Search. Hosted annually by Jean-Michel Cousteau, the expedition gives a small number of participants the chance to find out what it is like to be on a Cousteau expedition (The Cousteau Society, 930 West 21st Street, Norfolk, Virginia, USA 23517).

Other especially spectacular diving destinations with abundant marine life include Saba, Dominica and the Turks and Caicos. **Saba**, a tiny Dutch island, only 5 miles long, is truly one of the most protected places for divers. The entire reef surrounding the island was established as a marine park in 1987 and this conservation effort has led to an abundance of 'tame' fish. Saba diving is known for several deep pinnacles including Third Encounter, Twilight Zone and Shark Shoal. For the less adventurous and experienced, sites like Diamond Rock and Tent Reef offer the thrill of seeing large French Angels swimming up to the divers. The sport has been developing with both land-based and liveaboard diving boat facilities available, as well as a decompression chamber facility.

Dominica, 'The Nature Island', or 'The Water Island', is a lush, mountainous island with rugged topside and underwater terrain. It is diving for the adventurous and not for the diver who wants easy diving although there are a few beginner sites. This is one of few islands left where black coral abounds and can be seen along the wall drop-offs starting at 60 ft. For the more experienced the

Atlantic East coast offers some spectacular wall dives. Dominica was introduced to the diving world only a few years ago and there are not many dive shops.

The **Turks and Caicos Islands**, which consist of over 40 lovely sand islands and cays, are located on the Turks Island Passage, a 22-mile channel which is 7,000 ft deep connecting the Atlantic Ocean and the Caribbean Sea. This contributes to the abundance of marine life and large pelagic fish seen in these waters and spectacular wall diving in the channel. The islands are surrounded by coral reefs that cover over 200 square miles. Visibility is usually 100 ft or more and marine life plentiful. A wild Atlantic bottle nosed dolphin, JoJo, occasionally interacts with swimmers, snorkellers, divers and boaters and has actually been made a national treasure of the TCI. There is also a dolphin rehabilitation project, Into the Blue, in Providenciales, which has so far released three dolphins from UK zoos, but they have no contact now with people. The strong attitude towards conservation is reinforced by Protection of Reefs and Islands from Degradation and Exploitation (PRIDE), based at the Sea Island Centre, a commercial conch farm. PRIDE is a US-based foundation which has helped in numerous conservation projects. There are several dive shops on Providenciales and Grand Turk, mostly catering for small groups of divers, and there are three or four liveaboard boats in the islands' waters at any one time.

The **Grenadines** in the South Eastern Caribbean offer pristine diving, although facilities are limited. Grenada and tiny sister island of Carriacou offer limited diving facilities, as does Bequia, although nearby St Vincent is more developed for scuba diving.

Tobago is another unspoiled destination which is worth visiting. This small island is close to the South American coast and large marine life is encouraged by the flow of plankton-rich water from the continent's rivers. Manta ray are especially attracted by the plankton and at Speyside (also called Manta City) where currents meet they are seen on nearly every dive. Most diving is along the W and N coast.

Barbados is among the more developed islands in the Caribbean and the surrounding reef life is not as unspoiled as on some of the less developed islands. However, there are some thriving reefs and within the last few years the island has become known as a wreck diving destination. Five shipwrecks have been intentionally sunk as diving sites, offering interesting underwater photography. In addition, the island is the base for the regional organization, **The Eastern Caribbean Safe Diving Association**. This association helps to maintain a decompression facility for the Leeward and Windward islands and is attempting to establish minimum safe operating standards for dive shops, initially in the E Caribbean and eventually, regionally. For more information write ECSDA, Box 86 WRD, Welches Post Office, Barbados.

Bonaire, just off the South American coast, has long been known as a 'hot spot' for diving, and is one of the few islands (like the Caymans) which has devoted itself to scuba diving. A far-sighted government established a marine park way back in 1979 when conservation was not even being discussed by most diving destinations. Neighbouring Curaçao has now joined her in this reputation, with an expansion of diving facilities and exciting diving sites. Aruba is not likely to equal her sister islands as she lacks the reefs which surround Bonaire and Curaçao, although diving is available. Bonaire, being very experienced in offering diving, has a wide selection of about a dozen dive operations, including photo and marine life education facilities. Diving sites are also varied with reef, wreck and wall dives. In fact, the Marine Park Guide for Bonaire lists over 50 dive sites. The town pier, right off the capital, has long been a favourite night dive and the pilings are covered in soft sponges and invertebrate life.

Curaçao offers the reef diving of Bonaire and a couple of wreck dives of interest. The freighter, *Superior Producer* (rather deep at 100 ft) is intact and has a variety of growth including beautiful orange tubastera sponges.

While the reefs of **Aruba** may not be as prolific as her sister islands, there is an interesting wreck site, with which few other sites around the island compare in marine life. The *Antilla*, a 400 ft German ship, is in 70 ft (and less) of water. Her massive hull has provided a home for an amazing variety and size of fish life and night dives are truly a thrill.

Most Caribbean destinations offer some form of scuba diving, although not all operations are safety minded. While scuba diving is exciting and thrilling, it can also be dangerous, particularly for beginners who are not aware of what to look for in a safe diving operation. Proper instruction from a recognized scuba instructor is a must. Not all diving shops in the Caribbean adhere to the recommended safety standards, so it is important to ensure the level of training an instructor has and request to see certificates of instructor training if they are not displayed.

Good health is a must, but the myth that one needs to be a super man or super woman is not true. Important health aspects are healthy lungs, sinus and the ability to equalize your ears (by gently blowing air into the eustachian tube while blocking your nose). A medical exam by a physician trained in hyperbaric (diving) medicine is recommended and required by many instructors. A good basic swimming ability is necessary, although you do not need to be an Olympic swimmer. For female divers, smaller, lighter scuba tanks are available at some dive shops which makes the cumbersome, heavy gear easier to handle.

Most scuba training organizations offer several types of diving courses. A 'resort course' provides diving instruction in a condensed version (about 3 hrs) with a minimum of academic knowledge, one confined water session (usually in a swimming pool) and one scuba dive. This type of course is done by many tourists who do not have the time to do a full certification course, which requires written exams, classroom lectures, several confined water sessions and several scuba dives. For the serious diver, however, a full certification course should be taken.

It is not possible to provide here a comprehensive list of diving facilities on each island; see the **Diving and Marine Life** sections of the country chapters for further information and addresses. For information on the liveaboard boats mentioned for the Cayman Islands, contact The Aggressor Fleet, PO Drawer K, Morgan City, LA 70881-000K, T (504) 385-2416, F (504) 384-0817 or (USA & Canada) (800) 348-2628.

The above information has been compiled for us by Martha Watkins Gilkes, a freelance diving journalist based in Antigua and author of The Scuba Diving Guide to the Caribbean *(MacMillan).*

WINDSURFING

Whether you are an accomplished windsurfer or merely wishing to give it a try the Caribbean offers the windsurfer warm clear water, trade winds and a wealth of locations to choose from. Throughout the Caribbean there are hundreds of pristine windsurfing locations, many undeveloped. Bring your own gear and have an adventure, or sail with the many schools across the islands. The strongest steadiest winds are June and July, this is when the trades are at their most constant. Winter brings either howling winds or flat calm and is unpredictable. In summer the gentle breezes provide good learning conditions. Each island has different winds and conditions, there is something for everyone, even if you just want to sit on the beach and watch.

Antigua Steady winds and lots of good locations, at present there is only one dedicated school, although hotels often have learner boards. Best wind Nov-Feb, June-July. Patrick's Windsurfing Place at *Lord Nelson Hotel*, T (809) 458-3425, F (809) 458-3612.

Aruba Well known as a centre for great windsurfing, flat waist deep water on the leeward side with strong wind make this an ideal location for learners and advanced windsurfers, the perfect family windsurf vacation. Best wind May-July. Sailboard Vacations, T (800) 252-1070, (2978) 21072, F (802) 985-9100; Roger's Windsurfing Place, T (800) 225-0102, (2978) 21918; Vela Highwind Centres, T (800) 223-5443, F (415) 525-2086.

Barbados Sun, sand, wind and waves make Barbados one of the favourite locations for many pro windsurfers on the World Tour. For those not willing to try the waves, flat water can be found at Oistins Bay. Best wind and wave conditions Dec-Jan and June. Silver Rock Windsurfing, T (809) 428-2866; Vela Highwind Centres, T (800) 223-5443, F (415) 525 2086.

Bequia Bequia is a beautiful island, but though the wind blows and the sun shines, there is only one windsurf school run by Basil, a Bequian with a big smile. Good location for learners or advanced sailors with flat water and wave sailing, well off the beaten track. Best winds Nov-Feb, June-July. Paradise Windsurfing, T (809) 458-3425, F (809) 458-3612.

Bonaire Good winds and locations for all levels of sailors from flat water to gentle waves. Best winds Dec-August. The Sailboard Centre, T (800) 253-6573, F (407) 489-7963; Windsurfing Bonaire, T (809) 599-75363.

British Virgin Islands The centre for windsurf cruising, with over 50 small islands scattered within 40 miles and steady trades, the islands are perfect for flat water cruising and blasting. Already a popular yachting centre, the two sports fuse with international events such as the Hi Ho (hook in and hold on), a week long windsurf race and yacht cruise. Also the home of *Catariba*, a 70 ft catamaran built specifically for windsurfing vacations, packed with the latest gear, sleeping up to 20 guests. Good sailing for all levels. Best winds Dec-Jan, June-July. Boardsailing BVI, T (809) 494-4022, F (809) 495-1626, *Catariba*, T (800) 936-3333, (508) 465-4100, F (508) 465-5334, Hi-Ho (Windsurfing Tortola) T (809) 494-0337, F (809) 494-6488; Bitter End Yacht Club, T (809) 494-2745.

The Caymans Famous for its diving, the Caymans also offers good windsurfing, the E end is popular for beginners to advanced and everything in between, flat water on the inside and bump and jump further out. Best wind Nov-March. Cayman Windsurfing, T (809) 947-7492, F (809) 947-7902; Sailboards Caribbean, T 949-1068, F (809) 949-1068.

Dominican Republic Voted by many top sailors as one of the most exciting places to sail in the Caribbean, Cabarete, on the N coast, offers everything a windsurfer could want: flat water for beginners and great wavesailing on the outside with thermally affected winds that mean you can take the morning off. Lots of schools and hotels on the strip of beach and some of the best gear in the Caribbean. Best wind Jan-Mar and June-August. Carib Bic Centre, T (800) 635-1155, F (809) 586-9529, Sea Horse Ranch, T (800) 635-0991, F (809) 571-2374, many more, contact the Tourist Board (see also page 361).

Grenadines Great location with no facilities, take your own gear and hire a yacht out of Grenada or St Vincent, or visit Basil at Bequia (see above) the only rental centre in the area.

Nevis A windsurfer's paradise waiting to be discovered, good flat water and wavesailing, definitely no crowds, the island is small enough to offer all conditions for every skill level. Best wind Dec-Jan, June-July. *Mount Nevis Hotel and Beach Club*, T (800) 756- 3847, F (212) 874-4276; Nevis Windsurfing, T (809) 469-9682.

Puerto Rico Great wave sailing spot, the Caribbean's answer to Maui. The location is The Shacks at Isabela on the NW point of the island. Thermal winds make this a winter spot for the committed wave sailor, gentler sailing is offered in the San Juan area and in the summer. Best waves and wind Dec-April, slalom July-September. Lisa Penfield Windsurfing, T (809) 796-2188, F (809) 796-2188; Windsurfing Del Caribe, T (809) 728- 7526,(809) 791-1000, F (809) 728-7526.

St Barts Small exclusive island with some good windsurf spots for beginners and advanced, and it is quiet. Best wind Dec-February. St Barts BIC Centre, T (590) 277-122, F (590) 278-718; Wind Wave Power, T (590) 278-257, F (590) 277-276.

St Croix A great sailing spot and often overlooked, the guys here are good wave sailors and slalom racers as the island boasts all conditions at many locations. Best wind Jan-Feb and July. Mistral School at Chenay Bay, T (809) 773-4810; Off the Beaten Path Vacations, T (800) 253-0622, F (809) 773-6116.

St Lucia A beautiful destination for any visitor and for the windsurfer it offers uncrowded sailing and plenty to do on no wind days. Best to bring your own gear if you are an advanced sailor, although there is limited good gear to rent at Windsurf Cas-en-Bas. Best winds Dec-June. Windsurf Cas-en-Bas, T (800) 876-3941, F (804) 693-2411.

St Martin Ever fancied windsurfing naked across flat tropical waters? Orient Bay (Baie Orientale) is probably the only place in the world you can do this without getting arrested. Aside from the novelty of sailing naked, St Martin offers good learning and advanced slalom sailing. Best winds Dec-Jan and July. Surface, T (590) 879-324; Tropical Wave T (590) 873-709.

St Thomas Everything you expect from a Caribbean windsurf vacation, with shopping malls. St Thomas boasts a lively local windsurfing community, flat water and lots of races and events to attend. Best wind Dec-Jan and July, join the fun at the Caribbean Team Boardsailing Championships in July. Caribbean Boardsailing, T/F (809) 776-3486; West Indies Windsurfing T/F (809) 775-6530.

Trinidad & Tobago Situated in the prime trade wind zone, Tobago's Pigeon Point is the place to go, unexplored and beautiful with some excellent sailing spots. You will probably need to take your own gear. Best wind Dec-May. Windsurf Association of Trinidad & Tobago, T/F (809) 659-2457.

Turks & Caicos Flat turquoise waters and steady winds make this an ideal learner and intermediate destination, perfect for a family diving and windsurf vacation. Best winds Feb-Mar intermediate, Oct-Nov for beginners. Windsurfing Provo, T (809) 946-5490, F (809) 946-5936.

The above information has been compiled for us by Nicolette Clifford, a journalist based in Tortola, British Virgin Islands.

WALKING

The Caribbean provides ideal conditions for medium-distance walking in the tropics. Small islands avoid the very high temperatures which are common in India, Africa, or the South American mainland. Distances are manageable; a hard day's walk will take you from coast to coast on the smaller islands, and a few days is enough for a complete circuit. The scenery is varied: peasant farms with fruit trees, rain forests, and high mountains. Mountain streams and waterfalls which would be ice-cold in temperate countries are perfect for bathing. The sea is never far away. Nor are road transport, comfortable accommodation, rum shops and restaurants. Nevertheless, the illusion of remoteness can sometimes be complete. And much of the nastier *mainland* wildlife can't swim, so there are no large carnivores and few poisonous snakes on the islands.

There are some tips to note for people more used to walking in temperate countries.

Maps Good large scale maps (1: 25,000 or 1: 50,000) are available for all the Commonwealth islands. These can be obtained from the local Lands and Surveys department on each island; and usually from Edward Stanford Ltd, 12/14 Long Acre, London WC2E 9LP, or The Map Shop, 15 High Street, Upton- upon- Severn, Worcestershire, (T 01684 593146). The Ordnance Survey (Romsey Road, Southampton, UK, T 01703 792763, F 01703 792404) publishes a series of colourful World Maps which includes some holiday destinations. They contain comprehensive tourist information ranging from hotels and beaches to climbing and climate. Each map is produced in association with the country concerned. Relevant titles so far are: Barbados, St Lucia, Cayman Islands, British Virgin Islands, St Vincent, Dominica. Contact International Travel Maps for travel in Latin America, 345 West Broadway, Vancouver BC V5Y 1PB, Canada, T (604) 879-3621, F (604) 879-4521. There are also good large scale Serie Bleu maps of Guadeloupe and Martinique (1:25,000, 7 maps of Guadeloupe, No 4601G-4607G) issued by the Institut Géographique National, Paris, which include all hiking trails. Footpath information on maps is not always reliable, however.

The interior of Guyana is largely uncharted; beyond the coastal belt the vegetation of the rain forest can be very thick. Most maps of this area can be hard to follow as the only features are the rivers, which change according to season (ie islands becoming part of the land, etc). Always take a guide in these parts.

Clothing Lightweight cotton clothing, with a wide brimmed hat to keep off the sun. Shorts are more comfortable, but can leave the legs exposed to sunburn or sharp razor grasses; ditto short sleeved shirts. It is best to carry short and long, and change en route as appropriate. Rain comes in intense bursts. Raincoats are not particularly comfortable. A better technique is to strip down to light clothes and dry off when the rain stops. (A small, collapsible umbrella may be useful and can also provide protection against the sun.) In the rainy season in the Guianas, leather footwear is of little use as it will be permanently wet. Use trainers instead.

Timing An early start is ideal, preferably just before sunrise. This will give several hours walking before the sun becomes too hot. Public transport starts running surprisingly early in most places.

Water Carry a large thermos. This can keep water ice-cold through a full day. Refilling from mountain streams is generally safe if purification tablets are used, but be careful of streams *below* villages especially in islands like St Lucia and Martinique where there is some bilharzia, and of springs in cultivated areas where generously applied pesticides may have leached into the groundwater.

Sunburn Remember that the angle of the sun in the sky is what counts, not the temperature. So you may get burnt at midday even if you feel cool, but are unlikely to have trouble before 1000 or after 1500. Forearms can get burnt, and so can the back of your legs if you are walking away from the sun. It is a good idea to walk W in the morning and E in the afternoon to avoid strong sun on the face.

Snakes The only islands where these are a worry are Trinidad, St Lucia, and Martinique. Trinidad has several dangerous species, and also has African killer bees. All three islands have the venomous Fer de Lance. This snake, however, is usually frightened off by approaching footsteps, so snakebites are rare, but they can be fatal. The Fer de Lance prefers bush country in dry coastal areas. Ask and accept local advice on where to go, and stick to well marked trails. Some other islands have boa constrictors, which can bite but are not poisonous. In Trinidad, beware of the coral snake; visitors with children should take care because the snake looks like a colourful bracelet coiled on the ground. Snakes are also found in the interior jungles of the Guianas; walk with a guide. Most snakes will only attack in the breeding season if they feel the nest is threatened. Large centipedes (sometimes found in dry coastal areas) can also give a very nasty bite.

Marijuana Farmers In remote mountain areas in most islands these people are likely to assume that outsiders have come either to steal the crop or as police spies. On most islands they are armed, and on some they set trap guns for the unwary. Again, the best way to avoid them is to keep to well marked trails, and accept local advice about where to go.

Details of walks are to be found in each country chapter, but here is an indication of what is possible on a selection of islands:

Jamaica Spectacular scenery especially in the Blue Mountains and in the Cockpit country. Marijuana growers are a real problem in the remote areas, but the main trails in the Blue Mountains are

safe. Jamaica Camping and Hiking Association and Ministry of Tourism have a useful *Hikers Guide to the Blue Mountains*.

Haiti Another story altogether. Walking is the normal means of transport in rural areas, so there are masses of well-trodden trails, but it is better to walk with a group. Maps are rudimentary and small scale. Few people speak French in remote areas – try to pick up some Créole. Make sure you carry basic supplies, particularly water. Hiring a guide should be no problem.

Guadeloupe Network of waymarked trails on the mountainous half (Basse Terre) in the Parc Naturel and up La Soufrière. Contact the Organisation des Guides de Montagne de la Caraïbe (Maison Forestière, 97120 Matouba, T 80 05 79) for a guide and/or the booklet *Promenades et Randonnées*.

Martinique The *Parc Naturel Régional* (Caserne Bouillé, Rte de la Redoute de Matouba, T 73 19 30) organizes group hikes, usually on Sundays, and publishes a useful *Guide des Sentiers Pedestres à la Martinique*. Good trails on Mont Pelée and along the N coast.

Dominica Probably has the best unspoiled mountain scenery in the Caribbean. Some of the long distance trails are hard to follow, though. Guides readily available. Try the path via Laudat to the Boiling Lake.

St Lucia Very well marked E-W trail through Quillesse forest reserve. Other walks organized by the Forestry Department. Also a good trail up Gros Piton. See St Lucia chapter for details.

St Vincent Spectacular but sometimes difficult trail across the Soufrière volcano from Orange Hill to Richmond. Guide advisable. North coast trail past Falls of Baleine is spectacular, but hard to follow. Marijuana growers.

Grenada Very accessible mountain and rainforest scenery. Good network of signposted trails linking Grand Etang, Concord waterfall, and other points. The mountains to the SE of the Grand Étang Forest Reserve are less well marked and you may need a local guide, but the walking is spectacular with marvellous views.

Barbados Very safe and pleasant walking, especially on the E coast, but little really wild scenery. Barbados National Trust (T 426 2421) organizes regular Sunday hikes, morning at 0600, afternoon at 1500.

Trinidad Some fine scenery, but marijuana growers are a real problem, particularly in the Northern Range and you are advised always to walk in a group. Well marked trails are safe. Those at the Asa Wright Nature Centre are recommended (T 667-4655, F 667-0493). Trinidad Field Naturalists Club (1 Errol Park Road, St Anns, Port of Spain, T 624-3321) organizes long distance hikes, and visits to caves etc.

Tobago Safe and pleasant walking; distances are not too great. The scenery is varied: hills, woodland and unspoilt beaches.

Guyana The Ministry of Tourism is cautious about backpackers walking alone in the interior of the country for safety reasons. In addition, in the interests of ecotourism, visitors are asked to use local guides in order to limit damage to the rain forests.

Useful Addresses For groups organizing a serious hiking/camping expedition in the Caribbean, contact Mr David Clarke, Caribbean Regional Consultant, Duke of Edinburgh's Award, The Garrison, Bridgetown, Barbados (T 436 8954, F 431 0076). He is generally able to provide advice and to supply the address of a local organization on most islands with expedition experience.

The above information has been compiled for us by Mark Wilson, teacher of geography and journalist, currently based in Trinidad.

The John Brooks Travel Awards
The Dominican Republic: Colouring the Nation

THE JOHN BROOKS Memorial Fund was set up in 1990 to honour the memory of John Brooks (Editor of the *South American Handbook* from 1972 to 1989). In 1994 the fund was used to provide three bursaries for travel to Latin America and the Caribbean to students who had recently completed a degree in Latin American Studies in the United Kingdom. David Howard, Jesus College, Oxford, wrote this essay on his return after visiting Cuba, Haiti and the Dominican Republic.

Colour plays a major role in the construction of the Caribbean societies, adding a chromatic scale to all levels of social interaction. Emancipation freed the Caribbean from the strict colour lines that demarcated society under slavery, although racial-ethnic differences remains as important, if less rigid, social markers today. The legal strata of citizens, freemen and slaves readily translated themselves into the social hierarchy of whites, browns and blacks. Colour exists as a social, rather than simply biological, construction which tends to correlate with social mobility and economic status. Elites tend to be lighter-coloured than the rest of the population. The saying 'money lightens' holds true for most parts of the Caribbean region. Ambitions of 'marrying lighter' express the widely recognised view that marriage to a lighter partner may enhance social status, or increase the opportunities for one's offspring by 'im-

proving the colour' of a darker-skinned parent. Aesthetically, white is right for a successful, beautiful image.

Issues of colour and race are salient throughout the region. The Caribbean's population of thirty-five million come from diverse origins, but generally share similar experiences of European colonialism, the plantation economy, dependency, migration and insularity. However, such generalities hide the complexities of differing colonial regimes, forms of labour recruitment and contemporary social and political histories. The transportation of slaves from Africa, and the later arrival of indentured labour from Asia, drastically transformed island societies, as has the immigration of other nationalities such as the Lebanese, Syrians, the Chinese and the Italians. The influence of the United States during the twentieth century has been culturally, politically and economically significant throughout the region – television and transnational migrants trade images of North American lifestyles and tastes, while the United States has grown to dominate the region's politics and economy.

Images of the Caribbean often focus upon anglicised views of the 'West Indies' as former British sugar colonies transformed into independent isles of cricket and tourism, sidelining other colonial influences. The Hispanic Caribbean tends to be neglected in popular Caribbean imagery, yet over half of the region's population speaks Spanish and the most popular sport in the region is baseball. Attempts to categorise the plural societies of the Caribbean describe the Spanish-speaking countries, Cuba, Puerto Rico and the Domincan Republic, as having lighter-skinned populations due to varying demographic histories. The relatively late development of the sugar industry limited the number of African slaves brought to these countries, and in the case of Cuba, the additional immigration of Spanish settlers at the beginning of the present century noticeably increased the white presence. Of the three countries, the Dominican Republic differs as a result of sharing a land border with Haiti, a frontier that has heightened the importance of colour and nation in Dominican society.

National pride divides the Caribbean into a plethora of independent, rival identities. The Dominican Republic and Haiti share the island of Hispaniola, and an ongoing history of intense rivalry and mutual distrust. Haiti plays a fundamental role in the construction of a Dominican national identity which suggests that the Dominican Republic is in essence a white, Hispanic nation, juxtaposed against the 'blackness' of its neighbour. Nationalism and racism have formed the basis of recent election campaigns in the Dominican Republic. The main rival of the elderly, white President Balaguer in recent years has been Dr Peña Gómez, a black politician with Haitian parentage. The political campaigns are a bitter forum for thinly disguised racial politics.

In terms of colour or racial groups, some have stated that the Dominican population of seven-and-a-half million constitutes a society of 15% black, 10% white, 70% brown or mulatto and 5% other groups – however, such clearly defined categories become meaningless, confusing or blatantly inaccurate depending on the viewpoint of the observer. Colour permeates the structure of the Dominican society at all levels. The negation of 'blackness' and a strong anti-Haitian sentiment incorporate a subjugation and denial of an African ancestry, and have led to the creation of an *indio* myth as an alternative form of racial or national identity. Many Dominicans describe themselves in terms of various shades of *indio*, despite the complete demise of the indigenous Amerindian population in the the sixteenth century. Dominican *indias* and *indios*, women and men, define themselves in a variety of ways: as clear or dark, chocolate, coffee or cinammon coloured. Defining a person or population as *indio* escapes the use of derrogatively-perceived racial terms such as black or mulatto.

An aspiration to be racially defined by lighter colour terminology, especially among the most affluent classes, has given rise to expressions such as *blanca tropicalizada* and *blanco con negro detrás de la oreja* meaning 'white with some, unnoticeable and largely ignored, African ancestry' or literally, 'white with black behind the ear'. A strong emphasis on white *hispanidad* remains.

So why does this urge to 'lighten' remain? Colour matters – while lacking the black-and-white rigidity of race in the United States, Dominican society operates along subtle colour lines. Lightness still opens more doors. *Para ser blanco es una profesión* – 'if you're white you'll get the job' is an often-stated and proven maxim in the Dominican Republic, translatable to all parts of the Caribbean region.

Bahamas

THE BAHAMAS is a coral archipelago consisting of some 700 low-lying islands, and over 2,000 cays (pronounced "keys"). The highest hills, on Cat Island, are less than 400 feet and most islands have a maximum height of 100 feet. The total area of the islands is about 5,400 square miles, roughly the same as Jamaica. The whole archipelago extends for about 600 miles SE from the Mantanilla shoal off the coast of Florida to 50 miles N of Haiti. Some of the smaller cays are privately owned but most of them are uninhabited. Nassau, the capital, on New Providence Island, is 184 miles by air from Miami. Freeport, on Grand Bahama island is 60 miles from Florida. The other islands, known as the "Family Islands", or "Out Islands", include Bimini, the Berry Islands, Abaco, Eleuthera (these two are particularly attractive), the Exumas, Andros, Cat Island, Long Island, San Salvador, Rum Cay, Inagua, Acklins and Crooked Island.

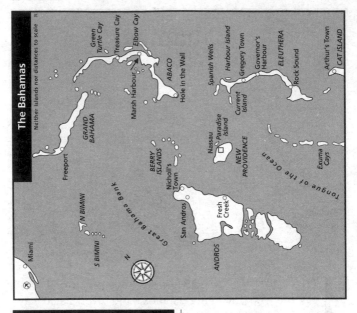

The Bahamas

Neither islands nor distances to scale

Green Turtle Cay · Treasure Cay · Elbow Cay · ABACO · Hole in the Wall · Marsh Harbour · Spanish Wells · Harbour Island · Gregory Town · Governor's Harbour · ELEUTHERA · Rock Sound · Arthur's Town · CAT ISLAND · Current Island · GRAND BAHAMA · Freeport · BERRY ISLANDS · Nicholl's Town · Nassau · Paradise Island · NEW PROVIDENCE · Exuma Cays · Tongue of the Ocean · Great Bahama Bank · N BIMINI · S BIMINI · Miami · San Andros · Fresh Creek · ANDROS · N

HORIZONS

The islands are made up of limestone over 5,000 metres deep, most of it Oolite, laid down for more than 150 million years on a gradually sinking sea bed. New material accumulated constantly and the seas of the Bahamas Platform remained remarkedly shallow, often only a few metres deep. From the air, the different shades of turquoise, ultramarine and blue in these shallow waters are spectacular. On land, the soil is thin and infertile except for a few pockets of fertile soil. In many places, bare limestone rock is exposed at the surface while much land is swampy, impenetrable and uninhabitable. There are many large cave systems, including the impressive blue holes, formed when sea levels were lower and since flooded. There are no rivers or streams on any of the islands, but there is some fresh water, found close to the surface but resting on underlying salt water. If wells are drilled too deep, they produce brackish or salt water. Andros has a surplus of fresh water, which is barged to Nassau. Most people drink bottled water.

About 15 island areas have been developed. They have a total population of about 276,000; about 183,000 live in New Providence and 50,000 in Grand Bahama. The weather can be pleasant in the winter season although cold fronts from the North American continent can bring strong N winds, heavy rain and surprisingly low temperatures. The summer months are hot, humid and often windless, with frequent thunderstorms. In Aug 1992 Hurricane Andrew hit the Bahamas, making over 1,200 homeless, killing four people and causing damage of over US$250mn. North Eleuthera was badly damaged and although most resorts soon reopened, houses took longer to rebuild. However, there is now little evidence of the storm and business is back to normal.

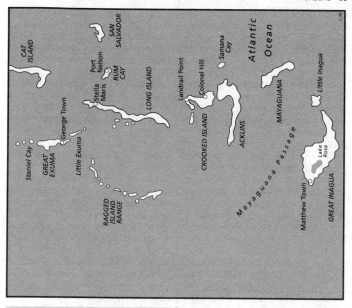

HISTORY

The first inhabitants were probably the Siboneys, fishermen who migrated from Florida and the Yucatán. The Indians Columbus found in the southern Bahamas were Arawaks, practising a culture called Tainan. They called themselves Lukku-cairi, island people, and became known as Lucayans. They were primitive farmers and fishermen, but produced the best cotton known to the Arawaks. The island of Guanahani is generally credited with Columbus' first landfall in the New World on 12 October 1492. Columbus called Guanahani San Salvador but it was not until 1926 that the Bahamas Parliament officially renamed Watling Island, an island which best fitted his rather vague description, as San Salvador. Columbus visited Rum Cay, which he named Santa María de la Concepción, Long Island, which he called Fernandina, and several other islands and cays, but finding no gold he set off for brighter horizons. The lack of mineral deposits

meant that the islands held little interest for the Spanish and there is no evidence of permanent settlement. However, the development of Hispaniola and Cuba led to shortages of labour on those islands and to the depopulation of the Bahamas as the Lucayans were captured and carried off as slaves. By 1520 about 20,000 had been captured for use in the plantations, mines or pearl fisheries in the Spanish colonies and the Bahamas were uninhabited. The islands and cays became feared by navigators and many ships were wrecked there, including a whole fleet of 17 Spanish ships off Abaco in 1595.

It was after founding their first colonies in Virginia that the English realized the strategic importance of the Bahamas, and in 1629 the islands received their first constitution as part of the Carolinas. In fact, the first settlers came from Bermuda with the aim of founding a colony free from the religious and constitutional troubles of Charles I's England. Then William Sayle, who had been

Governor of Bermuda, published in London in 1647 *A Broadside Advertising Eleuthera and the Bahama Islands*. As a result of this publicity, a company of Eleutherian Adventurers was formed and a party of about 70 settlers and 28 slaves, led by Sayle himself, set out for Eleuthera. Their ship was wrecked on the reefs. The party managed to land but most of the stores were lost and the settlers barely managed to survive by trading ambergris.

From this time on, the life of the Bahamas was largely influenced by their proximity to the North American mainland and their place on the sea routes. Piracy, buccaneering and the slave trade were features of the next two centuries. Pirates began to make the Bahamas their base after 1691 when they were thrown out of Tortuga. Conditions there were perfect, with creeks, shallows, headlands, rocks and reefs for hiding or making surprise attacks. By 1715 there were about 1,000 pirates active in the Bahamas, of whom the most notorious was Blackbeard, who wore his beard in plaits and was renowned for his cruelty. The colony was very poor and survived on the fortunes of shipping, both legal and illicit. In 1739 during the War of Jenkins' Ear, privateering brought a boom in trading activity but peace returned the islands to poverty. A revival of trade during the Seven Years' War was welcomed but peace once more brought depression to Nassau. When not involved in piracy or privateering, many of the inhabitants lived off wrecks, and great was their enthusiasm when whole fleets were destroyed.

A new form of piracy began after the abolition of the British slave trade, when illegal slave traders used the Bahamas as a base to supply the southern states of the mainland. This was followed during the 1861-65 American Civil War by the advent of blockade runners, shipowners and adventurers drawn by the prospect of vast profits. New, fast ships were developed which were unable to carry large cargoes and needed to find a safe, neutral port within two or three days' steaming. Nassau was again ideal, and the port prospered, the harbour and shops being packed with merchandise. The captains and pilots of the blockade running ships became as famous as their pirate predecessors. The end of the war provoked a severe and prolonged recession, with the cotton warehouses lying empty for 50 years. The inhabitants turned again to wrecking but even this livelihood was denied them when lighthouses and beacons were introduced, leaving few stretches of dangerous waters.

In 1919, with the advent of Prohibition in the United States, Nassau became a bootleggers' paradise, but with the repeal of Prohibition, this source of wealth dried up and the islands had little to fall back on. The Thirties, a time of severe depression, ended in disaster in 1939 when disease killed off the sponges which had provided some means of livelihood. Once again, it was war which brought prosperity back. This time, however, foundations were laid for more stable conditions in the future and the two bases of prosperity, tourism and offshore finance, became firmly established. Nevertheless, the Bahamas' location and the enormous difficulty in policing thousands of square miles of ocean has attracted both drug trafficking and the laundering of the resulting profits. About 11% of the cocaine entering the USA has been officially estimated to pass through the Bahamas. The Bahamas Government, in full cooperation with the US anti-narcotics agencies, has stepped up efforts to eradicate the trade.

For three centuries the merchant class elite of Nassau, known as the 'Bay Street Boys', influenced government and prevented universal adult suffrage until 1961. In the 1967 elections, an administration supported by the black majority came to power, led by Lynden (later Sir Lynden) Pindling, of the Progressive Liberal Party (PLP), who retained power until 1992. In the first half of the 1980s allegations were made that he was involved in the drugs trade, but they were never conclusively proven. This and subsequent scandals led to the resignation or removal of a number of public officials, and contributed, together with economic decline, to the growing distrust and unpopularity of the Government.

General elections were held in Aug 1992 and a landslide victory was won by the Free National Movement (FNM), led by Hubert Ingraham. Mr Ingraham, a former PLP minister, had been dismissed from his post as Housing Minister after he supported a move for the resignation of Sir Lynden in 1984. Subsquently expelled from the party, he was elected as an Independent in 1987, joining the FNM in 1990. The new Prime Minister promised an improved climate for investment and tourism and an end to political patronage. A series of inquiries were held into the finances of state corporations including Bahamasair, and the Hotel Corporation, where corruption and misuse of public funds were alleged.

GOVERNMENT

The Bahamas became independent, within the Commonwealth, in July 1973. The new Constitution provided for a Governor General to represent the British monarch who is head of state, a nominated 16-member Senate and an elected, 49-member House of Assembly, with a parliamentary life of a maximum of 5 years. The Free National Movement (FNM) holds 32 seats while the Progressive Liberal Party (PLP) holds 17. Sir Orville Turnquest, former Attorney General and Minister of Foreign Affairs, was appointed Governor General at the end of 1994.

THE ECONOMY

The economy of the Bahamas is based on tourism, financial services and shipping registration. Visitors are attracted throughout the year and since 1986, total

Bahamas: fact file

Geographic

Land area	13,939 sq km
forested	32.4%
pastures	0.2%
cultivated	1.0%

Demographic

Population (1995)	276,000
annual growth rate (1990-95)	1.5%
urban	86.0%
rural	14.0%
density	27.4 per sq km
Religious affiliation	
Protestant	55.2%
Anglican	20.1%
Roman Catholic	18.8%
Birth rate per 1,000 (1994)	18.9
	(world av 25.0)

Education and Health

Life expectancy at birth,	
male	67.7 years
female	75.5 years
Infant mortality rate	
per 1,000 live births (1994)	33.5
Physicians (1992)	1 per 714 persons
Hospital beds	1 per 250 persons
Calorie intake as %	
of FAO requirement	108%
Literacy	95%

Economic

GNP (1993 market prices)	
	US$3,059mn
GNP per capita	US$11,500
National debt (Dec 1994)	
	US$1,463mn
Tourism receipts (1994)	US$1,333mn
Inflation (annual av 1989-94)	4.3%
Radio	1 per 2.0 persons
Television	1 per 4.5 persons
Telephone	1 per 3.4 persons

Employment

Population economically active	
(1993)	136,900
Unemployment rate	10.7%
% of labour force in	
agriculture	4.7
trade, restaurants, hotels	26.8
manufacturing	3.6
construction	5.6
Military forces	850

Source *Encyclopaedia Britannica*

arrivals have exceeded 3 mn a year, mostly from the USA, of whom over half are cruise ship passengers or day trippers. In 1995, 3.5mn people visited the Bahamas, of which 1.9mn were cruise ship passengers. Also, since 1986, annual total visitor expenditure has exceeded US$1,100mn, about 13% of all tourist spending in the Caribbean region. Stopover tourists spend an average of US$794 per head while cruise ship passengers average US$60-70. In 1990 and 1991 the Gulf war and US recession took their toll on the Bahamian tourist industry with many airlines and hotels shedding staff and fiscal problems becoming more acute. Average hotel occupancy fell to 62% in 1990, 57% in 1993 and 62% in 1994, as US stopover visitors (82% of the total) declined. Room rates fell as over capacity in the hotel industry became critical. By 1994 prospects for the industry were improving, with a 5% increase in North American stopover visitors. The sale of most of the state-run hotels to private investors was expected to improve quality and revenue.

Agriculture is much less important than tourism, contributing only 1.5% of gdp, according to an agricultural census in 1994. A third of farmers are women, the average age is 59, and half of all farm labourers are Haitian. Emphasis is on fruit farming, taking advantage of the lack of frost and competing with the Florida citrus growers. Economic activity is principally restricted to the two main islands although on the Family Islands tourist facilities are being developed and agriculture extended.

Some steps have been taken to encourage light industries, notably salt, pharmaceuticals, rum and beer production, and substantial investment has taken place in the free-trade zone of Freeport, Grand Bahama. The financial sector, with its banks, insurance companies and finance companies, has developed since the 1920s, but since the mid-1980s has suffered from competition from other offshore centres such as the Cayman Islands and Barbados and from pressure from US bank regulators to reduce secrecy. The Bahamas shipping registry is the fifth largest in the world, with 1,500 vessels and a gross tonnage of 25.6 million at end-1995 compared with 1 million in 1983. As far as foreign trade is concerned, exports are mostly re-exports of oil products and there are also sales of rum, pharmaceuticals, crawfish, fishery products, fruits and vegetables. Imports are of food, consumer goods and crude oil (mainly kept in bunkers for re-export).

The new government elected in 1992 aimed to reform and revive the economy. Of immediate importance was public finance and efforts were made to put the Treasury in order. Government expenditure had previously been allowed to expand unrestrained and many accounts were found to be overdrawn without proper documentation. Salaries and allowances of MPs and Senators were cut and several other reforms were instituted into public sector pay and conditions. In an attempt to attract foreign investment, the Government joined the World Bank affiliate, the Multilateral Investment Guaranty Agency, and began studies into the establishment of a securities market to aid the divestment of state enterprises. Among the first of many companies to be sold were a hotel and a fish-landing complex, while inquiries were held into the loss-making Bahamasair, the Bahamas Hotel Corporation and the Bahamas Telecommunications Corporation. By 1996 nearly all the state hotels had been sold and the Government was preparing for the privatization of the electricity company and the telephone company, while Bahamasair was looking for a foreign partner.

NEW PROVIDENCE

New Providence is in the centre of the Bahamas archipelago, surrounded by Andros to the W, the Berry Islands to the N, the arc of the Eleutheran cays starting

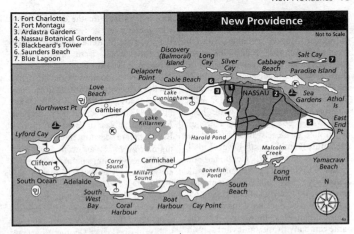

New Providence

Not to Scale

1. Fort Charlotte
2. Fort Montagu
3. Ardastra Gardens
4. Nassau Botanical Gardens
5. Blackbeard's Tower
6. Saunders Beach
7. Blue Lagoon

Discovery (Balmoral) Island
Long Cay
Silver Cay
Cabbage Beach
Salt Cay
Paradise Island
Delaporte Point
Cable Beach
NASSAU
Sea Gardens
Athol Is
Love Beach
Lake Cunningham
Northwest Pt
Gambier
Lake Killarney
East End Pt
Lyford Cay
Harold Pond
Malcolm Creek
Clifton
Corry Sound
Carmichael
Bonefish Pond
Long Point
Yamacraw Beach
South Ocean
Adelaide
Millars Sound
South Beach
N
South West Bay
Coral Harbour
Boat Harbour
Cay Point

off the NE tip and the Exuma Cays to the E and SE. It is one of the smallest major islands, at only 80 square miles, yet over half of the population lives here. The centre of Nassau has some fine historic buildings and there are some good beaches, but most of the island is covered by sprawling suburbia, scrubby woodland or swamp. Tourism is the principal industry, followed by banking, with the main developments at Nassau, Cable Beach and Paradise Island. Paradise Island, just off the N coast, is 826 acres of tourist resort. Once known as Hog Island, a legacy of New Providence settlers who used it as a pig farm, it was developed in the 1950s by Huntington Hartford as a resort. The name was changed after a bridge was built to connect the island with Nassau and the first casino licence was granted. For a history of the island, read *Paradise Island Story*, by Paul Albury (Macmillan Caribbean).

Diving and marine life

The variety of reefs and cays makes the Bahamas ideal for new or experienced divers. A great number of wrecks add spice to life underwater, including some that have been planted by film crews off the SW corner of New Providence, which attract scuba divers eager to see where the underwater scenes of James Bond films (the James Bond wreck was damaged by Hurricane Andrew and the front part collapsed, but it is still being dived), or Walt Disney's *20,000 Leagues Under the Sea*, were filmed. Just off Paradise Island there is a series of caves and a 19th century wreck, while to the W of New Providence there are dramatic walls and drops leading to the mile-deep 'Tongue of the Ocean'. Marine conservation is not as highly developed as in some of the other Bahamian islands where dive tourism is promoted, although there are 50 permanent moorings and seven dive operations, all offering PADI certification courses and trips to wrecks, reefs and walls, as well as other activities. Shark feeding and swimming with dolphins are two popular dives. The former involves sitting on the ocean floor and watching a dive master, clad in chain mail or other protective gear, feed several large sharks. Critics claim that more sharks are attracted to the dive site than is perhaps natural and are becoming dependent upon daily handouts. On the S coast, serving the *South Ocean* hotel, Stuart Cove's Dive South Ocean is particularly recommended (T 362 4171, F 362 5227), but the others include Bahama Divers Ltd (T 393 5644/6054, F 393 6078, East

Bay St), Dive, Dive, Dive Ltd (T 362 1143/1401, F 362 1994, Coral Harbour, Nitrox certification available), Sun Divers Ltd (T 325 8927, F 325 7788, at the *British Colonial Hotel*, serves the cruise ships as well as hotels, can take out 70 snorkellers or 25 divers on 55-foot boats), Diver's Haven (T 393 0869, F 393 3695, East Bay St), Nassau Scuba Centre (T 362 1964/1379, F 362 1198, Coral Harbour, an affiliate of Neal Watson's Undersea Adventures) and Sunskiff Divers Ltd (T 361 4075, T/F 362 1979, Coral Harbour, specialty diving). The cost of a 2-tank scuba dive with all equipment and transport included is about US$55-65. A learn-to-dive package costs much the same and enables you to dive with the same company throughout your stay on the island. Snorkelling trips for non-divers are US$20-25. Shark dives cost US$75 or more; you can see silky sharks, bull sharks and reef sharks. Stuart Cove's Dive South Ocean also offers a Shark Awareness certification course for US$210.

Beaches and watersports

Beaches are best near the hotels where the seaweed is cleaned off. The nicest ones are Love Beach (W), the E end of Paradise Island beach (hotel security guards often try to keep people off the beach at weekends; use hotel car park and walk through hotel as if you are a guest), South Ocean Beach (the sea here is very shallow) and beaches on the small islands off New Providence. One of the best and longest beaches is Lyford Cay, which is behind barriers in an exclusive housing area for the rich and famous in the W, but not impossible to enter with enough confidence. It is unwise to go to a beach where you might be on your own. Watersports include waterskiing (no tuition), parasailing, windsurfing and snorkelling. Some of the larger hotels offer full facilities to guests and non-guests. Prices about US$25 for 15 mins for waterskiing, while windsurfing can be US$12 an hour. Parasailing is US$30 for 7 mins and jet skiing US$25. Snorkelling equipment

hire is US$10-25 for the day. For those who prefer a less active encounter with the sea, glass-bottomed boats leave several times a day from Prince George Wharf in downtown Nassau.

Hartley's Undersea Walk, for those not keen to dive but wanting to see coral reefs up close, at 0930 and 1330, US$40 (T 393 8234). Check in at the houseboat, *Full Circle*, at Nassau Yacht Haven, East Bay St, before boarding the 57-foot catamaran *Pied Piper*. You walk down a 12-foot ladder wearing a helmet into which air is pumped so you can breath normally. The *Atlantis* Submarine goes down off Lyford Cay and will tour wrecks as well as reefs, weather permitting. The office is on Woodes Rodgers walk opposite Prince George Wharf and the cruise ships. The tour takes 3 hrs, of which 50 mins are on the submarine, Mon-Sat, 0930-2130 on the hour, every hour, US$68 adult, US$34 child, T 356 3842/5. The *Seaworld Explorer* is a semi-submarine which descends 10-15 feet and is reached by a shuttle boat which leaves from Captain Nemo's dock. Two trips daily except Sun and Wed of 1½ hrs, 1100 and 1500, US$26 adults, US$18 children, T 323 8426, 356 2548.

For island cruises, the Calypso Blue Lagoon trip and Rose Island excursions aboard large MVs with three decks are recommended (daily at 1000 except Wed, T 363 3577, US$35 for the day with lunch, although it is unlikely to be as good as in the brochure pictures, no complimentary snorkelling equipment). The Swim With The Dolphins Experience is at Blue Lagoon, Salt Cay, reached by tender from several cruise ships or on a day excursion with Calypso 1 and 11, reservations required, T 363 1653/1003. You get a 15-mins lecture on the dolphins, then you wade (US$30) or swim (US$85) with the dolphins; a full-day trip including lunch, drinks, beach, equipment, is US$59 or US$114. *Flying Cloud* catamaran cruises depart from Paradise Island West Dock for sunset, half-day, dinner or Sun cruises for

US$25-50 including snorkelling gear and transport from hotels (T 393 1957). Sea Island Adventure also do boat trips to Rose Island with lunch, snorkelling etc (T 325 3910, 328 2581), while *Yellow Bird* (250 passengers) and *Tropic Bird* (170 passengers) catamarans cater to cruise ships with 3-hr cruises. Top Sail Yacht Charters (T 393 0820/5817) have three boats and offer an all-day cruise from *British Colonial Hotel* dock 0945, Paradise Island ferry dock 1015, arriving Rose Island 1200, depart 1400, snorkelling included, US$49, private charters from US$370.

Powerboat Adventures go further in a high-speed boat; day trip departing from Captain Nemo's dock 0900, with lavish picnic to the Exuma Cays for US$149, including seeing iguanas on Allan's Cay, a nature trail walk and drift snorkelling (T 326 1936, 327 5385, Mon-Fri 0800-2000). Out Island Safaris (seaplane and boat, Captain Paul Harding, T 393 2522/1179) also offers day trips to other islands, eg Harbour Island, the Exumas, Hope Town, with scuba, snorkelling and lunch. A captained boat for fishing trips is US$300 for 4 hrs or US$600 for a day for up to 6 people (T 363 2335, Captain Jesse Pinder, or T 322 8148, F 326 4140, Captain Mike Russell of Chubasco Charters, or T 393 4144, 363 2003, Captain Philip Pinder, excellent), or arranged through hotel tour desks for US$60 per person for a half day.

Other sports

The most popular and well-developed sport on dry land is probably **golf**. There are four world class courses on New Providence: Cable Beach Golf Course (T 327 8617), South Ocean Golf Club (T 362 4394), Paradise Island (T 363 3925) and the private Lyford Cay Golf Course. Green fees vary: at the *South Ocean* in winter they are US$55 for guests, US$70 non-guests including cart, US$20 for 18-hole club rental, lessons US$30 for 30 mins, US$60 for 1 hr, club storage and daily cleaning US$10/week; at the Cable Beach Golf Club green fees

are US$60 pp in winter, US$55 pp in summer, with US$40 per cart and US$25 club rental; Paradise Island charges US$135 pp with cart, or US$86 for guests of member hotels, US$20 club rental.

There are over 100 **tennis** courts in the Nassau/Cable Beach/Paradise Island area and many of them are lit for night time play until 2200 (with an extra charge). Most of the larger hotels have tennis courts, usually free for guests. The Racquets Club, on Independence Drive (T 323 1854) has squash courts at about US$7 per hour. Very popular with Bahamians, it has European-sized squash courts. The Radisson Resort Sports Centre charges US$6 an hour for guests, US$10 for others, and has racquet-ball, squash and tennis available. Smarter, but the squash courts are smaller, being converted racquet-ball courts.

You can go **horse riding** for US$45 an hour, including transport, along the beach at Happy Trails, Coral Harbour (T 362 1820).

Cricket is played every Sat and Sun during the cricket season (5 Mar-27 Nov) at Haynes Oval, West Bay St, Nassau. Matches begin at 1200. For further details contact Sydney Deveaux of the Bahamas Cricket Association, T 322 1875.

Gambling at Paradise Island and *Crystal Palace* casinos, 1000-0400. Enquire about lessons free of charge. Fascinating to see the massed ranks of flashing fruit machines and the many games tables. Bahamians are not allowed to gamble in the casinos.

FESTIVALS

Junkanoo is a loud and boisterous national festivity loosely derived from African customs, celebrated on New Providence at 0300 on 26 Dec and 1 Jan (see under Grand Bahama for details of celebrations on that island). While the exact origins of Junkanoo are unknown, it is thought to have its roots in slave celebrations on their only days off in the year, at Christmas. John Canoe is said to have been a popular slave leader. Wild costumed rushers dance in Bay Street until dawn beating cowbells and shak-shaks, and blowing whistles. As in Carnival in many countries, local businesses sponsor groups who spend the whole year making their costumes. There is a Junkanoo Museum on Prince George Dock, by the cruise ships, open daily from 1000, closes 1300 Mon, Thur; 1600 Wed, Sun; 1800 Tues, Fri, Sat, US$2 adults, US$0.50 children, T 356 2731, where previous years' costumes are stored. Small Junkanoo displays can be seen on certain days in many of the large hotels. Parades with a military spirit and fireworks celebrate **Independence Day** on 10 July.

NASSAU

Nassau is the capital of the Bahamas. It looks comfortably old-fashioned with its white and pink houses: by-laws forbid skyscrapers. Bay Street is the main shopping street, which is packed with cruise ship visitors seeking duty free bargains during the day, but deserted at night. The new Government has taken steps to clean up the Bay Street area and on one occasion made the street a pedestrian mall for a day with stalls selling food and wares and lots of music. **Parliament Square** is typical of the colonial architecture with the Houses of Assembly, the old Colonial Secretary's Office and the Supreme Court clustered around a statue of Queen Victoria. On the N side of the square, more government buildings overlook the bust of Sir Milo B Butler, the first Bahamian Governor-General. To the right, surrey rides can be taken through the town for US$5 pp (horses rest 1300-1500 May-Oct, 1300-1400 Nov-April). Walking up Parliament Street you pass the Cenotaph on the left and the *Parliament Inn*, built in the 1930s, on the right. The octagonal pink building bordering on Shirley Street is the **Public Library**, built in 1798, which was once used as a prison. Inside you can climb stairs and look out

from the balcony, but unfortunately the old dungeons below are no longer open to the public. Open for consulting books, records, documents and artifacts, Mon-Thur 1000-2000, Fri 1000-1700, Sat 1000-1600, T 322 4907.

Opposite the library is the site of the *Royal Victoria Hotel*, the first hotel in the Bahamas, built in 1859-61, which closed in 1971. It was built by the Government to accommodate the influx of visitors during the American Civil War, but sold in 1898, after when it changed hands several times. There is not much to see and it looks like a park with some lovely tall trees providing shade, while much of it is used as a car park. On Elizabeth Ave on the corner with Shirley Street is the **Bahamas Historical Society**, which organizes monthly talks and houses a small museum (open Mon-Fri 1000-1600, Sat 1000-1200, closed Thur, T 322 4231). There is a collection of old pictures, historical documents, a few old household items and things brought up from the sea, not all of which are well-labelled; it is an old-fashioned display with little information. Nearby is the **Queen's Staircase**. The 66 steps (102-foot climb) at the end of a gorge (thought to have been cut out of the limestone by slaves in 1790, the canyon is now lined with palm trees and there is an attractive waterfall alongside the steps) lead to the ruined **Fort Fincastle**. Be careful to ignore men offering information on the history of the area unless you want to pay for it. They are very persistent, even when confronted with this text. The Fort itself was built in 1789 in the shape of a ship's bow. The Water Tower beside the fort was declared a water landmark in 1993. Take the lift (US$0.50) or the stairs to the top to see the shape of the fort. This is the highest point on the island (216 feet above sea level) and gives some lovely views of the island. There is another guide at the top who also expects a tip. The area is heavily visited by cruise ship tours and there are lots of souvenir stalls.

Government House in traditional Bahamian pink (built 1801) is pretty. Gregory's Arch is an overpass to Government House. On alternate Sat mornings at 1000, the Royal Bahamian Police Force Band plays in front of the **Christopher Columbus Statue** at the top of the flight of stairs. **Balcony House** on Market Street is the oldest wooden residence in Nassau, built in the 18th century. Open Mon, Wed, Fri, 1000-1600, closed 1300-1400, donations required, T 326 2568/2566. On West Hill Street is a plaque set in the rock which claims the site as being that of the oldest church in Nassau. Further along the street you pass several old houses including the Postern Gate on the left and the Sisters of Charity Convent on the right. Turning down the steps to Queen Street you pass by some of the oldest and prettiest houses in Nassau (no 16 is said to be 200 years old). The **St Francis Xavier Catholic Cathedral** is on West Street and down the hill is the quaint **Greek Orthodox Church** in blue and white. **Christ Church Cathedral** (built 1837) stands on the corner of George's Street and immediately to the S is **Lex House**, thought to have housed the Spanish Garrison in 1782-83.

Vendue House on Bay Street, close to the *British Colonial Hotel*, was the site of slave auctions, and has now been restored (with a grant from Bacardi to commemorate 1492) and converted into the **Pompey Museum**. It has drawings, artifacts and documents relating to slavery and emancipation in the Bahamas. The collection is limited but well displayed and interesting. Upstairs there is a permanent art exhibition of paintings by Mr Amos Ferguson, who uses house paints. Open Mon-Fri 1000-1630, Sat 1000-1300, adults US$1, children under 12, US$0.50. The renowned **Straw Market** has the offices of the Ministry of Tourism above. Almost all the straw work is imported from East Asia and is no longer native (better prices upstairs); they also sell carvings, jewellery and T-shirts. Bargain with the saleswomen but do not expect to get more than 15% off the originally stated price. Running behind the market is the enormous **Prince George Wharf** which can take up to 11 big cruise ships at once (peak time Sat). A duty free shopping area is planned here and construction work to increase facilities for visitors is under way. The **Junkanoo Museum** on the waterfront shows the colourful costumes used in the parades, see **Festivals**. Highly rec, good chance to see the workmanship up close. Guided walking tours of old Nassau start from Rawson Square, daily at 1000 and 1400, US$2, contact the Tourist Information Centre, T 326 9772.

EXCURSIONS

Go W along Bay Street, past Nassau Street and continue to the Road Traffic Centre where you turn left to **Fort Charlotte**, built in 1787-89 out of limestone. It has a dry moat and battlements. The fort was manned during the Napoleonic Wars but never saw action. The soldiers left some interesting graffiti. Look down on the cricket field, the guns (not original cannon), Arawak Cay and the W end of Paradise Island. Guides will fill you in on the history for a small tip or just wander at leisure. The guides have Ministry of Tourism name badges and are not as pushy as at Fort Fincastle.

Coral Island (T 328 1036, open 0900-1800, entry US$16 adults, US$11 children, annual membership US$21 adults, US$15 children, under 4s free) is on the 16-acre island, Silver Cay, reached by a bridge from the man-made Arawak Cay (made when the harbour was dredged to allow cruise ships in), which is in turn reached by a bridge (where conch sellers congregate). A US$3 bus runs from Cable Beach, a US$3 boat goes from Woodes Rodgers dock (daily except Thur, 1015, 1230, 1530, return 1200, 1500, 1700), or a US$3 bus from Paradise Island. Highlights include descending the observatory tower to

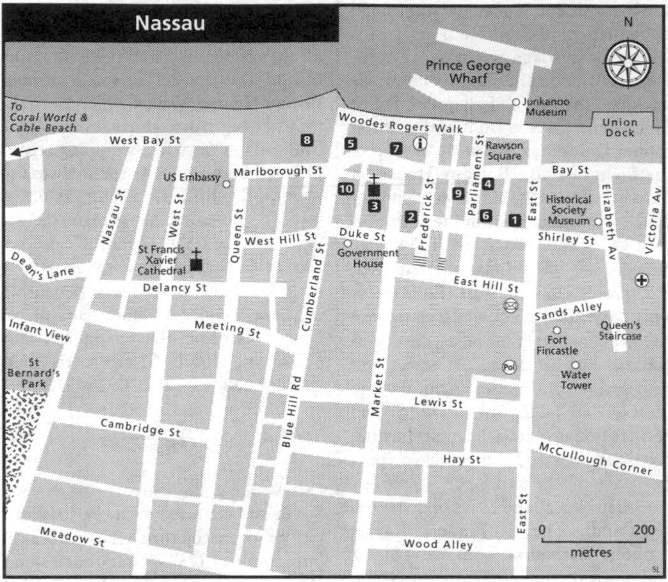

Nassau

[Map of Nassau showing streets and landmarks including Prince George Wharf, Junkanoo Museum, Union Dock, Woodes Rogers Walk, West Bay St, Marlborough St, US Embassy, Bay St, Rawson Square, Parliament St, Frederick St, East St, Historical Society Museum, Elizabeth Av, Victoria Av, Shirley St, Nassau St, West St, Queen St, West Hill St, Duke St, St Francis Xavier Cathedral, Government House, East Hill St, Sands Alley, Queen's Staircase, Dean's Lane, Delancy St, Fort Fincastle, Infant View, Meeting St, Cumberland St, Blue Hill Rd, Water Tower, St Bernard's Park, Market St, Lewis St, Cambridge St, Hay St, McCullough Corner, Meadow St, East St, Wood Alley. Scale 0 to 200 metres. To Coral World & Cable Beach.]

view the sea below (lots of fish and masses of lobsters), wandering through the excellent indoor exhibits of reef ecology, watching sting ray and sharks feed and selecting your own oyster with a pearl inside. The only drawback is the small size of the pools housing turtles, rays and sharks. A snorkelling trail has been added, US$12 for hire of mask, snorkel and fins, and mandatory life jacket. It is open 0930-1600, off a small beach overlooking Arawak Cay, where there are plenty of rest rooms and sun beds. Allow half a day for a visit. There is a restaurant, gift shops and also stands with sea biscuits and sand dollars for sale.

Going up Chippingham Road you come to the **Nassau Botanic Gardens** (open Mon-Fri, 0800-1600, Sat-Sun 0900-1600, adults US$1, children US$0.50), where there are 18 acres of tropical plants, and **The Ardastra Gardens and Zoo** (open daily, 0900-1700, last admission 1630, adults US$7.50, children US$3.75, T 323 5806/7232).

Trained, parading flamingoes march just after 1100, 1400, and 1600, but can be a disappointment. There are also parrots and some other animals, but not really enough to warrant the term zoo.

Going W along the coast, Saunders Beach is bordered by casuarina trees and Brown's Point looks across to the *Crystal Palace* (and *Radisson Resort*) at **Cable Beach**, which at night is a multi-coloured sight when the dayglo lights are switched on. Leaving Cable Beach you soon come to Delaporte Point (once a slave village) and Sandy Port residential areas. Further on are some local bars (*Nesbits* is very popular in the evenings) where you can buy drinks and native conch salad before you get to some limestone caves. There is an inscription commemorating the first visit by the British Royal Family in 1841. Just beyond is Conference Corner where Macmillan, Kennedy and Diefenbaker planted trees in 1962. At this point Blake Road leads to the airport while West Bay Street

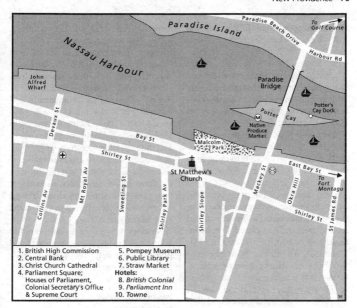

1. British High Commission
2. Central Bank
3. Christ Church Cathedral
4. Parliament Square;
   Houses of Parliament,
   Colonial Secretary's Office
   & Supreme Court
5. Pompey Museum
6. Public Library
7. Straw Market
Hotels:
8. *British Colonial*
9. *Parliament Inn*
10. *Towne*

continues past Orange Hill Beach and Gambier Village, another slave village. *Travellers Rest*, a bar and restaurant, overlooks the sea, and is very pleasant to watch the sunset (excellent daiquiris and minced lobster). Love Beach further on the right is probably one of the best beaches on New Providence. Park on the side of the road and walk down between the apartments, you can not see the beach from the road.

Continuing as far W as you can go you reach Lyford Cay, a private residential area for the rich, protected by barriers. Turn left at the roundabout for Clifton, a stretch of rocky coast now being developed for a power station and industry. This road leads to South West Bay where you can turn right to visit the *South Ocean* hotel and beach front (a good stop for a swim and a drink) before returning E. After two miles there is a signpost to **Adelaide Village**. This settlement is one of the oldest, founded when illegal slave traders were intercepted by the Brit-

ish Navy in the 19th century and the human cargo was taken to the Bahamas. The traditional houses are brightly painted, the beach is quite good, though the water is shallow, and the bars prepare fresh fish or conch salad. Continue E on Adelaide Road and you come to the Coral Harbour roundabout. To the right, the Bahamas Defence Force has its base. Coral Harbour was designed as a second Lyford Cay, exclusive, with security barriers, but when it was built in the 1960s there was considerable local opposition to it becoming a select ghetto. The development company went bankrupt leaving it incomplete. The shell of the hotel still stands and the area is now an upper middle class subdivision. At the roundabout you can turn off for the airport or join Carmichael Road and you will pass the Bacardi Company, open weekdays until 1600. At the end of Carmichael Road turn left to go along Blue Hill Road and join Independence Drive at the roundabout (with the cock on top).

Here on the N side is the new Town Centre Shopping Mall. In this area you will see many examples of the Government's low-cost housing. Rows of rectangular houses have been painted and adapted by their owners to make each one individual. Notice also that cemeteries are built on hills, where you can dig down six feet and not hit water; elsewhere water is too close to the surface.

Continue E on Independence until you come to traffic lights with another mall. At Marathon Mall turn right on to Prince Charles Drive and follow this to the sea. Turn left and you will be on Eastern Road, which hugs the coast and has many impressive homes overlooking the sea. **Blackbeard's Tower**, an old lookout point, is now closed. **Fort Montagu** (and beach), constructed in 1741, is famous for having been captured briefly by Americans during the Revolution. It is a rather smelly area where conch and fish are sold. If you turn left into Shirley Street and immediately left again into Village Road, you will come to **The Retreat** (opposite Queen's College), the headquarters of the Bahamas National Trust and an 11-acre botanical park. Guided tours (20 mins) US$2, Tues-Thur at 1150. Members of the BNT (PO Box N4105) are entitled to discounts at several tourist destinations locally (eg Coral Island, Power Boat Adventures, Ardastra Gardens) and free admission to National Trust properties worldwide. The BNT celebrated its 35th anniversary in 1994. It publishes a newsletter, *Currents*.

Returning to East Bay Street you will pass the *Club Waterloo* and the *Nassau Yacht Club* before reaching the toll bridge which crosses over to **Paradise Island**. Scooters cross for US$0.50, taxis and hired cars are US$2, cars with local licence plates US$0.50, pedestrians US$0.25. You pay the toll when taking a taxi across. Alternatively there is a water taxi, US$2, to the Calypso Dock on Paradise Island. Stop at the **Versailles Gardens and Cloisters** on the way to the golf course. The gardens with various statues were allowed to fall into disrepair for a while, but were restored in 1994. The cloisters were brought in pieces from France and date back to the 14th century. The gazebo looking across to Nassau is a favourite spot for weddings. The *Atlantis Resort* with its aquarium and waterscapes is worth a visit; you could spend half a day walking the pathways among turtle habitats, the predator pool and the aquarium (see the huge jewfish), including one with a glass tunnel where sharks swim all round you (all for free). Paradise has some lovely stretches of beach on the N side, including Cabbage Beach and Victoria Beach to the E at the edge of the golf course.

Potters Cay, next to the Paradise Island toll bridge, has the main fish and produce market. Try freshly made conch salad or scorched conch, very spicy and fresh.

Island information – New Providence

● Airports

Nassau International Airport, about 14 miles from Nassau. Taxi to Cable Beach US$10, to Nassau US$15-16 and to Paradise Island US$23. Third and subsequent extra passengers should be charged US$2, but drivers sometimes try to charge everyone a separate full fare. This is illegal. Make sure meter is used. Paradise Island Airport is nearer to Nassau and receives flights from Miami and Fort Lauderdale. Taxi to Paradise Island hotels US$7, to Nassau US$10 and to Cable Beach US$16. There is no public bus service to or from either airport, though some hotels have buses. For the return journey to Nassau Airport there is a bus from Nassau to Clifton (US$1.50); it leaves on the hour from Bay and Frederick Streets (Western Transportation Company) and will drop you 1½ miles from the airport, but this is not a recommended option.

Plenty of left luggage space is available in lockers outside the doors mid-way between the domestic and international ends of the terminal, they take 4 US quarter coins.

● Transport

Taxis are abundant but expensive. The rates are government-controlled: US$2 for the first

¼mile for 1-2 passengers, then US$0.30 for each subsequent ¼mile. You will be charged US$2 extra for additional passengers and for more than 2 pieces of luggage. To avoid over-charging, agree a price beforehand, or check that the meter is used. Taxi drivers in Nassau may "take you for a ride" otherwise. Taxis can be hired by the hour, US$20/hr for up to 5 passengers, larger taxis for 7 or more cost US$23/hr. Tipping is not necessary but 15% is normally expected. For a limousine service, Romeo's Executive Limousine Service is highly rec. Run by Bahamahost guide, Romeo Farrington, who has a white stretch limo and a fleet of lovely Bentleys, used for official visitors, special occasions or just sightseeing tours in style, T 327 6400/5280, PO Box GT-2280. For radio-dispatched taxis T 323 5111/4 or 323 4555.

Buses called 'jitneys', are good value at US$0.75, carrying from 9-44 people and going all over New Providence Island between 0630 and 2000. Make sure you have the exact fare, as by law the driver keeps the change. If you want to see some of the island catch any bus in town and it will bring you back about an hour later. They can be crowded and dirty but service is regular. Most buses run on one-way circular routes, which can be confusing. Route 10 goes out to Cable Beach along the coast road (leaving from beside *Best Western British Colonial Hotel*), route 16 goes along Eastern Rd to Fox Hill and Western Transportation buses go to *South Ocean* from Queen Street (US$1.75). A bus runs between hotels and the golf course on Paradise Island (blue and white striped bus, US$0.50, 30 min intervals between 0800-0130) but no buses go over the bridge. To cross to Paradise Island from Woodes Rogers Walk take the Paradise Express boat for US$2, it leaves when full and stops at several docks on Paradise Island.

● **Car hire**

A small car can cost US$70 a day or US$400-450 a week. Prices depend on the model and features. Avis (T 326 6380 or 377 7121 at airport); Hertz (T 327 6866); Dollar (T 325 3716) and Budget (T 377 7406) have offices at the airport and at other locations but local firms can be cheaper. Orange Creek Rent-a-Car has Suzuki runabouts for US$39 (T 323 4967). Large cash deposits can be required if you have no credit card. Scooters can be hired, Gibson's Scooter Rentals T 325 2963, US$30-45. Helmets are provided and it is mandatory that you wear them. Bicycles can be hired for

US$10/day with US$10 deposit. Traffic for such a small island is busy and roads are not well maintained. Take care.

● **Accommodation**

Hotel prices			
L1	over US$200	**L2**	US$151-200
L3	US$101-150	**A1**	US$81-100
A2	US$61-80	**A3**	US$46-60
B	US$31-45	**C**	US$21-30
D	US$12-20	**E**	US$7-11
F	US$4-6	**G**	up to US$3

The 2 main resort areas on New Providence are **Cable Beach**, which stretches 3 miles W of Nassau along the N coast, and **Paradise Island**, 5 mins across Nassau harbour and reached by a toll bridge. The benefit of staying at Cable Beach is that the jitney service into town is very easy to use, while from Paradise Island you need a taxi. Other hotels are in the town and suburbs. There is a great variety of accommodation, ranging from small guest houses, offering only rooms, to luxury hotels and sprawling resorts. Prices vary according to the season. Standards at hotels are now improving, helped by the privatization of state hotels and greater competition, but even so, service is slow at reception desks. Watch out for room tolls (4%), resort levies (4-6%), fuel surcharges and compulsory maid gratuities which are added to the basic price quoted. Up to date rates available at the Tourist Information Centres in Nassau, or write to the Tourist Offices listed under Information for travellers. You can usually pick up a cheaper package deal in the USA than by arranging a hotel on arrival.

In **Nassau** the largest hotel is **L3** *Best Western British Colonial* conveniently located at the beginning of Bay Street, built in 1923 on site of Fort Nassau, the cannon outside were found when the foundations were dug (T 322 3301, 800 528 1234, F 322 2286, room rates depend on view), economic difficulties forced the closure of 75 of its 325 rooms in 1993 with 80 staff redundancies, being refurbished 1995, good package deals year round, dive shop on site, watersports, small beach, view of cruise ships; **A2** *Parliament Inn*, 18 Parliament Street (T 322 2836, F 326 7196, PO Box N-4138, inc continental breakfast), central, old wooden building, small but adequate rooms with bathrooms, *Pick-a-Dilly* Daiquiri bar and restaurant downstairs, live music some evenings; the **B** *Diplomat Inn*,

Delancey Street on top of the hill (T 325 2688) is a budget hotel in a less salubrious area; nearby on West Bay Street close to the junction with Nassau Street, are a cluster of middle range hotels along the road overlooking Long Walk Beach: **A2** *El Greco* (T 325 1121, PO Box N4187), rec; **A2** *Ocean Spray* (T 322 8032/3, PO Box N3035); *Olympia*. A 10-min walk from the beach in the same area is the **A3** *Parthenon* on West Street (T 322 2643), clean and central. Further W off West Bay Street on St Alban's Drive is **A2** *Colony Club* (T 325 4824, F 325 1240, 100 rooms) extra beds in room for small charge, children under 10 free. Guest houses include **C** *Aliceanna's* on Hay Street (T 325 4974, PO Box N1336, clean, fan, bad area); **B** *Mignon* on Market Street (T 322 4771); **A2** *Towne Hotel* on George Street (T 322 8450, F 328 1512, PO Box N4808); **C** *Morris* on Davis Street (T 325 0195) and **C** *Olive's* on Blue Hill Road (T 323 5298).

Heading away from Nassau along **Cable Beach** are an all-inclusive resort, *Breezes*, a SuperClubs resort for singles and couples over 16, 400 rooms, refurbished 1995, a/c, TV, phone, pool, games room, fitness centre, outdoor sports and watersports, in UK T 01749 677200, F 677577, in Nassau T 327 5356, F 327 5155, PO Box CB13049; **L1-L2** *Forte Nassau Beach Hotel* (T 327 7711, F 327 8829, PO Box N7756), 6 restaurants, free tennis and non-motorized watersports, *King & Knights* native show club; **L1-L2** *Crystal Palace Resort and Casino*, managed by the Marriott chain under franchise to the Ruffin Hotel Group (T 327 6200, F 327 6459, PO Box N8306, suites up to US$25,000/night), this huge landmark hotel is usually lit up in dayglo orange, yellow, purple and magenta at night and contains shops, bars, restaurants and a casino the size of a football pitch, renovation planned; **Radisson Cable Beach Casino and Golf Resort**, next door, adjacent to casino (PO Box N-4914, T 327 6000, 800-777 7800, F 327 6987), 2 wings extend from central lobby and restaurant area, curving around lagoons and pools, long walk to some rooms down dark corridors, lots of packages, children's activities, all facilities but rather impersonal. Further along the beach *Sandals Royal Bahamian*, PO Box N10422, T 327 6400, F 327 1894, couples only, 196 rooms, all-inclusive, lots of sports, more rooms to come and **L3-A1** *Henrea Carlette Hotel* (T 327 7801) 1-2 bedrooms. *Compass Point Beach Club*, on Love Beach, PO Box CB 13842, West Bay Street, Nassau, T 327 4500, F 327 3299, opened 1995, 20 rooms in wooden cabanas, cottages on stilts or huts, all brightly painted in multi colours, fan, TV, CD, radio, restaurant, part of Chris Blackwell's Island Outpost chain.

On **Paradise Island**, Sun International Hotels owns the huge **L1-L3** *Atlantis Resort*. The 1,147 rooms inc suites and villas are located in the *Beach Tower*, *Coral Tower* and *Reef Club*, prices vary between seasons and at weekends as well as whether you have a sea view. The feature of the new resort is the 14-acre waterscape and free form pool area with aquarium, 30,000 sq ft casino, 18-hole golf course, tennis courts, lots of restaurants inc *Lagoon Bar and Grill* reached by underwater glass walkway with fish swimming all round you, T 363 3000, T 800-321 3000, F 363 3524, lots of package deals available, inc golf, air fares. A new 1,000-room hotel is to be built by 1998, expanding the casino and creating an ocean theme park. Other large hotels include *Radisson Grand Resort*, being refurbished 1994/95 after change of management from Sheraton, 342 rooms, tennis, pool, etc; *Club Méditerranée*, 312 rooms, children from 12 years, large tennis centre with 20 courts, watersports, PO Box 7137, T 363 2640-4, F 363 3496; **A1** *The Pink House* (inc breakfast) is a very small, smart hotel in the grounds of the *Club Med* (T 363 3363, F 393 1786); **L1** *Club Land'Or* (T 363 2400, F 363 3403), is a good suites and time share hotel, with good restaurant. At the opposite end of the spectrum the **A2** *Yoga Retreat* (PO Box N-7550, T 363 2902, F 363 3783), **C** for tent space, very strict, no onions, not allowed to skip meditation, guests cook and wash up. Paradise Island Vacations represents several hotels and offers air-inclusive packages, T 800-722 7466 or in Dade 891 3888.

On **Silver Cay**, **L1** *The Villas On Coral Island* (PO Box N-7797, T 328 1036, 800-328 8814, F 323 3202, children under 12 free), built in a row along rocky coastline but very private and enclosed, each of the 22 suites has small pool, bed sitting room, small kitchenette/dining area, large bathroom, luxury furnishings, nice décor, leafy surroundings, unlimited access to Coral Island and the snorkelling trail, honeymoon and lovers' packages.

L1-L3 *South Ocean Golf and Beach Resort* is set in 195 acres on the S coast, with the main hotel, attractively situated in the middle of the 18-hole, PGA-rated, par 72, 6,707-yard golf course, 250 rooms refurbished by new owners 1995, ocean front rooms with jacuzzi in a separate section between main hotel and sea convenient for dive shop, a/c, TV, fans, several restaurants and bars, nightclub, 2 pools, exercise room, games, jogging trail, watersports, tennis, golf/diving packages available, children's programmes, PO Box N-8191 (Adelaide Rd) South Ocean, T 362 4391, F 362 4728, T 800-241-6615. 250 rooms are to be added to meet requirements for a casino licence.

● **Places to eat**

A 15% gratuity will be added to every food and drink bill although service can be very slow and poor. Lunch is always cheaper than dinner and can be taken until 1700. For al fresco dining try *Passin' Jacks* or the *Poop Deck* on East Bay, *Traveller's Rest* near Gambier Village (always enjoyable), or *Sugar Reef* (T 323 8394/8426, open 1200-2230), Deveaux Street on the waterfront, name clearly written in white on red roof, popular with yachties who lunch there at 1230 on Thurs. Middle range places with bars and open air meals include *Coconuts* (indoors) and *Le Shack* (same place but outside), East Bay Street between Paradise Bridge and Nassau backing onto the harbour, where you can get exotic cocktails, Bahamian food and hamburgers (T 325 2148); *Tamarind Hill* on Village Road, European and Bahamian, rec, good food, live music Wed, Fri, Sat, 1930-2230 (T 393 1306) and *Pick-a-Dilly*, with live music Wed-Sat evenings, happy hour 1700-1800, on Parliament Street. *Charley Charley's*, Delancey Street serves hearty German fare while *Café Delancey*, on same street is middle range, rec. Cheap, cheerful and Bahamian are *The Shoal*, on Nassau Street, *Briteleys*, and *Three Queens* on Wulff Road, the first 2 are better than the *Three Queens*. Opposite the Central Bank, through arch down Market Street is *Palm Tree*, which has very good native cooking and does takeaway. Both the *Blue Lagoon* (a trio) on Paradise Island and the *Cellar* in town have music. *The Rose-lawn Café* on Bank Lane, off Parliament Square serves food after 2200. *Vesuvio's* on West Bay Street is a good Italian restaurant; *East Villa* on East Bay Street is a Chinese restaurant (T 393 3377/3385). Most hotels have expensive and formal restaurants but they also have good value buffets (US$12-20): Sun brunch at *Café Martinique* on Paradise Island is excellent. At the *Boat House* next door you can cook your own steak, lobster etc

on a tableside grill. *Blue Marlin* is one of only 2 restaurants on Paradise Island not owned by a hotel (T 363 2660), lunch and dinner, steel band most nights, cheaper than hotels. For a special meal visitors are often encouraged to go to *Graycliff*, West Hill Street, in a colonial mansion (also a hotel, **L1**, T 322 2796), but service and food have declined, poor reports. *The Sun and...* (T 393 1205, closed Mon) and the *Blue Lagoon* in *Club Land'Or* (for fish) are rec (over US$50 pp). Also expensive but good are *Ocean Club* (check your bill) on Paradise Island and *Buena Vista* on Delancey Street (T 322 2811/4039, reservations required, men wear jackets, popular with business people, pianist, also 10-12 guest rooms).

● **Nightlife**

Some clubs have a cover charge or a 2-drink minimum. The *Atlantis Paradise Island Resort & Casino* has a 30,000 square foot casino with 800 slot machines and a casino show nightly except Sun in *Le Cabaret Theatre*, times of shows vary, acts are changed every few months, generally of excellent quality, good live music with large troupe of dancers and singers, well choreographed, enjoyable; also *The Joker's Wild Comedy Club*, mostly US comedians and entertainers perform Tues-Sat, T 363 3000. The *King and Knights* at *Forte Nassau Beach Hotel* has a good native show, with steel drums etc. Native shows generally do not mean native to the Bahamas, but borrow from the culture of Trinidad and Jamaica with Junkanoo added. *Blue Marlin*, a restaurant/bar and night club on Paradise Island, offers a native revue similar to that at *King and Knights*, every night except Mon, starts 2115, lasts about 1½ hrs. *Bahamen's Culture Club*, Nassau Street, has Bahamian and Caribbean recording artists. Live bands can be heard at the *Waterloo*, East Bay (where you can bungee jump from 40 feet over the indoor swimming pool), and the *Ritz*, Bay Street (popular with Bahamians). Several restaurants have live music, see above. *We Place*, Thompson Avenue, US$4, is full of Bahamians and very lively at weekends. *The Zoo*, West Bay Street, Tues-Sat, 2 restaurants, dancing areas, state of the art private lounges, theme bar, multi-faceted club caters for wide clientèle, from young parties to the sophisticated executive. Discos can be found in most of the larger hotels. Dinner cruises in the harbour on the *Majestic Lady*, Bay Street, nightly for US$35 (T 322 2606). *The Village Lanes*, Village Road for bowling at US$2.75 a game during the day, US$3 after 1700 (T 393 2427). The *Dundas Centre for the Performing Arts*, Mackey Street, regularly has shows and plays by local groups (T 322 2728).

● **Warning**
There is a 'crack' cocaine problem in New Providence. Partly for this reason armed robberies are frequent. The majority of tourists are not affected and Nassau is less dangerous than Kingston or Port of Spain. However visitors should be extremely careful, particularly at night or when venturing off the beaten track. Do not be lulled into a false sense of security.

● **Shopping**
Shops are open 0900-1700, Mon-Sat, but some close at 1200 on Thur. As there is no sales tax and many items are duty free, buying imported goods can save you about 20-50%, but shop around. *Bernard's* has some fine china, the *English Shops* and *Linen and Lace* have Irish linen. Look in the *Perfume Shop* for French perfume. Try *John Bull* for watches and cameras. For unusual gifts look in *Marlborough Antiques*, West Bay, *Coin of the Realm*, Charlotte Street, or *Best of the Bahamas*, E of the square. For clothing see the *Androsia* boutique in *Mademoiselle's*, batik fashions from Andros. There are also international names like *St Michael*, *The Body Shop*, *Benetton*, *Gucci* and *Greenfire Emeralds* from Colombia all in Nassau. In general, however, buy everything you could possibly need before you arrive as regular import duties are high. Most of the smarter, tourist-oriented shops are on (or just off) Bay Street. For everyday shopping most people use suburban centres, of which the most convenient is in the Mackey Street-Madeira Street area. Super Value supermarkets have good variety of breads and salad bar (sold by the pound). The main fish and produce market is on Potters Cay (see above). Other fresh fish markets are Montague Foreshore, next to the Sailing Club and on West Bay Street, opp Fort Charlotte and at the entrance to Coral Island. The best book shop is probably the book department of the Island Shop on Bay Street, but most cater for 'holiday reading'. Service in shops is often poor, be prepared to wait.

● **Film developing**
Try the Island Colour Lab in the Island shop, opp the Straw Market, on Bay Street or Mr Photo chain on the Market Range off Bay Street. Others have lost films.

● **Tourist office**
In the straw market, extremely helpful. Ask for the monthly *What's On* and the *Tourist News*. Another, *Best-Buys*, is in your hotel or at the airport. There is also an information booth in Rawson Square (T 326 9772/9781) and at the airport which will help you find accommodation. A Ministry of Tourism hotline for urgent assistance or complaints is T 325 6694, Mon-Sat 0900-1700, T 325 6694, Sun and holidays 0900-1300. The tourist office has a list of churches (and church services).

● **Tourist agencies**
Majestic Tours (T 322 2606, 326 5818, F 326 5785, PO Box N-1401, Hillside Manor, Cumberland Street, one of the main agents for trips to Cuba) and Happy Tours (T 322 4011) arrange day trips to 'deserted' islands or cays, although the Blue Lagoon trip (see page 74) is probably better value. The many organized excursions offer the visitor an easy way of getting about but you can sometimes do the same thing by yourself for a lot less. As well as drives to places of interest, tours include visits to beaches on the Family Islands and trips aboard a catamaran with stops for swimming and sunbathing.

GRAND BAHAMA

The nearest to the USA and, with Great Abaco, the most northerly of the major Bahamas islands, is where the most spectacular development has taken place. Thanks to a fresh water table under the island it has no water problem. The pinewoods which this natural irrigation supports were, indirectly, the beginning of the present prosperity. Early in the 1940s, an American millionaire financier, Wallace Groves, bought a small timber company and developed it into an enterprise employing 2,000 people. In 1955, the Bahamas Government entered into an agreement with him as president of the Grand Bahama Port Authority Ltd, granting to the specific area, called **Freeport**, owned by the Port Authority, certain rights and privileges which apply to that area only and to no other section of the Colony. Most important, the area was to be free of taxes and with certain concessions on several imported goods. In

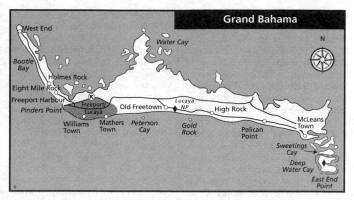

Grand Bahama

West End
Bootle Bay
Holmes Rock
Eight Mile Rock
Freeport Harbour
Pinders Point
Freeport
Lucaya
Williams Town
Mathers Town
Peterson Cay
Water Cay
Old Freetown
Lucaya NP
Gold Rock
High Rock
Pelican Point
McLeans Town
Sweetings Cay
Deep Water Cay
East End Point
N

return, Groves would pay for government services within the area, promote industry and dredge a deepwater harbour. By 1961 a large cement works was under construction and the harbour housed a thriving ship bunkering terminal. Seeing the potential for a tourist industry, Groves made a further agreement with the Government in 1960. He formed the Grand Bahama Development Company and purchased a large area of land which was to become **Lucaya**. He also built a luxury hotel and casino, the first of its kind in the Bahamas.

So successful was this that the population of the island grew from 9,500 in 1963 to 35,250 in 1967 and 41,035 in 1990. In the same period, the total investment rose from US$150mn to US$577mn and the tonnage of cargo handled increased ten times to 1.25mn tons. In 1969, however, the Government decided to introduce controls on the expansion of Freeport, and the vertiginous growth process has since slowed down. Official Bahamianization policies meant that many foreigners left or were forced to leave when their entry permits were not renewed. Today, Freeport's population consists mainly of Bahamians from the other islands who have been drawn there to find work. The Freeport/Lucaya area is isolated from the rest of the island and most tourists never venture into the settlements.

There is a marked division between the wealthy, Americanized and manicured tourist area and the rest of the island which looks like a Family Island.

Flora and fauna

Grand Bahama is mostly covered in scrub or Caribbean pines. The Royal and Cabbage palms found on the island have been imported, the former coming originally from Cuba. In the N there are marsh and mangrove swamps. Much of the coast supports the attractive seagrape tree and it is not unusual to see children collecting grapes from the trees. Common flowers and trees are the yellow elder, the national flower of the Bahamas, the lignum vitae, the national tree, hibiscus, bougainvillea, oleander, poinciana and poinsettia. Common fruit trees include avocado, lime, grapefruit, mango and custard apple. There is not a great deal of wildlife on Grand Bahama, although you may see racoons, snakes, lizards and frogs. Birds include pelicans, herons, egrets, owls, woodpeckers, magpies, humming birds (mostly Cuban Emeralds), the rare olive-capped warbler, cranes and ospreys. Watch out for poison wood which is found in the bush and pine copses around beaches and causes a very unpleasant rash over the body.

Diving and marine life

The paucity of wildlife on land is compensated by the richness of the marine life offshore. Rays often spring from the water in pairs, but be careful not to stand on them when snorkelling as they have a powerful whiplash sting. The spotted eagle rays are particularly beautiful when seen from above. Sea horses and moray eels are also common along the coral reef. It is illegal to break off coral or harvest starfish and there are fines for offenders. Shell collectors will find sand dollars and sea biscuits on the beaches. Conch usually has to be dived for but the beaches are often littered with empty shells. Scuba diving is popular, with attractions such as Treasure Reef, where more than US$1mn in sunken treasure was discovered in 1962, and Theo's Wreck, a deliberately sunk steel hulled freighter. The Underwater Explorers Society (UNEXSO) in Port Lucaya (T 373 1244, PO Box F-42433) has a deep training tank and recompression chamber, and offers PADI and NAUI certification courses. A one-day resort course is US$79, a certification course is US$325. A one-tank dive is US$29, a 3-dive package US$79 including tank, weights and belt. Other packages are available including accommodation at local hotels. Snorkelling trips are US$15 including equipment. They rent underwater photographic equipment, film processing is available daily and video tapes of your dive or dolphin encounter are sold. The Dolphin Experience (US$19pp) is a popular programme, usually booked well in advance. You take a boat from the UNEXSO dock to Sanctuary Bay, about 25 mins, where large pens have been put in the lagoon to house the captive bottlenose dolphins. After a lecture on dolphins you can get into the water with them to touch them. Very well organized so as not to worry the animals. Sessions at 1000, 1100 and 1400. You can also dive with the dolphins. Two dolphins are released from the pens, follow the dive boat out to the ocean, where they swim with the divers and return home afterwards (US$99). You can also enrol as a dolphin trainer for a day (US$159). Membership of UNEXSO is US$50 (discounts for students or families) and US$25 a year thereafter, entitling you to a newsletter, various discounts and invitations to participate in diving expeditions (PO Box 22878, Fort Lauderdale, FL 33335).

Other dive operators include Xanadu Dive Centre at the *Xanadu Hotel* (T 352 5856, 1-800 336 0938, F 352 4731), which offers one dive at US$32, 2 dives US$55, 3 dives US$75 or a 3-day package for US$250, including tank, weights, mask, snorkel and fins. A liveaboard is available for charter, sleeps 16, price depends on what you want to do. Certification courses and resort courses are offered. Both UNEXSO and Xanadu offer shark dives. They take it in turns to dive the same site, so the sharks are fed nearly every day with frozen fish from Canada, just like the dolphins. The fish is free of parasites, but not their natural diet. There is also the *Deep Water Cay Club* at East End, with no certification courses available. The *Deep Water Cay Club* is primarily a bone fishing lodge. Their boats fish over 200 square miles of flats and creeks. Accommodation is in cottages and cabins, there is a restaurant and private air strip, PO Box 1145, Palm Beach, Florida, 33480, T 407-684 3958, F 407-684 0959.

For the non-diver, there is now a submarine at Port Lucaya which has the advantage of a transparent hull giving much better visibility than some other submersibles in the Caribbean. Contact Deepstar Submarine, Comex Submarines Ltd, 22 Seahorse Plaza, Seahorse Rd, PO Box F 40393, Freeport, T 373 7934, F 373 8667. The tender, *Albatross*, leaves from UNEXSO, and joins the submarine for a dive about 1½ miles offshore on the deep reef.

Beaches and watersports

The island has several natural advantages over others in the group. It has miles of S-facing beaches sheltered from northerly winds and enjoys the full benefit of the Gulf Stream. Generally, beaches can be classed as tourist or local, the former having sports and refreshment facilities as well as security and regular cleaning. The more remote beaches, on the other hand, are usually completely empty, unspoiled by commercialism and very peaceful, their only drawback being that there is often considerable domestic waste and rubbish washed ashore, probably emanating from the garbage collection ships on their way to Florida.

Do exercise caution on the beaches as crime is common and most beaches have a security guard because of the high incidence of robbery and assault. Walking on beaches at night is definitely not a good idea and there is not necessarily safety in numbers. Also theft from parked cars is common so do not leave valuables in your car. Fortune Beach and the National Park Beach are both areas in which to be careful. Topless sunbathing is frowned upon by the Bahamians and skinny dipping is against the law.

Coral Beach, next to the hotel of the same name, is popular with windsurfers, cleaned regularly and has a small bar. Beach facilities are for hotel residents only and this policy is sporadically enforced with vigour. **Xanadu Beach** serves the *Princess Towers/Xanadu Hotel* and various watersports are available through Paradise Watersports (T 352 2887), including jet skis (US$22 for 15 mins, US$40/½ hr with US$50 deposit), water-skiing (US$15 for 1½ miles), paddle boats, catamarans, snorkelling equipment (there is a good reef here within easy reach), fishing and parasailing. Use of jet skis and boats is limited to a cordoned area. Hair braiding is done on the beach by local children who have fixed prices according to the number of plaits and length of hair (generally US$1 per plait). Watch out for scalp burn afterwards. There is a straw market and a bar which has very loud live music on Sun. Drinks or conch

salad can be bought more cheaply if you walk just beyond the boundary fence where locals bring ice boxes of cold sodas. The *Glass Bottom Boat* operates from Xanadu Marina, tickets on sale on the beach. Make sure the sea is calm, it can be very rough outside the marina and then water visibility is poor and most passengers get seasick.

The **Lucayan Beach** area includes the beaches for the big resort hotels which are clean, with bar and sports facilities including parasailing. Windsurfers, hobie cats, Boston whalers, snorkelling equipment, water skis (about US$15 for 2 miles) and wave runners can all be hired here. At nearby Port Lucaya, Reef Tours operate the *Mermaid Kitty*, a glass bottomed boat which sails several times a day, US$12 for 1½ hrs. They also have 2-hr snorkelling trips, US$15 pp. Various booze cruises depart daily as well as a trimaran sunset trip

On the road to West End past Eight Mile Rock are two good beaches for shelling, **Bootle Bay** and **Shell Bay**. At West End, the beach at the *Jack Tar Holiday Village* (closed 1990) is rather small. There are good coral heads here, close enough to wade to.

One of the nicest beaches on the island with attractive palms and a few broken down old umbrellas is **Taino Beach**, which is over a mile long and has an excellent stretch of coral for snorkelling very close to the shore. The *Taino Beach Resort* on the first part of the beach has expensive condominiums which can be rented on a short term basis. Further along past the *Stone Crab Restaurant* is the *Surfside Bar/Restaurant*. The *Club Fortuna Beach Resort* has been built with Italian investment in this area. **Fortune Beach** is sometimes used for tourist beach parties which are noisy and to be avoided. The main attraction of the beach is the restaurant *Blackbeards*. The beach is a bit rocky especially at low tide. Take care in this area, it is best to park near the restaurant as there have been many cars broken into in the rather lonely car park further along. The walk from William's Town along the beach is very pleasant, the vegetation being lush, mostly mangrove, sea grapes and tall grasses along the shore. The beach is used by Pinetree Riding Stables and occasionally local churches hold services here. Other beaches on the island include **Smith's Point** and **Mathers Town** just outside Freeport. Here you will find two popular bars: *Club Caribe* (Mathers Town) and the *White Wave Club* (Smith's Point).

Peterson's Cay is the archetypal one tree desert island and because of this can be crowded. Some tour companies run day trips to snorkel and eat lunch here. You can hire a boat to get there from Port Lucaya (Reef Tours, US$75/3 hrs with US$200 deposit), the approach is a bit tricky because of the reef. Directly opposite is **Barbary Beach**, pleasant and backed by a wide pine copse (good for hanging hammocks). An old church here called the Hermitage was built in 1901 by an ex-trappist monk,

Of the less commercial beaches, **Gold Rock Beach** is probably the most beautiful on the island, about 20 miles E of Freeport and part of the Bahamas National Trust. En route to it you cross the Grand Lucayan Waterway, a canal built in the 1960s when development was booming. Barely used today, the canal bisects the island and the abandoned building sites are a reminder of what Freeport could have become had the planned development taken place. Once past the canal turn right and further along this road is a deserted, never-used film studio. If you take the left turn before the studio you come to a signposted road for the crossing to **Water Cay**. It is not always easy to get a boat across. If you take the left turn but carry on, the road becomes overgrown and pot holed, and the area is littered with small planes shot down by drug enforcement officers or abandoned by drug traffickers. Fat Albert, a barrage balloon full of

radar equipment is supposed to have put a stop to aircraft landing on the road undetected. Another detour before reaching Gold Rock is to take the first turning after the film studio to Old Free Town, where there are blue holes and Mermaid's Lair, an opening to an underwater cave system. Further inland is a sink hole, the Owl Hole. Back on the road, turn off when you see the sign for the Lucayan National Park. There is a car park and a map. The 50-acre park was set up by workers from Operation Raleigh and a subsequent expedition laid the foundations (but nothing more) for a visitors centre. A Lucayan village and burial ground have been found here. The park contains the largest charted underwater cave system in the world. You can see two caves and climb to a lookout point. As well as bromeliads and orchids there are hundreds of bats in the first cave in the breeding season; also a rare water centipede found only in these waters. Across the road from the caves is a 1,000-yard board walk through mangrove swamp which leads to Gold Rock Beach. The beach is best seen at low tide as the sea goes out a long way and there is not much room to sit when the tide is in. The beach stretches for over a mile and is usually deserted. There are dunes and a large rock sticks out of the water giving the beach its name. It is excellent for shell collecting, but horseflies are very persistent so bring insect repellent. The picnic area is often too strewn with rubbish to be pleasant. Occasionally the area is cleaned.

Another wide, beautiful beach is **Pelican Point**, at the E end of the island, backed by Royal Palms and a very pretty and colourful village. There are fishing boats on the beach and it is not uncommon to see people gutting or cooking fish here. Pelicans can be seen flopping by. Roads out to the East End are poor and in places 4-wheel drive is preferable.

Kayaking can be done with Kayak Nature Tours run by Mrs Moultrie from Hawksbill Creek, Queen's Cove, along

N shore through mangrove creeks or Gold Rock Creek in the National Park, US$75 for all-day trip including lunch and transport; 16-foot kayaks, single or double, no experience necessary, minimum age 10, T 373 2485.

Other sports

There is no shortage of **golf courses** on Grand Bahama. At the *Bahama Princess Hotel and Golf Club* there are two PGA championship courses, the 6,420-yard Emerald and the 6,450-yard Ruby, with 162 bunkers between them (also tennis courts and a 6-mile jogging trail). The length of each hole is changed daily by moving the holes on the putting green. Reservations for starting times are essential and in peak season, winter, times are often booked a month in advance. Green fees US$51 in summer, or US$46 for guests inc cart, club rental US$22, T 352 6463. Carts are mandatory. The *Bahama Reef Golf and Country Club* offers a 6,768-yard championship course (swimming pool), and the *Fortune Hill Golf and Country Club* a 3,453-yard, 18-hole scenic course (T 373 4500, US$26 green fee, US$36 cart hire, US$13 club rental). The oldest is the *Lucaya Golf and Country Club*, built in 1963 where there is an 18-hole, 6,488-yard PGA-rated championship course (PO Box F-40333, Lucaya, T 373 1066, F 373 7481, green fees US$40-80 inc cart, club rental US$25), discounts are available through the large hotels and there is a booking booth at Port Lucaya. You can play **tennis** at the *Clarion Atlantik Beach* (guests US$1 per day, US$100 annual membership), the *Princess Country Club* (US$5/hour daytime, US$10/hour nightime), *Princess Tower* (same rates), *Lucayan Beach* and *Lucaya Marina* (guests free, no night play) and the *Xanadu Beach Hotel* (non-guests US$5/hour). The Grand Bahama Tennis and Squash Club (T 373 4567) has courts available from 0930-2400 but you have to be a member.

Horse riding is available at Pinetree Stables (T 373 3600, PO Box F-2915), US$35 for 1½-hrs trail and beach ride with guide (20 horses, rider's weight limit 200lbs), lessons can also be arranged with BHS and AIRA instructor (no credit cards). There is a Rugby and Hockey Club (Pioneers Way), which organizes various social events. The YMCA next to the Rugby Club can give information about watching local basketball and softball matches. Volleyball is a popular sport and many beaches and residential street corners have nets. Bowling is available at Sea Surf Lanes, Queen's Highway. There is a Super-Cross Motor Cycle dash in the autumn. Aerobics classes are available at most of the major hotels. There are several jogging routes but watch out for dogs. The Conchman Triathlon (swim/cycle/jog) is held in November. The GB5000 road race is in Feb, a 5-km flat race from *Princess Country Club*, with a 1-mile fun run/walk and a run for children. Contact the Grand Bahama Island Promotion Board, T 352-8356, for information and registration. UNEXSO organizes a conch diving competition for locals at Port Lucaya.

Festivals

Junkanoo is held on 1 Jan in Freeport. Beginning from the Ranfurly Circle, dancing outside *Princess Hotel* 0400 onwards with drums, cowbells, whistles, brass instruments and foghorns. Scrap gangs, impromptu groups, join in with the rushin'. Much smaller than Nassau's but worth seeing. Go to Ranfurly Circle early to see the participants flame heating their goat skin drums to stretch them. The **Goombay** Summer Festival consists of a series of events at the International Bazaar or in the Lucaya area. On 10 July, **Independence Day**, a Junkanoo parade is held at 0400 in West End and also on the first Mon in Aug, which is a holiday to commemorate the emancipation of the slaves. A mini Junkanoo is held weekly as part of the Goombay Festival and many of the hotels include a small Junkanoo as part of their native show. Other events are also held during the festival, get a calendar of events from the Tourist Office in the Bazaar or major hotels.

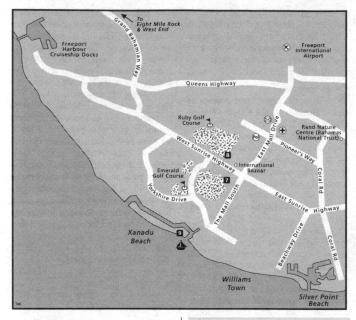

On **Discovery Day**, 12 Oct, a fair is held at McLean's Town, including a conch-cracking competition started by a British couple in the 1940s. The aim is to see who can remove the most conch from their shell in 10 mins. The women's competition has many machete-wielding experts who bring a lot of partisan support. There is also a swimming race to a nearby islet and back, which attracts a lot of local competition. The plaiting of the Maypole is an interesting Caribbean version of the English tradition, with children dancing round the pole to the beat of Reggae songs. Although much of the road to McLean's Town has been paved, the road is very poor in parts. Minibuses run regularly from Ranfurly Circle (US$2). If you rent a car it is sometimes difficult to park. Look out for details of local fairs in the Freeport News and at the Ranfurly Circle.

FREEPORT

Freeporters have a reputation of being less friendly than other Bahamians, but this is often blamed on the design of the town and the lack of community spirit. Avenues are large and buildings are spaced far apart, there are few corner shops or neighbourhood bars and it is hard to go anywhere without a car. In downtown Freeport there are a few small shopping malls (see under Shopping). If you take East Mall Drive out of town towards the airport you will pass the Rand Memorial Hospital and the excellent Wallace Groves Library. On the other side of the road is a bright pink pseudo classical building which is the Grand Bahama Port Authority Building. East Mall Drive connects with the Ranfurly Circle (named after 1950s British Colonial Governor) and the **International Bazaar**, a 10-acre integrated shopping complex on East Mall and West Sunrise Highway, with streets built in various

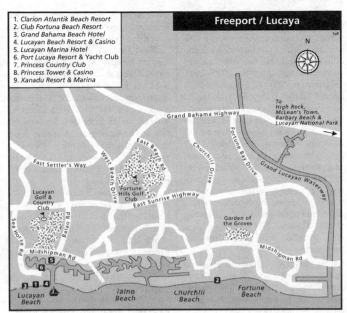

Freeport / Lucaya

1. Clarion Atlantik Beach Resort
2. Club Fortuna Beach Resort
3. Grand Bahama Beach Hotel
4. Lucayan Beach Resort & Casino
5. Lucayan Marina Hotel
6. Port Lucaya Resort & Yacht Club
7. Princess Country Club
8. Princess Tower & Casino
9. Xanadu Resort & Marina

assorted national styles with international merchandise and food. There is also a straw market, open Mon-Sat 0900-1600 and an Arts and Crafts Village behind it, also open Mon-Sat. To the rear of the International Bazaar, the other side of the street from Colombian Emeralds (where you can tour the factory) and the Straw Market, is a perfume factory in a replica of an old Bahamian mansion, which you can tour briefly and even mix your own perfume (T 352 9391, F 352 9040, orders in USA 1-800 628 9033, PO Box F-770, Freeport), open Mon-Fri, 1000-1730. Just over a mile E of Ranfurly Circle you come to another roundabout. Turn right to get to the Lucaya area, where there is the **Port Lucaya** shopping and entertainment complex and a number of hotels, casino, marinas. At the Market place there is another straw and crafts market. UNEXSO is based here. In the evenings live music is played at the bandstand by the waterwalk.

EXCURSIONS

The Hydroflora Gardens on East Beach Drive, 5 mins drive from Ranfurly Circle adjacent to the Palace disco, contain four acres of tropical plants grown hydroponically. Although the garden is on pure oolite rock, growth of up to five feet a year is achieved by this method. Open Mon-Sat 0900-1730, US$1 entry or US$2 guided tour, T 352 6052.

The Garden of Groves is a 12-acre botanical garden of flowers, birds (the flamingoes have been killed by dogs), pools and waterfalls. The centrepiece is a stone replica of the original church built for the loggers on Pine Ridge, and is a popular place for weddings. Gardens located on Magellan Drive, eight miles out of Freeport, 1000-1700 except Wed, free. Closed holidays. Times subject to change according to how much voluntary help is available, T 352 4045 for up to date information.

The Rand Nature Centre, East Settlers Way, opposite the Catholic High School, two miles out of town, is a 100-acre forest with a few flamingoes, hummingbirds and the rare olive capped warbler. Open Mon-Fri 0900-1600, guided tours 1000 and 1400, admission US$5 (children US$3), T 352 5438, PO Box F-3441, Freeport. Highly recommended for its explanation of the ecology of a Bahamian forest. Run by the Bahamas National Trust since 1992, work is being done on more educational programmes, more trail development and an improved self-guided tour. A replica of a Lucayan village is under construction. Special birdwatching walks are offered on the first Sat of each month at 0700, 1½ hrs, US$5 unless you are a BNT member, bring binoculars and field guide.

NB Be careful of wild dogs on the island and if out walking or jogging always carry a stick. If bothered, local people stoop as if to pick up a stone. This gives some breathing space.

Away from Freeport are the villages of Seagrape, Pine Ridge and Water Cay. West of Freeport: **Eight Mile Rock** (eight miles from Freeport) is the name given to eight miles of rock stretching E and W of Hawksbill Creek. The name refers to the town W of the creek. The Rock, as locals call it, has a strong sense of community not found in Freeport. The coastal road is prettier than the road directly through EMR although if you pass through the town you can see the original wooden clapboard dwellings raised off the ground, some with verandahs where the inhabitants sit chillin' and rapping. Local bar, *The Ritz*, very friendly, but see below under **Bars**. Sample Mr Wildgoose's tequila. Along the coastal road is a boiling hole and the Catholic church in Hepburn Town with walls shaped like praying hands. East of Hawksbill Creek are the settlement areas of Pinders Point, Lewis Yard and Hunters. Off Pinders Point is a boiling hole called the Chimney, which causes a vortex. Below is a large cave system but you need to go with a very experienced cave diver to see it.

West End, 21 miles from Freeport, was supposedly the first settlement on Grand Bahama. It enjoyed prosperity as a haven for rum-runners during the American prohibition era. The coastal road is pleasant with local fishermen hooking conch from their boats on one side and bars, shops and houses in pastel shades on the other. At the most westerly point is the *Jack Tar Hotel Village*, brainchild of Sir Billy Butlin (closed in 1990), but now abandoned.

Driving E from Freeport, you can see evidence of the aborted development plans, with many half-built plots, now mostly covered by bush, and roads which lead to nowhere. 15 miles E of Freeport, towards High Rock, is the 42-acre **Lucaya National Park**, with about 250 plant species, caves, plus a path through a Mangrove swamp, built in Mar 1985 by volunteers from 'Operation Raleigh'. Continuing E you get to High Rock (20 miles) (*Ezekiel Pinder's Restaurant* has an ocean view – almost) and Pelican Point (10 miles further), excellent deserted beach. The road on to **McLean's Town** (see **Festivals**, above) and East End is poor, but passable. From McLean's Town you can get a boat across to Sweetings or Deep Water Cay. Neither has vehicular traffic. It is possible to rent cottages. There is a guest house on Deep Water Cay and the *Traveller's Rest Bar* on Sweetings Cay. East End Adventures run 4WD tours to Sweetings Cay and Lightbourne's Cay via the Lucaya National Park and McLean's Town, US$100 pp, US$50 for children under 12, including lunch, T 373 6662, 352 6222 (after hours).

Island information – Grand Bahama

● **Transport**

Getting to see most of Grand Bahama without a car is difficult. Cars can be rented at the airport or in Freeport on a daily (US$70 for a compact car, plus insurance of about US$12 a day) or weekly (US$420) basis, as can jeeps

(US$90/day), mopeds (US$20/day) and bicycles. Five Wheels Car Hire, T 352 7001; Hertz, T 352 3297; Dollar Rent A Car, T 352 9308. Check the telephone yellow pages for many more. **Taxi** fares are fixed and cabs are metered (see page 80), but expect additional charges for extra passengers and more than 2 pieces of luggage. Taxis are available at the airport; expect to share as they leave when full and they are big taxis. Fare to International Bazaar US$5. Fare to Lucaya US$11, 15 mins. Taxis from the Harbour to the International Bazaar cost US$8 and to Port Lucaya US$14, based on a full taxi. Be sure to establish the fare in advance especially when there are people going to different destinations in the same taxi. Report any problems to the Ministry of Tourism. A strict rotation system is used and buses are not allowed into the harbour area. Public **buses** run from Freeport to Lucaya (US$0.75) and less frequently from Freeport to High Rock, Eight Mile Rock (US$1), Holmes Rock (US$2), West End (US$3) and East End. Check for timetable details. Buses drive fast and recklessly. There are routed stops but usually drivers will stop wherever you shout "bus stop coming up" loud enough to be heard over the music. Buses do not generally leave the bazaar or centre until full. Many hotels have a complimentary bus service for guests to the beach or in to Freeport.

● **Accommodation**

Hotel prices

L1	over US$200	L2	US$151-200
L3	US$101-150	A1	US$81-100
A2	US$61-80	A3	US$46-60
B	US$31-45	C	US$21-30
D	US$12-20	E	US$7-11
F	US$4-6	G	up to US$3

See note on Hotels under New Providence. Price lists can be obtained from the tourist office in the Bazaar or in Lucaya. In the Lucaya area, 5 miles from the airport, 3 miles from Downtown, there are 3 large hotels in a row along the beach all now owned by Sun and Sea Estates Ltd and under renovation in 1996: the **L1-L2** *Lucayan Beach Resort and Casino*, 243 rooms, rates depend on view but gambling, diving or golf packages work out cheaper, emphasis is on the casino, tennis and lots of watersports, convention facilities, several restaurants and bars, T 373 7777, F 373 6916, T 1-800-772 1227, PO Box F-40336, Lucaya; the nicest of the 3 is **L1-L3** *Clarion*

Atlantik Beach and Golf Resort, opp the Market Place, 123 elegant rooms and 52 luxury split-level suites of different sizes, 3 rooms for disabled, a/c, phone, TV, nice views, dining rooms overlook pool, beach bar, conference facilities, free use of tennis courts next door, golf, dive and other packages available, T 373 1444, F 373 7481, in USA 1-800 622 6770, in Canada 1-800 848 3315, PO Box F-42500; **L1-L3** *Grand Bahama Beach Hotel/Flamingo Beach Resort*, 500 rooms, standard, superior, ocean front and suites, major refurbishment and redesign in 1996, price depends on view, children under 12 free when sharing with adult, golf packages available, T 373 1333, F 373 8662/2396, 1-800-813 8426, in USA T 1-800-848-6770, in Canada T 1-800-848-3315, PO Box F 2496.

L1-A3 *Port Lucaya Resort and Yacht Club*, hotel adjoining existing marina opened 1993/94 with pool, jacuzzi, bars, restaurant, on reclaimed land jutting out into harbour, rooms and 1-2 bedroom suites, slips for 50 boats of 40-125 feet surround the resort, T 373 6618, F 373 6652, PO Box F 42452, the adjoining marina caters for all sizes of yachts including a luxury, private dock, all services and facilities, for information on dockage call Jack Chester, T 373 9090, F 373 5884. West along the coast is the **L1-L3** *Xanadu Beach and Marina Resort*, where Howard Hughes, the recluse, used to live on the top floors. There is a small study/library dedicated to him on the ground floor of the tower, which has a pink ring of apartments on top. Alongside is a lower rise block of rooms and restaurants. The rooms are decorated in heavy pink paint, shut your balcony doors, security lax, service and facilities poor value for price, small pool, bar, 3 tennis courts with pro, dive shop and watersports centre on site, nice beach, 67 slips in marina, T 352 6782/3, F 352 5799, PO Box F-2438. Inland on West Sunrise Highway by the Ranfurly Circle is the **L1-L3** *Bahamas Princess Resort and Casino*, comprising the mock-Moorish *Princess Tower*, with *Princess Casino* next door and *Princess Country Club* on the other side of the road, 400 rooms in the *Tower* with top 2 floors keyed off for gamblers, 565 rooms in the low-rise *Country Club*, where blocks of rooms and suites fan out from the large, landscaped pool with waterfalls, tunnels, rocks and hot tub, 9 restaurants, 12 tennis courts, 2 golf courses, beach shuttle, convention facilities, children's activities, packages available, children under 12 free when sharing with adults, T 352 6721, F 352 6842, PO Box F-40207, in USA T 800-223-1818.

L1 Club Fortuna Beach, on S side of island, 4 miles E of Port Lucaya, Italian resort, all-inclusive, 204 rooms with garden or ocean view, a/c, phone, cable TV, 2 big beds, sailing, windsurfing, kayaking, tennis, archery, bicycles, aerobics, golf putting green, volley ball, children's playground, scuba diving at extra cost, dive shop on site, nightly entertainment, T 373 4000, 1-800-847 4502, F 373 5555, PO Box F-42398.

Less expensive hotels are **A2 The New Victoria Inn** off Midshipman's Drive (40 rooms, 2-bedroom suite, pool, transport to beach, shops, casino, T 373 3040, F 373 8374, PO Box F-1261) and **A1-A2 Castaways** next to the Bazaar off the Ranfurly Circle (130 rooms on 4 floors, poolside or noisy roadside, TV, a/c, phone, small bathroom, courtesy transport to beach, avoid overpriced excursions, T 352 6682, F 352 5087, PO Box F-42629), but none can be rec for service. Self catering apartments are available at many resorts. To stay with a Bahamian family, write to the Grand Bahama Island Promotion Board, Freeport (see below, **Tourist Office**), for details of the People To People Programme; see also under **Information for travellers**. Vigilance is advised in Freeport. Never leave screen doors open at night, there have been a number of armed robberies and sexual assaults where intruders have just walked in through screen doors left open.

● **Places to eat**

The hotels have several expensive restaurants which serve native/international cuisine. Buffet brunches on Sun are rec, you can eat as much as you like at *Princess Towers, Xanadu Hotel* and *Lucayan Beach Resort* (US$18 including as much champagne as you can drink). Many restaurants, particularly those in hotels, do Early Bird Specials from 1730-1830, the EBS for US$13 at *La Trattoria* in the *Princess Towers* is good value. Beach front restaurants: *Pier One*, at Freeport Harbour, where they feed the sharks around 2100, and *The Stoned Crab* on Taino Beach are both expensive, romantic, with good views. *Surside Restaurant* further down on Taino Beach is a wooden structure on stilts, popular with Bahamians, cheap special most evenings; *Blackbeard's* on Fortune Beach, friendly, reasonably priced menu, mosquitos and no see'ums can be troublesome if you eat outside; *The Buccaneer*

Club at Deadman's Reef has a courtesy bus (call 349 3794) but if you use it you will be presented with a higher priced menu on arrival, about 40-mins drive from Freeport, Wed night specials, closed in Oct, interesting guest signature book. Other popular restaurants include: *Freddie's Native Restaurant* in Hunters Settlement, open 1100-2300 but phone in advance, food basic but freshly prepared, tasty and cheap with fish dishes for US$8; *The Traveller's Rest* in Williams Town has good cheap breakfasts, Johnny Cake and soused fish are popular; *The Outriggers* at Smith's Point, just outside Lucaya at the far end of Taino Beach, distinctly Bahamian flavour, phone to check menu, fish fry outdoors on Wed night, T 373 4811; nearby is *Mama Flo's*, similar, even more popular for fish fry on Wed when there is lots of loud music and barbecues; *The Native Lobster Hut*, Sergeant Major Drive, pea soup; *Scorpios*, Explorers Way, reasonably priced native food, favourable reports. For Italian food, *Silvano's* on Ranfurly Circus, *Luciano's* in Port Lucaya good, book a table outside to see fireworks over the square on Sat evenings at 2030-2100, noisy music though. *Pisces*, near *Lucayan Towers*, popular for its pizzas and cocktails, run by Bahamian George and Scottish Rosie. *Islander's Roost*, opp International Bazaar, open air dining patio, live entertainment, variety of Bahamian and American dishes, mascot Bella the parrot oversees all. For oriental dishes there are at least 3 Chinese restaurants in the International Bazaar, the one at the entrance is not rec. The *Phoenix* (*Silver Sands Hotel*) serves kebabs and curries and has an unusual bar. The *Ruby Swiss Restaurant* on West Sunrise (seafood) is expensive but service is good. *Fat Man's Nephew* in Port Lucaya is reasonably priced, good view of bandstand, open 1200-2400 except Tues 1700-2400 and Sun 1700-2300, T 373 8520. (*Fat Man* in Pinder's Point used to be popular but the owner, Fat Man, was gunned down by an armed robber.) *The Bahama Beach Club*, just W of the *Xanadu Hotel*, has a superb view of the sea, usually only bar snacks available, but watch newspapers for specials, eg Fish Fry on Fri, barbecue on Sat at 1900, nice local atmosphere; the *Brass Helmet*, upstairs at UNEXSO, a slightly different menu from normal, reasonable prices, breakfast, lunch and dinner, good and popular with divers. For sandwiches and salads at lunchtime, *Kristi's* in the Bain Building, West Atlantic Drive, Downtown, takeaway or eat in, open Mon-Sat 0800-1600, T 352 3149. Although some restaurants are efficient and friendly, be prepared for indifferent service and long waits in many. A poll showed that 51% of tourists were dissatisfied with service in local hotels and restaurants. Restaurants open and close with alarming speed, check the local newspapers for new ones or special offers. A cheap alternative is to go to one of the many cook outs, usually of a high standard. Often the proceeds go to a good cause, such as someone's hospital bills. Taino Beach hosts cook outs but best to look in local press for details.

● **Bars and nightlife**
There are a large number of bars in Freeport, most have a Happy Hour between 1700-1900. Most of the restaurants mentioned above have bars. While Bahamians are usually very friendly towards visitors and local bars are interesting and rewarding if you meet the local characters, be alert for any violent incidents which may suddenly arise. The *Pub on the Mall, Britannia Pub* and the *Winston Churchill* are all English style pubs. The *Winston Churchill* sells draught Courage, serves pizzas, fish 'n' chips, and hosts the Gong Show on Wed (starts around 2330, open 1100-0200, T 352 8866). *Pussers Pub* in Port Lucaya with an English style pub menu is in a very pleasant location overlooking the waterfront and band stand where live calypso music is played most nights. Pussers Painkiller is rec. *Sandpipers* on Coral Beach is a country and western style bar. Most hotels have native shows. The *Yellow Bird Club* close to the International Bazaar has limbo, drums, fire dancing and a glass eater, T 352 2325, 373 7368. The *Lucayan Beach Resort and Casino* has a casino show, Mon-Sat, 2045 and 2245, US$24.95 pp inc 2 drinks and tip, dinner/show packages, small cast of dancers, awful comedian, theatre half-empty for *Carnivale Lucaya* show, T 373 7777. The casino is advertised as the only casino on the beach, but you will not notice the sea when you are inside the 20,000 sq ft gaming hall with its 550 slot machines. The casino show at the *Princess* is much better, larger cast, well-choreographed, bright and lively. The huge casino has 20,000 sq ft of gaming space with 450 slot machines, 40 black jack tables, 8 dice tables, 8 roulette tables, 2 money wheels, 70 assorted video machines. At the *Xanadu Hotel* most weekends you can hear live jazz. *WRLX 5000*, Queen's Highway, plays music

from the 1960s. Most of the Freeport bars sponsor darts teams. The league is taken seriously and on Tues and Thur there are matches. Dominoes are also popular, particularly in the smaller bars. For cheaper drinks in a less touristy environment, *Outriggers, Surfside* and *The Traveller's Rest* are rec. *The Ritz* in Eight Mile Rock has a number of hammocks outside which overlook the sea (rubbish spoils the view), there has been some night-time violence at the bar, better to go during the day. Others include *The Ruby Swiss* on East Sunrise Highway, lively 0100-0400 when casino workers gather there after their shift ends, *Café Valencia* in the International Bazaar, also known as a croupiers' hangout, does not get going until after midnight. *The Bahama Mama* bar in the E corner of the Port Lucaya complex is one of the most popular bars, attracting local, expatriate and tourist customers giving it a lively, cosmopolitan atmosphere, interesting music, busy from 2300 onwards, a good place to meet people.

● **Discos**
At most of the large hotels, with 2 drinks in entrance fee. If you want to know which disco is 'in', ask the English croupiers at the casinos as they closely monitor the night life. *Goombay Land* behind *The Palace* has roller skating and go-karts, very popular with local youth, entrance US$5.

● **Shopping**
Many items are tax exempt in the bonded area of Freeport/Lucaya and bargains include perfume, linens, sweaters, china, cameras, emeralds, watches, leather goods and alcoholic drinks. The 2 main shopping areas are the International Bazaar and Port Lucaya. The International Bazaar is off Ranfurly Circle. Built in 1967, the 10-acre complex was designed by a film special effects expert, with shops designed in national styles and selling corresponding food and goods, although the overall effect is very American. The entrance is a giant Torri gate, the Japanese symbol of welcome. Port Lucaya was the brainchild of Count Basie, who used to live on Grand Bahama. The atmosphere is usually friendly and there is live music most evenings. There are many different shops to buy souvenirs as well as a straw market. The Rastafarian Shop has some interesting souvenirs and there is a Bahamian Arts and Crafts stall in the centre of the complex, one row back from the central bandstand. In downtown Freeport there are a few small

shopping malls; Regency has a Marks & Spencers, Body Shop behind it; 17 Centre behind the main Post Office. Close by are a Winn Dixie and a Woolley's which have a virtual monopoly of the grocery supplies.

● **Tourist office**
In Freeport, Bazaar, Port Lucaya Market Place, as well as in any large hotel. The Tourist Information Centres in Freeport/Lucaya can give a brochure listing all licensed hotels in the Bahamas and their rates. The Grand Bahama Island Promotion Board can be contacted through PO Box F40650, Freeport, T 352 8356, F 352 7840, or in Florida, One Turnberry Place, 19495 Biscayne Boulevard, Suite 809, Aventura, Fl 33180, T (305) 935-9461, (800) 448-3386, F (305) 935-9464.

● **Vendors**
A Vendors Committee has been set up for hair braiders, conch sellers and peddlers, to control and regulate their operation and prevent complaints of hassling by tourists. A photo identification card is to be worn by all vendors and they will generally wear Androsia batik tops. They must have a permit and to have completed a Bahamahost programme. Hair braiding is US$2-3 per braid.

THE FAMILY ISLANDS

The **Family Islands**, which are often called the Out Islands, are very different in atmosphere from New Providence and Grand Bahama. The larger islands are up to a hundred miles long, but have only a few thousand inhabitants. Sea and sky come in every possible shade of blue; there are wild cliffs and miles of white sand beaches. Inland, pine forests grow in the northern islands, dry woodland in the central ones and sparse scrub vegetation in the southern islands. Red-coloured salt ponds were once the basis of a thriving salt industry on the S islands, but the land offered few other economic possibilities, though one other product was Cascarilla bark, used to flavour Vermouth and Campari. Before the drugs-and-tourism boom of the 1980s, most people earned their living from the sea. The villages have brightly painted, traditional-style houses and whitewashed churches. People are generally friendly and helpful and the way of life is much more Bahamian and less Americanized.

Thousands of yachts visit the islands, mainly during the winter season. The sea is clean and clear and ideal for swimming, snorkelling and scuba diving. Most of the islands have relatively few tourists, although Eleuthera and one or two others have big, resort-type hotels with marinas and sports facilities. Most islands have at least one Bahamasair flight a day and at least one mailboat a week. If you are travelling in a group, a small charter plane may be much more convenient and only a little more expensive. Some islands also have a direct flight from Miami or another Florida airport; this cuts out the need for an unreliable, time-consuming connection in Nassau. Travel is restricted to one main road per island, usually called the Queen's Highway.

ABACO

The Abaco islands (population 11,000), are a chain of islands and cays covered in pine forests, stretching in a curve for 130 miles from **Walker's Cay** in the N to Hole in the Wall in the S. The Taino name for Abaco was Lucayoneque, although the first Spanish reference to it was Habacoa, a name also used for Andros. The Spanish did not settle, but by 1550 they had kidnapped all the Indian inhabitants for slavery elsewhere and the islands remained uninhabited for 200 years, despite a brief French attempt at settlement in 1625 and visits by pirates and fishermen. In 1783 over 600 loyalists left New York for Abaco, settling first at Carleton (N of Treasure Cay beach but no longer visible) and then moving to Marsh Harbour. Other groups settled further S but all found it hard to make a living on the small pockets of soil and of the 2,000 who arrived in the 1780s, only about 400 (half white and half black) were left in 1790. Wrecking was a profitable pastime and Abaco was ideally placed on a busy

Revolution Abaco style

The 1967 elections resulted in a victory for Lynden Pindling's party the Progressive Liberal Party (PLP), which represented the black majority of the Bahamas. Abaco, which was 50% white, voted for the opposition. In the early 1970s some Abaco residents formed the Greater Abaco Council which was opposed to Bahamian independence. When independence became a reality in 1973, the Abaco Independence Movement tried to assert Abaco's independence from the rest of the Bahamas. This breakaway movement by white residents caused the islanders to split into two camps and there were bitter conflicts. According to local storytellers, there was going to be a revolution, but there was confusion over whether it was planned for Wed or Thur, then some men went fishing and, well .... Support for the main opposition party, the Free National Movement (FNM), remained strong in Abaco. In 1992 it was elected to government and its Prime Minister, Hubert Ingraham, lives near Coopers Town.

shipping route to take advantage of its reefs and sand banks. Sponge, pineapple, sisal, sugar and lumber were later developed but never became big business. Wrecking also declined after the construction of lighthouses. The lighthouse on Elbow Cay at Hope Town was built in 1863, after the wreck in 1862 of the *USS Adirondack*, despite sabotage attempts by local people. By 1900 Hope Town was the largest town in the Abacos, with a population of 1,200 engaged in fishing, sponging, shipping and boat building. The boats made in Abaco were renowned for their design and the builders became famous for their construction skills. Boats, though made of fibreglass, are still made on Man-O-War Cay today. The inhabitants of Abaco continued to live barely at subsistence levels until after the Second World War, when the Owens-Illinois Corporation revived the lumber business, built roads and introduced cars. An airport was built at Marsh Harbour and banks arrived. When the pulpwood operation ended in the 1960s sugar replaced it but was short lived. Nowadays the major agribusiness is citrus from two huge farms which export their crop to Florida. Abaco has developed its tourist industry slowly and effectively and has a high employment rate. Resorts are small and the atmosphere is casual and friendly even in the most luxurious hotels.

The main centre on Abaco is Marsh Harbour, which is the third largest town in the Bahamas. Its name reflects the swampy nature of much of Greater Abaco. The scrub and swamp give the island a rather desolate appearance, but like many islands, life revolves around the offshore cays and the coastal settlements. The area S of Marsh Harbour owes its development and particularly its roads to lumber companies. There are miles and miles of pine forests, secondary growth after the heavy logging earlier this century. Nobody lives S of Sandy Point although there is a lighthouse at Hole in the Wall. Roads are better in the N, where they are mostly paved, while in the S they are dirt.

Guy Fawkes Day is celebrated on 5 Nov with parades through the streets led by the Guy to a big bonfire in the evening (no fireworks).

Flora and fauna

Like other northern Family Islands, Abaco is mostly covered by secondary growth stands of Caribbean pine, interspersed with hammocks or coppices of hardwoods such as mahogany and wild coffee. The Bahama parrot, extinct on all other islands bar Inagua, survives in these coppices, 42 breeding pairs have been counted. A captive breeding programme is now in progress and fledglings will be released back into these areas. In the wild, the parrot nests around Hole in the Wall and the area is to be made a reservation for them. Friends of the Environment, an environmental protection group, headquarters on Treasure Cay, Abaco, runs guided excursions to see the parrots (US$40 per person), and also has plenty of other, interesting information on the fauna of the Abacos, T 367 2847. A herd of wild horses roams the citrus groves and pine forests in the N. They are a hardy breed of work horses descended

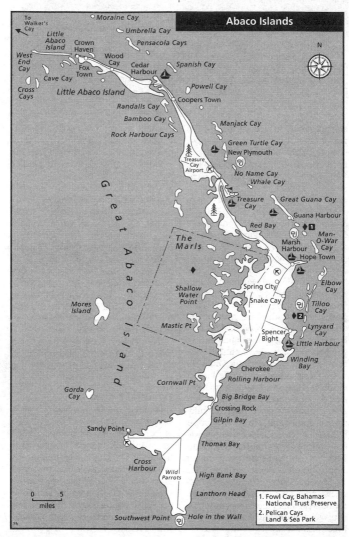

Abaco Islands

To Walker's Cay

Moraine Cay
Umbrella Cay
Little Abaco Island
Crown Haven
Pensacola Cays
Wood Cay
West End Cay
Cross Cays
Cave Cay
Fox Town
Cedar Harbour
Spanish Cay
Little Abaco Island
Powell Cay
Coopers Town
Randalls Cay
Bamboo Cay
Manjack Cay
Rock Harbour Cays
Green Turtle Cay
New Plymouth
Treasure Cay Airport
No Name Cay
Whale Cay
Great Guana Cay
Treasure Cay
Guana Harbour
Red Bay
Man-O-War Cay
The Marls
Marsh Harbour
Hope Town
Great Abaco Island
Shallow Water Point
Spring City
Snake Cay
Elbow Cay
Tilloo Cay
Mores Island
Mastic Pt
Lynyard Cay
Spencer Bight
Little Harbour
Cherokee
Rolling Harbour
Winding Bay
Cornwall Pt
Gorda Cay
Big Bridge Bay
Crossing Rock
Gilpin Bay
Sandy Point
Thomas Bay
Cross Harbour
Wild Parrots
High Bank Bay
Lanthorn Head
Southwest Point
Hole in the Wall

0   5
miles

1. Fowl Cay, Bahamas National Trust Preserve
2. Pelican Cays Land & Sea Park

from those used in the sawmills which closed in the 1920s and 1930s, abandoning the animals.

Diving and marine life

Life revolves around the sea and Abaco is sometimes called the 'sailing capital of the world', with good marina facilities at the *Treasure Cay Marina*, one of the largest tourist resorts in the Family Islands, the *Conch Inn Resort and Marina* (a 75-slip marina can accommodate boats up to 140 feet), the Boat Harbour Marina by the *Great Abaco Beach Hotel* (160 slips, boat hire, services, showers, laundromat, will hold mail, T 367 2736, VHF 16) and the *Green Turtle Yacht Club and Marina*. Marsh Harbour Regatta is 22 June to 4 July. Marsh Harbour is the starting place/drop off for many sailing charter companies. Charters can be arranged by the day or week, through numerous agencies (such as Sun Sail at Marsh Harbour, ABC at Hope Town or JIC Boat Rentals and Charter at Treasure Cay, T 367 2507), or more cheaply by private arrangement with boat owners. Ask at local marinas such as the *Jib Room*. Prices from $80 per day. Fishing charters are around US$200/half day, US$300/day.

The diving is good, don't miss Pelican Cay Land and Sea Park, which is an underwater wildlife sanctuary with no fishing or spear fishing allowed and Fowl Cay Bahamas National Trust Preserve with similar restrictions. Many areas are now officially protected and fish life is abundant, green turtles and porpoises numerous in and around harbour areas. Fishing is strictly controlled in reef areas although the coral still shows signs of previous damage by bleaching and careless sailors. Three of the best reefs for diving or snorkelling are Sandy Cay Reef (part of Pelican Cay Park), Johnny's Cay Reef and Fowl Cay Reef at each of which there are several dive sites and a few permanent moorings for small boats. If you like exploring wrecks, the 110-year old *USS Adirondack* with her rusting cannon is worth a visit. If it is windy or the sea rough there is unlikely to be any diving because of poor visibility in the shallow waters. Inland you can dive into Devil's Hole. Specialist dive operations include Dive Abaco at Marsh Harbour (*Conch Inn Marina*, T 367 2787, VHF 16, 800-247 5338, dives 0930, 1430, one tank US$45, 2 tanks US$60, snorkel trip US$30, one boat, one dive master, no back-up), Divers Down at Treasure Cay (T 367 2570 ext 126, one tank US$50, 2 tanks US$70, snorkelling US$30), Walker's Cay Dive Shop and Brendal's Dive Shop at Green Turtle Cay, who can offer introductory courses and a wide variety of facilities. For offshore snorkelling, Captain Nick's Tours, from the *Jib Room* marina and restaurant, runs trips out to local reefs and beauty spots, including Pelican Cay. Snorkel gear is available for hire.

Marsh Harbour lacks good beaches, but Mermaid's Cove on the road to the Point is a pretty little beach with excellent snorkelling. The best beach on Great Abaco is probably that at Treasure Cay, where there is a large, sandy bay backed by casuarina trees and a friendly beach bar. On the cays there are lots of lovely sandy beaches with few people on them, many of which are best reached by boat.

Other sports

You can play tennis at *Bluff House* (guests free), *Great Abaco Beach Hotel* (guests free) or *Green Turtle Club* (US$5/hour). *Walker's Cay Hotel and Marina* (T 305-522 1469), a 100-acre resort, has tennis courts as well as a range of water activities, including windsurfing (US$15/hour). *Treasure Cay Beach Hotel and Villas* on a 3-mile beach, has a 6,972-yard, 18-hole championship golf course (T 367 2570, green fees US$40, cart US$25 and club rental US$12.50), tennis, windsurfing (US$15/hour) and waterskiing (US$10/15 mins). Other places where you can windsurf include *Abaco Inn* (US$30/day), at Hope Town, *Elbow Cay Club* (US$25/day), the *Green Turtle Yacht Club* (free for guests), *Hope Town Harbour Lodge* (US$20/day), *Pinder's Cottages* (US$20/day).

MARSH HARBOUR

The town straggles along the flat S shore of a good and busy yachting harbour. It has the major airport about three miles from the town and is the commercial centre of Abaco. As you drive in from the airport you pass government offices, supermarkets and lots of churches and liquor stores. The town has a large white population, but at the last census 40% were found to be Haitian, most of whom lived in the districts of Pigeon Pea and The Mud and worked as domestic servants in the white suburbs. Many Haitians have since been repatriated however. Shops are varied and well stocked and Barclays and CIBC banks are both represented. The only traffic lights on the island are outside Barclays. BaTelCo is a yellow building off Queen Elizabeth Drive. The Tourist Office is nearby. The two main food stores are Golden Harvest and Abaco Market. The Bahamas Family Market on Front Street sells mainly fruit and vegetables grown on Abaco. The Marsh Harbour Dental Clinic (Dr Hornaday, T 367 3167) is near Abaco Market.

EXCURSIONS

The roads are better in the northern half of the island and it is easy to drive the 26 miles to *Treasure Cay*, a self-contained resort approached by a long drive through the grounds, past the golf course. There is a nice beach here and lots of watersports available at the marina. The main road continues past Treasure Cay airport and several small communities, where most of the workers for *Treasure Cay* live, to **Coopers Town**. 20 miles from Treasure Cay, it has lots of little painted wooden houses and an air of bustling importance. It is the seat of the commissioner for N Abaco and about 900 people live here. The Prime Minister, Hubert Ingraham, lives in the area. In 1993-94 a new health clinic was built, the biggest on the island with doctors, dentists and nurses working there. There is no harbour but

along the waterfront are wooden jetties where fishermen clean their catch, leaving piles of conch shells. Offshore on Powell Cay (uninhabited), there are some lovely beaches, good shelling and the *Shipwreck Bar and Grill*. The paved road carries on another 15 miles to Crown Haven, the end of the island.

South of Marsh Harbour it is 56 miles to Sandy Point, through citrus groves, or you can fork left to Hole in the Wall, the area where parrots breed. On the way you can visit Spencer Bight and the abandoned Wilson City, a company town founded in 1906 by the Bahamas Timber Company but closed in 1916. In its heyday there was a saw mill and dock facilities and it boasted electricity and an ice plant, both rarities at that time. At **Little Harbour** you find the highest point in Abaco, which is 120 feet. Little Harbour is a small, pretty and protected anchorage, famed for the Johnston family's artwork in bronze, ceramics and jewelry. Their work is on display in two galleries open 1030-1200, 1400-1500 or by appointment, closed Sun. Pete Johnston also has *Pete's Pub*, where there are moorings and you can eat at the open air bar on the beach (hot dogs, hamburgers, lobster). There is a nice walk to the old lighthouse and snorkelling is good over the small reef at the E entrance to the harbour. There are caves where the Johnstons lived when they first came to Little Harbour. If you go on Independence Day, 10 July, there is a free for all on the beach, everyone chips in, roast wild pig a feature.

ELBOW CAY

The name Elbow Cay is rarely used, people refer to the settlement of **Hope Town**, marked by a striped lighthouse from the top of which you can get lovely views (built by the British Imperial Lighthouse Service in 1863, it is one of the last hand-powered Kerosene-fuelled beacons still in use, open Mon-Fri 1000-1600) or **White Sound**, SW of the town, where there are a couple of resorts. Hope Town is very picturesque, set around a charming harbour, cluttered with jetties and brightly painted wooden houses. There are no cars allowed along the narrow

Elbow Cay

Cook's Cove

Anna Cay

Eagle Rock

Parrot Cays

Light House

Hope Town Harbour

Cemetery

White

Sound

Aunt Pats Bay

Atlantic Ocean

Tahiti Beach

0   0.5
miles

1. Wyannie Malone Museum
2. Captain Jack's Bar
3. Harbour's Edge Restaurant
4. Abaco Inn
5. Club Soleil Resort & Hope Town Hideaways
6. Hope Town Harbour Lodge
7. Sea Spray Villas & Marina

streets edged by white picket fences and saltbox cottages. Visit the Wyannie Malone Historical Museum which has a collection of old furniture, genealogies and memorabilia from the town. The museum is staffed by volunteers. If it is not open, call Peggy Thompson at *Hope Town Hideaways*. The town's jail is no longer used as such, but is filled with visitor's brochures. There are several places to eat and drink in the town, there are grocery stores, bakeries and gift shops. A lovely beach runs along the ocean side of the island and Tahiti Beach is at the extreme end in the SW. Bicycles can be hired but it is a rough ride down to the S. Dave's Dive Shop and Boat Rentals, T 366 0029, VHF 16, next to Hope Town Lower Ferry Dock, rents Boston Whalers, US$65/day, or larger boats, US$80-90, which are an easier way of getting around. Dave also rents diving gear and tanks.

● **Accommodation & places to eat** There are several bars and restaurants: *Captain Jack's* has tables on its own jetty, lovely views across the water to the mangroves, breakfast 0830-1030, lunch and dinner 1100-2100, happy hour 1700-1830, T 366 0247. *Harbour's Edge*, bar open from 1000, free transport for dinner, good food, open air or indoors, Sat night live band, weather permitting, pool table, satellite TV, bicycle rental US$8/day, friendly, happy hour 1700-1800, T 366 0087/0292, VHF 16, closed around Oct for 6 weeks. **L3** *Hope Town Harbour Lodge*, renovated and refurbished 1994, bar and pool the other side of the hill overlooking beach, lunch by pool, no prebooking in restaurant, rooms with harbour view in main hotel, or with ocean view, T 366 0095, 800-3167844, F 366 0286, lovely location, friendly. **L2** *Hope Town Villas*, run by Michael and Patty Myers, 2 clapboard cottages, one overlooking lighthouse, the other nearer the beach, US$850/week, fully equipped, T 366 0030, F 366 0377. On the other side of the water, reached by boat, is **L3** *Club Soleil Resort*, restaurant on waterfront, good menu, fish, chicken, champagne Sun brunch, always full, reservations needed, try their drink Tropical Shock, 6 rooms, bright, cheerful, TV, VCR, a/c, fridge, all overlook harbour, balcony, German and Dutch also spoken, own boat for deep sea fishing, T 366 0003, F 366 0254. A walkway connects with **L1-L2** *Hope Town Hideaways*, an attractive cluster of 4 villas, run by Chris and Peggy Thompson, T 366 0224, F 366 0434, very friendly, lovely location but you have to go everywhere by boat, each villa has 2 master bedrooms, full kitchen/diner, a/c, fans, TV, music centre, telephone, videos, games, beautifully decorated, small man-made beach and infants' sand play area, rental boats US$75-95/day, cheaper for longer, 12 large slips, power and water, no restaurant but local cooks can be contracted if you do not want to go next door. On White Sound, **L3** *Abaco Inn* overlooks the calm water and also the ocean, there is a dirt road from Hope Town, or you can hire a boat or charter a ferry, small rooms harbour side or ocean side, wonderful view, a/c, fan, hammocks, restaurant and pool overlook ocean, bar overlooks harbour, nude bathing area, snorkelling gear and bicycles free for guests, small children not encouraged, no evening entertainment, T 366 0133, 800-468 8799, F 366 0113, run by John Goodloe, usually full. **L2-A1** *Seaspray Resort and Villas*, also on White Sound, boats for hire, 1-2 bedroom villas have spacious living area, full kitchen, small bedrooms, a/c, US$550-950/week, min 3-nights, run by Monty and Ruth Albury, Monty's mother runs a bakery and will cook Bahamian meals if required, pool, windsurfing, sunfish, motorboats US$65-95/day, snorkelling, sailing and fishing trips, freshwater pool, games room with pool table, quiet, villas spread out, free Hope Town shuttle, T 366 0065, F 366 0383.

MAN-O-WAR CAY

This cay is a boat building and repair centre with New England Loyalist origins, where, until recently, blacks were not allowed to stay overnight. Nearly everyone on the island can trace their family back to Pappy Ben and Mammy Nellie, a young couple who settled there in the 1820s. There are two boatyards now, Edwin's Boat Yard, which specializes in boat repair and building fibreglass outboard boats, and Albury Brothers Boat Building, which makes smaller, fibreglass runabouts. Albury's Ferry is based here. It is very pretty, with a good beach on the E side and snorkelling at the N point. The

Marina offers full services, T 365 6008, VHF 16, and a gift shop. There are a couple of small places to eat, but they really cater for the takeaway trade, and a couple of grocery stores. No alcohol is sold on the island, you have to go to Marsh Harbour for that. L2-L3 *Schooner's Landing Resort*, 2-bedroom condos on the beach, a/c, minimum 3 nights' stay, US$850 a week, T 365 6072, F 365 6285, manageress Brenda Sawyer can arrange sailing, diving, snorkelling, fishing, boat rentals etc. Contact Bill and Sherry Albury for rental cottages, US$450-650/week, T 365 6009. The CIBC bank is open Thur only. There are no cars, people use golf carts and scooters. Sundays are graveyard quiet.

GREAT GUANA CAY

The population of Great Guana Cay is only about 100. There are a few shops, including a grocery and a liquor store, and most services are available. A wide, sandy beach extends nearly the length of the ocean side of the island, about 5½ miles, although the N end has been developed for use of Treasure Cay visitors. For snorkellers there is a reef just off the beach at High Rocks, SE of Guana Harbour. You can stay at the L3 *Guana Beach Resort and Marina* T 367-3590, 800-227 3366, F 305-751-9570, P O Box 474, small, informal, 15 rooms, 1-2 bedroom villas, own beach off the harbour cove and 5-mins walk from ocean beach, pool, docks and marina offering full service and yacht management programme. The restaurant is open daily 0730-1000 for indoor or outdoor dining. Guests are picked up by boat from *Conch Inn*, Marsh Harbour, at 0930 and 1600 or by arrangement.

GREEN TURTLE CAY

The picturesque and quaint village of **New Plymouth** can be reached from Treasure Cay airport by a short taxi ride (US$3 pp, min US$5) and then a ferry from Treasure Cay Dock (US$8, children 2-11 US$4, one-way, to Black Sound, White Sound, Bluff Cay or Coco Bay,

Green Turtle Cay

North End

N

Coco
Bay

Bluff
Cay

Atlantic
Ocean

Bluff House
Marina

White

Big
Bluff

Sound

Long
Bay
Cay

Long Bay

Black Sound

Gillam
Bay

0   0.5

miles

1. Alton Lowe Art
   Studios
2. New Plymouth:
   - Post Office
   - Albert Lowe Museum
   - New Plymouth Inn
3. Bluff House Club
4. Green Turtle Club
   & Marina
5. Linton Cottages
6. Roosters Rest

the public. In the village the only place to stay is the **L3** *New Plymouth Club and Inn*, a restored colonial building with 9 rooms, pool, restaurant and bar, good food, Bahamian dishes, cocktails 1830, dinner 1945, also breakfast, lunch and Sun brunch, T 365 4161, F 365 4138, PO Box 462. Further E along the coast, are *Sea Star Cottages* at Gillam Bay, on the beach, from US$500/week, T 365 4178, PO Box 282, and then **L2** *Linton Cottages*, a bit N, 1-2 bedrooms, on the ocean, fans, T 365 4003. Overlooking White Sound and beautifully sheltered is **L1-L3** *Green Turtle Club and Marina*, deluxe accommodation with all watersports, 35 rooms, in yellow wooden villas, beautifully furnished in hardwoods, clean, fresh, the beach at Coco Bay is a 5-mins walk, lots of repeat guests, T 365 4271, F 365 4272, P O Box 270, Brendal's Dive Shop on site does scuba, snorkelling, island excursions, and bicycle rentals, T 365 4411, VHF 16, there is also a gym, boat rental, bone fishing and deep sea fishing, PO Box 462, New Plymouth. **L1-A1** *Bluff House Club & Marina* has a marvellous view of the sea, pool, tennis, Boston whalers and sailboats US$50-80/day, bicycles, relaxed atmosphere, rustic, painted villas on small beach, rooms, suites and villas 1-3 bedrooms, 6 high seasons, lots of repeat business, great food and view at casual beach bar up hill, reservations needed for candlelit dinners at excellent restaurant upstairs, no locks, no TV. Boat rides to New Plymouth 3 mornings a week and for Sat night dance. Day trips to other cays with Lincoln Jones, barbecued lobster on the beach for lunch. Fishing and diving arranged. 20-mins walk to Coco Bay, a 3-mile beach. Popular with honeymooners, a secluded and friendly resort, T 365 4247, F 365 4248. *Coco Bay Cottages*, 4 cottages, US$500-800d/week, US$100/week per extra person, each with 2 bedrooms, comfortably furnished, in 5 acres of beach front property, fruit trees, snorkelling equipment available, T 365 4063/4464. To rent cottages sleeping up to 8 people per cottage, phone Sid's Grocery Store in New Plymouth, but take mosquito repellent in summer and autumn.

ferry is timed to meet planes, but can be chartered any time). The Albert Lowe Museum chronicles the British settlers who came in the 18th century and their shipbuilding skills. The Memorial Sculpture Garden is also worth a visit. The island has some lovely beaches, ideal for shelling, and boats are easily rented (US$50/day) for exploring other cays. On New Year's Day, the inhabitants celebrate the capture of Bunce, a legendary figure said to have lived in Abaco's pine forests.

• **Accommodation & places to eat** *Miss Emily's Blue Bee Bar* is worth a visit. Located in the centre of the settlement, next to the netball pitch, it is bursting with memorabilia of previous famous and infamous customers and serves unforgettable and very strong cocktails. *Laura's Kitchen*, near the ferry dock, open 1 100-1500, 1830-2100, T 365 4287, VHF 16. *Rooster's Rest*, on the outskirts, painted red, is a bar, restaurant and club, Gully's Roosters play there 2-3 nights a week, going to other clubs on other nights. Nearby, on Black Sound, the Alton Lowe art gallery is open to

SPANISH CAY

Spanish Cay is a private 185-acre island off Cooper's Town which has recently been developed as a resort. There is a 5,000-ft runway (Island Express flies from Fort Lauderdale) and a full-service marina. Transport on the island is by golf cart, or walk. L1-L2 *Spanish Cay Inn* has 5 suites and 7 apartments, a restaurant and store overlook the marina, another restaurant is at the tip of one of the 5 beaches, tennis, snorkelling, diving and fishing available, T 365 0083, 1-800-688 4752, 201-539 6450, F365 0466, 201-593 6106, reservations essential. The cay can be reached from Abaco at Coopers Town, where the resort's ferry will pick you up from the government dock. Taxi from Treasure Cay airport to Coopers Town US$30 for two people.

WALKER'S CAY

Walker's Cay was named after Judge Thomas Walker, who was banished to the island in the 18th century. It is the furthest N of all the Abaco cays and is dominated by the L1-A1 *Walker's Cay Hotel and Marina*, which offers sailors, fishermen and divers lots of facilities and hosts several fishing tournaments. Yachtsmen approaching Abaco from the N clear customs and immigration here. There are restaurants, bars, tennis and two pools for when you are on land, 62 rooms or suites and 4 villas. Enquire about package deals with airfares from Fort Lauderdale if you do not want to tour other cays, T 352 5252, F 352 3301, 800-432 2092. You can visit the fish farm on Walker's Cay, the Aqua Life Mariculture Project, the largest in the world breeding tropical fish.

Island information – Abaco

● **How to get there**

There are airstrips at Marsh Harbour, Treasure Cay, Spanish Cay and Walker's Cay. American Eagle, Gulfstream (Marsh Harbour T 367 3415), Island Express and Airways International fly daily from Miami. Airways International (T 305-887 2794), Gulfstream International and Island Express (T 954-359 0380, 1-800 682 9828, F 954-359 2752, in Marsh Harbour T 367 3597, in Treasure Cay T 365 8697) fly from Fort Lauderdale. Gulfstream also from Jacksonville Tallahassee, Tampa and West Palm Beach. US Air Express (Piedmont Airlines) flies from Orlando, Tampa and West Palm Beach. Bahamasair flies twice daily from Nassau and most days from West Palm Beach. Walker's Cay is served only by Walker's International from Fort Lauderdale. Look out for package deals to the various resorts with Bahamasair. Charter planes include Abaco Air, T 367 2266, 367 2205, 359 6357, PO Box 492, Marsh Harbour, VHF 74; Cherokee Air, T 367 2089, 367 2613, 367 2530, PO Box 485, Marsh Harbour. A taxi from Marsh Harbour airport to the ferry dock costs US$12 for 2; from Treasure Cay airport to the ferry for Green Turtle Cay US$3 pp, min US$5.

Albury's Ferry Service runs from Sandy Crossing, 2 miles E of Marsh Harbour to Hope Town and Man-O-War Cay, US$8 single, US$12 day return. Separate boats leave each cay at 0800 and 1330, returning from the mainland at 1030 and 1600. Albury's boats can also be chartered to these 2 cays and to other islands. For 5 or more, a charter to Hope Town or Man-O-War works out at US$10pp each way, to Guana Cay for 6 or more US$12pp, or US$70 for 1-5 pax. All day excursions to Treasure Cay, Guana Cay, Hope Town, Man-O-War, Little Harbour and Green Turtle Cay, T 367 2306, 365 6010, VHF 16, CB 11.

Green Turtle Cay is reached from the ferry dock at Treasure Cay, US$8 pp, you can be dropped off wherever you are staying. Great Guana Cay can be reached by the *Guana Beach Resort* boat from *Conch Inn*, Marsh Harbour. The *Spanish Cay Inn* ferry picks up guests from Coopers Town.

Car rental can be arranged in Marsh Harbour or Treasure Cay with a number of companies: Safari Kar Rental has jeeps, T 367 2278, pick up and delivery; H & L Car Rental; Birona's Car Rental; Ula's Car Rental; Cornish Car Rentals.

● **Accommodation**

Hotel prices

L1	over US$200	**L2**	US$151-200
L3	US$101-150	**A1**	US$81-100
A2	US$61-80	**A3**	US$46-60
B	US$31-45	**C**	US$21-30
D	US$12-20	**E**	US$7-11
F	US$4-6	**G**	up to US$3

At **Marsh Harbour**, **L3** *Abaco Town By the Sea Resort*, 2-bedroom villas, short walk to water, convenient for restaurants, US$840-1,120/week, winter, 1-6 people, T 367 2221, F 367 2227, PO Box 486; **L2-L3** *Great Abaco Beach Hotel*, 20 rooms, villas **L1**, also new wing opened 1994, 2 pools, tennis, beach, attached to Boat Harbour Marina with 180 slips, nice location, comfortable rooms, inadequate telephone system, no staff on duty after 2100, T 367 2158, F 367 2819, 800-468 4799, PO Box AB 20511; **A1** *Conch Inn*, 9 rooms, full marina facilities, pool, restaurant, dockside bar and cable TV, well located and a yachtie meeting place, T 367 4000, F 367 4004, PO Box AB20469; *Pelican Beach Villas*, 6 villas, 2 bedroom, 2 bath, US$975/week, fully equipped, a/c, phone, on beach, need car to get to shops, boat dock, hammocks, T 367 3600, F 912-437 6223; *Lofty Fig*, villas, nice looking, opp water, near *Conch Inn*, US$400/week, T 367 2681; **A2** *Ambassador Inn*, cheaper but not well located, T 367 2022, F 367 2113, PO Box 484.

The **L2-A2** *Treasure Cay Resort* has 64 rooms, 32 suites, 8 Treasure homes **L1** for 2-6 people, there are also 600 homes owned by non-residents, 18-hole golf course, tennis, fishing, watersports on site, marina, restaurants, bars, shops, bank, doctor, pleasant resort, gradually being remodelled, more needs to be done, lovely beach close by, T 367 2570/2577, 800-327 1584, PO Box AB 22183, a 35-room hotel and 12 acres which were once part of the resort have been sold for redevelopment to Sandals.

At **Coopers Town** there is a guest house above *M & M* restaurant and disco, owned by Hiram Mackintosh, basic but clean, caters mostly for travelling Bahamians, 3 singles **B** with shared bathroom, 1 double **A3**, can sleep 3, T 365 0142/3. Further N on **Wood Cay**, off Little Abaco, is **A2** *Tangelo Hotel*, 12 rooms, TV, a/c, fans, restaurant, bar, taxi from Treasure Cay airport will cost US$50 for 2 people, but if you call the hotel in advance they will provide bus for US$10 for 2 people, T 365 2222.

18 miles S of Marsh Harbour at **Casuarina Point**, is *Different of Abaco*, a bonefishing lodge and home of Great Abaco Bone Fishing Club, in a nature park with flamingoes, iguanas and donkeys, 8 rooms, 8 bonefishing boats, good restaurant open from 0900, T 327 7921/2, T/F 366 2150, F 327 8152, VHF 16, PO Box 20092. At Sandy Point there are 2 hotels: *Oeisha's Resort* and *Pete and Gay's Guest House*, which cater to an increasing number of bonefishermen using local fishermen as guides, very casual, all doors left unlocked.

● **Places to eat**

At **Marsh Harbour** there are several restaurants within walking distance of each other,

look out for special menus and happy hours on different days. *Mangoes* restaurant and marina, patio bar from 1130, lunch 1130-1430, dinner 1830-2100, good food, about US$25 for dinner, T 367 2366; *Wally's*, nearby, other side of road, good Bahamian food, popular happy hour, Wed 1600-1800, open lunch Mon 1130-1400, Tues-Sat 1130-1500, dinner Mon by reservation only, Sat 1800-2100, bar daily except Sun 1100-1700, music, boutique, T 367 2074; the *Jib Room* at Marsh Harbour Marina on N side of harbour, very long walk, coffee and croissants from 0830, lunch daily 1130-1500, daily special activities for dinner, huge ribs on Wed US$12 rec, happy hour Thur 1830-1930 all drinks US$1, closed Tues, T 367 2700, F 367 2033, PO Box AB 20518; *Sapodilly's*, waterfront, deli, beer and wine, picnic baskets, provisioning, breakfast and lunch from 0830 Mon-Sat, 0930 Sun, T 367 3498, VHF 19.

On the way NW from Marsh Harbour on the outskirts of **Treasure Cay**, is *Macy's* restaurant and bakery, open daily 0800-2300, local meals as well as burgers and sandwiches for lunch, steak US$16, lobster US$18 for dinner, cracked conch US$12, also deliver, VHF 16. There are several restaurants and bars in the resort itself, *Island Boil*, a yellow wooden shack near Treasure Cay ferry serves Bahamian dishes, fish for breakfast, cheap, used by locals, tourists, air arrivals. At **Coopers Town**, *M & M* restaurant and disco serves local dishes with peas 'n' rice and a converted van, *Mac's Rolling Kitchen*, goes out to Treasure Cay and nearby settlements for lunches; *Conch Crawl*, is a shack and pier, the fresh conch salad is made in front of you, fish fries and barbecues on different nights, sit inside or outside, T 365 0423; *Aunt Evie's* fresh home made bread can be bought nearby; there are lots of jetties along this stretch of coast, all with piles of conch shells underneath.

South of Marsh Harbour at **Spring City** is *Spring City Pub*, a bar open from 1830 with own special drink, finger food, conch fritters etc. At Little Harbour *Pete's Pub* has burgers, chicken etc, and Pete has now opened a gourmet restaurant as well, all part of the Johnston family's complex of foundry and art galleries.

● **Tourist office**

Ministry of Tourism, Abaco Tourist Office, PO Box AB 0464, Marsh Harbour, Abaco, T 367 3067, F 367 3068.

ANDROS

The Spanish called the island La Isla del Espíritu Santo, but its present name is said to come from the British commander Sir Edmund Andros. At 104 miles long and 40 miles wide, Andros (population 8,155) is the largest island in the Bahamas, with pine and mahogany forests, creeks and prolific birdlife. According to Indian legend, the forests house the 'chickcharnie', a mythical, three-fingered, three-toed, red-eyed creature who hangs upside down and can cause good or bad luck. It is also blamed when tools or other things go missing. In fact, a large, three-toed, burrowing owl of this description did inhabit the forests until the early 16th century when it became extinct. More recent legend has it that the pirate, Sir Henry Morgan lit a beacon (bonfire) on the top of Morgan's Bluff, the highest point on the island at 67 feet. This lured passing ships on to the treacherous reef close by. Sir Henry and his pirates then ransacked the ships and hid their treasure in the caves below. Both the Bluff and the caves are now signposted; the caves are in fact quite small and rather a disappointment. The area is nowadays more important for the docks, from where water is barged to Nassau. The mailboat comes in at the old harbour.

There are two separate islands, North and South Andros, with the central regions (middle bights)

accessible by boat from either direction. No roads connect the different parts and unless you have a boat you have to fly between them. The main settlements in the N are **Nicholl's Town**, **Lowe Sound**, **Conch Sound**, **Red Bays**, **Mastic Point** and **Fresh Creek** (previously known as Andros Town and Coakley Town). **Mangrove Cay** is in central Andros, while in the S are **Congo Town**, **Deep Creek** and

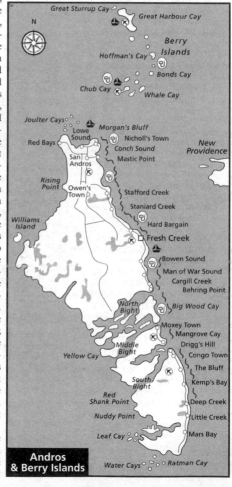

Andros & Berry Islands

ex-Prime Minister Sir Lynden Pindling's constituency at **Kemp's Bay**. The settlements in the far N have suffered a setback as a result of a crackdown on drugs trafficking. Several hotels and other businesses are now closed.

Near Fresh Creek, you can visit the Androsia clothing factory which makes batik fabrics in tropical colours and watch the whole process from the wax painting to the drying of the dyed cloth. Ask in the shop for a factory tour. Henry Wallace is a rastafarian wood carver, usually to be found chipping away to the beat of reggae music. He is also the curator of a small museum of the island's culture and history, near the mailboat dock in Fresh Creek (the old health clinic buildings), worth a visit. South of Fresh Creek is the Atlantic Underwater Testing and Evaluation Center (Autec), a joint venture between the USA and the UK for underwater testing of weapons and consequently top secret.

Nicholl's Town has a lively Junkanoo on Boxing Day (very early morning) and New Year's Eve, and Goombay Festival on every Thur in July and Aug from 1900 onwards on Seaview Square. There are many government administration buildings, schools, clinic, BaTelCo office, in what is a straggling, spread-out town with no apparent centre. Conch Sound is very close, almost an extension of Nicholl's Town; between the two are shops, a bakery, auditorium, laundry and disco.

Red Bays (population under 200) is the only settlement on the W coast of the island and is about 5 mins' drive from Red Bays beach, where there are a few small motor boats moored but nothing else. Long isolated and reached only by boat it is now connected by a good paved road cutting across the wild interior of the island. Originally a Seminole Indian settlement many of the people have distinctly Indian features and a true out island life style. The village welcomes visitors. Contact Rev Bertram A Newton for his history of Red Bays. Locally caught sponges and hand made baskets can all be bought very cheaply. Mrs Marshall is the local bush granny and community celebrity. Usually found weaving in the centre of the village she will show how baskets are made, and explain local culture, politics and bush medicine to visitors. Mr Russell always has plenty of sponges for sale (and illegally caught turtle and iguanas, don't buy these) and also works as a bonefishing guide. There is only one telephone in Red Bays, T 329 2369 and leave a message for the person you want to contact.

Fauna and flora

Andros has an extensive creek system which is largely unexplored. In S Andros the 40-square-mile area beyond the $\frac{1}{2}$ mile long ridge is also uninhabited and rarely visited. The large pine forests and mangrove swamps are home to a variety of birds and animals. In the S there are wild bird reserves which allow hunting in the season (Sept-Mar). Sightings of the Bahamian parrot have been reported in S Andros, while rare terns and whistling tree ducks, roseatte spoonbills and numerous different herons have been seen in the N and central areas. Green Cay, one of the many small islands off Andros (20 miles E of Deep Creek) has the world's second largest population of white crowned pigeons. These pigeons are prey to hunters from Sept to Mar each year (hunting season). The W side of Andros is undeveloped and other than Red Bays in the NW corner there are no settlements on this side, making it ideal for wildlife; large rock iguanas up to six feet long and hundreds of flamingos live here. During May to Aug the Andros land crabs migrate from the pine forests to the sea. These enormous crabs are to be found everywhere during this time. Many are caught and exported to Nassau.

Beaches and watersports

In the N, Nicholl's Town has the best beach. A wide, golden beach runs the length of the N coast, almost to Morgan's Bluff. It is ideal for swimming and excellent snorkelling spots are to be found directly off the beach. Lowe Sound, Conch Sound and Mastic Point all have good beaches. A very pleasant, $2\frac{1}{2}$-mile walk from Nicholl's Town to Morgan's Bluff along a leafy overgrown road (in fact the first road built on the island) leads to the caves at Morgan's Bluff and offers beautiful views of this part of the coast. Further S near Fresh Creek is Staniard Creek where there is an attractive palm-fringed beach with white sand and pleasant settlement close by. Sand bars, exposed at the mouth of Staniard Creek at low tide, are excellent shelling spots. Somerset beach is just S of Fresh Creek, signposted from the main highway. It is a spectacular spot, especially at low tide and another excellent shelling beach. At Victoria Point in central Andros there is a graveyard right on the water's edge. In some parts of Andros on Easter Monday at 0200-0600 there is a candlelight vigil by gravesites at which Easter hymns are sung. The E side of Mangrove Cay has spectacular beaches all lined with coconut groves. In S Andros along the 28-mile stretch from Mars Bay to Drigg's Hill are beautiful palm-lined beaches with occasional picturesque settlements.

Diving and marine life

Visitors mostly come for the unspoiled beaches, the diving in on pristine reefs in 80°F water with excellent visibility and extraordinary bonefishing. Development has been concentrated on the E coast facing one of the world's largest underwater reefs. This huge barrier reef, the second largest in the Western Hemisphere, plunges 6,000 feet to the Tongue of the Ocean, an exciting drop-off dive. Wreck dive sites include the *Lady Gloria*, an old mailboat sunk recently off Morgan's Bluff, and the *Potomac*, a steel-hulled barge which sank just after the war and is now home to many huge, friendly grouper and parrot fish, as well as some impressive barracuda. Andros has 197 blue holes, of these 50 are oceanic, the rest inland. Formed by water erosion then flooded at the end of the last ice-age,

the oceanic holes actually connect to the intricate inland underwater cave system. As tide rushes in and out ideal feeding grounds are created and consequently the oceanic blue holes harbour prolific and diverse marine life and are excellent dive sites at slack tide. The inland blue holes can be very deep (up to 350 feet) and contain a lens of freshwater 40-100 feet deep floating on seawater. Beautiful to swim in: Charlie's blue hole, near Nicholl's Town is clearly signposted as is Church's blue hole, just N of Fresh Creek. Marine life in the inland blue holes is limited, though the rare crustacean *Remepedidia* and the blind cave fish *Lucifuga* have been found. Earthwatch is currently conducting a detailed study on the mosquito fish, one of the few colonists of the blue holes on North Andros. On South Andros two popular blue holes are the Giant Doughnut near Deep Creek, S of Kemps Bay, and Inland Blue Hole Lissy near the Bluff, S Andros. Legends abound about blue holes, serpents known as Luska, originally a part of Seminole Indian legends are thought to drag unsuspecting swimmers and fishermen below. Caution should be exercised at some of the holes as they are extremely deep. The underwater cave system on Andros is considered to have some of the world's longest, deepest and most stunning caves. A 1991 expedition discovered remains of a Lucayan burial site in one of the blue holes of South Andros. Intact Lucayan skulls were recovered, as well as femurs and hip bones.

Small Hope Bay Lodge is the place to go for diving, just N of Fresh Creek and a short boat journey from the barrier reef, wrecks, caves and an ocean blue hole. A well-run operation with several decades of experience in Andros, they cater for beginners as well as specialty divers and have an excellent safety record. Most guests are on all-inclusive packages, otherwise diving is US$45 for a single tank dive, US$10 for a second tank, US$50 night dive, US$10 snorkelling. Specialty diving is tailored to individual requirements. This dive operation is one of the more conservation-minded in the Bahamas; no shark feeding here. Liveaboard dive boats also cruise around Andros and Stuart Cove's Dive South Ocean occasionally come over from Nassau and dive in Andros waters. For ecological tours Forfar Field Station, at Blanket Sound N of Fresh Creek, runs guided diving, snorkelling and inland excursions, mainly for high school students or college groups from the USA, T 368 6160/6129 for details. Cheap accommodation may also be available.

Small Hope Bay Lodge also does bonefishing (US$300/day boat and guide for 2 people or US$380/day reef fishing for up to 4), but the best place for serious fishermen and women is the Cargill Creek area, where there are lots of guides. At *Charlie's Haven* boats are about the same price including guide (T 368 4087), while at *Cargill Creek Fishing Lodge* boats and guides are more expensive; you have the option of staying at Grassy Camp further S (L1), or do a one-day Grassy Cay trip for US$800 (maximum 5 people). There is also *Andros Island Bonefish Club* (known locally as Rupert's Place) where deep sea fishing can be arranged.

All sportfishing is catch and release. The usual weight of bonefish is 5-7 lbs but on most days you will find fish of 12 lbs and over. There are around 100 square miles of flats in the N and middle bights which are fished by Cargill Creek resorts. Most are fished infrequently and you see hardly anyone else. The W side of the island can also be fished, depending on the weather and tide, but it will cost an extra US$50/day for fuel as it is 1½ hrs from Cargill Creek. You can still see traditional Bahamian wooden sailboats here, made by local craftsman Ronald Young, although nowadays he makes mostly fishing boats. On Christmas Day, Columbus' Discovery Day and Easter Monday sailboat races, featuring locally-made Bahamian sloops, are held at Lowe Sound,

Nicholl's Town and sometimes Conch Sound. Ask locals for details. Regattas also combine cook-outs, local music and dancing. On Independence Day there is a sailboats race in the Regatta.

Island information – Andros
● **How to get there**
Airports are at Fresh Creek (also referred to as Andros Town), Mangrove Cay (both central), San Andros (N) and Congo Town (S). Boats can dock at Mastic Point (N), Fresh Creek (central) and Congo Town (S). Bahamasair has daily flights to Andros Town and San Andros from Nassau. Flights to Mangrove Cay with Congo Air twice daily from Nassau, some via South Andros which also receives twice daily flights from Nassau. For mailboat schedules and fares see **Information for travellers, Ferries**. *Small Hope Bay Lodge* runs its own charter flights from Fort Lauderdale to Fresh Creek/Andros Town, US$200 pp round trip, children under 12 half price, 1 hr, T 305-359 8240, 800-223 6961, F 305-359 8241 or phone the Lodge on Andros. Most settlements are linked by paved roads with plenty of potholes to keep you awake. Taxis are available. A taxi from the airport at Fresh Creek to *Small Hope Bay Lodge* is US$15 (fare usually inc in all-inclusive package), to Cargill Creek US$30. Cars and scooters can be rented. In Kemps Bay Mr Rahming rents cars and also provides a charter service to any of the Family Islands (T 329 2569). In Lowe Sound R & M Rentals (T 320 2526), in Fresh Creek Berth Rent A Car (T 368 2101) and at San Andros airport Cecil Gaitor has cars for hire. *Small Hope Bay Lodge* will organize car hire for US$50-75/day. The *Donna Lee Motel & Store*, Nicholl's Town, rents out bicycles, scooters and cars. It is often possible to hire cars for the day from private individuals, ask locally, taxi drivers have details. Gasoline is US$2.65/gallon.

● **Accommodation**

Hotel prices

L1	over US$200	L2	US$151-200
L3	US$101-150	A1	US$81-100
A2	US$61-80	A3	US$46-60
B	US$31-45	C	US$21-30
D	US$12-20	E	US$7-11
F	US$4-6	G	up to US$3

From N to S: **A2** *Green Windows Inn*, 5 mins walk to beach, pool, T 329 2194, F 329 2016; **A2** *Donna Lee Motel*, opp the school in

Nicholl's Town, 10 basic but adequate rooms with shared bathrooms, 2 suites, horseriding, restaurant for breakfast, lunch and maybe dinner, live music Fri, Sat, T 329 2194, F 329 2515; at Mastic Point, **B** *Oliver's Guest House*, 7-8 rooms with bathroom, breakfast, dinner, in town, 300 feet from waterfront, mostly Bahamian guests and divers, T 329 3001; in Red Bays there is no hotel, but George Woodside has an apartment to rent, T 329 2369, the only phone in the settlement and leave a message. Staniard Creek is a settlement of small, mostly single storey houses with a clinic and school, reached by rutted road across swamp (turn off main road by BaTelCo); **A3-B** *Quality Inn*, also known as *Dicky's Place*, owned by Richard Riley, remote, small, refurbished 1993, jetty, on creek short way from sea, cheaper rooms in main house, or better rooms in new annex, food and drinks available; **B** *Central Andros Inn*, the other side of the creek, owned by the Munroes, rooms with bath or shared bathroom, basic, painted yellow, meals if ordered, mostly local business, T 368 6209; **L1** *Small Hope Bay Lodge*, between Staniard Creek and Fresh Creek, the nicest place to stay and highly rec, specializes in diving and fishing but still good if only one partner dives/fishes, informal, cabin accommodation among trees right on seafront, all inclusive with 3 hearty meals, drinks, taxes, service and scuba lesson, rustic but comfortable, good beds and lots of towels, fans, no phones, TV or a/c, sailboat, windsurfers, hot tub, bicycles, books, games, children's toys, run by Birch family since 1960s, very friendly, staff and guests mingle at meals and after dinner, excellent service, T 368 2014, F 368 2015, Box CB11 817, Nassau, or PO Box 21667, Ft Lauderdale, Fl 33335-1667, T 305 359 8240, 800-223 6961, F 305 359 8241; in Fresh Creek, *Landmark Hotel* (*Skinny's*), has sea view but run down, T 368 2082; **A2-B** *Chickcharnie* overlooks harbour, lovely view, 75-ft dock, restaurant, bar, foodstore, rooms with shared bath and fan, or with bath and a/c, or new rooms with view, Bahamian decor, T 368 2025; **L2-L3** *Lighthouse Yacht Club and Marina*, the other side of the creek, opened 1991, appalling service, unfriendly and usually empty but otherwise lovely location on waterfront, attractive buildings with luxury yachts moored at dock, big, tiled rooms, a/c, cool, TV, fridge, phones, bar, restaurant, tennis, bicycles, pool, ping pong, 12 rooms, 8 villas, 18 boat slips with fuel available, T 368 2305-8, F 368 2300;

just outside Fresh Creek is *Coakley House*, a luxury villa in 2 acres with 120-ft dock, owned and managed by *Small Hope Bay Lodge*, bare rental US$250/day, US$1,500/week, low season, US$350/1,800 peak inc transfers, tax and service, or fully inclusive with maid/cook and *Lodge* diving/fishing/restaurant facilities from US$770/2 people/2 nights, shops and restaurants in walking distance.

Around Behring Point and Cargill Creek the lodges offer fishing and nothing else, all guests are expected to be anglers: **L1** *Andros Island Bonefish Club* (*Rupert's Place*) owned by Rupert Leadon, 12 rooms with 2 double beds, a/c, some with fan and fridge, inc meals, 4-night package with fishing US$960 pp double occupancy, 2-3 months reservation needed, 80-90% repeat guests, comfortable but not luxurious, friendly, most fishermen go out by 0730, return 1600, shower, cocktails, supper 1900, bed by 2100, T 368 5167/5200, F 368 5235; **L1-L2** *Cargill Creek Fishing Lodge*, next door, 7 double rooms, 4 singles, 3 cottages with 2 bedrooms, US$630 (sleep 4), TV, pool, 10% discount for Autec employees, T 368 5129, F 329 5046; **L2** *Charlie's Haven*, 10 basic double rooms with bathroom, inc meals and tax, Charlie teaches flyfishing and guides, self serve bar, good menu, new rooms added 1994, T 368 4087; **L1** *Nottage Cottage*, inc 3 meals, 10 twin-bedded rooms with bathroom, a/c, TV, 2-bedroomed cottage US$90 pp, overlooks water, local guides can be arranged for fishing, T 368 4293. On Lisbon Creek, Mangrove Cay, is **A3** *Longley's Guest House*, run by Bernard Longley (T 369 0311); **A2** *Trade Wind Villas*, run by Mrs Bowley (T 329 2040); on the border of Congo Town and Long Bay, **L1-L3** *Emerald Palms-By-The-Sea*, (T 369 2661, F 369 2667, PO Box 800) modern with balconies facing the sea, swimming pool, tennis court and boats for charter; **B** *Congo Beach Hotel*, (T 329 4777), friendly, daily happy hour, rec. At Kemps Bay Mr Rahming (T 329 4608) who runs the local gas station and food store has rooms and beach houses to let, clean but the noise of slamming dominoes may keep you awake. He is a Seventh Day Adventist so the store is closed on Sat and sells no pork or alcohol. He has cars to rent and also does a good, cheap haircut.

● **Places to eat**
Andros has an exportable surplus of crabs, so crab dishes are very popular. May-July is the crab season. Try baked Andros crab, which uses

the crab's own fat to cook it in, also Vetol's crab'n'rice and stewed crab cooked with conch. Andros is relatively undeveloped and some restaurants may need advance warning. For a cheap meal look out for cook outs. In Congo Town, B Paul runs the *Jungle Club* and has barbecues frequently. Good, cheap conch fritters at the snack bar on Driggs Hill dock. Rec restaurants include *Rupert's Fish Camp*, Cargill Creek, very good local game fish, candlelit verandah overlooks sea; *Seaview Restaurant and Bar* is nearby; *Dig Dig's* is an excellent restaurant at Cargill Creek, on side of main road, T 368 5097 for reservations in evening, 1 hr's notice enough at lunch time, highly rec; the *Small Hope Bay Lodge* serves large, filling meals, well cooked; *Chickcharnie Hotel* in Fresh Creek; *Skinnys Landmark* serves Bahamian meals and is very popular locally, lively disco at weekends, many American Servicemen from AUTEC, local politicians etc among regular clientele; the *Bannister's Restaurant* with turtle pen in Lisbon Creek; at Morgan's Bluff, *Willy's Place* specializes in local seafood dishes, lunch US$5, dinner US$8, reservations T 329 2433. In Nicholl's Town: *Rolle's* takeaway serves best local food on island, cracked conch, chicken etc; *Rumours* restaurant, bar and disco, Fri, Sat, 2100-0300, T 329 2398. Rec bars include *Mr Sands'* in Little Creek, cheap and friendly; *Hole in the Wall*, in Mathers Town is good, as is Rev Henfield's *Beach Restaurant/Bar* in Nicholl's Town. At Kemps Bay, *Dudley's Pink Pussy Cat Club* has a rake'n'scrape band and traditional stepping dancing with Rosita on saw and Ben on drums.

BERRY ISLANDS

There are 30 Berry Islands (population 634) which offer beautiful opportunities for divers and snorkellers. Most are the private homes of the wealthy or inhabited only by wildlife. **Bullock's Harbour** in Great Harbour Cay is the main settlement in the area, Great Harbour Cay is the largest cay in the Berry chain at just two miles across. First settled by ex-slaves in 1836, the cay proved difficult to farm. L1-L2 *The Great Harbour Cay Club* is here, with villas and town houses, T 367 8838, 800-343 7256, 305-921 9084, F 367 8115, 305-921 1044. There are facilities

for yachts and a 9-hole golf course. Cruise ships drop anchor off Great Sturrup Cay and passengers can spend the day on the deserted beach there.

The only other spot in the Berry Islands which caters for tourists is **Chub Cay**, which was severely damaged by Hurricane Andrew in 1992. The L2 *Chub Cay Club* (T 325 1490, F 322 5199) has its own airstrip, tennis courts, restaurant, marina and extensive dive facilities offered by Chub Cay Undersea Adventures. There is a deep water canyon at Chub Cay where you can find a variety of colourful reef fish and open water marine life. Staghorn coral can be seen in the shallow waters near Mamma Rhoda Rock. Less natural, but still fascinating is the submarine deliberately sunk in 90 feet of water off Bond Cay, named after James himself.

Many of the cays do not welcome uninvited guests. Interesting wildlife can be found on Frozen Cay and Alder Cay. Terns and pelicans can be seen here and although they are privately owned, sailors may anchor here to observe the birds. Hoffman's Cay, now deserted, was originally home to a thriving farming settlement. Ruins of houses, a church and a graveyard still stand. Paths also lead to a deep blue hole. A golden road runs along the length of the E coast of the island. On Little Whale Cay, Wallace Groves, the founder of Freeport, has his own home and airstrip.

Great Harbour Cay has its own airport served by Island Express from Fort Lauderdale.

BIMINI

Once thought to be the site of the lost city of Atlantis, the Bimini chain of islands (population 1,638), only 50 miles from Florida, is divided into North and South Bimini and a series of cays. Ernest Hemingway lived on Bimini in 1931-37 at Blue Marlin Cottage and his novel *Islands in the Stream* was based on Bimini. A display of Hemingway memorabilia can be seen

Chalk's

Chalk's seaplanes are a popular and exciting feature of travelling to Bimini and conjure up a certain nostalgia for pre-war adventure travel. Founded in 1919 by Arthur B 'Pappy' Chalk on the docks of the *Royal Palm Hotel* in Miami, the company is now the largest seaplane airline in the world. Famous passengers in the 1930s included Ernest Hemingway, who travelled frequently to Bimini along with many other Americans escaping Prohibition, and the Cuban dictator, Gerardo Machado, who fled a coup in 1933 in a chartered Chalk's plane. His occupation on the manifest was listed as 'retired'.

at the *Compleat Angler Hotel and Museum*. On South Bimini is the legendary site of the Fountain of Youth, sought by Ponce de León in 1512. The pool known as the Healing Hole is claimed to have some beneficial effects. In 1994, a Spanish treasure ship, believed to be the *Santigo El Grande*, which sank in 1766 while heading for Spain laden with gold, silver and emeralds, was discovered off the southern tip of Bimini.

There are more bars than shops on Bimini, service is minimal, car rental non-existent. It is not a glamorous resort, although there are plenty of luxury yachts moored there. The airplane wrecks at the edge of the airfield at **Alice Town** on North Bimini are mostly the results of unsuccessful drugs running attempts en route from Colombia to Miami. Bimini has been claimed as an important success in the fight against drug running to the US mainland; Gun Cay has become the centre for drug interdiction operations and is full of US DEA personnel. Bimini suffered flood damage caused by Hurricane Andrew in 1992 but soon recovered.

Alice Town is the capital of Bimini although most people live in **Bailey Town** to the N along the King's Highway. Alice Town has a lot of bars and a straw market, if little else. Heading N from Alice Town you come to *The Anchorage*, a restaurant on the highest point on the island with good views of the sea. The beach in either direction is excellent with white sand and good surfing waves. Above the beach is a pathway which passes the picturesque Methodist Church (1858) and leads to Bailey Town.

Cat Cay, to the S, was hit by Hurricane Andrew in Aug 1992, with winds of 180mph, gusting to 250mph. Damage to island property was estimated at US$100mn. First developed in 1932 it had a golf course, 68 houses for the rich and their staff, and lots of expensive yachts.

Diving and marine life

Bimini is famous for big game fishing. Fishing is excellent all year round although 7 May-15 June is the tuna season (blue fin). June and July are best for blue marlin, winter and spring for white marlin. Blue marlin are the favourite target, averaging between 150 and 500 lbs, but which can exceed 1,000 lbs. The S Biminis, Cat Cay and Gun Cay are the places to catch billfish and bluefin. There are lots of fishing tournaments and the Ministry of Tourism promotes over 40 annually, including the Bacardi Billfish Tournament, the Bimini Benefit Tournament, the Bahamas Championship Tournament and the Bahamas Billfish Championship series. *The Bimini Big Game Fishing Club* caters for most fishermen's needs and can arrange fishing trips with guides. It has 180 slips, charter/boat rental, all supplies and a large walk-in freezer for daily catches. Fishing can also be arranged through the *Compleat Angler Hotel*, Brown's Marina or Weech's Bimini Dock.

Scuba diving is recommended, particularly over the Bimini Wall to see the black coral trees, or to the lovely reefs off Victory Cay. Bimini Undersea Adventures, run by Bill and Nowdla Keefe, has a comprehensive list of facilities and can also offer sailing, fishing and tennis (T 347 3089, F 347 3079, in the USA 800-348 4644).

Island information – Bimini
● **How to get there**
Bahamasair does not have flights to Bimini, but Chalk's International has flights from Miami, Fort Lauderdale and from Nassau to Alice Town with sea planes which land in the harbour. Sky Unlimited also flies from Nassau. For mailboat details see **Information for travellers, Ferries**.

● **Accommodation**
L1-L3 *The Bimini Big Game Fishing Club* (T 347 3391, F 347 3392, PO Box 523238, Miami, FL33152), owned by Bacardi, is the main hotel (cottages **L2** rec) and social centre (beware the Beastwhacker, a cocktail of champagne and Bacardi rum) and has swimming pool and tennis courts as well as a marina with charter boats and all facilities for deep sea fishing or bonefishing. **L2-A1** *Bimini Blue Water Resort* (T 347 3166, F 347 3293, PO Box 627), rooms, 3-bedroomed cottage, suites also include Hemingway's Marlin Cottage, private beach, swimming pool and 32-slip marina; **A3** *Brown's Hotel and Marina* (T 347 3227, PO Box 601), 2-bedroomed cottage **A1**, near beach; **A2** *Compleat Angler Hotel* (T 347 3122, PO Box 601), in town, popular bar; **A2** *Admiral Hotel* (T 347 3347), in Bailey Town; **A2** *Sea Crest*, (T 347 3071, P O Box 654), Alice Town, managed by Alfred Sweeting; **L3** *Bimini Reef Club and Marina*, South Bimini, T (901) 758 2376.

● **Places to eat**
After dark activities consist of drinking and dancing. *The End of the World Bar* in Alice Town has long opening hours and the back looks out to the harbour; *Yama's Bar*, run by former boxer Billy Yama Bahama Butler; *The Red Lion Pub* is rec for its seafood, as is *Captain Bob Smith's* and *The Big Game Restaurant* on the sea front in Alice Town. The *Calypsonians* play weekly at *The Compleat Angler*, worth seeing, and *Glen Rolle and the Surgeons* provide musical entertainment at *All My Children Hotel*. Other rec nightspots are the *Hy Star Disco* and *Brown's Hotel Bar*, both in Alice Town.

CAT ISLAND

Named after Arthur Catt, a British pirate who was in league with Henry Morgan and Edward Teach (Blackbeard), Cat Island (population 1,678) boasts Lucayan Indian caves near **Port Howe**, as well as the usual underwater sites of interest and beauty. Fifty miles long, it was once called San Salvador, and is a contender for the site of Columbus' first landfall. It has rolling hills and the highest point in the Bahamas, Mount Alvernia, 206 feet above sea level. The island is a centre for the practice of Obeah, a Bahamian voodoo incorporating both bush medicine and witchcraft, which is indicated by bottles and other small objects hanging from the branches of the trees.

Most development has taken place in the S. **New Bight** is the capital and shares an impressive bay with the quaint Old Bight, the site of an early 19th century attempt to establish a cotton plantation. You can see the ruins of Pigeon Bay Cottage, an old plantation house just outside Old Bight. New Bight has a few shops. The annual regatta is held here in August. Above the village you can climb Mount Alvernia and visit Father Jerome's Hermitage. The Stations of the Cross are carved along a winding path leading to the Hermitage, built by Father Jerome, an Anglican priest who converted to Roman Catholicism and designed several churches on Cat Island and Long Island. Fernandez Bay, three miles N of New Bight and home to *The Fernandez Bay Village Resort*, has one of the island's best beaches, a secluded cove with excellent sands. A dive shop, Cat Island Sea Club, is on site, offering PADI istruction to all levels, T 474 4821. On the most southerly tip of the island are two beaches with facilities: *The Cutlass Bay Club Beach* (tennis, waterskiing) has its own airstrip and a good restaurant. World famous bonefishing flats are within wading distance of the beach. Close by along the crumbling cliff tops are the impressive ruins of the Richman

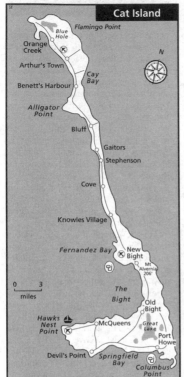

Cat Island

Flamingo Point
Blue Hole
Orange Creek
Arthur's Town
Cay Bay
Benett's Harbour
Alligator Point
Bluff
Gaitors
Stephenson
Cove
Knowles Village
Fernandez Bay
New Bight
Mt Alvernia 206'
The Bight
Old Bight
Hawks Nest Point
McQueens
Great Lake
Port Howe
Devil's Point
Springfield Bay
Columbus Point

0   3
miles

N

Hill plantation, with ruins of slave quarters, an overseer's house and a plantation house. The original plantation stretched from the ocean to the inland lake. Another interesting ruin is Colonel Andrew Deveaux' mansion at Port Howe. Granted land on Cat Island for delivering Nassau from the Spanish, he set up a briefly prosperous cotton plantation here. Early settlers in Port Howe lured ships on to the rocks in order to loot their cargoes. Today Port Howe is famous for its coconuts and pineapples, while the bread, cooked in Dutch or Rock wood-fuelled ovens, is said to be the Bahamas' tastiest. The Cat Island Dive Centre at *The Greenwood Beach Resort*, Port Howe offers scuba diving.

Run by Uwe Hinrichsen, it attracts German and other European visitors (T/F 342 3053).

The main settlement in the N of the island is **Arthur's Town**, but other than an airstrip there is not much else; there are no restaurants and only one shop which does not sell much. Local people rely on the weekly mailboat from Nassau for groceries. There are bars but none serves food. Two miles inland is a small lake surrounded by mangrove thickets. Islanders refer to it as a blue hole and tell stories of its supernatural inhabitants. The beaches in the N are excellent. Northside Beach, reached by dirt road, stretches for 20 miles but has no facilities at all and has the ubiquitous debris. Orange Creek is an attractive inlet three miles N of Arthur's Town. Along the nearby shores are the 'white sand farms' with small scale farming of beets, potatoes and carrots.

Flora and fauna

Uninhabited **Conception Island** and its adjoining reefs, between Cat Island and Long Island, is a land and sea park visited by migrating birds and nesting turtles, protected by the Bahamas National Trust. Many great and little blue herons can be seen at Hawksnest Creek bird sanctuary. In inland ponds it is possible to find the Cat Island turtle (*pseudyms felis*). Unfortunately, the turtles are a source of very rich meat and their numbers have recently dwindled. Near the settlement of Gaitors you can visit large caves full of bats. There are more bat caves S of Gaitors, near Stephenson. Farming is mostly subsistence, using slash and burn to grow crops such as red corn, guinea corn, cassava, okra, peas, beans, sugarcane, watermelons, pineapples, coconuts and bananas. Pot hole farming uses small amounts of soil in deep limestone holes to cultivate plants like the banana tree.

Island information – Cat Island
● **How to get there**
Bahamasair has flights to Arthur's Town from

Nassau 3 times a week, one of which goes via Rock Sound and another via San Salvador. There is also an airport at New Bight which is more convenient for most hotels. Some hotels have their own airstrips. For details on mailboats see **Information for travellers, Ferries**. Transport is difficult in the N as there are no taxis or buses and few cars for hitching lifts.

● **Accommodation**
L1-L2 *Fernandez Bay Village*, New Bight, 10 1-3 bedroomed cottages, most watersports available, diving, snorkelling, fishing, sailing, paddle tennis, volley ball, waterskiing, bicycles, beach bar, restaurant, hammocks, relaxed, unpretentious, T 342 3043, 800-940 1905, F 342 3051, PO Box 2126, flights can be arranged through Tony Ambrister (T 305-764 6945/792 1905); **A1** *Greenwood Beach Resort*, at Port Howe on 8-mile beach, German-run, good snorkelling, scuba diving from the beach, pool, satellite TV, T/F 342 3053, T 800-343 0373; **A2** *The Bridge Inn*, New Bight, with disco, reasonable accommodation, good food, T 342 3013, F 342 3041; *Orange Creek Inn*, 3 mins from airport, free transport, 16 rooms with kitchenettes, laundromat, store, T 354 4110/11; at Bennet's Harbour ask for Mrs Stracchan who lets rooms occasionally.

● **Places to eat**
The Bahamas' biggest goat farm is near New Bight. Goat meat is used in a local dish called 'souce stew', cooked with potatoes, onions and a lemon lookalike fruit called souce. The restaurant at the *Fernandez Bay Resort* is elegant and expensive. *Greenwood Inn* has Bahamian and European menu. *Pilot Harbour* on waterfront at Old Bight, VHF 16, Bahamian specials, cocktails. *Ambrister's Place*, Dumfries, is rec. Bars in Arthur's Town: *Miss Nelly's* (pool table), the *Hard Rock Café* and *Mr Pratt's Bar* (dominoes); also *Lovers' Boulevard Disco and Satellite Lounge* is popular and has a good local band playing Rake'n'Scrape.

CROOKED ISLAND

Crooked Island, Long Cay (joint population 423) and **Acklins** (population 428) comprise Crooked Island District, stretching three sides round the Bight of Acklins and bordered by 45 miles of treacherous barrier reef. At Crooked Island Passage, coral reefs can be found in very shallow water, falling sharply in walls housing sponges of every shape and colour. Although at 92 square miles, Crooked Island is larger than New Providence it is sparsely populated and the population is declining because of emigration. Tourism is not very developed and there is no electricity or running water in most of the settlements. Once as many as 40 plantations thrived here, but as in other islands, the crops failed because of poor soil and the industry declined. Nowadays, two valuable exports from the Crooked Island and Acklins District are aloe vera for use in skin preparations and the cascarilla bark which is sold to Italy for the production of Campari. Remains of the plantation era can be seen in Marine Farm and at Hope Great House in the N of the island. Bird Rock Lighthouse in the N is said to be the site of one of Columbus' original anchor spots on his first voyage. Close by is **Pittstown** where you can see the Bahamas' first General Post Office built in the era of William Pitt. It is now the restaurant of the hotel L3-A1 *Caribe Bay Limited*, formerly *Pittstown Point Landings* (14 rooms in cottages, T 344 2507, 800-752 2322, F 704-881 0771), which has its own airstrip, beaches, fishing, snorkelling, windsurfing and diving facilities. Gun Bluff, near the hotel was thought to have been a pirate's lookout, cannons have been found close by. In the surrounding area many North Americans have winter residences. Two miles away is **Landrail Point**, the main centre of the island, which has a hotel/restaurant and store. The people here are Seventh Day Adventists so no pork or alcohol is sold and everything closes on Sat. *Mrs Gibson's Lunch Room* is recommended for its freshly baked bread and simple Bahamian dishes.

Further S at **Cabbage Hill** are *T & S Guest Houses* run by the Rev Thompson, who also runs the A3 *Crooked Island Beach Inn* (T 336 2096, fishing available), near the beach and airport, and is the Bahamasair representative. The capital of

Crooked Island is **Colonel Hill**. There is a restaurant/baker's/guesthouse here run by Mrs Deleveaux, called *Sunny Lea*. Rooms have a good view of Major Cay Harbour. Close to the sheltered lagoon near Major Cay is a large cave; bromeliads can be seen at its entrance.

The main airport is at **Major Cay**; Bahamasair has two flights a week from Nassau, one of which is via Spring Point, Acklins. The *Windward Express* mailboat docks at the harbour in Landrail Point once a week, see **Information for travellers, Ferries**.

Acklins is a few miles from Crooked Island and a ferry operates between the two islands, docking at **Lovely Bay** twice a day. The island is 192 square miles and was named La Isabella by Columbus before being known as Acklins Cay and then just Acklins. Archaeological evidence points to a large Indian community once existing between Jamaica Cay and Delectable Bay (possibly the largest in the Bahamas). Today, Acklins is not very developed; there are roads to the settlements, but they are not paved. Atwood Bay is recommended as one of the Family Islands' most beautiful curved bays.

The main settlement on Acklins is **Spring Point**, which has an airport and Bahamasair has scheduled flights twice a week from Nassau, one flight goes via Crooked Island. The *Airport Inn* run by Curtis Hanna is a popular meeting place, with rooms to rent and a restaurant/bar. At nearby Pompey Bay it is still possible to see rock walls which were plantation demarcation boundaries. Pompey was once prosperous and busy; today most of the town is deserted and a tall church on the coast is abandoned. There is also a guesthouse at Pinefield run by the Williams family.

To the S of Acklins is a group of uninhabited cays sometimes referred to as the **Mira Por Vos Cays**. The most southerly is called **Castle Island** and is distinguished easily from afar by its tall battery operated lighthouse. There is a large seabird population here. South, North Guana and Fish Cay are all noted as havens for wildlife. **Long Cay** is the largest of the cays in this area and is inhabited. Long Cay was once known as Fortune Island and enjoyed great prosperity in the 19th century as a clearing house for ships between Europe and the Americas. The advent of the steamship made the use of Long Cay port redundant. Today you can see reminders of its former prosperity in the large unused Catholic

Crooked Island & Acklins

church, various civic buildings and the relics of a railway system. On the S end of this island there is a large nesting ground for the West Indian flamingo.

ELEUTHERA

This was the first permanent settlement in the Bahamas when Eleutheran Adventurers came from Bermuda and American colonial loyalists fled the mainland during the American Revolution (see **History** above). Their descendants still live here, living in houses painted in pastel colours. The first black settlers were slaves and free Africans from Bermuda. Eleuthera (population 10,600) is only about one mile wide but 110 miles long, with lovely pink sand beaches, particularly on the Atlantic side, coves and cliffs. The main road which runs down the backbone of the island is called the Queen's Highway and makes exploring by car easy and direct. In 1992 Hurricane Andrew hit the island, causing extensive damage. Some resorts stayed closed for the winter season, some went out of business, while others soon reopened. Many homes were destroyed and they took longer than the resorts to be repaired. On Current Island 24 of the 30 houses were smashed; in Gregory Town half the settlement was left homeless; on Harbour Island most homes were badly damaged and in Bogue the storm left three dead. To a visitor now, however, there is little evidence of the hurricane although at Hatchet Bay there are still wrecked boats left high and dry some distance from the sea.

Just N of Gregory Town is the **Glass Window Bridge**, where you can compare the blue Atlantic Ocean with the greenish water of the Caribbean on the other side, separated by a strip of rock just wide enough to drive a car across. Nearby are two small farming communities, Upper and Lower Bogue. **The Bogue** was once known as the bog because of its marshy ground. During the hurricane in 1965 the sea flooded the land and now there are salt water pools where you can find barracuda, grouper and snapper which were washed there by the tide. Also in the N is The Cave, which contains some impressive stalagmites and stalactites and the Preacher's Cave, where the Adventurers took shelter. The latter is reached by a rough unpaved track about 10 miles N of North Eleuthera; there is a pulpit carved out of rock from when the cave became a place of worship. Rock Sound Water Hole Park is an ocean or blue hole well stocked with grouper and yellowtail, while the walls are encrusted with flat oysters. Swimming is dangerous. Fishing is restricted.

Fauna and flora

Eleuthera is visited by many migrant birds. At Hatchet Bay, a few miles S of the Glass Window, there are ring necked pheasants. The Schooner and Kinley Cays in the Bight of Eleuthera are uninhabited but have large populations of white crowned pigeons. On Finlay Cay there are also sooty terns and noddy terns. The cays are protected by the Wild Bird Act. Local indigenous flowers include yellow elder, poincianas and hibiscus. Lizards, chicken snakes and feral goats and pigs are common. North of Hatchet Bay you can visit a bat cave where there are thousands of roosting leaf-nosed bats.

Diving and marine life

At the end of 1993, the Plateau became the sixth underwater national park in the Bahamas. It is a pretty site with mini walls and lots of fish in an area about ³/₄ mile by ½ mile. Funds for permanent moorings are being sought and the park is policed by dive operators. The usual regulations apply, with no fish feeding, no reef touching, no collecting and no spear fishing. The Plateau is about a mile from the Glass Window, 7 miles from Harbour Island. If you like exciting diving, try riding the Current Cut on the incoming tide, which propels you between islands at a speed of about seven

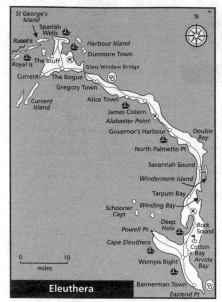

St George's Island
Spanish Wells
Russell Is
Harbour Island
Dunmore Town
Royal Is The Bluff
Glass Window Bridge
Current The Bogue
Gregory Town
Current Island
Alice Town
James Cistern
Alabaster Point
Governor's Harbour
Double Bay
North Palmetto Pt
Savannah Sound
Windermere Island
Tarpum Bay
Schooner Cays Winding Bay
Deep Hole
Powell Pt
Rock Sound
Cape Eleuthera
Cotton Bay
Wemyss Bight
Arvida Bay
Bannerman Town
Eastend Pt

0   10
miles

Eleuthera

knots. Surfing is also good here. A 300-year old shipwreck at Yankee Channel lies in only ten feet of water, while on the shallow, sharp reefs to the N called the Devil's Backbone, there is the wreck of a train where a barge once sank with its cargo on its way to Cuba, and a 19th century passenger steamship. Four miles S of Royal Island is an old freighter, sunk by fire while loaded with a cargo of bat guano, now used as a landmark by sailors. The guano is an excellent fish food and the wreck is home to enormous fish, with Angel fish weighing up to 15 lbs and parrot fish of 20-30 lbs. A remarkable dive or snorkel site. Unfortunately, illegal bleach used by craw fishermen has spoiled many W side reefs.

Diving and other watersports can be arranged with Valentine's Dive Centre on Harbour Island, which is where *Club Med* sends its guests as the diving is not so good around Governor's Harbour. There are two boats, plenty of staff, full training courses and full service with

rental, repair or purchase of dive gear (T 333 2080/2142, 800-323 5655, F 333 2135, PO Box 1, Harbour Island). Alternatively, try *Romora Bay Club* (T 333 2325, T/F 333 2500, PO Box 146, Harbour Island), where the dive operation is run by Jeff Fox and his diving dog. There are two boats taking out groups of 12-14 divers for single tank dives only, US$28 inc tank and weights, resort course US$55-65, full PADI certification available. If the wind is NNE there is no diving.

Sailing boats are recommended to use a local pilot along the notoriously dangerous stretch of coast between Harbour Island and Spanish Wells. *Valentine's Yacht Club*, Harbour Island, has a 50-slip marina taking boats of up to 140 feet and offering full services but no charter yachts. A regatta held to celebrate Discovery Day in Nov results in Valentine's bursting at the seams. Also on Harbour Island is the new *Harbour Island Club and Marina* with 32 slips for 50-60-foot boats. Full service facilities are gradually coming on stream, contact Roger Ironside for details (T/F 333 2427, VHF 16, PO Box 43). At Spanish Wells there is the *Spanish Wells Yacht Haven* (T 333 4255, VHF 16), with 30 slips, and several boat yards for repairs. On the W side of Eleuthera, *Marine Services* of Eleuthera (T/F 335 0186, VHF 16), with 20 slips, and *Hatchet Bay Yacht Club* are at Hatchet Bay. Round Cape Eleuthera is *Davis Harbour Marina*, with 40 slips (T 3134 6303/6101, VHF 16). This is also the centre for the deep sea and bonefishing charter companies. Harbour Island, Hatchet Bay, Governor's Harbour, Rock Sound and Cape Eleuthera are all ports of entry.

Beaches and watersports

There are excellent beaches on the E side of South Eleuthera. The W coast, however, is a little rocky. Many of the easterly beaches are backed by coconut palms or rocky cliffs with cedars. Three miles N of Alice Town in North Eleuthera there is a bushy and bumpy road off the main road which leads to Surfers Beach. It has the best surfing waves in the Bahamas and is frequently visited by surfing enthusiasts. Harbour Island has a beautiful pink sand beach which is said to be one of the most photographed beaches in the world. Lighthouse Beach at Cape Eleuthera has three miles of good beach.

Other sports

There is a 7,068-yard, 18-hole, par 72, championship golf course right by the sea at the *Cotton Bay Beach and Golf Club*, which also provides facilities for diving, snorkelling sailing and fishing. Green fees, US$100 pp inc cart, T 334 6103. You can play tennis at the *Club Méditerranée* (also windsurfing etc, free for guests), the *Coral Sands Hotel*, the *Dunmore Beach Club, Pink Sands Lodge, Romora Bay Club* (diving, fishing, sailing, snorkelling), *Rainbow Inn* or *Pineapple Cove* (Gregory Town).

EXCURSIONS

Gregory Town is the main settlement in the N of the island and the home of pineapple rum. A pineapple festival is held in June/July, the date changes annually. Pineapples here take 18 months to grow, making them sweeter than plants grown in 6 months with the help of commercial chemicals. All the farms are small and there are no large plantations. The pineapple slips were washed away by Andrew but by 1993/94 things were back to normal. Half the settlement was left homeless and water and electricity were cut off. There is a beach with good surfing. It is 20 mins drive from the airport. Locally-made stained glass can be seen and bought at the Simba studio gallery and shop.

Governor's Harbour is one of the oldest settlements in the Bahamas with several interesting colonial period houses. The harbour is picturesque and is linked by a causeway to Cupid's Cay, the original settlement. A new cruise ship pier was built in 1991 but is unusable as no deep water channel was dredged. On 10 Nov a Guy Festival celebrates Guy Fawkes Day and parades are held, culminating in an evening bonfire. Tourism is dominated here by *Club Méditerranée* (T 332 2270, PO Box 80), on the Atlantic beachfront, which also runs a watersports centre on the harbour side. Keen divers are taken by *Club Med* instructors to dive with Valentine's Dive Centre at Harbour Island, where the diving is better.

In the S, **Windermere Island**, linked to the mainland by a small bridge, was an exclusive resort popular with the British Royal Family. The resort is closed now but opulent holiday homes remain. **Tarpum Bay** is the home of MacMillan-Hughes' Art Gallery and Castle. It used to be a big pineapple centre and there are many examples of wooden colonial houses in good repair.

Further S is **Rock Sound**, the largest settlement on the island with a population of about 1,100. It was first known as New Portsmouth and then Wreck Sound. Rock Sound is surrounded by limey, bush covered hills. It has a large modern shopping centre, three churches and many bars.

A few farming villages exist in the extreme S with more stretches of beach and fishing. One such is **Bannerman Town**, once known as the Pearl of the South. In the 1930s it was a prosperous sponge fishing centre with 20 or more sponging schooners anchored off the W shore. Today the settlement is like a ghost town with large churches in ruins and few people. Those who have stayed eke out a living by farming goats and pineapples and catching land crabs to send to Nassau. At the most southerly point of the island, **Cape Eleuthera** and

Point Eleuthera are sometimes likened to the opposite points on the tail of a fish. On Cape Eleuthera there is a lighthouse which was repaired by the Raleigh Expedition in 1988. At one time the keeper, Captain Finby, was also the local obeah man. Legend has it that he slept with a ghost called the White Lady, who visited him nightly. Lighthouse Beach is three miles long. At Eleuthera Point there is a good cliff top view of Cat Island and Little San Salvador. Be careful as the edges are badly eroded. From here you can also see nesting stacks of fairy terns, shark and barracuda channels and the spectacular blues, greens, yellows, reds and browns of fringing reefs. A lone tarpon known as Tommy cruises off this beach often in less than four feet of water.

SPANISH WELLS

On St George's Cay, an island off the N of Eleuthera (a short ferry ride), Spanish Wells gets its name from the use of the cay by Spanish ships as a water supply. $1\frac{3}{4}$ miles long and $\frac{1}{2}$ mile wide, until the hurricane disaster of 1992 it was reputed to have the highest per capita income of the Bahamas islands, with the wealth coming from fishing the spiny Bahamian lobster (known locally as bugs) as well as tourism. Most of the boats were wrecked by the storm and the fishermen lost their livelihoods. The population of 1,291 are descended from the original settlers, the Eleutheran Adventurers from Bermuda and the British Loyalists from the mainland, and are all white. The Spanish Wells Museum in a restored wooden house with shutters has exhibits of the island's history and culture, open 1000-1200, 1300-1500, Mon-Sat. To get to Spanish Wells from North Eleuthera airport, take a Pinders Taxi to the ferry dock, then ferry to the island (about US$10 for 2 people, any other taxi will work out at least double that rate).

A number of local fishermen can be hired as fishing guides off nearby **Russell** and **Royal Islands** (inhabited by a group of Haitians), payment by negotiation. Royal Island was once developed as a sheep farm by an estranged English dignitary. The old house still stands and paths weave through the overgrown grounds and gardens. Visitors can hire bicycles, but there are no cars.

HARBOUR ISLAND

This is the most desirable place to stay in North Eleuthera (population 1,216). From the airport it is a quick taxi ride, US$3 pp, to the dock and from there water taxis wait to take passengers on a 10-min ride to the island (US$4 pp one-way or US$8 for only one person). Taxis from the harbour to most resorts cost US$3 pp. **Dunmore Town**, named after Lord Dunmore, Governor 1786-1797, is a mixture of pastel coloured cottages, white picket fences and a number of small hotels and restaurants. It was the capital of the Bahamas for a time and once an important shipyard and sugar refining centre. Rum making was particularly popular during Prohibition. The three mile pink sand beach is popular. Bicycles can be rented at the dock. Fishing trips are easily arranged (US$85/half day). Reggie does taxi tours of the island for day trippers and he and his wife Jena run a regular taxi service, recommended, T 333 2116.

● **Accommodation & places to eat** A nice place to eat is *Harbour Lounge*, in an old wooden building overlooking the ferry dock with a bar and indoor or outdoor dining, good food but not cheap, bar food all day and late, Sun brunch in high season (T 333 2031). *Arthur's Bakery* does lunch and breakfast as well as being a bakery. *Miss Mae's Tearoom* is principally a gift shop selling prints, textiles etc but you can get salads and other food in the courtyard at lunchtime, there is an ice cream parlour and also a 2-bedroom apartment to rent upstairs, US$750/week, contact through *Ocean View Club*. *Ma Rubie's* restaurant at *Tingum Village* is good for native food but is particularly noted for its cheeseburgers, apparently among the world's top ten, there are also 12 rooms **A2** and a 3-bedroom, 2-bath cottage **L2,** under 12s free, 3 mins from beach (T 333 2161, PO Box 61). **L2** *Romora Bay Club* has timeshare units for rent with a wide variety of units scattered around the property, all decorated differently, dive packages available with dive shop on site, sailing, tennis, fishing available, day trips for couples with picnic hamper to deserted Jacob or Man Island, bicycles, bar, restaurant on hill top, one sitting for dinner (T 333 2325, F 333 2500, T 800-327 8286, PO Box 146). **L3-A1** *Valentine's Yacht Club and Inn*, in town has rooms which get heavily booked during regatta, pool side or garden side, pool, jacuzzi, tennis, 2 restaurants and all the facilities of the marina and dive shop, friendly (T 333 2080/2142, F 333 2135, T 800-323 5655, PO Box 1). On the other side of the island overlooking the pink sand beach, there are several lovely places to stay. **L1-L2** *Runaway Hill Club*, built as a private home in the 1940s, now extended and run by Roger and Carol Becht, lovely bar, restaurant, pool and deck all overlooking the sea, 10 luxury rooms, all different in size and character, casual but smart, men wear jackets for candlelit dinner (T 333 2150, F 333-2420, PO Box EL 27031) **L1-L2** *Ocean View Club*, only open for winter season, split level overlooking sea, 9 rooms, those upstairs are larger, lovely old furniture, designer decorated, lower rooms smaller, children under 12 half price, meals US$60 pp, large chessmen on patio, F/T 333 2276. **L1** *Pink Sands*, renovated to high luxury standard after Hurricane Andrew, cottages, tennis, on the beach, lovely location (T 333 2030, F 333 2060, PO Box 87). **L2-L3** *Coral Sands*, right on the beach with 14 acres stretching over the hill to Dunmore Town, concrete block painted blue and yellow, cottages in gardens, 33 rooms inc 8 suites, beach bar, restaurant, twice weekly evening entertainment, tennis lit for night play, watersports, games room, library (T 333 2320/2350, F 333 2368, 800-468 2799).

NB All the major hotels close in the autumn for some weeks so plan ahead if visiting Sept-November.

Island information – Eleuthera
● How to get there

There are airports at Governor's Harbour (8 miles from the town, US$20 taxi fare for 2 people), North Eleuthera and Rock Sound. Bahamasair have scheduled flights daily from Nassau to all three. Governor's Harbour and North Eleuthera are served also by Airways International, Gulfstream International, US Air Express (Piedmont Airlines) and American Eagle from Fort Lauderdale and/or Miami.

Four mailboats call at Eleuthera. See **Information for travellers, Ferries**, or ask the harbour master or shopkeepers about mailboat sailings.

Car hire from all 3 airports and in town costs US$45-50/day, Ross Garage – U Drive It Cars (Harbour Island, T 333 2122); ASA Rent-A-Car Service (T 332 2575); Governor's Harbour Car Rental Service (T 332 2575); Hilton Johnson (near Hatchet Bay, T 332 0241/335 6241); Wendell Bullard Taxi and Car Rental (North Eleuthera, T 335 1165); also Ethel Knowles at *Ethel's Cottages*, at Tarpum Bay. You can also hire mopeds. There are some public buses.

● Accommodation

Hotel prices

L1	over US$200	L2	US$151-200
L3	US$101-150	A1	US$81-100
A2	US$61-80	A3	US$46-60
B	US$31-45	C	US$21-30
D	US$12-20	E	US$7-11
F	US$4-6	G	up to US$3

Gregory Town: **A3** *Cambridge Villas*, in Gregory Town, run by Mr and Mrs Cambridge, painted yellow, 21 double rooms, 2-bedroomed apartments **A1-A2** sleep 4-8, also triple and quad rooms (T 335 5080, F 335 5308, PO Box 1548), pool, transport to Golden Key beach for swimming or elsewhere for surfing, bar/restaurant, music some nights, rental cars available; **L3-A1** *The Cove Eleuthera*, also known as *Pineapple Cove*, rooms in scattered cottages on headland with rocky cove one side, sandy cove the other, triples available, children under 12 free, large airy dining room, rather spartan but relaxed, some rooms need refurbishment, small pool, tennis, snorkelling, sea kayaks, volley ball, badminton, hammocks, T 335 5142, 800-552 5960, F 335 5338, PO Box 1548) is just outside the town within walking distance. At **Hatchet Bay**, **L3-A1** *Rainbow Inn*, a/c rooms with fan, deck, kitchenette, or 3-bedroomed villa, T/F 335 0294, PO Box EL 25053, has tennis, swimming pool and a good restaurant, 2-storey cottages became bungalows after hurricane, rocky outlook, good snorkelling, caves, fantastic view, Rainbow beach 1 mile, two beaches just other side of hill, bicycles for guests, live entertainment Wed evenings in nautical bar, popular, run by Ken Keene, friendly host; nearby is *Hilton & Elsie Island House*, 1-2 bedroom apartments US$500-700/week, rental car US$200/week, on hill, great view of island, Rainbow beach close or walk 1 mile to Eden beach on other side if rough, good kitchens, ideal for families, food stores in nearby Hatchet Bay or Rainbow Bay, T 335 6241, 332 0241, Hilton is a taxi driver and does car rentals.

Governor's Harbour and the S: *Club Mediterrannée*, T 332 2271, F 332 2691, 288 rooms, children's programmes, marine sports complex 10 mins away by shuttle on Caribbean coast, diving and golf at extra cost; N of the town near North Palmetto Point on the ocean beach is **L2-A1** *Unique Village*, with rooms, apartments or 2-bedroom villas, restaurant, bar, satellite TV, children under 18 free in summer, under 12 in winter, all with sea views, T 332 1830, F 332 1838; **A1-A2** *The Cigatoo Inn* (T 332 2343, PO Box 86), 6 miles from the airport, sits on top of a hill with good views of the bay, be prepared for loud music; **A1-A2** *Laughing Bird Apartments* (US$65-80d, T 332 2012/1029, F 332 2358, PO Box EL 25076) efficiency units and a guest house for 1-4 people, in town, overlooking the beach, managed by nurse Jean Davies and her British architect husband Dan. **Tarpum Bay: A2-A3** *Hilton's Haven* near beach and Rock Sound airport, bicycles, car rental, bar/restaurant with Bahamian specials, rec (T 334 4231/4125); **L3-A2** *Cartwrights Ocean View* room or cottage (T 334 4215), rec; **A2** *Ethel's Cottages*, on the waterfront, families welcomed, Mrs Ethel Knowles also rents out cars (T 334 4233, PO Box 27). **L1** *Winding Bay Beach Resort*, all inclusive, on a secluded lagoon is a less formal resort (T 334 2020, F 334 4057, PO Box 93). **Rock Sound: A3** *Edwina's Place*, run by Edwina Burrows, modest accommodation but highly rec, T 334 2094, PO Box 30; **L1-L2** *Cotton Bay Beach and Golf Club*, 77 rooms on 2 miles of sandy beach, packages available, upmarket with its Robert Trent Jones 18-hole golf course designed by Arnold Palmer around the beach and ponds, and excellent tennis with 4 all-weather courts and pro-shop, croquet, snorkelling, most watersports are available here, inc deep sea fishing, very good food, closed Sept-Oct, T 334 6101/6156, F 334 6082, 800-334 3523, PO Box EL26028; **L2** *Club Eleuthera*, Rock Sound, all-inclusive resort, overlooks ocean, 36 rooms, set in 37 acres, restaurant, bar, pool, watersports, volleyball, tennis, bicycles, ping pong, chess and other games, golf at *Cotton Bay Club* is extra, T 334 4055/56, F 334 4057, PO Box 126093; **L2-L3** *Palmetto Shores Vacation Villas*, at South Palmetto Point, 12 miles S of the airport, 1-3 bedroom villas, a/c, tennis, snorkelling gear, watersports, rental cars or scooters, T/F 332 1305, PO Box EL25131.

● **Places to eat**

The pineapples on Eleuthera are said to be the world's sweetest (see above, Gregory Town). In Gregory Town they produce a pineapple rum called 'Gregory Town Special' which is highly rec. Pineapple upside down pudding is a common dish. Other local dishes include Cape Eleuthera's conch chowder, which is a substantial meal, the best is supposed to be from Mary Cambridge in Gregory Town. Hulled bonavas (a type of bean which tastes like split pea soup) or hulled corn soup with dumplings of rice. This is eaten traditionally after a special church service on Good Friday. On New Year's Eve traditional fare includes Benny Cake, pig's feet or mutton souse, or cassava/potato bread. In many of the smaller settlements such as James Cistern, outdoor or Dutch ovens are still used to bake bread. Most of the resorts have their own restaurants. Others which have been rec are *Cambridge Villas*, in Gregory Town, good seafood, fairly expensive; in Governor's Harbour, *Blue Room* (T 332 2736) is a restaurant/bar/disco, as is *Ronnie's* in Cubid's Cay, free transport to yacht or hotel at night; there are plenty of Bahamian places to eat in Governor's Harbour, fairly smart are *Buccaneer* (open Mon-Sat, no credit cards, T 332 2500, on New Bond Street on top of hill) and *Sunset Inn* (on water, open daily from 0800, pool table, satellite TV, juke box), smarter is *Kohinoor*, three miles outside town on hilltop, open Tues-Sun for lunch and dinner, local and American dishes, happy hour 1600-1800, T 332 2668. *Lady Blanche's Lifesaver Restaurant* in Upper Bogue serves the best cracked conch in the area, run by hospitable family, prices reasonable; for very cheap, tasty food try a takeaway meal of barbecue ribs or chicken for less than US$5 at roadside stands in James Cistern; *Big Sally's Disco*, just N of Rock Sound, cocktails, bar snacks, dancing; *Cush's Place* (between Gregory Town and Hatchet Bay) does cookouts Sat and Sun afternoons with music and dancing, US$10; Lida Scavella in Hatchet Bay does cheap food, her pastries are rec; *Hatchet Bay Yacht Club* has good food, videos and music; outside Palmetto Point is *La Rastic*, a reasonably priced restaurant/bar with traditional fare, no credit cards,

T 332 1164; a popular bar in this area is *Mate and Jenny's Pizza*, try conch pizza, good cocktails, T 332 2504; in Rock Sound, *Edwina Burrows'* restaurant is highly rec, good food reasonably priced, popular barbecue dishes; *Sammy's Place* is another rec restaurant and bar, open daily 0800-2200, T 334 2121. *The Islander* is a popular, friendly bar; several bars in Wemyss Bight and Green Castle sell spirits in half pint glasses very cheaply; rec in Deep Creek are *Bab's Place* and *Mr Pratt's Bar*; *The Waterfront Bar* in Rock Sound is cheap, no food, while *The Ponderosa* and *The Dark Side* are bars and cheap fast food restaurants.

● **Tourist office**

Ministry of Tourism, Eleuthera Tourist Office, Governors Harbour, Eleuthera, T 332 2142, F 332 2480.

THE EXUMAS

The chain of 365 Exuma cays and islands stretches for 90 miles although the majority of the 3,539 inhabitants live on **Great Exuma** and **Little Exuma** at the S end. The island of Barreterre (pronounced Barra Terry) can be reached from Great Exuma by a bridge. There is a ferry to Stocking Island from Great Exuma and another to Lee Stocking Island from Barreterre. Great Exuma is long and narrow, covered with scrub and dry woodland. The soil is pitifully thin but there are aromatic shrubs, curly-tailed lizards and songbirds and a few wild peacocks. Around the villages are a few patches of what the Lands and Surveys map accurately calls 'casual cultivation'. The main industry is tourism, based on yachting and a few hundred winter visitors who own houses on the island. In 1994 the government approved a US$90mn residential and resort development covering 518 acres on Exuma. A US$35mn hotel is to be built in the first phase and there will eventually be a marina, golf course and casino as well.

The islands were virtually uninhabited until after the American Revolution, when Loyalists from the S colonies were given land and brought their slaves to grow cotton. During the late 18th century the British Crown granted Denys Rolle, an Englishman, 7,000 acres of land and he set up cotton plantations at Rolletown, Rolleville, Mt Thompson, Steventon and Ramsey. Following the emancipation of the slaves and poor cotton harvests because of the exhaustion of the soil, it was believed that Rolle's son gave away his lands to his former slaves, who were also called Rolle as was customary at the time. However, no deeds have been found confirming transfer of title and longstanding squatter's rights provide an adequate title to the land for many. Today, half the population bears the surname Rolle and two of the largest settlements are Rolleville and Rolletown.

The Exuma cays are in general isolated communities which are difficult to get to (the exception being Staniel Cay). Their inaccessibility has attracted undesirable attention; Norman's Cay was for some time the drug smuggling centre of Carlos Lehder, the Colombian drug baron deported from the Bahamas in 1982 and now in prison in the USA. In 1993 the cay was confiscated by the Government and put up for sale. Recent attempts to control drug smuggling include mooring Fat Albert, an airship full of radar equipment, over Great Exuma, and low flying helicopters also monitor activity.

Diving and marine life

The Exuma Cays begin at Sail Rocks about 35 miles from Nassau. Much of the Exuma chain is encompassed in the **Exuma Cays Land and Sea Park**, an area of some 176 square miles set up by the Bahamas National Trust to conserve all underwater life and for boating, diving and observation of wildlife. There is a warden's residence on Waderick Wells Cay. On the northerly Allen Cays can be seen the protected Rock Iguanas which grow up to two feet long and are known as Bahamian Dragons, but they are extremely tame. The park stretches between Wax Cay and Conch Cut, 22 miles away and offers more delights for underwater explorers, with beautiful coral and

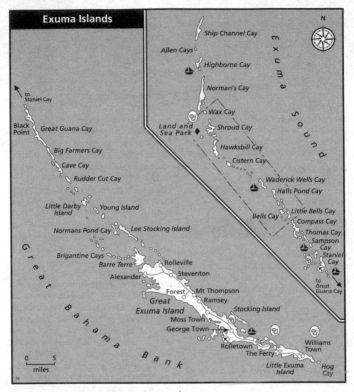

Exuma Islands

N

to Staniel Cay

Black Point — Great Guana Cay

Ship Channel Cay

Allen Cays

Highborne Cay

Norman's Cay

Wax Cay

Land and Sea Park

Shroud Cay

Hawksbill Cay

Cistern Cay

Big Farmers Cay

Cave Cay

Rudder Cut Cay

Waderick Wells Cay

Halls Pond Cay

Little Darby Island

Young Island

Little Bells Cay

Bells Cay

Compass Cay

Normans Pond Cay

Lee Stocking Island

Thomas Cay

Sampson Cay

Staniel Cay

Brigantine Cays

Barre Terre

Rolleville

Steventon

to Great Guana Cay

Alexander

Forest

Mt Thompson

Ramsey

Great Exuma Island

Stocking Island

Moss Town

George Town

Williams Town

Rolletown

The Ferry

Little Exuma Island

Hog Cay

Exuma Sound

Great Bahama Bank

0   5
miles

limestone reefs, blue holes and shipwrecks. Worth visiting are the underwater valley at Ocean Rock, the huge caves filled with black coral called the Iron Curtain, or Thunderball Grotto at Staniel Cay, where part of the James Bond film and the Disney film *Splash*, were made. Watch out for dangerous currents. Individual and package diving can be arranged with Exuma Fantasea, run by Madelaine and Ed Haxby, who are environmentally conscious. Ed is a marine biologist, is PADI licensed and has been researching the marine environment in the Bahamas for 20 years. He can be contacted through hotels which offer diving packages or in George Town T/F 336 3483, PO Box 29261. Get in touch with Ed Haxby for information on a stromatolite reef on the E (Atlantic) shore of Stocking Island. This is a growing reef of layered limestone, a living fossil and the oldest evidence of life on earth.

Beaches and watersports

Stocking Island is a long thin island about a mile from the mainland at Elizabeth Harbour, George Town. Its shape and position provide a natural protection for the harbour. It has good beaches and a burger bar and is famous for its Mysterious Cave, but this can only be reached by divers. A boat leaves the *Peace and Plenty Hotel* in George Town at 1000 and 1300, roundtrip US$8, free for guests, or boats can be hired from Exuma Fantasea (most watersports available) in George

Town to visit the reefs off Stocking Island. **The Three Sisters Rocks** which rise out of the water some 100 feet from the shore, are situated between two very good beaches: Jimmy Hill, which is a long empty beach good for swimming, and the beautiful bay of Ocean Bight. Other recommended beaches are the Tropic of Cancer Beach, 15 miles E of George Town, Cocoplum Beach, 20 miles N of George Town, Jollie Hall Beach, two miles W of George Town (no land access) and Out Island Inn Beach, George Town.

The Visiting Yachts Regatta is held in early Mar and on the fourth Thur in April the Family Island Regatta is held at George Town when working boats compete for the title of 'Best in the Bahamas'. During Aug there is a series of smaller regattas at Black Point, Barreterre and Rolleville.

For details of sportfishing, contact Bob Hyde, Director of Sportfishing at *Peace and Plenty Hotel*, T 800 525 2210, 345-5555, F 345-5556, who runs a bonefishing school and trains flyfishing guides; there is a bonefishing lodge with certified guides and three areas to fish. In Oct the Bonefish Bonanza Tournament is held at *Peace and Plenty Hotel*, George Town. In Nov a second Bonefish Bonanza Tournament is held at the *Peace and Plenty*.

There are several marinas in the Exumas. Exuma Fantasea Marina in George Town near *Club Peace and Plenty*, for motor boats up to 30 feet, rentals and sales of Boston Whalers, dive shop on site, T 336 3483; Exuma Docking Service, 52 slips, usual services, bar, fuel, showers etc, T 336 2578, VHF 16; Happy People Marina, Staniel Cay, 6 slips, 6 feet depth, showers, laundry, grocery, restaurant, T 355 2008; Staniel Cay Yacht Club, 4 slips, all services, tackle and bait, hotel, repairs, T 355 2024, VHF 16; Highborne Cay, fuel, electricity, supplies, restaurant, bar, VHF 16; Sampson Cay Colony, 30 slips, 7 feet depth, all services, charters and boat rentals, hotel, wet and dry storage, T 355 2034, VHF 16.

EXCURSIONS

The main town on **Great Exuma** is **George Town**, a pleasant little town built on a strip of land between a round lake and the sea. A narrow channel allows small boats to use the lake as a harbour but yachts moor offshore, often several hundred at a time in the peak winter months. The large and beautiful bay is called Elizabeth Harbour and is yet another contender for the site of Columbus' harbour that could "hold all the ships in Christendom." The main building is the Government Administration Building, pseudo colonial, pink and modelled on Nassau's Government House. Opposite is a large tree under which women plait straw and sell their wares. There are several pretty buildings, St Andrew's Church (Anglican), blue and white on the top of a little hill and the *Peace and Plenty Hotel* in an old cotton warehouse which was formerly the site of a slave market. There is a good range of shops and the supermarket is well stocked. The Sandpiper shop has an interesting array of clothes and souvenirs.

To the S of George Town is **Rolletown**, a small village on a hill overlooking the sea. Many old houses are painted in bright blues, yellows and pinks. There is a small cemetery in which are buried settlers from the 18th century in three family tombs: husband, wife and small child of the Mackay family. **The Ferry** is a small settlement by the beautiful strait which separates Great and Little Exuma, but there is a bridge there now, not a ferry.

North of George Town there is a thin scatter of expatriate holiday houses and a few shops along the Queen's Highway. East of the road are several fine beaches, including Hoopers Bay and Tar Bay. The airport turning is N of George Town. Small villages are Moss Town, Mount Thompson, Steventon and Rolleville. Moss Town was once an important sponging centre. Close by you can see The Hermitage, brick tombs dating back to just after the American War of Independence, not to be confused with the Hermitage or Cotton House close to Williams Town on Little Exuma. Mt Thompson was once the farming centre of Exuma and is important for its onion packing house. Some of the cottages in **Rolleville**, 16 miles NW of George Town, were originally slave quarters. The town overlooks a harbour and was the base of a group of rebellious slaves who attempted to escape and thereafter refused to work except in the mornings, until emancipation. Unfortunately, quite a large area of N Exuma is disfigured by roads which were laid out as part of a huge speculative land development scheme in the 1960s. Almost all the lots are still empty, but Cocoplum Beach and the coastal scenery are unspoilt. At the N end of the island is a bridge to Barreterre, with more fine scenery and places to eat lunch. At **Lee Stocking Island**, just offshore, the Caribbean Marine Research Centre is involved in research into the tilapia, a freshwater fish brought from Africa which can grow in salt water. This can be visited by prior appointment.

A bridge leads to **Little Exuma**, which is 12 miles long and one mile wide. An attractive cove is Pretty Molly Bay, next to the abandoned *Sand Dollar Hotel*. A mermaid story is based on Pretty Molly, a slave girl who sat on the rocks at night and gazed by the light of the moon towards Africa. Near Forbes Hill is the 'Fort', built in 1892 and said to be haunted. On Good Friday a nearby tree is said to give off a substance the colour of blood. **Williams Town** is the most southerly of the settlements on Exuma. Salt used to be made in the lagoon. Perched on the cliff top here is a tall white obelisk which not only guided passing ships safely in the 19th century, but was an advertisement that salt and fresh water could be picked up here. The Cotton House, near Williams Town, is the only plantation owner's house still standing in the Exumas. It is at the end of a driveway marked by a pair of trees, but is tiny, not grand. Slave quarters can be seen close by.

THE CAYS

Staniel Cay has excellent beaches with a half mile of sand dunes on the ocean side of the cay and good watersports facilities. On Staniel Cay during Bahamian Independence Day weekend on 10 July, there is a bonefishing festival, entrance fee US$20. The Staniel Cay Yacht Club provides free food in the evening and a rake'n'scrape band plays traditional music. The morning before the contest there is a sailing regatta for working Bahamian sailboats. A Bahamian sailboat regatta is held on New Year's Day. The Royal Entertainers Lounge serves food and drinks.

Farmer's Cay to the S of Staniel Cay has a lively annual festival called The Farmer's Cay First Friday in February Festival at which there are races, dancing games and the Bahamas' only Hermit Crab Race. Further S on **Darby Island** is an old mansion which is probably the remains of a large coconut plantation.

Forty miles off Staniel Cay on the edge of the Tongue of the Ocean is **Green Cay**, home to the world's second largest population of white crowned pigeons.

Island information – The Exumas
● **How to get there**
There is an international airport at Moss Town with an 8,000 foot runway, 2 miles from George Town, and another airport at George Town with an 8,000 foot runway, but this is closed to commercial traffic. Confusingly the Exuma International Airport at Moss Town carries the (GGT) George Town code. American Eagle flies daily from Miami into Moss Town in high season, 5 times a week in summer, Bahamasair flies from Fort Lauderdale, Nassau, Deadman's Cay and Stella Maris, Long Island. Mr Harry Nixon runs a charter service, Nixon Aviation and Harken Air (PO Box 3, Airport, George Town, T 336 2104). Bahamasair flights from Nassau through George Town to Long Island are often booked up well in advance. For details on mailboat sailings, see **Information for travellers, Ferries**.

● **Transport**
Taxis are expensive but plentiful. The fare from the airport to George Town is US$22. Hitching is easy. Cars can be rented from George Town, ask at *Peace and Plenty Hotel*. Buses run between Rolleville and George Town. Christine Rolle runs Island Tours from George Town, leaving at 1000 and 1400, including a native lunch, visits to various settlements and to Gloria, the 'shark lady,' on Little Exuma, who catches sharks and sells the teeth as souvenirs. Bicycles can be rented from *Two Turtles* shop or several hotels.

● **Accommodation**
L1-L3 *Coconut Cove*, a mile W of George Town, newest hotel, 9 beach or garden rooms, one suite **L1**, about 20% less in summer, diving/honeymoon/pilots packages available, a/c and fans, minibar, beach towels and robes provided, transport to town and to Stocking Island, boat rentals, pool, popular Mon barbecue, T 336 2659, F 336 2658, PO Box EX 29299; **A1-A2** *Two Turtles Inn*, 200 yards from harbour in George Town, 14 rooms, rooms large enough for 4, a/c, TV, some have kitchenettes, barbecue on Fri nights (T 336 2545, F 336 2528); **L2-L3** *Club Peace and Plenty*, T 336 2551/2, F 336 2253, 800-525 2210, PO Box 29055, dive, fishing, photography, honeymoon packages available, 300 yards from harbour, the pink building was once the slave market and sponge warehouse, 35 rooms/suites, a/c, all rooms have balcony overlooking harbour, entertainment some evenings, pool, sailboats, bicycles, restaurant, bar. The hotel also has a quieter *Beach Inn*, 16 rooms, marble baths, fans, balcony, pool, sailboats, restaurant, bar at end of pier, one mile E out of George Town, complimentary shuttle from *Peace and Plenty*, lots of water sports, T 336 2250, F 336 2253, and a *Bonefish Lodge*, 8 rooms in a timber building close to the fishing grounds overlooking blue hole, 10 miles E of *Peace and Plenty*, restaurant/bar, games room, all fishing facilities, certified guides; **L2-L3** *Regatta Point*, on a point just outside George Town, private beach, 5 apartments for 2-4 people, kitchens, bicycles, sunfish, dock, run by Nancy Bottomlea, T 336 2206, F 336 2046; *Pirates Point* villas, private beach, just S of George Town, US$490/week (T 336 2554); **B** *Marshall's Guesthouse*, (T 336 2571), John Marshall (grocery shop in George Town) has apartments to rent by week/month; also apartments at Sea Watch,

an isolated position 10 miles N of George Town on fine beach, T 336 4031. **A1** *Palms At Three Sisters Beach Club and Hotel*, Mount Thompson, 12 rooms or 3 villas, on beach, satellite TV, live music Fri, Sat nights, restaurant, T 358 4040, F 358 4043, 800-253 2711, PO Box EX 29196. **L2** *Staniel Cay Yacht Club*, has own private airstrip, accommodation in waterfront properties, 4 cottages, houseboat cottage, inc all meals and use of skiff and outboard motor, larger cottage sleeps 4, beach, marina, scuba diving gear available, T 355 2011/2024, F 355 2044, 800-825 5099.

● **Places to eat**
The main hotels in George Town have good restaurants, *Peace and Plenty* (dance with local band Sat nights), and *Two Turtles* (barbecue Fri nights, very lively and good value but take your own cutlery if you want to cut up your steak, plastic only provided, happy hour 1700-2300, US$1.50 for spirit and mixer, frequented by visitors and ex-pats). For sandwiches and light meals, *Ruth's Deli*, in George Town, open Mon-Sat 0900-1700, no credit cards, T 336 2596 *Eddy's Edgewater*, T 336 2050, specializes in Bahamian food, fried conch is rec, open Mon-Sat 0730-2300, no credit cards; *Sam's Place*, run by Mr Sam Gray, manager of the marina, T 336 2579, at dock, open daily from 0730 (expensive); *La Shante*, Forbes Hill, good, open daily 1000-0200, happy hour Sun 1800-1900, 3 a/c rooms to rent, guided bonefishing, T 345 4136; *Silver Dollar*, George Town, traditional Bahamian cooking, T 336 2615, no credit cards; *Central Highway Inn*, T 345 7014, on the road 6 miles NW of George Town, Bahamian specialities; *Rodriguez Neighbourhood Bar/Restaurant & Lounge*, at Harts, a settlement 13 miles outside George Town, largest night club on Exuma, on waterfront, live band Fri, disco Sat, Sun, famous for its conch fritters. Others doing mainly peas'n'rice type dishes are *Iva Bowes* and *Three Sisters* in Mt Thompson, *Kermit Rolle's*, in Rolleville is by appointment only but he also has a good restaurant opp the airport building, *Kermit's Airport Lounge*, for breakfast, lunch or dinner, takeaway service, T 345 0002, VHF 16; and *Fisherman's Inn*, Barreterre, very good. *Staniel Cay Yacht Club*, restaurant is open to non-guests if prior notice is given, T 355 2011/2024, VHF 16, breakfast 0800, lunch 1300, dinner 1900 one sitting, box lunches available. Discos at *Cousins*, up hill from *Club Peace and Plenty*, late night

music and bar; *Paramount Club* (Moss Town),
Oasis (Queen's Highway near Mt Thompson),
Flamingo Bay (George Town).

● **Tourist office**
Ministry of Tourism, Exuma Tourist Office,
Cousins Building, Queens Highway, George
Town, Exuma, T 336 2430, F 366 2431.

INAGUA

Inagua (Great and Little), population
985, is the most southerly of the Bahamas
Islands and the third largest. Little
Inagua is uninhabited now, but the 49-
square mile island is reputed to hide the
treasure of Henri Christophe, one-time
ruler of Haiti. On a clear day, Great
Inagua is visible from both Cuba and
Haiti. The highest points on the island
are Salt Pond Hill at 102 feet and East
Hill at 132 feet. Vegetation is sparse because of low rainfall, the buffeting trade
winds and lack of fresh water, but this has
granted ideal conditions for salt production leading to a development and prosperity not enjoyed by any of the
surrounding islands. It is thought that
the name Inagua comes from the Spanish
lleno (full) and *agua* (water): *henagua*.
This was apparently the name of the
island when the first salt farmers settled
there. In 1803 records show only one
inhabitant, but the success of the salt
industry meant that by 1871 the population had risen to 1,120. Although trade
barriers in the USA caused the decline of

the salt trade in Inagua for many years,
the industry was revitalized in the 1930s
with the establishment of the Morton
Salt Company, which now utilizes 12,000
acres. Morton Bahamas Ltd installed a
power plant which supplies electricity to
all homes in **Matthew Town**. Inagua has
the best telecommunications system in
the Family Islands and nearly everyone
has a telephone. For a while the island
supported a cotton plantation; although
a shortlived enterprise, wild cotton can
still be found growing on Inagua today.
Outside Matthew Town you can still see
the ruins of the cotton mill and the narrow plantation roads, as well as the ruins
of a prison from the days when the community was large enough to need one.

Flora and fauna
The SE side of the island is rocky and
because of the effects of the sea and wind,
the trees do not grow more than a foot
tall. Further inland trees have a better
chance of maturing. Many cactii are
found in this rocky part of Inagua, in
particular the dildo cactus and the
woolly-nipple. On Little Inagua, although it is largely overgrown, it is possible to see some of the only natural
palms in the Bahamas. The whole of
Little Inagua is a Land and Sea Park and
is a Bird Sanctuary.

Inagua has a restricted access National Park which is home to a wide
range of birds including the world's largest flamingo colony on Lake Rosa
(sometimes called Lake Windsor), a 12-
mile stretch of marshy wildlife sanctuary. Almost half of Great Inagua is
included in the 287-square-mile park.
Visitors should contact the Bahamas
National Trust in Nassau (PO Box N-
4105, T 393 1317). A basic but comfortable camp has been established on the
W side, 23 long miles by jeep from Matthew Town. National Trust wardens will
accompany you on tours of the area and
it is possible to view the flamingos close
up. At certain times of the year they cannot be approached. Jimmy Nixon, one of
the original wardens, is recommended as

a guide. Early spring is the breeding season when large numbers of flamingoes congregate on the lake. At the Union Creek camp on the NW side of the island is a breeding and research area for Green and Hawksbill turtles, called Turtle Sound. It is ideal for observing sea turtles at close quarters. On the E side of the island are mangrove swamps which are the nesting grounds for many birds including cormorants, pelicans and the rare reddish egret. Here you can also see the white tailed tropic bird and inland, the Bahamas parrot, the most northerly species of parrot in the world.

Beaches

Apart from the rocky SE side of the island, Inagua has many deserted and unspoiled beaches. Those which are used by locals include Cartwright's beach, with bar/restaurant, within easy reach of Matthew Town, Farquharson's Beach and Matthew Town Beach, which is pleasant and conveniently located. Man of War Bay has a lovely beach with some shade.

Sports

It is possible to play tennis and basketball in Matthew Town, but the most popular pastime is hunting. You can arrange to go on a wild boar hunt with Herman Bowe (known as the Crocodile Dundee of the Bahamas, who prefers to hunt barefoot) or Jimmy Nixon (the excellent National Trust guide). On Emancipation Day (1 Aug) and other public holidays, wild boar is roasted on the beach and there are wild donkey races. Rodeos take place on an ad hoc basis.

Island information – Inagua

● How to get there

The airport is on Great Inagua. Bahamasair have 3 scheduled flights a week from Nassau, one of which comes via Mayaguana. The mailboat takes 2 days from Nassau, see **Information for travellers, Ferries**.

● Transport

A taxi from the airport to Matthew Town costs about US$4. There are taxis but no buses. Mr Harry Ingraham runs a fleet of 3 tour buses called Great Inagua Tours, rates negotiable. Most roads are paved, except for those leading into the interior. Taxis cannot be used for birdwatching tours because of the state of the roads. If you want to see the island properly you will need transport, particularly if you travel to the N side of the island. Local people are very friendly and helpful and will organize a sightseeing/wildlife trip. Jeeps for hire from Mr Burrows at Matthew Town Service Station, rates negotiable but expect to pay at least US$40/day. To get out to the camps arrange transport with the warden in Matthew Town (about US$10). To arrange fishing expeditions or trips around the island contact the local repair man, Cecil Fawkes (nicknamed the old Red Fox), whose boat is called *The Foxy Lady*, or Mr Cartwright. There is no set rate, prices are negotiated. There is a marina and boats can moor here and refuel.

● Accommodation

There are several guest houses in Matthew Town. The **B** *Main House*, T 339 1267, F 339 1265, has 4 rooms. There is also the **B** *Ford's Inagua Inn*, T 339 1277, with 6 rooms and a few small private guesthouses such as *Walkine's*, T 339 1500 (enquire locally for information). There are 2 camps, *Union Creek* in the NW and *Flamingo Camp*, 23 miles from Matthew Town, with basic accommodation. Bunks cost about US$10 a night and reservations should be made with The Bahamas National Trust, PO Box N4105, Nassau (T 323 1317 or 323 2848).

● Places to eat

Eating out is cheaper than Nassau or Grand Bahama. For a typical Bahamian meal of macaroni, coleslaw, ribs or chicken and potato salad, expect to pay US$6-7. Local dishes include roast wild boar, baked box fish, crab meat 'n rice and roast pigeon and duck. A popular local drink is gin and coconut, which is made with fresh coconuts on special occasions. *Topps Restaurant and Bar*, run by the Palacious brothers is rec for its seafood dishes, fresh boiled fish is served for breakfast; also rec is *The Hide Out Club*, run by Mr Cox, which is a popular dance and drinking spot; *Pride*, run by Mr Moultry is very friendly. Nightlife revolves around the local bars, which periodically have live music and dancing.

Matthew Town has a Bank of the Bahamas Ltd (open 0930-1430 Mon-Thur, 1030-1830 Fri) and 6 churches.

NB Mosquitoes can be a problem at some times of the year, avoid May. Credit cards are not generally accepted, take plenty of cash with you.

LONG ISLAND

Long Island (population 3,107) lies SE of Little Exuma and is 57 miles long and 4 miles across at its widest. Columbus made a stop here and changed its name from the Arawak name Yuma to Fernandina, after Ferdinand, the King of Spain. The island has a variety of communities from different ethnic backgrounds, from Europe, Africa and North America. Most islanders live on the W side where the hills and dunes offer some protection from the sea. There are paths and dirt tracks to the E side, mostly used by fishermen. Villages to the S are rather neglected, with poor roads and no telephone service. The landscape is diverse, with tall white cliffs at Cape Santa Maria with caves below, old salt pans near

Long Island

Clarence Town, dense bush over much of the island and scattered areas of cactii. It has a rocky coastline on one side and lovely beaches and crystal clear water on the other, with the usual friendly fish and lots of convenient wrecks. One, a German freighter sunk in 1917, lies in 25 feet of water only 200 yards from the beach at Guana Cay, S of Salt Pond. Beaches in the S are good but rather hard to get to. Long Island is a major producer of vegetables and cattle and is known for its pot-hole farming which gives hearty supplies of tomatoes, bananas and onions. The *Stella Maris Resort Club* in the N is the biggest employer, but there are not enough jobs and most young people leave to work in Nassau or Grand Bahama.

The main settlements are **Deadman's Cay** and **Clarence Town** further S. Most tourists stay at **Stella Maris**, which is supposed to have the best yachting marina in the southern Bahamas. From a lookout tower here it is possible to see right across the island and to see the nearby ruins of the Adderly Plantation House. The town of **Simms** is the home of the best straw work in the Bahamas, made by Ivy Simms and her workers. The mailboat calls here and there is a high school, magistrate's court and Commissioner's office. The settlement of Clarence Town in the S half of the island is very pretty and boasts two white, twin-spired churches built on opposite hilltops by Father Jerome (see under Cat Island). St Paul's is the Anglican church and St Peter's the Catholic. Both are still in use today. There are many caves to explore and ruins of old plantation houses: Adderly's near Stella Maris and the remains of a cotton gin and plantation gate posts at Dunmore. At Glenton's, N of Stella Maris, archaeologists have found the remains of an Arawak village, and at Hamilton, S of Deadman's Cay, caves have been discovered with Arawak drawings and carvings.

Diving and marine life

The Stella Maris Marina is the only full-service marina in the area and is a port of entry. There are 12 slips and all facilities including repairs, T 336 2106, VHF 16, and facilities for diving, snorkelling, reef, bone and deep sea fishing and boat charters. At Clarence Town dock you can get fuel, water, ice and supplies. At Harding's Supplies Center on Salt Pond you can also find showers and a laundry. There are safe anchorages at Cape Santa Maria, Salt Pond and Little Harbour. Cape Santa Maria has lovely beaches, caves and bays but do not anchor there if there is a strong N or W wind. A lagoon just beyond the W end of the cape can accommodate boats of 60 feet with depths of six feet. Diving and snorkelling are also good in this area and the Cape Santa Maria Fishing Club operates from here. On the E coast, good anchorages are at Clarence Town (groceries and other supplies) and Little Harbour (no facilities). The annual Long Island Regatta at Salt Pond is held in May. Locals compete for best seaman award, the fastest boat and the best kept boat over 5 years old. The Regatta is popular and accompanied by authentic Bahamian food and traditional rake'n'scrape music.

Island information – Long Island

● How to get there

There are 2 airports at Stella Maris and at Deadman's Cay. Island Express flies several times a week from Fort Lauderdale to Stella Maris. There are 6 Bahamasair flights a week from Nassau to Stella Maris, one via Deadman's Cay and 3 from George Town. The drive from Deadman's Cay to Stella Maris is about 2 hrs along a rough potholed road. Taxis are available and private cars often negotiate to carry passengers too. Taxis are generally expensive. If you are going to Stella Maris it is better to get a flight to the airport there if possible, from where it is only 20 mins, US$3 pp, to the resort. The main road connecting all the main settlements on the island is the Queen's Highway, which is notoriously bad, particularly in the S where the potholes are said to be the size of a car in places. Avoid night driving.

● Accommodation

The **L1-L3** *Stella Maris Resort Club* is one of the top 5 resorts in the Caribbean (T 336 2106, 800-426 0466, PO Box LI-30105). It has rooms, 1-bedroom apartments/cottages and 2-bedroom villas. A shopping centre has a bank and post office. There are 3 pools and 5 beaches along with tennis, volley ball, table tennis, bicycles, diving, windsurfing (guests free) and waterskiing (US$25). Bicycles are free for guests; cars can be rented from US$50/day plus mileage. Free transport to Deal's Beach with use of sailboats, free daily snorkelling excursions. Glass bottom boat trips can be taken for US$20. Cave parties are held once a week and a Rum Punch party every Wed. 25 different diving areas offer a lot of variety for the experienced or the beginner and there is a shark reef with shark feeding. Fishing trips can be arranged: during Nov and Dec huge shoals of grouper make fishing easy in the waters around Long Island. The blue hole close to the harbour at Clarence Town is good for line fishing. **L1-L2** *Cape Santa Maria Beach Resort* on the island's N point, T/F 357 1006, T 800-663 7090, closed mid-Sept to mid-Nov, taxi from Stella Maris airport about US$20; **A3** *Thompson's Bay Inn* at Hardings near Salt Pond (T 337 0000, PO Box 30123), rec, small and friendly, 8 rooms, pool, fishing, disco lounge, serves native food. There are also a few guest houses, *Knowles Cottages*, guest house in Clarence Town; *Hamilton's Guest House* in Hamilton; **B** *Carroll's Guest House* (T 337 1048) at Deadman's Cay; *O and S Guest House* at Simms.

● Places to eat

Two island dishes to try are wild hog with onion and spices and grouper roe with liver. *Thompson's Bay Inn* has a good restaurant but reservations essential. *The Blue Chip Restaurant and Bar* in Simms is rec. *The Harbour Bar and Restaurant* at Clarence Town has Bahamian dishes, as does *Mario's*, 7 miles S of Stella Maris, breakfast, lunch and dinner, reservations needed for dinner; *Sabrina's*, at Burnt Ground Village, is by appointment only, cheap and simple, occasional disco. In Hard Bargain in the S, the *Forget Me Not Club* has a popular bar and restaurant. In Mangrove Bush the Knowles family run the hillside tavern and bar. They also sell fresh fish at *Summer Seafood* close by.

MAYAGUANA

Mayaguana (an Arawak name), located 50 miles E of Acklins and 60 miles N of Inagua, is the least developed (population 308) and most isolated of the Family Islands although there are now three Bahamasair flights a week (Mon, Wed and Fri) from Nassau, 2 of which come via Inagua. The main settlement is **Abraham's Bay**, a small town with a few shops and one bar/restaurant run by the Brown family who also own the guesthouse. There are two other settlements, **Betsy Bay** and **Pirate's Well**, which are both very isolated. Several people will rent you a room in their homes for US$30-60; fresh water and food can sometimes be hard to come by, young coconuts are recommended if short of water. Take mosquito repellent. Most people earn their living from fishing or farming and many leave for Nassau and Freeport to look for work. In 1993 the Government approved a tourist development by a Californian group in E Mayaguana. About half of the 50,000-acre project will be a botanical garden and park. If it is implemented it will provide employment but no doubt change the island considerably.

The island is on a direct route to the Caribbean and as such is sometimes visited by yachtsmen, although it is not a port of entry. There is a very large reef around the NW side of the island and excellent diving, although a liveaboard dive boat is necessary. Twenty miles from Mayaguana are the Plana and Samana Cays, notable for their interesting wildlife, where you can see the Bahama hutia, thought to be extinct until the mid-1960s. A cross between a rat and a rabbit, this rodent's flesh is said to be similar to pork.

RUM CAY

Some 35 miles S of San Salvador, this small island (population 53) is approximately 20 miles square. First known as Mamana by the Lucayan Indians, the cay was later renamed Santa María de la Concepción by Columbus. Spanish explorers once found a lone rum keg washed up on a shore and changed the name again to Rum Cay. In the N there is an interesting cave which has Lucayan drawings and carvings. Various artefacts from the Arawak period have been found by farmers in the fertile soil which the Indians enriched with bat guano. In common with other islands, Rum Cay has experienced a series of booms and busts. Pineapple, salt and sisal have all been important industries, but competition and natural disasters, such as the 1926 hurricane, have all taken their toll and today tourism is the main source of employment. Plantation boundaries known as 'margins' can be seen all over the island, which date from the beginning of the 19th century when Loyalists settled here. Nearly everybody lives in **Port Nelson** where cottages can be rented. Settlements such as Port Boyd, Black Rock and Gin Hill are now deserted and overgrown.

This former pirates' haven is surrounded by deep reefs and drop-offs. There is staghorn coral at Summer Point Reef and good diving at Pinder's Point. At the Grand Canyon, huge 60-foot coral walls almost reach the surface.

SAN SALVADOR

Known as Guanahani by the original Lucayan inhabitants, this island (population 486) claims to be the

Mayaguana

Pirate's Well
Blackwood Point
Betsy Bay
Upper Point
Flamingo Pond
Salt Pond
Long Bay
Broken Bay
Abraham's Bay
Horse Pond Bay
Low Point
Booby Cay
Southeast Point
0   3
miles

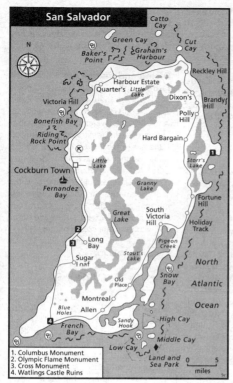

San Salvador

Catto Cay
Green Cay
Cut Cay
Baker's Point
Graham's Harbour
Reckley Hill
N
Harbour Estate
Quarter's Little Lake
Dixon's
Brandy Hill
Victoria Hill
Polly Hill
Bonefish Bay
Riding Rock Point
Hard Bargain
Little Lake
Cockburn Town
Storr's Lake
Fernandez Bay
Granny Lake
Fortune Hill
Great Lake
South Victoria Hill
Holiday Track
Long Bay
Pigeon Creek
North
Sugar Loaf
Stout's Lake
Old Place
Snow Bay
Atlantic
Montreal
Blue Holes
Allen
Ocean
High Cay
French Bay
Sandy Hook
Middle Cay
Low Cay
Land and Sea Park

0   5
miles

1. Columbus Monument
2. Olympic Flame Monument
3. Cross Monument
4. Watlings Castle Ruins

erected in 1892 to commemorate the 400th anniversary of Columbus' landing. It is the oldest monument, but judging by the rocky setting it is the most unlikely of the putative landfall spots.

The island is about 12 miles long and six miles wide with a network of inland lakes (with names like Granny Lake and Old Granny Lake) which were once the main transport routes. For a good view, climb the lookout tower E of the airport on Mount Kerr, at 140 feet the highest point on the island. Until the 1920s San Salvador was known as Watling's Island after the legendary pirate John Watling, who was said to have built Watling's Castle on French Bay in the 17th century. Archaeologists have now proven that the ruins are the remains of a loyalist plantation. You can see the stone ruins including the master's house, slave quarters and a whipping post. Access to the ruins is via the hill to the W of the Queen's Highway near the bay.

first place that Columbus landed in the New World and is cognisant of its history. Four sites vie for recognition as the first landing place and celebrations marked the quincentennial anniversary in 1992. One of the sites where Columbus may have come ashore is Long Bay. There is a bronze monument under the sea where he was supposed to have anchored and a white cross on the shore where he was said to have landed. Jewelry and pottery dating back to the Lucayan Indians have been found on the beach here. Close by is the Mexican Monument commemorating the handing over of the Olympic flame to the New World for the 1968 Olympics in Mexico. At Crab Cay in the E is the Chicago Herald Monument,

In the 1950s and 1960s, the US military leased land from the British Crown and built a submarine tracking station at **Graham's Harbour** in the N. Roads, an airport, a Pan American Base and a US Coast Guard Station were also built. The withdrawal of the military in the late 1960s led to unemployment and emigration. The building at Graham's Harbour is now occupied by the College of the Finger Lakes' Bahamian Field Station, a geological and historical research institute. Further development took place under the Columbus Landing Development Project, which built houses, condominiums, roads and a golf course around Sandy Point. In the 1990s, *Club Med* built a resort near Cockburn Town, known as *Columbus Isle*, which has provided some jobs. In 1995, *Club Med* was granted a casino licence, the first ever to be awarded to any of the Family Islands. The largest settlement is **Cockburn** in the NW, once known as Riding Rock because of the tidal movement on rocks off the bay which give the impression that the rocks are moving up and down.

Flora and fauna

San Salvador is famous for its reefs, beautiful bays, creeks and lakes. At Pigeon Creek in the SE there is a large lagoon, edged by mangroves, which is a nursery for many different kinds of large fish, including sharks. White Cay and Green Cay, off Graham's Harbour, are designated land and sea parks. White Cay has tall white cliffs on one side where there are large numbers of Brown Boobies. They are docile and you can get very close (once making them easy prey for hunters). Green Cay also has a large bird population. Manhead Cay off the NE is home to a rare species of iguana over one foot in length. There are large rock formations on the N side of the cay, access is possible from the S but is not easy, involving a climb up a rocky hill. Frigate birds can sometimes be seen here. Some subsistence farming using old slash and burn methods is still done on San Salvador.

Beaches and watersports

French Bay is a popular beach with excellent shelling and snorkelling. There are large reefs of elk and staghorn coral in less than 50 feet of water, some of which are exposed at low tide. Overlooking French Bay are the ruins of Watling's Castle, now better known as the Sandy Point Estate. Going S following the Queen's Highway along the bay you come to the Government Dock and further on Sandy Point. Both spots are recommended for their privacy and good reefs for scuba divers and snorkellers. The entire E coastline, with the exception of the creek areas, is uninhabited and has fine beaches of white sand. East of Dixon Lighthouse past the sand dunes is East Beach, a mile-long stretch of excellent sands.

Diving and marine life

Fishing, diving and sailing are all popular. There are shallow reefs, walls, corals and several wrecks to interest scuba divers and underwater life here is said to be some of the most spectacular in the Bahamas. *Club Med Columbus Isle* has scuba diving, contact Steve Schwartz, T 331 2000/2222. Island Water Sports at *Riding Rock Inn* has a full range of watersports activities on offer, an eight slip marina and daily scuba excursions. There are facilities for taking and developing underwater colour photographs (T 332 2631). On Discovery Day, 12 Oct, there is a dinghies race.

EXCURSIONS

North of Cockburn on the Queen's Highway is the small settlement of **Victoria Hill** where the New World Museum is owned by the local historian Ruth Wolper. There are interesting Lucayan artifacts, most of which came from the remains of an Indian settlement at Palmetto Grove, named after the silver top palmettos found there. **Dixon Hill Lighthouse**, which was built in Birmingham in the 19th century and rebuilt in 1930 is on the NE coast, still on the Queen's Highway. Mrs Hanna, the keeper, gives tours of the lighthouse, which is run by candle power and clockwork and is one of the few remaining hand operated lighthouses. South of the lighthouse and past East Beach you get to Crab Cay and the Chicago Herald Monument (see above).

Island information – San Salvador

● **How to get there**
There are scheduled Bahamasair flights from Nassau to Cockburn Town several times a week, one of which comes via Arthur's Town, another via The Bight. Bahamasair also has 2 flights a week from Miami. For details of

mailboat sailings see **Information for travellers, Inter Island Travel**. If you avoid the bush and water it is perfectly feasible to walk around San Salvador. The Queen's Highway encircles the island and there are no other main roads. You can hire cars, enquire in Cockburn Town. Mopeds are not available. There is a bus tour which visits the main points of interest, ask at *Riding Rock Inn*.

● **Accommodation**
Club Med Columbus Isle, said to be one of the nicer *Club Med* resorts, comfortable, well-integrated into surroundings, usual facilities and more, 148 rooms, a/c, TV, phone, mini-fridge, no children under 12, casino approved, fishing and diving at extra cost, T/F 331 2458, in USA T 800 CLUB-MED, 602-948 9190, F 602-948 4562, PO Box 4460, Scottsdale, Arizona 85261. **L3-A1** *Riding Rock Inn and Marina*, N of Cockburn Town, has 48 rooms, swimming pool and a restaurant overlooking the bay (T 367 2106), write to 1170 Lee Wagner Blvd 103, Fort Lauderdale, FL 33315 for details, T 800-272 1492, F 305-359 8254. **A1** *Ocean View Villas*, for accommodation in cottages.

● **Places to eat**
Riding Rock Inn is considered expensive at US$30, but it has a rake'n'scrape band once a week featuring Bernie the Band Leader (also Bernie the airport manager). *Dixie Hotel and Restaurant*, Dixon Hill and *Ocean Cabin*, Cockburn Town, are both reasonable. *Harlem Square Rip Club* is rec, friendly, Fri night disco. The local dish is crab'n'rice, made from the plentiful land crabs found on the island, average cost US$5-7.

Information for travellers

BEFORE TRAVELLING

● **Documents**
US citizens do not need passports or visas but for stays of up to 3 weeks they must carry a certified birth certificate or voter's registration card, along with a photo ID issued by a competent authority such as a driver's licence or military identification; for longer, a valid passport is required. Visitors may stay for up to 8 months but must have sufficient funds for their stay and an onward or return ticket. Passports are required by all other nationalities, but visas are not needed by nationals of Commonwealth and West European countries, South Korea, Israel and Japan (length of permitted stay varies between 3 and 8 months), nor by most Latin American nationals if staying no longer than 14 days. Colombians without a US visa need a Bahamian visa. Nationals of Haiti and communist countries need a visa. You will need a certificate of vaccination against yellow fever if you are coming from an infected area. To enter the Bahamas for business purposes the permission of the Immigration Department, Nassau, must be obtained. It is advisable to apply in writing to: Director of Immigration, Immigration Department, PO Box N3002, Nassau. No expatriate can be employed in a post for which a suitably qualified Bahamian is available, nor can a permit application be considered if the prospective employee is already in the country, having come in as a visitor.

● **Climate**
The sunshine and warm seas attract visitors throughout the year but winter, from Dec to April, is the high season. Temperatures are around 20°C (68°F). Summer temperatures average 30°C (86°F). Humidity is fairly high, particularly in the summer. The rainy season is May-Oct, when the showers are usually short but heavy. June-Nov is the official hurricane

season, the last major one to hit the Bahamas being Andrew in Sept 1992.

MONEY

● Currency
The unit of currency is the Bahamian Dollar (B$) which is at par with the US dollar. Both currencies are accepted everywhere. There is no restriction on foreign currency taken in or out; Bahamian currency may be exported up to B$70 pp. Notes of B$ 100, 50, 20, 10, 5, 3, 1 and 50c; coins of B$5, 2, 1, 50c, 25c, 15c, 10c, 5c and 1c.

● Credit cards
All major credit cards are accepted on New Providence and Grand Bahama. Not all the hotels and restaurants on the Family Islands take credit cards, although most take American Express, Mastercard and Visa.

GETTING THERE

AIR

Most flights to the Bahamas originate in the USA. Connecting flights by Bahamasair go out from Nassau like spokes of a wheel to the Family Islands although many airlines now fly direct from Florida to the Family Islands.

● To Nassau
From the USA: American Eagle from Miami and Tampa; Bahamasair flies from Miami, Fort Lauderdale and Orlando; Carnival Air Lines from Fort Lauderdale, and New York; American Trans Air from Boston, Chicago, Los Angeles, Orlando; Chalk's International from Miami (also to Bimini); Delta from Atlanta, Dallas, Fort Lauderdale, Memphis, Portland, New York (La Guardia), Orlando; USAIR from Charlotte, Miami, and Philadelphia (in high season), and West Palm Beach; Gulfstream International Airlines from Miami, Fort Lauderdale, Jacksonville, Orlando, Tampa.

From Canada: Air Canada flies from Toronto.

From Europe: British Airways have two flights a week from London (Gatwick); AOM French Airlines fly once a week from Paris and Condor have scheduled flights and charters from Germany.

From the Caribbean: Turks and Caicos Airways connects Providenciales with Nassau, while Air Jamaica flies from Kingston and Montego Bay and on to Chicago.

● To Freeport
From the USA: American Eagle from Miami; Bahamasair from Fort Lauderdale and Miami. Laker Airways (Bahamas) from Baltimore, Cincinnati, Cleveland, Fort Lauderdale, Memphis, New York, Raleigh/Durham, Richmond and West Palm Beach; Gulfstream International Airlines from Fort Lauderdale, Gainesville, Orlando, Miami, West Palm beach and Tampa. Comair from Fort Lauderdale, Jacksonville.

From the Caribbean: Turks and Caicos Airways flies from Providenciales twice a week.

There are also several commuter airlines serving some of the **Family Islands** direct from airports in Florida including Gulfstream International Airlines (in Miami T 305-871 1200, 800-992 8532, F 305-871 3540), Airways International (T 367 3193, 305-526 2000, F 305-871 6522), Island Express (T 367 3597, in USA 954-359 0380, F 954-359 2752), Walkers International (T 305-359 1400, F 305-359 1414), US Air Express (T 800-622 1015), Chalk's International (Fort Lauderdale T 305-359 7980, F 305-359 5240, Miami T 305-371 8628, Bimini T 347 3024, Nassau T 363 1687). Tickets can be booked through computer systems but are normally purchased on the spot at the airport, routing and timing subject to last minute alteration depending on demand. See text for details of services to each island. Laker Airways (T 352 3389) has charter flights to Freeport from Florida with some flights timed so that gamblers can do a day-trip to the *Princess Casino*. Other charter airlines include Cleare Air (T 377 0341, F 377 0342), Congo Air (T 377 8329, F 377 7413, Fort Lauderdale T 305-456 5611, F 305-985 0855) and Island Air Charters (T 305-359 9942, 800-444 9904). Private pilots should ask the Tourist Office for the Air Navigation Chart or contact the Private Pilot Briefing Centre, T 800-327 7678 in the USA.

SEA

● From the USA to Freeport
Sea Escape boat return trip to Freeport from Fort Lauderdale, including meals and entertainment, costs US$120 return. Journey is 5 hrs one-way; leaves from Freeport port area and carries 1,200 passengers. A catamaran, *Cloud 10*, owned by Party Cruise Line, may start a high speed service from Port Everglades, Fort Lauderdale, to Freeport. The new boat, built to withstand rough seas, will hold 345 passengers (and/or freight), take 2 hrs, depart

twice daily and cost only US$59 round trip inc taxes (T 305-776 9696, F 305-938 1877).

● **Ports of entry**
(Own flag) **Abaco**: Walker's Cay, Green Turtle Cay, Marsh Harbour, Sandy Point. **Andros**: Morgan's Bluff, Fresh Creek, Mangrove Cay, Congo Town. **Berry Islands**: Great Harbour Cay, Chub Cay. **Bimini**: Alice Town, Cat Cay, Gun Cay. **Eleuthera**: Harbour Island, Hatchet Bay, Governor's Harbour, Rock Sound. **Exuma**: George Town. **Grand Bahama**: West End, Freeport Harbour, Port Lucaya, Lucaya Marina, Xanadu Marina. **Inagua**: Matthew Town. **Long Island**: Stella Maris. **New Providence**: Nassau (any yacht basin). **Ragged Island**: Duncan Town. **San Salvador**: Cockburn Town.

● **Boat documents**
Complete duplicate copies of Maritime Declaration of Health, Inwards Report for Pleasure Vehicles and crew/passengers lists required. The vessel will be issued with a one-year cruising permit. During regular working hours, the only charge is for transportation for the clearing officer. Individuals will be given 60 days clearance with extensions obtained at a port of entry. A boat with a cruising permit may import parts duty free.

● **Radio communications**
Morning ham net 0745-0845 7268; Nassau and George Town have VHF net. Exuma Markets in George Town will accept and hold faxes and mail for boats.

ON ARRIVAL

● **Airlines**
American Airlines T 1-800-433 7300; US Air T 377 8888, 800-423 7714; Air Canada T 327 8411; Bahamasair T 377 3223 in Nassau, T 352 8341 in Freeport, 800-222 4262 in the USA; Delta Airlines/Comair, T 377 1043, 800-221 1212; Gulfstream International, T 352 8532. See also above, **Getting there**.

● **Banks**
There are several hundred banks licensed to do banking or trust business in the Bahamas. Some of the largest commercial banks include: Royal Bank of Canada at Nassau, the airport, Abaco, Andros (Fresh Creek), Bimini, Grand Bahama, Harbour Island, Long Island, Lyford Cay, and Spanish Wells; Lloyds Bank (Bahamas); Barclays Bank Plc, also at Grand Bahama, Eleuthera, Abaco; Scotiabank, also at Abaco, Grand Bahama, Exuma, Long Island; Canadian

Imperial Bank of Commerce also at Grand Bahama, Andros (Nicholl's Town), Abaco; Bank of the Bahamas Ltd, Grand Bahama, Andros and Inagua; Citibank.

● **Embassies and consulates**
US Embassy, Mosmar Building, Queen Street, PO Box N-8197, T 322 1181/3; **British High Commission** Bitco Building, East Street, T 325 7471; **Canada**, T 393 2123/4; honorary consulates: **Denmark** and **Norway, T 322 1340, F 328 8779; France**, T 326 5061; **Germany**, T 322 8032 (office), 324 3780 (residence); **Israel**, T 322 4130; **Japan**, T 322 8560; **The Netherlands**, T 323 5275; **Spain**, T 362 1271; **Sweden**, T 327 7944; **Switzerland**, T 322 1412. There is a **Haitian** Embassy, East and Bay Streets, T 326 0325; consulate of the **Dominican Republic**, T 325 5521.

● **Emergency numbers on New Providence**
Police T 322 4444; Ambulance T 322 2221; Hospital T 322 2861; Med Evac T 322 2881; BASRA T 322 3877. The Police have offices at East Bay T 322 1275, Paradise Island T 363 3160, Cable Beach T 327 8800 and downtown T 322 3114.

● **Fishing**
Annual fishing permits: US$20 per boat for hook and line. Lobster season from 1 August-31 March. Conch must have fully formed lip to be taken. Hawaiian slings are permitted for spearfishing. Spearfishing is not permitted within 1 mile of New Providence, 1 mile S of Freeport, Grand Bahama, nor within 200 yards of the Family Islands. Within Bahamas National Parks you may not fish, take lobster, conch, coral or shells etc.

● **Hours of business**
Banks: in Nassau, Mon-Thur 0930-1500, Fri 0930-1700; in Freeport, Mon-Fri 0900-1300 and Fri 1500-1700. Shops 0900-1700 Mon-Sat. Government offices 0900-1730 Mon-Fri.

● **Official time**
Bahamas time is 5 hours behind GMT, except in summer when Eastern Daylight Time (GMT - 4 hours) is adopted.

● **Public holidays**
New Year's Day, Good Friday, Easter Monday (very busy at the airport), Whit Monday, Labour Day (first Fri in June, a parade is organized by the trade unions), Independence Day (10 July), Emancipation Day (first Mon in Aug), Discovery Day (12 Oct), Christmas Day, Boxing Day.

● **Religion**

There are about 20 denominations represented in the Bahamas, of which those with the largest congregations are the Baptists, Roman Catholics and Anglicans. There is a synagogue in Freeport and a Mosque in Nassau. The Tourist Office publishes a leaflet called *Bahamas Places of Worship*, with a full list of addresses and services.

● **Scuba diving**

In addition to the land-based dive operators mentioned in the text, there are several live-aboard boats which cruise the Bahamas and offer less crowded and unspoilt sites: Blackbeard's Cruises, contact Bruce Purdy, PO Box 66-1091, Miami Springs, FL 33266, T 800-327 9600, 305-888 1226, F 305-884 4214; Bottom Time Adventures Inc, contact AJ Bland, Elizabeth Longtin, PO Box 11919, Fort Lauderdale, FL 33339-1919, T 800-234 8464, 305-921 7798, F 305-920 5578; Coral Bay Cruises, contact Lori Lachnicht, Thomas Conlin, 2631 E Oakland Park Blvd 108, Fort Lauderdale, Fl 33306, T 800-433 7262, 305-563 1711, F 305-563 1811; Crown Diving Corporation, contact Edward Guirola, *M/V Crown Islander*, 2790 North Federal Hwy, Boca Raton, FL 33431, T 800-447 2290, 407-394 7450, F 407 368 5715; Nekton Diving Cruises, contact Lynn A Oetzman, 1057 SE 17th Street, Suite 202, Fort Lauderdale, FL 33316, T 305-463 9324, F 305-463 8938; the first Bahamian owned and operated boat, Out Island Voyages, contact James or Marilynn Nottage, PO Box N7775, Nassau, T 809-328 8007/6; Sea Fever Diving, contact Tom Guarino, Cynthia Herod, PO Box 398 276, Miami Beach, FL 33139, T 800-443 3837, 305 531 3483, F 305 531 3127; Sea Dragon, contact Dan Doyle, Sue Ford, SW 717 Coconut Drive, Fort Lauderdale, FL 33315, T 305-522 0161, 809-359 2058. All the above are BDA members.

● **Shopping**

For those who want to pick up a bargain, prices of crystal, china and jewellery are cheaper than in the USA. You can find designer clothes and other goods from all over the world at the International Bazaar in Freeport. Local products include straw items, Androsia batik printed silk and cotton, shell jewellery and wood carvings. Bargaining is expected in the markets. Duty free shopping was introduced on 11 categories of goods on 1 January 1992; the Bahamas Duty Free Promotion Board was formed to monitor the system and ensure that

merchants participating in the scheme sell authentic goods.

● **Tipping**

The usual tip is 15%, including for taxi drivers. Hotels and restaurants include a service charge on the bill, sometimes a flat rate per day, or a percentage.

● **Voltage**

120 volt/60 cycles.

ON DEPARTURE

● **Departure tax**

Airport and security tax is US$16 from Nassau and US$18 from Freeport except for children under the age of 3. US immigration and customs formalities for those going to the USA are carried out at Nassau and Paradise Island airports. Harbour departure tax is US$15.

ACCOMMODATION

Accommodation ranges from luxury hotels and resorts with every conceivable facility, to modest guest houses or self-catering apartments and villas. Some of the larger properties have T 800 reservations numbers in the USA and Canada. You will often get a cheaper package if you book from abroad. These packages often include restaurants, tours, day trips and airfare and are cheap enough for you to discard the bits you do not want. In restaurants, visitors on a package can pay 25-50% less than locals.

FOOD AND DRINK

Conch, crab, grouper, snapper, dolphin (not the Flipper variety) and other seafood are on all the menus. Conch is the staple diet of many Bahamians. It is considered an aphrodisiac and a source of virility, especially the small end part of the conch which is bitten off and eaten from the live conch for maximum effect. Conch is prepared in a variety of ways; conch fritters and cracked conch are both coated in batter and fried, while conch salad is made from raw, shredded conch, onion, lime, lettuce and tomatoes. It can be bought daily from vendors who let you choose your conch from their truck and will 'jewk' it from the shell and prepare it for you in salad. Although delicious, conch has been linked to major outbreaks of food poisoning, so treat with caution. Bahamian cuisine is tasty, if a little predictable. The standard fare at most parties/cookouts is peas'n'rice, barbecue ribs and chicken wings, conch salad or fritters, potato salad, coleslaw and macaroni. Bahamian potato salad and macaroni are far richer than their English/Italian counterparts. The Bahamas have some good fruit: sapodilla, mango, breadfruit, sugar apple and pawpaw. Try soursop ice cream, coconut tarts and sugar bananas, which have an apple flavour. Guava duff is a popular sweet, a bit like jam roly poly pudding topped with guava sauce (often flavoured with rum). Tap water can be brackish; fresh water can be bought at the supermarket. The local beer brewed in Nassau, Kalik, is worth trying, it has won several international prizes. The local rum is Bacardi; the Anejo variety is OK. Bahama Mammas, Yellowbirds and Island Woman are all popular rum-based cocktails. Many bars have their own special cocktails.

GETTING AROUND

AIR TRANSPORT

Bahamasair operates scheduled **flights** between Nassau and the Family Islands. Service is reported to be improving. Charter flights and excursions available through them and several private companies, see Prestel for details. Seaplanes fly to those islands which have no landing strip. Inter-island travel is difficult given that nearly all flights originate in Nassau. To fly from Abaco to Eleuthera with Bahamasair, for example, you have to change planes in Nassau, often with a wait of several hours and a wasted day. Each island is developing direct transport links with the USA rather than with each other. Bahamasair now has a scheme for multiple island destinations (Discover the Bahamas) from Miami, Orlando or Nassau, based on the number of flights you want to take, valid 21 days, eg from Miami, 4 flights US$180; from Orlando 8 flights US$380; from Nassau 6 flights US$125.

LAND TRANSPORT

● **Motoring**

Visitors are permitted to drive on a valid foreign licence or International Permit for up to 3 months. Beyond that they need a local licence issued by the Road Traffic Department in Nassau. Traffic keeps left, although most cars are left-hand drive. Strict speed limits: Nassau and Freeport 30 mph; elsewhere 40 mph. Gasoline costs US$2.52 a gallon. The roads are not in good condition and are congested in town; drivers pay scant attention to the laws.

On many of the Family Islands bicycles and mopeds are appropriate. These can be hired in Nassau, Freeport and in many other places through hotels; helmets should be worn. Approximate rates: bicycles US$10 per day, US$40 per week; mopeds: US$30-45 per day. Scooters and light motorcycles can also be hired. Helmets are mandatory. Remember, though, that rates for car and bike hire tend to vary, according to season. Minimum age for hiring in Exuma is 25.

FERRIES

The Family Islands can also be reached by regular **ferry boat** services. A car ferry service, Sea Link, sails between Nassau and Freeport, Nassau and Eleuthera and Nassau and Abaco, departing Thur 1000 for Freeport, returning Fri 0700, departing Fri 1500 for Eleuthera, returning Sun, departing Tues 1800 for Marsh Harbour, returning Wed 1800, 7 hrs. Fares in 1995 were US$250 for cars (inc return fare for 2 passengers), US$60 return adults, children half price. Reservations 3-4 days in advance needed from Island Vacation, West Bay Street; ferry docks at East Bay Street, Nassau Shipyard (T 327 5444).

A colourful way of travelling between the islands is on the **mail boats**, which also carry passengers and merchandise. They leave from Potter's Cay Dock, just below the Paradise Island Bridge in Nassau, and Woodes Rogers Walk; their drawback is that they are slow and accommodation on board is very basic, but they do go everywhere, usually once a week. The Bahamas Family Islands Association has a helpful brochure listing fares (US$20-50) and schedules, but do not expect the boats to leave according to the timetable. For the latest information listen to the radio on ZNS, which lists the daily schedule with last minute changes broadcast at lunchtime, or ask for information at the Dock Master's office on Potter's Cay, T 393 1064.

We give here the name of the boat, its destination and travel time: *Bahamas Daybreak III*, to North Eleuthera, Spanish Wells, Harbour Island, Bluff, 5½ hrs; *Captain Moxey*, to South Andros, Kemp's Bay, Long Bay Cays, Bluff, 7½ hrs; *Central Andros Express*, to Fresh Creek, Staniard Creek, Blanket Sound, Bowne Sound, 3½ hrs; *Sea Hauler*, to Cat Island, Bluff, Smith's Bay, 10 hrs; *North Cat Island Special*, to North Cat Island, Arthur's Town, Bennet's Harbour, 14 hrs; *Maxine*, to San Salvador, United Estates, Rum Cay, 18 hrs; *Grand Master, Seahauler, Lady*

Roslyn, Captain Moxey, to Exuma, George Town, Mt Thompson, 14 hrs; *Abilin,* to Long Island, Clarence Town, 18 hrs; *Champion II,* to Abaco, Sandy Point, Bullock Harbour, Moore Island, 11 hrs; *Lisa J II,* to North Andros, Nichol's Town, Mastic Point, Lowe Sound, 5 hrs; *Lady Francis,* to Exuma Cays, Staniel Cay, Black Point, Farmer's Cay, Barraterre; *Deborah K,* Abaco, Marsh Harbour, Hope Town, Treasure Cay, Green Turtle Cay, Coopers Town, 12 hrs; *Harley & Charley,* to Governor's Harbour, Hatchet Bay, 5 hrs; *Mangrove Cay Express* to Mangrove Cay, Lisbon Creek, 5½ hrs; *Lady Gloria* to Mangrove Cay, Behring Point, Cargill Creek, 5 hrs; *Current Pride* to Current Island, Upper and Lower Bogue, Eleuthera, 5 hrs; *Emmette and Cephas* to Ragged Island, 21 hrs; *Bahamas Daybreak III,* to Rock Sound, Davis Harbour, South Eleuthera, 7 hrs; *Nay Dean,* to North Long Island, Salt Pond, Deadman's Cay, Stella Maris, 14 hrs; *Marcella III,* to Grand Bahama, Freeport, High Rock, Eight Mile Rock, West End, 12 hrs; *Windward Express,* to Crooked Island, Acklins, Mayaguana, Inagua; *Spanish Rose,* to Spanish Wells, 5½ hrs; *Eleuthera Express,* to Rock Sound, 5 hrs; *Challenger,* to North Andros; *Lady Margo,* also to North Andros; *Eleuthera Express,* Spanish Wells, Harbour Island, 5 hrs; *Bimini Mack,* to Bimini, Cat Cay, 12 hrs.

● **Yacht charter**
A pleasant way of seeing the islands is to charter your own yacht and several companies offer boats with or without crews. Abaco Bahamas Charters (ABC) is based in Hope Town. Bahamas Yachting Service (BYS) is based in Marsh Harbour, Abaco, T 305-467 8644 or toll free 800-327 2276 in North America, prices start from about US$50 per person per day. Moorings bases its bareboat charters at Marsh Harbour and has crewed yacht charters in George Town, Exuma. Contact the Bahamas Reservation Service (see below) for the Bahamas Marina Guide, marina reservations, known as 'book-a-slip', with details of over 50 marinas in the Bahamas and confirmation of boat slip reservations down as far as Grand Turk. Most resort islands have boats to rent.

COMMUNICATIONS

● **Postal services**
Main post office is at East Hill Street, Nassau. Letters to North America and the Caribbean US$0.55, to Europe and South America US$0.60; to Africa, Asia and Australia US$0.70. All postcards US$0.40. Air mail to Europe takes 4 to 8 days, surface mail takes a couple of months. There is no door to door mail delivery in the Bahamas, everything goes to a PO Box. Parcels must be opened at the Post Office with customs officials present. Stamp collectors can contact the Bahamas Philatelic Bureau at East Hill Street, PO Box N8302, Nassau, for current mint stamps and first day covers.

● **Telephone services**
There is a public telephone, cable and telex exchange open 24 hrs in the BaTelCo Office on East Street, near the BITCO building in Nassau. International calls can be made and faxes sent/received from here; also Prince George Dock, Shirley Street, Blue Hill Road, Mall at Marathon, Golden Gates and Fox Hill (0700-2000). BaTelCo's mailing address is PO Box N3048, Nassau (T 323 4911). Grand Bahama, New Providence and most of the other islands have automatic internal telephone systems. Direct dialling is available from New Providence and most of the other islands all over the world. The code for the Bahamas is 809 but on 1 Oct 1996 a new number 242 will be phased in. International calls are expensive: US$5 a minute to the UK through the operator, US$2.50 to the Caribbean. Credit card facilities. Phone cards are now quite widely available in denominations of US$5, US$10 and US$20. A call to the UK with a phone card is US$4/minute. Not all phones take cards. Facilities are available at most BaTelCo offices in Nassau and Freeport, Nassau and Freeport airports and several of the Family Islands. Videoconferencing facilities at BaTelCo's offices in the Mall at Marathon, Nassau and in Freeport.

MEDIA

● **Newspapers**
There are 3 daily newspapers: the *Nassau Guardian* (circulation 12,500), *The Tribune*, published in the evening (12,500) and the *Freeport News* (4,000). There are lots of tourist magazines, eg *Dining and Entertainment Guide, Nassau, Cable Beach, Paradise Island; What-To-Do, Freeport Lucaya; Getaway, Bahamas Out Islands; The Cruising Guide to Abaco, Bahamas* (annual); *Abaco Life.*

● **Radio**
The local commercial radio stations are ZNS1, owned by the Government and covering all the Bahamas, ZNS2 and ZNS3 covering New

Providence and the N Bahamas. The local commercial television station is ZNS TV 13. Transmissions from Florida can be picked up and satellite reception is common.

ENTERTAINMENT

● **Cinemas**
There is one 2-screen cinema in Freeport and a cinema in Governor's Harbour, Eleuthera.

TOURIST INFORMATION

● **Local tourist office**
The Bahamas Ministry of Tourism, Market Plaza, Bay Street, PO Box N3701, Nassau, Bahamas, T 322 7500, F 325 5835. There are representatives of the Bahamas Tourist Office on Abaco, Eleuthera, Exuma and throughout the USA.

● **Tourist offices overseas**
Canada: 1255 Phillips Square, Montreal, Quebec, H3B 3G1, T 514-861 6797, and 121 Bloor Street E, Toronto, Ontario, M4W 3M5, T 416-363 4441
France: 60 rue Saint Lazare, 75009 Paris, T 1 45 26 62 62, F 1 48 74 06 05.
Germany: Leipziger Strasse 67d, D 60487, Frankfurt am Main, T 069 97 08340, F 069 970 83434, info-line T 01030 813 118.
Italy: Via Cusani 7, 20121, Milano, T 02-720 22526, Toll free 02 1678 77225, F 02-72023123.
Japan: 4-9-17 Akasaka, Minato-Ku, Tokyo, T 813-470 6162.
Sweden: Gumshornsgatan 7, S-11460 Stockholm, T 8-6632850, F 8-6605780.
UK: 3 The Billings, Walnut Tree Close, Guildford, Surrey, T 01483 448900, F 01483 448990.
USA: in New York they are at 150 East 52nd Street, 28th floor N, NY 10022, T 212-758 2777; also in other major US cities. See page 96 for the Grand Bahama Island Promotion

Board addresses. The Bahama Out Islands Promotion Board is at 1100 Lee Wagener Boulevard, Suite 204, Fort Lauderdale, FLB3315, T 305-359 8099, 800-688 4752, F 305-359 8098.

● **People-to-People**
The People-to-People programme is a recommended way to meet local Bahamians. Fill in a form from the Ministry of Tourism giving age, occupation and interests and you will be matched with a Bahamian. Each experience is different but it might lead to a meal in a Bahamian home, a tour of out of the way places or a trip to church. They also hold a tea party at Government House in Jan-Aug on the last Fri of each month and can arrange weddings. T 326 5371, 328 7810, F 328 0945 in Nassau or 352 8044, F 352 2714 in Freeport, or ask at your hotel. The programme is also available in Eleuthera (T 332 2142, F 332 2480), Abaco (T 367 3067, F 367 3068), San Salvador, Exuma (T 336 2430, F 366 2431) and Bimini.

● **Maps**
The Lands and Surveys Department on East Bay Street, Nassau, PO Box 592, has an excellent stock of maps, including a marine chart of the whole archipelago for US$10 and 1:25,000 maps covering most of the islands for US$1 per sheet (several sheets per island). These are also available from Fairey Surveys, Maidenhead, Berks, UK. A good, up-to-date street map of New Providence is available from most Bahamian bookstores for US$2.95.

● **Further reading**
Out-island Doctor by Evans Cottman (Hodder and Stoughton) gives a picture of the 1940s; an interesting comparison can be made with *Cocaine Wars* by Paul Eddy et al (Bantam), a fascinating study of the 1980s.

Cuba

THE ISLAND OF CUBA, 1,250 km long, 191 km at its widest point, is the largest of the Caribbean islands and only 145 km S of Florida. The name is believed to derive from the Arawak word 'cubanacan', meaning centre, or central. Gifted with a moderate climate, afflicted only occasionally by hurricanes, not cursed by frosts, blessed by an ample and well distributed rainfall and excellent soils for tropical crops, it has traditionally been one of the largest exporters of cane sugar in the world.

HORIZONS

THE LAND

About a quarter of Cuba is fairly mountainous. To the W of Havana is the narrow Sierra de los Organos, rising to 750m and containing, in the extreme W, the strange scenery of the Guaniguánicos hill country. South of these Sierras, in a strip 145 km long and 16 km wide along the piedmont, is the Vuelta Abajo area which grows the finest of all Cuban tobaccos. Towards the centre of the island are the Escambray mountains, rising to 1,100m, and in the E, encircling the port of Santiago, are the most rugged mountains of all, the Sierra Maestra, in which Pico Turquino reaches 1,980m. In the rough and stony headland E of Guantánamo Bay are copper, manganese, chromium and iron mines. About a quarter of the land surface is covered with mountain forests of pine and mahogany. The coastline, with a remarkable number of fine ports and anchorages, is about 3,540 km long.

PEOPLE

Some 66% of Cubans register themselves as whites: they are mostly the descendants of Spanish colonial settlers and immigrants; 12% are black, now living mostly along the coasts and in certain provinces, Oriente in particular; 21% are

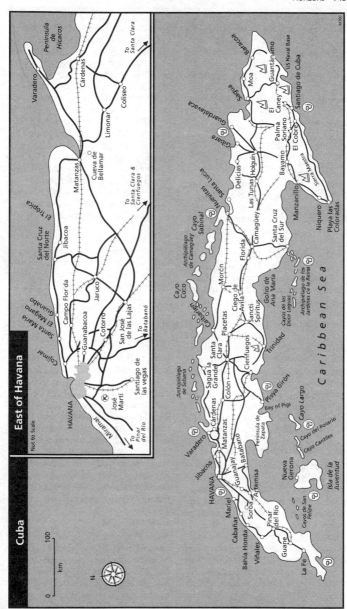

mixed and about 1% are Chinese; the indigenous Indians disappeared long ago although there is evidence of Amerindian ancestry in some Cubans. Some 73% live in the towns, of which there are nine with over 50,000 inhabitants each. The population is estimated at 11.0 million, of which 2.1 million live in Havana (the city and that part of the province within the city's limits).

HISTORY

SPANISH CONQUEST

Cuba was visited by Columbus during his first voyage on 27 October 1492, and he made another brief stop 2 years later on his way to Jamaica. Columbus did not realize it was an island; it was first circumnavigated by Sebastián de Ocampo in 1508. Diego de Velázquez conquered it in 1511 and founded several towns, including Havana. The first African slaves were imported in 1526. Sugar was introduced soon after but was not important until the last decade of the 16th century. When the British took Jamaica in 1655 a number of Spanish settlers fled to Cuba, already famous for its cigars. Tobacco was made a strict monopoly of Spain in 1717. The coffee plant was introduced in 1748. The British, under Lord Albemarle and Admiral Pocock, captured Havana and held the island in 1762-63, but it was returned to Spain in exchange for Florida.

INDEPENDENCE MOVEMENT

The tobacco monopoly was abolished in 1816 and Cuba was given the right to trade with the world in 1818. Independence elsewhere, however, bred ambitions, and a strong movement for independence was quelled by Spain in 1823. By this time the blacks outnumbered the whites in the island; there were several slave rebellions and little by little the Créoles (or Spaniards born in Cuba) made common cause with them. A slave rising in 1837 was savagely repressed and the poet Gabriel de la Concepción Valdés

was shot. There was a 10-year rebellion against Spain between 1868 and 1878, but it gained little save the effective abolition of slavery, which had been officially forbidden since 1847. From 1895 to 1898 rebellion flared up again under José Martí and Máximo Gómez. The United States was now in sympathy with the rebels, and when the US battleship *Maine* exploded in Havana harbour on 15 February 1898, this was made a pretext for declaring war on Spain. American forces (which included Colonel Theodore Roosevelt) were landed, a squadron blockaded Havana and defeated the Spanish fleet at Santiago de Cuba. In December peace was signed and US forces occupied the island. The Government of Cuba was handed over to its first president, Tomás Estrada Palma, on 20 May 1902. The USA retained naval bases at Río Hondo and Guantánamo Bay and reserved the right of intervention in Cuban domestic affairs, but granted the island a handsome import preference for its sugar. The USA chose to intervene several times, but relinquished this right in 1934.

DICTATORSHIP

From 1925 to 1933 the 'strong man' Gerardo Machado ruled Cuba as a dictator. His downfall was brought about by Fulgencio Batista, then a sergeant. Corrupt, ineffectual governments held office in the 1940s, until Batista, by then a self-promoted general, staged a military coup in 1952. His harshly repressive dictatorship was brought to an end by Fidel Castro in Jan 1959, after an extraordinary and heroic 3 years' campaign, mostly in the Sierra Maestra, with a guerrilla force reduced at one point to 12 men.

COMMUNISM

From 1960 onwards, in the face of increasing hostility from the USA, Castro led Cuba into communism. All farms of over 67 ha have been taken over by the state. Rationing is still fierce, and there are still shortages of consumer goods. However, education, housing and health services have been greatly improved. Infant mortality fell to 9.4 per 1,000 live births in 1994, compared with 19.6 in 1980. It is claimed that illiteracy has been wiped out. Considerable emphasis is placed on combining productive agricultural work with study: there are over 400 schools and colleges in rural areas where the students divide their time between the fields and the classroom. Education is compulsory up to the age of 17 and free.

US RELATIONS

Before the Revolution of 1959 the United States had investments in Cuba worth about US$1,000mn, covering nearly every activity from agriculture and mining to oil installations; it took 66% of Cuba's exports and supplied 70% of the imports in 1958. Today all American businesses, including banks, have been nationalized; the USA has cut off all imports from Cuba, placed an embargo on exports to Cuba, and broken off diplomatic relations. Promising moves to improve relations with the USA were given impetus in 1988 by the termination of Cuban military activities in Angola under agreement with the USA and South Africa. However, developments in Eastern Europe and the former USSR in 1989-90 provoked Castro to defend the Cuban system of government; the lack of political change delayed any further rapprochement with the USA. Prior to the 1992 US presidential elections, President Bush approved the Cuban Democracy Act (Torricelli Bill) which strengthened the trade embargo by forbidding US subsidiaries from trading with Cuba. Many countries, including EC members and Canada, said they would not allow the US bill to affect their trade with Cuba and the UN General Assembly voted in November in favour of a resolution calling for an end to the embargo. The defeat of George Bush by Bill Clinton did not, however, signal a change in US attitudes, in large part because of the support given to the Democrat's campaign by Cuban exiles in Miami.

1990'S CRISIS AND CHANGE

In an effort to broaden the people's power system of government introduced in 1976, the central committee of the Cuban Communist Party adopted resolutions in 1990 designed to strengthen the municipal and provincial assemblies and transform the National Assembly into a genuine parliament. In Feb 1993, the first direct, secret elections for the National Assembly and for provincial assemblies were held. Despite calls from opponents abroad for voters to register a protest by spoiling their ballot or not voting, the official results showed that 99.6% of the electorate voted, with 92.6% of votes cast valid. All 589 official candidates were elected.

Economic difficulties in the 1990s brought on by the changes in the former Soviet economy and Eastern Europe, together with higher oil prices because of the Gulf crisis, forced the Government to impose emergency measures and declare a special period in peace time. Rationing was increased, petrol became scarce, the bureaucracy was slashed and several hundred arrests were made in a drive against corruption. As economic hardship continued into 1993, Cuba was hit on 13 March by a winter storm which caused an estimated US$1bn in damage. Agricultural production, for both export and domestic consumption, was severely affected. In mid-1994, economic frustration and discontent boiled up and Cubans began to flee their country. Thousands left in a mass exodus to Florida on any homemade craft they could invent. It was estimated that between mid-Aug and mid-Sept 30,000 Cubans had left the country, compared with 3,656 in the whole of 1993. In contrast, the number of US visas issued in Jan-Aug was 2,059 out of an agreed maximum annual quota of 20,000. Eventually the crisis forced President Clinton into an agreement whereby the USA was committed to accepting at least 20,000 Cubans a year, plus the next of kin of US citizens, while Cuba agreed to prevent further departures.

As the economic crisis persisted, the government adopted measures (some of which are outlined below) which opened up many sectors to private enterprise and recognized the dependence of much of the economy on dollars. The partial reforms did not eradicate the imbalances between the peso and the dollar economies, and shortages remained for those without access to hard currency.

Cuba then intensified its economic liberalization programme, speeding up the opening of farmers' markets throughout the country and allowing farmers to sell at uncontrolled prices once their commitments to the state procurement system were fulfilled. Importantly, the reforms also allowed middlemen to operate. It had been the emergence of this profitable occupation which had provoked the Government to close down the previous farmers' market system in 1986. Markets in manufactured goods and handicrafts also opened and efforts were made to increase the number of self-employed.

Cuba's foreign policy initiatives in 1994-95 succeeded in bringing international pressure to bear on the USA over its trade embargo. In its third and worst defeat in 1994, the USA lost a resolution in the UN General Assembly which called for an end to the embargo by 101 votes to 2. In 1995 it lost again by 117 votes to 3. The European Parliament meanwhile adopted a resolution which described the 1992 Torricelli Act as contrary to international law and called for its repeal. The Russian parliament passed a similar motion. However, right wingers in the USA continued to push for further economic pressure on Cuba.

In 1996, another US election year, Cuba faced another crackdown by the US administration. In Feb, Cuba shot down 2 light aircraft piloted by Miami exiles allegedly over Cuban air space. The attack provoked President Clinton into reversing his previous opposition to key elements of the Helms-Burton bill to tighten and internationalize the US embargo on Cuba and on 12 March he signed into law the Cuban Liberty and Solidarity Act. The new legislation allows legal action against any company which benefits from properties expropriated by the Cuban government after the Revolution. It brought universal condemnation: Canada and Mexico (Nafta partners), the EU, Russia, China, the Caribbean Community and the Río Group of Latin American countries all protested that it was unacceptable to extend sanctions outside the USA to foreign companies and their employees who do business with Cuba. The effect on the Cuban leadership was to push them into reverse on both political and economic liberalization. Speeches by Fidel and Raúl Castro criticized 'ideological penetration' from the USA and Europe and formal negotiations with the EU for an economic cooperation agreement were stalled.

GOVERNMENT

In 1976 a new constitution was approved by 97.7% of the voters, setting up municipal and provincial assemblies and a National Assembly of the People's Power. The membership of the Assembly was increased to 589 in 1993, candidates being nominated by the 169 municipal councils, and elected by direct secret ballot. Similarly elected are numbers of the 14 provincial assemblies. The number of Cuba's provinces was increased from six to 14 as a result of the decisions of the First Congress of the Communist Party of Cuba in Dec 1975. Dr Fidel Castro was elected President of the Council of State by the National Assembly and his brother, Major Raúl Castro, was elected First Vice-President.

THE ECONOMY

Following the 1959 revolution, Cuba adopted a Marxist-Leninist system. Almost all sectors of the economy were

Self-employment – Cuban style

When the Cuban government realized it would have to lay off thousands of workers in state enterprises in order to achieve some sort of efficiency, it hit upon self-employment as a convenient way to mop up surplus labour. Initially cautious, Cubans accepted the scheme as the only way to increase their income from the average state employee's monthly salary of 200 pesos. Craft markets and street vendors appeared on street corners and many families opened their doors to feed tourists and Cubans with small restaurants, known as *paladares*, a term coined from a Brazilian soap opera. The boom was short-lived, however. As soon as the new entrepreneurs started to make money, the authorities saw an opportunity to tax and control them. Restaurant owners have to buy a licence to operate, they are limited to 12 chairs in their *paladar* and are not permitted to employ anyone other than relatives, who also have to buy a licence. In Feb 1996, tax payments were increased sharply from 500 to 1,000 pesos for restauranteurs, 100 to 400 pesos for taxi drivers and 45 to 500 pesos for car mechanics. No wonder that the number of registered self-employed fell in one month from 208,000 to 205,694. The Government, however, maintains that self-employment is here to stay and is aiming to triple the number to 600,000.

state controlled and centrally planned, the only significant exception being agriculture, where some 12% of arable land was still privately owned. The country became heavily dependent on trade and aid from other Communist countries, principally the USSR, encouraged by the US trade embargo. It relied on sugar, and to a lesser extent nickel, for nearly all its exports. While times were good, Cuba used the Soviet protection to build up an impressive, but costly, social welfare system, with better housing, education and health care than anywhere else in Latin America and the Caribbean. The collapse of the Eastern European bloc, however, revealed the vulnerability of the island's economy and the desperate need for reform. A sharp fall in gdp of 35% in 1990-93, accompanied by a decline in exports from US$8.1bn (1989) to US$1.7bn (1993), forced the Government to take remedial action and the decision was made to start the complex process of transition to a mixed economy.

Transformation of the unwieldy and heavily centralized state apparatus has progressed in fits and starts. The Government is keen to encourage self-employment to enable it to reduce the public sector workforce, but Cuban workers are cautious about relinquishing their job security. Some small businesses have sprung up, particularly in the tourism sector (see box). Free farm produce markets were permitted in 1994 and these were followed by similar markets at deregulated prices for manufacturers, including goods produced by state enterprises and handicrafts. Cubans are now allowed to hold US dollars and in 1995 a convertible peso at par with the US dollar was introduced, which is fully exchangeable for hard currencies.

Although commercial relations with market economies were poor in the late 1980s, because of lack of progress in debt rescheduling negotiations, Cuba has made great efforts in the 1990s to improve its foreign relations. The US trade embargo and the associated inability to secure finance from multilateral sources has led the Government to encourage foreign investment, principally in joint ventures. All sectors of the economy, including sugar and real estate, are now open to foreign investment and in some areas majority foreign shareholdings are allowed. About US$1,500mn was registered between 1990-94, in areas such as tourism, oil and mining. Some 400 foreign companies are now established in Cuba, with capital from 38 countries in 26 economic sectors. The leading investors are from Spain, Canada, France, Italy and Mexico, in that order. Bilateral investment promotion and protection agreements have been signed with 12 nations including Italy, Spain, Germany and the UK.

Structure of production

Sugar is the major crop, providing about 70% of export earnings. However, the industry has consistently failed to reach the targets set. Cuba's dream of a 10 million tonne raw sugar harvest has never been reached. Poor weather and shortages of fertilizers, oil and spare parts cut output to 3.3 million tonnes in 1994-95, but it was expected to recover to 4.5 million in 1995-96. A recovery to 7-8 million tonnes is planned by 1998. Sugar mills have been converted to use bagasse as fuel, but the canefields use large quantities of oil for machinery to cut and transport the cane. Earnings from sugar exports are devoted to purchasing oil. Trade agreements with the ex-USSR, involving oil and sugar, survived US pressure on Russia to end oil shipments in order to receive US aid.

Citrus is now the second most important agricultural export contributing about 4% of revenues. Cuba became a member of the International Coffee Agreement in 1985 and produces about 22,000 tonnes of **coffee** a year but exports are minimal. **Tobacco** is a traditional crop with Cuban cigars world famous, but this too has suffered from lack of fuel, fertilizers and other inputs. Production fell to about 13,800 tonnes, a third of previous levels, but is recovering with the help of Spanish credits and importers from France and Britain. The 1996 crop was expected to increase to some 34,500 tonnes, from which about 65 million cigars will be produced for export, earning over US$100mn.

Diversification away from sugar is a

Cuba: fact file

Geographic

Land area	110,861 sq km
forested	23.7%
pastures	27.0%
cultivated	30.4%

Demographic

Population (1995)	11,068,000
annual growth rate (1990-95)	0.8%
urban	72.8%
rural	27.2%
density	99.8 per sq km
Religious affiliation	
Roman Catholic	39.6%
Non religious	48.7%
Birth rate per 1,000 (1993)	14.0
	(world av 25.0)

Education and Health

Life expectancy at birth,	
male	73.9 years
female	77.6 years
Infant mortality rate	
per 1,000 live births (1994)	9.4
Physicians (1992)	1 per 231 persons
Hospital beds	1 per 134 persons
Calorie intake as %	
of FAO requirement	123%
Population age 25 and over	
with no formal schooling	39.6%
Literacy (over 15)	95.7%

Economic

GNP (1991 market prices)	
	US$17,000mn
GNP per capita	US$1,580
Public external debt (1989)	
	US$6,800mn
Tourism receipts (1993)	US$216mn
Inflation	na
Radio	1 per 3.0 persons
Television	1 per 4.4 persons
Telephone	1 per 31 persons

Employment

Population economically active	
(1988)	4,570,236
Unemployment rate	6.0%
% of labour force in	
agriculture	20.4
mining and manufacturing	21.8
construction	9.8
Military forces (1995)	105,000

Source Encyclopaedia Britannica

major goal, with the emphasis on production of **food** for domestic use because of the shortage of foreign exchange for imports. The beef herd declined from an average 5.2 million head in 1979-81 to 4 million in the first half of the 1990s because of the inability to pay for imports of grains, fertilizers and chemicals. Production is now less intensive, with smaller herds on pastures, and numbers are beginning to rise again. Similarly, milk production is also increasing. The opening of farmers markets in 1994 has helped to stimulate diversification of crops and greater availability of foodstuffs, although shortages still remain.

The sudden withdrawal of **oil** supplies when trade agreements with Russia had to be renegotiated and denominated in convertible currencies, was a crucial factor in the collapse of the Cuban economy. Although trade agreements involving oil and sugar remain, Cuba has had to purchase oil from other suppliers, such as Iran and Colombia, with extremely limited foreign exchange. As a result, Cuba has stepped up its own production to 1,287,000 tons in 1994, providing 27% of electricity generation. Foreign companies have been encouraged to explore for oil on and off shore and investment has borne fruit. Two Canadian companies have found oil in Cárdenas Bay, E of Havana, in a well capable of producing 3,750 barrels a day. Nevertheless, shortages of fuel remain, which, combined with a lack of spare parts for ex-Soviet and Czechoslovakian generating plants, does result in power cuts and unreliable public transport.

Mining is a sector attracting foreign interest and at the end of 1994 a new mining law was passed. A Mining Authority was created and a tax system set up. 40,000 sq km have been allocated for mining ventures and all were expected to have been allocated by the end of 1995. Major foreign investors included Australian (nickel), Canadian (gold, silver and base metals) and South African (gold, copper, nickel) companies. Nickel and cobalt production declined by 11.3% to 26,362 tonnes in 1994, but with greater investment output rose to 43,900 tonnes in 1995 and an expected 46,000 in 1996, nearly half of which came from the Moa Bay plant run as a joint venture between Canadian interests and the Cuban state. Cuba has one small gold mine at Castellanos in Pinar del Río province which produced 200 kg in 1995 and was expected to increase that to 300 kg in 1996. New, Canadian-backed projects in Pinar del Río at the Hierro Mantua site will produce gold and copper, and on Isla de Jurentud, gold and silver.

Tourism is now a major foreign exchange earner and has received massive investment from abroad with many joint ventures. New hotel projects are coming on stream and many more are planned. An estimated 5,000 new or renovated rooms were to come into use in 1996, bringing the total available to foreign visitors to 33,600. Most of the development has been along the Varadero coast, where large resort hotels attract package tourism. By the year 2000, Cuba aims to have 49,556 hotel rooms, of which 32,162 will be in beach resorts and 10,074 in cities. Despite political crises, numbers of visitors have risen steadily from 546,000 in 1993 to 630,000 in 1994, 741,700 in 1995 and an expected 1 million in 1996. Gross earnings in 1995 were US$1,100mn, with net receipts of US$330mn. The target is for 2,550,000 tourists a year bringing earnings of about US$3.1bn.

Recent trends

There has been considerable success in reducing the fiscal deficit, which was bloated by subsidies and inefficiencies. A deficit of 5,000mn pesos in 1993 was cut to 775mn in 1995 and 580mn in 1996, less than 3% of gdp, reflecting subsidy reductions. Nevertheless, the public accounts were strong enough to allow spending increases in 1995 for education, health, social assistance and housing construction, to prevent further loss of the progress made after the revolution. More reforms are planned, which may include the removal of subsidies from almost all state enterprises, new legislation on property ownership and commercial practice, development of the tax system and restructuring of the banking system. Financial services will have to be overhauled to cater for the accumulation of capital by owners of small businesses, who currently have to operate in cash. Discussions are in progress on the transformation of the Banco Nacional into a central bank.

There are signs that the Cuban economy has turned the corner, although these have yet to be felt by the population in general. In 1994 gdp showed a small growth rate of 0.7%, exports rose by about 3.5% and the black market exchange rate for the US dollar strengthened from 130 to 40 pesos. In 1995 gdp grew stronger by 2.5% and the exchange rate strengthened further to 20 pesos = US$1. 1996 was expected to be a good year with forecast increases in output of nickel, oil, fertilizers, tobacco, sugar, steel and cement as well as greater tourism earnings.

CULTURE

The Cuban Revolution has had a profound effect on culture both on the island itself and in a wider context. Domestically, its chief achievement has been to integrate popular expression into daily life, compared with the pre-revolutionary climate in which art was either the preserve of an elite or, in its popular forms, had to fight for acceptance. The encouragement of painting in people's studios and through a national art school, and the support given by the state to musicians and film-makers has done much to foster a national cultural identity. This is not to say that the system has neither refrained from controlling what the people should be exposed to (eg much

Western pop music was banned in the 1960s), nor that it has been without its domestic critics (either those who lived through the Revolution and took issue with it, or younger artists who now feel stifled by a cultural bureaucracy). Furthermore, while great steps have been made towards the goal of a fully-integrated society, there remain areas in which the unrestricted participation of blacks and women has yet to be achieved. Blacks predominate in sport and music (as in Brazil), but find it harder to gain recognition in the public media; women artists, novelists and composers have had to struggle for acceptance. Nevertheless, measures are being taken in the cultural, social and political spheres to rectify this.

The major characteristic of Cuban culture is its combination of the African and European. Because slavery was not abolished until 1886 in Cuba, black African traditions were kept intact much later than elsewhere in the Caribbean. They persist now, inevitably mingled with Hispanic influence, in religion: for instance *santería*, a cult which blends popular Catholicism with the Yoruba belief in the spirits which inhabit all plant life. This now has a greater hold than orthodox Catholicism, which lost much support in its initial opposition to the Revolution. In 1994 Cardinal Jaime Ortega was appointed by the Vatican to fill the position left vacant in Cuba since the last cardinal died in 1963.

MUSIC

Music is incredibly vibrant on the island. It is, again, a marriage of African rhythms, expressed in percussion instruments (batá drums, congas, claves, maracas, etc), and the Spanish guitar. Accompanying the music is an equally strong tradition of dance. A history of Cuban music is beyond the scope of this book, however there are certain styles which deserve mention. There are four basic elements out of which all others grow. The *rumba* (drumming, singing about social preoccupations and danc-

Death of a film maker

🐋 1996 marked the end of the notable and prolific career of Tomás Gutiérrez Alea, who died on 16 April at the age of 67. He was an internationally admired and respected film maker and a moving force in the founding of the Cuban Film Institute (ICAIC) in 1959. In the 1960s he directed *Historias de la Revolución* (1961), *Las Doce Sillas* (1962), *Cumbite* (1964), *Muerte de un Burócrata* (1966) and the award-winning *Memorias del Subdesarrollo* (1968), which made the *New York Times* list of the year's top 10 films. He continued to live in Cuba, making films which generated debate about the Cuban revolution, the bourgeoisie and the bureaucracy, with a satirical sense of humour. In 1993 he dealt with another taboo when he made *Fresa y Chocolate* about a gay man struggling for acceptance in a macho society. The film won a Silver Bear at the Berlin Film Festival and was submitted to the US Oscar awards foreign film category.

ing) is one of the original black dance forms. By the turn of the century, it had been transferred from the plantations to the slums; now it is a collective expression, with Sat evening competitions in which anyone can partake. Originating in eastern Cuba, *son* is the music out of which *salsa* was born. *Son* itself takes many different forms and it gained worldwide popularity after the 1920s when the National Septet of Ignacio Piñeiro made it fashionable. The more sophisticated *danzón*, ballroom dance music which was not accepted by the upper classes until the end of the last century, has also been very influential. It was the root for the *cha-cha-cha* (invented in 1948 by Enrique Jorrín). The fourth tradition is *trova*, the itinerant troubadour singing ballads, which has been transformed, post-Revolution, into the *nueva trova*, made famous by singers such as Pablo Milanés and Silvio Rodríguez. The new tradition adds politics and everyday concerns to the romantic themes.

There are many other styles, such as the *guajira*, the most famous example of which is the song 'Guantanamera'; *tumba francesa* drumming and dancing; and Afro-Cuban jazz, performed by internationally renowned artists like Irakere and Arturo Sandoval. Apart from sampling the recordings of groups, put out by the state company Egrem, the National Folklore Company (Conjunto Folklórico Nacional) gives perform-

ances of the traditional music which it was set up to study and keep alive.

In Vedado, the National Folklore Company, Calle 2 entre Calzada y 5ta, sometimes stage 'Rumba Saturday' at 1500, 1 peso.

LITERATURE

The Cuban Revolution had perhaps its widest cultural influence in the field of **literature**. Many now famous Latin American novelists (like Gabriel García Márquez, Mario Vargas Llosa and Julio Cortázar) visited Havana and worked with the Prensa Latina news agency or on the *Casa de las Américas* review. As Gordon Brotherston has said, "an undeniable factor in the rise of the novel in Latin America has been a reciprocal self-awareness among novelists in different countries and in which Cuba has been instrumental." (*The Emergence of the Latin American Novel*, Cambridge University Press, 1977, page 3.) Not all have maintained their allegiance, just as some Cuban writers have deserted the Revolution. One such Cuban is Guillermo Cabrera Infante, whose most celebrated novel is *Tres tristes tigres* (1967). Other established writers remained in Cuba after the Revolution: Alejo Carpentier, who invented the phrase 'marvellous reality' to describe the different order of reality which he perceived in Latin America and the Caribbean and which now, often wrongly, is attributed to many other writers from the region (his novels include *El reino de este mundo, El siglo de las luces, Los pasos perdidos,* and many more); Jorge Lezama Lima (*Paradiso,* 1966); and Edmundo Desnoes (*Memorias del subdesarrollo*). Of post-revolutionary writers, the poet and novelist Miguel Barnet is worth reading, especially for the use of black oral history and traditions in his work. After 1959, Nicolás Guillén, a black, was adopted as the national poet; his poems of the 1930s (*Motivos de son, Sóngoro cosongo, West Indies Ltd*) are steeped in popular speech and musical rhythms. In tone they are close to the work of the *négritude* writers (see under Martinique), but they look more towards Latin America than Africa. The other poet-hero of the Revolution is the 19th-century writer and fighter for freedom from Spain, José Martí. Even though a US radio and TV station beaming propaganda, pop music and North American culture usurped his name, Martí's importance to Cuba remains undimmed. 19 May 1995 was the centenary of his death in action against Spanish forces which was commemorated around the world by Cuban *aficionados.*

FLORA AND FAUNA

The National Committee for the Protection and Conservation of National Treasures and the Environment was set up in 1978. There are six national parks, including three in Pinar del Río alone (in the Sierra de los Organos and on the Península de Guanahacabibes), the swamps of the Zapata Peninsula and the Gran Piedra near Santiago. The Soledad Botanical Gardens near Cienfuegos house many of Cuba's plants. The Royal Palm is the national tree. Over 200 species of palms abound, as well as flowering trees, pines, oaks, cedars, etc. Original forest, however, is confined to some of the highest points in the SE mountains and the mangroves of the Zapata Peninsula.

There are, of course, a multitude of flowers and in the country even the smallest of houses has a flower garden in front. The orchidarium at Soroa has over 700 examples. To complement the wide variety of butterflies that can be found in Cuba, the buddleia, or butterfly bush, has been named the national flower. In fact, about 10,000 species of insect have been identified on the island.

Reptiles range from crocodiles (of which there is a farm on the Zapata Peninsula) to iguanas to tiny salamanders. Cuba claims the smallest of a number of animals, for instance the Cuban pygmy frog (one of some 30 small frogs), the almiqui (a shrew-like insectivore, the world's smallest mammal), the butterfly or moth bat and the bee humming-bird (called locally the *zunzuncito*). The latter is an endangered species, like the *carpintero real* woodpecker, the cariara (a hawk-like bird of the savannah), the pygmy owl, the Cuban green parrot and the *fermínia*. The best place for bird-watching on the island is the Zapata Peninsula, where 170 species of Cuban birds have been recorded, including the majority of endemic species. In winter the number increases as migratory waterbirds, swallows and others visit the marshes. The national bird is the forest-dwelling Cuban trogon (the *tocororo*).

Also protected is the manatee (sea cow) which has been hunted almost to extinction. It lives in the marshes of the Zapata Peninsula. Also living in the mangrove forests is the large Cuban land crab. Many species of turtle can be found around the offshore cays.

DIVING AND MARINE LIFE

Cuba's marine environment is pristine compared with most Caribbean islands, where there has often been overharvesting and overdevelopment of the dive industry. The majority of coral reefs are alive and healthy and teeming with assorted marine life. The Government has established a marine park around the Isla de la Juventud and much marine life is protected around the entire island, such as the hawksbill turtle, the manatee and coral.

The main dive areas are Isla de la Juventud, Havana, Varadero, Faro Luna, Santa Lucía and Santiago de Cuba. New areas are being developed as hotels are built around the island. Most areas offer a variety of diving, including reefs and walls and an assortment of wrecks, from remains of ancient Spanish ships to many modern wrecks sunk as dive sites. Cuban diving is a new frontier in the Caribbean and has much to offer the adventurous diver.

Varadero sites include the *Neptune*, a 60m steel ship lying in only 10m. This is home to a number of fish including 4 massive green moray eels and 4 very large, friendly French angel fish. The wreck is broken up, but there are places where the superstructure is interesting to explore and there are good photo sites. Among the many reef dive sites in the area are Clara Boyas (Sun Roof), a massive 60 sq metres coral head in 20 metres of water with tunnels large enough for 3-4 divers to swim through. These connect with upward passages where the sunlight can be seen streaming through. Playa Coral is a barrier reef W of Varadero with a large variety of fish and coral.

Faro Luna, S of Havana, has over 18 reef sites and a variety of modern wrecks, including 7 sunk as diving sites just outside the harbour. One of the best is *Camaronero II*, only 5 mins from the dive shop. Others are the cargo ships, *Panta I* and *II*, sunk in 1988, the *Barco R Club* in 8m, the *Barco Arimao* in 18m and the steel fishing boat *Itabo* in 12m.

Santiago de Cuba offers a great deal of diving with 4 dive shops: Bucanero, Daiquiri Dive Centre, Siqua Dive Centre and Sierra Mar. Popular wreck sites near the Siqua Dive Centre include the 30-m passenger ship, *Guarico*, lying in 15m. She lies on her port side with the mast covered in soft sponges. A ferry/tug wreck lies upside down in 35m of water and the two vessels together span

around 150m. The metal structure is covered with large yellow and purple tube sponges. The 35-m *Spring Coral* lies in 24m. Most of the structure is still intact with a great deal of marine growth offering many photo opportunities. An unusual site dived by Bucanero and the Daiquiri Dive Centre is the Bridge. In 1895 a large bridge broke and fell into the sea in 12m, along with a train. Later a ship sunk and was blown into the bridge underwater, adding to the mass of structures. The Sierra Mar Dive Shop offers a special wreck dive on the *Cristóbal Colón*, a Spanish ship lying on a slope in 9-27m. She was sunk, along with 4 others around 1895 by the US Navy during the Spanish American War. The other 4 are in shallow water and are ideal for a snorkel.

Santa Lucía on the Atlantic side of the island has 2 dive shops and offers one of the most interesting wrecks dived. The 66-m *Mortera* sank in 1905 on a slope of 7-27m and is home for a host of marine life, including 8 massive bull sharks, who have been hand fed by the dive masters from Sharks Friend Dive Shop since the early 1980s (very exciting to watch). Other wrecks include the *Sanbinal*, in 17m and the British steel ship, *Nuestra Senora de Alta Gracia*, sunk around 1973 and completely intact, allowing divers to penetrate the entire ship, entering the engine room where all the machinery is still in place. An exciting historical site is Las Anforas, under an old fort dating from 1456. The fort was attacked several times by pirates and artifacts from Spanish ships are scattered across the sea bed. Four anchors were seen on one dive, with the largest being at least 2m.

All dive shops are government owned in Cuba, but run as joint ventures with foreign investors. There are 3 main companies, the largest (14 dive shops) is Cubanacan (Marlin). The others are Puerto Sol and Gaviota. Most staff speak Spanish, English and often other languages. Diving is usually done as part of all-inclusive packages, although dives can be booked direct with dive shops for around US$35, including all equipment. Most companies use European dive gear. In Europe for details on dive packages contact Cubanacan UK Ltd, Skylines, Unit 49, Limeharbour, Docklands, London E14 9TS, T 0171 537 7909, F 537 7747.

You should be prepared with all spares needed for diving and photography (batteries, film etc) as these are either not available or excessively expensive. In the summer months, on the S of the island, tiny jelly fish may abound and can cause nasty stings on areas not covered by a wet suit. A tropical hood is a good idea to protect the neck and face in jelly fish season. A well-stocked first aid kit is recommended, for although the medical profession is well-trained, supplies are limited. Havana has a Hyperbaric Medicine Centre and Varadero has a chamber at the main hospital at Cárdenas, both staffed by doctors trained in hyperbaric medicine.

Dives can sometimes be delayed for a variety of reasons, including limited available fuel, Coast Guard clearance to depart port, etc, so patience is needed.

FESTIVALS

Festivals of dance (including ballet), theatre, jazz, cinema and other art forms are held frequently. Annual festivals in Havana which receive international recognition include ballet (April), traditional Cuban music (May), cinema (Dec) and the international jazz festival (Dec). Tickets (in dollars) are usually available from the box office at the place of performance and although little information about the events is published it is worth checking with the tourism desk in major hotels. Last minute changes and cancellations are common.

Carnival was prohibited by the revolutionary government because of its religious associations, but in Feb 1996 it took place again and will be an annual event. Festivities are mostly along the Malecón, which is closed to traffic. Dancing to rap, techno, salsa, rock, reggae etc, very lively if something of a drunken brawl. Celebrations take place Fri-Sun nights during February. A lack of resources means there are no elaborate costumes as in other countries' carnivals.

HAVANA

Havana, the capital, is situated at the mouth of a deep bay; in the colonial period, this natural harbour was the assembly point for ships of the annual silver convoy to Spain. Its stategic and commercial importance is reflected in the extensive fortifications, particularly on the E side of the entrance to the bay (see below). Before the Revolution, Havana was the largest, the most beautiful and the most sumptuous city in the Caribbean. Today it is rather run-down, but thanks to the Government's policy of developing the countryside, it is not ringed with shantytowns like so many other Latin American capitals. With its suburbs it has 2.1 million people, half of whom live in housing officially regarded as sub-standard. Many buildings are shored up by wooden planks. Some of it is very old, the city was founded in 1515, but the ancient palaces, plazas, colonnades, churches and monasteries merge agreeably with the new. The old city is being substantially refurbished with Unesco's help, as part of the drive to attract tourists, and has been declared a World Heritage Site by the United Nations. There are good views over the city from the top floor restaurant and bar of *Hotel Habana Libre* and of the *Hotel Sevilla*.

The centre is divided into five sections, three of which are of most interest to visitors, Habana Vieja (Old Havana), Central Havana and Vedado. The oldest part of the city, around the Plaza de Armas, is quite near the docks where you can see cargo ships from all over the world being unloaded. Here are the former palace of the Captains-General, the temple of El Templete, and La Fuerza, the oldest of all the forts. From Plaza de Armas run two narrow and picturesque streets, Calles Obispo and O'Reilly (several old-fashioned pharmacies on Obispo, traditional glass and ceramic medicine jars and decorative perfume bottles on display in shops gleaming with polished wood and mirrors). These two streets go W to the heart of the city: Parque Central, with its laurels, poincianas, almonds, palms, shrubs and gorgeous flowers. To the SW rises the golden dome of the Capitol. From the NW corner of Parque Central a wide, tree-shaded avenue, the Paseo del Prado, runs to the fortress of La Punta; at its N sea-side end is the Malecón, a splendid highway along the coast to the W residential district of Vedado. The sea crashing along the seawall here is a spectacular sight when the wind blows from the N. On calmer days, fishermen lean over the parapet, lovers sit in the shade of the small pillars, and joggers sweat along the pavement. On the other side of the six-lane road, buildings which look stout and grand, with arcaded pavements, balconies, mouldings and large entrances, are salt-eroded, faded and sadly decrepit inside.

Further W, Calle San Lázaro leads directly from the monument to General Antonio Maceo on the Malecón to the magnificent central stairway of Havana University. A monument to Julio Antonio Mella, founder of the Cuban Communist Party, stands across from the stairway. Further out, past El Príncipe castle, is Plaza de la Revolución, with the impressive monument to José Martí at its centre. The large buildings surrounding the square were mostly built in the 1950s and house the principal government ministries. The long grey building behind the monument is the former Justice Ministry (1958), now the HQ of the Central Committee of the Communist Party, where Fidel Castro has his office. The Plaza is the scene of massive parades and speeches marking important events.

From near the fortress of La Punta a tunnel runs E under the mouth of the harbour; it emerges in the rocky ground between the Castillo del Morro and the fort of La Cabaña, some 550m away, and a 5-km highway connects with the Havana-Matanzas road.

The street map of Old Havana is marked with numerals showing the places of most interest to visitors.

1. **Castillo del Morro** was built between 1589 and 1630, with a 20-m moat, but has been much altered. It stands on a bold headland, with the best view of Havana; it was one of the major fortifications built to protect the natural harbour and the assembly of Spain's silver fleets from pirate attack. The flash of its lighthouse, built in 1844, is visible 30 km out to sea. The castle is open to the public, Wed-Sun, 1000-1800, as a museum with a good exhibition of Cuban history since Columbus. On the harbour side, down by the water, is the Battery of the 12 Apostles, each gun named after an Apostle. It can be reached by bus through the tunnel to the former toll gates.

2. **Fortaleza de la Cabaña**, built 1763-1774. Fronting the harbour is a high wall; the ditch on the landward side, 12m deep, has a drawbridge to the main entrance. Inside are Los Fosos de los Laureles where political prisoners were shot during the Cuban fight for independence. Open to visitors at the same hours as El Morro.

The National Observatory and the railway station for trains to Matanzas are on the same side of the Channel as these two forts.

3. **Castillo de la Punta**, built at the end of the 16th century, a squat building with $2\frac{1}{2}$-m thick walls, is open to the public, daily 1400-2200. Opposite the fortress, across the Malecón, is the monument to Máximo Gómez, the independence leader.

4. **Castillo de la Fuerza**, Cuba's oldest

building and the second oldest fort in the New World, was built 1538-1544 after the city had been sacked by buccaneers. It is a low, long building with a picturesque tower from which there is a grand view. Inside the castle is a mu-

seum, open Mon, Thur-Sun, 0930-1700. The downstairs part is used for art exhibitions. The Castillo reopened (1994) after renovation. **NB** There are two other old forts in Havana: **Atarés**, finished in 763 n a h overlooking the SW end

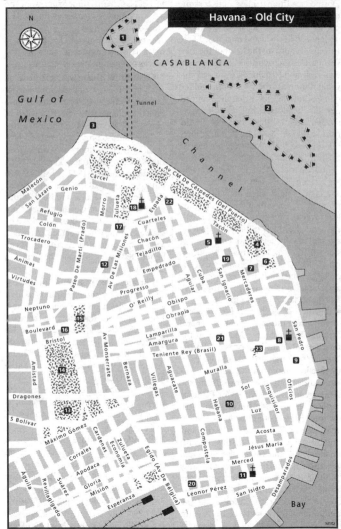

Havana - Old City

N

CASABLANCA

Gulf of Mexico

Tunnel

C h a n n e l

Malecón
San Lázaro
Refugio
Colón
Trocadero
Ánimas
Virtudes
Neptuno
Boulevard
Bristol
Amistad
Dragones
S Bolívar
Aguila
Revillagigedo

Genio
Cárcel
Morro
Zulueta
Paseo De Martí (Prado)
Av De Las Misiones
Av Monserrate
Bernaza
Villegas
Aguacate
Habana
Compostela

Av CM De Céspedes (Del Puerto)
Cuarteles
Chacón
Tejadillo
Empedrado
Progresso
O' Reilly
Obispo
Obrapia
Lamparilla
Amargura
Teniente Rey (Brasil)
Muralla
Sol
Luz
Acosta
Jesús María
Merced
Leonor Pérez
San Isidro

Espada
Tacón
Aguiar
Cuba
San Ignacio
Mercaderes
Oficios
Inquisidor
San Pedro
Desamparados

Maximo Gómez
Cárdenas
Economía
Zulueta
Corrales
Apodaca
Gloria
Misión
Esperanza
Suárez
Egido (AV De Bélgica)

Bay

M162

of the harbour; and **El Príncipe**, on a hill at the far end of Av Independencia (Av Rancho Boyeros), built 1774-1794, now the city gaol. Finest view in Havana from this hill.

5. **The Cathedral**. Construction of a church on this site was begun by Jesuit missionaries at the beginning of the 18th century. After the Jesuits were expelled in 1767 the church was later converted into a cathedral. On either side of the Spanish colonial baroque façade are belltowers, the left one (W) being half as wide as the right (E). There is a grand view from the latter. The church is officially dedicated to the Virgin of the Immaculate Conception, but is better known as the church of Havana's patron saint, San Cristóbal, and as the Columbus cathedral. The bones of Christopher Columbus were sent to this cathedral when Santo Domingo was ceded by Spain to France in 1795; they now lie in Santo Domingo. The bones were in fact those of another Columbus. The Cathedral is open Mon-Fri 0900-1130 and Sat 1530-1730. Several days a week there is a handicraft market on the square in front of the Cathedral, and in adjacent streets.

6. **Plaza de Armas**, has been restored to very much what it once was. The statue in the centre is of Céspedes. In the NE corner of the square is the church of El Templete; a column in front of it marks the spot where the first mass was said in 1519 under a ceiba tree. A sapling of the same tree, blown down by hurricane in 1753, was planted on the same spot, and under its branches the supposed bones of Columbus reposed in state before being taken to the cathedral. This tree was cut down in 1828, the present tree planted, and the Doric temple opened. There are paintings by Vermay, a pupil of David, inside. On the N side of the Plaza is the **Palacio del Segundo Cabo**, the former private residence of the Captains General, now housing the Feria Cubana del Libro. Its patio is worth a look.

7. On the W side of Plaza de Armas is the former **Palace of the Captains General**, built in 1780, a charming example of colonial architecture. The Spanish Governors and the Presidents lived here until 1917, when it became the City Hall. It is now the **Museo de la Ciudad**, the Historical Museum of the city of Havana (open Tues-Sun 0930-1700, US$3, T 61-0722) and rec to visit. It is best to go at 1130 when the upper floor is open. The building was the site of the signing of the 1899 treaty between Spain and the USA. The arcaded and balconied patio is well worth a visit. The museum houses a large collection of 19th-century furnishings which illustrate the wealth of the Spanish colonial community. There are no explanations, even in Spanish. Outside is a statue of Ferdinand VII of Spain, with a singularly uncomplimentary plaque. Also in front of the museum is a collection of church bells. The former Supreme Court on the N side of the Plaza is another colonial building, with a large patio.

8. **The church and convent of San Francisco**, built 1608, reconstructed 1737; a massive, sombre edifice suggesting defence rather than worship. The three-storeyed tower was both a landmark for returning voyagers and a lookout for pirates. Having been restored to the Franciscan order, it is now open to the public on Sun mornings or at other times immediately after services. Most of the treasures were removed by the government and some are in museums.

9. The Corinthian white marble building on Calle Oficinas S of the Post Office was once the legislative building, where the House of Representatives met before the Capitol was built.

10. **The Santa Clara convent** was built in 1635 for the Clarisan nuns. The quaint old patio has been carefully preserved; in it are the city's first slaughter house, first public fountain and public baths, and a house built by a sailor for his love-lorn daughter. You can still see the nuns' cemetery and their cells.

11. **La Merced church**, built in 1746, rebuilt 1792. It has a beautiful exterior and a redecorated lavish interior.

12. **The Museo Nacional Palacio de Bellas Artes** (T 62-0140). It also has a large collection of relics of the struggle for independence, and a fine array of modern paintings by Cuban and other artists. Its huge collection of European paintings, from the 16th century to the present, contains works supposedly by Gainsborough, Van Dyck, Velázquez, Tintoretto, Degas, et al. There are also large chambers of Greek, Roman, Egyptian sculpture and artefacts, many very impressive. Descriptions are in Spanish only and labels, on small cards, may be hard to read. The museum also has

Havana Orientation Map

1. Airline Offices
2. Monument to General Antonio Maceo, & Torre San Lázaro
3. Philatelic Museum & Ministry of Communications

Hotels:
4. Capri
5. Caribbean
6. Deauville
7. Habana Libre
8. Meliá Cohiba
9. Nacional
10. Sevilla

temporary exhibitions. Open Wed-Sun 0900-1700.

13. **Parque Fraternidad**, landscaped to show off the Capitol, N of it, to the best effect. At its centre is a ceiba tree growing in soil provided by each of the American republics. In the park also is a famous statue of the Indian woman who first welcomed the Spaniards: La Noble Habana, sculpted in 1837. From the SW corner the handsome Avenida Allende runs due W to the high hill on which stands Príncipe Castle (now the city gaol). The **Quinta de los Molinos**, on this avenue, at the foot of the hill, once housed the School of Agronomy of Havana University. The main house now contains the **Máximo Gómez museum** (Dominican-born fighter for Cuban Independence). Also here is the headquarters of the young writers and artists (Asociación Hermanos Saiz). The gardens are a lovely place to stroll. North, along Calle Universidad, on a hill which gives a good view, is the University.

14. **The Capitol**, opened May 1929, has a large dome over a rotunda; it is a copy, on a smaller scale, of the US Capitol in Washington. At the centre of its floor is set a 24-carat diamond, zero for all distance measurements in Cuba. The interior has large halls and stately staircases, all most sumptuously decorated. Entrance for visitors is to the left of the stairway. The Capitol now houses the **Museo Nacional de Historia Natural**, which is open Tues-Sat 1015-1745, and Sun 0915-1245, T 62-0553.

15. **Parque Central**.

16. **Gran Teatro de la Habana**, a beautiful building.

17. **Presidential Palace** (1922), a huge, ornate building topped by a dome, facing Av de las Misiones Park; now contains the **Museo de la Revolución** (T 62-4091). Open Tues-Sat 1300-1800, Sun 1000-1300, entrance US$3, cameras allowed, US$3 extra. (Allow several hours to see it all, explanations are all in Spanish.) The history of Cuban political

development is charted, from the slave uprisings to joint space missions with the ex-Soviet Union. The liveliest section displays the final battles against Batista's troops, with excellent photographs and some bizarre personal mementos, such as a revolutionary's knife, fork and spoon set and a plastic shower curtain worn in the Sierra Maestra campaign. The yacht *Granma*, from which Dr Castro disembarked with his companions in 1956 to launch the Revolution, has been installed in the park facing the S entrance, surrounded by planes, tanks and other vehicles involved, as well as a Soviet-built tank used against the Bay of Pigs invasion and a fragment from a US spy plane shot down in the 1970s.

18. **The Church of El Santo Angel Custodio** was built by the Jesuits in 1672 on the slight elevation of Peña Pobre hill. It has white, laced Gothic towers and 10 chapels, the best of which is behind the high altar.

19. **Museo de Arte Colonial**, Plaza de la Catedral (in the former Palacio de los Condes de Casa Bayona), open 0900-1300 (closed Tues), contains colonial furniture and other items, plus a section on stained glass, exquisite (T 61-1367).

20. **Museo Casa Natal de José Martí**, Leonor Pérez 314 entre Picota y Egido, opposite central railway station (Tues-Sat 1000-1800, Sun 0900-1245, T 61-3778).

21. **Museo Histórico de Ciencias Carlos J Finlay**, Calle Cuba 460 entre Amargura y Brasil (Mon-Sat, 0800-1130, 1330-1730).

22. **Palacio Pedroso**, now the **Palacio de la Artesanía**; see **Shopping** below.

23. **La Plaza Vieja**, an 18th century plaza, undergoing restoration since Feb 1996 as part of a joint project by UNESCO and Habaguanex, a state company responsible for the restoration and revival of old Havana. The former house of the Spanish Captain General, Conde de Ricla, who retook Havana from the English and restored power to

Spain in 1763 can be seen on the corner of San Ignacio and Muralla. As restoration continues, 18th century murals are being uncovered on the external walls of the buildings, many of which boast elegant balconies overlooking the plaza. Art exhibitions in the colonial house on the corner of San Ignacio and Brasil.

Other museums

Museo de Educación, Casa Conde de Lombillo, Plaza de la Catedral, 0900-1600, T 20-8054; **Museo Napoleónico**, San Miguel No 1159 esq Ronda (Tues-Sat 1100-1830; Sun 0900-1300, T 79-1412), houses paintings and other works of art, a specialized library and a collection of weaponry (T 79-1412); **Museo de Artes Decorativas**, Calles 17 y Este Vedado (Tues-Sat 1100-1830, T 32-0924); **Postal Museum**, Ministry of Communications, Plaza de la Revolución (Mon-Fri 1000-1700, Sun 0900-1300, T 70-5193); also **Numismatic Museum** (Calle Oficios 8 between Obispo and Obrapía, T 63-2521, Tues-Sat 1300-2200, Sun 0900-1300). **Museo de Finanzas**, Obispo y Cuba, in the old Ministry of Finance building, has a beautiful stained-class ceiling in the foyer, Mon-Fri 0830-1700, Sat till 1230 only. **Vintage Car Museum**, Oficios y Jústiz (just off Plaza de Armas; there are a great many museum pieces, pre-revolutionary US models, still on the road especially outside Havana, in among the Ladas, VWs and Nissans), **Casa de los Arabes** (with restaurant) opposite, on Oficios between Obispo and Obrapía, open Tues-Sat 1330-2030; **Casa de Africa**, on Obrapía 157 between San Ignacio and Mercaderes (Tues-Sun 1300-2000); small gallery of carved wooden artefacts and handmade costumes. **Museo Nacional de la Música**, Cárcel 1, entre Habana y Aguilar, Habana Vieja; small and beautifully furnished old house; interesting collection of African drums and other instruments from all around the world, showing development of Cuban *son* and *danzón* music (Tues-Sat 1000-1800, Sun 0900-1200, T 61-9846).

Suburbs

The western sections of the old city merge imperceptibly into Vedado. West of it, and reached by a tunnel under the Almendares river, lies **Miramar**, some 16 km W of the capital, and easily reached by bus. Miramar was where the wealthy lived before the Revolution; today there are several embassies and government buildings, and also many old, abandoned villas.

The Cuban pavilion, a large building on Calle 23, Vedado, is a combination of a tropical glade and a museum of social history. It tells the nation's story by a brilliant combination of objects, photography and the architectural manipulation of space.

The **National Arts College**, located in the grounds of the former Havana Country Club in Cubanacan, SW of Miramar, houses schools for different arts and was designed by Ricardo Porro. Architects will be interested in this 'new spatial sensation'.

The **Cementerio Colón** should be visited to see the wealth of funerary sculpture, including Carrara Marbles; Cubans visit the sculpture of Amelia de Milagrosa and pray for miracles; entry US$1.

Pabexpo completed in Jan 1989, a sprawling new facility SW of Havana, past Lenin Park, near the botanical gardens, features a score of pavilions showing Cuba's achievements in industry, science, agriculture and the arts and entertainment. Open weekdays Wed-Fri 1400-1600 and Sat-Sun 1000-1800 (times subject to change). Special trains leave from main terminal in Old Havana. Information on times (and special buses) from hotels.

South of the centre, in Cerro district, is the **Estadio Latinoamericano**, the best place to see baseball (the major league level, entrance free).

● Jardín Botánico Nacional de Cuba

Km 3½, Carretera Rocío, S of the city, beyond Parque Lenín (take Bus 4, if running, from the end of the Prado to Vivara, then take Bus 31 and ask; taxi to Varadero US$80). Open daily

0900-1700 (1000-1800 in summer), US$0.30, T 44-5525. The garden is well-maintained with excellent collections; it has a Japanese garden with tropical adaptations. Rosa Alvarez, one of the guides, is knowledgeable and speaks some English.

● **Zoo**
Parque Zoológico Nacional, Calzada de Varona Km 3.5, Boyeros, Wed-Sun, 0900-1515, T 44-7602. Parque Zoológico de la Habana, Av 26, Vedado (open Tues-Sun 0900-1800).

● **Cigar factory**
Partagas on Calle Inglaterra behind the Capitolio, gives tours twice daily, in theory, at 1000 and 1300, US$10 including drink and pack of small cigars. The tour lasts for about an hour and is very interesting. You are taken through the factory and shown the whole production process from storage and sorting of leaves, to packaging and labelling (explanation in Spanish only). Four different brand names are made here; Partagas, Cubana, Ramón Allones and Bolívar (special commission of 170,000 cigars made for the Seville Expo, Spain, 1992). These and other famous cigars can be bought at their shop here, and rum, at good prices (credit cards accepted). Cigars are also made at many tourist locations (eg Palacio de la Artesanía, the airport, some hotels).

● **El Bosque De La Habana**
Worth visiting. From the entrance to the City Zoo, cross Calle 26 and walk a few blocks until you reach a bridge across the Almendares. Cross this, turn right at the end and keep going N, directly to the Bosque which is a jungle-like wood.

● **Aquaria**
National Aquarium, Calle 60 and Av 1, Miramar, specializes in salt-water fish and dolphins, entrance US$2, while the Parque Lenín aquarium has fresh-water fish on show.

Beaches and watersports

The beaches in Havana, at Miramar and Playa de Marianao are rocky and generally very crowded in summer (transport may also be difficult and time consuming). The beach clubs belong to trade unions and may not let non-members in. Those to the E, El Mégano, Santa María del Mar and Bacuranao, for example, are much better (see also **East from Havana**). To the W of Havana are Arena Blanca and Bahía Honda, which are good for diving and fishing but difficult to get to unless you have a car.

The Marina Hemingway, 20 mins by taxi from Havana (see **West from Havana**), at Santa Fe, hosts annual fishing tournaments. Fishing and scuba diving trips can be arranged here as well as other watersports and land-based sports. The Offshore Class 1 World Championship and the Great Island speedboat Grand Prix races have become an annual event in Havana, usually held during the last week in April, attracting power boat enthusiasts from all over the world.

Local information
● **Accommodation**

Price guide			
L1	over US$200	L2	US$151-200
L3	US$101-150	A1	US$81-100
A2	US$61-80	A3	US$46-60
B	US$31-45	C	US$21-30
D	US$12-20	E	US$7-11
F	US$4-6	G	up to US$3

(Payment for hotels used by tourists is in US$). Foreign tourists should obtain a reservation through an accredited government agent (see **Travel agents** at the end of this chapter). Always tell the hotel each morning if you intend to stay on another day. Do not lose your 'guest card' which shows your name and room number. Tourist hotels are a/c, with 'tourist' TV (US films, tourism promotion), restaurants with reasonable food, but standards are not comparable with Europe and plumbing is often faulty or affected by water shortages.

The Vedado hotels (the best) are away from the old centre; the others reasonably close to it. Several important hotel renovation projects are in progress in Old Havana. A huge colonial building on the Plaza de Armas was due to open end-1996 as the luxury *Hotel Santa Isabel*, which will be the best situated hotel in the old city. *Hotel Ambos Mundos*, Calle Obispo on the corner of San Ignacio (also due to open end-1996) is well-located: Hemingway lived here for 10 yrs before moving to La Vigia in 1939. The *Parque Central* on park of same name was also due to open end-1996.

L1-L2 *Nacional de Cuba* (Gran Caribe), Calle O esq 21, Vedado, T 33-3564, F 33-5054, 467 rooms, some package tours use it at bargain rates, generally friendly and efficient service, faded grandeur, superb reception hall, note the vintage Otis high speed lifts (high speed, that is, when they appear). The hotel's tourist bureau is also efficient and friendly; **L2** *Meliá Cohiba* (Sol Meliá), Paseo entre 1 y 3, Vedado, T 33-3636, F 33-4555, 462 rooms, 120 suites, shops, gym, healthclub, pool, gourmet restaurant, disco, piano bar; **L3** *Victoria* (Gran Caribe), 19 y M, Vedado, T 32-6531, F 33-3104, 31 rooms, small, quiet and pleasant, tasteful if conservative, rec; **A1** *Habana Libre* (Gran Caribe), L y 23, Vedado, T 30-5011, F 33-3145, 606 rooms, prices depend on the floor number, ugly exterior but most facilities are here, eg hotel reservations, excursions, fancy shops, Post Office, airlines nearby, a US$30mn refurbishment in 1996 was expected to improve the interior, the buffet breakfast has been rec, as have the pizzas, but restaurant service is terrible, although this may change with new management (Tryp, of Spain) in 1996; **A1** *Habana Riviera* (Gran Caribe), Paseo y Malecón, Vedado, T 30-4051, F 33-3739, 330 rooms, 1950s block, Mafia style, comfortable, does a good breakfast; **A2** *Inglaterra* (Gran Caribe), Prado 416 esq San Rafael y San Miguel, T 62-7071, F 62-6715, 86 rooms, next to Teatro Nacional, old style, regal atmosphere, beautifully restored, balconies overlook Parque Central, highly rec, helpful staff, several of whom speak English, lovely old tiled dining room, also *Ristorante La Stella* (Italian), open to non-guests, snacks available in pleasant inner courtyard, piano music at meal times in *Restaurante Colonial*, the bar often has music or shows at 2200, US$5 cover; **A2** *Presidente* (Gran Caribe), Calzada y G, Vedado, T 32-7521, F 33-3753, 142 rooms, 1940s furniture, pool, TV, restaurant OK; **A2** *Plaza* (Gran Caribe), Ignacio Agramonte No 267, T 62-2006, F 33-8591, 186 rooms, comfortable, street front rooms very noisy, ask for one in the inner courtyard, good breakfast, poor dinner, service generally poor; **A2** *Sevilla* (Gran Caribe), Trocadero 55 y Prado, T 33-8560, 33-8580, F 33-8582, recently restored, 188 rooms on edge of Old Havana, pool, shops, sauna and massage, tourism bureau, buffet restaurant on ground floor, elegant restaurant on top floor with great night time views over Vedado and the Malecón; **A2** *Capri* (Horizontes), 21 y N, Vedado, T 32-0511, F 32-0525, 215 rooms, showing their age, a/c, pool, cabaret, shops,

currency exchange, parking, car rental; **A3** *Hostal Valencia* (Horizontes), Oficios 53 esq Obrapía, T 62-3801, Old Havana, joint Spanish/Cuban venture modelled on the Spanish *paradores*, 12 rooms, each named after a Valencian town, tastefully restored building, nicely furnished, good restaurant (see below); **A3** *Vedado* (Habaguanex), Calle O, No 244, T 32-6501, 191 rooms, a/c, pool, restaurants, nightclub; **A3** *Deauville*, Galiano y Malecón, T 62-8051, 148 rooms, noise from Malecón, poor food. **B** *St John's*, O, entre 23 y 25, Vedado, T 32-9531, 94 rooms, a/c, pool, nightclub; **B** *Colina* (Horizontes), L y 27, Vedado, T 32-3535, 84 rooms, hot water, street noise, small rooms, poor breakfast, not rec, popular with airport Cubatur desk; **B** *Lincoln* (Islazul), Galiano 164 esq Virtudes, T 62-8061, 135 rooms, friendly, TV, hot water, a/c, radio, clean, good value, guests are mostly Cuban honeymooners; **B** *Lido* (Horizontes), Consulado entre Animas y Trocadero, T 62-7000/2046, F 62-7000, 65 rooms, a/c, good, central, slightly dodgy area at night with prostitutes heckling, but 1 block from main street, very friendly reception and cafetería, bar on roof terrace, sometimes live music, rec.

The cheaper hotels are usually hard to get into; often full. **C** *Caribbean* (Horizontes), Paseo Martí 164 esq Colón (bus 82 from Vedado), T 62-2071, lobby full of smoke and prostitutes, 36 rooms, hot water (sporadic supply), fan and TV, popular with travellers, clean, old city, rec, but avoid noisy rooms at front and lower floors at back over deafening water pump, and beware of theft from rooms, small cafe serves mostly sandwiches and eggs at a low price; **D** *Isla de Cuba*, 169 Máximo Gómez, T 62-1031, refurbished, great character, central, rec; nearby is **C-D** *New York* at 156 Dragones, T 62-7001, OK; **D** *Bruzón* (Islazul), on Calle Bruzón No 217, with P Dulces y Independencia, near the Plaza de la Revolución and the bus station, T 70-3531, fan, bath, TV in some rooms, no hot water, drinking water on each floor, back rooms noisy from bus station, staff from sleepy to helpful, aggressive lady in charge of breakfasts, poor restaurant.

It is quite impossible for tourists to stay in 'peso hotels' in Havana. However Cubans may offer you their apartment or a room for about US$20-25/day and cook for you for US$5/day. It is not allowed but appears to be tolerated by the Government. See **Information for travellers**. Ask hustlers around the Prado and

Plaza de Armas. Private homes are, like hotels, mostly dirty with cockroaches, things don't work, there is cold water only, once a day, and the lights often go off. A torch is useful. The families will usually offer you cheap transport too.

If you have a car, the eastern beaches are good places to stay for visiting Havana. The hotels are usually booked up by package tours but you can rent an apartment on the beach away from the main tourist area for US$30. The office is at the end of the main road running along the beach nearest to Havana and furthest from the main hotel area.

● **Places to eat**

Restaurants are not cheap. The choice of food is limited to 'dollar' restaurants, recognizable by the credit card stickers on the door, where meals are about US$20-25, paid only in US dollars. Check the bill carefully as overcharging is common in some Havana 'dollar' restaurants, also the bill may not record what you actually ate. As a rule, in Havana, outside the hotels, the 'dollar' places have been the only option, but since 1995 it has been legal for private houses to operate as restaurants, charging for meals in dollars or pesos. Known as *paladares*, they are licensed and taxed and limited to 12 chairs as well as having employment restrictions (see box, above). A *paladar* thus offers no competition for state establishments but some very good family-run businesses have been set up, offering a 3-course meal for US$6-8 pp, excellent value. *Doña Eutimia*, Callejón del Chorro, just off Plaza Catedral in Old Havana, highly rec, open daily 1200-2400; in Vedado try *Doña Nieves*, Calle 19, entre 2 y 4, T 30-6282, open Tues-Sun, 1200-2400, rec. Also in Vedado, *El Helecho*, Calle 6 entre Línea y 11. Two more typically friendly *paladares* are to be found opp *Hotel Meliá Cohiba* in Paseo entre 3 y 5, Vedado.

La Bodeguita del Medio, Empedrado 207, near the Cathedral, was made famous by Hemingway and should be visited if only for a drink (*mojito* – rum, crushed ice, mint, lemon juice and carbonated water – is a must, US$4), food poor, expensive at US$35-40 for 2 but very popular, open 1030-0100, T 61-8442. *Floridita*, on the corner of Obispo and Monserrate, next to the Parque Central, T 63-1111, open 1200-0100, was another favourite haunt of Hemingway. It has had a recent face-lift and is now a very elegant bar and restaurant reflected in the prices (US$6 for a daiquiri), but well worth a visit if only to see the sumptuous

decor and 'Bogart atmosphere'. *El Patio*, San Ignacio 54 esq Empedrado, Plaza Catedral, nearby, is rec for national dishes, open 1200-2300, T 61-8511 and *La Mina*, on Obispo esq Oficios, Plaza de Armas, open 24 hrs, T 62-0216, traditional Cuban food but both have uneven service, waits can be long and cooking gas shortages are common; nearby, *Oasis*, Paseo Martí 256-58, in Arab Cultural Institute, cold a/c, very good hummus and lamb dishes, T 61-4098, open 1000-2400; and *D'Giovanni*, Italian, Tacón between Empedrado and O'Reilly, lovely old building with patio and terrace, interesting tree growing through the wall, but food very bland. Handicrafts shop in doorway specializes in miniature ornaments. In Old Havana, *La Zaragozana*, Monserrate entre Obispo y Obrapía, oldest restaurant in Havana, international cuisine, good seafood, rec; *Al Medina*, Oficios, entre Obrapía y Obispo, Arab food in lovely colonial mansion, also Mosque and Arab cultural centre off beautiful courtyard; *Torre de Marfil*, Mercaderes, entre Obispo y Obrapía, good, inexpensive Cantonese menu, open lunch and dinner. *Hostal Valencia* restaurant *La Paella* features the best paella in Havana, good food, charming; *El Tocororo* (national bird of Cuba), excellent food at US$40-50 a head, Calle 18 y Av 3a, Miramar, T 33-2209, open Mon-Sat 1230-2400, old colonial mansion with nice terrace, rec as probably the best restaurant in town, manager Erasmo attends guests personally and deserves his reputation as best chef in Cuba; *La Cecilia*, Calle 5a No 11010e/110 y 112, Miramar, good international food, mostly in open air setting, rec, open 1200-2400, T 33-1562. *La Divina Pastora*, fish restaurant, Fortaleza de la Cabaña, open 1200-2400, T 62-3886, dollars only, expensive, food praised; *Los XII Apostoles*, nearby on Vía Monumental, fish and good criollo food, good views of the Malecón. *Las Ruinas*, Calle 100 esq Cortina Presa in Parque Lenín, Cuba's most exclusive restaurant, and aptly named for its prices, is most easily reached by taxi; try to persuade the driver to come back and fetch you, as otherwise it is difficult to get back, open 1200-2200, T 44-3336. *El Conejito*, Calle M esq 17, Vedado, T 32-4671, open 1800-2200, specializes in rabbit, and *La Torre* (17 y M, at top of Edificio Fosca, T 32-5650, open midday-midnight, poor food but good view), are quite expensive. *Restaurante 1830*, Vedado, at far W end of Malecón, overlooks bay, excellent seafood, relatively inexpensive, open air show in gardens at 2200, rec; *El Ranchón*, Av 19 y 140, Playa, T 23-5838, good barbecued chicken, meats, typical *criolla* cuisine; *La Ferminia*, Av 5, entre 182 y 184, Playa, T 33-6555, international, elegant, lovely gardens, expensive. In the *Habana Libre Hotel*, try *El Barracón*, traditional Cuban with good fish and seafood at lobby level, open 1200-midnight, T 30-5011, and *Sierra Maestra* restaurant and *Bar Turquino* on the 25th floor (spectacular views of Havana which makes the food acceptable, service bad). Along and near La Rampa there are some cheaper pizzerías and self-service restaurants. *Hanoi*, on Av Brazil, Cuban food, and *La Azucena China* on Calle Cienfuegos, Chinese food, both charge US$1-2 for a main course. On Paseo and Calle 1, near the *Riviera*, there is a cafetería in the 'Diploferretería' (dollar hardware store), open 1000-2200 every day for sandwiches (usual limited selection), beer and soft drinks, quicker and cheaper than hotel cafés. At Marianao beach there are also some cheaper bars and restaurants. Inside the hard currency shopping centre, Av 5 and Calle 42 in Miramar, is an outdoor fast-foodery and an indoor restaurant, the latter with moderate dollar prices.

A visit to the *Coppelia* ice-cream parlour, 23 y L, Vedado, is rec, but even ice-cream is rationed. Open 1000-midnight officially but sometimes mornings only, residents have to start queuing at 0500 with their ration books if it is their day for ice-cream but there is virtually no queue for those with dollars. To get an ice-cream, pay first, collect a dish and then the ice. The parlour found movie fame in *Strawberry and Chocolate*. Alternatively, sample the Coppelia ice-cream in the tourist hotels and restaurants.

● **Bars**

Visitors find that ordinary bars *not* on the tourist circuit will charge them in dollars, if they let foreigners in at all. If it is a local bar and the Cubans are all paying in pesos, you will have to pay in US dollars. Even so, the prices in most places are not high by Caribbean standards.

The best bar in Old Havana is *La Bodeguita* (see above, also for *La Floridita*). *Lluvia de Oro*, by the harbour, Calle Obispo esq a Habana, good place to drink rum and listen to rock music, also food, open 24 hrs. Try a *mojito* in any bar.

● **Banks**

Banco Nacional and its branches. (See also under **Currency** below.)

● **Entertainment**

Casa De La Trova: San Lázaro, entre Belascoán y Gervasio. There are Casas de la Trova around the country, they are houses where traditional Cuban music can be heard for free, thoroughly recommended.

Cinemas: best are *Yara* (opp *Habana Libre* hotel, T 32-9430); *Payret*, Prado 503, esq San José, T 63-3163. Many others.

Jazz: *Maxim Club*, Calle 10, T 33981, free entry, music starts at 2100, worth arriving early, rec but beware of 'friends' drinks appearing on your bill; *Coparrun*, *Hotel Riviera* (big names play there), jazz in the bar rec.

Nightclubs: the *Tropicana* (closed Mon, Calle 72 No 4504, Marianao, T 33-7507, F 33-0109, 2000-0200) is a must; book with Havanatur, Rumbos Tour or through a tourist hotel, US$30-55, depending on seat, drinks extra. Despite being toned down to cater for more sober post-revolutionary tastes, it is still a lively place with plenty of atmosphere, open-air (entry refunded if it rains). Drinks are expensive: a bottle of rum is US$60; payment in dollars. Bringing your own bottle seems acceptable. Foreigners showing their exchange paper at the door may be admitted without booking if there is room. Next door is *Arcos de Cristal*, with live music till 0200. All the main hotels have their own cabarets, make a reservation. *Capri* is rec, at US$15 and longer show than *Tropicana* but the drinks are expensive at US$40 for a bottle of best rum. *Aché* in the *Meliá Cohiba* and next door *Palacio de Salsa* in the *Riviera*. Also *Pico Blanco (Rincón del Feeling)* at *Hotel St John's*; the *Commodore* disco (US$10), crowded, Western-style, free to *Hotel Neptune* guests; *La Finca* at Playas del Este. The *Cabaret Nacional*, San Rafael y Prado, costs US$10 for 2 shows (first with dancing, second a band, with everyone dancing between the 2); you must enter with a Cuban and leave passport details at the door.

Theatres: *Teatro Mella*, Línea entre A y B, Vedado, T 3-8696, specializes in modern dance; more traditional programmes at *Gran Teatro de la Habana* on Parque Central next to *Hotel Inglaterra*, T 61-3078. The Conjunto Folklórico Nacional dance company sometimes performs here, highly rec, US$0.60. Havana has some very lively theatre companies.

● **Post & telecommunications**

Post Office: there is a post and telegraph office in the *Hotel Habana Libre* building. Also on Calle Ejido next to central railway station and under the Gran Teatro de La Habana. For stamp collectors the Círculo Filatélico is on Calle San José 1172 between Infanta and Basarrata, open Mon-Fri, 1700-2000, and there is a shop on Obispo 518 with an excellent selection (Cuban stamps are very colourful and high quality).

Telephones & cable offices: Calle Obispo 351, T 6-9901/5; Telegraph in *Habana Libre* building. Ministerio de Comunicaciones, Plaza de la Revolución, T 70-5581. The international telephone, telex and fax centre in the *Habana Libre* is open round the clock (also see **Travel agents** below).

● **Shopping**

Local cigars and rum are excellent. Original lithographs and other works of art can be purchased directly from the artists at the *Galería del Grabado*, Plaza de la Catedral (Mon-Fri 1400-2100, Sat 1400-1900). On Sat afternoons there are handicraft stalls in the Plaza. Reproductions of works of art are sold at *La Exposición*, San Rafael 12, Manzana de Gómez, in front of Parque Central. Tourist trinket markets have sprung up, especially around the Cathedral, Che Guevara and religious *Santería* items lead the sales charts. There is a special boutique, the *Palacio de la Artesanía*, in the Palacio Pedroso (built 1780) at Calle Cuba 64 (opp Parque Anfiteatro) where the largest selection of Cuban handicrafts is available; the artisans have their workshops in the back of the same building (open Mon-Sat 0900-2000, T 61-9796) it has things not available elsewhere: jewellery, Cuban coffee, local and imported liqueurs, soft drinks, T-shirts, postcards and best retail selection of cigars (2 cigar-makers in attendance, lower prices than at factory); Visa and Mastercard accepted, passport required. The *Caracol* chain, formerly 'Intur-shops' in tourist hotels (eg *Habana Libre*) and elsewhere, which sell tourists' requisites and other luxury items such as chocolates, biscuits, wine, clothes, require payment in US$ (or credit cards: Mastercard, Visa) and will generally cash travellers' cheques and give change in US$ cash. *La Maison* is a luxurious mansion on Calle 16, 701 esq 7 in Miramar, with dollar shops selling cigars, alcohol, handicrafts, jewellery and perfume. There is sometimes live music in the evening in lovely open-air patio, and fashion shows displaying imported clothes sold in their own boutique, free entry. The large department stores are along Galiano (Av Italia) near San Rafael and Neptuno. Large diplomatic store, *Diplomercado*, at Miramar (Av 5 esq 24 y

26) accepts all foreign currencies (no pesos) and has a variety of goods (including foodstuffs) at prices way below the government Intur dollar shops. Rationed goods are distinguished by a small card bearing the code number and price but a great deal is now sold freely and these articles bear only the price. Most stores are open only in the afternoon. Queues can be long and the selection limited.

If buying food, go to the Diplomercado; if there is no bread, there is a good *panadería* next door. There are tourist food shops in the hotels *Habana Libre* and *Riviera*, but they do not sell fresh food. The International Press Centre (open to the public) on La Rampa sells items like chocolate for dollars in a shop to the right of the entrance.

Markets Farmers are allowed to sell their produce in the city at *mercados campesinos*, or *agromercados*. You can pay for food in dollars or pesos but change will be given in pesos. There are markets at the corner of Infantes y San Lázaro, in Vedado at Calle 19 y B and in the Cerro district near the Latino baseball stadium at Calzada de Montes, which has a wide range of produce.

Bookshops International bookstore at end of El Prado, near Parque Fraternidad and Capitol, English, French, German books but selection poor and payment has to be in dollars. Other good bookshops near Parque Central and *La Moderna Poesía* on Calle Obispo esq Bernaza, T 62-2189 (books are very good value). *Librería La Bella Habana*, in the Palacio del Segundo Cabo, O'Reilly 4 y Tacón, T 62-8092, open Mon-Fri 0900-1630, has both Cuban and international publications. Universal (San Rafael) and El Siglo de las Luces (Neptuno), both near Capitolio, are good places to buy *son, trova* and jazz (rock) records.

● **Photography**

films developed at *Publifoto*, Edificio Focsa, Calle M entre 17 y 19, and *Photoservice*, Calle 23 esq P, Vedado, 0800-2200, camera repairs 0800-1700, T 33-5031 (another branch in Varadero, *Hotel Cuatro Palmas*, 1a entre 61 y 62, open 0900-1900.

● **Travel agents**

There is a large number of state owned travel agencies, which cooperate fully with each other and have bureaus in all the major hotels (see **Information for travellers**).

Guides Many Cubans in Havana tout their services in their desperate quest for dollars and it can be easier to accept one of them to prevent being pestered all the time. Both male and female single travellers have recommended using a guide as long as you are careful who you choose. Lots of Cubans speak English and are keen to practise it. You may find, however, that if you choose a female guide the police will assume she is a prostitute and prohibit her from accompanying a male foreigner into a hotel.

● **Transport**

The economic crisis and shortage of fuel has led to severe transport problems. There is now very little local traffic, there are long queues at petrol stations and public transport has dwindled. Tourists are expected to use dollar transport, such as taxis or hired cars (when available), or not travel at all. Organized tours out of town are rarely more than day trips. Always check when booking that departure is definite, agencies will cancel through lack of passengers or fuel. You must have 4-6 people to get a tour started but arranged tours can be better than tackling the problems of public transport.

Taxis A fleet of white 'Turistaxis' with meters has been introduced for tourists' use; payment in US$: sample fare, Ciudad Vieja to Vedado US$3.50. If you ask your hotel to book a taxi for you they are more likely to call for the luxury variety (US$2 call-out charge). Some ordinary taxis are only allowed to operate in a restricted area (indicated by a sign in the window). If you want to go further afield look for one without a sign. The newer taxis have meters which should be set at No 1 during the daytime and at No 2 at night (2300-0700); they carry a maximum of 4 passengers (drivers may take a fifth if he/she is prepared to hide when passing the police). In the older taxis there are no meters and there is normally a fixed charge between points in or near the city. The fare should be fixed before setting out on a journey. **Ordinary taxis** are not allowed to accept US dollars; latest reports indicate that peso taxis have stopped running completely. Beware of unofficial taxis at the airport arrival gate who will overcharge. **Private cars** also wait at the airport, bus and train stations and will negotiate a price (their preference is for dollars).

Buses Town buses used to be frequent and cheap but the crisis since 1993 means that they are scarce and crowded. The **out-of-town bus services** leave from the Terminal de Omnibus Interprovinciales, Av Rancho Boyeros (Independencia), but they suffer the same problems. See **Information for travellers** for advance booking addresses.

Trains Trains leave from the Estación Central in Av Egido (de Bélgica), Havana, to the larger cities. The Estación Central has what is claimed to be the oldest engine in Latin America, *La Junta*, built in Baltimore in 1842. It is easier to get a seat on a train than on a bus, but all public transport out of Havana is heavily booked in advance and difficult to get on. Staff at the train station have been said to be unhelpful in providing information on departures, with little interest in helping you travel. *Ferrotur*, Calles Arsenal y Egido, use side entrance, official government outlet for dollar tickets, is very helpful. Tickets to Santiago easily purchased from LADIS ticket office at opp end of platform from main building, pay in US$, carriage, a/c, spacious, food and drink on board. For details of services, **see below**. A long distance dollar taxi may well do the same journey in a fraction of the time for the same cost as the train, eg Havana-Pinar del Río, US$15 one way, 2 hrs or less by taxi, 7-8 hrs by train.

Bicycle hire From **Panataxi**, car-park in corner of O'Reilly and Cuba, T 81-0153, US$1 per hour, US$12 per day. *Hotel Neptune*, charges US$3 for the first hour then US$1 for each subsequent hour. Also *Hotel Riviera* and *Palacio del Turismo*, Obispo 252. Check the bicycle carefully (take your own lock, pump, even a bicycle spanner and puncture repair kit; petrol stations have often been converted into bicycle stations, providing air and tyre repairs). Cycling is a good way to see Havana, especially the suburbs; some roads in the Embassy area are closed to cyclists. The tunnel underneath the harbour mouth has a bus designed specifically to carry bicycles and their riders. Take care at night as there are few street lights and bikes are not fitted with lamps.

● **Airport**

José Martí, 18 km from Havana. A new terminal is to be built by 1998 to allow 3 million passengers a year. Turistaxi to airport, US$16-18 depending on time of day or night and destination. Small Lada taxis are US$10-12. The Cubatur desk will book a taxi for you from the airport. The duty free shop at the airport is good value. City buses run from Terminal 4 (Air Cubana terminal) to town, ask around. To catch a bus to the airport from town, the M2 buses leave from Plaza Fraternidad, but are always full, long queues, difficult with luggage.

EAST FROM HAVANA

BEACH RESORTS

An easy excursion, 15 mins by taxi, is to **Cojímar**, the seaside village featured in Hemingway's *The Old Man and the Sea*. He celebrated his Nobel prize here in 1954 and his bust is here. The coastline is dirty because of effluent from tankers, but it is a quiet, pretty place to relax. *La Terraza* is a restaurant with a pleasant view, reasonably priced seafood meals; photographs of Hemingway cover the walls. Further E is the pleasant little beach of **Bacuranao**, 15 km from Havana. At the far end of the beach is a villa complex with restaurant and bar. Another 5 km E is **Santa María del Mar**, with a long, open beach which continues eastwards to **Guanabo** (4 train departures daily), a pleasant, non-touristy beach but packed at weekends. Cars roll in from Havana early on Sat mornings, line up and deposit their cargo of sun worshippers at the sea's edge. The quietest spot is **Brisas del Mar**, at the E end. Tourism bureaux offer day excursions (min 6 people) for about US$15 pp to the Playas del Este, but its worth hiring a non-government taxi for the day for US$20-25.

● **Accommodation A2** *Tropicoco Beach Club*, Av Sur y Av Terrazas, Santa María del Mar, T 2531/2541; price inc beer, rum, 3 meals, wonderful view of beach but food boring after 2 days, nothing to do but drink and bathe, 188 rooms; **A3** *Itabo*, Laguna Itabo entre Santa María del Mar y Boca Ciega, T 2581, 198 rooms, good accommodation, poor food, dirty pool; **B** *Hotel Atlántico* (Gran Caribe), Av Las Terrazas, Santa María del Mar, T 3308, F 33-5502, 92 rooms, also has an *Aparthotel* (opposite the hotel is the self-catering complex's shop selling fresh food, inc eggs, bread, cheese and meat). It may be possible to find 'black market' apartments in Guanabo for US$15 a night with kitchen; ask around; **C** *Villa Playa Hermosa*, 5 Av y Calle 470, T 2774, Guanabo, 33 rooms or chalets, good value, often used by party faithful and honeymooners, pizzería, good quality, US$1-2, rich French pastries US$1, well worth the culinary experience, rents bikes (in poor condition).

Guanabacoa

Guanabacoa is 5 km to the E of Havana and is reached by a road turning off the Central Highway, or by launch from Muelle Luz (not far from No 9 on the map) to the suburb of Regla, then by bus (if running) direct to Guanabacoa. It is a well preserved small colonial town; sights include the old parish church which has a splendid altar; the monastery of San Francisco; the Carral theatre; and some attractive mansions. The **Museo Histórico de Guanabacoa**, a former estate mansion, has an unusual voodoo collection in the former slave quarters at the back of the building, Calle Martí 108, between San Antonio and Versalles, T 90-9117. Open Mon and Wed to Sat 1000-1800.

Santa María del Rosario

A delightful colonial town, founded in 1732, 16 km E of Havana. It is reached from Cotorro, on the Central Highway, and was carefully restored and preserved before the Revolution. The village church is particularly good. See the paintings, one by Veronese. There are curative springs nearby.

San Francisco de Paula

Hemingway fans may wish to visit his house, 11 km from the centre of Havana, where he lived from 1939 to 1960 (called the **Museo Ernest Hemingway**, T 91-0809, US$5, open Mon-Sat 0900-1600, Sun 0900-1230). The signpost is opposite the Post Office, leading up a short driveway. Visitors are not allowed inside the plain whitewashed house which has been lovingly preserved with all Hemingway's furniture and books, just as he left it. But you can walk all around the outside and look in through the windows and open doors, although vigilant staff prohibit any photographs unless you pay US$5 for each one. There is a small annex building with one room used for temporary exhibitions, and from the upper floors there are fine views over Havana. The garden is beautiful and tropical, with many shady palms. Next to the swimming pool (empty) are the gravestones of Hemingway's pet dogs, shaded by a flowering shrub. Hemingway tours are offered by hotel tour desks for US$35.

Some 60 km E of Havana is **Jibacoa** beach, which is excellent for snorkelling as the reefs are close to the beach. (D *Camping de Jibacoa*, cabins for 4 or 2. Food is rather expensive.)

MATANZAS

The old provincial town of **Matanzas** lies 104 km E of Havana along the Vía Blanca, which links the capital with Varadero beach, 34 km further E (many small oilwells producing low-grade crude are passed en route). It is a sleepy town. Walk along the riverside at dusk to watch the fishermen and take in the tranquility and murmur of fellow observers.

The old town is on the W bank of the estuary, the new town on the E; both the rivers Yumurí and San Juan flow through the city. In Matanzas one should visit the **Museo Farmacéutico** (Milanés, 4951 entre Santa Teresa y Ayuntamiento, T 3179, Mon-Sat 1000-1800, Sun 0900-1300), the **Museo Provincial** (Milanés entre Magdalena y Ayllón, T 3195, Tues-Sun 1500-1800, 1900-2200), and the cathedral, all near Parque La Libertad. There is a wonderful view of the surrounding countryside from the church of Montserrat. Bellamar Cave is only 5 km from Matanzas.

- **Accommodation** B *Hotel Canimao*, Km 3½ Carretera Matanzas a Varadero, T 6-1014, good restaurant; **B-C** *Hotel Louvre*, variety of rooms and prices, opt for the a/c room with bathroom and balcony overlooking the square, beautiful mahogany furniture, rather than the small, dark, cupboard room in the bowels of the hotel.

- **Transport** There used to be frequent buses but the journey via the Hershey Railway is more memorable (4 trains daily, 3 hrs, from the Casablanca station, which is reached by public launch from near La Fuerza Castle). Those who wish to make it a day trip from Havana can do so, long queues for return tickets, best to get one as soon as you arrive.

From Matanzas one can continue on a good dual carriageway to **Varadero**, 144 km from Havana, Cuba's chief beach resort with all facilities. It is built on a 20-km sandspit, the length of which run two roads lined with about a dozen large hotels, some smaller ones, and many chalets and villas. Many of the villas date from before 1959. It is undergoing large scale development of new hotels and cabins and joint ventures with foreign investors are being encouraged with the aim of expanding to 30,000 rooms by the turn of the century. The southern end is more downmarket, with hustlers on the beaches by day and prostitutes in the bars at night. The northern end is where the Sol/Meliá hotels are; you can use their facilities if you have dollars even if you are not staying there. In Varadero all hotels, restaurants and excursions must be paid in US dollars. Book excursions at any hotel with a Travel Agency office. Despite the building in progress it is not over exploited and is a good place for a family beach holiday. The beaches are quite deserted, if a bit exposed, but there is not a lot to do. Distances are large. Avenida 1, which runs NE-SW the length of the spit, has a bus service; calle numbers begin with lowest numbers at the SW end and work upwards to the NE peninsula. There is a **Municipal Museum** at Calle 57 y Av de la Playa. The **Centro Recreativo Josone**, Av 1 y Calle 59, is a large park with pool, bowling, other activities and a café.

Festival

Each Nov a festival is held in Varadero, lasting a week, which attracts some of the best artists in South America. Entrance US$2-10 per day.

Excursions

From Varadero it is possible to explore the interesting town of **Cárdenas**, where the present Cuban flag was raised for the first time in 1850. The sea here is polluted with oil and the air smells of phosphorous.

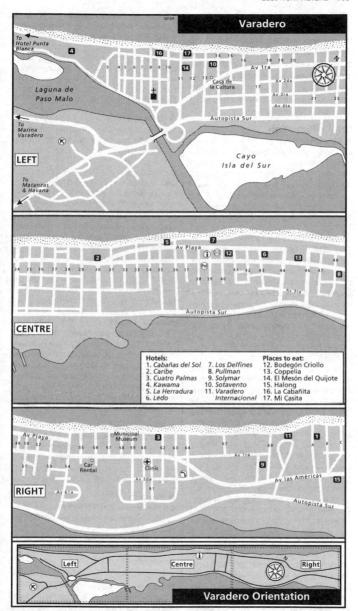

Varadero

M104

To
Hotel Punta
Blanca

Laguna de
Paso Malo

To
Marina
Varadero

To
Matanzas
& Havana

LEFT

Av 1ra
Av 2da
Av 3ra
Av 4ta

Casa de
la Cultura

Autopista Sur

Cayo
Isla del Sur

Av Playa

Autopista Sur

CENTRE

Av 1ra

Hotels:
1. Cabañas del Sol
2. Caribe
3. Cuatro Palmas
4. Kawama
5. La Herradura
6. Ledo
7. Los Delfines
8. Pullman
9. Solymar
10. Sotavento
11. Varadero
    Internacional

Places to eat:
12. Bodegón Criollo
13. Coppelia
14. El Mesón del Quijote
15. Halong
16. La Cabañita
17. Mi Casita

Av Playa
Municipal
Museum

Car
Rental

Clinic

Av 1ra

Av 2da

Av las Américas

RIGHT
Av 61a

Autopista Sur

Left   Centre   Right

Varadero Orientation

Another excursion is to **Neptune's Cave** (thought a more appealing name than the old one, Cepero), which is S of the town of **Carboneras**, half-way between Matanzas and Varadero. It has an underground lagoon, stalagmites and stalactites, evidence of Indian occupation and was used as a clandestine hospital during the war of independence.

Local information
● Accommodation
(All prices high season, double. Hotels can be booked in the tourist office.) A Cuban-Spanish joint venture has opened three resort hotels managed by Sol/Meliá Hotels of Spain: **L2** *Meliá Las Américas*, T 33-7600, F 33-7625, 5 stars, 250 rooms, golf, tennis, watersports, horse riding, disco; **L2** *Sol Palmeras*, T 33-7013, F 33-7162, 375 rooms, 4 stars, same facilities, and the **L2** *Meliá Varadero*, T 33-7013, F 33-7162, 490 rooms, 5 stars, tennis, watersports, disco, nightclub, spa, sauna, jacuzzi. Jamaican investors have built the 160-room, all-inclusive *Club Varadero Superclubs Resort* for singles and couples, no children under 16, lots of activities and sports, to be followed by a 250-room hotel later. At the S end: **L3** *Paradiso*, attached to *Puntarena* (Gran Caribe), T 6-3917 (Paradiso), 6-3919 (Puntarena), F 33-7074, with all resort facilities, 3 pools, watersports, all shared by both hotels, 518 rooms in total, 5 stars, good restaurants, fresh seafood, rec. **L3** *Varadero Internacional* (Gran Caribe), Av Las Américas, T 33-7038/9, F 33-7246, 2 grades of rooms, 371 in total, all facilities (including 5 restaurants); **A2** *Acuazul*, Av 1 entre Calles 13 y 14, T 63918, 156 rooms, with pool; **B** *Varazul*, Av 1 entre Calles 14 y 15, T 63918, aparthotel, 69 rooms, quiet; **B** *Villa Sotavento*, dependency of *Acuazul*, Calle 12 between Av 1 and Av Playa, T 63918, 130 rooms, next to beach, clean, with bath, breakfast, US$5, buffet, very good; **B** *Club Kawama Complejo Turístico*, Carretera de Kawama y Calle 0, T 33-7155/6, F 33-7334, 202 rooms. **L3** *Cuatro Palmas Resort* (Gran Caribe), Av 1 entre 60 y 62, T 6-3912/2893, F 33-7004, 343 a/c rooms, also in bungalows and villas, very pleasant, pool, tennis, bicycle and moped hire, tourism bureau, Post Office, lots of services; **A2** *Villa Punta Blanca*, T 33-7090/7083, F 33-7004, 320 rooms, made up of a number of former private residences with some new complexes;

B *Caribe*, Av de la Playa y Calle 30, T 6-3310, 124 rooms; **B** *Pullman*, Calle 49 No 4904 y Av 1, T 6-2575, best value for the independent traveller, only 15 rooms, very popular; **C** *Ledo*, Calle 43 y Av de la Playa, T 6-3206, under reconstruction; **A3** *Villa La Herradura*, Av Playa entre 35 y 36, T 6-3703, well-equipped suites, balcony, restaurant, bar, *Caracol* shop, etc; **B** *Los Delfines*, Av Playa y Calle 39, T 6-3815.

● Places to eat
Recommended restaurants, all between US$9-15, are *Mi Casita* (book in advance), Camino del Mar entre 11 y 12, T 63787, meat and seafood, open 1800-2300, *La Cabañita* Camino del Mar esq Calle 9, T 62215, meat and seafood, open 1900-0100, *Halong*, Camino del Mar esq Calle 12, T 63787, Chinese, open 1900-2300, *El Mesón del Quijote* (Spanish) at *Villa Cuba*, Cra Américas, T 63522, open 1500-2300 and buffets at the restaurant of hotel *Kawama*. *Albacora*, at *Hotel Copey*, Calle C entre Av 62 y 63, T 63811, open 1200-1245, disappointing, all dishes except *pescado*, US$12-18, but if you want fish you may be told 'no hay'; *Las Américas*, Av Las Américas, T 66162, open 1200-2215, international food, beautiful setting, food good one night, inedible the next; *La Terraza* cafetería at the *Internacional* for the best lunches, T 33-7038, open 1200-2300; *Bodegón Criollo*, Av Playa esq Calle 40, T 62180, open 1200-0100, pleasant atmosphere, popular, no vegetarian food. *Coppelia*, Av 1 entre Calle 44 y 46, T 62866, open 1000-2245, in town centre, ice cream US$0.90. It is now easier to buy food in Varadero because the new Aparthotels (*Varazul*, *La Herradura*) have a small food store.

● Services
Bank: Banco Financiero Internacional, Av Playa y C 32, T 6-3144; cash advance service with credit cards. **Phones**, telex and telegrams: C 64 y 1 Av, T 6-2103. **Clinic**: 1 Av y C 61, T 6-2122. **Police**: C 39 y 1 Av, T 116.

● Transport
Car hire Havanautos, T 33-7341 at airport, or through many hotels. **Moped rental** US$5 per hour, US$15 3 hrs, US$24 for 24 hrs, a good way to see the city. **Bicycle hire** from hotels, US$1/hour. Horse drawn vehicles sometimes act as **taxis**.

A cheap method of getting to Varadero is to take the **train** to Matanzas (see above), then a taxi to Matanzas bus terminal from where you catch a bus, about 1 hr (state destination, take ticket, wait for bus and then your number to be called, and run for the bus). About 5½ hrs in all, if buses are running. Bus station in Varadero is at Calle 36, but there is a wait of several days. There is an **airport**; bus to hotels US$10 pp.

SANTA CLARA

300 km from Havana and 196 km from Varadero, **Santa Clara** is a pleasant university city in the centre of the island. It was the site of the last battle of the Cuban revolution before Castro entered Havana, and the Batista troop train captured by Che Guevara can be seen near the cathedral.

● **Accommodation** There are two hotels, **B** *Motel Los Caneyes*, Av de los Eucaliptos y Circunvalación, T 4512 (outside the city), chalet-style cabins, hot showers, good buffet, supper US$12, breakfast US$4, excellent value, and **C** *Santa Clara Libre*, central, on Parque Vidal, T 27548/27550, reasonable lunch. At **Corralillo** is **D** *Hotel Elguea*, at the spa of that name, a/c rooms, bath, sports facilities, T 68-6298/6387.

CIENFUEGOS

Cienfuegos, on the S coast, is an attractive seaport and industrial city 80 km from Trinidad and 70 km from Santa Clara. Interesting colonial buildings around the central Parque Martí.

● **Accommodation** There is one hotel, 45 mins' walk from station, **B** *Jagua* (Gran Caribe), Punta Gorda, Calle 37 No 1, T 6190/6362-66, F 33-5056, 145 a/c rooms with view over bay, comfortable, palatial restaurant next door, gorgeous decor, live piano music, simple but good food in snack bar (expensive restaurant next door). Many of the hotels are out of town or booked solid by Cubans. **B** *Hotel Pasacaballo*, Carretera a Rancho Luna, Km 22, T 096-212, and **B** *Rancho Luna*, Km 16, T 0432-5929, 048120/3, F 33-5057, 24 rooms with balcony, salt water pool, scuba diving, are seaside complexes with cafeteria etc.

PLAYA GIRON

From Cienfuegos take a taxi to **Playa Girón** and the **Bay of Pigs** (1½ hrs). Ask the driver to wait while you visit the beach and tourist complex, and the site of national pilgrimage where, in 1961, the disastrous US-backed invasion of Cuba was attempted.

● **Accommodation** **C** *Villa Horizontes Playa Girón*, T 59-4118, 292 rooms, a/c with bath, good self-service meals, bar pool, disco, tourist information desk, shop.

ZAPATA PENINSULA

Further W from Girón is the **Zapata Peninsula**, an area of swamps, mangroves, beaches and much bird and animal life. It is the largest ecosystem in the island and contains the Laguna del Tesoro, a 92 sq km lagoon over 10m deep. It is an important winter home for flocks of migrating birds. There are 16 species of reptiles, including crocodiles. Mammals include the jutia and the manatee, while there are over 1,000 species of invertebrate of which more than 100 are spiders. Access from Playa Larga or Guamá, inland. There is a crocodile farm at the Zapata Tourist Institute in **Guamá**, which can be visited. Varadero hotels and tourist agencies organize day excursions for US$39 pp which includes lunch, English-speaking guide and a boat ride on the lagoon. If you go on your own, entrance to the crocodile farm is US$3 and the boat trip to Guamá island US$10.

● **Accommodation** **B** *Horizontes Villa Guamá*, Laguna del Tesoro, T 59-7125, 59 a/c rooms with bath, phone, TV, restaurant, bar, *cafetería*, nightclub, shop, tourist information desk; **C** *Villa Horizontes Playa Larga*, at Playa Larga, T 59-7219, 59 a/c rooms with bath, radio, TV, restaurant, bar, nightclub, shop, birdwatching and watersports.

TRINIDAD

Trinidad, 133 km S of Santa Clara is a perfect relic of the early days of the Spanish colony: beautifully preserved streets and buildings with hardly a trace of the 20th century anywhere. It was founded in 1514 as a base for expeditions into the 'New World'; Cortés set out from here for Mexico in 1518. The five main squares and four churches date from the 18th and 19th centuries; the whole city, with its fine palaces, cobbled streets and tiled roofs, is a national monument and since 1988 a UNESCO World Heritage Site. The **Museo Romántico**, next to the church of Santíssima Trinidad on the main square, is excellent. It has a collection of romantic-style porcelain, glass, paintings and ornate furniture displayed in a colonial mansion, with beautiful views from the upper floor balconies. No cameras allowed, open Tues-Sat 0900-1200, Sun 0900-1300, T 4363. **Museo Municipal de Historia** is on Calle Simón Bolívar 423, an attractive building but rather dull displays, open Mon-Fri 1000-1800, Sun 0900-1300, T 4460. Other museums worth visiting include the **Museo de Arqueología Guamuhaya**, Simón Bolívar 457, Plaza Mayor, T 3420; **Museo de Arquitectura**, Desengaño 83, T 3208; **Museo Nacional de Lucha Contra Bandidos**, Calle del Cristo esq a Boca, all open Tues-Sat 0900-1200, Sun 0900-1300, T 4121. **NB** Admission to most museums is US$3-4.

One block from the church is the *Casa de la Trova*, open weekend lunchtimes and evenings, entry free. Excellent live Cuban music with a warm, lively atmosphere. There are mostly Cubans here, of all age groups, and it's a great place to watch, and join in with, the locals having a good time. All drinks paid for in dollars. Another venue for live music is *La Canchanchara*, Calle Real 70, T 4345. Open 0900-1900, cocktails, no food. More touristy than *Casa de La Trova* (cigar and souvenir shop), but good traditional music at lunchtimes. *Restaurant El Jigüe*, Calle Real esq a Boca, T 4315, lunch only, live music, good food and atmosphere.

Excursions

Nearby are the excellent beaches of **La Boca** (8 km), a small fishing village, restaurant on beach, some buses or taxi. Inland from Trinidad are the beautiful, wooded Escambray mountains. There is

no public transport but day trips are organized to **Topes de Collantes National Park** by the *Hotel Ancón*, for US$43 pp. Their tour includes lunch, cocktail (at 1000) and visits coffee plantations, a crystal clear swimming pond and a pretty waterfall. Half-way up the mountainside, the paved road gives way to dirt track. Passengers transfer from air-conditioned mini-bus to Russian 6WD lorry, an exhilarating experience! You can see hummingbirds and the tocororo, the national bird of Cuba. A great day out. There is also a huge hospital in the mountains, which offers special therapeutic treatments for patients from all over the world, and a hotel C *Los Helechos*, T 40117, details about both places at the *Hotel Ancón*, T 4011/3155.

Local information
● Accommodation
Hard to find accommodation, particularly in summer. **B** *Motel Horizontes Las Cuevas*, Finca Santa Ana, T 419-4013/9, on a hill 10 mins' walk from town (good road), chalets with balconies, 84 very comfortable rooms with a/c, phone, radio, hot water, and very clean, 2 swimming pools, bar, discotheque (most rooms are far enough away not to be disturbed by noise), dollar shop, restaurant (good self-service meals), very good value, rec. Campsites at Ancón beach (see below) and La Boca (5-bed apartments). Camping at Base Manacal in the mountains: tent or small hut for US$5 per day; take No 10 bus from Cienfuegos. Rooms in private houses are available as in Havana.

● Places to eat
The best restaurant/café/bar is in a beautifully restored yellow colonial building on Plaza Santa Ana, big old windows with view of plaza, good food and service. There are also a couple of dollar tiendas in the centre selling souvenirs, postcards and imported snacks. The price of beer in some restaurants drops from US$2 to US$0.60 after 1700 when the tourist tours leave. Family-run restaurants, *paladares* have opened. On the road to Cienfuegos, *Hacienda María Dolores*, serving creole food, 0900-1600, has a collection of tropical birds, cockfighting and a fiesta on Thur, 1800-2300.

● **Transport**
Bus From Havana: a/c buses at 0335 (arrive 0905) and 1220 (arrive 1750), if running. From Santa Clara to Cienfuegos there are several buses daily; from Santa Clara to Trinidad only 2. Transport to the E of Cuba is difficult from Trinidad as it is not on the Carretera Central. Best to go to Sancti Spiritus (see below) and bus from there, about 1½ hrs through beautiful hilly scenery. As elsewhere, severe shortages and huge queues, trucks and tractors with trailers may be laid on as a back-up. If you can get on a tour bus returning to Havana, the fare, inc lunch, will be US$25 pp.

Train From Estación 19 de Noviembre (on Tulipán) to Cienfuegos, number 1301 departs 2146 arrives 0440, number 1303 departs 0725 arrives 1420, 7 hrs to travel 250 km.

Taxi Cienfuegos-Trinidad US$75; tour US$30 pp inc lunch.

PLAYA ANCON

13 km from Trinidad is **Playa Ancón** not a town as such, just two resort hotels. The beach is lovely, pure white sand and clean turquoise water, highly recommended.

● **Accommodation** *Ancón (Gran Caribe)*, T 4011/3155, is B with a/c, though they encourage you to take the daily package A1 inc three meals, drinks and such extras as snorkels, bicycles and horse riding. Good restaurant, snack bar and many facilities, inc scuba diving and watersports, popular for families; **B** *Horizontes Costa Sur*, 11 km from Trinidad, T 419-6100/2524, 131 rooms, a/c, bath, phone, restaurant, bar, nightclub, pool, shop, good value, car rental and taxis.

SANCTI SPIRITUS

Sancti Spiritus, about 80 km E of Trinidad and 90 km SE of Santa Clara, can be reached by road from Cienfuegos, Santa Clara or Trinidad (2 hrs over a mountain road through the Escambray). In the San Luis valley, between Trinidad and Sancti Spiritus are many 19th century sugarmills. Among them is the 45-m Manacas-Iznagas tower (entry US$1), with a café nearby. It is one of Cuba's seven original Spanish towns and has a wealth of buildings from the colonial period. Refreshments in town available at the *Casa de las Infusiones*.

● **Accommodation** The nearest tourist hotel is the **B** *Horizontes Zaza*, T 412-6012/5334, 10 km outside the town on the Zaza artificial lake, 128 a/c rooms with bath, phone, restaurant, bar, nightclub, pool, shop, car rental, rather run down but service and food praised by Cubans.

● **Transport Train** Daily train from Havana, 0645, 9 hrs, US$13 (1995), each carriage has a conductor to control seat reservations. The train seats are very comfortable, though the journey is hot and stuffy through flat countryside, endless fields of sugar cane and a few villages. Buffet car on board (serving tinned grapefruit juice, bread with oil, rice and beans), intriguing queueing system with cards, giving priority to pregnant mothers, the elderly, the disabled and children.

Ciego de Avila

The next province E is **Ciego de Avila**, largely flat, with mangrove swamps on the coasts and cayes to the N. 2 km outside the province's capital is B *Hotel Ciego de Avila*, T 2-8013, with good food. At Morón on Av Tarafa, N of Ciego de Avila, is B *Morón*, T 3901/3904, very smart, renovated 1994, 144 rooms with balcony, pool, games room, good a/c and food.

CAYO COCO

Cayo Coco has become a focal point in the Government's ecotourism interests. It is a large island of mostly mangrove and bush which shelter many migratory birds as well as permanent residents. The Atlantic side of the island has excellent beaches, particularly Playa Flamenco (15 mins' drive from hotels), with some 5 km of white sand and shallow, crystal-line water. Beach bar and horses for hire. Anyone looking for solitude can explore Playa Prohibida, appropriately named as the Government has banned construction here in the interests of ecology. Day trips and 2-night packages from Havana.

● **Accommodation** *Hotel Tryp Cayo Coco*, Spanish and Cuban, 458 rooms, 5 restaurants, 2 bars, piano bar, 2 snack bars, 2 pools, shops, disco, watersports, volleyball, floodlit tennis, beach a bit disappointing but facilities well planned; second hotel alongside under construction 1996. A joint French-Cuban venture is to construct 1,300 rooms on the cay by 2001. There is also a hotel on **Cayo Guillermo**, W of Cayo Coco, *Cayo Guillermo*, in the Gran Caribe chain, T 30-1012/1160, F 33-5221, 80 rooms, a/c, bath, restaurant, watersports, scuba diving, etc. The 13 sq km cay with 5 km of beach is protected by a long coral reef which is good for diving with plentiful fish and crustaceans, while on land there are lots of birds.

CAMAGUEY

The **Museo Casa Natal Ignacio Agramonte** in the large city of **Camagüey**, halfway between Santa Clara and Santiago, is one of the biggest and most impressive museums in the country (Av Ignacio Agramonte 59, T 9-7116, open Mon, Wed, Sat 1300-1600, Sun 0800-1200).

● **Accommodation** B *Hotel Camagüey*, Av Ignacio Agramonte, T 8-2490, good condition, good buffet restaurant; **B** *Puerto Príncipe*, Av de los Mártires 60 y Andrés Sánchez, La Vigía (in town), T 82490/82469; **B** *Gran Hotel*, Maceo 67, T 92093/4.

Several resort hotels have been built at **Santa Lucía** near **Nuevitas**, on the coast N of Camagüey, and at **Marca del Portillo**, on the coast S of Camagüey. Nuevitas was the original site of Camagüey, founded in 1514 by Diego de Velázquez as Santa María del Puerto del Príncipe. Constant pirate attacks forced the town to be moved inland.

Holguín, a provincial capital in the E, near Santiago, has the **B** *Hotel Pernik*, Av Jorge Dimitrov y Av XX Aniversario, T 48-1011, F 4141, plentiful food; C *Motel El Bosque*, Av Jorge Dimitrov, T 48-1012/1140, and C *Motel Mirador de Mayabe*, Alturas de Mayabe, T 42-2160/3485, 24 rooms.

From Holguín the beautiful Atlantic resort of **Guardalavaca** (B *Hotel Guardalavaca*, pool, rec, T 30121-4), with good beach, can be reached by bus.

On the road from Holguín to Baracoa is the small town of **Mayarí** on the river of the same name. Inland and up in the hills the soil turns to a deep red; known as *mocarrero*, it is 85% iron. Visit the scientific station at the **Jardín de Pinare National Park**. There are trails in the park through 12 different eco-systems. The **Salto de Guayabo** is 85m high, one of the highest waterfalls in Cuba, and there is a tremendous view across the fall, down the valley to the Bahía de Nipe.

● **Accommodation** *Pinares de Mayarí*, rustic timber and stone, isolated, pool, nature trails, pine trees, lake, 25 rooms, restaurant, bar, billiards, horse riding.

SANTIAGO DE CUBA

Santiago de Cuba, near the E end of the island, 970 km from Havana and 670 km from Santa Clara, is Cuba's second city and 'capital moral de la Revolución Cubana'. It is a pleasant colonial Caribbean city, with many balconies and *rejas* (grills), for instance on Calles Aguilera and Félix Pena. Of the several museums, the best is the **Museo de Ambiente Histórico Cubano** located in Diego de Velázquez' house (the oldest in Cuba, started by Cortés in 1516, completed 1530), at the NW corner of Parque Céspedes. It has been restored after its use as offices after the Revolution and is in two parts, one 16th century, one 18th century (each room shows a particular period; there is also a 19th-century extension; open Mon-Sat 0800-1800, Sun 0900-1300, free). On the S side of Parque Céspedes is the Cathedral (1522). Two blocks E of the Parque, opposite the Palacio Provincial is the **Museo Emilio Bacardí** (exhibits from prehistory to the Revolution downstairs, paintings upstairs), open Tues-Sat 0900-1800, Sun 0900-1300, T 2-4240. Visit the **Moncada barracks museum** and the **Museo Casa Natal de Frank País** (General Banderas 226), leader of the armed uprising in Santiago on 30 November 1956, who was shot in July 1957. The national hero, José Martí, is buried in Santa Efigenia cemetery, just W of the city. The **Museo de la Lucha Clandestina** has an exhibition of the citizens' underground struggle against the dictatorship. It was originally the residence of the Intendente, then was a police HQ. It is at the top of picturesque Calle Padre Pico (steps), corner of Santa Rita, and affords good views of the city (T 2-4689). Another historical site is the huge ceiba tree in the grounds of the *Motel San Juan* (formerly *Leningrado* hotel), beneath which Spain and the USA

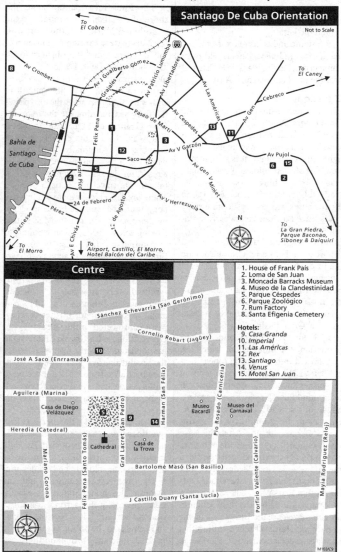

Santiago De Cuba Orientation

Not to Scale

To El Cobre

To El Caney

Av Crombet

Av J Gualberto Gomez
Grajales
Av Patricio Lumumba
Av Libertadores
Av Las Américas
Av Cespedes
Paseo de Marti
To Cebreco
Av Gen Cebreco

Bahía de Santiago de Cuba

Felix Pena

Av Pujol

Av V Garzón
Saco
Av Gen V Minet

Padre Pico

24 de Febrero

Pérez

Av V Herrezuela

L Dacnesse

Av E Chivás

de Agosto

To El Morro

To Airport, Castillo, El Morro, Hotel Balcón del Caribe

To La Gran Piedra, Parque Baconao, Siboney & Daiquiri

N

Centre

1. House of Frank País
2. Loma de San Juan
3. Moncada Barracks Museum
4. Museo de la Clandestinidad
5. Parque Céspedes
6. Parque Zoológico
7. Rum Factory
8. Santa Efigenia Cemetery

Hotels:
9. Casa Granda
10. Imperial
11. Las Américas
12. Rex
13. Santiago
14. Venus
15. Motel San Juan

Sánchez Echevarria (San Gerónimo)

Cornelio Robart (Jagüey)

José A Saco (Enrramada)

Aguilera (Marina)

Casa de Diego Velázquez

Heredia (Catedral)

Mariano Corona

Félix Pena (Santo Tomás)

Gral Lacret (San Pedro)

Harman (San Félix)

Pío Rosado (Carnicería)

Museo Bacardí

Museo del Carnaval

Cathedral

Casa de la Trova

Bartolomé Masó (San Basilio)

Porfirio Valiente (Calvario)

Mayía Rodriguez (Reloj)

J Castillo Duany (Santa Lucia)

N

M103/C9

signed the surrender of Santiago on 16 July 1898; at the Loma de San Juan nearby are more monuments of the Hispano-Cuban-American war (only worth visiting if staying at the *San Juan*, or going to the zoo and amusement park behind the hotel).

For stamp and coin collectors, the *círculo filatélico* and *numismático* is held every Sun morning on the Plaza de la Catedral near the hotel reservations office.

Excursions

Excellent excursions can be made to the **Gran Piedra** (32 km E) a viewpoint from which it is said you can see Haiti and Jamaica on a clear day, more likely their lights on a clear night. It is a giant rock weighing 75,000 tonnes, 1,234m high, reached by climbing 454 steps from the road ('only for the fit'). Santiago-La Gran Piedra buses are no use because daily buses leave La Gran Piedra early morning and return in the evening (the *Turismo Buró* in any hotel will arrange a tour, good value). 2 km before La Gran Piedra are the **Jardines de la Siberia**, on the site of a former coffee plantation, an extensive botanical garden; turn right and follow the track for about 1 km to reach the gardens. The **Museo Isabelica** is 2 km past La Gran Piedra (Carretera de la Gran Piedra Km 14), a ruined coffee plantation, the buildings of which are now turned into a museum (open Tues-Sat 0900-1700, Sun 0900-1300) housing the former kitchen and other facilities on the ground floor. Upstairs is the owners' house in authentic 19th-century style. On view in the ground floor are instruments of slave torture. After the slave revolt in Haiti, large numbers of former slave owners were encouraged to settle in the Sierra de la Gran Piedra. Here they built 51 *cafetales*, using slave labour. During the Ten Years War (1868-78) the revolutionaries called for the destruction of all the *cafetales*. This influx led to the impact of Haitian/French culture on Santiago, especially in music. The owner, Victor Constantin Cuzeau, named the

plantation after his lover and house slave, but when Céspedes freed the slaves he fled and Isabelica was thrown by the former slaves into a burning oven.

The Ruta Turística runs along the shore of the Bahía de Santiago to the Castillo del Morro, a clifftop fort with the **Museo de la Piratería**, a museum of the sea, piracy and local history (open Tues-Sun 0900-1800, T 9-1569). Recommended, even if only for the view. Turis-taxi to El Morro, US$5.50-6 round trip with wait. Transport along the road passes the ferry at Ciudadmar to the resorts of **Cayo Granma** and La Socapa in the estuary (hourly, 5 cents each way). Cayo Granma was originally Cayo Smith, named after its wealthy owner; it became a resort for the rich. Now most of its 600 inhabitants travel to Santiago to work. There are no vehicles; there is a fish restaurant and bar (try the house speciality in the restaurant) in an idyllic setting looking across the bay towards Santiago.

Another excursion can be made to **Siboney**, the nearest beach to Santiago, pleasant and unpretentious (no dollar facilities). Take bus 214 from near bus terminal. Very crowded at weekends. Even nicer is **Junagua** beach, bus 207, along the same road; further development is projected in this area. 13½ km E of Santiago is **La Granja Siboney**, the farmhouse used as the headquarters for the revolutionaries' attack on the Moncada barracks. It now has a museum of uniforms, weapons and artefacts as well as extensive newspaper accounts of the attack (open Tues-Sun 0900-1700, T 9836, entry US$1). Further E is **Parque Bacanao**, a wonderful amusement park in which you can visit **El Valle Prehistórico** (with lifesize replicas of dinosaurs), an old car and trailer museum (free, recommended) and the Daiquirí Beach and Hotel, basic facilities, quiet, lovely setting, beautiful beach. There are buses Nos 14, 35 & 62 (if running) to the public beaches in the park. Beyond the Parque, on the coast, is an aquarium/dolphinarium.

10 mins from the centre of Santiago there is a rum factory, open to visitors, US$6 for a guided tour with English-speaking guide, including free sample. From Santiago, it is possible to visit **El Cobre** (bus No 3) where the shrine of Cuba's patron saint, the Virgen de la Caridad del Cobre, is located (there is a hotel and reasonable restaurant). Built over a copper mine, there is a moving shrine set up by the relatives of the 'raft' people. Interesting collection of personal offerings at foot of the statue, including a gold model of Fidel Castro.

Festivals

The Festival de Caribe runs from 16 to 19 April, with traditional African dancing and beautiful costumes. There is daily live music and singing every weekend at the Casa de la Trova at Calle Heredia 206-8, US$1 for tourists, free for locals, cheap drinks (but hope that there is no modern music at the Casa de Estudiantes Josué País García next door to drown out the more traditional thing).

Local information

● Accommodation

C *Motel San Juan*, Km 1 Carretera a Siboney, T 4-2434, too far out of town, turistaxi US$3.95, a complex with cabins, very nice rooms, excellent value, pool, bar and several restaurants, high quality by Cuban standards, accepts pesos, queues at weekends and during festivals; **B** *Las Américas*, T 4-2011, Av de las Américas y Gen Cebreco, not so far out of town, lively, rec (turistaxi US$2.35), expensive restaurant with poor breakfast (although cheap sandwiches and spaghetti are available), discotheque, non-residents may use swimming pool, bicycle hire; not far away is **L3** *Hotel Santiago*, Av Las Américas entre 4 y Av Manduley, T 4-2612/2654, F 4-1756, 5-star, clean, good service, excellent breakfast buffet US$7, good *La Cubana* restaurant, highly rec, open 1200-2100, swimming pool, tennis, sauna, discotheque; and **B** *Balcón del Caribe*, next to Castillo del Morro, T 9-1011, overlooking the sea, quiet, pool, basic food, cold water in bungalows, pleasant but inconvenient for the town. **C** *MES*, Calle L and 7 Terraza (about 5 blocks N of *Las Américas*), T 4-2398, TV and fan, 2 rooms share bath and fridge. **E** *Libertad*

on Plaza Mart, good value if slightly downmarket, very noisy fans; *Casa Granda* on Parque Céspedes has a café, open 2000-0300, good. You can reserve beach accommodation in Santiago, eg a Siboney apartment, 2 rooms, 4 people, Mar Verde, crowded at weekends, a *cabaña*, basic, 3 people. Private homes are available, as in Havana, for about US$20 for a room with bathroom and breakfast. Also look out for private restaurants.

● **Banks & money changers**

Possible to get US dollar cash advance on Visa at Banco Financiero Internacional.

● **Entertainment**

Club Tropicana Santiago at *Hotel Santiago*, local version of Havana show.

● **Shopping**

Diplomercado outside airport; take passport.

● **Telephones**

For calls outside Santiago, Centro de Comunicaciones Nacional e Internacional, Heredia y Félix Pena, underneath the cathedral.

● **Transport**

Train Havana-Santiago every other day at 1659; Santiago-Havana, every other day at 1859: LADIS ticket office at station, US$35 single for foreigners, 15-21 hrs, food and drink on board but nothing special; train Santiago-Camagüey 1810, arrives 2300, also Tues, Thur, Sat 1000, arrive 1500, US$13 one-way. No tourist taxis at the station, only local drivers, who charge, for example, US$4 to *Hotel Las Américas*.

Bus Terminal near Plaza de la Revolución for reservations.

Taxis For private/unofficial taxis, ask around the park at Av Victoriano Garzón and Plácido. Motorbike transport can be arranged at Parque Céspedes for about 20 pesos.

GUANTANAMO

80 km from Santiago on the Baracoa road, Guantánamo is close to the US base of the same name (which cannot be easily visited from Cuba). Trains are met at the station by very practical horse-drawn carts, definitely not designed for tourists. Pesos needed for this journey. Peter Hope, English speaking Public Relations Officer, can arrange tours to Mt Malones, where you can view the US base through Soviet binoculars.

● **Accommodation C** *Guantánamo*, Plaza Mariana Grajales, T 3-6015, a very Soviet atmosphere, clean, a/c, bar and restaurant, telephone service to Havana and beyond.

BARACOA

150 km E of Santiago, close to the most easterly point of the island, is an attractive place surrounded by a fruitful countryside. It is the wettest region in Cuba with annual rainfall of 2m in the coastal zone to 3.6m in the middle and upper Toa Valley. White water rafting is possible down the Río Toa, with different levels of difficulty. It is well worth the trip from Santiago (4 hrs drive) for the scenery of the last section of road, called La Farola, which winds through lush tropical mountains and then descends steeply to the coast. The church is built on the site of Columbus' house, it contains a relic: the remains of his cross.

● **Accommodation   B** *Horizontes El Castillo*, Calixto García, Loma del Paraíso, T 214-2103/2125, 35 a/c rooms with bath, phone, TV in lobby lounge, rec, friendly staff, food OK, nice views, good swimming pool; **A1-B** *Horizontes Porto Santo*, T 214-3578/3590, 36 rooms, 24 *cabañas* or suites, a/c, bath, restaurant, bar, shop, swimming pool, car hire, near runway of small airport.

● **Transport** The taxi base is in front of the hospital. Bus to Guantánamo takes 4 hrs. The Cubana office is on Plaza Martí.

Guardalavaca (see page 174) on the N coast is a lovely drive through the mountains from Santiago. Take a day driving to Frente II (eat at *Rancho México*), down to Sagua and across to Guardalavaca. You can stay at Don Lino beach, which is small but pleasant, where there are comfortable huts (US$14) with refrigerator for cooling beer. Restaurant food is basic.

West from Santiago runs a wonderful coastal road along the **Sierra Maestra** with beautiful bays and beaches, completely deserted, some with black sand. It is only possible to visit by car. At **La Plata**, about 150 km from Santiago, is a little museum about the Cuban guerrillas' first successful battle. There is no

curator so ask the local people to open it. En route you pass **Las Coloradas**, the beach where *Granma* landed. You can make a circular route back to Santiago via **Manzanillo**, **Bayamo** (both in Granma province; in Bayamo B *Hotel Sierra Maestra*, Km 7½, on Santiago road, T 48-1013, a/c, bath, restaurant, pool and other usual facilities) and **Palma Soriano**.

WEST FROM HAVANA

The western end of the island is dominated by the Cordillera de Guaniguanico. The eastern end of the range, known as the Sierra del Rosario, contains the Pan de Guajaibón, at 699m its highest point. UNESCO has classified 20,000 ha as a Biosphere Reserve covering an area of mesophytic tropical forest with over 50 bird species and several reptiles, including a water lizard found only in the Sierra del Rosario.

West from Havana a dual carriage highway has been completed almost to **Pinar del Río**, the major city W of Havana. The province of Pinar del Río produces Cuba's best cigars.

SOROA

If travelling by car on this route, you can make a detour to **Soroa** in the Sierra del Rosario, 81 km SW of the capital. It is a spa and resort in luxuriant hills. As you drive into the area, a sign on the right indicates the **Mirador de Venus** and **Baños Romanos**. Past the baths is the *Bar Edén* (open till 1800), where you can park before walking up to the Mirador (25 mins). From the top you get fine views of the southern plains, the palm-covered Sierra and the tourist complex itself; lots of birds, butterflies, dragonflies and lizards around the path; many flowers in season.

The road continues into the complex where there is an orchidarium with over 700 species (check if they are in bloom before visiting, guided tours between 0830-1140, 1340-1555 daily, US$2) and the *Castillo de las Nubes* restaurant (1200-1900, entrées US$5-6), a mock castle. Across the road from the orchidarium is a waterfall (250m, paved path, entry US$1), worth a visit if you are in the area.

● **Accommodation** At the resort, **B** *Horizontes Villa Soroa*, T 82-2122, 49 cabins and 10 houses, a/c, phone, radio, TV, VCR, some have private pool, restaurant *El Centro* (quite good), disco, bar, Olympic swimming pool, bike rental, riding nearby and handicrafts and dollar shops. Despite the ugly, gloomy cabins, it's a peaceful place and would be more so without the loud juke box.

Nearer Pinar del Río another detour N off the main road is to the spa of **San Diego de los Baños**, also in fine scenery in the Sierra de los Organos.

PINAR DEL RIO

The city has many neoclassical villas with columns, but is not especially interesting for tourists.

● **Accommodation** At the E entrance to the city is the **B** *Hotel Pinar del Río*, Calle Martí final, T 5070-7, swimming pool, nightclub etc.

● **Transport** For travel to Pinar del Río, train from Havana's Estación 19 de Noviembre/del Occidente, rather than bus, is recommended (leaves Havana 0500, book 1300 day before, leaves Pinar del Río 1702, 8 hrs); slow but comfortable. Shared taxi from Havana US$4 pp.

VINALES

North of Pinar del Río, on a road which leads to the N coast and eventually back to Havana is **Viñales**, a delightful small town in a dramatic valley. Stands of palm and tobacco fields with their drying barns (*vegas*, steep, thatch-roofed buildings which you can enter and photograph with ease) lie amid sheer and rounded mountains (*mogotes*) reminiscent of a Chinese landscape, especially at dawn and dusk. These massifs were part of a cave system which collapsed millions of years ago and, on some, remnants of stalactites can still be seen.

Viñales itself is a pleasant town, with trees and wooden colonnades along the main street, red tiled roofs and a main square with a little-used cathedral and a Casa de Cultura with art gallery.

Excursions 2 km N is the **Mural de la Prehistoria**, painted by Lovigildo González, a disciple of the Mexican Diego Rivera, between 1959 and 1976; tourist restaurant nearby. 6 km beyond Viñales is the **Cueva del Indio** which can be approached from two ends, neither far apart. Inside, though, you can travel the cave's length on foot and by boat (US$2 for foreigners), very beautiful. There is a restaurant at the cave (also at a smaller cave nearer Viñales).

● **Accommodation** **B** *Horizontes Los Jazmines*, Carretera de Vinales Km 25, 3 km before the town, in a superb location overlooking the valley, T 829-3265, 62 rooms and 16 *cabañas*, nightclub, good restaurant, bar with snacks available, shops, swimming pool, riding, easy transport, T 829-3265, 62 rooms and 16 *cabañas*, nightclub, good restaurant, bar with snacks available, shops, swimming pool, riding, easy transport; **B-C** *Horizontes La Ermita*, Carretera de la Ermita Km 2, 3 km from town with magnificent view, T 829-3204, 62 rooms, a/c, phone, radio, shop, tennis court, wheelchair access, food (not always usable), good food, rec as beautiful, the farmers in the valley below are friendly and hospitable, they may invite you for a meal of their own fruit and vegetables or offer a home grown cigar; **B** *Horizontes Rancho San Vicente*, Valle de San Vicente, near Cueva del Indio, T 829-3200, 34 rooms in a/c cabañas, bar, restaurant, nightclub, shop, tourist information desk, nice pool, pleasant. Book your hotel before you arrive as everywhere is often full.

● **Transport** Turistaxi from Havana to *Motel Los Jazmines* takes 2½ hrs, there may be a bus back to the capital, 3½ hrs.

Offshore, N of Viñales is **Cayo Levisa**, part of the Archipiélago de los Colorados, with a long, sandy beach and reef offshore with good snorkelling and scuba diving (lots of fish). One small hotel, *Cayo Levisa* (Gran Caribe) with 20 cabins, a/c, restaurant, bar, shop, waterskiing, windsurfing and sailing.

VINALES TO HAVANA

From Viñales to Havana along the coast road takes about 4 hrs by car. It is an attractive drive through sugar and tobacco plantations, pines, the mountains inland, the coast occasionally visible. All the small houses have flower gardens in front. You pass through **La Palma**, **Las Pozas** (which has a ruined church with a boring new one beside it), **Bahía Honda** and **Cabañas**; many agricultural collectives along the way. After Cabañas the road deteriorates; either rejoin the motorway back to the capital, or take the old coast road through the port of **Mariel** to enter Havana on Av 5.

Near Mariel is **El Salado** beach, small, secluded, with calm, clear water, although some parts are rocky. Taxi from Havana US$25. There is a reasonably-priced restaurant, part of a small hotel used by German holidaymakers; the hotel has good value tours. Taxis back to Havana can be ordered at the hotel, but you may have to wait.

Off Avenida 5 is the Marina Hemingway tourist complex, in the fishing village of **Santa Fe**. In May and June the marina hosts the annual Ernest Hemingway International Marlin Fishing Tournament and in Aug and Sept the Blue Marlin tournament. The resort includes the hotel *El Viejo y El Mar*, a Canadian-Cuban joint venture, four restaurants (*La Cora*, *Fiesta*, *Papa's* and *Los Caneyes*), bungalows and villas for rent, shopping, watersports, facilities for yachts, sports and a tourist bureau. Excursions include a day trip to the Castillo del Morro in Old Havana with swimming and lunch (US$30); a snorkelling excursion along the reef W of Havana with equipment and lunch (US$35); by yacht to the beaches E of Havana with swimming and lunch (US$45). Shorter trips available as well as scuba diving and fishing trips, T 33-1909. VHF radio channels 16, 72, or 55B 2790.

THE ISLANDS

In the Gulf of Batabanó is the **Isla de la Juventud** (Isle of Youth), 97 km from the main island, reached by daily Cubana flights or hydrofoil, the *Kometa*. At about 3,050 sq km, it is not much smaller than Trinidad, but its population is only 60,000. It gets its present name from the educational courses run there, particularly for overseas students. Columbus, who landed there in 1494 called the island Evangelista and, until recently, it was called the Isla de Pinos. It was a pirate's haunt and *Treasure Island* by R L Stevenson is believed to have been inspired by its legends. From the 19th century until the Revolution its main function was as a prison and both José Martí and Fidel Castro served time there. It was here that Castro wrote his famous speech ending with the words, "History will absolve me". The prison building is a Panopticon, devised in 1791 by Jeremy Bentham, to give total surveillance and control of its inmates and built by Gerardo Machado in 1932 (closed by Castro in 1967). The building is now decaying but you can wander around the rotundas and guard towers, see the numbered cells and imagine the horrors of incarceration there.

Today the main activities are citrus-growing, fishing and tourism. Cuba's largest known gold deposit is on the island; the Delita property is a gold-silver project expected to start operations in 1998 with Canadian investment. There are several beaches and ample opportunities for water sports. The capital is **Nueva Gerona**. There is a museum in the old Model Prison (El Presidio) and four others. Main tourist hotel is A2 *El Colony*, 83 rooms, T 98181.

CAYO LARGO

Cayo Largo, E of Isla de la Juventud, is a westernized island resort reached by air from Havana (US$94 day trip) and Varadero, or by light plane or boat from Juventud, or by charter plane from Grand Cayman. Snorkelling and scuba diving can be done at Playa Sirena, 10 mins' boat ride from the hotels. Very tame iguanas can be spotted at another nearby cay, **Cayo Rico** (day-trips available for US$37 from Cayo Largo). Hotel expansion is planned to cater for watersport tourism. **Cayos Rosario** and **Avalos**, between Juventud and Largo, have not yet been developed.

Island information
● **Accommodation**
There are several hotels here at present, all in the Gran Caribe chain, T 79-4215, F 52108, with all facilities shared and included in the package cost (prices quoted are high season per person and include 3 meals and free use of all water sports and other activities). **L3** *Villa Capricho*, 60 rooms in *cabañas*, **L3** *Isla del Sur*, 62 rooms, **L3** *Pueblito* (*Villa Coral*), 72 rooms and suites, **L3** *Hotel y Villa Pelícano*, 144 rooms, and **A2** *Club* (*Villa Iguana*), 114 rooms. The hotels and the thatched *cabañas* are low-lying and pleasantly spread out in gardens by the beach.

● **Places to eat**
There are several restaurants attached to the hotels, including a highly recommended Italian place and a good pizzería. As with many Cuban resort hotels restaurants are run on a self-serv- ice buffet basis and food is reported to be plentiful and fresh.

Information for travellers

BEFORE TRAVELLING

● **Documents**
Visitors from the majority of countries need only a tourist card to enter Cuba, as long as they are going solely for tourist purposes. A tourist card may be obtained from Cuban embassies, consulates, or approved travel agents (price in the UK £10 from the consulate, £12-13 from travel agents, some other coun- tries US$15). From some countries (eg Canada) tourist cards are handed out by the tour op- erator or on the plane and checked by visa control at the airport; the first one is free but replacements cost US$10. Nationals of other countries without visa-free agreement with Cuba, journalists and those visiting on other business must check what visa requirements pertain (in the UK a business visa costs £25, plus US$13 for any telex that has to be sent in connection with the application). The US gov- ernment does not normally permit its citizens to visit Cuba. US citizens should have a US licence to engage in any transactions related to travel to Cuba, but tourist or business travel are not licensable, even through a third country such as Mexico or Canada. They should con- tact Marazul Tours, 250 West 57th St, Suite 1311, New York City, 10107 New York, T 212- 582 9570, or Miami T 305-232 8157 (infor- mation also from Havanatur, Calle 2 No 17 Miramar, Havana, T 33-2121/2318). Many travellers do conceal their tracks by going via Mexico, or Canada, when only the tourist card is stamped, not the passport. The Cuban Con- sulate in Mexico City refuses to issue visas unless you have pre-arranged accommodation and book through a travel agent; even then, only tourist visas are available, US$20. In Mérida, a travel agent will arrange your docu- ments so you do not need to go to a Consulate for a visa. In the USA, the Cuban interests

section is at 2630 16th St NW, Washington DC 20009, T 202-797 8518, and will process applications for visas. Visas can take several weeks to be granted, and are apparently difficult to obtain for people other than businessmen, guests of the Cuban Government or Embassy officials. However, a British citizen was able to obtain a Tourist Card there in half an hour (US$26, photographs essential). When the applicant is too far from a Cuban consulate to be able to apply conveniently for a visa, he may apply direct to the Cuban Foreign Ministry for a visa waiver.

Visitors travelling on a visa must go in person to the Immigration Office for registration the day after arrival. The office is on the corner of Calle 22 and Av 3, Miramar. (If buses are running, take no 132 from the old city centre, get off at second stop after the tunnel; also bus 32 from La Rampa or *Coppelia* icecream parlour in Vedado, alight at same stop.) When you register you will be given an exit permit.

Travellers coming from or going through infected areas must have certificates of vaccination against cholera and yellow fever.

The Cuban authorities do not insist on stamping your passport in and out. They will stamp your tourist card instead. 'Souvenir' stamps can be put in your passport if you wish.

British business travellers should get 'Hints to Exporters: Cuba', from DTI Export Publications, PO Box 55, Stratford- upon-Avon, Warwickshire, CV37 9GE. US citizens on business with Cuba should contact Foreign Assets Control, Federal Reserve Bank of New York, 33 Liberty St, NY 10045. Another useful leaflet 'Tips For Travelers to Cuba' is available from the Passport Office, US Department of State, Washington DC 20524.

● **Customs**
Personal baggage and articles for personal use are allowed in free of duty; so are 200 cigarettes, or 25 cigars, or 1 lb of tobacco, and 2 bottles of alcoholic drinks. Visitors importing new goods worth between US$100 and US$1,000 will be charged 100% duty, subject to a limit of 2 items a year. No duty is payable on goods valued at under US$100. Many things are scarce or unobtainable in Cuba: take in everything you are likely to need other than food (say razor blades, soap, medicines and pills, insecticides against mosquitoes, tampons, reading and writing materials and photographic supplies).

● **Climate**
Northeast trade winds temper the heat. Average summer shade temperatures rise to 30°C (86°F) in Havana, and higher elsewhere. In winter, day temperatures drop to 19°C (66°F). Average rainfall is from 860 mm in Oriente to 1,730 mm in Havana; it falls mostly in the summer and autumn, but there can be torrential rains at any time. Hurricanes come in June-October. The best time for a visit is during the cooler dry season (Nov to April). In Havana, there are a few cold days, 8°-10°C (45°-50°F), with a N wind. Walking is uncomfortable in summer but most offices, hotels, leading restaurants and cinemas are air-conditioned. Humidity varies between 75 and 95%.

● **Health**
Sanitary reforms have transformed Cuba into a healthy country, though tap water is generally not safe to drink except in Havana; bottled and mineral water are recommended.

Medical service is no longer free for foreign visitors in Havana and Varadero, where there are clinics that charge in dollars. Visitors requiring medical attention will be sent to them. Emergencies are handled on an ad hoc basis. Check with your national health service or health insurance on coverage in Cuba. Charges are generally lower than those charged in Western countries. According to latest reports, visitors are still treated free of charge in other parts of the country, with the exception of tourist enclaves with on-site medical services.

The Cira García Clinic in Havana (Calle 20 No 4101 esq 43, Playa, T 33-2811/14, F 33-1633, payment in dollars) sells prescription and patent drugs and medical supplies that are often unavailable in chemists. Bring all medicines you might need as they can be difficult to find.

Between May and Oct, the risk of sunburn is high, sun blocks are rec when walking around the city as well as on the beach. In the cooler months, limit beach sessions to 2 hrs.

● **Working in Cuba**
Those interested in joining International Work Brigades should contact Cuba Solidarity Campaign, c/o The Red Rose, 129 Seven Sisters Rd, London N7 7QG, or 119 Burton Rd, London SW9 6TG.

MONEY
● **Currency**
The monetary unit is the peso Cubano, US$1=1 peso. Watch out for pre-1962 peso

notes, no longer valid. There are notes for 3, 5, 10, and 20 pesos, and coins for 5, 20, and 40 centavos and 1 peso. You must have a supply of 5 centavo coins if you want to use the local town buses (10 centavos) or pay phones (very few work). The 20 centavo coin is called a *peseta*. In 1995 the Government introduced a new freely 'convertible peso' at par with the US dollar with a new set of notes and coins. It is fully exchangeable with authorized hard currencies circulating in the economy.

● **Exchange**
As a result of currency reforms the black market exchange rate has fallen from 130 pesos Cubanos = US$1 in May 1994 to 20 pesos = US$1 in May 1996. Official Casas de Cambio usually offer about 17 pesos to the dollar. The 'peso convertible' is equally valuable on the black market. Cubans are allowed to hold US$ but not to have a dollar bank account. There is very little opportunity for foreigners to spend pesos Cubanos and you are advised to change only the absolute minimum, if at all. Food in the markets (*agromercados*), on trains, postcards, stamps and books, but not in every shop, can be bought in pesos. Visitors on pre-paid package tours are best advised not to acquire any pesos at all. Bring US$ in small denominations for spending money, dollars are now universally preferred. US dollars are the only currency accepted in all tourist establishments. The visitor should be careful to retain the receipt every time money is changed officially; this will enable Cuban pesos remaining at the end of the stay to be changed back into foreign currency (to a maximum of US$10 equivalent).

Travellers' cheques expressed in US or Canadian dollars or sterling are valid in Cuba. TCs issued on US bank paper are not accepted so it is best to take Thomas Cook. Don't enter the place or date when signing cheques, or they may be refused. You can occasionally get US dollars change when paying a hotel bill with TCs, but you can not cash TCs for US dollars, nor even for Cuban pesos.

There is a branch of the Banco Nacional at the 42nd St 'diplomatic' shopping centre in Havana for changing money legally. It is useful for changing non-dollar currencies into dollars and also for changing TCs. Visitors have difficulties using torn or tatty US dollar notes.

● **Credit cards**
Credit cards acceptable in most places are Visa, Master, Access, Diners, Banamex (Mexican) and Carnet. No US credit cards accepted so a Visa card issued in the USA will not be accepted. American Express, no matter where issued, is unacceptable. Many restaurants which claim to accept credit cards make such a performance that it is not worthwhile. A master list of stolen and rogue cards is kept at the *Habana Libre* and any transaction over US$50 must be checked there; this can take up to 3 hrs. You can obtain cash with a credit card at branches of the Banco Financiero Internacional, but best to bring plenty of cash as there will often be no other way of paying for what you need.

GETTING THERE

AIR

From Europe: Cubana flies London Stansted-Havana once a week on Thur. Cubana flies from Berlin (Sat), Brussels (Sun), Rome (Wed) and Paris (Sat and Sun, also AOM French Airlines Mon and Fri), Iberia and Cubana from Barcelona and Madrid (Cubana also from Gran Canaria), LTU from Dusseldorf. Cubana and Aeroflot from Moscow. Aeroflot's flights go via Shannon (Eire) and Stockholm. Aeroflot flights continue on to Lima and Santiago. It is essential to check Aeroflot's flights to make sure there really is a plane going. Since Havana no longer enjoys the close relationship with Moscow that it used to have, these flights are now reported to be increasingly unreliable. There are also flights to Varadero from Amsterdam (Martinair), Dusseldorf (LTU), Montréal (Cubana), Frankfurt (Condor) and Paris (AOM French Airlines). There are also lots of charter flights.

From North America: Cubana from Montréal, Cubana and Mexicana de Aviación from Mexico City with some Mexicana flights via Mérida, AeroCaribe also flies from Oaxaca via Tuxtla Gutierrez, Villahermosa, Mérida and Cancún, Cubana and AeroCaribe also from Cancún.

From Central and South America: Cubana and Viasa from Caracas, Cubana and Lacsa from San José, Costa Rica (good service, convenient connections between San José and Miami), Cubana from Buenos Aires, Cubana from São Paulo via Rio de Janeiro, Cubana Copa and Aeroflot from Panama and Cubana and Aeroflot from Santiago de Chile; from Colombia, Intercontinental de Avación flies from Bogotá via Cartagena, Aerorepública and SAM from Bogotá (also Cubana) via Barranquilla; Cubana from Quito and Guayaquil.

From the Caribbean: Cubana flies from Kingston, Jamaica and Fort-de-France and Pointe-à-Pitre in the French Antilles.

From Africa: Taag-Angola Airlines flies once a week from Luande, via Sal, Cape Verde.

The frequency of these flights depends on the season, with twice weekly flights in the winter being reduced to once a week in the summer. Some of the longer haul flights, such as to Buenos Aires, are cut from once every 2 weeks in winter to once a month in summer. There are charters to Cancún, Mexico, and between Santiago de Cuba and Montego Bay, Jamaica. Regular charters between Cayo Largo and Grand Cayman. The Cuban air charter line AeroCaribbean has an arrangement with Bahamasair for a daily service Miami-Nassau-Havana, changing planes in Nassau; the Cuban tourist agency Amistur organizes the service. Martinair has charters from Amsterdam to Varadero and Holguín. At certain times of year there are special offers available from Europe; enquire at specialist agents. There are also many combinations of flights involving Cuba and Mexico, Venezuela, Colombia and the Dominican Republic; again ask a specialist agent.

Mexicana de Aviación organizes package tours. Several Canadian tour operators have departures from Toronto and Montréal and run package tours to Cuba for all nationalities. Package tours also available from Venezuela, the Bahamas and Jamaica (see **Travel agencies** below).

SEA

See **Shipping** in Introduction and hints for Sprante Shiffahrts regular service from Amsterdam to Cuba. No other passenger ships call regularly.

● **Ports of entry**

Havana, Cienfuegos and Santiago receive tourist cruise vessels. There are several marinas, including the Hemingway, Tarará and Veneciana (in Havana), Acua, Chapelín, Gaviota (in Varadero), and Cayo Largo. Arriving by yacht, announce your arrival on VHF channel 16, 72 or 55B.

ON ARRIVAL

● **Airlines**

All are situated in Havana, at the seaward end of Calle 23 (La Rampa), Vedado: eg Cubana, Calle 23, esq Infanta, T 78-4911/4961, F 3-6190; Aeroflot, Calle 23, No 64, T 70-6292,

F 33-3288. Iberia, T 33-5064/5060, F 33-5041/2; Mexicana, T 33-3531/2, F 33-3729, Viasa, T 33-3130/3228, F 33-3611. Lacsa has an office in the *Habana Libre* which sells tickets for cash only, T 33-3114/3187, F 33-3728. If staying at Old Havana, allow sufficient time if you need to visit an airline office before going to the airport.

● **Clothing**

Generally informal. Summer calls for the very lightest clothing. A jersey and light raincoat or umbrella are needed in the cooler months.

● **Embassies and consulates**

All in Miramar, unless stated otherwise: **Argentina**, Calle 36 No 511 between 5 and 7, T 33-2972/2549, F 33-2140; **Austria**, Calle 4 No 101, on the corner with 1st, T 33-2825, F 33-1235; **Belgium**, Av 5 No 7408 on the corner with 76, T 33-2410, F 33-1318; **Brazil**, Calle 16 No 503 between 5 and 7, T 33-2139/2786, F 33-2328; **Canada**, Calle 30 No 518, on the corner with 7, T 33-2516/2527, F 33-2044; **UK**, Calle 34, No 702, T 33-1771, F 33-8104 or 33-9214 Commercial Section, open Mon-Fri 0800-1530; **Germany**, Calle 28 No 313, between 3 and 5, T 33-2539, F 33-1586; **France**, Calle 14 No 312 between 3 and 5, T 33-2132/2080, F 33-1439; **Mexico**, Calle 12 No 518 between 5 and 7, T 33-2383/2498, F 33-2719, open 0900-1200, Mon-Fri; **Netherlands**, Calle 8 No 307 between 3 and 5, T 33-2511/2, F 33-2059; **Peru**, Calle 36 No 109 between 1 and 3, T 33-2477, F 33-2636; **Sweden**, Av 31, No 1411, T 33-2563, F 33-1194; **Switzerland**, Av 5, No 2005, T 33-2611, F 33-1148; **Venezuela**, Calle 36A No 704 corner of 42, T 33-2662, F 33-2773; **Greece**, Av 5, No 7802, Esq 78, T 29-2395, 21-5060, 29-0054. In Vedado, **The US Interests Section** of the Swiss Embassy, Calzada between L and M, T 33-3550/9; **Italy**, Paseo No 606 between 25 and 27, T 33-3334, F 33-3416; **Japan**, Calle N No 62, on the corner with 15, T 33-3454/3508. In the old city, **Spain**, Cárcel No 51 on the corner of Zulueta, T 33-8025-6, F 33-8006; **Denmark** and **Norway** are at the Prado No 20, Apartment 4C, T 33-8128, F 33-8127.

● **Hours of business**

Government offices: 0830-1230 and 1330-1730 Mon to Fri. Some offices open on Sat morning. Banks: 0830-1200, 1330-1500 Mon to Fri, 0830-1030 Sat. Shops: 1230-1930 Mon to Sat, although some open in the morning one day a week. Hotel tourist (hard currency) shops generally open 1000-2100.

● **Official time**
Eastern Standard Time, 5 hrs behind GMT; Daylight Saving Time, 4 hrs behind GMT.

● **Photography**
It is forbidden to photograph military or police installations or personnel, port, rail or airport facilities.

● **Public Holidays**
Liberation Day (1 Jan), Victory of Armed Forces (2 Jan), Labour Day (1 May), Revolution Day (26 July and the day either side), Beginning of War of Independence (10 Oct).

● **Sale of possessions, gifts, etc**
Tourists willing to take risks can earn extra spending money by taking along consumer goods to sell to Cubans. It has been reported that you need to guard your clothes more closely than your camera and a T-shirt is greatly appreciated as a gift (you may be asked to sign it, to show that it *is* a gift). Cubans are now rationed to one pair of new trousers a year. Any foreigner sitting in the Parque Central with a flight bag at his side is soon approached by buyers. One can usually get about 3 times what was paid for the articles. Also appreciated as gifts are household medicines, cosmetics and, for children, pens, chewing gum and sweets. Soap and cigarette lighters are in short supply. It's inadvisable to bring in too many of a single item or you may have trouble at Customs. Walking in Havana involves a constant escort of small children, or even teenagers, asking for chewing gum and small change. You need to be equipped with pockets full of little gifts or a very hard heart.

● **Security**
In general the Cuban people are very hospitable. The island is generally safer than many of its Caribbean and Latin neighbours, but certain precautions should be taken. Visitors should never lose sight of their luggage or leave valuables in hotel rooms (most hotels have safes). Do not leave your things on the beach when going swimming. Pickpocketing and purse-snatching on buses is quite common in Havana (especially the old city) and Santiago. Also beware of bagsnatching by passing cyclists. In the capital, street lighting is poor so care is needed when walking or cycling the city at night. A wire across a dark street will send you flying and your bicycle will be stolen. The police are very helpful and thorough, but you may have to insist on a written police report for insurance purposes. In the event of a crime, make a note of where it happened. Visitors should remember that the government permitting Cubans to hold dollars legally has not altered the fact that the local population will often do anything to get hard currency, from simply asking for money or dollar-bought goods, to mugging. Latest reports suggest that foreigners will be offered almost anything on the street 'from cigars to cocaine to chicas'. Prostitution is common, beware of AIDS. Cubans who offer their services (whether sexual or otherwise) in return for dollars are known as *jineteros*, or *jineteras* (because they 'ride on the back' of the tourists). Take extra passport photos and keep them separate from your passport. You will waste a lot of time getting new photos if your passport is stolen.

● **Shopping**
Essentials, rent and most food, are fairly cheap; non-essentials are very expensive. Everything is very scarce, although imported toiletries and camera film (Kodak print only, from Mexico), are reasonably priced. Take your own toilet paper. A sandwich in a restaurant or bar costs about US$4, a coffee costs US$1. The price of a bottle of rum ranges from US$2 for poor quality to US$4-5 for a 5-year-old rum. In the dollar shops prices range from US$5-7 for 3-5-year-old rum. A beer costs US$0.75-1.50 in both restaurants and shops. Compared with much of Latin America, Cuba is expensive for the tourist, but compared with many Caribbean islands it is not dear.

● **Tipping**
Tipping customs have changed after a period when visitors were not allowed to tip in hotels and restaurants. It is now definitely recommended. Tip a small amount (not a percentage) in the same currency as you pay for the bill (typically US$1-2 on a US$25 meal). At times taxi drivers will expect (or demand) a tip. Turistaxis are not tipped, but the drivers still appreciate a tip. If you want to express gratitude, offer a packet of American cigarettes. Leaving basic items in your room, like toothpaste, deodorant, paper, pens, is recommended.

● **Voltage**
110-230 Volts. 3 phase 60 cycles, AC. Plugs are usually of the American type, an adaptor for European appliances can be bought at the Intur shop at the *Habana Libre*. In some tourist

hotel developments, however, European plugs are used, check in advance if it is important to you.

● **Weights and measures**
The metric system is compulsory, but exists side by side with American and old Spanish systems.

ON DEPARTURE

It is advisable to book your flight out of Cuba before actually going there as arranging it there can be time-consuming. Furthermore, it is essential to reconfirm onward flights as soon as you arrive in Cuba, otherwise you will lose your reservation. Independent travellers should have tickets stamped in person, not by an agent and, for Mexico, should make sure they have a Mexican tourist card and that Cuban departure tax is collected. The airport departure tax is US$12.

ACCOMMODATION

● **Hotels**
Accommodation for your first few days should be booked in advance of travelling. You have to fill in an address on your tourist card and if you leave it blank you will be directed to the reservations desk at the airport, which is time consuming. A voucher from your travel agent to confirm arrangements is advisable. It is best to book hotel rooms before visiting any of the provinces otherwise you may have to return to Havana. This can be done abroad through travel agencies, accredited government agencies, or through Turismo Buró desks in main hotels. It's a good idea to book hotel rooms generally before noon. In the peak season, Dec to Feb, it is essential to book in advance. At other times it is possible to book at hotel reception. Prices given in the text are high season (15 Dec-15 Mar); low season prices are about 20% lower. After 31 Aug many hotels go into hibernation and offer limited facilities, eg no restaurant, no swimming pool. All hotels are owned by the government, solely or in joint ventures with foreign partners.

● **Camping**
Official campsites are opening up all over the island; they are usually in nice surroundings and are good value. One such is El Abra International Campsite halfway between Havana and Varadero, which has extensive facilities (car hire, bicycles, mopeds, horses, watersports, tennis etc) and organizes excursions.

Note Cuba is geared more to package tourism than to independent visitors and this has become more evident with the local petrol shortage. Camping out on the beach or in a field is forbidden. Lodging with a family is possible (at US$10-25 per day) but technically illegal at time of writing. We have received many recommendations for places to stay but are unable to publish names and addresses of private homes and restaurants at this stage. The rules may change soon, with private operators permitted, subject to health and hygiene regulations and incorporation into the tax system. Because of rationing it is difficult to buy food in the shops. Also be prepared for long waits for everything: buses, cinemas, restaurants, shops etc. Service has improved somewhat in Havana tourist facilities with foreign investment and the passage of new legislation allowing employees to be sacked if they are not up to the job. Officials in the tourist industry, tour guides, agencies and hotel staff are generally efficient and helpful 'beyond the call of duty'. Take care with unofficial guides or 'friends' you make; if they take you to a bar or nightclub or restaurant you will be expected to pay for them and pay in dollars. This chapter catalogues a great many difficulties for the independent traveller, but if on a package, with a couple of days in Havana and a few days on the beach, the visitor should have no problems at all. Similarly, if travelling independently in a rented vehicle, there should be no problems.

FOOD AND DRINK

Visitors should remember that eating is often a problem and plan ahead. It is generally impossible to have an evening meal and go on to a concert or the theatre (performances start at 2030 or 2100 in Havana).

Breakfast can be particularly slow although this is overcome in the larger hotels who generally have buffets (breakfast US$3, lunch and dinner US$10-20). If not eating at a buffet, service, no matter what standard of restaurant or hotel, can be very slow (even if you are the only customers). Look out for the *oferta especial* in small hotels which gives guests a 25% discount on buffet meals in larger hotels. Also, the 'all-you-can-eat' vouchers for buffets in tourist hotels do not have to be used in the hotel where bought. Breakfast and one other meal may be sufficient if you fill in with street or 'dollar shop' snacks.

In Havana the peso food situation is dire. Outside Havana, including Havana province, shortages are not so bad. Self-catering is extremely difficult as supermarkets (as opposed to *Diplomercados*) are not accessible without ration cards. The dollar shops have imported supplies. The opening of farmers' markets improved food supply gradually during 1995-96. Cubans are rationed to one small round bread a day and local products such as rice, beans, sugar and coffee, although available to dollar holders are severely rationed to Cuban families. Milk is allowed only for children up to the age of 7; fish is a luxury and beef an impossibility.

For vegetarians the choice is very limited, normally only cheese, sandwiches, spaghetti and omelettes. Generally, although restaurants have improved in the last few years, the food in Cuba is not very exciting or enjoyable. There is little variety in the menu and menu items are frequently unavailable. Always check restaurant prices in advance and then your bill. Private restaurants are better; these are now licensed, subjected to health inspections and regulations, and taxed, which may limit their scope in the short term. The national dish is *arrozmoro* (rice mixed with black beans), roast pork and yucca (manioc). Salads in restaurants are mixed vegetables which are slightly pickled and not to everyone's taste. The local beer, Hateuy, is worth trying, named after an Indian chief ruling when the Spanish arrived.

GETTING AROUND

AIR TRANSPORT

Cubana de Aviación services between most of the main towns. From Havana to Camagüey (US$52 one way), Holguín (US$60), Baracoa (US$79), Guantánamo (US$73), Manzanillo (US$60), Moa (US$73), Nueva Gerona/Isla de Juventud (US$17), Bayamo (US$60), Ciego de Avila (US$44), Las Tunas (US$57), and Santiago (US$68); also flights to Cayo Coco, Varadero, all have airports. Return fare is twice the single fare. Tourists must pay airfares in US$; it is advisable to prebook flights at home as demand is very heavy. It is difficult to book flights from one city to another when you are not at the point of departure, except from Havana, the computer is not able to cope. Airports are usually a long way from the towns, so extra transport costs will be necessary. Delays are common.

Although theoretically possible to get a scheduled flight as listed above, it is often only possible for tourists to travel on excursions: day trips or packages with flights, accommodation, meals and sightseeing.

LAND TRANSPORT
● Motoring
Petrol, if you can find it, costs US$1 per litre and must be paid for in US$. If possible, get the rental company to fill the car with fuel, otherwise your first day will be spent looking for petrol. Get clear directions on which filling stations will serve foreigners: some accept only pesos, some do not have 'Especial' fuel, some have no electricity to pump the fuel. Hiring a car is recommended, in view of difficulties of getting seats on buses and trains and you can save a considerable amount of time but it is the most expensive form of travel. Breakdowns are not unknown, in which case you may be stuck with your rented car many kilometres from the nearest place that will accept dollars to help you. Be careful about picking up hitch-hikers, although it can be an interesting and pleasant way of meeting Cubans.

● Car hire
Through state rental companies at the International Airport, *Hotels Capri* and *Victoria* in Havana, at *Tropicoco Beach Club*, Santa María del Mar (T 2531), at Varadero beach (eg *Paradiso* and *Puntarena Resort*, *Barlovento*, *Villa Tortuga*, *Club Herradura* and others), *Hoteles Ancón* and *Costasur*, *Motel Las Cuevas*, *Hotel Zaza*, in Trinidad province, *Hotel Porto Santo*, Baracoa and an increasing number of other hotels (see text). Maximum 4 passengers allowed; vehicles can be returned to any depot but you will be charged extra. Minimum US$45 a day (or US$60 for a/c) with free mileage, and US$9 a day optional insurance. The overall cost may work out at around US$65-70 a day. Buggies are available, mostly for use on the beach, at US$30 a day plus US$0.15 each km after the first 100 km. Visa, Mastercard, Eurocard, Banamex, JCB and Carnet accepted for the rental, or US$250 deposit; you must also present your passport and home driving licence. Fly and drive packages can be booked from abroad, eg in the UK, Journey Latin America, T 0181-747-8315, can organize rentals of Suzuki Samurai jeeps (or equivalent).

● Bus
The local word for bus is *guagua*. The urban bus fare throughout Cuba is 10 centavos and

the exact fare is required. In the rush hours they are filled to more than capacity, making it hard to get on if you have managed to get on. Buses are running but fuel shortages limit services. Tickets can only be bought in pesos Cubanos. In busy areas there is an horrendous queuing system, which you are unlikely to get through without assistance. When entering the bus station, purchase a 5 centavo ticket with a number. This is your place in the queue. As each bus becomes available, a man calls out numbers in batches of 5 (eg 405-410-415 etc). If your number is included, push to the front, wave frantically, and the ticket is exchanged for a pass, a guaranteed place (not necessarily a seat!). Cubans queue professionally and make a profit out of selling numbers near the top of the queue and passes. One traveller obtained his pass and his fare with a Mexican T shirt (US$3) after finding his number was 400 down the line. Dollars will also do.

● **Bus reservations**
Tickets between towns must be purchased in advance from: Oficina Reservaciones Pasajes, Calle 21, esq 4, Vedado (main booking office for buses and trains from Havana to anywhere in the country, one-way only, open Mon to Fri 1200-1745, organized chaos); Plazoleta de la Virgen del Camino, San Miguel del Padrón; Calzada 10 de Octubre y Carmen, Centro; Terminal de Omnibus Nacional, Boyeros y 19 de Mayo (all in Havana). Look for notices in the window for latest availabilities, find out who is last in the queues (separate queues for buses and trains, sometimes waiting numbers issued, see above, **Bus**), and ask around for what is the best bet. Maximum 3 tickets sold per person. Seat reservations are only possible on a few long distance routes (eg Havana-Trinidad Express) but you still need pesos Cubanos or a Cuban entrepreneur to obtain one.

● **Taxis**
The best you can do is avoid the most expensive tourist taxis. See **Transport** under Havana. **Dollar tourist taxis** can be hired for driving around; you pay for the distance, not for waiting time. On short routes, fares start at US$1. Airport to Havana (depending on destination), US$16-18, to Playas del Este US$25, to Varadero US$71; Havana to Varadero US$65; Varadero airport to Varadero hotels US$13; Santiago de Cuba airport to *Hotel Las Américas* US$8, to *Balcón del Caribe* US$5. Taxis can work out cheaper than going on organized tours, eg US$60 pp to tour the

Viñales area but US$25 (206 km) Havana-Viñales by taxi, US$15 (183 km) Havana-Pinar del Río. Shorter journeys are comparatively more expensive: Pinar del Río-Viñales US$10 (23 km). Cubans are not allowed to carry foreigners in their vehicles, but they do; private taxis are considerably cheaper, eg airport to Havana centre US$8-12, from Havana to Santa María del Mar beach US$8-10, from Santiago to the airport US$3.

● **Train**
Recommended whenever possible, although delays and breakdowns must be expected. Be at station at least 30 mins before scheduled departure time, you have to queue to reconfirm your seat and have your ticket stamped. Fares are reasonable, eg US$13 to Sancti Spiritus (for Trinidad), 9 hrs. See above for latest booking procedure. Alternatively *Ferrotur*, Calles Arsenal y Egido, near Estación Central, T 62-1770, Havana, very helpful (and escort you and your luggage to the train), or at the Tourist Desk in the *Habana Libre*, *Inglaterra* and *Plaza* hotels sell train tickets to foreigners, in dollars; eg to Santiago de Cuba US$70 return, US$35 one way. Tourists will find it is only possible to pay for rail tickets in dollars. See the text above for details. Bicycles can be carried as an express item only.

NB In major bus and train terminals, ask if there are special arrangements for tourists to buy tickets without queuing; payment would then be in dollars. You can waste hours queuing and waiting for public transport. Travel between provinces is usually booked solid several days or weeks in advance. If you are on a short trip you may do better to go on a package tour with excursions. Trains and some buses are air-conditioned, you may need a warm jersey. All train carriages are smokers; there is no food service.

COMMUNICATIONS

● **Language**
Spanish, with local variants in pronunciation and vocabulary. English is becoming more commonly used; it is a university entrance requirement and encouraged by the influx of Canadian tourists.

● **Language study**
Any Cuban embassy will give details, or, in Santiago, contact Cecilia Suárez, c/o Departamiento de Idiomas, Universidad de Oriente, Av Patricio Lumumba, Código Postal 90500, Santiago de Cuba. Spanish courses at the

University of Havana cost US$300-350 depending on the level and begin the first Mon of every month. For language combined with social study, contact Projecto Cultural EL1, PO Box 12227, 6000 Luzern, Switzerland, T/F 4141360 8764, 3-week courses all year at the University of Havana.

● **Postal services**

When possible correspondence to Cuba should be addressed to post office boxes (Apartados), where delivery is more certain. Stamps can only be bought at Post Offices, or at certain hotels. All postal services, national and international, have been described as appalling. Letters to Europe, for instance, take at least 4-5 weeks, up to 3 months. Many Cubans will stop you in the street and ask you to bring letters out of Cuba for them. Telegraphic services are adequate. You can send telegrams from all post offices in Havana. Telegrams to Britain cost 49 centavos a word. The night letter rate is 3.85 pesos for 22 words.

● **Telecommunications**

Local telephone calls can be made from public telephones for 5 centavos. A telephone call to Europe costs US$18 for the first 3 mins, US$6/minute thereafter. The cost of phoning the USA is US$4.50/minute from Havana, US$3 from Varadero. Many hard currency hotels and airports (including Havana departure lounge and Santiago) have telephone offices where international calls can be made at high prices. No 'collect' calls allowed and only cash accepted. Collect calls to some places, including London, are possible from private Cuban telephones. At least one Havana hotel, the *Nacional*, can arrange for you to direct dial foreign countries from your room. Telephone sockets (for computer users) are standard US type. The cost of these calls is high, connections are hard to make and you will be cut off frequently. In 1994 the US Federal Communications Commission approved applications from 5 US companies to provide direct telephone services to Cuba and for AT&T to expand its existing service.

MEDIA

● **Newspapers**

Granma, mornings except Sun and Mon; *Trabajadores*, Trade Union weekly; and *Juventud Rebelde*, now also only weekly. *Granma* has a weekly English edition, *Granma International*, main offices: Avenida General Suárez y Territorial, Plaza de la Revolución, La Habana 6, T 70-8218, Telex: 0511 355; in UK 928 Bourges Boulevard, Peterborough PE1 2AN. *El País* is the Mexican edition of the Spanish newspaper, available daily, 2 days late. Foreign (not US) newspapers are sometimes on sale at the telex centre in *Habana Libre* and in the *Riviera* (also telex centre, open 0800-2000). The previous day's paper is available during the week. Weekend editions on sale Tues.

TOURIST INFORMATION

● **Local tourist office**

The Government has a decentralized system for receptive tourism and there is a large number of state-owned travel agencies/tour companies, which cooperate fully with each other and with the tourism bureaux in the major hotels. Their main function is to sell excursions and package tours. Individual tourism is made complicated and frustrating.

● **Tourist offices overseas**

The Cuba Tourist Office also has offices in: **Canada**, 440 Blvd René Levesque, Suite 1402, Montréal, Quebec H2Z 1V7, T (514) 875-8004/5, F 875-8006; 55 Queen St E, Suite 705, Toronto, M5C 1R5, T (416) 362-0700/2, F 362-6799. **France**, 280 Bd Raspail, 75014 Paris, T 14-538-90-10, F 14-538-99-30; **Italy**, Via General Fara 30, Terzo Plano, 20124 Milan, T 66981463, F 6690042; **Spain**, Paseo de la Habana No 28 iro derecha, 28036 Madrid, T 411-3097, F 564-5804; **Switzerland**, Gesellschaststrasse 8, 3012 Berne, Case Postale 52725, T/F 31 3022111; **UK**, 167 High Holborn, London WC1V 6PA, T 01891-880-820, 0171-379-1706, F 0171-379-5455.

Russia, Room 627, Hotel Belgrado, Kutuzovskii 14KB7, Moscow, T 2-48-2454/3262, F 2-43-1125.

Argentina, Paraguay 631, 2° piso A, Buenos Aires, T 311-4198, T 311-5820; **Mexico**, Insurgentes Sur 421 y Aguascalientes, Complejo Aristos, Edificio B, Local 310, México DF 06100, T 574-9651, F 574-9454.

● **Travel agents abroad**

In the UK, agents who sell holidays in Cuba include Regent Holidays, 15 John St, Bristol BS1 2HR, T (0117) 9211711, F (0117) 9254866, ABTA members, holding ATOL and IATA Licences; South American Experience Ltd, 47 Causton St, Pimlico, London SW1P 4AT,

T 0171-976 5511, F 0171-976 6908, ATOL, IATA; Progressive Tours, 12 Porchester Place, Marble Arch, London W2 2BS, T 0171-262 1676, F 0171-724 6941, ABTA, ATOL, IATA. Cubanacan UK Ltd, Skylines, Unit 49, Limeharbour Docklands, London E14 9TS, T 0171-537-7909, F 0171-537-7747. Check with these agents for special deals combined with jazz or film festivals. Cubanacan SA, Calle 148/11 y 13, Playa, Aptdo Postal 16046, Zona 16, Havana, T 7-219-457/200-569/336-006, operates all diving packages (**see p 11**), as well as Veracuba excursions by bus or fly/drive packages; Club Amigo all-inclusives; Servimed health organization for special treatments; Cubacar car hire; Tropicana Club; Pabexpo and ExpoCuba at Havana International Conference Centre. A recommended agent in Eire for assistance with Aeroflot flights is Concorde Travel, T Dublin 763232; Cubatur agent is Cubatravel, T Dublin 713385. See above under **Documents** for Marazul Tours in the USA. If travelling from Mexico, many agencies in the Yucatan peninsula offer packages, very good value and popular with travellers wanting to avoid Mexico City. A 1-week charter air fare on Cubana from Mérida costs US$180 inc visa and airport taxes. From Canada, Air Canada Vacations has year-round packages or air tickets only to Varadero, from economy to first class hotels; Canadian Holidays (division of Canadian Airlines) to Varadero and other destinations inc ecological tour of Sierra Maestra; Alba Tours, year-round packages up to 4 weeks to all parts of the island, or flights only; Magna Holidays books individual travel and custom tours out of Toronto; several more inc Fiesta Sun, Hola Holidays (Cuban) offer individual travel arrangements from Canada. From Venezuela, Ideal Tours, Centro Capriles, Plaza Venezuela, T (010 582) 793-0037/1822, have 4-day or 8-day package tours depending on the season, flight only available. From Jamaica, UTAS Tours offer weekends in Cuba for US$199 inc flight, hotel etc, PO Box 429, Montego Bay, T (809) 979-0684, F 979-3465.

● **Local travel agents**

Several state-owned tour companies offer day trips or excursion packages inc accommodation to many parts of the island as well as tours of colonial and modern Havana. Examples (one day, except where indicated): Viñales, inc tobacco and rum factories, US$39; Guamá, US$39; Cayo Coco (by air), US$89; Soroa, US$29; Varadero, US$27; Cayo Largo (by air), US$94; Trinidad (by air), US$79; Trinidad and Cienfuegos (2 days), US$109; Santiago de Cuba (by air), US$159 inc 1 night's accommodation. Tours can also be taken from Varadero, eg to Trinidad, US$59 inc lunch; Pinar del Río, 2 days, US$105. Guides speak English, French or German; the tours are generally rec as well-organized and good value. A common complaint from individual tourists is that, when they sign up for day trips and other excursions (eg Cayo Largo), they are not told that actual departure depends on a minimum number of passengers. The situation is made worse by the fact that most tourists are on pre-arranged package tours. They are often subject to long waits on buses and at points of departure and are not informed of delays in departure times. Always ask the organizers when they will know if the trip is on or what the real departure time will be.

● **Maps**
Mapa Turístico de la Habana, Mapa de la Habana Vieja, and similar maps of Santiago de Cuba, Trinidad, Camagüey and Varadero are helpful, but not always available. The best shop for maps of all kinds inc nautical maps is *El Navegante*, Mercaderes entre Obispo y Obrapía in Old Havana.

ACKNOWLEDGEMENTS

The editor is most grateful to Tom Clough for his help in revising and updating this chapter, and to the following for their support and assistance during his visit to Cuba in 1996: Manuel García and Rosendo González, of Publicitur, Havana; Rafael Fernández Moya, of Habaguanex; and special thanks to Dalia Rosales, who made it all possible.

Cayman Islands

THE BRITISH CROWN COLONY of the Cayman Islands consists of Grand Cayman and the sister islands of Cayman Brac and Little Cayman, in the Caribbean Sea. None of the islands has any rivers, but vegetation is luxuriant, the main trees being coconut, thatch palm, seagrape and Australian pine.

HORIZONS

Grand Cayman, the largest of the three islands, lies 150 miles S of Havana, Cuba, about 180 miles WNW of Jamaica and 480 miles S of Miami. Grand Cayman is low-lying, 22 miles long and 4 miles wide, but of the total 76 square miles about half is swamp. A striking feature is the shallow, reef-protected lagoon, North Sound, 40 miles square and the largest area of inland mangrove in the Caribbean. **George Town**, the capital of the islands, is located on the W side of Grand Cayman. **Cayman Brac** (Gaelic for 'bluff') gets its name from the high limestone bluff rising from sea level in the W to a height of 140 feet in the E. The island lies about 89 miles ENE of Grand Cayman. It is about 12 miles long and a little more than a mile wide. **Little Cayman** lies five miles W of Cayman Brac and is 10 miles long and just over a mile wide with its highest point being only 40 feet above sea level. **Owen Island**, an islet off the SW coast of Little Cayman, is uninhabited but visited by picnickers.

The total population of mixed African and European descent is estimated at 31,900, of which nearly 30,000 live on Grand Cayman, most of them in George Town, or the smaller towns of West Bay, Bodden Town, North Side and East End. The population of Cayman Brac has fallen to 2,000. Little Cayman is largely undeveloped with only about 60 residents and frequented by sports fishermen. The Cayman Islands are very exclusive, with strict controls on who is allowed to settle there, although the proportion of Caymanians in the resident population fell from 79% in 1980 to 63% by 1994. Consequently the cost of living is extremely high. On the other hand, petty crime is rare and the islands are well looked after (described as "a very clean sandbank").

National symbols

New national symbols were adopted in 1996 after a ballot of Caymanians' preferences. The national flower is the wild banana orchid, the national tree is the silver thatch palm and the national bird is the Cayman parrot. Postage stamps are to be issued to commemorate their adoption.

HISTORY

The Cayman Islands were first sighted by Columbus in May 1503 when he was blown off course on his way to Hispaniola. He found two small islands (Cayman Brac and Little Cayman) which were full of turtles, and he therefore named the islands Las Tortugas. A 1523 map of the islands referred to them as Lagartos, meaning alligators or large lizards, but by 1530 they were known as the Caymanas after the Carib word for the marine crocodile which also lived there.

The first recorded English visitor was Sir Francis Drake in 1586, who reported that the *caymanas* were edible, but it was the turtles which attracted ships in search of fresh meat for their crews. Overfishing nearly extinguished the turtles from the local waters. The islands were ceded to the English Crown under the Treaty of Madrid in 1670, after the first settlers came from Jamaica in 1661-71 to Little Cayman and Cayman Brac. The first settlements were abandoned after attacks by Spanish privateers, but British privateers often used the Cayman Islands as a base and in the 18th century they became an increasingly popular hideout for pirates, even after the end of legitimate privateering in 1713. In November 1794, a convoy of 10 Jamaican merchantmen was wrecked on the reef in Gun Bay, on the E end of Grand Cayman, but with the help of the local settlers there was no loss of life. Legend has it that there was a member of the Royal Family on board and that

in gratitude for their bravery, King George III decreed that Caymanians should never be conscripted for war service and Parliament legislated that they should never be taxed.

From 1670, the Cayman Islands were dependencies of Jamaica, although there was considerable self-government. In 1832, a legislative assembly was established, consisting of eight magistrates appointed by the Governor of Jamaica and 10 (later increased to 27) elected representatives. In 1959 dependency ceased when Jamaica became a member of the Federation of the West Indies, although the Governor of Jamaica remained the Governor of the Cayman Islands. When Jamaica achieved independence in 1962 the Islands opted to become a direct dependency of the British Crown.

In 1991 a review of the 1972 constitution recommended several constitutional changes to be debated by the Legislative Assembly. The post of Chief Secretary was reinstated in 1992 after having been abolished in 1986. The establishment of the post of Chief Minister was also proposed. However, in November 1992 elections were held for an enlarged Legislative Assembly and the Government was soundly defeated, casting doubt on constitutional reform. The 'National Team' of government critics won 12 of the 15 seats, and independents won the other three, after a campaign opposing the appointment of a Chief Minister and advocating spending cuts. The unofficial leader of the team, Thomas Jefferson, had been the appointed Financial Secretary until March 1992, when he resigned over public spending disputes to fight the election. After the elections Mr Jefferson was appointed Minister and leader of government business; he also holds the portfolios of Tourism, Aviation and Commerce in the Executive Council.

GOVERNMENT

A Governor appointed by the British Crown is the head of Government. The present Constitution came into effect in 1993 and provides for an Executive Council to advise the Governor on administration of the islands. The Council is made up of five Elected and three Official Members and is chaired by the Governor. The former, called Ministers from February 1994, are elected from the 15 elected representatives in the Legislative Assembly and have a range of responsibilities allocated by the Governor, while the latter are the Chief Secretary, the Financial Secretary, and the Attorney General and the Administrative Secretary. The Legislative Assembly may remove a minister from office by nine votes out of the 15. There is no Chief Minister. There have been no political parties since the mid-1960s but politicians organize themselves into teams. The Chief Secretary is the First Official Member of the Executive Council, and acts as Governor in the absence of the Governor.

THE ECONOMY

Structure of production

The original settlers earned their living from the sea, either as turtle fishermen or as crew members on ships around the world. In 1906 more than a fifth of the population of 5,000 was estimated to be at sea, and even in the 1950s the government's annual report said that the main export was of seamen and their remittances the mainstay of the economy. Today the standard of living is high with the highest per capita income in the Caribbean. The islands' economy is based largely on offshore finance and banking, tourism, real estate and construction, a little local industry, and remittances of Caymanians working on ships abroad. Apart from a certain amount of meat, turtle, fish and a few local fruits and vegetables, almost all foodstuffs and other necessities are imported. The cost of living therefore rises in line with that of the main trading partners.

The Cayman Islands is the largest offshore centre in the world. In 1995 there were 550 licensed banks with assets of US$464bn, nearly 32,000 registered companies and 377 offshore insurance companies, with assets of US$4.5bn; the banking sector employs more than a tenth of the labour force.

Cayman Islands: fact file

Geographic

Land area	264 sq km

Demographic

Population (1992)	28,100
annual growth rate (1987-92)	4.2%
urban	100%
rural	0%
density	106.4 per sq km
Religious affiliation	
Presbyterian	35.6%
Church of God	24.9%
Birth rate per 1,000 (1990)	17.9
	(world av 27.1)

Education and Health

Life expectancy at birth	77.1 years
Infant mortality rate	
per 1,000 live births (1990)	6.1
Physicians (1990)	1 per 669 persons
Hospital beds	1 per 384 persons
Literate males (over 15)	97.5%
Literate females (over 15)	97.6%

Economic

GNP (1989 market prices)	US$357mn
GNP per capita	US$13,770
Public external debt (1988)	US$185mn
Tourism receipts (1990)	US$326mn
Radio	1 per 1.5 persons
Television	1 per 5.7 persons
Telephone	1 per 1.4 persons

Employment

Population economically active (1991)	
	16,700
% of labour force in	
agriculture	1.4
mining, manufacturing	
and public utilities	3.2
construction	16.0
trade, hotels and restaurants	30.2

Source Encyclopaedia Britannica

Legislation has been approved for the establishment of a stock exchange. It will initially focus on a listing facility to attract mutual funds. There is also a large shipping registry, with 920 ships on the register in 1996, with a gross tonnage of 595,087.

Tourism revenues have risen sharply in recent years. The slowdown in the US economy in 1991, however, brought a sharp drop in air arrivals and hotel occupancy fell to 60% from 68% in 1990, although cruise ship visitors soared by 31% to 474,747, with the introduction of calls by the cruise liner *Ecstasy* which carries 2,500 passengers. Since 1991 the market has improved. By 1995 cruise ship passenger arrivals were 682,885. Stopover visitors numbered a record 361,444 in 1995 having risen steadily each year. Tourism provides about 35% of jobs and 70% of gross domestic product. Spending by visitors in 1995 was estimated at US$40mn by cruise ship passengers and US$433mn by stopover visitors. In 1995 a new 350-room Westin hotel was built and completed for the winter season 1995/96. The largest hotel on the island and the first new beach hotel built since 1989, it is called the *Casuarina Resort*.

Recent trends

There was a rapid rise in construction activity in the 1980s to meet demand and tourist accommodation doubled in 10 years. As a result, spectacular rates of economic growth were recorded: 15.6% in 1987, 15.2% in 1988, 10.6% in 1989, slowing to 8.0% in 1990. There was full employment and labour had to be imported to meet demand. The slowdown of the 1990s brought a huge fall in public and private construction projects and unemployment rose to a record 7.6% by 1992. The government budget went into deficit, the public debt rose from US$7mn at end-1990 to US$21.3mn at end-1991, the loss-making, state-owned airline, Cayman Airways accumulated a deficit of US$32.7mn by end-1991 and the Government proposed building a US$32mn hospital. The new Government elected in 1992 called for a reduction in spending, cancelled the hospital project, cut the size of the civil service and recapitalized Cayman Airways. By 1993 Cayman Airways had reduced its debt to less than US$6mn, and by closing unprofitable routes and cutting staff and other costs it managed to reduce its loss to about US$1mn, with all routes meeting their direct costs.

In 1994/95 the Government had to cope with the economic burden of Cuban migrants (see **Cuba** chapter). The costs of maintaining the Tent City with hundreds of refugees had absorbed about 1.5% of the annual budget, or around US$3 million, by March 1995. Over a hundred Cubans were granted residence visas because of Caymanian family connections, but several hundred more were transferred to the US base at Guantánamo, for which the USA charged a daily fee of US$10 per head. The EU awarded the Cayman Islands a grant of ECU95,000 (US$122,600 eq) for food and medicines for the Cubans which remained at the camp on the island.

FAUNA AND FLORA

There are around 200 species of birds, including the Antillean grackle, the smooth-billed ani, the green-backed heron, the yellow-crowned night heron and many other heron species, the snowy egret, the common ground dove, the bananaquit and the Cayman parrot. The endangered West Indian whistling duck can be seen on Grand Cayman and Little Cayman. If you are interested in birdwatching, go to the mosquito control dykes on the West Bay peninsula of Grand Cayman, or walk to the Cistern at East End. The previous Governor is a keen birdwatcher and in 1993 he set up a fund to establish the **Governor Michael Gore Bird Sanctuary** on 3½ acres of wetland on Grand Cayman, where you can see 60 local species. There are nesting colonies of the red-footed booby and the

Sir Turtle

Turtles have always played a large part in the islands' folklore, dating back to 1503 when Columbus named them Las Tortugas. Generations of sailors stocked up on turtle meat while in the area and today there is a turtle farm, designed to replenish wild stocks and satisfy demand for the table. In 1963 Suzy Soto designed the 'Sir Turtle' logo, of a peg-leg, swashbuckling, pirate turtle. She sold it in the 1970s to the Department of Tourism for the grand sum of US$1, and it is now used intensively as a mascot and symbol for the Cayman Islands. There is even a racehorse in the UK called 'Sir Turtle', a hurdler sponsored by the Department of Tourism's British office and owned by Adrian Pratt, who had a good time on holiday in the islands.

magnificent frigate bird on Little Cayman and a walk across Cayman Brac is rewarding. There is a Parrot Reserve on Cayman Brac. *Birds of the Cayman Islands*, published by Bradley, is a photographic record; it costs £22.

Indigenous animals on the islands are few. The most common are the agouti, a few non-poisonous snakes, some iguana and other small lizards, freshwater turtle, the hickatee and two species of tree frogs. *Oncidium calochilum*, a rare orchid, indigenous to Grand Cayman with a small yellow flower about half an inch long, is found only in the rocky area off Frank Sound Drive. Several other orchid species have been recorded as endemic but are threatened by construction and orchid fanciers. There is protection under international and local laws for several indigenous species, including sea turtles, iguanas, Cayman parrots, orchids and marine life. For a full description of the islands' flora see George R Proctor, *Flora of the Cayman Islands*, Kew Bulletin Additional Series XI, HMSO (1984), 834 pp, which list 21 endemic plant taxa including some which are rare, endangered or possibly extinct.

The National Botanic Park, now renamed the **Queen Elizabeth II Botanic Park** (officially opened by the Queen in 1994), is off Frank Sound Road, Grand Cayman. A mile-long trail has been cleared and an entrance garden created. Plans have been drawn up for a Heritage Garden, with endemic plants within the park. Over 200 plants have been labelled so far, several of which are rare. Orchids bloom in May-June and there are breeding areas for the Grand Cayman Blue Iguana, the Grand Cayman parrot and the Cayman anole lizard. There is a Visitor Centre, café, information desk and giftshop and a typical Caymanian cottage and garden has been built (T 947 9462, F 947 7873).

Several animal sanctuaries have been established, most of which are RAMSAR sites where no hunting or collecting of any species is allowed. On Grand Cayman there are sanctuaries at Booby Cay, Meagre Bay Pond and Colliers Bay Pond; on Cayman Brac at the ponds near the airport and on Little Cayman at Booby Road and Rookery, Tarpon Lake and the Wearis Bay Wetland, stretching E along the S coast to the Easterly Wetlands.

DIVING AND MARINE LIFE

The Cayman Islands are world-famous for their underwater scenery. There are tropical fish of all kinds in the waters surrounding the islands, especially in the coral reefs, and green turtles (*chelonia mydas*) are now increasing in numbers, having been deliberately restocked by excess hatchings at the Grand Cayman Turtle Farm. A project at the Turtle Farm to reintroduce the endangered Kemp's ridley species of turtle has shown initial success with some reproduction in captivity.

Since 1986, a Marine Parks plan has been implemented to preserve the beauty and marine life of the islands. Permanent moorings have been installed along the W coast of Grand Cayman where there is concentrated diving, and also outside the marine parks in order to encourage diving boats to disperse and lessen anchor damage to the reefs. There are now 205 permanent mooring sites around all three islands, 119 around Grand Cayman (32 on the North Wall), 41 around Cayman Brac and 45 around Little Cayman. These parks and protected areas are clearly marked and strictly enforced by a full-time Marine Conservation Officer who has the power to arrest offenders. Make sure you check all rules and regulations as there have been several prosecutions and convictions for offences such as taking conch or lobsters. The import of spearguns or speargun parts and their use without a licence is banned. Divers and snorkellers must use a flag attached to a buoy when outside safe swimming areas. For further information call Natural Resources, T 949 8469.

Many of the better reefs and several wrecks are found in water shallow enough to require only mask, snorkel and fins; the swimming is easy and the fish are friendly. However, each island has a wall going down to extraordinary depths: the N wall of Cayman Brac drops from 60 to 14,000 feet, while the S wall drops to 18,000 feet. The deepest known point in the Caribbean is the Cayman Trench, 40 miles S of Cayman Brac, where soundings have indicated a depth of 24,724 feet. *The Cayman Divers Guide* illustrates the major dive sites on all three islands with a fish index and photo review.

The dive-tourism market is highly developed in the Cayman Islands and there is plenty of choice, but is frequently described as a cattle market with dive boats taking very large parties. Many companies offer full services to certified divers as well as courses designed to introduce scuba diving to novices; there are several highly qualified instructor-guides. There is a firm limit of a depth of 110 feet for visiting divers, regardless of training and experience and the 69 member companies of the CIWOA will not allow you to exceed that. The best months for diving are April-October. A complete selection of diving and fishing tackle, underwater cameras and video equipment is available for hire. The tourist office has a full price list for all operators. There is also the liveaboard *Cayman Aggressor III* (US$1,495/week all-inclusive), which accommodates 18 divers and cruises around Grand Cayman and Little Cayman. Contact Aggressor Fleet Limited, PO Drawer K, Morgan City, LA 70381, or PO Box 1882G, Grand Cayman, T 949 5551, 1-800-348-2628, (504) 385 2416, F (504) 384 0817. A smaller liveaboard taking 10 divers maximum (US$1,295-1,595/week all-inclusive) is the *Little Cayman Diver II*, which operates only around Little Cayman, T 1-800-458-BRAC, (813) 932-1993, F (813) 935-2250, PO Box 280058, Tampa, FL33682-0058.

BEACHES AND WATERSPORTS

The beaches of the Cayman Islands are said to be the best in the Caribbean. Various companies offer glass-bottomed boats, sailing, snorkelling, windsurfing, water skiing, water tours and a host of other activities. You can hire wave runners, aqua trikes and paddlecats, take banana rides and go parasailing. When waterskiing, there must be a minimum of two people in the boat so that one person can look out for hazards. There is year-round deep sea game fishing for blue marlin, white marlin, wahoo, yellow fin tuna and smaller varieties, and shore-fishing in all three islands.

FESTIVALS

Pirates' Week is the islands' national festival and takes place in the last week of

October. Parades, regattas, fishing tournaments and treasure hunts are all part of the celebrations, which commemorate the days when the Cayman Islands were the haunt of pirates and buccaneers (T 949 5078). **Batabano** is Grand Cayman's costume carnival weekend, which takes place in the last week of April or beginning of May. Cayman Brac has a similar celebration, known as **Brachanal**, which takes place on the following Saturday. Everyone is invited to dress up and participate, and there are several competitions. At Easter there is a regatta with several sailing classes, power boat races and windsurfing. The **Queen's Birthday** is celebrated in mid-June with a full-dress uniform parade, marching bands and a 21-gun salute. **Million Dollar Month** during June is when fishermen from all over the world come to compete in this month-long tournament (T 949 5587). Also in June, **National Aviation Week** attracts private pilots and flight demonstrations over Seven Mile Beach.

GRAND CAYMAN

Grand Cayman is a prosperous island with a very British feel. Driving is on the left and the roads are in good order. The island is green with luxuriant vegetation, especially at the E end where there are pastures and grazing cows. North Sound is a 40-square mile lagoon with mangroves, although dredging schemes and urban growth threaten the mangrove habitat and the reefs. Some low-key but sophisticated development has taken place along the N coast around Cayman Kai, a very attractive area with lovely beaches and good swimming and snorkelling. Most of the tourist development, however, is along Seven Mile Beach on West Bay, where there are hotels, condominiums, clubs, sports facilities, banks, restaurants and supermarkets.

Diving and marine life

Snorkelling and dive sites abound all round the island and include shallow dives for beginners as well as highly challenging and deep dives for the experienced. Off the W coast there are three wrecks, arches, tunnels, caves, canyons and lots of reef sites close to shore which can be enjoyed by snorkellers and divers. Along the S coast the coral reefs are rich and varied with depths ranging from 15 feet to thousands of feet. The East End wall has pinnacles, tunnels and a coral formation known as The Maze, a 500-foot coral formation of caverns, chimneys, arches and crevices. There are several wrecks here also. Along the N coast you can dive the North Wall. Near Rum Point Channel experienced divers can dive the Grand Canyon, where depths start at 70 feet. The canyons, collapsed reefs, are 150 feet wide in places. Other sites in this area towards Palmetto Point include the aptly-named Eagle Ray Pass, Tarpon Alley and Sting Ray City. Sting Ray City is a popular local phenomenon, where it is possible to swim with and observe large groups of extremely tame rays. Sting Ray City is better dived but half a mile away is the sandbar where sting rays also congregate, usually over 30 at a time. The water here is only 1-3 feet deep and crystal clear, so you hop out of your boat and the rays brush past you waiting to be fed. Their mouths are beneath their head and the rays, 3 feet across, swim into your arms to be fed on squid. A glass bottom boat leaves from the Rum Point Club to the sandbar and a nearby reef, 1100-1230, 1500-1630, US$25, T 949 9098. From Morgan's Harbour boats charge US$30.

The Tourist Office lists 32 dive operations on Grand Cayman, offering a wide range of courses and dive sites. Many are at more than one location, attached to hotels. All are of a high standard but you may want to make your choice according to the number of divers per boat. The most popular and accessible dive sites are off South Sound or North West Point, where the wall or mini walls are close to shore and an easy swim. Boat dives are to the many sites along Seven Mile Beach or the North Wall, which is much more dramatic but generally a

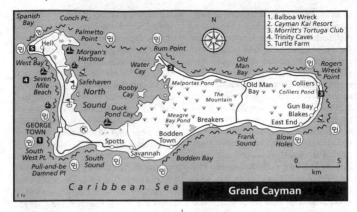

Grand Cayman

little rougher. Prices for a certification course start at US$280, rising to US$400; for qualified divers, a 2-tank dive costs US$50-65 and a Stingray City dive US$40-50. Snorkelling trips are also available, US$20-37.

An additional refinement: Atlantis Research Submersibles Ltd, PO Box 1043GT, Grand Cayman, T 949 8296, F 949 8574, operates a 20-foot research submarine, taking 2 passengers (fare US$275 pp, 5 dives a day Monday-Saturday) to the 800-foot-deep Cayman Wall or to the wreck of the *Kirk Pride* at 780 feet. A larger submarine with room for 48 passengers is operated by Atlantis Submarine, PO Box 1043GT, Grand Cayman, T 949 7700; fares are US$69 for a 1-hour day or night dive (children 4-12 half price), both to 100 feet along Cayman Wall. For US$29 you can take a 1-hour ride in *Seaworld Explorer*, an underwater observatory which feels like a submarine but you are down only 4 feet. A diver will attract fish within view by feeding them (T 949 8534, F 949 7538, PO Box 1544).

There are at least 14 companies on Grand Cayman offering **fishing**. The Tourist Office can give you a full list with prices, which depend on the type of boat you choose. Deep sea fishing boats can be chartered for a half day (US$350-600) or full day (US$475-1,000). Reef and

bone fishing is about US$250-500 for a full day including all equipment, bait and lunch.

Beaches and watersports

West Bay Beach, now known as Seven Mile Beach, has dazzling white sand and is lined by hotels and tall Australian pines. Beaches on the E and N coasts are equally good, and are protected by an offshore barrier reef. On the N coast, at the *Cayman Kai Beach Resort,* there is a superb public beach with changing facilities; from here you can snorkel along the reef to Rum Point. The beaches around Rum Point are recommended for peace and quiet but Red Sail Sports at Rum Point also ensure lots of entertainment, with wind surfers, sail boats, wave runners and water skiing as well as glass bottomed boat tours to see the sting-rays and scuba diving. There are lockers, changing rooms, showers, restaurants and bar. You can cross the North Sound by ferry (120 passengers, 30 mins, departs 1000, 1200, 1600 Mon-Thurs, 1000, 1200, 1800 Fri-Sun, returns 1100, 1500, 1830 Mon-Thurs, 1100, 1530, 2115 Fri-Sun, US$15 round trip, children under 12 free, T 949 9098) from the *Hyatt Hotel* to *Rum Point Club* (also under Hyatt management). Around Rum Point at Water Cay and Finger Cay there are picnic sites on the lagoon. Take insect repellent. South of George Town there are good beaches for swimming and snorkelling at Smith's Cove and Sand Cay. In Frank Sound, Heritage Beach, just W of Cottage Point, is owned by the National Trust.

For information about sailing contact the Cayman Islands Yacht Club, PO Box 30 985 SMB, Grand Cayman, T 947 4322, F 947 4432, with docking facilities for 154 boats, 7-foot maximum draft. Kaibo, PO Box 96BT, North Side, T 947 1056, has 12 slips, 40-foot maximum length, 7-foot maximum draft. Morgan's Harbour Marina and Restaurant, PO Box 815G, T 949 3948, F 949 3822, also offers the usual facilities. For a social sailing club there is the Grand Cayman Yacht Club, Red Bay Estates, where the sailing pro is Matthew Whittaker, T 947 7913, PO Box 30513 SMB.

Cayman Windsurf is at *Morritt's Tortuga Club*, East End, T 947 7492, F 947 6763, and at Safehaven West Bay Road, T 949 8334, with a full range of BiC boards and UP sails and instruction available. Red Sail Sports (T 947 5965) and Sailboards Caribbean (T 949 1068) also offer rental and instruction. Windsurfing at the East End is highly rated for people of all abilities. Beginners are safe within the reef, while outside the reef experienced sailors can try wave jumping or wave riding. Winds are brisk nearly all the year, with speeds of 15-25 knots. Lots of hotels' watersports operators offer windsurfing, sunfish, wave runners and other equipment.

Other Sports

Jack Nicklaus has designed the Britannia **golf** course for the *Hyatt-Regency Grand Cayman* hotel, T 949 8020 for starting times. There is a nine-hole Championship course, an 18-hole executive course and an 18-hole Cayman course played with a special short-distance Cayman ball, but it can only be laid out for one course at a time; the executive has 14 par threes and four par fours, so it is short, while the short-distance ball with local winds is a tourist gimmick. To play the executive course with hire of clubs and

compulsory buggie will cost you about US$90. The Links, the new 18-hole championship golf course is now open at Safehaven, with a par 71 course and a total yardage of 6,525 from the championship tees, although every hole will have five separate tee areas to accommodate all levels of players. 18 holes with cart/buggie costs US$80. The club house is open daily with restaurant and bar open to golfers and non-golfers. Practice facilities include an aqua range, two putting greens, sand trap and pitching green (night lights). The golf pro is Derek Nash, T 949 6828/5988, 0700-1800. You can hire clubs, US$1, take lessons or just practice, US$8/50 balls (you can buy balls at the bar if the clubhouse is closed).

There are three **squash** courts at the Cayman Islands Squash Racquets Association at South Sound, also courts at Downtowner Squash Club in George Town. For information on matches contact John MacRury (T 949 2269). Most of the larger hotels have their own **tennis** courts but the Cayman Islands Tennis Club next door to the squash courts at South Sound has six floodlit tennis courts and a club pro. For match information contact Scott Smith (T 949 9464). For **soccer**, contact Tony Scott (T 949 7339) of the Cayman Islands Football Association. **Cricket** matches are played at the Smith Road Oval near the airport (although location may change with extension of runway); there are five teams in the Cayman Islands Cricket Association's league, details on matches from Ian Burgess (T 949 8721) of the Cayman Islands Cricket Association. **Rugby** is played every Saturday between September and May at the Cayman Rugby Football Club at South Sound, for information phone Campbell Law (T 949 9876).

GEORGE TOWN

The largest town and capital of the islands is George Town (*pop* over 15,000), which is principally a business centre, dominated by modern office blocks. However, many of the older buildings are being restored and the Government is trying to promote museums and societies to complement beach and watersports tourism. The **Cayman Islands National Museum**, in the restored Old Courts Building in George Town, opened in 1990 and is well worth a visit. There are exhibits portraying the nation's seafaring history, an audio visual presentation and a natural history display. Open 0900-1700 Monday-Friday, 1000-1400 Saturday, 1300-1700 first Sunday of each month, closed first Monday of each month, CI\$4 adults, CI\$2 children aged 6-18, T 949 8368. There is a museum shop and *Jailhouse Café* for refreshments. The **Cayman Maritime and Treasure Museum** (T 947 5033) on West Bay Road near the *Hyatt Regency*, has a collection of gold and silver relics from sunken Spanish ships, open Monday-Saturday 0900-1700, US\$5 adults, US\$3 children 6-12.

An archaeological dig on the waterfront on the site of Fort George has been sponsored by the Cayman National Trust. Unfortunately only a small part of the walls remains, much was demolished in 1972 by a developer who would have destroyed the lot if residents had not prevented him. The National Trust has designed a walking tour of George Town to include 28 sites of interest, such as Fort George, built around 1790, the Legislative Assembly, the war and peace memorials and traditional Caymanian architecture. A brochure and map (free) is available from the National Trust (PO Box 10, T 949 0121, F 949 7494) or the Tourist Office.

EXCURSIONS

Some of the many things of interest to visit in Grand Cayman include a tour round **Cayman Turtle Farm**, which houses over 12,000 green turtles. Located at North West Point, this is the only commercial turtle farm in the world. Most of the turtles are used for meat locally since the USA banned the import of turtle meat, but many thousands of hatchlings and year-old turtles are released into the wild each year to replenish native stocks. Those at the farm range in size from 2-ounce hatchlings to breeding stock weighing around 400 pounds. Polished turtle shells are sold here for about US\$100, but their import into the USA is prohibited. A new flora and fauna section of the farm includes three 10-foot crocodiles of the type which used to inhabit the islands and gave their name to the Cayman Islands; there is also the Cayman green parrot, ground iguanas and agouti (known as the Cayman rabbit). Open daily 0830-1700, US\$5 adults, US\$2.50 children aged 6-12, T 949 3893/4.

West Bay is a colourful area with pretty old houses dating back to the seafaring days. The National Trust has a self-guided walkers' booklet of the area, directing you along lanes and paths and giving illustrated information about the district. The Pink House, built in 1912, is included in all tour itineraries as a typical Caymanian home. Originally home to the Bothwell family, it is now open to the public. Its traditional sand yard is raked every morning according to custom. **Hell**, situated near West Bay, is a bizarre rock formation worth visiting. Have your cards and letters postmarked at the sub-post office there. The Post Office is open Mon-Fri 0830-1300, 1400-1530, Saturday 0830-1130.

On the S coast at Savannah, just off the main coastal road, **Pedro St James Castle** is being excavated, restored and developed into a national landmark. The castle appears to have been a private residence (although pirate legends abound) and a variety of late 18th century artifacts have been unearthed. There are caves in **Bodden Town**, believed to have been used by pirates, where you can see bones and stocks, and a line of unmarked graves in an old cemetery on the shore opposite, said to be those of buccaneers. There are also caves on the other islands but these are

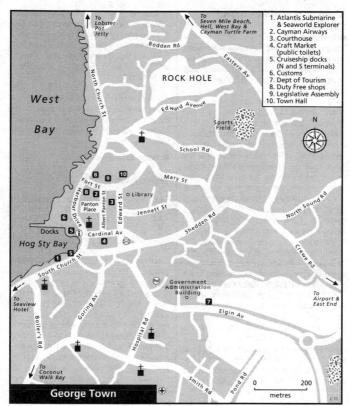

1. Atlantis Submarine & Seaworld Explorer
2. Cayman Airways
3. Courthouse
4. Craft Market (public toilets)
5. Cruiseship docks (N and S terminals)
6. Customs
7. Dept of Tourism
8. Duty Free shops
9. Legislative Assembly
10. Town Hall

George Town

0   200

metres

C·11

not as accessible. Continuing E just after Half Moon Bay you will see blowholes: waterspouts that rise above the coral rock in unusual patterns as a result of water being funnelled along passages in the rock as the waves come rolling in. At the E end of the island there is a good viewing point at the **Goring Bluff lighthouse**. A trip to **Gun Bay** at the E end of the island will show you the scene of the famous 'Wreck of the Ten Sails', which took place in 1788 (see above under **History**).

The National Trust organizes guided village walks and has opened a nature trail, the Mastic Trail, a 2-mile walk through farmlands, woodlands and mangroves, T 949 1996.

For a pleasurable day's outing, arrange a boat trip to North Sound for US$35 or so. This will include snorkelling, fishing and a good look at marine life on a barrier reef. Your guide will cook fish, fresh marinated conch or lobster for you, delicious and highly recommended. You can also take a moonlit cruise aboard a tall ship, *Blackbeard's Nancy*, at 1800, T 949 8988, with a sunset buffet dinner cruise on Mon, Wed, Thur, Sat, US$50; a cocktail cruise on Tues, US$30, or a happy hour cruise on Fri, US$15.

Island information – Grand Cayman

● Transport

There is a regular **bus** service between West Bay and George Town that stops at all the hotels on Seven Mile Beach, CI$1.50 each way. Buses also run to East End, CI$2.50 every hour. Both routes start from Panton Place and run 0600-1900, they can be flagged down anywhere. The bus to East End passes the S end of airport runway, from where it is a 15-min walk to terminal. **Taxis** are readily obtainable at hotels and restaurants. You can usually find taxis stationed at the *Holiday Inn* on West Bay Road. In George Town there are always lots of taxis at the dock when the cruise ships come in, otherwise hailing a taxi is most easily done in the vicinity of the Post Office. Fares are based on a fixed place-to-place tariff rather than a meter charge and vary according to how many people there are and how much luggage there is. For going a long distance (ie across the island) they are expensive. From the airport to George Town is US$8, based on up to 4 passengers with 2 pieces of luggage each; to the *Holiday Inn*, US$12; to Governor's Harbour, US$15; to Silver Sands, US$16; to Mount Pleasant, US$19.50; to Spanish Cove and Bodden Town, US$21.50; to East End, US$39; to Rum Point US$48 and Water Cay, US$50.

For **car hire**, Avis, National and Hertz are represented and there are a number of good local companies as well. Rental firms issue visitors with driving permits on production of a valid driving licence from the visitor's country of residence. The minimum driving age is 21 at some places, 25 at other companies, check. Ace Hertz, PO Box 53, T 949 2280, F 949 0572, standard jeep US$52 a day in winter, US$45 in summer, compact car US$27-34; Andy's Rent A Car Ltd, PO Box 277 WB, West Bay, T 949 8111, F 949 8385, cheapest automatic car US$35 in winter, US$25 in summer, weekly rates US$210 or US$150; Just Jeeps, PO Box 30497 SMB, North Church Street, George Town, T 949 7263, F 949 0216, US$45-65; Cico Avis, PO Box 400, T 949 2468, F 949 7127, smallest standard car US$40 winter/summer, jeeps, automatics and mini vans available, minimum 2-day rental, one day rental 25% extra, if paid in US dollars, add 25% for conversion; Coconut Car Rentals Ltd, PO Box 1991 GT, T 949 4037, F 949 7786, from US$40/30 a day winter/summer or US$240/180 a week, jeeps US$52/47, US$312/282. Collision damage waiver ranges from US$8-15 a day.

Bicycles (cheapest US$10/day), scooters (US$20-25/day) can also be rented, from Bicycles Cayman, North Church Street, T 949 5572, or Cayman Cycle Rentals, PO Box 1299 SMB, T 947 4021, at *Coconut Place*, *Hyatt Regency* and *Treasure Island*. Bicycles are also available at Rum Point.

Driving is on the left. Be careful of buses whose doors open into the centre of the road. Island tours can be arranged at about US$60 for a taxi, or US$10 pp on a bus with a minimum of 20 persons. Check with your hotel for full details.

● Accommodation

Price guide

L1	over US$200	**L2**	US$151-200
L3	US$101-150	**A1**	US$81-100
A2	US$61-80	**A3**	US$46-60
B	US$31-45	**C**	US$21-30
D	US$12-20	**E**	US$7-11
F	US$4-6	**G**	up to US$3

There are about 50 hotels along **Seven Mile Beach**. All the major chains are represented, offering all types of luxury accommodation. The newest is **L1** *Westin Casuarina Resort*, PO Box 30620, T 945 3800, F 945 3804, T 800 228 3000, 343 rooms, a/c, TV, phone, mini-bar, fan, marble bath, 2 pools, swim-up bar, tennis, dive shop, watersports, next to golf course. 200 yards from the beach is **A1-A2** *Cayman Islander Hotel*, PO Box 30081, T 948 0990, F 949 7896, pool, relaxed, good value breakfast, 64 nice rooms, dive shop, a/c, TV, phones. Away from Seven Mile Beach, there are hotels on Grand Cayman at Spanish Bay, Conch Point, Rum Point, North Side, East End, Half Moon Bay and Bodden Bay. At East End, **L1-L3** *Morritt's Tortuga Club* is new and upmarket, suites and town houses, on beach, excellent windsurfing, pool with waterfalls and bar, full dive operation, packages available, PO Box 496, T 947 7449, F 947 7669; on the North coast and rec for diving the N wall, **L1-L3** *Cayman Kai Resort*, PO Box 201 Northside, T 947 9055, F 947 9102, peaceful, on beautiful beach, dive packages available, lodges or beach villa. There are lots of guest houses catering for divers in the suburbs S of George Town. A rec guest house is **A2** *Adam's Guest House*, PO Box 312G, on Melmac Ave, ¾ mile S of George Town, T 949 2512, F 949 0919 run by Tom and Olga Adams, excellent accommodation, 4 rooms, US$10 additional person, a/c or fan, very helpful, about 300 yards from

Parrots Landing dive shop, no credit cards, TCs accepted. A pleasant small hotel in this area is **A2 Seaview**, PO Box 260, T 949 8804, F 949 8507, 15 rooms, a/c, fans, saltwater pool, piano bar, award-winning restaurant, Cayman Diving School on site, excellent snorkelling and off-shore diving, credit cards accepted. Three others in this price range (no credit cards) include **A2 Grama's Bed and Breakfast**, PO Box 198, T 949 3798, N of Seven Mile Beach, rate includes breakfast, tax and gratuity, a/c or fan, pool; **A2 Ambassadors Inn**, PO Box 1789, T 949 7577, F 949 7050, 1 mile S of town, on South Church St, walking distance from Smith Cove, on site diving operation, a/c, fans, pool, friendly, helpful, rec, and **A1-A2 Eldemire's Guest House**, PO Box 482G, T 949 5387, F 949 6987, room, studio or apartment, 1 mile from town, ½ mile from beach. Cottages, basic, may cost US$600-700 a week, and rates are usually by night, not per person. For longer stay visitors, a 2-bedroom, furnished house can be found away from the tourist areas in, say, Breakers or Bodden Town for US$600-1,000 a month.

● **Places to eat and drink**
There are dozens of restaurants on Grand Cayman ranging from gourmet standards where a jacket and tie is required, to smaller places serving native dishes. Fish, seafood and turtle meat are local specialities. In George Town, there are many restaurants catering for the lunchtime trade of the office workers and a number of fast-food places, takeaways and delicatessens. Prices obviously vary according to the standard of restaurant, but for dinner, main courses start at about US$10 and range upward to US$60 or more for a full meal including wine. Lunch prices can be around US$7-US$10 and breakfast from about US$5. During the high season it is advisable to reserve tables for dinner. People tend to eat early so if you reserve a table after 2000 you are likely to finish with the restaurant to yourself.

Good restaurants include: **The Wharf**, on the outskirts of George Town on the way to Seven Mile Beach, T 949 2231, lunch Mon-Fri, 1200-1430, dinner daily 1800-2200, beautiful waterfront setting, quite a large restaurant, reservations advisable; **Lantana's**, at the Caribbean Club on West Bay Road, fine, sophisticated dining, excellent food, try the garlic soup, T 947 5595 for reservations; **Crow's Nest**, about 4 miles S of George Town, T 949 9366, open lunch Mon-Sat, 1130-1430,

dinner daily 1800-2200, a local's favourite, small, glorious position, dining on the patio overlooking the sea or inside, moderate prices, reservations essential; **Pappagallo**, Barkers, West Bay, Italian cuisine, expensive, on 14-acre bird sanctuary overlooking natural lagoon, eat inside the haphazardly thatched building or in outside screened patio, excellent food and extensive wine list, reservations essential, T 947 3479, open daily 1800-2300; **Cracked Conch**, Selkirk Plaza, West Bay Road, T 947 5217, lively, take aways very popular; **Spanish Cove**, Barkers, West Bay, T 949 3765; **Almond Tree**, North Church Street, T 949 2893, outdoor dining, lobster specials Mon and Thur, all you can eat for US$14 on Wed and Fri, open lunch and dinner; **Grand Old House**, South Church Street, T 949 9333; **Lobster Pot**, North Church Street, T 949 2736; **Welly's Cool Spot**, North Sound Road, T 949 2541, has native food at reasonable prices. **Richard Fish** at the Seven Mile Shops, deli-type restaurant serves breakfast through to 0200, inexpensive, own baked bread and local dishes; **Eats Diner**, Cayman Falls, West Bay Road, T 947 5288, for breakfast; **Holiday Inn** hot breakfast buffet. All of these restaurants are near George Town or on Seven Mile Beach on the W side of Grand Cayman. Good sandwiches from **Coconut Place Delicatessen**. **Casanova Café** on the waterfront, old Fort Building, George Town, T 949 7633; **Champion House, I** and **II**, both on Eastern Avenue, George Town, T 949 2190 (*I*), 949 7882 (*II*), cheap, local food, rec; **Dominique's**, Fort Street, T 949 5747; **Island Taste**, South Church Street, T 949 4945, rec, upstairs outdoor patio overlooking harbour, excellent food. Bakeries include the **Coffee Grinder**, Seven Mile Shops, T 949 4833; **Caribbean Bakery and Pastry Shop**, West Bay.

For local colour visit **Farmers**, off Eastern Avenue near school. **Cayman Arms** on Harbour Drive is fairly typical 'pub', popular with expatriates. Open air bars are **Sunset House** and **Coconut Harbour** on South Church Street. In down town George Town, the **Hog Sty Bay Café**, T 949 6163, has a patio overlooking the harbour; **Big Daddy's** in Seven Mile Shop, West Bay Road, T 949 8511, and **Lone Star Bar and Grill**, next to the Hyatt Hotel, West Bay Road, T 949 5575, are favourites with sports fans, showing international sporting events nightly; **West Bay Polo Club**, T 949 9892, sports bar, speciality nights, eg sushi on Tues, always popular.

● **Nightlife**

Sharkey's nightclub, Cayman Falls on West Bay Road, T 947 5366, popular Mon nights, dancing to disco and reggae. *Rumheads Nightclub* features local groups such as Cayman Edition, as well as rock, reggae and other Caribbean music, also on West Bay Road, T 949 7169. Others include *Apollo II Club*, North Side, T 947 9568; *McDoom's Club Inferno*, Hell, West Bay, T 949 3263. The *Treasure Island Resort* has its own nightclub, *Silvers*, T 949 7777. *The Barefoot Man* at the *Holiday Inn*, calypso and a dash of country music, Wed-Sat. Another entertainment option is *Coconuts Comedy Club* at the *Holiday Inn*, T 945 7000, nightly except Mon and Thur, 2130, US$15. There is also a comedy cruise aboard the 72-ft *Carib Express*, Sat and Sun, 1700-1930, US$18, cash bar, T 945 7000. The Cayman National Theatre Company, T 949 5477, puts on plays and musicals at the Harquail Cultural Center on West Bay Road; the season runs from Oct to June, T 949 5477. The Cayman Drama Society use the Prospect Play House, a small theatre on the road to Bodden Town. There is a **cinema** on West Bay Road with two screens, 2 showings a night Mon-Sat, CI$6 adults, CI$2.75 children, T 949 4011.

CAYMAN BRAC

Settlement of Cayman Brac has been determined by **the Bluff**, which rises from sea level at the W end to a sheer cliff at the E end. Most building first took place on the flatter land in the W, where the sea is a little calmer, and then spread along the N coast where the Bluff gives shelter. The first three families of settlers arrived in 1833, followed by two more families in 1835. These five families, Ritch, Scott, Foster, Hunter and Ryan, are still well-represented on the island today. They made a living from growing coconuts and selling turtle shells and from the 1850s started building boats to facilitate trading. In 1886 a Baptist missionary arrived from Jamaica and introduced education and health care.

There are three roads running E-W, one along the N shore, one along the S coast and a third (unpaved) in the middle which runs along the top of the

Bluff to the lighthouse. Up here it is sometimes possible to spot various orchids and there is a 180-acre **Parrot Reserve**. A hiking trail has been cleared by the Cayman Brac National Trust, which protects the parrots' nesting sites but you should be able to see the birds. From the airport the N shore road leads to **Cotton Tree Bay**, where in 1932 a hurricane flooded the area, killing more than 100 people and destroying virtually every house. The coconut groves were devastated and many people left the island at this time. Demand for turtle shell went into decline as the use of plastic increased and many men found that the only opportunities open to them were as sailors, travelling around the world on merchant ships.

Stake Bay is the main village on the N coast and it is well worthwhile visiting the small, but interesting Cayman Brac museum. Open Monday – Friday 0900-1200, 1300-1600, Sunday 0900-1200, T 498 4222, admission free. Further E at Creek, *La Esperanza* is a good place to stop for refreshment, in a glorious setting with good views and welcome sea breeze. At Spot Bay at the extreme E, follow a track up towards the lighthouse. Here you will find Peter's Cave and a good viewpoint. This can also be reached from the road which runs along the top of the Bluff. From the end of the N coast road you can walk through the almond trees to the beach, from where you get an excellent view of the Bluff from below. Little Cayman can be seen in the distance. Along the S coast, the best beaches are at the W end, where there are two dive resorts. There is a pleasant public beach with shade and toilets at South East Bay. Bat Cave and Rebecca's Cave are in this vicinity and can be visited. Holiday homes are being built along this coast. These do not seem to need the shelter of the N coast as do the locals. Tourism is now the mainstay of the economy but construction of homes for foreigners has pushed up the price of land out of the reach of many local

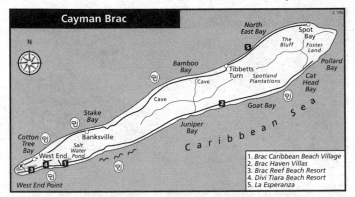

Cayman Brac

North East Bay
Spot Bay
The Bluff
Foster Land
Bamboo Bay
Tibbetts Turn
Spotland Plantations
Pollard Bay
Cave
Cat Head Bay
Cave
Goat Bay
Stake Bay
Juniper Bay
Cotton Tree Bay
Banksville
Salt Water Pond
West End
West End Point

Caribbean Sea

1. Brac Caribbean Beach Village
2. Brac Haven Villas
3. Brac Reef Beach Resort
4. Divi Tiara Beach Resort
5. La Esperanza

families. Most young adults leave the island for a career in financial services in Grand Cayman or other jobs further afield.

Diving and marine life

Cayman Brac is also blessed with spectacular reef and wall diving with excellent visibility. Most of the sites are around the W end, with both shallow reef snorkelling and diving and deeper wall diving a bit further out. There are also a few wrecks among the 40 or so named dive sites. Three dive operations are based on Cayman Brac, offering diving at both Cayman Brac and Little Cayman sites, certification and resort courses, photo/video services and equipment rental. Reef Divers is at *Brac Reef Beach Resort* (T 948 1429, PO Box 56, West End) and Peter Hughes Dive Tiara is at the *Divi Tiara Beach Resort* (T 948 1553, F 948 1316, PO Box 238, Stake Bay). Both offer PADI, NAUI, NASDS and SSI training. Brac Aquatics is an independent dive operation serving private rental homes and condos as well as hotels (PO Box 89, West End, T 948 1429). A 2-tank dive costs US$63 with Reef Divers US$65 with Brac Aquatics and US$61 with Dive Tiara.

Island information – Cayman Brac
● **Transport**
There is no bus service. An island tour by taxi costs about CI$15, Elo's Taxi and Tours, T 948 0220, rec, Hill's Taxi and Tours, T 948 0540, Maple Edward's Taxi and Tours, T 948 0448.

Brac Hertz, T & D and Four D's for car hire (about US$35-40/day for a car), B&S Motor Ventures for moped and bike hire, T 948 1546.

● **Accommodation**
At West End Point there are the **L3** *Brac Reef Beach Resort* (PO Box 56, T 948 1323, F 948 1207, 40 rooms, packages available) and **L2-A1** *Divi Tiara Beach Resort*, (T 948 1553, F 948 1316, T 800 367 3484, 70 rooms, facilities for the handicapped, packages available) both with full watersports and diving facilities, while there are also the **A1-A2** *Brac Airport Inn*, T 948 1323, 2 miles from town, 7 rooms or 3 suites with kitchenettes, a/c, TV, guests have full use of *Brac Reef* facilities and *Blackie's Seaview Hotel*, very basic island hotel, not resort-type, 9 rooms, a/c, fans, pool, bar, restaurant, T 948 8232. A condominium development, **L1-L2** *Brac Caribbean Beach Village*, on the S coast, W end, PO Box 4, Stake Bay, T 948 2265, F 948 1111, in USA (800) 791-7911, a/c, fans, on beach, reef protected, credit cards accepted, 15 units all 2-bedroomed, restaurant, pool, dive packages, laundry, maid service available, satellite TV, child and teenage discounts; *Seafarer Condominiums*, on SW coast, 8 beach front, one-bedroomed units, a/c, fans, verandah, daily and weekly rates, T 948 2265, no credit cards. Cayman Villas, T 947 4144, F 949 7471, have two properties for rent, **L2** *Reefside Retreat*, sleeps 4, ocean front; **L1-L2** *Brac Villa*, sleeps 8, walking distance to beach. **L2** *Brac Haven Villas*, PO Box 89, Stake Bay, T 948 2473, F 948 2329, small development of 6 units, each 1-bedroomed, inc car rental, on beach, a/c, fan, TV, maid service, babysitting, pool, credit cards accepted.

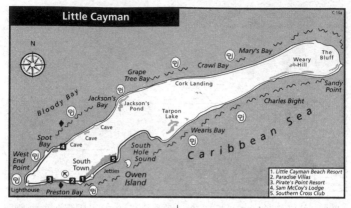

Little Cayman

C.104

Mary's Bay
The Bluff
Weary Hill
Crawl Bay
Grape Tree Bay
Cork Landing
Sandy Point
Jackson's Bay
Jackson's Pond
Charles Bight
Bloody Bay
Tarpon Lake
Cave
Wearis Bay
Spot Bay
Cave
Cave
South Hole Sound
Caribbean Sea
West End Point
South Town
Jetties
Lighthouse
Preston Bay
Owen Island

1. Little Cayman Beach Resort
2. Paradise Villas
3. Pirate's Point Resort
4. Sam McCoy's Lodge
5. Southern Cross Club

● **Places to eat**

On Cayman Brac there are a few restaurants; *Blackie's*, at the Youth Centre, South Side, T 948 0232, good ice cream; *Edd's Place*, West End, T 948 1208, open from 0700, restaurant and bar, Chinese seafood and local dishes, phone for transport; *La Esperanza*, T 948 0531, seafood, one of the nicest, tables at water's edge as well as a/c dining room, transport available, open Mon-Fri, 0900-0100, Sat 0900-2400, Sun 1200-2400 and *Lagoon*, T 948 7523, both at Stake Bay; *Sonia's*, White Bay, T 948 1214, island food; *Aunt Sha's Kitchen*, T 948 1581, island style, local dishes, rec.

LITTLE CAYMAN

The first inhabitants of Little Cayman were turtlers who made camp on the S shore. After them, at the beginning of the 20th century, the population exploded to over 100 Caymanians living at **Blossom** on the SW coast and farming coconuts. Attacks of blight killed off the palms and the farmers moved to the other two islands. In the 1950s, some US sport fishermen set up a small fishing camp on the S coast known as the Southern Cross Club, which is still in operation today as a diving/fishing lodge. Since then, a handful of similar small resorts have been built but the resident population remains tiny.

Little Cayman is small and low-lying with large areas of dense mangrove

swamps, ponds, lagoons and lakes. It is the ideal habitat for about 10,000 red-footed boobies and numerous iguanas. The best beach for swimming and snorkelling is at **Sandy Point** at the E tip of the island. Look for a red and white marker opposite a pond, a sandy path leads down to the beach. Other beaches are at **Jackson's Point** on the N side and on **Owen Island** in South Hole Sound. This privately owned island 200 yards offshore, is freely used by residents and visitors alike and is accessible by row boat. Popular with picnic parties.

Diving and marine life

Underwater visibility around Little Cayman averages 100-150 feet all year and diving is excellent. There are dive sites all round the island, but the most popular spot is in the Marine Park in Bloody Bay, a 2-mile stretch between Spot Bay and Jackson's Point off the N coast. Bloody Bay wall, a mile-deep vertical drop is one of the major dive sites worldwide and is highly rated by marine biologists and photographers. Unlike the walls around the other islands, which begin at a depth of about 65 feet and drop down about a mile, the Bloody Bay wall begins at only 15-20 feet, which means you can snorkel over the drop-off. Shore diving from Jackson's Point is also spectacular, with coral heads rising from a 40-foot sandy bottom to about 10 feet of the surface. *Sam McCoy's Dive Lodge* is at the W end of Spot Bay. There is also a Marine Park off the S coast opposite the airport, with *Pirate's Point Dive Resort* at one end. Diving can be arranged with *Pirate's Point*, *Sam McCoy's* or *Southern Cross Club*. Two newer dive operations are Paradise Divers (T/F 948 0004) and Reef Divers Little Cayman Beach Resort, South Sound (T 948 1033, F 948 1040). A 2-tank dive costs US$55-63.

The bonefishing around Little Cayman is some of the best and just offshore. The 15-acre Tarpon Lake is home to the game fish from which the pond gets its name. Fishing is offered at *Sam McCoy's* (T 948 0026, F 949 6281), where bonefishing and tarpon is US$80/half day and deep sea fishing is US$300/half day and US$475/full day. At *Southern Cross Club* (T 948 1099) deep sea fishing is US$175/half day and US$350/day, while a half day of bonefishing for two people with guide is US$90. *Little Cayman Beach Resort* also offers bonefishing at US$20/hr and deep sea fishing for US$500/day.

Island information – Little Cayman
● Transport
The airport consists of a wooden shack and a grass runway. Jeep hire is available here with McLaughlin Rentals, T 948 1000, daily and weekly rates, best to book in advance as last minute prices can be high. Roads are unpaved.

● Accommodation
Accommodation consists of diving lodges, a few private cottages and homes plus 10 rooms at the *Southern Cross Club*. **L1** *Sam McCoy's*, (T 948 0026/949 2891, F 949 6821, inc transport, diving, 3 meals, fishing costs extra (see above), small scale, low key, 12 rooms, no credit cards; **L1** *Pirates Point*, (T 948 1010, F 948 1011, 10 rooms, all inclusive with or without diving, fishing, a/c, fan, TV, phone, owned by a cordon bleu chef, highly rec, very relaxing, friendly; **L2** *Suzy's Cottage*, sleeps 4, weekly rates available, contact Cayman Villas, T 947 4144, F 949 7471; *Sefton's Cottages* (US$1,295/ week for a house, US$910/ week for an apartment in winter, US$1,190 and US$805 in summer) or **L1** *Southern Cross Club*, under new management and totally renovated 1996, T/F 948 1099, inc 3 meals, scuba, fishing, no credit cards, all in the W end of the island. The 32-room **L2-L3** *Little Cayman Beach Resort*, Blossom Village, T 948 1033, F 948 1040, T 1 800 327 3835, credit cards accepted, a/c, TV, on beach, dock facilities, tennis, basketball, volleyball, pool, jacuzzi, fishing, diving, facilities for the handicapped, all-inclusive dive packages available, under same ownership as *Village Inn*, Blossom Village, by the airport, 8 apartments, US$125, a/c, fans, T 949 1064 or 948 7423. Most offer full accommodation and diving and fishing facilities. Blossom Villas, T/F 948 1001, have condos and cottages, **L1-L2** *Lighthouse Point Condos*, sleep 4, maid service, diving offered, handicap accessible; **L1-L2** *Sea View Villas*, sleep 6, maid service, diving. **L1** *Sunset Cottage*, sleeps 4, same facilities. **L1-L3** *Paradise Villas*, PO Box 30, T 948 0001, F 948 0002, small, duplex, 1-2-bedroom cottages with kitchens, on the shore, restaurant *Hungry Iguana* next to pool.

Information for travellers

MONEY

● **Currency**
The legal currency is the Cayman Islands dollar (CI$).

● **Exchange**
The exchange rate is fixed at CI$1 to US$1.20, or CI$0.80 to US$1, although officially the exchange rate is CI$0.83 to US$1. US currency is readily accepted throughout the Islands, and Canadian and British currencies can be exchanged at all banks. There is no exchange control.

● **Credit cards**
Personal cheques are not generally welcome and credit cards are not accepted everywhere; do not assume that your hotel will accept them. Travellers' cheques are preferred.

BEFORE TRAVELLING

● **Documents**
No passports are required for US, British or Canadian visitors. However, proof of citizenship such as voter registration or 'British Visitor's Passport' is required, as well as an outward ticket. Married women using their husband's name should also show their marriage certificate. Passports but not visas are required for citizens of West European and Commonwealth countries, Israel, Japan, Argentina, Bahrain, Brazil, Chile, Costa Rica, Ecuador, El Salvador, Guatemala, Mexico, Oman, Panama, Peru, Saudi Arabia and Venezuela. If you are from any of these countries you may be admitted to the Cayman Islands for a period of up to 6 months providing you have proof of citizenship, sufficient resources to maintain yourself during your stay, and a return ticket to your country of origin or another country in which you will be accepted.

Visas are required by nationals of communist countries and all countries not included in the above list. Luggage is inspected by customs officials on arrival; no attempt should be made to take drugs into the country.

● **Climate**
The Cayman Islands lie in the trade-wind belt and the prevailing NE winds moderate the temperatures, making the climate delightful all year round. Average temperatures in winter are about 24°C and in summer are around 26°-29°C. Most rain falls between May and October, but even then it only takes the form of short showers.

● **Health**
Although Grand Cayman is sprayed regularly, it is advisable to bring plenty of insect repellent to combat mosquitoes and sandflies, particularly when there is rain. Little Cayman has to

GETTING THERE

AIR
● **From Europe**
British Airways has a twice weekly scheduled flight from London Gatwick operated by Caledonian Airways; the Tues flight is via Nassau, the Fri flight is non-stop but returns via Nassau.

● **From North America**
The national flag carrier, Cayman Airways, has regular services between the islands and Miami, Houston, Atlanta, Orlando (3 times a week) and Tampa in the USA (no charge for carrying diving gear). Grand Cayman is also served from Miami by American Airlines and Northwest Airlines. Northwest also flies from Atlanta and Memphis via Miami. American Airlines also flies direct from Atlanta and San Juan, Puerto Rico. US Air flies from Washington DC, Baltimore, Boston, Cleveland, New York, Charlotte, Pittsburgh and Philadelphia. American Transair flies from Chicago, Indianapolis and Seattle. With Air Jamaica Cayman Airways shares a service to Kingston.

● **From the Caribbean**
Regular charter flights also from Grand Cayman to Cayo Largo, Cuba, but you can not travel further to visit Cuba itself.

SEA
The islands are not served by any scheduled

passenger ships but there are cargo services between the islands and Miami and Tampa in the USA, Kingston in Jamaica and Costa Rica. The port at George Town comprises the S wharf, with a depth of 24 feet, and the W wharf, with a depth of 20 feet. The port at Creek, Cayman Brac, is equipped to handle the same class of vessels but Little Cayman has only a small facility. There is a small jetty at Spotts, Grand Cayman, which caters for cruise ships when the weather is too bad to land at George Town.

ON ARRIVAL

● Airports

Air communications are good and there are 2 international airports, the Owen Roberts International Airport on Grand Cayman and the Gerrard-Smith Airport on Cayman Brac. Owen Roberts International Airport is situated less than 2 miles from the centre of George Town and only 10 mins' drive from most of the hotels on Seven Mile Beach.

● Airlines

Cayman Airways, T 949 2311. For information on flights to Cayman Brac, T 948 1221. Air Jamaica, T 949 2300. American Airlines, T 949 8799. Island Air, T 949 0241/5252, F 949 7044. Northwest Airlines, T 949 2955/6. United Airlines T 949 7724. US Air T 949 7488. Charter companies: Executive Air Services, T 949 7766.

● Banks

Most of the major international banks are represented in George Town, Grand Cayman but not all are licensed to offer normal banking facilities. Those which include Bank of Nova Scotia, Barclays Bank International, Canadian Imperial Bank of Commerce and Royal Bank of Canada. Commercial banking hours are 0900 to 1430 Mon to Thur, and 0900 to 1300 and 1430 to 1600 on Fri. Barclays Bank and the Cayman National Bank have branches on Cayman Brac.

● Hospitals

Medical Care on Grand Cayman is good and readily available. There is a 52-bed government hospital in George Town (T 949 8600, out-patients appointments T 949 8601) and a 12-bed hospital in Cayman Brac. All hospital beds are in single rooms. Out-patients pay a fixed charge per visit. Primary care is provided through 4 district health centres in Grand Cayman. There is also a clinic on Little Cayman.

Cayman Islands Divers, the local branch of the British Sub-Aqua Club, operates the only re-compression chamber, behind Cayman Clinic, off Crew Road in George Town (T 555).

● Official time

Eastern Standard Time, 5 hours behind GMT, for the whole year.

● Public holidays

New Year's Day, Ash Wednesday, Good Friday, Easter Monday, Discovery Day (third Monday in May), the Monday following the Queen's official birthday (June), Constitution Day (first Monday in July), the Monday after Remembrance Sunday (November), Christmas Day and Boxing Day.

● Security

The Cayman Islands are safe to visit and present no need for extra security precautions. However, drugs related offences have increased sharply, with 894 arrests in 1993 compared with 606 in 1992 and about 80% of all thefts estimated to be drugs linked. The islands have become a major trans-shipment point.

● Shopping

As a free port, there is duty-free shopping and a range of British glass, china, woollens, perfumes and spirits are available. US citizens are entitled to a US$400 exemption after being away from the USA for 48 hours.

Black coral carvings and jewellery are widely available. Note that since the 1978 Cayman Islands Marine Conservation Law prohibited the removal of coral from local waters, manufacturers turned to Belize and Honduras for their supply. All the Central American countries are now members of CITES, so if you must buy it it would be worth checking the source of the coral in case it has been procured illegally. Caymanite is a semi-precious gem stone with layers of various colours found only in the Cayman Islands. Local craftspeople use it to make jewellery.

The day's fish catch can be bought from the fishermen most afternoons opposite the Tower Building just outside central George Town. Otto Watler makes and sells honey in Savannah, sign on the right just after the speed limit notice. Pure Art, on South Church Street (also at *Hyatt Regency* and Queens Court, West Bay Road), sells the work of over 50 local artists and craftsmen and women; paintings, prints, sculptures, crafts, rugs, wallhangings etc, open Mon-Sat 1000-1600. On Cayman Brac, NIM Things sells items made locally, including caymanite jewellery, straw bags and crochet, open 0900-1900 at Spot Bay, E end of the Main North Side Road.

The Book Nook (which sells *Caribbean Islands Handbook* among other books, toys, gifts and games), is at Galleria Plaza, West Bay Road, T 947 4686, and Anchorage Centre, T 949 7392, PO Box 1551, Grand Cayman, F 947 5053.

● **Warning**
Care must be taken when walking on a road, especially at night; they are generally in poor condition, narrow and vehicles move fast.

ON DEPARTURE

● **Departure tax**
There is a departure tax of US$10 for all visitors aged 12 and over payable either in Cayman or US currency when you leave the Islands.

ACCOMMODATION

The winter season, running from 16 Dec to 15 April, is the peak tourist season. Visitors intending to come to the island during this period are advised to make hotel and travel arrangements well in advance. There are substantial reductions in May-Nov, with cut rates or even free accommodation for children under 12. Most hotels offer watersports, scuba diving and snorkelling, and many have tennis courts, swimming pools and other facilities. Accommodations are many and varied, ranging from resort hotels on the beach to small out-of-the-way family-run guest houses. There is also a wide variety of cottages, apartments (condominiums) and villas available for daily, weekly or monthly rental. A full list of tourist accommodation and prices, including hotels, cottages, apartments and villas, is available from Cayman Islands Department of Tourism at the addresses shown at the end of this section. The Cayman Islands Hotel Reservations Service represents 52 properties in the Cayman Islands and can be contacted abroad through the Tourist Office. A government tax of 6% is added to the room charge and most hotels also add a 15% service charge to the bill in lieu of tipping.

FOOD AND DRINK

The range of restaurants is wide and all international styles are available. There is fast food through to gourmet. Caymanian recipes use predominantly seafood. Cayman-style fish is sautéed with tomato, onion, pepper and piquant seasoning. Conch is available as chowder, fritters, marinated etc. Try Caymanian Rum Cake for dessert.

GETTING AROUND

AIR TRANSPORT
Cayman Airways and Island Air provide interisland services from Grand Cayman to Cayman Brac and Little Cayman and return (US$99 day return, or US$122 round trip to one island, US$142 to both sister islands).

COMMUNICATIONS

● **Postal services**
Airmail postal rates are divided into 3 groups. Group A: the Caribbean, USA, Canada, Central America and Venezuela, first class 30 cents, second class, post cards, airletters 20 cents. Group B: Europe, Scandinavia, West Africa, South America, first class 40 cents, others 25 cents. Group C: East Africa, the Arabian subcontinent, Asia and the Far East, first class 55 cents, others 30 cents.

● **Telecommunications**
The Cayman Islands have a modern automatic telephone system operated by Cable and Wireless, which links them with the rest of the world by satellite and by submarine cable. International telephone, telex, telegram, data transmission and facsimile facilities are available and about 108 countries can be dialled directly. There is also a telephone route to the UK via Mercury. Public international telephone booths and a telegram counter are at the Cable and Wireless offices at Anderson Square, open from 0815-1700. The international code for the Cayman Islands is 1-809, followed by a 7-digit local number but there are plans to change the international code to 345. For overseas credit card calls (Visa and Mastercard) dial 110.

MEDIA

● **Newspapers**
The *Daily Caymanian Compass* is published 5 days a week with a circulation of 25,000.

TOURIST INFORMATION

● **Local tourist office**
Cable and Wireless, in conjunction with the

Department of Tourism, provide a Tourist Hotline. By dialling 949 8989 you can find out this week's events and local information. Further information may be obtained from the Cayman Islands Department of Tourism, The Pavilion, Cricket Square, Elgin Avenue, George Town, PO Box 67, George Town, Grand Cayman, BWI, T (809) 949 0623, F 949 4053, toll free 1-800-346-3313, open 0830-1700.

● **Tourist offices overseas**
Belgium/Netherlands/Luxembourg: Associated Travel Consultants, Leidsestraat 32, 1017 PB Amsterdam, Netherlands, T 20 6261 197, F 20 6274 86 9.

Canada: c/o Earl B Smith, Travel Marketing Consultants, 234 Eglinton Avenue East, Suite 306, Toronto, Ontario, M4P IK5 T (416) 485-1550, F (416) 485-7578.

Germany/Austria/Switzerland: Marketing Services International, Walter Stöhrer and Partner GmbH, Postfach 170446, Liebigstr 8, 60323 Frankfurt/Main 1, T 69-726342, F 69-727714.

Italy: G & A Martinengo, Via Fratelli, Ruffini 9, 20123 Milano, T 02-4801 2068, F 02-4635 32.

Japan: International Travel Produce Inc., c/o Shuwa Dai-2, Tsukiji Residence 4-3-12-201, Tsukiji, Chuo-Ku, Tokyo 104, T (03) 3546-1754, F 3545-8756.

UK: 6 Arlington Street, London SW1A 1RE, T 0171 491 7771, F 0171 409 7773. The London office is also the European headquarters for Cayman Airways, providing air reservations and tickets as well as a hotel reservations service (free). The Public Relations office for both organizations is Sugden McCluskey Associates, 50 Sulivan Road, London SW6 3DX, T 0171 371 8900, F 0171 371 8116.

USA: 6100 Blue Lagoon Drive, Suite 150, Miami, Fl 33126-2085, T (305) 266-2300, F (305) 267-2932; 9525 W Bryn Mawr Ave,

Suite 160, Rosemont, Illinois 60018, T (708) 678-6446, F (708) 678-6675; Two Memorial City Plaza, 820 Gessner, Suite 170, Houston, Texas 77024, T (713) 461-1317, F (713) 461-7409; 420 Lexington Avenue, Suite 2733, New York, NY 10170, T (212) 682 5582, F (212) 986-5123; 3440 Wilshire Boulevard, Suite 1202, Los Angeles, California 90010, T (213) 738-1968, F (213) 738-1829. There are also offices in Atlanta, T (404) 934-3959; Baltimore, T (301) 625-4503; Boston, T (617) 431-7771; Dallas, T (214) 823-3838; San Francisco, T (415) 991-1836; and Tampa, T (813) 934-9078.

● **Maps**
The Ordnance Survey produces a 1:50,000 scale map of the Cayman Islands with an inset map of George Town in its World Map Series. For information contact Ordnance Survey, Romsey Road, Maybush, Southampton SO9 4DH, T 0703 792000, F 0703 792404.

● **Further reading**
The Cayman Islands Government Information Services (third floor, Tower Building, Grand Cayman, T 949 8092, F 949 8487) publishes a series of booklets including one on *Marine Parks Rules and Sea Code in The Cayman Islands* and several on banking, captive insurance, company registration, residential status, work permits, living in the Cayman Islands etc. The Department of Tourism publishes *The Cayman Islands Ours & Yours* annually, giving hotel and transport prices as well as other useful information.

ACKNOWLEDGEMENTS

The editors are most grateful to Naomi Landau for updating this chapter.

Jamaica

JAMAICA lies some 90 miles S of Cuba and a little over 100 miles W of Haiti. With an area of 4,244 square miles, it is the third largest island in the Greater Antilles. It is 146 miles from E to W and 51 miles from N to S at its widest, bounded by the Caribbean. Like other West Indian islands, it is an outcrop of a submerged mountain range. It is crossed by a range of mountains reaching 7,402 feet at the Blue Mountain Peak in the E and descending towards the W, with a series of spurs and forested gullies running N and S. Most of the best beaches are on the N and W coasts, though there are some good bathing places on the S coast too.

HORIZONS

Jamaica has magnificent scenery and a tropical climate freshened by sea breezes. The easily accessible hill and mountain resorts provide a more temperate climate, sunny but invigorating. In fact, it would be hard to find, in so small an area, a greater variety of tropical natural beauty.

Over 90% of Jamaicans are of West African descent, the English settlers having followed the Spaniards in bringing in slaves from West Africa. Because of this, Ashanti words still figure very largely in the local dialect, which is known as Jamaica Talk. There are also Chinese, East Indians and Christian Arabs as well as those of British descent and other European minorities. The population is approximately 2.5 million. There is considerable poverty on the island, which has created social problems and some tension.

Jamaicans are naturally friendly, easy going and international in their outlook (more people of Jamaican origin live outside Jamaica than inside; compare the Irish). The Jamaicans have a 'Meet the People' programme which enables visitors to meet Jamaicans on a one-to-one basis.

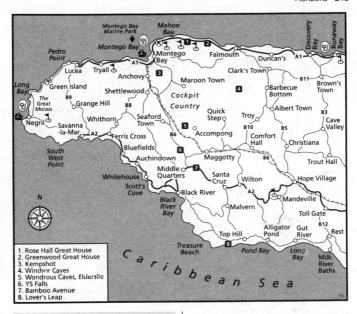

1. Rose Hall Great House
2. Greenwood Great House
3. Kempshot
4. Windsor Caves
5. Wondrous Caves, Elderslie
6. YS Falls
7. Bamboo Avenue
8. Lover's Leap

HISTORY

THE COLONY

When Columbus landed on Jamaica in 1494 it was inhabited by peaceful Arawak Indians. Evidence collected by archaeologists suggests that the tribe had not lived on the island much before the year 1000. Under Spanish occupation, which began in 1509, the race died out and gradually African slaves were brought in to provide the labour force. In 1655 an English expeditionary force landed at Passage Fort and met with little resistance other than that offered by a small group of Spanish settlers and a larger number of African slaves who took refuge in the mountains. The Spaniards abandoned the island after about five years, but the slaves and their descendants, who became known as Maroons, waged war against the new colonists for 80 years until the 1730s although there was another brief rebellion in 1795. The Cockpit Country, or 'Look Behind Country,'

where the Leeward Maroons hid and around Nanny Town where the Windward Maroons hid is still the home of some of their descendants.

After a short period of military rule, the colony was organized with an English-type constitution and a Legislative Council. The great sugar estates, which still today produce an important part of the island's wealth, were planted in the early days of English occupation when Jamaica also became the haunt of buccaneers and slave traders. In 1833 emancipation was declared for slaves (although a system of apprenticeship remained until 1838) and modern Jamaica was born. The framework for Jamaica's modern political system was laid in the 1930s with the foundation in 1938 of the People's National Party (PNP) by Norman W Manley, and the Jamaica Labour Party (JLP) by his cousin, Sir Alexander Bustamante in 1944. These two parties had their roots in rival trade

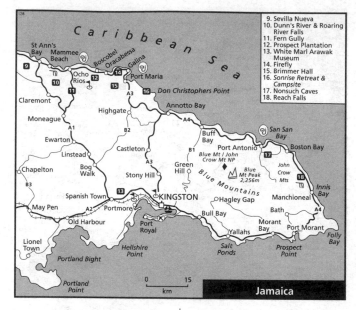

9. Sevilla Nueva	
10. Dunn's River & Roaring River Falls	
11. Fern Gully	
12. Prospect Plantation	
13. White Marl Arawak Museum	
14. Firefly	
15. Brimmer Hall	
16. Sonrise Retreat & Campsite	
17. Nonsuch Caves	
18. Reach Falls	

unions and have dominated Jamaican politics since universal adult suffrage was introduced in 1944.

INDEPENDENCE

In 1958, Jamaica joined the West Indies Federation with nine other British territories but withdrew following a national referendum on the issue in 1961. On 6 August 1962, Jamaica became an independent member of the Commonwealth.

THE MANLEY LEGACY

After 23 years as leader of the PNP, eight of them as Prime Minister in the 1970s and three as Prime Minister from 1989, Michael Manley, son of the party's founder, retired in March 1992 because of ill health. During Manley's first two terms in office between 1972 and 1980 he endorsed socialist policies at home and encouraged South-South relations abroad. He antagonized the USA by developing close economic and political links with Cuba. State control of the economy failed to produce the desired results and Mr Manley was rejected by the electorate. The conservative JLP led by Edward Seaga, held office for the next nine years. By 1989 however, Manley's political thinking had changed dramatically and he was re-elected with policies advocating the free market. Before his retirement he oversaw the reduction in the size of the state, deregulation of the economy and close relations with the IMF. He was succeeded by the Party Chairman, former deputy Prime Minister and Finance Minister P J Patterson who overwhelmingly defeated his only rival in an election at a special party meeting. Mr Patterson promised to maintain Mr Manley's policies and deepen the restructuring of the economy.

THE 1990'S

General elections were held early on 30 March 1993 and the incumbent PNP was returned for a second term with a larger than expected majority, winning 55 of the

"He huffed and he puffed ..."

Most of the earlier historical landmarks have been destroyed by hurricanes and earthquakes. Very few traces, apart from place names, therefore remain of the Spanish occupation. In 1692 an earthquake destroyed Port Royal which, because of being the base for English buccaneers such as Henry Morgan, had become famed as the most splendid town in the West Indies. In 1907 another earthquake damaged much of Kingston. Some of the historic buildings which are still standing, including the 18th century churches at Port Royal, St Ann's Bay and Montego Bay, are now in the care of the National Trust Commission. The Great Houses are a reminder of the British settlers; some have been converted into hotels or museums. Jamaica has the best preserved historical records in the Caribbean, held at the Institute of Jamaica, Kingston, and the Spanish Archives, Spanish Town. The copperplate slave returns (officially required from 1817) make fascinating reading, recommended for tracing family history, access free. In September 1988, Hurricane Gilbert travelled the length of the island causing extensive damage in all areas. There is hardly any sign of Gilbert now.

60 seats. Despite the landslide victory, the elections were marred by violence in which 11 people died, malpractices and a turnout of only 58%. The JLP boycotted parliament for four months while it demanded electoral reform and an inquiry into the election day events. It also refused to contest by-elections, two of which were held in the next 12 months and won by the PNP. Some concessions were made by the Government. The police force is to be reorganized to remove direct political control and local government elections have been postponed pending electoral reform. The reform is being drafted by the Electoral Advisory Committee but has been repeatedly delayed. Both parties have equal representation on the committee. General elections are due by 1998 but will not be held on the voter's list used in 1993.

The traditional two-party system was shaken up in 1995 by the launch of a third party, the National Democratic Movement (NDM), by Bruce Golding, the former chairman of the JLP. Mr Golding called for constitutional reform and the introduction of a republican system, arguing that the Westminster system concentrated too much power in the hands of the Prime Minister. Many JLP members defected to the new party and political tension increased with

confrontations between JLP and NDM supporters. Growing disaffection with the Government because of its unpopular economic policies also increased support for the new party.

GOVERNMENT

Jamaica is a constitutional monarchy. A Governor-General represents the British monarch, who is Head of State, and the Government is made up of a Prime Minister, (who nominates the Cabinet), a 60-seat House of Representatives and a 21-seat Senate. All citizens over 18 are eligible for the vote. The judicial system is on British lines.

THE ECONOMY

Structure of production

Once one of the more prosperous islands in the West Indies, Jamaica went into recession in 1973 and output declined steadily throughout the 1970s and 1980s. Gdp per head fell considerably in real terms although by 1989-92 economic output was beginning to pick up. At the core of Jamaica's economic difficulties lay the collapse of the vital bauxite mining and alumina refining industries. Bauxite and alumina export earnings provided 46% of all foreign exchange receipts and 28%

Jamaica: fact file

Geographic

Land area	10,991 sq km
forested	17.0%
pastures	23.7%
cultivated	20.2%

Demographic

Population (1995)	2,520,000
annual growth rate (1990-95)	1.0%
urban	50.2%
rural	49.8%
density	229.3 per sq km
Religious affiliation	
Protestant	55.9%
Non-religious	17.7%
Roman Catholic	5.0%
Other, inc Rastafarian	21.4%
Birth rate per 1,000 (1994)	23.7
	(world av 25.0)

Education and Health

Life expectancy at birth,	
male	71.4 years
female	75.8 years
Infant mortality rate	
per 1,000 live births (1989)	27.0
Physicians (1994)	1 per 6,335 persons
Hospital beds	1 per 492 persons
Calorie intake as %	
of FAO requirement	114%
Population age 25 and over	
with no formal schooling	3.2%
Literacy (over 15)	98.4%

Economic

GNP (1993 market prices)	US$3,927mn
GNP per capita	US$1,190
Public external debt (1993)	
	US$3,604mn
Tourism receipts (1994)	US$915mn
Inflation (annual av 1988-93)	35.5%
Radio	1 per 2.5 persons
Television	1 per 5.2 persons
Telephone	1 per 9.5 persons

Employment

Population economically active (1994)	
	1,090,500
Unemployment rate	15.4%
% of labour force in	
agriculture	20.0
mining	0.6
manufacturing	8.7
construction	6.1
Military forces	3,320

Source *Encyclopaedia Britannica*

of gdp in 1980 but by 1984 these shares had fallen to 33% and 20% respectively. Nevertheless, Jamaica is the world's third largest producer of bauxite after Australia and Guinea, and higher output and prices have now improved the outlook for the industry. In 1994 bauxite production rose to 11.6mn tonnes and alumina production increased to a record 3.2mn tonnes, but in 1995 it fell because of labour disputes at alumina refineries in support of wage claims, despite production capacity increases. Nevertheless, higher prices raised earnings from US$623mn in 1994 to US$718mn in 1995.

Manufacturing, which contributes over 18% to gdp, is mostly agricultural processing, such as rum, beer, cigarettes and foodstuffs. However, garments exported to the USA and other miscellaneous manufactured articles have seen considerable expansion, rising by 23.2% to US$262mn in 1994. Several manufacturing plants have closed because of competition from imports as markets have been liberalized.

By comparison with manufacturing, agriculture is a less important sector in terms of contribution to gdp, though it generates far more employment. Sugar is the main crop, and most important export item (US$99mn in 1993) after bauxite and alumina. Four state-owned sugar mills were sold in 1993 to the Sugar Company of Jamaica, leaving only one remaining in government hands. The Company is investing US$70mn in 1995-2000 to expand output from 120,000 to 220,000 tonnes a year and will rehabilitate Jamaica's only sugar refinery to raise production of refined sugar to 30,000 tonnes a year. However, drought in 1995 meant that imports of sugar were needed to meet domestic demand once export quotas had been met. Other export crops include bananas, coffee, cocoa and citrus fruits. An agricultural development plan for 1994-2000 aims to raise agricultural exports from US$194mn in 1993 to US$400mn.

Crime and tourism

🐦 The impact of tourism on a population of less than 2½ million is massive, both economically and socially. Bad publicity abroad or a natural disaster, such as Hurricane Gilbert, can have a devastating effect. The crime rate is high but most of the serious crime is around Kingston, principally in West Kingston. Many country districts and N coast resorts are fairly safe and in fact less dangerous than US tourist cities such as Miami, Orlando and Washington DC. Partly because of crime, all-inclusive resorts have become particularly important in Jamaica. A large proportion of tourists never leave these hotels except on an organized tour or to return to the airport.

Tourism is the second foreign exchange earner and Jamaica is the third most popular destination in the Caribbean after the Bahamas and Cancún. Stopover arrivals grew by an annual average of 8% and cruise visitors by 14% in the first half of the 1980s until, in 1987, combined stopover and cruise arrivals passed the million mark for the first time. In the 1990s numbers have continued to rise and hotel capacity has increased.

Recent trends

The Government turned to the IMF for support in 1976 and has since been a regular customer. In compliance with IMF agreements, the Government had to reduce domestic demand commensurate with the fall in export earnings, by devaluing the currency and reducing the size of its fiscal deficits. Jamaica has rescheduled its debt to creditor governments and also to foreign commercial banks. Some debt forgiveness has also been granted. By end-1994 debt had fallen to US$3.5bn, the lowest since end-1986, through repayments, renegotiations and cancellations. Paris Club debt is US$1.6bn, which became a heavy burden in 1996 with the resumption of payments of principal as well as interest.

A 15-month SDR 82mn standby credit facility was agreed with the IMF in January 1990 with targets to reduce the budget and current account deficits and eliminate payment arrears. Several tax increases were announced, together with the sale of hotels and other government assets and the ending of some unprofitable Air Jamaica routes (Air Jamaica has since been privatized and the loss-making Trans-Jamaican airline was put up for sale in 1995). The Jamaican dollar was devalued, the foreign exchange market was deregulated, and interest rates and credit ceilings were kept high to reduce consumption, close the trade gap and rebuild foreign reserves.

A further standby agreement was negotiated in 1991, together with loans from the World Bank and the InterAmerican Development Bank, which aimed to cut the budget deficit still further. In December 1992 an IMF 3-year Extended Fund Facility (EFF) replaced the Standby. The economy showed signs of growth but recovery was fragile. During the political leadership handover, uncertainties caused the currency to fall rapidly, but tighter monetary policies and private business sector support enabled it to recover soon afterwards and hold steady. Inflation was cut from an annual rate of 105% at the end of 1991 to only 17% in 1992, but cuts in fiscal spending led to a reduction in health and education services as well as in the size of the civil service and the poor were worst hit. The lack of adequate housing is a perennial problem, commonly solved by poor Jamaicans by squatting.

The 1993/94 budget granted wage increases to public employees, to be financed by higher taxes, including a rise in the general consumption tax (GCT) from 10% to 12.5% and a rise in the cruise ship passengers levy from US$10 to US$15. Further tax increases were announced in the 1994/95 budget, with a rise in petrol tax and a doubling of the departure tax. The 1995/96 budget reflected continued tight fiscal and monetary policies. Taxes were raised again, with the GCT up from 12.5% to 15%. The Government faced pressure for higher spending on wages, with public sector disputes in 1994-96. Nevertheless, the external accounts showed considerable improvement with a current account surplus of US$127mn in 1994 compared with a deficit of US$212mn in 1993. Targets set by the IMF were met in Sept 1995. Net international reserves rose from a deficit of US$803mn in 1980 to a surplus of US$460mn in 1995, while the fiscal accounts similarly improved from a deficit of 17% of gdp in 1980 to a cash surplus. The IMF agreement expired at end-1995 and the Government did not renew it. Despite these results, however, confidence at home deteriorated. The exchange rate again showed volatility as labour disputes became widespread and inflation jumped to 25.5% in 1995, twice the official target. The Government was forced to bail out some ailing financial companies to avoid a crisis in the banking sector.

The 1996/97 budget further increased taxes and a campaign was launched to cut tax evasion. Debt servicing remained a heavy burden, with amortization taking 52% of capital spending and interest payments 41% of current spending. A new industrial development policy aims to raise gdp growth from 0.5% in 1995 to 5% a year with per capita income rising to US$4,000 by 2010. Tourism, mining, manufacturing and food production have been highlighted as the key sectors.

CULTURE

The predominant religion is Protestantism, but there is also a Roman Catholic community. There are followers of the Church of God, Baptists, Anglicans, Seventh Day Adventists, Pentecostals and Methodists. The Jewish, Moslem, Hindu and Bahai religions are also practised. It is said that Jamaica has more churches per square mile than anywhere else in the world. To a small degree, early adaptations of the Christian faith, Revival and Pocomania, survive, but the most obvious local minority sect is Rastafarianism see box, page 219).

Kingston is the main cultural centre of Jamaica. There are two important institutes which can be visited: the African Caribbean Institute (ACIJ, on Little North Street) is involved in research into African traditions in Jamaica and the Caribbean; the Institute of Jamaica (East Street) has historical sections, including Arawak carvings, the National Library, science museum and occasional lectures and exhibitions. The National Gallery of Jamaica (Orange Street and Ocean Boulevard) has a large collection of Jamaican art; there are about a dozen other galleries in the city. The National Dance Theatre has an annual summer season; throughout the year plays and concerts are staged. The local press has full details of events in Kingston and other centres.

FLORA AND FAUNA

Jamaica has been called the Island of Springs, and the luxuriance of the vegetation is striking (its Arawak name, Xaymaca, meant land of wood and water). There are reported to be about 3,000 species of flowering plants alone, 827 of which are not found anywhere else. There are over 550 varieties of fern, 300 of which can be found in Fern Gully (see below). The national flower is the dark blue bloom of the lignum vitae. There are many orchids, bougainvillea, hibiscus and other tropical flowers. Tropical hardwoods like cedar and mahogany, palms, balsa and many other trees, besides those that are cultivated, can be seen. Cultivation, however, is putting

Dreadlocks to reggae: jammin' in Jamaica

Followers of the Rastafarian cult are easily recognizable by their long dreadlocks; they are non-violent and do not eat pork. They believe in the divinity of the late Emperor of Ethiopia, Haile Selassie (Ras Tafari). Haile Selassie's call for the end of the superiority of one race over another has been incorporated into a faith which holds that God, Jah, will lead the blacks out of oppression (Babylon) back to Ethiopia (Zion, the Promised Land). The Rastas regard the ideologist, Marcus Garvey (born 1887, St Ann's Bay), as a prophet of the return to Africa (he is now a Jamaican national hero). In the early part of the twentieth century, Garvey founded the idea of black nationalism, with Africa as the home for blacks, be they living on the continent or not.

The music most strongly associated with Rastafarianism is reggae. According to O R Dathorne, "it is evident that the sound and words of Jamaican reggae have altered the life of the English-speaking Caribbean. The extent of this alteration is still unknown, but this new sound has touched, *more than any other single art medium*, the consciousness of the people of this region" (*Dark Ancestor*, page 229, Louisiana State University Press, 1981). The sound is a mixture of African percussion and up-to-the-minute electronics; the lyrics a blend of praise of Jah, political comment and criticism and the mundane. The late Bob Marley, the late Peter Tosh, Dennis Brown and Jimmy Cliff are among the world-famous reggae artists, and many, many more can be heard on the island. Over the last few years, traditional reggae has been supplanted by Dance Hall, which has a much heavier beat, and instead of Marley's rather thoughtful lyrics, it is all about guns and sex, Shabba Ranks, Buju Banton and so on. Closely related to reggae is dub poetry, a chanted verse form which combines the musical tradition, folk traditions and popular speech. Its first practitioner was Louise Bennett, in the 1970s, who has been followed by poets such as Linton Kwesi Johnson, Michael Smith, Oku Onora and Mutabaruka. Many of these poets work in the UK, but their links with Jamaica are strong.

Two novels which give a fascinating insight into Rasta culture (and, in the latter, Revival and other social events) are *Brother Man*, by Roger Mais, and *The Children of Sysiphus*, by H Orlando Patterson. These writers have also published other books which are worth investigating, as are the works of Olive Senior (eg *Summer Lightning*), and the poets Mervyn Morris, the late Andrew Salkey and Dennis Scott (who is also involved in the theatre).

much of Jamaica's plant life at risk. Having been almost entirely forested, we have an estimated 6% of the land is virgin forest. A great many species are now classified as endangered.

This is also a land of hummingbirds and butterflies; sea-cows and the Pedro seal are found in the island's waters. There are crocodiles, but no wild mammals apart from the hutia, or coney (a native of the island and now an endangered species), the mongoose (considered a pest since it has eliminated snakes and now eats chickens) and, in the mountains, wild pig. The Jamaican iguana (*Cyclura collei*), of the lizard family Iguonidae, subspecies Iguaninae, was thought to have died out in the 1960s, but in 1990 a small group was found to be surviving in the Hellshire Hills.

Good sites for birdwatching are given in the text below; the three main areas are the Cockpit Country, the Blue Mountains and Marshall's Pen. The national bird is the doctor bird hummingbird, with a tail much longer than its body, one of Jamaica's endemic species. There are 25 species and 21 subspecies of birds which are found nowhere else. Many migratory birds stop on Jamaica on their journeys N or S. *Birds of Jamaica: a photographic field guide* by Audrey Downer and Robert Sutton with photos by Yves-Jacques Rey Millet, was published in 1990 by Cambridge University Press.

In 1989 the Government established two pilot national parks, the first in Jamaica, under the Protected Areas Resource Conservation (PARC) project. The Blue Mountain/John Crow Mountain National Park encompasses almost 200,000 acres of mountains, forests and rivers. Efforts are being made to stem soil erosion and restore woodland lost in Hurricane Gilbert, while developing the area for ecotourism and provide a livelihood for local people. The other national park is the Montego Bay Marine Park, which aims to protect the offshore reef from urban waste, over-fishing and hillside erosion leading to excessive soil deposition. All coral reefs are now protected and the sale of both black and white coral is banned. Also forbidden is the hunting of the American crocodile, the yellow- and black-billed parrot and all species of sea turtle.

DIVING AND MARINE LIFE

Although established in 1989, the Montego Bay Marine Park (see above) was officially opened in July 1992. It stretches from the E end of the airport to the Great River and contains three major ecosystems, seagrass bed, mangroves and coral reefs. Non-motorized watersports such as diving, snorkelling and glass bottom boat tours are permitted, but do not touch or remove anything.

There are several conservation groups involved in marine ecology. In St Ann, Friends of the Sea is a non-profit, non-governmental organization, formed in 1992, which concentrates on education and public awareness and draws attention to what is happening on land which might affect what happens underwater. The Negril Coral Reef Preservation Society was formed in 1990. It has installed permanent mooring buoys for recreational boats and works on educational programmes with schools with slide shows, videos and environmental fun days. Together with the National Resource Conservation Authority and the Negril community, it is working on forming a marine park in conjunction with protected coastal and terrestrial habitats, aimed at protecting the coral reefs and improving fish stocks for fishermen.

Around Negril there are lots of reef dive sites and there is a variety of coral, sponges, invertebrates and other marine life. Sea turtles, octopus, starfish and lots of fish can be seen here. Off Montego Bay and Ocho Rios there is wall diving quite close to shore and a few wrecks. Off Port Antonio fish are attracted to fresh water springs which provide good feeding grounds.

Nearly all dive operators are based along the N coast at hotels. They must be licensed by the Jamaica Tourist Board and most are members of the Jamaica Association of Dive Operators (JADO). They offer introductory and certification courses at all levels. Dive packages are available with the hotels where they are located. Contact the Tourist Board for a full list of operators and map of dive sites. Diving can be included in a hotel package, but if you are doing it independently, a 2-tank dive costs on average US$55. Dives are limited to 100 feet.

In 1994 the Government announced that it is to privatize 21 beaches currently owned by nine parish councils. A 'tourism action plan' will select public beaches which can be made 'commercially viable'.

Deep sea fishing for white marlin, wahoo, tuna and dolphin (not the mammal) can be arranged at N coast hotels. There is a famous Blue Marlin tournament at Port Antonio in October. A half-day charter costs US$300-350 for up to 6 people, plus a 10% tip for the crew, who will also expect to keep half the catch.

SPORT

Apart from the sports associated with the main resorts (tennis, riding, diving, and other water sports), golf is played at the Constant Spring (18 holes, green fee US$10, T 924-1610) and Caymanas Clubs (18 holes, green fee US$20, T 997-8026, c/o Liguanea Club) (Kingston), the Manchester Club (Mandeville, 9-hole, first opened in the middle of the 19th century, green fee US$5, T 962-2403), Sandals Golf and Country Club, formerly known as Upton (Ocho Rios, 18 holes, green fee US$30, golf and restaurant free for Sandals guests, T 975-0119/22), SuperClubs Golf Club (18 holes, green fee US$50, free for guests at *Breezes Runaway Bar*, the only golf school open to the public, T 973-2561), Ironshore Golf and Country Club (another Sandals course, free for guests, 18 holes, green fee US$40, Tel 953-2800), Half Moon Club (advance booking necessary for this championship course, 18 holes, green fee US$85, T 953-2731) and Wyndham Rose Hall Golf Club (18 holes, green fee US$60, T 953-2650) (all E of Montego Bay) and Tryall Golf, Tennis and Beach Club (Par 71, 6,407 yards in 2,200-acre resort complex, green fee US$125, between Montego Bay and Negril, T 956-5660/3). The Tryall course is probably the best known and hosts the annual Johnny Walker World Championship. Advance bookings are essential. A new course near Negril is the Negril Hills Golf Club (T 957-4638), Par 72, 6,333 yards, 18 holes in the hills.

The island's main spectator sport is cricket. Test matches are played in Kingston. For details on matches ring Jamaica Cricket Association, T 967-0322. **Tennis** can be played at the Eric Bell Tennis Centre, Kingston. For track and field meets phone Jam Amateur Athletics Association. **Horse racing** at Caymanas Park, T 925-7780/925-3312, every Wednesday and Saturday and most public holidays. **Polo** is played on Saturday afternoons at Drax Hall, near Ocho Rios, entrance free. International tournaments at Chukka Cove, Runaway Bay and Caymanas Polo Club, Kingston. **Riding** lessons and trail rides also available at Chukka Cove, which has probably the best facilities, T 972-2506. Hotels can arrange riding with local stables too. A 3-hr beach ride costs about US$50, while a 2-3 day trek into the mountains costs US$285-500. For Football phone the Jamaica Football Federation, T 929-0484.

FESTIVALS

Carnival has come only recently to Jamaica and is held around Easter time with floats, bands and mass dances, at various locations around the islands, attended by thousands. You can get very fit dancing for six hours a night for seven nights. Byron Lee, the leading Jamaican calypsonian, spends a lot of time in Trinidad over Carnival period and then brings the Trinidad calypsoes back to Jamaica. Some Trinidadian costumes (although not the really spectacular ones) are recycled for Jamaica's carnival. The annual reggae festival, Sun Splash, is normally held in the middle of August, usually in Montego Bay, in the Bob Marley Centre. Also in August, the celebrations around Independence Day (1 August) last a week and are very colourful. The annual International Marlin Tournament at Port Antonio in October attracts anglers from all over the world and includes festivities other than fishing. The Tourist Board publishes a twice-yearly calendar of events which covers the whole spectrum of arts and sports festivals.

KINGSTON

The capital since 1870 and the island's commercial centre, **Kingston** has a population of over 750,000 (part of St Andrew's Parish is included in the metropolitan area, which helps swell the figure). It has one of the largest and best natural harbours in the world. Following the earthquake of 1907 much of the lower part of the city (Down Town) was rebuilt in concrete. On the waterfront there are some notable modern buildings including the Bank of Jamaica and the Jamaica Conference Centre which also houses the National Gallery. Most of the new shops and offices are scattered over a wide area of N and E Kingston. Crossroads and Halfway Tree are referred to as midtown areas. Many shopping plazas are further

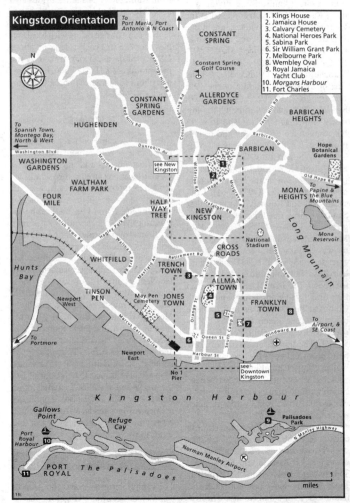

Kingston Orientation

To Port Maria, Port Antonio & N Coast

1. Kings House
2. Jamaica House
3. Calvary Cemetery
4. National Heroes Park
5. Sabina Park
6. Sir William Grant Park
7. Melbourne Park
8. Wembley Oval
9. Royal Jamaica Yacht Club
10. *Morgans Harbour*
11. Fort Charles

CONSTANT SPRING

Constant Spring Golf Course

CONSTANT SPRING GARDENS

ALLERDYCE GARDENS

BARBICAN HEIGHTS

HUGHENDEN

To Spanish Town, Montego Bay, North & West

Washington Blvd

Manning Hill Rd

Red Hills Rd

Constant Spring Rd

Dunrobin Av

Waterloo Rd

Hope Rd

Musgrave Rd

Jacks Hill Rd

Barbican Rd

BARBICAN

Hope Botanical Gardens

WASHINGTON GARDENS

Molynes Rd

see New Kingston

Old Hope Rd

MONA HEIGHTS

To Papine & the Blue Mountains

WALTHAM FARM PARK

FOUR MILE

Spanish Town Rd

Hagley Park Rd

Maxfield Av

HALF WAY TREE

Trafalgar Rd

NEW KINGSTON

Mona Reservoir

Long Mountain

WHITFIELD

Retirement Rd

CROSS ROADS

National Stadium

Mountain View Av

Hunts Bay

TINSON PEN

Newport West

May Pen Cemetery

TRENCH TOWN

JONES TOWN

Orange St

3

ALLMAN TOWN

4

FRANKLIN TOWN

8

To Airport, & SE Coast

To Portmore

Marcus Garvey Drive

5

South Camp Rd

7

Windward Rd

Newport East

6

Queen St

Harbour St

No 1 Pier

see Downtown Kingston

K i n g s t o n   H a r b o u r

Gallows Point

Refuge Cay

Palisadoes Park

9

Port Royal Harbour

10

N Manley Highway

PORT ROYAL

11

T h e   P a l i s a d o e s

Norman Manley Airport

0   1
miles

N again along the Constant Spring Road. The old racecourse was redeveloped in the 1960s as the New Kingston district, which contains most of the big hotels and many banks and financial institutions.

Among older buildings of note in the Down Town area are **Gordon House** (on Duke Street), which dates from the mid-18th century and houses the Jamaican legislature. Visitors are allowed into the Strangers' Gallery but must be suitably dressed (jackets for men and dresses for women). There is also the early 18th century parish church S of Parade, where Admiral Benbow is buried. **Parade** (Sir William Grant Park) is at the heart of the city centre; it is an open oasis amid the densely-packed surroundings. The name derives from the British soldiers' parades here during colonial rule. Now it is at the junction of the main E-W route through the Down Town area (Windward Road/East Queen Street-West Queen Street/Spanish Town Road) and King Street/Orange Street which runs N to Cross Roads. At Cross Roads, the main route forks, left to Half Way Tree (recently renamed Nelson Mandela Park), straight on up Old Hope Road to Liguanea. These two roads encompass New Kingston.

The Parish Church at St Andrew at **Half Way Tree** dates from 1700. Half Way Tree, so called because it was a half-way stage on the road between the harbour and the hills, is a busy traffic junction which takes some negotiating in a car. Hope Road, on the N edge of New Kingston, runs E from Half Way Tree. Just off it are **Devon House**, a former 'great house', built by Jamaica's first millionaire in the 1880s, at the corner of Trafalgar and Hope Roads, now renovated, complete with antique furniture, with craft shops and refreshment stalls (open Tues-Sat, 1000-1700, small admission fee to look inside the main house, US$2 for a guided tour, but the shops and restaurants in the grounds are open to all and well worth a visit). Not far away is **King's House**, the official residence of the Governor-General and, nearby, **Jamaica House**, the Prime Minister's residence.

About 10 blocks E of Devon House, off Hope Road, is the **Bob Marley Museum**, entry US$3 including obligatory guided tour, which takes an hour, including 20-minute audio visual presentation (open 0930-1700, Mon, Tues, Thur, Fri, 1230-1800, Wed, Sat). The house where Marley used to live traces back to his childhood and family, with paintings, newspaper cuttings, posters and other memorabilia. He died tragically of brain cancer at the age of 36, having survived a controversial assassination attempt (the bullet-holes in the walls have been left as a reminder). There is an Ethiopian restaurant in the garden serving some of his favourite vegetarian dishes. Marijuana plants grow profusely throughout the grounds and ganja is smoked openly in and around the restaurant and bar by staff Photography is totally banned within the museum and grounds.

Further E, along Old Hope Road, are the **Hope Botanical Gardens** (open 0830-1830, free). The land was first acquired by Major Richard Hope in 1671 and 200 years later the Governor of Jamaica, Sir John Peter Grant, bought 200 acres and created a botanical gardens. In 1961 a zoo was opened alongside the gardens (US$0.35). After extensive damage in 1988 by Hurricane Gilbert, plans have been made to transform the small, traditional zoo into a showcase for the different natural habitats of Jamaica and its indigenous animals.

Local information – Kingston
● Airport
The airport for Kingston is the Norman Manley (with restaurant, good tourist office, offering much information, maps and up-to-date hotel and guest house lists), 11 miles away, up to 30 mins' drive. There is an exchange desk in the arrivals lounge which will change cash or TCs (at a slightly lower rate than banks). You can also change back excess Jamaican dollars into US$ at the bank in the departure lounge, when

you leave. There are several reasonable shops in the departure lounge which will accept Jamaican currency (except for duty free goods). Allow plenty of time to check in for a flight; there are 9 separate security, baggage or documentation checks before you board. Bus No SR8 leaves West Parade for the airport, US$0.35, but the service is infrequent, so allow for waiting time. To get to New Kingston by bus involves a change of bus (to No. 27) Down Town. The recognized service from town to airport is JUTA, taxi/minibus, which charges US$17 to New Kingston (taxi despatcher gives you a note of fare before you leave, can be shared). Alternatively, if you have not got much luggage, take taxi to Port Royal, US$9, ferry to Kingston (see below, **Port Royal**) and then taxi to New Kingston, US$5-6.

● Accommodation

Price guide

L1	over US$200	L2	US$151-200
L3	US$101-150	A1	US$81-100
A2	US$61-80	A3	US$46-60
B	US$31-45	C	US$21-30
D	US$12-20	E	US$7-11
F	US$4-6	G	up to US$3

A full list is available from Tourist Board: addresses in **Information for travellers**. *Morgan's Harbour* is conveniently close to the airport and has complimentary transport there and back, 10 mins (see Port Royal); all the other main hotels are in or near New Kingston: **L1-L2** *Jamaica Pegasus* (Trust House Forte), 81 Knutsford Boulevard (PO Box 333, T 926-3690/9, F 929-5855), 350 rooms; **L1-L2** *Wyndham New Kingston*, 77 Knutsford Boulevard (PO Box 112, Kingston 10, T 926-5430/9, F 929-7439), 300 rooms; **L1** *Fort Belle Hotel and Suites*, opened 1996, 132 rooms designed for business travellers, suites have phones, fax and computer terminal, pool, tennis, squash, gym, jogging trail, T 968-0936; **L2** *Terra Nova*, 17 Waterloo Road (T 926-2211, F 929-4933), 35 rooms, popular with business travellers; **A2** *Mayfair*, 4 West King's House Circle (adjoining the Governor General's residence), PO Box 163, T 926-1610, F 926-7741, beautiful setting, balconies look towards mountains, 32 good rooms, food and service; **A2** *Four Seasons*, 18 Ruthven Road, PO Box 190, T 929-7655, F 929-5964, run by Mrs Stocker, German, long-time knowledgeable resident, in a converted Edwardian house and gardens, good cooking, rec; and a number

of others. Among the cheaper hotels is **A3-B** *The Indies*, 5 Holborn Road (T 926-2952, F 926-2879), (television US$6 extra), breakfast and lunch available, comfortable, pleasant patio, garden. Next door is the popular **B** *Johnson Holborn Manor* (ex Mrs Johnson's Guest House), 3, Holborn Road, with breakfast and shower, fan, clean, safe and quiet, very convenient for business in New Kingston, 3 good places to eat within 50 yards, luggage storage available, friendly, new annex, rec; **B** *Ivy Whiteman's Guest House*, 14 Monterey Drive, T 927-5449, bed and breakfast, very nice and helpful, clean, quiet, kitchen, beautiful garden, run by 5 sisters, take bus up Hope Road heading for Papine, get out at Hope Blvd, walk up Hope Blvd 15-20 mins and ask, Monterey Road is on left; **A3** *Sandhurst*, 70 Sandhurst Crescent, Kingston 6 (T 927-7239). **B-C** *Retreat Guest House*, 8 Devon Road, T 926-2565, 4 rooms, among the cheapest, safe area after dark; **C** *Chelsea Guest House*, Chelsea Avenue. About 25 mins from Kingston is **A1** *Ivor Guest House* and restaurant, Jack's Hill, Kingston 6, T/F 977-0033, 972-1460, high up in the hills overlooking Kingston and set in its own extensive grounds, 3 double bedrooms, free transport to/from Kingston, charge for airport pickup, lunches US$12, dinners US$16 by reservation only, Helen Aitken, highly rec. About 40 minutes from Kingston is *Pine Grove*, see under Eastern Jamaica and the Mountains. The YMCA, opp Devon House on Hope Road, has a good swimming pool, many sports facilities and a cheaply priced restaurant.The Tourist Board can arrange Bed and Breakfast for you, which usually costs US$25-60 a night.

● Places to eat

A great many places to eat in Down Town Kingston, New Kingston and the Half Way Tree area. There are plush establishments, inside and outside the hotels, and small places. The *Pegasus Hotel* does a good lunch and dinner special at US$5.50 and US$6.50 respectively. For the impecunious, meat patties may be had at US$0.25 each. Be warned that around the waterfront most places close at 1700. On Holborn Road, opp the *Indies Hotel* is the *Indies Pub*, which is reasonable, and next door is the *Three Little Bears* with patisserie attached, cheap cakes and coffee, excellent lobster in the main restaurant and quite palatable Jamaican wine, main course for lunch under US$4, evening meal US$8-18, buffet Fri and

New Kingston

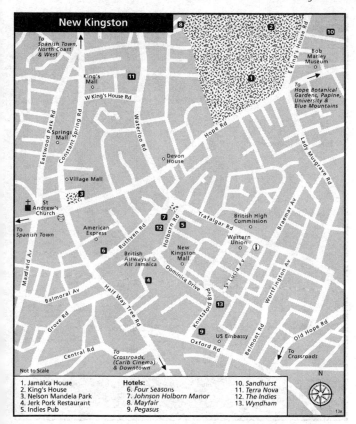

1. Jamaica House
2. King's House
3. Nelson Mandela Park
4. Jerk Pork Restaurant
5. Indies Pub

Hotels:
6. Four Seasons
7. Johnson Holborn Manor
8. Mayfair
9. Pegasus

10. Sandhurst
11. Terra Nova
12. The Indies
13. Wyndham

Not to Scale

Sun excellent value at US$8; *Kohinoor*, 11 Holborn Road, very good Indian food, good service, nice atmosphere, US$20 for 3-course dinner and drinks for 2. On Chelsea Avenue (in the same area) is *Jerk Pork*, popular with locals. Nearby are Mexican and Indian restaurants, both very good but not cheap. The *Lychee Restaurant* in the New Kingston Shopping Mall, on Dominica Drive, serves excellent Chinese food, moderately priced, several other eating places here, from takeaway pattie bakery to upmarket restaurant, popular lunch spot for office workers; *Norma*, 8 Belmont Road, Kingston 5, T 929-4966, very good; *Heathers*, Haining Road, very pleasant to sit outside, Middle Eastern and Jamaican dishes, US$3.25-9; around the corner in Altamont Road, *Hot Pot*, very

cheap, serves good Jamaican food in a pleasant patio, also a take-out box for just over US$1, difficult to find it without asking for directions. On Knutsford Boulevard there are lots of vans selling a satisfying lunch for US$1-1.50, often less, depending on what you eat. Many outlets of international takeaway chains all over the city, *Burger King* and *Kentucky Fried Chicken*, etc, as well as Jamaica's own variation, *Mothers*, also widespread. At *Devon House* (see page 223), there is a plush expensive restaurant, a reasonably-priced snack bar and delicious ice-cream at *I Scream*.

● **Entertainment**

Amusements in Kingston include cinemas and theatres. There is a good School of Drama and

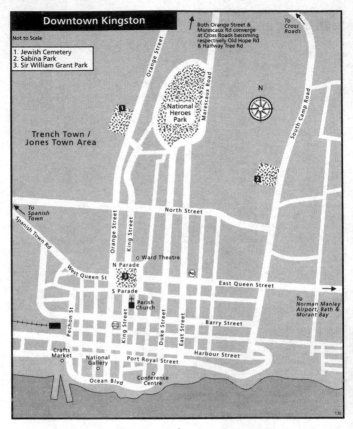

Downtown Kingston

Not to Scale

1. Jewish Cemetery
2. Sabina Park
3. Sir William Grant Park

Both Orange Street & Mareseaux Rd converge at Cross Roads becoming respectively Old Hope Rd & Halfway Tree Rd

To Cross Roads

Orange Street

Mareseaux Road

South Camp Road

National Heroes Park

Trench Town / Jones Town Area

N

To Spanish Town

Spanish Town Rd

North Street

Orange Street

King Street

o Ward Theatre

N Parade

West Queen St

S Parade

Pechon St

Parish Church

King Street

Duke Street

East Street

East Queen Street

To Norman Manley Airport, Bath & Morant Bay

Barry Street

Crafts Market

National Gallery

Port Royal Street

Harbour Street

Ocean Blvd

Conference Centre

several theatre and dance companies. Jamaica Dance Theatre is well known. Theatres include Ward Theatre (N Parade), Little Theatre (St Andrew), The Barn, New Kingston Playhouse, Green Gables, Creative Arts Centre. Watch the press for details of performances.

● **Nightlife**

Most hotels have dancing at weekends. The *Jamaica Vacation Guide* (at hotels, tourist offices) has the latest information. Clubs and discos include *Godfather's* in New Kingston, *Mingles* at *Courtleigh Hotel*, *Illusions* on Constant Spring Road, *24 Carat* at Manor Park, *Bleachers* on Constant Spring Road, all quite safe. So is *Peppers* on Waterloo Road, a good open air drinking spot, *the* place to go at night.

Devon House is a good place for a quiet evening drink under the trees. *Centre Pole* at Mary Brown's Corner on Constant Spring Road is rowdy and raunchy but fairly safe too. Tourists are strongly advised not to try, unless they have Jamaican friends, to probe deeply into real Jamaican night life, at least in towns. For genuine local dances and songs, see the advertisements in the local press.

● **Beaches**

The swimming at Kingston is not very good. The sea at Gunboat beach, near the airport, is dirty. Better at Port Royal (see below). 'Hellshire', S of Port Henderson, is a locals' favourite, but is difficult to reach. At Port Henderson is the *Rodney Arms* restaurant.

● **Shopping**

In Down Town Kingston, the Jamaica Crafts Market and many shops at W end of Port Royal Street have local crafts. Off W Queen Street is an interesting local market, selling fish, fruit and general produce. Down Town is where Jamaicans shop for bargains, but be careful, particularly in the market, it can be dangerous and you need to be thick skinned to get through, even if you do not get robbed. Most shops are in the plazas along Constant Spring Road and in Liguanea. There is a smart little shopping centre in New Kingston. Reggae music shops can be found close together along Orange Street, just N of Parade. The best book-shop, particularly for Caribbean fiction, is The Book Shop, The Springs, 15-17 Constant Spring Road, T 926-1800. Also very good is the Kingston Bookshop at 70B King Street, T 922-4056, and at the Pavilion Shopping Mall, Half Way Tree, T 968-4591. Bookland on Knutsford Boulevard, has a wide range of US magazines and newspapers and also *The Times*. There are various duty-free concessions for visitors. There is a **laundry** in Chelsea Avenue.

● **Transport**

Bus travel in Kingston costs between US$0.20 and US$0.30. A free map of Kingston bus routes is available from Jamaica Omnibus Services Ltd, 80 King Street. Travelling by bus is not safe after dark. Take a taxi to the bus station although you will still get hassled and pestered during the short walk to the bus. Do not walk out of the bus station; the area is notorious. Crossroads, Pechon Street and Half Way Tree are the main bus stops, but buses coming from town are usually full by the time they reach Crossroads or Half Way Tree. Fares from Kingston are: US$1.40 to Mandeville, US$2.75 to Montego Bay, US$1.50 to Negril, US$1.25 to Ocho Rios, US$2 to Port Antonio, 3 hrs, you are lucky if you get a seat. The buses are invaded by touts as they approach the bus station. (See also **Information for travellers**.)

PORT ROYAL

Port Royal (*pop* 2,000), the old naval base, lies across the harbour from Kingston, beyond the international airport, some 15 miles by excellent road. It can also be reached by boat from Victoria Pier; they leave 7 times a day, take 20 minutes and cost US$0.20. Port Royal was founded in 1650, captured by the English and turned into a strategic military and naval base. Merchant shipping developed under naval protection and the town soon became prosperous. It also attracted less reputable shipping and in 1660-92 became a haven for pirates such as Henry Morgan, with gambling and drinking dens and brothels protected by the 6 forts and 145 guns. The 'wickedest city in the world', with a population of 8,000, soon provoked what was thought to be divine retribution. On 7 June 1692 an earthquake hit E Jamaica, coursing along the Port Royal fault line and bringing with it massive tidal waves. The port, commercial area and harbour front were cut away and slid down the slope of the bay to rest on the sea bed, while much of the rest of the town was flooded for weeks. About 5,000 people died (of drowning, injuries or subsequent disease) and the naval, merchant and fishing fleets were wrecked. The town was gradually rebuilt as a naval and military post but has had

Kingston's bus fiasco

In March 1995 small, independent operators were replaced by three franchise holders. The change was designed to end years of chaos in the bus service and the franchisees were expected to lease vehicles owned by small operators. However, implementation of the new bus system was a fiasco. One company was short of 200 buses while another had 200 more than needed. Passenger frustration led to riots and road blocks at Half Way Tree and the Police had to use tear gas to disperse the crowds in some areas. The system was abandoned and the Government took over responsibility for operating and financing bus services in the Kingston area. A new company, Kingston Metropolitan Transport Ltd, was registered and 300 new buses ordered.

to withstand 16 hurricanes, 9 earth-quakes, 3 fires and a storm (which in 1951 left only 4 buildings undamaged).

Nelson served here as a post-captain from 1779 to 1780 and commanded Fort Charles, built in 1655, key battery in the island's fortifications. Part of the ramparts, known as Nelson's Quarterdeck, still stands (US$2). The Giddy House was the Royal Artillery store, built in 1888 but damaged by the 1907 earthquake which caused it to tilt at an angle of 45°. The Victoria Albert battery complex was a boiler house and underground armoury with late 19th century guns to protect the harbour and tunnels. The old Naval Hospital was built in 1819 of prefabricated cast iron sections brought all the way from England, one of the earliest constructions of this type and built on a raft foundation. The old gaol can also be seen. This dates from the early 18th century and was used as a women's prison in the 19th century. St Peter's Church, though the restoration is unfortunate, is of historic interest, as is the Historical Archaeological Museum (admission US$0.30). The museum is little more than one room and the Fort Charles remains are more informative and substantive.

- **Accommodation L3** *Morgan's Harbour* at Port Royal is a favourite holiday centre (T 967-8030/8040/8060, F 967-8073), 40 rooms, 5 suites, a/c, TV, balcony, seaview, seminar rooms, gift shop, scuba diving (packages available), with water ski-ing, fresh and salt water swimming pools, beach cabins, a good sea-food restaurant, and dancing, closest hotel to airport. Boats may be hired for picnic bathing lunches on the numerous nearby cays or at Port Henderson. There is a full service marina at *Morgan's Harbour* with customs clearance, 24-hr security and fishing boats for hire.

SPANISH TOWN

Spanish Town, the former capital founded in 1534, some 14 miles W of Kingston by road or rail, is historically the most interesting of Jamaica's towns and in desperate need of funds for renovation. Bus from

Half Way Tree and from Orange Street. Its English-style architecture dates from the 18th century. Well worth seeing are the Cathedral Church of St James, the oldest in the anglophone West Indies dating back to 1714; in need of renovation is the fine Georgian main square with, of special note, the ruins of the King's House built in 1762 and burnt down in 1925 (the façade has been rebuilt and now houses the Jamaican People's Museum of Craft, open Mon-Fri, 1000-1700, US$0.20); a colonnade (paint peeling off) and statue commemorating Rodney's victory at the Battle of the Saints (see under Guadeloupe and Dominica); the House of Assembly and the Court House. There is a museum with interesting relics of Jamaican history and accurate portrayal of life of the country people. The park in the centre is overgrown with weeds and the gates are padlocked. Outside town, on the road to Kingston is the White Marl Arawak Museum, open Mon-Fri, 1000-1600, US$0.10. Restaurant: *Miami*, Cumberland Road, near the market area; food is delicious, especially the pumpkin soup.

EASTERN JAMAICA AND THE MOUNTAINS

Behind Kingston lie the **Blue Mountains** with Blue Mountain Peak rising to a height of 7,402 feet. This is undoubtedly one of the most spectacular and beautiful parts of Jamaica and an area which must be visited by keen bird watchers and botanists as also by those who like mountain walking. It is possible to explore some of the Blue Mountains by ordinary car from Kingston. Drive towards Papine and just before arriving there visit the Botanical Gardens at Hope with a splendid collection of orchids and tropical trees and plants. After leaving Papine and just after passing the *Blue Mountain Inn* (good restaurant and night club), turn left to Irish Town and thence to Newcastle, a Jamaica Defence Force training camp at 4,000 feet with magnificent views of Kingston and Port Royal. If

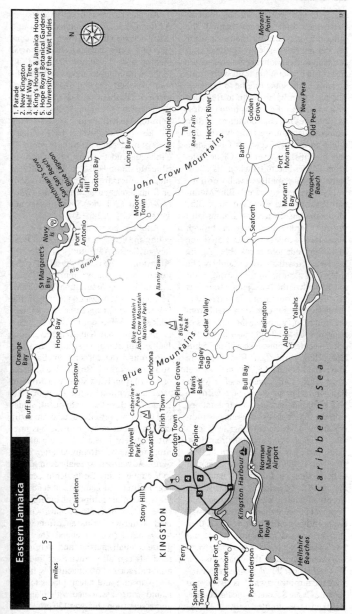

Eastern Jamaica

1. Parade
2. New Kingston
3. Half Way Tree
4. King's House & Jamaica House
5. Hope Royal Botanical Gardens
6. University of the West Indies

N

miles
0   5

Morant Point

Frenchman's Cove
San San Beach
Blue Lagoon

Orange Bay
Buff Bay
Hope Bay
Chepstow
St Margaret's Bay
Navy Is
Port Antonio
Fairy Hill
Boston Bay
Long Bay
Manchioneal
Reach Falls
Hector's River

Rio Grande

Castleton

Stony Hill

Hollywell Park
Newcastle
Catherine's Peak
Cinchona
Pine Grove
Irish Town
Mavis Bank
Gordon Town
Papine

Blue Mountains

Nanny Town

Blue Mountain / John Crow Mountain National Park
Blue Mt Peak

John Crow Mountains

Moore Town

Cedar Valley

Hagley Gap

Bull Bay

Bath
Seaforth
Morant Bay
Prospect Beach

Easington
Albion
Yallahs

Golden Grove
Port Morant
New Pera
Old Pera

KINGSTON

Ferry
Passage Fort
Portmore
Spanish Town
Port Henderson

Kingston Harbour
Norman Manley Airport
Port Royal

Hellshire Beaches

Caribbean Sea

energetic you may climb the road to Catherine's Peak directly behind the camp (about 1 hour for the moderately fit). Beyond Newcastle lies Hardwar Gap and Holywell National Park. This whole area is full of mountain trails with innumerable birds, some unique to Jamaica. The road then winds down to Buff Bay with a turning off to the right to Clydesdale and the Cinchona botanical garden. Unfortunately you are unlikely to be able to get an ordinary car past Clydesdale and perhaps not even to Clydesdale. From Clydesdale to Cinchona is about an hour's walk uphill but well worth it.

If you wish to go towards Blue Mountain Peak, you drive straight on at Blue Mountain Inn (instead of turning left), through Gordon Town and on through Mavis Bank 4 miles to Hagley Gap (if the Mahogany Vale ford is passable). Again, however, you will almost certainly not be able to get a car up to the starting point for the walk to the Peak. Public transport up the Blue Mountains is infrequent. There are some buses to Mavis Bank from the square in Papine on the outskirts of Kingston, US$0.60 but you will need to ask. To get to Papine, take a 70 or 75 bus along Hope Road. Taxis from Papine to Mavis Bank about US$7.50. Only 4-wheel drive vehicles are advisable after Mavis Bank (no shortage of people offering to take you), and there are no petrol stations en route. There are two walking possibilities from Mavis Bank: either look for a 4WD to Hagley Gap and walk from there to the starting point of the trail to the Peak (3½ miles uphill through villages), or walk the short cut from Mavis Bank. You may need to be guided for the first part (plenty of guides, Linford Morrison rec, lives near Police Station), across two small rivers and on to the path, which is then straight forward, a reasonably hard but lovely walk for 2 hours. Keep going when you eventually reach the village. Ask for *Whitfield Hall* or *Wildflower Lodge* (see below), the turning for which is just beyond Penlyne Castle School, by the Post Office. It is then a few minutes' walk.

An alternative solution is to stay at A2 *Pine Grove Hotel* about half an hour's drive beyond Gordon Town. This consists of a series of cottages with central feeding and the atmosphere of a ski lodge with double rooms with bathroom, kitchen area and couch. The proprietors, Barbara and Radwick, live there and are extremely welcoming and helpful. Apart from giving advice they will also provide 4-wheel drive vehicles at very moderate cost to take guests to Cinchona and the start of the trail to Blue Mountain Peak, etc. They will also pick up guests from the airport (US$50) or from Kingston (address: *Pine Grove Hotel*, c/o 62 Duke Street, Kingston, T 922-8708, F 922-5895).

Another possible solution for the young and active is to contact Peter Bentley of Sense Adventures at Box 216, Kingston 7, who is also President of the Jamaican Alternative Tourism, Camping and Hiking Association (JATCHA). The office is at Maya Lodge and Hiking Centre, Juba Spring, Peter's Rock Road, Jack's Hill, Kingston, T 927-2097. Buses or pickups from Kingston leave from Jack's Hill Road opposite Texaco station, round the corner from Barbican Square where bus SR6 from Duke Street or bus 14 from King Street will drop you after a circuitous route through New Kingston. Buses are infrequent; someone will probably offer to take you up by car for rather more than the bus fare. Alternatively, it is a 3½-mile walk uphill, not to be attempted after dark. Sense Adventures specializes in hiking in the mountains, birdwatching, canoeing, rafting and camping, it lends out tents and other equipment and it is possible to stay or camp at Maya. Organized, island-wide trips range from ½ day to 9 days (recommended for good guides, small parties and very good food). It can also provide information about all sorts of other activities, itinerary planning and cheap places to stay island wide; assistance with planning and reservations for over 150 properties is offered for US$15 including all the camping areas. A room or cabin at *Maya Lodge*, C, hostel style E pp, camping in own tent F pp, in hired tent E (all plus 12½% to fund projects), restaurant, menu repetitive, 15 acres of land in jungle setting, many paths for hikes around area, highly recommended. For a short tour of an organic farm ask for Willy, who will show you round his farm, interesting, reasonable rates, but only attempt it if you can walk up and down a steep hill and have old shoes. Willy is often used by foreign journalists as a guide.

There are two lodges close to the point where the Blue Mount Peak trail begins. John Algrove (8 Almon Crescent, Kingston 6, T 927-0986) owns *Whitfield Hall Hostel*, a large wooden lodge with no electricity but gas for the kitchen and paraffin lamps, D pp, capacity 40, hostel or private room accommodation, cold showers only. No meals unless you order them in advance, but kitchen with stoves and crockery, etc, for guests' use. Very peaceful and homely with comfortable lounge, log fire and library (visitors' books dating back to the 1950's), staff friendly and helpful. If the hostel is full, camping is permitted, F pp. A couple of minutes' walk before *Whitfield Hall* is *Wildflower Lodge*, known locally as the White House. It charges the same prices for dormitory or private room as *Whitfield Hall*, but is a bit more modern and the food is better, breakfast US$3, evening meals US$5 but hard to tell the difference, substantial and excellent vegetables from the garden, T 929-5394/5 or write 10 Ellesmere Road, Kingston 10. Both lodges will arrange 4WD transport from Kingston or Mavis Bank and offer guides and horses for walking or riding excursions.

The walk to Blue Mountain Peak (6½ miles from Whitfield Hall) takes 3 to 4 hours up and 2 to 3 hours down. The first part is the steepest. Some start very early in the morning in the hope of watching the sunrise from the Peak. As often as not, though, the Peak is shrouded in cloud and rain in the early morning making it a depressing experience. You can leave in early daylight and almost certainly reach the top before it starts clouding over again (mid to late morning). In this case you do not need a guide as the path is straightforward). The trail winds through a fascinating variety of vegetation, coffee groves and banana plantations on the lower, S slopes, to tree ferns and dwarf forest near the summit (with some explanatory and mileage signposts). The doctor bird (national bird of Jamaica) is quite common, a beautiful swallow-tailed hummingbird. Quite hard to spot at first but recognizable by its loud buzz, especially near the many flowering bushes. You must take your own food and torch, sweater and rainproof if you set out in the darkness. There are two huts on the Peak where one can overnight in some discomfort (empty concrete buildings with no door). There is a campsite with cabins, water and a shower at Portland Gap, about one hour up. Snacks and drinks are available at the ranger station; the rangers are very helpful. Another trail, to Mossman Peak, starts at Portland Gap, but is currently overgrown after 15 mins, having not recovered from Hurricane Gilbert. In high season up to 500 people walk up Blue Mountain Peak every day, while in low season there will be only a handful. Considering the numbers, it is remarkably unspoiled and the views are spectacular.

Bath at the E end of the island is another place from which one can make attractive trips into the **John Crow Mountains** (named after the ubiquitous turkey buzzards). There is a modest but cheap hotel (*Bath Spa*) dating from 1727 whose main attraction is that it contains natural hot water spring baths which are most relaxing at the end of a long day. There are two passes above Bath, called the Cuna Cuna Pass and the Cornpuss Gap, which lead down to the source of the Rio Grande River on the N slopes of the mountain range. Both are tough going particularly the Cornpuss Gap. It is absolutely essential to take a local guide. The N slopes of the mountain range are the home of the unique and extremely rare Jamaican butterfly, *papilio homerus*, a large black and yellow swallowtail. It can best be seen in May/June. Nearby, but not easily accessible, is the magnificent Pera beach between Port Morant and Morant Lighthouse. Near the lighthouse is another good beach but, like nearly all the beaches along the E coast round to Port Antonio, there is a dangerous undertow in certain spots. **L3** *Goldfinger's Guesthouse* in Morant Bay, cars to rent, clean, friendly, good cooking. *Golden Shore Beach Hotel*, 2 miles E of Morant Bay, 15 rooms, 8 with a/c, 7 with fan, bathrooms, TV, hot water, bar, restaurant, T 982-9657, Windward Drive, PO Box 8 Lyssons, St Thomas. Just before reaching Manchioneal from Bath there is a road off to the left which leads to the Reach Falls or Manchioneal Falls (about 3 miles). Well worth a visit if you have a car or are prepared to walk (45 minutes with views of rolling forested hills) from the main road. No facilities at the Falls, there may be an entry charge of US$0.50. Pretty tiers of smooth boulders, the highest fall about 15 feet, through a lush, green gorge. Buses from main road to Port Antonio infrequent, every 1-2 hours. Further NW along the coast from Manchioneal are **B** *Herman's Holiday Homes*, H Doswell, Long Bay, Portland, 3 minutes to the beach, nice, clean, comfortable, helpful (also, 2 bedroom cottage, US$270 a week per couple). Several other cottages and guesthouses have been built on the beach at Long Bay, including *Rose Hill Cottage*, *Casa Pecaro*, *Seascape*, *Nirvana*, *Coconut Isle* and *Rolling Surf* (T 0993 2856, Desmond Goldbourne in Port Antonio).

PORT ANTONIO

Once the major banana port where many of the island's first tourists arrived on banana boats, **Port Antonio** (*pop* 14,000) dates back to the 16th century. Its prosperity has for many years been in gentle decline, but it has an atmosphere unlike any other town in Jamaica with some superb old public buildings. The rainfall in this part of the island is very high and in consequence the vegetation very lush. Boston Bay, Fairy Hill Beach, San San Beach, the Blue Lagoon (also known as the Blue Hole) and Frenchman's Cove Beach are notable beauty spots to the E of the town. Boston Bay is renowned for its local jerk food pits; several unnamed places by the roadside serving hot spicy chicken, pork or fish, chopped up and wrapped in paper, cooked on planks over a pit of hot coals, very good and tasty. Also worth visiting is Nonsuch Cave, a few miles to the SE, where there are fossils and evidence of Arawak occupation, Somerset Falls and Folly, an elaborate, turn-of-the-century mansion built in the style of Roman and Greek architecture, now in ruins (partly because the millionaire American's wife took an instant dislike to it). The Folly is about half an hour's walk around the bay from the town. Take a right fork off the path before going into a clump of trees on the peninsula (leading towards lighthouse inside military camp). It is a ghostly, crumbling old mansion in an open field with lovely views shared with grazing cows. A makeshift bar has been set up inside and it looks as though squatters have moved in. There is no public transport to Nonsuch Cave, return taxi fare US$10 including waiting time. Entry US$5, open 0900-1700 daily, stalactites, gift shop and lunch area. For Somerset Falls, take a bus to Buff Bay (any westbound Kingston bus) and walk 5 minutes from there, entry US$1.

In the harbour it is possible to visit the 68-acre Navy Island, at one time owned by Errol Flynn, which has beaches (one nudist) and a moderately expensive restaurant. Return boat fare US$2, ferry operates 24 hours. Accommodation at the **L1** *Navy Island Marina Resort* in 14 rooms or individual

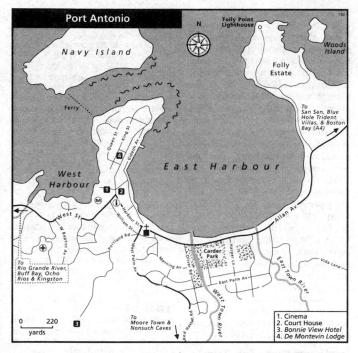

Port Antonio

1. Cinema
2. Court House
3. Bonnie View Hotel
4. De Montevin Lodge

0   220
     yards

To San San, Blue Hole Trident Villas, & Boston Bay (A4)

To Rio Grande River, Buff Bay, Ocho Rios & Kingston

To Moore Town & Nonsuch Caves

villas. Restaurant, pool and bar open to non-guests, open view of bay. 'Errol Flynn Gallery' has display of movie stills and screenings of his golden oldies. The beaches on the island all belong to the resort but are open to non-guests. Snorkelling available (at the nudist beach), US$2 for half-day hire, but there are strong currents and not many fish. Many other sports and other activities on offer, including a complete wedding ceremony in the resort chapel. Reservations, T 993-2667, F 993-2041.

Flynn also saw the potential as a tourist attraction for the bamboo rafts which used to bring bananas down the Rio Grande River. Expert raftsmen now take tourists on these rafts down the river. One boatman is Keith Allen, with a registered licence, who can be contacted in Port Antonio at the Huntress Marina,

but if you just turn up at Berrydale there are always rafters ready and willing to take you. Each raft (US$40 per raft from the ticket office, but if you arrive before it opens at 0800 or if you arrive by local bus, you can sometimes negotiate a fare of as little as US$25 with a rafter) takes two passengers and the trip takes 1½-2 hours (depending on the river flow) through magnificent scenery and with an opportunity to stop en route. Before you start make it clear who is buying the drinks. A driver will take your car down from the point of embarkation to the point of arrival. This is known as Rafter's Rest and is on the main coastal road. Recommended as a place to have a moderately priced lunch or drink in pleasant surroundings even if you are not proposing to raft. The return taxi fare is US$10, there are also buses,

US$0.25, to Berrydale, the setting-off point, though infrequent. Returning from St Margaret's, downstream, is easier as there are plenty of buses passing between Annotto Bay and Port Antonio. The Rio Grande valley is also well worth exploring, including a trip to the Maroons (descendants of escaped slaves) at Moore Town, but the roads are rough and public transport minimal. Ask for Colonel Harris there who is the leader of the Maroons and is recommended for guided tours. No telephone contact and no accommodation, return taxi fare US$15. To the W of the Rio Grande lie the N slopes of the Blue Mountains, many parts of which are still virtually unexplored. Nanny Town, the home of the Maroons, was destroyed by the British in 1734 and then 'lost' until the 1960s. There is recent archaeological evidence at Nanny Town to suggest that the Maroons originally took to the mountains and lived with (and possibly later absorbed) Arawak peoples. There have been some dramatic discoveries of Arawak wooden carvings which are now on display at the National Gallery.

Local information – Port Antonio
● **Accommodation**

Two up market hotels are **L1-L2** *Trident Villas and Hotel Jamaica*, PO Box 119, T 993-2602/2705, T/F 993-2590, 26 rooms/suites with sea view, antique furniture, private, tennis, croquet, pools, restaurants, afternoon tea, and *Jamaica Palace*, rates on request, Williams Field, PO Box 277, T 993-2020, F 993-3459. On Titchfield Hill, 5 mins' walk from the town are **B** *De Montevin Lodge*, 21 Fort George Street (PO Box 85, T 993-2604), inc breakfast, shared bath, more expensive rooms have private bath, charming and cosy old Victorian house, restaurant serves set meals, US$8-10, very good value, and **A3-C** *Ivanhoe* nearby, some with shared bath, patio with bay view. Opp the *De Montevin* also on Titchfield Hill is **D** *Sunnyside Guest House*, shared bath, basic but quite clean and quiet, rec and good views of the bay. Several nearby private houses also take guests. In the town centre are **D** *Hope View Guest House*, 26 Harbour Street, T 993-3040, with bath, small, friendly;

Triff's Inn, 1 Bridge Street, T 993-2162, F 993-2062, rates on application, modern, clean, pleasant lounge area; on top of a hill overlooking both bays is **L2-A1** *Bonnie View*, set in its own working plantation, PO Box 82, T 993-2752, F 993-2862, charming rooms, many with excellent views, bar and restaurant, very good meals, probably the best place to stay in town, horse riding and other activities also available. Outside Port Antonio on the Kingston road are *Goblin Villas*, kitchen, no restaurant; **L1-L3** *Dragon Bay Beach Resort*, tennis, good restaurant, rec, 90 rooms, PO Box 176, T 993-3281/2, F 993-3284. **L2** *Fern Hill Club* at San San, 31 rooms and spa suites, cottages, pool, jacuzzi, restaurant, golf, tennis nearby, watersports, windsurfing, sailing, diving, snorkelling, horseriding. At Frenchman's Cove, *Mocking Bird Hill*, PO Box 254, Port Antonio, T 993-7267/7134, F 993-7133, 15 mins from town, 5 mins' walk from beach, 10 rooms in Caribbean style villa in 7 acres of parkland, pool, gardens, nature trail, restaurant with Jamaican cuisine and international, Gallery Carriacou and gift shop exhibits owner's art, German, French, English and Spanish spoken.

● **Places to eat**
Huntress Marina on a jetty in the harbour, mainly a bar popular with yachting fraternity, but good breakfast-evening meals also served, cold beer; *Coronation Bakery*, near Musgrave Market on West Street, good for cheap patties and spice buns; *Cream World*, good for ice-cream, cakes and cheap snacks; *Stop Group Jerk Centre* on the bay out of town towards the folly, bar and jerk pork, chicken and fish, also music and dance until late.

● **Cinema**
Shows recent films, 2 for US$1.

● **Post Office**
Located by the clock tower in town centre.

● **Tourist Office**
Upstairs in City Centre Plaza on Harbour Street (T 993-3051/2587, F 993-2117), quite helpful, have timetables for local buses ("soon come"), which leave regularly when full, but at uncertain hours, from sea-front behind Texaco station.

ROADS INTO THE INTERIOR
Between Port Antonio and the **Buff Bay** area there are several roads into the interior from such places as Hope Bay and

Orange Bay. It is worth a detour if you have a car, but well off the beaten track and public transport is minimal. However, just to the E of Buff Bay there is a new development called Crystal Springs with beautifully laid out gardens, a variety of fish in the clear waters of the streams, an aviary, a bird sanctuary and masses of orchids. There is a moderately priced restaurant, three cottages to rent (L3) and camping sites (tent can be rented). Take any bus between Port Antonio and Kingston (US$0.40, about 45 minutes from Port Antonio), signposted at a turn-off between Orange Bay and Buff Bay (marked Spring Garden on Discover Jamaica road map). About 1½ miles along a flat paved road there is a small swimming pool surrounded by palms and flowering tropical plants. An idyllic spot, not busy during the week. Admission about US$1.50 including a complimentary drink of coconut water. Well worth a visit and a good base for exploring the foothills of the Blue Mountains. Contact Pauline Stuart of Stuarts Travel Service, 40 Union Square, Kingston, T 926-4291 (or King's Plaza, Kingston 10, T 929-4222), for up to date information. From Crystal Springs the road goes on to Chepstow and thence to Claverty Cottage and Thompson Gap; spectacular scenery, waterfalls in the valleys and very remote. It is possible to walk from Thompson Gap over the Blue Mountains via Morces Gap and down to Clydesdale, but this is a full day's trip and only to be undertaken with an experienced local guide and there is a problem of getting transport to meet you at Clydesdale. It is also possible to take a bus for part of the way up the Buff Bay valley and then walk on either to Clydesdale or over the Hardwar Gap to Newcastle. Both very long trips and only for the really fit.

THE NORTH COAST

The Kingston to Port Maria road (the Junction Road) passes through Castleton Gardens (in a very tranquil setting, well worth a visit by botanists, ask Roy Bennett to be your guide if available). The journey takes about two hours and there are plenty of minibuses. **Port Maria** itself is a sleepy and decaying old banana port but not without charm and lots of goats. East of Port Maria in Robin's Bay there is a camping and cottage resort on the beach, **A1-A3** *Sonrise Beach Retreat* (formerly Strawberry Fields), standard or 'deluxe' cabins with or without bath and tent sites, bath house, T/F 999-7169, two miles from village, transport essential or arrange pick-up with resort, meal plans and eco-tour packages available, restaurant, nature trails, trampoline, volley ball, ping pong. A few miles to the W of Port Maria lies the attractive looking **A1-A2** *Casa Maria* hotel which has seen better days, PO Box 10, T 994-2323, F 994-2324. Close to the hotel is *Firefly*, Noel Coward's Jamaican home, now owned by the Jamaican National Trust. Worth a visit if only for the magnificent view (entrance fee US$10, open 0900-1600 Mon-Sat). Noel Coward's other property, *Blue Harbour*, is half a mile from the hotel, and is where he used to entertain film stars, royalty etc. It is now a guest house with accommodation for up to 15 in the 2-bedroomed Villa Grande, the 1-bedroomed Villa Chica and the 4-roomed Villa Rose, all much as Coward left it although there has been some hurricane damage. Prices range from L3-A3 depending on season and number of guests, excellent Jamaican cooking or use of kitchen, fans, salt water pool, coral beach, good snorkelling and scuba, gardens, lovely views, PO Box 50, Port Maria, St Mary, T 994-2262 or in USA T 505-586-1244. At Galina, about 2 miles further W, there is the prominently signposted C *Blue Rock Estate Guest House* on the cliff edge. It was badly damaged by Hurricane Gilbert and is still pretty shambolic but it has a certain charm and a friendly Jamaican atmosphere. Recommended for young, low budget visitors, food prices to match, owner's wife is Canadian. Ten minutes further on by car lies Oracabessa, another old banana port with a half completed marina and *Golden Eye*, the house where Ian Fleming wrote all the James Bond books. To the W of Oracabessa is Boscobel, where the air strip for Ocho Rios is located. Opposite the air strip are numerous houses for rent.

OCHO RIOS

On a bay sheltered by reefs and surrounded by coconut groves, sugar cane and fruit plantations, is **Ocho Rios**, which has become very popular, with many cruise ships making a stop here. It is 64 miles E of Montego Bay, and claims some of the best beaches on the island. The beach in town is safe and well-organized with facilities, 200 yards from Main Street where most of the shops and vehicle hire companies can be found. **Shaw gardens** are an easy walk from the town centre, being up the hill on the edge of town. Nice gardens, recommended, entrance US$3, open 0730-1730 daily. The scenery of the surrounding area is an added attraction. Most spectacular are the beauty spots of **Fern Gully**, a marvel of unspoilt tropical vegetation, **Roaring River Falls**, which has been partially exploited for hydroelectric power, and **Dunn's River Falls**, tumbling into the Caribbean with invigorating salt and fresh water bathing at its foot. Worth a visit, take 5-minute bus ride, US$0.20, from Ocho Rios, or one hour's drive from Montego Bay, open 0800-1700 daily, entry fee US$5, locker US$1, bath shoes US$5 (rental) but not necessary if you move with care. (Beware of pseudo guides who hang around and take you somewhere totally different, then try to sell you marijuana.) The minibus from Kingston to Ocho Rios costs US$2 and follows a spectacular route, up the gorge of the Rio Cobre, then across Mount Diablo. Faith's Pen, right on the top, is an enormous collection of huts selling food and drink, great for a stop but you may not get on another bus as they normally pass full. The last section of road whizzes round a series of blind corners as you go through Fern Gully. Driving time is 1 hour 50 minutes once the bus has started. Alternatively, take a minibus from the Texaco petrol station on Da Costa Drive, Ocho Rios, for US$0.30 to Fern Gully. Lots of minibuses for return journey.

Historical attractions in the area include **Sevilla Nueva**, some nine miles to the W, which was where the Spanish first settled in 1509. The ruins of the fort still remain. The site is being investigated by the University of California at Los Angeles and the Spanish Government. Offshore, marine archaeologists, from the Institute of Nautical Archaeology at Texas A & M University, are investigating the St Ann's Bay area for sunken ships. Salvaged timbers are believed to have come from two disabled caravels, the *Capitana* and the *Santiago de Palos*, abandoned at Sevilla Nueva probably in 1503 during Columbus' last visit to Jamaica.

There are numerous plantation tours available to tourists all along the N coast. Details are widely publicized. Probably the most attractive, informative and certainly most accessible, is the Prospect Plantation Tour (T 974-2058, US$10, 1030, 1400, and 1530 daily), a short distance to the E of Ocho Rios nearly opposite the *Sans Souci Lido*. Harmony Hall art gallery just E of Ocho Rios is worth a visit.

Beautifully sited, near Ocho Rios, is the *Sandals Golf and Country Club* (formerly Upton, all-inclusive, really good food and good value for people who want to be packaged): golf links (US$30 green fee), tennis, riding and swimming. The *Lion's Den* is a friendly club frequented by Rastafarians; rooms available, good food, clean. West of Ocho Rios is Mammee beach, which is beautiful and less crowded than Ocho Rios, though there is no shade there. There is much fashionable night life in and around Ocho Rios.

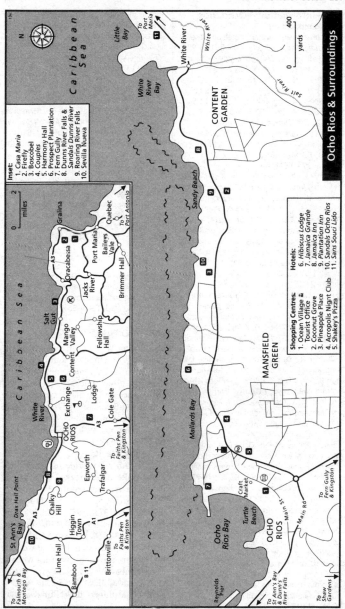

Ocho Rios & Surroundings

Inset:
1. Casa Maria
2. Firefly
3. Boscobel
4. Couples
5. Harmony Hall
6. Prospect Plantation
7. Fern Gully
8. Dunns River Falls & Sandals Dunns River
9. Roaring River Falls
10. Sevilla Nueva

Shopping Centres:
1. Ocean Village & Tourist Office
2. Coconut Grove
3. Pineapple Place
4. Acropolis Night Club
5. Shakey's Pizza

Hotels:
6. Hibiscus Lodge
7. Jamaica Grande
8. Jamaica Inn
9. Plantation Inn
10. Sandals Ocho Rios
11. Sans Souci Lido

Caribbean Sea

Little Bay
To Port Maria
White River
White River Bay
CONTENT GARDEN
Salt River
Sandy Beach
MANSFIELD GREEN
Mallards Bay
Craft Market
Turtle Beach
Ocho Rios Bay
OCHO RIOS
Main St
Main Rd
To Fern Gully & Kingston
To Shaw Gardens
To St Ann's Bay & Dunn's River Falls
Reynolds Pier

N

Caribbean Sea

To Falmouth & Montego Bay
St Ann's Bay
Drax Hall Point
A3
Chalky Hill
Higgin Town
A1
Lime Hall
Bamboo
B 11
Brittonville
To Faiths Pen & Kingston
Trafalgar
Epworth
OCHO RIOS
White River
Exchange
Lodge
Cole Gate
A3
To Faiths Pen & Kingston
Content
Mango Valley
Fellowship Hall
Salt Gut
Jacks River
Oracabessa
Galina
A3
Port Maria
Baileys Vale
Brimmer Hall
Quebec
To Port Antonio

0   miles   2

0   yards   400

Local information – Ocho Rios
● **Accommodation**

The Tourist Board lists many hotels and resorts: **L1** *Jamaica Inn*, PO Box 1, T 974-2514, F 974-2449, 45 rooms, FAP, pool, private beach; **L1-L2** *Plantation Inn*, PO Box 2, T 974-5601, F 974-5912, 63 rooms, 15 suites, 2 cottages, pool, beach, tennis, facilities for disabled, watersports, diving, fishing etc; and **L1** *Sans Souci Lido*, PO Box 103, T 974-2353, F 974-2544, a SuperClubs all-inclusive resort for couples, lots of facilities, watersports, 111 rooms and suites. Mid-price inns include **A1** *Hibiscus Lodge*, 88 Main Street, PO Box 52, T 974-2676, F 974-1874, pool, jacuzzi, tennis. **A3-B** *Jeff's House*, 10 Main Street, T 974-2664, owned by Jeffrey and Pearl McCoy, a/c, restaurant good, clean, cheap, kind and helpful, no credit cards; **A3** *Big Daddy's Pier View Apartment Motel*, 19 Main Street, T 974-2607, clean, quiet, good service, pool with sundeck, ask to see rooms, not all same size, avoid ones near noisy fountain, close to beach and town centre; **A3** *Little Pub Inn*, 59 Main Street, T 974-2324, inc breakfast, small, nice rooms,a/c, show time Wed, Fri, Sat, US$5 for guests, US$10 for others; **C** *Hunter's Inn*, 86 Main Street, T 974-5627, Swedish proprietors, rec, fan, bathroom, clean, restaurant, games room, billiards; **B** *De-Lo's Villa*, 21a Shaw Park Road, T 974-6151, ask for Monica, rec; about 1 mile from town centre, you can camp at Milford Falls, **D**, right by the waterfall, take Kingston road out of Ocho Rios, turn right at sign to Shaw Park Gardens then fork left up Milford Road, stop at George Barnes' shop on right, he will take you there and provide you with information, food and drink, he has a tent or a rustic cabin with 1 bed to rent, nice place to get away from city hustle. There are all-inclusive resorts E of Ocho Rios which are very good if you want that sort of holiday: *Boscobel Beach* is a SuperClubs resort set up for family holidays (PO Box 63, T 975-7330, F 975-7370), **Couples** is for honeymooners (T 975-4271, F 975-4439). The new **L1** *Renaissance Jamaica Grande Resort* (PO Box 100, T 974-2201/9, F 947-5378, in USA T (800) 228-9898) has received lots of favourable publicity but has been described to us as a barracks and the food criticized, maybe it depends on your expectations, 720 rooms, pool complex with waterfalls, children's programmes, convention facilities, singles packages, watersports, yacht charter, fishing, diving. **A1-L3** *Club Jamaica Beach Resort*, another all-inclusive is on Turtle Beach in Ocho Rios, 95 rooms, a/c, TV, phone, pool, watersports, diving, lots of games, exercise facilities, nightclub, PO Box 342, T 974-6632/142, F 974-6644, in USA T 1-800-818-2964. There are also **L1** *Sandals Ocho Rios*, Main Street, PO Box 771, T 974-5691/6, F 974-5700, and *Sandals Dunn's River*, Mammee Bay, T 972-0563/71, F 972-1611. West of Ocho Rios, about 1½ miles W of St Ann's Bay town in an area called Seville Heights is **D** *Joyce's Holiday Resort*, 40 Hibiscus Drive, T 972-1228, room with shared bath in family home, clean, safe, meals can be arranged, rec.

● **Places to eat**

On Main Street are *The Lobsterpot*, US$12-15 for lobster supper, very good, and *Jerk Pork*, same price for barbecued pork, fish or chicken; *Shakey's Pizza*, Main Street, nice bar and patio, fast, friendly service, smallest pizza from US$5.50. *Bill's Place* on Main Street is good for a drink or two. *The Acropolis* night club is lively and fairly safe.

● **Watersports**

Scuba diving with Fantasea, at *Sans Souci*, T 974-5344 and at *Boscobel*, T 975-7330, and Resort Divers Ltd, T 974-5338.

WEST TO FALMOUTH

Continuing W along the coast is **Runaway Bay**, an attractive and friendly resort. It is named for the Spanish governor Ysasi, who left quickly for Cuba in a canoe when he saw the English coming. Only five miles away is **Discovery Bay** where Columbus made his first landing. The Columbus Park has exhibits and relics of Jamaican history. From Runaway Bay, the Runaway Caves can be visited with a boat ride on the underground lake in the Green Grotto. Among the hotels in this area is the **A1** *Runaway Bay HEART Country Club* (PO Box 98, T 973-2671, F 973-2693), which is a hotel training centre. The **L2-L3** *Ambiance Jamaica*, T 973-2066, F 973-2067, has been described as adequate for fine weather but lacking in indoor facilities when it rains. Scuba diving here is with Sundivers Runaway Bay, T 973-2346. Golf is available at SuperClub's Runaway Bay Golf Club, where green fees are US$50.

There are several L1 all-inclusive resorts here too, including *Breezes Runaway Bay* (SuperClubs, lots of activities, golf, tennis, scuba diving, for couples and singles, 238 rooms and suites, PO Box 58, Runaway Bay, T 973-2436, F 973-2352), *Eaton Hall Beach Hotel*, *Club Caribbean* and *Franklyn D Resort*.

Falmouth is a charming small town about 20 miles E of Montego Bay. It has a fine colonial court house (restored inside), a church, some 18th century houses, and Antonio's, a famous place to buy beach shirts. There is good fishing (tarpon and kingfish) at the mouth of the Martha Brae, near Falmouth, and no licence is required. It is possible to go rafting from **Martha Brae** village. Expert rafters guide the craft very gently for the 1-hour trip to the coast (US$34 from Montego Bay in a 2-person raft, lunch and transfers, 0900-1700, or take local bus from Montego Bay to Falmouth, US$0.50, hitch hike or walk 6 miles to upper station; end station is about 3 miles from Falmouth). Jamaica Swamp Safaris (a crocodile farm) has a bar and restaurant. Entrance US$6 for adults to see lazy crocodiles with equally laid back guides. Two James Bond films were made here. Some 10 miles inland is the 18th century plantation guest house of Good Hope amongst coconut palms (T 954-3289): de luxe accommodation in the superb setting of a working plantation, as well as day tours and horse riding – some of the best riding in Jamaica – and its own beach on the coast. Scuba diving is available with Caribbean Amusements at *Fisherman's Inn* and *Trelawny Beach Hotel*, T 954-3427.

THE COCKPIT COUNTRY

This is a strange and virtually uninhabited area to the S of Falmouth and to the SW of Montego Bay. It consists of a seemingly endless succession of high bumps made of limestone rock. The tourist office and hotels in Montego Bay organize day trips to Maroon Town (no longer occupied by Maroons) and Accompong, the headquarters of the Maroons who live in the Cockpit Country area. Older locals can accurately describe what happened at the last battle between the Maroons and the British forces. Ask to see the 'Wondrous Caves' at Elderslie near Accompong. If you have a car take the road on the E side of the Cockpit Country from Duncans (near Falmouth) to Clark's Town. From there the road deteriorates to a track, impassable after a few miles even for 4WD vehicles, to Barbecue Bottom and on to Albert Town. The views from Barbecue Bottom are truly spectacular (the track is high above the Bottom) and this is wonderful birding country. If you wish to go on foot into the Cockpit Country make your way, either by car or on foot (no public transport), to the Windsor Caves due S of Falmouth. They are full of bats which make a spectacular mass exit from the caves at dusk. There are local guides to hand. The underground rivers in the caves (as elsewhere in much of Jamaica) run for miles, but are only for the experienced and properly equipped potholer. There is a locally published book called *Jamaica Underground* but the local caving club seems moribund at the time of writing. Mr Stephenson is a guide who has been recommended at the town of Quick Step; many caves and good walks in the area. It is possible to walk from the Windsor Caves across the middle of the Cockpit Country to Troy on the S side (about eight hours). It is essential to have a local guide and to make a preliminary trip to the Windsor Caves to engage him. Convince yourself that he really does know the way because these days this crossing is very rarely made even by the locals. It is also vastly preferable to be met with transport at Troy because you will still be in a pretty remote area.

MONTEGO BAY

About 120 miles from Kingston, situated on the NW coast, is **Montego Bay** (*pop*

92,000), Jamaica's principal tourist centre with all possible watersport amenities. Known familiarly as Mo' Bay, it has superb natural features, sunshine most of the year round, a beautiful coastline with miles of white sand and deep blue water never too cold for bathing (20°-26°C average temperature) and gentle winds which make sailing a favourite sport. There are underwater coral gardens in a

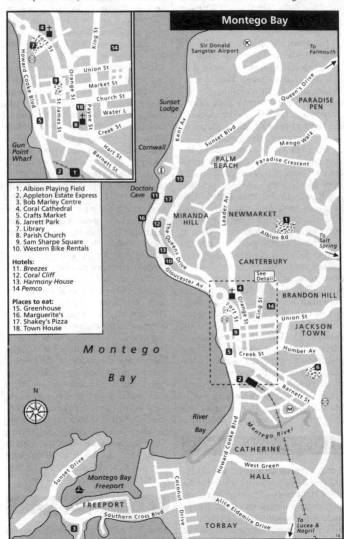

Montego Bay

1. Albion Playing Field
2. Appleton Estate Express
3. Bob Marley Centre
4. Coral Cathedral
5. Crafts Market
6. Jarrett Park
7. Library
8. Parish Church
9. Sam Sharpe Square
10. Western Bike Rentals

Hotels:
11. *Breezes*
12. *Coral Cliff*
13. *Harmony House*
14. *Pemco*

Places to eat:
15. Greenhouse
16. Marguerite's
17. Shakey's Pizza
18. Town House

Security

Constant importuning is a major problem downtown and tourists are constantly hassled and hustled. Knife attacks and other muggings by thieves are also frequently reported to us. The unfortunate consequence of this is that tourists avoid the town centre and stay in the tourist strip, where the selling is not unpleasant, or, worse, stay confined to the all-inclusive resorts. If you do go into town, do not be fooled by those who 'just want to talk', nor by 'do you recognize me? Its Tony from the hotel'. Answer, 'which hotel?'

sea so clear that they can be seen without effort from glass-bottomed boats at the Doctor's Cave, which is also the social centre of beach life (there is an admission charge of about US$1.50, which protects you from itinerant vendors). Doctor's Cave is the beach for relaxed sun bathing, while Cornwall is more sun 'n' fun, or beach 'n' boogie, with beach contests etc. Scuba diving can be arranged through Seaworld, at *Cariblue Beach Hotel*, *Holiday Inn* and *Wyndam Rose Hall*, T 953-2180; Poseidon Divers, at *Toby Inn*, *Reading Reef Club* and *Marguerite's Restaurant*, T 952-3624; The Scuba Connection, *Sea Gardens Hotel*, T 952-4780. A single dive costs about US$45, a snorkelling trip US$25.

Montego Bay caters also for the rich and sophisticated. Visitors enjoy the same duty-free concessions as in Kingston. Gloucester Avenue, by Doctor's Cave, is one of the busiest streets for tourists, lined with duty-free shops, souvenir arcades and several restaurants and hotels. Prices are fairly high but can be negotiated. Rum is cheaper here than at airport duty free shops.

Of interest to the sightseer are the remaining battery, cannons and powder magazine of an old British fort (Fort Montego, landscaped gardens and crafts market) and the 18th century church of St James in Montego Bay (built in 1778 and restored after earthquake damage in 1957). There are a few Georgian buildings, such as the *Town House Restaurant*, 16 Church Street (good local art gallery next door), and the Georgian Court at the corner of Union and Orange Streets. The centre of town is Sam Sharpe

Square, named after the slave who led a rebellion in 1831-2. The Burchell Memorial Church, established in 1824 by the Baptist missionary, Thomas Burchell, was where Samuel Sharpe served as a deacon.

If you are staying in town, rather than at the hotel strip, there are beaches close by, either public ones with no services or private (US$0.50-2.00 admission) with food, drinks, tennis, boat hire, snorkelling, shower, changing rooms etc. Walk from the traffic circle in the middle of town towards the hotels and the beach will be on your left. Mosquitoes can be a problem at certain times of the year or when the drains need cleaning out. Take repellent and coils.

Local information – Montego Bay
● **Airport**

The Donald Sangster international airport is only 2 miles from the town centre. For those landing here who want to go to Kingston, there is a transfer service by Martins minibus which takes 5 hours. It is also possible to get to the Norman Manley airport, Kingston, by taking the minibus from the town centre to Pechon Street, Kingston, from where the airport buses leave; US$4.50, 3 hrs. Do not buy at the airport duty free shop; everything is half the price at ordinary shops in town.

● **Transport**

There is no need to take the expensive tourist buses, except that the regular buses get crowded. They only depart when full. The regular buses are fast, very frequent and cheap, about US$2 from Montego Bay to Negril with a 30-second transfer in Lucea. There are more buses Montego Bay-Lucea than Lucea-Negril, which often causes a bottleneck. A taxi Lucea-Negril costs about US$20. Buses from Kingston depart from Pechon Street, near the railway station, roughly every hour from 0600 to 1500, US$2.80. It is possible to get to Montego Bay from Port Antonio all along the N coast, a scenic journey involving changes in Annotto Bay (then shared taxi, US$1 per person, mad rush to squeeze into clapped-out Ladas, the locals give no quarter to slow tourists), Port Maria US$1, and Ocho Rios. Ochos Rios-Montego Bay by bus takes 2 hours, US$1.50. The bus station for Kingston and Ocho Rios is NE of the downtown area, where Queen's Drive joins Gloucester Avenue. The bus station for Negril is at the other end of town, off Barnett Street (beware pickpockets). UTAS Tours, T 952-3820, 979-0684, F 979-3465, offer 12-hr day trip to Kingston via Dunns River Falls and Ocho Rios, US$60 for driver in a/c car; also 9-hr tour to Negril, US$21, with sunset drink at Rick's Cafe, Negril. **Taxi**: airport to town US$7 or 20-min walk airport to Doctor's Cave. **Bicycle** rentals through Western Bike Rentals and Sales Ltd, 27 Gloucester Avenue, T 952-0185, US$8/24 hours, bikes a bit battered.

● **Accommodation**

Price guide

L1	over US$200	L2	US$151-200
L3	US$101-150	A1	US$81-100
A2	US$61-80	A3	US$46-60
B	US$31-45	C	US$21-30
D	US$12-20	E	US$7-11
F	US$4-6	G	up to US$3

There are over 40 hotels, guest houses and apartment hotels listed by the Tourist Board and many more which are not. In the super-luxury range are *Round Hill Hotel and Villas*, 10 mins W of Montego Bay on 98-acre peninsula, originally a coconut and pineapple plantation, popular with the rich and famous, T 952-5150/5; *Half Moon Golf, Tennis and Beach Club*, on 400 acres adjoining beach, 340 rooms and 5-7 bedroomed villas with staff, golf, tennis, riding stables, squash, fitness centre etc, T 953-2211; **L1-L2** *Coyaba Beach Resort and Club*, 50 rooms, beach, gardens, pool, fishing pier, tennis, watersports, restaurants, bar, hammocks on the shore, T 953-9150/3. There are several large, lavish resorts in the area, inc a 516-room **L2** *Holiday Inn* and the 420-room **L2-L3** *Seawind Beach Resort*, while Sandals have 3 all-inclusive resorts, *Sandals Inn*, *Sandals Montego Bay* and *Sandals Royal Caribbean*. SuperClubs have *Breezes Montego Bay* on Doctor's Cave

Beach, T 940-1150, F 940-1160, 124 rooms and suites, tennis, watersports, fitness centre, entertainment, scuba and golf at extra cost. The weekly rate at these places can rise to US$6,000 in high season.

The **A2** *Coral Cliff*, 365 Gloucester Avenue, PO Box 253, T 952-4130, F 952-6532 (a US$7 cab ride from the airport) is rec, with a beautiful veranda, restaurant, bar, pool and friendly service; **A2** *The Guest House*, 29 Gloucester Avenue, T 952-3121, F 979-3176, beautiful house with wide balcony overlooking sunset in the bay, get room at back to avoid traffic noise, inc huge nutritious breakfast, run by Irish and Canadian, very friendly; **L3-A2** *Montego Bay Club*, Gloucester Avenue, T 952-4310, F 952-4639, dominant 12-storey apartment hotel in centre of tourist area overlooking Doctor's Cave Beach, rec; **B** *Ocean View Guest House*, 26 Sunset Boulevard, PO Box 210 (T 952-2662), 10 mins' easy walk from the airport, cheaper without a/c, many rooms overlook the bay, all clean, with bath, back-breaking mattresses (no advance bookings, but on arrival, ask tourist board to phone the hotel who will arrange free transport from the airport); **B** *Upper Deck Condominiums*, Sewell Avenue, Queen's Drive, T 979-2424, rec, ask for Dawn; **C** *Ridgeway Guest House*, 34 Queen's Drive, PO Box 1237, T 952-2709, F 979-1740, 5 mins' walk from airport, with bath and fan, friendly, clean, family atmosphere (cheaper rates for longer stays). **B** *The View Guest House*, Jarrett Terrace, T 952-3175, F 979-1740, homely atmosphere, some rooms with excellent view over bay, very friendly staff, huge breakfasts, try the Jamaican variety with saltfish, ackee etc, swimming pool, highly rec, but unfortunately unsafe areas between it and the beach; **C** *Mrs Craig's Guest House*, on Church Street, near Police Station, no sign, ask directions, noisy with uncomfortable mattresses and terrible showers but safe and cheap; **C-D** *Linkage Guest House*, Church Street, also near the Police Station, fan, shared bath, breakfast; *Pemco Hotel*, Union Street, on the way up to Brandon Hill, 20 mins' walk from Doctor's Cave Beach, can arrange accommodation at good rates (T 952-4000, Mr Samuel Clarke); **B** *Mountainside Guest House*, Queen's Drive, near the airport, behind the *Cotton Tree Restaurant*, enquire at the restaurant, very pleasant, clean rooms, balcony, good views, private bathroom, mosquito coils provided, noisy in early evening because of restaurant, but quiet at night, friendly and helpful. *Datura Villa*, in hills overlooking Montego Bay, T (508) 580-9974 in USA, exquisite location, staff and food rec, ask for the master bedroom, Mr Chisholm can be contracted as guide/chauffeur at US$100/day for 2-3 couples. There is a YMCA at Mount Salem with sports facilities available to members.

● **Places to eat**

Service at restaurants can be begrudging but the food is excellent. On the way into town from the airport there are several reasonably-priced restaurants; rec is the *Pork Pit* next to *The Guest House* on Gloucester Avenue, jerk chicken, pork and ribs sold by weight, service basic, and the *Toby Inn*, very good for cheap barbecued chicken and pork, cheap drinks, live band, romantic atmosphere, rec; *Baba Joe's* (Barbara Joe's), Kent Avenue, near airport on way to Whitehouse Village, just past Sandals, excellent fish, local style, about US$8 for meal with beer; *Cotton Tree*, Queen's Drive, near airport, free pick-up service, mainly seafood but very good vegetarian food on request, T 952-5329 for reservation; *Orlan Caribe Vegetarian Restaurant*, 71 Barnett Street, tidy, comfortable, low prices, sole vegetarian restaurant. There are several restaurants along Gloucester Avenue, including *Shakey's*, for pizza and breakfasts (deliveries, T 952-2665), not too good; *Patsy's Place*, 100m from *The Guest House*, small, good local dishes, excellent curried goat, cheap; *Walter's Bar and Grill*, 39 Gloucester Avenue, T 952-9391, local food, nice garden, good value; *The Greenhouse*, opp St James Place shopping arcade, good food and inexpensive; *Cascade*, in the *Hotel Pelican*, (T 952-3171), seafood specialities at moderate prices; *Marguerite's*, on the sea-front, has 2 restaurants, one posh with a/c and another simpler next door on a patio; *Le Chalet*, 32 Gloucester Avenue, T 952-5240, clean, friendly, Chinese, Jamaican (good curried goat), European menu at ¼ price of neighbouring *Pelican* and *Marguerite's*, free hotel transfers; *Town House* (see above), T 952-2660, highly rec for mildly pungent stuffed lobster US$30, other dishes also good, US$12.50-27; *Natives Jerk Centre*, Market Street, garden, outside bar, jerk chicken or pork, fish dishes with rice 'n' peas, rec, about US$7 for meal with beer; *Smokey Joe's*, St James Street, just beyond Woolworths towards Courts, good local restaurant, about US$6 for soup, main course and beer. Most restaurants are happy for guests to bring their own wine and will provide chillers and glasses.

● **Nightclubs**

The Cave (at *Seawinds Hotel*, drinks reasonable, beer and spirits US$2), the Cornwall beach gang seems to carry on here, at *Casa Montego Hotel*, *The Rum Barrel*, the *Cellar* and the *Reef Club*. The *Keg Club*, Barnett Street, opp fire station, roof top club, view of Mo' Bay and Freetown, US$5 entrance. Many others. Every Mon Gloucester Avenue is closed to traffic 1900-2400 for a street carnival and market. Many reggae bands and entertainers perform in the street. Vendors have stalls offering every conceivable souvenir at low prices.

EXCURSIONS

Out of town, to the E, the great houses of Rose Hall and Greenwood may be visited. The latter was built by the forefathers of the poet, Elizabeth Barrett Browning, in 1780-1800 (US$8, 0900-1700 daily). Rose Hall was started 10 years earlier, in 1770, by John Palmer. A lively legend of witchcraft surrounds the wife of one of his descendants, Anne Palmer, (US10 adults, US$4 children, 0900-1600 daily).

Inland, seven miles from Montego Bay off the Maroon Town road (turn off E ½mile before the village of Johns Hall), is the recommended A3 *Orange River Lodge*, an old Great House overlooking the Orange River Valley, which has guest rooms, hostel accommodation in bunk beds, US$10pp, and camping, US$5pp, bring own tent, beautiful location, excellent food, friendly staff, excursions arranged through Sense Adventures, also shuttle service to Montego Bay. Good walking in the area, you can swim in the river or go canoeing and birdwatching is good, T 979-2688 at Lodge or PO Box 822, 34 Font Street, Montego Bay, T 952-7208, F 952-6241. Southeast of Montego Bay is the Arawak rock carving at Kempshot, while to the SW is the bird sanctuary at Anchovy (Rocklands Feeding Station, don't miss this, the doctor bird humming birds will even perch on your finger, knowledgeable guides; open to visitors after 1530, but members of birdwatching societies will be admitted any time. Children under five are not admitted). The road to Anchovy is too rough for ordinary cars. Three miles to the W of Anchovy is Lethe, the starting point for rafting down the Great River. Ten miles from Montego Bay on the Savanna-La-Mar road is the Montpelier Great House, on the site of the old Montpelier sugar factory which was destroyed during the 1831 rebellion, call Pat Ottey, T 952-4299, for bed and breakfast, US$15-25, children welcome. South of Anchovy, about 25 miles from Montego Bay, is Seaford Town, which was settled by Germans in the 1830s. Only about 200 of their descendants survive. Write to Francis Friesen, Lamb's River Post Office.

Lucea is a charming spot on the N coast where the *Tamarind Lodge* serves excellent Jamaican food. Visit the Rusea School, endowed by a refugee Frenchman in the 18th century, in a lovely location but badly damaged by Hurricane Gilbert. Between here and Montego Bay (bus, US$0.88) is Tryall, with one of the best (and certainly the most expensive) golf courses on the island. The course is home to the Jamaica Classic, an LPGA Tour event and is set in a 2,200 acre resort complex. Green fees are US$125 in winter, hire of cart US$27, clubs US$20, caddy US$15. Tennis is also available and there is a clubhouse, beach bar and restaurant. To stay at the L1 *Tryall Golf Tennis and Beach Club* is expensive, T 956-5600/5, F 956-5673. Continuing around the island's W end, the road passes through **Green Island** before reaching Negril (29 miles from Lucea).

At Green Island, an Anglo-Jamaican couple, David and Nicki Reynolds, run Adventure Tours (see page 258), an island-wide alternative tour company for those who want to see behind some of the gloss. Generally tailor-made, tour prices start from about US$300/3 days including food, lodging and landrover transport. Find David five nights a week at the *Pickled Parrot* in Negril playing his

sound system Ark Force (ska/rock steady/reggae), or at the Negril Yacht Club; or bus to Green Island, ask for Orange Bay and the Post Office there will dirct you. Mobile phone T 999-9857, in UK F 0171 243 8969.

NEGRIL

Negril, on a seven-mile stretch of pure white sand on the W end of the island, is far less formal than other tourist spots but is still a one-industry town. The town is at the S end of Long Bay; at the N is the smaller Bloody Bay, where whalers used to carve up their catch. The Negril Area Environmental Protection Trust (NEPT) hopes to have the coastal area declared a national marine park and a grant has been awarded by the European Union (for information T 957 4473). The main part of the town has resorts and beaches but no snorkelling and you have to take a boat. In the West End of the village are beautiful cliffs and many fine caves, with great snorkelling but no beaches. In between is an area with neither beaches nor cliffs. There is clothes optional bathing at certain hotels, which is still quite rare in non-French Caribbean islands. Watersports are a particular attraction and there are facilities for tennis and riding (Babo's Horseback Riding Stable and Country Western Riding Stables, US$30-35, daily). There is a dive shop at *Hedonism II*, T 957-4200, free for guests, and Sundivers Negril, a PADI 5-star facility at *Poinciana Beach Resort*, diving lessons 0900 and 1200, resort course US$60, guided boat dives 3 times daily, US$30 single tank, US$45 – 2 tanks (also at *Rock Cliff Resort*). Negril Scuba Centre is at *Negril Beach Club* and at *Negril Inn*, while Resort Divers are at *Swept Away* and *Grand Lido*.

By the *Poinciana Beach Resort* is the Anancy Family Fun and Nature Park with boating lake, minigolf, go-karts, fishing pond, nature trail, video arcade and historical exhibitions, open Monday-Friday 1300-2200, Saturday-

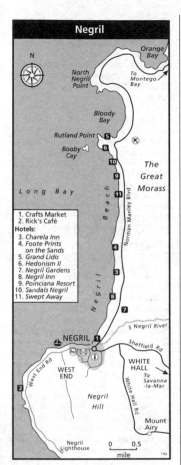

Negril

N

Orange
Bay

North
Negril
Point

To
Montego
Bay

Bloody
Bay

Rutland Point

Booby
Cay

The
Great
Morass

Long Bay

Norman Manley Blvd

Negril Beach

1. Crafts Market
2. Rick's Café
Hotels:
3. Charela Inn
4. Foote Prints
   on the Sands
5. Grand Lido
6. Hedonism II
7. Negril Gardens
8. Negril Inn
9. Poinciana Resort
10. Sandals Negril
11. Swept Away

S Negril River

NEGRIL

Sheffield Rd

West End Rd

WHITE
HALL

To
Savanna
-la-Mar

WEST
END

White Hall Rd

Negril
Hill

Mount
Airy

Negril
Lighthouse

0   0.5
mile

Sunday 1000-2200, no admission fee, you pay for what you do.

Hawkers ('higglers') are annoying and reported to be worse than at Montego Bay. They will interrupt whatever you are doing to push their drugs, hair braiding, aloe etc. Politely decline whatever they are offering (if you do not want it), they do not want to be shrugged off or ignored, but neither do they want to hold a long conversation with you. Fruit is readily available although not ready

to eat; ask the vendor to cut it up and put it in a bag for you. To avoid the worst of the higglers go to the end of the beach near the crafts market where there are no stalls or bars. There are toilets and showers (US$0.30). Behind the bay is the Great Morass, which is being drained for development.

Inland, up in the hills, a golf course has been built: the Negril Hills Golf Club (T 957-4638, F 957-0222) is a new, 18-hole, Par 72, 6,333 yd course, with clubhouse, restaurant, pro shop and tennis.

Local information – Negril
● Transport
The orange minibuses are the cheapest way to travel around the town. There are buses to Negril from both Savanna-la-Mar (about ¾ hour) and Montego Bay. From Montego Bay the fare is about US$2; there are also taxi and colectivo services (see under **Montego Bay** for tours). From the Donald Sangster airport minibuses run to Negril; you must bargain with the driver to get the fare to US$5-7.

● Accommodation
There is a local rule that no hotel in Negril should be taller than the tallest palm tree to minimize the visual and environmental impact of tourism. Many Tourist Board listed establishments, ranging from the (SuperClubs) **L1** *Hedonism II* 280-room all-inclusive adult resort (T 957-4200, F 957-4289, PO Box 25); **L1** *Grand Lido*, another SuperClubs resort at S end of 2-mile sandy beach of Bloody Bay (P O Box 88, T 957-4010, F 957-4317), all-inclusive, couples only, superb food, service and setting, clothes optional, pool and jacuzzi beside its nude beach area, guests can also use the facilities at *Hedonism II*, a short walk across Rutland Point; **L1** *Sandals Negril*, all-inclusive, T 957 4216, Sandals is due to open another all-inclusive, *Beaches Negril*, in 1996; **L1** *Swept Away*, all-inclusive, sports complex, T 800-545 7937, 957-4061, F 957-4060, to several less expensive hotels on Norman Manley Boulevard: **L3** *Negril Gardens Hotel*, PO Box 58, T 957-4408, 800-752-6824, F 957-4374, 65 suites with balconies, gardenside or beach; **L3** *Negril Inn*, PO Box 59, T 957-4370, F 957-4365; **L2-L3** *Foote Prints on the Sands*, PO Box 100, T 957-4300, F 957-3152, 30 rooms, a/c, on beach, cheaper packages sometimes available; **L1** *Poinciana Beach Resort*, PO Box 44, T 957-4256/4100, F 957-

4229, all-inclusive, 130 rooms and villas, scuba diving at extra cost, bicycle rental, 2 pools, gym, jacuzzi, tennis, ping pong, basketball and lots of other sports and watersports, children's programmes, free pass to the Anancy Family Fun and Nature Park opp the resort; **L2-L3 Charela Inn**, on the beach (PO Box 33, T 957-4648/4650/4277, F 957-4414), is rec. *Firefly Beach Cottages*, Norman Manley Blvd, on the beach and therefore not very private (PO Box 54, T/F 957-4358), from a basic cabin for 2, **B**, to studios, **A2**, or 1-3 bedroomed cottages, or luxury villa, **L1-L3**, cabins fall to **D** in summer, gymnasium, min 1 week rental in winter, 3 nights in summer; *Whistling Bird Beach Cottages*, T 957-4403, or in the USA PO Box 7301, Boulder, Colorado 80306, T (303) 442-0722, family business run by Julie and Tim Boydston, 1-3 room cottages US$680-1,500/week, 25% less in summer, full service, private dining room and bar, gardens, hammocks, families welcome. Hotels to the W of centre are about 10-20 mins' walk, and are in a better area for mixing with the locals. **A3-C Tigress 1**, West End Road, cheaper rooms with fan, no hot water, shared bathrooms, higher priced rooms with a/c, hot water, private bath, all with kitchen facilities, good security, bar and pool in nice gardens, 20 mins' walk to beach and walking distance from town centre, friendly, clean, well-maintained, lots of repeat business; **L1-L3 Rock Cliff**, West End, PO Box 67, T 957-4331, F 957-4108, on rocky promontory; **L3-B Mariner's Inn and Diving Resort**, West End, T 957-4348, on cliffs, 52 rooms, PADI and NAUI instructors for diving, kayaking, riding, volleyball; **A1-A2 Ocean Edge Resort**, also on cliffs, PO Box 71, T 957-4362, F 957-4849, 30 rooms; **L3-A3 Addis Kobeb Guest House and Cottages** (PO Box 78, T 957-4485) room in house, entire house (6 rooms) or cottages, 20% less in summer, long term rates negotiable, wooden houses, hammocks outside, shady gardens, restaurant next door. **A3-B Emerald Hotel**, Westland Mountain Rd, c/o Negril PO, T 957-4814, F 957-0000, chalets, small pool, inc breakfast, TV, gardens with hammocks, short walk to beach. **L3-A1 Negril Cabins**, rec, Norman Manley Blvd, on Bloody Bay, across the road from the beach, cabins on stilts, 26 new and more expensive rooms, pool, swim-up bar, private beach, restaurant, piano bar, beach parties, children's programme, security guards keep away 'higglers', PO Box 118, T 957-4350, 800-382-3444, F 957-4381; **D Captain Nemo's**, US$20, just across the street from Joe's Caves, an excellent snorkelling area. Accommodation is available at the Yacht Club, West End Road, PO Box 34, T 999-5732. **B-D Lighthouse Park** on Negril's cliffs, campsite, cabins, tent site **E**, rec. The East End is the more expensive part of town, but there are a few cheap cabins: **C Roots Bamboo** is very neat; **D Coconut International**, on the beach, basic cabin, dirty, no fan; next door is *Gloria's Sunset*, Jamaican family-run, clean, friendly, helpful, security guards at night, variety of accommodation, bar, restaurant, rec. This whole beach is lined with clubs and is noisy. None of the cabins has any services, nor do they provide blankets, but they are right on the beach. When choosing a cabin check to see whether it has a fan, whether there is a mesh or screen to keep out mosquitoes (if not, buy 'Destroyers', 8-hour incense to keep bugs away) and whether it looks safe (many get broken into). Locals living along the beach will often let you camp on their property.

● **Places to eat**

For entertainment try the *White Swan*, where the locals go. *The Dolphin*, next to *New Providence Guest House*, is good. *The Yacht Club* and *Wharf Club* both have restaurants, the latter being cheaper. *Peewee's Restaurant*, in the West End of Negril, has excellent seafood and other dishes at reasonable prices. *Erica's*, restaurant and *The Tigress*, both near West End; latter is cheaper than many and good. *The Hungry Lion*, on the West End road, vegetarian and fish dishes, excellent food and service, relaxing, moderately priced; *Rick's Café*, the 'trendy' place to watch the sunset, full ocean view from cliff top setting but pricey with it, Red Stripe beer or cocktail US$3, plastic bead money used, full restaurant next door, expensive, with even better view of sunset. *Cool Runnings*, with a chef/owner, is also rec. *The Office*, on the beach, open 24 hours, provides a good choice of Jamaican food, reasonably priced and friendly service, a good place to meet the locals. Eating cheaply is difficult but not impossible. The native restaurant-food stalls are good and relatively cheap; the local patties are delicious. Street hawkers will sell you jerk chicken for US$4-5, which is good but barely enough to whet your appetite. *The Bread Basket*, next to the banks at the mall in town is rec, but even better is the *Fisherman's Club* supermarket, just off the beach in the main part of town near *Pete's Seafood*, which is a restaurant as well as a market and serves good local, filling meals for about US$4.

● **Entertainment**

Live reggae shows in outdoor venues most nights, featuring local and well known stars. Entrance is usually US$5-7, good fun, lively atmosphere, very popular. Nice bars are located along the beach, usually with music, unnamed bar next to *Coconut International* rec, friendly service. For a pleasant drink in beautiful surroundings try the bar at the *Rock Cliff Hotel* on the West End Road, friendly barman who mixes great fruit punches and cocktails.

● **Banks**

Two banks (including National Commercial Bank) and *bureau de change* in the shopping centre in town.

● **Tourist office**

In Adrija Plaza, T 957-4243.

EAST TO SAVANNA-LA-MAR

About 18 miles E of Negril, on the coast, is **Savanna-la-Mar**, a busy, commercial town with shopping, banks etc, but no major attractions for tourists. It does not have a good beach, nor good quality restaurants and accommodation. Regular concerts are held at the remodelled St Joseph's Catholic Church (T 955-2648). Talented local musicians play under the auspices of Father Sean Lavery, formerly a professor of music at Dublin University, recommended. It can easily be reached by minibus from Negril and there are hourly buses from Montego Bay (US$2). The Frome sugar refinery, five miles N of Savanna-la-Mar, will often allow visitors to tour their facilities during sugar cane season (generally November-June). Another interesting and unusual outing in this part of Jamaica is to the 6-mile long Roaring River and the Ital Herbs and Spice Farm, two miles N of Petersfield, from where it is remarkably well signposted. The Farm, owned by an American, Ed Kritzler, employs organic methods. There is a cave at Roaring River and the Farm is about half a mile further on. It is a very scenic area with interesting walks and tumbling streams suitable for bathing. A good restaurant serves fish and vegetable dishes at the Farm, best to order lunch before exploring. Totally basic accommodation in a hut available, popular but it is suggested you look before you book.

THE SOUTH COAST

Outside Savanna-la-Mar, the main S coast road (A2) passes by Paradise Plantation, a huge private estate with miles of frontage on Bluefields Bay, a wide protected anchorage with unspoiled reefs and wetlands teeming with birds. Just after Paradise, you come to Ferris Crossroads, where the A2 meets up with the B8 road, a well-maintained N-S connection and about 40 minutes drive to Montego Bay via Whithorn and Anchovy. For the next four miles the A2 hugs the coast along a beautiful stretch of road to *Bluefields*, where there is a lovely white sand beach mainly used by local Jamaicans and guests of the upmarket *Villas on Bluefields Bay*. This beach front resort offers exclusive, luxury, fully-staffed accommodation, US$750- 2,000 per adult per week depending on season, children under 12 US$250, includes food, drinks, transfers, staff and sporting facilities, each villa has a secluded waterfront and pool. Information and bookings through the owners, Deborah and Braxton Moncure, 726 N Washington Street, Alexandria, Virginia 22314, USA (T (202) 234-4010, F (703) 549-6517). There is no mass tourism either in Bluefields or in the adjacent village of Belmont, where plenty of reggae is always playing at the numerous fishermen's bars, but there are a few expatriate homes which might sometimes be available for rent: *Oristano*, the oldest home in W Jamaica, dating back to the 1700s, owned by the Hon William Fielding, an Englishman who does beautiful drawings of the Jamaican greathouses, P O Box 1, Bluefields, Westmoreland Parish; *Two Pelicans*, built right on the side of the main road, this 1950s home is a waterfront cliffhanger with good views, contact the American owners, Steve and Linda Browne, T (301) 924-3464; *Horizon*, a cottage in Belmont, owned by American Mary Gunst, T (603) 942-7633.

The S coast is known as the best part of Jamaica for deep sea fishing and boat trips go out from Belmont to the reefs or to off-shore banks. Snorkelling is also good because the sea is almost always very calm in the morning. The Blue-fields Great House, now privately owned, was the place where Philip Gosse lived in the 1830s when he wrote his famous book, *Birds of Jamaica*, and re-portedly contains the first breadfruit tree planted in Jamaica by Captain Bligh after his expedition to the South Pacific. The next six miles of coast SE of Bluefields is one of the most beautiful, unspoiled coasts in Jamaica, but see it now, a 300-room *Sandals South Coast* resort is being built at Auchindown. However, much of the land is being left untouched on the resort's property. A bird sanctuary has been designated and a section of beach set aside as a turtle nesting area. Just beyond here, A3 *Natania's*, a guest house and seafood restaurant at Little Culloden, White House, has been highly recommended. It is on the sea and has 8 rooms (16 beds), food extra but good and at reasonable prices. The owner is Peter Probst; ad-dress: Natania's, Little Culloden, White House PO, Westmoreland, T/F 963-5342. Transport from Montego Bay can be arranged, as also local tours, deep sea fishing and water sports. A few miles further on, A3 *South Sea View* guest house has 8 bedrooms, British manager, John Ackerman, White House PO, Westmoreland, T 965-2550.

The A2 road passes through Scotts Cove, where you leave Westmoreland and enter the parish of St Elizabeth. It proceeds to the town of Black River, travelling inland from there to Middle Quarters, YS Falls and Bamboo Avenue, after which it ascends to the old hill station of Mandeville.

BLACK RIVER

Black River is one of the oldest towns in Jamaica. It had its heyday in the 18th century when it was the main exporting harbour for logwood dyes. The first car imported into Jamaica was landed here. Along the shore are some fine early 19th century mansions, some of which are being restored.

At Black River, you can go by boat from across the bridge up the lower stretches of the Black River, the longest river in Jamaica (10 miles, duration 1$\frac{1}{2}$-2 hours, US$15 pp, drinks included, 3 boats, 25 people per boat, tours 1100, 1400, 1600 on Mon, Sat, other days 0900, 1100, 1400, 1600). You should see croco-diles (called alligators in Jamaica, most likely at midday when they bask on the river banks) and plenty of bird life in beautifully tranquil surroundings with a very knowledgeable guide (contact South Coast Safaris, Hotel Street, PO Box 129, Mandeville, T 962-0220/2513). If you want to avoid large tour parties, go with a local, whose boats are through the fish market. The boats are smaller, open, slower, quieter and go further up river, which means you see more. They stop at a 'countryside bar' rather than the one the tour companies use. The trip takes about 2 hrs and costs US$27 for 2 including boatman and guide.

Local information – Black River

● **Transport**

To get to Black River from Mandeville by bus involves a change in Santa Cruz.

● **Accommodation**

B-C *Waterloo Guest House*, in a Georgian building (the first house in Jamaica with electric light), old rooms in the main house, or more expensive in the new annex, all with showers, very good restaurant (lobster in season), rec. **B-C** *Hotel Pontio*, 49 High Street (PO Box 35, T 965-2255), with or without a/c, restaurant, rec. Two miles E of Black River is the **B** *Port of Call Hotel*, 136 Crane Road, T 965-2360/2410, a bit spartan but on the sea. Also, **C** *Bridge House Hotel*, Crane Rd, shady gar-den with hammocks leads down to beach, good Jamaican food, US$8-10 for a meal, staff friendly, bar, TV, lounge, ask for odd num-bered room at front to avoid noise from club down beach.

● **Places to eat**

Bayside, near bridge, excellent steamed fish with rice and peas for US$6, usually all gone by 1300; *Caribbe*, near bus station, very good steamed fish and curried goat for US$6 with beer; *Superbus*, an old bus near bus station, good cheap food, eg fried chicken with trimmings and beer for US$3.

THE ROAD TO MANDEVILLE

On the S coast past Black River is **Treasure Beach**, a wide dark sand beach with body surfing waves and one of the most beautiful areas on the island. It is largely used by local fishermen as it is the closest point to the Pedro Banks. There is one small grocery shop and a van comes to the village every day with fresh fruit and vegetables. Accommodation on the beach includes the 20-room L3 *Treasure Beach Hotel*, T 965-2305, F 965-2544; A2 *Old Wharf Resort*, suites, pool, tennis, beach, children's activities, Sandy Bay, PO Box 189, Mandeville PO, T 962-4471, F 962-2858; B *Four M's Cottage*, T/F 965-2472, T 965-0131, Box 4, Mountainside PO, 4 rooms; and several houses you can rent: Sparkling Waters, Folichon, Caprice, and Siwind (PO Box 73, Black River), with its own cove. B *Ital Rest* is a wooden guesthouse, hard to find, known to locals and bus drivers, verandah decks with mountain and sea views, very clean with helpful owners, kitchen available, highly recommended. Camping is possible in the grounds and 'Ital Rest II' is due to open soon. This area is quite unlike any other part of Jamaica, still relatively unvisited by tourists and well worth a visit. The local people are very friendly and you will be less hassled by higglers than elsewhere. To the E of Treasure Beach lies Lovers' Leap, a beauty spot named after the slave and his lover (his owner's daughter) who jumped off the cliff in despair, and Alligator Pond.

If you stay on the A2 instead of turning off at Black River, the road comes to Middle Quarters, on the edge of the Black River Morass (a large swamp); hot pepper shrimp are sold by the wayside, but insist that they are fresh (today's

catch). Just after Middle Quarters is the left turn which takes you to the beautiful YS Falls (pronounced Why-Ess), an unspoiled spot in the middle of a large private plantation and well worth visiting. There is a 15-minute walk from where you park your car. You can bathe but there are no changing rooms or other facilities; plan a morning visit as there is no shelter in case of afternoon rain. Further along the main road is the impressive 2½-mile long Bamboo Avenue (badly hit by Gilbert but now recovering). The Jamaica Tourist Board is building a travellers' halt, which will have food and toilets. North of Bamboo Avenue is Maggotty, on the (closed) railway line from Montego Bay to Kingston and close to the Appleton Estate, where tours of the rum factory are offered (for information contact Jamaica Estate Tours Ltd, T 997-6077, F 963-2243, or T 963-2210/2216, T 952-6606, Montego Bay. Regular tour parties come from Montego Bay and Negril hotels). Opposite the Maggotty train depot is the Sweet Bakery, run by Patrick and Lucille Lee, who can arrange accommodation in a Great House (B) or at a rustic campsite (D-E), very friendly and helpful, local trips organized, Mrs Lee is an excellent cook.

MANDEVILLE

After Bamboo Avenue, the A2 road goes through Lacovia and Santa Cruz, an expanding town on the St Elizabeth Plain, and on up to **Mandeville**, a beautiful and peaceful upland town with perhaps the best climate in the island. It is very spread out, with building on all the surrounding hills and no slums (population 50,000). In recent years Mandeville has derived much of its prosperity from being one of the centres of the bauxite/alumina industry (though industrial activity is outside the town).

The town's centre is the village green, now called Cecil Charlton Park (after the ex-mayor, whose opulent mansion, Huntingdon Summit, can be visited with prior arrangement). The green looks a bit like New England; at its NE side stands a Georgian courthouse and, on the SE, St Mark's parish church (both 1820). By St Mark's is the market area (busiest days are Monday, Wednesday and Friday – the market is supposed to be moved elsewhere) and the area where buses congregate. West of the green, at the corner of Ward Avenue and Caledonia Road, is the Manchester Club (T 962-2403), one of the oldest country clubs in the West Indies (1868) and the oldest in Jamaica. It has a 9-hole golf

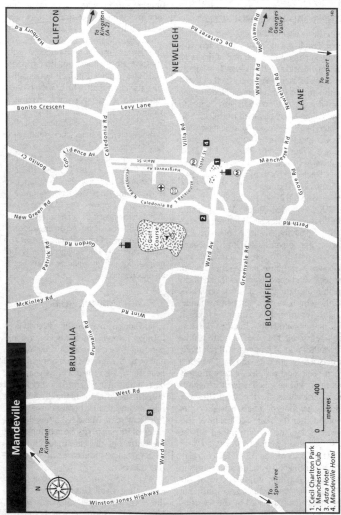

Mandeville

1. Cecil Charlton Park
2. Manchester Club
3. Astra Hotel
4. Mandeville Hotel

course (18 tee boxes, enabling you to play 18 holes) and tennis courts (you must be introduced by a member). Also, horse riding can be arranged, T Ann Turner on 962-2527.

Local information – Mandeville
● **Accommodation**

Diana McIntyre-Pyke, the proprietress of the small, family run **L3-A3** *Astra Hotel* (62 Ward Avenue, PO Box 60, T 962-3265/3377, F 962-1461) and her staff provide a highly efficient and cheerful information service about everything to be done in the area, the restaurant is good and service friendly, but the highly rec hotel is some way from the town centre. Even if not staying at the *Astra*, you can seek information on the following there: community tourism (meeting the local community), tourism in central and S Jamaica, an island-wide bed and breakfast programme, villa rentals, staying with local families, and tours of Mandeville, free for guests.

In the centre is the **A1-A2** *Mandeville Hotel*, 4 Hotel Street (PO Box 78, T 962-2138, F 962-0700), TV, spacious, pool, restaurant, excursions arranged, good. Cheaper accommodation is available at **C** *Rodan's Guest House*, 3 Wesley Avenue (T 962-2552), with bath, basic, no fan, uncomfortable beds. **B** *Kariba Kariba*, Atkinson's Drive, near New Green roundabout on Winston Jones highway, first right off New Green Road, 45 mins' walk from centre, on bus route, T 962-3039, bath, fan, 5 rooms or suites, inc breakfast, TV lounge, bar, dining room. The owners, Derrick and Hazel O'Conner, are friendly, knowledgeable and hospitable, they can arrange for you to meet local people with similar interests and offer tours. Derrick is developing a 12-acre farm at Mile Gully (opportunity for work if you wish) and plans to develop a small campsite, bar, accommodation and other facilities.

● **Places to eat**

Technically a restaurant, but also rec for its décor (of old cars and licence plates) and atmosphere is *Bill Laurie's Steak House*, 600 feet above the town, good for views, steaks, conversation (closed Sun). *Pot Pourri*, on second floor of the Caledonia Mall, just N of the Manchester Club, clean and bright, good food and service; *International Chinese Restaurant*, Newport Road; *Hunger Hut*, 45 Manchester Road, cheap, excellent food and service (owner, Fay, grew up in England and likes a chat).

● **Shopping**

Westico Health Foods, by the West Indies College, run by Seventh Day Adventists; they also run a vegetarian restaurant behind the church in the town centre, opening hours erratic. Craft Centre, sponsored by the Women's Club of Manchester, on Manchester Road.

● **Banks**

Bank of Novia Scotia; National Commercial Bank.

EXCURSIONS

Although some way inland Mandeville is a good place from which to start exploring both the surrounding area and the S coast. (In fact, by car you can get to most of Jamaica's resorts, except those E of Ocho Rios or Kingston, in two hours or less.) Birdwatchers and those interested in seeing a beautiful 'great house' in a cattle property should contact Robert Sutton at Marshall's Pen (T 962-2260, US$10 for Great House tour by appointment only). Robert is the island's top ornithologist (23 of Jamaica's endemic bird species have been observed here). The *Astra Hotel* can arrange a visit. Also around the town you can visit the High Mountain Coffee and Pioneer Chocolate Factories, a factory making bammy (a delicacy from cassava root), the Alcan works, and local gardens.

There are interesting excursions N to Christiana (at about 2,800 feet, **A3** *Hotel Villa Bella*, 18 rooms and suites, restaurant, in six acres with orchard of ortaniques and bananas, nature walks, riding, special interest groups catered for, PO Box 473, Christiana, T 964-2243, F 964-2765, SW to the Santa Cruz mountains, and S to Alligator Pond on the coast. East of Alligator Pond is Gut River, where you can sometimes see alligators and manatees; cottages can be rented near the very picturesque river flowing into the sea (contact through *Astra Hotel*). Boat and fishing trips can be made to Pigeon Island, with a day on the island for swimming and snorkelling.

From Mandeville it is about 55 miles E to Kingston on the A2, bypassing May Pen, through Old Harbour then on to Spanish Town and Kingston. Before the May Pen bypass, a road branches S to **Milk River Bath**, the world's most radioactive spa. The baths are somewhat run down, but the medical properties of the water are among the best anywhere (US$0.60, 20 mins, open 0800-2130, Sun-Mon). About three miles from the baths is a marine conservation area, Alligator Hole, where manatees (sea cows) can sometimes be seen. Local boatmen will do their best to oblige.

Information for travellers

BEFORE TRAVELLING

● Documents

Canadian and US citizens do not need passports or visas for a stay of up to 6 months, if they reside in their own countries and have some proof of citizenship (eg a birth certificate, certified by the issuing authority with an embossed seal, together with a voter's registration card). Residents of Commonwealth countries (except Nigeria, which requires a visa), Austria, Belgium, Denmark, Finland, France, Iceland, Eire, Israel, Italy, Luxembourg, Mexico, Netherlands, Norway, Spain, Sweden, Switzerland, Turkey and Germany, need a passport and an onward ticket for a stay not exceeding 6 months. Citizens of all other countries must have a visa, passport and onward ticket. Immigration may insist on your having an address, prior to giving an entry stamp. Otherwise you will have to book a hotel room in the airport tourist office (friendly and helpful). For visa extensions, apply to Ministry of Social security and Justice, Kingston Mall, 12 Ocean Blvd, Kingston, T 922-0800.

● Climate

In the mountains, the temperature can fall to as low as 7°C during the winter season. Temperatures on the coast average 27°C, rising occasionally to 32° in July and August and never falling below 20°. The humidity is fairly high. The best months are December to April. Rain falls intermittently from about May, with daily short tropical showers in September, October and November.

MONEY

● Currency

The Jamaican dollar (J$) is the local currency but foreign currency up to US$100 is legal tender for purchases of goods and services, with change given in J$.

● **Exchange**

The Jamaican dollar floats on the foreign exchange market. The only legal exchange transactions are those carried out in commercial banks, or in official exchange bureaux in major hotels and the international airports. It is illegal to buy, sell or lend foreign currency without a licence. Banks pay slightly more for US$ travellers cheques than for cash. Retain your receipt so you can convert Jamaican dollars at the end of your stay. Most banks and exchange bureaux, inc at the airport, will not accept US$100 bills because of forgeries.

Note that if using credit cards the transaction will be converted from the agreed J$ rate into US$ before you sign, be sure to verify exact rate that is being used, often a 5-10% downward adjustment can be instantly obtained by this enquiry. Rates in Negril can be worse than in Montego Bay.

GETTING THERE

AIR

From Europe British Airways and Air Jamaica fly direct, between London and Kingston and Montego Bay with lots of connections from other European cities. LTU International Airways has a weekly flight to Montego Bay from Dusseldorf. Martinair Holland has a weekly flight from Amsterdam to Montego Bay. Condor flies weekly from Frankfurt to Montego Bay. There are many charter flights from Europe which change according to the season, check with travel agent.

From North America Air Jamaica has services to Kingston and/or Montego Bay from Atlanta, Baltimore, Chicago, Fort Lauderdale, Los Angeles, Miami, New York, Orlando, Philadelphia. Air Canada flies from Toronto to Kingston and Montego Bay. American Airlines flies from Atlanta, Boston, New York and Miami daily to Montego Bay and from New York, Orlando and Miami daily to Kingston with lots of connections to other cities through Miami. TWA flies from St Louis, Missouri to Montego Bay, US Air flies to Montego Bay from Baltimore, Boston, Charlotte, Hartford and New York. Continental from New York and Northwest Airlines from Fargo, Minneapolis and Tampa to Montego Bay. American Trans Air flies from Milwaukee and Orlando to Montego Bay. Enquire in Florida about cheap flights from Fort Lauderdale and Orlando.

From the Caribbean and Latin America

Cayman Airways and Air Jamaica connect the Caymans and Jamaica. BWIA flies to Kingston from Antigua, Barbados, Trinidad and Sint Maarten, while ALM flies to Kingston from Curaçao. There is a Cubana flight 3 times a week from Havana to Kingston. Tropical Airlines flies from Santiago de Cuba to Montego Bay 4 times a week and from Varadero 3 times. Air Jamaica fly from Kingston and Montego Bay to Nassau. Copa flies Panama City-Kingston and Montego Bay 3 times a week. SAM flies to Montego Bay from Bogotá via Barranquilla twice a week.

SEA

It is extremely difficult to book a passage by ship to other Caribbean islands. There are cruise ship ports in Ocho Rios, Montego Bay, Port Antonio and Kingston. About 11 cruise lines call.

ON ARRIVAL

● **Airports**

Details of the 2 international airports are given under Kingston and Montego Bay. Montego Bay airport is the only one really within walking distance of most hotels. The Kingston airstrip is at Tinson Pen which is only 2 miles from the centre of town on Marcus Garvey Drive, but those at Ocho Rios and Port Antonio are a long way out of town. There is no sales tax on air tickets purchased in Jamaica but there is a stamp duty which rises according to the value of the ticket.

● **Airlines**

Air Jamaica head office: The Towers, Dominica Drive, Kingston 5, T 929-4661 (opens at 0830), offices in Montego Bay, T 952-4300, Negril, T 957-4210, Ocho Rios, T 974-2566; British Airways is also in The Towers, T 929-9020/5, 952-3771 (Montego Bay). BWIA, 19 Dominica Drive, Kingston 5, T 929-3771/3, 924-8364 (airport), 952-4100 (Montego Bay). American Airlines, T 924-8305 (Kingston), 952-5950 (Montego Bay).

● **Banks**

The central bank is the Bank of Jamaica. National Commercial Bank of Jamaica, 77 King Street, Kingston and branches all over the island; the same applies to the Bank of Nova Scotia Jamaica Ltd (head office: Duke and Port Royal Streets, Kingston). Citibank, 63-67

254

Security

The per capita crime rate is lower than in most North American cities, but there is much violent crime. This is particularly concentrated in downtown Kingston but can be encountered anywhere on the island. You are advised not to walk any street in Kingston after dark. There are large areas of W Kingston where you should not go off the main roads even by day and even in a locked car. The motive is robbery so take sensible precautions with valuables. When in need of a taxi you are recommended to go into a shopping mall or hotel and have one ordered, rather than hail one in the street. Gang warfare increased before the 1993 elections and has been exacerbated by the US policy of deporting Jamaican criminals, who return to Kingston to shoot it out with local gangs. There were 777 murders in 1995, the highest number since 1980, when 857 were recorded.

Beware of pickpockets in the main tourist areas and be firm but polite with touts. Do not wear jewellery. Do not go into the downtown areas of any towns especially at night. Avoid arriving in a town at night. Take a taxi from bus stations to your hotel. Travellers have reported being threatened for refusing to buy drugs and Jamaicans can get aggressive over traffic accidents, however minor, or even if you refuse to give a lift to a hitch hiker. Observe the obvious precautions and you should have no problem. The vast majority of Jamaicans welcome tourists and want to be helpful but the actions of the minority can leave you with the impression that dollar-spending tourists are not wanted.

Emergency telephone numbers: Fire/Ambulance 110, Police 119.

Knutsford Boulevard, Kingston; and other local banks. A string of ATM's has been installed in main centres from which you can withdraw cash from Visa and Mastercards. Immediate money transfers can be made via the Western Union Bank, behind the National Commercial Bank at the top of Knutsford Boulevard, or through American Express, at Stuarts Travel Services, 9 Cecilio Avenue (T 929-3077).

● **Clothing**
Light summer clothing is needed all the year round, with a stole or sweater for cooler evenings. Some hotels expect casual evening wear in their dining rooms and nightclubs, but for the most part dress is informal. Bathing costumes, though, are only appropriate by the pool or on the beach.

● **Drugs**
Marijuana (ganja) is widely grown in remote areas and frequently offered to tourists. Cocaine (not indigenous to Jamaica) is also peddled on the N (tourist) coast and in Kingston. Possession of either drug is a criminal offence and on average well over 50 foreigners are serving prison sentences in Jamaica at any given moment for drug offences. The police may stop taxis, cars etc in random road checks

and search you and your luggage. Airport security is being continually tightened (sniffer dogs, etc) to prevent drug exports. You have been warned.

● **Embassies and consulates**
British High Commission is at 26 Trafalgar Road, Kingston 5, T 926-9050, F 929-7869, PO Box 575. Twenty six other countries represented. **The British Council** has an office in the First Life Building, 64 Knutsford Boulevard, PO Box 575, Kingston 5, T 929-6915, 929-7049, F 929-7090, with an information library, mainly on education, British newspapers available.

● **Hours of business**
Offices: usually open from 0900-1700 Mon to Fri. **Shop**: hours vary between 0830 and 0930 to 1600 and 1730, depending on area, Mon to Sat; there is half-day closing (at 1200) on Wed in Down Town Kingston, on Thur in uptown Kingston and Montego Bay, and on Fri in Ocho Rios. **Banking hours**: are 0900-1400 Mon to Thur, 0900-1500 on Fri (there may be some local variations).

● **Official time**
Eastern Standard Time, 5 hours behind GMT and an hour behind the Eastern Caribbean.

● **Photography**
Film is reasonably easily obtained but take spares of essentials such as Lithium batteries as they are difficult to find and expensive. Glare and UV light is constant, take suitable filters. Do not photograph Jamaicans without their permission, the men, particularly in Kingston, can get aggressive.

● **Public holidays**
New Year's Day (1 January), Ash Wednesday, Good Friday and Easter Monday, Labour Day (4th Mon in May), Independence Day (1st Mon in August), National Heroes Day (3rd Mon in October), Christmas and Boxing Day (25-26 December).

● **Shopping**
In the craft markets and stores you can find items of wood (by Rastafarians and Maroons), straw, batik (from a number of good textile companies) and embroidery; the hand-knitted woollen gold, red, green Rasta caps (with or without black dreadlocks affixed) are very cheap; jewellery from Blue Mountain Gems, near Rose Hall, Montego Bay area; for art and ceramics, Devon House gallery, Chelsea Galleries on Chelsea Road, Gallery 14, Old Boulevard Gallery, Contemporary Art Centre in Liguanea; Blue Mountain coffee is excellent, cheaper at airport duty free shop than in supermarkets or tourist shops.

Please remember to check with legislation (and your conscience) before buying articles made from tortoiseshell, crocodile skin, and certain corals, shells and butterflies. Many such animals are protected and should not therefore be bought as souvenirs. It is illegal to take or possess black or white coral in Jamaica; sea turtles are protected and you should refuse to buy products made from their shells. The closed season for lobster fishing is April-June, so if lobster is on the menu check where it has come from.

Some shopkeepers offer a 10-15% discount on all goods but in fact merely refrain from adding the tax when payment is made. Street vendors never add tax.

● **Tipping**
Hotel staff, waiters at restaurants, barmen, taxi drivers, cloakroom attendants, hairdressers get 10-15% of the bill. In places where the bill already includes a service charge, it appears that personal tips are nonetheless expected. In some areas you may be expected to give a tip when asking for local information.

● **Voltage**
110 volts, 50 cycles AC; some hotels have 220 volts.

● **Weights and measures**
On 31 Mar 1996 Jamaica introduced the metric system of weights and measures, under legislation passed at the end of 1995.

ON DEPARTURE

● **Departure tax**
There is an airport departure tax of J$500, payable in Jamaican or US dollars, for all those who have been in the island over 24 hours. Cruise ship passengers pay a US$15 tax.

ACCOMMODATION

Because Jamaica is a major tourist destination there are a great many hotels and restaurants, particularly in the tourist areas. Full and up to date information is available at all tourist information centres. We only mention those which have recently been recommended for whatever reason. The brochure *Elegant Resorts* features most of the hotels in the top price-range which have reciprocal arrangements. All-inclusive resorts are extremely popular in Jamaica and development has been led by SuperClubs and Sandals, with hotels mainly along the N coast; some allow children but most are for couples. As a result of their popularity, other hotels have been forced to discount their rates, so bargains can be found. SuperClubs can be contacted in the USA on T 1-800-859-SUPER or (305) 925-0925; in the UK T 01749 677200, F 01749 677577.

Visitors on a low budget should aim to arrive at Montego Bay rather than Kingston because the former is the island's tourism capital with more cheap accommodation. Get hold of the Tourist Board's list of Hotels and Guest Houses, which gives rates and addresses, and also a copy of *Jamaica Vacation Guide* (both free). For bed and breakfast possibilities throughout Jamaica, contact the *Astra Hotel*, Mandeville (T 962-3265/3377, telex 2426 Jamhotels, Diana McIntyre-Pike).

Information/reservations for self-catering villas and apartments can be done through the Jamaica Association of Villas and Apartments (JAVA), see below, who represent over 300 private houses. Renting a villa may be an attractive option if you do not intend to do much travelling and there are 4/6 of you to share the costs (about US$1,000-1,500 per week for a nice villa with private swimming pool and fully staffed). You will, however, probably have to rent a car as you will have to take the cook shopping, etc. You can go ever more up-market and pay US$2,000-14,000 a week for a fully staffed luxury villa through Elegant Resorts Villas International, T 993-2287.

Accommodation is subject to a 15% value added tax called the General Consumption Tax, which may or may not be included in a quoted room rate; you have to check.

Larger hotels have introduced strict security to prevent guests being bothered by hustling.

FOOD AND DRINK

● **Food**
Local dishes, fragrant and spicy, are usually served with rice. There are many unusual and delicious vegetables and fruits such as sweet-sop, soursop and sapodilla. National specialities include codfish ('stamp-and-go' are crisp pancakes made with salt cod) and ackee; curried goat; and jerked pork, highly spiced pork which has been cooked in the earth covered by wood and burning coals. Chicken is cooked in the same way and all along the roadsides are signs advertising jerk pork or jerk chicken. Patties, sold in specialist shops and bars, are seasoned meat or lobster in pastry; normally very good value. Curried lobster is a delightful local speciality. Stew peas is chunks of beef stewed with kidney beans and spices and served with rice. Along the coast, fish tea is a hotch potch of the day's catch made into a soup, US$1 a cup.

● **Drink**
Local rum (white or brown, overproof and underproof), and the cocktails which combine it with local fruit juices, or mixed with Ting, the carbonated grapefruit soft drink; Tia Maria, the coffee liqueur and quite a lot of other liqueurs; Red Stripe lager, with which, the locals say, no other Caribbean beer compares, about US$1 at road side bar, considerably more in a hotel. Try the Irish Moss soft drink. All rums are very cheap duty free, typically US$13 for a 3-pack.

GETTING AROUND

AIR TRANSPORT

There are internal flights by Tropical Airlines between Montego Bay, Kingston, Negril and Ocho Rios. There is also an airport at Port Antonio. Charges are reasonable (US$50

Kingston-Montego Bay return) but using this method of travel is not very satisfactory unless you can arrange to be met at your destination.

LAND TRANSPORT
● **Motoring**
Driving times and distances of major routes: Kingston to Montego Bay 117 miles, 3 hours, to Ocho Rios 55 miles, 2 hours, to Port Antonio 68 miles, 2 hours; Montego Bay to Negril 50 miles, 1½ hours, to Ocho Rios 67 miles, 2 hours; Ocho Rios to Port Antonio 67 miles, 2½ hours. The speed limit is 30 mph in built up areas, 50 mph on highways.

Try to avoid driving outside towns at night. Roads, even on the coast, are twisty and in the mountains extremely so, add potholes and Jamaican drivers and you are an accident waiting to happen. Plan ahead because it gets dark early. Even in daylight driving is dangerous; the coastal road from Kingston to Port Antonio is in a particularly bad condition and the drivers awful. Between 1989 and 1993 there were over 42,000 accidents in which 2,441 people died. The introduction of highway patrols and a ticketing system for driving offences helped to reduce the number of accidents from 8,574 in 1994 to 7,379 in 1995. Breath tests from drunk driving are being considered. Ask car hire firms or hotels for estimates of journey times but remember that distances stretch when overtaking is difficult. Petrol stations often close on Sun; note that fuel is paid for in cash.

● **Car hire**
Undoubtedly a rented car is the most satisfactory, and most expensive, way of getting about. All the major car rental firms are represented both at the airports and in the major resort areas. There are also numerous local car rental firms which are mostly just as good and tend to be cheaper. The Tourist Board has a list of members of the Jamaica U-Drive Association, Newlin Street, Ocho Rios, T 974-2852. Be prepared to pay considerably more than in North America or Europe (starting from about US$65/day plus CDW of US$9-12 and tax of 12½%). Many companies operate a 3-day minimum hire policy. Island Car Rentals is a well known firm, airport office T 924-8075, 924-8389, Montego Bay T 925-5771, Kingston T 926-8861. Praise Tours & Auto Rentals Ltd, 72 Half Way Tree Road, Kingston 10, T 929-3580/6961/6931, F 929-3555, good deals on longer rentals, no trouble with refunds,

airport transfers, rec. Don's Car Rental, headquarters 1 Worthington Avenue, New Kingston, Kingston 5, T 926-2181, F 926-0866, also offices at Negril Aerodrome, T 957-4366, *Trident Hotel*, Port Antonio, T 993-2241 and *Shaw Park Hotel*, Ocho Rios, T 974-7726, rates from US$46/day, US$276/week for small Ford in low season, US$50 and US$300 respectively in high season, buses with driver from US$102/day. In the resort areas of Montego Bay, Ocho Rios and Negril, jeeps are available for about US$90 a day, motorbikes and scooters from US$30 and bicycles from US$5. Watch out for sunburn.

● **Buses**
Public road transport is mostly by minibus. This is cheap but overcrowded and generally chaotic and only to be recommended for the young and fit ("Step Up!" shouted by the conductors means please move down the bus, there is plenty of room at the back!). Be prepared also for a certain amount of physical abuse from the bus company front men as they compete for your custom. Country buses are slow and sometimes dangerous. There are also minibuses which ply all the main routes and operate on a 'colectivo' basis, leaving only when full.

● **Taxis**
There are taxis, with red PP licence plates, in all the major resort areas and at the airports. Some have meters, some do not. Only the JUTA taxis have officially authorized charges to all destinations, with others (Yellow Cab, Checker Cab etc), the important point is to ask the fare before you get in. It can be around US$2 for a short hop, US$3-4 from New Kingston to Down Town, US$7 from Down Town to Mona Campus. All taxis should charge the same to the airport. The tourist information centres should also be able to help in this respect. Some 'non-tourist' taxis operate like minibuses, ie have a set route and can be flagged down. They will cram about 6 passengers into a small Lada, but if you do not want to share you can hire it all to yourself. Negotiate the fare in advance. To take a taxi for long distance is expensive; a JUTA taxi from Kingston to Ocho Rios for example could cost US$90, rather more than a day's car hire, although you could negotiate a fare less than half that with a smaller taxi company.

● **Train**
There was a train, called 'The Diesel', between Kingston and Montego Bay through some spectacular hilly scenery for much of the journey, especially around the edge of the Cockpit Country. Although out of operation in 1994 the line may reopen one day. Kingston station is in a deserted, not very safe-looking area, take a taxi. The line between Kingston and Port Antonio was damaged in a hurricane some years ago, and there are no plans to repair it.

COMMUNICATIONS

● **Postal services**
There are post offices in all main towns. Post offices handle inland and overseas telegrams. Postcards and letters to Europe, Asia and Oceania J$1. The sorting office on South Camp Road, Down Town Kingston, has a good and helpful philatelic bureau.

● **Telecommunications**
Cable, telephone, fax and telex services are operated by Telecommunications of Jamaica (70% owned by Cable & Wireless). It has main offices in Kingston and Montego Bay, but calls can easily be made from hotels. 'Time and charge' phone calls overseas cost the same in hotels as at the phone company, but there is a 15% tax and a J$2 service charge. In fact, making an international call is often easier from a hotel. Anywhere else you need a 10-digit access number, without which you cannot even make a collect call from a private phone. The only other method is a card phone, if you can find one which is working and you are prepared to queue. You can buy telephone cards at supermarkets J$50 but check that it is valid for the year you want to use it, several people have been sold out of date cards (particularly around Jan/Feb) and there is no refund. The international telephone code for Jamaica is 809. Although Telecommunications of Jamaica has a monopoly on phone, fax and telex services until 2006, competition is allowed in other areas such as electronic mail, teletext and videotext.

MEDIA

● **Newspapers**
The daily paper with the largest circulation is *The Daily Gleaner*, which also publishes an evening paper, *The Star* and the *Sunday Gleaner*. *The Jamaica Herald* is a livelier daily than *The Gleaner*, also the *Sunday Herald*. The other daily is the *Observer*. *Money Index* is a financial weekly, in Montego Bay *The Western*

Mirror is weekly. *Lifestyle* is a monthly glossy magazine, *Jamaica Journal* is a quarterly with interesting but academic articles.

ENTERTAINMENT

Apart from the performance arts mentioned above, most large hotels and resorts have evening entertainment, usually including calypso bands, limbo dancers, fire eaters, etc.

TOURIST INFORMATION

● **Local tourist office**
Circulates detailed hotel lists and plenty of other information. Head office at ICWI Building, 2 St Lucia Avenue, Kingston 5, PO Box 360, T 929-9200/19, F 929-9375. Other offices in Jamaica: at the international airports; Cornwall Beach, Montego Bay, PO Box 67, T 952-4425 or T 952-2462, airport, nights, holidays, F 952-3587; Ocean Village Shopping Centre, Ocho Rios, PO Box 240, T 974-2582/3, T 974-2570, F 974-2559; City Centre Plaza, Port Antonio, PO Box 151, T 993-3051/2587, F 993-2117; Adrija Plaza, Negril PO, Westmoreland, T 957-4243, F 957-4489; Hendricks Building, 2 High Street, Black River PO, T 965-2074/5, F 965-2076.

● **Tourist offices overseas**
Overseas offices: **New York**: 801 Second Avenue, 20th Floor, New York, NY 10017, T (212) 856-9727, F 856-9730; **Chicago**: 500 N Michigan Avenue, Suite 1030, Chicago, IL 60611, T (312) 527-1296, F 527-1472; **Miami**: Suite 1100, 1320 South Dixie Highway, Coral Gables, Fl 33146, T (305) 665-0557, F 666-7239; **Los Angeles**: 3440 Wilshire Boulevard, Suite 1207, Los Angeles, CA 90010, T (213) 384-1123, F 384-1780; **Toronto**: 1 Eglinton Avenue East, Suite 616, Toronto, Ontario M4P 3A1, T (416) 482-7850, F 482-1730; **London**: 1-2 Prince Consort Road, London SW7 2BZ, T (0171) 224 0505, F 224 0551; **Frankfurt**: Pan Consult, Falkstrasse 72-74, D-60487 Frankfurt 90, Germany, T (069) 70 74 065, F (069) 70 1007; **Paris**: 32 rue de Ponthieu, 75008 Paris, T 45 61 90 58, F 42 25 66 40; **Rome**: c/o Sergat Italia SRL, via Monte dei Cenci 20, 00186 Roma, T (6) 686-9112, F 687-3644; **Tokyo**: Chigusa Building, 6th Floor, 1-5-9 Nishi-Shinbashi Minato-ku, Tokyo 105, T 03-3591 3841, F 03-3591 3845.

The Jamaica Association of Villas and Apartments (JAVA), Pineapple Place, Ocho Rios, Box 298, T 974-2508, F 974-2967, has information on villas and apartments available for rent; also 1501 W. Fullerton, Chicago, IL 60614, T (312) 883-1020, F (312) 883-5140 or toll free (800) 221-8830. In the UK, The Caribbean Centre, 3 The Green, Richmond, Surrey, TW9 1PL, T 0181 940 3399, F 0181 940 7424, handles accommodation reservations and car rental arrangements.

● **Local travel agents**
Stuart's Travel Service Ltd, King's Plaza, Constant Spring Road, Kingston, T 929-4222/5, also at Spanish Town, Maypen, Linstead, Browns Town, Ocho Rios, Port Antonio and Montego Bay, members of IATA and Amex representative. Pauline Stuart is an exponent of alternative tourism. Sense Adventures, Box 216, Kingston 7, T 927-2097, F 929-6967, for expeditions, adventure travel and camping, see page 230. Adventure Tours, David and Nicki Reynolds, Orange Bay, Green Island, Hanover, T 999-9857, for tailor-made tours, town and country, historic sites and adventure travel (see page 244). UTAS Tours, T 952-3820, 979-0684, F 979-3465, offer weekends in Havana: Juta Tours, T 926-1537; Caribic Tours, T 979-9387.

● **Maps**
The *Discover Jamaica* road map (American Map Corporation) costs US$1 but is widely available free from Tourist Offices. It has plans of Kingston, Montego Bay, Negril, Mandeville, Ocho Rios, Port Antonio and Spanish Town. The ITM Road Map of Jamaica (1:250,000, International Travel Map Productions, PO Box 2290, Vancouver, BC, V6B 3W5, Canada) also includes plans of Kingston, Montego Bay, Spanish Town, Mandeville, Port Antonio and Ocho Rios. Good clear series of 1:50,000 maps covering Jamaica in 20 sheets from Survey Department, 23½ Charles Street, PO Box 493, Kingston.

● **Further reading**
Tour Jamaica by Margaret Morris is probably the best general guide to Jamaica for a traveller and widely available locally (US$7). The *Insight Guide to Jamaica*, besides being a general guide, delves more deeply into history, culture, etc, and is beautifully illustrated (US$14). Many other books about different aspects of Jamaica are also on sale, for example, *A to Z of Jamaican Heritage*, in the Heinemann Caribbean series. For ornithologists the standard work is *Birds of the Caribbean* by James Bond (after whom Ian Fleming named his James Bond).

Ray Chen has published 2 magnificent books of photos (Periwinkle Press) and also does photos for postcards and posters. *Jamaica In focus, A Guide to the People, Politics and Culture*, by Marcel Bayer was published in 1993 as part of a series by Latin American Bureau (Research and Action) Ltd, 1 Amwell Street, London EC1R 1UL; also published in Jamaica and the Caribbean by Ian Randle Publishers, 206 Old Hope Road, Kingston 6, and in a Dutch language edition by Royal Tropical Institute, 63 Mauritskade, 1092 AD Amsterdam, and Novib, The Hague, the Netherlands.

Turks and Caicos Islands

THE TURKS AND CAICOS ISLANDS lie 575 miles SE of Miami, Florida, directly E of Inagua at the S tip of the Bahamas and N of Hispaniola. They comprise about 40 low-lying islands and cays covering 193 square miles, surrounded by one of the longest coral reefs in the world.

HORIZONS

The Turks and the Caicos groups are separated by the Turks Island Passage, a 22-mile channel over 7,000 feet deep which connects the Atlantic and the Caribbean, contributing to the area's profusion of marine life. Generally, the windward sides of the islands are made up of limestone cliffs and sand dunes, while the leeward sides have more lush vegetation. The S islands of Grand Turk, Salt Cay and South Caicos are very dry, having had their trees felled by salt rakers long ago to discourage rain. The other islands have slightly more rain but very little soil and most of the vegetation is scrub and cactus.

Only eight islands are inhabited. The main islands of the Turks group, Grand Turk and Salt Cay, shelter two fifths of the colony's 7,901 'belongers', as the islanders call themselves, but only a third of the total resident population of 13,000. The rest of the population is scattered among the larger Caicos group to the W: South Caicos, Middle (or Grand) Caicos, North Caicos, and Providenciales, the most populous, known locally as 'Provo'. Pine Cay and Parrot Cay are resort islands. East and West Caicos, inhabited from 1797 to the mid-19th century, are now the private domain of wild animals. East Caicos is home to swarms of mosquitoes and wild

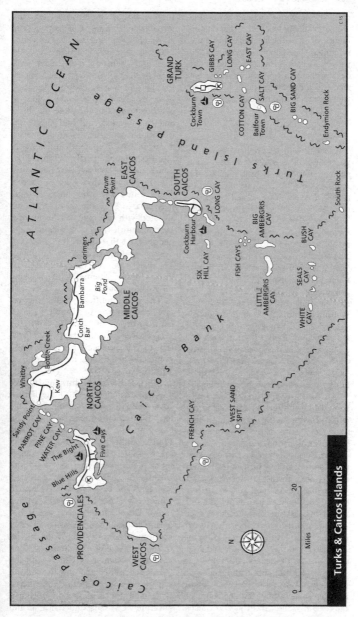

ATLANTIC OCEAN

Turks Island Passage

GRAND TURK

GIBBS CAY
LONG CAY
EAST CAY
Cockburn Town
COTTON CAY
SALT CAY
Balfour Town
BIG SAND CAY
Endymion Rock

EAST CAICOS

Drum Point

SOUTH CAICOS

LONG CAY

Cockburn Harbour

SIX HILL CAY

FISH CAYS

BIG AMBERGRIS CAY

BUSH CAY

South Rock

Lorimers

Bambarra

Big Pond

MIDDLE CAICOS

Conch Bar

LITTLE AMBERGRIS CAY

SEALS CAY

WHITE CAY

Caicos Bank

Whitby

Bottle Creek

Kew

NORTH CAICOS

Sandy Point
PARROT CAY
PINE CAY
WATER CAY
The Bight
Five Cays
Blue Hills

FRENCH CAY

WEST SAND SPIT

PROVIDENCIALES

WEST CAICOS

Caicos Passage

N

20

Miles

0

Turks & Caicos Islands

cattle, while West Caicos harbours land crabs, nesting pairs of ospreys and flamingoes. Most of the smaller cays are uninhabited. The people of the Turks and Caicos are welcoming and friendly. The development of tourism on Provo has changed attitudes there, however, and friendliness is not universal.

HISTORY

The islands' first dwellers were the peaceful Tainos, who left behind some ancient utensils and little else. By the middle of the 16th century not one Lucayan, as Columbus named them, remained. Like the Lucayans in the Bahamas islands, they were kidnapped for use as slaves or pearl divers, while many others died of imported diseases. The discovery of the islands, whether by Columbus in 1492 or later by Ponce de León, is hotly disputed. There is a very convincing argument that Columbus' first landfall was on Grand Turk, not Watling Island in the Bahamas, now officially named San Salvador. The infamous Caicos Banks S of the Caicos group, where in the space of 1,000 yards the water depth changes from 6,000 to 30 feet, claimed many of the Spanish ships lost in the central Caribbean from the 16th to the 18th century. The islands were named after the Turk's Head 'fez' cactus found growing on the islands. The name Caicos comes from the Lucayan, *caya hico*, meaning string of islands.

The Bermudan traders who settled the islands of Grand Turk, Salt Cay, and South Caicos in the 17th century used slaves to rake salt for sale to British colonies on the American mainland, and fought pirates and buccaneers for over 200 years. During the American Revolution, British loyalists found refuge on the islands, setting up cotton and sisal plantations with the labour of imported slaves. For a while, cotton and sisal from the islands were sold in New York and London, solar salt became the staple of the economy, and the Turks and Caicos

thrived, but all these products encountered overwhelming competition from elsewhere. The thin soil was an added disdvantage and a hurricane in 1813 marked the demise of cotton plantations.

Following an alternation of Spanish, French and British control, the group became part of the Bahamas colony in 1766. Attempts to integrate the Turks and Caicos failed, rule from Nassau was unpopular and inefficient and abandoned in 1848. Links with Jamaica were more developed, partly because London-Kingston boats visited frequently. The Turks and Caicos were annexed to Jamaica in 1874. After Jamaica's independence in 1962, they were loosely associated with the Bahamas for just over 10 years until the latter became independent. At that point, the Turks and Caicos became a British Crown Colony. The Anglican Church maintained its links with the Bahamas, which is where the Bishop resides.

The main political parties were established in 1976: the People's Democratic Movement (PDM) and the Progressive National Party (PNP). From time to time independence is raised as a political issue but does not have universal support.

The isolation of the Turks and Caicos and the benign neglect of the British government led to increasing use of the islands as refuelling posts by drug smugglers en route from South America to Florida until preventive action was taken in 1985. In that year the islands found themselves in the news headlines because of corruption and narcotics scandals. The Chief Minister, Norman Saunders and Stafford Missick, Minister for Development, were arrested in Miami on drugs charges and accused of accepting bribes to allow drugs planes to land and refuel on South Caicos. Saunders resigned as Chief Minister, was found guilty and imprisoned, although he has now returned to the islands and to politics. Constitutional government was suspended in 1986 and direct rule from the UK was imposed while investigations continued into malpractice by other public officials.

In March 1988, general elections restored constitutional government. These were won by the PDM, and Oswald Skippings took office as Chief Minister. The April 1991 elections brought the PNP, led by Washington Missick, back to power with eight seats (4,866 votes) while the PDM were reduced to five (4,542 votes). Economic austerity measures and civil service job cuts made the PNP unpopular with the electorate. In the latest elections, held in January 1995 the PDM won by 171 votes and now holds eight seats over the PNP's four. The thirteenth seat is held by Norman Saunders, who stood as an independent (winning by six votes) after failing to win the PNP nomination. The Chief Minister is Derek Taylor, leader of the PDM since the 1991 election defeat when Oswald Skippings resigned. The latter was named Minister of Communications, Transport, Tourism, Information and Caricom affairs.

In 1996 the Government and the opposition joined forces to try to oust the Governor, Martin Bourke, after a number of incidents, the latest of which involved an interview for an insurance journal, with some defamatory remarks about drugs smuggling through the islands. All members of the Legislative Council petitioned for his removal but had it rejected by the Foreign and Commonwealth Office. However, the Governor's term was not renewed when it expired in Sept 1996.

GOVERNMENT

The Turks and Caicos are a British Dependent Territory. The British monarch is Head of State, represented by a Governor. The Executive Council chaired by the Governor is formed by six ministers, the Financial Secretary, the Attorney General and the Chief Secretary, the last two being British government appointments. The Legislative Council has 13 elected members and 2 party-appointed members.

THE ECONOMY

The traditional economic activity, salt production, ceased in 1964, and for two decades there was little to generate legal income apart from fishing, government employment and some tourism. National resources are limited, even water has to be strictly conserved. Agriculture is almost non-existent and limited to subsistence farming of corn, pigeon peas, sweet potatoes and some livestock. Small scale fishing is important for job creation. Practically all consumer goods and most foodstuffs are imported. There is a rice milling plant on Grand Turk which has provided a few jobs. The lack of a manufacturing base and any major employment activities led in the 1960s and 1970s to thousands of local people emigrating to the nearby Bahamas or the USA to seek work. This trend has now been reversed as the economy has improved and the population is rising. Belongers have returned and unskilled labour, much of it illegal, comes from Haiti and the Dominican Republic.

One area of growth in the 1980s was that of offshore companies, over 12,000 of which were registered in the islands by 1993. There is no income tax, no company tax, no exchange control and no restriction on the nationality or residence of shareholders or directors. New legislation and the creation of the Offshore Finance Centre Unit (OFCU) were designed to regulate and promote the growth of offshore finance and encourage banking, insurance and trust companies. Five international banks have been granted offshore licences and some 1,350 offshore insurance companies have been licensed. A project to promote jurisdiction was started in the 1990s with several conferences to publicize the industry, which has a reputation for being well-administered and scandal-free.

Budgetary aid from the UK for recurrent expenditure was eliminated in fiscal year 1986/87 and the islands are aiming to be self-financing. Capital aid remains, augmented by financial assistance from the European Community, the European Investment Bank and the Caribbean Development Bank. In 1992 the British Government approved a capital aid package of US$43mn over three years, the largest ever awarded by the UK in the Western Hemisphere. Included in the aid was an award of US$2mn for 'good government'. The 1994 Public Sector Reform made sweeping cuts in the civil service and redundancies saved an estimated US$2mn a year. A 3-year British aid package for 1994/95 to 1996/97 granted a further £21mn for the islands.

The main area of economic growth and revenue for the islands is tourism. Investment has taken place in infrastructure, particularly airfields, hotels and marinas. The opening of a *Club Méditerranée* in 1984 doubled the number of visitors to the Turks and Caicos in two years. By 1991, the annual number of visitors reached 54,616, from 11,900 in 1980, but numbers declined in 1992, partly because of the collapse of Pan Am. Nevertheless, the arrival of American Airlines' twice daily flight to Providenciales from Miami and numerous North American charters pushed tourist numbers up to 78,957 in 1995. 23,000 of those visitors came primarily for the diving, a rise of 80% over 1994. American continues to be the only international carrier. The news that Sandals was to take over the *Royal Bay Resort* in 1996 was a further filip to the industry.

FAUNA AND FLORA

The islands support 175 resident and migrant species of birds, including flocks of greater flamingoes, frigate birds, ospreys, brown pelicans, the ruby throated humming bird, the belted kingfisher, white billed tropic birds, black-necked stilts, snowy plovers, peregrine falcons, red-tailed hawks, northern harriers, Baltimore orioles and scarlet tanagers and many others. There are lizards, iguanas, two species of snake, including a pygmy boa, and two species of bat. A system of National Parks, Nature Reserves and Sanctuaries has been set up; entrance to Sanctuaries is by permit only. The Turks and Caicos National Trust (Box 261, Grand Turk, T 946 1723) plans to develop and protect the Princess Alexandra National Park on Providenciales' N shore. The S parts of North, Middle and East Caicos have been designated a wetland of international importance under the Ramsar Convention to protect waterbirds, lobster, conch, flora and a fish nursery.

DIVING AND MARINE LIFE

Marine life is varied and beautiful and can be enjoyed by snorkellers and sailors as well as scuba divers. Colourful fish and grouper can be seen on the coral and close to the shore you can find green turtles, loggerhead turtles and manta and spotted eagle rays.

A bottle-nosed dolphin, known as Jo Jo, frequents the Princess Alexandra Marine Park along the N coast of Providenciales in the Grace Bay area, although he is also found occasionally in other locations. He used to be attracted by boats and humans, apparently enjoying swimming and playing with people, while often coming in very close to the shore. However he has not been seen as often as in the past and it is speculated that he may have a mate or may be getting tired of human pressure. If you are fortunate enough to see or swim with him, remember that he is a protected wild animal: do not touch him. For more information contact Jo Jo's warden at VHF 'Sea Base' channel 68 or 73 or T/F 941 5617; the Jo Jo Dolphin Project is supported by the Bellerive Foundation.

In January-March, hump back whales migrate through the deep Turks Island Passage on their way S to the

Silver and Mouchoir Banks breeding grounds N of the Dominican Republic. Beyond the reef are the game fish such as tuna, blue marlin, wahoo, snapper, bill fish and barracuda. Because there is no soil run off from the islands, water visibility is excellent. Great care is being taken to conserve the reefs and the coral is in very good condition. The islands have become one of the most highly regarded diving locations in the region. Laws to conserve marine resources are strict. Do not take live coral, sea fans or other marine life. No spearguns are allowed.

There are 13 dive operations on Provo, offering courses (resort course approx US$125, full certification US$375) and dive packages. The standard cost of a two tank dive is US$60. Several companies are based at Turtle Cove: Flamingo Divers, PO Box 322, Providenciales, T/F 946 4193, T 800-204-9282, caters for small groups of experienced or novice divers, PADI and SSI instruction. Provo Turtle Divers, PO Box 219, T 946 4232, 1-800-328 5285, F 941 5296, *Turtle Cove Inn* at Turtle Cove marina and at *Ocean Club Resort*, Grace Bay, run by the very knowledgeable and long-time resident, Art Pickering, is also recommended for small groups of experienced divers at similar prices. Turtle In Divers, a full-service dive centre with 45-ft catamaran , accommodating 49 passengers, excellent for handicapped divers, T 941 5389. *Silver Deep*, Admiral's Club, T 941 5595, F 946 4527, 21 ft dive boat, seafood barbecue on the beach, native captain. Caicos Adventures, by Banana Boat, T 941-3346, 36 ft custom boat trips to West Caicos, French Cay for small groups, full service, NAUI/CMAS. On Grace Bay are: Dive Provo, located at the *Turquoise Reef Resort*, PO Box 350, T 946 5029/5040, F 946 5936, 3 boats, windsurfing, kayaks. *Club Med* also has a dive boat for in-house guests, T 946 5500, but caters for large parties. *Le Deck* Diving Centre, instruction in 5 languages, 23-ft

boat, full service plus windsurfing and sailing, T 946 5547, 800-528-1905, F 946 5770. Provo Aquatic Adventures, *Royal Bay Resort* (to become Sandals in 1997), T 946 8000, F 946 8001, small groups, 21-ft boat, native PADI divemaster. At Leeward Marina is: *J & B Tours*, T 946 5047, F 946 5288, 24-ft dive boat, courses.

There is a recompression chamber at Menzies Medical Practice on Provo, T 946 4242, DAN insurance is accepted. Some of the best diving is off the wall at Northwest Point, West Caicos and French Cay.

On Grand Turk there are two dive organizers. Blue Water Divers Ltd is on Front Street, next to the museum, PO Box 124, Grand Turk, T/F 946 2432. Mitch Rolling and Dave Warren offer a complete range of courses and special day trips with two small boats (bimini tops for shade). Sea Eye Diving, run by Cecil Ingham and Connie Rus, is a larger operation with underwater photography and a range of watersports on offer. They can be found at two locations on Duke Street, one next to the *Salt Raker Inn* and the other next to the *Sitting Pretty*. They have five boats, maximum 12 divers per boat, NAUI and PADI instruction, US$55 per dive, frequent cay trips, dive packages with accommodation available, PO Box 67, T/F 946 1407. The highlight of diving here is the wall off Cockburn Town, which drops suddenly from 40 feet to 7,000 feet only ¼ mile offshore. There are 25 moored sites along the wall where you can find coral arches, tunnels, canyons, caves and overhangs.

On Salt Cay, Porpoise Divers is based at the *Mount Pleasant Guest House*, run by Brian Sheedy, T 946 6927 (see under Salt Cay). The main dive boat is an ex-landing craft and divers swim up the ramp, making it suitable for disabled divers, although there is also a purpose-built 30-ft dive boat. A 2-tank dive is US$50, but most people stay at the guest house and take a 5-day package for US$795 which includes three meals, transfers and unlimited day and night diving. There are seven moored dive sites and off Great Sand Cay there is an 18th century British shipwreck, the *Endymion*, still loaded with cannon. A wall chart telling her story is on sale at gift shops on the islands and at the Museum on Grand Turk. She was found in 1991 by Brian Sheedy with the help of a local historian, Josiah Marvel, and the only way to visit her is with Porpoise Divers. The wreck lies in about 25 ft of water with the remains of two other ships nearby: a Civil War steamer and a ship dating from around 1900. The coral is prolific and the fish plentiful and huge. The best time for a visit is May-November.

On the W side of the Turks Island Passage the wall along the E shores of South Caicos and Long Cay also drops gradually or steeply from a depth of about 50 feet, with many types of coral and a variety of fish of all sizes. Grouper, barracuda, turtles, black durgeon, sharks and rays are all common. The disadvantage is that being on the windward side, the sea is sometimes rough, making boat dives difficult. Snorkelling is rewarding with several shallow reefs close to the shore. On South Caicos *Club Carib* Dive and Watersports offers 2-tank dives for US$50, excellent diving and snorkelling with eagle rays 5-10 minutes offshore, T 946 3444, F 946 3446, packages available. On North Caicos *Club Vacanze* at *Prospect of Whitby Hotel* will arrange diving and snorkelling at US$50 per dive and US$15 per snorkel, T 946 7119, F 946 7114.

There are live-aboard boats for those who want to spend a week doing nothing else but diving. *Sea Dancer* (Peter Hughes Diving, 1390 S Dixie Highway, Suite 2213, Coral Gables, Fl 33146, T 800-9-DANCER or 305-669-9391) operates from the Caicos Marina Shipyard, has accommodation for 18 people and offers 5 dives a day around French Cay, West Caicos and Northwest Point. *Aquanaut*, T 946 4048, a 50-ft motor catamaran sleeps 4 to 6 experienced diving guests. The *Ocean Outback* at Sapodilla Bay, Provo, T 941 5810, owned and operated by Captain Bill Rattey Jr, exuberant host and excellent chef, is a 70-ft rather shabby liveaboard cruising mostly along the N reef and West Caicos, also does day-trips with the help of smaller boats exploring Silly Cay, settlers ruins, pirate caves and carvings, barbecue on deserted beach, at reasonable prices (Box 1163, Dania, Fl 33004, T 305-923-3483, T/F 809-941 5810). *The Turks and Caicos Aggressor*, contact the Aggressor Fleet Limited, PO Drawer K, Morgan City, LA 70381, T (504) 385 2416, 1-800-348 2628, F (504) 384 0817.

All divers must have a valid certificate; there are plenty of training courses for novices. The best months for diving are April-November. The sea is often rough in February-March. For detailed descriptive information consult the *Diving, Snorkelling, Visitor's Guide to the Turks and Caicos Islands*, by Captain Bob Gascoine.

BEACHES AND WATERSPORTS

There are 230 miles of white sand beaches round all the islands surrounded by coral reefs and azure water. Grace Bay on Provo is the longest stretch of sand, at 12 miles, and despite the hotels it is possible to find plenty of empty space, but *no* shade. There is rarely any shade on the beaches. Most watersports can be arranged through the hotels. There are restrictions on motorized watersports in the marine park and jetskis have been banned.

Several tour operators represent all-day sails, scuba dives or snorkelling trips or you can contact the captains direct or through your hotel. **Sailing** trips include: *Sea 'N' Double*, 36-ft catamaran, day charter, snorkelling, T 941 3117; *Aquanaute*, Turtle Cove Marina, T 946 4240, VHF Eagle Ray, 60-ft trimaran with glass bottom viewing room; *Beluga*, Leeward Going Through, T/F 946 4396, VHF 68, 37-ft catamaran, private full and half-day sails; *Caicos Sol*, Sapodilla

Bay, T 946 4965, VHF 16, 51-ft fibreglass ketch yacht, snorkelling, lunch, to French Cay and West Caicos; *Minx*, Turtle Cove Marina, T 946 5122, 41-ft trimaran, up to 6 people, day, sunset, overnight trips; *My Choice*, Turtle Cove Marina, T 946 4203, VHF 16, 41-ft sailing sloop, day/sunset cruises with Captain Ron; *Tao*, Turtle Cove Marina, T 946 4783, VHF 77, 56-ft trimaran, full or half-day cruise, sunset or glow worm; *Two Fingers*, Grace Bay, T 946 4783, VHF 77, 36-ft catamaran, full and half-day cruises, snorkelling; Galio Exploration's *Karina V*, 1938 heritage cruising yacht, French cuisine, diving, snorkelling, through J & B Tours, T 946 5047. See also *Ocean Outback*, under **Diving and Marine Life**.

Windsurfing Provo at *Turquoise Reef Resort*, Grace Bay, T 946 5040, offers sailing and kayaking as well as windsurfing. Parasailing with Turtle Parasailing, *Turtle Cove Inn*, costs 'US$50 a fly', T/F 941 5389.

There are marinas on Provo at Turtle Cove, Leeward Going Through and Caicos Shipyard (which also has dry storage). South Caicos also has a marina. There are no bareboat charter fleets.

Fishing is popular: Provo and Pine Cay have the best bonefishing but it is also possible at South Caicos, Middle Caicos, North Caicos and Salt Cay. May is the prime time. Fishermen have not organized themselves into offering packages, so you have to find your own accommodation and fishing guide. Shop around before, committing US$250-300/day because experienced visitor fishermen have reported a lack of skill, professionalism and simple amenities among local guides. On Providenciales, choices are: Captain Barr Gardiner, 'Hammerhead' Joe Stubbs, 'Black Diamond' Earl Musgrove. Leeward Going Through Marina is the best place to find and talk to fishermen, or try to reach them on the radio, VHF 16. J & B Tours will arrange full and half-day fishing, T 946 5047; *Gilley's* restaurant will cook

your catch. *Silver Deep*, Arthur Dean includes fishing in his itinerary, T 941 5595.

There is sport fishing aboard the *Sakitumi* with Captain Bob Collins, T 946 4203 to leave a message, VHF Channel 16 'Sakitumi'. Other charters include *Fairtide* 40-ft Egg Harbour, Turtle Cove Marina, T 946 4684, F 946 4283 (also bonefishing); *I'se the B'ys*, Captain Fred Healey, Turtle Cove Marina, T 941 3698, full or half day charters; *Ricochet*, 45-ft Hatteras, Captain John Brant, Turtle Cove Marina, T 941 3891; *Silver Deep*, native Captain Arthur Dean, bone and bottom fishing, T 941 5595. On Grand Turk fishing can be arranged through Ossie (Oswald) Virgil, of Virgil's Taxis at the airport, or PO Box 78, T 946 2018. On Middle Caicos fishing and boating is arranged through the District Commissioner's Office, T 946 6100, with Dotis Arthur and her husband, Cardinal. On South Caicos a bonefish specialist is Julius 'Goo the Guide' Jennings, US$20/hour, who can be contacted through the *Club Carib*, T 946 3444, F 946 3446.

A US$10 sport fishing licence, for pole fishing only, is required from the Fisheries Department, Grand Turk, T 946 2970, or South Caicos, T 946 3306, or Provo, T 946 4017. Ask your guide whether the fishing licence is included in his package. Spear fishing is not allowed. An international billfishing tournament is held annually coinciding with the full moon in July, T 946 4106, F 946 4771.

OTHER SPORTS

An 18-hole championship **golf** course opened November 1992 (black tees 3,202 yards, white tees 2,865 yards). Owned by the water company, it is located within walking distance of the *Club Med*, *Turquoise Reef*, *Grace Bay Club*, *Ocean Club* and *Columbus Slept Here Bed & Breakfast*. Most hotels offer 3-5 day packages of green fees and mandatory carts, otherwise it costs US$80 pp, T 946 5991, F 946

5992, licensed snackbar. An amateur open golf championship is held in October. There are **tennis** courts on Grand Turk at the *Coral Reef* and on Provo at *Club Med*, *Erebus Inn* and the *Turquoise Reef*. There are also courts on Pine Cay and North Caicos at *The Prospect of Whitby*. A small but active squash community welcomes visitors and can be contacted at Johnston Apartments, Kings Court, T 946 5683/4201/4606. Island Network sports and fitness centre with aqua/land aerobics is at *Erebus Club*, contact Darlene, T 946 4240. *Fun & Fit Health Club*, next to NAPA on Leeward Highway, offers weights and machines, aerobics, personal training and nutrition advice. There is a certified fitness trainer, T 941 3527, ask for Lisa.

FESTIVALS

Most events are linked to the sea and land-based acitivities are tacked on to regattas or fishing tournaments. In Providenciales the billfishing tournament (see above) is a big event with lots of parties every night. Provo Day festivities follow Emancipation Day in August and a carnival procession starts in Blue Hills and ends Down Town, with floats, band and dancing. Festivities culminate in the choosing and inauguration of Miss Turks and Caicos Islands, who competes in international beauty pagents. On Grand Turk a fishing tournament and the Cactus Fest are held in Aug, with competitions for sports, costumes, bands and gospel; there is a float parade, dancing and an art exhibition. On North Caicos, Festarama is in July; on Middle Caicos, Expo is in August; on South Caicos the Regatta with associated activities is in May.

GRAND TURK

Grand Turk (*pop* 3,691) is the seat of government and the second largest population centre, although it has an area of only seven square miles. The island was called Amuana by the Lucayans, Grand

Saline by the French and Isla del Viejo by the Spanish. The E coast is often littered with tree trunks and other debris which have drifted across from Africa, lending credence to the claim that Columbus could have been carried here, rather than further N in the Bahamas chain. Grand Turk is not a resort island although there are hotels and dive operations which concentrate mostly on the wall just off the W coast. The vegetation is mostly scrub and cactus, among which you will find wild donkeys and horses roaming (there are plans to establish a donkey sanctuary with the aid of a British charity). Behind the town are old salt pans, with crumbling walls and ruined windmills, where pelicans and other waterbirds fish. More abandoned salt pans can be seen around the island, particularly towards the S.

Cockburn Town, the capital and financial centre, has some very attractive colonial buildings, mostly along Duke Street, or Front Street, as it is usually known. The government offices are in a nicely restored, small square with cannons facing the sea. The oldest church on Grand Turk is **St Thomas' Anglican church** (inland, near the water catchment tanks), built by Bermudan settlers. After a while it was considered too far to walk to the centre of the island and **St Mary's Anglican church** was built in 1899 on Front Street overlooking the water. The **Victoria Library**, built to commemorate 50 years of Queen Victoria's reign, is also an interesting building, pink, with shutters. Walking N along Front Street you come to **Odd Fellows Lodge**, opposite the salt pier, which is thought to be one of the oldest buildings on the island and was probably the place where the abolition of slavery was proclaimed in 1832.

Continue N to the **Turks and Caicos National Museum** opened in 1991 in the beautifully renovated Guinep Lodge (entrance US$5 for non-residents, US$2 residents, US$0.50 students, open Monday-Friday 1000-1600, Saturday

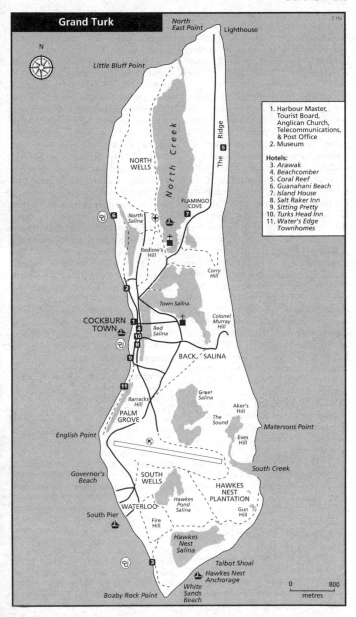

Grand Turk

North East Point
Lighthouse
Little Bluff Point

1. Harbour Master,
   Tourist Board,
   Anglican Church,
   Telecommunications,
   & Post Office
2. Museum

Hotels:
3. *Arawak*
4. *Beachcomber*
5. *Coral Reef*
6. *Guanahani Beach*
7. *Island House*
8. *Salt Raker Inn*
9. *Sitting Pretty*
10. *Turks Head Inn*
11. *Water's Edge Townhomes*

N

NORTH WELLS

North Creek

The Ridge

FLAMINGO COVE

North Salina

Bedlow's Hill

Corry Hill

Town Salina

COCKBURN TOWN

Red Salina

Colonel Murray Hill

BACK SALINA

Great Salina

Aker's Hill

The Sound

Matersons Point

Barracks Hill

PALM GROVE

English Point

Eves Hill

South Creek

Governor's Beach

SOUTH WELLS

WATERLOO

Hawkes Pond Salina

HAWKES NEST PLANTATION

Gun Hill

South Pier

Fire Hill

Hawkes Nest Salina

Talbot Shoal

Hawkes Nest Anchorage

White Sands Beach

Boaby Rock Point

0   800
metres

C 15a

1000-1300, for further information contact the curator, Brian Riggs, Box 188, Grand Turk, T 946 2160). The exhibition on the ground floor is of the early 16th century wreck of a Spanish caravel found on the Molasses Reef between West Caicos and French Cay in only 20 feet of water. The ship is believed to have been on an illegal slaving mission in the islands, as evidenced by locked leg irons found on the site. A guided tour is highly recommended although not essential. Upstairs there is an exhibition of local artifacts, photos, stamps, coins, a few Taino beads, figures and potsherds; expansion is planned, the museum is still growing. A local historian, the late Herbert Sadler, compiled many volumes on the theory of Columbus' landfall and local history, some of which are on sale at the museum.

There is now an attractive walkway beside the salinas behind the town. There is a shaded viewing spot for birdwatchers and palm trees have been planted all along Pond Street to improve the view. Elaine Huard runs an animal sanctuary (United Humanitarians) at her home on Duke St, where she usually has up to 40 dogs and cats. She brings vets from Canada 3 times a year to provide free sterilizations, medicines and general care for the domestic and stray animals on the island. Her dedicated voluntary work has made her something of a national institution and she is always pleased to receive visitors. Donations welcome.

The Governor's residence, **Waterloo**, S of the airport, was built in 1815 as a private residence and acquired for the head of government in 1857. Successive governors and administrators have modified and extended it, prompted partly by hurricane damage in 1866 and 1945, and by the Queen's visit in 1966. In 1993 the building was again renovated and remodelled; the works were so extensive they constituted a near rebuilding of the historic residence. Governor's Beach is one of the nicest

beaches and excellent for snorkelling, with isolated coral heads rising out of the sand and a wide variety of fish and invertebrates.

Further S is an ex-USAF base, known as South Base, which is now used as government offices, and beyond there some pleasant beaches on the S coast, with good snorkelling at White Sands beach by the point. US Navy, NASA and Coast Guard bases were once important for the economy of Grand Turk; John Glenn, the first American to orbit the earth, splashed down off Grand Turk in the 1960s. In 1994 a US-financed land base was built to process Haitian refugees under an agreement with the British and Turks and Caicos governments. It was barely used and all that remains is some barbed wire in the S and a large area of cleared scrubland.

North of Cockburn Town a paved road leads along The Ridge up the E side of the island to the 1852 lighthouse and another abandoned US base, from where there are good views out to sea. A channel at the N point gives access to North Creek, an excellent hurricane shelter for boats. The island's carnival takes place in late August.

Island information – Grand Turk
● **How to get there**
Airlines and schedules tend to change frequently. Most visitors to Grand Turk arrive with American Airlines to Provo and then shuttle over on a small aircraft. This works quite smoothly, but note that you won't arrive in Grand Turk until about 2100, and the return connection leaves at 0700 to meet the 1000 American Airlines flight. TCA flies from Cap Haitiën in Haiti twice a week and Puerto Plata in the Dominican Republic three times a week. More destinations have been applied for. SkyKing flies to Jamaica and Cap Haitiën (the Dominican Republic and Cuba on request). TCA (T 946 4255), SkyKing (T 946 1520) and Inter Island Airways (Provo, 941 5481, also office and aircraft based at Grand Turk airport, efficient even at very short notice) operate frequent inter-island flights and it is often possible to turn up on the day you want to travel and catch the next flight. Reservations

are rec, however, particularly when going to Provo. For those arriving by sea, there is a safe harbour and marina at Flamingo Cove, North Creek, run by Leah and Kirk, T 946 2227.

● **Transport**
There are no buses on Grand Turk and taxis are the only form of public transport (US$4 from the airport to the *Kittina Hotel*, the nearest). Jeeps or cars can be rented from Tropical Auto Leasing, US$55/day, everything included except fuel, T 946 1000, Sunshine Auto Leasing, by airport, T 946 1588, rec, Dutchie's Car Rental, Airport Rd, T 946 2244, rec, or C J Car Rental, T 946 2744. If you rent a bicycle, jeep or car, note that the islanders completely ignore the 20 mph speed limit in town (and 40 mph outside), particularly on Pond Street rec to stay on Front Street/Duke Street route through town and exercise caution elsewhere. Fatal accidents have occurred.

● **Accommodation**

Price guide

L1	over US$200	L2	US$151-200
L3	US$101-150	A1	US$81-100
A2	US$61-80	A3	US$46-60
B	US$31-45	C	US$21-30
D	US$12-20	E	US$7-11
F	US$4-6	G	up to US$3

In an old Bermuda-style building on Duke Street, built by Bermudan ship-wright Jonathon Glass in the 1840s, facing the beach is the very friendly, relaxed and unpretentious **L3-A3** *Salt Raker Inn*, run by Jenny Smith, 12 rooms, some basic, budget rooms, others more comfortable, most with sea view, dive packages, PO Box 1, T 946-2260, F 946-2432; also good but under new ownership in 1996 is the **A1-A3** *Turks Head Inn* on Duke Street, built in 1869 also by Jonathon Glass, first as a private house but later used as a doctor's dispensary, the American Consulate and once a guest house for the British Government, set back from the beach surrounded by tall trees, 6 rooms, with wooden floors, beds and balconies, fully equipped 2-bedroom apartment available, dive packages with Blue Water Divers or Sea Eye, PO Box 58, T 946-2466, F 946 2825; **L2-A1** *Sitting Pretty*, rooms on ground floor, renovated under new ownership 1996, open directly onto the sand, suites available with kitchenette, PO Box 42, T 946 2232, F 946 2877; **A2** *Sadler's Seaview Apartments*, Duke Street, S of Cable and Wireless,

2 apartments with fan, TV, patio, fully equipped kitchens, laundry and maid service, small beach across the road, contact Marjorie Sadler, PO Box 31, T 946 2569/2374, F 946 1523; also on Front Street, Angela and Douglas Gordon have a large guest suite with sea view, **A2** *Beachcomber House*, also referred to as 'The Gordons', behind the government buildings, close to beach and restaurants, inc superb breakfast, with homemade bread and muffins, and huge afternoon tea, no tax or service charges, dive packages available, PO Box 110, T 946 2470, open Nov-April only, in UK T 01673 838548 for bookings during summer months when the Gordons are off the island; **L1** *Water's Edge Townhomes*, S of town, T 946 2055, F 946 2911, three 2-storey houses on beach; **L3** *Arawak Inn*, right on the beach at SW end of island, new in 1995, 15 spacious suites, clean, nicely furnished, well-equipped kitchens, porches, private, all with sea view, charming beach bar/restaurant, unpretentious, beach is quiet and empty, pool, dive packages available, PO Box 190, T 946 2276/7, F 946 2279; N of town on Lighthouse Rd, **L2-A2** *Island House*, opened 1996, 7 different suites with kitchen and barbecue, TV, phone, a/c, fan, on edge of North Creek, pool, laundry facilities, maid service, bicycles and golf carts available, diving, fishing etc can be arranged, contact Colin and Lucy Brooker, PO Box 36, T/F 946 2646; **L3-A2** *Coral Reef*, has an extensive wooden deck running all round the hotel, on the E coast away from the town, lovely colours in the sea but debris washed up frequently, rather dark studios and one-bedroom apartments with kitchenette although all sea-facing, PO Box 156, T 946 2055/7, F 946 2911, pool, lit tennis court, fitness centre; **L2-L3** *Guanahani Beach Hotel*, on the broad, sandy Pillory Beach on the W coast N of the town, refurbished, landscaped and improved in 1995, 16 twin-bedded rooms, 2 apartments, all with sea view, balcony, TV, a/c, fan, pool, dive packages with Sea Eye Diving, PO Box 178, T 946 2135/2666, F 946 2668/1460.

● **Places to eat**
The best restaurants and bars are at the hotels. The outdoor *Salt Raker Inn* is rec for good food and pleasant company, it is a popular meeting place and fills up on Wed and Sun barbecue nights when Mitch and Dave, from Blue Water Divers, play the guitar and sing; the *Turks Head Inn* is also a gathering place with

a friendly bar and good food; *Water's Edge*, between the two, is a reasonably priced, good restaurant open 1100-2300, closed Mon, T 946 1680; *Ocean View Hotel*, rec for good food, atmosphere, indoor or patio dining, friendly watering hole, the only pizza on the island; the *Guanahani* has a restaurant where the fish is excellent; for local food and lunch specials try *Touch of Class* on the road S, a/c, TV, bar, filling, tasty portions; the *Poop Deck* is a tiny bar, set back from the road in the centre of town by the sea, local food and hamburgers at lunchtime, chicken and chips in the evenings; local food also at *Regal Beagle* on the road N of town on the W side of North Creek, a favourite lunch place; the best conch fritters are at *Peanut's* snack bar on the waterfront, not to be missed.

SALT CAY

Seven miles S of Grand Turk, Salt Cay (population 208) is out of the past, with windmills, salt sheds and other remnants of the old salt industry and little else. The island was first visited by the Bermudans in 1645; they started making salt here in 1673 and maintained a thriving salt industry until its collapse in the 1960s. Production ceased all together in 1971. The main village is **Balfour Town**, divided into North Side and South Side, noted for its Bermudan buildings and pretty cottages with stone walls around the gardens. The White House dominates the skyline; built in the 1830s of Bermudan stone brought in as ballast, by the Harriott family during the height of the salt industry. The Methodist Church nearby, one of several churches on the island, is over 125 years old. Look into some of the ruined houses and you will find salt still stored in the cellars. Plant life was curtailed during the salt raking days to prevent rainfall. Snorkelling is good and diving is excellent; there are seven moored dive sites along the wall, with tunnels, caves and undercuts. In January-March you can often see the humpbacked whales migrating through the channel as they pass close to the W coast.

Island information – Salt Cay

● **How to get there**

There is a paved airstrip for small aircraft, around which a fence has been erected to keep out the donkeys. The island is served by TCA, with 2 5-minute flights Mon, Wed, Fri from Grand Turk, one at 0645 and one at an indeterminate time (about 1530) in the afternoon, making a day trip possible. Alternatively, charter a flight, or get a seat on someone else's charter, which costs the same if you can fill the aircraft, or contact the District Commissioner's Office on Salt Cay (or Brian Sheedy at *Mount Pleasant Guest House*) for details of ferries. The only public transport on the island is the taxi van run by Nathan Smith (T 946 6920), airport pickup and touring; there are very few vehicles of any sort.

● **Accommodation**

The most expensive and exclusive hotel is the architect-designed and owned **L1** *Windmills Plantation* on a 2½-mile beach, which appeals to people who want to do nothing undisturbed, 8 suites, inc all food and drink, meals taken family style, local recipes, saltwater pool, no children, diving can be arranged with Porpoise Divers, reservations (min 3 nights) *The Windmills Plantation*, 440 32nd Street, West Palm Beach, FL 33407, T 800-822 7715, F 407 845 2982, on Salt Cay T 946 6962; at the other end of the scale is the cheerful **A1** *Mount Pleasant Guest House*, owned by amiable host Brian Sheedy, who also runs Porpoise Divers, a salt raker's house built in 1830, can sleep 25 (but only take 12 on the dive boat) in 4 simple rooms in the main house, 2 with shared bath, and in a separate annex/guesthouse which has 3 basic rooms downstairs with kitchen and living room and a dormitory with 7 beds upstairs, 5-night dive package US$795, 9 nights US$995 inc 3 excellent meals, transfers and unlimited diving, processing facilities for dive photos, video/TV, library, bicycles, horses for riding or driving, outdoor restaurant/bar with the best food on the island, rec as 'even on a rainy day it is a pleasure to be a guest at the *Mount Pleasant Guest House*, which has such interesting guests!' T 946 6927; Mrs Irene Leggatt runs the small **A3** *Halfway House* on the sea shore in Balfour Town, 3 rooms, 2 bathrooms, pleasant, clean, good homemade breakfast US$5, lunch, dinner by reservations, T 946 6936; the **L2-L3** *Castaways* villas along the beach N of *Windmill Plantation* are also available for rent

Nov-May, T 946 6921 or (315) 536-7061. Leon Wilson, the Legislative Council PDM Representative for Salt Cay, runs a small, friendly bar, *One Down And One To Go*, with iced beer and Guinness stout, dominoes, pool table, table tennis.

SOUTH CAICOS

The nearest Caicos island, 22 miles W of Grand Turk (*pop* 1,198), South Caicos was once the most populous and the largest producer of salt, but is now the main fishing port, having the benefit of the most protected natural harbour. As a result, yachts frequently call here and there is a popular annual regatta held at the end of May. Excellent diving along the drop off to the S, snorkelling is best on the windward side going E and N. The beaches here are totally deserted and you can walk for miles beachcombing along the E shore. Boat trips can be organized with fishermen to the island reserves of Six Hill Cays and Long Cay. Further S are the two Ambergris Cays, Big and Little, where there are caves and the diving and fishing are good.

Cockburn Harbour is the only settlement and is an attractive if rather run down little place with lots of old buildings, a pleasant waterfront with old salt warehouses and boats of all kinds in the harbour. The District Commissioner's house, currently unoccupied, stands atop a hill SE of the village and can be recognized by its green roof. The School For Field Studies is in the 19th century *Admiral's Arm Inn*, and attracts undergraduate students from abroad to the island to study reef ecology and marine resources, but otherwise there are very few visitors. Wild donkeys, cows and horses roam the island and several have made their home in an abandoned hotel construction site along the coast from the Residency. The salinas dominate the central part of the island and there is a 'boiling hole', connected to the sea by a subterranean passage, which was used to supply the salt pans. It makes an interesting walk and you may see flamingoes.

Island information – South Caicos

● **How to get there**

TCA and SkyKing connect South Caicos with Providenciales, North Caicos, Middle Caicos and Grand Turk. There are a few taxis on the island, US$4 from the airport to *Club Carib* hotel.

● **Accommodation**

L2-A1 *Club Carib Beach Resort*, a 2-storey, functional, adequate place to sleep, 16 rooms, also **L3-A2** *Club Carib Harbour Resort* in town, 24 rooms, a/c bonefishing can be arranged through the manager, T 946 3251, F 946 3446; a few people in the town rent out rooms.

● **Places to eat**

Club Carib will give you an excellent dinner, but it is not always open; *Muriel's* is in the front of an unprepossessing house one block from the *Club Carib*, filling native recipes, breakfast by prior arrangement, T 946 3210; *Myrna Lisa*, also local food, has been rec; *Love's* has local dishes; *Café Columbus* for drinks and conversation with English bartender, Jack, good selection of beer, frozen yoghurt.

EAST CAICOS

Originally named Guana by the Lucayans, East Caicos has an area of 18 square miles, making it one of the largest islands and boasting the highest point in the Turks and Caicos, Flamingo Hill at 156 feet. A ridge runs all along the N coast, but the rest of the island is swamp, creeks, mangrove and mudflats. Jacksonville, in the NW, used to be the centre of a 50,000 acre sisal plantation and there was also a cattle farm at the beginning of the 20th century, but the island is now uninhabited. There is an abandoned railway left over from the plantation days and feral donkeys have worn paths through the scrub and sisal. Caves near Jacksonville, which were once mined for bat guano, contain petroglyphs carved on the walls and there is evidence of several Lucayan settlements. Splendid beaches including a 17-mile beach on the N coast where turtles come to lay their eggs, but accommodation for mosquitoes only.

Bring repellent. There is good snorkelling and diving around Lorimer's Cut, but the reefs and banks make access difficult. Off the N coast, opposite Jacksonville, is Guana Cay, home to the Caicos iguana.

MIDDLE CAICOS

Also known as Grand Caicos (population 272), this is the largest of the islands, with an area of 48 square miles. Its coastline is more dramatic than some of the other islands, characterized by limestone cliffs along the N coast, interspersed with long sandy beaches shaded by casuarina pines or secluded coves. The S part of the island is swamp and tidal flats. There are three settlements linked by the newly paved King's Road, **Conch Bar**, where there is an airstrip, a primary school and guesthouses, **Bambarra** and **Lorimers**. Visit the huge caves in the National Park at Conch Bar where there are bats, stalactites, stalagmites and underwater salt lakes with pink shrimp, which link up with the sea. Ask in Conch Bar for a guide, for added local colour. Cardinal Arthur arranges cave tours and boat trips. There are also caves between Bambarra and Lorimers, which were used by the Lucayan Indians and were later mined for guano. Archaeological excavations have uncovered a Lucayan ball court and a settlement near Armstrong Pond, due S of Bambarra, but these are not easily accessible. Evidence of the Lucayan civilisation dates back to 750 AD. Loyalist plantation ruins can also be explored. Bambarra beach is an empty, curving sweep of white sand, fringed with casuarina trees. Middle Caicos regatta is held here and there are small thatched huts which serve as restaurants for the very popular end-August Expo (some litter remains), but otherwise there are no facilities. A sand bar stretches out to Pelican Cay, half a mile out, which you can walk at low tide, popular with wading birds. The view from Conch Bar beach is marred by a rusting barge in shallow water, but there is afternoon shade at the W end under a cliff where the reef meets the land. A pretty cove, popular with day trippers, is Mudjeon Harbour, just W of Conch Bar, protected by a sand bar and with shade under a rocky overhang. The reef juts out from the land again here before branching out westwards along the rocky coastline which can be quite spectacular in the winter months with crashing waves. South of Middle Caicos there is a Nature Reserve comprising a frigatebird breeding colony and a marine sinkhole with turtles, bonefish and shark. The blue hole is surrounded by sandy banks and is difficult to get to, but it shows up on the satellite photo of the islands on display in the museum in Grand Turk.

Ask the District Commissioner's office, T 946 6100, for information and assistance, including boat tours and cave tours.

Island information – Middle Caicos
● **How to get there**
TCA and SkyKing fly from Grand Turk, South Caicos, North Caicos and Providenciales. Private pilots will also stop off if flying to North Caicos, or you can charter a plane. A ferry service for cargo and passengers runs between Provo, Middle and North Caicos, operated by owners of Blue Horizons Development, contact Dale T 946 6141, F 946 6139 for times and days (probably only Sat) the *Dale Marie* runs. Hired scooters (eg from Whitby Plaza, US$25 pp plus US$5 tax) may be taken on board for day trips and overnight stays on Middle Caicos. Carlon Forbes runs a taxi service and fares are based on US$2 per mile for 2 people, eg Conch Bar to Bambarra US$14, to Lorimers US$20.

● **Accommodation**
In Conch Bar: **A3-B** *Taylor's Guesthouse*, simple with 4 bedrooms, communal kitchen, bathroom and sitting/dining room, not always clean rooms or linens, fans, bring own food, T 946 6118, in USA T (305) 667-0966; Stacia and Dolphus Arthur run **A3** *Arthur's Guesthouse* next to Arthur's Store, one double, one twin-bedded room, private bath, kitchen; George and Martha Volz' **L3** *Villa* is a 3-bedroom house let for 3-day min, week or month,

Dec-April, contact 1255 Carolyn Drive, Southampton, PA, 18966, T 215-322 0505, F 215-322 0593, or through District Commissioner's office, Dolphus Arthur, T 946 6100. *Eagles Rest Villas*, 2 villas on 5 miles of beach, sometimes for rent, amenities offered are not always available, T 946 6122, in USA (215) 255 4640, F (813) 793 7157, weekly rates US$850-1,200.

● **Places to eat**
Most people are self-catering, it is best to bring your own food although canned foods and sodas are available from the few small stores in Conch Bar. Annie Taylor is known for her cooking and runs a restaurant on demand in her house, the conch stew is at US$18 for 2 is rec. *Carrie's Restaurant and Bar*, in Conch Bar, lunch, dinner, picnic lunches, ask locally.

NORTH CAICOS

The lushest of the islands, North Caicos has taller trees than the other islands and attracts more rain. Like Middle and East Caicos, the S part of the island is comprised of swamp and mangrove. There is one Nature Reserve at Dick Hill Creek and Bellefield Landing Pond, to protect the West Indian whistling duck and flamingoes, and another at Cottage Pond, a fresh/salt water sinkhole, about 170 feet deep, where there are grebes and West Indian whistling duck. Pumpkin Bluff Pond is a sanctuary for flamingoes, Bahamian pintail and various waders. Three Mary's Cays is a sanctuary for flamingoes and is an osprey nesting site. Flocks of flamingoes can also be seen on Flamingo Pond, but take binoculars. There is a viewing point at the side of the road, which is the only place from where you can see them and at low tide they can be a long way off. There is also good snorkelling at Three Mary's Cays and Sandy Point beach to the W is lovely. There is a rough road to Three Mary's Cays suitable for scooters. The beaches are good along the N coast where the hotels are, although the best is a seven-mile strip W of Pumpkin Bluff, where there has been no development so far. It can be reached by walking along the beach or via a dirt road past the *Club Vacanze/Prospect of Whitby* car park.. A cargo ship foundered on the reef in the 1980s, and is still stuck fast, making it of snorkelling interest.

The population has declined to 1,275 inhabitants living at the settlements of Bottle Creek, Whitby, Sandy Point and Kew. **Kew**, in the centre, is a pretty, scruffy but happy little village with neat gardens and tall trees, many of them exotic fruit trees, to provide shade; there are three churches, a primary school, a shop and two bars. **Bottle Creek**, in the E, has a high school, clinic and churches; the paved road ends here and a rough road requiring 4-wheel drive continues to Toby Rock. The backstreets of Bottle Creek run alongside the creek and here you can see the importance of water conservation, with people carrying buckets to and from the municipal water tap at the rain catchment area, while donkeys, goats and dogs roam around. The area is poor, but many people are building themselves bigger and better homes. **Whitby**, on the N coast, is rather spread out along the road, but this is where the few hotels are. Several expatriates have built their homes along Whitby Beach. Sandflies can be a problem in this area, particularly if there is not enough wind, take insect repellent. **Sandy Point**, in the W, is a fishing community. North Caicos is the centre of basket making in the islands and there are several women, including Clementine Mackintosh, Eliza Swan and Cassandra Gardiner, who are expert in their craft. Prices do not vary much from those in the shops in Providenciales or locally. Eliza Swan is based in Whitby and makes beautiful bags and baskets using many colours and designs. Wades Green Plantation, just to the W of Kew, is the best example of a Loyalist plantation in the islands, with many ruins, including a courtyard and a prison. Archaeologists from the University of California in Los Angeles carried out excavations in 1989. The boutiquesection of *Papa Grunts* restaurant in the Whitby Plaza sells T-shirts, crafts and non-prescription drugs at lower prices than on Provo.

You are advised to bring small denomination US dollar notes as there is no bank and it is difficult to cash US$50 or US$100.

Island information – North Caicos
● **How to get there**
TCA flies from Provo and there are flights via Middle Caicos and South Caicos to Grand Turk. Charters can be arranged from Provo, or private pilots (Blue Hills Aviation, Flamingo Air Service and Inter Island Airways, T 946-5481) have 3 or 4 flights a day US$25 one way. There is a ferry service between North and Middle Caicos, for details see above, **Island information – Middle Caicos**. For day trips or overnight stays you can rent a one or 2 seater motor scooter at Whitby Plaza, island map supplied. Rates are US$25pp plus US$5pp tax per 24 hrs, for weekly rates seventh day free, credit card deposit required, T/F 946 7301/7184. There are car hire facilities on North Caicos with Saunders Rent A Car, VHF Channel 16 'Sierra 7', or Gardiners Auto Service, US$35 for half day, US$70 for full day, plus US$10 tax. A taxi costs US$10 from the airport to Whitby for one person, US$12 for 2, US$15 for 3. Taxi from Sandy Point to Whitby is US$20. A tour of the island by taxi costs US$80-100, the drivers are friendly and knowledgeable but some tend to run their own errands while working.

● **Accommodation**
All accommodation is in the Whitby beach area on the N coast. **L2** *The Prospect of Whitby*, long-established hotel now owned by Club Vacanze of Italy and nearly all guests are on an all-inclusive Italian package, renovated 1994, luxury accommodation, very little English spoken by Italian staff, T 946 7119, F 946 7114, pool, tennis; **L2-A1** *Pelican Beach Hotel*, friendly, relaxed, few facilities, 14 rooms, 2 suites, the older rooms face the beach, run by Clifford Gardner, T 946 7112, F 946 7139; **L2** *Ocean Beach*, 10 condominiums, T 946 7113/2876 or contact the Canadian office at PO Box 1152, Station B, Burlington, Canada, T 416-336 8276, F 416-336 1232. The only guesthouse, **A1** *Jo Anne's Bed and Breakfast*, belongs to Jo Anne James Selver, who also runs a tourist shop and restaurant in Whitby, set back 300 ft from the beach with purple sea fans outside, it is light and airy, comfortable rooms, private bath, fans, screened veranda, T/F 946 7301, after 2030, whole house for rent by reservation, 6 nights min, 4 adults, she also has **A1** *Whitby Plaza Bed & Breakfast*, 2 new 2-room suites to rent 5 min walk from Whitby beach, sea view from deck, and **A3** hotel rooms, clean, fans, comfortable, share bath, hot showers, breakfast at *Papa Grunt's* on premises.

● **Places to eat**
Good food at the *Pelican Beach Hotel*; Italian at the Club Vacanze *Prospect of Whitby*, reservations necessary. *Papa Grunt's Seafood Restaurant*, Whitby Plaza, open 0830, last sitting for dinner 1930, credit cards accepted, indoor or screened verandah dining, native and American cuisine, seafood, chef Delphine makes everything to order, appetizers US$5, entrées US$8.75, takeaway service, closed Sun. Simple local restaurants include *Club Titter's Restaurant and Bar*, near the airport, and *Aquatic* restaurant and bar, but not always open.

PARROT CAY

A luxury, 50-room hotel was built in 1992 on this 1,300-acre private island, but it has not yet opened. Cotton used to be grown here and there are the remains of a plantation house. The wetlands and mangroves are to be preserved to protect wildlife.

DELLIS CAY

Dellis Cay is uninhabited but frequently visited for its shells. A popular excursion is to be dropped off there for the day for shelling by a local charter boat out of Leeward Marina, no facilities.

PINE CAY

Pine Cay is an 800-acre private resort owned by a group of homeowners who also own the exclusive 12-room L1 *Meridian Club*. No children under six allowed to stay in the hotel and lots of restrictions on where they are allowed if brought to a villa. The homes, which are very comfortable, with spectacular views, can be rented from US$2,960/week to US$4,815 for 10 days, per couple. A hurricane in 1969 left Pine Cay five feet under water for a while and since then the houses have been built slightly back from the beach and many of them are on stilts. There is a fairly well-stocked commissary or you can eat in the hotel; golf carts are used to get around the island. Note that the island is on the same time as Miami. Open November-June, reservations can be made through Resorts Management Inc, The Carriage House at 201½ East 29th St, New York NY 10016, T 800-331 9154, 212-696 4566, F 212-689 1598, locally T/F 946 5128. Non-motorized watersports and tennis are available and excursions to other cays can be arranged. May is a popular time for bonefishing. Day trippers are not encouraged although visitors may come for lunch at the restaurant by prior reservation as long as they do not use the facilities; the homeowners value

their privacy and put a ban on visitors if they feel there have been too many. Pine Cay benefits from a few freshwater ponds and wells, so water is no problem here and the vegetation is more lush than on Provo. On the other hand mosquito control is a constant problem. Nature trails have been laid out around the ponds and through the trees. Water Cay is a nature reserve and although classified as a separate island, is joined to Pine Cay by sand dunes created during the 1969 hurricane. There is an airstrip, guests usually charter a flight, and a dock if they prefer to come in with the *Meridian Club's* exclusive shuttle boat.

LITTLE WATER CAY

Little Water Cay is the nearest island to Provo. Iguanas live here but they have become quite aggressive because of constant pressure by people and their offerings of potato chips and lettuce. Do not feed them. Take pictures instead. Charter boats can be arranged from Leeward Going Through Marina. Many day sail charters visit regularly.

PROVIDENCIALES

'Provo' (*pop* over 6,000 with many Haitians, Dominicans, French, Germans, Canadians, Americans) is 25 miles long and about three wide. Twelve-mile Grace Bay on the N shore has only seven hotels and condominiums so you can walk and snorkel without seeing another soul. The Princess Alexandra Marine Park incorporates the reef offshore. Development of the island began in 1967 although it had been settled in the 18th century and there were three large plantations in the 19th century growing cotton and sisal. The three original settlements, The Bight (meaning Bay), Five Cays and Blue Hills, are fragmented and have not grown into towns as the population has increased. Instead shopping malls have been built along the Leeward Highway (Market Place, Plantation Hills, Central

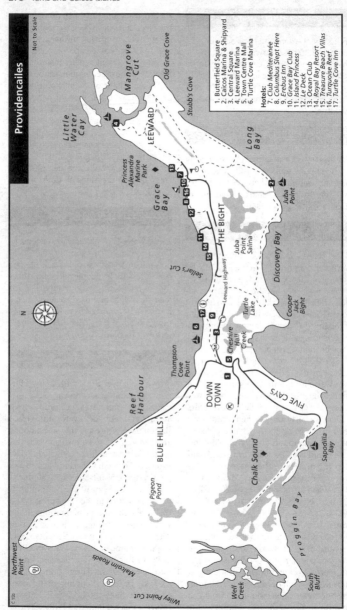

Providenciales

Not to Scale

1. Butterfield Square
2. Caicos Marina & Shipyard
3. Central Square
4. Leeward Marina
5. Town Centre Mall
6. Turtle Cove Marina

Hotels:
7. Club Mediterranée
8. Columbus Slept Here
9. Erebus Inn
10. Grace Bay Club
11. Island Princess
12. Le Deck
13. Ocean Club
14. Royal Bay Resort
15. Treasure Beach Villas
16. Turquoise Reef
17. Turtle Cove Inn

Square, retail stores, restaurants, lawyers and business offices). The Office of the Chief Secretary, Immigration, Customs, banks, lawyers, supermarkets, travel agent are **Down Town**. **Turtle Cove** calls itself 'the heart of Provo', with a couple of hotels, a marina, dive operators, boat charters, deep sea fishing, 7 restaurants, the Tourist Office, hairdressing and a few boutiques.

On the S side of the island, South Dock is the island's commercial port. The Caicos Marina and Shipyard on the S coast is a disappointment to sailors because the advertised facilities and major services are not available and it is many miles from shopping supplies. To the W, Sapodilla Bay offers good protection for yachts. Chalk Sound, a National Park inland from Sapodilla Bay, is a shallow lagoon of marvellous turquoise colours, dotted with rocky islets.

At the NE end, a deep channel known as Leeward Going Through is a natural harbour and a marina with fuel, water, ice and restaurant has been built here. There is a conch farm at the Island Sea Centre at Leeward, open for hatchery tours 0900-1700, US$6 adults, US$3 children under 12, T 946 5330, F 946 5849, also gift shop.

Northwest Point, a marine park offshore, has good beaches, diving and snorkelling. In 1993 a French television company shot a series of underwater game shows here and a treacherous road was bulldozed through to the beautiful beach. They left several tiki huts which offer much needed shade for a day on the beach. Two other good places to snorkel in the Grace Bay area are just to the E of Turtle Cove, where rays and turtles can be seen on Smith's reef near the entrance to the marina, and just W of *Treasure Beach Villas*, by the White House, where there is a variety of life, including grouper, ask anybody for directions.

Inland, along Seasage Hill Road in Long Bay, is The Hole, a collapsed limestone, water-filled sinkhole next to a house called *By the Hole*. A tunnel to the right hand side gives access to the main pool. Do not attempt to descend. Ruins of Loyalist and Bermudian settlers' plantations and houses can be seen at Cheshire Hall, Richmond Hills, and along the Bight road. On the hill overlooking the *Mariner Hotel* at Sapodilla Bay a pole marks the location of stones engraved with initials and dates in the 18th century possibly by shipwrecked sailors or wreckers.

Island information – Providenciales
● How to get there
American Airways twice daily from Miami (T 800-433 7300, or locally T 941 5700). TCA has flights from the Bahamas, the Dominican Republic and Haiti. TCA operates internal flights within the Turks and Caicos islands, see above. Charter companies at Provo airport are TCA, T 946 4255, F 946 2081; Blue Hills Aviation, T 941 5290/946 4388, F 946 4644 (day/overnight trips to Cuba); Inter Island Airways, Lyndon Gardiner, T 941 5481; Flamingo Air Services, T 946 2109/8, is based in Grand Turk; Provo Air Charter, T 946 4879, offers day trips to Grand Turk, US$119pp, group of 4; TCI Sky King, T 946 4594, F 946 4604, internal flights and day trips to Grand Turk, Cuba, Haiti, Bahamas.

● Transport
Most roads are paved, contributing to fast, erratic driving by residents; speed limits (40 mph highway, 20 mph in town) are not observed, dangerous overtaking is common; if on a bicycle, scooter or in a rental car, particularly at night, be warned. Leeward Highway is especially risky. Hired cars are not generally well serviced, exchanges are common. An economy car, quoted at US$39/day will work out to US$61.50 with taxes and insurance. Deposits are at least US$400. A 'gold' credit card qualifies for an exemption of US$11.95/day CDW. **Provo Rent A Car**, PO Box 137, T 946 4404, F 946 4993, at the airport and *Turquoise Reef Resort*, Suzukis, rec. **Budget**, Down Town, Town Centre Mall, open Mon-Sat, 0800-1700, T 946 4709, F 941 5364, worldwide reservations 800-527 0700, Suzukis, Mitsubishis, one day free for weekly rental. **Tropical Auto Rental**, Tropicana Plaza and *Ocean Club Condos* at Grace Bay, T 946 5300/5357, F 946 5456, **Turks & Caicos National Car Rental**, Airport Road, T/F 946

4701, not always reliable vehicles delivery. **Rent-a-Buggy**, Leeward Highway, T 946 4158, Suzuki jeeps, VW Thing, **Provo Fun Cycles** at Ports of Call across from *Turquoise Reef*, single scooters US$25/day, doubles US$39, packages, also bicycles, T 946 5868; **Sunrise Auto Rental**, jeeps and scooters, Leeward Highway and *Club Med*, T 946 4705. Scooter Bob's, Yamaha, Leeward Highway and *Ocean Club Resort*, Grace Bay, T 946 4684, F 946 4283, 50cc US$30 1-2 days, US$25 3 days or more; 80cc US$40 1-2 days, US$30 3 days or more; credit cards, free pick up and delivery, also canoes US$40/day. Taxis charge US$2 per mile but are soon to be metered, a ride for one person from the airport to the *Turquoise Reef Resort* is US$12-15, and a round trip to a restaurant or Downtown can be US$40. Tours and shopping trips about US$25/hr. Complaints have not lowered the rates. There are usually taxis at the large hotels, otherwise phone for one. Paradise Taxi Co, T 941 3555; Nell's Taxi, T 941 3228, 946 4971; Island's Choice Taxi, T 946 5481; Provo Taxi Association T 946 5481. Stafford Morris' Blue Bus, pickup and delivery almost anywhere, US$3 pp each way say Down Town to Grace Bay, T 941 3598 or flag him down.

● **Accommodation**

Price guide

L1	over US$200	L2	US$151-200
L3	US$101-150	A1	US$81-100
A2	US$61-80	A3	US$46-60
B	US$31-45	C	US$21-30
D	US$12-20	E	US$7-11
F	US$4-6	G	up to US$3

When confirming rates and availability, check whether 8% tax and 10-15% service are included. **L2-A1** *Erebus Inn*, on hillside overlooking Turtle Cove, 26 rooms, larger than those in other hotels, and a few basic chalets with wonderful view liked by divers, dive packages available, all watersports at the marina, gym and fitness centre on site, pool, tennis, 2 rooms fully equipped for ham radio operators, T 946-4240, F 946-4704; **L2-A1** *Turtle Cove Inn*, 32 rooms, poolside or ocean view, smallish rooms but comfortable, suite with kitchenette available, not on beach, docking facilities, all watersports, at the marina, cable TV, 2 restaurants, T 946-4203, F 946-4141, T 800-887-0477; along the N shore on the beach heading E are **L2-L3** *Treasure Beach Villas*, run down, 18 self-catering apartments, 1-2 bedrooms, no restaurant, swimming pool, T 946-4325, F 946-4108; **L1-L3** *Royal Bay Resort and Villas*, luxury beachfront resort, 200 rooms and villa suites, facilities for handicapped, free form pool, 3 restaurants, all watersports, downwind of *Smokey's* all-night local bands several nights a week, to become a Sandals' all-inclusive, couples only resort in 1997, T 941 3600, F 941 8001; **L3-A2** *Island Princess*, 80 rooms, only a few with a/c, run down, airless rooms, next door to *Smokey's* all-night bands, T 946-4260, F 946-4666; **L1-L3** *Le Deck Hotel and Beach Club*, 26 rooms and condos, dive shop, golf packages, restaurant, lovely bougainvillea in the courtyard, pool, watersports inc equipment rental, unfriendly management, T 946-5547, F 946-5770, T 1-800-528 1905. **L1** *Grace Bay Club*, on beach, luxury accommodation, 21 elegant condos, a/c, phone, TV, watersports, tennis, pool, jacuzzi, all amenities, French restaurant, beach bar, T 946 5757, F 946 5758; **L1-L3** *Turquoise Reef Resort and Casino*, 228 a/c rooms and suites, mostly used by charter package holiday business, in receivership in 1996, the grounds are attractive, service has been criticized but is friendly in bar and restaurants, three restaurants, tennis, diving, Port Royale casino, boutiques, T 946-5555, F 946-5522; **L1-L3** *Club Méditerranée Turkoise*, Grace Bay, stays on daylight savings time all year, 298 all-inclusive rooms, no children under 12, rooms stark but comfortable, keen young organizers, lots of watersports, communal dining, diving and golf arranged at extra cost, T 946-5500/5491-7, F 946-5501, T 800-258-2633. **L1-L3** *Ocean Club Beach and Golf Resort*, condos on the beach, comfortable, well-equipped, balconies, some with good views the length of Grace Bay, spacious deck around pool with daytime snack bar, next to Provo Golf Club, packages available, free transport to airport, bike rentals, PO Box 240, T 946 5880, F 946 5845, T 800-457 8787. The only bed and breakfast home on the island is Louise Fletcher's, **A2** *Columbus Slept Here*, one double room, private bathroom, share owner's kitchen, make your own breakfast, small self-catering apartments downstairs, friendly, personal service, weekly and monthly rates, 200 yards to Grace Bay beach, golf, restaurants, snorkelling, casino nearby, T/F 946 5878, PO Box 273. *Bed & Breakfast Hospitality Center*, Box 364, T/F 941 5860, phone service only as Reservation Service Organization host in Caribbean with attendant membership fees and commissions, sometimes reservation agent for various vacation rentals with breakfast. **L1-L3** *Platinum Resort Villas* at Leeward, a/c, TV, phone, 1-4 bedroomed villas with kitchens, sleep 2-8, T 946 5539, F 946 5421. **A2** *Airport Inn*, 2 mins to airport, close to banks, groceries, restaurants, a/c, TV, special rates for pilots, businessmen, 15% discount if you book room and rental car, T/F 946 4701. In the Sapodilla area there are self-catering villas: *Casuarina Cottages*, 3 units, US$750-1,000 a week, T 946 4687, F 946 4895. Other 3-5 bedroomed rental villas with pools and modest-to-luxury accommodation available through Elliot Holdings & Management, PO Box 235, T 946 5355, F 946 5176; Turks & Caicos Realty, PO Box 279, T 946 4474, F 946 4433; Alpha Omega, T 946 4702, F 941 3191.

● **Places to eat**

In the Turtle Cove area: *Alfred's Place*, on Suzy Turn Road, lunch and dinner, European and island food, open 1100-2400, Tues-Sun, popular, T 946 4679; *Banana Boat*, dockside at Turtle Cove marina, Caribbean bar and grill, colourful, cheerful, T 941 5706; *Tiki Hut*, at *Turtle Cove Inn*, breakfast, lunch and dinner, chicken or ribs every Wed night, US$10, extremely popular with ex-pats, T 946 5341; *The Terrace*, 'creative' conch, seafood, lunch, dinner, T 946 4763, closed Sun; *Sharkbite Bar and Grill*, Admiral's Club, on the water, 1100-0200 daily, Caribbean night Tues, US$12, live music, T 941 5090; *Erebus*, spectacular view, breakfast, lunch, dinner, mostly French, 'native' food Tues, T 941 5445; next door to *Jimmy's Bar*, sunset drinks, happy hour, T 941 5575, popular with ex-pats, darts, games.

Down Town: *Tasty Temptations*, next to the dry cleaners, French breakfasts, sandwiches, fresh salads for lunch, good coffee, deli, open 0630-1500, closed Sun, T 946 4049; *Sweet T's Meals On Wheels*, next to Texaco service station, native dishes, open nearly all day, every day. A *KFC* is next to Texaco in Butterfield Square, open 1100-2300, closed Sun, reportedly not up to chain standards.

East along Leeward Highway: at Market Place, the *Pasta House*, lunch and dinner, all-you-can-eat US$15 Mon and Thurs, closed Sun, reasonable prices, healthy food, T 941 3482; *Mackie's Café*, native style breakfast and lunch daily, 0800-1900, fresh seafood; *Hey José Cantina*, near the Tourist Shoppe, Central Square Shopping Centre, Leeward Highway, consistently excellent service, great food, best margaritas, Mexican/American, tacos, huge pizza etc, 1200-1500, 1800-2200, closed Sun, take aways, T 946 4812; *Top O' The Cove Deli*, Leeward Highway, next to Napa auto at Suzie Turn, 'Little bit of New York-style deli', subs, bagels, order lunch by phone/fax 946 4694, beer, wine, picnic food, open 0630-1530 daily; *Dora's Restaurant and Bar*, near PPC power station, open from 0730 until very late, local recipes, filling, eat in or take away, live band and seafood buffet some nights, T 946 4558; at Provo Plaza, E of WIV, TV satellite dishes, *Winkey's Catering*, native and 'worldwide' cuisine; *Pizza Pizza*, due to open mid-1996.

Within walking distance of the *Turquoise Reef Resort* (where there are 3 restaurants): **Prestancia**, Turkish Restaurant and Bar, elegant kebabs, pizza, baby lamb chops, lobster, baklava, food and service impeccable, not cheap but value for money, T 946 5900, F 941 3111; *China Restaurant*, T 946 5377, Mandarin cuisine, Chinese chef, a/c, open daily 1100-1400, 1800-2200, no lunch Sun; further E, *Caicos Café & Grill*, home made pasta with French flair, grilled fish and seafood, service personal but slow, go early or late to avoid crowds, open-air, open daily 1200-2400,

T 946 5278; *Island Kitchen*, 0700-2400, open daily, native style, conch, peas/rice, reasonable; *Lone Star Bar and Grill*, Tex Mex and 'gringo' style, lunch, dinner, open daily, T 946 5832; *Island Dreams Café*, speciality teas, coffee, ice cream, mornings, midday, late, closed Sun; *Bella Luna Ristorante*, across from *Turquoise Reef*, breakfast US$8.50, all you can eat, 0730-1030, dinner 1830-2200, chef Michelangelo presents pasta, veal, you name it, rave reviews for food and service, T 946 5214; *Coco Bistro*, past *Caicos Café*, E of *Turquoise Reef* near *Club Med*, behind Sunshine Nursery in mature palm trees, indoor dining/bar, or outdoors under the palms, Mediterranean cooking, specials every night, 1200-2400, congenial hosts and service, T 946 5369; *Hong Kong Restaurant*, E of *Turquoise Reef*, a/c, Chinese eat in, take away, moderate prices, excellent meals inc vegetarian and conch dishes, Nine Star beer, T 946 5678; *Fairways Bar & Grill*, opp *Ocean Club*, Provo Golf Course Clubhouse, T 946 5991, breakfast and lunch, Wed lunch specials, Fri happy hour, popular with doctors, lawyers, business people and visiting golfers.

At Leeward Going Through at the E end of Providenciales is *Gilley's at Leeward*, open from 0700-2100, by the marina, breakfast, lunch specials, good food, friendly, superb service, meet local fishermen, arrange outings, boat trips, elegant, romantic dinners, T 946 5094.

Grace Bay, along the beach W to E: *Royal Bay Resort and Villas*, 4 expensive restaurants from gourmet to lounge cocktails and pastries in the lobby, T 946 8000; *Island Princess Hotel*, in-house restaurant *Confetti's*, native style, Fri seafood buffet, 0700-2400, T 946 4260; *Smokey's*, next to *Island Princess*, beachfront lunch/dinner, US$5 glass of wine, menu board with no posted prices, ask, live bands many nights, T 941 3466; *Le Deck Restaurant*, 3 meals, Sun buffet US$25 all-you-can-eat, drinks and dessert extra, slow service, rec in season, T 946 5547; *Bonnie's Bistro and Bar*, the 'round house' between Lower Bight Road and *Le Deck*, Bonnie Arthur Williams, a Turks Islander serves lunch and dinner, in or out, superb seafood dishes inc conch and lobster, also vegetarian and lowfat cooking, very popular, T 946 4072; E of *Turquoise Reef* at the exclusive, expensive *Anacaona* restaurant and bar on the beach, thatched roof elegance, nouvelle cuisine with Caribbean flair, exclusive and expensive, live music some evenings, guests only, reservations

rec, T 946 5050; *Ocean Club's Cabana Bar & Grill*, T 946 5880, lunch, drinks, only, poolside, expensive, indifferent service; adjacent to *Ocean Club*, *Gecko Grille*, Ocean Club Plaza, pretentious, bar opens 1630-2400, dining 1800-2200 daily, T 946 5885.

In Blue Hills settlement: *Pub On the Bay*, not to be missed, indoor or tiki hut dining on the beach, great native dishes, lobster, conch, buffets, sometimes live band, open mid-morning until late, T 941 3090; further along Blue Hills Road, *Henry's Roadrunner Restaurant*, Blue Hills, everybody's favourite for all you can eat Wed buffet and seafood specialities, stewed fish/grits/Johnny cake Sat/Sun mornings, VHF Channel 16, T 941 3699, open daily.

At or near the airport: *Gilley's* is the only place to eat at the airport, a/c, noisy, local hangout, indifferent service, daily specials, fast food, T 946 4472, within walking distance is *Fast Eddie's*, Airport Road, Wed night buffet, live music if enough reservations, open 0730-2300, slot machines, T 941-3176; *Where Its At* has Jamaican specialities, T 946 4185, generous portions, daily specials, 0630-2300.

WEST CAICOS

Rugged and uninhabited but worth visiting for its beautiful beach on the NW coast and excellent diving offshore. The E shore is a marine park. Once frequented by pirates, there are many wrecks between here and Provo. Inland there is a salt water lake, Lake Catherine, which rises and falls with the tides and is a nature reserve, home to migrant nesting flamingoes, ducks and waders. The ruins of Yankee Town, its sisal press and railroad are a surface interval destination for scuba divers and sailors.

FRENCH CAY

An old pirate lair, now uninhabited, with exceptional marine life. It has been designated a sanctuary for frigate birds, osprey and nesting seabirds. Visitors come almost daily aboard the *Caicos Sol* to swim, explore and snorkel. It operates out of the old Aquatic Centre, at Sapodilla Bay, enquire locally, consult newspapers, *Times of the Islands*, for the adverts.

Information for travellers

AIR

Ports of entry for aircraft are Providenciales, South Caicos and Grand Turk, but the major international airport is on Providenciales. There are also airstrips on North Caicos, Middle Caicos, Pine Cay and Salt Cay.

American Airlines flies twice daily from Miami to Provo, with one of the flights originating in New York. Turks & Caicos Airways (TCA) flies from Nassau, Freeport, Santo Domingo and Puerto Plata (Dominican Republic) and Cap Haitiën into Provo and provides connecting flights between Grand Turk, Salt Cay, South Caicos, Middle Caicos, North Caicos and Providenciales. SkyKing also flies to Jamaica alternate Weds, Cap Haitiën daily except Sun, Dominican Republic, Bahamas and Cuba on request.

SEA

There is no scheduled passenger service (cargo comes in regularly from Florida) and no port is deep enough to take cruise ships although some occasionally stop outside the reef and shuttle in passengers for half a day.

● **Ports of entry**
(British flag) Providenciales: Turtle Cove Marina, Caicos Shipyard, Leeward Marina, Sapodilla Bay; Grand Turk; South Caicos; Salt Cay. Clear in and out with Customs and immigration, VHF 16.

● **Boat documents**
On arrival, Customs will grant 7 days immigration clearance. Go to town to the Immigration Office (closed 1230-1430) to obtain a 30-day extension. Fuel and alcoholic drink may be purchased duty free with clearance to leave the country.

● **Radio communications**
Evening weather report on VHF from Blue Water Divers on Grand Turk; *Mystine* on SSB.

● **Airlines**
TCA, T 946 4255, domestic emergency T 941 5353, F 946 5338. American Airlines T 1-800-433 7300 or locally, T 941 5700.

● **Banks**
There are banks on Grand Turk and Providenciales. Barclays Bank is on Grand Turk, T 946

● **Documents**
US and Canadian citizens need only birth certificate or proof of identity to enter Turks and Caicos. All others need a valid passport; a visa is not necessary except for nationals of communist countries. Onward ticket officially required. Visitors are allowed to stay for 30 days, renewable once only. The immigration office is on Grand Turk, T 946 2939.

● **Climate**
There is no recognized rainy season, and temperatures average 75°-85°F from November to May, reaching into the 90°s from June to October, but constant tradewinds keep life comfortable. Average annual rainfall is 21 inches on Grand Turk and South Caicos but increases to 40 inches as you travel westwards through the Caicos Islands where more lush vegetation is found. Hurricane season is normally June-October. Hurricane Kate swept through the islands November 1985; Hugo and Andrew missed in 1992; there were several near misses in 1995 and Bertha passed through in 1996.

● **Health**
There are no endemic tropical diseases and no malaria, no special vaccinations are required prior to arrival. Aids exists.

MONEY

● **Currency**
The official currency is the US dollar. Most banks will advance cash on credit cards. Most hotels, restaurants and taxi drivers will accept travellers' cheques, but personal cheques are not widely accepted. Take small denomination US dollars when visiting an island without a bank, as it is often difficult to get change from a US$50 or US$100 note.

2831, F 946 2695, at Butterfield Square, PO Box 236, Provo, T 946 4245, F 946 4573, and an agency service is held on South Caicos on Thur, T 946 3268. Scotiabank is at the Town Centre Mall, PO Box 15, Provo, T 946 4750/2, F 946 4755, and at Harbour House, PO Box 132, Grand Turk, T 946 2506/7, F 946 2667.

● **Clothing**
Dress is informal and shorts are worn in town as well as on the beach. Nudity is illegal although condoned by local hoteliers at *Club Med, Turquoise Reef Resort* and *Le Deck*, all on Grace Bay. The islanders find it offensive and flaunting local protocol may elicit unwelcome stares and remarks. Islanders love to dress up in the evenings when they frequent live band nights at hotels or discos.

● **Hospitals**
On Provo, Menzies Medical Practice, Leeward Highway, Jon Delisser Building, open 0830-1700 Mon-Fri, 0830-1200 Sat, recompression chamber and Dr Euan Menzies, T 946 4242. Dr Sam Slattery, T 941 5252. Optometrist, Dr John Malcolm, T 941 5842. Dentist, Dr Robert McIntosh, T 946 4321. The government clinic on Provo is New Era Medical Centre, Blue Hills, Dr Steve Bourne, T 941 5455, 24 hrs. Myrtle Rigby Health Complex, Leeward Highway, near Down Town, T 941 3000, Dr Ajibabe Adeladan. Ambulance services available and emergency medical air charter to USA or Nassau, full life support can be arranged, T 999 or any doctor. On Grand Turk there is a small, understaffed hospital on the N side of town and a government clinic in town, open 0800-1200, 1400-1630. Dr D O Astwood, T 946 2451, Dr L Astwood, T 946 3287. The other islands organize emergency air evacuation to Grand Turk hospital.

● **Laundry**
On Provo there is a laundry/dry cleaners in Butterfield Square, Down Town.

● **Public holidays**
New Year's Day, Commonwealth Day, Good Friday, Easter Monday, National Heroes Day (end May), the Queen's birthday (second week in June), Emancipation Day (beginning of August), National Youth Day (end Sept), Columbus' Day and Human Rights Day (both in October), Christmas Day and Boxing Day.

● **Security**
There is little personal security problem on most islands but it is not advisable to walk around alone at night or on deserted beaches. On Provo, take normal precautions about leaving valuables in your room or on the beach. Crime is on the increase and traffic is fast and aggressive. Personal security is much better on Grand Turk and the other islands and a haven compared with most other Caribbean countries.

● **Voltage**
110 volts, 60 cycles, the same as in the USA.

ON DEPARTURE

It is worth checking in early when returning to Miami, to avoid long queues. Airport departure tax is US$15.

ACCOMMODATION

● **Hotels**
There is a 10% service charge and 9% tax added to the bill. Hotels on Provo are aiming for North American standards and are expensive. Cheap to inexpensive, value for money accommodation is hard to find. Hoteliers may quote a price, only to forget it on check out. Rack rates will not include tax and service, be sure to check what you are quoted.

● **Camping**
Camping is possible on beaches on most islands, but no water or sewage facilities and not encouraged. Contact the District Commissioner's office on each island for permission. If planning to stay on a deserted island take everything with you and leave nothing behind. A very basic, private campsite was started on North Caicos in 1993 but you have to take all your own gear.

FOOD AND DRINK

Good, moderate to expensive meals in restaurants and bars are good quality. Watch out for specials with no posted prices. Wine by the glass at US$5 is unreasonable. With over 50 restaurants and delis on Provo alone, prices are variable but local restaurants with native cuisine are reasonable. Seafood, lobster, conch with peas'n'rice is standard island fare. Many restaurants feature vegetarian meals and low fat cooking. All food is imported from Miami, occasionally from the Dominican Republic, and therefore not cheap. Many restaurants charge a 10% gratuity and/or 8% government tax. Check your bill carefully and tip, or not, accordingly.

GETTING AROUND

AIR TRANSPORT

Flight time from Grand Turk to the furthest island (Provo) is 30 mins. SkyKing (Grand Turk T 946 1520, South Caicos T 946 3376, Provo T 946 4594, F 941 5127) and Inter Island Airways (T 941 5481) also provide frequent flights between the islands. Private charters are readily available within the island group and can easily be arranged by asking around at Grand Turk or Provo airport, as charter pilots wait to see if they can fill a plane in the mornings. See page 279 for telephone numbers of charter companies. On other islands they are easily arranged by phone.

LAND TRANSPORT
● **Motoring**
Drive on the left. Rental cars are available on Grand Turk, North and South Caicos and Provo although demand often exceeds supply on Provo. Most roads are fairly basic, although those on Provo have been upgraded and paved, and all parts are easily accessible. Maximum speed in urban areas is 20 mph and outside villages 40 mph, but on Provo driving is erratic and no one (except visitors) pays heed to speed limits, not even the Traffic Department. There is no control. Local drivers do not dim their headlights at night. Pedestrians and cyclists should be especially careful on the roads at night because of speeding, dangerous drivers. Watch out for donkeys on Grand Turk.

● **Bicycles**
Bicycles and motor scooters can be rented from some hotels but can be relatively expensive compared with cars. Helmets are not mandatory but should be worn. Tourists invite trouble riding in bathing suits and barefeet.

● **Taxis**
There are no buses. On-island transport is restricted to expensive taxi service with a basic fare of US$2/mile, although drivers are not always consistent. Complaints are frequent. Taxis can be hired for island tours, agree the price before hand.

COMMUNICATIONS

● **Telecommunications**
Grand Turk, Provo and South Caicos have a modern local and international telephone service, with Cable and Wireless offices in Grand Turk and Provo. Telephone services on the North and Middle Caicos and Salt City are improving. The international code is 809. There are two exchanges, 946 and 941. The small volume of international calls means that costs are high; a call to the UK/Canada costs US$3.30 a minute at peak time (US$2.70 off-peak), 1 minute min charge; to USA and Caribbean costs US$2.59-1.95 a minute, all plus 10% government tax. The local phone book has a list of charges to anywhere in the world. Phone cards are available from Cable and Wireless and from many outlets inc Provo airport in US$5, US$10 and US$20 denominations plus 10%, The Cable and Wireless Public Sales Office in Grand Turk and Provo has a public fax service, F 946 2497/4210. Credit card calling, T 1-800-877-8000, 3 minute min; USA direct, T 872 from hotel room or 01-800-872-2881 from card phone. Paging service is popular among businesses.

ENTERTAINMENT

● **Nightlife**
The Port Royal Casino at the *Turquoise Reef Hotel* offers black jack, craps, roulette, money wheel, Caribbean stud poker, T 946 5508, F 946 5554.

Local bands play mostly calypso, reggae and the traditional island music with its Haitian and African influences. On Provo, ask hoteliers and residents when and where live bands and karaoke sing alongs are held at various watering hole, such as the *Island Princess, Pub on the Bay, Alfred's Place, Smokey's, Le Deck, Turquoise Reef, Casablanca Palace* etc. *Club Med* has nightly dinner/show for guests and visitors who phone for reservations (T 946 5500). Night life does not start until 2200-2300. On Grand Turk, the *Salt Raker Inn* for music on Wed and Sun nights.

TOURIST INFORMATION

● **Local tourist office**
Turks and Caicos Islands Tourist Board, PO Box 128, Pond Street, Grand Turk, Turks & Caicos Islands, T 946 2321/2322, T 800-241 0824, F 946 2733. On Provo the Tourist Office is at Turtle Cove, PO Box 174, T 946 4970, F 941 5494. Various maps and guidebooks have been published inc *Where, When, How, Providenciales; Your Monthly Entertainment Guide*, placed in hotels and selected shops, free of charge; *Times of the Islands; International*

Magazine of the Turks and Caicos, quarterly, US$4.

● **Tourist offices overseas**
USA: Trombone Associates Inc, 420 Madison Avenue, New York NY 10017, T (212) 223-2323, F 223-0260, T 1-800-241-0824.
UK: c/o Morris Kevan International Ltd, International House, 47 Chase Side, Enfield, Middlesex, EN2 6NB, T 0181-364 5188, F 0181-367 9949.

● **Local travel agents**
Marco Travel Services, Down Town, T 946 4393, F 946 4048, for reconfirmation of tickets, emergency check cashing, travel services, travellers' cheque sales, Amex representative. Provo Travel Ltd, run by Althea Ewing, at Central Square, Leeward Highway, T 946 4035, F 946 4081, helpful. Island Travel T 941 5195, Down Town, near shell station, specializes in travel and shopping packages for TCI residents, international bookings and tours. On Grand Turk: T & C Travel Ltd, at *Hotel Kittina*, Box 42, T 946 2592, F 946 2877, run by Daphne James, friendly, reliable.

ACKNOWLEDGEMENTS

We are most grateful to Louise Fletcher, *Columbus Slept Here*, Provo, for another thorough and exhaustive revision of this chapter; to JoAnne James Selver for help on North Caicos and also to Angela Gordon, *Beachcomber House*, Grand Turk, for her corrections and additions to the Grand Turk section.

Hispaniola

ONE MIGHT EXPECT that a relatively small island such as Hispaniola (from Spanish 'Isla Española' – the Spanish island) lying in the heart of the Caribbean would be occupied by one nation, or at least that its people should demonstrate ethnic and cultural similarities. This is not so. Hispaniola, with an area of just over 75,800 sq km, not much more than half the size of Cuba, is shared by two very different countries, the Dominican Republic and Haiti. The original indigenous name for the island, Quisqueya, is still used in the Dominican Republic as an 'elegant variation'. Hispaniola is mountainous and forested, with plains and plateaux. Haiti, with 27,700 sq km, has a population of 6.6 million increasing at an annual rate of 1.7%. The Dominican Republic is much larger in area, 48,443 sq km, including some offshore islands, but its population is not much more at 7.8 million, growing at 1.9% a year. In the Dominican Republic, 65% of the population is urban, yet only 31% in Haiti live in towns.

Columbus visited the N coast of Hispaniola, modern Haiti, on his first visit to the West Indies, leaving a few men there to make a settlement before he moved on to Cuba. Columbus traded with the native Tainos for trinkets such as gold nose plugs, bracelets and other ornaments, which were to seal the Indians' fate when shown to the Spanish monarchs. A second voyage was ordered immediately. Columbus tried again to establish settlements, his first having been wiped out. His undisciplined men were soon at war with the native Tainos, who were hunted, taxed and enslaved. Hundreds were shipped to Spain, where they died. When Columbus had to return to Spain he left his brother, Bartolomé, in charge of the fever-ridden, starving colony. The latter sensibly moved the settlement to the healthier S coast and founded Santo Domingo, which became the capital of the Spanish Indies. The native inhabitants were gradually eliminated by European diseases, murder, suicide and slavery, while their crops were destroyed by newly introduced herds of cattle and pigs. Development was hindered by the labour shortage and the island became merely a base from which to provision further exploration, being a source of bacon, dried beef and cassava. Even the alluvial gold dwindled and could not compete with discoveries on the mainland. Sugar was introduced at the beginning of the sixteenth century and the need for labour soon brought African slaves to the island. In 1512 the Indians were declared free subjects of Spain, and missionary zeal ensured their conversion to Christianity.

The Haitians are almost wholly black, with a culture that is a unique mixture of African and French influences. Haiti was a French colony until 1804 when, fired by the example of the French Revolution, the black slaves revolted, massacred the French landowners and proclaimed the world's first black republic. Throughout the 19th century the Haitians reverted to a primitive way of life, indulging in a succession of bloody, almost tribal wars. Even today, nowhere else in the Caribbean do African cults, particularly voodoo, play such a part in everyday life. The standard of living is the lowest in the Americas.

The Dominicans are a mixture of black, Amerindian and white, with a far stronger European strain (but see **Introduction** to the Dominican Republic, below). Their culture and language are hispanic and their religion Roman Catholic. Economically, the country is much more developed, despite a stormy political past and unsavoury periods of dictatorship, particularly under Generalísimo Trujillo (1930-61). Nevertheless, in a material sense the country prospered during the Trujillo era and the standard of living is much higher than it is in Haiti.

The climate is tropical but tempered by sea breezes. The cooler months are between December and March.

HAITI

The Republic of Haiti occupies the western third of the island. Haitian Créole is the only language of 85% of its inhabitants. It evolved from French into a distinct language. The other 15% speak Créole and French. About 95% are of virtually pure African descent. The rest are mostly mulattoes, the descendants of unions between French masters and African slaves. The mulattoes became the ruling class, called the élite. In the last 50 years their economic preeminence has been weakened by Arab immigrants while an emerging black middle-class took over the state sector. Haiti is an Indian word meaning 'high ground'. It is the Caribbean's most mountainous country. Except for a few small, mainly coastal plains and the central Artibonite River valley, the entire country is a mass of ranges. The highest peak is the 2,674m La Selle, SE of the capital. Little remains of Haiti's once luxuriant forest cover, cut down for fuel or to make way for farming. With soil erosion and desertification far advanced, Haiti is an ecological disaster. The main regions still regularly receiving abundant rainfall are the SW peninsula and the eastern two thirds of the northern seaboard. Haiti has two rainy seasons: April-May and September-October.

HISTORY

The birth of a colony

In the 17th century the French invaded from their base on Tortuga and colonized what became known as Saint Domingue, its borders later being determined by the Treaty of Ryswick in 1697. The area was occupied by cattle hunting buccaneers and pirates, but Governor de Cussy, appointed in 1684, introduced legal trading and planting. By the eighteenth century it was regarded as the most valuable tropical colony of its size in the world and

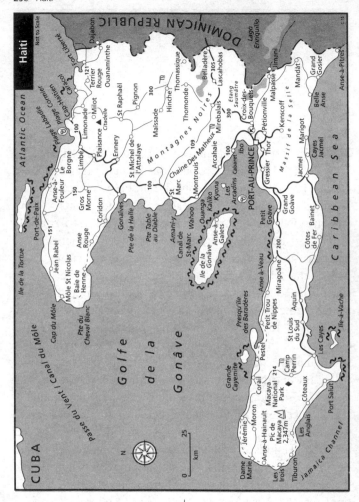

Haiti

Not to Scale

DOMINICAN REPUBLIC

Atlantic Ocean

CUBA

Golfe de la Gonâve

Caribbean Sea

was the largest sugar producer in the West Indies. However, that wealth was based on slavery and the planters were aware of the dangers of rebellion. After the French Revolution, slavery came under attack in France and the planters defensively called for more freedom to run their colony as they wished. In 1791 France decreed that persons of colour born of free parents should be entitled to vote; the white inhabitants of Saint Domingue refused to implement the decree and mulattoes were up in arms demanding their rights. However, while the whites and mulattoes were involved in their dispute, slave unrest erupted in the north in 1791. Thousands of white inhabitants were slaughtered and the northern plain was put to the torch. Soon whites, mulattoes and negroes were all fighting with shifting alliances and mutual hatred.

Toussaint Louverture

Out of the chaos rose a new leader, an ex-slave called François-Dominique Toussaint, also known as Toussaint Louverture, who created his own roaming army after the 1791 uprising. When France and Spain went to war, he joined the Spanish forces as a mercenary and built up a troop of 4,000 negroes. However, when the English captured Port-au-Prince in 1794 he defected with his men to join the French against the English. After 4 years of war and disease, the English withdrew, by which time Toussaint was an unrivalled leader among the black population. He then turned against the mulattoes of the W and S, forcing their armies to surrender. Ordered to purge the mulatto troops, Toussaint's cruel lieutenant, Jean-Jacques Dessalines, an African-born ex-slave, slew at least 350. Mulatto historians later claimed that 10,000 were massacred. The same year, torrential rain broke the irrigation dams upon which the prosperity of the area depended. They were never repaired and the soil was gradually eroded to become a wilderness. By 1800 Toussaint was politically supreme. In 1801 he drew up a new constitution and proclaimed himself governor general for life. However, Napoleon had other plans, which included an alliance with Spain, complicated by Toussaint's successful invasion of Santo Domingo, and the reintroduction of the colonial system based on slavery. In 1802 a French army was sent to Saint Domingue which defeated Toussaint and shipped him to France where he died in prison. The news that slavery had been reintroduced in Guadeloupe, however, provoked another popular uprising which drove out the French, already weakened by fever.

19th century revolution

This new revolt was led by Dessalines, who had risen to power in Toussaint's entourage and was his natural successor. In 1804 he proclaimed himself Emperor of the independent Haiti, changing the country's name to the Indian word for 'high land'. Dessalines was assassinated in 1806 and the country divided between his rival successors: the negro Christophe in the N, and the mulatto Pétion in the S. The former's rule was based on forced labour and he managed to keep the estates running until his death in 1820. (He called himself Roi Henri Christophe and built the Citadelle and Sans Souci near Milot, see below; for a fictionalized account of these events, read Alejo Carpentier's *El reino de este mundo – The Kingdom of This World*, arguably the first Latin American novel to employ the technique of *lo real maravilloso*.) Pétion divided the land into peasant plots, which in time became the pattern all over Haiti and led to economic ruin with virtually no sugar production and little coffee. Revolution succeeded revolution as hatred between the blacks and the ruling mulattoes intensified; constitutional government rarely existed in the nineteenth century.

US intervention

At the beginning of the 20th century, the USA became financially and politically involved for geopolitical and strategic reasons. Intervention in 1915 was provoked by the murder and mutilation of a president, but occupation brought order and the reorganization of public finances. Provision of health services, water supply, sewerage and education did not prevent opposition to occupation erupting in an uprising in 1918-20 which left 2,000 Haitians dead. By the 1930s the strategic need for occupation had receded and the expense was unpopular in the USA. In 1934 the USA withdrew, leaving Haiti poor and overpopulated with few natural resources. Migrants commonly sought work on the sugar estates of the neighbouring Dominican Republic, although there was hatred between the two nations. In 1937 about 10,000 Haitian immigrants were rounded up and massacred in the Dominican Republic.

The Duvalier dynasty

In 1957 François (Papa Doc) Duvalier, a black nationalist, was elected president and unlike previous autocrats he succeeded in holding on to power. He managed to break the mulattoes' grip on political power, even if not on the economy. In 1964 he became President-for-Life, a title which was inherited by his 19-year-old son, Jean-Claude (Baby Doc) in 1971. The Duvaliers' power rested on the use of an armed militia, the Tontons Macoutes, to dominate the people. Tens of thousands of Haitians were murdered and thousands more fled the country. However, repression eased under Jean-Claude, and dissidence rose, encouraged partly by US policies on human rights. Internecine rivalry continued and the mulatto elite began to regain power, highlighted by the President's marriage to Michèle Bennett, the daughter of a mulatto businessman, in 1980. Discontent began to grow with the May 1984 riots in Gonaïves and Cap Haïtien, and resurfaced after the holding of a constitutional referendum on 22 July 1985 which gave the Government 99.98% of the vote. Several months of unrest and rioting gradually built up into a tide of popular insistence on the removal of Duvalier, during the course of which several hundred people were killed by his henchmen. The dictatorship of the Duvaliers (father and son) was brought to a swift and unexpected end when the President-for-Life fled to France on 7 February 1986.

Democracy and the army

The removal of the Duvaliers left Haitians hungry for radical change. The leader of the interim military-civilian Government, General Henri Namphy, promised presidential elections for November 1987, but they were called off after Duvalierists massacred at least 34 voters early on polling day with apparent military connivance. New, rigged elections were held in January 1988, and Professor Leslie Manigat was handed the presidency only to be ousted in June when he tried to remove Namphy as army commander. Namphy took over as military president, but 4 months later he himself was ousted in a coup that brought General Prosper Avril to power. Dissatisfaction within the army resurfaced in April, 1989, when several coup attempts were staged within quick succession and lawlessness increased as armed gangs, including disaffected soldiers, terrorized the population. Nevertheless, the USA renewed aid, for the first time since 1987, on the grounds that Haiti was moving towards democratic elections, promised for 1990, and was making efforts to combat drug smuggling. Under General Namphy, cocaine worth US$700mn passed through Haiti each month, with a 10% cut for senior army officers. However, Avril's position was insecure; he moved closer to hardline Duvalierists and arrests, beatings and murders of opposition activists increased. Foreign aid was again cut off in January 1990 when Avril imposed a state of siege and the holding of elections looked unlikely. Finally, in March, General Avril fled the country after a week of mass demonstrations and violence. Following his resignation, Haiti was governed by an interim President, Supreme Court judge, Ertha Pascal-Trouillot.

1990 Elections and coup

Despite poor relations between Mme Pascal-Trouillot and the 19-member Council of State appointed to assist her, successful elections were held on 16 December 1990. The presidential winner, by a landslide margin of 67% to 15%, was Father Jean-Bertrand Aristide; his nearest rival was the former finance minister Marc Bazin. The electoral campaign was marked by the candidacy of Roger Lafontant, a Duvalierest and former 'security official' of Baby Doc. A warrant for his arrest did not prevent Lafontant running for the presidency; only the failure of his coup attempt against Mme Pascal-Trouillot in January 1991 brought him to justice.

President Aristide ('Titide'), a Roman Catholic priest who was expelled from the Salesian order in 1988 for 'incitement to hatred, violence and class struggle', was sworn in on 7 February. His denunciations of corruption within the government, church and army over the previous decade had won him a vast following. Among his immediate steps on taking office were to start investigations into the conduct of Mme Pascal Trouillot and many other officials, to seek the resignation of six generals, to propose the separation of the army and police and to garner urgently-needed financial assistance from abroad for the new administration. Aristide's refusal to share power with other politicians, his attacks on the interests of the armed forces and the business elite and the actions of some of his militant supporters provoked his overthrow on 30 September 1991 by sections of the army sympathetic to Lafontant (who was murdered in his cell during the rising). Aristide fled into exile. Harsh repression was imposed after the deposition of Aristide; at least 2,000 people were said to have died in the first 6 months, almost 600 during the coup itself. People began fleeing in small boats to the United States' Guantánamo naval base on Cuba in an exodus that had reached 38,000 by May 1992. The USA brought it to an end by immediately repatriating everyone without screening political asylum claims.

International pressure

International condemnation of the coup was swift, with the Organization of American States, led by the USA, imposing an embargo. While the EC and other nations did not join in the embargo, they did follow the OAS in suspending aid and freezing Haitian government assets. The sanctions hurt, but not sufficiently to promote a formula for Aristide's return; this was partly because of Washington's misgivings about his radical populism.

The election of Bill Clinton to the US presidency in 1992 with the prospect of more decisive US action on restoring Aristide to power prompted United Nations involvement. Former Argentine foreign minister Dante Caputo was appointed UN special envoy for Haiti in December 1992. With Washington making it clear it was ready to step up sanctions, Caputo persuaded the army commander, General Raoul Cedras, to agree in February 1993 to the deployment of 250 civilian UN/OAS human rights monitors throughout Haiti. Further UN pressure was applied in June 1993 with the imposition of an oil embargo and a freeze on financial assets. As a result, an accord was reached in July whereby Aristide would return to office by 30 October, Cedras would retire and Aristide would appoint a new army chief and a prime minister.

As the 30 October deadline approached, it became clear that Aristide would not be allowed to return. In mid-October, the Haitian rulers humiliated the USA by refusing to allow a ship to dock carrying a 1,300-strong UN non-combat mission. Oil and arms sanctions were reimposed, yet Aristide supporters continued to be killed and harassed. Aristide's appointed cabinet resigned in mid-December as the régime showed no signs of weakening. In fact, as smuggled fuel from the Dominican Republic flowed in, Cedras and his collaborators set their sights on staying in power until the end of Aristide's term of office, February 1996.

Meanwhile, tensions between Aristide and the Clinton administration grew as the USA appeared unable, or unwilling, to break the impasse. Pressure from the US Black Caucus and from Florida politicians eventually persuaded Clinton to take more positive action. The policy of returning boat people was stopped. Tough worldwide sanctions, including a cessation of commercial flights, were initiated in May 1994 and the Dominican Republic was approached to control sanctions breaking. These measures led to a state of emergency in Haiti, but not an end to defiance.

Aristide's return

Despite the lack of wholehearted support in the USA, an occupation of Haiti by 20,000 US troops, first proposed in June, began on 19 September 1994. Aristide returned to the presidency on 15 October to serve the remainder of his term, aided first by a 6,000 strong US force, then by 6,000 UN troops which replaced the Americans in March 1995.

General Cedras and his chief-of-staff, General Philippe Biamby, were talked into exile in Panama, while the third leader of the regime, police chief Michel François, fled to the Dominican Republic. In the months after the regime's demise, Aristide set about reducing the influence of the army and police and the USA began to train new recruits for a new police force. By April 1995, the absence of a fully-trained police force and of an adequate justice system contributed to a general breakdown of law and order. Many people suspected of robbery or murder were brutally punished by ordinary Haitians taking the law into their own hands. 'Zenglendo' thugs, often thought to be demobilized soldiers, were involved in the killing of political figures and others. The fear of violence disrupted preparations for legislative and local elections, held over two rounds in June and July 1995.

The elections gave overwhelming support to Aristide's Lavalas movement in the Senate (all but one of the seats up for election) and the Lower House (71 of the 83 seats) but the turn out was very low and the results were bitterly contested. 23 of the 27 competing parties denounced the election because of irregularities reported by international observers.

Economic reform under Aristide was slow and there was dissent within the Cabinet. Progress on judicial reform progressed but investigations into recent killings stalled. The US Senate consequently blocked disbursement of aid. Mob violence and extra-judicial killings continued, with the new police force unable to do anything about it.

René Préval

Presidential elections were held on 17 December 1995 and for the first time power was transferred from one elected Haitian president to another. René Préval, a close aide of Aristide's, won a landslide victory with 87% of the vote, although only 25% of the electorate turned out and most opposition parties boycotted the event. He was inaugurated on 7 February 1996 and Rony Smarth was later sworn in as Prime Minister. The new Government aimed to introduce a new privatization plan for nine state companies, based on the Bolivian system whereby companies invest in, rather than buy, a minority share of the state entity. Agreement on a structural adjustment programme was reached with the IMF in May but was likely to be hampered by a hostile Congress. Haiti was treated as a political football in the US Senate, which was absorbed in its own presidential race. Aid only dribbled in, leaving civil servants and police unpaid and mounting violence in the streets. The UN Peacekeeping Force was asked to stay for a further 5 months from 1 July as the new police force was still unready to take over.

GOVERNMENT

Under the terms of the July 1993, UN-brokered agreement to restore democracy, Haiti has two legislative houses, a 27-seat Senate and an 83-seat Chamber of Deputies. The parliament in this form, with the elected president as chief of state, came into effect in October 1994.

THE ECONOMY

Structure of production

Haiti is the Western Hemisphere's poorest country and among the 30 poorest in the world. 75% of the people fall below the World Bank's absolute poverty level. It is overpopulated. It lacks communications, cheap power and raw materials for industry. Its mountainous terrain cannot provide a living for its rural population.

Haiti: fact file

Geographic

Land area	27,700 sq km
forested	5.1%
pastures	18.0%
cultivated	33.0%

Demographic

Population (1995)	6,589,000
annual growth rate (1990-95)	1.7%
urban	30.7%
rural	69.3%
density	237.9 per sq km
Religious affiliation	
Roman Catholic (inc Voodoo)	80.3%
Birth rate per 1,000 (1994)	40.0
	(world av 26.0)

Education and Health

Life expectancy at birth,	
male	43 years
female	47 years
Infant mortality rate	
per 1,000 live births (1994)	109.0
Physicians (1992)	1 per 10,060 persons
Hospital beds	1 per 1,201 persons
Calorie intake as %	
of FAO requirement	75%
Population age 25 and over	
with no formal schooling	59.5%
Literate males (over 15)	59.1%
Literate females (over 15)	47.4%

Economic

GNP (1992 market prices)	
	US$2,479mn
GNP per capita	US$370
Public external debt (1993)	
	US$617.6mn
Tourism receipts (1993)	US$46mn
Inflation (annual av 1989-94)	23.9%

Radio	1 per 24 persons
Television	1 per 260 persons
Telephone	1 per 164 persons

Employment

Population economically active (1990)	
	2,679,140
Unemployment rate (1994)	70.0%
% of labour force in	
agriculture	57.3
mining	0.9
manufacturing	5.6
construction	1.0

Source *Encyclopaedia Britannica*

Until the embargo, the main economic problem was chronic low agricultural productivity, compounded by low world commodity prices. 1% of the population controls 40% of the wealth. The average farm size is less than 1 ha. Only a third of the land is arable, yet most of the people live in the country, using rudimentary tools to grow maize, rice, sorghum and coffee. Deforestation has played havoc with watersheds and agriculture. Only a fraction of the land is now forested, yet charcoal continues to supply 70% of fuel needs. Agriculture generates 38.6% of the gdp but employs more than half the workforce. Coffee is the main cash crop, providing 9% of exports. Sugar and sisal output has slumped as population pressure has forced farmers to switch to subsistence crops.

Industry and commerce is limited, and heavily concentrated in Port-au-Prince. Until the embargo, assembly operations turned out baseballs, garments and electronic parts for export to the USA. After the lifting of the embargo, factories were slow to reopen because of civil unrest and electricity shortages. In addition, a 40% increase in the minimum wage, to US$2.57 a day, made Haiti's pay level marginally higher than the Dominican Republic, to which many offshore companies had relocated. Vegetable oils, footwear and metal goods are still produced for domestic consumption. Manufactured goods make up two thirds of total exports. Tourism all but disappeared in the 1980s, at first because of a scare about AIDS, then because of the political instability. Many hotels were forced to close.

Recent trends

The 1987 aid cut-off by major donors hit the economy hard and gdp began to slip. Aid resumed in 1990 as the prospects of elections improved. By mapping out very orthodox economic policies, the Aristide government secured pledges of more than US$400mn in international aid in July and August 1991, but it never materialized because of the coup the following month.

The 3 years following the coup were marked by import and export embargos, the suspension of foreign aid amounting to US$150-180mn a year and the freezing of assets abroad. There were huge job losses in the formal sector of 50,000 (35,000 in the export assembly industries alone) and of a similar amount in the informal sector. Foreign exchange earnings plummeted; the electricity and telephone systems deteriorated; prices for foodstuffs and other essential items rose sharply. The only areas to benefit were contraband and drug smuggling (56 kg of cocaine passed through Haiti in 1992, 157 kg in 1993 and 716 kg in 1994). Remittances by the 1.5 million Haitians living abroad, put at about US$150mn a year, were not affected.

The return of Aristide and the lifting of the trade embargo led to hopes of economic recovery. The Paris Club group of lending countries cancelled US$75mn of bilateral debt and the forgiveness of debt arrears renewed access to suspended aid. International donor agencies pledged a total of US$1.2bn in various packages, but also required Haiti to follow set economic guidelines. A reform programme was drawn up, including the privatization of nine of 33 state enterprises but opposition to it delayed implementation. Electricity supply, one of the sectors due for divestment, did not improve in 1995, which hampered a return to growth in other areas. It was left to the Préval Government in 1996 to push ahead with unpopular economic reform under the aegis of the IMF in order to release aid blocked due to lack of progress.

CULTURE

Although Haiti wiped out slavery in its 18th century revolution, its society still suffers from the racial, cultural and linguistic divisions inherited from slavery. Toussaint's tolerant statesmanship was unable to resist Napeolon's push to reimpose slavery. It took the tyranny and despotism of Dessalines and Christophe. Haitian despots stepped into the shoes of the French despots. The new, mulatto ruling class considered its French language and culture superior to the blacks' Créole language and Voodoo religion, which it despised. The corruption and despotism of the black political class created by Duvalier suggest that, despite its profession of *noirisme*, it internalized the mulatto contempt for its own race.

Religion

Voodoo (French: Vaudou) is a blend of religions from West Africa, above all from Dahomey (present-day Benin) and the Congo River basin. Like Cuba's Santería and Brazil's Candomblé, it uses drumming, singing and dance to induce possession by powerful African spirits with colourful personalities. Called *loas* in Haiti (pronounced lwa), they help with life's daily problems. In return, they must be 'served' with ceremonies, offerings of food and drink, and occasional animal sacrifice in temples known as *ounphors*.

The essence of Voodoo is keeping in harmony with the *loas*, the dead and nature. Magic may be used in self-defense, but those in perfect harmony with the universe should not need it. Magic in the pursuit of personal ambitions is frowned on. The use of black magic and sorcery, or the use of attack magic against others without just cause, is considered evil. Sorcerers, called *bokors*, exist but they are not seen as part of Voodoo. The *loas* punish Voodoo priests (*oungans*) or priestesses (*mambos*) who betray their vocation by practicing black magic. Many Haitians believe in the existence of *zombis*, the living dead victims of black magic who are supposedly disinterred by sorcerers and put to work as slaves.

Voodoo acquired an overlay of Catholicism in colonial times, when the slaves learned to disguise their *loas* as saints. Nowadays, major ceremonies coincide with Catholic celebrations such as Chistmas, Epiphany and the Day of the Dead. Lithographs of Catholic saints are used to represent the *loas*.

The role of attack and defence magic in Haiti's religious culture expanded during the slave revolts and the independence war. Many rebel leaders were *oungans*, such as Mackandal, who terrorized the northern plain with his knowledge of poisons from 1748 to 1758, and Boukman, who plotted the 1791 uprising at a clandestine Voodoo ceremony. Belief in Voodoo's protective spells inspired a fearlessness in battle that amazed the French. As a result, many Haitian rulers saw Voodoo as a threat to their own authority and tried to stamp it out. They also thought its survival weakened Haiti's claim to membership of the family of 'civilized' nations. François Duvalier enlisted enough *oungans* to neutralize Voodoo as a potential threat. He also coopted the Catholic church hierarchy. He had less success with the Catholic grass roots which, inspired by Liberation Theology, played a key role in his son's 1986 fall and Aristide's election in 1990.

After several ruthless campaigns against Voodoo, most recently in the early 1940s, the Catholic church has settled into an attitude of tolerant coexistence. Now the militant hostility to Voodoo comes from fundamentalist Protestant sects of American origin which have exploited their relative wealth and ability to provide jobs to win converts.

Language

The origins of Haitian Créole are hotly disputed. Is Créole basically a French-derived lingua franca of seafarers in the 17th and 18th centuries that reached Haiti already evolved? Or is it the product of the transformation of French in Saint Domingue by African slaves who needed a common language, one the slave-owners were forced to learn in order to speak to their slaves? The evidence points both ways.

More important is how Créole and French are used now. All Haitians understand Créole and speak it at least part of the time. Use of French is limited to the élite and middle class. The illiterate majority of the population understand no French at all. There is almost no teaching in Créole and no attempt is made to teach French as a foreign language to the few Créole-only speakers who enter the school system. Since mastery of French is still a condition for self-advancement, language perpetuates Haiti's deep class divisions. All those pushing for reform in Haiti are trying to change this. Radio stations have begun using Créole in the last 10 years. Musicians now increasingly sing in Créole. The 1987 constitution gave Créole equal official status alongside French. Even élite politicians have begun using Créole in speeches although some speak it poorly. Aristide's sway over the people is due in part to his poetic virtuosity in Créole. A phonetic transcription of Créole has evolved over the last 50 years, but little has been published except the Bible, some poetry and, nowadays, a weekly pro-Aristide newspaper, *Libète*. Créole is famed for its proverbs voicing popular philosophy and reflecting Haiti's enormous social divisions. The best teach yourself book is *Ann Pale Kreyòl*, published by the Créole Institute, Ballentine Hall 602, Indiana University, Bloomington IN 47405, USA. It is hard to find in Haitian bookshops. **NB** In the text below, 'Cr' means Créole version.

The arts

Haitian handicraft and naive art is the best in the Caribbean. Even such utilitarian articles as the woven straw shoulder bags and the tooled-leather scabbards of the peasant machete have great beauty. The *rada* Voodoo drum is an object of great aesthetic appeal. Haiti is famed for its wood carvings, but poverty has pushed craftsmen into producing art from such cheap material as papier maché and steel drums, flattened and turned into cut-out wall-hangings or sculpture. Haitian naive art on canvas emerged only in response to the demand of travellers and tourists in the 1930s and

40s, but it had always existed on the walls of Voodoo temples, where some of the best representations of the spirit world are to be found. Weddings, cock-fights, market scenes or fantasy African jungles are other favoured themes. Good paintings can range from one hundred to several thousand dollars. Mass-produced but lively copies of the masters sell for as little as US$10. Negotiating with street vendors and artists can be an animated experience, offering insights into the nation's personality. (See **Shopping** sections below.)

Exposure to white racism during the US occupation shook some of the mulatto intellectuals out of their complacent Francophilia. Led by Jean Price Mars and his 1919 pioneering essay *Ainsi parla l'oncle* (Thus Spoke Uncle) they began to seek their identity in Haiti's African roots. Peasant life, Créole expressions and Voodoo started to appear together with a Marxist perspective in novels such as Jacques Romain's *Gouverneurs de la rosée* (Masters of the Dew). René Depestre, now resident in Paris after years in Cuba, is viewed as Haiti's greatest living novelist. Voodoo, politics and acerbic social comment are blended in the novels of Haiti's youngest successful writer Gary Victor, a deputy minister in the Aristide government before the coup.

Music and dance

Nigel Gallop writes: The poorest nation in the western hemisphere is among the richest when it comes to music. This is a people whose most popular religion worships the deities through singing, drumming and dancing. The prime musical influence is African, although European elements are to be found, but none that are Amerindian. The music and dance (and in Haiti music is almost inseparable from dance) can be divided into three main categories: Voodoo ritual, rural folk and urban popular. The Voodoo rituals, described above, are collective and are profoundly serious, even when the *loa* is humorous or mischievous. The hypnotic dance is accompanied by call-and-response singing and continuous drumming, the drums themselves (the large Manman, medium-sized Seconde and smaller Bula or Kata) being regarded as sacred.

During Mardi Gras (Carnival) and Rara (see below), bands of masked dancers and revellers can be found on the roads and in the streets almost anywhere in the country, accompanied by musicians playing the Vaccines (bamboo trumpets). Haitians also give rein to their love of music and dance in the so-called Bambouches, social gatherings where the dancing is *pou' plaisi* (for pleasure) and largely directed to the opposite sex. They may be doing the Congo, the Martinique or Juba, the Crabienne or the national dance, the Méringue. The first two are of African provenance, the Crabienne evolved from the European Quadrille, while the Méringue is cousin to the Dominican Merengue. Haitians claim it originated in their country and was taken to the Dominican Republic during the Haitian occupation of 1822 to 1844, but this is a matter of fierce debate between the two nations. In remote villages it may still be possible to come across such European dances as the Waltz, Polka, Mazurka and Contredanse, accompanied by violin, flute or accordion.

Haitian music has not remained impervious to outside influences during the 20th century, many of them introduced by Haitian migrant workers returning from Cuba, the Dominican Republic and elsewhere in the region (as well as exporting its own music to Cuba's Oriente province in the form of the Tumba Francesa). One very important external influence was that of the Cuban Son, which gave rise to the so-called 'Troubadour Groups', with their melodious voices and soft guitar accompaniment, still to be heard in some hotels. Jazz was another intruder, a result of the US marines' occupation between 1915 and 1934. Then in the 1950s two equally celebrated composers and band leaders, Nemours Jean-Baptiste and Weber Sicot, introduced a new style of recreational dance music, strongly influenced by the Dominican Merengue and known as Compact Directe ('compas') or Cadence Rampa. Compas (the s is not pronounced) dominated the music scene until the past few years, when it has become a much more open market, with Salsa, Reggae, Soca and Zouk all making big inroads. A number of Haitian groups have achieved international recognition, notably Tabou Combo and Coupé Cloué, while female singers Martha-Jean Claude and Toto Bissainthe have also made a name for themsleves abroad. One excellent troubadour-style singer who has been well-recorded is Althiery Dorival. Also highly recommended is the set of six LPs titled 'Roots of Haiti', recorded in the country, but distributed by Mini Records of Brooklyn. Finally, no comment on Haitian music would be complete without reference to the well-known lullaby 'Choucounne' which, under the title 'Yellow Bird', is crooned to tourists every night on every English-speaking Antillean island.

Mike Tarr adds: A musical revolution came with the emergence of 'voodoo beat', a fusion of Voodoo drumming and melody with an international rock guitar and keyboard sound. Its lyrics call for political change and a return to peasant values. With albums out on the Island label, and US tours behind them, Boukman Eksperyans is the most successful of these bands. People who have ignored Voodoo all their lives are possessed at Boukman concerts. Other 'voodoo beat' bands of note are Ram, Boukan Ginen, Foula, Sanba-Yo and Koudjay.

FLORA AND FAUNA

Deforestation and soil erosion have destroyed habitats. Haiti is therefore poor in flora and fauna compared with its eastern neighbour. Three sites are worth visiting. One is Lake Saumâtre, 90 minutes E of the capital. Less brackish than Enriquillo, across the Dominican border, it is the habitat of more than 100 species of waterfowl (including migratory North American ducks), plus flamingoes and American crocodiles. The N side of the lake is better, reached via the town of Thomazeau (see under **Excursions from Port-au-Prince**).

The other two are mountain parks. Relatively easy to reach is Parc La Visite, about 5 hours' hike from the hill resort of Kenscoff behind Port-au-Prince. On the high Massif de la Selle, with a mixture of pine forest and montane cloud forest, it has 80 bird species and two endemic mammals, the Hispaniolan hutia (*Plagiodontia aedium*) and the nez longue (*Solenodon paradoxus*). North American warblers winter there. It is also a nesting-place for the black-capped petrel (*Pteradoma hasitata*). See under **Excursions from Port-au-Prince**. Harder to reach is the Macaya National Park, at the tip of the SW peninsula, site of Haiti's last virgin cloud forest. It has pines 45m high, 141 species of orchid, 102 species of fern, 99 species of moss and 49 species of liverwort. Its fauna include 11 species of butterfly, 57 species of snail, 28 species of amphibian, 34 species of reptile, 65 species of bird and 19 species of bat. In addition to the hutia, nez longue and black-capped petrel, its most exotic animals are the Grey-crowned Palm Tanager (*Phaenicophilus poliocephalus*) and the Hispaniolan trogan (*Temnotrogan roseigaster*). The endangered Peregrine falcon (*Falco pergrinus*) winters in the park. From Les Cayes, it takes half a day to get to a University of Florida base on the edge of the park which has basic camping facilities. Allow another 2 days each way for the 2,347m Pic de Macaya. See under **Southwest from Port-au-Prince**. Paul Paryski (T 23-1400/1), a UN ecosystems expert, will give advice.

Leaf doctors, voodoo priests and sorcerers have a wealth of knowledge of natural remedies and poisons to be found in Haiti's surviving plant life. They do not share their knowledge readily. In his book *The Serpent and the Rainbow*, Harvard ethnobotanist Wade Davis gives a racy account of his attempts to discover which natural toxins sorcerers are thought to use to turn their victims into *zombis*.

Almost any tree is liable to be chopped down for firewood or charcoal; a few very large species are not because they are believed to be the habitat of *loas*. Chief among them is the silkcotton tree, 'mapou' in Creole. Haiti has no poisonous snakes or insects.

FESTIVALS

The standard of the Port-au-Prince carnival has fallen since the Duvaliers left. Nowadays few people wear costumes and the floats are poorly decorated. There is a cacophony of music blaring out from both stands and passing floats. Excitement is provided by the walking bands (*bandes-à-pied*), cousins of the Rara bands that appear after carnival (see below). Circulating on foot, drawing a large dancing, chanting crowd in their wake, they specialize in salacious lyrics and political satire. Beware, when crowds moving in different directions pass, there is boisterous pushing and occasional knife fights. The safest place to watch is from one of the stands near the *Holiday Inn*. Carnival climaxes on the 3 days before Ash Wednesday, but the government lays on free open-air concerts in different parts of the city during the 3 or 4 weekends of pre-carnival. Members of the élite

prefer the carnival at Jacmel, 2-3 hours from the capital, where the tradition of elaborate, imaginative masked costumes still thrives. The music at Jacmel is unremarkable, however.

Carnival is immediately followed by Rara, dubbed the 'peasant carnival'. Every weekend during Lent, including Easter weekend, colourfully attired Rara bands emerge from voodoo societies and roam the countryside. They seek donations, so be ready with a few small notes. Beating drums, blowing home-made wind instruments, dancing and singing, some bands may have a thousand or more members. A good place to see it is the town of Leogane near the capital on Easter Sunday. Beware, the drinking is heavy and fights are common.

The Gede (pronounced gay-day) are *loas* who possess Voodooists on 1-2 November (All Saints and Day of the Dead). They can be seen in cemeteries or roaming the streets, dressed to look like corpses or undertakers. The lords of death and the cemetery, they mock human vanity and pretension, and remind people that sex is the source of life. They do this by dancing in a lewd fashion with strangers, causing much hilarity. For pilgrimages, see Saut d'Eau, Plaine du Nord and Limonade in the text below.

TRAVEL HINTS

Haiti is especially fascinating for the tourist who is avid for out-of-the-way experience. In order that you may make the most of your visit, we offer the following hints. Although it is one of the poorest countries in the world, most of whose

Forts

Haiti abounds with ruined forts. Those on the coast were built by the French or English in the 17th and 18th centuries. Those inland were built by the Haitians after winning independence from France in order to deter any attempt to recover the former colony. Having no navy, the Haitian strategy for an invasion was to put the plains to the torch and retreat into the mountains behind a line of fortresses. The strategy was never tested, but the Cacos guerrillas did use some of the forts during their 1918-20 fight against the US occupation.

citizens suffer from one kind of oppression or another, Haiti is proud of having been the only nation to have carried out successfully a slave rebellion. Haitians at all levels are very sensitive to how they are treated by foreigners, commonly called 'blanc'. If you treat them with warmth and consideration, they will respond with enthusiasm and friendship. There is no hostility towards 'blanc'; if you feel threatened it is probably the result of a misunderstanding.

Eye contact is very important; it is not avoided as in some other countries. Humour plays an important role in social interactions; Haitians survive by laughing at themselves and their situation. This, sadly, became a very difficult proposition during the events following the overthrow of President Aristide. Haitians are physical, touching and flirting a lot.

It is important to recognize the presence of each person in a social encounter, either with a handshake or a nod. When walking in the countryside, you usually wish *bon jour* (before 1200) or *bon soir* to anyone you meet. *Salud* is another common greeting, at any time of day. Coffee or cola are often offered by richer peasants to visitors (Haitian coffee is among the best in the world). Do not expect straight answers to questions about a peasant's wealth, property or income.

It is assumed that each 'blanc' is wealthy and therefore it is legitimate to try to separate you from your riches. Such attempts should be treated with humour, indignation or consideration as appropriate.

Guides Young men and boys offer their services as guides at every turn and corner. It seems that it's worthwhile taking one (for about US$10-30 a day, depending where you go) just to prevent others pestering you. Most guides speak English and it is easier to get around with one than without. If you hire a guide you can also visit places off the beaten tourist track and avoid some of the frustrations of the public transport system. Max

Church, a pastor who has been training English/French/Créole-speaking guides, can be called on 34-2622, Port-au-Prince. However, if you take guides you must realize that they expect you to buy them food if you stop to eat.

Secondly, and more important, the guides are often 'on commission' with local shop- and stall-keepers, so that even if you ask them to bargain for you, you will not necessarily be getting a good price; nor will they necessarily go where you want to go. If you don't want a guide a firm but polite *non, merci* gets the message across. It is best to ignore altogether hustlers outside guesthouses, etc, as any contact makes them persist.

PORT-AU-PRINCE

What **Port-au-Prince** lacks in architectural grace, it makes up in a stunning setting, with steep mountains towering over the city to the S, La Gonâve island in a horseshoe bay on the W, and another wall of mountains beyond a rift valley plain to the N. Over the years the city has spilled out of its original waterfront location, climbing further into the mountains behind. A rural exodus has swollen the population from 150,000 in 1954 to 1.5 million now. The worst shantytowns (*bidonvilles*) are in a marshy waterfront area N of the centre, but most of the city is very poor. Enormous mounds of rotting garbage are a common sight. The commercial quarter starts near the port and stretches inland, to the E, about 10 blocks. It lacks charm or interest, except the area beside the port that was remodelled for the city's 1949 bicentennial. Known as the Bicentenaire (more formally, Cité de l'Exposition), it contains the post office, foreign ministry, parliament, American embassy and French Institute. It is now very run down.

The central reference point for visitors is the large, irregularly-shaped park called the Champs de Mars which begins to the E of the commercial quarter. The NW corner is dominated by the white, triple-domed presidential palace. It was built in 1918 on the site of a predecessor that was blown up in 1912 with its president inside. In the 1991 coup, President Aristide made a stand inside the present building. Just to the NE is the colonnaded, white and gold army high command building, where soldiers nearly lynched Aristide after dragging him out of the palace. (He was saved by the French ambassador, the American ambassador, or General

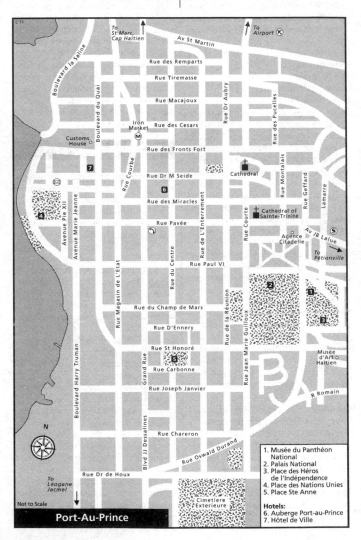

1. Musée du Panthéon National
2. Palais National
3. Place des Héros de l'Indépendance
4. Place des Nations Unies
5. Place Ste Anne

Hotels:
6. Auberge Port-au-prince
7. Hôtel de Ville

Port-Au-Prince

Cedras, depending on whose story you believe.) Immediately behind the palace, to the S, is a large, mustard-yellow army garrison that was once the fief of the ill-famed Colonel Jean-Claude Paul, indicted in Miami in 1987 for drug smuggling and poisoned the following year.

Immediately to the E of the palace, on Place des Héros de l'Independence, the subterranean Musée du Panthéon National (MUPANAH) houses historial relics, including the rusted anchor of Columbus's flagship, the *Santa María*. Don't miss an 1818 oil painting of King Henri Christophe by Welshman Richard Evans, director of Christophe's Fine Arts Academy at Sans Souci. Two blocks N and two W, at the corner of rue Courte and the busy rue Pavée, the Sainte Trinité Episcopal Cathedral has astounding biblical murals by the greatest naïve artists, including Philomé Obin, Castera Bazile and Riguaud Benoit. Done in 1949, they are considered the crowning achievement of Haitian art. The adjoining complex has a gift shop and a school whose students give excellent choral and classical music concerts (details from Sister Anne-Marie, T 22-5638). The pink and white stone Catholic Cathedral is four blocks to the N.

At the intersection of rues Capois and Légitime, the Musée d'Art Haïtien (T 22-2510) has Haiti's finest naive art collection, plus a craft shop and a small restaurant in its garden. The Maison Défly, the house next door on Légitime, built by an army commander in 1896, is in the Victorian 'gingerbread' style, characterized by steep roofs and gables, round turrets, high ceilings, balconies and rich fretwork embellishment. Not a distinguished example, it contains a museum with period furniture, 0900-1300 Monday to Saturday. The rue Capois has several hotels, restaurants and shops. At the southern end of rue Capois, 1 km from the Champs de Mars, is the *Hotel Oloffson*, a much more imposing example of a gingerbread. West

of rue Capois are leafy neighbourhoods climbing into the foothills where the well-off built residences in the 19th century, and gingerbreads abound.

Local information – Port-au-Prince
● Accommodation

Price guide			
L1	over US$200	L2	US$151-200
L3	US$101-150	A1	US$81-100
A2	US$61-80	A3	US$46-60
B	US$31-45	C	US$21-30
D	US$12-20	E	US$7-11
F	US$4-6	G	up to US$3

Hotels L3-A2 *Oloffson* (see above, rue Cadet Jérémie at intersection with rue Capois, T 23-4000/23-4102, F 23-0919), model for Hotel Trianon in Graham Greene's *The Comedians*, eccentrically managed by Haitian-American musician Richard Morse, Haiti's most charming hotel but you pay for the atmosphere, the rooms are not worth the price, haunt of writers, journalists and film-makers, voodoo beat or folklore several nights a week, Thurs buffet and live music well worth the money, pool, never lacks electricity, most rooms a/c, CP; **A1** *Holiday Inn* (T 23-9800/93, F 22-0822), 10 rue Capois, central location on Champs de Mars, jungly gardens, pool, tolerable restaurant, own generator, all rooms a/c, CP; **A2** *Visa Lodge* (T 49-1201/2/3/4, 46-2662) businessman's hotel in industrial zone near airport, pool, good restaurant, own generator, EP; **A3** *Prince* (T 45-2764/5), corner of rue 3 and ave N, Pacot, quiet hillside neighbourhood 15 minutes' walk from taxis, own generator, all rooms a/c; **A3-B** *Park* (T 22-4406) 25 rue Capois, near *Holiday Inn*, cheaper to pay in gourdes, safe, central, be prepared to wait an age for breakfast, no generator; **D** *Palace* (T 22-3344), rue Capois at SE corner of Champs de Mars, no generator, unfriendly, cheap, dirty and sleazy; **C-F** *Auberge Port-au-Prince*, 148 rue du Centre, where buses from Dominican Republic disgorge their passengers amid hordes of vendors, no frills, no theft, rooms with bath or inside room, fan, ground floor bar serves lunch but closes around 1900, good view from roof.

Guesthouses A3 *Sendral's* (T 45-6502), rue Mercier, Bourdon, near *Hotel Villa St-Louis*, own generator, rooms with private bath and fan, CP; **A3** *La Griffonne* (T 45-4095/3440), 21 rue Jean Baptiste, Canapé Vert, quiet neighbourhood 5 minutes' walk from ave John Brown, own generator, rooms with private bath and a/c, MAP; **A3** *Coconut Villa* (T 46-1691), rue Berthold, Delmas 19 (poor location in dusty, northern suburb), own generator but turned off during day, rooms with private bath and a/c, CP; **B** *May's Villa* (T 45-1208), 28 Debussy, quiet neighbourhood at top of ave John Paul II (Cr: Tijo), 10 minutes' walk from nearest taxis, view, has a generator, but room lights only come on with city power at about 2100, rooms with private bath and fan, CP; **D** *Acropolis*, Blvd Dessalines, between rues Paul VI and Champ de Mars, no water in pool, bar/restaurant at back.

Note Most of the best hotels are in Pétionville, which is treated separately, although just 15 minutes away. Only the most expensive hotels and guesthouses have air-conditioning plus sufficiently powerful in-house generators able to cope with the long electricity blackouts in the city. Some have a generator to give partial power eg to the bar but not to guest rooms. Water is also rationed, and many of the cheaper, central hotels lack both water and electricity much of the time.

Tax, service charge and even energy surcharge are sometimes added to hotel bills. These extras have been included in the prices given here, which are very approximate because of exchange rate vagaries. While hotels are accommodating UN and NGO personnel, prices are usually quoted in US dollars and in consequence are high. Where possible, it is cheaper to pay in gourdes bought from money changers. Paying by credit card also works out more expensive.

Check rooms in advance in the cheaper hotels, service may be deficient.

● **Places to eat**
Almost the only places to eat out at night in Port-au-Prince proper are the *Oloffson* or *Holiday Inn*, or a row of terrace cafés selling barbecued chicken at the SE corner of the Champs de Mars (starting near Rex theatre). Bars in this area will probably try and short change you if they think you're a guest at the *Holiday Inn*. Well-off Port-au-Princiens go up to Pétionville to dine out. The following restaurants are open during the day only and close about 1600: *Table Ronde*, 7 rue Capois (half block from Holiday Inn), good lunch, front veranda excellent for street watching, popular with politicians; *Café Terrasse*, rear of Air France Bldg, 11 rue Capois and rue Ducoste,

excellent lunch, favoured by international aid agency staffers; *Rotisserie Lifran*, Av Delmar, just below the Imperial Cinema and Citibank, delicious barbecue chicken, good value; *Plaisance*, 3 rue Pavée, near corner of Geffrard, créole lunch in quiet garden on busy intersection; *Chez Nenel*, 18 rue Pavée, a block and a half from Ave Marie Jeanne, créole lunch, closed Sat and Sun; *Tiffany* (T 22-3506/0993), Blvd Harry Truman, N of Tele-Haiti; *Chez Yvane* (T 22-0188), 19 Blvd Harry Truman, S of Tele-Haiti, créole lunch in new a/c premises; *La Perle*, 80 rue Pavée, between Dessalines and rue des Miracles, pleasant, cool, enormous sandwiches, also spaghetti, omelettes, rec; *Paradis de Amis*, 43 rue Pavée, between Centre and Dessalines, rec for club sandwiches, omelettes, ice cream, a/c, popular with locals, cheap, large portions, spaghetti costs US$2.

Drinks, such as cold beers, water, juice, rum, can be bought at the *Supermarket de la Bonne Foie*, 52 rue Dr Marselly Seide, open Mon-Sat 0730-1600, small, friendly, English spoken, rec; also at *Supermarket Express* up on the hill on John Brown, cold beer and Guinness, UN customers.

● **Shopping**
Art and craft Some galleries have a near monopoly on certain artists, so don't expect to see a cross-section of all the major artists in any one, good gallery. The paintings hung at the *Oloffson* are for sale. *Galerie Carlos Jara* (T 45-7164) has a fine collection at 28 rue Armand Holly, Debussy, 10 minutes' drive up-hill from the *Oloffson*. The *Nader* family has two galleries: one at 258 rue Magasin de l'Etat, in the downtown inferno (T 22-0033/69); the other at 18 rue Bouvreuil (T 45-0565/4552) in the leafy Croix Desprez neighbourhood; *Galerie Issa* (T 22-3287), 17 ave Chile (300m from *Oloffson*) is more like a wholesale warehouse, but cheap if you know what you are looking for. A similar warehouse-type place for a variety of handicrafts and some paintings at reasonable prices, is run by Edner Pierre-Pierre on Av Delmas, across from Scotia Bank. Mass produced copies of the Haitian naive masters are sold very cheaply around the post office, near the port. Vendors sell first-class Voodoo flags outside the Musée d'Art Haïtien. Souvenir sellers also close to the *Holiday Inn*.

Gingerbread (T 45-3698), 52 ave Lamartinière (Cr: Bwa Vèna) is a gingerbread house where ironwork, papier-maché, Voodoo flags, and horn carvings are sold, 1000-1600 Monday to Friday, 1000-1300 Saturday; *Comité Artisanat Haïtien* (T 22-8440), 29 rue 3 (near *Oloffson*) is a cooperative selling handicraft from all over Haiti at good prices 0900-1600 Monday to Friday, 1000-1200 Saturday; *Ambiance*, 17 rue M, Pacot, has Haitian jewellery and pottery; *Rainbow Art Gallery* (T 45-6655/6039), 9 rue Pierre Wiener, Bourdon, sells handicraft and paintings.

Postcards, newspapers etc can be bought at *Librairie RM Auguste*, Blvd Dessalines, between rue des Miracles and rue Pavée. Also good selection outside Post Office.

● **Nightlife**

The *Oloffson* has a voodoo beat concert or a folklore show 3 nights a week, RAM performs Thur, the place to be. Otherwise, the best nightlife is to be found in Pétionville (see separate section). There is a red-light district on the SW Carrefour road that has been badly eclipsed by AIDS and political turmoil. The central part of the establishments consist of spacious, breezy, outdoor discothèques. The Dominican beer on offer is excellent and cheap, but the Dominican prostitutes and loud Dominican merengue music may have scant appeal. The city's western limits, around Mariani, have several ill-lit waterfront nightclubs, such as *Le Lambi*, where couples dance groin-to-groin to live compas bands and the men eat plate after plate of spicy, fresh-caught lambi (conch) to boost their virility.

● **Caution**

Shantytown dwellers don't welcome obvious sightseers and people with cameras. The area between the Champs de Mars and the waterfront is deserted after dark and should be avoided. It is safe to go to most places by car or taxi at night, but don't go about on foot except in Pétionville's restaurant and bar district. Remember that frequent power cuts plunge entire neighbourhoods into darkness. Drivers must always carry a licence as police blocks are common at night.

Watch out for pickpockets in markets and bus terminal areas and inside buses. (See also under **Security** in **Information for travellers**).

Be careful of traffic when walking around town. Street vendors crowd the pavements, forcing pedestrians into the path of vehicles. Many people have been knocked down and injured.

● **City public transport**

Shared taxis, called **Publiques** or simply taxis, are flagged down. They charge a basic fare (Cr: kous) of US$0.20 that may double or treble (de kous, twa kous) depending on how far off the beaten track you go. A red ribbon tied to the inside rear-view mirror identifies them. Language skills are needed. They stop work at about 1930.

Camionettes (minibuses) and **Taptaps** (open-backed pickups with a brightly painted wooden superstructure) have fixed routes and fares (about US$0.15). They are difficult to manage with luggage. They rarely circulate after 2030. Camionettes to Pétionville leave from ave John Brown, US$0.20.

A regular **taxi** is hard to find. Nick's Taxis (T 57-7777), based in Pétionville, is the only radio taxi company. It charges according to the meter. A passing Publique that is empty can be persuaded to do a private job (Cr: flete). The driver removes the red ribbon.

Chauffeurs-Guides are cab drivers who cater to foreign visitors. Usually found outside the biggest hotels such as the *Holiday Inn*, or at the airport, their cars can be used like regular taxis or hired by the hour, half-day, day or for a tour. The drivers usually speak French, plus a little English. They can be booked through the Association des Chauffeurs-Guides (T 22-0330) 18 blvd Harry Truman. Prices have been hiked to make the most of the US dollars brought in by US, UN and NGO personnel.

● **Street names**

Several major Port-au-Prince thoroughfares have two names, the official one used for maps and the telephone book, and the one commonly used in speech. Often the taxi drivers only know the second. Boulevard Jean-Jacques Dessalines is also known as Grand' Rue (Créole: Gran Ri); Avenue Lamartinière is Bois Verna (Cr: Bwa Vèna); ave Jean Paul II is Turgeau (Cr: Tijo); ave John Brown is Lalue (Cr: Lali); ave Paul VI is rue des Casernes (Cr: Ridekazèn); ave Martin Luther King is Nazon (Cr: Nazon).

● **Voodoo**

Seeing a Voodoo ceremony or dance during a short visit is not easy. They are not announced in newspapers or on the radio. Never go unless accompanied by a Haitian, or someone already known there. Most middle and upper-class Haitians do not attend ceremonies and won't know where or when they are happening. They may even be discomfited by your interest. Befriend poor, working-class Haitians and tell them about your interest. You may strike lucky. To increase you chances, time your stay to coincide with 2 November (Day of the Dead), Christmas, New Year or Epiphany (6 January). There are many ceremonies around these dates. If invited, take a bottle or two of rum or whisky and be ready to give generously if there is a collection. Sometimes, on the contrary, a wealthy 'oungan' (priest) or 'mambo' (priestess) will insist on lavishing drinks and food on the visitor. Don't refuse. To take pictures with a still camera or video, ask permission. You may be asked to pay for the privilege. TV crews are usually asked to pay substantial amounts. An oungan may always be consulted in his 'ounphor' (temple) even if there is no ceremony. Be ready to plead poverty if the sum requested seems exhorbitant.

Max Beauvoir (T 34-2818/3723), an oungan intellectual with fluent English, has initiated foreigners. He has a 'peristyle' (Voodoo dancehall) at Mariani, on the western edge of the city. Purists questioned the authenticity of the regular voodoo dances he used to lay on for tourists, but he is unquestionably an authority and talks readily to visitors. Aboudja (T 45-8476, or through the *Oloffson*), an English-speaking TV news cameraman, has been initiated as an oungan although he does not practice regularly. He acts as voodoo consultant for visiting journalists and TV crews.

● Cinemas
Cheap and interesting: the best are *Imperial* (a/c), Delmas; *Capitol* (a/c), 53, rue Lamarre; *Paramount*, Champs de Mars. Popular foreign films (British, US, French) are shown; non-French films are dubbed into French.

● Clubs
Pétionville Club (T 57-7575/1437), near US ambassador's residence at the end of rue Métreaux, a turning off rue Panaméricaine, between Port-au-Prince and Pétionville, a social and sports club. Visitors may use nine-hole golf course. For other facilities (tennis courts, racketball, gym, pool, restaurant) a 1-year temporary membership costs US$125. *Bellevue*, near Argentine Embassy on Panaméricaine, Bourdon, a social club with tennis courts. *Turgeau Tennis Club* on ave Jean-Paul II (Cr: Tijo) near corner Martin Luther King (Cr: Nazon) has a few courts. *Jotac* near airport has tennis courts, gym and restaurant.

● Banks
Promobank, corner of Lamarre and ave John Brown, also a branch at Blvd du Quai and rue Eden; **Banque de Boston**, rue des Miracles (place Geffrard); **Scotiabank**, route de Delmas (beneath Canadian embassy) and branch on rue des Miracles near corner of Blvd Dessalines; **Citibank**, route de Delmas. Also several small Haitian banks such as **Sogebank** and **Banque de L'Union Haïtienne**. There are long queues in most banks for any kind of service.

● Exchange
The best rate is obtained from street money changers (Fr: cambistes), who rarely cheat or steal. Find them on rue Pavée, at the airport, or near the market in Pétionville. It is perfectly legal. Check the rate on page 2 of the daily *Le Nouvelliste* newspaper. You may prefer to go in a car and do it through the window. The cambiste hands over the agreed sum in gourdes for you to count before you surrender the equivalent US dollar amount. They take only cash.

Currency dealers working out of offices give almost as good a rate. They also take TCs. Try Daniel Fouchard (T 23-1739) 14 rue des Miracles, Banque de Boston Bldg. Many importers and big retailers give a good rate for cash, TCs and even personal cheques on US bank accounts. Try Didier Rossard (T 22-5163), upstairs at 115 Place Geffrard; M or Mme Handal at Express Market, ave John Brown, six blocks down from Villa St-Louis. (See also **Currency** in **Information for travellers**.)

● Libraries
Institut Haitiano-Americain (T 22-3715/2947) corner of rue Capois and rue St-Cyr, next to *Holiday Inn*, 0800-1200, 1300-1700 Monday to Friday. The director is helpful to visiting travellers. Institut Français (T 22-3720), corner of Blvd Harry Truman and rue des Casernes, Bicentenaire, 1000-1600 Tues to Fri, 0900-1700 Sat; also has art exhibitions, concerts and plays.

● Travel agents
Agence Citadelle (T 23-5900) place du Marron Inconnu, sightseeing tours in a/c buses, travel to Dominican Republic and Cuba (owner Bobby Chauvet is a leading Haitian ecologist); *Horizons Tours*, 192B ave John Brown, T 45-8208, tours to Cuba; *Agence Martine*, 17 rue de Miracles, flights to Miami; *ABC Tours*, rue Pavée, near Sainte-Trinité, courteous, helpful; *Chatelain Tours* (T 23-2400/69) rue Geffrard; *Continental Travel* (T 22-0604) 105 rue Pavée; *Magic Island Tours*, 82 rue Pavée, corner of Rue du Centre, unhelpful; *Southerland Tours* (T 22-1600) 30 ave Marie Jeanne.

Because of the collapse of tourism, sightseeing tours are set up only on request.

● **Travel to the provinces**
Fairly conventional-looking **buses** (Cr: bis) and/or colourfully converted trucks and pick-ups (Cr: taptap) provide inter-city transport. The place where buses and taptaps leave from is called a *station*. For example, to get directions to the departure point for buses to Cap Haïtien, ask for the *station Au Cap*. Most of the *stations* are somewhere on or between blvd Jean-Jacques Dessalines and the waterfront. There are no fixed departure times. Buses leave when they are packed. Roads are bad and journeys are long and uncomfortable. In trucks, it is worth paying more to sit up front with the driver.

There are **flights** to Jérémie, Cap and Hinche.

PETIONVILLE

Just 15 minutes from Port-au-Prince, but 450m above sea level, **Pétionville** was once the capital's hill resort. Now it is considered a middle-to-upper-class suburb with many chic restaurants and boutiques. Three roads lead up from Port-au-Prince. The northernmost, the Delmas Road, is ugly and dusty. Prefer the Panaméricaine, an extension of Avenue John Brown (Cr: Lali), which is serviced by camionettes, and the southernmost Route Canapé Vert, which has the best views.

In Pétionville, the main streets are parallel to each other, one block apart, Lamarre and Grégoire, on the six blocks between the Panaméricaine and the place St Pierre. Most of the shops, galleries and restaurants are on or between these two streets or within a couple of blocks of them.

Local information – Pétionville
● **Accommodation**
Hotels A1 *Montana* (T 57-1920/21), rue Cardozo (a turning off the Panaméricaine at the entrance to Pétionville), an oasis of luxury, best views over Port-au-Prince, especially from poolside restaurant, EP all a/c; **A2** *El Rancho* (T 57-2080/1/2/3), rue José de San Martín, just off the Panaméricaine, casino, nightclub, sauna,

spa, EP all a/c; **A2** *Villa Créole* (T 57-1570/1, F 57-4935), just beyond the *El Rancho* on José de San Martín, tennis court, pool, good view, EP all a/c; **A3** *Kinam* (T 57-0462 57-6525) mock Gingerbread house, pool, handy location; **C** *Caraïbe*, central, 13 rue Leon Nau, Nerette, PO Box 15423, T 57-2524, 12 rooms with large baths, a/c, honour system bar, restaurant, TV lounge, pool, built in 1920s, charming, good value.

Guest houses *Doux Séjour* (T 57-1560), 32 rue Magny (quiet street five blocks from Place St Pierre) weekly rates US$100s, US$140d rooms with fan and bathroom; *Marabou* (T 57-1934), 72 rue Stephen Archer, just behind St Pierre church, haggle for good rate for long stay; **C** *Ife* (T 57-0737), 30 rue Grégoire (a busy street), CP; **C** *Villa Kalewes* (T 57-0817), 99 rue Grégoire (at the upper, quiet end of the street), CP, pool.

● **Places to eat**
Plantation (T 57-0979), impasse Fouchard (turning off rue Borno) excellent French chef, good wine, rec; *Le Souvenance*, 8 rue Gabart at the corner of Aubran, gourmet French cuisine, rec, pricey; *Chez Gerard* (T 57-1949), 17 rue Pinchinat (near Place St Pierre), French, pricey; *Les Cascades* (T 57-5704), 73 rue Clerveaux, French; *La Voile* (T 57-4561), 32 rue Rigaud between Lamarre and Faubert, good; *La Belle Epoque* (T 57-0984), 21 rue Grégoire, good French cuisine in a pretty house; *Bolero* (T 57-1929), 18 rue Louverture between Grégoire and Lamarre, lobster, salads and pastas, lively bar scene, popular with expats; *Coin Des Artistes* (T 57-2400), 59 rue Panaméricaine, beneath Festival Arts Gallery, grilled fish and lobster; *Steak Inn* (T 57-2153), rue Magny, beautiful, large garden, live music at weekend; *Arc-En-Ciel* (T 57-2055), 67 rue Grégoire, French and German; *Le Grégoire* (T 57-1669), 34 rue Grégoire, Viet and Thai, quiet. On the Kenscoff road the *Altitude 1300* is the place where the bourgeoisie go at weekends, with the best of créole cuisine.

● **Shopping**
Pétionville has many elegant boutiques, galleries, bookshops and delicatessen. Rec is La Promenade at the intersection of Grégoire and Moïse (SE corner of Place St Pierre), a garden turned into small shopping promenade with an outdoor cafe, 1000-1800.

Art and handicrafts *Galerie Bourbon-Lally* (T 57-6321/3397), 24 rue Lamarre, corner of rue Villate, owned by Englishman Reynald Lally, good choice of naive art; *Galerie Monnin* (T 57-4430), 19 rue Lamarre, in same house as Café des Arts; *Galerie Marasa* (T 57-1977), 11 rue Lamarre, hand-painted boxes, trays: *Expressions* (T 57-0112), 75 rue Clerveaux, one of the Nader family galleries; *Festival Arts Gallery* (T 57-6233), 59 rue Panaméricaine, Haitian artists who have moved on from primitivism; *Galata* (T 57-1114), rue Faubert, mainly handicrafts, especially weavings, metalwork; *Fleur De Canne* (T 57-4266) 34 bis, rue Gabart, good quality craft in a charming store.

● **Nightlife**
Café Des Arts (T 57-7979), 19 rue Lamarre (same house as Galerie Monnin) open 1900 until late, dining and live music; *Bambu*, corner of rues Lamarre and Chavannes, especially when they have live bands; *Faces*, in the *Hotel El Rancho*, also Sat evening live jazz; *Blackout*, popular bar hangout round the corner from the *Bolero;* the *Garage*, a couple of blocks below the *Kinam*, features the most popular local bands at weekends; not far away, the *Lakol* also often has some of the most famous groups performing.

EXCURSIONS NEAR PORT-AU-PRINCE

Beaches Haiti's best beaches are far from the capital, on the Caribbean and Atlantic coasts. The Gulf of La Gonâve beaches, the only ones that can be reached within an hour's drive, are second rate. Those W of the capital are especially poor. The best of what's available is to the N. They tend to be gravelly or gritty, with a backdrop of arid, deforested mountainside, but the calm, clear, shallow water is excellent for children.

Closest is **Ibo Beach**, on an island near Km 30 of the Route Nationale 1. A sign painted on the side of a house shows the turnoff, which is 4 km after the flour mill and 500m before the cement works. The boat-ride is US$2. The beach is small, but it has white sand and shade. Good, basic meals are served on the beach. A hotel consisting of many chalets is closed.

The **Côte Des Arcadins**, a 20-km stretch of beach hotels, begins 60 km N of the capital. They all have pools, bars and restaurants, and charge US$2 admission to day visitors. They may be crowded with wealthy Port-au-Princiens at weekends. The Arcadins are three uninhabited, sandy cays 3 km offshore which are surrounded by reefs. The diving is excellent. (At the time of writing, no diving excursions were available, but check with Bobby Chauvet of *Citadelle Tours*). The first, and quietest hotel, is *Kyona Beach*; followed by A3 *Kaliko Beach* (T 22-8040, F 23-0588), MAP, good lunch, horse-riding. Ouanga Bay is next, then *Wahoo Beach* (T 22-9653), clean, well-run and crowded. At Km 77, 1 km after the town of Montrouis, A2 *Moulin sur Mer* (T 22-1844/1918) is a converted 18th century plantation house and sugar mill where people usually stay a night or two (a/c MAP). *Club Med*, 500m beyond Moulin sur Mer, has been closed since 1987, but is ready to reopen when conditions permit. Amani-Y Beach, about 5 km before St Marc, is a small, pretty beach with a restaurant and bar that have been closed for several years.

Other Excursions The asphalt road to Kenscoff, in the mountains behind Port-au-Prince, starts just to the W of the Pétionville police station, on the Place St Pierre. After 10 minutes, there is a turnoff on the right at United Sculptors of Haiti, which sells good woodcarvings. It skirts a huge quarry and climbs to **Boutilliers**, a peak topped by radio and television masts that dominates the city. Next to the quarry, visit the Barbancourt rum company's mock castle to taste fruit-flavoured rum liqueurs for free. In about 20 minutes, the main Kenscoff road reaches **Fermathe** where the large Baptist Mission has a snack bar with fine views S, and a store selling handicraft and souvenirs (taptaps and camionettes from near the market in Pétionville). Climb up a trail to Fermathe from Pétionville in 3 hours by setting off from rue Montagne Noire. A turnoff near the Mission leads to Fort

Jacques and Fort Alexandre (10 minutes by car or an easy 45 minutes' walk), two forts on adjoining summits built after the defeat of Napoleon. The views N over the Cul de Sac plain are breathtaking. Fort Jacques is restored.

30 minutes (15 km) from Pétionville, but 1,500m above sea level, **Kenscoff** is a hill resort where members of the élite retire to their country homes in July and August to escape the heat. (Camionette from Pétionville US$0.50. *Hotel Florville* for refreshments or meals.) Market on Fri. Hire a guide for a 2-3 hour hike via the village of Godet to the summit above Kenscoff that is topped by a radio mast, or the summit just to the W, called Morne Zombi. The ridge just to the E of the radio mast can be reached by a surfaced road in poor condition. It offers views S over a rugged, dark massif that boasts Haiti's highest peak, the 2,674m La Selle.

From the ridge, a 5-hour hike along a trail heading towards the village of **Seguin** brings you to **Parc La Visite**, a nature park covering part of the massif. It has pine woods, montane cloud forest at higher altitudes, dozens of big limestone caves (one 10 km long), and strange karst-formation rocks locals call 'broken teeth' (Cr: kase dan). See under **Flora and fauna** for wildlife. Camp at a disused saw mill (Cr: siri) by the trail, where water is available from a fountain. Bring thick clothes and sleeping bags; temperatures can fall to freezing at night. A waterfall is a short hike away. For longer hikes and fine views, head E with a guide and climb the 2,282m Pic Cabaio or the 2,100m Pic La Visite (another camping site). The park keeper, Jean-Claude, rents horses. Seguin lies on a sloping plateau on the massif's southern face, about 1 hour beyond the park. From Seguin, a 5-hour hike gets you to the S-coast village of Marigot, from where you can bus back to Port-au-Prince via Jacmel in 4 hours.

The lush, densely-populated coastal Leogane Plain, 45 minutes W of the capital, offers a look at rural life. E and W of the town of **Leogane**, the plain is dotted with small villages and criss-crossed by bumpy lanes. Turn right down any of the side-roads off the Route Nationale 2 after it crosses the big, stony Momance River, then wander at random.

Wildlife enthusiasts should visit **Lake Saumâtre** (see **Flora and fauna**), at the eastern end of the Cul de Sac plain near the Dominican border. The newly improved road from Croix-des-Bouquets to the border crossing at Malpasse skirts the lake's southern side. The northern side offers more chance of seeing its wildlife. On Route Nationale 3 heading NE from Port-au-Prince towards Mirebalais, fork right at the Thomazeau turnoff to the lakeside villages of Manneville and Fond Pite. It takes 90 minutes.

SOUTH OF PORT-AU-PRINCE

Set off on the Route Nationale 2, the highway heading W toward Les Cayes, and turn S at the Carrefour Dufour intersection (Km 40) for a scenic, French-built mountain road to the lush S coast.

JACMEL

The port of **Jacmel** is Haiti's prettiest, but run down, city. Its name derives from an Indian word meaning 'rich land'. Quiet, with 10,000 inhabitants, Jacmel has changed little since the late 19th century when it was a booming coffee port and its wealthy merchants built New Orleans-style mansions using cast-iron pillars and balconies imported from France or the United States. The charm of its Victorian architecture is matched by a setting at the head of a 3 km wide horseshoe bay, with streets winding down three small hills to a palm-fringed, black-sand beach.

Begin a visit with refreshments on the S-facing upper veranda of the *Manoir Alexandre*, a turn-of-the-century patrician home that is now a guest house. It has Jacmel's best view plus fine antiques. Two blocks to the E is an iron market built in 1895. (Saturday is market day.) The street below the *Manoir Alexandre*, rue Seymour Pradel, has another old residence, now an American-owned art gallery called *Salubria*. Closer to the beach, on rue Commerce, more 19th-century homes have been turned into galleries or handicraft stores. The Boucard family residence at the corner of Grand' Rue and Commerce, is especially fine. At the other end of Commerce, near the wharf, note the Vital family warehouse dating from 1865. The nearby prison was built in the 18th century. Members of a small expatriate community frequent *La Choubouloute*, a basic beach bar with simple meals 100m W of the wharf. Jacmel's handicraft speciality is boxes, trays, place mats and other objects covered with parrots or flowers, hand-painted in bright colours.

● **Accommodation A2** *La Jacmelienne* (T 88-3451, Port-au-Prince office: 22-4899), a modern, two-storey hotel on the beach with pool, MAP, fans, no a/c, often no water either, all rooms with sea view; **B** *Manoir Alexandre* (T 88-2511), C.P., lots of character but no bathroom in rooms; **D** *Guest House Douge*, 39 Grand' Rue, character but even more basic, C.P.

● **Exchange** Best rates at *Matekha* hardware shop on the square one block from the Iron Market, rec by UN/NGO personnel.

● **Transport** In Port-au-Prince, small buses leave from the station Jacmel near the customs house on rue du Quai and rue des Fronts Forts, taking 2-3 hours (US$1.50).

A hurricane swallowed up most of Jacmel's beach and what is left is dirty. A good dirt road leads E to fine white-sand beaches. The first is **Cyvadier**, a tiny cove down a side-road at Km 7. A quiet, French Canadian-run hotel, C *Cyvadier Plage*, offers rooms with ceiling fans, C.P. At Km 15, just before Cayes Jacmel, is Raymond-les-Bains, a beach alongside the road. No facilities except showers. Beware, it has a slight undertow, like most beaches on the S coast. Just after Cayes Jacmel, at Ti Mouillage, the road runs beside two beaches. The

first has a basic restaurant. Small beach homes can be rented at the second. From Marigot, a pretty coastal village 10 km further on, a 4WD can climb a rough trail to the village of Seguin (see under Excursions from Port-au-Prince).

A 12-km track into the hills SW of Jacmel leads to **Bassin Bleu**, a series of natural pools and waterfalls descending a limestone gorge in tiers. The big, deep, blue-green pools are framed by smooth rocks and draped with creeper and maidenhair fern. It takes 2-3 hours each way on foot or horse-back (horses for hire in Jacmel). Take a guide, fixing a price in advance. There are excellent views over Jacmel bay on the way. If it has not rained, a good driver can nurse a 2WD or 4WD three quarters of the way. The Jacmel guide hands over to a local guide for the last km which is steep and, at one point, requires the aid of a rope. This means an additional small fee.

WEST OF PORT-AU-PRINCE

The southwestern peninsula is the wettest, greenest, most beautiful part of Haiti; its rugged western tip has forests, rivers, waterfalls and unspoilt beaches.

The Route Nationale 2 to Les Cayes is asphalted all the way and very scenic. For the first 92 km it runs along the N coast of the peninsula. At Km 68 is the town of **Petit Goave** (Cr: Ti Gwav). Visit the *Relais de l'Empereur* (T 22-9557), once the residence of Emperor Faustin 1 (1849-56). The hotel is no longer operating, but the caretaker will show you around.

Just 2 km down a turn-off at Km 92 is the smugglers' port of **Miragoane**, a pretty town of narrow streets that wind around a natural harbour or climb up a hill capped by a neo-gothic church. Small, rusting freighters unload contrabrand rice, cement, bicycles, TV sets and second-hand clothes shipped from Miami. A 4WD is needed for the dirt road that continues along the N coast, fording rivers and passing fishing vil-

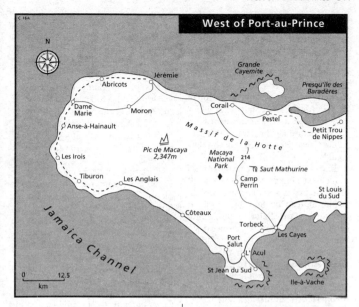

West of Port-au-Prince

lages, as far as Petit Trou de Nippes. At Petite Rivière de Nippes, 15 km along this road, a 3-hour trek inland on foot or horseback (take a guide) brings you to one of Haiti's four great waterfalls, **Saut De Baril**.

After Miragoane, the main road crosses the peninsula's spine and reaches the southern, Caribbean coast at Aquin (Km 138) where you can bathe in several rivers. At **Zanglais**, 6 km farther on, there are white sand beaches near the road. (Beware of slight undertow at any beach on the S coast.) Just beyond Zanglais a ruined English fort is visible on a small offshore island, with the remains of a battery emplacement just opposite, on the mainland.

On a wet, coastal plain 196 km W of Port-au-Prince, Haiti's fourth city, **Les Cayes** (Cr: Okay), is quiet, but not without charm (B *Hotel Concorde*, T 86-0277, rue Gabions des Indigènes, rooms with bath/fan, EP). In Port-au-Prince, buses leave mornings from the station Aux Cayes near the post office for the 4-hour trip. Fare US$4. Visible from the waterfront is **Ile-à-Vache** (*pop* 5,000), a 20-km-long island that was Henry Morgan's base for a 1670 raid against Panama. It has Indian remains and good beaches on the southern side near La Hatte, the biggest village. Visit it by renting a boat with outboard (about US$25 for the day) or take the daily ferry leaving at around 1600, and pay to sleep in someone's home. Or camp, after asking permission.

Fortresse des Platons, a huge ruined fortress on a 600m summit overlooking the coastal plain, can be visited in a 1-day excursion from Les Cayes. It was built in 1804 at Dessalines' behest. Take the coast road SW out of the city. Just after Torbeck, a rough road heads inland up a river valley via Ducis to the village of Dubreuil (trucks from Les Cayes). From Dubreuil, the fortress is a 2-3 hour hike up a steep trail with great views. Carry on the same trail via Formond to enter the **Macaya National Park**, which has Haiti's last virgin cloud forest surrounding the 2,347m Pic Macaya. See under **Flora and fauna** for the park's vegetation and wildlife. A University of Florida base at Plaine Durand (2 hours beyond the fortress) has basic camping facilities. Hire guides for hikes into the lower montane rain forest. Only the very fit should attempt the hike to the top of the Pic Macaya. It entails climbing a 2,100m ridge and then descending to 1,000m before tackling the peak itself. Allow at least 2 days each way and take a guide.

Beyond Torbeck, the coast road goes as far as **St Jean du Sud** where a small off-shore cay is suitable for camping. Before St Jean du Sud, fork right at L'Acul for **Port Salut**, a 90-minute drive from Les Cayes (two buses a day). This small village has a wild, 800m-long, palm-lined beach that is one of the most beautiful in Haiti. C *Arada Inn*, owned by Swiss resident Christian Deck, offers clean rooms with fans, breakfast and dinner; or rent rooms from locals. Grilled lobster lunches available in a basic restaurant near the beach.

The adventurous should take the coastal route from Les Cayes to Jérémie, around the peninsula's tip, a remote, rugged, lush region that has changed little in 200 years. It has wild rivers, sand beaches, mountains falling steeply into the sea, and some of Haiti's last rain forest. Allow 4 days. Les Cayes buses or taptaps may go as far as Les Anglais, depending on the state of the road. A 4WD may even get to Tiburon. Thereafter, you must hike from Anse d'Hainault or even Dame Marie before finding road good enough to be serviced by taptaps out of Jérémie. Alternatively, try getting a ride on sloops that carry merchandise and passengers along the coast. Residents in small villages all the way will cook meals and rent beds for a few dollars. 'Pripri', rafts made of bamboo lashed together and steered by a pole, ply the rivers. Anse d'Hainault and Abricots (25 km W of Jérémie) have good beaches.

The scenic, hair-raising, 97-km mountain road from Les Cayes to Jérémie, across the Massif de la Hotte, can be done in 5 hours. But it may be impassable after rain. 1 hour's drive brings you to **Camp Perrin** (several guesthouses), a hill resort at the foot of the 2,347m Pic de Macaya. Rent horses for a 2-hour ride to **Saut Mathurine**, Haiti's biggest waterfall. It has good swimming in the deep, green pool at its base.

Fork right off the Jérémie road at the Kafou Zaboka intersection for **Pestel**, a picturesque port dominated by a French fort, 4 hours' hard drive from Les Cayes. Worth seeing any time of the year, but especially for the Easter weekend regatta, when many Rara bands come. Charter a boat to tour nearby fishing villages such as Les Basses (Cr: Obas) on the Baradères peninsula and Anse-à-Maçon on the offshore island of Grande Cayemite with its splendid view of the Massif de la Hotte and distant Pic Macaya.

With crumbling mansions overgrown by rampant vegetation, **Jérémie** (*pop* 20,000) is famed for its poets, eccentrics and isolation. Two bus companies stopped services from Port-au-Prince in early 1993 because the road got so bad. Some buses are still running, however, leaving from Jean-Jacques Dessalines near rue Chareron (US$8). The 12-hour overnight ferry ride is not recommended. At least 800 (maybe as many as 1,500) Jérémie residents drowned when an overloaded ferry, the *Neptune*, sank on its way to Port-au-Prince in February 1993. MAF and Caribintair have a total of six flights a week from Port-au-Prince. They may be booked up to 10 days ahead. On a hill above the town, with a shady garden, is C *Hotel La Cabane* (MAP). Anse d'Azur, 4 km W of the town, is a white-sand beach with, in the rocky headland at one end, a big cave into which you can swim.

NORTH OF PORT-AU-PRINCE

The seaboard N of the capital is arid or semi-arid most of the way to Gonaïves, and all round the NW peninsula as far as Port-de-Paix. From Port-de-Paix to the Dominican border, it is quite lush and green. The Route Nationale 1 is asphalted to Cap Haïtien, but is badly potholed for the 65 km between Pont Sondé and Gonaïves. It hugs the coast for most of the first 85 km, skirting the foot of the Chaine des Matheux mountains. Cabaret (Km 35) is the former Duvalierville. Its ugly, modernistic buildings and pretensions of becoming Haiti's Brasilia were lampooned in *The Comedians*. L'Arcahaie (Km 47) is where Dessalines created the blue and red Haitian flag by tearing the white out of the French tricolor. Outside L'Arcahaie, a dirt road heads E high into the Chaine des Matheux to a region where coffee and indigo was grown in colonial times. A dozen ruined plantation houses survive. The turnoff is just before the point where the highway crosses the small Mi Temps River. Sailboats leave at mid-morning from Montrouis (Km 76) for the 22-km crossing to Anse-à-Galets (one guesthouse), the main town on barren La Gonâve Island.

At Km 96, after the Côte des Arcadins beaches, the RN1 reaches the port of St Marc (E *Hotel Belfort*, 166 rue Louverture, clean, basic). Several fine gingerbread houses are on streets to the E of the main street. A pretty valley runs inland SE as far as Goavier.

The highway crosses the River Artibonite at Pont Sondé, entering a region of rice paddies irrigated by canals. Fork right at the Kafou Peyi intersection, 2 km N of Pont Sondé, for **Petite Rivière de L'Artibonite** (Cr: Ti Rivyè), a picturesque town built by Christophe on a steep-sided ridge overlooking the River Artibonite. Its Palace of 365 Doors was Christophe's provincial headquarters. In 1802, there was a key battle at the Crète-à-Pierrot fort (5 minutes' walk above the town) in which Leclerc sacrificed 2,000 men to dislodge a force of 1,200 led by Dessalines.

About 8 km after L'Estère, a right turnoff runs SE 25 km to Marchand, a town at the foot of the Cahos mountains that was briefly Dessalines' capital. Hike into the surrounding hills to visit seven big ruined forts built by Dessalines. Near the town is a spring with a natural swimming pool. Dessalines told his soldiers that bathing here made them immune to French bullets. The house of Dessalines' wife, Claire Heureuse, still survives in the town. You can also see the foundations of his own home. After the Marchand turnoff, the RN1 crosses a semi-desert called Savane Désolée.

Amid saltpans and arid, brackish lowlands, **Gonaïves** at Km 171 is an ugly, dusty town of 70,000 (Haïti's third largest). It is called the City of Independence because Dessalines proclaimed Haiti's independence here in 1804. The unrest that toppled Jean-Claude Duvalier in February 1986 also began here. C *Chez Elias* is a safe, clean guesthouse (T 74-0318), rue Egalité opposite Teleco, rooms with fan and bathroom, MAP. At *Chez Frantz* (T 74-0348), avenue des Dattes, the rooms are often all taken by long-term residents, but the food is Gonaïves' best. *Rex Restaurant*, rue Louverture, half a block from the market, has Créole food and hamburgers. Buses (US$3, 4 hours) leave Port-au-Prince mornings from the intersection of Blvd La Saline and Jean-Jacques Dessalines. In Gonaïves, mopeds operate as taxis, charging US$0.20 a ride.

After Ennery at Km 201, the RN1 climbs steeply up to the Chaine de Belance watershed and enters the green, northern region. **Limbé** at Km 245, has a museum created by Dr William Hodges, a Baptist missionary doctor who runs the local hospital and supervises archaeological digs along the N coast (see La Navidad under **Excursions from Cap Haïtien**). Fort Crète Rouge,

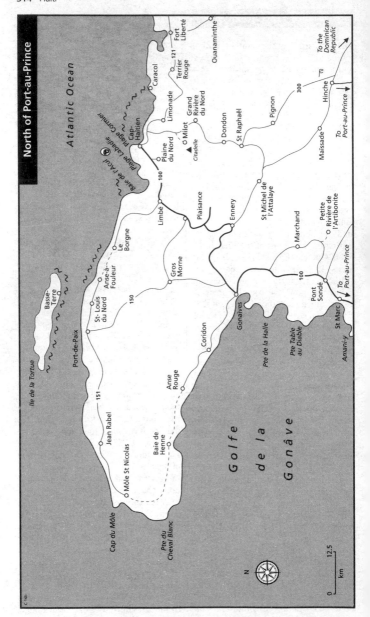

North of Port-au-Prince

above Limbé, is one of the many fortresses built by Christophe.

A rugged side-road from Limbé down to **Le Borgne** (Cr: Oboy) on the coast offers spectacular views. The 20 km either side of Le Borgne abound with white-sand beaches. The high, green mountains right behind add to their beauty, but the coast is densely inhabited and the beaches are often used as a public latrine. From Le Borgne to St Louis du Nord, the road is very bad but not impassable for 4WD.

After Limbé, the main highway descends quickly, offering fine views over L'Acul Bay, where Columbus anchored on 23 December 1492, 2 days before his flagship sank.

CAP HAITIEN

Cap Haïtien, Haiti's second city, with 100,000 inhabitants, has a dramatic location on the sheltered, SE side of an 824m high cape, from which it gets its name. It was the capital in colonial times, when it was called Cap Français. Its wealth and sophistication earned it the title of 'Paris of the Antilles'. The colony's biggest port, it was also the commercial centre of the northern plain, the biggest sugar producing region. Nowadays it usually referred to simply as Cap, or Okap in Créole. It was burned to the ground three times, in 1734, 1798 and 1802, the last time by Christophe to prevent it falling intact into the hands of the French. It was destroyed again by an 1842 earthquake that killed half the population. The historic centre's architecture is now Spanish influenced, with barrel-tile roofs, porches, arcades and interior courtyards.

Vertières, an outlying district on the Port-au-Prince road, is the site of the battle at which Dessalines's army definitively routed the French on 18 November 1803, forcing them to leave the island for good 12 days later. There is a roadside monument.

Local information – Cap Haïtien
● **Accommodation**
(Note: Cap Haïtien gets electricity only 1900-2300) **A3 Mont-Joli** (T 62-0300/26, Port-au-Prince: 22-7764), on hillside above town, pool, tennis court, good restaurant, own generator runs 1000-1200 and 1730-0600, rooms with private bath and a/c, EP; **A3 Roi Christophe** (T 62-0414), corner of 24 and B, central location in colonial house first built in 1724 as the French governor's palace (Pauline Bonaparte stayed here) lush gardens, pool, own generator (not big enough for a/c) runs 0600 until city power comes on; more expensive with a/c, cheaper with fan, CP, rec; **A2 Beck** (T 62-0001), in the mountainside, residential Bel-Air district, woodland setting, two pools, constant water, own generator, private beach at Cormier, German owner, rooms with private bath and fan, MAP; **C Brise De Mer** (T 62-0821), 4 Carenage (on waterfront at northern edge of town), friendly but reportedly not very safe, own generator (but not on all the time), rooms with private bath and fan, MAP. **D Columbia**, rue 5, 3-K, fan, clean, safe, very helpful owner speaks English.

● **Places to eat**
Cap 2000, rue 5 and Boulevard (not far from waterfront) sandwiches, icecream; *Sacade*, rues 18 and B, cheap.

● **Shopping**
Ateliers Taggart (T 62-1931), rue 5 near Boulevard (by *Cap 2000*) all kinds of handicrafts, especially weavings and metalwork, rec, 1000-1700 Mon to Fri; *Galerie Des Trois Visages*, excellent art gallery next to *Ateliers Taggart*. A tourist market by the port has handicrafts and naive paintings. Bargain hard.

● **Exchange**
BNP, good for changing TCs; also **Banque Union Haïtien** changes TCs, open until 1300.

● **Post Office**
Ave B at rue 17.

● **Travel agent**
Cap Travel, 84 rue 23A, T 62-0517.

● **Tourist bureau**
Rue 24, Esplanade.

● **Car rental**
Hertz (T 62-0369). Check price quotes very carefully. Don't leave your passport as deposit.

● **Transport**
Buses leave Port-au-Prince from the station Au

Cap opp the big Texaco garage at the junction of Delmas Road and Blvd La Saline between 0630 and 0830, when full. The 274 km trip usually takes 6-7 hours. Fare US$5.80. It may be necessary to change in Gonaïves, 3½ hours, US$2, then take another bus to the capital. There are two principal taptap stations in Cap: Barrière Bouteille at southern end of town, for all destinations to Port-au-Prince, and Port Metalique, at A2, also S end of town, cross bridge for station for all destinations to Milot (outside *Hotel Bon Dieu Bon*), Hinche, Fort Liberté, Ouanaminthe and the border.

MAF and Caribintair both have six **flights** a week from Port-au-Prince. A Cap-based air taxi service, Marien Air (T 62-0527/0742) offers flights to Port-au-Prince, the Dominican Republic, Turks and Caicos, Bahamas and Jamaica.

Ruins The rich, alluvial plain to the S and E of Cap boasted a thousand plantation houses during the last years of the colonial period. ISPAN (T 62-2459), rue 15 and rue B in Cap, is a good source of information on these nearby colonial ruins, as well as Sans Souci and the Citadelle.

Beaches The beaches in the town itself are dirty and lack charm. Excellent beaches on the N side of the cape can be reached in 20 minutes by car. The first is **Cormier Plage**, site of the recommended A1 *Hotel Cormier Plage* (T 62-1000), simple chalet or room in main building, including breakfast and dinner, excellent food, own generator turned on 0730-1100 and 1630-2330. Scuba diving with equipment for 10. Good wrecks and coral reefs. Run by charming French couple: Jean-Claude and Kathy Dicqueman. If you call ahead, they will pick you up from airport. Book ahead, because tour groups from Dominican Republic sometimes fill the place up. Take mosquito repellent.

5 minutes further W (30 minutes on foot), is **Labadie** beach, a fenced-off sandy peninsula once used by Royal Caribbean Lines as a private beach for its visiting cruise ships. The public may enter to use its facilities (pool, restaurants, water sports) for US$3.

Just beyond Labadie Beach is Belli Beach, a small sandy cove with a very basic hotel, E, used as a bordello for the cruise ship crews. This is the end of the road, but boats, some with outboards, can be rented here to visit nearby Labadie village, dramatically located at the foot of a cliff, and other beaches further along the coast. Fix a price before boarding. Labadie village (about US$3 by boat, also reachable by scrambling over the rocks) has two guest houses, *Dessa Motel* and *Maison Amitié*, with basic rooms on the beach, both F. Employees will buy and cook food for a price that must be negotiated.

Farther still, about 10 km W of Cap, is L3 *Club Roche Sauvage* (T 62-2765) an all-inclusive, 144-bed resort with its own 300m beach. Spa and diving extra. Round trip air-and-sea transfer from Port-au-Prince another US$85 pp. Beyond Roche Sauvage is Labadie Shore, Crown Cruise Line's answer to Labadie Beach.

EXCURSIONS FROM CAP HAITIEN

The massive, mountain-top fortress of **La Citadelle** was built by King Henri Christophe between 1805 and 1820 to deter any French reinvasion (see under **History**). With walls up to 40m high and 4m thick, and covering 10,000 sq m, 20,000 people were pressed into its construction. It is dizzily perched atop the 900m high Pic La Ferrière, overlooking Cap and the entire northern plain, and controlling access to the Central Plateau. Its garrison of 5,000 soldiers (plus the royal family and its retinue) could have held out for a year. Haitians call it the eighth wonder of the world. It is indeed impressive, and has breathtaking views. Restoration work has been under way for years and is well advanced. Behind the fortress, at the end of a 1.5 km level ridge with sheer drops on both sides, is the Site des Ramiers, a complex of four small forts which controlled the rear access. Worth visiting just for the views.

To get to the Citadelle, take the 25 km asphalt road S from Cap to the village of **Milot** in a publique (US$1) or taptap (US$0.30). Taptaps leave Cap in the morning. Hotels like the *Mont Joli* offer jeep tours for about US$60 pp, but don't count on the guide's information being correct. From Milot it is a steep 5-km hike through lush countryside up to the fortress (about 90 minutes, start early to avoid the heat; to find the road up to the Citadelle you need to walk through Sans Souci Palace). Wear stout shoes and be protected from the sun. Horses can be rented for about US$5 (dangerous in wet weather). Hire a guide even if you don't want one, just to stop others importuning (fix the fee in advance). Prices of refreshments at the Citadelle are higher than elsewhere (US$0.80 for a coke), but someone has had to carry them up there. Those with their own vehicle drive to a car park two thirds of the way up, reducing the walk to 1.5 km. Admission is US$1.

At Milot itself are the ruins of Christophe's royal palace, **Sans Souci**. More than a palace, it was an embryo administrative capital ranging over 8 ha in the foothills beneath the Citadelle. Christophe sited his capital inland because of the difficulty of defending coastal cities against the overwhelming naval might of France and Britain. It included a printing shop, garment factory, distillery, schools, hospital, medical faculty, chapel and military barracks. Begun in 1810, inaugurated in 1813, ransacked after Christophe shot himself in the heart with a silver bullet in 1820, it was finally ruined by the 1842 earthquake that destroyed Cap. The admission to the Citadelle covers Sans Souci. Try not to go any day there are cruise ships at Cap or the nearby beaches. If planning to visit both sites, arrive before 1300 to have enough time, as they close at 1700. There are no buses or taptaps back to Cap after 1700.

Morne Rouge, 8 km SW of Cap, is the site of Habitation Le Normand de Mezy, a sugar plantation that spawned several famous rebel slaves. (Leave Cap by the RN1 and take a dirt road running N from a point about 75m W of the turnoff to the town of Plaine du Nord.) Its ruins include two aqueducts and bits of walls. Voodoo ceremonies are held under a giant tree in the village. Among its rebel progeny was Mackandal, an African chief's son who ran away, became a prophetic oungan and led a maroon band. After terrorizing the entire northern plain by poisoning food and water supplies, he was captured and burned alive in January 1758. **Bois Caiman** was the wood where slaves met secretly on the night of 14 August 1791 to hold a Voodoo ceremony and plan an uprising. (It is near the Plaine du Nord road, about 3 km S of the RN1. Ask locals to guide you once you are in the area.) Their leader was an oungan and slave foreman from Le Normand de Mezy called Boukman. The uprising a week later was the Haitian equivalent of the storming of the Bastille. Slaves put plantation houses and cane fields to the torch and massacred hundreds of French settlers. It began the only successful slave revolt in history and led to Haiti's independence. Little is left of the wood now except a giant ficus tree overgrowing a colonial well credited with mystic properties.

The town of **Plaine du Nord**, 12 km SW of Cap, is a pilgrimage centre every year on 24-25 July, the Catholic festival of St James, who is identified with the Voodoo spirit Ogou. Voodoo societies come from all over Haiti, camp in the streets and spend the 2 days in non-stop drumming and dancing. Many are possessed by Ogou and wallow in a much-photographed mud pool in one of its streets. On 26 July, the feast day of St Anne, most of the Voodoo societies at Plaine du Nord decamp to nearby **Limonade**, 15 km SE of Cap, for another day and night of celebrations. A dirt road on the NW side of Limonade leads to Bord De Mer De Limonade, a fishing village where Columbus' flagship, the

Santa María, struck a reef and sank on Christmas Day, 1492. Columbus used wood from the wreck to build a settlement, **La Navidad**, which was wiped out by Taino Indians after he left. Its location was discovered by American archeologist William Hodges while digging at the site of Puerto Real, a city founded years later on the same spot. The untrained eye will detect nothing of either settlement now, but the Hodges museum in Limbé, 20 km SW of Cap, has relics.

Fort Liberté, 56 km E of Cap, is a picturesque, French-designed town on a large bay with a narrow entrance. It is dotted with French forts that can be reached by boat. The best is Fort Dauphin, built in 1732. The bay was the site of the Caribbean's largest sisal plantation until nylon was invented. (Two hotels: *Cirene*, used as a military base in 1995; *Bayaha*, overlooking bay, modern.) There are direct taptaps Cap-Fort Liberté, but it may be easier to return to Cap from the main road, which is 4 km from the centre of Fort Liberté. **Ounaminthe** (*Hotel Paradis*, basic, on main street) is northern Haiti's chief border crossing. (Taptaps for US$2 from the station nordest in Cap; US$1.10 from Fort Liberté.) The Dominican frontier town, Dajabón, is just 2 km from the Ounaminthe taptap station. The crossing is straightforward and the Haitain border office is very helpful. Buses leave Dajabón for many Dominican cities. The River Massacre, which forms the border, had this name long before the massacre of thousands of Haitians in the neighbouring part of the Dominican Republic under Trujillo in 1937, when the river was said to have been red with blood for days. The bridge across the river is packed with money changers and *motoconchos* (not necessary for transport to Haitian border post, which is about 1 km from Dominican side).

For the rugged, the dirt road forking left 5 km before Milot could be an alternative route back to Port-au-Prince via Hinche and the Central Plateau (see under **Northeast of Port-au-Prince**). A 4WD is needed. It takes 2-3 hours. By public transport it takes much longer, up to 2 days to the capital. Vehicles tend to be old, it is very dusty and the worst stretch is from near Milot to Hinche. The first town is Grand Rivière du Nord, where another of Christophe's fortresses, Fort Rivière, sits atop a ridge to the E. It was used by the Cacos guerrillas who fought the US occupation from 1918 to 1920. The Americans captured the Cacos leader Charlemagne Peralte near here. Dondon has caves inhabited by bats. One is close to the town. The other, 90 minutes on foot or horseback up a river bed to the W of the village, has heads carved in relief on its walls, presumably by the original Indian inhabitants. In the rainy season, cars cannot ford the river near St Raphaël, but you can walk, with locals helping for a small fee.

NORTHWEST

Except for Tortuga island and a coastal strip running E from Port-de-Paix, the NW peninsula is Haiti's driest, most barren region. In recent years, especially since the 1991 coup, it has teetered on the brink of famine.

The 86-km mountain road from Gonaïves to Port-de-Paix via Gros Morne fords several rivers and takes 4 hours in a 4WD, needed for travel anywhere in the NW. (Minibuses from Gonaïves, big buses from Port-au-Prince, leaving from beside the station Au Cap.) **Port-de-Paix** once made an honest living exporting coffee and bananas. Now it specializes in importing contraband goods from Miami. Vendors tout the wares on all its unpaved streets. In 1992-93, its small freighters also ferried illegal immigrants into Miami. Despite the smuggling, it is safe to spend a night (D *Hotel Bienvenue*, T 68-5138, basic, EP).

Half an hour's drive to the E by a good, dirt road is St Louis du Nord, a pretty coastal town from where sailing boats cross the 10-km channel to **Tortuga**

Where the buccaneers came from

The French and English freebooters who began settling on Tortuga Island in 1630 were drawn by the S coast's coves, beaches and small anchorages, and a protective line of reefs with few openings. Pirate raids had led Spain to withdraw from the N and W coasts of Hispaniola in 1605, leaving livestock that multiplied and was hunted by the freebooters. Because they smoked the meat on 'boucans', an Indian word for spit, they became known as buccaneers.

Island, the Caribbean's biggest pirate base in the 17th century. Nearly 40 km long, 7 km wide and 464m above the sea at its highest point, its smooth rounded shape reminded seafarers of the back of a turtle. (Tortuga in Spanish and La Tortue, its Haitian name, in French.)

Its present population of 30,000 is spread all over the island. The biggest S-coast villages, Cayonne and Basse-Terre, are less than 1 km apart. A ferry-boat leaves Cayonne for St Louis du Nord at 0800 and returns at about 1000, charging locals US$0.50 each way. Foreigners may have to pay up to US$10, depending on their negotiating skills. Boats crossing at other times charge more. From Cayonne there is a narrow cement road up to Palmiste serviced by a single taptap, one of the four or five cars on the island. From Palmiste, the biggest village on the rounded spine, there are spectacular views of the corniche coastline stretching from Cap to Jean Rabel, and the towering mountains behind. The best view is from the home of French Canadian priest Bruno Blondeau (T 68-5138/6709), the director of a Catholic Church mission who has effectively governed the island since 1977. He runs 35 schools and has built all 55 km of its road. His order also operates a small, basic hotel (F pp, EP).

The best beach, 2 km long, is at Pointe Saline, at the western tip (34 km from Palmiste, 2 hours by car). This is also the driest part of the island and there is little shade. La Grotte au Bassin, 6 km E of Palmiste, is a large cave with a 10m high precolumbian rock carving of a goddess. There are two other big caves: Trou d'Enfer, near

La Rochelle ravine, and La Grotte de la Galerie, 1 km E of Trou d'Enfer.

The largest historic ruin on the island is a 15m high lime kiln (four à chaux), built at the end of the 18th century. Fort de la Roche, 1639, was once Tortuga's biggest fortress (70m high). Its masonry foundations can be seen at a spring where women wash clothes on the hillside above Basse-Terre. Three cannon and a bit of wall remain from Fort d'Ogeron, built in 1667.

A coast road runs W from Port-de-Paix along the N coast of the peninsula as far as Môle St Nicolas and then returns to Gonaïves via the S coast. **Jean Rabel** is a tense town which was the site of a peasant massacre in July 1987. At least 150 died in the clash, said to have been engineered by local Duvalierist landlords seeking to crush the attempts of Catholic priests to organize landless peasants. From Jean Rabel round to Baie de Henne, the landscape is arid, windy and dusty. Old people say they can remember when it was still green and forested.

Columbus first set foot on the island of Hispaniola at **Môle St Nicolas**. It has several ruined forts built by the English and French. General Maitland's surrender of Môle to Toussaint in 1798 marked the end of a 5-year British bid to gain a toehold on this end of the island. Strategically located on the Windward Passage, just 120 km from Cuba, Môle was long coveted as a naval base by the United States. The hinterland has Haiti's lowest rainfall and little grows. The main occupation is making charcoal and shipping it to Port-au-Prince. Because few trees are left, charcoal makers now dig up roots. The peninsula's S side, especially from Baie de Henne to Anse Rouge, is a mixture of barren rock and desert, but the sea is crystal clear. There are few inhabitants. With salt pans on either side, Anse Rouge ships sacks of salt instead of charcoal.

NORTHEAST OF PORT-AU-PRINCE

Grandly called the Route National 3, the 128-km dirt road NE from Port-au-Prince to Hinche requires a 4WD and takes at least 5 hours (much longer by public transport). It starts by crossing the Cul de Sac plain via Croix-des-Bouquets. Here, a newly improved road branches off SE through a parched, barren region, skirting Lake Saumâtre (see **Flora and fauna** and **Excursions from Port-au-Prince**) before reaching the Dominican border at Malpasse (see **Travel to the Dominican Republic** in Information for travellers). On the N side of the plain, the RN3 zig-zags up a steep mountainside called Morne Tapion (great views back over Port-au-Prince) to reach Mirebalais, a crossroads at the head of the Artibonite valley. It is Haiti's wettest town. The road E leads to Lascahobas and the frontier town of Belladère, the least used of Haiti's three border crossings into the Dominican Republic. The road W heads down the Artibonite valley. Before it gets too bad, a left turnoff leads up into the hills to the charming village of **Ville-Bonheur** with its church built on the spot where locals reported an appearance of the Virgin in a palm tree in 1884. Thousands of pilgrims come every 15 July. The Voodooists among them hike 4 km to visit the much-filmed **Saut d'Eau** waterfall. Overhung by creepers, descending 30m in a series of shallow pools separated by mossy limestone shelves, the fall seems enchanted. The Voodooists bathe in its waters to purify themselves and light candles to enlist the help of the ancient spirits believed to live there.

The RN3 heads N out of Mirebalais on to the Central Plateau, where the military crackdown was especially harsh after the 1991 coup because peasant movements had been pressing for change here for years. After skirting the Peligre hydroelectric dam, now silted up and almost useless, the road passes Thomonde and reaches the region's capital, **Hinche**. The *Foyer d'Accueil* is an unmarked guest house above a school that is behind the blue and white church on the E side of the main square (F pp, basic rooms with fan, rarely any power, EP). The *Hotel Prestige*, also unmarked, at 2 rue Cité du Peuple, near the market, has not so good rooms for the same price. In Port-au-Prince, buses leave from the station Au Cap at the intersection of blvd La Saline and route de Delmas. MAF operates about two flights a week. East of Hinche, **Bassin Zim** is a 20m waterfall in a lush setting 30 minutes' drive from town (head E on the Thomassique road, then fork N at Papaye). The cascade fans out over a rounded, sloping, limestone rockface. At its foot is a 60m wide natural pool with deep, milky-blue water that is perfect for swimming.

Information for travellers

BEFORE TRAVELLING

● **Documents**

All visitors need passports except Americans and Canadians, who need only proof of citizenship. Visas were not needed for nationals of USA, Canada, EC and Caricom countries, Argentina, Austria, Finland, Israel, Liechtenstein, Mexico, Monaco, Norway, South Korea, Sweden and Switzerland. Visas issued at the Haitian Embassy in New York (60 East 42nd Street 1365, New York, NY 10017) take 1 hour, two photos required, US$18, valid for 3 months. Visitors must have an onward ticket. All visitors, except cruise ship passengers, must complete an embarkation/disembarkation card on the plane; this is valid for 90 days, and may be extended. It is no longer necessary to have a *laissez-passer* before visiting the interior, but you must have some form of identification to satisfy the many police controls. It may also be wise to obtain a letter from the Tourist Office or police in Port-au-Prince confirming that you are a tourist.

For **Tourist information**, see page 326, below.

● **Customs**

Baggage inspection is thorough and drug-enforcement laws are strict. There is no restriction on foreign currency. You may bring in one quart of spirits, and 200 cigarettes or 50 cigars. There are no export limitations.

● **Climate**

The climate is generally very warm but the cool on- and off-shore winds of morning and evening help to make it bearable. In coastal areas temperatures vary between 20° and 35°C, being slightly hotter in April-September. The driest months are December-March. In the hill resorts the temperature is cooler.

● **Health**

Prophylaxis against malaria is essential. Tap water is not to be trusted (drink only filtered or treated water) and take care when choosing food. The local herb tea can help stomach troubles. Hepatitis is common in some areas.

Good professional advice is available for the more common ailments. Ask friends, associates, or at the hotel desk for referrals to a doctor suited to your requirements. Office hours are usually 0730-1200, 1500-1800. A consultation costs about US$10-15.

Hospital care and comfort varies. Pharmacies/chemists can fill out prescriptions and many prescription drugs may be bought over the counter. A note on prostitution: there are no laws in Haiti to suppress it. Activity seems to be evident only at night with the commonly known areas being along the main roads in Carrefour and street corners in Pétionville. After hours the prostitutes move into the dive-type joints, targeting foreigners. With regard to casual sex, there is a red alert in Haiti over Aids.

MONEY

● **Currency**

The unit is the gourde (Cr: goud), divided into 100 centimes (Cr: kòb). Coins in circulation are for 5, 10, 20 and 50 centimes, notes for 1, 2, 5, 10, 25, 50, 100, 250 and 500 gourdes. Some 100 gourde notes are plastic, faded, smeared and look like forgeries; they are not. They have 'American Banknote Company' printed on them. Small denomination notes are in appalling condition and there is always a shortage of them. Try to break down large notes whenever possible. 500 gourde notes are next to useless unless you can break them down at a bank or spend them at expensive hotels: ask for smaller denominations. Coins are few and far between.

● **Exchange**

The gourde was tied at 5 to the dollar during the US occupation. In the 1980s it began to trade at a slightly lower value on a parallel market, but the official rate was kept until 1991, when the Aristide government severed the tie and let the gourde float. From 7.5 to the dollar at the time of the September 1991 coup, it fell to 15 in 1995.

So far, so good. Now it gets complicated. Money changers express the rate as a percentage increase on the old official rate of 5 to 1. Thus, 6 to 1 is 20%, 7 to 1 is 40%, and 13 to

1 is 160%. Haitians routinely refer to their own money as dollars, based on the old 5 to 1 rate. Thus, 5 gourdes is called a dollar, 10 gourdes is 2 dollars, 25 gourdes is 5 dollars, etc. Prices in shops are usually in Haitian dollars, therefore multiply by 5 to get the price in gourdes. Visitors must constantly clarify whether the price being quoted is in Haitian or American dollars, or gourdes, now increasingly used on bills. US coins co-circulate with local coins. They are treated as if the old 5 to 1 rate was still in force. Thus, a US penny is treated as 5 kòb, a nickel is 25 kòb, and so on.

The fall of the gourde has triggered inflation, but inflation has lagged far behind the rising value of the US dollar. This means that Haiti is currently a bargain for the visitor, except in those places catering for UN or NGO personnel which charge in dollars. The best exchange rate is obtained from money changers, whether those on the street or those working out of offices. It is perfectly legal (see **Money Exchange**, Port-au-Prince).

It is foolish to come to Haiti with any currency other than US dollars or French francs. Currencies like sterling can be changed, but only at a massive loss.

● **Credit cards**
Visa, Mastercard and American Express are widely accepted. Beware, card users will not get a good rate.

GETTING THERE

AIR

To Port-au-Prince
From Europe: Air France flies weekly from Paris.

From North America: American Airlines flies from New York and Miami. Other airlines from Miami include ALM, Halisa Air, Haiti National Airlines (Hanair), Haiti TransAir and Surinam Airways. Air Canada flies from Montreal.

From Central America: Copa flies from Panama City.

From the Caribbean: ALM from Curaçao; Air France from Guadeloupe via Martinique; Air Guadeloupe from Guadeloupe and St Martin; Air France from Santo Domingo; Air Guadeloupe, American Airlines and American Eagle from San Juan. There are charter flights to/from Cuba.

From South America: Surinam Airways from Paramaribo.

To Cap Haïtien
Turks and Caicos Airways fly 4 times a week from Providenciales. There are also several unscheduled or charter flights, see the Turks and Caicos chapter.

Note that flights from Miami are frequently overbooked. If you are not on a tight schedule, but have a confirmed seat, you may be asked to give your seat to a passenger with no confirmation in return for credit vouchers to be used on another flight within 12 months. Your original ticket will still be valid for the next flight, or for transfer to a different flight.

SEA
Cruise ships stopped calling at Port-au-Prince years ago, partly because of passenger reaction to begging. Royal Caribbean and Crown cruise lines have leased private beaches near Cap Haïtien for 1-day stopovers, but they suspended visits after the 1991 coup.

ON ARRIVAL

● **Airport**
On the northern edge of Delmas, 13 km outside Port-au-Prince (information: T 46-410516). Arrival can be pandemonium, especially if more than one flight is being accommodated at once. Knowledge of French helps; just get on with your affairs and try not to be distracted. The so-called 'supervisors' at the airport are in fact taxi-drivers, touting for business. Porters charge US$0.50 per bag. Once through the squash inside you emerge into a squash outside, of taxi drivers and people awaiting friends. Taxi into town, US$15-20, depending on how hard you bargain, or take a seat in a taptap (open-backed truck), extra charged for large bag. To get to the airport cheaply take a shared taxi from the turning off Ave Saint Martin (see map – was called Ave François Duvalier) for 3-4 km to rue Haile Sellassie where taptaps marked 'Airport' gather; US$0.15 from here, 10 km.

Information Office at the airport is very helpful. The downstairs snackbar is cheap and friendly. Not so the upstairs restaurant at the W end of the terminal. The public area has a bookstore and a handicraft shop. Duty free goods and more crafts are on sale in the area reserved for departing passengers. Officials will allow camera film to be passed through outside the X-ray machinery. In the baggage claim hall for arriving passengers, there is a *bureau de change* that gives almost as good a rate as that available from street changers outside.

● **Airlines**
Air Canada (T 46-0441/2); Air France (T 22-1700/1086), 11 rue Capois, corner rue Ducoste, near *Holiday Inn*; ALM (T 22-0900) 69 rue Pavée, corner rue du Peuple; American Airlines (T 23-1314), ave Pie XII, near post office, always packed with people (also T 46-0110 at the airport); Copa, 35 ave Marie Jeanne, T 23-2326, or airport T 46-0946; Haiti Trans Air (T 23-4010/20/9258), rue Capois near *Holiday Inn*.
Lynx Air in Cap Haïtien is 62-1386.

● **Clothing**
As in most other countries in the Caribbean beachwear should not be worn away from the beach and poolside. Dress is casual but never sloppy; Haitians appreciate good manners and style. Above-the knee hems for women are considered risqué but acceptable. Men always wear a shirt, but a tie is not necessary in the evening.

● **Embassies and consulates**
Austria, Blvd du Quai, between rue Pavée and rue des Miracles; **British Consulate** (T 57-3969, F 57-4048), *Hotel Montana*, rue Cardozo, Pétionville (PO Box 1032, Port-au-Prince); **Canada** (T 23-2358/ 4919/ 9373, F 23-8720), Bank of Nova Scotia Bldg, Route de Delmas, Delmas 18; **Denmark**, above Copa, on ave Marie Jeanne at rue Paul VI and Blvd Harry Truman; **Dominican Republic** (T 57-1650/0383), 121 rue Panaméricaine (50 m down rue José de San Martín), Pétionville; **France** (T 22-0951/2/3, F 22-0963), 51 rue Capois at the SW corner of the Champs de Mars, near *Hotel Palace*; **Germany** (T 57-3128/0456); **Honduras**, 167 rue du Centre, where buses leave for Santo Domingo; **Norway**, ERF building, rue Paul VI at rue Magasin de l'Etat; **US Embassy** (T 22-0200), Blvd Harry Truman, Bicentenaire; **US Consulate** (T 22-0200), 22 rue Oswald Durand.

● **Hospitals**
Recommended hospitals (all in Port-au-Prince) are *Canapé Vert*, rue Canapé Vert (45-1052/3/0984); *Adventiste de Diquini*, Carrefour Road (T 34-2000/0521), *Hospital Français de Haiti*, rue du Centre (T 22-2323); *St Francois de Salles*, rue de la Révolution (T 22-2110/0232).

● **Hours of business**
Government offices: 0700-1200, 1300-1600 (0800-1200, 1300-1800 Oct-April); banks: 0900-1300 Mon to Fri; shops and offices: 0700-1600 (an hour later Oct-April).

● **Official time**
Eastern standard time, 5 hours behind GMT; 4 hours behind early April to late October (dates vary each year).

● **Public holidays**
New Year and Ancestors (1-2 January), Mardi Gras (the 3 days before Ash Wednesday), Americas Day (14 April), Good Friday, 1 May, Flag and University Day (18 May), Assumption (15 August), Deaths of Henri Christophe and Dessalines (8 and 17 October), United Nations Day (24 October), All Saints (1 November), Armed Forces Day (18 November), Discovery of Haiti (5 December), 25 December. Corpus Christi and Ascension are also public holidays.

● **Security**
Despite all the political turmoil since 1986, security is not major a problem for the foreign visitor. In fact, Haiti has much less crime than most Caribbean countries. Take normal precautions. Carry handbags securely and do not leave belongings in sight in a parked car.
During any political unrest it is advisable to limit your movements in the daytime and not to go out at night. Streets are usually deserted by 2300. Foreigners are not normally targeted at such times, but seek local advice.

● **Shopping**
The Iron Markets sell only food items, charcoal, etc. The Iron Market in Port-au-Prince would be a fascinating place to visit but for the hustlers who will latch on to you and make the experience hell. Try out your bargaining skills at the Iron Markets in Jacmel and Cap Haïtien. Haitians may tell you that many of the items for sale in the few tourist shops can be bought far cheaper in markets. That may be true for them, but market vendors jack up prices for the foreigner, who will have to haggle skilfully to bring them down. People always ask for a discount in shops, except at food shops. All handicrafts can be bought at a discount. See above under **Culture** for best buys, and under towns for individual establishments.

Film processing services are the same as in the USA, but the price of film is high; transparency developing is considerably less.

● **Tipping**
Budget travellers, particularly outside Port-au-Prince, are a rarity. Expect to be the subject of much friendly curiosity, and keep a pocketful of small change to conform with the local custom of tipping on every conceivable occasion. Even cigarettes and sweets are accepted. Hotels generally add 10% service charge. Baggage porters at hotels usually get US$0.50 per bag. Do not fail to reward good service since hotel and restaurant staff rely on tips to boost their meagre salaries. Nobody tips taxi, *publique, camionette* or *tap-tap* drivers, unless exceptional service has been given.

● **Voltage**
110 volt, 60 cycle AC. Electricity supply is unpredictable as there are insufficient funds to maintain the service. Only if sufficient rain falls to operate the hydroelectric facility will the capital have power and water. It is hoped that resources will be found to improve supply. Only the best hotels have sufficiently powerful generators to make up the deficiency (see **Where to stay** section). As the *Oloffson* is on the same circuit as the Presidential Palace, it is never blacked out.

● **Weights and measures**
The metric system is used.

ON DEPARTURE

● **Departure tax**
Visitors must pay a US$25 departure tax in US currency and a 10-gourde security tax in Haitian currency. Do not buy international flight tickets in Haiti, especially not at the airport: sales tax is very high and the application of exchange rates may be very arbitrary.

● **Travel to the Dominican Republic**
See **Documents** in the Dominican Republic chapter, and check with the Dominican Consulate (see below) for those who need a visa. A *laissez-passer* from Haitian Immigration, on Avenue John Brown, is necessary to leave Haiti by land, although the crossing has been done without it. Ask a travel agency to get it for you. Give them 2 days' warning, two photos and US$15. Taptaps and trucks ply the road to the border at Malpasse/Jimaní. Repaired and improved in 1993-94 (to transport smuggled fuel), it can be done in 1 hour. The Ounaminthe/Dojabón crossing in the North is easily reached from Cap Haïtien and is straightforward. You should not pay anything on leaving Haiti, but travellers have been asked for anything between US$10 and US$40 before their papers will be stamped. It is US$14 to reenter Haiti. Visitors arriving in the Dominican Republic pay US$10. Mopeds ferry you between the Haitian and Dominican border posts for US$1. There are regular buses from the Dominican frontier town of Jimaní to Santo Domingo (6 hours) and from Dajabón via Montecristi and Santiago de los Caballeros. Rental cars are not allowed to cross the border, but you could safely leave one at the border for a few hours during a quick excursion to Jimaní. Dominican buses leave Port-au-Prince most mornings for their return trip to Santo Domingo via Malpasse, but they have no fixed time or departure point (the trip can take up to 10 hours, with 2 hours at the border). Ask at the *Hotel Palace* on rue Capois, where many Dominicans stay. Buses also leave from rue du Centre, between *Auberge Port-au-Prince* and rue des Miracles, around 3-4 a day, mostly 25-seater a/c Mitsubishis, US$20. A new service introduced in 1995 is operated by Tartan Tours in Port-au-Prince (Terrabús in Santo Domingo): buses run between Port-au-Prince and Santo Domingo, and Cap Haïtien and Santiago de los Caballeros. Luz Tours, T 23-1059, and Kenya Express (also T 23-1059) have weekly buses to Santo Domingo. Haitian travel agencies sometimes offer 3 or 4 day inclusive bus tours into the Republic.

Air France has one flight a week to Santo Domingo. No *laissez-passer* is necessary to leave by air.

WHERE TO STAY

● **Hotels**
Details are given in the main text.

● **Camping**
Camping in Haiti is an adventure. The dramatic scenery is very enticing but access to much of it is over rough terrain and there are no facilities, leaving exploring to the rugged. Campers have to take everything and create, or find their own shelter.

Peasant homes dot the countryside and it is almost impossible to find a spot where you will be spared curious and suspicious onlookers. It is best to set up camp or lodging before dark. To prevent misunderstanding, it is important to explain to the locals your intentions, or better yet, talk to the local elder and ask assistance or protection. Creating a relationship with the locals will usually ensure cooperation and more privacy. Offer to pay a small amount for use of the land.

FOOD AND DRINK

● Food

Most restaurants offer Créole or French cuisine, or a mixture of both. Haiti's Créole cuisine is like its Caribbean cousins, but more peppery. Specialities include *griot* (deep-fried pieces of pork), *lambi* (conch, considered an aphrodisiac), *tassot* (jerked beef) and rice with *djon-djon* (tiny, dark mushrooms). As elsewhere in the Caribbean, lobster is widely available.

Pétionville has many good French restaurants. Some are French-managed or have French chefs, and are undeniably first class.

Haiti's wide range of micro-climates produces a large assortment of fruits and vegetables. It is popular to buy these in the regions where they grow and are freshest (prices can be bargained 40% below shop prices). The French influence is obvious in butcher shops where fine cuts of meat, cold cuts, paté and cheeses can be bought. The bakeries sell French croissants, together with Créole bread and meat pasties. American influence is felt in the supermarkets. Most common are US-brand foods along with smaller amounts of Haitian, French and Middle Eastern brands.

● Drink

Haiti's Barbancourt rum is excellent. Rum punch is popular. The local beer, Prestige, may be too sweet for some palates. The Dominican beer, Presidente, is the best of the foreign beers sold in Haiti, but Beck's is more widely available. Soft drinks include Séjourne, Couronne and Sékola (banana).

GETTING AROUND

AIR TRANSPORT

Mission Aviation Fellowship (T 46-3993) and Caribintair (T 46-0737/78, 49-0203) have flights every day except Sunday to Cap Haïtien (US$50 round trip). They also run two or three flights a week each to Jérémie (US$70 round trip). MAF additionally flies Tues, Thur and Sat to Hinche (US$40 round trip). Book and pay through travel agents. Flights leave from Aviation Générale, a small domestic airport 1 km E of the international airport.

Caribintair also operates as a charter/air taxi company, and has three flights a week to Santo Domingo. Marien Air (T 62-0527/0742), a Cap-based air taxi service run by Paul Takeo Hodges, flies anywhere in Haiti. It also offers flights to Port-au-Prince, the Dominican Republic, Turks and Caicos, Bahamas and Jamaica.

LAND TRANSPORT

See **Travel to the provinces** under Port-au-Prince.

● Motoring

Driving in Haiti is a hazardous free-for-all, but some find it exhilarating. The streets are narrow, with many sharp bends and full of pedestrians in the towns. There are few signs. Vehicles swerve unexpectedly to avoid potholes. Cars often don't stop in an accident, so, to avoid paying the high insurance excess, keep a pen and paper handy to take down a number if necessary.

Fuel is usually available in the big provincial towns, but power cuts may prevent stations from pumping at certain times of the day.

For driving to Cap Haïtien, Les Cayes and Jacmel, an ordinary car is fine, but for Jérémie, Port-de-Paix or Hinche, a 4WD is nessary. Foreigners may use a national driving licence for 3 months, then a local permit is required.

● Car hire

A small Japanese saloon car such as a Nissan Sunny, with a/c, rents for about US$45/day, US$250/week, unlimited mileage. A 4WD such as a Nissan Pathfinder is US$65/day, US$400/week. This includes insurance, but with a high excess, ranging from US$250 to US$750, depending on the company. It is cheaper to pay for the rental in gourdes (cash) than by credit card.

Avis (T 46-4161/2640/96), Hertz (T 46-0700/2048) and Budget (T 46-2324) all have bases near the airport, and have desks in a small, shared office just opposite the airport terminal, open 0800-1700. Smaller companies include Sunshine Jeep (T 49-1155), Secom (T 57-1913) and Sugar (T 46-3413). Hertz is the only company with a base in Cap Haïtien.

● Hitchhiking

Foreigners do not normally hitch. There are many young Haitian men who stick out a thumb asking for a 'roue libre', especially from foreigners. Use your discretion.

COMMUNICATIONS

● Telecommunications

Always bad, the telephone system deteriorated even more during the 1991-94 embargo.

Fewer than a third of calls get through. The Haitian international operator (dial 09) is hard to raise. The *Oloffson*, *Holiday Inn*, *Montana* and *El Rancho* hotels have AT&T 'USA Direct' telephones for collect calls to the USA or calls anywhere in the world with an AT&T credit card, but even these connections can be problematic.

In 1990 all telephone numbers in Haiti changed; an extra digit was added to the prefix, thus: in Port-au-Prince 2- became 22-, 3=23, 4=34, 6=46, 7=57, 8=48, 9=49 and 5 became 45 (Turgeau), or 55 (Laboule). In Cap Haïtien 2- became 62-; Port de Paix 8=68; Gonaïves 4=74; Jérémie 4=84, Jacmel 8=88.

MEDIA

● **Newspapers**
Le Nouvelliste is the better of the two daily French-language newspapers; conservative, but tries to be impartial. Three weekly newspapers are published in French, all very one-sided, but on different sides. The pro-Aristide weekly *Libète* is the only Créole newspaper.

● **Radio**
Radio stations use a mix of French and Créole. Metropole and Tropic are best for news. The satellite-beamed Radio France Inter is rebroadcast locally on FM 89.3. The BBC World Service can be heard on 15220 (early morning) and 7325 (evenings). Voice of America is on 11915 (mornings) and 9455 evenings.

● **Television**
A commercial TV station, Tele-Haiti, retransmits American, French, Canadian and Latin American stations (including CNN) to cable subscribers, electricity permitting.

ENTERTAINMENT

Until the mid-1980s, Haiti used to be a very good place for night spots. With the drop in tourism and Haitians hesitating to be out late at night in uneasy times, many places have had to shut or curtail their level of entertainment. The few that survive offer a good evening's enjoyment and plenty of personality. Following French custom, entertaining starts late in the evening, about 2030-2100. Night clubbing starts around 2330 and continues into the small hours.

TOURISM INFORMATION

● **Local tourist office**
The Tourist Office is in the Département du Commerce et de l'Industrie, upstairs, at 8 rue Légitime (T 509-686150), half a block from the Musée d'Art Haïtien, but it has poor information and no maps or brochures. Supplementary information may be sought from the Hotel and Tourism Association, at the *Hotel Montana*, or from travel agencies.

ISPAN (Institute for the Protection of the Nation's Heritage) has information on ruined forts and plantation houses, corner of Ave Martin Luther King and Cheriez, Pont Morin (T 45-3220/3118). Also at Rue 15-B, Cap Haïtien (T 62-2459).

● **Further reading**
History: *The Black Jacobins*, by CLR James (about Toussaint); *Papa Doc and the Tontons Macoutes*, by Bernard Diederich and Al Burt.

Voodoo: *The Drum and the Hoe*, by Harold Courlander; *Divine Horsemen* by Maya Deren; *The Serpent and the Rainbow* by Wade Davis; *Mama Lola* by Karen McCarthy Brown.

Travelogue: *Bonjour Blanc* by Ian Thomson (by a recent British visitor)

Fiction: *The Comedians* by Graham Greene (set during Papa Doc's time); *The Kingdom of This World* by Alejo Carpentier (about Mackandal and Christophe).

Dominican Republic

T HE DOMINICAN REPUBLIC occupies the eastern two-thirds of Hispaniola. The country is mountainous, but despite having the highest mountain on the island and in the Caribbean, Pico Duarte (3,175m), it is less mountainous than Haiti. Within a system of widespread food production are large sugar and fruit plantations.

The Republic is building up its tourist trade, and has much to offer in the way of natural beauty, old colonial architecture, attractive beaches, modern resorts and native friendliness. Its population is mostly a mixture of black, white and mestizo, and is Spanish-speaking. These English terms should, however, be qualified: 'blanco' (white) refers to anybody who is white, white/Indian mestizo, or substantially white with either or both Indian or African admixture; 'indio claro' (tan) is anyone who is white/black mixed, or a mestizo; 'indio oscuro' (dark Indian) is anyone who is not 100% black (ie with some white or Indian admixture); 'negro' is 100% African. Negro is not a derogatory term. There is a certain aspiration towards the Indian; this can be seen not only in the use of the original name for the island, Quisqueya (and Quisqueyanos), but in place names (San Pedro de Macorís, from the Macorix tribe, the other Indian inhabitants being the Taíno and the Ciguayo) and in given family names (Guainorex, Anacaona, etc). An introduction to the Indians of the region is given in the **Pre-Columbian Civilizations** chapter.

HISTORY

For the general history of the island of Hispaniola after the arrival of the Spaniards, see the beginning of this chapter.

Although the Spanish launched much of their westward expansion from Santo Domingo, their efforts at colonizing the rest of the island were desultory. Drake sacked Santo Domingo in 1586, the French gained control of the western part of the island in 1697 and, by the mid-18th century, the number of Spaniards in the eastern part of the island was about one-third of a total of 6,000. Since there was little commercial activity or population of the interior, it was easy prey for Haitian invaders fired with the fervour of their rebellion at the turn of the 19th century. Between 1801 and 1805, followers of Toussaint L'Ouverture and Dessalines plundered the territory. Sovereignty was disputed for the next 17 years, then, in 1822, Haiti took control for a further 22 years.

After the declaration of the Dominican Republic's independence in 1844, by the writer Duarte, the lawyer Sánchez and the soldier Mella, the country underwent yet another period of instability, including more Haitian incursions and, in 1861, a four-year re-annexion with Spain. Independence was regained in the War of Restoration (la Restauración), but with no respite in factional fighting or economic disorder. Apart from the dictatorship of Ulises Heureaux (1882-84, 1887-99), governments were short-lived. The country must be one of the very few where a Roman Catholic archbishop has served as head of state: Archbishop Meriño was President from 1880 to 1882.

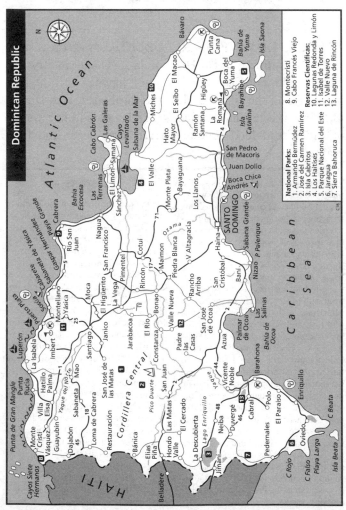

Dominican Republic

National Parks:
1. Armando Bermúdez
2. José del Carmen Ramírez
3. Isla Cabritos
4. Los Haitises
5. Parque Nacional del Este
6. Jaragua
7. Sierra Bahoruca
8. Montecristi
9. Cabo Francés Viejo

Reservas Científicas:
10. Lagunas Redonda y Limón
11. Isabel de Torres
12. Valle Nuevo
13. Laguna de Rincón

In 1916, the USA occupied the Dominican Republic, having managed the country's customs affairs (on behalf of US and European creditors) since 1905. When the USA left in 1924, the Republic had a fully organized army, whose commander, Rafael Leonidas Trujillo Molina, became President in 1930. Thus began one of the most ruthless dictatorships ever seen in the Dominican Republic. With either himself or his surrogates at the helm (Héctor Trujillo, 1947-60, and Joaquín Balaguer, 1960-62), Trujillo embarked on the expansion of industry and public works, the introduction of the national currency and the liquidation of the country's debts. Nevertheless, his methods of government denied any form of representation and included murder, torture, blackmail and corruption. During his reign, in 1937, an estimated 10,000 Haitian immigrants were slaughtered, prolonging the hatred between the two republics which had begun in the early 19th century.

Trujillo was assassinated in 1961. President Balaguer immediately set about eradicating his family's influence, but in 1962 Balaguer was defeated in elections by Dr Juan Bosch of the Partido Revolucionario Dominicano (PRD). After seven months he was ousted by a military coup led by Colonel Elías Wessin y Wessin. The PRD, with the support of a group of young colonels, tried to win back constitutional government in 1965, but were prevented from doing so by the army, backed by the USA and the Organization of American States. New elections were held in 1966; they were won by Balaguer, at the head of the Partido Reformista Social Cristiano (PRSC). He remained in office until 1978, forging closer links with the USA, but not without facing coup attempts, right-wing terrorism and left-wing guerrilla incursions.

A PRD President was returned in 1978, Antonio Guzmán, whose chief aims were to reduce army power and eliminate corruption. A month before leaving office in 1982, he discovered that members of his family, who had held office under him, had been involved in corruption, so he killed himself. His successor, Dr Salvador Jorge Blanco, also of the PRD, presided over severe economic difficulties which led to rioting in 1984 in which 60 people died. The party split over the handling of the economy, helping Joaquín Balaguer to win a narrow majority in the 1986 elections giving him a fifth presidential term. The 1990 elections were contested by two octogenarians, Dr Balaguer (83) and Dr Juan Bosch (80), now of the Partido de la Liberación Dominicana (PLD). Dr Balaguer won a sixth term of office by a very narrow majority, which was subjected to a verification process after Dr Bosch alleged fraud had taken place in the capital. The May 1994 elections had the same outcome, after Balaguer had decided very late in the campaign to stand for re-election. His chief opponent was José Francisco Peña Gómez of the PRD. First results gave Balaguer the narrowest of victories. Peña Gómez, supported by many outside observers, claimed that fraud had taken place and the election was reviewed by a revision committee appointed by the Central Electoral Junta. The committee found numerous irregularities, but its findings were ignored by the Junta which awarded victory to Balaguer, once again by the narrowest of margins. To defuse the crisis, Balaguer signed a pact with Peña Gómez allowing for new elections in November 1995; Congress rejected this date, putting the new election back 6 months to 16 May 1996. Peña Gómez and the PRD, angry at Congress' decision, boycotted Balaguer's inauguration. The USA, which had expressed serious misgivings about the 1994 elections, did send its ambassador to the inauguration.

Almost at once campaigning began for the 1996 presidential election. The PRD selected Peña Gómez again while the PLD chose Leonel Fernández as its candidate, to replace Juan Bosch who had retired. Within the PRSC, jockeying for the candidacy was beset by scandals and power struggles, exacerbated by the absence of an appointment by Balaguer himself.

Violent demonstrations and general strikes against economic hardship occurred in 1987, 1990 and 1991, in the last instance following the signing of an IMF accord. As a result of the government's structural adjustment programme, however, improvement was recorded in most productive sectors, the level of reserves and the rate of inflation. Positive economic results did not prevent spending on health and education lagging behind other public sectors. Unemployment remained high and many Dominicans were tempted by better opportunities in the USA and Puerto Rico. In 1995 there was speculation over whether the government would seek a new structural adjustment programme from the IMF. Renewed economic problems, compounded by the continuing failure of the electricity industry (see **Economy** below), forced the government to raise taxes and support the peso. At the same time, unauthorized increases in public transport fares led to riots in March and June 1995. With the PRD accusing the PRSC of fuelling the protests in order to create instability and thus undermine the 1996 elections, with growing revelations of corruption in government departments and with infighting unabated in the PRSC, the political climate was tense.

Relations between the Dominican Republic and Haiti became very strained in 1991 after President Balaguer ordered the deportation of all illegal Haitian immigrants under the age of 16 and over 60. Many from outside these age groups left, putting pressure on the resources of President Aristide's government. Attitudes to the overthrow of Aristide were ambivalent because the Dominican Republic officially supported the Organization of American States' trade embargo while politicians vocally and traders in practice defied it. Soon after Aristide's return to power, legitimate trade with Haiti resumed and various meetings at ministerial level took place. Balaguer and Aristide also met briefly. In 1996, Haiti's new president, René Préval, paid his first official visit abroad to the Dominican Republic. Agreements were signed for joint projects in the border region.

In the first round of the 1996 elections, Peña Gómez received 46% of the vote, compared with 39% for Leonel Fernández. However, in the second round, Balaguer gave his support to Fernández, in an effort to keep Peña Gómez (who suffered racial abuse because of his Haitian ancestry) from the presidency, and he won 51% of the vote. Balaguer was expected to continue to influence the new government's policies through Congress, where the PLD has only 12 deputies and the support of the PRSC will be needed to pass legislation, at least until the 1998 congressional elections.

GOVERNMENT

The Dominican Republic is a representative democracy, with legislative power resting in a bicameral Congress: a 30-seat Senate and a 120-seat Chamber of Deputies. Senators and deputies are elected for a four-year term, as is the President, in whom is vested executive power.

THE ECONOMY

Structure of production
There are six main agricultural regions: the N, the Cibao valley in the N central area, Constanza and Tiero, the E, the San Juan valley, and the S. Cibao is the most fertile and largest region, while the eastern region is the main sugar-producing area. Sugar is traditionally the main crop. Until 1984, the US import quota system, of which the Dominican Republic was the largest beneficiary, provided a preferential market for over half

the country's sugar exports as well as a cushion against the slump in world sugar prices. Major adjustments in US consumption patterns, particularly the switch by Coca Cola and Pepsi to High Fructose Corn Syrup, prompted the USA to cut quotas drastically. By 1988, the Dominican Republic's quota had been cut to 25% of previous levels and quota cuts continued. Diversification out of sugar cane, the conversion of some cane lands into tourist resorts, the expulsion of Haitian cutters and a slump in productivity led the country to import sugar in 1992. Each season, from 1990 to 1995, the volume and value of sugar production and exports has fallen. Exports of sugar in 1995 were US$125mn, while the other traditional crops of coffee, cocoa and tobacco earned US$81mn, US$54mn and US$15mn, respectively. Non-traditional products have been gaining in importance. These include fruit and vegetables, plants and cut flowers, marine products, processed foods, cigars and other agroindustrial products.

Since 1975 gold and silver mining has been of considerable importance. The Pueblo Viejo mine's oxide ores are running out, and high productivity costs together with accumulated debts in 1992-93 forced the state mining company, Rosario Dominicana, to suspend a large part of its operations for 14 months from March 1993. Resumption of full operations led to exports worth US$19mn in 1994, compared with US$26mn in 1992. By 1995 exports were US$65mn and were expected to rise further in 1996. The country also produces ferronickel, which has overtaken sugar as the major commodity export earner. Reserves are estimated at 10% of total world deposits. Ferronickel mining was also suspended in the first three months of 1993 because of unfavourable market conditions. This contributed to an accumulated decline of 40% in the mining sector in 1993. The mining sector in 1994, however, registered growth of 88% as improved world markets prompted the mining companies to reopen.

Dominican Republic: fact file

Geographic

Land area	48,443 sq km
forested	12.4%
pastures	43.2%
cultivated	30.0%

Demographic

Population (1995)	7,823,000
annual growth rate (1990-95)	1.9%
urban	64.6%
rural	35.4%
density	161.5 per sq km
Religious affiliation	
Roman Catholic	91.2%
Birth rate per 1,000 (1993)	30.0
	(world av 25.0)

Education and Health

Life expectancy at birth,	
male	60.0 years
female	64.0 years
Infant mortality rate	
per 1,000 live births (1993)	66.0
Physicians (1993)	1 per 2,511 persons
Hospital beds	1 per 608 persons
Calorie intake as %	
of FAO requirement	101%
Population age 25 and over	
with no formal schooling	48.0%
Literate males (over 15)	82.0%
Literate females (over 15)	82.2%

Economic

GNP (1993 market prices)	
	US$8,039mn
GNP per capita	US$1,080
Public external debt (1993)	
	US$3,763mn
Tourism receipts (1994)	US$1,148mn
Inflation (annual av 1989-94)	23.9%
Radio	1 per 6.6 persons
Television	1 per 11 persons
Telephone	1 per 14 persons

Employment

Population economically active (1991)	
	2,758,000
Unemployment rate (1994)	28.0%
% of labour force in agriculture	22.0
mining	0.2
manufacturing	11.7
construction	4.3
Military forces	24,500

Source *Encyclopaedia Britannica*

Other sources of income are the industrial free zones, almost 30 in number, with 469 companies and 165,000 employees, where manufactured goods are assembled for the North American market (generating US$550mn in 1995), and remittances from Dominicans resident abroad.

The largest foreign exchange earner nowadays is, however, tourism, with annual receipts exceeding US$1.5bn (1995), twice the amount generated by exports of goods. The industry employs about 5% of the labour force, 44,000 in direct jobs and 110,000 indirectly. New hotel projects brought the number of hotel rooms to about 30,000 in 1995, compared with 11,400 in 1987. Tourist arrivals by air (including Dominicans resident overseas) in 1995 were put at 2.1 million, compared with 1.9 million in 1994. The average hotel occupancy rate also increased from 72% in 1994 to 77% in 1995. The largest single source of tourists is Germany, which sent 450,000 holiday makers on 988 charter flights in 1995.

Recent trends

In the first half of the 1980s, a combination of fiscal and external account problems brought about a sharp decline in the rate of gdp growth and led the Government to turn to the IMF for financial assistance. The Government agreed to reduce its fiscal deficit and take a number of other austerity measures, including a gradual devaluation of the peso. It failed to meet targets, so the programme was suspended in early 1984. Government measures to remove subsidies, as part of the austerity package agreed with the IMF, led to riots in Santo Domingo in April 1984. A one-year standby loan facility worth RD$78.5mn was eventually approved in April 1985 but not renewed because of political opposition. Despite the widespread unpopularity of policies designed to satisfy IMF demands, President Balaguer in 1990-91 negotiated a new IMF agreement. Having repaid debts worth US$81.6mn to the IMF,

World Bank and other multilateral agencies, an IMF standby agreement was approved in August 1991. The terms of the accord, which included the unification of the exchange rates, an end to price controls, balancing state corporation budgets and a commitment to pay outstanding foreign debt arrears, were greeted by a series of general strikes. Agreement with the IMF did, however, permit the rescheduling of US$905mn of debt with the Paris Club group of foreign governments in November 1991, with further successful renegotiations of official debt in 1992. The IMF signed a new US$44mn standby facility in July 1993. In February 1994, commercial bank creditors signed an agreement to reschedule US$1.04bn of debt.

The major problems confronting the Government in 1990 were the high rate of inflation, unofficially estimated at 100% a year, and the disruptive electricity crisis, which had got steadily worse for several years. By 1995 the same problems, and others, resurfaced. Inflation, pushed by heavy government spending on public works and increasing subsidies, was reduced to 4.6% in 1992 and 2.7% in 1993 as a result of a curtailment of spending, both in a refusal to increase public sector wages and after the completion of major public works. Increased government expenditure in 1994 contributed to inflation of 14.3%. In September 1994 the Central Bank introduced a series of measures, including the curtailment of government spending, to stabilize the peso against the dollar. The official rate was modified from 12.50 to 12.85 pesos = US$1. The main aim of the Bank's action was to reduce a government deficit which had risen to 691mn pesos in 1994. A fiscal surplus of 1,720mn pesos was achieved in 1995, helping inflation to come down to 9.2%. Gdp rose by an estimated 4.8% as a result of a further growth in services, eg tourism and communications, although the official figures were disputed by independent economists who pointed to the increase in unemployment (45,000 workers were sacked in 1995) and rising poverty.

CULTURE

Music and dance

The most popular dance is the *merengue*, which dominates the musical life of the Dominican Republic; a great many orchestras have recorded *merengue* rhythms and are now world-famous. The traditional *merengue* is played by a 3-man group called a *perico ripiao*, or *pri-prí*, which consists of a *tambora* (small drum), an accordion and a *güira* (a percussion instrument scraped by a metal rod, or, as originally used by Indians, a gourd scraped with a forked stick). Since the 1970s the *merengue* has got much faster, with less formal steps. There is a *merengue* festival in the last week of July and the first week of August, held on the Malecón in Santo Domingo and there are plans to make this the major festival of the year for the whole country. Puerto Plata holds its *merengue* festival in the first week of October and Sosúa has one the last week of September.

Other popular dances are the *mangulina*, the *salve*, the *bambulá* (from Samaná), the *ritmo guloya* (especially in San Pedro de Macorís, see also that section below), the *carabiné* (typical of the region around Barahona), and the *chenche matriculado*. Salsa is very popular in dance halls and discos (every town, however small, has a discothèque). *Bachata* is Dominican 'country music', usually songs of unrequited love, to the accompaniment of virtuoso guitar, percussion, *güira* and bass.

Literature

In the colonial period, Santo Domingo encouraged the development of literature within the framework of the first seats of learning in Spanish America. The early colonists expressed their inspiration most readily in poetry and the verses of Elvira de Mendoza and Leonor de Ovando are frequently cited as examples of that time. Among the many Dominican poets famed within the country in subsequent years are Gastón Fernando Deligne, Fabio Fiallo and the national poet, Pedro Mir, author of *Hay un país en el mundo*. The two dominant political figures of the latter half of the twentieth century, Joaquín Balaguer and Juan Bosch, are also well known for their literary output, Balaguer in many styles, especially poetry, Bosch in short stories. Of the present generation of writers, Frank Moya Pons and Bernardo Vega stand out as writers of mainly historical works.

Painting

The first major representations of the country in painting came after 1870 with the establishment of a national identity through the Restauración movement and the consolidation of independence from Haiti. The first important painter was Alejandro Bonilla while the Spaniard José Fernández Corredor is credited with the foundation of the first painting school in the country. From this period the artists Arturo Grullón, Luis Desangles (Sisito), Leopoldo Navarro and Abelardo Rodríguez Urdaneta stand out. The last named is famous as painter, sculptor and photographer. In the 1930s, Jaime Colson, Yoryi Morel and Darío Suro were precursors of *costumbrismo* (art of customs and manners). Contemporary painters have followed the various styles which have prevailed throughout the art world. Those who have gained an international reputation are Iván Tovar, Ramón Oviedo, Cándido Bidó, José Rincón Mora and Paul Giudicelli. Exhibitions of Dominican art are held frequently in Santo Domingo galleries, for example the Voluntariado de las Casas Reales, Galería Nader, Museo de Arte Moderno, El Pincel, La Galería, and others. For additional details on Dominican painters, consult *Arte contemporáneo dominicano*, by Gary Nicolás Nader, and *Antología de la pintura dominicana*, by Cándido Gerón.

For details on theatres and other sites of cultural interest, see below under Santo Domingo, Puerto Plata and Sosúa.

FLORA AND FAUNA

The government has adopted 6 generic categories for environmental protection: areas for scientific research, national parks, natural monuments, sanctuaries, protected areas and wildernesses. They include many lagoons, river estuaries, islands and bays.

There are 13 national parks and 9 scientific reserves in the Dominican Republic, all under the control of the Dirección Nacional de Parques (DNP, address below): **Armando Bermúdez** and **José del Carmen Ramírez**, both containing pine forests and mountains in the Cordillera Central are the only remaining areas of extensive forest in the republic; it is estimated that since the arrival of Columbus, two-thirds of the virgin forest has been destroyed. The reasons for the loss are fire and the establishment of smallholdings by landless peasants. By setting up these parks the gloomy prediction of 1973, that all the Dominican Republic's forest would vanish by 1990, has been avoided. In addition, a pilot reforestation project has been started near San José de las Matas, the Plan Sierra. The **Isla Cabritos** National Park in Lago Enriquillo is the smallest in the system; it is a unique environment, between 4 and 40m below sea level. Its original vegetation has been lost either to timber collection or to the goats and cattle which once grazed it. Now covered in secondary vegetation, 106 species of plant have been identified, including 10 types of cactus. The island has a large crocodile population, an endemic species of iguana, and other reptiles. 62 species of bird have been identified, 5 aquatic, 16 shore and 41 land birds; 45 are native to the island. Among the birds that can be seen (or heard) are the tiny manuelito (*myiarchus stolidus*) and the great hummingbird (*anthracothorax dominicus*), the querebebé (*chordeiles gundlachii*), best heard at dusk, and the cu-cú (*athene cunicularia*), which sings at night and dawn and excavates a hole in the desert for its nest.

Los Haitises, on the S coast of Samaná Bay (Bahía de San Lorenzo), is a protected coastal region, whose land and seascape of mangrove swamps, caves and strange rock formations emerging from the sea (*mogotes*) is unmatched in the republic. In Los Haitises you can visit the Cueva del Angel, cayes on which live many birds and humid tropical forest, as well as the mangroves. The **Parque Nacional del Este** is on the peninsula S of San Rafael del Yuma and includes the Isla Saona. It has remote beaches, examples of precolumbian art in a system of caves and is the habitat of the now scarce paloma coronita (crowned, or white-headed dove, *columba leucocephala*), the rhinoceros iguana and of various turtles. In the NW the **Montecristi** national park, on the Haitian border, contains marine and land ecosystems, the coastal Laguna de Saladillo, dry subtropical forest and the Cayos Siete Hermanos. In the SW, the **Sierra de Bahoruco** is a forested highland which has, among other plants, 52% of the orchids found in the republic; it also has many species of birds. At the southernmost tip of Barahona, also in the SW, is **Jaragua** national park, which includes the Isla Beata; on the mainland it is principally dry forest. Also designated national parks are a number of panoramic roads, botanical and zoological gardens (such as those in Santo Domingo, see below), aquaria and recreational parks, and sites of historic interest (La Vega Vieja and La Isabela).

The Reservas Científicas include lakes, patches of forest and the Banco de la Plata (Silver Banks), to which humpbacked whales migrate from the Arctic yearly for the birth of their young. Trips are organized to see the whales on about 50 boats; contact the DNP (see also Samaná page 362).

The National Parks Office (DNP) is at Avenida Independencia 539 esquina Cervantes, Santo Domingo (Apartado Postal 2487, T 221-5340). To visit the main forest reserves you must obtain a permit from the DNP or from the authorized administration office of each park for RD$50 (US$3.95). Note that to visit Los Haitises or Isla Cabritos, prices from DNP do not include the boat fare, usually US$24 extra per boat. The DNP publishes a book, *Sistema de areas protegidas de República Dominicana*, which describes each park and details how to reach it (US$12).

The DNP is studying a scheme to protect the **El Pomier** caves, in San Cristóbal, under threat from limestone quarrying. The caves are of enormous archaeological value, with over 4,000 wall paintings and 5,000 rock drawings. Cave No 1 contains 590 pictograms, making it superior to any other cave painting site in the Caribbean. The caves also house large numbers of bats. There is a campaign to have the site declared a UNESCO world heritage site and encourage tourism rather than quarrying.

Ecoturisa (Santiago 203, B, Santo Domingo, T 221-4104/6, F 689-3703) is promoting ecotourism in the Republic; in 1992 it won the Thompson World Aware award. Part of its profits go towards the non-profit organization, Fundación Prospectiva Ambiental Dominicana. The Foundation proposes new areas for protection, education and study, while Ecoturisa sets up tours to areas already under protection or of special interest. Ecoturisa rarely sells tours direct to clients; its programmes are available through tour companies and hotels. Tours can be designed especially for small groups and all arrangements with DNP can be made.

The Jardín Botánico Nacional and the Museo de Historia Natural, Santo Domingo, have a full classification of the republic's flora. Of interest are the 67 types and 300 species of orchid found in this part of Hispaniola; there are a number of gardens which specialize in their cultivation. The most popular are *oncidium henekenii, polyradicium lindenii* and *leonchilus labiatus*. The Jardín

Botánico holds an orchid show each year. The national plant is the caoba (mahogany). There is a wide variety of palms, some of which grow only on Hispaniola.

The Dominican Republic is becoming a popular bird-watching destination. The national bird is the cotica parrot, which is green, very talkative and a popular pet. It is, however, protected. Among other birds that can be seen, apart from those mentioned above, are other parrots, hummingbirds, the guaraguao (a hawk), the barrancolí and the flautero.

Of the island's mammals, the hutia, an endemic rodent, is endangered. Similarly in peril is the manatee, which may be seen at Estero Hondo; details from Ecoturisa.

BEACHES AND WATERSPORTS

According to Unesco, the Dominican Republic has some of the best beaches in the world: white sand, coconut palms and many with a profusion of green vegetation. The main ones are described in the text below. The beaches vary enormously in development, cleanliness, price of facilities, number of hawkers and so on. Boca Chica and Juan Dolio, for instance, are very touristy and not suitable for anyone seeking peace and quiet (except out of season); for that, Bayahibe would be a much better bet (although development is under way here). The best-known beaches are in the E of the republic, including: Boca Chica, Juan Dolio, Playa Caribe, Guayacanes and Villas del Mar in San Pedro de Macorís; Minitas (La Romana), Bayahibe, Macao, Bávaro, Puerto Escondido (Higüey); Anadel, Cayo Levantado, Las Terrenas, Playa Rincón and Portillo in Samaná and Sánchez; Playa el Bretón at Cabrera, Playa Grande in the Province of María Trinidad Sánchez and Laguna Gri-Gri at Río San Juan, where you can also visit the beaches of Puerto Escondido, Punta Preciosa in the Bahía Escocesa and Cabo

Francés Viejo. NE of Puerto Plata, recommended, although in many cases fully developed, beaches include Cabarete, Ermita, Magante, Playa Grande and Sosúa. At Puerto Plata itself are Playa Dorada, Costámbar, Cofresí, Long Beach, Boca de Cangrejos, Caño Grande, Bergantín, Playa de Copello and Playa Mariposa. Towards the NW and the Haitian border there are beaches at Bahía de Luperón, Playa de El Morro, Punta Rucia, Cayos los Siete Hermanos and Estero Hondo. The Montecristi area, outside the national park, is due for development.

In the S the best beaches are Las Salinas, Monte Río, Palmar de Ocoa, Najayo, Nigua, Palenque, Nizao and those S and W of Barahona. The majority of beaches have hotels or lodgings, but those without are suitable for camping.

Watersports such as deep-sea fishing, diving and surfing can be arranged at the Náutico Clubs in Santo Domingo and at Boca Chica beach. Güibia Beach, on the Malecón, Santo Domingo, has good waves for **surfing**. Demar Beach Club, Andrés (Boca Chica, T 523-4365) operates fishing, sailing, diving and water skiing charters, windsurfing, snorkelling and canoeing. All watersports can be arranged through Actividades Acuáticas, P O Box 1348, Santo Domingo, T 688-5838, F 688-5271 (you will be referred to their offices at Boca Chica, T 523-4511, or Puerto Plata, T 320-2567). There is excellent **scuba diving** at the underwater park at La Caleta, the small beach near the turn-off to the airport, on the Autopista de las Américas; snorkelling and diving is good all along the S coast. Hotels on the N coast also offer diving and snorkelling facilities. For expert divers there are many sunken Spanish galleons on the reefs offshore. For full information on diving contact the Dirección Nacional de Parques, T 221-5340.

Cabarete, near Sosúa, is one of the best **windsurfing** places in the world, attracting international competitors to tournaments there. Other centres are Boca Chica and Puerto Plata; most beach hotels offer windsurfing facilities. The Cabarete Race Organization, made up of all the windsurfing operations in the area (Surf Resort, CariBic, Fanatic, Vela/Spinout, Sport Away, Happy and Surf & Sport), organizes Cabarete Race Week (16-22 June 1997) as a non-profit event. Lots of competitions, fiestas and other events, F 571-3346, Mike Braden, for information.

For renting boats and yachts, contact the Secretaría de Turismo. There are no marinas at present but plans are being prepared. For independent yachtsmen the Dominican Republic is an excellent place to reprovision if cruising the islands. Laundry is taken in by local women.

Several international **fishing** tournaments are held each year, the catch being blue marlin, bonito and dorado. There is an annual deep-sea fishing tournament at Boca de Yuma, E of La Romana, in June. For information about fishing contact Santo Domingo Club Náutico, Lope de Vega 55, T 566-1682, or the Clubes Náuticos at Boca Chica and Cabeza de Toro. Parasailing is practised at the *Hotel Playa Dorada*, Puerto Plata, T 586-3988 (same number for deep-sea fishing), and on Sosúa beach.

OTHER SPORTS

Golf The best course is at Los Cajuiles at the *Casa de Campo Hotel* in La Romana; the *Santo Domingo* and *Hispaniola* hotels in Santo Domingo can arrange guest passes. There are also golf courses at the Santo Domingo Country Club and at Playa Dorada, near Puerto Plata. Several more golf courses are being built at new resorts around the country. **Tennis** can also be played at the Santo Domingo Country Club and at the tennis centre which can be found by the Autopista 30 de Mayo. **Athletics** facilities can be found at the Centro Olímpico Juan Pablo Duarte in the heart of Santo Domingo. **Target shooting** at the Polígono de Tiro on Avenida Bolívar.

The national sport is **baseball**, which is played from October to January, with national and big league players participating. The best players are recruited by US and Canadian teams; about half of the 300 professional Dominican players in the USA come from San Pedro de Macorís. There are five professional stadia, including the Quisqueya. **Polo** matches are played at weekends at Sierra Prieta, 25 minutes from Santo Domingo, and at Casa del Campo (T 523-3333). The **basketball** season is from June to August. **Boxing** matches take place frequently in Santo Domingo.

FESTIVALS

In Santo Domingo, Carnival at the end of February, notable for the parade along the Malecón on 27 February; there are other parades on 16 August. The *merengue* festival in July (see **Culture** above), including festivals of gastronomy, cocktails, and exhibitions of handicrafts and fruit. Puerto Plata has a similar, annual *merengue* festival at the beginning of October on the Malecón La Puntilla, as does Sosúa, in the last week of September. In the Parque Central, there are year-end celebrations from 22 December to 2 January. Carnival in Santiago de los Caballeros in February is very colourful; its central character is the piglet, which represents the devil. On the Sundays of February in Montecristi there are the festivals of the *toros* versus the *civiles*. Each town's saint's day is celebrated with several days of festivities of which one of the most popular is the Santa Cruz de Mayo fiesta in El Seibo in May. Holy Week is the most important holiday time for Dominicans, when there are processions and festivities such as the *guloyas* in San Pedro de Macorís, the mystical-religious *ga-ga* in sugar cane villages and the *cachúas* in Cabral in the SW.

The fourth floor of the Museo del Hombre Dominicano, Santo Domingo (see below), has an excellent exhibition of the masks and costumes that feature in the various carnivals around the country. Generally the masks are of animals or devils, or a combination of the two, and are designed to be as hideous as possible. The costumes are very brightly coloured.

Throughout the year there are many festivals and events, cultural, agricultural, commercial and sporting. Most are held in Santo Domingo or Puerto Plata, although golf and polo tournaments are held at Casa de Campo, La Romana.

SANTO DOMINGO

Santo Domingo (*pop* 2.1mn), the capital and chief seaport, was founded in 1496 by Columbus' brother Bartolomé and hence was the first capital in Spanish America. For years the city was the base for the Spaniards' exploration and conquest of the continent: from it Ponce de León sailed to discover Puerto Rico, Hernán Cortés launched his attack on Mexico, Balboa discovered the Pacific and Diego de Velázquez set out to settle Cuba. Hispaniola was where Europe's first social and political activities in the Americas took place. Santo Domingo itself holds the title 'first' for a variety of offices: first city, having the first Audiencia Real, cathedral, university, coinage, etc. In view of this, Unesco has designated Santo Domingo a World Cultural Heritage site (Patrimonio Cultural Mundial). In the old part of the city, on the W bank of the Río Ozama, there are many fine early 16th century buildings. Restoration of the old city has made the area very attractive, with open air cafés and pleasant squares near the waterfront Avenida del Puerto.

Under the title of the **Quinto Centenario**, Santo Domingo played a prominent role in the celebration of the five hundredth anniversary of Christopher Columbus' landfall in the Caribbean (1492-1992). The Government undertook an extensive programme of public works, principally restoration work in the colonial city. A series of commemorative coins in limited editions was struck, available from the Centro de Información Numismática, Casa del Quinto Centenario, Isabel la Católica 103, T 682-0185, F 530-9164, Santo Domingo.

Places of interest

Catedral Basílica Menor de Santa María, Primada de América, Isabel La Católica esquina Nouel, the first cathedral to be founded in the New World. Its first stone was laid by Diego Colón, son of Christopher Columbus, in 1514; the architect was Alonzo Rodríguez. It was finished in 1540. The alleged remains of Christopher Columbus were found in 1877 during restoration work. In 1892, the Government of Spain donated the tomb in which the remains rest, behind the high altar, until their removal to the Faro a Colón (see below). The cathedral was fully restored for 1992, with new gargoyles and sculptures at the gates showing the indigenous people when Columbus arrived. The windows, altars and roof were all returned to their colonial splendour. Open to the public 0900-1200, 1500-1630.

Torre del Homenaje inside Fortaleza Ozama, reached through the mansion of Rodrigo Bastidas (later the founder of the city of Santa Marta in Colombia) on Calle Las Damas, which is now completely restored and has a museum/gallery with temporary exhibitions. It is the oldest fortress in America, constructed 1503-07 by Nicolás de Ovando, whose house in the same street has been restored and turned into a splendid hotel.

Museo de las Casas Reales, on Calle Las Damas, in a reconstructed early 16th century building which was in colonial days the Palace of the Governors and Captains-General, and of the Real Audiencia and Chancery of the Indies. It is an excellent colonial museum (often has special exhibits, entry US$0.50); open Tues-Sun 1000-1700; entry US$0.75, T 682-4202. The Voluntariado de las Casas Reales has exhibitions of contemporary Dominican art.

Alcázar de Colón at the end of Las Damas and Emilio Tejera, constructed by Diego Colón in 1510-14. For six decades it was the seat of the Spanish Crown in the New World; it was sacked by Drake in 1586. Now completely restored, it houses the interesting **Museo Virreinal** (Viceregal Museum). Open 0900-1700 daily; entry US$0.75.

Casa del Cordón, Isabel La Católica esquina Emiliano Tejera, built in 1509 by Francisco de Garay, who accompanied Columbus on his first voyage to Hispaniola. Named for the cord of the Franciscan Order, sculpted above the entrance. Now the offices of the Banco Popular; free guided tours during working hours.

Monasterio de San Francisco (ruins), Hostos esquina E Tejera, first monastery in America, constructed in the first decade of the 16th century. Sacked by Drake and destroyed by earthquakes in 1673 and 1751.

Reloj de Sol (sundial) built 1753, near end of Las Damas, by order of General Francisco de Rubio y Peñaranda; by its side is **Capilla de Nuestra Señora de Los Remedios**, built in the early 16th century as the private chapel of the Dávila family.

La Ataranza, near the Alcázar, a cluster of 16th century buildings which served as warehouses. Now restored to contain shops, bars and restaurants.

Hospital-Iglesia de San Nicolás de Bari (ruins), Hostos between Mercedes and Luperón, begun in 1509 by Nicolás de Ovando, completed 1552, the first stone-built hospital in the Americas. Also sacked by Drake, it was probably one of the best constructed buildings of the period, it survived many earthquakes and hurricanes. In 1911 some of its walls were knocked down because they posed a hazard to passers-by; also the last of its valuable wood was taken. It is now full of pigeons.

Convento de San Ignacio de Loyola, Las Damas between Mercedes and El Conde. Finished in 1743, it is now the

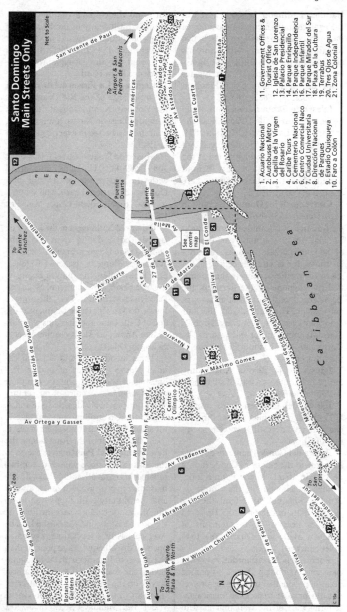

Santo Domingo **339**

Santo Domingo Main Streets Only

1. Acuario Nacional
2. Autobuses Metro
3. Capilla de la Virgen del Rosario
4. Caribe Tours
5. Cementerio Nacional
6. Centro Comercial Naco
7. Ciudad Universitaria
8. Dirección Nacional de Parques
9. Estadio Quisqueya
10. Faro a Colón
11. Government Offices & Tourist Office
12. Iglesia de San Lorenzo
13. Palacio Presidencial
14. Parque Enriquillo
15. Parque Independencia
16. Parque Infantil
17. Parque Mirador del Sur
18. Plaza de la Cultura
19. Terrabus
20. Tres Ojos de Agua
21. Zona Colonial

National Pantheon. It was restored in 1955 and contains memorials to many of the country's heroes and patriots. It also contains an ornate tomb built before his death for the dictator Trujillo, the 'Benefactor of the Fatherland', but his remains do not lie there. Open Tues-Sun 0900-1700, free, T 682-0185.

Iglesia de Santa Bárbara, off Mella to the left near Calle J Parra, near the end of Isabel La Católica. Built in 1574, sacked by Drake in 1586, destroyed by a hurricane in 1591, reconstructed at the beginning of the 17th century. Behind the church are the ruins of its fort, where one can get good views.

Convento de los Dominicos, built in 1510. Here in 1538 the first university in the Americas was founded, named for St Thomas Aquinas; it now bears the title of the Universidad Autónoma de Santo Domingo. It has a unique ceiling which shows the medieval concept that identified the elements of the universe, the classical gods and the Christian icons in one system. The Sun is God, the four evangelists are the planetary symbols Mars, Mercury, Jupiter and Saturn. The University itself has moved to a site in the suburbs.

Iglesia de la Regina Angelorum, built 1537, contains a wall of silver near one of its altars.

Iglesia del Carmen, built around 1615 at side of Capilla de San Andrés, contains an interesting wooden sculpture of Christ.

Puerta del Conde (Baluarte de 27 de Febrero), at the end of El Conde (now a pedestrian street) in the Parque Independencia. Named for the Conde de Peñalva, who helped defend the city against William Penn in 1655. Restored in 1976, near it lie the remains of Sánchez, Mella and Duarte, the 1844 independence leaders.

Puerta de la Misericordia, Palo Hincado and Arzobispo Portes, so named because people fled under it for protection during earthquakes and hurricanes. It forms part of the wall that used to surround the colonial city, into which are now built many of the houses and shops of Ciudad Nueva. It was here on 27 February 1844 that Mella fired the first shot in the struggle for independence from Haiti.

Capilla de La Virgen del Rosario, on the other side of the Río Ozama, near the Molinos Dominicanos at the end of Avenida Olegario Vargas. It was the first church constructed in America, restored in 1943.

Museo de Duarte, Isabel La Católica 308, T 689-0326. Contains items linked with the independence struggle and Duarte, the national hero, whose home it was (open 0900-1700, Mon-Fri, US$0.75).

Other old buildings are the Iglesia de las Mercedes, dating from 1555; the Puerta de San Diego, near the Alcázar; the Palacio de Borgella, Isabel la Católica, near Plaza Colón; the ruins of Fuerte de la Concepción, at the corner of Mella and Palo Hincado, built in 1543; the ruins of Fuerte de San Gil, Padre Billini, near the end of Calle Pina; and the ruins of Iglesia de San Antón, off Mella esquina Vicente Celestino Duarte.

The Ciudad Vieja and adjacent Ciudad Nueva (the area of middle-class housing of the 19th century, complete with *pulperías* – turn-of-the-century stores) are practically deserted on Sunday, a good time to stroll around and take in the architecture and atmosphere in peace.

At the mouth of the Río Ozama, the new **Avenida del Puerto** gives access to the Antigua Ceiba, where Columbus moored his caravelles, the Plaza de Armas, the city's original drainage system and the old city wall. Steps lead up to the Alcázar de Colón where the Plaza de España has been established. The Avenida has in a short time become an open-air discothèque, more popular than the Malecón. Together with the inauguration of the Avenida del Puerto is a boat service on the Río Ozama for sightseeing upstream (operated by Mar C por A in the vessel *Sea*, Monday-Friday 1800-2200,

Saturday 1600, US$4, happy hour from 1800-2000, drinks two for the price of one). Water sports and speed-boat races can also be seen. The eastern bank of the Ozama is to be restored with a new footpath, the Vereda del Almirante, an amphitheatre and a new tourist harbour. All commercial shipping will be diverted to Río Haina.

Parks

Among the attractive parks are the Central Olímpico (see above) in the city centre, Parque Independencia (a peaceful haven amid all the traffic, with the Altar de la Patria, containing the remains of the country's founders, Juan Pablo Duarte, Francisco del Rosario Sánchez and Ramón Matías Mella), Parque Colón, Parque Mirador del Este (Autopista de las Américas, a 7 km-long *alameda*) and Parque Mirador del Sur (Paseo de los Indios at Mirador Sur, 7 km long, popular for walking, jogging, cycling, picnics) Parque Mirador del Norte has been constructed on the banks of the Río Isabela, near Guarícano and Villa Mella. There is a boating lake, picnic areas, restaurants, jogging and cycling trails. On Avenida José Contreras are many caves, some with lakes, in the southern cliff of Parque Mirador del Sur. Along this cliff the Avenida Cayetano Germosén has been built, giving access to a number of caves used at one time by Taino Indians. One such Lago Subterráneo has been opened as a tourist attraction, entry US$0.40 (0900-1730). The road, lined with gardens, links Avenidas Luperón and Italia.

The **Jardín Botánico Nacional**, Urbanización Los Ríos (T 565-2860, open Tues-Sun 0900-1700, admission US$0.75, children US$0.35 and the Parque Zoológico Nacional, La Puya (T 562-3149, open daily 0900-1700, US$0.40). The Botanical Gardens are highly recommended (the Japanese Garden especially); horse-drawn carriages and a small train tour the grounds (US$0.80, children US$0.55). There is an **Acuario Nacional**, Avenida España, on the coast E

of the city, open daily 0900-2000, US$0.80, very popular, very good; it has a café serving pizzas (there is a bus from Avenida Independencia, by the park). Quisqueya Park, César Nicolás Penson, is a recreational park for children, entry US$0.40. The Parque Infantil at Avenidas Bolívar y Tiradentes is to be remodelled.

The **Faro a Colón** (Columbus Lighthouse), built at great cost (and not without controversy) in the Parque Mirador del Este, is in the shape of a cross. Where the arms of the cross intersect is the mausoleum containing the supposed remains of Columbus. The navy mounts a permanent guard over the tomb. Spotlights project a crucifix of light into the night sky, spectacular on a cloudy night, less so when it is clear. Until the lighthouse has its own solar-powered generators, the lights are lit Friday to Sunday 2000-2200 and on holidays. One of the rooms inside the lighthouse is a chapel, in others different countries have mounted exhibitions (the British exhibit concentrates on the entries for the competition to design the lighthouse: the competition was won by a British design). Many rooms are empty and the Taino museum on the second floor has yet to be mounted. (Open Tues-Sun 1000-1700; US$0.80, half price for children, T 592-5217, photography inside permitted; guides are free, but give a tip; shorts above the knee not allowed.) The interior of the arms of the cross are open to the sky so that when it rains the only shelter is around the mausoleum, where there are no seats. Around the building gardens have been laid out.

The **modern city** is very spread out because, until recently, there was no high-rise building. The outer city has fine avenues, especially Avenida George Washington (also known as the Malecón) which runs parallel to the sea; it often becomes an open-air discothèque, where locals and foreigners dance the *merengue*. The annual *merengue* festival is held here. The spectacular monument to Fray Antón de Montesinos

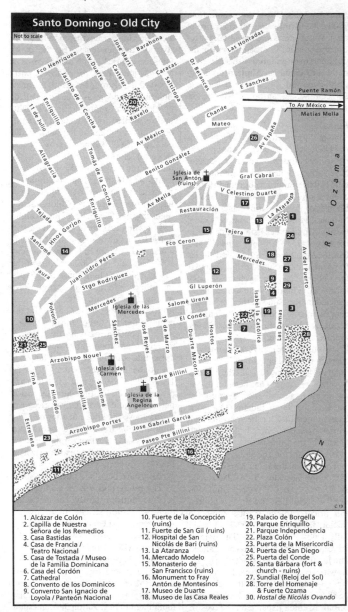

Santo Domingo - Old City

Not to scale

1. Alcázar de Colón
2. Capilla de Nuestra
   Señora de los Remedios
3. Casa Bastidas
4. Casa de Francia /
   Teatro Nacional
5. Casa de Tostada / Museo
   de la Familia Dominicana
6. Casa del Cordón
7. Cathedral
8. Convento de los Dominicos
9. Convento San Ignacio de
   Loyola / Panteón Nacional
10. Fuerte de la Concepción
    (ruins)
11. Fuerte de San Gil (ruins)
12. Hospital de San
    Nicolás de Bari (ruins)
13. La Ataranza
14. Mercado Modelo
15. Monasterio de
    San Francisco (ruins)
16. Monument to Fray
    Antón de Montesinos
17. Museo de Duarte
18. Museo de las Casa Reales
19. Palacio de Borgella
20. Parque Enriquillo
21. Parque Independencia
22. Plaza Colón
23. Puerta de la Misericordia
24. Puerta de San Diego
25. Puerta del Conde
26. Santa Bárbara (fort &
    church - ruins)
27. Sundial (Reloj del Sol)
28. Torre del Homenaje
    & Fuerte Ozama
30. *Hostal de Nicolás Ovando*

is at the eastern end of Avenida George Washington. A new exhibition centre has been built on Avenida George Washington opposite the Parque Eugenio María de Hostos, and cultural events and shows take place here.

The continuation (Prolongación) of Avenida México, which runs parallel to Avs Bolívar and 27 de Febrero, has many modern buildings, while Expreso Quinto Centenario, in the Villa Juana and Villa Francisca districts, is a new roadway which has rejuvenated these parts of the city. Other important avenues are Independencia, Bolívar, Abraham Lincoln, Winston Churchill, Núñez de Cáceres, 27 de Febrero, John F Kennedy, Juan Pablo Duarte, Ramón Matías Mella and General Gregorio Luperón.

Gazcue is a quiet, attractive residential area with expensive homes built in the 1930s and 1940s, stretching W of the Zona Colonial as far as Avenida Máximo Gómez. The coral pink Palacio Presidencial with a neo-classical central portico and cupola, built by Trujillo, is at the intersection of Doctor Delgado and Manuel María Castillo. It is used by the President, but guided tours of the richly decorated interior can be arranged, T 686-4771 ext 340 or 360. Opposite the Palacio's grounds, at Avenida México y 30 de Marzo, are the government offices. The 1955/56 World's Fair (Feria de Confraternidad) buildings now house the Senate and Congress.

Museums

The national museum collection, which includes a wonderful display of Taino artefacts and the ethnography section mentioned under **Festivals** above, is in the **Museo del Hombre Dominicano** (US$0.80, 1000-1700, closed on Mon, T 687-3622), which forms part of the Plaza de la Cultura, founded by Joaquín Balaguer on Avenida Máximo Gómez. It also includes the ultra-modern national theatre and national library; the **Museo de Arte Moderno** (open 1000-1700, US$0.80, closed Mon, T 685-2153), the Cinemateca Nacional, the **Museo de Historia Natural** (T 689-0106, US$0.80, open Tues-Sun 1000-1700, café open 0700-1900) and the **Museo de Historia y Geografía** (open 1000-1700, US$0.75, T 689-0106). The **Museo de la Familia Dominicana** is housed in the Casa de Tostada (Calle Padre Billini esq Arzobispo Meriño), an early 16th century mansion (Mon-Fri, 0900-1700, US$0.80, T 689-5057). The Banco Central has a **Museo Numismático y Filatélico**, open Mon-Fri 0830-1530, free, T 688-6512. The Fundación García Arévalo, in the

The mystery of Columbus' bones

After his death in 1506, Columbus was buried in Valladolid, Spain. In 1509 his body was apparently removed to Sevilla, thence together with that of his son Diego to Santo Domingo sometime in the 1540s. When France took control of Hispaniola in 1795, Cuba (still part of Spain) requested Columbus' remains. An urn bearing the name 'Colón' was disinterred from beneath the altar, sent to Havana and then back to the Cathedral in Sevilla in 1898, when Cuba became independent. In 1877, however, during alterations and repairs in Santo Domingo cathedral, the cache of urns beneath the altar was reopened. One casket bore the inscription 'Almirante Cristóbal Colón', both outside and in. Experts confirmed that the remains were those of Columbus; the Spanish ambassador and two further experts from Spain were dismissed for concurring with the findings. A second pair of Spanish experts denied the discovery, hence the confusion over where the admiral's bones lay. The urn that was opened in 1877 is that which is now given pride of place in the Faro a Colón.

With thanks to Joe Hollins, Stockbridge, UK.

7 Up building, Avenida San Martín, near Lope de Vega, has an exhibition of prehispanic art and civilization, T 540-7777 for an appointment. For archaeologists there is the Instituto de Investigaciones Históricas, José Reyes 24. At José Reyes 6, in the Zona Colonial, is the **Instituto de la Porcelana** (T 689-1766). At the entrance to the airport is La Caleta Archaeological Museum (**Museo Ceremonial La Caleta**) with its display of Taino and Arawak ceramics and a Taino burial site (entry free). Roadside sellers offer copies of statues.

Three bridges cross the Río Ozama: the nearest to the sea is Mella (originally nicknamed La Bicicleta because it is so narrow, but now with a new bridge beside it to ease congestion), next is Duarte, and further inland Sánchez. On the road to the airport are the Tres Ojos de Agua, two water-filled caves and a sunken lake which are worth a visit. To reach the last-named you must take the raft across the second cave; it is supposed to have two crocodiles in it, put there by the Botanical Gardens, but they didn't reproduce (no one bothered to check their sex).

Local information – Santo Domingo
● Accommodation

Price guide

L1	over US$200	L2	US$151-200
L3	US$101-150	A1	US$81-100
A2	US$61-80	A3	US$46-60
B	US$31-45	C	US$21-30
D	US$12-20	E	US$7-11
F	US$4-6	G	up to US$3

Hotels (prices are double, high season and do not include taxes, normally 23%).

On the Malecón are the **L1-A1** *Hotel V Centenario Intercontinental*, Av George Washington 218, T 221-0000, F 686-3287, 5 stars, very well-appointed with restaurants, pools, gym, etc. A little further from the colonial centre are **L3-A1** *Sheraton*, Av George Washington 365, T 221-6666, F 687-8150, 260 rooms, a/c, pool, tennis, gym, casino, and **L1-L3** *Jaragua Renaissance Resort & Casino*, Av George Washington 367, T 221-2222,

F 686-0528, the latter being much more glitzy than the former. The *Jaragua* has a large spa and health club, tennis, free form pool, casino with entertainment, meetings facilities, executive floor, business centre, 5 restaurants and 300 deluxe a/c rooms and suites. **L2-A1** *Embajador*, a member of the Spanish Occidental chain (with other hotels in the country), is rec, Av Sarasota 65, T 221-2131, F 532-4494, 316 rooms, a/c, pool, tennis, casino. **A2** *Naco*, Av Tiradentes 22, T 562-3100, F 544-0957, 106 rooms, a/c, pool, casino; nearby is the newer **L2-A3** *Plaza*, T 541-6226, F 541-7251, suites with kitchenette, very comfortable, cable TV, pool, gym, gourmet restaurant, coffee shop (if you wish to self-cater, ask hotel for utensils and tableware and buy food in nearby supermarket), rec. **A2-A3** *Hostal Nicolás de Ovando*, Calle Las Damas 53, T 687-3101, a restored 16th century mansion in the oldest part of the city, is warmly rec for comfort, lovely public areas, friendly service, a/c, pool, quiet and atmosphere, standard of rooms varies, some are beginning to deteriorate, hot water problems, attractive swimming pool (not regularly cleaned), with view over Rio Ozama. **L3** *Gran Hotel Lina*, Av Máximo Gómez y 27 de Febrero, T 563-5000, F 686-5521, a/c, pool, highly rec and has a good restaurant, well-equipped, 5 star. **L2-L3** *Santo Domingo*, Av Independencia y Av Abraham Lincoln, T 221-1511, F 535-1511, a/c, pool, colonial style, plush and charming, main restaurant open 5 days a week for lunch, otherwise for receptions, *Café Tal*, less well-staffed; **A2-A3** *Hispaniola*, Av Independencia y Abraham Lincoln, T 221-2131, F 535-4050, a/c, pool. **L3-A1** *Dominican Fiesta/Concor*, Av Anacaona, T 562-8222, F 562-8939, a/c, pool; **A3-B** *Comodoro*, Av Bolívar 193, T 687-7141, T/F 541-2277, a/c, pool, reasonable, with fridges in rooms. **A3-B** *Cervantes*, Cervantes 202, T 686-8161, F 686-5754, a/c, 180 rooms, family-run, with pool; **B** *Comercial*, Calle El Conde esq Hostos, T 682-2814, central, with fans, TV, bath and a fair restaurant, friendly, clean, good value.

There are several apart-hotels: **B** *Aladino*, H Pieter 34, T 567-0144, fan and a/c; **A3** *Plaza Colonial*, Julio Verne 4, T 685-9171, F 686-2877, big, bare apartments, close to Zona Colonial, pool; *Casa de Huéspedes Sterling*, Av Bolívar 5 y Parque Independencia, T 688-5773, next to Codetel office, self-catering apartments, weekly or monthly basis, fully equipped, friendly, clean, negotiate price, US$256/month high season, rec. **B** *Plaza Florida*, Av Bolívar 203, T 541-3957, F 540-5582;

A3 *Delta*, Av Sarasota 53, T 535-0800; from **B** *Petit Apart-Hotel Turístico*, Aníbal de Espinosa 70, T 681-5454, with restaurant, terrace, disco.

Other hotels include: on Av George Washington, **A1-A3** *Napolitano*, T 687-1131, F 687-6814, a/c, pool, casino; next door is **C** *Palmeras del Caribe*, Cambronal 1, T 689-3872, nice rooms but small, pleasant garden, use of fridge, adjoining café; **A3** *Continental*, Av Máximo Gómez 16, T 689-1151, F 687-8397, inc taxes and breakfast, pleasant area, pool; **B** *Royal*, Av Duarte y 27 de Febrero, T 685-5400, fully a/c, small pool, good restaurant, *guaguas* leaving to N and W across the street. In the old city, **A3** *Hostal Nicolás Nader*, Duarte y General Luperón, T 687-6674, inc taxes, small, old building, friendly, personal service, pleasant; **A3** pp *Casa Vapor*, Av Francia y Dr Delgado (basic price), near Presidential Palace, in a house dating from Trujillo's time, in the shape of a ship, includes restaurant, *Café Francés*, *Terraza del Puerto*, *Sport Vapor* and *Cafetería La Proa*; **A2** *Palacio*, Macorís y Ureña, T 682-4730, with fan.

Cheaper hotels include: **C** *Alameda*, Calle Cervantes opposite *Cervantes*, T 685-5121, restaurant; **D** *Aída*, El Conde and Espaillat, T 685-7692, a/c (less without), fairly quiet (but record shop below may be noisy in day), very central, popular, often full; **D** *Independencia*, Estrella casi esquina Arzobispo Nouel, near Parque Independencia, price for single room, soap, towels etc provided, clean, convenient location, rec, some rooms without windows, also has a club, bar (noisy all night), language school (across the street) and art exhibitions; **C** *Montesino*, José Gabriel García III, Zona Colonial, T 688-3346, overlooking Malecón and Montesino's statue, 4 rooms, with bath, **D** with shared bath, fan, use of kitchen, will negotiate longer stays, highly rec; **C** *Señorial*, Av Presidente Vicini Burgos 58 (Parque Eugenio María de Hostos), T 687-4367, F 687-0600, Swiss run, a/c, good electricity and water supply, colour TV, friendly, clean and informal, good Italian food, popular with Swiss-Italian visitors, see the 1952 map on the wall; **D** *Luna del Norte*, Benito González 89, T 687-0124/2504, clean, friendly, rec, restaurant; **D** *Radiante*, Av Duarte 7 between Av Mella and Benito González, with bath, key deposit charged; **F** *Benito*, Benito González near market, with bath, cheaper without, not rec; **E** *Macau*, Benito González, near Av Duarte, dirty, very basic, Chinese run, as is the

restaurant downstairs; **E-F** *Ferdan*, Francisco Henríquez 107 y Carvajal, T 221-7710, just off Av Duarte, buses to Boca Chica leave outside, and to airport 2 blocks away, large clean rooms with bath, foreigners given rooms with windows, large discounts for long stays but you will be given room on top floors where generator does not reach and suffer power cuts. There are dozens of cheap hotels, especially around the Mercado Modelo; those on Av Duarte are usually used by prostitutes; have a good look round them before making any decision. For cheap rooms in hotels or *casas de pensión*, or for apartments for rent for longer stays in or outside the capital, look in the classified section of daily paper, *Listín Diario*. Rooms in the private house of Doña Hilkka, Abreu 7, near Iglesia San Carlos, central, cheap, charming. Business travellers can often get cheaper rates than posted by requesting '*la tarifa comercial*'.

● **Places to eat**

At main hotels, eg *Alcázar* at the *Santo Domingo*; the *Lina*; *La Piazzeta* at the *Hispaniola* (Italian specialities); *Le Gourmet* at the *Comodoro*. Many of the hotels have '*bufets ejecutivos*' at lunch time.

Recommended restaurants include *Ché Bandoneón*, on El Conde between Damas y Parque Colón, Argentine owned, outdoor terrace, Argentine, criollo and French food, tangos, T 687-0023; *La Cocina*, next door at No 56, is also good, créole food, both stay open till after midnight; at No 60 is *L'Avocat* café-restaurant. *Mesón de la Cava*, Parque Mirador, situated in a natural cave, good steaks, dancing, very popular so reserve in advance, T 533-3818; *Lago Enriquillo*, also in Parque Mirador, Chinese and international. *Jai-Alai*, Av Independencia 411, for seafood and local specialities, attentive service, T 685-2409; also for seafood, *Sully*, Charles Summers y Calle Caoba, T 562-3389, some distance from centre, excellent. *Fonda La Ataranza*, La Ataranza 5, T 689-2900, popular for créole and international cuisine; *Café St Michel*, Lope de Vega 24, T 562-4141, good Caribbean and French cooking; *La Fromagière*, 27 de Febrero at Plaza Criollo, T 567-9430, French and international, reasonable; *Juan Carlos*, Av Mejía Ricart, near Olympic stadium, very good value. *Café Coco*, Sánchez 153, Zona Colonial, T 687-9624, a small restaurant owned and run by 2 Englishmen, excellent food and service, menu changes daily, highly rec, open

1200-1500, 1830-2230, closed Sun pm and all day Mon; *Plaza Toledo*, Isabel la Católica 163, Plaza María de Toledo, combination café and art gallery owned by American Betty Marshall; *Asadera las Argentinas*, Av Independencia between Av Abraham Lincoln and Máximo Gómez, excellent Argentine food; *Cappuccino*, Av Máximo Gómez 60, Italian owned restaurant and café, great Italian food, suave, prices to match. *Sheherezade*, Roberto Pastoriza 226, T 227-2323, Arabian and Mediterranean food; *Jardín de Jade*, José María Heredia 6, T 686-3226, Oriental cooking; *Fellini*, Roberto Pastoriza, esq Winston Churchill, Mediterranean cuisine; *Café Berimbau*, Abraham Lincoln, esq Gustavo Mejía Ricart, Brazilian food; *David Crockett*, Gustavo Mejía Ricart 34, esq Alberto Larancuet, T 565-8898, 547-2999, grill, excellent, around US$20-25 pp.

Vesuvio I, Av George Washington 521, very expensive, not worth it, more touristy than *Vesuvio II*, Av Tiradentes 17, Italian and international cuisine; *Maniquí* in the Plaza de la Cultura is good. *Lucky Seven*, Av Pasteur y Casimiro de Moya, good for seafood and steaks, popular haunt for baseball fans.

Veneto Ice Cream on Av Independencia; *Las Pirámides*, Rómulo Betancourt 351, and *Il Capo del Malecón*, Av George Washington 517 (other branches at Av Tiradentes and Jardines del Embajador), both good for pizzas. *Aubergine*, Av Alma Mater y Av México, German food; *La Esquina de Tejas*, Av 27 de Febrero 343, offers Spanish cuisine; also Spanish, *Boga Boga*, Plaza Florida, Av Bolívar 303, US$15-20. For good Chinese food try *Marios*, 27 de Febrero 299, very popular, or *La Gran Muralla*, Av 27 de Febrero. *Pacos Café*, El Conde, near Parque Independencia, local food at reasonable prices but waiters expect you to tip as well as pay 10% service. For the local dish *mofongo* (see under **Food and Drink** below), *Palacio del Mofongo* Av George Washington 509, T 688-8121, or *Casa del Mofongo*, 27 de Febrero y Calle 7 Eva Mo, T 565-1778 (a long way from the centre); *Bariloche*, El Conde 203, self-service food from about 1145, look at what is on offer then buy ticket at cash register, lasagne only US$1, *menú del día* US$3, huge portions; *La Cafetería Colonial*, El Conde 253, good for coffee after meal at *Bariloche*, freshly ground; *Petrus*, El Conde 357 between 19 de Marzo y Sánchez, portion of pizza US$1.20, sandwiches, hamburgers, drinks; *Atenas*, Benito González 79, close to many cheaper hotels, off Av Duarte,

local food, meat, rice and beans US$2, avoid table by footpath.

Two good vegetarian restaurants are *Ananda*, Casimiro de Moya 7, T 562-4465, and *Vegetariano*, Calle Luperón 9 (open 0800-1500). Also *Ojas*, Calle Jonas Salk 2, T 682-3940 and *El Terrenal*, Malecón y Estrelleta, T 689-3161, some vegetarian dishes. *Vita Naturaleza*, Mercedes 255, sells health products (by small park at junction with Luperón).

The Village Pub, in Calle Hostos 350, opposite the ruins of Hospital San Nicolás de Bari, is a good place for snacks and drinks in a pub-type atmosphere, in the colonial city; and so is *La Taberna* (classical music) at Padre Billini with Las Damas. *Chez Duke*, Arzobispo Nouel y Arzobispo Meriño, French Canadian jazz place, cosy patio. In the Plaza España are *Drake's Pub*, *Museo de Jamón* (ceiling covered with hams) and *Bachata Rosa*, named after the popular album of Juan Luis Guerra, 2 huge screens with music videos. *Ortolio II*, Av W Churchill y G M Ricart, behind *Burger King*, great for live jazz/rock music.

There are numerous pizzerias which are good value: *Domino's* has several delivery outlets and there is a *Pizza Hut* on the corner of Av 27 de Febrero and Av Abraham Lincoln; there is a *Burger King* on Av Churchill with Gustavo Mejía, a *Wendy's* on 27 de Febrero and other Americanized fast food chains; also try a *chimichurri* (spiced sausage), throughout the city stalls sell sandwiches, *chimichurris*, hot dogs and hamburgers. Several small restaurants specialize in roast chicken, *pollo al carbón*, with a tasty *wasa kaca* sauce; the best of these is *Pollo Caribe* on Av Winston Churchill, just below Av Sarasota. Many fast food places offer dishes for about US$2-3, which would cost US$8 in a hotel restaurant. There are also take-away places where a meal costs about US$2.50. Cheapest are probably the Chinese restaurants, but in many cases the hygiene is dubious (the same applies to other basic restaurants). Several *cafeterías* serving local lunches around Mercado Modelo. *France-Croissant*, Av Sarasota 82 y Dr Defillo, French bakery, tastiest pastries in the country, unsweetened wholemeal bread available, small café.

The Asociación Nacional de Hoteles y Restaurantes, Asonahores, T 688-7542, publishes a guide to the best restaurants in the capital, *Guía de Restaurantes*.

● Banks and Exchange

Officially possible only in banks and cambios, many along Isabel La Católica, but check which banks accept which TCs, see **Information for travellers**. Do not change money on the street; you will undoubtedly be cheated and you also run the risk of imprisonment. Casa de Cambio Quisqueya, Sánchez 205, off El Conde, gives a slightly better rate than banks.

● Casinos

Hotels Dominican Concorde, Santo Domingo, San Gerónimo, Sheraton, El Embajador, Naco, Jaragua, Lina and Maunaloa Night Club, Centro de los Héroes.

● Concerts

Concerts and other cultural events are often held at the National Theatre, the Casa de Francia, corner of Las Damas and El Conde, where Cortés lived for a while (run by the French Embassy, also art gallery and library, open to non-members), and the Casa de Teatro (see below).

● Discothèques

Omni in Hotel Sheraton, rock, merengue, salsa and ballads; Hípocampo in Hotel El Embajador; Disco Piano in Hotel El Napolitano; Jet Set and Opus, Av Independencia; Shehara and Bella Blu (next to Vesuvio I) on George Washington; Punto Final, Av Pasteur. Tops (Hotel Plaza Naco, US$2.50 entry, high above city, rec), El Final, Magic Disco, Jet Set and Xappil. Club 60, Máximo Gómez 60, rock, merengue and ballads; Neon in Hotel Hispaniola, upmarket, occasionally has live Latin jazz; Sentimiento, I lostos 99, down market with lots of merengue, very dark. For Cuban son music: El Rincón Habanero, Sánchez Valverde y Baltazar de los Reyes in Villa Consuelo, working class enthusiasts of Cuban son dance between tables to old records of 1940s and 1950s; Secreto Musical Bar, one block away, Baltazar de los Reyes and Pimentel, similar, headquarters of Club Nacional de los Soneros, rock, merengue, salsa and ballads; La Vieja Habana, in Villa Mella on the northern outskirts of town, owner called Generoso. Café Capri, Av Tiradentes, live bands performing most nights, Wed jazz night; Café Atlántico, Av Abraham Lincoln, 1 block below Av 27 de Febrero, popular with the 20-something crowd, also serves Mexican food.

● Night Clubs

Salon La Fiesta in the Jaragua Hotel; El Yarey in the Sheraton; Embassy Club in the Hotel El Embajador; Napolitana; Maunaloa Night Club and Casino; Hotel San Gerónimo Independencia; La Azotea in Hotel Concorde; Salón Rojo, Hotel Comodoro, Av Bolívar; Night Club Herminia; Las Vegas, Babilon, Fuego Fuego, Piano Bar Las Palmas in Hotel Santo Domingo, Piano Bar Intramuros, Primera Clase and Tablao Flamenco.

Also Instrumental Night Club on Autopista Las Américas; Exodus, George Washington 511; Le Petit Chateau, Av George Washington Km 11½, nude shows. Herminia's, Av Máximo Gómez y Calle Félix Evaristo Mejía, and Félix, 1 block away, good for unattached men, armed security guards, vigilant taxi drivers but beware pickpocketing by the ladies.

Guácara Taína, Paseo de los Indios, between Avenida Cayetano Germosén and Parque Mirador, has shows of Taino dancing in a deep natural cave with stalactites and indigenous pictographs, spectacular setting, from 1700-0200, US$4-12 (also disco, all types of music, a/c, 2 dance floors, Happy Hours and fashion shows, many recs).

To hear pericos ripiaos, go on Friday or Saturday night to the eating places (colmados) near the Malecón in Ciudad Nueva section of the city; the groups move from place to place.

● Theatres

Teatro Nacional, Plaza de la Cultura, Av Máximo Gómez; Palace of Fine Arts, Av Independencia and Máximo Gómez; Casa de Teatro, small drama workshop, Calle Padre Billini and, in Barrio Don Bosco, Teatro Nuevo (performances all year). The Anglo Dominican Theater Society, funded by the British Council and local businesses, puts on shows; details from the Honorary British Consul (address in **Information for travellers**).

● Hospitals

Clínica Abréu, Av Independencia y Beller, and adjacent **Clínica Gómez Patiño** are rec for foreigners needing treatment or hospitalization. Fees are high but care is good. 24-hr emergency department. Other reputable clinics are **Centro Médico UCE** and **Clínica Yunén** on Av Máximo Gómez, and **Clínica Abel González**, Av Independencia. For free consultation and prescription, **Padre Billini hospital**, Calle Padre Billini y Santomé, Zona Colonial, efficient, friendly.

● Language School

Escuela de Idiomas de la Universidad APEC, Av Máximo Gómez 72, Apartado Postal 59-2, Santo Domingo, T 687-3181, offers Spanish courses, either 1 or 2 hrs daily, Mon to Fri, for a term.

● **Libraries**

Biblioteca Nacional, in the Plaza de la Cultura, has a fine collection and is a good place for a quiet read. Instituto Cultural Dominico-Americano, corner of Av Abraham Lincoln and Calle Antonio de la Maza; English and Spanish books. The National Congress has a good library, as do some of the universities: Pontífica Universidad Católica Madre y Maestra, and the Instituto Tecnológico de Santo Domingo and the Universidad Autónoma de Santo Domingo.

● **Pharmacy**

Farmacía San Judas Tadeo, Independencia 33 y Bernado Pichard, T 689-6644, open 24 hrs all year, home delivery, cosmetics, magazines, cafetería outside.

● **Post Office**

In Zona Colonial, Arzobispo Portes 510, entre Cambronal y El Número, T 685-6920. The new Correo Central is in La Feria, Calle Rafael Damirón, Centro de los Héroes, opp *Fantasy* Night Club and Teatro Mauna Loa. Open 0700-1800, Mon-Fri; also certain hours on Sat. Lista de correo (poste restante) keeps mail for two months. There are post offices on the 2nd floor of the government building El Haucal, tallest building in the city, on Av Padre Castellanos, near Av Duarte, and in *Hotel Embajador*.

To ensure the delivery of documents worldwide, use a courier service: American Airlines (T 542-5151); DHL Dominicana (T 541-7988); Servicio de Documentos y pequeños paquetes (T 541-2119); Emery Worldwide (T 688-1855); Federal Express (T 567-9547); Internacional Bonded Couriers (T 542-5265).

● **Telephones**

International and long distance, also Telex and Fax: Codetel, Av 30 de Marzo 12, near Parque Independencia, and 11 others throughout the city (open 0800-2200); a convenient central office is at El Conde 202. Cheaper is the Tricom office on Av Máximo Gómez between Bolívar and Independencia. The Palacio de las Comunicaciones next to the Post Office (at Isabel La Católica y Emiliano Tejera) does not handle phone calls.

● **Episcopal Church**

Av Independencia 253, service in English, 0830 Sun; also Iglesia Episcopal San Andrés, on Marcos Ruiz.

● **Shopping**

Duty-free at Centro de los Héroes, La Ataranza, shops in *Embajador, Sheraton* and *Santo Domingo* hotels; departure lounge at airport; all purchases must be in US dollars. The Mercado Modelo, on Avenida Mella esquina Santomé, includes gift shops and is the best place in the city for handicrafts (see **Best Buys** in Information for travellers); you must bargain to get a good price. There are also 'speciality shops' at Plaza Criolla, 27 de Febrero y Máximo Gómez. Calle El Conde, now reserved to pedestrians, is the oldest shopping sector in Santo Domingo; Avenida Mella at Duarte is a good spot for discount shopping and local colour. A flea market, Mercado de las Pulgas, operates on Sunday in the Centro de los Héroes and at the Mercado de Oportunidades, 27 de Febrero. In contrast are the modern complexes at Plaza Naco and the new US style shopping mall at the corner of Av 27 de Febrero and Av Abraham Lincoln; also Plaza Caribe, at 27 de Febrero y Leopoldo Navarro.

Bookshop *Macalé*, Calle Arzobispo Nouel 3, T 682-2011, near Cathedral, open daily inc Sunday, has a wide selection of books, especially on the Republic's history.

● **Tours**

There are several tours of the city, taking in the duty-free shops, nightlife, etc. Rec travel agents in Santo Domingo for sightseeing tours include: *Metro Tours* (T 566-7126), *Domitur* (T 544-0929), *Prieto Tours* (T 685-0102), *Viajes Barceló* (T 685-8411). *Servicio Turístico de Helicóptero Dominicano* offers helicopter tours over Santo Domingo, office on the Malecón, T 687-1093/3093, US$46-110. Companies that offer tours around the republic are given in **Information for travellers**. **NB** See warnings at the end of this chapter about unofficial guides.

● **Buses**

Public transport buses (Onatrate), commonly called *guaguas*, run throughout the city, fares are RD$2.50 (US$0.20), but the service is very limited, therefore crowded. Exact change is needed. Private companies (eg Caribe Tours) operate on some routes, charging RD$3.

● **Taxis**

Carros públicos, or *conchos*, are shared taxis normally operating on fixed routes, 24 hrs a day, basic fare RD$2 (US$0.20). *Públicos* can be hired by one person, if they are empty, and are then called *carreras*. They can be expensive (US$3-4, more on longer routes); settle price before getting in. Fares are higher at Christmas time. *Públicos/conchos* also run onlong-distance routes; ask around to find the cheapest. You can get to just about anywhere by bus or *público* from Parque Independencia, but you have to ask where to stand. *Conchos* running on a shared basis are becoming scarcer, being replaced by *carreras*. Radio taxis charge between US$3-5 on local journeys around Santo Domingo (US$10 per hr) and are safer than street taxis, call about 20-30 mins in advance: Aero Taxi, T 686-1212; Anacaona Taxi, T 530-4800; Enlace Taxi, T 688-8881; Apolo Taxi, T 537-7772/531-3800; Express Taxi, T 537-7777; Oriental Taxi, T 549-5555. The 30-mins ride from Las Américas International airport to Santo Domingo should cost no more than US$14 in a radio taxi, but more in a *carrera*. Most hotels have a taxi or limousine service with set fares throughout the city and to the airport. There are motorcyclists who offer a taxi service, known as *motoconchos*, RD$3 (US$0.25), they sometimes take up to three passengers on pillion; they raise the noise level (in most towns) very considerably.

● **Car Hire**

Many places at the airport, on the road to the airport and on Malecón. There are many more agencies than those listed: National (T 562-1444, airport T 542-0162); Budget (T 562-6812); Nelly (José Contreras 139, T 544-5800); Dollar (JF Kennedy y Lincoln, T 685-1519); Patsy (T 686-4333); Hertz (T 221-5333); Avis (Sarasota y Lincoln, T 535-7191); Thrifty (T 687-9369); Honda (JF Kennedy y Pepillo Salcedo, T 567-1015/6); McDeal (T 688-6518); Auto Rental (T 685-7873); Rentauto (27 Febrero, T 566-7221); Ford (Máximo Gómez y JF Kennedy, T 565-1818). See also under **Information for travellers**.

● **Airport**

Aeropuerto La Américas, 23 km out of town, T 549-0450/80, has been modernized, very clean and smart. Immediately on arrival there is a tourist office on your right (reported as only interested in selling expensive tours), and just past that an office selling tourist cards (a blackboard indicates who needs a card, see **Documents** in **Information for travellers**). You must check if you need a card, otherwise the long queue to get through immigration will be wasted. In the customs hall is a bank for exchanging dollars; it is open Sunday and at night (good rates). On leaving do not forget to fill in a departure form to present to immigration, nor that you have to pay departure tax of US$10. Pesos can be changed back into

dollars, but this may involve going downstairs to the bank in the customs hall. In the departure area are lots of duty-free shops, one small café (dollars only) and limited seating. Upstairs there are good facilities with a burger restaurant which has plenty of seating and a good view of the airport.

The price of a taxi or minibus to town is given above (can be shared); it may be less if you bargain with drivers in the car park (though this is not easy) or telephone a radio taxi in advance (numbers given above). Leaving the airport on the ground floor, the same floor as immigration and customs, you find the expensive, individual taxis. Upstairs, outside the second floor, colectivo taxis cram up to 6 passengers into the vehicle; much cheaper. If arriving late at night it may be better to go to Boca Chica (see **East from Santo Domingo**), about 10 km from the airport, taxi about US$15. Aerobus (T 412-0220/1, F 412-0223) runs a/c 24-passenger buses from the Terrabus terminal at Plaza Criolla, off 27 de Febrero and Av Máximo Gómez to the airport every hour 0600-2100, US$5, but you can only get a seat from the airport into town by pre-booking and receiving a voucher in New York (T 718-681-4477), Miami (T 305-383-2381) or Montréal (T 514-322-8888). This is to avoid opposition from taxi unions. To get to the airport cheaply take a 'Boca Chica Express' bus from José Martí y París, near Parque Enriquillo, to the cargo terminal, 3-4 mins walk to the passenger terminal, US$1.50, buses every few minutes in either direction. Alternatively take any minibus heading E from Parque Enriquillo which will pass the turn-off to the airport; alight at the turning and walk 1½ km or take one of the many *motoconchos* waiting at the junction. This option can be done in reverse when heading into the city. Various tour agencies also run minibuses to the airport; check with your hotel. Herrera airport (T 567-3900) for internal flights to Santiago, Puerto Plata, Barahona and La Romana (allow plenty of time).

NORTH FROM SANTO DOMINGO

The Carretera Duarte runs N from Santo Domingo, now a 4-lane highway all the way to Santiago de los Caballeros. Around **Bonao** are rice paddies. The town is also known as Villa de las Hortensias. There are cheap hotels near the market and on the highway are many *paradas*, *posadas* and *plazas turísticas*. The area is renowned for its *queso de hoja*, fresh balls of moist white cheese. Several places along the Carretera Duarte sell this typical cheese with bread or crackers.

LA VEGA

Further N is **La Vega**, a quiet place in the beautiful valley of la Vega Real, in the heart of the Cibao. La Vega's cathedral is a modern, concrete building. The exterior looks a little like a turreted castle while the huge bell tower slightly resembles a ship's prow surmounted by a cross. The interior is spacious, with round stained-glass windows and lights suspended from a wooden ceiling. There is a Codetel office on the square.

● Accommodation

Hotels on the highway: *América*, at the Santo Domingo end of town, looks very rundown; **C** *Guarícano*, by the Río Camú at Santiago end of town, with a/c, a bit noisy from traffic and nearby discos, nothing special, cold water, overpriced. International artists appear at the *Astromundo* discothèque. In town: on Núñez de Cáceres, **D** *Astral*, a/c; opposite is **D** *San Pedro*, no 87, T 573-2844, a/c, cheaper without, very dirty, insecure; in the same block is *Santa Clara*, even more down market; on Restauración, near Núñez de Cáceres is *Quinta Patio*, with reasonable restaurant; on same street near the highway is *Nueva Ilusión* restaurant and amusements.

● Transport

Transport for Santo Domingo and Santiago can be caught on the highway; Expreso del Valle from Av Independencia in Santo Domingo, US$3, frequent. To Jarabacoa (45 mins, US$1) from Restauración y 27 de Febrero, opposite Ali Tours. Metrobus in La Vega, T 573-7099.

Further along the road from La Vega on the right is the turn for Santo Cerro, an old convent where the image of Virgen de las Mercedes is venerated. From there one can get a view of the valley of La Vega Real. If one continues along the road to the other side of the hill and into the valley the ruins of La Vega Vieja can be seen. It was founded by Columbus but destroyed by an earthquake in 1564; undergoing restoration.

JARABACOA

Continuing along the highway, on the left, is the turn for Jarabacoa. The road winds through some beautiful pine forests to the town itself, which is a popular summer hill resort in a valley in the mountains. The climate is fresh, with warm days and cool nights. On the road between La Vega and Jarabacoa are several Centros Vacacionales. The town itself is quite modern, with plenty of plots of land for sale. Nearby is the good *balneario* (swimming hole) of La Confluencia, in the Río Jimenoa (nice campsite, crowded at holiday times). The Jimenoa waterfalls are worth seeing, 10 km from town; a new bridge across the river has eased access, you may need a guide to cllimb the falls (if going in your own car, the guards at the control post will look after it). Closer to town, off the Constanza road, are the Baiguate falls (3.5-4 km, an easy walk, there is a signpost to the falls, 2nd turn on the right after *Pinar Dorado*). The first turn on the right after this hotel, by the *Parada Baez*, goes into the hills through the irrigated fields where vegetables and flowers are grown (look for herons in the channels), it comes to a dead end on private property. Horses for hire (US$3.25/hr) and bicycles from *Rancho Baiguate* (gift shop, bar, snacks), close to *Pinar Dorado*.

Local information – Jarabacoa
● Accommodation

11 km from town on the La Vega road, *La Montaña*, T 682-8181, friendly, clean, highly rec, but need own transport to make excursions from it; **B** *Pinar Dorado*, on road towards Constanza, about 20 mins walk from centre, price inc tax, nice rooms, a/c, hot water, good atmosphere and buffet meals, dinner à la carte, well-kept grounds, pool (T 574-2820); *River Resorts*, 1 km from town on La Vega road, 3-room cabins, TV, kitchen, pool, T 574-4688, **A3** per cabin, **D** for 1 room if available. **D** *Plaza Ortiz*, Mario Galán entre Sánchez y Duarte, T 574-6188, hotel, restaurant, disco; **E** *Doña Ligia*, on Mella, T 574-2739; **F** pp unmarked hotel on corner of Independencia and El Carmen, without bath; **E** *Junior*, with fan and shower, clean; nearby is *Dormitorio*, basic, clean, friendly, with a good *comedor*.

● **Places to eat**

The town has several restaurants; try the *Rincón Montañés* on Calle Gaston F Deligne, near El Carmen; *Basilia*, not as expensive as it looks, nice food; *Don Luis*, on square; *Jaraba-deli-bar-b-q*, opp Esso station, very good value, fast, rec. Several other *comedores* and *cafeterías*.

● **Services**

Banks on Calle Mario Galán. Codetel on road to La Vega. Market on M Galán. Tourist office opp cemetery at entrance to town, T 574-4883/4, 0800-1700 daily, very helpful.

● **Transport**

Conchos in town US$0.50. To Santo Domingo, Caribe Tours, T 574-4796, opp Inversiones de los Santos on Independencia, 0730 and 1500 in each direction, arrive 30 mins in advance (even earlier for the 0730 Mon bus), tickets sold only on day of departure, US$4.15, 2¾ hrs. To La Vega from Esso station, US$1; if you want to go to the capital or Santiago, they will let you off at the right place (coming from La Vega, *guaguas* charge an extra US$0.50 to drop you at *Hotel Pinar Dorado*). To Constanza, opp Shell station every hour or so, US$2.50. No transport anywhere after 1800, very little after 1500.

To Constanza is much easier via Bonao, from where the road is paved all the way; the road from Jarabacoa is very bad until El Río, the junction with the Bonao road. A new road will run from Jarabacoa to La Ciénaga, via Manabao, for access to Pico Duarte (see below).

CONSTANZA

Beyond Jarabacoa, on the same road, is **Constanza**, where the scenery is even better than in Jarabacoa, with rivers, forests and waterfalls. In winter, temperatures can fall to zero and there may be frosts. The valley is famous for food production, potatoes, garlic, strawberries, mushrooms and other vegetables, and for growing ornamental flowers.

● **Accommodation**

E *Mi Cabaña*, clean, bath, good, T 539-2472; others are *La Casa*, hotel and restaurant, *Sobeyola* and *Lorenzo*, average price in cheaper, basic hotels E-F.

● **Transport**

There are direct buses from Santo Domingo, Santiago and La Vega, return from Constanza at 0600 or earlier (buses will often pick you up at your hotel if you inform them in advance). Expreso Dominicano, Av Independencia, 100m W of Parque Independencia, to La Vega every hour 0700-1800, get off at junction for Constanza. You can get to/from the Santo Domingo-Santiago highway by taking a *público* or *guagua* (US$2.50) to/from Constanza. Constanza can also be reached by taking a bus to Bonao from either Santo Domingo or Santiago, then *guagua*. The last 1½ hrs of the trip to Constanza is through the finest scenery in the Republic. From Jarabacoa, see above. From Constanza you can use the *guagua* hopping system to get to Las Terrenas via San Francisco de Macoris, Nagua and Sánchez, US$1.50 for each stage.

Steve Morris recommends a route from the W to Constanza by public transport, avoiding Santo Domingo, across country and more time consuming but much more exciting and through spectacular scenery. He started in Neiba, near Lago Enriquillo (see below), took a *guagua* to Cruce de Ocoa, 2½ hrs, US$1.50, and from there to San José de Ocoa (NE of Azua), 45 mins, US$0.70. (*Hotel Marien*, on the main square, without bath, clean, good value.) He writes: 'Although what could hardly be called a road exists between San José de Ocoa and Constanza, there is no regular transport connecting the two towns. Apparently a gentleman named Pepe occasionally takes his jeep through the mountains to Constanza; the only hope is to get to La Isla gas station early in the morning and let everyone know that you want to get to Constanza. There is a regular bus service to Rancho Arriba and from there you can hire a motorcyclist to take you along a horrendous road to Piedra Blanca on the Santo Domingo-Santiago highway. Once on the highway it is very easy to get to Constanza.'

In the Cordillera Central near Jarabacoa and Constanza is **Pico Duarte**, at 3,175m the highest peak in the Caribbean. Before climbing it one must inform the army in Constanza; you must also purchase a permit from the Dirección Nacional de Parques at La Ciénaga de Manabao for US$3.95. (It is advisable to take a guide, who will tell you that mules are necessary for the ascent, but it can be done without them. An organized climb with DNP, Nuevos

Horizontes, Maritisant, T 585-7887, costs about US$78, September and October.) The climb takes two days and the walk from the tropical rain forest of the National Park through pine woods is pleasant. There are two huts on the path, which is clearly marked; they are lacking in 'facilities'. Take adequate clothing with you; it can be cold (below 0°C) and wet; also take torch, food and matches. The driest time is December to February. The last *carro* leaves Manabao for Jarabacoa at 1600, so aim to climb the peak well before lunch on the second day. The National Park itself is a 4 km walk from La Ciénaga, which is reached by a road passing through some magnificent scenery from Jarabacoa.

SANTIAGO DE LOS CABALLEROS

Santiago de Los Caballeros is the second largest city in the Republic (*pop* 690,000, 1994) and chief town of the Cibao valley in the N-central part of the country. The streets of the centre are busy, noisy, with lots of advertising signs; E of the centre it becomes greener, cleaner and quieter. The Río Yaque del Norte skirts the city with Avenida Circunvalación parallel to it. In 1494 Columbus ordered a fort to be built on the banks of the Río Yaque del Norte at a place called Jacagua; the resulting settlement was moved to its present site in 1563, but was destroyed by an earthquake. It is now a centre for tobacco and rum. On Parque Duarte are the Catedral de Santiago Apóstol, a neoclassical building (19th century) containing the tombs of the tyrant Ulises Heureux and of heroes of the Restauración de la República; the Museo del Tabaco (open Tues-Sat 0800-1200, 1500-1800), the Centro de Recreo (one of the country's most exclusive private clubs) and the Palacio Consistorial. Also on Parque Duarte is the Plaza de la Cultura y Oficina Regional de Patrimonio Cultural, which holds art exhibitions (closes 1230 on Sat).

Other places worth visiting are the Pontífica Universidad Católica Madre y Maestra (founded 1962, with good 50m swimming pool), the Museo Folklórico Tomás Morel, open 0900-1700 (free), and the Monumento a los Héroes de la Restauración, at the highest point in the city (panoramic views of the Cibao valley, remodelled in 1991 to include a *mirador*). Behind the monument is the newly-constructed theatre, built at an estimated cost of US$25mn. Calle El Sol is the main commercial street, with both vendors and the main shops. The Instituto Superior de Agricultura is in the Herradura on the other side of the Río Yaque del Norte (km 6).

Local information – Santiago de Los Caballeros
● **Accommodation**

A2 *El Gran Almirante*, Av Estrella Sadhalá, Los Jardines, on road N, T 580-1992, F 241-1492, popular with business visitors, quite good. **A2** *Camino Real*, T 581-7000, Del Sol y Mella, has good restaurant and night club, no parking facilities. **B** and over: *Matum*, Av Monumental, T 581-3107/8682, has night club, swimming pool open to non-residents US$2; *Don Diego*, Av Estrella Sadhalá, on road N, T 575-4186, has restaurant and night club. **B-C** *Ambar*, also on Av Estrella Sadhalá, T 575-1957; *Mercedes*, Calle 30 de Marzo 18, T 583-1171, hot water, a/c or fan, phone, central so a bit noisy, tatty, but friendly, fast laundry (5 hrs). **F** *Dorado*, Av Salvador Cucurullo 88, T 582-7563, with bath, basic, friendly. Many other cheap hotels on S Cucurullo, 4 blocks N of Parque Duarte on 30 de Marzo (many *guaguas* start from this junction).

● **Places to eat**

Pez Dorado, El Sol 43 (Parque Colón), T 582-2518 (Chinese and international), has a fine tradition of good quality food in generous portions. At the upper end of the price range is *El Café*, Av Texas esq Calle 5, Jardines Metropolitanos, the favourite of businessmen and upper class society. Strongly rec is *La Taberna Verde*, Prolongación Av 27 de Febrero 262, 5-minute drive from centre, in Urbanización El Dorado, good quality cuisine, service and décor. Rec for pasta and steaks is *Mezzaluna*, Av 27 de Febrero 77. Nearby is *Don Miguel*, Av 27 de Febrero 40, specializing in Cuban and local cuisine. Others include *El Sol* (upstairs in Mercado Modelo Turístico,

T 583-0767); *Yaque* (Restauración), US$4 plus for a good meal. For good value, open-air eating, rec are *Mac-Selo*, Juan Pablo Duarte III, and *La Pista*, behind the monument. For fast food, rec are *Pollos Victorina*, Av 27 de Febrero esq Maimon, for chicken; *Gyros Burger*, in the Las Bromelias commercial centre on Av Juan Pablo Duarte, for burgers; *De Nosotros Empanadas*, El Sol 1, near the monument, for delicious savoury pasties.

The restaurants of the hotels *El Gran Almirante*, *Camino Real* and *Don Diego* are good.

For the most spectacular view across the Cibao Valley, try *Camp David Ranch*; get there by driving (or take a taxi, fare about US$10) to Km 7 on Carretera Luperón, the turn-off is on the right, unsigned, before the *El Económico* supermarket; a 10-min climb up a winding, paved road leads to the ranch. The food quality is erratic, but the view is breathtaking. Next door is *El Generalísimo*, a piano bar decorated with classic cars from the Trujillo era. Some 10 bedrooms and suites have been added, reasonably priced in our **C** range. (With thanks once again to David Beardsmore.)

● **Discothèques**
La Nuit, in *Hotel Matum*; *El Alcazar*, in basement of *El Gran Almirante* hotel; *La Mansión*, Autopista Duarte, *La Antorcha*, 27 Febrero 58; and *Las Vegas*, Autopista Navarrete Km 9, all modern. *Champion Palace* is a huge disco for 2,000 people, open daily.

● **Shopping**
The Mercado Modelo Turístico is at Calle Del Sol and Avenida España. Cheap amber at Calle El Sol 60, rec. Outside town, on the main road N and S, are many potteries where ceramics can be bought very cheaply (how you get them home is another matter).

● **Services**
Banks: Scotiabank on Parque Duarte, others on El Sol between San Luis and Sánchez. Post office on the corner of El Sol and San Luis. Beware of the moneychangers outside: reports of short-changing have been received. **Telephones:** Codetel is at the junction of Estrella Sadhalá and J P Duarte; take Carro A from the Parque.

● **Tourist Information**
There is a Tourist Office in the basement of the Town Hall (Ayuntamiento), Av Juan Pablo Duarte; it has little information available, only Spanish spoken.

● **City Transport**
All *carros públicos* have a letter indicating which route they are on, eg M runs on E Sadhalá to the Autopista Duarte roundabout; *carros* cost US$0.20, a *motoconcho* US$0.15 and an *autobus* US$25. Many congregate at El Sol y 30 de Marzo on Parque Duarte.

● **Buses**
Guagua to La Vega US$2 from the roundabout where Autopista Duarte joins Estrella Sadhalá. Caribe Tours (Av Sadhalá y Calle 10, T 583-9197) bus to Puerto Plata US$4.15; it is easier to take Caribe Tours than Metro to Puerto Plata or the capital because Metro only takes passengers on standby on their Santo Domingo-Puerto Plata route. Metro terminal Maimón y Duarte, T 582-9111, a block or so towards the centre on Duarte from the roundabout at E Sadhalá (opposite direction from Codetel); 6 buses daily Santo Domingo-Santiago. Línea Gladys, Calle Las Carreras 57, opp Pan de Moca Rosaura, leaves 1300 Mon-Sat for Samaná via La Vega, arrives about 1630, T 582-2134. *Guaguas* to Moca leave from Autopista Duarte, near intersection with Av Estrella Sadhalá. *Guaguas* to San José de las Matas leave from the Puente Hermanos Patiño, by the river not far from the centre, US$1.50. Transporte del Cibao, Restauración casi esquina J P Duarte, runs buses up to Dajabón in the NW near the Haitian border, 2½ hrs, US$2.30. For other services see **Information for travellers**.

EXCURSIONS FROM SANTIAGO DE LOS CABALLEROS

An interesting day trip is to **Moca**, E of Santiago, which is a coffee and cacao centre and one of the richer regions of the country. The Iglesia Corazón de Jesús dominates the town; the tower can be climbed. The view is well worth the recommended US$1 tip to the church official. Tourist information may be found at the Town Hall at the corner of Independencia and Antonio de la Maza. It is not recommended that you stay the night, there is only one hotel, *La Niza*, on J P Duarte towards Santiago, which does not charge by the hour.

Outside Moca on the road towards the Autopista Duarte, lies **El Higüerito** where they make faceless dolls. Every shack is a doll factory and you can bargain for better prices than in Santo Domingo or Puerto Plata. The road leading from Moca to Sabaneta on the coast is extremely beautiful, winding through lush green hills. At the crest of the hillside, about halfway between Moca and Sabaneta is a lovely restaurant called *El Molino*, "it has the most glorious chicken crêpes and a view to match, don't forget your camera". (The restaurant *Vista del Cumbre*, higher up the hill, is not as good.) You can go from Moca to Sosúa by *guaguas*, changing at the Cruce de Veragua/Sabaneta. A very recommendable trip with a magnificent view from the summit just before you cross over the mountains, of Santiago, Moca and even La Vega. The scenery is so good it is worth taking a taxi (eg US$15 to Sabaneta, rather than squashing into a *guagua*. Metrobus has buses Santo Domingo-Moca twice daily, via La Vega (T Moca 578-2541).

San José de las Matas

To the SW of Santiago is the pleasant, mountain town of **San José de las Matas**. It has tree-lined streets, mostly modern buildings and a breezy climate. Nearby are the *balnearios* (bathing spots) of Amina, Las Ventanas and Aguas Calientes, all about 5-6 km away. There is fishing in the Represa del Río Bao.

● **Accommodation**   **A2** *La Mansión*, T 581-0393/5 or Santo Domingo 221-2131, F 532-4494 (Occidental chain), 30 mins' walk from town, set in 12 sq km of pine woods, spacious rooms with fridge, a/c and heating, fully-equipped cabins with 2 or 3 rooms, restaurant with buffet meals, local food, plenty of salads, pool, very quiet, spa and health resort owned by Aveda of the USA with sauna, massage, gym, natural products; riding, mountain biking, walking excursions, trips to Santiago, Pico Duarte and the coast. In town, on the main square, *Oasis*, with disco, pizzería and ice creams. On the dual carriageway into town, **E** *Los Samanes*, T 578-8316, bath, basic, clean, local food in restaurant; nearby is *El Primitivo*. There are several restaurants and cafés.

Post Office is just uphill from *Oasis*; opp the post office is a path to a *mirador* with benches. Codetel at Padre Espinosa y Félix Saychuela.

● **Transport**   For Santiago transport congregates at the bottom end of the dual carriageway (carretera a Santiago), opp Texaco (another Texaco in town centre), US$1.50 via Jánico. If driving from Santiago, the best road goes via Jánico: after crossing the Puente Hermanos Patiño, turn immediately left through Bella Vista for Jánico. The road that is signed to San José de las Matas goes towards Mao. It is paved; after about 6 km an unsigned road turns left, going over the hills through Jaqui Picado, 31 km to the junction on the Jánico-San José road, 5 km before San José; lovely views, but a very rough route.

From **Jánico**, the site of Columbus' first inland fort, Santo Tomás, can be visited, although there are no remains to be seen, just a memorial stone and a flagpole in a beautiful meadow with palms, above a little river. In Jánico seek out a *motoconcho* driver who knows the way and pay about US$5 for the trip, up and down steep hills, along narrow paths and river beds. There is a small sign in Jánico on the road.

To the NW of Santiago a Highway runs through the Yaque del Norte valley to the Haitian border. One route to Haiti turns S to **Mao** (Hotels **D** *Cahoba*, T 572-3357, also *Céntrico*, T 572-2122, *San Pedro*, T 572-3134, *Marién*, T 525-3558) and continues through Sabaneta to the border town of Dajabón (see below). Instead of turning S to Mao, you can continue to **Montecristi**, a dusty little town at the western end of the republic's N coast. One can visit the house of Máximo Gómez, the Dominican patriot who played an important role in the struggle for Cuban independence and in the Dominican Restoration. Columbus rejected his original idea to make his first settlement here and the town was in fact founded in the 16th century, rebuilt in the 17th. In the 19th century it was a major port exporting agricultural produce. The town has an interesting old clock. Very near Montecristi is a peak named **El Morro** (in the national park) which has a beach (very rocky) at the foot of its E side. There are mangroves and turtles which can be seen in the clear water. The **Cayos Siete Hermanos**, a sanctuary for tropical birds, with white beaches, are a good excursion. There has been some destruction of the offshore reefs.

● **Accommodation** *Chic*, Benito Monción 44, T 579-2316; *Santa Clara*, Mayobanex 8, T 579-2307; *Cabañas Las Carabelas*, J Bolaños, T 579-2682. Restaurants: *La Taberna de Rafúa*, Duarte 84, T 579-2291; *Heladería y Pizzería Kendy*, Duarte 92, T 579-2386; *Mi Barrita*, Duarte 86, T 579-2487.

There is also a road S from Montecristi 34 km to **Dajabón**, opposite the Haitian town of Ouanaminthe. This border crossing is very straightforward and informal and gives easy access to Cap Haïtien and La Citadelle. Many willing guides and *motoconcho* drivers hang around and will take travellers between the border posts, but it is not far to walk. Caribe Tours run buses from Santo Domingo to Dajabón, several daily, via Santiago and Montecristi. If you want to join one of these buses in Santiago it may be full. Caribe Tours' terminal in Dajabón is 2 blocks straight, then 2 blocks right to the border post. South of Dajabón is the *balneario* at Loma de Cabrera, rec to visit if you are in the area.

At the town of Navarrete on the Santiago-Montecristi Highway, a road branches N, bifurcating at **Imbert** (where there is a cheese factory and a Codetel office; Cristina Clare, Calle Ezekiel Gallardo A78, rents a hut (*bohío*) at the rear of her house, F, she will cook for you).

LUPERON

The NE fork goes to Puerto Plata (see below), the NW road to the N coast at **Luperón**, which has fine beaches, suitable for water sports. It is also a good haven for yachts; the marina offers electricity and water connections for boats and there are several markets selling fish, meat and vegetables.

● **Accommodation**
A1 *Hotel Luperón Beach Resort*, in Casa Marina Luperón, T 581-4153, F 581-6262

(high season price), and *Hotel Luperón*, Calle Independencia, T 571-8125. **E** *La Morena*, Calle Juan P Duarte 103, opposite Esso station, near Codetel, with bath and fan. *Restaurant La Marina*, Independencia 47, T 571-8066, lunch and dinner, local specialities, credit cards accepted. Frequent electricity and water cuts here.

West of Luperón by a new road is **La Isabela**. Here, on his second voyage (1493), Columbus founded the first European town in the Americas, with the first *ayuntamiento* and court, and here was said the first mass. Only the layout of the town is visible. The restoration and archaeological excavation of La Isabela is being undertaken by the Dirección Nacional de Parques. There is a hotel by the ruins. To get there either take a tour from Puerto Plata, or take a *carro público* from Villanueva y Kundhard, Puerto Plata, to La Isabela village, US$3.50, then a *motoconcho* to the ruins, US$7.25 return including wait at ruins, a lovely trip. Martisant, T 585-7887, runs group tours for US$92.

Between La Isabela and Montecristi are the beaches of Punta Rucia at Estero Hondo. Besides the beaches there are mangroves and interesting flora and fauna. Lodging at **L1** *Hotel Discovery Bay*, T 685-0151/562-7475, F 686-6741, all inclusive, no children under 16, watersports and other activities provided.

PUERTO PLATA

Puerto Plata, the chief town on the Atlantic coast (which is also known as the Amber Coast) was founded by Ovando in 1502. It is 235 km from the capital. The older scenic road from Santiago to Puerto Plata is now in poor condition. The centre of town has many old, wooden houses, some new buildings and plenty of colour. A visit to the colonial **San Felipe** fortress, the oldest in the New World, at the end of the Malecón is recommended. Just 1,000m past Puerto Plata, you can catch a *teleférico* (cable car) to the summit of **Loma Isabel de Torres**, an elevation of 779m. There is a statue of Christ that looks out over all of Puerto Plata; it also houses craft shops, a café and there are botanical gardens with a lovely view of the coast and mountains. The fare is US$0.80, daily except Wednesday (when not closed for maintenance); or you can take your chances with horses, bikes or even a car, but be prepared, the road is impassable at some points. *Motoconcho* from town to *teleférico* US$1. The **Museum of Dominican Amber**, Duarte 61, houses a collection of rare amber; guided tours Mon-Fri 0900-1800, Sat-Sun 0900-1700, T 586- 2848, Amber Museum Shop at Playa Dorada Plaza. The mountains behind Puerto Plata contain the world's richest deposits of amber, which is a fossilized tree resin. The cathedral is worth a visit, as are the ruins of the Vieja Logia and the Parque Central. A new **Museum of Taino Art**, Beller y San Felipe, 1st floor above *artesanía* shops, only contains replicas, but is interesting (open daily, more replicas on sale in the shops below).

If you are led into a shop by a local boy, tour guide or taxi driver, you will more than likely be paying a hidden commission on the price of your purchase, even after you bargain. If you want a guide, call the Association of Official Tour Guides, on 586-2866. Fishing: contact Santiago Camps (T 586-2632) for equipment and boat hire. A tourist train, the Ambar Tour Train, runs (not on rails) from Playa Dorada Plaza to San Felipe fort, The Amber Museum, a rum factory, the Parque Central and gift shops, 3 times daily, US$11.50, 2½-hr trip, safe, tickets from Discount Plaza, *Heavens Hotel* (Playa Dorada), *Bayside Hill* (Costambar), *Sand Castle* (Sosúa), or T 586-4082.

To the W is the Costambar resort area, which has not been a success (*Bayside Hill Club*, Naco group, 9-hole golf course, beach, closed 1996 because of noise and soot from nearby power station) and Cofresí beach (several hotels, cabins, B pp and more at weekends). At the E end of town is Long Beach, 2 km from the centre, US$0.15 by bus, but it is crowded at weekends, rather dirty, and

it is best to be on your guard. Just E of Puerto Plata, 4 km from the airport, is the beach resort of **Playa Dorada** with an exceptional golf course, and other sporting facilities. The Playa Dorada Resort is an umbrella name for a complex of 14 large hotels. Already the resort has 3,319 rooms and there are plans to build many more. **Montellano**, to the E of Playa Dorada, about half way to Sosúa, is the town in which all the processing of sugar cane is done for the N coast. It is undeveloped as a tourist town, but there are tours of the cane processing plant. For the adventurous, it has a great discothèque called *Las Brisas*, on the river, that all the locals visit, especially on Sunday afternoons. A bottle of rum, bucket of ice and 2 colas will cost about US$4. The town is a bit primitive, but the disco is not; guaranteed to have a great time, dancing merengue, salsa and some American music.

Local information – Puerto Plata and Playa Dorada

● **Accommodation**

At Puerto Plata: **A1** *Puerto Plata Beach Resort and Casino*, the sort of place found in package tour brochures and so difficult to get in to, T 562-7475, F 566-2436, meals not included, B pp basic low season price. **A1-3** *Montemar*, short walk to seafront, Occidental group, PO Box 382, T 586-2800, F 586-2009, all facilities, taxi from centre US$5; **B** *Hostal Jimessón*, John F Kennedy 41, T 586-5131/364-2024, close to Parque Central, old colonial building, C-D low season, lobby furnished with antiques, clean, a/c, cold water, pleasant, no restaurant; **D** *Castilla*, with shower and fan, on José del Carmen Ariza in centre of town, T 586-2559, unhelpful staff, dirty, restaurant, not rec; around corner, and preferable is **D** *Atlántico*, 12 de Julio 24, T 586-2503, with bath, fan, mosquito net, clean, simple, colonial building, friendly, back rooms quiet, rec (almost opposite Caribe Tours bus terminal); *El Condado*, Av Circunvalación Sur, T 586-3255; **A3** *Puerto Plata Latin Quarter*, on sea front, modern, T 586-2588, F 586-1828, pool, good value in low season. **E** *Swedish Guest House*, Av Circunvalación Sur 15, T 586-5086, Krystyna Danielsson, 9 rooms with toilet and shower, garden, clean, backpackers welcome, rooms can be rented for long periods, decorated with Krystyna's beautiful appliqué work, opp Mercado San Luis, convenient for *guaguas*, close to hospital, good *pizzeria* almost next door. At Plaza Anacaona, 30 de Marzo 94-98, are **C** *Hotel /Restaurant El Indio*, T/F 586-1201, with breakfast and fan, clean, restaurant serves good breakfast and fish, rec, very good value, Mexican music on Sat; a patio with native plants, palm trees and hummingbirds; and a Red Cross emergency station. Ask for Pedro Brunschwiler (who speaks German, English and Spanish) if you want to go scuba diving, horse riding or on adventure trips. Plaza Anacaona's owner, Wolfgang Wirth (who also speaks German, English and Spanish) is very helpful; he is the founder of the Dominican Red Cross.

E *Pensión Ilra*, Calle Villanueva, T 586-2337, good food, friendly; **E** *Alfa*, with shower, pleasant but watch out for mosquitoes, friendly, safe, clean, T 586-2684; **E** *Andy's Guest House*, rec, one of many of similar price range, breakfast US$1 extra; some houses also available from US$22 a week. There are cheap hotels at Long Beach, but catering mostly for short stay.

At Playa Dorada: **L1-L2** *Jack Tar Village* hotel, prices fall to A3 pp low season, all inclusive, PO Box 368, T 586-3800/530-5817, F 586-4161, US style and US prices, casino; **L3** *Heavens*, full board (B pp basic low season price), PO Box 576, Playa Dorada, T 586-5250, F 686-6741, helpful and friendly staff, lots of activities around pool, *Andromeda Bar*, very popular disco, lots of excursions and trips; *Playa Dorada* (an Occidental hotel), PO Box 272, T 320-3988, prices start at **A2**, low season, casino; **A2** *Paradise Beach Resort*, formerly *Eurotel*, T 320-3663, F 320-4858 (**C** low season), also has a casino; *Dorado Naco*, PO Box 162, prices from A3 basic low season, T 586-2019; **L3-A1** *Villas Doradas Beach Resort* (also Occidental) 207 rooms, or 5 individual houses with kitchenettes, T 320-3000, F 320-4790 (low season); *Villas Caraibe*, *Playa Dorada Princess* (T 530-5871, B pp low season), **L3** *Flamenco* (T 320-5084, Occidental), *Puerto Plata Village* (T 320-4012, F 320-5113), and the newest resort, **L3-A3** *Playa Naco*, T 320-6226, touted as the most beautiful of all the hotels, it houses a fully-equipped fitness centre. Many establishments in Playa Dorada offer all inclusive accommodation; the average price for a room is over US$100. Contact the Asociación de Proprietarios de Hoteles y Condominios de Playa Dorada, T 320-3132, telex ITT 346-0360, F 320-5301.

● **Places To Eat**
The food is superb at all the main hotels; there is every variety of cuisine. In the Playa Dorada Shopping Mall is *Hemmingway's Café*, T 320-2230, good food and music, a/c, good service, fun at night and during the day. *Los Pinos*, international cuisine, T 586-3222; *De Armando*, in city centre, near Parque Central, expensive; *Pizzería Roma*, T 586-3904; *Roma II*, best pizza, Calle Beller; *Costa Brava*, 12 de Julio 31, Spanish, pleasant, guitarists; *La Carreta*, Calle Separación; *El Canario*, 12 de Julio; *Valter*, on Hermanas Mirabel, seafood and Italian specialities, good food and service (T 586-2329). *El Sombrero*, Playa Cofresí, Autopista Santiago-Puerto Plata; *Papillón*, Villas Cofresí, fine dining and atmosphere, moderately priced, 3 km from town in Royal Palm forest. Opp the baseball stadium is *Pizzería Internacional*. *Cafetería Los Bonilla*, La Javilla, good food, *merengue* music. *La Canasta*, 2 blocks N of main square, good for lunches; *Neptuno*, on the Malecón, T 586-4243, for good seafood; *Jardín Suizo*, on sea front, very good food; *Willy's Sportscenter*, also on sea front, good local dishes; *Español Pollo al Carbón*, for inexpensive and delicious roast chicken, on Calle Circunvalación. *Jade Garden*, in Villas Doradas Beach Resort, for Chinese food; *Otro Mundo*, Playa Dorada Commercial Plaza, for something different, has a mini-zoo with many tropical birds, offers free transport from and to your hotel, T 543-8019; *Eddy's Pub*, Av Colón, near harbour, American burgers. *Pepe Postre* bakery chain in Puerto Plata/Montellano area, good breads, yoghurt, etc. *El Cable*, *La Paella*, *Infratur* and the *Beach Club Restaurant*, all at Long Beach.

● **Discothèques**
Andromeda in *Heavens Hotel* (the most popular), *Charlie's* in *Jack Tar Village Casino* and *Crazy Moon* in *Paradise Beach Resort*; all three are popular and offer a mix of *merengue*, *salsa* and international pop music. All have cover charges, about US$2. *Tropimal* is very popular, good mix of locals and tourists, *merengue* music.

● **Casinos**
There are five casinos on the N coast. *Jack Tar Village*, *Playa Dorada Hotel*, *Paradise Beach Club*, *Playa Chiquita Resort* and *The Puerto Plata Beach Resort*. Only the last named is right in Puerto Plata, the other three are in the Playa

Dorada complex, and the *Playa Chiquita* is in Sosúa. The casinos feature black jack, craps, roulette and poker. *Playa Chiquita* offers baccarat and bingo, sessions played twice nightly at 1930 and 2230. Also a game called Caribbean poker, very popular, check the rules before you begin to play. There are slot machines but these can be played **only** in US dollars. If you play other games in US dollars, you win in US dollars, if you play in pesos, you win in pesos. Do not change your foreign money to pesos in the casino, the rate given is very unfavourable. *Jack Tar Village Casino* offers novices a one hour lesson in black jack or craps at 2130 nightly, free of charge.

● **Shopping**
The Playa Dorada Complex has the first real shopping mall on the N coast. Prices are slightly inflated, but the quality of all items, especially the locally-made ceramics, jewellery, and clothing, is superior to most sold by beach or street vendors. The mall includes a Benneton, a selection of Tiffany lamps and some very original jewellery. Souvenirs can also be bought on the beach, or in downtown Puerto Plata, where there is shop after shop to sell you trinkets.

● **Tourist Information**
There is a tourist office on the Malecón (No 20) which has plenty of useful information.

● **Useful Phone Numbers**
Police, 586-2331; Centro Médico Antera Mota, 586-2342; Codetel (telephone office) 586-3311, on J F Kennedy, half a block E of square; association of tourist guides, 586-2866; US consular agency, 586-3676.

● **Motorcycle Rental**
US$20-30 a day, from any rental agency. Make sure to lock your motorcycle or scooter, as bike theft is big business in the area and there is no theft insurance on motorbikes.

● **Local Transport**
Públicos in the city RD$3/US$0.25; *guaguas* RD$3/US$0.25; *carreras* US$3-4; *motoconchos*, US$0.20. *Carreras* from Puerto Plata to Playa Dorada, US$15 (tourists), US$5 (Dominicans); to Sosúa, see below; from the airport to Playa Dorada US$14 (have small change handy when taking a taxi, drivers often say they have none). Bus to Nagua, US$5.20, 3½ hrs. *Conchos* from Puerto Plata to Playa Dorada, US$0.10, *motoconchos* between US$0.35-1.

A *carro público* to/from the capital costs US$6, but is not the most comfortable way to travel. Metrobus (T 586-6062, Beller y 16 de Agosto), 4 a day, and Caribe Tours (T 586-4544, 12 de Julio y José Carmen Ariza in centre) run a/c coaches to/from Santo Domingo, 4 hrs (for fares see **Information for travellers**). To Samaná, there is a *guagua* daily at about 0500, passing Cabarete at 0600, 4½ hrs, US$7.75; at other times of day you have to change buses at least 3 times.

● **Airport**
Gregorio Luperón international airport, T 586-0219 serves the entire N coast. It is 20 mins from Puerto Plata, 7 mins from Sosúa and 15 from Cabarete. Taxi from airport to Puerto Plata or Cabarete US$19, to Sosúa US$9. Small bank at airport for exchange. Do not panic at the airport when approached by Dominicans in overalls attempting to take your bag. They are baggage handlers trying to make a living. Proper tipping is about US$2 per bag.

EAST TO SOSÚA AND THE NORTH COAST

28 km E of Puerto Plata is **Sosúa**, a little town that has a beautiful and lively 1 km beach, perfect for diving and water sports. There is a smaller public beach on the E side of town, referred to as the 'playita', where you will be less bothered by vendors. It is located by *Hotel Sosúa-by-the-Sea*. Sosúa is popular with Europeans, Americans and Canadians and is becoming increasingly busy and scruffy. The main street (correctly named Calle Pedro Clisante, but only ever referred to as Main Street, or Calle Principal in Spanish) is lined with all variety of shops, restaurants and bars. The unusual European atmosphere stems from the fact that the El Batey side of town (the side that houses most of the hotels and restaurants) was founded by German Jewish refugees who settled here in 1941. A synagogue and memorial building are open to the public. Although many of the original settlers have moved away, services are still held, and in 1991 a 50th year anniversary party brought settlers and their relatives from all over the world for a reunion. The original houses are now lost among the modern developments. The western end of the

Dominican Republic North Coast

0   20
km

town is referred to as Los Charamicos (the two ends are separated by the beach); this is the older side of town, where the Dominicans themselves generally live, shop and party.

Note Sosúa, although crowded with tourist spots, is a small town. Little or no attention is paid to street names or numbers. The quiet road between El Batey and Playa Chiquita should be treated with caution at night. Dress is very informal. Although it is considered impolite to wander the streets in bathing attire, dress for dinner at any location is comfortable and Caribbean.

Local information – Sosúa
● **Accommodation**
A2 *Casa Marina Beach Club*, T 571-3690, high season (B low), but special offers may be available, located on the Little Beach, pool, restaurant, excellent value. **A2** *Sosúa-by-the-Sea*, T 571-3222 (high season price), owned and operated by Austrian-Canadians, on Little Beach, immaculate, beautiful a/c rooms, good restaurant, pool, bar, includes breakfast and dinner (also sells timeshares); **A3** *Playa Chiquita Beach Resort*, T 571-2800 (**L3** full board), slightly out of the way, located on own private beach, good restaurant, accommodation and service, and casino, has shuttle to town and beach. **A3** *Corallilos*, unpretentious, perched on a cliff with breathtaking view of beach, B low season, T 571-2645; **B** *Auberge du Village*, Calle Dr Rosen 8, American-run guest house 5 mins walk from

beach, small pool, breakfast, rec, T 571-2569, F 571-2865 (postal address EPS – D #02-5548, Miami, FL 33102). **A2** *One Ocean Place*, El Batey, T 571-3131, restaurant, pool, 10 mins' walk to beach; *Hotel Sosúa*, T 571-2683, F 586-2442, in town centre, 3 mins from main beach, restaurant, pool, quiet; *Sandcastles Beach Resort*, T 530-5817/571-2420, F 571-2000, just outside Sosúa, private beach, restaurants, self-contained, shuttle buses into Sosúa, prices from A3 pp in double. **A3** *Charlie's Cabañas*, 27 cabins, quiet, tropical, ocean front pool, on a cliff overlooking the sea, 5 mins to beach, special rates for groups, T 571-2670; **A3-B** *Nuevo Sol*, T 571-2124, on main street; **A1-A3** *La Esplanada*, T 571-3333, Spanish owned, near casino; *Condos Carolina*, T 571-3626, units with kitchen and sitting room, 1 and 2 bedrooms, variable prices; *Coconut Palms Resort*, T 571-1625, F 571-1725, beautiful resort, scenic hilltop view, 8 km outside Sosúa, all units with kitchen facilities, shuttle bus to town and beach, variable rates. For the budget-minded (prices **B-D** depending on season): *Jardín del Sol*, T/F 571-3553, family-run, clean, pool, near town; *Margaritaville*, T/F 571-3553, on hilltop, clean, scenic, shuttle to town; **B** *Tropix*, T 571-2291 (address: EPS-D#274, Box 02-5548, Miami, FL 33103), near centre of town, clean, some traffic noise, beautiful pool and landscaped beautiful garden, impeccable service, good food, use of kitchen facilities, rec. **C** *Koch's Guest House*, El Batey, use of kitchen, breakfast extra. There are many other hotels, guest houses and villas for rent, ask around locally. Try in Los Cerros for rooms to rent, from F to C. If you are looking for a place to stay for longer than the average charter flight, or would like to get a group together to stay in a house, or have any questions regarding rentals in the Sosúa/Cabarete area, call *Sosúa Central Rental*, T/F 571-3648.

● **Places to eat**
On the Waterfront, excellent food and a spectacular sunset overlooking the sea, all-you-can-eat barbeque on Fri night, pleasant entertainment nightly in *Charlie's Cabañas Hotel*, on the lookout point, down from the Codetel offices, T 571-3024; *The Spaghetti House*, Main Street, terrific pasta meals (especially for garlic lovers), reasonable prices, no reservations necessary, special pizza ovens; *Don Juan*, in centre of Main Street, Spanish food, *paella*, excellent seafood, tables on the boulevard; *Marco Polo Club*, La Puntilla, overlooking Sosúa beach, Italian, or set-price, 6-course French meal, great view, antipasto buffet table, T 571-3128; *El Destino*, on City Hall Street (Calle Ayuntamiento, follow the Clock Tower), vegetarian, owners read palms or cards for you with dinner, or make an appointment for a full reading; *Pavillion*, also on Calle Ayuntamiento, great European food, steaks, salad bar, and an ice cream crêpe, worth the walk, follow the signs for it all over town; *Caribbean*, Main Street, glassed-in, a/c, lovely atmosphere, good European and Caribbean cuisine. *Caribae*, seafood specialities, organically grown vegetables and a shrimp farm on the premises, El Mirador hill; *Tropix*, homestyle cooking, one special per night, friendly, tranquil, check hotels for weekly menu listings, T 571-2291 for reservations. Fast Food: *Sammy's*, good burgers and good chicken wings, in the heart of Sosúa, where the locals meet to see and be seen; *PJ's International*, satisfying breakfasts, terrific chef's salad and schnitzel burger for lunch, on corner of Main Street; *Dundee's Burgers*, Calle Alejo Martínez, in front-of-school yard, open 1900-0700, the place to go after a night of revelling, Dundee, the American-Dominican owner, is a local fixture. *Hotel Sosúa-by-the-Sea* serves the best value buffet breakfast in town. For delicious baked products go to the *German Bakery (Panadería Alemán)*, in Villas Ana María, residential area. *The Big Squeeze* makes fresh juices out of all and any fruits and vegetables, inexpensive, delicious, on City Hall Street.

● **Bars And Nightclubs**
Tree Top Lounge, Main Street, 2nd floor, British-owned, pub atmosphere, has lots of games (backgammon, cards, scrabble, etc), rec. *Casablanca*, on Main Street, great place for dancing and partying, mostly American music. *La Roca*, last spot on Main Street before the beach, Sosúa's oldest bar/disco/eatery, beautiful decor, comfy couches, good food and music; *Moby Dick Disco*, by far the most popular disco, a/c, cover charge. *Barock* and *Pyramide* both in the same building at the corner of Calle Dr Rosen and Main Street, dancing until the small hours. *Tropic Disco*, on rooftop of Plaza del Fuente, biliard table, darts board, dance floor, good sound system; *Marinero*, Main Street, ground floor, local entertainment.

● **Services**
Codetel, Calle Dr Alejo Martínez, near corner with Dr Rosen. Next to the bank on the small square at Calle Dr Martínez and Duarte is the *Viva Art Gallery*. Sosúa Business Services, for all typing, faxing, phoning, photocopying needs, on Main Street, upstairs from *Casablanca Bar*, T 571-3452. *Salón Tres Hermanas*, Av Pedro Clisante 31, El Batey, very friendly hairdressers, does plaiting, uses natural cosmetics, helpful with sunburn.

● **Police**
T 571-2293.

● **Transport**
A *público* from Puerto Plata costs US$4, a taxi will cost about US$15.50 and is far more comfortable. *Guaguas*, overcrowded minibuses, charge about US$1.30 and leave Puerto Plata's main square or, more frequently, from the hospital on Circunvalación Sur (Caribe Tours charge US$1.60). In Sosúa, transport congregates by the Texaco station and the junction of Calle Dr Rosen and the Carretera. The most popular form of transportation within Sosúa is *motoconcho* (motorcycle taxi), pay 6 pesos during the daylight hours and 12 pesos at night, pp, to anywhere in town. A *concho* (car) costs RD$3/US$0.25; *carreras* US$3.75-5. For organized tours by plane to Haiti, Samaná, Turks and Caicos, Santo Domingo, contact Columbus Air, T 571-2711 or 586-6991. Car and bike rentals are everywhere, shop around for prices, and once again be cautioned as to theft (eg Asociación de Renta Moto Sosúa Cabarete, US$28-35 for 1-2 days, US$5-7.25 hourly, depending on type).

Several places do horse riding tours, but make sure that the group is not too large, they can be as big as 40 riders, which is not much fun.

CABARETE

12 km E of Sosúa is **Cabarete**, nowadays the windsurf capital of the world, having hosted the World Windsurf Championship. International competitions are held annually in June (see **Beaches and Watersports**). The 2 km curving bay has a strip of hotels and guest houses catering for windsurfers' needs. Conditions vary according to season: in summer there are constant trade winds but few waves, in winter there are days with no wind, but when it comes the waves are tremendous. February and March are the best months, November and December are the worst. Boards rent for US$40/day, US$195/week, with variations, make sure insurance is available. The main places are *MB*, at *Auberge du Roi Tropical* (headquarters of the championship organizers, see below), T 571-0957; *Carib BIC*, T 586-9519, F 586-9529; Nathalie Simon; and others. There are many kilometres of white sand beach lined with coconut palms and a lagoon with many waterbirds, and waterskiing. Taxi fares: Cabarete-Sosúa US$8.25 (*guagua* US$0.50-1), airport US$20, Puerto Plata US$25.

● **Accommodation & places to eat** **L3** *Punta Goleta Beach Resort* for package tours (PO Box 272, Puerto Plata, T 535-4941, basic price, full board). Another development is *Camino del Sol*, T 571-2858, E of the town. **A2** *Auberge du Roi Tropical*, T 571-0770, F 571-0680, popular, *MB* windsurf centre, mountain bikes, pool. Opposite is **A1-2** *Casa Laguna*, T 571-0725, **A3-B** in low season; **A2** *Cita del Sol*, T 571-0720, B in low season, French Canadian, *P'tit Quebec* restaurant; **B** *Kaoba*, T 571-0837, F 571-0879, with fan and hot water, reductions for over 2 weeks, bungalows, good value, separate restaurant for breakfast and evening meal; these three are across the road from the beach. Similarly, **B-C** *Banana Boat Motel*, T 571-0690, F 571-3346, quiet, central, kitchen facilities, laundry, rec. On beach, **L3-B** *Cabarete Beach Hotel*, T 571-0755, F 571-0831, good buffet breakfast, *Mariposa* restaurant. **B** *GiGi Beach*, at

Sosúa end of town, T 571-0722, with fan, no restaurant, windsurf shop. **C** *Casa Blanca*, T/F 571-0934, on main road, sea view, opp Rent-a-Moto, 9 rooms, 7 apartments with kitchenette, clean, friendly; **C** *Caribe Surf*, at end of beach, owned by Swiss, Teddy Muller, new, modern, clean, reasonably priced; 100m away, *Chez Michel* restaurant offers full breakfast for US$3 and full gourmet evening meal for US$7.50. There are many more hotels and rooms for rent, just ask around when you arrive. Note that many places charge much more for 'walk-in' customers than for tour groups. Cabarete has many restaurants, eg *Julio's*, *Casa del Pescador*, most specializing in fast food and with views of the beach.

RIO SAN JUAN

On the NE coast, **Río San Juan**, is a friendly town with a lagoon called Gri-Grí (*guagua* from Sosúa US$3.10, 1¼ hrs, may have to change in Gaspar Hernández). Boats take visitors through the mangrove forests and to see caves and rocks, and to the natural swimming pool called the Cueva de las Golondrinas (US$16 without swim, US$24 with swim, US$1.60 pp if more than 10 people). Also worth visiting from the town is Puerto Escondido beach. You can walk beyond *Hotel Bahía Blanca* between mangroves and the sea to the mouth of Gri-Grí, many birds in the mangroves.

● **Accommodation & places to eat** Nicest hotel is **A2-B** *Bahía Blanca*, T 589-2563, F 589-2528, lovely location right on the sea, clean, lots of balconies, some meals included; next best is *Río San Juan*, on main street, Duarte, at brow of hill, T 589-2379/2211, many price variations from C, a/c, disco, pool, good restaurant and there is a good pizzeria, *Cachalotte*, opp (the hotel offers boat trips on the lagoon). **D** *Santa Clara*, Padre Billini y Capotillo, opp Mini Market, with bath and fan, F without; **F** *San Martín*, friendly but very dirty. *Cheo's Café Bar*, Padre Billini, casi Libertad, pizzas, seafood, meat; *Bar/Restaurant La Casona*, fish and creole food, good value, friendly, purified drinking water, near Laguna Gri-Grí; several other eating places, mostly *pizzerias*.

Transport stops at the junction of Duarte and the main road.

Further to the E is **Playa Grande**, 60 km from Puerto Plata, another beautiful new resort which is being developed, in conjunction with Playa Dorada, at a cost of many millions of dollars (lots of hawkers on the beach). The many tour companies in Sosúa offer tours to Gri-Grí and Playa Grande. 5 km E of Playa Grande is *Club Paradise*, T (813)949-9327, F (813)949-1008, a 'clothing optional' resort, with beautiful, secluded beaches, self-sufficient complex, watersports and entertainment.

Between Río San Juan and Samaná, the coast road runs through Cabrera to **Nagua**, a dirty fishing village on the shores of the Bahía Escocesa. Several small and medium-sized hotels: *Hotel San Carlos*; *Hotel Corazón de Jesús*; B *Hotel Carib Caban*, 8 km S of Nagua, studio (less in smaller room), pleasant, directly on beach, restaurant with Austrian food (hire a motorcycle to get there, US$2, T 584-3145). Puerto Plata-Nagua, three buses, 3½ hrs, US$5.20; Nagua-Santo Domingo, 3½ hrs, US$4 (Metrobus, T 584-2177, twice a day); Río San Juan-Nagua, US$3.10, Nagua-Samaná also US$3.10.

The scenery along the N coast from Sosúa to Samaná is exceptionally beautiful. The road has been repaved all the way from Sosúa to Samaná. **Sánchez** is a pleasant, unspoilt little place with some basic accommodation. Much of the architecture is 19th century. It was at one time a prosperous sea port and had a railway which ran to San Francisco de Macorís and La Vega. Bus Santo Domingo-Sánchez, Caribe Tours 3 a day, US$5.

THE SAMANÁ PENINSULA

On the peninsula of **Samaná** is the city of the same name. Columbus arrived here on 12 January 1493, but was so fiercely repelled by the Ciguayo Indians that he called the bay the Golfo de las Flechas (the Gulf of Arrows). Samaná Bay, as it is now called, is very picturesque, fringed with coconut palms and studded with islets. The present town of Santa Bárbara de Samaná was founded in 1756 by families expressly brought from the Canary Islands. The city, reconstructed after being devastated by fire in 1946, shows no evidence of this past, with its modern Catholic church, broad streets, new restaurants and hotels, and noisy motorcycle taxis. In contrast to the Catholic church, and overlooking it, is a more traditional Protestant church, white with red corrugated-iron roofing, nicknamed locally 'La Churcha'. Traditional dances, such as *bambulá* and the *chivo florete* can be seen at local festivals (4 December, the patron saint's day; 24 October, San Rafael). An airport for the peninsula is at Arroyo Barril (8 km from town, good road, but only 25 mins' flying time from Santo Domingo), which is being upgraded to take international traffic. Many Caribbean-cruising yachts anchor at Samaná, taking advantage of the calm waters.

Humpback whales return to Samaná Bay every year between December and March to mate and calve. Various tours go whale-watching (some are given under **Excursions** below), certainly worthwhile if you are in the area at that time of year.

Local information – Samaná
● **Accommodation**

L2 *Gran Bahía*, T 562-6271, F 562-5232, 96-room, charming luxury resort on coast road, 10 mins, 8 km E of town, all facilities available, C pp low season, small beach, good food and service, compact golf course, water sports, shuttle service to Cayo Levantado; **L2-A2** *Hotel Cayo Levantado*, on the island, 10 mins by boat from Samaná, white beaches, 28 rooms, 4 *cabañas*, restaurant, beach bar, T 223-8704, F 538-2985; **B** pp and up *Cayacoa*, T 538-2426, F 538-2985, on a hill overlooking the town, view of the bay, beautiful gardens, watersports, very nice; **B** *Tropical Lodge*, on Malecón, T 538-2480, 8 rooms, basic but clean; **C** *Nilka*, Santa Bárbara y Colón, T 538-2244, 10 rooms, with a/c (cheaper with fan), all with bath, popular; *Guest House Alcide*, T 538-2512; *Cocoloco*, near rotunda, T 240-6068, 6 rooms, clean, helpful German owner, who is also a guide to the National Park, good barbecue;

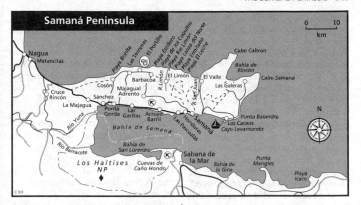

B *Cotubanamá*, T 538-2557, excellent, breakfast US$3, good value. There are other hotels, eg *King*, T 538-2404, *Casa de Huéspedes*, T 538-2475 and *Ursula*, T 538-2402.

● **Places to eat**
Going E along the Malecón: *Típico El Coco*, *L'Hacienda*, T 538-2383, grill and bar; *Le Café de Paris*, pizzeria, good crêperie, cocktails, loud music; *La Mata Rosada*, *Camilo* (on corner of Parque), local and not-so-local food, reasonable (takes credit cards). Also on Malecón: *La France*, T 538-2257, French owned, excellent, highly rec; *Samaná Sam's Saloon*, No 5, almost opp. *Morgan's*, on roundabout near the market place, run by American Wally, good value, good for local information. Chinese restaurant on the hill, excellent. At the dock, *El Marino* and *La Serena*.

The local cuisine is highly regarded, especially the fish and coconut dishes.

● **Other Services**
Petrol station at the dock, open 0700-2200. Banco Hispano Dominicano on Malecón. Banco del Cambio, behind Samaná Tours, changes cheques. Banco del Comercio gives cash against Visa, 5% commission, open 0830-1500 Mon-Fri. Post Office behind *Camilo*, just off Parque; Codetel, Calle Santa Bárbara, 0800-2200 daily. Tourist information at Richard Tours at *Samaná Sam's* and Samaná Information Service, T 538-2451; both on Malecón, and closed out of season; also Samaná Tours, good maps and information, closed Sunday; alternatively, T 538-2219, or 538-2206 (Ayuntamiento), or 538-2210 (provincial government).

● **Transport**
Concho or *guagua* in town RD$3/US$0.25; *carreras* US$3.50-4. From the capital either by bus direct, 4½ hrs via *San Francisco de Macorís* (10-min stop by a park with trees whose trunks are painted red, white and blue, **F** *Hotel Joya*, near Plaza Mayor, quiet, clean, friendly), Nagua and Sánchez (return bus to capital, Caribe Tours on Malecón, 2-3 a day each direction; Metrobus, T 538-2851, leaves Santo Domingo 0700 daily, returns from Samaná 1400), or by bus or *público* to San Pedro de Macorís, then another to **Sabana de la Mar** (**D** *Hotel Villa Suiza*, pool, run down; **E** *Hotel Brisas de la Bahía*), and cross by boat (foot passengers only, 5 return trips a day, US$2.10 one way, beware overcharging of tourists) from Sabana to Samaná at 0900, 1100, 1430, 1500, 1700 (safety conditions leave something to be desired). To Santiago, Línea Gladys, bus leaves 0715 Mon-Sat from farmers' market, arrives 1100, fills up on way to Sánchez, will stop in La Vega on request. The road from Sabana de la Mar to Hato Mayor is good, the scenery beautiful, and from Hato Mayor to San Pedro de Macorís (see below) it is also good.

EXCURSIONS FROM SAMANÁ

There are several beautiful offshore islands. **Cayo Levantado** is a popular picnic place, especially at weekends when the beach is packed. The white sand beach is nice, though, and there are good views of the bay and the peninsulas on either side. There is a hotel on the island;

good drinks and fish lunches are for sale. Public boats go there from the dock in Samaná (US$4 return, buy ticket at Malecón No 3, not from the hustlers on the pier, 2-4 trips daily outward 0900-1100, return 1500-1700); alternatively, take a *público* or *motoconcho* 8 km out of town to Los Cacaos (US$3) to where two companies, Transportes José and Simi Báez, run boats to the island and will pick you up later for US$10-15 (the latter company also does fishing and whale-spotting trips). Tours with Santo Domingo agencies range from US$61.50 (Turinter, Insular) to US$77 (Martisant).

At the eastern end of the peninsula is **Playa Galeras**, 26 km (1 hr, US$1.50 by *guagua*), worth a visit. The 1 km beach is framed by the dark rock cliffs and forested mountains of Cape Samaná and Cape Cabrón.

● **Accommodation**

Villa Serena, next to the shore, T 223-8703, F 538-2545, Canadian-owned, 11 rooms, private terrace overlooking sea, a/c and fans, gourmet restaurant, tours organized; *Marea Beach*, French-owned, T 538-2545 and **B** *La Marinique*; several fish restaurants, good atmosphere. The area will soon be dominated by the *Cala Blanca* resort development, with time share apartments and plans for golf courses, sports centres etc.

20 minutes away by boat, or 40 minutes by jeep along a very rough track is the deserted Playa Rincón, dominated by the cliffs of 600m high Cape Cabrón. The whole peninsula is beautiful, but many beaches are accessible only by boat (and the Samaná boatmen charge the earth). Others are reached by a dirt road, negotiable by ordinary cars. Check locally before swimming at deserted beaches where there can be strong surf and an undertow. Drownings have occurred near El Valle.

Visits to the **Parque Nacional de Haitises**, across the bay, can be arranged by launch for US$60, US$15 from Samaná, eg *Hotel Cayacoa* or from Sabana de la Mar, or ask at Samaná Tourist Information; various companies organize tours to Los Haitises and to caves in the area (eg Ecoturisa, see under Santo Domingo; Martisant, T 585-7887, US$38.50, others, eg Turinter, Prieto, T 685-0102, Insular, US$61.50; in Sabana de la Mar, Juan Julio Rodríguez, Calle Duvergé 24, or at the pier, offers trips to Los Haitises and to see whales). The DNP, from whom permits must be obtained, also organizes tours; see above, **Flora and Fauna**. Tour companies and boat owners organize whale-watching trips from mid-January to March, from about US$25 pp, an incredible experience. For reputable tour guides and people who care about the regulations which prevent boats from disturbing the whales too much, phone Kim Beddall, T 538-2494, owner of *Victoria II*, concise, interesting, friendly tours.

LAS TERRENAS

On the N coast of the peninsula is **Las Terrenas**, with some of the finest beaches in the country, from which, at low tide, you can walk out to coral reefs to see abundant sea life. The region is frequently visited by divers, drawn by its excellent reefs, sponges and underwater caves. Insect repellent is necessary at dawn and dusk to combat the sandflies. Many people go there by private plane, but it is reachable by a newly-paved 17 km road from Sánchez which zig-zags steeply up to a height of 450m with wonderful views before dropping down to the N coast. The road Samaná-Las Terrenas is being paved (mid-1995) and is due for completion in 1996. Las Terrenas village is developing rapidly to cope with the influx of tourists: the wooden houses are being replaced by concrete ones; in high season (November-January, July-August) there is a lot of traffic noise; the beaches, except Playa Bonita, are crowded and hawkers sell their wares to the visitors, but they are mostly clean and remain beautiful. Out of season it is very pleasant. Horseriding can be arranged through *El Portillo* or *Trópico Banana* (Frank Hofenbrect's stables) on healthy, well-schooled animals, for beach or mountain rides.

Local information – Las Terrenas
● **Accommodation**

Most hotels are small; those on the beach have prices ranging up to **A2**, but those in town or behind those on the beach can be very cheap. **A3** *Trópico Banana*, T 240-6110, 25 rooms, breakfast inc, tennis, pool, fans, screened windows, balconies, one of the larger guesthouses, good value food, popular bar with live merengue nightly; **A3** *Isla Bonita*, Western end, near *Trópico Banana* on beach, 8 rooms, clean, good view, very good restaurant, Italian chef, hotel rooms may close, check by fax to Codetel, F 240-6070. On Playa Bonita (see below) are **A2-A3** *Atlantis*, T 240-6111, F 240-6205, breakfast inc, restaurant serves Dominican food; **B** *Punta Bonita Cabañas*, T 240-6011 and **B** *Acaya*, nice atmosphere, good breakfast and restaurant, recommended; *Palo Coco*, on main road at entrance to Las Terrenas, expensive, good. **B** *La Hacienda*, beautiful gardens, balcony, bath, view, kitchen facilities; **B** *Kanesh*, at end of W track to beach, new, run by friendly Sri Lankans, inc excellent breakfast, some rooms cheaper, rec. *Cacao Beach*, 190 rooms, biggest hotel, T 530-5817, E of *Trópico Banana*, prices from B (low season, inc 2 meals), sailing boats for rent; *Plantation Club*, E of *Cacao Beach*, price inc 3 meals and drinks, and, similar, **A2** *El Portillo*, 5 km E of cemetery, T 240-6100, cabins, no a/c, secluded, used by Spanish package holidays, own airstrip, good snorkelling, watersports, tennis, horseriding, bicycles, entertainment, 100 rooms in large grounds on huge beach, uncrowded, all-inclusive; all 3 are on beach and have swimming pools. **C-E** *L'Aubergine*, T 240-6167, F 240-6070, price depends on room and number of people, run by French Canadians, near *Cacao* and beach, very good, restaurant closed Sunday; **B-D** *Villa Caracol*, along from *L'Aubergine*, clean, friendly, quiet; **C** *Papagayo*, on beach road, good, bath, clean, fans, screened windows, breakfast inc, small bar and restaurant; **C** *Casa Robinson*, next door, F 240-6070 at Codetel, small suites with kitchenettes and balconies; **C** *Los Pinos*, Swiss run, family atmosphere, clean, excellent, huge breakfast, helpful; *Cabañas La Esmeralda*, on beach just W of cemetery, similar price range. **D-E** *Dinny*, on the beach, clean, central, noisy, near the main junction, ask for quieter room away from road. Ask for Doña Nina, turn right for 800m along the beach in Las Terrenas, basic cabins F, very friendly, but insecure. Each hotel has its own electricity generator and water supply.

● **Places To Eat**

Chez Paco, French, very good; the best Spanish restaurant is in *Hotel Palo Coco*; the best Italian is in *La Isla Bonita* in a garden setting; the best German is *El Colibrí*, which also serves good beef (next to *Hotel Cacao Beach*); *Restaurante Canne à Sucre*, on beach W of cemetery, tasty pastas and crêpes; *Pizza Coca*, good, back of *Hotel Atlantis*; *Cocoloco*, cheap langosta; *Chez Sarah*, French specialities from Guadeloupe and Martinique, delicious; *Dinny* serves excellent breakfast with *jugos* and lots of fresh fruit; *Casa Azul*, Spanish run, sandwiches, salads, Spanish tortilla, hamburgers, good for lunch or dinner, on beach by main junction; *La Salsa*, thatched roof restaurant on the beach near *Trópico Banana*, French-owned, grilled meats with little dishes of different sauces, also very good seafood, large portions, inexpensive, rec for food and service; *Mami*, on the main road, créole food, cheap, rec; *Louisianne*, small café run by Austrians, lovely spot, does a fine sandwich. At the point between Playas Bonita and Cosón (see below) is *Queenie's*, owned by Reyna, who serves excellent meals, good value, friendly, rec. Small places along main street may have only 1-2 items on menu but food is usually good and much cheaper than a restaurant. Popular disco is *Mambo Bar*, next to *Papagayo*, open weekends only.

● **Services**

For tourist information and hotel booking service go to *Sunshine Services*, Calle del Carmen, T/F 240-6164, run by Germans/Swiss; Spanish, English, German, French and Italian spoken. Lots of information and help, also car, bicycle and motorbike rental, excursions, fishing trips. *Agencia de Viajes Vimenca*, Remeses Vimenca, on the main road, exchanges money at the best rates in town. Codetel has a phone and fax office. Supermarket Frank will change dollars cash and TCs. In many shops they sell 'express' stamps which are more expensive but the delivery time is not much shorter. There is a petrol/gasoline station. Motorbikes and mountain bikes can be hired.

● **Watersports**

The *Cacao Beach* rents sailboats. There are several dive shops, inc at *Trópico Banana*, T 589-9410, courses available. *Las Ballenas* restaurant rents ocean going kayaks and other craft at W end of beach. Windsurfing and sailing are mostly only available at the all-inclusive resorts.

● **How To Get There**
Guagua Samaná-Sánchez US$1.50, then another to Las Terrenas, US$1.25, or taxi US$30 (or hire a motorbike in Samaná, US$25/day, the roads are suitable). Bus from Santo Domingo, Calle Juan B Vicini 133, opp Huacalito, 1400, 5 hrs, US$5; Las Terrenas-Santo Domingo at 0630; alternatively go via Sánchez; to Puerto Plata at 0700. Note that *guaguas* which meet arriving Caribe Tours buses in Sánchez overcharge for the journey to Las Terrenas (US$4.75-9.50); instead take a *motoconcho* for US$0.50 to the *guagua* stop in the heart of the town and negotiate for a fare of US$1.10-1.50. You can get along the coast from Cabarete to Las Terrenas via Río San Juan, Nagua and Sánchez, US$1.50 for each stage by *guagua*.

Where the road reaches the shore, at the cemetery in Las Terrenas village, a left turn takes you along a sandy track that winds between coconut palms alongside the white sand beach for about 5 km, past many French and Italian-run guesthouses and restaurants. At the end of the beach, walk behind a rocky promontory to reach Playa Bonita, with hotels, guesthouses and restaurants; there are apartments beside *Hotel Atlantis*. Beyond the western tip of this beach is the deserted Playa Cosón, a magnificent 6 km arc of white sand and coconut groves ending in steep wooded cliffs (1½ hr walk or US$1 on *motoconcho*), an Italian development is planned here. A right turn at Las Terrenas takes you along a potholed road about 4 km to the largest hotel in the area, *El Portillo* (see above). 10 km further on is **El Limón**, a farming village on the road across the peninsula to Samaná. From El Limón you can hike for an hour into the hills to a 50m high waterfall and swim in a pool of green water at its foot. Behind the falls is a small cave. The landscape between the village and the falls is beautiful, with many different fruits growing in the woods. If taking a guide to the falls, fix the price in advance (the falls can be deserted, do not take valuables there). *Motoconcho* Las Terrenas – El Limón US$2.50, but they will try to charge

US$5-10. Motorcycles can be hired in Las Terrenas for US$15-20/day, also bicycles, but they have no brakes.

EAST FROM SANTO DOMINGO

BOCA CHICA

About 25 km E of Santo Domingo is the beach of **Boca Chica**, the principal resort for the capital. It is a reef-protected shallow lagoon, with many kilometres of white sand. Offshore are the islands of La Matica and Piños. Tourist development has been intensive and, at weekends, the place is invaded by the citizens of Santo Domingo (and by attendant hawkers, disreputables and prostitutes). There are a great many hotels, aparthotels and restaurants but the centre is rather seedy and charmless. It is worth considering staying here if arriving at the airport late at night, rather than looking for a hotel in the capital. Prices are generally higher here than at the N coast resorts. At the W end of the beach is the marina of the Santo Domingo Club Náutico (see above, **Beaches and Watersports**). A few km SW of Boca Chica is La Caleta, with a small, often rough beach. It is right by the airport. Here is La Caleta Archaeological Museum, see under Santo Domingo.

Local information – Boca Chica
● **Accommodation**
A2 *Boca Chica Beach Resort*, T 563-2200; **A1-2** *Sun Set*, T 523-4580, F 523-4975; **L1-3** *Hotel Hamaca*, T 523-4611, F 523-6767, PO Box 2973, Santo Domingo, 5-star, vast resort hotel; on same road as *Sun Set* and *Hamaca* (Calle Duarte at eastern end of town) is **B** *Mesón Isabela*, T 523-4224, F 523-4136, in room, more in apartment without tax, French-Canadian and Dominican owned, bar, pool, family atmosphere, quiet, personal service, breakfast, light lunches on request, access to private beach, cookers in some rooms; next door is **B** *Neptuno's Club Guest House* (for restaurant, see below), with bath, free coffee, very satisfactory. **B-C** *La Belle*, Calle Juan Bautista Vicini 9, T 523-5959, F 523-5077, on corner of highway, very nice, a/c, pool, colour TV, permanent water and electricity. **B** *Villa Sans*

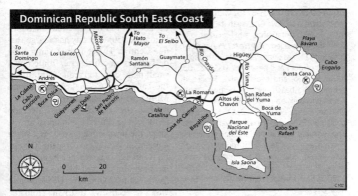

Dominican Republic South East Coast

Soucy, Juan Batista Vicini 48, T 523-4461, F 523-4136, with tax, clean, beautiful, pool, restaurant, bar, rec; opp is **C** *Mozart*, rooms remodelled but airless, friendly; **B** and up *Las Kasistas del Sol*, Primera y 2 de Junio, away from beach, T 523-4386, F 523-6056, pool, restaurant, clean, beautiful setting, good service, friendly; **D** *Don Paco*, Duarte 6, T 523-4816, central, clean, friendly. The cheapest guest houses are on Av Las Américas heading towards the airport, about 1½ km from beach.

● **Places to eat**
L'Horizon is excellent and *Buxeda* is rec for seafood, especially *centolla* – crab; also rec is *Neptuno's Club*, almost opp *Sun Set*, seafood, German-owned, menu is German and English, very expensive, 0900-2230, closed Mon. On the beach *fritureras* sell typical dishes, among them the famous *yaniqueques* – Johnny cakes. There is a good all-night, palm-covered burger hut where people gather for late-night satellite TV entertainment. For cheaper meals go to Andrés, the next village, 2 km away.

● **Exchange**
Banco Popular will change TCs at good rates. There are several exchange houses.

● **Nightlife**
There are numerous quaint bars for couples on Calle Duarte. In the same area is plenty of variety for unattached males, but beware of pickpockets; otherwise safe.

● **How To Get There**
Taxi Santo Domingo-Boca Chica US$25, US$11.50 from the airport, *guagua* US$0.85 from either Parque Enriquillo or Parque Independencia, or the corner of San Martín and Av París but not after dark. If driving from the capital, look carefully for signposts to whichever part of Boca Chica you wish to go.

JUAN DOLIO

The Guayacanes, Embassy and **Juan Dolio** beaches, E of Boca Chica, are also popular, especially at weekends when they can be littered and plagued with hawkers (much cleaner and very quiet out of season). The whole area is being developed in a long ribbon of hotels and resorts, but with little apparent planning. On the road between the beach and the highway are Jerry's Dive Center and Calypso Divers, also at *Punta Garza*, T 526-1242, F 526-3814, also runs excursions; Diving Center Playa Caribe, also at *Hotel Talanquera*; Jungle Tours for trips all over the island. Venus Tours, rec. Buses going along the S coast will drop you, and pick you up again, at the various turn-offs to the beaches.

● **Accommodation & places to eat**
Here too are plenty of hotels: *Embassy* beach resort; **B** *Sol-y-Mar* (Calle Central 23, Guayacanes, T 526-2514, French-Canadian run, overpriced restaurant); *Playacanes* beach resort, T 529-8516. In Juan Dolio: **A2** *Marena Beach Resort*; *Tamarindo Sol Club*, T 529-8471, prices from **A2**; **B** and up *Punta Garza* bungalows, T 529-8331. *Metro Hotel y Marina*, T 526-2811, F 526-1808, from **A3** pp without tax, very nice; on the road to *Metro* are **A2** *Talanquera* (T 541-1166) and **A3** and

up *Decámeron* (T 685-5715, with casino). Near *Metro* is La Llave Plaza with Italian, German, Spanish restaurants, a minimarket, gift shop and travel agent. **A3** *Hotel Playa Real* (T 529-8471) has Sunday buffets with dancing, use of pool and beach for US$9.25 pp (US$2.50 pool and beach only). The road between the beach and the highway is in poor condition; on it are **B** *Ramada Guesthouse*, T 526-3310, F 526-2512, meals US$18.50 FAP, pool, disco bar, water sports; opp is *Marco's* restaurant and bar, German. There is a good selection of modern, modestly-priced apartments for rent, by day, week, month or year, eg *Yamina*, T 526-1123/526-1411 (operated by Villas del Mar Realty, reliable).

East of Juan Dolio is the new resort of Villas del Mar, with **L1-A1** *Renaissance Capella Beach Resort* (T 809-526-1080), pools, lots of watersports, inc scuba diving and fishing, tennis, bikes, games room, restaurants, golf packages. There are also several apartment developments.

Inland from this stretch of coast, if you want a change from sea bathing, there is the recommended *balneario* at Bayaguana, some 45 km from the capital.

San Pedro de Macorís (*pop* 86,950), on the Río Higuamo, is a quiet sea port whose economy is heavily dependent on the sugar estates which surround it. Tourist development is also under way here. Facing the river is the cathedral, by which is the bus terminus. In the city is the Universidad Central del Este and a baseball stadium. There is a marked cultural influence from immigrants from the Leeward and Windward Islands, especially in the dances called *guloyas*. Another name is *momise*, which derives from the English mummer tradition; dance-dramas known as *la danza salvaje* (the wild dance), *la danza del padre invierno* (the dance of Father Winter, which imitates the St George and the Dragon legend) and *la danza de El Codril* take place on 29 June, St Peter, and other festivals. For further information T 529-3600 (Ayuntamiento) or 529-3309 (provincial government). (Hotel: D *Macorix*, T 596-3950.)

LA ROMANA

East of San Pedro is **La Romana**, population 101,350). The city has a large Parque Central. The church of Santa Rosa de Lima is on a little rise, fronted by a small park, close to Parque Central. On the Parque are Codetel, Ayuntamiento Municipal and Colón cinema. One block behind the church is the Mercado Modelo. The central commercial area is large, the town spread out. It is a sugar town, with railways to carry the harvest. La Romana can be reached by air (international airport) and by bus or *público* from Santo Domingo (US$4.55 and US$5 respectively). If driving from the capital, at the western edge of La Romana, by a large stadium, the road forks three ways: sharp right for Higüey and Parque Nacional del Este; the middle road, bearing right, for the town centre; straight on for Guaymate. *Concho* or *guagua* in town RD$2.50-3/US$0.25; *motoconcho* US$0.20; *carrera* US$3.50-4.50.

● **Accommodation** **B** *Olimpo*, Av Padre Albreu esq Pedro A Lluberes, T 550-7646, new, mock-Greek décor, clean, restaurant; **D** *Frano*, Av Padre Abreu, 21 rooms, with a/c, less without, inconveniently located away from main plaza and restaurants; 500m away is **E** *Bolívar*, as good; *Hotel y Cabañas Tío Tom*, 4.5 km before town on road from capital, T 556-6212/5, F 556-6201, 2 standards of cabin, **C** with fan and **B** with a/c, bar, good but restaurant below average, separate pizzería, pool, hot water, disco, taxi from La Romana US$8.45; about 2 km closer to town is **D** *Andanamay*, T 556-6102, with bath and fan; **D** *San Santiago*, Calle Hernández, with bath; **E** *Pensión de Aza*, Ramón Bergés y A Miranda, at plaza, without bath, basic; **G** *dormitorio*, dark, basic, but OK, from SE corner of market go 2½ blocks W and it's on the right. Good restaurant, *La Pasarella*, on main plaza.

Casa de Campo, 10 km to the E of La Romana, is the premier tourist centre in the republic, P O Box 140, La Romana, T 523-3333, F 523-8548: hotel, villas, bars, restaurants and country club with many sporting facilities (on land and sea), including golf courses and polo fields, in 7,000 acres; prices start at A1, low season, rising to L1 (US$255-995), high season. The Playa Minitas beach is within the complex. An international artists' village in mock-Italian style has been established at Altos de Chavón, near La Romana, in a spectacular hilltop setting; there is a free bus every 15 mins from *Casa de Campo*. Taxi from La Romana US$15. There are several restaurants, expensive shops, a **Museo Arqueológico Regional**, open 0900-1700 (free) and an amphitheatre which was inaugurated with a show by Frank Sinatra (many international stars perform there, as well as the best Dominican performers).

Off La Romana is the **Isla Catalina**, to which Costa Lines run excursions for the day (they call it Serena Cay), travel agents also run tours for US$30-68 including lunch, supper and drinks; T 585-7887, Martisant, cheapest, or Turinter, Insular, Prieto (T 685-0102), most expensive. Cruise ships also call at the island, disgorging some 98,000 passengers in a winter season. New rules were announced in 1996 to protect the ecology of the island, which is under the permanent supervision of the Dominican Navy and the Ministry of Tourism. All works that may affect the vegetation have been prohibited and work on building sun shades for tourists has been suspended, although Costa Cruise Line is still permitted to expand the beach area for its passengers' use. The island's flora and fauna is to be catalogued with a view to incorporating it into the Sistema Natural de Areas Protegidas.

Although inland the SE part of the island is dry, flat and monotonous, the beaches have fine, white sand with some of the best bathing in waters protected by reefs and excellent diving.

The Río Chavón area E of La Romana and Casa de Campo was declared a protected zone at the end of 1995 to safeguard a large area of red and black mangroves.

BAYAHIBE

About 25 km E of La Romana is **Bayahibe**, a fishing village on a small bay. It is reached by a road which turns off the highway to Higüey (*carro público* La Romana-Bayahibe US$2.50, or take a Higüey bus to the turnoff and take a *motoconcho*, US$1). The fishing village is now accommodating tourism, with excursions, lodgings and cafés. Small wooden houses and the green wooden church of the village are on a point between the new buildings and an excellent, 1.5 km curving white sand beach fringed with palms. Plenty of fishing and pleasure boats are moored in the bay. A coral reef with sponges is popular with divers. Marco's shop does boat trips to Saona and Catalina islands, US$25 pp, 5 passengers, full day, about 1 hr each way in boat. Santo Domingo travel agency trips to Saona range from US$31 (Martisant) to US$58 (Turinter, Prieto) to US$67 (Ecoturisa, T 221-4104, Insular). Sun and Fun Island Tours, T/F 223-5749, telecommunications centre, rentals, *cabañas*, excursions. Scuba Libre for diving.

● **Accommodation**
B-C *Club Bayahibe*; **D** *Pensión Rae*, price per room, separate baths; *cabañas* for rent, Doña Olga's are good, **C-D**; at certain times almost all rooms are taken up by European tour companies. About 10 km SE is **Dominicus**, an Italian-run tourist complex with its own beach, T 529-8531 (prices start at A3 pp). Sandflies can be a nuisance.

● **Places to eat**
Restaurante La Punta, seafood; *Café Caribe*, breakfasts and other meals; *Adrian* café and restaurant; *La Bahía*, on the beach.

Further E is **Boca de Yuma**, an interesting fishing village. There are some caves and a nice beach outside the village. There are a couple of hotels and a few small restaurants. **B-C** *Club El 28*, T 223-0503, 6 cabañas with bath, full board available, 5 hotel rooms, **E**, fan, pool, horses, Italian restaurant, quiet, friendly, family atmosphere, beautiful. A repaved road runs from Boca de Yuma inland to Higüey; along this, about 2 km

N of San Rafael de Yuma, is the restored residence of Ponce de León (1505-1508).

HIGUEY

Higüey has the Basílica de Nuestra Señora de la Altagracia (patroness of the Republic), a very impressive modern building to which every year there is a pilgrimage on 21 January; the statue of the virgin and a silver crown are in a glass case on the altar. People wearing shorts are not allowed to enter. The old 16th century church is still standing. Codetel near the Basilica. Market.

● **Accommodation**

B *Hotel Naranjo*, T 554-3400, F 554-5455, on road to El Seibo, a/c café, restaurant, disco, conference centre. *El Topacio*, T 554-5910. Plenty of cheap hotels on Calle Colón; also *Brisas del Este*.

● **Transport**

Buses from Santo Domingo cost US$4.55, *públicos* US$5.50; bus from La Romana US$3.10.)

Due E from Higüey, on the coast again, is **Punta Cana** which has some beautiful beaches and good diving; the all-inclusive resorts in the area are quite spread out. The resorts are first class but the fenced in luxury contrasts with the standard of living of the local people. Independent visitors find it difficult to find a public beach as hotels will not allow non-residents through their property. A good road, beside which are some pretty houses, runs to Punta Cana international airport, but some of the side roads are in bad condition. There is a *Club Méditerranée* (T 687-2767, F 687-2896, P O Box 106, Higüey, 334 rooms, children's clubs, circus school, 10 tennis courts, pool, windsurfing and lots of other land and watersports). **L3** *Punta Cana Beach Resort* (T 686-0084, F 687-8745, P O Box 1083), MAP, beautiful beach, good diving, but sparse public transport. Most people staying there arrive by plane and only leave the resort on a tour bus; a taxi to Higüey costs US$7.80, *Club Med's* bus to Higüey US$8.35, and there is transport provided

for employees. The *Punta Cana Yacht Club* has villas and one-bedroom apartments, golf course under construction, T 565-3077.

Continuing round the coast, there are many other beaches to be visited, with white sand and reef-sheltered water. Another resort on the eastern tip, *Bávaro Beach* and *Bávaro Gardens* has the largest hotel in the country with 1,000 rooms on a 2 km beach, tennis, boutiques, diving, evening salsa and merengue entertainment, T 686-5773, F 686-5771, P O Box 1, Higüey, to which charter flights go. Hotel rates from A2 pp half board. There is a *Meliá* hotel at Bávaro (T 530-5817, **L1-A1** per room, depending on season, good); also a guesthouse near Bávaro, **D** *El Galeón del Pirata*, restaurant. Take a taxi from Higüey. If exploring the eastern tip, Spanish is essential.

A road runs W from Higüey to Hato Mayor, via El Seibo. As far as Cruce El Pavón it is in very good condition, passing through cattle and agricultural land. The 'living fences' are in pink blossom in January. After El Pavón there are huge sugar cane fields with oxen, trains, *bateyes* where the cutters live and much poverty. The road is rough either side of **El Seibo** (also spelt El Seybo). El Seibo is a quiet little town with painted houses, like many others in the region. It has an old, white church. (**D** *Hotel Santa Cruz*, T 552-3962, on hill above road to Hato Mayor; F *Las Mercedes*, clean, quiet, pleasant, no generator; the town's water supply depends on the electricity supply.) A *guagua* can be taken to El Llano (US$0.65), from where you can either return to El Seibo, or continue on foot to Miches on the coast (two days, lovely scenery).

Hato Mayor (Codetel and church on square) is a junction for routes between Santo Domingo and Higüey, Sabana de la Mar and San Pedro de Macorís. 2 blocks from the square is a Shell station at Duarte y San Antonio. By the station, on Duarte, *guaguas* leave for Santo Domingo, US$2, and San Pedro de Macorís, US$0.90; on San Antonio they leave for Sabana de la Mar, US$1.55. Driving to Santo Domingo, either take the road to San Pedro de Macorís and turn W along the coast, or take the inland route, Ruta 4, which turns W before San Pedro. This again is sugar country; note the large steam engine in the open space at Ingenio Consuela. Ruta 4 crosses the Río Higuamo by a big bridge with traffic lights by the national cement works. The road continues through sugar cane fields to the capital.

WEST FROM SANTO DOMINGO

The far SW of the Republic is a dry zone with typical dry-forest vegetation. A new highway has been built from the capital, cutting journey times to half what they used to be. Tourist development is proceeding apace and by the mid- to late-1990s a number of resorts should be operating. For the time being, exploring by car is the best way to enjoy this relatively untouched area.

To the W of Santo Domingo is **Haina**, the country's main port and an industrial zone. It has a teachers' vacation centre and a country club with swimming pool.

SAN CRISTÓBAL

Further W one can visit **San Cristóbal** in the interior, 25 km from the capital, the birthplace of the dictator Rafael Leonidas Trujillo. Trujillo's home, the Casa de Caoba (now rapidly disintegrating, but open 0900-1700) may be reached by *público* from behind the market, or by motorcycle taxi (US$0.35), though you may have to walk the last kilometre, uphill. You can also visit El Palacio del Cerro, the luxury residence which he built but never lived in. Both buildings are being restored. Also due for restoration are the Iglesia Parroquial and the Ingenio Diego Caballero, a colonial sugar mill at Boca de Nigua. Other attractions are the Palacio del Ayuntamiento in

which the republic's first constitution was signed, the Iglesia de Piedras Vivas, the caves at El Pomier (with Taino petroglyphs) and the Santa María caves, where African-influenced stick and drum festivals are held. The local saint's day festival is from 6-10 June. Nearby are La Toma natural pools, for scenery and swimming, and the beaches at Palenque, Nigua and Najayo. At the last named are the ruins of Trujillo's beach house.

● **Accommodation**
San Cristóbal, Constitución, cheaper, former has a disco, and there are others in town: **E** *Las Terrazas*, a government-owned hotel in the centre, is best avoided, nothing works; on the road to Santo Domingo are a couple of small hotels, **E** *La Ruta*, with small breakfast, has a helpful owner. A famous local dish is *pasteles en hojas*, made from plátano, minced meat and other ingredients.

● **Transport**
Minibus Santo Domingo-San Cristóbal from the Malecón, US$0.85, *público* US$1.30; radio taxi US$14-20; La Covancha company organizes group transport (27 passengers) to San Cristóbal, La Toma and Palenque Beach.

From San Cristóbal the road runs W to **Baní**, birthplace of Máximo Gómez, 19th century fighter for the liberation of Cuba. The town is a major producer of sugar cane, coffee, vegetables, bananas and salt. The parish church is Nuestra Señora de Regla (festival, 21 November). *Hotel Brisas del Sur* (T 522-3548); cheaper hotels to be found near the market on Máximo Gómez; *Disco Sur*, on three floors, in the centre; minibus from Santo Domingo, US$2. The local goats' milk sweets from Paya, 5km E of the town centre on main road, are renowned throughout the country, eg from *Las Marías*. Las Tablas, a village nearby, was one of the last places to conserve indigenous ways of life. *Restaurant Rancho Escondido*, Km 2.5 on Carretera Sánchez highway to Santo Domingo.

Don't bother with the Baní beach (although at Los Almendros a tourist development is being built), better to carry on to **Las Salinas**. Of the two roads

W out of Baní, take the one to Las Calderas naval base for Las Salinas. There is no problem in going through the base; after it, turn left onto an unmade road for 3 km to the fishing village of Las Salinas, passing the unique sand dunes of the Bahía de Calderas. The bay is an inlet on the Bahía de Ocoa, shallow, with some mangroves and good windsurfing and fishing. In the village is **B** *Las Salinas High Wind Center*, hotel, restaurant, windsurf centre, price per room. Beyond the village are the saltpans which give it its name and then the point surrounded by a grey sand beach (one bar, calm waters, no facilities). Across the inlet are the undeveloped white sand beaches of Corbanito; fishermen will go across for US$2, apparently.

The fishing village of **Palmar de Ocoa** (99 km from Santo Domingo) hosts a fishing tournament each year; it is reached by a road branching off the Baní-Las Salinas road, going along the northern shore of the Bahía de Calderas. Poor roads go to Corbanito, no development whatsoever. Palmar has lots of summer houses, a grey sand, pebbly beach, calm waters and a newly-built, poor village behind the summer houses. There is no large-scale tourist development. The setting is beautiful, looking across the bay to the mountains inland.

The main road W, in excellent condition, carries on from Baní through Azua to Barahona. **Azua** de Compostela was founded in 1504 on the orders of Fray Nicolás de Ovando; at one time Puerto Viejo was an alternative port to Santo Domingo. An important victory by Dominican troops against the Haitian army took place here on 19 March 1844. The main beach is Monte Río. Hotels: *Altagracia*, T 521-3813; *Brisas del Mar*, T 521-3813; also **F** *La Familiar*, T 521-3656, with shower and fan; *Hotel Restaurant San Ramón*, T 521-3529 (none is of high quality). Restaurants: *El Gran Segovia*, *José Segundo*, *Mi Bosquecito Bar*, *Patio Español*. Santo Domingo-Azua is 2 hrs by *guagua*, US$4.15, *público* US$3.55,

and Azua has good bus connections for Barahona, under 2 hrs, US$4.15, San Juan and Padre Las Casas.

BARAHONA

On the square in **Barahona** is the Sede Principal de la República of 1913 (re-modelled). It is a clean town with brightly painted houses. The province of Barahona produces coffee (excursions can be made to Platón or Santa Elena), sugar, grapes, salt, bananas and other fruits, also gypsum and seafood. Barahona's domestic airport has been upgraded to international (Aeropuerto María Montés). The road which passes the airport is lined with flamboyant trees and goes to the sugar factory; see the yellow railway engine on the way. There is a tourist information office in the *Hotel Fundacipe*.

● **Accommodation A1** *Hotel Riviera Beach*, newly-built by Occidental outside town with own beach, T 524-5111, F 524-5798, good comfortable rooms, many with balconies, buffet meals, pool and poolside bar; **C** *Hotel Caribe* on same road, but closer to town, T 524-2185, excellent open-air restaurant (*La Rocca*) next door; **C** *Hotel Guaracuyá*, T 524-2211, is rec, being clean and on its own beach at Saladilla (the dawns here are spectacular), with a/c, less with fan. In town, **E** *Hotel Barahona*, Calle Jaime Mota 5, T 542-3442, with fan, restaurant, simple; **C** *Micheluz*, Av 30 de Mayo 28, T 524-2358, with a/c, cheaper with fan, cold water, restaurant, opp is **F** *Mencía*, small, central, basic, clean, friendly, fan; **C** *Las Magnolias*, Anacaona 13, T 524-2244, with a/c, **D** with fan; *Ana Isabel*, Anacaona y Padre Billini, T 524-5422, central, no restaurant, fan or a/c; several smaller hotels.

● **Places to eat** *Las Mercedes* restaurant on corner of Jaime Mota and seafront road; *Brisas del Caribe* seafood restaurant near airport, excellent food and service, reasonable prices, pleasant setting, popular at lunchtime, T 524-2794; good juices on one corner of Parque Central; *José*, comida criolla and video, on Jaime Mota. 2 discos, *Imperio* next to *Riviera Beach*; *Costa Sur* with restaurant almost opp *Riviera Beach*.

• **Transport Air** A new, international airport was opened in 1996. The María Montez airport, named after a Dominican Hollywood actress of the 1940s and 1950s, is designed to promote tourism development in the area. **Bus** Journey time from the capital is 3 hrs. Minibus fare is US$3, *público* US$4, Caribe Tours runs 2 buses a day (group transport also available with Metro Tours, La Covacha and Taxi Raffi). *Concho* or *guagua* in town RD$3/US$0.25; *carrera* US$3-4.

Be careful when swimming at the small, public beach at Barahona, as there are frequently stinging jelly fish, it is also filthy, as is the sea, and theft is common. About 70% of the coral reef off Barahona is reported to be dead. Those with a car can visit other, more remote beaches from Barahona (public transport is limited to *públicos*). A new road has been built S of Barahona, running down the coast through some of the most beautiful scenery in the republic, mountains on one side, the sea on the other, leading to Pedernales on the Haitian border (146 km). All along the southern coast are many white sand beaches which offer the best snorkelling and scuba diving in the Republic. The first place is the pebble beach of **El Quemaito**, where the river comes out of the beach, the cold fresh water mixing with the warm sea; offshore is a reef. There is a *parador*. The road proceeds, coming right down to the sea before **San Rafael** (about 40 mins from Barahona) where a river runs out onto a stony beach. The forest grows to the edge of the beach. Where the road crosses the river is a *pensión* with a swimming hole behind it (the swimming hole is safer than the sea as enormous waves surge onto the beach). Construction is under way here. At weekends it gets very crowded. Between San Rafael and **El Paraíso** rooms are available for rent. As the road approaches El Paraíso, see the changing colours where underground rivers flow into the sea. At El Paraíso, 31 km from Barahona, are a Texaco station and **D** *Hotel Paraíso* (no phone, big rooms with bath, clean, TV). At Los Patos another river flows into the sea; *comedores*, disco. Note that most of these beaches have domestic animals, so there are droppings on the sand. There are cool, fresh-water lagoons behind several of the other beaches on this stretch of coast. Limón lagoon is a flamingo reserve.

At the village of **Enriquillo**, 54 km S of Barahona, a new dock has been constructed (**G** *Hotel Dajtra*, on main road, basic; the only place with light at night is a disco where half the village hangs out, its prices are 'normal'). One must explore for oneself: the area is not developed for tourism, yet. It is scheduled for development when Punta Cana is finished. Between Enriquillo and Pedernales the beaches are all sandy.

William E Rainey, of Berkeley, California, writes: "South from Barahona between Baoruco and Enriquillo there is wet tropical forest with rushing mountain streams and fruit stands in little roadside settlements. At Enriquillo you enter the Barahona Peninsula lowlands and the terrain grows markedly drier. Continuing W from Oviedo to Pedernales the road is in good condition and the surrounding habitat, particularly near Pedernales, is tropical thorn scrub with abundant cacti growing on karstic limestone.

"The entire country is dotted with checkpoints adjacent to roadside military installations; at most of these the traffic is simply waved through. At the checkpoint in Pedernales (perhaps because gringos were an anomaly there) there were brief interrogations each time we passed (with automatic weapons pointed at us by uniformed teenagers). The last time we passed this point, one of them initiated a detailed search of our gear. Fortunately, this entertainment was cut short by a senior officer who apologized. It was, on balance, a minor aggravation, but one likely to be experienced by travellers near the Haitian border."

Pedernales is the most westerly town of the republic, on the Haitian border.

Beautiful beaches include Cabo Rojo (usually deserted, little shade) and Bahía de las Aguilas, where there is abundant fishing. Here is the **Parque Nacional Jaragua** in which are the islands Beata and Alto Velo; many iguanas.

N of Pedernales a road runs through lush and hilly countryside along the Haitian border to Duvergé, where it joins the road to Jimaní (see below). There are frequent and friendly military checkpoints but hardly any traffic and impassable without a capable 4WD. The views are magnificent, particularly of Lago Enriquillo to the N.

Inland from Barahona, near the Haitian border, is **Lago Enriquillo**, whose waters, 30m below sea level, are three times saltier than the sea. It has a wealth of wild life including crocodiles (best seen in the morning), iguanas and flamingoes. The crocodiles and iguanas can best be seen on the largest of the three islands in the lake, which make up the **Cabritos National Park** (see **Flora and Fauna** above), which is also where the crocodiles lay their eggs and spend their nights. A large colony of flamingoes overwinters at the lake. You need to purchase a Dirección Nacional de Parques (DNP) permit (US$3.95) to visit the island and only groups with a guide are permitted to go there (2 boatmen do trips and charge according to number of passengers, from about US$9 pp for a large group, inc the permit. Ask at Bocas del Chacón, 3 km W of the park entrance, for the captain). The two smaller islands are Barbarita and La Islita. To visit the lake it is best to have one's own transport if short of time because, even though public transport runs both on the N and S shores, there is no guarantee of travelling on (or returning) the same day. Note that there is a filling station in Duvergé but no fuel elsewhere in this area. There is no accommodation on the lake shore.

If not in one's own car, you can either take a tour from the capital (eg Martisant, T 585-7887, US$54 pp in a group,

or contact Ecoturisa or the DNP), or take a *guagua* from Av Duarte y Av 27 de Febrero to Neiba, US$2.60 (also reached by *guagua* from Barahona, US$2), and then make a connection for La Descubierta, US$1.30. Alternatively take a bus from Santo Domingo to Jimaní (US$6.50, La Experiencia and Riviera companies; the journey takes 8 hrs) and get off at La Descubierta. Before Neiba is Galván, in a banana-growing area; the landscape is very flat (very depressing on the rare occasions that it rains). **Neiba** is known for its grapes, sold on the main square in season; *Hotel Comedor Babei* on square, *Hotel Comedor Dania* on a street off the road going E out of town. Between Galván and Neiba is Balneario Las Marías.

The road around the lake is fully paved. A portion of the Parque Nacional Isla Cabritas is on the N shore at La Azufrada, before La Descubierta. At **La Azufrada** is a swimming pool of sulphurous water, good for the skin. The pool is clean but the surroundings are littered. A path along the beach gives views of the lake and of Las Caritas, a line of rocks with precolumbian petroglyphs (an even better place to see them is signposted on the road). **La Descubierta**, at the NW end, is a pleasant village with a celebrated *balneario*, Las Barías. The water is very cold; it is surprising how such an arid area can produce so much water to feed the lake. After La Descubierta are the springs and *balneario* of Bocas del Chacón (a *parador* is under construction).

Jimaní, at the western end of the lake (not on the shore) is about 2 km from the Haitian border. It is a spread out town of single-storey housing; C *Hotel Jimaní* on square, appears to be converted military accommodation, no hot water, little service but nice pool and ice cold beer. *Restaurant Los Lagos*, Duarte y Restauración, excellent *chivo y gandules* (goat and beans), stays open late as town's main meeting place, also has disco *Krystal*. Cabins are being built on the road into town from the lake's N shore. If you go to the border you will see queues of trucks waiting to cross; Haitians sell Barbancourt rum and perfumes. Customs officers in Jimaní are not above taking items from your luggage. The road around the S side of the lake goes through El Limón and La Zurza, another sulphurous *balneario*. From the lake to Barahona, the road goes through Duvergé, La Colonia (with a statue of Enriquillo, "the first fighter for independence in the New World"; he was a cacique whose land stretched from Haiti to Azua and who fought against the Spaniards) and Cabral. At Cabral is a turning marked Polo; the road climbs to a spot, with good views of Lago Rincón, where the road appears to slope upwards, but if you put your car in neutral, or place a ball or can on the road it seems to run uphill. The place is called the **Polo Magnético**; university studies have shown it to be an optical illusion, but it is a source of great discussion. Get a local to show you the best spots. From Cabral the road runs through very dry, low-lying land (there is a project to protect the dry forest, also experimental agricultural projects).

San Juan de la Maguana, in a rich agricultural area, is on the main road to the Haitian border at Comendador. Soldiers frequently patrol this route. Visit the Corral de Los Indios, an ancient Indian meeting ground several km N of the San Juan. (Hotels: *Tamarindo*, T 541-2211; D *Maguana*, T 557-2244.)

Information for travellers

BEFORE TRAVELLING

● Documents

Citizens of the following countries do not need a tourist card to enter the Dominican Republic: Argentina, Ecuador, Israel, Japan, Liechtenstein, Norway, South Korea, Sweden, UK, Uruguay. All others need a green tourist card, which costs US$10, purchased from consulates, tourist offices, airlines on departure (eg American at Miami), or at the airport on arrival before queueing for immigration. The time limit on tourist cards is 60 days, but if necessary extensions are obtainable from Immigration, Huacal Building, Santo Domingo (T 685-2505/2535). The easiest method of extending a tourist card is simply to pay the fine (US$2 for each month over 3 months) at the airport when leaving. Check all entry requirements in advance if possible.

All visitors should have an outward ticket (not always asked for).

● Customs

The airport police are on the lookout for illegal drugs. It is also illegal to bring firearms into the country. At the land border with Haiti bags are searched and things go missing, keep a close eye on everyone, not just on customs officials.

Duty-free import of 200 cigarettes or one box of cigars, plus one litre of alcoholic liquor and gift articles to the value of US$100, is permitted. Military-type clothing and food products will be confiscated on arrival. Currency in excess of US$10,000 may not be taken out of the country without special permission.

● Climate

The climate is tropical. The rainy months are May, June, August, September and November. The temperature shows little seasonal change, and varies between 18° and 32°C. Only in December does the temperature fall, averaging about

20°C. Humidity can be high, particularly in coastal areas, making physical activity difficult.

● **Health**
It is not advisable to drink tap water. All hotels have bottled water. The supply of drinking water in Santo Domingo was improved in 1992. The local greasy food, if served in places with dubious hygiene, may cause stomach problems. Hepatitis is common. It is also advisable to avoid the midday sun.

MONEY
● **Currency**
The Dominican peso (RD$) is the only legal tender. The peso is divided into 100 centavos. There are coins in circulation of 25 and 50 centavos and 1 peso, and notes of 5, 10, 20, 50, 100, 500 and 1,000 pesos.

● **Exchange**
In 1991, new legislation outlawed all exchange transactions except those in branches of the major banks. You will be given a receipt and, with this, you can change remaining pesos back into dollars at the end of your visit (maximum 30% of dollars changed; cash obtained against a credit card does not count). Do not rely on the airport bank being open. Most European currencies can be changed at the Banco de Reservas (and some other banks); Scandinavian currencies are very hard to change. If stuck at weekends and wishing to avoid street changers, most hotels will offer to change money if you ask casually "Is there anywhere open to change dollars?" The rates are generally the same as in banks; cash only. The black market usually offers rates higher than the official rate; illegal money changers on the street approach foreigners (do *not* use them, sometimes they work with a policeman who will demand a large bribe not to imprison you).

● **Credit cards**
Nearly all major hotels, restaurants and stores accept most credit cards. Several banks will give cash against Visa or American Express cards, usually with 5% commission. Thomas Cook Mastercard refund assistant points are Vimenca, Av Abraham Lincoln 306, Santo Domingo, T 532-7381, and the Banco del Comercio Dominicano in Puerto Plata (T586-2350, Duarte y Padre Castellanos) and La Romana (T 556-5151, Trinitaria 59).

GETTING THERE

AIR
To Santo Domingo
From North America: American and Apa International fly from Miami and New York; Continental and TWA also from New York. American fly daily from Atlanta, Boston, Hartford, Nashville and Orlando; from other US cities, connections in Miami or San Juan, Puerto Rico.

From Europe: Iberia flies from Madrid several times a week and has connecting flights from most European and Spanish cities, eg Amsterdam, Barcelona, Bilbao, Brussels, Frankfurt, London, Milan, Rome, Zurich. Air France from Paris 3 times a week; also from Martinique, Guadeloupe, Port-au-Prince and Cayenne. TAP from Lisbon twice a week. Martinair flies from Amsterdam once a week. LTU flies once a week from Dusseldorf; Condor flies once a week from Frankfurt.

From the Caribbean: ALM has flights from Curaçao and Sint Maarten. TCA from Providenciales; Air Guadeloupe from Pointe-à-Pitre, Port-au-Prince; Copa, American Eagle, Apa, Air Guadeloupe, Aces, American Airlines all from San Juan, American Eagle also from Mayagüez.

From Central America: Copa from Panama City, San José, Guatemala City.

From South America: Aces from Bogotá; Viasa and Aerotour Dominicano from Caracas; Copa from Guayaquil; Copa and Iberia from Lima; Iberia from Quito; other capital cities are connected through Miami.

To Puerto Plata
From North America: American Airlines from Atlanta, Detroit, Miami, New York, Raleigh/Durham; Apa International also from Miami.

From Europe: Martinair from Amsterdam; Condor from Berlin, Cologne/Bonn, Dusseldorf, Frankfurt, Hamburg, Hanover, Munich and Stuttgart, LTU from Dusseldorf, Frankfurt and Hamburg.

From the Caribbean: TCA from Providenciales; American Eagle from San Juan.

To Punta Cana
From North America: Aerolíneas Argentinas from Miami.

From Europe: Martinair from Amsterdam;

Condor from Berlin, Cologne/Bonn, Dusseldorf, Frankfurt, Hamburg, Hanover, Munich and Stuttgart. LTU from Dusseldorf, Frankfurt and Hamburg.

From the Caribbean: Viasa from Sint Maarten. American Eagle and Aerolíneas Argentinas from San Juan.

From South America: Lan Chile from Bogotá and Santiago; Aerolíneas Argentinas from Buenos Aires; Viasa from Caracas.

There are also many charter flights from European and North American cities, which are usually cheaper than scheduled flights but frequency varies according to the season. Cubana de Aviación has been authorized to start scheduled services from Cuba after several years of operating charter services.

SEA

There are cargo and passenger shipping services with New York, New Orleans, Miami and South American countries. Many cruise lines from USA, Canada and Europe call at the Dominican Republic on itineraries to various ports on Caribbean islands or the mainland. Agencies which handle cruises include Emely (T 682-2744, for Festival, Holidays, Jubilee, Sur Viking).

● **Ports of entry**
Luperón, Puerto Plata, Samaná.

● **Boat documents**
Customs fees US$10 pp. 30 days immigration clearance. Declare weapons and check in with Customs officials ashore at each port of entry. Do not depart from anchorage before sunrise after picking up weapons.

ON ARRIVAL

● **Airport information**
Details of airports are given in the text above. There are several: Las Américas (Santo Domingo), Gregorio Luperón (Puerto Plata), Arroyo Barril (Samaná), Cibao (Santiago), Punta Aguila (La Romana), Punta Cana (Higüey) and María Montéz (Barahona).

● **Airline offices**
In Santo Domingo: Air Canada, Kennedy y Lope de Vega, T 586-0251; Air France, Av George Washington 101, T 686- 8419; ALM, L Navarro 28, T 687-4594; American, El Conde next to Iberia, T 542-5151; Avianca, R Pastoriza 401, T 562-1797; Carnival, T 563-4691/5300/8900; Continental, Edificio IN

TEMPO, T 562-6688; Copa, Edificio IN TEMPO, T 562-5824; Iberia, El Conde 401, T 686-9191; LTU, T 567-2236; Martinair, M Gómez 688, T 688-6661; TAP, Plaza Merengue on Av 27 de Febrero, esq Tiradentes, T 472-1441; Air Guadeloupe is represented by AIRP Tours, Calle Luis Alberti 7, T 412-1872, 566-6150, F 563-2163, 541-3260; TWA is represented by Quisqueya Air, Av Francia 54, Suite 103, T 680-6073, 689-6985; TCA, T 586-0286; Viasa, L Navarro 28, T 566-0698.

● **Banks**
The Central Bank determines monetary policy. Among the commercial banks in the Republic are Scotiabank (Santo Domingo, Santiago, and Puerto Plata), Chase Manhattan (Santo Domingo and Santiago), Citibank (Santo Domingo and Santiago), Banco de Reservas, Banco Popular, Banco Metropolitano, Banco Central, Bancrédito, Intercontinental, Banco Dominicano Hispano, Banco Mercantil and others. Obtaining money from banks with a Visa card is easy.

● **Clothing**
Light clothing, preferably cotton, is best all year round. It is recommended to take one formal outfit since some hotels and nightclubs do not permit casual dress.

● **Embassies and consulates**
Argentina, Máximo Gómez 10, T 682-2977; **Austria**, Calle Primera 3, T 532-2591; **Brazil**, Winston Churchill 32, T 532-0868; **Canada**, Máximo Gómez 30, T 685-1136; **Chile**, Av Anacaona, T 532-7800; **Colombia**, Salvador Sturia 21, T 562-1670; **Costa Rica**, Augustín Lara 22, T 565-6467; **Denmark**, Duarte Highway, Km 6.5, T 562-1333; **Ecuador**, Rafael Augusto Sánchez 17, T 563-8363; **El Salvador**, José Brea Peña 12, T 565-4311; **France**, George Washington 353, T 689-2161; **Germany**, J T Mejía y Calle 37, T 565-8811; **Guatemala**, Pedro Henríquez Ureña 136A, T 567-0115; **Honduras**, Salvador Sturia 22, T 565-5112; **Israel**, P Henríquez Ureña 80, T 686-7359; **Italy**, Manuel Rodríguez Objío 4, T 689-3684; **Jamaica**, José Contreras 98, T 532-1079; **Japan**, Av Winston Churchill, Torre BHD, piso 8, T 567-3365; **Mexico**, Arzobispo Merino 265 y Mercedes, T 565-2565; **Netherlands**, Mayor Enrique Valverde, T 565-5240; **Norway**, Av Mella 468, T 689-6355; **Panama**, Benito Monción 255, T 688-1014; **Paraguay**, Calle A Lara 19, T 562-4814; **Peru**, VD Ordoñez 16, T 565-5851; **Spain**, Independencia

1205, T 533-1424; **Sweden**, Máximo Gómez 31, T 685-2121; **Switzerland**, José Gabriel García 26, T 689-4131; **UK** Honorary Consul, Maureen Tejada, St George School, Abraham Lincoln 552, T 586-8464, F 562-5015 (a British Embassy is due to open in Santo Domingo in September 1995); **Uruguay**, Calle B, Brium 7, T 682-5565; **US Embassy** and Consulate, César Nicolás Penson, T (embassy) 221-2171, (consulate) 541-2111; **Venezuela**, Av Anacaona 7, T 535-0514.

● **Hours of business**
Offices: 0830-1230, 1430-1830; some offices and shops work 0930-1730 Mon-Fri, 0800-1300 Sat. Banks: 0830-1700 Mon-Fri. Government offices 0730-1430. Shop hours are normally 0800-1900, some open all day Sat and mornings on Sun and holidays. Most shops in tourist areas stay open through the siesta and on Sun.

● **Official time**
Atlantic Standard Time, 4 hours behind GMT, 1 hour ahead of EST.

● **Public holidays**
New Year's Day (1 January), Epiphany (6 January), Our Lady of Altagracia (21 January), Duarte Day (26 January), Independence Day (27 February), Good Friday (although all Semana Santa is treated as a holiday), Labour Day (1 May), Corpus Christi (60 days after Good Friday), Restoration Day (16 August), Our Lady of Las Mercedes (24 September), Christmas (25 December).

● **Religion**
Roman Catholicism is the predominant religion. There are also Episcopalian, Baptist, Seventh Day Adventist, Presbyterian and Methodist churches in the main towns. There is a synagogue on Avenida Sarasota, Santo Domingo; call the Israeli Embassy (686-7359) for details of services. There is also a synagogue on Av Alejo Martínez in Sosúa, services are held every other Friday night. Voodoo, technically illegal, is tolerated and practised mostly in the western provinces.

● **Security**
There are well-trained guides who speak two or more languages in Santo Domingo, who are courteous and do not push themselves on you. However, outside the historic buildings in Santo Domingo, on the beaches and at other tourist attractions, visitors will be approached by unofficial English-speaking guides, sellers of rum, women or black market pesos. The last three are undoubtedly a rip-off and probably the only value in taking an unofficial guide is to deter others from pestering you (similarly, hiring a lounger chair on the beach). Beware of drug-pushers on the Malecón in Santo Domingo and near the Cathedral in Puerto Plata. Unofficial guides often refuse to give prices in advance, saying 'pay what you want' and then at the end, if they are not happy with the tip, they make a scene and threaten to tell the police that the customer had approached them to deal in drugs etc. Guides also collaborate with street money changers to cheat the tourist. On no account change money on the streets. Be careful with 'helpers' at the airports, who speed your progress through the queues and then charge US$15-20 for their services. Single men have complained of the massive presence of pimps and prostitutes. Be prepared to say 'no' a lot.

It must be stressed that these problems do not occur in rural areas and small towns, where travellers have been impressed with the open and welcoming nature of the Dominicans.

Violent crime against tourists is rare but, as anywhere, watch your money and valuables in cities late at night and on beaches. The streets of Santo Domingo are not considered safe after 2300. Purse snatchers on motorcycles operate in cities.

● **Shopping**
The native amber is sold throughout the country. Do not buy amber on the street, it will as likely as not be plastic. Real amber fluoresces under ultra violet light (the shop in the Amber Museum in Puerto Plata has a UV light); it floats in salt water; if rubbed it produces static electricity; except for the very best pieces it is not absolutely pure, streaks, bits of dirt, etc, are common. Larimar, a sea-blue stone, and red and black coral are also available (remember that black coral is protected). Other items which make good souvenirs are leather goods, basketware, weavings and onyx jewellery. The ceramic *muñeca sin rostro* (faceless doll) has become a sort of symbol of the Dominican Republic, at least, as something to take home. There are excellent cigars at very reasonable prices.

● **Tipping**
In addition to the 10% service and 13% VAT charge in restaurants, it is customary to give an extra tip of about 10% in restaurants, depending on service. Porters receive US$0.50

per bag; taxi drivers, *público* drivers and garage attendants are not usually tipped.

● **Voltage**
110 volts, 60 cycles AC current. American-type, flat-pin plugs are used. There are frequent power cuts, often for several hours, so take a torch with you when you go out at night. Many establishments have their own (often noisy) generators.

● **Weights and measures**
Officially the metric system is used but business is often done on a pound/yard/US gallon basis. Land areas in cities are measured by square metres, but in the countryside by the *tarea*, one of which equals 624 square metres.

ON DEPARTURE

● **Departure tax**
There is a departure tax of US$10, payable by all. There is a 20% tax on air tickets bought in the Dominican Republic.

● **Travel To Haiti**
No special permit is needed, just a passport or visa (check if you need one, US$40, half-price if it is not your first visa, takes 3 days). Haitian Embassy, Juan Sánchez Ramírez, on corner with José Deseridio Velverde, T 686-5778, Santo Domingo, 0830-1400. By plane to Port-au-Prince takes $1/2$ hr, US$50 approximately. By bus: a bus goes once a day, sometimes twice, from outside the Haitian embassy, leaving when full, US$18 one way, US$36 return (if it leaves in the afternoon, it stops overnight in Jimaní), Kenya Express, T 566-1045, leaves Sat 1100, Chuchula, T 540-1151, Luz Tours, T 542-2423, leaves Tues at 1000 (1200 more likely). Be quick on arriving at Embassy, get through gates ignoring hangers on and cries of 'passport', unless you want to wait in the street and pay someone else US$10 to take your passport in. All the passports are processed together. Payments may be required. Do not wear shorts. A second option is from *Domitorio San Tomé*, Calle Santomé, beside Mercado Modelo, Santo Domingo (T 688-5100, ask for Alejandro), US$32. Terrabús has a service between Santo Domingo and Port-au-Prince US$73 return, T 531-2777, 472-1080. Alternatively, take a minibus to Jimaní from near the bridge over the Río Seco in the centre of Santo Domingo, 6-8 hrs; get a lift up to the Haitian border and then get overcharged by Haitian youths on mopeds who take you across 3 km of no-man's-land for US$3. From

Haitian immigration take a lorry-bus to Port-au-Prince, 3-4 hrs, very dusty. You can also take Dominican public transport to Dajabón, cross to Ounaminthe and continue to Cap Haïtien. If driving to Haiti you must get a vehicle permit at the Foreign Ministry (T 533-1424). The drive from Santo Domingo to Port-au-Prince takes about 6 hrs. Buy gourdes from money changers outside the embassy, or at the border, but no more than US$50-worth, rates are much better in Haiti. Also take US$25 for border taxes, which have to be paid in dollars cash.

Flights between Santo Domingo and Port-au-Prince are operated by Air France (one a week).

● **To Cuba And Puerto Rico**
Lots of travel agents do package tours to Cuba, eg Elvira's Travel, Av 27 de Febrero 279, T 687-8017, open 0800-1900; Emely Tours, San Francisco de Macorís 58, Don Bosco, Santo Domingo (T 687-7114/18, F 686-0275); Arbaje Tours, T 535-4941, 535-5495, check special offers, eg 2 for the price of one. Details of other options can be found in the morning papers. There are also short cruises to Puerto Rico, eg with Diamond Cruises, for about US$120 pp.

WHERE TO STAY

● **Hotels**
Hotels are given under the towns in which they are situated. Note that 5-star hotels charge an average of US$140, plus 23% tax. In aparthotels, the average price is US$130 for two. In more modest guest houses, a weekly or monthly rate, with discount, can be arranged. All hotels charge the 23% tax; the VAT component is 13%.

The better hotels have a high occupancy rate and it is best to book in advance, particularly at holiday times. Standards in the five-star hotels are not equivalent to those, say, in the Bahamas.

FOOD AND DRINK

● **Food**
Local dishes include *sancocho* or *salcocho prieto* (a type of stew made of six local meats and vegetables, often including *plátanos*, *ñame* and *yautia*), *mondongo* (a tripe stew), *mofongo*, ground *plátano* with garlic and *chicharrón de cerdo* (pork crackling), usually served with a soup, a side dish of meat and avocado (very filling), *chicharrón de pollo* is

small pieces of chicken prepared with lime and oregano, *locrio de cerdo* or *pollo* (meat and rice), *cocido* (a soup of chickpeas, meat and vegetables), *asopao de pollo* or *de camarones*, *chivo* (goat). Also try *pipián*, goats' offal served as a stew. Fish and seafood are good; lobster can be found for as little as US$12. Fish cooked with coconut (eg *pescado con coco*) is popular around Samaná. The salads are often good; another good side dish is *tostones* (fried and flattened *plátanos*), *fritos verdes* are the same thing. *Plátano* mashed with oil is called *mangú*, often served with rice and beans. Sweet bananas are often called *guineo*. *Moro* is rice and lentils. *Gandules* are green beans, as opposed to *habichuelas*, very good when cooked with coconut. *Quipes* (made of flour and meat) and *pastelitos* (fried dough with meat or cheese inside) can be bought from street vendors; can be risky. *Casabe* is a cassava bread, flat and round, best toasted. *Catibias* are cassava flour fritters with meat. The most common dish is called *bandera dominicana*, white rice, beans, meat/chicken, *plátano* or *yuca* and, in season, avocado. The traveller should be warned that Dominican food is rather on the greasy side; most of the dishes are fried. Local food can often be obtained from private houses, which act as *comedores*. Basic prices, US$3-6.

● **Drink**

Juices, or *jugos*, are good; orange is usually called *china*, papaya is *lechosa*, passion fruit is *chinola*. *Agua de coco* is coconut milk, often served cold, straight from the coconut, chilled in an ice box. Local beers are Presidente (the most popular), Quisqueya and Heineken. There are many rums (the most popular brands are Barceló, Brugal, Bermúdez, Macorix and Carta Vieja). Light rum (*blanco*) is the driest and has the highest proof, usually mixed with fruit juice or other soft drink (*refresco*). Amber (*amarillo*) is aged at least a year in an oak barrel and has a lower proof and more flavour, while dark rum (*añejo*) is aged for several years and is smooth enough, like a brandy, to be drunk neat or with ice and lime. Brugal allows visitors to tour its factory in Puerto Plata, on Avenida Luis Genebra, just before the entrance to the town, and offers free daiquiris. In a discothèque, *un servicio* is a ⅓ litre bottle of rum with a bucket of ice and *refrescos*. In rural areas this costs US$3-4, but in cities rises to US$15. Imported drinks are very expensive. Many of the main hotels have a 'Happy Hour' from 1700-1900, on a 'two for one' basis, ie two drinks for the price of one with free snacks.

GETTING AROUND

AIR TRANSPORT

Several companies offer **air taxi or charter** services within the Republic, all based at Herrera airport. Alas Nacionales, T 542-6688; Transporte Aéreo SA, T 567-4549; Coturisca, T 567-7211. Dorado Air (T 686-1067) flies between Santo Domingo and Puerto Plata several times a day on Fri and Sat. Flights go to Santiago, Puerto Plata, Barahona, Portillo and La Romana daily.

LAND TRANSPORT

● **Motoring**

A valid driving licence from your country of origin or an international licence is accepted. Dominicans drive on the right. The main road from Santo Domingo to Puerto Plata, the Carretera Duarte, is very good, but crowded. Also good are the main road from Santo Domingo to the W, as far as Pedernales and Jimaní; similarly good are the main roads to the E, the coastal and inland routes to Higüey, the continuation to Punta Cana airport, Hato Mayor to Sabana de la Mar, and most of the NE coastal route from Puerto Plata to Samaná (details in the text above). Other roads and many city streets are in poor condition with lots of potholes, so avoid night driving. The speed limit for city driving is 40 kph, for suburban areas 60 kph and on main roads 80 kph. Service stations generally close at 1800, although there are now some offering 24-hr service (petrol/gasoline costs US$1.60 per gallon). Most police or military posts have 'sleeping policemen', speed humps, usually unmarked, outside them. In towns there are often 'ditches' at road junctions, which need as much care as humps. The operation of traffic lights depends on electricity supply, unless they are funded by a local business. In towns the lack of a right of way makes junctions difficult; proceed with caution. Local drivers can be erratic; be on the alert. Hand signals mean only 'I am about to do something', nothing more specific than that. Beware motorcyclists in towns. At night look out for poorly lighted, or lightless vehicles. There are tolls on all principal roads out of the capital: US$0.08 going E, US$0.04 going W. Road signs are very poor: a detailed map is essential, plus a knowledge of Spanish for asking directions.

Drivers can expect to be stopped by the police at the entrance to and exit from towns (normally brief and courteous), at junctions in towns, or any speed-restricted area. Charges, imaginary or otherwise, are common; often an on-the-spot fine of the price of a beer or two may do the trick. At other times a more serious charge with a visit to the *tribunal* is threatened; be patient and the policeman may offer an on-the-spot fine.

● **Car hire**

If renting a car, avoid the cheapest companies because their vehicles are not usually trustworthy; it is better to pay more with a well-known agency. Car rental is expensive because of high import tariffs on vehicles. Prices for small vehicles start at US$40/day but can be as much as US$90. Credit cards are widely accepted; the cash deposit is normally twice the sum of the contract. The minimum age for hiring a car is 25; maximum period for driving is 90 days.

Mopeds and motorcycles are everywhere and are very noisy. Most beach resorts hire motorcycles for between US$20 and 35 a day. By law, the driver of a motorcycle must wear a crash helmet; passengers are not required to wear one.

● **Bus hire**

A number of companies hire vehicles for group travel, which is fairly economical as long as you have a large enough number of friends. For instance *Transporte Turístico Tanya*, T 565-5691, 24-seat buses to Puerto Plata, US$195; *Autobuses Metro*, T 566-7126, 54-seaters to Puerto Plata, US$578; *Compañía Nacional de Autobuses*, T 565-6681, 25, 45 and 60 seaters, US$272, US$315, US$317 respectively to Puerto Plata. Other destinations also served. *LC Tours* and *La Covacha* run 30-seat minibus trips to the E of the country, including Samaná. Taxi companies (addresses under Santo Domingo) run trips to towns in the republic.

● **Buses**

Services from Santo Domingo: Autobuses Metro, first class (T 566-7126) operate from Av Winston Churchill and Hatuey, near 27 de Febrero and have buses to La Vega, Santiago (US$4.50), Puerto Plata (US$6.15), Nagua, Moca, San Francisco de Macorís and Castillo daily. In Puerto Plata, T 586-6063, Santiago, T 583-9111, Nagua, T 584-2259. Caribe Tours (T 221-4422) operates from Av 27 de Febrero at Leopoldo Navarro; most of their services (cheaper than Metro) are in a/c buses, rec (eg US$5.40 to Puerto Plata, US$3.85 to Santiago; they run to all parts except E of Santo Domingo.

Transporte del Cibao, opp Parque Enriquillo, to Puerto Plata, cheaper than other companies. Also to Santiago, Terrabús, US$4.50, and El Expreso, cheaper. La Covacha buses leave from Parque Enriquillo (Av Duarte and Ravelo) for the E: Higüey (US$4.55), Nagua, San Pedro de Macorís, Miches, etc. Expresos Moto Saad, Av Independencia near Parque Independencia runs 12 daily buses to Bonao, La Vega and Santiago (US$2.60). Línea Sur (T 682-7682) runs to San Juan, Barahona, Azua and Haiti. *Guaguas* for Azua, 2 hrs US$3, depart from Av Bolívar near Parque Independencia; easy connections in Azua for Barahona, San Juan and Padre las Casas. For bus offices in other towns, see text above.

Bus (*guagua*) services between most towns are efficient and inexpensive. In rural areas it can be easy to find a *guagua* (mini bus or pickup) but they are often filled to the point where you can not move your legs.

● **Taxis**

There are usually fixed *público* rates (see under Santo Domingo) between cities, so inquire first. Rates are given in the text. Many drivers pack a truly incredible number of passengers in their cars, so the ride is often uncomfortable but friendly and quite an experience. If travelling by private taxi, bargaining is very important. In Santo Domingo, Apolo Taxi is rec if you need to call a taxi, cheap, friendly and efficient.

Motorcyclists (*motoconchos*) also offer a taxi service and take several passengers on pillion. In some towns eg Samaná, motoconchas pull 4-seater covered rickshaws. Negotiate fare first.

● **Hitchhiking**

Hitchhiking is perfectly possible.

● **Boat**

If negotiating transport by **boat**, a *canuco* is a small dugout, a *yola* is a medium-sized rowing boat taking up to 10 passengers, a *bote* takes 20 or more.

COMMUNICATIONS

● **Postal services**

Don't use post boxes, they are unreliable. The postal system as a whole is very slow. For each 10 grams, or fraction thereof, the cost to Europe is 1 peso; to North America, Venezuela, Central America and the Caribbean, 50 centavos; to elsewhere in the Americas and Spain, 70 centavos; to Africa, Australia, Asia and Oceania, RD$1.50. It is recommended to use *entrega especial* (special delivery, with separate window at post offices), for 2 pesos extra, on overseas mail, or better still a courier service (see under Santo Domingo).

● **Telecommunications**
Operated by the Compañía Dominicana de Teléfonos (Codetel), a subsidiary of GTE. All local calls and overseas calls and faxes to the Caribbean, European Community, US and Canada may be dialled directly from any Codetel office (no collect calls to the UK, but they are available to many other countries). Through Codetel you call abroad either person-to-person or through an operator (more expensive, but you only pay if connected). Calls and faxes may be paid for by credit card. For phone boxes you need 25-centavo coins. Phone calls to the USA cost US$7.85, to Europe US$8.50, to Australia US$9.60 and Argentina US$14.80 (3 mins). AT&T's USA-Direct is available on 1-800-872-2881, US$1.45 for the first minute, US$1.06 additional and US$2.50 service charge. Canada Direct is 1-800-333-0111. Codetel publishes a bilingual Spanish/English business telephone directory for tourism (a sort of tourist's yellow pages), called the *Dominican Republic Tourist Guide/Guía Turística de la República Dominicana*, which contains a lot of information as well as telephone numbers. Emergency number: 711; information is 1411.

MEDIA

● **Newspapers**
There are 10 daily papers in all, seven in the morning, three in the afternoon. *Listín Diario* has the widest circulation; among the other morning papers are *El Caribe, Hoy, El Siglo* (has good foreign coverage). In the afternoon, *Ultima Hora* and *El Nacional* are published. The English-language *Santo Domingo News*, published every Friday, is available at hotels. *Touring* is a multilingual tourist newspaper with articles and adverts in English, German, French, Spanish and Italian. *La Información*, published in Santiago on weekdays, is a good regional paper carrying both national and international stories.

● **Radio and television**
There are over 170 local radio stations and 7 television stations. In the N coast area, Radio Fantasia (90.5 FM) is an all-American music station. Also 1 cable TV station broadcasting in English.

TOURIST INFORMATION

● **Local tourist office**
The head office of the Secretaría de Estado de Turismo is in the Edificio de Oficinas Gubernamentales, Avenida México esquina 30 de Marzo, Ala 'D', near the Palacio Nacional (PO Box 497, T 689-3655/3657, F 682-3806); it publishes a tourism guide called *La Cotica*, which is free (some places in Santo Domingo, around the cathedral, charge US$2.45 for it). There are also offices at Las Américas International Airport, in Santo Domingo in the colonial city, La Unión Airport at Puerto Plata, in Puerto Plata (Malecón 20, T 586-3676), in Santiago (Ayuntamiento, T 582-5885), Barahona, Jimaní, Samaná and Boca Chica. The Consejo de Promoción Turística (CPT), Desiderio Arias 24, Bella Vista, Santo Domingo, T 535-3276, F 535-7767, promotes the Dominican Republic abroad, under the new name of Dominicana (US mailing address EPS No A-355, PO Box 02-5256, Miami, FL 33102-5256). Asonahores (Asociación Nacional de Hoteles y Restaurantes), Av México 66, T 687-4676, F 687-4727.

● **Tourist offices overseas**
Outside the Dominican Republic, there are tourist offices in the **USA**: 1501 Broadway, Suite 410, New York, NY 10036, T (212) 575-4966, F (212) 575-5448; 2355 Salzedo Street, Suite 305, Coral Gables, Miami, Florida 33134, T 444-4592/3, F 444-4845; in **Canada**: 1650 de Maisonneuve Ouest, Suite 302, Montréal, Québec, H3H 2P3, T (514) 933-9008, F 933-2070; in **Puerto Rico**: Metro Tours, Ortegón esq Tabonuco, Caparra Hills, Guaynabo, PR 00657, T (809) 781-8665, F (809) 793-7935; in **Spain**: Núñez de Balboa 37, 4° Izquierda, Madrid 1, T (01) 431-5354; in **Germany**, Voelckerstrasse 24, D-6000 Frankfurt am Main 1, T (49-69) 597-0330, F 590982.

● **Local tour agents**
Martisant, Av Duarte y Padre Billini, T 585-7887, has tours to the national parks, also group travel, some with overnight stops in a hotel; *Chris Travel*, Santomé 352, T 689-7007, just off Av Mella at Mercado Modelo, helpful; *El Dorado*, Juan Sánchez Ramírez y Av Máximo Gómez, 1 block from Haitian Embassy; other companies include *Palmtours* at the *Hotel Sheraton*, T 682-3407, 682-3284, *Tanya*, T 565-5691, *Nuevo Mundo*, T 685-5615, *Juan Perdomo Travel, Ecoturismo*, T 563-0744,

Mundi Tours, T 536-738/-2, *Caria Tours,* T 685-3018 and *Omni Tours,* T 565-6591, F 567-4710, or Punta Cana T 686-5797, F 688-0764. In Puerto Plata, *Connex Caribe,* Plaza Turisol, T 586-6879, F 586-6099, offers a wide variety of tours in town, to Santo Domingo and all over the republic. Many other companies operate tours (some are mentioned, with prices, in the text above).

The Museo de Historia y Geografía in Santo Domingo organizes archaeological and historical tours in the the republic, visiting, for example, Cotuí, Bonao, Presa de Hatillo, Sánchez, Samaná, Pozo de Bojolo in Nagua, Lago Enriquillo and other places of interest. The tour is by bus, inc lunch; T 686-6668.

● **Maps**
A map of the Dominican Republic, with plans of Santo Domingo, Santiago, Puerto Plata, La Romana, San Pedro de Macorís and Sosúa, is available from bookshops and stationers. Texaco also produce a good (Rand McNally) map of the country, capital and Santiago. Maps tend to be a little optimistic about roads and features.

● **Further reading**
For a study of contemporary Dominican politics and economics see *Dominican Republic: Beyond the Lighthouse,* by James Ferguson (London: Latin America Bureau, 1992).

Living in Santo Domingo, published by The Santo Domingo News (CPS 1215, PO Box 149020, Coral Gables, FL 33114, USA) gives advice on the city; on sale in Santo Domingo bookshops or from above address, US$11.50 plus shipping.

ACKNOWLEDGEMENTS

Thanks go to Dania Goris for help with updating Santo Domingo.

Puerto Rico

THE COMMONWEALTH of Puerto Rico, the smallest and most easterly island of the Greater Antilles, is the first Overseas Commonwealth Territory (defined as a 'free and associated State') of the USA. Spanish is the first language but the citizenship is US and English is widely spoken (as is 'Spanglish'). In 1993, Spanish and English were made official languages (thereby restoring a 1902 statute which had been amended in 1991 making Spanish the sole official language). Puerto Rico lies about 1,600 km SE of Miami between the island of Hispaniola and the Virgin Islands, which give it some shelter from the open Atlantic, and is between longitudes 66° and 67° W and at latitude 18°30 N. Almost rectangular in shape, slightly smaller than Jamaica, it measures 153 km in length (E to W), 58 km in width, and has a total land area of some 8,768 square km.

HORIZONS

Old volcanic mountains, long inactive, occupy a large part of the interior of the island, with the highest peak, Cerro de Punta, at 1,338m in the Cordillera Central. North of the Cordillera is the karst country where the limestone has been acted upon by water to produce a series of small steep hills (*mogotes*) and deep holes, both conical in shape. The mountains are surrounded by a coastal plain with the Atlantic shore beaches cooled all the year round by trade winds, which make the temperatures of 28-30°C bearable in the summer. Temperatures in the winter drop to the range 21-26°C and the climate all the year round is very agreeable. Rain falls mainly from May to October, with most precipitation from July to October.

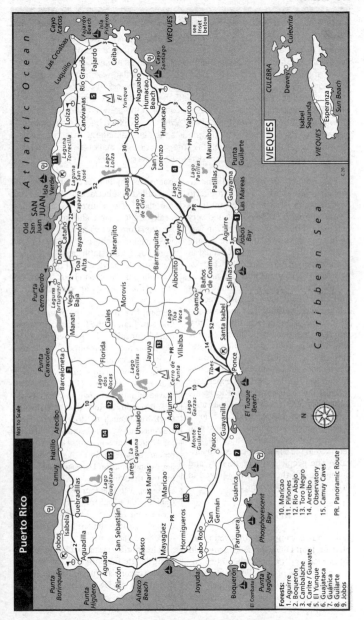

Puerto Rico

Not to Scale

Forests:
1. Aguirre
2. Boquerón
3. Cambalache
4. Carite / Guavate
5. El Yunque
6. Guajataca
7. Guánica
8. Guilarte
9. Jobos
10. Maricao
11. Piñones
12. Río Abajo
13. Toro Negro
14. Arecibo Observatory
15. Camuy Caves

PR. Panoramic Route

The flag

🔖 22 December 1995 was the 100th anniversary of the lone star flag of Puerto Rico, marked by hoisting it alone at the Ateneo Puertorriqueño, in clear violation of US law which states that the US flag should always be flown alongside state or other territorial flags. All over the island the flag was flown as a gesture of pride in Puerto Rican nationality. The flag was first used on 22 December 1895 and adopted as a national symbol. In 1898 the flag became the mark of resistance to the US invasion; the lone star was the 'guide of the patriots', and in the 1930s it was adopted by the Nationalist Party. When Puerto Rico became a Commonwealth in 1952 it was officially adopted as the national flag but after the Cuban revolution the US administration became suspicious of nationalists and people who displayed the flag were considered subversives.

The population is 3.6 million, although about another 2 million Puerto Ricans live in the USA. The country is a strange mixture of very new and very old, exhibiting the open American way of life yet retaining the more formal Spanish influences. This is reflected in the architecture, not just the contrast between the colonial and the modern but also in the countryside, where older buildings sit side by side with concrete schools and dwellings. It is also found in the cuisine, a plethora of fast food restaurants together with local cuisine which has its roots in the same hybrid culture of all the Caribbean. However, if you do not stray beyond the tourist areas around San Juan, you will not experience the real Puerto Rico. Puerto Ricans are sometimes referred to as Boricuas after the Indian name of the island (see below). Second generation Puerto Ricans who were born in New York, but who have returned to the island, are called Nuyoricans. The people are very friendly and hospitable but there is crime, linked to drugs and unemployment.

HISTORY

Columbus, accompanied by a young nobleman, Juan Ponce de León, arrived in Puerto Rico on 19 November 1493. Attracted by tales of gold, Ponce obtained permission to colonize Boriquén (or Boriken), as it was called by the natives. Boriquén (later altered to Borinquén in poetry) meant 'land of the great lord' and was called that because of the belief that the god, Juracan, lived on the highest peak of the island and controlled the weather from there. The word 'hurricane' is derived from this god's name. In 1508 Ponce de León established the first settlement at Caparra, a small village not far from the harbour of San Juan. A year later the Spanish Crown appointed him the first Governor. In 1521, however, the settlement was moved to the present site of Old San Juan as the former site was declared unhealthy. In that year Ponce de León was mortally wounded in the conquest of Florida.

Because of Puerto Rico's excellent location at the gateway to Latin America, it played an important part in defending the Spanish empire against attacks from French, English and Dutch invaders. After the Spanish-American war, Spain ceded the island to the United States in 1898. The inhabitants became US citizens in 1917, with their own Senate and House of Delegates, and in 1948, for the first time, they elected their own Governor, who is authorized to appoint his Cabinet and members of the island's Supreme Court. In 1952 Puerto Rico became a Commonwealth voluntarily associated with the United States.

The island's status is a matter of constant debate for both political and economic reasons as Puerto Rico is heavily dependent on US funding (see **Economy** section). The New Progressive Party (NPP) favours Puerto Rico's full accession to the USA as the 51st state. The Popular Democratic Party (PDP) favours enhancement of the existing Commonwealth status. Pro-independence groups receive less support, the Puerto Rican Independence Party (PIP) struggles to gain seats in Congress. A small guerrilla group, the Macheteros, demands that all US presence be removed from the island. A referendum on Puerto Rico's future status was held in 1991, but voters rejected the PDP administration's proposals to guarantee that they remain citizens of the USA regardless of any change in Puerto Rico's political status. The 1991 vote was seen as a rejection of the policies of the governing party and Governor Rafael Hernández Colón subsequently decided not to seek re-election in the 1992 elections. The elections were convincingly won by the pro-statehood NPP, who secured 36 seats in the House of Representatives and 20 in the Senate. The PDP won 14 seats in the House and six in the Senate, while the PIP won one in each chamber. An extra two seats were to be added to the opposition representation under a constitutional requirement that no party may hold more than two thirds of the seats in either house. The new Governor, Pedro Rosselló, took office in January 1993. Carlos Romero Barceló, of the NPP, who was Governor 1976-84, won the office of Resident Commissioner in Washington.

In November 1993 another referendum was held on the future political status of the island. Voter turnout was high, at 73.6%, of whom 48.4% voted for Commonwealth Status, 46.2% for statehood and 4.4% for independence. Although the result was close, it was seen as a set-back for the pro-statehood government.

GOVERNMENT

Puerto Rico is a self-governing Commonwealth in association with the USA. The chief of state is the President of the United States of America. The head of government is an elected Governor. There are two legislative chambers: the House of Representatives, 51 seats, and the Senate, 27 seats. Two extra seats are granted in each house to the opposition if necessary to limit any party's control to two thirds. Puerto Ricans do not vote in US federal elections, nor do they pay federal taxes, when resident on the island.

THE ECONOMY

Structure of production

Great social and economic progress has been made in the past 30 years, as a result of the 'Operation Bootstrap' industrialization programme supported by the US and Puerto Rican governments, which was begun in 1948. Accordingly manufacturing for export has become the most important sector of the economy, in place of agriculture. Until 1976, US Corporations were given tax incentives to set up in Puerto Rico and their profits were taxed only if repatriated. Industrial parks were built based on labour intensive industries to take advantage of Puerto Rico's low wages. In the mid-1970s, however, the strategy changed to attract capital intensive companies with the aim of avoiding the low wage trap. Nowadays about 70% of manufacturing income is repatriated; manufacturing produces about 40% of total output, but only 20% if remittances are excluded, about the same as in the 1950s. Investment has also fallen recently to 16% of gdp, having risen from 15% in 1950 to 30% in 1970.

The principal manufactures are textiles, clothing, electrical and electronic equipment, chemicals and pharmaceuticals. Dairy and livestock production is one of the leading agricultural activities; others are the cultivation of sugar, tobacco, coffee, pineapples and coconut. Tourism is another key element in the economy although it contributes only about 6.5% to gdp. The industry is profitable and a large employer. Over 2 million people visit Puerto Rico each year (over half are stayover visitors and the

Puerto Rico: fact file

Geographic

Land area	9,104 sq km
forested	20.0%
pastures	37.7%
cultivated	14.0%

Demographic

Population (1995)	3,725,000
annual growth rate (1990-95)	1.1%
urban	71.2%
rural	28.8%
density	409.2 per sq km
Religious affiliation	
Roman Catholic	85.3%
Birth rate per 1,000 (1994)	17.9
	(world av 25.0)

Education and health

Life expectancy at birth,	
male	69.6 years
female	78.5 years
Infant mortality rate	
per 1,000 live births (1993)	13.4
Physicians (1988)	1 per 349 persons
Hospital beds (1994)	1 per 381 persons
Calorie intake as %	
of FAO requirement	na
Population age 25 and over	
with no formal schooling	none
Literate males (over 15)	89.6%
Literate females (over 15)	89.7%

Economic

GNP (1993 market prices)	
	US$25,317mn
GNP per capita	US$6,700
Public external debt (1994)	
	US$15,258mn
Tourism receipts (1994)	US$1,737mn
Inflation (annual av 1989-94)	3.6%

Radio	1 per 1.5 persons
Television	1 per 4.4 persons
Telephone	1 per 2.6 persons

Employment

Population economically active (1994)	
	1,203,000
Unemployment rate	16.0%
% of labour force in	
agriculture	2.8
manufacturing	13.8
construction	4.5
Military forces (US)	3,518

Source *Encyclopaedia Britannica*

rest cruise ship passengers) and spend about US$1.7bn a year. There are several large projects designed to increase tourism. New, luxury hotels are being built in the San Juan area (see **Accommodation**) and colonial buildings are being renovated in old San Juan and converted into elegant hotels.

Recent trends

Despite the progress made to industrialize the country, the economy has suffered from US budget cuts. Some 30% of all spending on gnp originates in Washington and high unemployment is possible because of food stamps and other US transfers. Migration is a safety valve, and there are more Puerto Ricans living in New York than San Juan. The economy depends heavily on the tax incentives (known as Section 936) given to US mainland companies and on federal transfers. Puerto Rico is also used to channel loans to other Caribbean and Central American countries under the Caribbean Basin Initiative (CBI). President Clinton aimed to cut the Section 936 tax exemption for US companies and introduced legislation to Congress in 1993 to replace it with a more modest tax credit linked to wages paid by those companies in Puerto Rico rather than to profits. This was also likely to reduce sharply the amount of finance available to other CBI countries. It is estimated that 100,000 Puerto Ricans are employed by companies operating under Section 936 (of which 23,000 are in pharmaceuticals) and another 200,000 are indirectly employed. By 1993, Section 936 funds had been invested in nine CBI countries, with US$685mn provided for 46 projects and about 13,000 jobs. President Clinton's proposals were modified by the US Senate Finance Committee after much lobbying by Caribbean and Central American governments and companies, although the outcome represented a reduction in US budgetary spending.

The agreement between the USA, Canada and Mexico for the North American Free Trade Agreement

(NAFTA) also has implications for Puerto Rico because of competition for jobs and investment. Although wage levels are lower in Mexico, Section 936 gives companies in Puerto Rico an advantage in pharmaceuticals and hi-tec industries. In low-skill labour-intensive manufacturing, such as clothing and footwear, Mexico has the advantage. Puerto Rico currently employs 30,000 in the clothing industry.

CULTURE

Puerto Rico may be part of the United States, but its music and dance, and indeed its soul, are wholly Latin American. A visitor who sticks to the hotels and beaches will be largely subjected to rock music and salsa and to hear the real Puerto Rican music you should head for the countryside and especially to the hilly interior, the 'Montaña'. The island was Spanish until 1898 and the oldest musical tradition is that of the nineteenth century Danza, associated particularly with the name of Juan Morel Campos and his phenomenal output of 549 compositions. This is European-derived salon music for ballroom dancing, slow, romantic and sentimental. The Institute of Puerto Rican Culture sponsors an annual competition for writers of danzas for the piano during the Puerto Rican Danza Week in May. The peasants of the interior, the Jíbaros, sing and dance the Seis, of Spanish origin, in its many varied forms, such as the Seis Chorreao, Seis Zapateao, Seis Corrido and Seis Bombeao. Other variants are named after places, like the Seis Cagueño and Seis Fajardeño. Favoured instruments are the *cuatro* and other varieties of the guitar, the *bordonúa, tiple, tres* and *quintillo*, backed by *güiro* (scraper), *maracas, pandereta* (tambourine) and *bomba* (drum) to provide rhythm. One uniquely Puerto Rican phenomenon is the singer's 'La-Le-Lo-Lai' introduction to the verses, which are in Spanish 10-line *décimas*. The beautiful Aguinaldos are sung at Christmastime,

while the words of the Mapeyé express the Jíbaro's somewhat tragic view of life. Many artists have recorded the mountain music, notably El Gallito de Manatí, Ramito, Chuito el de Bayamón, Baltazar Carrero and El Jibarito de Lares. A popular singer is Andrés Jiménez, 'El Jíbaro', whose rustic songs of Puerto Rican folklore were honoured at Christmas 1993 by a concert with the Symphonic Orchestra of Puerto Rico and the Choir of the Conservatorio de Música de Puerto Rico, in which many traditional instruments were used.

Puerto Rico's best-known musical genre is the Plena, ironically developed by a black couple from Barbados, John Clark and Catherine George, known as 'Los Ingleses', who lived in the La Joya del Castillo neighbourhood of Ponce during the years of the First World War. With a four-line stanza and refrain in call-and-response between the 'Inspirador' (soloist) and chorus, the rhythm is distinctly African and the words embody calypso-style commentaries on social affairs and true-life incidents. Accompanying instruments were originally tambourines, then accordions and *güiros*, but nowadays include guitars, trumpets and clarinets. The Plena's most celebrated composer and performer was Manuel A Jiménez, known as 'Canario'.

There are relatively few black people in Puerto Rico and the only specifically black music is the Bomba, sung by the 'Cantaor' and chorus, accompanied by the drums called *buleadores* and *subidores* and naturally also danced. The Bomba can be seen and heard at its best in the island's only black town of Loíza Aldea at the Feast of Santiago in late July. Rafael Cepeda and his family are the best known exponents.

For a modern interpretation of traditional music, recordings by the singer/composer Tony Croatto are highly recommended, while Rafael Cortijo and his Combo have taken the Plena beyond the confines of the island into the wider world of Caribbean salsa.

There are several music festivals each

year, celebrating different styles and forms, including a Jazzfest in May and the Casals Music Festival in June.

The Jíbaro, mentioned above, is a common figure in Puerto Rican literature. The origin of the name is unknown, but it refers to the *campesino del interior*, a sort of Puerto Rican equivalent to the gaucho, native, but with predominantly hispanic features. The Jíbaro, as a literary figure, first appeared in the 19th century, with Manuel Alonso Pacheco's *El gíbaro* emerging as a cornerstone of the island's literature. In 29 'scenes', Alonso attempted both to describe and to interpret Puerto Rican life; he showed a form of rural life about to disappear in the face of bourgeois progress. The book also appeared at a time (1849) when romanticism was gaining popularity. Prior to this period, there had been a definite gulf between the educated letters, chronicles and memoires of the 16th to 18th centuries and the oral traditions of the people. These included *coplas, décimas, aguinaldas* (see above) and folk tales. The Jíbaro has survived the various literary fashions, from 19th century romanticism and *realismo costumbrista* (writing about manners and customs), through the change from Spanish to US influence, well into the 20th century.

One reason for this tenacity is the continual search for a Puerto Rican identity. When, in 1898, Spain relinquished power to the USA, many Puerto Ricans sought full independence. Among the writers of this time were José de Diego and Manuel Zeno Gandía. The latter's series of four novels, *Crónicas de un mundo enfermo* (*Garduña* – 1896, *La charca* – 1898, *El negocio* – 1922, *Redentores* – 1925), contain a strong element of social protest. As the series progresses, a new theme is added to that of local economic misery, emigration to New York, which booms after 1945. For a variety of domestic reasons, many fled the island to seek adventures, happiness, material wealth in the United States. While some writers and artists in the 1930s and 1940s, eg Luis Lloréns Torres, tried to build a kind of nationalism around a mythical, rural past, others still favoured a complete separation from the colonialism which had characterized Puerto Rico's history. For a while, the former trend dominated, but by the 1960s the emigré culture had created a different set of themes to set against the search for the Puerto Rican secure in his/her national identity. These included, on the one hand, the social problems of the islander in New York, shown, for example, in some of the novels of Enrique A Laguerre, *Trópico en Manhattan* by Guillermo Cotto Thorner, stories such as *Spiks* by Pedro Juan Soto, or plays like René Marqués' *La carreta*. On the other there is the Americanization of the island, the figure of the 'piti-yanqui' (the native Puerto Rican who admires and flatters his North American neighbour) and the subordination of the agricultural to a US-based, industrial economy. Writers after 1965 who have documented this change include Rosario Ferré and the novelist and playwright, Luis Rafael Sánchez. The latter's *La guaracha del Macho Camacho* (1976), an alliterative, humorous novel, revolves around a traffic jam in a San Juan taken over by a vastly popular song, *La vida es una cosa fenomenal*, a far cry from the Jíbaro's world.

FLORA AND FAUNA

Although less than 1% of the island is virgin forest, there are several forest reserves designed to protect plants and wildlife. In **El Yunque Tropical Rain Forest** (called The Caribbean National Forest) there are an estimated 240 types of tree (26 indigenous), and many other plants, such as tiny wild orchids, bamboo trees, giant ferns, and trumpet trees. The forest falls into four overlapping types: at the lowest level the rain forest, then thicket, palm forest and, at the highest altitudes, dwarf forest. The total area is

28,000 acres. Several marked paths (quite easy, you could walk 2-3 in a day, no guide needed), recreational areas and information areas have been set up, but note that Route 191, which some maps show traversing the forest, is closed beyond the Sierra Palma Visitors' Centre and there is no evidence of any intention to reopen it. It is also home to the Puerto Rican parrot, which has been saved from extinction. It is often seen around the picnic area behind the Visitors' Centre. Hurricane Hugo nearly wiped out the whole population and some say only 24 pairs are left alive. The whole forest is a bird sanctuary.

Other forest areas, some of which are mentioned in the text below are Guajataca in the NW; Río Abajo, between Arecibo and Utuado; Maricao, Guilarte, Toro Negro and Carite (Guavate), all on the transinsular Panoramic Route.

Mangroves are protected in **Aguirre Forest**, on the S coast near Salinas, at the Jobos Bay National Estuarine Research Reserve, at the W end of Jobos Bay from Aguirre, and at Piñones Forest, E of San Juan (also hit by Hurricane Hugo). Unlike the N coast mangroves, those on the S coast tend to die behind the outer fringe because not enough water is received to wash away the salt. This leaves areas of mud and skeletal trees which, at times of spring tide, flood and are home to many birds. In winter, many ducks stop on their migration routes at Jobos. Also at **Jobos Bay**, manatees and turtles can be seen. A short boardwalk runs into the mangroves at Jobos, while at Aguirre a man runs catamaran trips to the offshore cays, and there are some good fish restaurants; take Route 7710. For Jobos Bay take Route 703, to Las Mareas de Salinas (marked Mar Negro on some maps). Before going to Jobos, contact the office at Jobos, Box 1170, Guayama, Puerto Rico 00655, T 864-0105, or 724-8774 in San Juan.

The largest number of bird species can be found at **Guánica Forest**, W of Ponce, which is home to 700 plant species of which 48 are endangered and 16 exist nowhere else. (*Las aves de Puerto Rico*, by Virgilio Biaggi, University of Puerto Rico, 1983, US$12.95, is available in San Juan, eg the bookshop in Fort San Cristóbal; Herbert Raffaele's *Guide to the Birds of Puerto Rico and the Virgin Islands* is also recommended.) Guánica's dry forest vegetation is unique and the Forest has been declared an International Biosphere Reserve by UNESCO. Most of the trails through these and other forests are now marked, but it may be advisable to contact the wardens for directions before wandering off. Open daily 0900-1700, no admission charge; wear protective clothing and take drinking water, T 723-1770/1717.

One of the most notable creatures on Puerto Rico is the inch-long tree frog called a *coquí*, after the two-tone noise it makes.

Puerto Rico also has some of the most important caves in the W hemisphere. The Río Camuy runs underground for part of its course, forming the third largest subterranean river in the world. Near Lares, on Route 129, Km 9.8, the **Río Camuy Cave Park** has been established by the Administración de Terrenos (PO Box 3767, San Juan, T 893-3100), where visitors are guided through one cave and two sinkholes, open Tues to Sun, and holidays 0800-1600, last trip 1545, US$10 for adults, less for children, highly recommended, but entry is limited. There are fine examples of stalactites, stalagmites and, of course, plenty of bats. Keen photographers should bring a tripod for excellent photo opportunities. Also close is the privately-owned **Cueva de Camuy**, Route 486, Km 1.1; much smaller and less interesting, with guided tours, the area also has a swimming pool and waterslide, amusements, café, ponies, go-karts, entertainments, entry US$1, children US$0.50, open daily 0900-1700 (till 2000 Sunday). Also close is **Cueva del Infierno**, to which 2-3 hour tours can be arranged by phoning 898-2723. About 2,000 caves have been discovered; in them live 13 species of bat (but not in every cave), the *coquí*, crickets, an arachnid called the *guavá*, and other species. For full details contact the Speleological Society of Puerto Rico (Sepri).

BEACHES AND WATERSPORTS

Swimming from most beaches is safe; the best beaches near San Juan are those at Isla Verde in front of the main hotels; Luquillo to the E of San Juan is less crowded and has a fine-sand beach (Monserrate Beach Park) from where there are good views of El Yunque (controlled car parking, US$2 per car all day, if arriving by *público* from San Juan, ask to get off at La Playa de Luquillo, which is 1 km W of the town). There are showers, toilets and life guards, food kiosks and souvenir shops, it is peaceful during the week but noisy at weekends. The N coast Atlantic sea is rougher than the S waters, particularly in winter; some beaches are semi-deserted. There are 13 *balneario* beaches round the island where lockers, showers and parking places are provided for a small fee. Some have cabins, tent sites or trailer sites. *Balnearios* are open Tues-Sun 0900-1700 in winter and 0800-1700 in summer.

The most popular beaches for surfing are the Pine Beach Grove in Isla Verde (San Juan), Jobos (near Isabela in the NW, not the S coast bay), La Pared in Luquillo, officially listed as dangerous for swimming but used for surfing tournaments, Surfer and Wilderness beaches in the former Ramey Field air base at Punta Borinquén, N of Aguadilla and Punta Higuero, Route 413 between Aguadilla and Rincón on the W coast. Several international surfing competitions have been held at Surfer and Wilderness. The Condado lagoon is popular for windsurfing (there is a windsurfing school in Santurce, Lisa Penfield, 2A Rambla del Almirante, T 796-2188, with rentals at US$25 per hour and lessons starting at US$45 for 1½ hrs), as is Bo-

querón Bay and Ocean Park beach.

Puerto Rico's coastline is protected in many places by coral reefs and cays which are fun to visit and explore. Sloops can be hired at US$60 pp a day, with crew, and hold 6 passengers (eg Captain Jayne at Fajardo, T 791-5174).

There are four marinas at Fajardo, the Club Náutico at Miramar and another at Boca de Cangrejos in Isla Verde (both in San Juan) and one at the *Palmas del Mar Resort* near Humacao. There is a marina for fishing motor launches at Arecibo. The first phase of an ambitious marina project at Puerto del Rey, Fajardo, opened late 1988 and a second stage of expansion was under construction in 1994. Sailing is popular, with winds of about 10-15 knots all year round. Craft of all sizes are available for hire. There are several racing tournaments; a major international regatta is the Discover the Caribbean series in September and October. Power boats appeal to the Puerto Rican spirit and there are a lot of races, held mostly off the W coast from Mayagüez Bay to Boquerón Bay. A huge crowd collects for the Caribbean Offshore Race, with professionals and celebrities participating.

Deep-sea fishing is popular and more than 30 world records have been broken in Puerto Rican waters, where blue and white marlin, sailfish, wahoo, dolphin, mackerel and tarpon, to mention a few, are a challenge to the angler. An international bill fish competition is held in September, one of the biggest tournaments in the Caribbean. Fishing boat charters are available: eg Mike Benítez Fishing Charters Inc, at the Club Náutico de San Juan, PO Box 5141, Puerta de Tierra, San Juan, PR 00906, T 723-2292 (till 2100), 724-6265 (till 1700), F 725-1336, prices from US$125-1,200. Maikara Hunter do deep sea fishing, boating trips, charters, big and small game, Club Náutico de San Juan, Stop 9½, Fernández Juncos Avenue, Miramar, T 397-8028, rates from US$390-690. You can also fish in the many lakes inland. Contact the Department of Natural Resources (T 722-5938) for details.

DIVING AND MARINE LIFE

The shallow waters are good for snorkelling and while a boat is needed to reach deeper water for most scuba diving, divers can walk in at Isabela. Visibility is not quite as good as in some other islands because of the large number of rivers flowing out to the sea, but is generally around 70 feet. However, an advantage is that the fresh water attracts a large number of fish. Manatees can occasionally be seen and hump back whales migrate through Puerto Rican waters in the autumn. There are many companies all round the island offering boat dives, equipment rental and diving instruction, including Coral Head Divers, Marina de Palmas, *Palmas del Mar Resort*, Humacao (T 850-7208, 800-635-4529, F 850-4445, US$50-75), Mundo Submarino, Laguna Gardens, Isla Verde (T 791-5764, US$65), in San Juan, Carib Aquatic Adventures, San Juan Bay Marina, Miramar, (T 724-1882, 765-7444, F 721-3127, US$90-110). Diving also at some of the larger hotels. Companies in San Juan and to the E also dive Culebra and Vieques, but there are dive shops on those islands if you want to avoid long boat rides. Check how many divers are taken on the boats, some companies cater for small groups of 6-7 divers, but several of the larger operations take out parties of 40 or 80. *Qué Pasa* lists all the operators approved by the Tourism Company.

OTHER SPORTS

Golf There are 14 golf courses around the island of which six are professionally designed championship courses. The *Cerromar* and *Dorado Beach* hotels in Dorado have excellent 36-hole championship golf courses; among the 18-hole courses, *Berwind Country Club* accepts non-members on Tues, Thur and Fri, *Palmas del Mar* (Humacao), Club Riomar (Río Grande), and Punta Borinquén (Aguadilla, 9 holes) all have golf pros and are open to the public. **Tennis** Over 100 tennis courts are available, mostly in the

larger hotels. There are also 17 lit public courts in San Juan's Central Park, open daily, with tennis pro, T 722-1646. The *Palmas del Mar* resort, at Humacao, has 20 courts. **Cockfighting** The season is from 1 November to 31 August. This sport is held at the new, air-conditioned Coliseo Gallístico in Isla Verde, near the *Holiday Inn* (Route 37, Km 1.5). Saturday 1300-1900, T 791-1557/6005 for times. Admission from US$4 to US$10. **Horse Racing** El Comandante, Route 3, Km 5.5, Canóvanas, is one of the hemisphere's most beautiful race courses. Races are held all the year round (Wednesday, Friday, Sunday and holidays). First race is at 1430. Wednesday is ladies' day. Children under 12 not admitted at any time. **Riding** On mountain trails or beaches, riding is a good way to see the island. Puerto Rico also prides itself on its paso fino horses. There are over 7,000 registered paso fino horses on the island and several horse shows are held throughout the year which are well worth attending. The two best known are the Dulce Sueño Fair, Guayama, the first weekend in March, and the Fiesta La Candelaria, Manatí, the first weekend in February. At Palmas del Mar, Humacao, there is an equestrian centre T 852-6000 ext 12721) which offers beach rides and riding and jumping lessons. Hacienda Carabalí (T 889-5820, 889-4954), Route 992, Km 4, offers beach or hill riding and has paso fino horses, groups of up to 40 for trail rides. **Polo** is becoming popular and the Ingenio Polo Club hosts the Rolex Polo Cup on its 25-acre grounds by the Loiza River in March.

Popular spectator sports are boxing and baseball (at professional level, also a winter league at San Juan stadium, US$4 for a general seat, US$5 box seat, Tues is Ladies' Night), basketball, volleyball and beach volleyball. Running, competitive and non-competitive, is also popular. Puerto Rico is a member of the Olympic Committee. The island is making a bid to host the 2004 Olympic Games.

FESTIVALS

Everything is closed on public holidays. One of the most important is 24 June, though in fact the capital grinds to a halt the previous afternoon and everyone heads for the beach. Here there is loud *salsa* music and barbecues until midnight when everyone walks backwards into the sea to greet the Baptist and ensure good fortune. Every town/city has local holidays for crop-over festivals (pineapple, tobacco, sugar cane, etc) and for celebration of the town's saint. Check in *Qué Pasa* for an up-to-date listing, but call first and check in case the event has been postponed. These festivals can be great fun, especially the Carnival in Mayagüez late May. There is a festival somewhere every week.

SAN JUAN

Founded in 1510, **San Juan**, the capital (population about 1 million) spreads several km along the N coast and also inland. The nucleus is Old San Juan, the old walled city on a tongue of land between the Atlantic and San Juan bay. It has a great deal of charm and character, a living museum; the Institute of Culture restores and renovates old buildings, museums and places of particular beauty. The narrow streets of Old San Juan, some paved with small grey-blue blocks which were cast from the residues of iron furnaces in Spain and brought over as ships' ballast, are lined with colonial churches, houses and mansions, in a very good state of repair and all painted different pastel colours. Small yellow buses run around the old city all day, free, *paradas* (stops) are marked. They go to the forts and run every 5-8 mins from 0730-1930, reducing in frequency after then.

Some of the restored and interesting buildings to visit include **La Fortaleza**, the Governor's Palace, built between 1533 and 1540 as a fortress against Carib attacks but greatly expanded in the 19th century. It is believed to be the oldest executive residence in continuous use in the Western Hemisphere. Access to the official areas is not permitted (open 0900-1600 Monday-Friday; guided tours in English on the hour, in Spanish every half hour, T 721-7000 ext 2211). The **Cathedral** was built in the 16th century but extensively restored in the 19th and 20th. The body of Juan Ponce de León rests in a marble tomb (open daily 0630-1700). The tiny **Cristo Chapel** with its silver altar, was built after a young man competing in 1753 in a horse-race during the San Juan festival celebrations plunged with his horse over the precipice at that very spot (open Tues 1000-1600). Next to it is the aptly-named **Parque de las Palomas**, where the birds perch on your hand to be fed. **San Felipe del Morro** was built in 1591 to defend the entrance to the harbour, and the 11-ha **Fort San Cristóbal** was completed in 1772 to support El Morro and to defend the landward side of the city, with its five independent units connected by tunnels and dry moats, rising 46m above the ocean. Good views of the city (both open daily 0900-1700, admission free). The new **Plaza del Quinto Centenario**, inaugurated on 12 October 1992 to commemorate the 500th anniversary of Columbus' landing, is a modernistic square on several levels with steps leading to a central fountain with hundreds of jets (good view of El Morro, the cemetery and sunsets). The restored **Cuartel de Ballajá**, once the barracks for Spanish troops and their families, was also inaugurated 12 October 1992 with the **Museum of the Americas** on the second floor tracing the cultural development of the history of the New World (open Mon-Fri 1000-1600, Sat-Sun 1100-1700, guided tours available weekdays 1030, 1130, 1230 and 1400, T 724-5052, admission free). The **Dominican Convent** built in the early 16th century, later used as a headquarters by the US Army, is now the office of the Institute of Culture, with a good art gallery (Chapel museum open Wednesday-Sunday, 0900-1200, 1300-

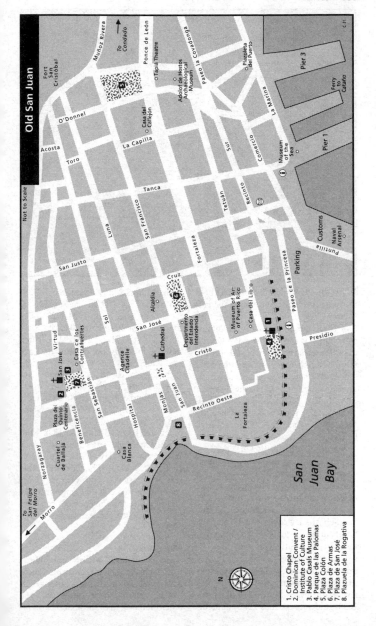

Old San Juan

Not to Scale

To San Felipe del Morro

Morro

Norzagaray

Cuartel de Ballajá

Casa Blanca

Beneficencia

San Sebastián

Plaza del Quinto Centenario

Vir-tud

San José

Casa de los Contrafuertes

Hospital

Sol

Agence Citadelle

San José

Monjas

San Juan

Recinto Oeste

La Fortaleza

Cathedral

Cristo

San Justo

Luna

San Francisco

Tanca

La Capilla

Alcaldía

Cruz

Departamento del Estado / Intendencia

Museum of Art of Puerto Rico

Casa del Libro

Fortaleza

Tetuán

Recinto

Presidio

Paseo de la Princesa

Parking

Muñoz Rivera

To Condado

Ponce de León

Acosta

Toro

O'Donnel

Casa del Callejón

Adolfo de Hostos Archaeological Museum

Tapiá Theatre

Paseo la Covadonga

Plazoleta del Puerto

Sur

Comercio

La Marina

Museum of the Sea

Pier 1

Pier 3

Ferry to Cataño

Customs

Naval Arsenal

San Juan Bay

N

1. Cristo Chapel
2. Dominican Convent / Institute of Culture
3. Pablo Casals Museum
4. Parque de las Palomas
5. Plaza Colon
6. Plaza de Armas
7. Plaza de San José
8. Plazuela de la Rogativa

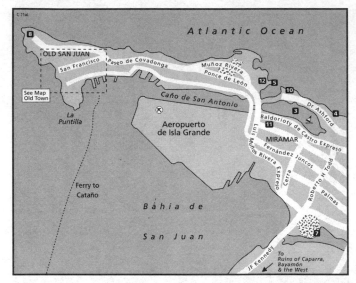

1630;cultural events are sometimes held in the patio, art exhibitions in the galleries, T 724-0700). The 16th-century **San José** church, originally a Dominican chapel, is the second oldest church in the Western Hemisphere and once the family church of Ponce de León's descendants. Ponce was buried here until moved to the Cathedral in the 20th century (open Monday-Saturday 0830-1600, Sunday mass at 1200). The early 18th century **Casa de los Contrafuertes** believed to be the oldest private residence in the old city, now has periodic art exhibitions on the second floor and a small pharmacy museum with 19th century exhibits on the ground floor (open Wednesday-Sunday, 0900-1630, T 724-5949). The **Casa Blanca**, 1 Calle San Sebastián, was built in 1523 by the family of Ponce de León, who lived in it for 250 years until it became the residence of the Spanish and then the US military commander-in-chief. It is now a historical museum which is well worth a visit (open Tues-Sun 0900-1200, 1300-1630, guided tours Tues-Fri by appoint-

ment, admission US$2 adults, US$1 children, T 724-4102). The **Alcaldía**, or City Hall, was built 1604-1789 (open Monday-Friday 0800-1600 except holidays, T 724-7171 ext 2391). The **Intendencia**, formerly the Spanish colonial exchequer, a fine example of 19th century Puerto Rican architecture, now houses Puerto Rico's State Department (open Monday-Friday 0800-1200, 1300-1630, T 722-2121). The **naval arsenal** was the last place in Puerto Rico to be evacuated by the Spanish in 1898, exhibitions are held in 3 galleries (open Wednesday-Sunday, 0900-1200, 1300-1630, T 724-5949). The **Casa del Callejón** is a restored 18th-century house containing two colonial museums, the architectural and the Puerto Rican Family (both closed for restoration, T 725-5250).

Museums

Apart from those in historic buildings listed above, there are the **Pablo Casals Museum** in an 18th century house beside San José church, with Casals' cello and other memorabilia (Tues-Sat 0930-1730,

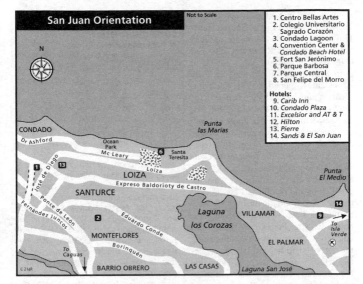

San Juan Orientation — Not to Scale

1. Centro Bellas Artes
2. Colegio Universitario Sagrado Corazón
3. Condado Lagoon
4. Convention Center & Condado Beach Hotel
5. Fort San Jerónimo
6. Parque Barbosa
7. Parque Central
8. San Felipe del Morro

Hotels:
9. *Carib Inn*
10. *Condado Plaza*
11. *Excelsior and AT & T*
12. *Hilton*
13. *Pierre*
14. *Sands & El San Juan*

entrance US$1 adults, US$0.50 children, T 723-9185); the **San Juan Museum of Art and History**, Norzagaray y MacArthur, built in 1855 as a marketplace, now a cultural centre with exhibition galleries, open Tues-Sun, 1000-1600, T 724-1875; the **Casa del Libro** is an 18th century house on Calle Cristo, has a collection of rare books, including some over 400 years old (Tues-Sat, except holidays, 1100-1630, T 723-0354); and the **Museum of the Sea** on Pier One, with a collection of maritime instruments and models (open when the pier is open for cruise ships, T 725-2532). The **Indian Museum** at Calle San José 109 on the corner of Luna concentrates on Puerto Rican indigenous cultures, with exhibits, ceramics and archaeological digs. Open Tues-Sat 0900-1600, no admission charge, T 724-5477 or 722-1709. Another museum in the old city is a military museum at **Fort San Jerónimo** (open Wednesday-Sunday, 0930-1200, 1300-1630, T 724-5949).

The metropolitan area of San Juan includes the more modern areas of Santurce, Hato Rey, and Río Piedras. **Río Piedras** was founded in 1714 but became incorporated into San Juan in 1951. On the edge of Río Piedras, the gardens and library of the former governor, Luis Muñoz Marín, are open to the public, Tues-Sat 0900-1300 (T 755-7979), with a museum showing his letters, photos and speeches.

The **University of Puerto Rico** at Río Piedras is in a lovely area. The **University Museum** (open Monday-Friday, 0900-2100, weekends 0900-1500, T 764-0000, ext 2452) has archaeological and historical exhibitions, and also monthly art exhibitions. The **Botanical Garden** at the Agricultural Experiment Station has over 200 species of tropical and subtropical plants, a bamboo promenade (one variety can grow 4 feet in a day), an orchid garden (over 30,000 orchids), and an aquatic garden (open daily 0900-1630, T 250-0000 ext 6580).

Hato Rey is the financial district of San Juan nicknamed 'the Golden Mile'. The **Luís Muñoz Marín Park** on Jesús T Piñero Avenue covers 86 acres, which can be toured by a 1 km cable car. Open Tues-Sun 0900-1700. The **Sacred Heart University** with the **Museum of Contemporary Puerto Rican Art** (Tues-Sat 0900-1600, Sun 1100-1700, T 268-0049) is in Santurce, as is the modern **Fine Arts Center**, opened in 1981, which has theatres and halls at the corner of De Diego and Ponce de León (T 724-4751). The residential area **Miramar** has several moderately priced hotels as well as some expensive ones. Miramar is separated from the Atlantic coast by the **Condado lagoon** and the Condado beach area, where the luxury hotels, casinos, night clubs and restaurants are concentrated. From Condado the beach front is built up eastwards through Ocean Park, Santa Teresita, Punta Las Marías and Isla Verde. Building is expanding along the narrow strip beyond Isla Verde, between the sea and the airport. Along this road, Avenida Boca de Cangrejos, there are lots of food trucks selling barbecued specialities.

Directions

Up until the 1950s tramcars ran between Río Piedras and Old San Juan along Avs Ponce de León and Fernández Juncos. To this day directions are given by Paradas, or tram stops, so you have to find out where each one is.

Excursions

A ferry, Old San Juan (Pier Two) – Hato Rey, Cataño, crosses every half hour, 0600-2100, T 788-1155, US$0.50, to Cataño where you can catch a *público* (US$1 pp), or bus 37 to the **Bacardi rum distillery**. There are free conducted tours around the plant Monday-Saturday, 0930-1030, 1200-1400, travelling from one building to the next by a little open motor train, T 788-1500, closed for Christmas holidays.

On Route 2, shortly before Bayamón, is the island's earliest settlement, **Caparra**, established by Ponce de León in 1508. Ruins of the fort can still be seen and there is a **Museum of the Conquest and Colonization of Puerto Rico** (open

daily 0900-1600, T 781-4795).

Local information
● **Accommodation**

Price guide			
L1	over US$200	L2	US$151-200
L3	US$101-150	A1	US$81-100
A2	US$61-80	A3	US$46-60
B	US$31-45	C	US$21-30
D	US$12-20	E	US$7-11
F	US$4-6	G	up to US$3

Most of the large San Juan hotels are in **Condado or Isla Verde** and overlook the sea, with swimming pools, night clubs, restaurants, shops and bars. Lots of new resorts are being built and others refurbished. New hotels in the luxury category coming on stream in 1996/97 include the *Westin Río Mar Beach Resort and Country Club*, the *Wyndham Old San Juan Hotel and Casino*, the *Embassy Suites Hotel and Casino*, the *Colony San Juan Beach Hotel*, the *Hampton Inn*, and the *Ritz-Carlton San Juan Hotel and Casino*. To get value for money, it may be advisable to avoid the luxury hotels on the sea front. There is plenty of cheaper accommodation within walking distance of the beaches and lots of beachfront apartments at very reasonable prices for stays of a week or more, look in the local newspaper, *El Nuevo Día* for notices, usually quote monthly rates but available for shorter stays. New guesthouses being built in 1996/97 include the *Casablanca Inn*, the *Shangri-La Resort*, the *Hostal Aibonito*, the *Palmas de Lucía Hotel* and the *Hospedería Vista Al Faro*.

Condado: **L1-L2** *Radisson Ambassador Plaza*, 1369 Ashford, T 721-7300, 233 rooms, suites, casino; **L1** *Caribe Hilton*, Ocean Front, Puerta de Tierra, on the old city side of Condado bridge, T 721-0303, luxury, expensive suites, 733 rooms, casino, set in 17 acres of gardens, many sporting facilities. On the Condado side of the bridge is the **L1** *Condado Plaza*, 999 Ashford, T 721-1000, also expensive, 587 rooms, suites, casino, with *Tony Roma's* restaurant, small beach, etc; **L1** *Condado Beach*, Ashford, next to the Convention Center, T 721-6888, suites, 245 rooms. Cheaper: **L3** *Condado Lagoon*, 6 Clemenceau, T 721-0170, 44 rooms, good, with good restaurant on the premises, *Ajili-Mojili*; **L3** *Dutn Inn and Tower*, 55 Condado Av, Condado, T 721-0810, 144 rooms, casino; good value are **A1** *El Canario by the Sea*, 4 Condado Av, T 722-8640, including continental breakfast, 25 rooms, close to beach, comfortable, and **A1** *El Canario Inn*, 1317 Ashford, T 722-3861, breakfast included, 1 block from the beach, good, clean, safe; **A3** *Aleli By The Sea*, with terrace on ocean front, good, friendly.

Ocean Park: **L3** *Hostería del Mar*, 1 Tapia Street, T 727-3302, on the beach; a guest house is **L2-A2** *Numero Uno on the Beach*, 1 Santa Ana, T 727-9687, 726-5010, safe behind barred doors and high walls, beach not safe after dark, with pool, friendly, mediocre food, overpriced bar drinks, unitemized bill on checkout; **A2** *Beach Buoy Inn*, 1853 McLeary, T 728-8119, F 268-0037, T 800-221-8119, also safe behind barred doors and high walls, but on busy road so some traffic noise, windows sealed in some rooms, no view but pleasant, complimentary breakfast with lots of coffee, Danish pastries and newspapers, helpful, parking, shopping close by, beach towels.

Isla Verde: **L1** *Sands Hotel and Casino*, on Route 37 (the main road through Isla Verde), 420 rooms, T 791-6100 and **L1** *El San Juan Hotel and Casino*, Ocean Front, 389 rooms, T 791-1000 are the 2 poshest hotels in Isla Verde, both refurbished 1996, look at the latter's lobby even if you do not stay; there is also a **L3** *Travel Lodge*, on Route 37, T 728-1300. **L1** *Holiday Inn Crowne Plaza*, T 253-2929, F 841-8085, Km 1.5 on Highway 187, resort, golf, tennis. **L3** *Carib Inn*, Route 187 (T 791-3535), in need of renovation, showing its age, pool, 2 restaurants, near airport; **A2** *Don Pedro*, Calle Rosa 4, T 791-2838, not far from airport, close to beach, pleasant, pool; **A2-A3** *La Casa Mathieson*, Uno 14, Villamar, Isla Verde T 726-8662, 727-3223, and *Green Isle Inn*, 36 Calle Uno, T 726-4330, 728-5749 are jointly owned, both charge the same, both near airport, and have swimming pools, cooking facilities, friendly, free transport to and from airport, rec; between the two is **A1-A2** *The Mango Inn*, Calle Uno 20, Villamar, T 726-5546, pool; **A3** *El Patio*, Tres Oeste 87, Bloque D-8, Villamar, T 726-6298, swimming pool, use of kitchen, rec; **A1-A2** *Casa de Playa*, Av Isla Verde 86, T 728-9779, on beach, inc continental breakfast, TV, bath, a/c, pleasant, restaurant and bar; **A1-A2** *Borinquen Royal*, Av Isla Verde 58, T 728-8400, also on beach.

In **Old San Juan**: **L1-L2** *Gran Hotel El Convento*, a converted Carmelite nunnery at Cristo 100, is a charming hotel with a Spanish atmosphere and the dining room is in the former chapel, under new management and renovated 1996, 54 rooms, swimming pool, nice garden in which to have a drink, T 723-9020. Nearby, in equally exquisite restored mansion is **L1** *Casa San José*, 159 Calle San José, T 723-1212, F 723-7620, T 1-800-223 6510, rates inc breakfast and evening cocktails, no children under 12, 10 rooms/suites, antique furniture, marble floors, very elegant. **B** *El Escenario*, Calle San Sebastián, very friendly, rec, good roof top views. Guest houses on Calle San Francisco, information from Joyería Sol, Tanca 207, fan, cooking and washing facilities, friendly and helpful, but absolutely filthy and like cells. Also in Old San Juan are **B-D** *Central*, Calle San José 202, T 722-2751, good location, but reportedly used by short stay visitors and drug dealers, very basic, ask for a room with fan away from a/c units, also ask for towels when checking in so you do not have to run up and downstairs again; **D** *Enrique Castro Guest House*, Tanca 205, T 722-5436, at Relojería Suiza Mecánico Cuarzo, 2nd floor (Box 947), welcoming, run by Enrique and his son, Vincente, communal showers, some with hot water, rooms a/c, washbasin, fridge, kitchen available, rooms without a/c can be uncomfortably hot; *Buena Vista Guesthouse by the Sea*, Gral Valle 2218, Sta Teresita, English, French spoken, with kitchen, near beach, airport pickup for a small charge. *The Caleta*, 11 Caleta de las Monjas, T 725-5347, furnished apartments run by Michael Giessler, about US$450/month, studios cheaper, coin laundry.

In **Miramar**: **L2-L3** *Excelsior*, 801 Ponce de León, T 721-7400, restaurant, bar, pool, rooms overlooking freeway are noisy; **A3** *Miramar*, 606 Av Ponce de León, T 722-6239, 'not chic', but clean and friendly, longer stays possible; **A3-B** *El Toro*, 605 Miramar, T 725-5150/2647, good value, pleasant, close to bus stop.

In **Santurce**: **L2-L3** *Pierre* (Best Western), 105 De Diego, T 721-1200, F 721-3118.

● **Places to eat**

All major hotels. In **Old San Juan**: *Fortaleza*, Fortaleza 252; for Puerto Rican cuisine, *La Tasca del Callejón*, Fortaleza 317; *Bistro*, Calle Cruz 152, a pleasant, small restaurant and bar with tasty local food at reasonable prices; *La Mallorquina*, San Justo 207, T 722-3261, the oldest restaurant in the Caribbean, rec; also on San Justo: *Café de Paris*, No 256; *Szechuan*, Chinese, No 257, and other cafés and *Taco Maker*, No 255. There are several Mexican places in the city, eg *Parián* on Fortaleza; *Taza de Oro*, Luna 254, near San Justo. *La Zaragozana*, San Francisco 356, T 723-5103, some Spanish specialities, highly rec; *Bodegón de La Fortaleza*, Fortaleza 312; *El Siglo XX*, Fortaleza 355, T 724-1849, 723-3321, consistently good, great breakfast, lunch and dinner, not expensive, excellent service, spectacular paella; *La Danza*, corner of Cristo and Fortaleza, T 723-1642; *La Bombonera*, San Francisco 259, restaurant and pastry shop, good value breakfast, 1960s atmosphere, antique coffee machine; *4 Seasons Café*, in *Hotel Central*, Plaza de Armas, for good value local lunches; *Tropical Blend*, juice bar in La Calle alley on Fortaleza; *El Batey* bar, Cristo 101, just behind El Convento, rec; *Cafetería Manolin*, Calle San Justo 258, a/c, packed with locals at breakfast, Puerto Rican food, lunch specials daily. *Nono's*, San Sebastián y Cristo, bar, burgers, salads, steaks, sandwiches, and nearby on San Sebastián (all on Plaza San José), *Patio de Sam* very good for local drinks (happy hour 1600-1900), and *Tasca El Boquerón*. On Av Ponce de León, *El Miramar*, good, but not cheap. *La Buena Mesa*, 605 Ponce de León, good, small, middle price range. Several bars and cafés on Plaza Colón in Old San Juan. There is a huge selection of restaurants in Condado, from the posh to all the fast food chain restaurants. Similarly, Isla Verde is well-served by the fast food fraternity; on the beach at Isla Verde is *The Hungry Sailor* bar and grill, sandwiches, tapas, burgers, with a snack bar next door. *Cecilia's Place*, Rosa St, Isla Verde.

For breakfast or lunch seek out the *fondas*, not advertised as restaurants but usually part of a private home, or a family-run eating place serving *criollo* meals which are filling and good value. Recommended in San Juan are: *Macumba*, 2000 Loíza; *Casa Juanita*, 242 Av Roosevelt, Hato Rey (try chicken asopao or pork chops con mangu); *Cafetería del Parking*, 757 José de Diego, interior, Cayey (specialities include mondongo, and boronia de apio y bacalao – cod and celery root); *D'Arcos*, 605 Miramar, Santurce, speciality is roast veal with stuffed peppers and white bean sauce, also try pega'o (crunchy rice).

THE INTERIOR

Out of the metropolitan area 'on the island' are a variety of excursions; as it is a small island it is possible to see forested mountains and desert-like areas in only a short time. However, because the public transport system is rather limited, it is difficult if not impossible to visit some places without a rented car (see **Information for travellers**, **Car hire** and **Warning**). The cool climate in the mountains has caused resort hotels to be built in several towns inland.

EASTERN TOUR

An interesting round trip through the E half of the island can be done by a series of públicos from San Juan - Río Piedras - Luquillo - Fajardo - Humacao- Yabucoa - Guayama - Cayey - Aibonito- Barranquitas - Bayamón - San Juan. If travelling by car, a variant between San Juan and El Yunque takes you on Route 187 from Isla Verde, outside San Juan, to Loíza along a stretch of the N coast, which includes the **Piñones State Forest**, sand blown and palm-lined road. Some parts are unspoilt, some parts pass through apartment blocks on the outskirts of towns, and the road is a popular rush-hour route. The bay at Vacía Talega is beautifully calm. The section which joins the coast to Route 3 at Río Grande is also tree-lined and attractive.

El Yunque (see also **Flora and fauna** above) is a tropical forest and bird sanctuary. Trails (very stony) to the various peaks: El Yunque (The Anvil) itself, Mount Britton, Los Picachos. In view of the heavy rainfall, another name for the forest is Rain Forest. Visitors need not worry unduly, as storms are usually brief and plenty of shelter is provided. (No buses through the national forests, unfortunately; El Yunque is reached via Route 3 from San Juan towards Fajardo, and then right on Route 191.)

At **Luquillo** there is a beach in town and a *balneario* W of town (see **Beaches and Watersports**); just by the latter is a row of restaurants on the slip road off the dual carriageway (Route 3). *Públicos* from San Juan to Luquillo are marked Fajardo, US$3, no return *públicos* after 1500. **Fajardo** is a boating centre with several marinas and a public beach at Seven Seas; beyond Seven Seas is Las Croabas beach. Offshore is an uninhabited, but much visited, coral island, Icacos. You can camp at Seven Seas Beach, but T 722-1551 first. **Las Cabezas de San Juan** is a nature reserve on the headlands (3 promontories) N of Fajardo on Route 987. A 19th century lighthouse contains a nature centre and its observation deck has a great view of El Yunque and surrounding islands. There are trails and boardwalks, guides and explanatory signs of the different ecological habitats. Open Fri-Sun, tours at 0930, 1000, 1030 and 1400, admission US$5 adults, US$2 children, T 722-5882, or T 860-2560 at weekends. Off Humacao Beach/*Balneario* is a tiny cay called **Cayo Santiago**, also known as Monkey Island. It is inhabited by over 500 tiny monkeys, which are protected. The island is closed to the public although there are sightseeing tours which get you close enough to see the monkeys through binoculars.

● **Accommodation** The only paradores on the E side are **A2** *Martorell* at Luquillo, 6A Ocean Drive, close to beach, inc breakfast, rooms in need of redecoration, shared bath, T 889-2710, F 889-4520, you pay for the location, advisable to reserve in advance here at any time; **A2** *Familia*, on Route 987, Km 4, Las Croabas, Fajardo, 28 rooms, T 863-1193. There is a campground on the beach (*balneario*) at Luquillo, US$17 with electricity, US$13 without, min stay 2 days, max 7 days, take own tent, occasional security but best to pick a time when other campers are around, eg weekends and holidays, shower, toilets, barbecue; **A2** *Las Delicias*, Fajardo Playa, on the dock, across street from post office and customs building, very good, nice staff, rec, T 863-1818, bar; in Fajardo try **B** *Guez House de Express*, near ferry dock, 388 Union, small, clean, T 863-1362. **L1** *Palmas del Mar Hotel*, Humacao, T 852-6000, hotel rooms or villa resort, 7 restaurants, 18-hole golf course, swimming pools and other sports.

THE SOUTHEAST

One of the prettiest parts of Puerto Rico, which should be visited, lies S of Huma-cao, between Yabucoa and Guayama. Here are the villages of **Patillas** (*público* from Guayama) and **Maunabo** (*público* from Patillas, and from Yabucoa), where you can camp on the beach. There are a number of restaurants in this area, especially on the coast, which sell good, cheap food. **Yabucoa** is the E starting point of the Panoramic Route which runs the length of the island. There is an extension to the Route around the Cerro La Pandura and the Puntas Quebrada Honda, Yaguas and Toro; this affords lovely views of the Caribbean coast and Vieques island. **Guayama**, the cleanest town in Puerto Rico, it claims, has a delightful square, on which are the church and the **Casa Cautiño**, built in 1887, now a museum and cultural centre. Route 3, the coastal road around the E part continues from Guayama to Salinas (see below), where it joins Route 1 for Ponce.

● **Accommodation** Near Maunabo, is **A3** *Playa Emajaguas Guest House*, off the Ruta Panorámica, Carr 901, Km 2.5, Box 834, Maunabo, T 861-6023, lovely view, short walk down private path to empty beach, owned by Victor Morales and Edna Huertos, 7 apartments with kitchens, friendly, helpful, tennis court, pool table, horses, highly rec, good seafood restaurants nearby; near Patillas, Km 112, Route 3, is **A2** *Caribe Playa*, right on the Caribbean, comfortable, restaurant (order dinner in advance), sea bathing and snorkelling in a small, safe area, very friendly and helpful (owner Esther Geller, manager Minerva Moreno), rec, T 839-6339 (USA 212-988-1801), Box 8490, Guardarraya, Patillas, PR 00723. Inland, N of Barranguitas is **A3** *Residencia Margarita*, restaurant, useful for people following the Panoramic route.

THE SOUTH AND WEST

A round trip through the W half of the island would take in Ponce, the second city (reached by motorway from San Juan via Caguas), Guánica, Parguera, San Germán, Boquerón, Mayagüez (the third city), Aguadilla, Quebradillas and Arecibo, with side trips to the Maricao State Forest and fish hatchery, the Río Abajo State Forest and Lake Dos Bocas, the precolumbian ceremonial ball-park near Utuado, and the Arecibo observatory (open for self-guided tours Tuesday to Friday at 1400-1500, T 878-2612 for groups, and on Sunday 1300-1630; the Fundación Angel Ramos Visitor Center opened in 1996).

Off the motorway which runs from San Juan to Ponce is **Baños de Coamo**, which was the island's most fashionable resort from 1847 to 1958; legend has it that the spring was the fountain of youth which Juan Ponce de León was seeking. (Take Route 153 from the motorway and then 546.) It has been redeveloped by Paradores Puertorriqueños and still has a thermal bath (see under **Accommodation**). About 45 mins SE of Coamo is Salinas, a fishing and farming centre. There are several good seafood restaurants on the waterfront.

● **Accommodation A3** *Baños de Coamo* at the end of Carretera 546, where there are thermal water springs (maximum 15 mins) and an ordinary pool (spend as long as you like), 48 rooms, T 825-2186, F 825-4739, PO Box 540, Coamo, Puerto Rico 00640, rec.

PONCE

Much renovation has taken place in the heart of the city; the Casas Villaronga and Salazar-Zapater have been restored (the latter to accommodate the Museo de Historia de Ponce), other houses are being repainted in pastel shades, streets have been made into pedestrian areas (eg the Paseo Peotonal Atocha and Callejón Amor), and the large, air-conditioned market on Vives and Atocha (N of the plaza) has been remodelled. The city is now very pleasant to walk around.

The cathedral is also worth a look, and so is the black and red fire-station, built for a fair in 1883. Both buildings stand back to back in the main square, **Plaza Las Delicias**, which has fountains and many neatly-trimmed trees. Also on the plaza is the **Casa Armstrong-Poventud** (or Casa de las Cariatides), facing the Cathedral, with the Instituto de Cultura Puertorriqueño (Región Sur) and tourist information centre (Monday-Friday 0800-1200, 1300-1630; the Instituto is open 0900-1200, 1300-1600 Tuesday to Sunday). East of the plaza is the **Teatro La Perla**, painted cream, white and gold, the city's cultural centre (19th century), restored in 1990, as was the Alcaldía on the Plaza.

On El Vigía hill is the **Observation Tower** (open Tuesday-Wednesday, 0900-1730, Thursday-Sunday 1000-2200, US$0.50). The walkway next to the Yacht and Fishing Club is a good place to be at the weekend: good atmosphere.

Museums

Ponce has a very fine **Museum of Art**, donated by a foundation established by Luis A Ferré (industrialist, art historian and Governor 1968-72) in a modern building designed by Edward Durrel Stone, with a beautiful staircase, now famous. It contains a representative collection of European and American art from the third century BC to the present day. As well as an extensive Baroque collection and fine examples of pre-Raphaelite painting, there is a small collection of precolumbian ceramics and two cases of beautiful Art Nouveau glass. Most of the best Latin American painters are exhibited and there are often special displays. There are three gardens, one Spanish, one American and one Puerto Rican. Open daily 1000-1700; entry US$3 for adults, US$2 for children under 12, T 848-0511/0505.

The **Ponce History Museum** on 51-53 Calle Isabela, near La Perla, opened in 1992 and has 10 exhibition halls with photographs, documents and memorabilia provided by locals, as well as models and other exhibits chronicling the city's history. Guided tours in English, Spanish or French. Open weekdays 1000-1700, weekends 1000-1800, closed Tues, US$3 adults, US$1 children, T 844-7071/7042.

Two other new museums have opened, the **Museo de la Música Puertorriqueña**, Calle Cristina 70, T 844-9722, open Tuesday to Sunday 0900-1200 and 1300-1730, catalogue US$3, and the **Museo Castillo Serrallés**, on El Vigía hill (T 259-1774), open Tuesday-Thursday 0930-1630, Friday-Sunday 1000-1700, US$3, children US$1.50, groups must reserve in advance. This fine, 1930s mansion has been restored by the Municipio.

Excursions

A short drive away on Route 503, Km 2.2, in the outskirts of the city, is the **Tibes Indian Ceremonial Center**. This is an Igneri (300 AD) and pre-Taino (700 AD) burial ground, with seven ball courts (*bateyes*) and two plazas, one in the form of a star, a replica of a Taino village and a good museum. The site was discovered in 1975 after heavy rain uncovered some of the stone margins of the ball courts. Under the Zemi Batey, the longest in the Caribbean (approximately 100 by 20m), evidence of human sacrifice has been found. Underneath a stone in the Main Plaza, which is almost square (55 by 50m), the bodies of children were found, buried ceremonially in earthenware pots. In all, 130 skeletons have been uncovered near the Main Plaza, out of a total on site of 187. All the ball courts and plazas are said to line up with solstices or equinoxes. The park is filled with trees (all named), the most predominant being the higuera, whose fruit is used, among other things, for making maracas (it's forbidden to pick them up though). Open Tues-Sun (and Mon holidays, when closed Tues), 0900-1600, admission US$2 for adults, US$2 for children; bilingual guides give an informative description of the site and a documentary is shown, T 840-2255.

Hacienda Buena Vista, at Km 16.8 on Route 10, N of the city, is another recommended excursion. Built in 1833, converted into a coffee plantation and corn mill in 1845 and in operation till 1937, this estate has been restored by Fideicomiso de Conservación de Puerto Rico. All the machinery works (the metal parts are original), operated by water channelled from the 360-metre Vives waterfall; the hydraulic turbine which turns the corn mill is unique. Reservations are necessary for the 2-hour tour (in Spanish or English), T 722-5882 (at weekends 848-7020), open Fri-Sun, tours at 0830, 1030, 1330 and 1530; groups of 20 or more admitted Wed and Thur; US$5 adults, US$1 children under 12.

At weekends trips can be made to the beach at **Caja de Muerto**, Coffin Island, the ferry leaves Ponce at 0900, returns 1600, T 848-4575, US$5.50 return, children US$3.50.

Local information
● **Accommodation**

A1-A2 *Hotel Meliá*, a/c, TV, bath and breakfast, small stuffy rooms, not nice, roof top and garden terraces (2 Cristina, just off main plaza, PO Box 1431, T 842-0261, F 841-3602); also the **L3-A1** *Ponce Holiday Inn*, Route 2, Km 221.2, W of the city, T 844-1200, F 841-8085, where there are tennis courts, pools, and golf arrangements made; to the E of the city, on Route 1, Km 123.5, near the junction with the autopista is **L3-A1** *Days Inn*, T 844-1200. Cheaper hotel near main square; **A3** *Hotel Bélgica*, 122 Villa St, T 844-3255, refurbished, tasteful, clean, huge rooms with balcony, some with 2 double beds, friendly, highly rec. There are about 5 other guesthouses.

● **Places to eat**

The restaurant of the *Meliá Hotel* is good (look out for the 'Breaded Lion' on the menu), there is a vegetarian restaurant in the Plaza del Mercado shopping centre, Calle Mayor, 4 blocks NE from main plaza. Fast food places on main plaza. Fast food places on main plaza.

● **Transport**

Most *carros públicos* leave from the intersection of Victoria and Unión, three blocks N of the plaza (fare to San Juan US$6-7; to Guayama, either direct or via Santa Isabel, US$3).

GUANICA

Going West from Ponce is **Guánica**, the place where American troops first landed in the Spanish-American war. It has an old fort from which there are excellent views. Although Guánica has a history stretching back to Ponce de León's landing in 1508, the first of many colonist landings in the bay, the town was not actually founded here until 1914. Outside

Guánica is a *balneario* with a large hotel alongside, *Copamarina*. Scuba diving is possible here with Dive Copamarina, T 821-6009, F 821-4119; the wall is close to the shore and there are drop-offs and canyons. For details on the Guánica Forest, see **Flora and fauna**.

LA PARGUERA

Further W is **La Parguera**, originally a fishing village and now a popular resort with two *paradores*, guest houses, fish restaurants, fast food outlets. Noisy on holiday weekends. Fishing, kayaking, mountain biking and other activities are offered. Nearby is **Phosphorescent Bay**, an area of phosphorescent water, occurring through a permanent population of minescent dinoflagellates, a tiny form of marine life, which produce sparks of chemical light when disturbed. 1 hour boat trips round the bay depart between 1930 and 1030, every ½ hr, US$4 pp, the experience is said to be rather disappointing, however, and it is best to go on a very dark night or even when it is raining.

● **Accommodation A1-A2** *Villa Parguera* (T 899-7777/3975, F 899-6040, 62 rooms, seaview) and **A3** *Porlamar* (T 899-4015, 18 rooms, on the canals, kitchen facilities).

SAN GERMAN

Inland from La Parguera, off the main Route 2, **San Germán** has much traditional charm; it was the second town to be founded on the island and has preserved its colonial atmosphere. It is an excellent base from which to explore the mountains and villages of S W Puerto Rico. The beautiful little Porta Coeli chapel on the plaza contains a small, rather sparse museum of religious art. (Open Wednesday-Sunday, 0830-1200, 1300-1630.) A university town: it can be difficult to get cheap accommodation in term time.

● **Accommodation A3** *Oasis*, T 892-1175/1110, F 892-1175 ext 200, 52 rooms, not as close to the beach as it claims, but is ideal for the hills, good food and service, pool, jacuzzi, gym, sauna, a/c.

BOQUERON

On the S side of the W coast is **Boquerón**, in Cabo Rojo district, which has an excellent beach for swimming. It is very wide and long, admission US$1, parking for hundreds of cars, camping, changing rooms, beach and first 30 yards of sea packed with bodies on holiday weekends. About 1½ km away across the bay is a beautiful, deserted beach, but there is no road to it. The small village is pleasant, with typical bars, restaurants and street vendors serving the local speciality, oysters. This is one of the cheapest spots on the island because it is a centre for the Compánia de Fomento Recreativo to provide holiday accommodation for Puerto Rican families.

South of the town is **Boquerón Lagoon**, a wildfowl sanctuary; also the **Cabo Rojo Wildlife Refuge**, with a visitors' centre and birdwatching trails. The **Cabo Rojo lighthouse** (Faro), at the island's SW tip is the most S point on the island with a breathtaking view; the exposed coral rocks have marine fossils and, closer inshore, shallow salt pools where crystals collect. Popular beaches in this area are **El Combate** (miles of white sand, undeveloped, but now a favourite with university students), S of Boquerón, and **Joyuda** (small island just offshore offers good snorkelling and swimming, but beach itself not spectacular) and **Buye** (camping US$8 a night) to the N.

● **Accommodation B** *Canadian Jack's Guest House*, PO Box 990, Boquerón, PR 00622, T 851-2410, with private bathroom, colour tv, clean and comfortable but noisy on Fri, Sat nights when the streets are crowded with people partying, Jack also rents hammocks overlooking the water, **E** pp per night, fantastic spot; **A2** *Boquemar*, T 851-2158, F 851-7600, 63 rooms; **A2** *Perichi's*, Carretera 102, Km 14.3, Playa Joyuda, T 851-3131, F 851-0560, 25 rooms, well-run, with good restaurant; **A3-B** *Centro Vacacional de Boquerón*, cheapest rates mid-week, fully self-contained apartments, with barbecues, front the beach. Foreigners are welcomed, but it is so popular with Puerto Ricans that you may have to make an application up to 3 months in advance. There are other hotels and a *parador*.

● **Places to eat** Joyuda is famous for seafood restaurants on the beach; inexpensive food, good quality, nice atmosphere, whole, grilled fish is a must, especially snapper (*chillo*).

MAYAGUEZ

Mayagüez a crowded city with little of interest to the tourist. There are botanical gardens, at the Tropical Agricultural Research Station, near the University of Puerto Rico, free admission, open Monday-Friday, 0730-1630. The city also has a zoo; open Tues-Sun, 0900-1630, adults US$1, children US$0.50. The tourist office is in the Municipalidad on Plaza Colón but has no tourist information available.

● **Accommodation A2-A3** *El Sol*, rec, T 834-0303, F 265-7567, 9 S R Palmer Este, 52 rooms, in city centre; **L1-L2** *Hilton*, casino, pool, T 831-7575; **A2-A3** *Palma*, on Méndez Vigo, T 834-3800, good, TV, bathroom, a/c; **C** *RUM Hotel* (hotel of the Recinto University of Mayagüez), safe, pool, library, T 832-4040 (similar prices at other branches of the University); *Colón*, Plaza Colón, a dump, no bath, ask for a quiet room, mainly rented by the hour; **A3** *El Embajador*, 111 E Ramos Antonini.

● **Places to eat** The *Vegetarian Restaurant*, Calle José de Diego, open 1100-1400; *Fuente Tropical*, same street, run by Colombians, good fruit shakes and hamburgers; *Recomeni*, Calle Vigo, good inexpensive food, open all hours, eat in or take away.

● **Transport** *Públicos* leave from a modern terminal in Calle Peral. Bus to San Juan US$10.

Mona Island, 80 km W of Mayagüez, is fascinating for historians and nature lovers, but can only be reached by chartered boat or plane. Originally inhabited by Taino Indians and then by pirates and privateers, it is now deserted except for its wildlife. Here you can see 3-foot iguanas, colonies of sea birds and bats in the caves. 200-foot high cliffs are dotted with caves, ascending to a flat table top covered with dry forest. The island is managed by the Department of National Resources

(T 722-1726), who have cabins to rent with prior permission. Camping is allowed at Sardinera Beach, US$1 per night. There are no restaurants or facilities. Take all your food and water with you and bring back all your rubbish.

RINCON

Going N from Mayagüez, you come to **Rincón**, on the westernmost point of the island. Here the mountains run down to the sea, and the scenery is spectacular. The town itself is unremarkable, but the nearby beaches are beautiful and the surfing is a major attraction. The beaches are called Steps, Dome (named after the nearby nuclear storage dome) and the Public Beach, with lifeguard. Humpback whales visit in winter. There are cottages to rent and there is also accommodation in Rincón and the neighbouring village of Puntas (see below). There are also some small bars and restaurants. Rincón can be reached by *público* from Mayagüez or (less frequent) from Aguadillas. Public transport is scarce at weekends.

● **Accommodation L1** *Horned Dorset Primavera*, excellent, Route 429, Km 3, T 823-4030/4050, no children under 12, 22 suites, restaurant, watersports; **A2** *Villa Cofresí* and, alongside it, Route 115, Km 12.3, **A1-A3** *Villa Antonio*, apartment (T 823-2645/2285, F 823-3380) on a good beach for swimming and near good surfing beaches; *The Lazy Parrot*, PO Box 430, Carrera 413, km 4.1, Barrio Puntas, T 823-5654, rooms sleep 4 in bunk beds, breakfast Tues-Sun. (At **Puntas**, Carmen's grocery store has rooms, basic, cooking facilities.)

NORTH COAST ROAD

Route 2, the main road in the N, runs through urban areas to some extent from Arecibo and completely from Manatí to San Juan. If you have the time it is much nicer to drive along the coast. Take Route 681 out of Arecibo, with an immediate detour to the Poza del Obispo beach, by Arecibo lighthouse. Here a pool has been formed inside some rocks, but the breakers on the rocks themselves send up magnificent jets of spray. The bay, with fine surf, stretches round to another headland, **Punta Caracoles**, on which is the **Cueva del Indio** (small car park on Route 681, US$1 charge if anyone is around). A short walk through private land leads to the cave, a sea-eroded hole and funnel in the cliff; watch out for holes in the ground when walking around. There are drawings in the cave, but whether they are precolumbian, or modern graffiti is not made clear. *Públicos* run along Route 681 from Arecibo. Rejoin Route 2 through Barceloneta. The State Forest of Cambalache is between Arecibo and Barceloneta.

The coast road is not continuous; where it does go beside the sea, there are beaches, seafood restaurants and some good views. Route 165, another coastal stretch which can be reached either through Dorado on the 693, or through Toa Baja, enters metropolitan San Juan at Cataño.

● **Accommodation** At **Arecibo** there are several hotels and guest houses around the main square, **B** *Hotel Plaza*; near Quebradillas, Route 2, Km 103.8, are **A1-A2** *El Guajataca* (T 721-2884, 895-3070, F 895-3589), beautifully located on a beach (dangerous swimming), 38 rooms, pool, entertainment, restaurant, bars; on the other side of the road, and higher up the hill at Km7.9, Route 113, is **A1-A2** *Vistamar*, T 895-2065, F 895-2294, 55 rooms, also with pool, restaurant and bar.

PANORAMIC ROUTE

Heading E from Mayagüez is the **Panoramic Route** which runs the whole length of Puerto Rico, through some of the island's most stunning scenery. It passes through the Cordillera Central, with large areas of forest, and there are several excursions to various countryside resorts. Despite the fact that you are never far from buildings, schools or farms, the landscape is always fascinating. In the evening the panoramas are lovely and you can hear the song of the *coquí*. No trip to the interior should miss at least some part of the Panoramic

Route, but if you want to travel all of it, allow 3 days. The roads which are used are narrow, with many bends, so take care at corners. The **Maricao State Forest** (Monte del Estado) is the most W forest on the Route; its visitors' areas are open from 0600 to 1800. It is a beautiful forest with magnificent views. As it approaches Adjuntas and the transinsular Route 10, the Panoramic Route goes through the **Bosque de Guilarte**, again with fine views, flowering trees, bougainvillaea, banks of impatiens (busy lizzie, miramelinda in Spanish), and bird song (if you stop to listen). After Adjuntas, the road enters the **Toro Negro Forest Reserve**, which includes the highest point on the island, **Cerro de Punta** (1,338m). The Recreation Areas in Toro Negro are open from 0800-1700. After this high, lush forest with its marvellous vistas, the road continues to Aibonito, around which the views and scenery are more open (mainly as a result of deforestation). Thence to Cayey and, beyond, another forest, Carite (also known as Guavate). Finally the road descends into the rich, green valley which leads to Yabucoa.

From various points on the Panoramic Route you can head N or S; eg Route 10 goes S from Adjuntas to Ponce, or N to Utuado (*Riverside* hotel, bargain for price) and then on to **Río Abajo State Forest** (open 0600-1800) where there are a swimming pool and various picnic spots. It is approached through splendid views of the karst hills and the **Dos Bocas Lake**. Free launch trips are offered on this lake at 0700, 1000, 1400 and 1700; they last 2 hours and are provided by the Public Works Department. Route 10 reaches the N coast at Arecibo.

The **Caguana Indian Ceremonial Park**, W of Utuado, dates from about 1100 AD, and contains ten Taino ball courts, each named after a Taino *cacique* (chieftain). The courts vary in size, the longest being about 85m by 20 (Guarionex), the largest 65 by 50 (Agueybana). These two have monoliths in the stones that line the level 'pitch', and on those of Agueybana there are petroglyphs, some quite faint. None of the monoliths is taller than a man. A path leads down to the Río Tanamá. The setting, amid limestone hills, is very impressive. It is believed to be a site of some religious significance and has been restored with a small museum in the landscaped park. It is on Route 111 to Lares, Km 12.3, open 0900-1700 (gate to the river closes at 1630), admission free. Further W of Utuado, **Lares** is a hilltop town (*públicos* go from one block from church) from where you can either carry on to the W coast at Aguadilla, or head N on one of the many routes to the Atlantic coast. Route 453 passes **Lago de Guajataca**, continuing as Route 113 to Quebradillas. Route 455 branches W off the 453, leading via a short stretch of the 119 to the 457 and 446 (good view at the junction of these 2). Route 446 traverses, as a single track, the **Bosque de Guajataca**, which has several easy paths into the forest which are nice to walk (25 miles in all) and three recreational areas (open 0900-1800). Permission to camp must be obtained from the Departamento de Recursos Naturales, office in the Bosque open Monday-Friday 0700-1530 (in theory). Route 129 goes to Arecibo, passing the Río Camuy Cave Park, with side trips to the Cueva de Camuy and the Arecibo Observatory (see above for all these). Driving on the country roads in the area between the Panoramic Route and the N coast is twisty but pleasant, passing conical limestone hills (*mogotes*) and farms set among patches of lush forest.

• **Accommodation**   **A3** *Hacienda Gripiñas*, an old coffee plantation house, 19 rooms, which lies in the mountains near Jayuya, N of Ponce, E of Utuado at Km 2.5, Route 527 (T 828-1717, F 828-1719); in the same area is *Casa Grande*, Barrio Caonillas, Route 612, Km 0.3, T/F 894-3939, 20 rooms in attractive mountain setting.

VIEQUES

Vieques, a peaceful, relaxing, low-key island of rolling hills, is located 11 km across the sea from Puerto Rico. Fajardo is the closest sea and air port. The island is about 34 km long by 6 km wide with a population of about 8,000 mostly concentrated in the main town of **Isabel Segunda**. There is an excellent historical museum at the beautifully restored fort, **El Fortín Conde de Mirasol** (open Wed-Sun 1000-1600, week days by appointment, T 741-1717, 741-8651 evenings), which was the last fort begun by the Spanish in the Western Hemisphere. There is another interesting exhibit at the **Punta Mulas Lighthouse** (T 741-5000, open daily 0800-1630). The island was named Graciosa by Columbus, after a friend's mother, but better known as Crab Island by pirates who frequented its waters.

The US Military owns two thirds of the island: the E third and W third, with the civilian population living on the middle strip. Both bases are open to the public upon presentation of any photo identification except on days when the red flag is up: when manoeuvers and/or bombing practice are underway. The US military presence has been greatly reduced and the military is expected to leave soon and return the land to the people. The military is heard but not much seen: planes and helicopters fly low but since only a handful of personnel are permanently stationed on the island, it is not a base town atmosphere. The land owned by the military is mostly untouched, creating a bird sanctuary and nature preserve.

Vieques has over 52 beaches in secluded coves, the few developed beaches have people and exuberant groups of picnickers, the rest are deserted. Public **Sun Beach** has picnic and camping areas (no shade in camping area).

Tourism is an infant industry on this island, with the small beach town of **Esperanza** being the main area of guest houses and tourist related restaurants, bars, dive companies (Blue Caribe Dive Center, SSI facility, full service, T 741-2522, PO Box 1574), etc. The museum in Esperanza has archaeological and

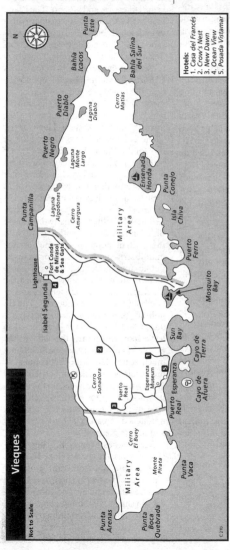

Vieques

Not to Scale

natural history exhibits and is open Tues-Sun, 1100-1500, T 741-8850. The biggest 'action' on the island is Saturday night in Esperanza, when everyone promenades along the sea front dressed in their finest, talking and flirting, before going to a nightclub or bar.

Small, hardy, island horses, most with paso fino blood lines (that means smooth gaits with no bouncing) are still used as transport, and wild horses roam the island. Renting a horse is an exciting way to explore the beaches and coves.

Mosquito Bay, also known as **Phosphorescent Bay** (the BBC broadcast a documentary about this in 1994), is a large, but very shallow bay, surrounded by mangrove trees and full of bioluminescent organisms. Sightseeing trips go at night (recommended are the tours that use non polluting electric boats or kayaks). The organisms glow when disturbed by the prop, paddle, fish or you swimming. The glow generated by a 13cm fish is about a 39cm circle of light brighter than a light bulb. Swimming in this glow is a wonderful experience.

Island information – Vieques

● **How to get there**

By air: Vieques Air Link (T 741-3266) and Isla Nena Air (T 741-6362) have flights from Fajardo (10 mins, T 863-3020), San Juan (30 mins, T 722-3736), International as well as Isla Grande and St Croix (30 mins, T 778-9858) multiple times a day. **By sea**: from Fajardo, the car, cargo and passenger ferry runs at 0400, 0930 and 1630, returning at 0600, 1330 and 1830, Mon-Fri. For passengers only from Fajardo 0930 and 1630, returning 0700 and 1630 Mon-Fri, and 0900, 1500 and 1800, returning 0700, 1300 and 1630 Sat-Sun, in Fajardo T 863-0705/0852, 1-800-981-2005, in Vieques T 741-4761, open for reservations 0800-1100, 1300-1500, reservations needed for cars only, passenger fare is US$2, crossing takes 1¼ hrs. At weekends the ferries are often full and advance reservations are rec.

● **Local transport**

Públicos meet you at the airport and ferry dock, posted rates (none higher than US$3.00), but some drivers will try to overcharge you, ask the price first. Jitney Taxi Service (T 741-0757) or Rafael Acevedo (T 741-4201) can be called for pick up, or let your hotel/guest house arrange transport for you. Car rentals available at Dreda Rent a Car (T 741-8397), Maritzas Car Rental (T 741-0078), VIAS Car Rental (T 741-8173) also has scooters, Sammy's (T 741-0106), Marco's (741-1388, 382-3054) or Island Car Rentals (T 741-1666). Horse rentals can be arranged by your guesthouse.

● **Accommodation**

Esperanza: B *Tradewinds*, T 741-8666, with bar, restaurant, rec, owned by Janet and Harry Washburn, PO Box 1012; **A3-B** *Bananas Guest House*, facing the ocean, popular, pleasant American restaurant, T 741-8700, some rooms a/c; **A1** *La Casa del Francés*, T 741-3751, F 741-2330, route 996, 18 rooms, classical sugar plantation Great House, designated historical landmark, bar, restaurant, pool, located 5 min walk out of Esperanza. Smaller and cheaper guest houses include: *Camar*, (T 741-8604), *La Central*, (T 741-0106), *Posada Vistamar*, (T 741-8716); *La Concha*, (T 741-2733). For apartments in Esperanza try *Acacia Apts*, 236 Acacia Street, T/F 741-1856, owned by Jürgen Meuser and Manfred Kissel, clean, cosy, friendly, rec, or *La Piña*, 222 Acacia Street, T/F 741-2953, owned by Elswith Petrakovic. In and around **Isabel Segunda:** *Vieques Inn*, downtown, (T 741-1500); *Casa La Lanchita*, oceanfront, (T 741-0023); **A3** *Sea Gate Hotel*, near the fort, 16 rooms high up on hill, good views (T 741-4661), pool, tennis; **A3** *Ocean View*, concrete block hotel right on water's edge next to ferry dock, 35 rooms with balconies, T/F 741-3696, Box 124, Chinese restaurant next door under same ownership. Inland is **A3** *Crow's Nest*, 10 rooms with

kitchenettes, set in rolling hillside, pool, restaurant (T 741-0033, F 741-1294, Box 1521, Route 201, Km 1.6) or **B** *New Dawn*, an unusual guesthouse built on 5 acres of land with horses grazing off the hugh veranda, is 5 km from the beach, frequently booked by women's groups for retreats, 2-storey wooden house, large deck and hammocks, rooms, dorms **D** pp, and tentsites **E**, all with shared bath and outdoor showers or you can rent the entire place (sleeps 20+) with or without a cook, for US$250/day, US$3,000/month, (T 741-0495), PO Box 1512. For villa rentals contact Connections, (T 741-0023). A new hotel was due to be built in 1996: **L3** *Casa de Playa Beach Village*, with 140 rooms and suites.

● **Places to eat**

Almost all of the island's restaurants are part of a hotel or guesthouse listed above. There are numerous small places offering take out or eat in sandwiches, hamburgers, barbecue chicken, etc. *Inn on the Blue Horizon* has *Café Blu* for fine dining, open 1800-2200, reservations rec, T 741-3318, and *Blu Bar* with happy hour 1600-1800 every day and lighter food 1200-2200. *Café Mar Azul*, bar on ocean front, open 0900-0100, later at weekends, happy hour 1700-1800, T 741-3400.

CULEBRA

Culebra, about seven miles long and three miles wide (pop 2,000), is another quiet, unspoilt island where there is little tourism. The main village, **Dewey** (called Pueblo by the locals) is attractively set between two lagoons. A visitor's information centre is in the City Hall. The climate and landscape is similar to that of the Virgin Islands, with tropical forest on the hills and palm groves near the beaches. About 40% of the land is park or national reserve, including many beaches. The **Culebra National Wildlife Refuge** (T 742-0115), comprising 23 offshore islands and four parcels of land on Culebra, protects large colonies of sea birds, particularly terns and boobies, and nesting sea turtles. Volunteers are welcomed to help Wildlife Refuge rangers count and protect nests and hatchlings.

There are good, sandy beaches, clear water and a coral reef. Aquaventuras (742-

3569) and Gene Thomas (742-3555) offer scuba diving, equipment is limited so it may be better to bring your own; snorkel rental from Jody's (T 742-3266); Kayak rental from Jim Peterson (T 742-3177); boat trips with Pat and Jack's (T 742-3516), Dion McCallum (T 742-3136), Captain Jody (T 742-3266), Aquaventuras (T 742-3374) and Ed Whiteway (T 742-0328).

Island information – Culebra

● **How to get there**

By air: Flamenco Airways flies several times a day from Isla Grande airport San Juan (30 mins, US$25 one way, T 723-8110) and Fajardo (15 mins, T 863-3366) to Culebra (T 742-3885) and St Thomas (T 777-9789). Tickets from the airport only. By ferry: Fajardo-Culebra, 1½ hr, US$2, Mon-Thur 1600, Fri-Sat, 0900 and 1600, Sunday 0800 and 1430; Culebra-Fajardo, 0700 weekdays, Fri also 1400, 1800, Sat, 0700, 1400 and 1730, Sun 1300 and 1630. The 1600 ferry from Fajardo (return 0700) takes cars as well as passengers. Reservations needed for cars. Fajardo ticket and information office is open 0800-1100, 1300-1500, T 863-0705/0852 (Culebra T 742-3161). (It is best to arrive in Fajardo in time for the last ferry if you are going to the islands; there is little to do in the town and it is not a cheap place). However, at weekends the ferries are usually full and it is best to reserve a ticket.

● **Local transport**

Bicycles can be hired at US$2 a day from Jody's (T 742-3266) La Loma (T 742-3565) and Richard and Kathy's Rentals; cars and jeeps from Prestige (742-3242), Richard and Kathy's Rentals (T 742-0062), Willy Solis (T 742-3537), Seaside (T 742-3171) and M & R (T 742-3372). Taxi service with Marcelino (T 742-0292) or Cito (T 742-2787).

● **Accommodation**

Bay View Villas, PO Box 775, T 742-3392/765-5711, two 2-bedroomed villas, US$1,200/week or US$1,000/week, well-equipped, good views overlooking Ensenada Honda, walking distance of Dewey; **L3** *Culebra Island Villas*, T/F 742-0333, or in USA 52 Marlow Ave, Bricktown, NJ 08724, T/F (908) 458-5591, 10 units all with kitchen, weekly rates US$350-625 in 1-bedroom apartment, US$595-895 in 2-bedroom villa, 10 mins walk from town, overlooks Ensenada Bay, good for

diving and snorkelling; **A2-A3** *Posada La Hamaca*, 68 Castelar, T 742-3516, well kept, only 9 units, book in advance; **B** *Coral Island Guest House*, PO Box 396, T 742-3177, on water front near ferry terminal, 5 bedrooms, sleeps 12, living room, kitchen, fans, US$240 weekly, group rates available, credit cards accepted, in the USA contact John Dinga, 17 Riverbank Road, Quincy, MA02169, T (617) 773-0565. There are also a few bed and breakfast places: *Arynar Villa*, T 742-3145; *Casa Katrina*, T 742-3565; *Casa Llave*, T 742-3559; *Villa Boheme*, Ensenada Honda, T 742-3508; *Club Seabourne Mini Resort*, T 742-3169, hotel, restaurant, bar, pool; *Tamarindo Estates Beach Resort*, pool, dock, snorkelling, T 742-3343.

● **Places to eat**

There are several small restaurants in Dewey, offering local dishes and seafood. Take aways available. Prices range from US$3-15. For those who are self catering, there are 7 grocery stores, a fish market and a liquor store. Everything is imported so prices are high.

Information for travellers

BEFORE TRAVELLING

● **Documents**
All non-US residents need a US visa, or a US visa waiver for participating countries.

● **Health**
'La monga' is a common, flu-like illness, nothing serious, it goes away after a few days. Avoid swimming in rivers: bilharzia may be present. There was an outbreak of dengue fever in 1995, take care not to get bitten by mosquitoes. The northwest coast is particularly risky.

MONEY

● **Currency**
United States dollar. Locally, a dollar may be called a *peso*, 25 cents a *peseta*, 5 cents a *bellón* (but in Ponce a *bellón* is 10 cents and a *ficha* is 5 cents). Most international and US credit cards are accepted.

● **Exchange**
Currency exchange at Banco Popular; Caribbean Foreign Exchange, 201B Tetuán, Old San Juan, T 722-8222, and at the airport; Deak international at the airport; Scotia Bank exchange only Canadian currency; Western Union for cable money transfer, Pueblo Supermarket, Old San Juan.

GETTING THERE

AIR

● **From Europe**
American Airlines from London Heathrow or Brussels via New York JFK, or Frankfurt via Miami with immediate connection to San Juan (T 749-1747); Condor from Manchester, Frankfurt and Cologne, Bonn; Iberia from Madrid and Barcelona (T 721-5630). British Airways from London Gatwick once a week.

● **From Latin America**
Most South and Central American countries are connected via Miami but there are also direct flights from Caracas (Lacsa), Bogotá (Aces), T 791-0580, Guayaquil (Copa), Lima (Copa), Panama City (Lacsa and Copa), Guatemala City (Copa), and San José (Copa and Lacsa).

● **From the Caribbean**
Anguilla, Antigua, Aruba, Barbados, Casa de Campo, Dominica, Fort-de-France, Grenada, Pointe-à-Pitre, Port au Prince, Port of Spain, Puerto Plata, Punta Cana, St Barts, St Croix, St Kitts, St Lucia, St Maarten, St Thomas, Santiago (Dominican Republic), Santo Domingo, Tortola and Virgin Gorda, with LIAT (T 791-3838), American Airlines, American Eagle, Air Guadeloupe, Aerolíneas Argentinas, Carib Air, Aerolineas Dominicanas (Dominair), Dolphin Airlines, Air St Thomas.

Caribbean Air Express is noted for lower fares, flying from San José in Costa Rica, Orlando in Florida, and Santo Domingo and Puerto Plata in the Dominican Republic. Another cheaper airline is APA International Air, between Santo Domingo and San Juan.

● **From the USA**
A great many US cities are served by American Airlines and American Eagle; Delta (T 721-1144, 800-221-1212); Carnival, Northwest Airlines, Continental, Tower Air, TWA (T 753-8928), US Air and United Airlines.

SEA

There are no boats to other Caribbean destinations, apart from cruise ships, which call at San Juan and Ponce.

● **Ports of entry**
Mayagüez, Ponce, Fajardo, San Juan (not Boquerón).

● **Boat documents**
Clearance required from Customs, Immigration and Agriculture. US$25 annual customs fee. US citizens must clear into Puerto Rico when coming from USVI. Boats and firearms must be registered after 60 days.

● **Marinas**
There is a liveaboard community at Boquerón. Ponce is a good place to provision, with wholesale houses, Sears, Walmart, nearby. Fajardo is headquarters for marinas, boat supplies and haul-out. Anchorages: Boquerón, La Parguera, Guánica, Ponce, Fajardo, Vieques, Culebra has

many (see Bruce Van Sant's *Guide to the Span-ish Virgin Islands*). Ponce Yacht Club (members) allows one night free to other Yacht Club members. Haul out: Isleta, Puerto del Rey, Palmas del Mar, Villa Marina. Get weather from VHF weather, VI Radio or local AM station.

ON ARRIVAL

● **Airports**
There are airport limousines to a number of hotels. The taxi fare to old San Juan is US$10-12, to Condado US$6 (make sure the taxi meter is used; note that drivers prefer not to go to old San Juan, the beach areas are much more popular with them). Bus M7 goes to the airport from old San Juan, as does M8 from Santurce, but drivers can refuse to take you if you have too much luggage. You can also get bus T1 to Isla Verde, from where a taxi will charge about US$4 pp (plus US$1 for luggage), or you can catch the M7 or M8. Services are not very frequent, however, so allow plenty of time.

● **Airlines**
A number of airlines have offices at Miramar Plaza Center, Av Ponce de León 954: British Airways and Delta (9th floor), Lacsa, US Air; others can be found at Ashford 1022, Condado: American, BWIA, LIAT (best to use their office at the airport for reconfirmation). Flamenco Airways are at San Juan (T 725-7707), Isla Grande (T 723-8110), Culebra (T 742-3885), Fajardo (T 863-3366) and St Thomas (T 777-9789).

● **Banks**
Banco Popular; Banco de San Juan; Banco Mercantil de Puerto Rico; and branches of US and foreign banks. Banco de Santander, of Spain, is the second largest bank in Puerto Rico.

● **Hospitals**
Government and private hospitals. Ambulance, T 343-2500. Emergency T 911.

● **Public holidays**
New Year's Day, Three Kings' Day (6 January), De Hostos' Birthday (11 January), Washington's Birthday (22 February), Emancipation Day (22 March), Good Friday, José de Diego's Birthday (16 April), Memorial Day (30 May), St John the Baptist (24 June), Independence Day (4 July), Muñoz Rivera's Birthday (17 July), Constitution Day (25 July), Dr José Celso Barbosa's Birthday (27 July), Labour Day (1 September), Columbus Day (12 October), Veterans' Day (11 November), Discovery of Puerto Rico (19 November), Thanksgiving Day (25 November), Christmas Day.

● **Religion**
Roman Catholic, Episcopal, Baptist, Seventh Day Adventist, Presbyterian, Lutheran, Christian Science and Union Church. There is also a Jewish community. At the Anglican-Episcopal cathedral in San Juan there are services in both Spanish and English.

● **Shopping**
Puerto Rico is a large producer of rum, with many different types ranging from light rums for mixing with soft drinks to dark brandy-type rums (see above). Hand made cigars can still be found in Old San Juan and Puerta de Tierra. The largest shopping mall in the Caribbean is Plaza las Américas in Hato Rey, others include Plaza Carolina in Carolina, Río Hondo in Levittown, Plaza del Carmen in Caguas and Mayagüez Mall in Mayagüez. There are more traditional shops, but also many souvenir shops in Old San Juan. Imported goods from all over the world are available. Local artesanías include wooden carvings, musical instruments, lace, ceramics (especially model house fronts,

Warning

Crime has increased and we have received several warnings from travellers. In 1994 there were 995 murders, an all-time record, most were linked to drugs trafficking. In 1995, 65% of all crimes were related to drugs trafficking. Female tourists should avoid the Condado beach areas at night and all areas of San Juan can be dangerous after dark. Even during the day do not walk alone, stay with a group or in a busy area. Take precautions against theft from your person and your car (see **Car hire**), wherever you are on the island. Violent car hijackings amounted to about 350 a month in 1993 and car theft was running at over 1,300 a month by 1994. Car hire is therefore not rec from a security point of view, taking the *públicos* is safer. Take advice locally, guided excursions or bus trips may be less hassle.

eg from La Casa de Las Casitas, Cristo 250), hammocks, masks and basketwork. There are several shops in San Juan, but it is more interesting to visit the workshops around Puerto Rico. Contact the Centro de Artes Populares (T 724-6250) or the Tourism Company Artisan Office (T 721-2400 ext 2201) for details. Many of the tourist shops in the old city sell Andean goods.

There are a number of bookshops in the metropolitan area: The Bookstore, in Old San Juan, 257 San José, T 724-1815, has an excellent selection of English and Spanish titles. The Instituto de Cultura Puertorriqueña, Plaza de San José, has a good book and record shop with stock of all the best known Puerto Rican writers (all in Spanish). Another record shop near here is Saravá, Cristo at the corner of Sol 101, local, Caribbean, jazz and 'world music'.

● **Tipping**
Service is usually included in the bill, but where no fixed service charge is included, it is recommended that 15-20% is given to waiters, taxi drivers, etc.

● **Tourist Zone Police**
The Puerto Rico Tourist Zone Police are at Vieques Street, Condado (T 722-0738 and 724-5210). They can help you settle problems with taxis. Emergency T 911.

● **Water**
Drought forced the imposition of water rationing in 1994 in greater San Juan and 10 other towns. Water remained in short supply in 1995 and despite emergency dredging of the Carraizo reservoir, which had lost 65% of its capacity because of silt, rationing was temporarily reimposed in May.

ON DEPARTURE

● **Departure tax**
None is payable, although LIAT demands a 'security tax' of US$5.

WHERE TO STAY

The summer season runs from 16 April to 14 December and is somewhat cheaper than the winter season, for which we give rates where possible. A 9% tax is charged on the room rate in hotels with casinos, 7% in those without casinos. A full list is given in the monthly tourist guide, Qué Pasa, published by the Puerto Rican Tourism Company.

There are 18 **Paradores Puertorriqueños** to put you up while touring, some old, most new, with prices at US$55-100d: the majority are to the W of San Juan; for reservations T 721-2884, or 1-800-981-7575, from the USA T 1-800-443-0266.

Tourism Marketing Group, T 721-8793, arranges Fly-Drive packages, with car hire and accommodation at paradores; rates depend on which paradores you choose, but 3 days, 2 nights, starts at US$165 pp in a double room, 6 days, 5 nights US$350 pp.

See above in the main text under Boquerón for details of Compañía de Fomento Recreativo family accommodation **A2-B**; there are 4 other such centres at Punta Santiago on the E coast (Route 3, Km 72.4, T 852-1660), Punta Guilarte near Patillas (Route 3 Km 126, T 839-3565), Villas de Añasco in the W (Route 115, Km 5, T 826-1600) and Monte de Estado in the Maricao Forest (Route 120, Km 13.1, T 873-5632).

● **Camping**
Camping is permitted in the Forest Reserves; you have to get a permit (free) from the visitor centres. Camping is also allowed on some of the public beaches, contact the Recreation and Sports Department (T 722-1551 or 721-2800 ext 225). There are tent sites at Añasco, Cerro Gordo, Luquillo, Sombé, near Lake Guajataca and Punta Guilarte, cabins at Boquerón, Punta Guilarte and Punta Santiago, tent and trailer site at Seven Seas. Since Hurricane Hugo, many beach camping facilities have been closed; phone ahead to check.

FOOD AND DRINK

● **Food**
Good local dishes are the mixed stew (chicken, seafood, etc), asopao; mofongo, mashed plantain with garlic served instead of rice, very filling; mofongo relleno is the mofongo used as a crust around a seafood stew. Sacocho is a beef stew with various root vegetables, starchy but tasty. Empanadillas are similar to South American empanadas but with a thinner dough and filled with fish or meat. Pastillas are yucca, peas, meat, usually pork, wrapped in a banana leaf and boiled. Tostones are fried banana slices. Rice is served with many dishes; arroz con habichuelas (rice with red kidney beans) is a standard side dish. Sometimes a local restaurant will ask if you want provisiones; these are root vegetables and are worth trying. Comida criolla means 'food of the island',

criollo refers to anything 'native'. Some local fruit names: *china* is orange, *parcha* passion-fruit, *guanábana* soursop, *toronja* grapefruit; juices are made of all these, as well as guava, tamarind and mixtures. *Papaya* in a restaurant may not be fresh fruit, but *dulce de papaya* (candied), served with cheese, a good combination. Guava is served in a similar manner.

As most food is imported, the tourist, picknicker, or anyone economizing can eat as cheaply in a restaurant as by buying food in a grocery store.

Outside San Juan a network of 42 restaurants, called *Mesones Gastronómicos*, has been set up. These places serve Puerto Rican dishes at reasonable prices. Most of the *Parador* restaurants are included; a full list is available for tourist offices. *Qué Pasa* magazine gives a full list of restaurants on the island.

● **Drink**

Local beers are Medalla (a light beer), Gold Label (a premium beer, very good but hard to find) and Indio (a dark beer); a number of US brands and Heineken are brewed under licence. Rums: Don Q is the local favourite, also Palo Viejo, Ron Llave and the world-famous Bacardi (not so highly regarded by puertorriqueños); Ron Barrilito, a small distillery, has a very good reputation. Many restaurants pride themselves on their *piñas coladas*. *Mavi* is a drink fermented from the bark of a tree and sold in many snack-bars. Home-grown Puerto Rican coffee is very good.

GETTING AROUND

AIR

Several local airlines operate services within Puerto Rico, including American Eagle, Flamenco and Vieques Air Link, and they have offices either at the Luis Muñoz Marín International Airport, or the Isla Grande airport (eg Flamenco and Vieques Air Link). There are 4 daily American Eagle flights between San Juan and Ponce. Flamenco Airways flies to Culebra and St Thomas from Fajardo and San Juan. Some charter or inter-island flights leave from the Isla Grande airport.

LAND TRANSPORT

● **Motoring**

The Rand McNally road map is rec (US$1.85); the Gousha road map costs US$2.95 at Texaco stations. A good map is essential because there are few signs to places, but frequent indications of Route numbers and intersections. Avoid driving in the San Juan metropolitan area as traffic can be very heavy. Car theft and burglar damage is a major problem in the San Juan area. Make sure you use all the security devices given you by the rental company. Many people actually recommend you do not stop at red lights after 2200, because of hold-ups, just pause, look and go.

● **Car hire**

The best and easiest form of transport if you want to see the island; public transport is not always easy and finishes early. There are many car rental agencies, including Hertz (T 791-0840), Isla Verde International Airport and 10 other locations; National (T 791-1805), Luis M Marín Airport. Budget (T 791-3685) at the airport. Target (T 783-6592/782-6381), not at airport, among the cheapest, will negotiate rates. L & M, Condado, (main office T 791-1345/1160), free pick-up, make sure you get it even for day hire. A small car may be hired for as little as US$25 (not including collision damage waiver, US$12.50, insurance is sometimes already covered by your credit card) for 24 hrs, unlimited mileage (national driving licence preferred to international licence), but rates vary according to company and demand.

● **Buses**

San Juan: there is a city bus (*guagua*) service with a fixed charge of US$0.25 for standard route, US$0.50 for longer. (No change given; make sure you have right money.) They have special routes, sometimes against the normal direction of traffic, in which case the bus lanes are marked by yellow and white lines. Bus stops are marked by white and orange signs or yellow and black notices on lampposts marked 'Parada'. From the terminal near Plazoleta del Puerto in Old San Juan, T1 goes through Miramar, past the Fine Arts Center in Santurce, to Isla Verde (Route 37); No 2 goes to Río Piedras via Condado, Av Muñoz Rivera and the University; No 46 goes to Bayamón along Av Roosevelt; A7 goes about every 2 hrs to Piñones, through Condado and Isla Verde (Av Ashford to Route 37); M7 goes through Condado to the airport. From behind Pier 2, No 8 goes to Puerto Nuevo and Río Piedras, No 12 to Río Piedras, and No 14 to Río Piedras via Av Ponce de León, Santurce, Hato Rey and the University. City buses run to a 30, or 45-min schedule and many do not operate after 2200.

● **Rail**

An urban rail system has been approved for Greater San Juan. Construction by a German consortium was to start in 1996 with completion due in 2001.

● **Taxis**

All taxis are metered, charge US$1 for initial charge and US$0.10 for every additional 1/10 mile; US$0.50 for each suitcase; US$1 is charged for a taxi called from home or business. Minimum fee US$3. Approximate fares: San Juan to Condado, US$4; Condado to Isla Verde, US$4.50-5. Taxis may be hired at US$12 an hour unmetered. Taxi drivers sometimes try to ask more from tourists, so beware, insist that the meter is used, and avoid picking up a taxi anywhere near a cruise ship. If they refuse, tell them you will call Puerto Rico Tourist Zone Police, T 722-0738, or the Public Service Commission, T 751-5050 ext 253, 254, and complain. They can revoke a taxi licence.

There are also shared taxis, usually Ford minibuses (*carros públicos*) which have yellow number plates with the letters P or PD at the end and run to all parts of the island. They usually carry about 10 people and are not particularly comfortable but often safer than hiring a car (see **Warning** below). The Río Piedras *terminal de públicos* handles all departures to the E. Many públicos for the W leave from *puntos* near parada 18 in Santurce. Also some leave from the main post office and others collect at the airport; elsewhere, ask around for the terminal. They do not usually operate after about 1700 and some connections do not operate after 1500, eg Río Piedras-Fajardo. They are also very scarce on Sun and public holidays. *Público* to Caguas costs US$1.25; Río Piedras-Fajardo 1½ hrs (US$3); to Ponce takes 2 hrs (US$6-7). A service referred to as *linea* will pick up and drop off passengers where they wish. They operate between San Juan, and most towns and cities at a fixed rate. They can be found in the phone book under Líneas de Carros. *Públicos* are a good way of getting around, provided you are prepared to wait up to a couple of hours for the car to fill up. It is not rec, however, if you want to get to out of the way places, such as the Arecibo Observatory, the Camuy Caves, or the Tibes Indian Ceremonial Centre, when a hired car is essential. If you hire a *público* for yourself it works out expensive, eg San Juan airport to Ponce US$75.

COMMUNICATIONS

● **Postal services**

Inside the new Post Office building in Hato Rey, on Av Roosevelt, there is a separate counter for sales of special tourist stamps. In Old San Juan, the Post Office is in an attractive old rococo-style building, at the corner of San Justo and Recinto Sur. You can buy stamps at hotels and at the airport. *Poste restante* is called General Delivery, letters are held for 9 days.

● **Telecommunications**

Operated by Puerto Rico Telephone Co, state-owned. Local calls from coin- operated booths cost US$0.10, but from one city to another on the island costs more (eg US$1.25 Ponce-San Juan). Local calls from hotel rooms cost US$2.60 and often a charge is made even if there is no connection. In 1996 a new international telephone code, 787, was adopted, to run in conjunction with the old 809 code until 31 January 1997, when 787 will be the sole code. 800 numbers can be used. The cheapest way to phone abroad is from Phone Home (run by Sprint), 257 Recinto Sur, Old San Juan, T 721-5431, F 721-5497, opp the Post Office by Pier 1, US$0.36/min to the USA, discounts on all other calls abroad, no 3-min minimum charge, fax, telex and telegram messages also sent and received. Overseas calls can be made from the AT&T office at Parada 11, Av Ponce de León 850, Miramar (opposite *Hotel Excelsior*, bus T1 passes outside, a chaotic place), from an office next to the Museo del Mar on Pier One, and from the airport. Three mins to New York, US$1.50 and to the UK, US$3. For Canada Direct, dial 1-800-496-7123 to get through to a Canadian operator. The blue pages in the telephone book are a tourist section in English, divided by subject.

MEDIA

● **Newspapers**

San Juan Star is the only daily English paper. There are 3 Spanish daily papers of note, *El Mundo, El Vocero* and *El Nuevo Día*.

● **Radio**

Two radio stations have English programmes.

ENTERTAINMENT

● **Nightclubs**
Jazz at The Place, Calle Fortaleza 154 in old San Juan, no admission charge, drinks about US$2. *Shannons Irish Pub*, Condado, T1 bus from airport passes it, live music (rock and roll), beer US$2.50, rec. *Caribe Hilton* is a favourite nightspot, also the other 4-5 star hotels, *Condado Beach*, *Regency* and *La Concha*.

TOURIST INFORMATION

● **Local tourist office**
The Puerto Rico Tourism Company, PO Box 4435, San Juan 00905, with Information Centres also at the international airport (T 791-1014, F 791-8033; next to the *Condado Plaza Hotel*, T 721-2400 (ext 2280); La Casita, near Pier One, Old San Juan, T 722-1709, F 722-5208; Rafael Hernández Airport, Aguadilla, T 890-3315, T 890-0220; Citibank Building, 53 McKinley East, facing plaza, Mayagüez, T 831-5220, F 831-3210; Casa Armstrong-Proventud, Plaza Las Delicias, Ponce, T 840-5695, F 843-5958. For details on museums, contact the Puerto Rico Institute of Culture, Museums and Parks Programs, T 724-5477.

● **Tourist offices overseas**
New York (T 800-223-6530, F 212-818-1866), **Los Angeles** (T 213-874-5991, F 874-7257), **Miami** (T 305-381-8915, F 381-8917), **France** (Express Conseil, 5 bis, rue du Louvre, 75001 Paris, T 331 4477 8800, F 42 60 05 45), **Spain** (Calle Serrano, 1-20 izda, 28001, Madrid, T 341-431-2128, 800-898920, F 577-5260), **Italy** (Gioco Viaggi, Via Dante 2/53, 1521 Genoa, T 3910 553 11669, F 553 1191, and Via Carroccio 12, 20123 Milan, T 392 894 02034, F 894 01508) **Tokyo** (Kasho Building 2-14-09, Nihombashi, Chuo-ku, Tokyo 103, T 03-3272- 3060/2445), **Germany** (Kreuzberger Ring 56, D-65205 Wiesbaden 32, T 49611-744-2880, F 724-089) and **Toronto** 2 Bloor Street West, Suite 700, Toronto, Ontario, M4W 3R1, (T 416-969-9025, F 969 9478). The Caribbean Travel Service, Av Ashford 1300, Condado, is happy to help. Out in the country, tourist information can be obtained from the town halls, usually found on the main plaza. Hours are usually Mon-Fri, 0800-1200, 1300-1430.

● **Further reading**
Two books which may be useful to visitors are *The Other Puerto Rico*, by Kathryn Robinson (Permanent Press, 1987), US$11.95, and *The Adventure Guide to Puerto Rico*, by Harry S Pariser (Hunter, 1989), US$13.95; they give more detail on the out of the way places than we have space for. *Qué Pasa*, a monthly guide for tourists published by the Tourism Company, can be obtained free from the tourist office. It is very helpful.

Virgin Islands

THE VIRGIN ISLANDS are a group of about 107 small islands situated between Puerto Rico and the Leeward Islands; the total population is about 115,000. Politically they are divided into two groups: the larger W group, with a population of 97,800 (1995 est), was purchased from Denmark by the USA in 1917 and remains a US Territory; the smaller E group constitutes a British Crown Colony, with a population of only 17,383. Apart from their historical background, having been discovered by Columbus on the same voyage and named by him after Ursula and her 11,000 virgin warriors, the islands have little in common. The two groups share the same language, currency and cost of living, but the US group is very much more developed than the British, and tourism has been a prime source of income for much longer.

The US Virgin Islands

THE US VIRGIN ISLANDS (USVI), in which the legacies of Danish ownership are very apparent, contain three main islands: St Thomas, St John and St Croix, lying about 40 miles E of Puerto Rico. There are 68 islands in all, although most of them are uninhabited. They have long been developed as holiday centres for US citizens and because of that are distinct from the British Virgin Islands, which have only recently started to develop their tourist potential. The population, mainly black, has always been English-speaking, despite the long period of Danish control, although some Spanish is in use, particularly on St Croix. The West Indian dialect is mostly English, with inflections from Dutch, Danish, French, Spanish, African languages and Créole.

HORIZONS

HISTORY

The islands were 'discovered' by Columbus on his second voyage in 1493 and, partly because of their number, he named them 'Las Once Mil Vírgenes' (the 11,000 virgins) in honour of the legend of St Ursula and her 11,000 martyred virgins. There were Indian settlements in all the major islands of the group and the first hostile action with the Caribs took place during Columbus' visit. Spain asserted its exclusive right to settle the islands but did not colonize them, being more interested in the larger and more lucrative Greater Antilles. European settlement did not begin until the 17th century, when few Indians were to be found. St Croix (Santa Cruz) was settled by the Dutch and the English around 1625, and later by the French. In 1645 the Dutch abandoned the island and went to St Eustatius and St Maarten. In 1650 the Spanish repossessed the island and drove off the English, but the French, under Philippe de Loinvilliers de Poincy of the Knights of Malta, persuaded the Spanish to sail for Puerto Rico. Three years later de Poincy formally deeded his islands to the Knights of Malta although the King of France retained sovereignty. St Croix prospered and planters gradually converted their coffee, ginger, indigo and tobacco plantations to the more profitable sugar, and African slavery was introduced. Wars, illegal trading, privateering, piracy and religious conflicts finally persuaded the French Crown that a colony on St Croix was not militarily or economically feasible and in 1695/6 the colony was evacuated to St Domingue.

A plan for colonizing St Thomas was approved by Frederik III of Denmark in 1665 but the first settlement failed. The Danes asserted authority over uninhabited St John in 1684, but the hostility of the English in Tortola prevented them from settling until 1717. In 1733 France sold St Croix to the Danish West India & Guinea Company and in 1754 the Danish West Indies became a royal colony. This was the most prosperous period for the Danish islands. After the end of Company rule and its trading monopoly, St Thomas turned increasingly toward commerce while in St Croix plantation agriculture flourished. St Thomas became an important shipping centre with heavy reliance on the slave trade. Denmark was the first European nation to end its participation in the slave trade in 1802. Illegal trade continued, however, and British occupation of the Virgin Islands between 1801 and 1802 and again between 1807 and 1815 prevented enforcement of the ban.

The Danish Virgin Islands reached a peak population of 43,178 in 1835, but thereafter fell to 27,086 by 1911. Sailing ships were replaced by steamships which found it less necessary to transship in St Thomas. Prosperity declined with a fall in sugar prices, a heavy debt burden, soil exhaustion, development of sugar beet in Europe, hurricanes and droughts and the abolition of slavery. In 1847 a Royal decree provided that all slaves would be free after 1859 but the slaves of St Croix were unwilling to wait and rebelled in July 1848. By the late 19th century economic decline became pronounced. The sugar factory on St Croix was inefficient and in the 20th

century the First World War meant less shipping for St Thomas, more inflation, unemployment and labour unrest. The Virgin Islands became a liability for Denmark and the economic benefits of colonialism no longer existed. Negotiations with the USA had taken place intermittently ever since the 1860s for cession of the Virgin Islands to the USA. The USA wanted a Caribbean naval base for security reasons and after the 1914 opening of the Panama Canal was particularly concerned to guard against German acquisition of Caribbean territory. In 1917, the islands were sold for US$25mn but no political, social or economic progress was made for several years. The islands were under naval rule during and after the War and it was not until 1932 that US citizenship was granted to all natives of the Virgin Islands.

A devastating hurricane in 1928, followed by the stock market crash of 1929, brought US awareness of the need for economic and political modernization. Several years of drought, the financial collapse of the sugar refineries, high unemployment, low wages and very high infant mortality characterized these years. In 1931 naval rule was replaced by a civil government. In 1934, the Virgin Islands Company (VICO) was set up as a long term development 'partnership programme'. The sugar and rum industry benefited from increased demand in the Second World War. VICO improved housing, land and social conditions, particularly in rural areas, but the end of the wartime construction boom, wartime demand for rum and the closing of the submarine base, brought further economic recession. However, the severance of diplomatic relations between the USA and Cuba shifted tourism towards the islands. Construction boomed and there was even a labour shortage. With immigrant labour, the population increased and by 1970 per capita income reached US$2,400, five times that of the Caribbean region as a whole, with about half of the labour force engaged

Hurricanes

In Sept 1995 the islands escaped the worst of Hurricane Luis but were hit by Hurricane Marilyn, causing damage estimated at US$3.5bn. St Thomas was the worst hit, with 5 deaths and a quarter of all homes destroyed. Many resorts suffered such extensive damage that they remained closed for repairs until summer 1996. Thousands of homes and businesses lost their roofs and much of the island had no electricity for weeks. At least 70 boats were destroyed. Looting broke out and a curfew was imposed. In July 1996 the hurricane season came early with the arrival of Bertha, but the 80 mph winds caused only relatively minor damage.

in tourist activities and tourism providing about 60% of the islands' revenues. With the shift from agriculture to tourism, VICO was officially disbanded in 1966, along with the production of sugarcane. Various tax incentives, however, promoted the arrival of heavy industry, and during the 1960s the Harvey Alumina Company and the Hess Oil Company began operating on St Croix. By 1970, the economy was dominated by mainland investment and marked by white-owned and managed enterprises based on cheap imported labour from other Caribbean islands.

On 17 September 1989, Hurricane Hugo ripped across St Croix causing damage or destruction to 90% of the buildings and leaving 22,500 people homeless. The disaster was followed by civil unrest, with rioting and looting, and US army troops were sent in to restore order. The territorial government, located on St Thomas, had been slow to react to the disaster on St Croix and was strongly criticized. Subsequently, a referendum endorsed the establishment of some sort of municipal government on each island which would be more responsive to that island's needs and legislation to that effect was introduced into the Legislature in July 1993. St Croix's feeling of neglect led to attempts to balance the division of power between the islands, but calls for greater autonomy grew. After some delay, a referendum was held in October 1993, which presented voters with seven options on the island's status, grouped into

three choices: continued or enhanced status, integration into the USA, or independence. However, the vote was inconclusive, with only 27% of the registered voters turning out, whereas 50% were needed for a binding decision. Of those who did, 90% preferred the first option, leaving the process of constitutional change in some disarray.

In 1993 the government of the USVI reached agreement with the Danish company, the East Asiatic Company Ltd, to buy the West Indian Company Ltd (WICO), whose major holdings on St Thomas included a cruise ship dock, the Havensight Shopping Mall, a 7.2-acre landfill, the former Danish consulate, Denmark Hill, and some undeveloped land. WICO had remained in Danish hands after the 1917 purchase of the islands by the USA and had retained the right to dredge, fill and develop submerged lands in the E part of St Thomas harbour, despite local opposition. The US$54mn sale was described locally as wiping out the last vestiges of Danish colonialism.

Governor Alexander Farrelly completed his second term of office at the end of 1994. The Republican Party campaigned on the back of the unpopularity of his government to try and win the November gubernatorial election but it was won by an independent, Roy Schneider, who promised a firm stance against crime.

GOVERNMENT

In 1936 the Organic Act of the Virgin

Islands of the United States provided for two municipal councils and a Legislative Assembly in the islands. Suffrage was extended to all residents of twenty one and over who could read and write English. Discrimination on the grounds of race, colour, sex or religious belief was forbidden and a bill of rights was included. Real political parties now emerged, based on popular support. In 1946, the first black governor was appointed to the Virgin Islands and in 1950 the first native governor was appointed. In 1968 the Elective Governor Act was passed, to become effective in 1970 when, for the first time, Virgin Islanders would elect their own governor and lieutenant governor. The Act also abolished the presidential veto of territorial legislation and authorized the legislature to override the governor's veto by a two-thirds majority vote. The USVI is an unincorporated Territory under the US Department of Interior with a Delegate in the House of Representatives who (since January 1993) has a vote in sittings of the whole House. An independent, Victor Frazer, was elected in 1994, replacing a Democrat, Ron de Lugo, who had held the seat since its creation in 1972. The Governor is elected every four years; there are 15 Senators; judicial power is vested in local courts. All persons born in the USVI are citizens of the United States, but do not vote in presidential elections while resident on the islands.

THE ECONOMY

USVI residents enjoy a comparatively high standard of living (the cost of living is the highest in the USA), unemployment is low, at around 4% (mostly on St Croix), but the working population is young and there is constant pressure for new jobs. The islands used to rely on the Martin Marietta alumina plant, and the Hess oil refinery, operating well below capacity, for employment and income, but nowadays the major economic activity is tourism. Over 2mn visitors come

every year, of which more than a third arrive by air but the majority are cruise ship passengers. Earnings from tourism are around US$800mn, about 70% of non-oil revenues. The number of hotel rooms is now around 5,000, generating jobs for two thirds of the labour force. There is a perennial conflict between the hotel industry, which provides employment,

US Virgin Islands: fact file	
Geographic	
Land area	352 sq km
forested	10.3%
pastures	75.3%
cultivated	10.7%
Demographic	
Population (1995)	97,800
annual growth rate (1990-95)	-0.8%
urban	37.2%
rural	62.8%
density	277.8 per sq km
Religious affiliation	
Protestant	46%
Roman Catholic	34%
Birth rate per 1,000 (1988)	22.0
	(world av 27.1)
Education and Health	
Life expectancy at birth,	
male	66.7 years
female	70.7 years
Infant mortality rate	
per 1,000 live births (1988)	13.1
Physicians (1985)	1 per 622 persons
Hospital beds	1 per 505 persons
Economic	
GDP (1987 market prices)	US$1,246mn
GNP per capita	US$11,740
Tourism receipts (1992)	US$792mn
Radio	1 per 1.0 persons
Television	1 per 3.1 persons
Telephone	1 per 1.7 persons
Employment	
Population economically active (1990)	
	47,400
% of labour force in	
agriculture	1.2
mining, manufacturing	
and public utilities	7.8
construction	12.0
trade, hotels, restaurants	21.8
Source Encyclopaedia Britannica	

fixed investment and pays taxes, and the cruise ship industry, which contributes comparatively little to the islands.

Industry is better developed than in many Caribbean islands and exports of manufactured goods include watches, textiles, electronics, pharmaceuticals and rum. The Hess Oil refinery operates at less than 400,000 barrels a day nowadays, compared with its previous peak capacity of 728,000 b/d, but investment of US$550mn has been made in a fluid catalytic cracking unit to produce unleaded gasoline from 100,000 b/d of heavy industrial fuel. Industrial incentives and tax concessions equivalent to those enjoyed by Puerto Rico, are designed to attract new investors with US markets to the islands. Over 30 large US corporations have set up manufacturing operations in the USVI and industrial parks are being built.

Agriculture has declined in importance since sugar production ended, and the poor soil prevents much commercial farming. Emphasis is placed on growing food crops for the domestic market and fruit, vegetables and sorghum for animal feed have been introduced. Fishing in the USVI waters is mostly for game rather than for commercial purposes. The islands' lack of natural resources makes them heavily dependent on imports, both for domestic consumption and for later re-exports, such as oil and manufactured goods. The trade account is traditionally in deficit, but is offset by tourist revenues and by US transfers. The government budget is also in deficit partly because of the high cost of public sector wages which account for 80% of spending. Revenue collections are inadequate and large sums of unpaid taxes are outstanding.

Damage from Hurricane Hugo, principally on St Croix which was declared a major disaster area, was estimated at US$1.25bn, equivalent to annual gnp. The islands were destined to receive US$600mn in federal assistance.

Reconstruction led to improvements in infrastructure and most hotels and houses were upgraded.

FLORA AND FAUNA

The Virgin Islands' national bird is the yellow breast (*Coereba flaveola*); the national flower is the yellow cedar (*Tecoma Stans*). Most of St John is a national park (see below). Also a park is Hassel Island, off Charlotte Amalie. The National Parks Service headquarters is at Red Hook, St Thomas. In Red Hook too is the Island Resources Foundation (T 775-6225, PO Box 33, USVI 00802; US office, 1718 P Street NW, Suite T4, Washington DC 20036, T 265-9712). This non-governmental office which is also a consulting firm, but non-profit-making, is open to serious researchers and investigators seeking information on wildlife, tourism and the environment; it has an extensive library. It may also be used as a contact base for those seeking specialist information on other islands. The Audubon Society is represented on St John by Peg Fisher at the At Your Service Travel Agency. *Virgin Islands Birdlife*, published by the USVI Cooperative Extension Service, with the US National Park Service, is available for birdwatchers. The National Park Headquarters has an excellent, reasonably priced selection of reference books for marine life, flora, fauna and island history.

On St Croix, the National Parks Service office is in the old customs building on the waterfront. Buck Island (see below) is a national marine park. In Christiansted, contact the Environmental Association, PO Box 3839, T 773-1989, office in Apothecary Hall Courtyard, Company Street. The Association runs hikes, boat trips and walks, and in March-May, in conjunction with Earthwatch and the US Fish and Wildlife Department, takes visitors to see the leatherback turtles at Sandy Point (T 773-7545 for information on trips). The association has made Salt River (see page 435) a natural park for wildlife, reef and mangroves. There are books, leaflets, etc, available at the association's office.

The mongoose was brought to the islands during the plantation days to kill rats that ate the crops. Unfortunately rats are nocturnal and mongooses are not and they succeeded only in eliminating most of the parrots. Now you see them all over the islands, especially near the rubbish dumps. There are many small lizards and some iguanas of up to 4 feet long. The iguanas sleep in the trees and you can see them and feed them (favourite food hibiscus flowers) at the Limetree beach. St John has a large population of wild donkeys which are pests; they bite, steal picnic lunches and ruin gardens. On all these islands, chickens, pigs, goats and cows have the right of way on the roads.

ST THOMAS

St Thomas lies about 75 miles E of Puerto Rico at 18°N, 40 miles N of St Croix. Thirteen miles long and less than 3 miles wide, with an area of 32 square miles and population of 51,000, St Thomas rises out of the sea to a range of hills that runs down its spine. The highest peak, Crown Mountain, is 1,550 feet, but on St Peter Mountain, 1,500 feet, is a viewpoint at Mountain Top. Various scenic roads can be driven, such as Skyline Drive (Route 40), from which both sides of the island can be seen simultaneously. This road continues W as St Peter Mountain Road, with a detour to Hull Bay on the N coast. Route 35, Mafolie Road, leaves the capital, Charlotte Amalie, heading N to cross the Skyline Drive and becomes Magens Bay Road, descending to the beautiful bay described below. It should be said that much of the island has been built upon, especially on its E half.

Beaches and watersports

There are 44 beaches of which Magens Bay on the N coast is considered to be the finest on the island and wonderfully safe for small children. There are changing facilities and you can rent snorkelling equipment (but the snorkelling is not the best on the island) and loungers. Other good beaches are at Lindbergh Bay (SW, close to the airport runway, good for plane spotters), Morningstar Bay (S coast near *Frenchman's Reef Hotel*, beach and watersports equipment for hire), Bolongo Bay, Sapphire Bay (E coast, good snorkelling, beach gear for rent) and Brewer's Bay (can be reached by bus from Charlotte Amalie, get off just beyond the airport). Hull Bay on the N coast is good for surfing and snorkelling. At Coki Beach (NE, showers, lockers, water skiing, jet skiing), a US$7.50 taxi ride from St Thomas, is the Coral World underwater observatory, recommended (open daily, US$12 entrance). The observatory is 20 feet under the sea and you get a good view of the reef around it. There is also a large aquarium, predator tank and other marine exhibits. On the beach snorkelling equipment can be rented for US$6, snorkelling is good just off the beach. Windsurfing lessons and rentals at Morningstar, Magens Bay, Sapphire Beach, Secret Harbour and the *Stouffer Grand*. West Indies Windsurfing will deliver rental equipment to wherever you are staying, T 775-6530, not only windsurfing boards but also sunfish and kayaks. Snorkelling gear can be rented at all major hotels and the dive shops. Sunfish sailboats for rent at Morningstar, Magens Bay and the *Stouffer Grand*. Parasailing at some hotels or call Caribbean Parasail and Watersports, T 775-4206, or Fat Boys Water Toys, T 777-3055, who have a variety of jet-skis etc to go fast and make a noise, or pedalos to go slowly and peacefully. There are few deserted beaches left on St Thomas, although out of season they are less crowded. The most inaccessible, and therefore more likely to be empty, are those along the NW coast, which need 4-wheel drive to get there. Otherwise for solitude take a boat to one of the uninhabited islets offshore and discover your own beaches.

St Thomas

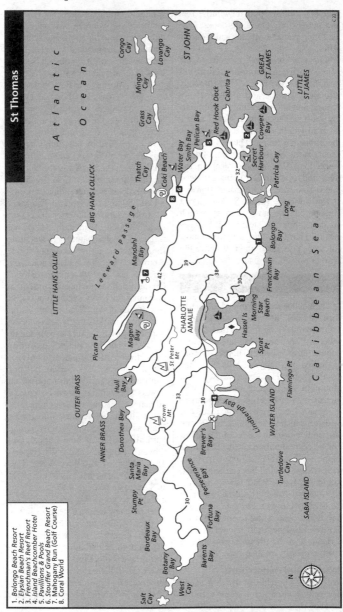

1. Bolongo Beach Resort
2. Elysian Beach Resort
3. Frenchman's Reef Resort
4. Island Beachcomber Hotel
5. Pavillions & Pools
6. Stouffer Grand Beach Resort
7. Mahogany Run (Golf Course)
8. Coral World

Atlantic Ocean

Leeward Passage

Caribbean Sea

CHARLOTTE AMALIE

ST JOHN

Congo Cay
Lovango Cay
Mingo Cay
Grass Cay
Cabrita Pt
GREAT ST JAMES
Cowpet Bay
Secret Harbour
Patricia Cay
LITTLE ST JAMES
Long Pt
Bolongo Bay
Frenchman Bay
Morning Star Beach
Hassel Is
Sprat Pt
Flamingo Pt
WATER ISLAND
Lindbergh Bay
Brewer's Bay
Turtledove Cay
SABA ISLAND
West Cay
Salt Cay
Botany Bay
Bordeaux Bay
Barents Bay
Fortuna Bay
Perseverance Bay
Santa Maria Bay
Stumpy Pt
Dorothea Bay
INNER BRASS
OUTER BRASS
Hull Bay
St Peter Mt
Crown Mt
Magens Bay
Picara Pt
LITTLE HANS LOLLIK
BIG HANS LOLLIK
Mandahl Bay
Thatch Cay
Coki Beach
Water Bay
Smith Bay
Pelican Bay
Red Hook Dock

30
33
42
39
30
38
30
32

Sailing of all types and cruises are available. Half day sails from US$40, full day from US$65 and sunset cruises from US$30 are offered by many boats, including *Coconuts* and *Daydreamer* (T 775-2584), two trimarans; *The Alexander Hamilton* (T 775-6500), a 65-ft traditional schooner; and *Spirit of St Christopher*, a 70-ft catamaran claiming to be the fastest sailboat in the Caribbean, lovely sailing, especially at sunset, half day US$45, sunset cruise US$30, T 776-1043. Power boats offering day trips are *Limnos* (T 775-3203) and Club Nautico Powerboats (T 779-2555). You can explore on your own by renting a small power boat from Nauti Nymph (T 775 5066), 21-ft runabouts; See An Ski (T 775-6265), 21-ft makos; or Calypso (T 775-2628), 22-ft, 6 passengers, US$150/day, 27-ft, 8 passengers, US$185/day, including fuel, boats equipped with VHF radios, ice chest, stereo, fish finder, snorkelling gear, very helpful with planning a route, also scuba, waterskiing and fishing gear can be provided. Virgin Islands Power (VIP) Yacht Charters, T 776-1510, 800-524-2015, F 776-3801, PO Box 6760, has the largest power yacht charter fleet and sport fishing fleet in the Caribbean, bareboat or crewed, US$3,000-5,000 a week in summer, US$4,000-6,100 in winter.

Charter yachts available in a wide variety of luxury and size, with or without crew, cost about the same as a good hotel. Virgin Islands Charteryacht League, T 774-3944 or (800) 524-2061 has a huge number of crewed yachts from US$2,300/week in summer to US$20,000/week in winter, bareboats US$2,950-6,100; other companies include: Bajor Yacht Charters, T 776-1954; Easy Adventures, T 775-7870; Proper Yachts, T 776-6256; Sailing Vacations, T 800-922-4880 or Travel Services, T 775-9035. Note that if you plan to sail in both the US and British Virgin Islands it is cheaper to charter your boat in the BVI. To get on a yacht as crew, either for passage or paid charter jobs, try 'Captains and Crew', at *Yacht Haven* in Charlotte Amalie, a placement service which charges US$15/year and a portion of your first pay cheque.

The annual Rolex Cup Regatta is held at St Thomas Yacht Club in April (T 775-6320).

Diving and marine life

The waters around the islands are so clear that snorkelling is extremely popular. *At-a-glance snorkeller's Guide to St Thomas* by Nick Aquilar describes 15 snorkel spots in detail. Spearfishing is not allowed and you may not remove any living things from underwater such as coral, live shells or sea fans. For divers, there are over 200 dive sites, caves, coral reefs, drop offs and lots of colourful fish to see, although be careful of short sighted barracuda if you swim into murky water. There are several wrecks of ships and even a wrecked plane to explore. Many of the resorts offer diving packages or courses and there are at least 15 dive companies. Equipment and instruction for underwater photography are available. A one-tank dive costs around US$40 while a 2-tank dive starts from US$55. Coki Beach Dive Club, T 775-4220 offers an introductory dive for US$25, cruise ships bring their guests here. Chris Sawyer Diving Centre, T 775-7320, 800-882-2965, specializes in quality service to small groups, great all day, wreck of the *Rhone* trip once a week. There are also several liveaboard sail/dive charters, worth contacting if you want to spend more time on and under the water: Regency Yacht Vacations (T 800-524-7676), VIP Yacht Charters (T 800-524-2015), Island Yachts (T 800-524-2019), Red Hook Charters (T 800-233-4938).

The Atlantis Submarine dives to 150 feet for those who can not scuba dive but want to see the exotic fish, coral, sponges and other underwater life. Located at Building VI, Bay L, Havensight Mall, St Thomas, T 776-5650 for reservations, or 776-0288 for information (also kiosk on waterfront, usually 6 dives daily). You have to take a 4-mile launch ride on the *Yukon III* to join the submarine at Buck Island. One-hour day dives US$58, night dives US$66, children 4-12 half price.

There is deep sea fishing with the next world record in every class lurking just under the boat. The USVI Fishing Club Tournament is in June, contact the American Yacht Harbour for details, F 776-5970. The Bastille Day Kingfish Tournament is in July and the USVI Open Atlantic Blue Marlin tournament is held in August every year (T 774-2752); other game fish include white marlin, kingfish, sailfish, tarpon, Alison tuna and wahoo. No fishing licence is required for shoreline fishing; government pamphlets list 100 good spots (T 775-6762). For sportfishing charters and information contact Blues Brothers Charters (T 775-7956), Charterboat Centre (T 800-866-5714), Cruzan Gold (T 775-3339), Poor Devil (T 776-8996), Red Hook Charter Office (T 800-233-4938), St Thomas Charter (T 775-3690), Fishing Fleet St Thomas Sportfishing (T 775-7990).

Sports

There are a few public tennis courts (2 at Long Bay and 2 at Sub Base), which operate on a first come first served basis, but the hotel courts at *Sugar Bay Resort, Bolongo Bay Resort, Bluebeard's Castle, Frenchman's Reef, Bolongo Lime Tree Tennis Center, Mahogany Run, Sapphire Beach* and *Stouffer Grand* are mostly lit for night time play and open for non-residents if you phone in advance to book. Rates range around US$10 for 45 mins. There is an 18-hole, 6,022-yard golf course with lovely views at Mahogany Run, green fee US$60 pp, cheaper after 1400 (T 800-253-7103). A miniature golf course is at Smith Bay, lots of fun, $4 for 18 holes. Horse riding can be arranged at Rosendahl Riding Ring, T 775-2636. Horse racing is a popular spectator sport.

Festivals

Carnival in April (T 776-3112 for precise date and events). Most spectacular. Dating back to the arrival of African slaves who danced bamboulas based on ritual worship of the gods of Dahomey, the festivities have since been redirected towards Christianity. Parades with costumed bands include the J'Ouvert Morning Tramp, the Children's Parade, Mocko Jumbis on stilts and steel bands (for information on Mocko Jumbi dancing, contact Willard S John, see below under St Croix **festivals**).

CHARLOTTE AMALIE

The harbour at **Charlotte Amalie** (*pop* 12,331), capital of St Thomas and also of the entire USVI, still bustles with colour and excitement, although the harbour area can be a startling contrast for the visitor arriving by sea from the British Virgin Islands. As the Fort Christian Museum (see below) puts it, "Oversized, architecturally inappropriate buildings have marred the scenic beauty of the harbour. Harbour congestion has become a major problem." One could add that the streets are congested, too. But as the museum also says, there are still a number of historical buildings. The town was built by the Danes, who named it after their King's consort, but to most visitors it remains 'St Thomas'. Beautiful old Danish houses painted in a variety of pastel colours are a reminder of the island's history.

There are also picturesque **churches**: one of the oldest synagogues in the Western Hemisphere (1833) is on Crystal Gade, an airy, domed building, with a sand floor and hurricane-proof walls; it has books for sale in the office, iced spring water and visitors are given a 10-minute introduction, free, worth a visit. In 1996 the Hebrew Congregation of St Thomas celebrated the 200th anniversary of its founding with lots of services and commemorative events. The Dutch Reformed Church is the oldest established church, having had a congregation since 1660 although the present building dates from 1846. The Frederick Lutheran Church dates from

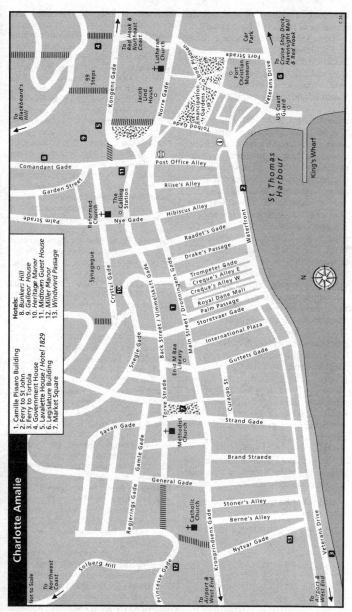

Charlotte Amalie

Not to Scale

1. Camille Pissaro Building
2. Ferry to St John
3. Ferry to Tortola
4. Government House
5. Lavalette House / Hotel 1829
6. Legislature Building
7. Market Square

Hotels:
8. Bunker Hill
9. Galleor House
10. Heritage Manor
11. Midtown Guest House
12. Miller Manor
13. Windward Passage

St Thomas Harbour

King's Wharf

To Blackbeard's Hill

To Red Hook & Northeast Coast

Lutheran Church

99 Steps

Jacob Lind House

Kongens Gade

Norre Gade

Toldbod Gade

Emancipation Garden

Fort Christian Museum

Fort Strade

Veterans Drive

US Coast Guard

Car Park

To Cruise Ship Dock, Havensight Mall & Red Hook

Comandant Gade

Garden Street

Palm Strade

Post Office Alley

Riise's Alley

Hibiscus Alley

The Calling Station

Reformed Church

Nye Gade

Raadet's Gade

Drake's Passage

Trompeter Gade

Creque's Alley E

Creque's Alley W

Royal Dane Mall

Palm Passage

Storetvaer Gade

International Plaza

Guttets Gade

Waterfront

Synagogue

Crystal Gade

Stiegle Gade

Back Street / Vimmelskft Gade

Main Street / Dronningens Gede

Enid M Baa Library

Curacao St

Torve Strade

Savan Gade

Gamle Gade

Methodist Church

Strand Gade

Brand Straede

Reglerings Gade

General Gade

Catholic Church

Stoner's Alley

Berne's Alley

Nytvar Gade

Kronprindsens Gade

Solberg Hill

Princesse Gade

To Northwest Coast

To Airport & West End

Veterans Drive

To Airport & West End

N

C.24

1820 and its parish hall was once the residence of Jacob H S Lind (1806-27).

There are several old fortifications to see: Bluebeard's Castle Tower and Blackbeard's Castle, the latter built in 1679 and lived in by the pirate and his 14 wives, now an inn and restaurant. The **Virgin Islands Museum**, in the former dungeon at Fort Christian (1666-80), is open Mon-Fri, 0830-1630 (T 776-4566 to check times), free, but donations welcome as much restoration work remains to be done; there are historical and natural history sections and an art gallery. In contrast to the red-painted fort is the green **Legislative Building**, originally the Danish police barracks (1874), open Mon-Fri. Government House, off Kongens Gade, was built in 1865-87. The Enid M Baa Library and Archive is on Main Street, it is another early 19th century edifice.

Two historical buildings which cannot be visited are the former Danish Consulate, on Denmark Hill and the house of the French painter, Camille Pissaro, on Main Street. The Dockside Bookshop in Havensight Mall (at the Cruise Ship Dock) has books and other publications on the Virgin Islands and the Caribbean in general. The Old Mill, up Crown Mountain Road from Sub Base traffic light is an old sugar mill open to the public. Estate St Peter Greathouse and Botanical Gardens has 500 varieties of plants, a stunning view and an art gallery for local artists.

On Wed and Fri, the heaviest cruise ship days, Main Street in Charlotte Amalie is closed to traffic.

Island information – St Thomas
● **Accommodation**

Price guide

L1	over US$200	L2	US$151-200
L3	US$101-150	A1	US$81-100
A2	US$61-80	A3	US$46-60
B	US$31-45	C	US$21-30
D	US$12-20	E	US$7-11
F	US$4-6	G	up to US$3

There are many hotels, guesthouses, apartments, villas and cottages on St Thomas, the cheaper places to stay are in town or up in the hills, while the newer, chain hotels on the beach are at the top of the range. Summer rates are about 33% cheaper than winter. There is a Hotel Association counter at the airport which can help you with reservations. Please note that non-inclusion does not imply non-recommendation. Resorts, apartments and condominiums are clustered around the E end, such as the **L1** *Renaissance Grand Beach Resort* on Water Bay (PO Box 8267, T 775-1510, F 775-2185), totally renovated and reopened Oct 1996 after hurricane repairs, 290 hill or beachside suites, well-appointed, 2 pools, 6 lit tennis courts, restaurants, bars, children's programmes, complimentary watersports, sailing can be arranged, conference facilities, lovely views over the resort's own beach to St John and the British Virgins; next door is **L1** *Point Pleasant Resort*, children sharing parents' room free under 21, 134 rooms in villas in 15 acres of gardens, pool, tennis, watersports, free use of car 4 hrs daily, 6600 Estate Smith Bay No 4, T 775-7200, F 776-5694. **L1-L2** *Elysian Beach Resort* on Cowpet Bay, 175 rooms and suites, fitness centre, tennis, pool, jacuzzi, watersports centre offering diving, kayaking, parasailing, T 755-1000, 800-753-2554, F 779-2400. On the S coast is **L1-L3** *Bolongo Bay Beach and Sports Club*, family resort, kids' offers, pool, beach, tennis, kitchen facilities, 5 restaurants, (PO Box 7337, T 779-2844, F 779-2844); among others, and overlooking the entrance to Charlotte Amalie harbour and above Morningstar Beach, the huge **L1-L2** *Frenchman's Reef* (a *Marriott* hotel, PO Box 7100, T 776-8500, F 776-3054), badly damaged by hurricane Marilyn but reopened, 420 rooms, 18 suites, all facilities, and its 96-room sister property **L1-L2** *Morning Star Beach Resort* alongside. West of Charlotte Amalie are **L1** *Emerald Beach Resort*, opened in 1991, pool, bar, restaurant, 'The Palms' rooms have ocean and airport view, tennis, watersports, 8070 Lindbergh Bay, T 777-8800, F 776-3426, and **L3** *Island Beachcomber* (PO Box 2579, T 774-5250, F 774-5615), smaller at 48 rooms, no pool, poor plumbing but pleasant, both on Lindbergh Bay, sheltered beach at end of airport runway. **L1-L3** *Magens Point Resort Hotel*, T 775-5500, 1-800-524-2031, F 776-5524, half a mile from the sea overlooking Magens Bay, 3 miles from Charlotte

Amalie, pool, tennis, adjacent to Mahogany Run Golf Course, sailing, fishing, diving packages available, 32 rooms and 23 suites; **L1 Pavilions and Pools**, 6400 Estate Smith Bay, T/F 775-6110, on Sapphire Beach, offers suites and kitchens and your own private pool, very romantic, rec. Two new luxury hotels with all facilities opened in 1992: **L1 The Grand Palazzo**, 6900 Great Bay, T 775-3333, F 775-4444, 152 rooms, very expensive and luxurious and **Sugar Bay Plantation Resort**, part of the Holiday Inn chain, near the Renaissance Grand, T 777-7100, F 777-7200, 300 rooms, also very expensive, 3 pools, watersports, tennis.

In Charlotte Amalie: **L1-L2 Bluebeard's Castle**, T 774-1600, F 774-5134, 170 rooms, sports, pool, free shuttle to Magens Bay Beach; **L2-L3 Blackbeard's Castle**, on Blackbeard's Hill, T 776-1234, 800-344-5771, F 776-4321, 20 rooms, restaurant. On the waterfront, Veterans' Drive heading towards the airport, is **L3 Windward Passage** (PO Box 640, T 774-5200, F 774-1231), with pool, restaurant, entertainment in modern block. In the centre, on Government Hill is **L1 A1 Hotel 1829**, another historical building, with pool, restaurant, very comfortable (PO Box 1576, T 776-1829, 800-524-2002, F 776-4313) only 15 rooms; next door, behind The Fiddle Leaf Restaurant, is **L3-A2 Galleon House**, (PO Box 6577, T/F 774-6952, T 800-524-2052), swimming pool, verandah, gourmet breakfast, but not wholly safe, missing safety bars on windows allowed theft, snorkel gear provided, discounts for senior citizens. **L3-A2 Heritage Manor**, Snegle Gade (just off Back Street), PO Box 90, T 774-3003, 800-828-0757, F 776-9585, small pool (in old baker's oven), honour bar, clean, comfortable, helpful, each room different, some with shared bath, some suites, rec; **A1 Bunkers' Hill Hotel**, 7A Commandant Gade, T 774-8056, F 774-3172, 2 sections, kitchens, TV, etc, pool, airport transfers, deli and shop, good value; two doors up the hill is a 9-room **Guest House** with no name, **B-C**, a/c, clean, T 777-9746; in same area but closer to centre, **A2-A3 Midtown Guest House** (PO Box 521, T 774-6677), not impressive, but reasonable rates, cash or TCs only; **A2-A3 Miller Manor** (PO Box 1570, T/F 774-1535), on the hill behind the Catholic Cathedral, clean, very friendly, a/c, kitchen facilities, rec; up Solberg Hill, going up from Miller Manor, is **A1-A2 Danish Chalet Inn**, T 774-5764, 800-635-1531, F 777-4886, helpful, honour bar, pool, short walk to town,

pleasant; **A3-B Beverley Hill Guesthouse**, T 774-2693, on road to airport, basic, friendly, but clean. **L2-L3** The **Ramada Yacht Haven**, 5400 Long Bay Road, T 774-9700, F 776-3410, watersports, pool, restaurant, next to marina; also at the marina, check the bulletin board for boats providing overnight accommodation for US$15-30 pp.

● **Places to eat**
There are many very good restaurants on the island, most of which are listed in Here's How and St Thomas This Week, or you can get details in your hotel. The large hotels all have their own restaurants, you will not be short of places to eat. **Hotel 1829**, on Government Hill, superb food and service, expensive, if you can't afford it go and have a look anyway, lovely old building and great view; **Café Normandie** in Frenchtown, T 774-1622, for great French cuisine, or **Entre Nous** at Bluebeard's Castle, T 774-4050; **The Chart House**, at Villa Olga in Frenchtown, T 774-4262, not cheap but excellent food, rec, fish, rib, lobster, extensive salad bar, also on St Croix; **Virgilio's**, between Main and Back streets, T 776-4920, up from Storetvaer Gade, Italian, good food and service; there are several places on Back Street, bars and bistros for breakfast, lunch or dinner; **Island Reef** on Garden Street specializes in Jamaican jerk chicken for lunch, or dinner, also all you can eat spaghetti on Wed; **Zorba's**, T 776-0444, Greek, next to **The Fiddle Leaf**, T 775-2810, both across park from Post Office; **Hard Rock Café**, T 777-5555, next to **The Green House**, on harbour front, Veterans Drive, T 774-7998, excellent restaurant at reasonable prices, attracts younger crowd, serves drinks, happy hour 1630, in season has a band, and dancing at 2100, cover charge US$4 if no dinner ordered, ladies' night Wed, open 0700-0230 for breakfast, lunch and dinner; as does **Drake's Inn**, restaurant and bar, Drake's Passage and Trompeter Gade (good value breakfast special - best 0630 to 0900 but doesn't open that early on Sun); breakfast also at **Burger King**; there are also **Kentucky Fried Chicken**, **Baskin-Robbins** ice cream, etc. **Upper Crust Bakery** behind The Green House, good for continental breakfast or quick lunch. There is a **Wendy's** hamburger restaurant on Veterans Drive by the cruise ship docks, with a small Heineken bar above. The area W of the Market Square is more local, with restaurants and bars, including **Long Look** vegetarian restaurant, on General Gade.

Bavarian Restaurant and Pub on Raphune Hill offers German cuisine and beer, live music Wed-Sat, T 775-3615; *Paradise Point* on the hill overlooking Charlotte Amalie, all you can eat buffet, happy hour 1600-1900 half price drinks, excellent view, great place to watch the sunset; *For the Birds* (T 775-6431) is a Tex-Mex style restaurant and bar outside town on the road to Red Hook, on Scotts beach, good view of Cays, Fri free buffet and happy hour 1600-1900, half price drinks, live band Thur, free drinks for ladies Thur and Sun, Sun is the big night, especially crowded during American colleges' spring break (March-early May). At Red Hook, inexpensive breakfast and lunch at *The Three Virgins*; waiting for the ferry is easy at *Piccola Marina Café-Bar*, lunch and dinner, right on the water. The *Fish Shack*, a seafood retailer, also serves lunch and dinner, T 776-7190; the *East Coast Bar and Grill* is the locals' pub with food, drinks, and conversation. At *Yacht Haven*, the *Gourmet Gallery* has excellent deli sandwiches on homemade bread to eat outside in the courtyard, also a great selection of domestic and international wines at reasonable prices (for the USVI). Award winning ribs from the *Texas Pit BBQ*, a mobile truck that shows up on the waterfront Tues-Thur 1830-2000. The *Squirrel Cage*, on Norre Gade next to World Wide Travel, cheap food, breakfast, lunch and dinner. *Wok on Water* in Frenchtown, T 777-8886 for excellent Vietnamese, Thai and Chinese food, right at the water's edge.

● **Nightlife**
St Thomas offers the greatest variety of nightlife to be found in the Virgin Islands. Bands and combos play nightly at most hotels. Several of the hotels offer limbo dancing 3 or 4 nights a week and the ubiquitous steel bands remain a great favourite with both visitors and inhabitants. At any time you will hear plenty of bass booming from the smart cars cruising the town's streets. Nightclubs include *Club Z* (all the action on Sat night), *Famous*, *JP's Steak House* (also known as the *Old Mill* bar, has a progressive music night on Thur, popular), *The Green House*, live rock and roll bands Mon-Sat, *Barnacle Bill's*, Frenchtown, live bands inc reggae every night, some comedy, poetry reading, Mon is talent night, very popular with locals and yacht crews, *The Limetree* has 3 nightclubs, a disco, a club with West Indian bands and *Iggie's*, a bistro (cheap, good and large portions) with pool tables, darts and a sing

along video machine, your chance to be a star. *Calypso Jack's*, on corner above Crystal Gade and Commandant Gade, good bar with live rock band at weekends. The Reichhold Centre for the Arts, part of the University of the Virgin Islands, has programmes with local or international performers.

Unfortunately, because of the increase in crime, you are not recommended to walk around downtown Charlotte Amalie at night, take a taxi. Between downtown and Havensight the police have put up signs advising you not to walk along the waterfront path.

● **Shopping**
Charlotte Amalie is packed with duty free shops of all description, and is also packed with shoppers. If you want to shop seriously, then this is the cheapest island of the 3 and has the largest selection. Nevertheless it is a good idea to have done your research at home and know what you want to buy. Local produce can be bought in the Market Square (most produce brought in by farmers on Sat 0530) and there are some small supermarkets and grocery stores. Solberg Supermarket on Solberg Hill has a launderette (US$2 a load). Large supermarkets: Pueblo Grand Union, Woolworths, E end of town, K-Mart has opened near Four Winds for inexpensive clothes, sporting goods, camping equipment and household goods. Check the prices in supermarkets; what you see on the shelf and what you are charged are not always identical. Good arts and crafts centre at Tillet Gardens, opp Four Winds Plaza, where you can watch the craftsmen at work.

● **Telephones**
The Calling Station, Bakery Square Mall, Nye Gade, for local and international calls, Mon-Thur 0730-1930, Fri-Sat until 2130, Sun 1000-1600; also video rentals. Red Hook Mail Services, upstairs at Red Hook Plaza. VI Telecom at the West Indian Co dock.

● **Transport**
Air Harry S Truman international airport; the taxi stand is at the far left end of the new terminal, a long way from the commuter flights from Puerto Rico and other islands. Taxi to town US$4.50 pp (US$4 for each additional passenger). There are public buses every 20 mins 0600-1900 from the terminal to the town, US$1.

Bus services (US$0.75 city fare, US$1 country fare, exact change) with a new fleet of 34-passenger, a/c buses, run from town to the university, to Four Winds Plaza and to Red Hook (every hour); new routes are being added, contact Mannassah bus liners (T 774-5678). Hourly open-air taxi-buses charge US$3 for the trip from Red Hook to Market Square.

Taxis Cabs are not metered but a list of fares is published in *St Thomas This Week* and *Here's How*; fares list must be carried by each driver. Rates quoted are for one passenger and additional passengers are charged extra; drivers are notorious for trying to charge each passenger the single passenger rate. Airport to Red Hook is US$10 for one, US$6.00 each additional passenger for extra person, town to Magens Bay is US$6.50 for one, US$4 for extra person. When travelling on routes not covered by the official list, it is advisable to agree the fare in advance. There are extra charges between 2400 and 0600 and charges for luggage. A 2-hr taxi tour for 2 people costs US$30, additional passengers US$12 each. VI taxi Radio Despatch, T 774-4550, Independent Taxi, T 776-1669, 24-hour Radio Dispatch Taxi Service, T 776-0496. Gypsy cabs, unlicenced taxis, operate outside Charlotte Amalie, they are cheaper but if you use one make sure you agree fare and route before you get in.

Car hire All types of wheels are available with rental firms plentiful. Car hire is about US$35/day, or from Budget US$42 with second day free and coupons for entry into local attractions.

Tours There are also group tours by surrey, bus or taxi. Island tours in an open bus cost US$12 pp, many leave from Main Street at about 1200; complete tours only are sold, Gaston Brown rec.

Helicopter To tour the islands by air, contact *Air Center Helicopters*, T 775-7335; *Antilles Helicopter*, T 776-7880; or *Seaborne Seaplane Adventures*, T 777-4491, US$79 pp.

Ferries There are a number of ferry boats to various destinations, including one from Red Hook to nearby St John (every hour from 0800 to 2400 plus 0630 and 0730 Mon to Fri, takes 20 mins, US$3 each way). Charlotte Amalie to St John, US$7, 45 mins; there is also a ferry from downtown to *Frenchman's Reef Hotel* and Morningstar beach, US$3 each way, leaving every hour 0900-1700, 15 mins, a nice way to go to the beach.

ST JOHN

Only 16 miles square, **St John** is about 5 miles E of St Thomas and 35 miles N of St Croix. The population is only 3,500, mainly concentrated in the little town of Cruz Bay and the village of Coral Bay. The population of St John fell to less than a thousand people in 1950 when 85% of the land had reverted to bush and second growth tropical forest. In the 1950s Laurence Rockefeller bought about half of the island but later donated his holdings to establish a national park which was to take up about two thirds of the predominantly mountainous island. The Virgin Islands National Park was opened in 1956 and is covered by an extensive network of trails (some land in the park is still privately owned and not open to visitors). Several times a week a Park ranger leads the Reef Bay hike, which passes through a variety of vegetation zones, visits an old sugar mill and some unexplained petroglyphs and ends with a ferry ride back to Cruz Bay. The trail can be hiked without the ranger, but the National Park trip provides a boat at the bottom of the trail so you do not need to walk back up the 3-mile hill. You should reserve a place on the guided hike at the Park Service Visitors' Centre, Cruz Bay (on N side of harbour) open daily 0800-1630, T 776-6201; information on all aspects of the park can be obtained here, there are informative displays, topographical and hiking trail maps, books on shells, birds, fish, plants, flowers and local history, sign up here for activities. There are 22 hikes in all, 14 on the N shore, 8 on the S shore. The trails are well-maintained and clearly signed with interpretive information along the way. Insect repellent is essential. A seashore walk in shallow water, using a glass bottomed bucket to discover sea life, is recommended. There is a snorkel trip round St John in which the boat takes you to 5-6 reefs not accessible by land (and therefore less damaged), a good way to see the island even if you do not snorkel.

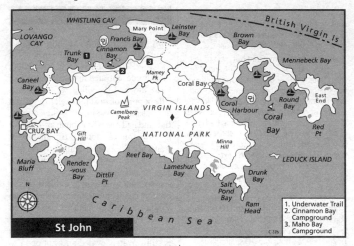

1. Underwater Trail
2. Cinnamon Bay Campground
3. Maho Bay Campground

St John

An informative, historical bus tour goes to the remote East End. There are evening programmes at Cinnamon Bay and Maho Bay camps, where rangers show slides and movies and hold informal talks. For detailed information on what to do and where to find it, *Exploring St John* covers hiking trails, 39 beaches and snorkel spots, historic sites and jeep adventures.

Beaches and watersports

Off Trunk Bay, the island's best beach, there is an underwater snorkelling trail maintained by the National Parks Service. Not surprisingly, the beach tends to get rather crowded (especially when tour groups come in); lockers for hire, US$2 (deposit US$5), snorkelling equipment US$6 (deposit US$40) return by 1600. Other good beaches include Hawk's Nest Bay, Caneel Bay, Cinnamon Bay (there is a small museum of historical photographs and pictures here), Salt Pond (excellent beach with good snorkelling and a spectacular hike to Ram's Head), Lameshur Bay (difficult road but worth it), Maho Bay (beach is 5 feet from the road, lots of turtles, sometimes tarpon, nice and calm) and Solomon Bay (unofficial nudist beach about half an hour's walk from the road). Reef Bay has excellent snorkelling.

In the National Park there are snack bars at Cinnamon Bay and Trunk Bay only. Bring water and lunch if you are hiking or going to other beaches which will not be so crowded.

Windsurfers can be rented at Cinnamon Bay and Maho Camps, sunfishes at Maho Camp. Coral Bay Watersports, T 776-6850, next to *Don Carlos*, rents sail and power boats, waterskiing, sport fishing and tackle, they also offer diving, snorkelling, kayaking and windsurfing. Half and full day sails and fishing trips can be arranged by Connections, T 776-6922, sailing also with Jolly Mon Day Sailing, T 776-6239, Noah's Little Arks (Zodiacs), T 693-9030, Proper Yachts, T 776-6256. You can rent a power boat with Ocean Runner Powerboats, T 693-8809. For one and 2 tank scuba dives, wreck dives and night dives: Low Key Watersports at Wharfside Village, specializes in small groups, maximum 6 people, also kayaking, T 800-835-7718; Cruz Bay Watersports, T 776-6234, across from *Joe's Diner*, offers a free snorkel map. Other dive operators are Cinnamon Bay Watersports, T 776-6330 (also kayaking and windsurfing), Paradise Watersports, T 776-6111, and Sea Trade Ltd, T 774-2001.

Sports

There is tennis at the large resorts and also 2 public courts available on a first come first served basis. Horseriding is available at Pony Express Riding Stables at Bordeaux Mountain, T 776-6494, where you can tour the sites of the National Park or go on a horticultural tour, US$40-100.

Carnival

St John's carnival is in the week of 4 July, but there are lots of events in the two preceding weeks.

Island information – St John
● Accommodation

Price guide

L1	over US$200	L2	US$151-200
L3	US$101-150	A1	US$81-100
A2	US$61-80	A3	US$46-60
B	US$31-45	C	US$21-30
D	US$12-20	E	US$7-11
F	US$4-6	G	up to US$3

L1 *Caneel Bay Plantation*, lots of packages available in a variety of rooms or cottages (PO Box 720, T 776-6111, 800-928-8889, F 693-8280), 171-room resort built in the late 1950's by Laurance Rockefeller, since 1993 managed by Rosewood Hotels and Resorts, renovation 1995/96 after the hurricanes, several restaurants, bars, dress smartly after sunset, 11 all-weather tennis courts, complimentary watersports for guests inc sunfish, windsurfers, also boat rentals, fishing and diving available, ferry service between Caneel Bay and downtown St Thomas, also to sister resort of *Little Dix Bay* on Virgin Gorda, BVI; **L1** *Hyatt Regency*, 285 rooms and suites in 34 acres, huge pool, conference facilities, watersports, tennis etc, PO Box 8310, T 693-8000, F 779-4985; **L1** *Gallows Point*, 50 suites, fans, pool, watersports, kitchen facilities (PO Box 58, T 776-6434, F 776-6520). Within walking distance of town are **L1-L3** *Battery Hill* (PO Box 458, T 776-6152, F 779-4044), 2-bedroom villas, pool, personal service, attentive management; and *Caribe Havens*, lovely views, US$750-2,100/week, (PO Box 455, T/F 776-6518). Cheaper places: **A1-A3** *Cruz Inn*, T 693-8688, F 693-8590 (PO Box 566), CP, shared bathroom, fan, West Indian style inn, helpful advice on what to do and see, great sunsets from the Bamboo Bar, music and

movies some nights, book swap; **A1-A2** *The Inn at Tamarind Court*, T/F 776-6378 (PO Box 350), inexpensive breakfast and dinner, bar, music and movies some nights, both are in Cruz Bay; **A1-A3** *Raintree Inn*, also in Cruz Bay, T/F 693-8590, (PO Box 566 also). At Cinnamon Bay (frequent taxibuses from Cruz Bay) there is a **A1-A2** campground and chalet site run by the National Park Service, usually full so book in advance, maximum stay 2 weeks; bare site **D**, a few shared showers, food reasonably priced in both the cafeteria and grocery store. Write to Cinnamon Bay Camp, PO Box 720, St John, USVI, 00831-0720, T 776 6330, 800-539-9998, F 776-6458. At Maho Bay (8 miles from Cruz Bay, regular bus service) there is a privately run campground, write to Maho Bay Camp, Box 310, Cruz Bay, St John, USVI 00830, T 776 6226, 800-392-9004, F 776-6504. **A1** 'tent cottages' are connected by a raised boardwalk to protect the environment, lots of steps, magnificent view from restaurant, lots of planned activities, attracts socially-conscious, environmentally-aware guests and staff, guests come back year after year, possible to work in return for your board. In 1993 they also opened the **L2** *Harmony Resort*, (same address, fax, T 776-6240), the world's first to operate on sun and wind power alone and largely built from recycled materials, 12 rooms, handicap access. The **C** *St John Hostel*, is located on Bordeaux mountain, midway between Cruz Bay, taxis don't like to go that far, but hitchhiking is easy (T 693-5544). There is a restaurant; also facilities for scuba diving and snorkelling and evening lectures on diving, sailing etc. It is possible to stay in private homes; contact Havens with Ambiance, PO Box 635, Cruz Bay. Virgin Island Bed and Breakfast Homestays (PO Box 191) T 779-4094/776-7836, also arrange rooms in private houses, **A1** and up. **L2-A1** *Serendip Condos*, PO Box 273, T/F 776-6646, fully equipped apartments. To rent a villa contact Vacation Vistas, run by Lisa Durgin, PO Box 476, T 776-6462, about a dozen houses to rent all round the island, some with pools, nearly all over US$1,000 a week for 2, 25-50% less in summer, honeymoon specials. *Catered to* has rental homes and luxury villas from US$1,200/week in winter for 2 people to US$4,850/week in winter for 6 people, run by Vacation Property Management Service, PO Box 704, Cruz Bay, St John, USVI 00830, T 776-6641, F 693-8191. Others include *Vacation Homes*, PO Box 272, Cruz Bay,

T776-6094, F 693-8455, US$800-5,000/ week; *Caribbean Villas and Resorts*, T 776-6152, 800-338-0987, F 779-4044, offers 1 and 2 bedroom apartments with pools for US$150/day in season.

● **Places to eat**
In Cruz Bay, *Fred's* (open 0800-2300 daily, live entertainment, T 776-6363) and *Hercules* serve inexpensive, filling, delicious West Indian food. Opposite the Post Office is the *Chicken B-B-Q*. For sandwiches and light meals, *Joe's Diner, Jumby's, Dockside Pub, Wendy's* and *Luscious Lick's* (vegetarian meals, also has ice cream). At the *Lime Inn* restaurant, seafood, steak, excellent lobster and pasta, all you can eat night on Wed, very popular with locals and visitors, T 776-6425; *The Barracuda Bistro* at Wharfside Village is a bakery, a deli, and a 'home cooking' type restaurant for breakfast, lunch and dinner, T 779-4944; *The Old Gallery*, West Indian and American food, 2 blocks E of ferry dock, Fri West Indian buffet, all you can eat, T 776-7544; *Morgan's Mango*, excellent seafood and steak, open air dining, great sauces, open evenings only, T 693-8141; *Paradiso*, Italian, at Mongoose Junction, dinner only, T 693-8899; *Mongoose Restaurant*, American, also at Mongoose Junction, serves breakfast, lunch and dinner, T 693-8677; *Ellington's* at Gallow's Point, continental and seafood, dinner only, closed Mon, T 693-8490; *Café Roma*, Italian food and good pizza, open evenings, also vegetarian dishes, T 776-6524; *Fish Trap*, seafood, pasta and steak at *Raintree Inn*, dinner only, closed Mon, T 693-9994; *JJ's Texas Coast Café*, on the park, very good Tex-Mex food, hearty meat and potato type specials, breakfast, lunch and dinner. For something special try the French cuisine at *Le Chateau de Bordeaux*, T 776-6611, mountain view. In Coral Bay, *Skinny Legs* has inexpensive grilled hotdogs, hamburgers, chicken, etc, plus horse shoes and darts to play with; *Shipwreck Landing*, continental cuisine; *Don Carlos* has Mexican food; *Sea Breeze*, different menu every night, popular with locals, inexpensive; *Lucy's*, West Indian and continental. *Caneel Bay* and *The Hyatt* have several restaurants and entertainment. *The Hyatt Regency* is rec for brunch, a treat, you will not need to eat for weeks after, very lush and exquisite, super service.

● **Nightlife**
Up to date information on events is posted on the trees around town or on the bulletin board

in front of Connections. In Coral Bay, *Shipwreck Landing* has jazz on Sun, a 2-day music festival in April; *Skinny Legs* has live music some nights, horse shoes, darts, and lots of special events. In Cruz Bay, the place to go and dance is *Fred's*, calypso and reggae Wed and Fri; guitar and vocals at *Pusser's* and at *JJ's*. Popular places to 'lime' (relax) are *JJ's*, the *Rock Lobster Bar, The Backyard* and sitting in Cruz Bay Park, watching the world go by. A disco the *Boom Boom Room* offers dancing to a DJ and videos until the small hours of the morning.

● **Shopping**
Scattered around Cruz Bay and concentrated in Wharfside Village and Mongoose Junction are shops selling souvenirs, arts and crafts and jewellery. Right in the Park is Sparkey's, selling newspapers, paperbacks, film, cold drinks, gifts. The St John Pharmacy is next to the Supermarket Deli, open 7 days a week. Small markets sell groceries, Pine Peace Market, Oscar's, the Supermarket Deli, Supernatural Foods and Marina Market. Joe's Discount Liquor has food and liquor. Food is expensive (rum is cheaper than water) and the selection is limited. If you are camping for a week, shopping at the big supermarkets on St Thomas is a good idea. Fresh produce is available at Nature's Nook, also fish and produce is sold from boats a couple of times a week at the freight dock. Love City Videos at the Boulon Centre, rents videos and VCRs.

● **Bank**
Chase Manhattan in Cruz Bay is the only bank, open 0900-1500, T 776-6881, cashes US$ TCs but will not exchange currency or process cash advances on credit cards, you must go to the St Thomas banks for that.

● **Telecommunications**
Connections (T 776-6922), as well as arranging sailing trips and villa rentals, is the place for business services, local and international telephone calls, faxes, Western Union money transfers, photocopying, wordprocessing, notary, VHF radio calls and tourist information (they know everything that is happening). Connections East (T 779-4994) does the same thing in Coral Bay.

● **Newspaper**
The St John newspaper, *Tradewinds*, is published bi-weekly, US$0.50. The funny, informative, free, St John Guidebook and map is available in shops and also at the ticket booth at the ferry dock.

● **Transport**
There are only 3 roads on St John although the
government map shows more roads that are
barely passable 4-wheel drive dirt tracks. The
island is covered with steep hills and it is hot.
Mountain bicycles (available from Cinnamon
Bay Watersports, T 776-6330 and Coral Bay
Watersports, T 776-6850) and long distance
backpacking are not recommended ways of
getting around, but you can always start walking and then catch a taxibus when it passes
you. The road from Cruz Bay to Coral Bay is
only 7 miles but it takes about 40 mins to drive
it. There are no buses on St John, you have to
use taxis or jeeps. Official taxi rates can be
obtained from St John Police Department or
by asking the taxi driver to show the official
rate card. A 2-hr island tour costs US$30 for
one or 2 passengers, or US$12 pp if there are
3 or more. Taxi from Cruz Bay to Trunk Bay,
US$3; to Cinnamon Bay US$4. Vehicles may
be rented, see **Information for travellers**
below. Hitchhiking is easy. It is almost impossible to persuade a taxi to take you to Coral
Bay, so hitchhike by waiting with everyone else
at the intersection by the supermarket deli.
There are 2 service stations, open 0800-1900,
both in Cruz Bay, may be closed on holidays.

Ferry to St Thomas: hourly 0700 to 2200 and
2315 to Red Hook, every 2 hrs 0715 to 1315,
1545 and 1715 to Charlotte Amalie (fares and
length of journey under St Thomas).

ST CROIX

With 84 square miles, St Croix is the
largest of the group (population 55,000),
lying some 75 miles E of Puerto Rico and
40 miles S of St Thomas. The name is
pronounced to rhyme with 'boy'. People
born on the island are called Cruzans,
while North Americans who move there
are known as Continentals. The E of the
island is rocky, arid terrain, the W end
is higher, wetter and forested. Columbus thought that St Croix looked like a
lush garden when he first saw it during
his second voyage in 1493. He landed at
Salt River on the N coast, which has
now been approved as a National Park
encompassing the landing site as well
as the rich underwater Salt River drop
off and canyon. It had been cultivated
by the Carib Indians, who called it

Ay-Ay, and the land still lies green and
fertile between the rolling hills.

Agriculture was long the staple of the
economy, cattle and sugar the main activities, and today there are the ruins of
numerous sugar plantations with their
Great Houses and windmills. **Whim Estate** is restored to the way it was under
Danish rule in the 1700s and is well
worth a visit; it is a beautiful oblong
building housing a museum of the period, and in the grounds are many of the
factory buildings and implements (open
Mon-Fri 1000-1500, US$5, T 772-0598).
There is a gift shop. **St George Botanical Garden**, just off Centreline Road
(Queen Mary Highway), in an old estate,
has a theatre as well as gardens amid the
ruined buildings. The 17-acre site was
built on a pre-Columbian settlement.
Open Tues-Sat 0900-1800, US$5. Ju-
dith's Fancy, from the time of the
French, is now surrounded by building
developments and has less to see than
the other two.

Today agriculture has been surpassed
by tourism and industry, including the
huge Hess oil refinery on the S coast.

Beaches and watersports

St Croix has it all: swimming, sailing,
fishing, and above all, diving. Good
beaches can be found at Davis Bay, Protestant Cay, Buccaneer, the Reef, Cane
Bay (good snorkelling), Grapetree Beach
and Cormorant Beach. Cramer Park on
the E shore and Frederiksted beach to
the N of the town, both have changing
facilities and showers. All beaches are
open to the public, but on those where
there is a hotel (*Buccaneer* – good snorkelling) which maintains the beach, you
may have to pay for the use of facilities.
Generally the N coast is best for surfing
because there are no reefs to protect the
beaches. On the NW coast, the stretch
from Northside Beach to Ham's Bay is
easily accessible for shell collecting (but
watch out for sea urchins at Ham's Bay
beach); the road is alongside the beach.
The road ends at the General Offshore
Sonorbuoy Area (a naval installation at

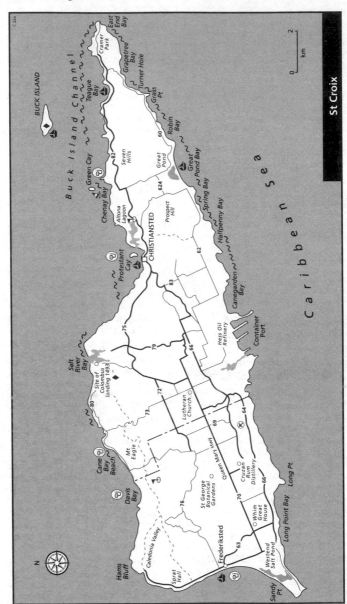

St Croix

Ham's Bluff), which is a good place to see booby birds and frigate birds leaving at dawn and coming home to roost at dusk. Shells can also be found on Sprat Hall beach (ask Judy or Jill at *Sprat Hall Plantation* for details).

Water skiing, jet skiing, windsurfing and parasailing are all on offer. For windsurfing instruction contact Mistral School, T 773-4810. At the *Chenay Bay Beach Resort* former World Champion Lisa Neuberger offers windsurfing lessons and board rental to beginners or experienced windsurfers. St Croix Water Sports, T 773-7060, has windsurfing, aqua bikes, waterskiing, sea kayaking, sailing, snorkelling and parasailing. There are several companies offering day sails on crewed yachts.

The Mumm's Cup Regatta is held in May, with 3 days of ocean racing off the E coast. Other races include the Hugo Memorial Race in September and the Harvest Moon Race in October. Contact the St Croix Yacht Club for details, T 773-9531.

Diving and marine life

At **Buck Island** there are guided tours on underwater snorkelling trails, the two main ones being Turtle Bay Trail and East End Trail. The fish are superb, but much of the coral is dead; it is hoped that it will come back. The reef is an underwater national park covering over 850 acres, including the island. Hawksbill turtles nest on Buck Island and, during a 1993 Buck Island National Monument Sea Turtle Research Programme, Sandy Point Leatherbacks were also observed nesting there. Half-day tours to Buck Island, including 1¼ hrs' snorkelling and ½ hour at the beach, cost between US$25 and US$35 and can be arranged through hotels or boat owners on the waterfront at Christiansted. (Mile Mark Charters, in *King Christian Hotel* complex, T 773-2628, 800-524-2012, take your own snorkelling equipment; Big Beard's, T 773-4482; Llewellyn, the Calypso King, takes 6 passengers, T 773-9027, as does Clydie; all trips, and these

are, must be approved by the National Parks Service.) Another attraction is the Salt River coral canyon.

Scuba diving is good around St Croix, with forests of elkhorn coral, black coral, brain coral, sea fans, a multitude of tropical fish, sea horses under the Frederiksted pier, drop offs, reefs and wrecks. Diving trips are arranged by several companies, many of which also charter boats out and offer sailing lessons. VI Divers, T 773-6045, 800-544-5911, are located in the Pan Am Pavilion in Christiansted, they offer introductory or certification courses, equipment rentals and a full diving service. Other dive companies include: St Croix Watersports (see above); Dive Experience, Christiansted, T 773-3307, 800-235-9047, good offers on prices and good equipment, including masks with prescription lenses; Cruzan Divers, 12 Strand St, Frederiksted, T 772-3701, 800-352 0107. Dive packages can be arranged with the *Buccaneer, Hibiscus Beach Hotel, Caravelle, Tamarind Reef, Westin Carambola* and other hotels. February, March and April are the months when you are likely to see hump backed whales near the islands. Boats sometimes go out to watch them.

Other sports

Most of the large hotels have tennis courts for residents, but you can also play at the *Buccaneer Hotel* (8 courts, US$5 per person for non-guests), the *Carambola* (4 grass courts, 2 lit for night play and another 5 clay courts at the golf club, pro US$50/hour, guests offered free ½ hour clinics Tues-Fri morning), the *Hotel on the Cay* (3 courts, US$5 per person), Chenay Bay, Club St Croix, The Reef Club (2 courts, US$5/hour) and others. There are 4 public courts at Canegata Park in Christiansted and 2 public courts near the fort in Frederiksted which can be used free of charge on a first come first served basis. Two 18-hole golf courses, one at the *Carambola* (T 778-5638), with pro shop, putting green and driving range, and the other at the *Buccaneer Hotel*

(T 773-2100), also with putting green and pro shop. There is also a 9-hole course at The Reef (T 773-8844), green fee US$12.50. **Horse riding**: Jill's Equestrian Stables (T 772-2880 or 772-2627), at Sprat Hall Plantation, 1½ miles N of Frederiksted, on Route 63, reserve one day in advance if possible for rides through the rain forest, past Danish ruins, for all levels of ability, US$50 for 2 hrs, no credit cards.

In April/May a Sports Festival Week is held, with at least three events open to all, followed the next week by the St Croix International Triathlon which attracts over 600 participants. Phone Tom Guthrie or Miles Sperber, T 773-4470, for details of running courses and tours. For the Virgin Islands Track and Field Federation, contact Wallace Williams (secretary), PO Box 2720, Christiansted, T 773-5715. For swimmers, the Finmen have open water swim meetings, T Bill Cleveland 773-2153, or look in the local papers. VI Cycling organize regular monthly rides and races, T John Harper 773-0079.

Festivals

St Croix's Festival lasts from Christmas week to 6 January. There is another festival on the Sat nearest to 17 March, St Patrick's Day, when there is a splendid parade. Mocko Jumbi dancing (on stilts) takes place at festivals and on other occasions; for information on Mocko Jumbi, contact Willard S John, PO Box 3162, Frederiksted, St Croix, USVI 00840, T 773-8909 (day), 772-0225 (evening). The St Croix Jazz and Caribbean Music and Arts Festival is held over 2 weeks in October, with lots of music and arts and cultural exhibits (contact Linda Vanterpool, T 778-3312).

CHRISTIANSTED

The old town square and waterfront area of **Christiansted**, the old Danish capital, still retain the colourful character of the early days. Overhanging second-floor balconies designed by the Danes to shade the streets serve as cool arcades for shoppers. Red-roofed pastel houses built by early settlers climb the hills overlooking Kings Wharf and there is an old outdoor market. Old Christiansted is compact and easy to stroll. The best place to start is the Visitors' Bureau, housed in a building near the Wharf which served a century ago as the Customs Scale House. Here you can pick up brochures.

Across the way is **Fort Christiansvaern**, which the Danes built in 1774 on the foundations of a French fort dating from 1645. Admission is free (open 0800-1645). See the punishment cells, dungeons, barracks room, officers' kitchen, powder magazine, an exhibit of how to fire a cannon, and the battery, the best vantage point for photographing the old town and harbour. The Fort and the surrounding historic buildings are run by the National Parks Service. In front of the Fort is the old customs house, now the National Parks Service office.

The **Steeple Building** is a minute's walk away. Built as a church by the Danes in 1734, then converted into a military bakery, storehouse and later a hospital, it is now a museum of the island's early history. Open 0930-1200, 1300-1500, US$2.

The area here is a treasury of old Danish architecture, and many of the original buildings are still in use. The West India and Guinea Co, which bought St Croix from the French and settled the island, built a warehouse on the corner of Church and Company Streets in 1749 which now serves as a post office, Customs House and public toilets.

Across the way from Government House on King St is the building where the young Alexander Hamilton, who was to become one of the founding fathers of the USA, worked as a clerk in Nicolas Cruger's countinghouse. Today the building houses the Little Switzerland shop.

Government House has all the hallmarks of the elegant and luxurious life of the merchants and planters in the days when 'sugar was king'. The centre

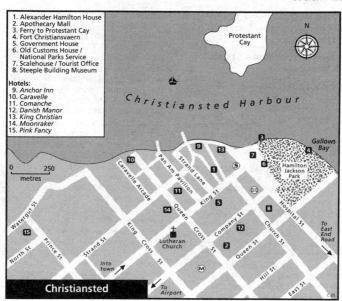

1. Alexander Hamilton House
2. Apothecary Mall
3. Ferry to Protestant Cay
4. Fort Christiansvaern
5. Government House
6. Old Customs House /
   National Parks Service
7. Scalehouse / Tourist Office
8. Steeple Building Museum

Hotels:
9. *Anchor Inn*
10. *Caravelle*
11. *Comanche*
12. *Danish Manor*
13. *King Christian*
14. *Moonraker*
15. *Pink Fancy*

Protestant Cay

Christiansted Harbour

Gallows Bay

Hamilton Jackson Park

0   250
metres

Caravelle Arcade
Pan Am Pavilion
Strand Lane
King St
Queen Cross St
Company St
Church St
Hospital St
Watergut St
Prince St
Strand St
King Cross St
North St
Queen St
Hill St
East St

Lutheran Church

Into town

To Airport

To East End Road

Christiansted

---

section, built in 1747 as a merchant's residence, was bought by the Secret Council of St Croix in 1771 to serve as a government office. It was later joined to another merchant's town house on the corner of Queen Cross St and a handsome ballroom was added. Visitors are welcome to view the ballroom, stroll through the gardens and watch the proceedings in the Court of Justice, open daily 1000-1600. Across Queen Cross Street from Government House is the Dutch Reformed Church.

Queen Cross St leads into Strand and the fascinating maze of arcades and alleys lined with boutiques, handicrafts and jewellery shops. Along the waterfront there are bars, restaurant pavilions and a boardwalk, rebuilt after the Hurricane destroyed the original. Just offshore is **Protestant Cay** (just called The Cay), reached by ferry for US$3 return for the pleasant beach, and the *Hotel on the Cay* with restaurants, pool, tennis, watersports.

Frederiksted, 17 miles from Christiansted, is the only other town on St Croix and although quiet, its gingerbread architecture has its own charm. Public taxis link the two towns and there are taxis from the airport to Frederiksted. Historic buildings such as **Victoria House**, 7-8 Strand Street, and the Customs House, have been repaired following hurricane damage. **Fort Frederik** (1752) is a museum; it was here that the first official foreign salute to the 13 US States was made in 1776 (see also **Sint Eustatius**). Also here was read the proclamation freeing all Danish slaves in 1848. Open Mon-Fri, 0830-1600, free. A new pier, to accommodate at least 2 cruise ships, was built in 1993. An aquarium, close to the pier, is open Wed-Sun, 1100-1600, US$3.

The rain forest to the N of town is worth a visit; although Hurricane Hugo caused much damage to the forest, it is recuperating. Two roads, the paved Mahogany Road (Route 76) and the unpaved Creque Dam Road (Road 58) traverse it.

Island information – St Croix
● **Accommodation**

Price guide

L1	over US$200	L2	US$151-200
L3	US$101-150	A1	US$81-100
A2	US$61-80	A3	US$46-60
B	US$31-45	C	US$21-30
D	US$12-20	E	US$7-11
F	US$4-6	G	up to US$3

The best resorts are: **L1-L2** *Buccaneer*, T 773-2100, 800-255-3881, F 778-8215, in the UK T 0800-373742, on Gallows Bay N coast, 340 acres, 150 luxury rooms, ocean front rooms refurbished 1996, 3 beaches, sports inc golf (see above), tennis, fitness centre, health spa, watersports centre, several restaurants, lots of packages available, and **L1-L2** *Westin Carambola Beach Resort and Golf Club*, on Davis Bay, T 778-3800, 800-228-3000, F 778-1682, N coast, formerly Radisson, now Westin's first Caribbean resort, 150 rooms in 25 2-storey villas, tennis with pro, golf packages available, pool, jacuzzis, snorkelling, scuba; closer to Christiansted are: **L1-L3** *Cormorant Beach* (hotel) and *Cormorant Cove* (condominium), first class, T 778-8920, F 778-9218. **L1-L3** *Chenay Bay*, PO Box 24600, T/F 773-2918, T (800) 548-4457, secluded, private one-room cottages with kitchenettes on nice N coast beach, windsurfing, honeymoon, family packages available, tennis, pool, snorkelling, kayaks, windsurfing school and board rental; **L3** *St Croix by the Sea*, N coast, 3 miles W of Christiansted, T 778-8600, F 773-8002, 65 rooms, salt water pool, beach, etc, families welcome, restaurants and bars; just W of Christiansted is **L1-L3** *Hibiscus Beach Hotel*, 38 beach front rooms, access for handicapped to beach, pool, restaurant, watersports in all-inclusive packages, lots of special deals offered, T 773-4042, 800-442-0121, F 773-7668. On the NE coast **L1-L3** *Tamarind Reef Hotel*, opened 1994, 46 rooms, half have kitchenettes, a/c, fan, TV, balcony, all with sea view, 2 beaches, pool, snorkelling, boardsailing, kayaking at hotel, or diving, fishing, sailing from adjacent Green Cay Marina, croquet and tennis lawn, T 1-800-619-0014; **L2** *Hotel on the Cay*, on Protestant Cay, see above, in Christiansted harbour, free ferry service, 55 rooms, pool, beach,

watersports, tennis, restaurants, PO Box 4020, T 773-2035, 800-524-2035, F 773-7046.

In Christiansted: **L3-A1** *King Christian*, 59 King's Wharf, T 773-2285, 800-524-2012, F 773-9411 (PO Box 3619), with 39 superior and minimum rooms, family-run, watersports on site run by manager's sons, honeymoon and dive packages, pool, convenient; **L3-A1** *Caravelle*, 44A Queen Cross St, T 773-0687, 800-524-0410, F 778-7004, 43 rooms, also good, pool, diving, transport to other sports facilities, diving packages available; **A3** *The Breakfast Club*, 18 Queen Cross Street, T 773-7383, newly remodelled, rooms with bath and kitchenette, gourmet breakfasts, nice view, manager is skillful golf player, highly rec; **L3-A3** *Club Comanche*, Comanche Walk, Strand St, T/F 773-0210, older style, no 2 rooms alike, cable TV, a/c, on waterfront, pool, shop, dive packages, family run, staff helpful, rec, also restaurant; **L3-A1** *King's Alley*, on waterfront, T 773-0103, 800-843-3574, F 773-4431; **L3-A1** *Anchor Inn*, also on waterfront with watersports, fishing charters and scuba diving available on hotel boardwalk, 58 King St, T 773-4000, F 773-4408, restaurant, pool, cable TV, refrigerator, a/c, etc, scuba diving packages available; **A1-A2** *Danish Manor*, 2 Company St, T 773-1377, F 773-1913, pool in old courtyard, renovated rooms. **L3** *Pink Fancy*, 27 Prince Street, T 773-8460, 800-524-2045, F 773-6448, 5 mins from shopping centre and waterfront, bar, pool, in 18th century townhouse.

In Frederiksted: **L3-A1** *Antilles Resorts at Frederiksted Hotel*, 20 Strand St, T 773-9150, 800-524-2025, F 778-4009, modern, pool, restaurant, bar, good, US$115-130; ½ mile from town, **L2-A1** *On The Beach Resort*, pool, 14 rooms, kitchenettes, restaurants, T 772-1205, 800-524-2018, F 772-1757; **A2-A3** *Prince Street Inn*, 402 Prince Street, T 772-9550, 800-771-9559, F 771-9550, another historic building, small, charming, each room unique, rec.

North of Frederiksted: **L1-L3** *Sprat Hall* (PO Box 695, T 772-0305, 800-843-3584), a former Great House, dating from the French Occupation, has antique furnishings, strictly no-smoking rooms in the old building, also has modern units, efficiency suites and a 2-bedroom cottage, excellent restaurant, beach bar serving lunch till 1530, highly rec, also has riding stables (see *Jill's* above) and can organize diving and fishing trips. On the N coast, **L2-L3** *Cane Bay Reef Club*, PO Box

1407, Kingshill, T/F 778-2966, 800-253-8534, 9 suites with balconies over the sea, pool, restaurant, bar, rough sea but short walk to beach, weekly rates cheaper; **L2-L3** *Waves At Cane Bay*, T 778-1805, 800-545-0603, PO Box 1749, Kingshill, 12 oceanfront studios with balconies and cable TV, natural grotto pool, beach, good snorkelling and scuba from property. South of Frederiksted is **L3-A1** *Cottages by the Sea*, PO Box 1697, T/F 772-0495, 800-323-7252, good beach, watersports, 6-day maid service, good. **A3** *Ackie's Guesthouse*, basic, kitchen facilities, in peaceful, rural location, though rather difficult to get to and from, it is a 15 min walk to the main road whence shared taxis run to Christiansted or Frederiksted. There are several rental agents for villas and condominiums: *American Rentals*, 2001 Old Hospital Street, Christiansted, T 773-8470, F 773-8472; *Island Villas*, 14 A Caravelle Arcade, Christiansted, T 773-8821, 800-626-4512, F 773-8823; *Tropic Retreats*, PO Box 5219, Sunny Isle, T 778-7550, 778-3557, all with a wide range.

● **Places to eat**
Restaurant life on St Croix includes charcoal-broiled steaks and lobsters, West Indian Créole dishes and Danish and French specialities. Do not miss the open-air Cruzan picnics. *Club Comanche*, Strand Street, T 773-2665, popular and good for lunches and dinners; *Chart House*, on the wharf, steaks, seafood, very good salad bar, T 773-7718; *Lunchería*, Mexican food, cheap margaritas on Company Street; also on Company Street are *Harvey's Bar and Restaurant*, local cuisine, T 773-3433; *The Captain's Table*, T 773-2026, seafood restaurant and *The Three Dolphins*; *The Smoothie Shop*, health food sandwich shop; *Stixx on the Waterfront*, Pan Am Pavilion, Sun brunch, lunch, dinner, steaks, pizzas, burgers, etc, popular bar; *Nelson's Bar and Restaurant*, in the arcade, nice, cheap; *Ship's Galley*, deli and food store, Strand St, good. There are many other restaurants and fast food places in Christiansted. In Frederiksted, *Star of the West* (Mrs Mary Pennyfeather), Strand Street, for Créole food (Blinky and the Road Masters play local music here each Sun), *Le Crocodile* French restaurant at *The Royal Dane Hotel*. For seafood and native dishes plus music, the *Blue Moon* or *Motown Bar and Restaurant*, rec, both on Strand Street. The out of town resorts have restaurants too. The restaurant at *Paradise Sunset Beach Hotel*, Ham's Bay, has been rec, great sunset too. The top restaurants participate in a 'Dine Around' programme.

● **Food**
Local dishes include stewed or roast goat, red pea soup (a sweet soup of kidney beans and pork), callalou (dasheen soup); snacks, Johnny cakes (unleavened fried bread) and pate (pastry filled with spiced beef, chicken or salt fish); drinks, ginger beer, *mavi* (from the bark of a tree).

● **Nightlife**
Most hotels provide evening entertainment on a rotating basis, the custom of many of the Caribbean islands, so it is sometimes best to stay put and let the world of West Indian music and dance come to you. The *Hibiscus Beach Hotel* hosts the Caribbean Dance Company on Fri at 2030, evocative, and a steel pan band on Wed at 1830, also electric mandolin on Thur and a jazz trio on Sat at 2000. Some restaurants also provide entertainment, eg *The Captain's Table*, *Tivoli Gardens* (Queen Cross and Strand Streets), *Calabash* (Strand Street) and *The Galleon* (Green Cay Marina, piano bar). *The Wreck Bar*, Hospital Street, has crab races on Fri, guitar on Wed, Green Flash rock Thur-Sat. *The Blue Moon*, 17 Strand Street, has live jazz every Fri and on full moons. *Two plus Two Disco*, Northside Road, W of Christiansted (closed Mon), live entertainment Fri and Sat, US$5 cover charge; snack bar from 1200 till 1800. Most cultural events take place at the Island Centre, a 600-seat theatre with an open air amphitheatre seating another 1,600, where drama, dance and music are performed.

● **Shopping**
St Croix Leap (Life and Environmental Arts Project), on Route 76, the Paved Rain Forest Road, is a woodworking centre, from which the artefacts may be bought direct. *Many Hands*, Pan Am Pavilion, sells only arts and crafts from the Virgin Islands. For special jewellery go to *Sonya's*, in Christiansted, and see her hand-wrought gold and silver things. The market in Christiansted is on Company Street, and has been on the site since 1735. Bookshops (all Christiansted): *Collage*, Apothecary Hall Upper Courtyard, bookshop, café and gallery, open Mon-Sat 1000-1800 (later Wed-Sat pm); *Jeltrup's* 51 ABC Company Street (on King Cross Street), both have good selection; *The Writer's Block*, King's Alley, for novels.

● **People to people programme**
If you wish to contact someone in a similar profession to your own, contact Geri Simpson, PO Box 943, Kingshill, St Croix, USVI 00851, T 778-8007.

● **Transport**
Air Alexander Hamilton international airport. Taxi airport-Christiansted US$5; airport-Frederiksted, US$4, taxi dispatcher's booth at airport exit. Bus airport-Christiansted every 1½ hrs, change buses at La Reine terminal.

Taxis A taxi tour costs US$20 pp, less for groups; contact St Croix Taxi and Tours Association, Alexander Hamilton Airport, T 778-1088, PO Box 1106, Christiansted, F 778-6887. Taxi vans run between Christiansted and Frederiksted.

Bus A bus service runs Christiansted-Frederiksted 0530-2130 every 30 mins (every hour on Sun), US$1, timetable from airport or bus driver.

Car hire The major car rental agencies are represented at the airport, in hotels and in both cities. Rent a 4WD car (US$40-50 a day) if you can afford it so you can drive along the scenic roads, eg to Ham's Bay or Point Udall. For scooter rental, A and B, 26 Friendensthal, Christiansted, T 778-8567. There is a distinct lack of road signs on St Croix, so if you use a car, take a good map with you.

Information for travellers

BEFORE TRAVELLING

● **Documents**
US citizens do not of course require passports for visits to the US Virgin Islands. British visitors to the US islands need passport and US visa (or waiver). Visitors of other nationalities will need passports, visas (or waiver for participating countries) and return/onward tickets.

● **Climate**
The climate in the Virgin Islands is very pleasant, with the trade winds keeping the humidity down. The average temperature varies little between winter (25°C or 77°F) and summer (28°C or 82°F). Average annual rainfall is 40 inches.

MONEY

● **Currency**
The US dollar. Credit cards are widely accepted in major tourist resorts and duty free shops, less so by local businesses.

GETTING THERE

AIR

From the USA there are flights to St Croix and/or St Thomas with American Airlines (Dallas, Miami, New York, Philadelphia, Washington), Delta (Atlanta), US Air (Baltimore). From Europe there are no direct flights, but American Airlines has a connecting flight via New York and connections can be made via Miami to St Thomas; there are also good connections from Puerto Rico, St Maarten and Antigua. Airlines operating on the St Croix/St Thomas-Puerto Rico (San Juan, Vieques or Fajardo) route include American Eagle, Dolphin Airlines, Vieques Air Link. Regional airlines link the USVI with other Caribbean islands and there are flights to Anguilla, Antigua, St Barthélémy,

St Kitts, Nevis, St Maarten and the BVI. There are lots of flights between St Croix and St Thomas. Seabourne Seaplane Adventures has a daily service between Christiansted Harbour and Charlotte Amalie, arriving at the Ramada Yacht Haven dock in 18 mins.

SEA

Ocean going ships can be accommodated at Charlotte Amalie in St Thomas and Frederiksted and the South Shore cargo port in St Croix. There are regular services between the USVI and the BVI (see the BVI **Information for Visitors**). Inter-Island Boat Services, *Sundance II*, between Cruz Bay, St John, and West End, Tortola, at least 3 times a day; also Water Taxi available, T 776-6597. *Native Son* between St Thomas and Road Town via West End, Tortola, or between Red Hook, St Thomas and St John to West End, several daily, T 774-8685. Smiths Ferry Services, T 775-7292, *M/V Daphne Elise* and *M/V Marie Elise*, between St Thomas and the BVI (both Tortola and Virgin Gorda), several daily, also between St John and Red Hook, St Thomas, and West End, Tortola, T 494-4430, 494-2355, 495-4495. *Speedy's Fantasy* and *Speedy's Delight* on the route Virgin Gorda-Road Town-St Thomas, T 774-8685. To St John: ferries run hourly from Red Hook or about every 2 hrs from the Charlotte Amalie Waterfront. For information on chartering your own boat, write to the Executive Director of the VI Charteryacht League, Homeport, St Thomas, USVI 00802.

● **Ports of entry**
Charlotte Amalie, St Thomas; Christiansted and Frederiksted, St Croix; Cruz Bay, St John.

● **Boat documents**
The USVI are a territory of the USA but constitute a separate Customs district. US boats and citizens do not have to clear in here when coming from Puerto Rico, but must when arriving from other Caribbean islands. There is an annual Customs fee of US$25. All aboard must go ashore to obtain entry into the USVI.

ON ARRIVAL

● **Banks**
US banking legislation applies. Bank of America, Citibank, Chase Manhattan, and First Pennsylvania Bank (Virgin Islands National Bank) are all represented and have several branches. Also Barclays Bank, Bank of Nova Scotia, Banco Popular de Puerto Rico, First Federal Savings and Loan of Puerto Rico.

● **Clothing**
Bathing suits are considered offensive when worn away from the beach, so cover up. There is even a law against it, you can get a fine for having your belly showing.

● **Embassies and consulates**
On St Thomas: Danish, T 774-1780; Dominican Republic, T 775-2640; Finnish, T 776-6666; French, T 774-4663; Norwegian, T 776-1780; Swedish, T 776-1900. On St Croix: Dutch, T 773-7100; Norwegian, T 773-7100.

● **Hospitals**
St Thomas has a 250-bed hospital, T 776-8311, St John has a 7-bed clinic, T 776-6252, and St Croix has a 250-bed hospital, T 778-6311. All 3 have 24-hour emergency services. Mobile medical units provide health services to outlying areas.

● **Hours of business**
Banks open Mon-Thur, 0900-1430, Fri 0900-1400, 1530-1700. Government offices open Mon-Thur, 0900-1700. Beware: banks, filling stations and government offices close for local holidays.

● **Official time**
Atlantic Standard Time, 4 hours behind GMT, 1 ahead of EST.

● **Public holidays**
New Year's Day, Three Kings Day (6 January), Martin Luther King Day (15 January), Presidents' Day (19 February), Holy Thursday, Good Friday, Easter Monday, Transfer Day (31 March), Memorial Day (28 May), Organic Act Day (18 June), Emancipation Day (3 July), Independence Day (4 July), Hurricane Supplication Day (23 July), Labour Day (beginning of September), Puerto Rico/Virgin Islands Friendship Day (mid-October), Hurricane Thanksgiving Day (mid- October), Liberty Day (1 November), Veterans' Day (11 November), Thanksgiving Day (mid-November), Christmas Day, 25 December.

● **Religion**
On St Croix: Apostolic, Baptist, Christian Scientist, Church of God, Episcopalian, Hindu, Jehovah's Witnesses, Jewish, Lutheran, Methodist, Moravian, Moslem, Presbyterian, Roman Catholic, Seventh Day Adventist. On St Thomas: Baptist, Christian Scientist, Episcopalian, Jehovah's Witnesses, Jewish, Lutheran, Methodist,

Moravian, Moslem, Presbyterian, Roman Catholic, Salvation Army, Seventh Day Adventist. On St Thomas: Apostolic, Baha'i, Baptist, Christian Scientist, Episcopalian, Jehovah's Witnesses, Jewish, Lutheran, Methodist, Moravian, Moslem, Presbyterian, Roman Catholic, Salvation Army, Seventh Day Adventist.

It is a simple procedure to get married in the USVI and you do not need to employ wedding consultants if you do not want them. You can obtain the relevant papers from any USVI Tourist Office, send them off about 3 weeks before your visit, then pick up the marriage licence at the Territorial Court on arrival. A recommended church in which to be married is the Frederick Lutheran Church in Charlotte Amalie, contact Pastor Coleman, PO Box 58, St Thomas, USVI 00804, T 776-1315/774-9524.

● **Security**
Take the usual precautions against crime, lock your car, leave valuable jewellery at home and be careful walking around at night. The Tourist Office recommends that you do not go to deserted beaches on your own, but always in a group. In 1996 the shooting on St Thomas of 3 tourists prompted the reistatement of a 2200 curfew for youths under 16 and increased police patrols.

● **Shopping**
The USVI are a free port and tourist related items are duty-free. Shops are usually shut on Sun unless there is a cruise ship in harbour. There are several local rums in white or gold: Cruzan (guided tours of the distillery, on St Croix, Mon-Fri 0900-1130, 1300-1615, but phone in advance, T 772-0799), Old St Croix and Brugal.

● **Tipping**
As in the mainland USA, tipping is usually 15% and hotels often add 10-15%.

● **Useful addresses**
Air Ambulance: 778-9177 (day), 772-1629 (night); recompression chamber 776-2686.
Ambulance: 922.
Fire: 921.
Police: 915.

● **Voltage**
120 volts 60 cycles.

● **Departure tax**
No departure tax at the airport (the price of US$5 is included in your ticket).

ACCOMMODATION

There is a 8% tax on all forms of accommodation in the US Virgin Islands. Hotels may also charge a US$1/night Hotel Association charge and/or a $2\frac{1}{2}$-3% energy tax.

GETTING AROUND

LAND TRANSPORT
● **Motoring**
Driving in Charlotte Amalie during business hours is a slow business. It is best to park and walk (municipal car park beside Fort Christian). Country speed limits are 35 miles an hour, in towns, 20 miles an hour, although the traffic is so heavy you will be lucky if you can go that fast. On St John the speed limit is 20 mph everywhere. Driving is on the left, even though the cars are lefthand drive. Donkeys, goats, chickens and cows have the right of way. There is a new seatbelt law that the police enforce with a vengeance (US$50 fine).

● **Car hire**
In St Thomas rental agencies include Budget (T 776-5774), Cowpet (775-7376), Avis (T 774-1468), Sun Island (774-3333), Discount (776-4858), VI Auto Rental (776-3616, Sub Base), Gassett (776-4600); most have an office by the airport. Rates range from US$40 to US$80 a day, unlimited mileage, vehicles from small cars to jeeps. Honda scooters, from A1's, T 774-2010, for example, range from US$25 to US$40 a day. On St John: Hertz, T 776-6695; Delbert Hill's Jeep Rental, T 776-6637; Budget, T 776-7575; Avis, T 776-6374; Cool Breeze, T 776-6588, St John Car Rental, T 776-6103; rates start from US$50/day. In St Croix: Avis, at the airport, T 778-9355/9365. Budget at the airport, T 778-9636, or Christiansted (*King Christian Hotel* 773-2285), also Hertz, T 778-1402, or *Buccaneer Hotel*, T 773-2100 Ext 737; Caribbean Jeep and Car Rental, 6 Hospital Street, Christiansted, T 773-4399; Green Cay Jeep and Car Rental, T 773-7227; Berton, 1 mile W of Christiansted, T 773-1516.

COMMUNICATIONS

● **Telecommunications**
Local telephone calls within the USVI from coin-operated phones are US$0.25 for each 5 mins. Cable, Telex, Fax, data and other business services are all available.

MEDIA

● **Newspaper**

The Daily News is published daily, US$0.50, and on Fri it includes the weekend section, a complete listing of restaurants, night clubs, music and special events for the week, for all 3 islands.

TOURIST INFORMATION

● **Local tourist office**

On St Thomas, the Tourist Information Centre at the airport is open daily 0900-1900. Offices at the town waterfront and at the West Indian Company dock are open 0800-1700 Mon-Fri (PO Box 6400, Charlotte Amalie, USVI 00804, T 774-8784, F 774-4390). On St Croix, there is a Tourism Booth at the airport in the baggage claim area and next to it the First Stop Information Booth. In Christiansted there is a Visitor's Bureau by the wharf in the Old Customs Scalehouse (open Mon-Fri 0800-1700, PO Box 4538, Christiansted, USVI 00822, T 773-0495, F 778-9259), and in Frederiksted the Visitors' Centre is opposite the pier in the Custom House Building, Strand Street, USVI 00840 (T 772-0357). There is also an office in Cruz Bay, St John (PO Box 200, Cruz Bay, USVI 00830, T 776-6450).

● **Tourist offices overseas**

There are offices of the USVI Division of Tourism in the **USA** at: 500 North Michigan Ave, Suite 2030, Chicago, IL 60611, T (312) 670-8784, F 670-8788/9; 2655 Le Jeune Rd, Suite 907, Coral Gables, FL 33134, T (305) 442-7200, F 445-9044; 1270 Av of the Americas, Suite 2108, New York, NY 10020, T (212) 332-2222, F 332-2223; 900 17th Street NW, Suite 500, Washington DC, 20006, T (202) 293-3707, F 785-2542; 225 Peachtree St, N E, Suite 760, Atlanta, GA 30303, T (404) 688-0906, F 525-1102; 3460 Wilshire Blvd, Suite 412, Los Angeles, CA 90010, T (213) 739-0138, F 739-2005.

In **Canada**: 33 Niagara Street, Toronto, MSVIC2, T (416) 362-8784, 800-465-8784, F 362-9841.

In **Brazil**: ITR-Representações Turisticas Internacionais Ltda, Ave São Luis, 112-14 Floor, São Paulo, SP, T (11) 257-9877, F 258-0206.

In **Germany**: Otto-Hahn-Str 23, D-50997 Cologne, T 49-2236 841743, F 2236 43045.

In **Italy**: Via Gherardini 2, 20145, Milan, T (02) 33105841, F 33105827.

In **Japan**: Discover America Marketing Inc, Suite B234B, Hibiya Kokusai Bldg 2-3, Uchisaiwaicho 2-chrome, Chiyoda-ku, Tokyo 100, T (3) 3597-9451, F 3597-0385.

In **Puerto Rico**: 1300 Ashford Ave, Condado, Puerto Rico 00907, T (809) 724-3816, F 724-7223.

In the **UK**: 2 Cinnamon Row, Plantation Wharf, York Place, London SW11 3TW, T 0171-978-5262, F 0171-924-3171. Hotel and restaurant lists, weekly guides and descriptive leaflets available.

● **Maps**

The Government offers a free road map (available at Tourist Information Offices) but considerable optimism was used in showing road classifications, especially on the St John map. Some of the 'paved highways' are really bad, unpaved roads which require hard, 4-wheel drive. Texaco issues a map of the US islands, as does Phillip A Schneider, Dept of Geography, University of Illinois at Urbana-Champaign, price US$3.95.

● **Further reading**

The publications, *St Croix This Week* and *St Thomas This Week* have regularly updated tourist information, including shopping news, ferry schedules, taxi fares, restaurants, nightlife and other tourist news.

A useful book is *The Settlers' Handbook for the US Virgin Islands*, Megnin Publishing (PO Box 5161, Sunny Isle, St Croix, USVI 00823-5161), US$7.95. *Exploring St Croix* by Shirley Imsand and Richard Philibosian costs US$10 and is very detailed on out of the way places and how to get to them, as is *Exploring St John* by Pam Gaffin, also US$10.

British Virgin Islands

THE BRITISH VIRGIN ISLANDS (BVI), grouped around Sir Francis Drake Channel, are less developed than the US group, and number some 60 islands, islets, rocks, and cays, of which only 16 or so are inhabited. They are all of volcanic origin except one, Anegada, which is coral and limestone. Most of the land was cleared years ago for its timber or to grow crops, and it is now largely covered by secondary forest and scrub. In the areas with greatest rainfall there are mangoes and palm trees, but generally the islands can look brown and parched, or green and lush just after rain. Mangrove and sea grape can be found in some areas along the shore.

The two major islands, Tortola and Virgin Gorda, along with the groups of Anegada and Jost Van Dyke, contain most of the total population of about 17,383, which is mainly of African descent. The resident population was only 10,985 in 1980 and most of the increase has come from inward migration of workers for the construction and tourist industries. About half the present population is of foreign origin. Everyone speaks English. While there are some large resorts in the BVI, there are no high-rise hotels, nightclubs and casinos, as found in some of the other islands which depend heavily on tourism. In fact, there is very little to do at all on land and nearly everything happens in the beautiful water which surrounds the islands. If you are keen on watersports and sailing and have adequate finance (the Virgin Islands are not cheap), you will enjoy island hopping.

HISTORY

Although discovered by the Spanish in 1493, the islands were first settled by Dutch planters before falling into British hands in 1666. In 1672 the Governor of the Leeward Islands annexed Tortola and in 1680 planters from Anguilla moved into Anegada and Virgin Gorda. Civil government was introduced in 1773 with an elected House of Assembly and a part-elected and part-nominated Legislative Council. Between 1872 and 1956 the islands were part of the Leeward Islands Federation (a British Colony), but then became a separately administered entity, building up economic links with the US

Virgin Islands rather than joining the West Indies Federation of British territories. In 1960 direct responsibility was assumed by an appointed Administrator, later to become Governor. The Constitution became effective in 1967 but was later amended in 1977 to allow the islands greater autonomy in domestic affairs. Mr H Lavity Stoutt, of the Virgin Islands Party (VIP), became Chief Minister in 1967-71 and again in 1979-83 and in 1986. At the most recent election in Feb 1995 the Virgin Islands Party, still led by Mr Lavity Stoutt, won a third consecutive term in office with six seats. The Concerned Citizens' Movement (CCM) and the United Party (UP) each won two seats. Three independents were elected and one formed an alliance with the VIP. However, Mr Stoutt died in May 1995 and the Deputy Chief Minister Ralph O'Neal was appointed interim Chief Minister. The VIP won the by-election after Mr Stoutt's death

In 1994, the British Government accepted a proposal from a constitutional review commission for the Legislative Council to be enlarged from nine to 13 seats. The four new members represent the territory as a single constituency. This plan created the first mixed electoral system in the UK, in which voters have one vote for their constituency member as usual, plus four votes for the new territory-wide representatives. The British government pushed it into effect before 6 December 1994, the last date for the dissolution of the legislature. There was considerable disquiet in the BVI and in the UK at the way in which it was rushed through without prior consultation and without the support of Mr Stoutt's government.

GOVERNMENT

A nearly self-contained community, the islands are a Crown Colony with a Governor appointed by London, although to a large extent they are internally self-governing. The Governor (David Mackilligin, appointed 1995) presides over the Executive Council, made up of the Chief Minister, the Attorney-General and three other ministers. A Legislative Council comprises 13 members elected by universal adult suffrage (of which nine represent district constituencies and four represent the whole territory), one member appointed by the Governor, a Speaker elected from outside by members of the Council, and the Attorney-General as an ex-officio member.

THE ECONOMY

The economy is based predominantly on tourism; the islands offer up-market tourism in quiet, unspoiled surroundings and earnings are around US$125mn a year. There are approximately 1,213 hotel rooms, half of which are on Tortola and a third on Virgin Gorda, the rest being scattered around the other islands, but nearly half of those visitors who stay on the islands charter yachts and only sleep on land for their arrival and for departure nights.

Tourism in the BVI was hit badly by the recession and in 1991 stopover arrivals were down by nearly 17% while cruise ship passengers declined by almost 19%, with the fall being registered in all markets. The yacht charter business saw several closures in 1991/92 because of declining demand, higher air fares and tax changes in the USA and France, which brought greater competition from the French Caribbean. A new charter yacht strategy was announced in 1992, removing import duty and introducing licences to encourage more business. The Government aimed to attract quality operators in a more highly structured environment with streamlined entry regulations. Crewed yachts have been pushed rather than increasing bare boat charters. In another development to promote the islands, the British Virgin Islands Film Commission was set up to encourage film production in the islands and the previous permit fee was lifted. Film crews were expected to bring considerable economic benefit through their use of local services and labour.

Since 1991 the tourism industry has shown improvement, particularly in the numbers of cruise ships calling. A new US$6.9mn, 550 ft cruise ship pier was inaugurated at Road Town, Tortola, which can accommodate two medium-size cruise liners. The Government is aiming to attract the upper end of the cruise market and not to encourage the very large ships. Tourist arrivals and earnings are now growing steadily at about 4-5% a year.

A growth industry of the last few years is the offshore company business, which has benefited from uncertainty in Hong Kong and Panama. International Business Company legislation passed in 1984 allows locally-registered foreign companies tax exemptions with little currency risk as the US dollar is the national currency. By the end of 1995 over 168,000 companies had been registered as IBCs and fees from new licences

generated substantial revenues. Diversification of the offshore financial centre is being sought; currently over one third of government revenue comes from this sector. In 1994 the Legislative Council passed an insurance law, designed to regulate all insurance business in the BVI including captive insurance and reinsurance. A commissioner of insurance will supervise the business and carry out the law's requirements. Further legislation is planned to cover mutual funds, insolvency, partnerships, limited duration companies and ship registration.

Industry on the islands is limited to small scale operations such as rum, sand or gravel, and desalination plants are being built. Farming is limited to fruit, vegetables and some livestock, some of which are shipped to the USVI. Fishing is expanding both for export, sport and domestic consumption. However, nearly all the islands' needs are imported.

Although the budget is in surplus, the Government is still receiving British

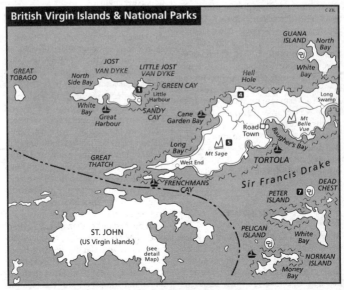

capital assistance, as well as funding from the EC, the Caribbean Development Bank and the Commonwealth Development Corporation. Loans have also been raised from commercial banks. The British government is now curtailing its capital funding and other sources of foreign finance are being explored.

DIVING AND MARINE LIFE

There is much to see around the Virgin Islands and considerable work is being done to establish marine parks and conserve the reefs. The Department of Conservation and Fisheries is in charge of the BVI's natural resources and a fisheries

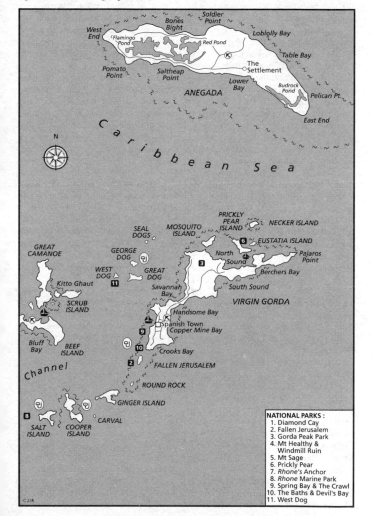

NATIONAL PARKS :
1. Diamond Cay
2. Fallen Jerusalem
3. Gorda Peak Park
4. Mt Healthy & Windmill Ruin
5. Mt Sage
6. Prickly Pear
7. *Rhone's* Anchor
8. *Rhone* Marine Park
9. Spring Bay & The Crawl
10. The Baths & Devil's Bay
11. West Dog

management plan aims to avoid overfishing and help conserve the reefs. The 17.5-km Horseshoe Reef off the S shore of Anegada is the third largest reef in the world (after the Great Barrier Reef and Belize) and now a Protected Area, with an anchor and fishing ban in force. The anchor ban is expected to remain indefinitely although permanent moorings will be put at popular dive sites. There are 80 visible wrecks around Anegada and many more covered by coral; about 300 ships are believed to have foundered on the reef.

Humpback whales migrate to the islands every year and the Department of Conservation and Fisheries is trying to estimate their numbers with the aim of designating the BVI waters as a marine mammal sanctuary. If you see any (mostly N of Tortola), let them know. Similarly, turtles are being counted with the help of volunteers in order to draw up environmental legislation to protect them. Leatherback turtles travel to N shore beaches to nest, but their numbers have been declining fast. Hawksbill and Green turtles are more common but still endangered. For several months of the year the killing of turtles or taking their eggs is prohibited and the export of turtle products is illegal. If you see turtle on the menu, or a turtle shell product, please do not buy it; even the legal killing damages the population.

There are over 60 charted dive sites, many of which are in underwater National Parks. They include walls, pinnacles, coral reefs, caverns and wrecks. The most visited wreck is that of the *Rhone*, sunk in 1867 in a storm and broken in two. The bow section is in about 80 ft of water and you can swim through the hull. The stern is shallower and you can see the prop shaft and the propeller (and an octopus). Another wreck is the 246-ft *Chikuzen* sunk in 1981 about 6 miles N of Tortola, where you will see bigger fish such as barracuda and rays. Most Caribbean and Atlantic species of tropical fish and marine invertebrates can be found in BVI waters, with hard and soft corals,

gorgonians and sea fans. Watch out for fire coral, sea urchins and the occasional bristle worm. Visibility ranges from 60-200 ft and the water temperature varies from 76°F in winter to 86°F in summer. Wet suits are not essential but most people wear them.

A moorings system has been set up to eliminate anchor damage to the coral and all users of the moorings must have a National Parks permit. These are available through dive operators, charter companies, government offices and the National Parks Trust, T 494-3904. They cost US$10-15, depending on the number of people on board, and the revenue goes towards maintenance and new moorings. As yet, there is no legislation to prohibit anchoring in areas other than in the Marine Parks, but it is actively discouraged. National Parks Trust moorings (of which there are currently 180 with another 70 planned) are located at The Caves, The Indians, The Baths, Pelican Island, Carrot Shoal, dive sites at Peter Island, Cooper Island, Ginger Island and Norman Island, The *Rhone's* anchor, the wreck of *The Rhone*, the wreck of *The Fearless*, Deadchest Island, Blonde Rock, Guana Island, The Dogs and other popular diving and recreational sites.

There are several dive shops around the islands which offer individual tours, package deals with hotels or rendezvous with charter boats. Rates depend on the distance to the dive site but are generally US$80-100 for two tanks, including equipment hire. A day's resort course and shallow dive costs about the same. Baskin in the Sun, established in 1969 and a PADI 5-star dive centre, is at *Prospect Reef Village Cay* and Soper's Hole. Packages can be arranged with all the major hotels and in fact they are often full with package business so book individual diving in good time. They win awards for excellence and readership surveys. They have three boats, 10 certified instructors and offer full service, Box 108, Road Town, T 494-2858, 800-233-7938,

F 494-4304 (operate from *Prospect Reef*), at Sopers Hole, T 495-4582, F 494-5853. Dive BVI Ltd, another PADI 5-star operation (also NAUI courses) is at Virgin Gorda Yacht Harbour, Leverick Bay and Peter Island, with five boats, Box 1040, Virgin Gorda, T 495-5513, 800-848-7078, F 495-5347. Blue Water Divers, with three boats, has been at Nanny Cay since 1980, Box 846, Road Town, T 494-2847, F 494-0198. Kilbride's Underwater Tours is at the *Bitter End Yacht Club*, North Sound, Box 46, Virgin Gorda, T 495-9638, 800-932-4286, F 495-7549. Underwater Safaris, with three boats is at *The Moorings*, Road Town (PO Box 139, T 494-3235, 800-537-7032, F 494-5322), and has a small shop on Cooper Island which is used as a surface interval between dives in the area, eg *The Rhone*. Air refills are available here. Underwater Safaris (and most other companies) will take you anywhere you want to dive, even if there is only one passenger on the boat, and each dive tour location is determined by the first people to book, although they normally only go to sites within 30 mins of Road Town. Underwater photography, camera rental, and film processing is offered by Rainbow Visions Photography, Prospect Reef, Box 680, Road Town, T 494-2749. They often join dive boats and take video film of you underwater. Great fun and excellent quality but expensive.

BEACHES AND WATERSPORTS

There are lovely sandy beaches on all the islands and many of them are remote, empty and accessible only from the sea. The clean, crystal-clear waters around the islands provide excellent snorkelling, diving, cruising and fishing. Most of the hotels offer a wide variety of watersports, including windsurfing, sunfish, scuba, snorkelling and small boats. Jet skis are banned.

'Bareboating' (self-crew yacht chartering) is extremely popular and the way most visitors see the islands. The BVI are one of the most popular destinations in the world for bareboaters. If you do not feel confident in handling a yacht, there are various options from fully-crewed luxury yachts to hiring a skipper to take you and your bareboat out for as long as you need. Navigation is not difficult, the water and weather are generally clear and there are many excellent cruising guides and charts for reference. Most of the islands offer at least one beautiful bay and it is possible even at the height of the season to find deserted beaches and calm anchorages. Bareboaters are not supposed to sail to Anegada because of the hazardous, unmarked route through the reef and generally only crewed yachts go there. If you are sailing independently, however, check the charts, ensure you approach in clear daylight when the sun is high, or call the *Anegada Reef Hotel* at Setting Point when you are within sight and they will direct you over the radio. Charter companies are too numerous to list here, there are many on Tortola and several more on Virgin Gorda. Contact the Tourist Office for a list of bareboats with prices. For crewed yachts, *The Moorings*, T 494-2331/2/3, F 494-2226; Caribbean Connections, T 494-3623; Virgin Islands Sailing, T 494-2774; Sail Vacations, T 494-3656, 800-368-9905, F 494-4731, or Paradise Yacht Vacations, T 494-0253/0333, will be able to match your needs with the hundreds of charter yachts available. Marinas are plentiful with yard services, haul out, fuel docks, water and showers.

Sailing and boardsailing schools offer 3-hrs to 1-week courses. The Nick Trotter Sailing School at the *Bitter End Yacht Club*, North Sound, T 494-2745, has sailing and windsurfing courses for all ages with a wide variety of craft, very popular, principally for guests because of its isolated location. Offshore Sailing School Ltd, at Treasure Isle Jetty, T 494-5119, T 800-221-4326, has courses on live-aboard cruising as well as learn-to-sail on dinghies. Thomas Sailing at Nanny Cay, T 494-0333, F 494-0334, has land-based and live-aboard courses.

The annual spring Regatta is held in Sir Francis Drake's Channel, considered one of the best sailing venues in the world. It is the second stage of the Caribbean Ocean Racing Triangle (CORT) series of regattas, so international yachtsmen and women compete alongside local islanders and sailors on hired bareboats. The Regatta Village (and parties) is at Nanny Cay. Contact the *BVI Yacht Club*, T 494-3286, for information. A cruising permit is required by everyone cruising in the BVI: 1 Dec-30 April, all recorded charter boats US$2 pp/day, all non-recorded charter boats US$4 pp/day; 1 May-30 Nov, US$0.75 and US$4 respectively. Dive boats, sport fishing boats etc should contact the Customs Department for cruising permit regulations. Permits are required if you want to use any National Parks Trust moorings, call The Trust office at T 494-3904.

Several companies offer snorkelling tours and there are lots of yachts offering daysails to all the little islands at around US$45-75 with snorkelling, beverages and sometimes lunch. *Patouche II* (T 494-6300), *Kuralu* (T 495-4381), *White Squall* (T 495-2564), *No Fear* (T 494-4000), and *Ppalu* (T 494-0608, F 494-4495) all offer popular day sails, but avoid them when the cruise ships are in town as they are often packed out.

Windsurfing is popular in the islands and there is an annual Hi-Ho (hook in and hold on) race which attracts windsurfers from all over the world. The week long event involves inter-island racing with accommodation on sailing yachts (contact Windsurfing Tortola, Nanny Cay, T 494-0337, F 494-6488). Boardsailing BVI is at Trellis Bay, Beef Island, T 495-2447, F 495 1626, and at Nanny Cay (a BIC Centre), T 494-0422, with schools and shops. Both schools have good equipment for beginners and advanced sailors.

Sport fishing is becoming more popular with many companies offering day trips aboard sport fishing boats: *Anegada Reef Hotel*, Anegada, US$500-900, T 495-8002; *Miss Robbie*, Fort Burt Marina, T 494-3193, US$450-750. A local permit is required for fishing, call the Fisheries Division for information, T 494-3429; spearfishing is not allowed, hunting on land is also banned and no firearms are allowed. There are areas known to house ciguatera (fish poisoning) around the reefs, so it is important to contact the Fisheries Division before fishing of any kind is undertaken.

OTHER SPORTS

There is a tennis club on Tortola and many hotels have their own courts. Golf has not been developed although a couple of the hotels have small practice courses. Horse riding can be arranged through the hotels, or T 494-2262, Shadow's Stables, or T 494-4442, Ellis Thomas, for riding through Mt Sage National Park or down to Cane Garden Bay, Tortola. Walking and birdwatching are quite popular and trails have been laid out in some places. Spectator sports include cricket and soft ball. Horse racing is held at Sea Cow's Bay, Tortola, one Sun a month and is a popular local event, worth seeing if you want to see the Virgin Islanders at leisure. Gyms include Bodyworks, T 494-2705, and Cutting Edge, T 495-9570. *Prospect Reef* has a healthclub called Healthy Prospects where you can do aerobics (called Body Images, T 494-4713), yoga, tennis and 9-hole pitch and putt, T 494-3311 ext 245.

FESTIVALS

The BVI Summer Festival is held over 2 weeks at the end of July and beginning of August. There is entertainment every night with steel bands, fungi and calypso music, a Prince and Princess show and a calypso show. During the year there are many regattas, such as the annual BVI Spring Regatta in April, Foxy's Wooden Boat Regatta in September and windsurfing events, which attract many extracurricular activities and lots of parties.

TORTOLA

The main island, with a population of about 14,000, or 81% of the total population of the BVI. Mount Sage, the highest point in the archipelago, rises to 1,780 ft, and traces of a primeval rain forest can still be found on its slopes. Walking trails have been marked through Mount Sage National Park. The S part of the island is mountainous and rocky, covered with scrub, frangipani and ginger thomas. The N has groves of bananas, mangoes and palm trees, and long sandy beaches.

Road Town, on the S shore, is the capital and business centre of the territory and is dominated by marinas and financial companies, many of which line the harbour. Main Street houses many of the oldest buildings, churches and the prison, and is the most picturesque street. Until the 1960s, Main Street was the waterfront road, but land infill has allowed another road, Waterfront Drive, to be built between it and the sea. A new dual carriageway is being built from Port Purcell to Wickhams Cay, which will later be extended to Fort Burt, so expect disruption in Road Town. Cruise ships now call frequently at a new dock in the Wickhams Cay area opened late-1994. There are many gift shops, hotels and restaurants catering for the tourist market. In 1992-93, very grand and imposing government offices were built on the waterfront overlooking the harbour entrance. Banks, offices, Cable and Wireless, the Tourist Office and a small craft village are also in this area. All these buildings are built on infilled land, called Wickhams Cay; the restaurant *Spaghetti Junction* was once a bar overlooking the water but is now some way back, divided from the sea by roads and office buildings. The Governor resides in **Government House** above Waterfront Drive overlooking the harbour (T 494 2345, F 494 4435). The house is in a classical style, painted white with green shutters and surrounded by beautifully tended gardens with a fine display of flamboyant trees in the front.

The 4-acre **Joseph Reynold O'Neal Botanic Gardens** near the Police Station in Road Town (free admission, donations welcomed) has a good selection of tropical and subtropical plants such as palm trees, succulents, ferns and orchids. There is a good booklet which gives a suggested route round the garden, pond, orchid house, fern house and medicinal herb garden. It is a peaceful place, luxuriant, with magnificent pergolas, recommended. The small BVI Folk Museum in a lovely old wooden building on Main Street behind *Pusser's Bar* was closed in 1996.

There are also communities at East End and West End. **West End** has more facilities for visitors. *Sopers Hole* is a port of entry (ferries to St Thomas, St John and Jost Van Dyke leave from here) and popular meeting place for people on yachts. *Pussers* is alongside the moorings and there are several shops, including a dive shop and some boutiques. All the buildings are painted in bright pinks and blues. It is very relaxing to sip cocktails on the dock and watch the yachts come and go. The *Jolly Roger*, on the opposite side of the bay is a popular yachtie hangout. The area is famous for being the former home of Edward Teach (Blackbeard the pirate).

The best beaches are along the NW and N coasts. **Smugglers Cove** and **Apple Bay**, West End, have fine sandy beaches. If you have no transport, Smugglers Cove is an hour's walk on a dirt road over a steep hill from West End. There is an old hotel with a bar which is often self-service; the beach is usually deserted. **Cane Garden Bay** is the best beach and yachts can anchor there. There are two reefs with a marked gap in between. The Callwood Rum Distillery at Cane Garden Bay still produces rum with copper boiling vats and an old still and cane crusher in much the same way as it did in the 18th century. Apple Bay is popular with surfers from November for a few months, as is the E end of Cane Garden Bay and Josiah's Bay. **Brewers Bay** is a long curving bay with

Tortola

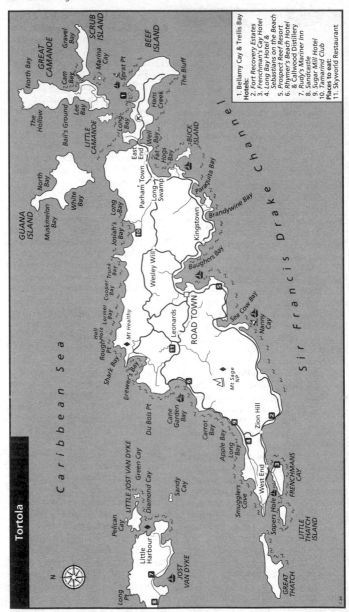

Hotels:
1. Bellamy Cay & Trellis Bay
2. Fort Recovery Estates
3. Frenchman's Cay Hotel
4. Long Bay Hotel & Sebastians on the Beach
5. Prospect Reef Resort
6. Rhymer's Beach Hotel & Callwood Distillery
7. Rudy's Mariner Inn
8. Sandcastle
9. Sugar Mill Hotel
10. Tamarind Club

Places to eat:
11. Skyworld Restaurant

Caribbean Sea

Sir Francis Drake Channel

GUANA ISLAND
GREAT CAMANOE
SCRUB ISLAND
BEEF ISLAND
LITTLE CAMANOE
JOST VAN DYKE
LITTLE JOST VAN DYKE
GREAT THATCH
LITTLE THATCH ISLAND

ROAD TOWN
Parham Town
Kingstown
Leonards
Wesley Will
West End
Zion Hill
East End

North Bay
Gravel Cay
Cam Bay
Lee Bay
Marina Cay
Sprat Pt
The Bluff
Hans Creek
The Hollow
Ball's Ground
Long Bay
BUCK ISLAND
North Bay
White Bay
Well
Fat Hogs Bay
Muskmelon Bay
Josiah's Bay
Long Bay
Long Swamp
Paraquita Bay
Brandywine Bay
Baughers Bay
Sea Cow Bay
Nanny Cay
Mt Sage NP
Cane Garden Bay
Du Bois Pt
Carrot Bay
Apple Bay
Long Bay
Smugglers Cove
Sopers Hole
FRENCHMANS CAY
Diamond Cay
Green Cay
Sandy Cay
Pelican Cay
Long Pt
Little Harbour
Shark Bay
Brewer's Bay
Hell Rough Hole Pt
Lormer Pt
Cooper Trunk Bay
Mt Healthy

N

plenty of shade and a small campsite in the trees by the beach. Josiah's Bay (another campsite) and Long Bay, East End, are also pleasant beaches. Carrot Bay is stony, there is no sand, but there are lots of pelicans and the village is pleasant, having a very Caribbean feel with several bars, palm trees and banana plants. Watch out for strong rip currents at some of the N shore beaches, and seek local advice before swimming, especially if the surfers are out.

Tortola is superb, but the full flavour of the BVI can only be discovered by cruising round the other islands (see above, **Beaches and watersports**). You can also take day trips on the regular ferry to Virgin Gorda, with lunch and a visit to The Baths included if you wish.

Island information – Tortola
● Accommodation

Price guide

L1	over US$200	L2	US$151-200
L3	US$101-150	A1	US$81-100
A2	US$61-80	A3	US$46-60
B	US$31-45	C	US$21-30
D	US$12-20	E	US$7-11
F	US$4-6	G	up to US$3

Road Town: L1-L3 *Treasure Isle*, on hillside overlooking the marina and Sir Francis Drake Channel, 40 rooms and 3 suites, pool, tennis, restaurant, a/c, TV, convenient for business travellers, used by people on crewed yacht charters for first and last night, helpful staff at front desk, PO Box 68, T 494-2501, F 494-2507; under same ownership and used by *Treasure Isle* for all watersports is the L1-A1 *Moorings/Mariner Inn*, at the dockside for bareboat charters, 36 standard rooms with kitchenette, 4 suites, fan, tennis, small pool by bar, briefing room for those setting out on yachts, informal and relaxed but well organized, Underwater Safaris dive shop on site, PO Box 139, T 494-2332, F 494-2226; L2-A1 *Village Cay Resort and Marina*, directly opp on the other side of the harbour, 18 clean, bright rooms, well-furnished although a bit sterile, TV, phone, cheaper rooms face inland, restaurant and bar overlooking yachts, good food, buffet with steel band Fri 1800-2300, also showers, toilets and launderette for sailors, PO Box 145, T 494-2771, F 494-2773; L1-A2 *Maria's*

By The Sea, by new government buildings, overlooks sea but no beach, older part is simple, all have kitchenette, a/c, TV, phone, double beds, new wing has bigger rooms, balconies, conference room, friendly, Maria's cooking rec, light and airy entrance with bar, pool, PO Box 206, T 494-2595, F 494-2420; L2-B *Sea View Hotel*, 12 rooms, 8 studios, 1 efficiency apartment, pool, quite noisy because of traffic but good value, PO Box 59, T 494-2483, F 494-4952; 200m further on is L2-A1 *Fort Burt*, on hillside opp Marina, was fort built by Dutch, first hotel on island built 1953, restaurant and bar, convenient location, good views, PO Box 243, T 494-4200, F 494-2547; L3-A3 *Hotel Castle Maria*, up the hill overlooking Road Town, 30 rooms, some triple and quads, kitchenette, a/c, cable TV, pool, restaurant, bar, car rentals, popular with local business travellers, PO Box 206, T 494-2553, F 494-2111. About the cheapest on the island is B *Wayside Inn Guest House*, Road Town, near library, 20 rooms, with fan, adequate but basic, shared bathrooms but not very clean, PO Box 258, T 494-3606.

South coast: heading W from Road Town you come to L1-A1 *Prospect Reef Resort*, a 15-acre resort specializing in package holidays, wide variety of rooms, studios, town houses and villas, some with sea view, some without, comfortable, welcoming, tennis, pitch and put, sea water pool, fresh water swimming lane pool, diving pool, health and fitness centre, Baskin in the Sun dive shop, marina, sailing, fishing, café and restaurant, conference centre for 150, car rental, complimentary sports equipment, boutiques, shuttle service, PO Box 104, T 494-3311, 800-356-8937, F 494-5595; L2-A3 *Nanny Cay Resort and Marina*, 42 rooms, a/c, TV, VCRs, kitchenette, phone, deluxe rooms have 2 queen-size beds, standard rooms are darker, smaller, restaurants, bars, boutiques, tennis, Blue Water Divers dive shop, car rental, windsurfing and sailing, used by short stay people going out on bareboat charters, PO Box 281, T 800-74 CHARMS, T 494-2512, F 494-0555; L1-L3 *Villas at Fort Recovery Estate*, 10 spacious and nicely furnished villas of different sizes on small beach, inc breakfast, built around 17th century Dutch fort, commissary, no restaurant, but à la carte room service available inc complimentary dinner and snorkel trip for stays of over 7 nights, yoga, massage, good snorkelling offshore, pool, car essential, PO Box 239, T 495-4354, 800-367-8455, F 495-4036; inexpensive is

A2-B *BVI Aquatic Hotel*, West End, 14 rooms, also 1-bedroom apartments in Road Town, US$280-550/week, T 495-4541/2114; **L1-L3** *Frenchman's Cay Hotel*, beautiful hillside location on the cay overlooking the S coast of Tortola, 9 villas, all with view, fans, phone, a quiet resort with lots of repeat business, small sandy beach with reef for snorkelling, hammocks, tennis (fee for non-guests), pool, library, games, short trail out to point, Sun beach

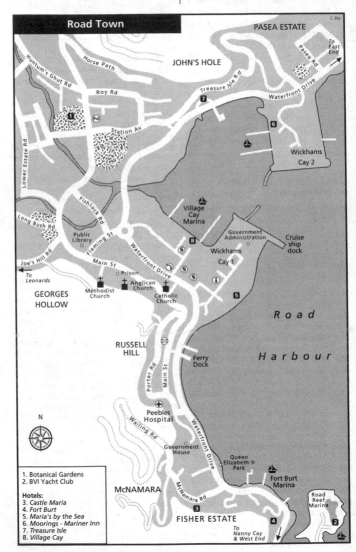

Road Town

PASEA ESTATE

C 26a

Huntum's Ghut Rd

Horse Path

JOHN'S HOLE

Pasea Rd

To East End

Roy Rd

Treasure Isle Rd

Waterfront Drive

7

Station Av

6

Lower Estate Rd

Fishlock Rd

Wickhams Cay 2

Long Bush Rd

Village Cay Marina

Public Library

8

Government Administration

Cruise ship dock

Fleming St

Waterfront Drive

Wickhams Cay 1

Joe's Hill Rd

Main St

Prison

To Leonards

GEORGES HOLLOW

Methodist Church

Anglican Church

Catholic Church

5

Road

Harbour

RUSSELL HILL

Ferry Dock

Porter Rd

Main St

N

Peebles Hospital

Walling Rd

Government House

McNAMARA

Waterfront Drive

McNamara Rd

Queen Elizabeth II Park

Fort Burt Marina

Road Reef Marina

1. Botanical Gardens
2. BVI Yacht Club

Hotels:
3. *Castle Maria*
4. *Fort Burt*
5. *Maria's by the Sea*
6. *Moorings - Mariner Inn*
7. *Treasure Isle*
8. *Village Cay*

FISHER ESTATE

To Nanny Cay & West End

4

2

barbecue, bar, restaurant, TV in clubhouse, PO Box 1054, West End, T 495-4844, 800-235-4077; **A2-B** *Jolly Roger Inn*, rec, a small inn and bar on waterfront at Sopers Hole, run by New Yorkers, live music at weekends so do not stay here if you want peace and quiet, convenient for ferries (see above), 6 brightly decorated, clean rooms, some with shared bathroom, fans, screens, singles, doubles, triples available, good breakfasts, busy restaurant and bar, meeting place, T 495-4559, F 495-4184.

West coast: heading NE, **A1-A2** *Smugglers Cove Beach Resort*, fans, kitchenettes, beach bar, snorkelling reef, PO Box 4, West End, T 495-4234; **L1-A3** *Long Bay Beach Resort*, 104 rooms, studios and villas spread along the beach and up the hillside, a/c, TV, phone, fridge, pool, tennis, pitch and put, car rental, 2 restaurants with vegetarian options, bars, surfboards, snorkelling equipment, nice beach, sandy with some rocks, level of sand can shift depending on season, PO Box 433, T 495-4252, in the USA T 800-729-9599, in the UK T 0800-373 742; **L2-A2** *Sebastian's On The Beach*, Apple Bay, located either side of road, informal and popular surfers' hangout, 8 comfortable beachfront rooms with balcony, 4 rear rooms which connect, 12 more rooms across the road at rear of office around patio, 2 rooms above office, 10% service, fans, fridge, payphones, grocery 0800-2200, restaurant/bar overlooking sandy beach, happy hour 1600-1800, blend own rum, surfboards and boogieboards for rent, PO Box 441, T 495-4212, 800-336-4870, F 495-4466; **L1-L3** *Sugar Mill Hotel*, Little Apple Bay, 21 rooms, most with kitchenettes, prestigious restaurant, beach bar, pool, no children in season, PO Box 425, T 495-4355, 800-462-8834, F 495-4696; along this stretch of coast there are lots of rental villas, many of which are advertised simply with a notice outside, usually about US$90/day; at the upper end of the scale, *Rockview Holiday Homes*, PO Box 263, T 494-2550, F 494-5866, have several villas for rent, the cheapest in winter at US$1,275/week and the most expensive at US$11,000/week, most have daily maid service, *Sunset House* has a cook as well; *Cliff Houses* offers various villas at US$800-1,800, T 495-4727, F 495-4958; private villas inc *Limeberry House*, 3 bedrooms with pool, T 494-2354, F 495-2900 and the 2-bedroom *Belmont House*, T 495-4477, F 495-4476; **A2-B** *Cane Garden Bay (Rhymer's) Beach Hotel*, Cane

Garden Bay, has 27 basic but clean rooms, most with double bed and single bed, right on sandy beach, beach towels provided, store and shop, laundromat, restaurant/bar on beach, watersports companies on either side of hotel, PO Box 570, T 495-4639, 495-4215, F 495-4820; **L1-A2** *Ole Works Inn*, Cane Garden Bay, built around 300-year-old sugar factory, on beach, 18 rooms, honeymoon tower, bar, restaurant, gift shop, T 495-4837, F 495-9618; **L3-A2** *Sunset Vacation Apartments*, 6 1-bedroom and 1 2-bedroom apartments, T 495-4751; **L3** *Clyne's Beach Suites*, 5 1-bedroom apartments, 40% less in summer, T 494-2888, 495-4543.

North coast: **L3-A1** *Tamarind Club*, small hotel with pool, nestled in trees, take insect repellent, close to 4 beaches, excellent restaurant, bar, 9 rooms with kitchenettes, 6 villas, fans, screens, PO Box 509, East End, T 495-2477, 800-313-5662.

East End: **L3-A2** *Seabreeze Yacht Charters*, PO Box 528, East End, 8 rooms for sailors, marina, yacht charters, pool, commissary, T 495-1560, F 495-1561

Camping: at *Brewer's Bay campsite* on N coast, bare site US$8, tent hire US$35 for 2 people, babysitters available, beach bar and simple restaurant, PO Box 185, T 494-3463; campground at Josiah's Bay.

There is lots of self-catering accommodation in what are variously known as houses, villas, apartments, guest houses, 'efficiencies' or 'housekeeping units'. Prices are usually set on a weekly basis according to size and standard of luxury, and there is often a 30%-40% discount in the summer. Contact the Tourist Office for a full list and individual brochures.

● **Places to eat**
Road Town: restaurants serving West Indian specialities inc *C & F Restaurant*, Purcell Estate, very popular with visitors and locals, excellent local food, slow but friendly service, T 494-4941; *Mario's*, Palm Grove Shopping Centre, West Indian specialities, clean, a/c, good service, generous portions, T 494-3883; *Oliver's*, Waterfront Drive near roundabout, clean, a/c, 0730-2300, good food, baby grand piano, bit of a jazz venue, T 494-2177; *Beach Club Terrace*, T 494-2272, at Baughers Bay, open 0800-2200; *Butterfly Bar and Restaurant*, Main Street, open 0700-2200 except Sun; *Roti Palace*, T 494-4196, Russel Hill, East Indian specialities from Trinidad and Guyana, huge rotis, rec. Recommended restaurants include *The Fish Trap*, T 494-3626, at the

Columbus Centre, behind Village Cay Marina, open lunch and dinner, open air, reservations rec, good seafood, inside is a popular yachtie bar open 1630-late serving good lower-priced bar meals, and *The Captain's Table*, a French restaurant on the waterfront by Village Cay Marina, T 494-3885, lunch Mon-Fri, dinner daily except Sat from 1800; next door is the *Hungry Sailor*, same great food but for a lot less, you eat on the patio though; *Pusser's Co Store & Pub* on Main Street, Road Town, T 494-3897, yachties' meeting place, good pub atmosphere, open 1100-2200, on ground floor bar, store and restaurant for simple dishes such as English pies and New York deli sandwiches, nickel beer on Tues and Thur, really is US$0.05 but not rec, 'pain killer' cocktails rec, strongest is 'brain killer', first floor restaurant, *The Outpost*, T 494-4199, serves steaks and Mexican food, dinner only, reservations rec, cheap drink specials Tues and Thur nights; *Tavern in the Town*, Road Town, next to Pussers, traditional English pub food and atmosphere, sells Newcastle Brown Ale, garden looks out across harbour, closed Sat, T 494-2790; *Cell 5 Lounge*, next door, T 494-4629, burgers, native dishes, tropical drinks, breakfast, lunch and dinner, notice outside says 'sorry, we do not cater to persons in a hurry'; *Capriccio del Mare*, Waterfront Drive overlooking water, Italian café serving excellent coffee and delicious, if overpriced, snacks and continental lunches, open 0800-2100, T 494-5369; *Spaghetti Junction*, Waterfront Drive opp Palm Grove shopping centre upstairs in small blue building, 1800-2300, T 494-4880; *BVI Steak and Chopp House*, in *Hotel Castle Maria*, overlooking harbour, good food, congenial hosts Tom and Fran, open daily 0730-1000, 1130-1400, 1800-2200, T 494-5433; *Virgin Queen*, Road Town, T 494-2310, homemade pizza plus West Indian and European food, a popular watering hole for English and American residents; *Rays of Hope*, Port Purcell, small health food store, café and take away, excellent vegetarian set lunch, Mon-Fri 1130-1530, get there early, they run out fast; *Marlene's Delicious Designs*, Waterfront Drive near Cable and Wireless, popular lunch spot for office workers serving sandwiches, cakes and local patties, cheap and delicious, open 0730-1800, T 494-4634.

Outside Road Town: *Brandywine Bay Restaurant*, East End, run by Cele and Davide Pugliese, 10 mins drive from Road Town, one of the most exclusive restaurants on Tortola,

indoor and outdoor dining, grills and Florentine food, cocktails 1730, dinner 1830-2100, closed Sun, reservations, T 495-2301, F 495-1203, Channel 16, anchorage 15-ft draft; *Bing's Drop Inn Bar and Restaurant*, at Fat Hog's Bay, East End, T 495-2627, home cooked dinners, excellent conch fritters, an after hours dance spot, late night menu, reservations; *Tamarind Club*, East End, excellent food, nice atmosphere, live music often, open 1200-1500, 1830-2130, closed Tues, T 495-2477; *The Struggling Man*, T 494-4163, Sea Cows Bay, between Road Town and Nanny Cay, West Indian, breakfast, lunch and dinner; *Mrs Scatliffe's*, T 495-4556, Carrot Bay, upstairs in a yellow and white building opp the Primary School, local cuisine, home grown fruit and vegetables, family fungi performance after dinner, lunch Mon-Fri 1200-1400, dinner daily 1900-2100, reservations essential; also in Carrot Bay, *Clem's By The Sea*, T 495-4350, West Indian specialities, goat stew, boiled fish and fungi, steel band, Mon, Sat, open 0900 until late; *The Sugar Mill*, in an old mill in Apple Bay, gourmet and elegant, dinner 1900, reservations, T 495-4355, hotel attached, breakfast and lunch at beach bar. There is also *Pusser's Landing* and *Jolly Roger* (fun, yachtie hangout, good pizza and burgers, good cheap breakfast, open 0700-2200, T 495-4559) at West End and many more excellent restaurants in the hotels and yacht clubs. At Cane Garden Bay you can 'Jump Up' (Caribbean music), almost every night at *Rhymers*, (serves breakfast, lunch and dinner, T 495-4639; folk music at *Quito's Gazebo*, T 495-4837, restaurant and beach bar at N end of Cane Garden Bay, lunch 1100-1500, rotis and burgers, dinner 1830-2130, buffets Sun, Tues, fish fry Fri, closed Mon. There are a number of small restaurants serving excellent food along the road going towards the rum distillery ruins; check in the late afternoon to make reservations and find out what the menu will be. 10 mins drive from Road Town or Cane Garden Bay is the *Skyworld Restaurant*, with a panoramic view of all the Virgin Islands, food and prices reasonable, open from 1000, rec for view, T 494-3567.

If you are self-catering, you can get reasonably priced food from K Mark's and other supermarkets at Port Purcell or at the 'Rite Way' supermarkets a little closer to town. At the entrance to the Moorings, Wickhams Cay II, is the Bon Appetit Deli, T 494-5199, where you can get cheese and wine as well as regular provisions; they also do sandwiches and lunch specials and party services. In Road Town is Fort Wines Gourmet Shop, a wine shop with a high class image but reasonable prices, you can also eat there, excellent light snacks (eg quiche) and wine by the glass.

● **Nightlife**

In Road Town, *Paradise Pub*, entertainment Mon-Sat, T 494-2608, dancing Thur-Sat, Trivial Pursuits Wed, they also serve lunches and dinners; the hotels organize live bands and movie nights. At East End is *Bing's Drop Inn Bar*, see above; *Pusser's Landing* at Frenchman's Cay has bands, Thur and Sun, T 495-4554; *Jolly Roger* at West End has live music most weekends and often has visiting bands, call for details, T 495-4559; *Bomba's Shack*, on the beach in Apple Bay has music Wed and Sun, famous full moon party every month, sleep before you go, the party goes on all night, T 495-4148; *Quito's Gazebo*, Cane Garden Bay, has live music nightly and the beat is quickened at weekends and holidays, making it a popular beach front dance spot, T 495-4837; *Tamarind Club* at Josiah's Bay has live music Fri and Sat and often has special party nights, T 495-2477.

● **Laundry**

Sylvia's Laundromat, next to Public Library on Flemming St, Road Town, T 494-2230; *Freeman's Laundromat*, beside Barclays Bank, Wickham's Cay, T 494-2285. Marinas usually have laundromats. See telephone listings for out of town laundries.

BEEF ISLAND

This island was famed as a hunting ground for beef cattle during the buccaneering days. The island is linked to Tortola by the Queen Elizabeth bridge. The main airport of the BVI is here. (Taxi to Road Town, US$15.) Long Bay beach is on the N shore. Also Trellis Bay which has an excellent harbour and bars. *The Last Resort*, run by Englishman Tony Snell, based on Bellamy Cay, provides a lavish buffet menu plus one-man show cabaret, happy hour 1730-1830, dinner 1930, cabaret 2130, ferry service available, reservations required, T 495-2520 or channel 16. Also Boardsailing BVI, (see **Beaches and watersports**) the

Conch Shell Point Restaurant (T 495-2285) and a painting and jewellery shop. L3-A1 *Beef Island Guest House* has 4 rooms on the beach, T 495-2303, F 495-1611, food available at its *De Loose Mongoose Bar*, 0800-1600, 1800-2100, mostly burgers and sandwiches. *Rama Villas* are 3 new, elegant rental homes, very spacious, light and airy, together sleep 14 or available separately, suitable for families or corporate retreat, pool, daily maid service, fax and teleconferencing facilities, overlooks Tortola, not on beach, PO Box 663, Road Town, T 494-5972, F 494-3782.

MARINA CAY

This tiny private island of 6 acres just N of Beef Island was where Robb White wrote his book *Our Virgin Isle*, which was made into a film starring Sidney Poitier and John Cassavetes. A charming cottage hotel, L1-L2 *Pusser's Marina Cay Hotel*, comprises most of the island, which is encircled by a reef, offering some of the best snorkelling in the BVI. Marina facilities (boats use mooring buoys and a dinghy dock), laundry, showers, diving, kayaking, sailing, snorkelling etc, there are 4 rooms and 2 villas available, MAP, T 494-2174 or VHF channel 16, PO Box 626, Road Town. Bar, restaurant, beach barbecue on Fri, Pussers Co Store, selling clothes and travel accessories. Daily ferry service from Trellis Bay jetty, 3 in morning, 5 in afternoon, ferries after 2100 on request. If sailing, enter from the N.

GUANA ISLAND

North of Tortola, Guana Island is an 850-acre private island and wildlife sanctuary as well as having a very expensive hotel, L1 *The Guana Island Club*, 15 rooms, tennis, restaurant, watersports, T 494-2354, 800-544-8262, PO Box 32, Road Town. The island is available for rent. The owners discourage visitors apart from guests, in order to keep the island a sanctuary for wildlife. A few flamingoes have been introduced to the island. They live in a small pond where the salinity fluctuates widely so their diets are supplemented with food and water if they need it. The birds used to live in a zoo, so they are fairly tame.

THE DOGS

Northeast of Tortola are The Dogs, small uninhabited islands. West Dog is a National Park. On Great Dog you can see frigate birds nesting. The islands are often used as a stopping off point when sailing from North Sound to Jost Van Dyke, and are popular with divers coming from North Sound. The dive sites are not spectacular but there are some interesting rock formations, with canyons and bridges. The best anchorages are on George Dog to the W of Kitchen Point and on the S side of Great Dog.

VIRGIN GORDA

Over a century ago, Virgin Gorda was the centre of population and commerce. It is now better known as the site of the geological curiosity called **The Baths**, where enormous boulders form a natural swimming pool and underwater caves. The snorkelling is good, especially going left from the beach. Climbing over and around the boulders is fun for the adventurous and there is an easy trail with ladders and bridges for those not so agile. However, exploring in the water with a mask and snorkel is the recommended way to do it. Unfortunately the popularity of The Baths with tour companies and cruise ships has led to overcrowding. There are many day trips from Tortola and when a cruise ship is in port you can not move on the beach. Choose carefully which day you visit.

The island is 7 miles long and has a population of about 5,000. The N half is mountainous, with a peak 1,370 ft high, while the S half is relatively flat. There are some 20 secluded beaches; the most frequented are Devil's Bay, Spring Bay, and Trunk Bay on the W coast. North of

the island is North Sound, formed to the S and E by Virgin Gorda, to the N by Prickly Pear Island, and to the W by Mosquito Island. On the SE tip is Copper Mine Point, where the Spaniards mined copper, gold and silver some 400 years ago; the remains of the mine can be seen. The rocky façade here is reminiscent of the Cornish coast of England. The amateur geologist will find stones such as malachite and crystals embedded in quartz. All land on Virgin Gorda over 1,000 ft high is now a National Park, where trails have been blazed for walking. Just off the SW tip of the island is Fallen Jerusalem, an islet which is now a National Park. There is a 3,000-ft airstrip near the main settlement, **Spanish Town**. The Virgin Gorda Yacht Harbour is here and besides the marina facilities with full yachting chandlery, there is a good supermarket, dive centre, bar/restaurant, a craft shop selling stamps, souvenir and clothes shops and phones, post box and taxis. **Bitter End** and **Biras Creek** are good anchorages and both have a hotel and restaurant. There is no road to either of them, you have to get a hotel launch from Gun Creek or the North Sound Express from Beef Island to *Bitter End Yacht Club*.

Island information – Virgin Gorda
● Accommodation

Price guide			
L1	over US$200	**L2**	US$151-200
L3	US$101-150	**A1**	US$81-100
A2	US$61-80	**A3**	US$46-60
B	US$31-45	**C**	US$21-30
D	US$12-20	**E**	US$7-11
F	US$4-6	**G**	up to US$3

In the S part of the island near The Valley and the airport are: **L1** *Little Dix Bay*, luxury 98-roomed chalet hotel, with 4 1-bedroom suites, on ½-mile beach, watersports arranged, tennis, health and fitness centre, hiking trails in surrounding hills, quiet, lovely gardens in extensive grounds, no TV or pool, strict dress code after sunset, 70% repeat guests in winter, honeymooners in summer, children's programme isolated from rest of resort, lots of packages available, PO Box 70, Virgin Gorda,

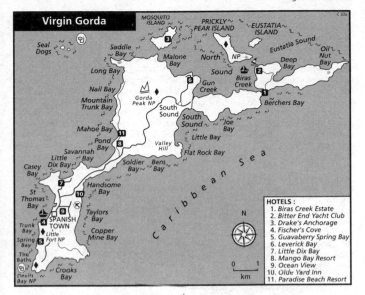

Virgin Gorda

MOSQUITO ISLAND
PRICKLY PEAR ISLAND
EUSTATIA ISLAND

Seal Dogs
Saddle Bay
Malone Bay
North Sound
Eustatia Sound
Deep Bay
Oil Nut Bay

Long Bay
Gun Creek
Biras Creek

Nail Bay
Gorda Peak NP
South Sound
Berchers Bay

Mountain Trunk Bay
Mahoe Bay
South Sound
Joe Bay
Little Bay
Flat Rock Bay

Savannah Bay
Pond Bay
Valley Hill

Casey Bay
Little Dix Bay
Soldier Bay
Bens Bay

St Thomas Bay
Handsome Bay
Taylors Bay

Trunk Bay
SPANISH TOWN
Copper Mine Bay

Little Spring Bay
The Baths
Crooks Bay

Caribbean Sea

N

0   1
km

HOTELS :
1. Biras Creek Estate
2. Bitter End Yacht Club
3. Drake's Anchorage
4. Fischer's Cove
5. Guavaberry Spring Bay
6. Leverick Bay
7. Little Dix Bay
8. Mango Bay Resort
9. Ocean View
10. Olde Yard Inn
11. Paradise Beach Resort

T 495-5555, F 495-5083, in USA T 800-928-3000 (Rosewood Hotels & Resorts, same as *Caneel Bay Resort*, St John), also owns and operates the airport and the Virgin Gorda Yacht Harbour, a large marina in St Thomas Bay offering most facilities; at the cheaper end of the range is **L1-A3** *Ocean View/The Wheelhouse*, 12 rooms, close to ferry and harbour, pink building, small rooms but adequately furnished, TV, fan, a/c, functional restaurant, bar, PO Box 66, T 495-5230; **L1-L3** *Fischer's Cove Beach Hotel*, St Thomas Bay, 12 studio rooms, some with fan, some a/c, or 8 cottages with kitchenette, less space, some beachfront, balcony restaurant overlooking sea open 0730-2200, beach barbecue when calm, PO Box 60, T 495-5252, F 495-5820; **L1-L3** *Diamond Beach*, Trunk Bay, 6 villas with 1-3 bedrooms, all with sea view, secluded location, PO Box 69, T 495-5452, 800-871-3551; **L1-L3** *Guavaberry Spring Bay*, well-equipped wooden cottages, beautiful location, friendly, sandy beach with shade 5 mins walk through grounds, to the S are The Baths, to the N the Crawl, a National Park enclosing a natural swimming pool and more boulders, highly rec, run by Tina and Ludwig Goschler, PO Box 20, T 495-5227; *Toad Hall*, luxury rental home, 3 bedrooms with garden

showers, private access to The Baths beach along spectacular wooden walkway, pool among the boulders, caves to explore, great for agile children, US$3,500-4,500/week, contact Stephen and Marie Green, PO Box 7, T 495-5397, F 495-5708; **L1-A1** *Olde Yard Inn*, convenient for airport, 14 rooms, 1 suite, a/c available, downstairs rooms rather dark, pool, jacuzzi, health spa, poolside restaurant, pleasant gardens, good food, library with piano, games room, croquet, hammocks, small shop, 10-15 mins on trail to beach, owned by Carol Kaufman, PO Box 26, T 495-5544, 800-653-9273, F 495-5968; N of The Valley up the W coast are two resorts which were built as one, so the villas are the same, **L1-L3** *Mango Bay* has 5 villas which can make 12 1-bedroomed units or the apartments can be connected to provide 2 or 3 bedrooms, very clean, light and airy, tiled floors, light colours, a/c on request, pretty shrubbery, narrow sandy beach, lovely sea view, jetty, Italian management, PO Box 1062, T 495-5672, F 495-5674; **L1-L3** *Paradise Beach* has 7 units in 3 houses, snorkelling and fishing gear available, dinghy, quiet, rental car inc, PO Box 1105, T 495-5871, 800-225-4255; on the N coast is **L1-L3** *Leverick Bay Hotel and Vacation Villas*, offering a wide variety of spacious accommodation from hotel rooms to villas and condominiums built up a hillside with a great view of the jetty and the bay, villas US$866-4,737/week inc tax and maid service, *Pussers* is on site and all the buildings are painted the bright multi-colours which are *Pussers'* emblem, use *Pussers'* restaurant or cross the water to *Drake's Anchorage* on Mosquito Island opp, tennis, watersports, Dive BVI operates from here, food store, laundry, shops, beauty therapy and massage, PO Box 63, T 495-7421, 800-848-7081; perhaps the most exclusive resort on the island is **L1 Biras Creek**, reached by launch from Gun Creek, or on the North Sound Express from Beef Island, on a spit of land overlooking both North Sound and Berchers Bay, luxury, beautifully decorated cottages and grand suites up to US$1,000/4 people spread along the Atlantic coast, can sleep maximum 84 people, no children under 6, those under 8 are not allowed in the dining room but have early dinner and babysitter, no phones or a/c, 2 floodlit tennis courts with pro, sailing trips and other watersports arranged, free watersports instruction, small pool overlooking ocean, nice little beach in sheltered bay with mangroves, very private, beach barbecues, good menu and wonderful view from the split level restaurant, popular with honeymooners, sailing packages with some nights on board available, PO Box 54, T 494-3555, F 494-3557, in the UK T 0800-373 742; **L1 The Bitter End Yacht Club and Resort**, North Sound, reached by launch from Gun Creek or the North Sound Express from Beef Island (US$18 one-way) or by yacht, lively, popular, action-packed for water lovers with a marina, sailing in all sizes of boats for all ages, yacht charters, windsurfing, diving, anything any water lover would want, plus instruction, stay on your boat, charter one of the 8 liveaboard yachts, or use the 100 rooms and chalets, comfortable big beds, very spread out along coastal hillside (used to be 2 resorts), can be a long walk from your room to the clubhouse but taxi service available, the older, cheaper rooms are closest, busy restaurant, reserve dinner at breakfast, shops, food stores, conference room, public phone system is archaic, free room for children in summer, PO Box 46, T 494-2746, 800-872-2392.

● **Places to eat**

For upmarket, elegant dining try *Biras Creek*, 5-course fixed price dinner plus 15% service, 1930-2100, dress smartly; *Little Dix Bay* has 3 full service restaurants open 0700-2100,

T 495-5555; *Bitter End Yacht Club* for the sailing fraternity, champagne breakfast US$15, buffet lunch US$20, dinner US$30; *Pirate's Pub and Grill*, on Saba Rock, North Sound, burgers, barbecue and sandwiches 1000-2000, channel 16, T 495-9537, F 495-9369; *Giorgio's Table*, Mahoe Bay, next to *Mango Bay* resort, authentic Italian food, 80% of ingredients imported from Italy, open 0900-2200, T 495-5684; *Olde Yard Inn*, international food in a garden setting; *Chez Michelle*, T 495-5510, international cuisine, 1830-2130, reservations; restaurants serving West Indian recipes include *Anything Goes*, The Valley, T 495-5062, curries and seafood, 1100-2200, take away and delivery locally; *Teacher Ilma's*, in the Valley at Princess Quarters, dinner only, reservations after 1600, T 495-5355; *Fischers Cove*, international and local food and beach barbecues, T 495-5252; also *Crab Hole*, South Valley, locals eat here, inexpensive West Indian food, curries, roti, callalou, conch, entertainment on Fri 0930-2400, T 495-5307; *Lobster Pot*, at *Andy's Chateau de Pirate*, T 495-5252, beach pig roast on Mon, seafood buffet on Thur, barbecue on Sat; *The Bath and Turtle*, Virgin Gorda Yacht Harbour, standard pub fare, open 0730-2130 daily, good place to wait for the ferry; *Pusser's* Leverick Bay, T 495-7369, breakfast and lunch 0800-1800 at beach bar, dinner 1800-2200 on the veranda, steaks, seafood, pies; *Mad Dog*, next to the parking lot at The Baths, drinks, sandwiches, T-shirts and friendly conversation, open 1000-1900; there is also a bar on the beach at The Baths also selling T-shirts, not always open, be sure to bring a bottle of water just in case, toilets round the back.

● **Nightlife**

Live music at *The Bath and Turtle* and *Little Dix Bay*, live music and/or DJ at *Pirate's Pub*, *Pussers* and *Bitter End*. Check the bulletin board at the Virgin Gorda Yacht Harbour for special events and concerts.

MOSQUITO ISLAND

Mosquito Island is privately owned by L1 *Drake's Anchorage Resort* and enjoys beautiful views over North Sound and Virgin Gorda and Prickly Pear Island. This 125-acre island is just NW of Leverick Bay and can only be reached by boat. There is a lovely beach at South Bay, sandy with boulders, and there are trails leading from the hotel to this and other quiet, sandy coves. The island can be rented in its entirety, or you can just use the hotel, which has 8 rooms, 2 villas and 2 suites, very expensive, rates include 3 meals and watersports, bars, restaurant, moorings, windsurfing, very quiet and relaxed atmosphere, PO Box 2510, Virgin Gorda, T 494-2254, 800-624-6651, restaurant open 0730-1000, 1200-1400, candlelit dinner seating time 1900, French-style menu, reservations essential for dinner.

PRICKLY PEAR ISLAND

Prickly Pear Island forms the NE edge of North Sound. It has a lovely beach at Vixen Point with a small beach bar, not always open, and a watersports centre. This is a great spot for volley ball, with a net permanently on the beach. There is no phone, call on the radio, VHF channel 16, Vixen Point.

NECKER ISLAND

This 74-acre, private island NE of Virgin Gorda is owned by Richard Branson, who wanted a Virgin island to add to his Virgin enterprise. It is available for rent, contact Necker Island (BVI) Ltd, 120 Campden Hill Road, London W8 7AR, T 0171-727 8000, F 0171-727 8343, toll free from USA (800) 231-1445. The house, in Balinese style, sleeps 20, is fully staffed and costs an arm and a leg. Lovely beaches, protected by a coral reef, tennis and water sports provided, private.

COOPER ISLAND

In the chain of islands running SW from Virgin Gorda is Cooper Island (*pop 9*), which has a beautiful beach and harbour at Manchioneel Bay with palm trees, coral reefs and **L2-A2** *Cooper Island Beach Club* (PO Box 859, Road Town, T 494-3721, in USA Parlmes Enterprises Inc, T 413-863-3162, 800-542

4624, F 413-863-3662). British owned and managed, there are 12 guest rooms with kitchen and bathroom, breakfast on request, lunch 1130-1430, dinner from 1830, reservations preferred, bar all day from 1000, do your grocery shopping on Tortola, electricity generator evenings only. The supply boat leaves Road Town Mon, Wed, Sat, other days use Underwater Safaris' dive boat from *The Moorings*, Road Town; they have a small dive shop on the island and use the beach club for surface intervals or to pick up divers from yachts anchored in the bay, dive equipment for sale or rent, airfill station, photographic services.

SALT ISLAND

Very few people visit this lovely island, there are no ferries and access is only by private boat. There are two salt ponds from which salt is gathered by two ageing residents. A bag of salt is still sent to the British monarch every year as rent for the island, the remainder is sold to visitors and local restaurants. The two old men who live there welcome visitors and will show you the salt forming and packing process. They have a hut from which they sell conch shells and shell necklaces. There is a small settlement on the N side as well as a reef-protected lagoon on the E shore. The population numbers about 20. The main reason people come here is for a rest stop between dives. The British mail ship *Rhone*, a 310-ft steamer, sank off Salt Island in a hurricane in 1867 and the site was used in the film *The Deep*. Those who perished were buried on Salt Island. The wreck is still almost intact in 20-80 ft of water and is very impressive. There are moorings provided at Lee Bay, just N of the *Rhone*, for those diving the wreck, to minimize anchor damage. The dive is usually divided between the bow section and the stern section; in the former you can swim through the hull at a depth of about 70 ft, be prepared for darkness. In calm weather it is possible to snorkel part of it.

DEAD CHEST

A tiny island in Salt Island Passage, between Salt Island and Peter Island, this is reputedly the island where the pirate Blackbeard abandoned sailors: "15 men on a Dead Man's Chest – Yo Ho Ho and a bottle of rum!".

PETER ISLAND

This 1,000-acre island has a tiny population and offers isolated, palm-fringed beaches, good anchorage and picnic spots. The exclusive, luxury, L1 *Peter Island Resort and Yacht Harbour* is built on reclaimed land jutting out into Sir Francis Drake Channel, forming a sheltered harbour with marine facilities. Built by Norwegians, there are chalet-type cottages, harbour rooms, or beach rooms, full board, a pool, tennis, horseriding, watersports, dress formally in evening, T 495-2000, in USA 800-346 4451, F 495-2500, PO Box 211, Road Town. Eight daily ferry departures from Tortola, private guest launch from Tortola or St Thomas, helicopter from St Thomas or San Juan.

NORMAN ISLAND

The island is uninhabited (apart from the floating bar/restaurant *William Thornton II*, T 494-2564 or VHF Channel 16, anchored in the Bight of Norman to the N of the island, the first *William Thornton*, a converted 1910 Baltic Trader sank in 1995; launch service from Fort Burt Marina, Road Town, daily at 1715), but reputed to be the 'Treasure Island' of Robert Louis Stevenson fame. On its rocky W coast are caves where treasure is said to have been discovered many years ago. These can be reached by small boats and there are several day trips on offer. There is excellent snorkelling around the caves and the reef in front slopes downward to a depth of 40 ft. Be careful with the wild cattle: their tempers are unpredictable. **The Indians** off the NW of

Norman Island are pinnacles of rock sticking out of the sea with their neighbour, the gently rounded **Pelican Island**. Together they offer the diver and snorkeller a labyrinth of underwater reefs and caves.

JOST VAN DYKE

Lying to the W of Tortola, the island was named after a Dutch pirate. It is mountainous, with beaches at White Bay and Great Harbour Bay on the S coast. Great Harbour looks like the fantasy tropical island, a long horseshoe shaped, white sandy beach, fringed with palm trees and dotted with beach bar/restaurants. Population about 300, very friendly with lots of stories to tell. Jost Van Dyke is a point of entry and has a Customs House. In January 1991, the island was provided with electricity for the first time and a paved road. It is surrounded by some smaller islands, one of which is **Little Jost Van Dyke**, the birthplace of Dr John Lettsome, the founder of the British Medical Society.

Island information – Jost Van Dyke
● **Accommodation**
L1 *Sandcastle*, at White Bay, owned by Darrell Sanderson, 4 wooden cottages, basic amenities but great for total relaxation, hammocks between palm trees on the beach, restaurant (must reserve dinner and order in advance to your specifications), snorkelling, windsurfing, reservations Suite 201, 6501 Red Hook Plaza, USVI 00802, T 495-9888 or 775-5262 or (USA) 803-237 8999, F 775 3590, *The Soggy Dollar Bar* is popular at weekends, most people arrive by boat and swim or wade ashore, aspires to be the birthplace of the infamous 'painkiller'; **L1-A3** *Rudy's Mariner Inn*, Great Harbour, 3 rooms, beach bar and restaurant, kitchenettes, grocery, water taxi, T 495-9282 or (USVI) 775 3558; **A2-B** *Harris' Place*, T 495-9302 or call VHF channel 16, 2 rooms, beach bar, restaurant, grocery, water taxi, live music, Harris calls his place the friendliest spot in the BVIs; *Sandy Ground Estates*, T 495-3391, PO Box 594, West End, Tortola, 8 luxury villas, provisioning, free water taxi from/to Tortola, US$1,200/ 780/week for 2 people.

Camping: *White Bay Campground*, nice site, right on beautiful, sandy, White Bay, tents US$35, or bare sites US$15 (3 people), T 495-9312.

● **Places to eat**

In Little Harbour: *Harris' Place*, open daily, breakfast, lunch and dinner, happy hour 1100-1500, pig roasts with live music Tues and Thur, lobster night on Mon, ferries from Tortola and St Thomas/St John arranged for these feasts, T 495-9302; *Sidney's Peace and Love*, Little Harbour, T 495-9271 or Channel 16, open from 0900, happy hour 1700-1830, pig roast Mon and Sat 1900, US$15, or all you can eat pig and ribs, US$20, barbecue rib and chicken Sun, Tues and Thur, US$15, otherwise lunch and dinner usual steak, fish, shrimp or lobster; *Abe's By The Sea*, pig roast on Wed, US$18, call VHF channel 16 for reservations, also has 3 rooms overlooking harbour, can be 1 apartment, **A2**, friendly family, T 495-9329, F 495-9529.

In Great Harbour: *Ali Baba's*, run by Baba Hatchett, W of the Customs House, breakfast, lunch and dinner, happy hour 1600-1800; *Rudy's Mariner's Rendezvous*, open for dinner until 0100, US$12.50-22.50, reservations T 495-9282 or channel 16; *Club Paradise* open daily, Mon lobster special US$20, Wed pig roast US$15, live entertainment regularly, lunch 1100-1500, dinner 1900-2200, T 495-9267, F 495-9633 or VHF channel 16; *Foxy's Bar*, friendly and cheap, lunch Mon-Fri rotis and burgers, dinner daily, reservations by 1700, T 495-9258, spontaneous calypso by Foxy, master story-teller and musician, big parties on New Year's Eve and other holidays, hundreds of yachts arrive, wooden boat regatta on Labour Day draws hundreds of boats from all over the Caribbean for a 3-days beach party, very easy to get invited on board to watch or race, special ferry service to USVI and Tortola; *Happy Laury's*, very good value for breakfast, happy hour is 1500-1700, try the Happy Laury Pain Killer. There is a pig roast on Jost Van Dyke every Fri.

For details of ferries see **Information for travellers**.

SANDY CAY

This small uninhabited islet just E of Jost Van Dyke is owned by Laurance Rockefeller. It is covered with scrub but there is a pleasant trail set out around the whole island, which makes a good walk. Bright white beaches surround the island and provide excellent swimming. Offshore is a coral reef.

ANEGADA

Unique among this group of islands because of its coral and limestone formation, the highest point is only 28 ft above sea level. There are still a few large iguanas, which are indigenous to the island. 20 flamingoes were released in 1992 in the ponds and 4 wild ones joined them 2 years later. In the spring of 1995 they bred 5 chicks, something of a record with flamingoes reintroduced into the wild. They are best seen from the little bridge over The Creek on the road from the *Anegada Reef Hotel* to the airport turn off. Hawksbill and Green Turtles nest all along the N shore; the Government has drawn up a conservation policy and the waters around the island are protected. The waters abound with fish and lobster, and the extensive reefs are popular with snorkellers and scuba divers who also explore wrecks of ships which foundered in years past. Some were said to hold treasure, but to date only a few doubloons have been discovered. Anegada has excellent fishing and is one of the top bone fishing spots in the world. From the wharf on the S shore, all the way round to the W end, across the entire N shore (about 11 miles) is perfect, uninterrupted, white sandy beach. Any fences on the beach are to keep out cattle, not people. Loblolly Bay is popular with day trippers, partly because it has a beach bar at either end (*The Big Bamboo* at the W end is busier and more accessible than *Flash of Beauty* at the E end), the only places where there is shade, but also for the reef just off shore where snorkellers can explore caverns and ledges and see coral, nurse sharks, rays, turtles, barracuda and shoals of colourful fish. The beach is generally deserted. Bring water and sun screen. The population numbers about 290, living mostly in **The Settlement**. This is a

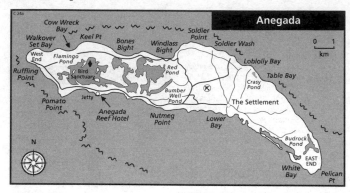

collection of wooden shacks and some newer houses, a smart new government building, a few bars, little shops, a bakery, jeep hire and church. A short stretch of concrete road leads from The Settlement to the airport turn off; all other roads on the island are sand. There is no public transport except taxis and the best way to get around is to hire a jeep, bicycle or walk (take an umbrella for the sun or walk in the early evening). The island is very quiet and relaxed. There is an airstrip 2,500 ft long and 60 ft wide, which can handle light aircraft. Day trips by boat from Tortola are available. There is no regular ferry service.

Island information – Anegada
● Accommodation
L1-L3 *Anegada Reef Hotel*, 12 rooms, where there is an anchorage, fishing packages, dive equipment, beach bar, restaurant, great service, famous lobster barbecue, rec, cash or TCs only, no credit cards, T 495-8002, F 495-9362 or by VHF Radio Channel 16, if arriving by yacht radio in advance for directions through the reef, jeep and bicycle hire, taxi service, boutique, closed Sept-Oct; **A1-A2** *Ocean Range*, in the settlement, single and adjoining rooms, kitchenettes available, sea view, T 495-8017/2019; *Anegada Beach Campground*, T 495-9466, US$20-36 prepared site, bare site US$7/day, plus 10% service, no credit cards, beach bar, restaurant, snorkelling, windsurfing; *Neptune's Treasure* has a campsite and tents available US$15-25/night, US$90-150/week, no cooking, T 495-9439.

● Places to eat
Pomato Point Beach Restaurant, T 495-9466, Channel 16, barbecue dinners, reserve by 1600; *Neptune's Treasure*, breakfast, lunch, dinner, camping available, delicious breads and chutneys, make sure you take some home, T 495-9439; *Big Bamboo*, see above, Aubrey and his wife serve delicious lobster and conch on the beach at Loblolly Bay, VHF channel 16; *Del's Restaurant and Bar*, in The Settlement, T 495-8014, West Indian food, lunch and dinner; *Banana Well Bar and Restaurant*, The Settlement, T 495-9461, breakfast, lunch and dinner, native dishes, seafood, sandwiches. Recommended to make dinner reservations before 1600 at all restaurants.

Information for travellers

BEFORE TRAVELLING

● **Documents**
An authenticated birth or citizenship certificate or voter's registration may suffice for US or Canadian citizens. All other nationalities need a valid passport and a return or onward ticket. Visitors from some countries, such as Guyana, require a visa. The Chief Immigration Officer is in Road Town, T 494-3701

● **Climate**
The temperature averages 84°F in summer and 80°F in winter. At night temperatures may drop about 10 degrees. Average annual rainfall is 40 ins.

MONEY

● **Currency**
The US dollar is the legal tender. There are no exchange control restrictions. Try to avoid large denominated TCs. Cheques accepted rarely, cash is king. There is a 10% stamp duty on all cheques and TCs.

● **Credit cards**
Credit cards are all right for most hotels and the larger restaurants, but not for the majority of the bar/restaurants. Credit cards are not accepted on Anegada.

GETTING THERE

AIR
There are international airports on Tortola, Virgin Gorda and (since 1995) Anegada, but no direct flights from Europe or from the USA.

● **From Europe**
Same day connections can be made through Puerto Rico (British Airways from London, Iberia from Madrid) or Antigua (BWIA or British Airways from London, BWIA from Zurich).

● **From the USA**
Connecting flights can be arranged through Puerto Rico or the USVI. American Eagle, Carib Air, Dolphin Airlines and LIAT fly several times a day from San Juan. LIAT flies to Tortola from Anguilla, Antigua, Barbados, Grenada, Dominica, St Kitts, St Maarten, St Lucia, St Thomas, Martinique, Trinidad and Tobago, Puerto Rico. Winair also flies from St Maarten to Tortola.

Virgin Gorda's air links are not especially good. In 1996 Air St Thomas (from St Thomas and San Juan with connections from St Barts, Fajardo and Culebra) were still flying in, T 495-5935. Dolphin Airlines also fly from St Thomas and San Juan via Tortola.

SEA
There are frequent connections with the USVI and within the BVI. To St Thomas or St John, US$18 one-way, US$32 return. *Inter-Island Boat Services*, *Sundance II* between Cruz Bay, St John, and West End, Tortola, 3 times a day Mon-Thur, 4 times on Fri, 3 times on Sat and Sun, T 495-4166; also Water Taxi available, T 776-6597. *Native Son Inc*, T 495-4617, between St Thomas and Road Town via West End, or between Red Hook, St Thomas and St John to West End, several daily. *Smiths Ferry Services*, *M/V Daphne Elise* and *M/V Marie Elise*, from St Thomas to West End and the Government Jetty, Road Town and on to The Valley, Virgin Gorda, several daily, also to West End from St John and Red Hook, St Thomas, 4 daily, T 494-2355, 495-4495. These two companies alternate their departure times by 30 mins. *Speedy's Fantasy* and *Speedy's Delight* on the routes Virgin Gorda-Road Town-St Thomas, Virgin Gorda-Road Town, T 495-5240 Virgin Gorda, or 774-8685 St Thomas.

● **Ports of entry**
(British flag) Port Purcell at Road Town is the principal port of entry with an 800-ft, deep water berth for cruise ships; a second 550-ft pier was built in 1994; Government Jetty, Road Town, is also used. There are others at West End (Soper's Hole), Tortola; St Thomas Bay, Virgin Gorda; and Great Harbour, Jost Van Dyke. Anegada is a new port of entry, customs and immigration can be cleared 0715-1715 Mon-Fri, 0800-1530 Sat-Sun.

● **Boat documents**
Customs clearance fee US$0.75, harbour dues US$7, US$10.50 for a boat registered under the name of a corporation.

ON ARRIVAL

● **Banks**

Bank of Nova Scotia, Road Town, T 494-2526; **Barclays Bank**, Road Town, T 494-2171, F 494-4315, with agencies in The Valley, Virgin Gorda; **Chase Manhattan Bank**, Road Town, T 494-2662; **Development Bank of the Virgin Islands**, T 494-3737; **Banco Popular**, Road Town, T 494-2117.

● **Clothing**

Island dress is casual and only the most exclusive restaurants require formal clothes. However, bathing suits are for the beach only, it is very offensive to locals to see bare chests and bellies, so cover up.

● **Hospitals**

Peebles Hospital is a public hospital with x-ray and surgical facilities. There are 12 doctors on Tortola and one on Virgin Gorda, two dentists and a small private hospital, the Bougainvillea Clinic which specializes in plastic surgery. Be careful in the sun, always use a sunscreen.

● **Hours of business**

Banks open Mon-Fri, 0900-1400, **Barclays** is open until 1500, **Chase Manhattan** until 1600, also Chase opens on Sat 0900-1200. Shops open Mon-Fri, 0900-1700. Government offices open Mon-Fri, 0830-1630.

● **Official time**

Atlantic Standard Time, 4 hrs behind GMT, 1 ahead of EST.

● **Public holidays**

New Year's Day, Commonwealth Day (2nd Mon in Mar), Good Friday, Easter Monday, Whit Monday in May, Queen's Birthday (2nd Mon in June), Territory Day (1 July), Festival beginning of Aug, St Ursula's Day (21 Oct), Prince Charles' Birthday (14 Nov), Christmas Day, Boxing Day.

● **Religion**

Methodist, Anglican (Episcopal), Roman Catholic, Seventh Day Adventist, Baptist, Church of God, Church of Christ, Jehovah's Witness and Pentecostal Churches, Hindu and Muslim.

● **Shopping**

The BVI is not duty-free. There are gift shops and boutiques in Road Town, Tortola and in Spanish Town, Virgin Gorda. The BVI Philatelic Bureau or Post Offices sell stamps for collectors. You can also buy BVI coins, but they are not used as a currency. *Samarkand*, on Main St, Tortola, sells gold and silver jewellery created by the local Bibby family with nautical themes; you can buy earrings of yachts, pelicans, etc, and they will make anything to order. *Sunny Caribbee Spice Co* (PO Box 286), is on Main St, *Skyworld Restaurant* and *Long Bay Hotel*, selling spices, herbs, preserves and handicrafts, mail order and shipping services available. *Pusser's Co Store* in Road Town and West End, Tortola, and Leverick Bay, Virgin Gorda, sells nautical clothing, luggage and accessories as well as Pusser's Rum. *Turtle Dove Boutique*, opposite Public Library in Road Town, has a good selection of gifts and is the only place selling a reasonable selection of books (other than romances and thrillers stocked by hotels). *Caribbean Handprints*, Main St, has a silk-screen studio and shop with local designs and clothing made on site. An open air market close to the Tourist Office offers a selection of T-shirts and other souvenirs.

● **Voltage**

110 volts, 60 cycles.

ON DEPARTURE

● **Departure tax**

There is a departure tax of US$10 if you leave by air and a US$8 departure tax by sea. There is a cruise ship passenger tax of US$7.

ACCOMMODATION

● **Hotels**

There is a 7% hotel tax and a 10% service charge in the BVI. Rates apply to double rooms, EP, winter-summer.

● **Camping**

Allowed only on authorized sites.

FOOD AND DRINK

There are lots of good restaurants across the island. The BVI Restaurant Guide, updated annually, gives menu listings of the best restaurants.

Fish dishes are often excellent, try snapper, dolphin (fish, not the mammal), grouper, tuna and swordfish, and don't miss the lobster.

Most things are imported and will cost at least the same as in Florida. Try local produce which is cheaper, yams and sweet potatoes rather than potatoes, for example.

Once the centre of rum production for the Royal Navy 'Pussers' (Pursers), rum is still available from *Pusser's* or supermarkets. Local rums of varying quality are also sold by hotels and restaurants.

GETTING AROUND

AIR TRANSPORT
Within the BVI there are flights: Anegada/Tortola, Virgin Gorda/Tortola with Virgin Islands Airways, Aero Gorda and other small airlines. Aero Gorda flies to Anegada Mon, Wed and Fri, US$27 one-way, or hire the whole plane, US$250, seats 8 people, T 495-2271. Fly BVI is a small charter airline which is often cheaper and more convenient than a scheduled flight if there are a few of you, to Anegada US$125 one-way T 495-1747, 800-1-FLY BVI, F 495-1973. Pack light, there is limited luggage space on the small aircraft. Alternatively take a day trip to Anegada, US$110 pp including taxi, air fare, lunch, contact Nikki and Barry Abrams, owners of Fly BVI.

LAND TRANSPORT
● **Motoring**
There are only about 50 miles of roads suitable for cars. Drive on the left. Maximum speed limit 30 mph, in residential areas 10-15 mph. Minimokes and jeeps can be hired on Tortola, Virgin Gorda and Anegada. Jeeps may be more useful for exploring secluded beach areas. Car rental offices (or the Police Headquarters) provide the necessary temporary BVI driving licence (US$10) but you must also have a valid licence from your home country.

● **Car hire**
It is advisable to book in advance in the peak season. Rates range from US$45/day in winter for a small car, US$35-60/day for jeeps, usually about US$10 less in summer.

Tortola: Airways Car Rentals, Inner Harbour Marina, T 494-4502, or Airport, T 495-2161, jeeps for US$40-50/day plus US$10 insurance; **Alphonso Car Rentals**, Fish Bay, T 494-3137, US$45-75/day, 20% less in summer; **Avis Rent-a-Car**, opp Botanic Gardens, Road Town, T 494-2193, US$35-50/day winter, US$25-40 summer, cheaper weekly rates; **Budget**, Wickhams Cay I, T 494-2639, US$35-50/day; **Caribbean Car Rental**, *Maria's Inn*, Wickhams Cay, T 494-2698, US$45-49/day; **Denzil Clyne Car Rentals**, West End, T 495-4900,

jeeps US$45-60/day in winter, US$40-60 in summer; **Hertz Car Rental**, West End, T 495-4405, US$45-55/day; **International Car Rentals**, Road Town, T 494-2516, US$40-57/day; **National Car Rental**, Duffs Bottom, Road Town, T 494-3197, US$40-58/day; **Rancal Rent-a-car**, *Long Bay Beach Resort*, T 495-4330, and *Prospect Reef*, T 494-4534, US$48-55/day in winter, package rates for resort guests.

Virgin Gorda: Andy's Taxi and Jeep Rental, The Valley, T 495-5511, US$50-55/day, guided tours US$30; **Hertz**, The Valley, T 495-5803, cars US$35-55, jeeps US$35-60/day; **L & S Jeep Rentals**, South Valley, T 495-5297, small or large jeeps, US$42-68/day; **Mahogany Car Rentals**, The Valley, T 495-5469, US$42-60; **Speedy's Car Rentals**, The Valley, T 495-5235, US$42-52/day.

Anegada: Anegada Reef Hotel, T 495-8000, F 495-9362, car rental and licence US$50-65/day, also bicycle hire, US$3/hr; **DW Jeep Rentals**, The Settlement, T 495-8018, US$40/day winter, US$35/day summer.

● **Bicycles**
All bicycles must be registered at the Traffic Licencing Office in Road Town and the licence plate must be fixed to the bicycle, cost US$5. *Last Stop Sports* in Nanny Cay rents and repairs quality mountain bikes, rental US$20/day, T 494-0564, F 494-0593.

● **Buses**
There is a local bus service on Tortola with cheap fares (US$1-4) but erratic timetable. Scheduled (but nowhere near actual) times are: Road Town to West End, 0700, 0835, 1000; West End to Carrot Bay, 0730, 0900, 1030. From Carrot Bay it goes to Road Town, East End and back to Road Town. In the afternoon it leaves West End at 1515 and 1645. Call **Scatos Bus Service** for information, T 494-5873/2365.

● **Taxis**
BVI Taxi Association, T 494-2875, island tours arranged. **Taxi stands**: in Road Town, T 494-2322; on Beef Island, T 495-2378. Taxis are easy to come by on Tortola and fares are fixed, ask for a list or get one from the Tourist Office. The fare from Beef Island Airport to Road Town, Tortola is US$15 or US$8 if shared.

FERRIES
The *North Sound Express* has 3 daily crossings Beef Island-North Sound (Bitter End), 30 mins,

US$20, with a bus service (not inc in fare) to and from Road Town waterfront (Pussers) and Beef Island ferry dock, T 495-2271. *The Virgin Gorda Ferry Service*, T 495-5240, between Road Town and The Valley, has 2 daily crossings. *Peter Island Ferry* has 8 daily crossings from the Peter Island Ferry Dock, Road Town, to Peter Island, T494-2561. *Jost Van Dyke Ferry Service*, T 494-2997, 4 crossings a day between West End and Jost Van Dyke Mon-Sat, 3 on Sun. Speedy's and Smith's also run ferries between Road Town and The Valley (see above in **Getting there**). Williams and Williams run a car ferry from Beef Island, T 494-2627/2726.

COMMUNICATION

● **Postal services**

There is a General Post Office in Road Town, branches in Tortola and Virgin Gorda and sub-branches in other islands. Postal rates for postcards are US$0.30 to the USA, US$0.35 to Europe and US$0,45 to the rest of the world; for aerogrammes US$0.35; for letters to the USA US$0.45, to Europe US$0.50, to the rest of the world US$0.75.

● **Telecommunications**

Direct dialling is available locally and worldwide. The code for the BVI is 809-49 followed by a 5-digit number. All telecommunications are operated by Cable & Wireless. Telephone, telex, facsimile transmission, data transmission and telegraph facilities are all available. Phone cards are available, US$5, US$10 and US$20, discount rates in evenings at weekends. To make a credit card call, dial 111 and quote your Visa or Mastercard number. Dial 119 for the operator or 110 for the international operator. Cable & Wireless is at the centre of Road Town at Wickhams Cay I, open 0700-1900 Mon-Fri, 0700-1600 Sat, 0900-1400 Sun and public holidays, T 494-4444, F 494-2506; also in The Valley, Virgin Gorda, T 495-5444, F 495-5702. They also operate Tortola Marine Radio, call on VHF channel 16, talk on 27 or 84. The CCT Boatphone company in Road Town offers cellular telephone services throughout the Virgin Islands for yachts, US$10/day, T 494-3825. To call VHF stations from a land phone, call Tortola Radio, T 116.

MEDIA

● **Newspapers**

The Island Sun is published on Fri, while the *BVI Beacon* comes out on Thur.

● **Radio**

Radio ZBVI broadcasts on medium wave 780 KHZ. Weather reports for sailors are broadcast hourly from 0730 to 1830 every day. There are three FM stations: Z ROD, Z Gold and The Heat.

TOURIST INFORMATION

● **Local tourist office**

The BVI Tourist Board Office is in the Social Security Building, Wickhams Cay, in Tortola: PO Box 134, Road Town, T 494-3134; there is also an office at Virgin Gorda Yacht Harbour, T 495-5181; some offices overseas can help with reservations. *The Limin' Times*, printed weekly, is a free magazine giving entertainment news: nightlife, sports, music etc. *The Restaurant Guide* is published annually and is a free menu guide. *The BVI Welcome* is a bimonthly colour tourist guide now on line as well, on the Internet at http://www.caribweb.com/caribweb/bvi. *The Tourism Directory* is published annually and is a detailed listing of services. The Tourist Board has these and many other brochures.

● **Tourist offices overseas**

In **Germany**: Sophienstrasse 4, D-65189 Wiesbaden, T 49 611 300262, F 49 611 300766. In the **UK**: 110 St Martin's Lane, London WC2N 4DY, T 0171-240-4259, F 0171-240-4270. In the **USA**: 370 Lexington Ave, Suite 313, New York, NY 10017, T (212) 696-0400 or (800) 835-8530; 1804 Union St, San Francisco, CA 94123, T (415) 775 0344.

● **Maps**

The Ordnance Survey publishes a map of the BVI in its World Maps series, with inset maps of Road Town and East End, Tortola, tourist information and some text; Ordnance Survey, Romsey Rd, Southampton, SO9 4DH, T 01703 792792. The Tourist Office distributes a road map, updated annually with some tourist information on resorts, restaurants and what to do.

ACKNOWLEDGEMENTS

The editors are most grateful to Naomi Landau for updating the BVI chapter.

Leeward Islands
Antigua

NTIGUA, with about 108 square miles, is the largest of the Leewards, and also the most popular and the most developed. The island is low-lying and composed of volcanic rock, coral and limestone. Boggy Peak, its highest elevation, rises 1,330 feet (399m). There is nothing spectacular about its landscape, although its rolling hills and flowering trees are picturesque, but its coast line, curving into coves and graceful harbours, with 365 soft white sand beaches fringed with palm trees, is among the most attractive in the West Indies. It had a population of around 63,900 in 1995, most of them of African origin although some are of English, Portuguese, Lebanese and Syrian descent.

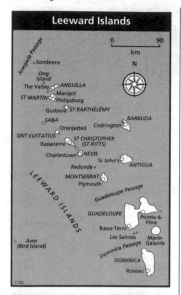

HISTORY

Antigua (pronounced Anteega) was first inhabited by the Siboney (stone people), whose settlements date back to at least 2400 BC. The Arawaks lived on the island between about AD 35 and 1100. Columbus landed on his second voyage in 1493 and named the island Santa María de la Antigua. Spanish and French colonists attempted to settle there but were discouraged by the absence of fresh water springs and attacks by the Caribs. In 1632 the English successfully colonized the island and, apart from a brief interlude in 1666 when held by the French, the island and its dependencies, Barbuda and uninhabited Redonda, remained British. Sir Christopher Codrington established the first large sugar estate in Antigua in 1674 and leased Barbuda to raise provisions for his plantations. Barbuda's only village is named after him. Forests were cleared for sugarcane

production and African slave labour was imported. Today, many Antiguans blame frequent droughts on the island's lack of trees to attract rainfall, and ruined towers of sugar plantations stand as testament to the destruction and consequent barrenness of the landscape. In the 17th and 18th centuries, Antigua was important for its natural harbours where British ships could be refitted safe from hurricanes and from attack. The Dockyard and the many fortifications date from this period. *Shirley Heights, The Story of the Red Coats in Antigua*, by Charles W E Jane, published by the Reference Library of Nelson's Dockyard National Park Foundation at English Harbour, Antigua, in 1982, gives a detailed account of the military history of the island and the building of the fortifications, price US$4.

The slaves were emancipated in 1834 but economic opportunities for the freed labourers were limited by a lack of surplus farming land, no access to credit, and an economy built on agriculture rather than manufacturing. Conditions for black people were little better than under slavery and in many cases the planters treated them worse. Poor labour conditions persisted and violence erupted in the first part of the twentieth century as workers protested against low wages, food shortages and poor living conditions. In 1939, to alleviate the seething discontent, the first labour movement was formed: the Antigua Trades and Labour Union. Vere Cornwall Bird became the union's president in 1943 and with other trade unionists formed the Antigua Labour Party (ALP). In 1946 the ALP won the first of a long series of electoral victories, being voted out of office only in 1971-76 when the Progressive Labour Movement won the general election. For a graphic account of the terrible conditions in which black people lived and worked during slavery and its aftermath, read *To Shoot Hard Labour (The Life and Times of Samuel Smith, an Antiguan Workingman*

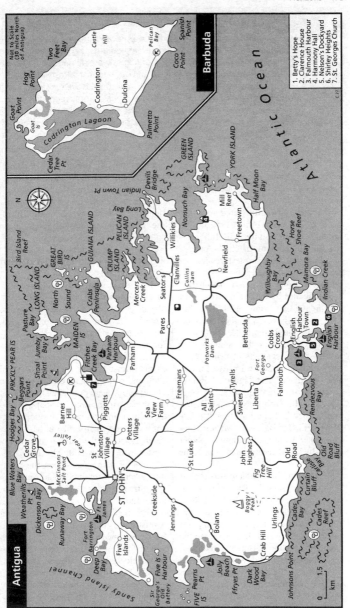

Barbuda

Not to Scale
(30 miles North
of Antigua)

1. Betty's Hope
2. Clarence House
3. Falmouth Harbour
4. Harmony Hall
5. Nelson's Dockyard
6. Shirley Heights
7. St. Georges Church

Antigua

Atlantic Ocean

Hurricane Luis

In Sept 1995 Antigua was pounded for 36 hrs by Hurricane Luis with winds of up to 175 mph, which left a trail of destruction estimated at EC$1bn, 2 dead, 160 injured and thousands homeless. About 75% of homes were damaged and there was extensive damage to hotels, port facilities and other tourist infrastructure. 10 days later, Hurricane Marilyn flooded the island. Water supplies were restored in a few weeks but electricity took longer. 21 hotels and guesthouses reopened fairly quickly, 16 more welcomed visitors in December. The Sandals resort stayed closed until early 1996, while the *Half Moon Bay Hotel* was not expected to open before Sept 1996 at the earliest, having received a direct hit by Luis.

1877-1982), by Keithlyn B Smith and Fernando C Smith, published by Karia Press, London, and Edan's Publishers, Toronto.

Antigua was administered as part of the Leeward Islands until 1959 and attained associated status, with full internal self-government in 1967. Antigua and Barbuda, as a single territory, became independent in November 1981, despite a strong campaign for separate independence by Barbuda. Vere C Bird became the first Prime Minister and in 1989, at the age of 79, he took office for the fourth consecutive time. The general elections were marked by some irregularities and allegations of bribery, but the ALP won 15 of the 16 seats for Antigua in the 17-seat House of Representatives, the remaining seats being taken by the United National Democratic Party and the Barbuda People's Movement, for Barbuda. Mr Bird appointed a largely unchanged cabinet which included several members of his family.

In 1990 the Government was rocked by an arms smuggling scandal which exposed corruption at an international level when allegations were made that Antigua had been used as a transit point for shipments of arms from Israel to the Medellín cocaine cartel in Colombia. Communications and Works Minister, Vere Bird Jr, the Prime Minister's son, became the subject of a judicial inquiry, following a complaint from the Colombian Government, for having signed authorization documents. His Cabinet appointment was revoked although he remained an MP. The Blom-Cooper report recommended no prosecutions although it undermined the credibility of the Government and highlighted the rivalry between the two sons, Vere Jr and Lester Bird. The report also recommended that Vere Bird Jr be banned for life from holding public office.

Repeated calls for the resignation of Prime Minister Vere Bird were ignored although several ministers resigned from his Government. Demonstrations were organized in 1992 by the newly-formed three-party United Opposition Front, seeking the resignation of the Prime Minister amid allegations of his theft and corruption. Fresh allegations of corruption were published in 1993 by the weekly opposition newspaper, *Outlet*, concerning property development contracts and misuse of public funds, resulting in a libel action issued by Lester Bird. *Outlet*, edited by Tim Hector, has for many years been the most outspoken critic of the Bird administration, frequently exposing corruption and fraud.

Vere Bird finally retired as Prime Minister in February 1994 at the age of 84. He was succeeded by his son, Lester, who led the ALP into the general elections held in March, winning its ninth out of 10 elections held since 1951. The Government's unpopularity was reflected in the vote and the ALP saw its representation cut from 15 to 11 seats in the House of Representatives. The Barbuda People's Movement retained its seat, while the United Progressive Party (formerly the United Opposition Front), led by Baldwin Spencer, won five seats, the largest number for any opposition party in the country's history. Tim Hector was appointed an opposition senator, having stood against Vere Jr in the election and lost. Vere Bird Jr, who is the chairman of the ALP, was not appointed to the new cabinet.

The new government was not free of allegations of corruption scandals (Ivor Bird, a younger Bird brother and general manager of the ZDK radio station was arrested and fined for taking possession of 12kg of cocaine at the airport) although Prime Minister Bird made efforts to portray a more professional administration. Economic adjustment was given priority and new tax policies sparked protest demonstrations and strikes (see **The Economy**).

In 1995, Hugh Marshall, a former trade minister launched a new party, the People's Democratic Movement.

GOVERNMENT

Antigua and Barbuda is a constitutional monarchy within the Commonwealth and the British Crown is represented by a Governor General. The head of government is the Prime Minister. There are two legislative houses: a directly elected 17-member House of Representatives and a 17-member Upper House, or Senate, appointed by the Governor General, mainly on the advice of the Prime Minister and the Leader of the Opposition. Antigua is divided into six parishes: St George, St John's, St Mary, St Paul, St Peter and St Phillip. Community councils on Antigua and the local government council on Barbuda are the organs of local government.

THE ECONOMY

The economy was long dominated by the cultivation of sugar, which was the major export earner until 1960, when prices fell

Antigua and Barbuda: fact file

Geographic

Land area	441.6 sq km
of which Barbuda	160.6
Redonda	1.3
forested	11.0%
pastures	9.0%
cultivated	18.0%

Demographic

Population (1995)	63,900
annual growth rate (1990-95)	0.0%
urban	36.2%
rural	63.8%
density	144.7 per sq km
Religious affiliation	
Protestant	73.7%
Roman Catholic	10.8%
Birth rate per 1,000 (1994)	17.3
	(world av 25.0)

Education and Health

Life expectancy at birth (1993),	
male	71.1 years
female	75.3 years
Infant mortality rate	
per 1,000 live births (1994)	18.5
Physicians (1991)	1 per 1,085 persons
Hospital beds	1 per 283 persons
Calorie intake as %	
of FAO requirement	105%
Literacy (over 15)	90%

Economic

GNP (1993 market prices)	US$425mn
GNP per capita	US$6,390
Public external debt (1994)	US$327mn
Tourism receipts (1993)	US$277mn
Inflation (annual av 1989-93)	2.4%
Radio	1 per 0.9 persons
Television	1 per 2.3 persons
Telephone	1 per 3.3 persons

Employment

Population economically active (1991)	
	26,753
Unemployment rate	na
% of labour force in agriculture	3.9
trade, restaurants and hotels	31.9
manufacturing	5.4
construction	11.6
Military forces	90

Source Encyclopaedia Britannica

dramatically and crippled the industry. By 1972 sugar had largely disappeared and farming had shifted towards fruit, vegetables, cotton and livestock. The economy is now based on services, principally tourism and offshore banking. Hotels and restaurants contribute about a quarter of gross domestic product and employ about one third of the work force. Tourism receipts make up about 60% of total foreign exchange earnings. 1995 arrivals were down 18.5% to 191,401, principally because of the hurricane damage, while cruise passenger numbers fell by 3.5% to 227,443.

There is some light industry which has been encouraged by tax and other incentives, but manufacturing for export is hampered by high wage and energy costs. A major expansion of tourist infrastructure has taken place, with development of harbour, airport, road and hotel facilities. This investment has not yet touched the bulk of the population and in rural areas small wooden shacks still constitute the most common form of dwelling, often alongside resorts and villa developments. Economic growth slowed in the early 1990s; political instability and corruption discouraged private sector investment, while government finances were weakened by high levels of debt, wages and tax evasion. Although growth was 5.5% in 1994, gdp declined by 3.8% when the hurricane struck in 1995.

The 1994/95 budget announced after the 1994 general elections increased taxation, notably on hotels and restaurants, and introduced an education levy on incomes. Current spending was increased by 24%, partly because of wage rises in the public sector, while capital spending included expenditure on economic infrastructure, such as roads and airport works. The new taxes and fees for government services were highly unpopular and provoked demonstrations and strikes. The Government also implemented the Caricom Comnon External Tariff on the same day, but later suspended it on a wide range of items because of its effect on the cost of living. The 1995/96 budget did not reverse any tax increases but included new capital projects: a new EC$40mn, 30-bed hospital, EC$18mn government offices and a EC$10-15mn housing programme.

The hurricane disaster of 1995 and its effect on the tourist industry had a knock-on impact on the fiscal accounts because of a sharp fall in tax revenues and increased spending demands. The Government turned to the IMF and World Bank for advice, and subsequently introduced an austerity plan which was reinforced by the 1996/97 budget. Spending cuts were announced for the public sector with a 2-year wage freeze although the Government rejected the IMF proposal for redundancies, abolition of price controls and privatizations.

FAUNA AND FLORA

Around 150 different birds have been observed in Antigua and Barbuda, of which a third are year-round residents and the rest seasonal or migrants. Good spots for birdwatching include McKinnons salt pond, N of St John's, where thousands of sandpipers and other water birds can be seen. Yellow crowned nightherons breed here. Potworks Dam is noted for the great blue heron in spring and many water fowl. Great Bird Island is home to the red-billed tropic bird and on Man of War Island, Barbuda, frigate birds breed. At Pasture Bay, on Long Island, the hawksbill turtle lays its eggs from late May to December. The Wide Caribbean Sea Turtle Conservation Network (Widecast) organizes turtle watches.

BEACHES AND WATERSPORTS

Tourist brochures will never tire of telling you that there are 365 beaches on Antigua, one for every day of the year, some of which are deserted. The nearest beach to St John's is Fort James which

Behind the façade

Many visitors regard Antigua as the ideal Caribbean holiday destination. The role of tourism in Antigua today is, however, one of the objects of a vehement attack in Jamaica Kincaid's book *A Small Place* (1988). Addressed to the foreign visitor, the essay proposes to reveal the realities underneath the island's surface. What follows is a passionate indictment of much of Antiguan government, society, the colonists who laid its foundations and the modern tourist. It is a profoundly negative book, designed to inspire the visitor to think beyond the beach and the hotel on this, or any other, island. Jamaica Kincaid was brought up on Antigua (she now lives in the USA), and memories and images from her childhood figure strongly in her other books to date. Another book which is interesting (if rather sensational at times) on Antigua, including its less attractive spots, is *Caribbean Time Bomb*, by Robert Coram (published by William Morrow, New York), who reveals what he calls "shocking truths" about the island.

is sometimes rough and has a milky appearance, lots of weed and not good for swimming. At other times it can be pleasant, with palm trees and a few boulders but crowded at weekends. It is rather secluded, do not go alone, drugs-users confrontations have been recorded there. Further but better is Dickenson Bay but there are hotels all along the beach which fence off their property and some pump sewage into the sea which can be smelly. Soldier's Bay, next to the *Blue Waters Hotel*, is shallow and picturesque. Instead of following the sign, park your car in the hotel car park, which has shade, walk left across the property, climb through the hole in the fence and in about three minutes you are there. Also good is Deep Bay which, like most beaches, can only be reached by taxi or car. There are several nice beaches on the peninsula W of St John's, past the *Royal Antiguan Hotel*. On Trafalgar Beach condominiums are being built on the rocks overlooking the small, sheltered bay. If you go through Five Islands village you come to Galley Bay, a secluded and unspoilt hotel beach which is popular with locals, especially joggers at sunset. The four *Hawksbill* beaches at the end of the peninsula, one of which is a nudist beach (free public entry, very secluded, security guard on duty, pleas-

ant atmosphere), are crescent shaped, very scenic and unspoilt. Take drinks to the furthest one as there are no facilities and you may have the place to yourself. Half Moon Bay, in the E, has a resort at one end, but there is plenty of room; the waves can be rough in the centre of the bay, but the water is calm at the N end. Near English Harbour is Galleon Beach, which is splendid, but again can only be reached by taxi or car or water taxi from English Harbour, EC$2. It has an excellent restaurant. Dark Wood Beach, on the road from St John's to Old Road round the SW coast, is very nice, quiet, with a bar and restaurant at the S end, reasonable food but not cheap.

Antigua offers sailing (sailing week at end-April, beginning of May, is a major yacht-racing event, with lots of noisy nightlife), water-skiing, windsurfing, parasailing, snorkelling and deep-sea fishing. Cocktail and barbecue cruises are reasonably priced. Shorty's Glass Bottom Boat at Dickenson Bay, takes people out to the coral reefs; there are also excursions to Bird Island, food and drink provided. Trips round the island with stops at smaller islands such as Bird Island, Prickly Pear Island, or even Barbuda or Montserrat, can be arranged on the catamarans *Kokomo Cat* (T 462 7245), *Wadadli Cats* (T 462 4792), *Loafer*

(T 462 2690) or *Sagitoo* (T 460 1244). *Sentio* is a luxury yacht for small groups, honeymooners, families, for special trips, beach exploring, overnight to Barbuda or sailing instruction T 464 7127. There is also, of course, the *Jolly Roger* (T 462 2064), a wooden sailing ship used for entertaining would-be pirates, with Wednesday lunchtime cruises from Jolly Beach, Thursday cocktail cruises from the *Royal Antiguan*, and Saturday night barbecue and dancing cruise, helped along with plentiful rum punch.

Races are held throughout the year. The Antigua Yacht Club holds races every Thur and anyone wishing to crew should listen to English Harbour Radio at 0900 on VHF 68/06 that morning. Jolly Harbour Yacht Club holds Sat races as well as the Red Stripe Regatta in Feb and Jolly Harbour Regatta in September. The Classic Regatta in mid-April is spectacular, with yawls, ketches, schooners and square-masted vessels displaying their sails. Antigua Sailing Week begins at the end of April with 5 days of races and noisy parties; 240 boats participated in 1995. The first Carib Cup Regatta was held in July 1995 with 5 teams of 3 boats competing.

A marina was built at Jolly Harbour in 1992, just S of Ffryes Point. Several day charter boats have moved there. For cruisers or bareboat charters Antigua offers good provisioning and marine supplies abound, with facilities to haul out boats as well. Haulout can be done at Antigua Slipway, Crabbs Marina or Jolly Harbour; there are several other marinas as well. Charter fleets include Sun Yachts and Nicholson's Yacht Charters. There are too many anchorages to list.

Lobster King, a 35-foot Bertram offers deep sea fishing charters, US$500 half day, US$900 full day, maximum 8 people, special price on Wednesday US$100 pp, T 462 4363; *M/Y Nimrod*, US$500 half day, US$900 full day, also scuba diving, based at Falmouth Harbour, T 464 0143; *Jacal* is a 25-foot

Mako, T 462 2650; *Legend* is a 35-foot Hatteras sport fishing boat, T 462 0256 ext 458 at Halcyon Cove Watersports; *Obsession* is a 45-foot Hatteras which leaves from Falmouth Harbour, T 462 3174.

Dickenson Bay is the only beach with public hire of watersports equipment but some hotels will hire to the public especially out of season, eg the *Club Antigua* hotel near Bolan's Village (bus from West End bus station). Halcyon Cove Watersports at the *Halcyon Cove Hotel* has waterskiing and small sailing craft for rent, T 462 0256. The *Sandals* all-inclusive resort on Dickenson Bay will admit outsiders, at EC$450 per couple 1000-1800 or EC$250 for the evening, giving you the use of all sports facilities, meals, bar etc. Patrick's Windsurfing School at the *Lord Nelson Beach Club* at Dutchman's Bay N of the airport (no frills accommodation and food), offers instruction to intermediate and advanced windsurfers, while beginners are taught at *Halcyon Cove Hotel* (T 462 3094/0256).

DIVING AND MARINE LIFE

There are barrier reefs around most of Antigua which are host to lots of colourful fish and underwater plant life. Diving is mostly shallow, up to 60 feet, except below Shirley Heights, where dives are up to 110 feet, or Sunken Rock, with a depth of 122 feet where the cleft rock formation gives the impression of a cave dive. Popular sites are Cades Reef, which runs for 2½ miles along the leeward side of the island and is an underwater park; Sandy Island Reef, covered with several types of coral and only 30-50 feet deep; Horseshoe Reef, Barracuda Alley and Little Bird Island. There are also plenty of wrecks to explore, including the *Andes*, in 20 feet of water in Deep Bay, the *Harbour of St John's* and the *Unknown Barge*, also in Deep Bay. Diving off Barbuda is more difficult unless you are on a boat with full gear and a compressor, as facilities are very limited. The water is fairly shallow, though, so snorkelling can be enjoyable. There is little information on the island about conservation and few warnings on the dangers of touching living coral.

Dive shops are located nearly all round the island and include: Aquanaut Diving Centre, at *St James's Club*, T 460 5000; Dive Runaway, *Runaway Beach Club*, T 462 2626, training sessions, PADI certification courses, equipment rental; Dive Antigua, *Halcyon Cove Hotel*, T 462 3483; Jolly Dive, *Club Antigua*, T 462 0061; Curtain Bluff Dive Shop, *Curtain Bluff Hotel*, T 462 8400 (certified hotel guests only); Dockyard Divers at Nelson's Dockyard, T 460 1178; Pirate Divers at *Lord Nelson*, T 462 9463; Long Bay Dive Shop, *Long Bay Hotel*, T 460 2005 (certified hotel guests only).

OTHER SPORTS

There are two **golf** courses: a professional 18-hole one at Cedar Valley, near St John's, T 462 0161, and a 9-hole course which may or may not reopen after hurricane damage at *Half Moon Bay Hotel*, T 460 4300. The opening of an 18-hole course at Jolly Beach was delayed until the second half of 1996. The Antigua Open is played at Cedar Valley in mid-March. Rental equipment available at both courses.

Many of the large hotels have **tennis** courts, the most prestigious of which are probably at *Half Moon Bay Hotel*, not open early 1996, T 463 2101. Also courts at the *Royal Antiguan Hotel*, T 462 3733, Deep Bay; *Hodges Bay Club*, T 462 2300; Temo Sports, English Harbour (sports complex with floodlit tennis courts, glass-backed squash courts, bar/bistro, equipment rental, open Mon-Sat 0700-2200, no credit cards, T 460 1781, VHF 68). *St James's Club* has floodlit courts, T 463 1113. There is a tennis and squash club open to the public next to the *Falmouth Harbour Beach Apartments*. The new Jolly Harbour development includes BBR Sportive, with lit tennis and squash courts (US$20/30 minutes) and a 25m swimming pool, open 0800-2100, food and drink available, T 462 6260, VHF Channel 68.

Riding is available through the hotels. Charlie's Horse Riding at Half Moon Bay offers trail rides, T 460 4372. Wadadli Riding Stables at Gambles Bluff, T 462 2721. *St James's Club* also arranges horseriding, T 463 1430. Spring Hill Riding Club, on the road to Rendezvous Bay, offers tuition from BHS qualified instructors, English style, floodlit schooling arena, cross country course, horses and ponies, beach rides, forest rides, picnic area, open daily from 0730, contact Janie Easton, T 460 1333.

Cricket is the national sport and Test Matches are played at the Recreation Ground. There are matches between Antiguan teams and against teams from neighbouring islands.

Horse racing takes place on public holidays at Cassada Park.

There is a Fitness Club in Hodges Bay, which offers aerobic classes, weight training rooms and other facilities (T 462 1540). The National Fitness Centre, off Old Parham Road behind the Price Waterhouse building, has a good gym, with weight and exercise machines, price negotiable for multiple visits. Open Mon-Fri 0600-1000, 1200-2000, Sat 0900-1400, aerobics classes in the evenings, T 462 3681.

Organized **hikes** are arranged frequently to historical and natural attractions and can be a good way of seeing the island. Once a month the Historical and Archaeological Society organize hikes free of charge, PO Box 103, St John's, T 462 1469. Hash House Harriers arrange hikes off the beaten track every other Sat at 1600, free of charge, contact David Owen, Hash Master, PO Box 124, St John's, T/F 462 2724, T 461 0853. For other walking and exploring, see **Tour operators** in **Information for travellers**.

FESTIVALS

Antigua's carnival is at the end of July and lasts until the first Tuesday in August. The main event is 'J'ouvert', or 'Juvé' morning when from 0400 people come into town dancing behind steel and brass bands. Hotels and airlines tend to be booked up well in advance. For information contact the Carnival Committee, High Street, St John's, T 462 0194. Barbuda has a smaller carnival in June, known as 'Caribana'. An annual jazz festival is held, usually in late May, with concerts at Fort James, the *Sandpiper Reef Hotel*, King's Casino and on the *Jolly Roger*. Contact the Tourist Office for a programme.

ST JOHN'S

Built around the largest of the natural harbours is **St John's**, the capital, with an estimated population of about 30,000. It is rather quiet and run-down but parts have been developed for tourism and the town is a mixture of the old and the new. Although parts of the town are tatty, it is generally safe to walk around even late at night. New boutiques, duty-free shops and restaurants are vying for custom. Redcliffe Quay is a picturesque area of restored historical buildings now full of souvenir shops and the only toy shop in town. Heritage Quay, opened in 1988, is a duty free shopping complex strategically placed to catch cruise ship visitors. It has a casino and a big screen satellite TV, a cool, pleasant place to have a drink. Most activity now takes place around these two quay developments, especially when there is a cruise ship in dock.

However, St John's does have interesting historical associations. Nelson served in Antigua as a young man for almost three years, and visited it again in 1805, during his long chase of Villeneuve which was to end with the Battle of Trafalgar. Some of the old buildings in St John's, including the Anglican Cathedral, have been damaged several times by earthquakes, the last one in 1974. A cathedral in St John's was first built in 1683, but replaced in 1745 and then again in 1843 after an earthquake, at which time it was built of stone. Its twin towers can be seen from all over St John's. It has a wonderfully cool interior lined with pitchpine timber. Donations requested.

The Museum and Archives at the former Court House in Long Street are worth a visit, both to see the exhibition of pre-Columbian and colonial archaeology and anthropology of Antigua and for the Court House building itself, first built in 1747, damaged by earthquakes in 1843 and 1974 but now restored. There is also Viv Richards' cricket bat, with which he scored the fastest century, various 'hands on' items and games. Entrance free, although donations requested; gift shop. Open Monday-Friday 1000-1500, Saturdays 1000-1300. (T 463 1060). You can also visit Viv Richards' childhood home on Viv Richards' Street. The Museum of Marine and Living Art, Gambles Terrace, opposite Princess Margaret School, T 462 1228, F 462 1187, exhibits of sea shells, shipwrecks and pre-Columbian history. Recommended weekly lectures, Thursday 1000, on the evolution of the earth and the formation of the continents and civilizations.

A short drive W of St John's are the ruins of Fort Barrington on a promontory at Goat Hill overlooking Deep Bay and the entrance to St John's Harbour. These fortifications were erected by Governor Burt, who gave up active duty in 1780 suffering from psychiatric disorders; a stone he placed in one of the walls at the Fort describes him grandly as 'Imperator and Gubernator' of the Carib Islands. The previous fortifications saw the most action in Antigua's history with the French and English battling for possession in the 17th century. At the other side of the harbour are the ruins of Fort James, from where you can get a good view of St John's. There was originally a fort on this site dating

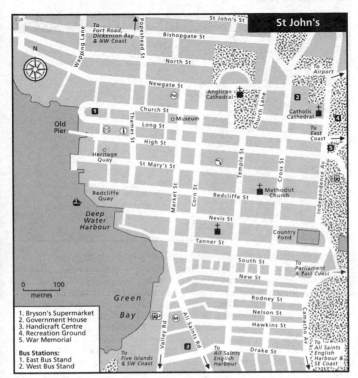

St John's

To Fort Road, Dickenson Bay & NW Coast

Popeshead St

St John's St

Wapping Lane

Bishopgate St

North St

To Airport

Newgate St

Church St

Thames St

Long St

High St

Anglican Cathedral

Church Lane

Catholic Cathedral

2

4

To East Coast

5

Old Pier

Museum

1

Pol

Heritage Quay

St Mary's St

Temple St

Cross St

Redcliffe Quay

Deep Water Harbour

Market St

Corn St

Redcliffe St

Methodist Church

Independence Av

Nevis St

Tanner St

Country Pond

South St

To Parliament & East Coast

New St

Green Bay

Valley Rd

All Saints Rd

Rodney St

Nelson St

Hawkins St

Camacho Av

To Five Islands & SW Coast

To All Saints English Harbour

Drake St

To All Saints English Harbour & SE Coast

3

0   100
metres

1. Bryson's Supermarket
2. Government House
3. Handicraft Centre
4. Recreation Ground
5. War Memorial

Bus Stations:
1. East Bus Stand
2. West Bus Stand

from 1675, but most of what can now be seen dates from 1749. To get there, head N out of St John's, turn W by *Barrymore Hotel* to the sea, then follow the road parallel to the beach to the end.

EXCURSIONS

On the other side of the island is **English Harbour**, which has become one of the world's most attractive yachting centres. Here 'Nelson's Dockyard' has been restored and is one of the most interesting historical monuments in the West Indies. It was designated a National Park in 1985 (Parks Commissioner, T 463-1379). Entrance US$1.60, children under 12 free. Souvenirs and T-shirts are on sale at the entrance. See *Admiral's Inn*, with its boat and mast yard, slipway and pillars still standing but which suffered earthquake damage in the nineteenth century. The *Copper and Lumber Store* is now a hotel bar and restaurant. There is a small museum, with gift shop in the same building. *Limey's Bar* has a good view of the harbour and is a nice place for a drink. Next to it is an art centre with work by local artists including Katie Shears, who specializes in flora and fauna. The Ralph A Aldridge shell collection in a wall case is fascinating, all the shells were found in Antiguan waters. On the quay are three large capstans, showing signs of wear and tear. Boat charters can be arranged from here; also a 20-30 minute cruise round the historic Dockyard for US$6 on *Horatio*, from outside the *Copper and Lumber*

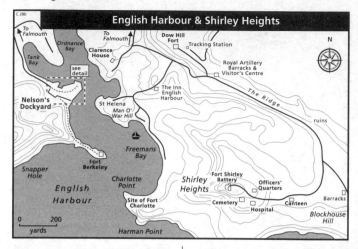

Store, depending on seasonal demand. A footpath leads round the bay to **Fort Berkeley** at the harbour mouth, well grazed by goats, wonderful views. Near the Dockyard, Clarence House still stands where the future King, William IV stayed when he served as a midshipman in the 1780s.

On the left of the road from English Harbour to Shirley Heights are the remains of the British Navy's magazines and a small branch road to the Dow Hill Interpretation Centre. There is a gift shop, restaurant, small museum with shell display and an audio visual room which puts on a display about every half hour on Antigua's history, highly recommended. Local guides also available.

At **Shirley Heights**, overlooking English Harbour, are the ruins of fortifications built in the 18th century with a wonderful view. Some buildings, like officers' quarters, are still standing, restored but roofless, which give an idea of their former grandeur. At the lookout point, or Battery, at the S end is a bar and restaurant. On Sundays a steel band plays 1500-1800, followed by reggae 1800-2200, very loud and popular, can be heard at the dockyard below. Barbecued burgers, chicken, ribs and salad. Great fun, recommended. An-

tiguans as well as tourists enjoy it. There is often some activity on Thursdays too.

Great George Fort, on Monk's Hill, above Falmouth Harbour (a 30-minute walk from the village of Liberta, and from Cobb's Cross near English Harbour) has been less well preserved. There is a museum of pre-Columbian artefacts in the Dow Hill tracking station building (formerly used in connection with the US Apollo space programme). It can be visited by prior arrangement, or on Thursday afternoons there are tours, starting from Nelson's Dockyard and taking in Dow Hill (check the details at Nicholson's travel agency). If advance notice is given, the Antigua Rum Distillery welcomes visitors.

Fig Tree Drive between Old Road and the Catholic church on the road going N from Liberta, is a steep, winding, bumpy road, through mountainous rainforest. It is greener and more scenic than most of the island, but the rainforest is scanty and can not be compared with islands like Dominica. If travelling by bicycle make sure you go *down* Fig Tree Drive from the All Saints to Liberta road, heading towards Old Road, the hill is very steep.

Boggy Peak, in the SW, is the highest

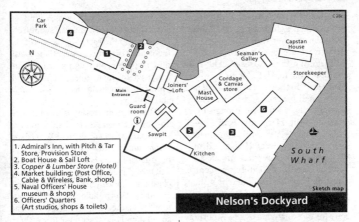

1. Admiral's Inn, with Pitch & Tar Store, Provision Store
2. Boat House & Sail Loft
3. Copper & Lumber Store (Hotel)
4. Market building; (Post Office, Cable & Wireless, Bank, shops)
5. Naval Officers' House museum & shops)
6. Officers' Quarters (Art studios, shops & toilets)

Nelson's Dockyard

point on the island and from the top you can get wonderful views over to Guadelupe, St Kitts, Nevis and Montserrat. It is a good walk up, or you can take a car. From Urlings walk (or take minibus) about ½-¾ mile in the direction of Old Town. There is a clear track on the left (ask the bus driver to drop you off there) which runs very straight then ascends quite steeply. When you get to the top, walk round the fence surrounding the Cable and Wireless buildings to get a good view in all directions. It takes over an hour to walk up (signs say it is a private road) and you are advised not to wander around alone.

A recommended excursion to the E coast, if you have a car, is to take the road out to the airport from St John's. Do not enter the airport but take the right fork which runs alongside it. After about 1½ miles take a right turn down a small road to St George's Church, on Fitches Creek Bay, built in 1687 in a beautiful location, interesting gravestones. From there, follow the rough road round the coast to **Parham**, which is interesting for being the first British settlement on the island and for having an unusual octagonal church, St Peter's, which dates from the 1840s. Lovely flamboyant trees surround the church and enhance its attractiveness. From

Parham take the road due S and then E at the petrol station through Pares to Willikies. On this road, just past Pares Village, is a sign to **Betty's Hope**, a ruined sugar estate built in 1650 and owned by the Codrington family from 1674-1944. Restoration was carried out by the Antigua Museum in St John's and it was officially opened in 1995. One of the twin windmills can actually be seen working, making it the only operational 18th century windmill in the Caribbean. There is a Visitors' Centre (open Tues-Sat 1000-1600) which tells the story of life on a sugar plantation. Well worth a visit. For a guided tour contact the Antigua Museum, T 462 3946 ext 14/16.

After Willikies the road is signed to the *Pineapple Beach Club* at Long Bay, but before you get there, take a right turn down a small road, which deteriorates to a bumpy track, to **Devil's Bridge** at Indian Town Point. The area on the Atlantic coast is a national park where rough waves have carved out the bridge and made blowholes, not easily visible at first, but quite impressive when the spray breaks through. Good view of Long Bay and the headland.

Returning through Willikies to Glanvilles, take a left turn shortly after St Stephen's Church down a small road S past Collins Dam. When you meet up with the main road (petrol station) turn left and then right towards St Phillips. The scenery after this village is quite attractive, there are several ruined sugar mills dotting the landscape. The road continues on to Half Moon Bay and tracks lead up the coast to Mill Reef and many small beaches and jetties. Alternatively, take a left turn through Freetown to visit **Harmony Hall** (T 460 4120), Brown's Bay Mill, at Nonsuch Bay, a restored Great House and mill which has been converted into a Caribbean art and craft exhibition centre. Open daily 1000-1800. There is a shop, bar and restaurant (Sunday barbecue, dinner by reservation only, rec), and a jetty for those arriving by sea. Moorings also available for anchoring in the bay. Harmony Hall broadcasts a daily weather service at 0900 on VHF Channel 68. There are two villas for rent with use of swimming pool.

Warning

Finding your way around is not easy: street names are rarely in evidence. The Ordnance Survey map, US$7.50, is recommended if you are exploring the island. It is a little dated, but there is nothing better. A map hand drawn by Brian Dyde is available from several locations and is adequate for driving around.

BARBUDA

Some 30 miles to the N is Barbuda, a flat coral island some 68 miles square, one of the two island dependencies of Antigua. The population is about 1,500 and most of them live in the only village on the island, Codrington, which stands on the edge of the lagoon.

The people of Barbuda are unusually tall, descended from the Corramante tribe in Africa and used by Codrington in his experiments in slave breeding. Barbuda has some excellent beaches and its seas are rich with all types of crustaceans and tropical fish. Palaster Reef is a marine reserve to protect the reef and

the shipwrecks (there are around 60 ships documented). You can swim from the beach to the reef. This is one of the few islands in the area where there is still much wild life, although much of it introduced by man: duck, guinea fowl, plover, pigeon, wild deer, pigs, horses and donkeys.

There is an impressive frigate bird colony in the mangroves in Codrington Lagoon, particularly on Man of War Island where hundreds of birds mate and breed in August-December. Local fishermen will take you out there; you can get quite close for photography or just to watch. Popular with ornithologists working nine months of the year in Antarctica, who spend their holidays coming to see 'their' frigate birds in Codrington Lagoon. Ask the guide to drop you at Palm Bay on the W side of the lagoon, and pick you up 4-5 hours later.

Meanwhile walk the 17 miles of beaches, up N or down S, but bring a hat and sunscreen. There are no beach bars or vendors, you will probably be the only person for miles. There is no shade except around Palm Beach where there is a lot of litter. The island has a Martello Tower and fort. The tower is 56 feet high and once had nine guns to defend the SW approach. It now has a swarm of killer bees in the cellar – take care. From Codrington, River Road runs 3 miles to Palmetto Point (with beautiful pink sand beaches), past Cocoa Point and on to Spanish Point, a half-mile finger of land that divides the Atlantic from the Caribbean Sea. There is a small ruin of a lookout post here and the most important Arawak settlements found in Barbuda.

One of Barbuda's main sources of income is the mining of sand. In 1993 a High Court injunction against the mining led to a severe cash crisis and public employees were not paid for several months. The injunction was imposed pending the resolution of a dispute between the Government and the island council over who has authority for sand mining. Mining of sand at Palmetto

Point allegedly damaged a pure water supply. The Minister of Agriculture and two businessmen were convicted of breaching the injunction, but the Minister was subsequently pardoned by the Governor General.

Barbuda is being developed as a tourist resort with attractions for snorkellers and skin-divers such as exploring old wrecks. The elkhorn coral and staghorn coral formations are very impressive. Take your own scuba equipment. Snorkelling equipment is available but is more expensive than on Antigua.

Island information – Barbuda
● Accommodation
There are two hotels, two villas and a few guesthouses, although more are planned. *Coco Point Lodge*, which charges US$750 double per night inc all meals and drinks and airfare from Antigua, is quiet and exclusive, islanders and non-guests are not admitted. In the USA T 212-980 1416. The *K-Club*, owned and designed by Italians, opened in 1991 Is even more expensive, 28 rooms, from US$1,100 a night inc local airfare, with its own 9-hole golf course (the grass was laid on soil cleared from the mangrove swamp so there are problems now with salt) as well as water sports, welcomes islanders and non-residents, open mid-Nov-end-May, no children under 12, T 460 0300, F 460 0305, in the UK T 0171 936 5000, or through Unique Hotels, T 01453 835801, F 01453 835525. **A3** *Nedd's Guest House* in Codrington, T 460 0059, has clean and airy rooms upstairs, call prior to arrival and fix room rate with Mr McArthur Nedd, use of kitchen, minimart downstairs, bakery just behind the guest house in the next street, no road name signs. Houses are also available for rent at about US$35-70, phone Evans at the car rental for help.

● Places to eat
The *Lagoon Café*, at the jetty where you embark for boat trips, is a night spot run by Norris Morris Harris, who also cooks at the *Jolly Beach*. Dim table lights, food difficult to see. If you prefer to have lobster or fish with a family, ask Mr Nedd to call George for you. Fix the price beforehand and George and his family will cook. Do not expect many 'mod cons' on Barbuda. Several small snack bars, ask locally. The *Codrington Tavern* in town is a nice spot

for meals and refreshments, run by Eric and Maxine Bunton, who run tours of all sorts and can arrange any request, T 460 0078.

● Transport
Excellent 1:25,000 maps should be available from the Codrington post office, or from the map shop in Jardine Court, St Mary's, St John's (good 1:50,000 maps of Antigua as well). It is safer to get one before you arrive in Barbuda, you can not rely on anything being in stock there. It is possible to hire jeeps (US$45/day inc insurance, from Eric Bunton, T 460 0078, or Williams and Thomas Car Rental, T 460 0047, on main road down S to Martello Tower) or horses in Codrington, otherwise everywhere is a long hot walk, so take liquid refreshment with you. Easily reached by air (taking 10 minutes, US$45 return), or (with some difficulty and at a high price, US$150) by boat from St John's. Charter boats do day trips but you will not see much of Barbuda. There are two airports. The main one is just S of Codrington, to which LIAT has regular flights, while Four Island Airways or Carib Aviation will arrange charters and day trips. The second airport is near Cocoa Point and only serves *Coco Point*. Day tours from Antigua include the Bird Sanctuary, Highland House, the Caves and the Martello Tower, contact Barbara Japal, Caribrep, T 462 0818, F 462 3529.

REDONDA

Antigua's second dependency, 35 miles to the SW and at half a mile square, little more than a rocky volcanic islet, is uninhabited. Columbus sighted the island on 12 November 1493 and named it after a church in Cadiz called Santa María de Redonda. He did not land, however, and thus did not formally claim the island. Neither did anyone else until 1865 when Matthew Dowdy Shiel, an Irish sea-trader from Montserrat, celebrated the birth of a long-awaited son by leading an expedition of friends to Redonda and claiming it as his kingdom. In 1872, the island was annexed by Britain and came under the jurisdiction of the colony of Antigua, despite protests from the Shiels. The Title of King was not disputed, however, and has survived to this day. The island was never inhabited although for some years guano was extracted by the Redonda Phosphate Company until the works were blown away by a hurricane.

In 1880 MD Shiel abdicated in favour of his son, Matthew Phipps Shiel, who became King Felipe of Redonda but emigrated to the UK where he was educated and became a prolific and popular novelist. His most well-known novel was *The Purple Cloud* (1901), which was later made into a film, *The World, the Flesh and the Devil*, starring Harry Belafonte. On his death in 1947 he appointed as his literary executor and successor to the throne, his friend John Gawsworth, the poet, who became Juan, third King of Redonda, but continuing to live in London. His reign was notable for his idea of an 'intellectual aristocracy' of the realm of Redonda and he conferred titles on his literary friends, including Victor Gollancz, the publisher, JB Priestley, Dorothy L Sayers and Lawrence Durrell. This eccentric pastime hit a crisis when declining fortunes and increasing time spent in the pub sparked a rash of new titles to all and sundry, a number of abdications in different pubs, and the succession was disputed. On one occasion, King Juan abdicated in 1967 in favour of his friend, Arthur John Roberts, who took the title of Juan II. He formed a Shiel Society and set up a charitable trust fund to assist young writers. However, controversy surrounded his accession as Mathew Phipps Shiel had left John Gawsworth the crown "as his possession, to be confirmed by him on his death unto such of his blood as he appoints". Abdication was not allowed. Not withstanding this minor detail, in 1989 King Juan II abdicated in favour of his friend and supporter, William Leonard Gates, an historian, lecturer and writer, who took the title of Leo, Fifth King of Redonda. His aim is to keep alive the Kingdom of Redonda and perpetuate the memory of M P Shiel, the novelist, while still fending off potential usurpers of his crown.

The other major claimant to the throne is the novelist Jon Wynne-Tyson, the literary executor of Gawsworth and Shiel. He is known as the 'Reluctant Monarch', but the members of his court (mostly the survivors of the Gawsworth reign) insist that by inheriting the crown on the death in 1970, rather than the abdication, of Gawsworth, his claim is paramount. He has also made history by visiting Redonda, the first monarch to do so since 1880.

Meanwhile, on Redonda, all is much the same for the goats, lizards and sea birds, who live an undisturbed life apart from the occasional bird watcher who might come to find the burrowing owl, now extinct on Antigua.

Information for travellers

don't sit under the tree in the rain as the dripping oil from the leaves causes blisters.

Some beaches, particularly those on the W coast, get jelly fish at certain times of the year, eg July/August.

MONEY

● **Currency**

Eastern Caribbean dollars are used, at a rate of EC\$2.70 = US\$1. It is advisable to change some currency at the airport on arrival. The airport bank is open 0900-1500, Mon-Thur, closes at 1330 on Fri just as American Airlines come in from New York, closed when BWIA flight comes in from Europe. US dollars are accepted in most places, but no one will know the exchange rate of other currencies. The conventional rate of exchange if you want to pay in US dollars is EC\$2.50=US\$1, so it is worth changing money in a bank. Credit cards are accepted, especially Visa and American Express, but small restaurants will take only cash or TCs. Always verify whether hotels, taxis etc are quoting you US or EC dollars, you can be cheated. Take care not to get left with excess EC\$ on departure, you will not be able to exchange them for another currency except at a very poor rate with a taxi driver.

BEFORE TRAVELLING

● **Documents**

A valid onward ticket is necessary. American, Canadian and British nationals need only proof of citizenship. Passports but not visas are required by nationals of other Commonwealth countries and British Dependent Territories, if their stay does not exceed 6 months. The following countries need valid passports but not visas: Argentina, Austria, Belgium, Brazil, Chile, Denmark, Finland, France, Germany, Greece, Ireland, Italy, Japan, Liechtenstein, Luxembourg, Malta, Mexico, Monaco, Netherlands, Norway, Peru, Portugal, Spain, Suriname, Sweden, Switzerland, Turkey and Venezuela. Nationals of all other countries require visas, unless they are in transit for less than 24 hrs. Visitors must satisfy immigration officials that they have enough money for their stay. You will not be allowed through Immigration without somewhere to stay. The Tourist Office can help you and you can always change your mind later.

● **Climate**

Antigua is a dry island with average rainfall of about 45 ins a year and although Sept-Nov is considered the rainy season, the showers are usually short. Temperatures range from 73°F (23°C) to 85°F (30°C) between winter and summer and the trade winds blow constantly.

● **Health**

Tiny sandflies, known locally as 'Noseeums' often appear on the beaches in the late afternoon and can give nasty stings. Keep a good supply of repellent and make sure you wash off all sand to avoid taking them with you from the beach.

Do not eat the little green apples of the manchineel tree, as they are poisonous, and

GETTING THERE

AIR

V C Bird airport, some 4½ miles from St John's, is the centre for air traffic in the area.

From Europe: British Airways (3 direct flights a week from London Gatwick, connections with Barbados, Port of Spain and St Lucia, T 462 0876/9), BWIA (1 flight a week from London Heathrow, 1 from Zurich), Condor (1 flight a week direct from Frankfurt), Air France (once a week from Paris).

From North America: American Airlines (from New York, T 462 0950), Continental (from Newark, NJ), BWIA (from New York, Miami) and Air Canada from Toronto, T 462 1147.

From the Caribbean: there are frequent air services to neighbouring islands (Anguilla, Barbados, Barbuda, Dominica, Martinique, Grenada, Jamaica, Montserrat, Nevis, Guadeloupe, Trinidad and Tobago, St Croix, St Kitts, St Lucia, St Maarten, St Thomas, St Vincent, Puerto Rico, Tortola) operated by LIAT (T 462 3142/3), BWIA (T 462 0262/3), Continental, American Airlines, BWIA, Cardinal

Airlines, Montserrat Airways. Carib Aviation arranges charters to neighbouring islands in planes carrying 5, 6 or 9 passengers and can often work out cheaper and more convenient than using LIAT. The office is at the airport, T 462 3147, 0800-1700, after office hours T 461 1650. They will meet incoming flights if you are transferring to another island, and make sure you make your return connection. Also day tours. The flight to Montserrat takes 18 mins. Montserrat Airways runs a charter shuttle service on a first come first served basis 0700-1800. LIAT fare to Montserrat is US$68 return, plus tax, to St Kitts US$100 return, or you can get a ticket, Antigua-St Kitts- Montserrat- Antigua for about US$160 inc all departure taxes.

SEA

● **Ports of entry**
(Own flag). All yachts must clear in and obtain a Cruising Permit in Antigua but may clear out of either Antigua or at the C & I office in Barbuda. Customs and Immigration offices are at English Harbour, Crabbs Marina, St John's and Jolly Harbour.

● **Boat documents**
Entry fees are US$2 for boats up to 20 ft, US$4 for 21 ft-40 ft, US$6 for 41 ft-80 ft. Monthly cruising permits are US$8 for boats up to 40 ft, US$10 for 41 ft-80 ft. There are additional fees for anchoring or stern to dockage in English Harbour and Falmouth, an EC$5 charge per person plus electricity and water used. Dinghies must show lights at night and barbecues are prohibited in the harbour.

ON ARRIVAL

● **Banks**
Scotia Bank, Barclays Bank, Royal Bank of Canada, Bank of Antigua, Antigua and Barbuda Investment Bank, Antigua Commercial Bank. Mosts banks take Mastercard and Visa. The Swiss American Bank of Antigua is open on Sat morning (also a branch in St John's). A tax of 1% is levied on all foreign exchange transactions but there may be additional charges on TCs. Casinos will change TCs without a fee. American Express is at Antours near Heritage Quay, staff helpful and friendly.

● **Embassies and consulates**
The British High Commission is at the Price Waterhouse Centre (PO Box 483), 11 Old Parham Road, St Johns, T 462 0008/9, F 462

2806. The US embassy in St John's was closed in the 1993/94 fiscal year; the visa section is in Barbados.

● **Hours of business**
Banks: 0800-1400 Mon-Wed; 0800-1300 Thur; 1500-1700 Fri. Bank of Antigua opens Sat 0800-1200. **Shops**: 0800-1200, 1300-1600 Mon-Sat. Thur is early closing day for most non-tourist shops. On Sun everything closes except churches and Kings Casino, although *Kentucky Fried Chicken* opens in the afternoon.

● **Official time**
Atlantic standard time, 4 hours behind GMT, 1 ahead of EST.

● **Public holidays**
New Year's Day, Good Friday, Easter Monday, Labour Day (first Mon in May), Whit Monday (end-May), Queen's Birthday (second Sat in June), Caricom Day, beginning of July (whole island closes down), Carnival (first Mon and Tues in Aug), Independence Day (1 Nov), Christmas Day and Boxing Day.

● **Security**
Normal precautions against theft should be taken. Vendors on the beach can be a problem but in 1995 joint army and police patrols were deployed on beaches to remove 'unlicensed vendors, vagrants and loiterers' after the fatal shooting of a holiday maker during a beach robbery. Generally, however, despite the poverty, Antigua is free from hassle for the traveller.

● **Shopping**
Market day in St John's is Sat. The market building is at the S end of Market Street but there are goods on sale all around. Avoid the middle of the day when it is very hot. In season, there is a good supply of fruit and vegetables, which are easy to obtain on the island. The Epicurean Supermarket, at Woods Estate outside St John's is a large, modern, fully stocked supermarket. The main supermarket in St John's is Bryson's, on Long Street. Hutchinson's is a drive-in supermarket on Old Parham Road beyond the roundabout. Most grocery stores open 0800-2200, although many close at 1300 on Thur. You can buy fish from the fishing boats at the back of the Casino or from Caribbean Seafoods in Cassada Gardens near the horse racetrack (T 462 6113), large selection of cleaned and ready to cook seafood, freshly caught (by their own fishing boat), vacuum packed and quick frozen. Heritage Quay (has

public toilets) and Redcliffe Quay are shopping complexes with expensive duty-free shops in the former, and boutiques. There are several shops on St Mary Street and others nearby, which stock clothing, crafts and other items from neighbouring islands, eg Caribelle Batik. Some tourist shops offer 10% reductions to locals: they compensate by overcharging tourists. Duty free shops at the airport are more expensive than normal shops in town. The Map Shop (St Mary Street) carries a good selection of Caribbean literature plus reference books and guides to history, culture, fauna and flora of the Caribbean. PC Book Revue, further up the road has lots of old issues of magazines.

● **Tipping**
Tips for taxi drivers are usually 10% of the fare. Porters expect EC$1/bag.

● **Voltage**
220 volts usually, but 110v in some areas, check before using your own appliances. Many hotels have transformers.

ON DEPARTURE

● **Departure tax**
There is an airport departure tax of EC$30.

Occasional boat services to St Kitts and Dominica; see boat captains at Fisherman's Wharf. There is a cargo boat to Dominica once a week and you can arrange a passage through Vernon Edwards Shipping Company on Thames Street; very basic facilities, no toilet.

ACCOMMODATION

There is a 10% service charge and 8.5% government tax at all hotels.

There are hotels, resorts and apartments all round the island and more are being built all the time. We have not space to mention them all, this is a selection of those on which we have received comments from correspondents. The greatest concentration of developments is in the area around St John's, along the coast to the W and also to the N in a clockwise direction to the airport. A second cluster of places to stay is around English Harbour and Falmouth Harbour in the SE of the island. Many may be closed September-October in preparation for the winter season. Full lists of hotels, apartments, villas and guesthouses should be available from the Tourist Office at the airport, although it is not always easy to get hold of. The Tourist Office will book you a hotel room on arrival if you have not already done so. There are lots of self-catering apartments available all round the island but a common complaint is that sufficient provisions are not available locally and you have to go into St John's for shopping.

Price guide

L1	over US$200	L2	US$151-200
L3	US$101-150	A1	US$81-100
A2	US$61-80	A3	US$46-60
B	US$31-45	C	US$21-30
D	US$12-20	E	US$7-11
F	US$4-6	G	up to US$3

In St John's: **L2-L3** *Heritage Hotel*, Heritage Quay, PO Box 1532, St John's, T 462 1247/8, caters to business travellers, discounts available; **A1-A2** *Barrymore*, on Fort Road, on the outskirts of the town, get a room away from Fort Road traffic, rooms basic but clean, T 462 1055, F 462-4062, PO Box 244; **A1-A2** *Courtsland*, Upper Gambles, PO Box 403, T 462 1395; **A3** *Joe Mike's Hotel*, in Corn Alley and Nevis St, T 462 3244 or 1142, F 462 6056, PO Box 136, special rates can be negotiated but not by phone, rooms OK, no balconies, weak a/c, no food but downstairs are fast food, restaurant and bar, casino, icecream parlour, cocktail lounge, beauty salon and mini-mart; **A3** *Roslyn's Guest House*, Fort Road, PO Box 161, T 462 0762, 3 double rooms, 1 triple room, 10 mins walk to shops, 15 mins' walk to beach, big garden with mango trees, friendly lady owner, rec; **A3** *Spanish Main Guest House*, Independence Avenue, opp the cricket oval, originally house of the American Consul, cheaper out of season, probably the best place to stay in town, T 462 0660: **A3-B** *Murphy's Apartments*, PO Box 491, All Saints Road, T 461 1183, run by Elaine Murphy, apartments somewhat aged, no breakfast, check price twice; **B** *Tyrone's Guesthouse*, All Saints Road, close to market and bus station, T 462 3554, T/F 462 1442, nice, clean, friendly, fan, balcony, downstairs supermarket and restaurant; **C** *Miami*, near market on Main Road, PO Box 300, T 462 0975, with bath, grubby; **C** *Palm View Guest House*, 57 St Mary's Street, no sign, T 462 1299, friendly, basic, no fan, can be hot, clean, good; **C** *Pigottsville Guest House*, at Clare Hall, PO Box 521, hurricane repairs under way 1996, no signs, about 2 miles from the airport and within easy walking distance of St John's, 20 rooms, T 462 0592; **D** *Montgomery*

Hotel, Tindale Road, usually plenty of room except during carnival and cricket matches, central but not a very nice part of town, noisy roosters across the street, scruffy and basic, small rooms, shared bath, rats in downstairs rooms, no water after midnight, cable TV, T 462 1164; **D-E** *Main Road Guest House*, near the market, about the cheapest but very basic, no fan, noisy, mice visit at night, take insect repellent, run by elderly Aunt Vi and her friendly family.

Outside St John's: **L1-L3** *Barrymore Beach Club* on Runaway Bay, 2 miles from St John's, which has rooms and apartments, rec, clean, comfortable, T 462 4101, F 462 4140, on 1½ miles of white sand beach; **L1-A2** *Runaway Beach Club*, on Runaway Bay, friendly, beachfront cabins, rooms or villas, 110V electricity, excellent beach restaurant, *The Lobster Pot*, T 462 1318, F 462 4172, PO Box 874; **L1-L3** *Siboney Beach Club*, good, small, PO Box 222, T 462 0806, F 462 3356; **L1** *Coral Sands* beach front cottages at Runaway Bay, 2-bedroomed or 3-bedroomed, reservations through Mrs Sonia King, PO Box 34, St John's, T 461 0925; **A1-A2** *Sand Haven Hotel*, PO Box 405, rebuilding 1996, on clean, sandy beach with shade from palm trees and sea grape, T 462-4491, 5-10 min beach walk from *Barrymore Beach Apartments*, vehicle hire needed. The **L1-L2** *Royal Antiguan*, 3 miles from St John's, depressing drive through tatty suburbs, 270 rooms, high rise, comfortable, good facilities, quiet in summer, casino, pool, tennis etc, PO Box 1322, T 462 3733, F 462 3732. Further round the coast **L1-L2** *Hawksbill Beach Resort*, 4 miles from St John's, 37 acres and 4 lovely beaches, good food, pleasant rooms, friendly staff, PO Box 108, T 462 0301, F 462 1515, tennis, table tennis, pool, watersports, 99 rooms.

At Dickenson Bay: **L1-A2** *Antigua Village* has villas with free watersports from a studio or beach front 2-bedroomed villa, there is a small store for provisions, nothing exciting, T 462 2930, F 462 0375, PO Box 649, St John's. **L1** *Sandals Antigua*, PO Box 147, T 462 0267, F 462 4135, couples only, all-inclusive, 189 comfortable rooms, several restaurants, diving, waterskiing, other watersports, tennis, jacuzzi, 4 pools. **L1-L3** *Rex Halcyon Cove Beach Resort and Casino*, PO Box 251, T 462 0256-8, F 462 0271, on the beach with full watersports facilities inc diving and fishing, and tennis.

On the N coast: **L1-L3** *Blue Waters*, T 462 0290, F 462 0293, P O Box 256, not open 1996, for sale; **A2-A3** *The Vienna Inn*, Hodges Bay, T 462 3554, T/F 462 1442, Austrian owned, nice, clean, fan, 8 rooms, 2 apartments, beach, swimming pool, garden, restaurant with creole and Austrian food.

In the southwest: **A1-A2** *Jolly Harbour Beach Resort, Marina and Golf Club*, PO Box 1793, T 462 6166, F 462 6167, a/c, 30 rooms, suites, with plenty of activities, watersports, pool, tennis, squash, exterior stark and in need of landscaping; **L1** *Club Antigua*, Jolly Beach, PO Box 744, St John's, T 462 8400/2, all-inclusive inc watersports, adjacent to marina, visitors may use all facilities inc food and drink for US$70 pp/day, US$40/half day.

At English Harbour: **L3-A2** *Admiral's Inn*, PO Box 713, T 460 1027, F 460 1534, 14 rooms of varying sizes in restored 17th century building, very pleasant, transport to the beach, complimentary sunfish and snorkelling equipment, excellent location, good food; **L1-A1** *Copper and Lumber Store* (restored dockyard building) PO Box 184, T 460 1058, F 460 1529, studios and suites available, boat transport to nearby beaches; **L1-L3** *The Inn at English Harbour*, set in 10 acres with lovely white sand beach, watersports provided, tennis and golf nearby, PO Box 187, St John's, T 460 1014, F 460 1603.

At Falmouth Harbour: **L3-A2** *Catamaran Hotel and Marina*, on narrow beach, friendly, T 460 1036, F 460 1506, PO Box 958; **L3-A1** *Falmouth Harbour Beach Apartments* (same management as *Admiral's Inn*) good value, 28 hillside or beach front studio apartments on or near private beach, very clean, friendly staff, inc use of boats and other watersports equipment, all apartments have lovely view of harbour, PO Box 713, St John's, T 460 1027/1094, F 460 1534.

In the east: **L1** *Half Moon Bay Hotel*, good setting, closed because of hurricane damage, may reopen winter 1996/97 with tennis, eventually the 9-hole golf course will be reclaimed, PO Box 144, St John's, T 460 4300, F 460 4306.

On Long Island: **L1** *Jumby Bay Resort*, secluded, luxurious, all inclusive and incredibly expensive, PO Box 243, St John's, T 462 6000, F 462 6020, US reservations: T 800 437 0049 or (212) 819 9490. The resort does not accept credit cards.

If you are changing planes and have to stop over, take a taxi into St John's where the accommodation is much better than near the airport. **A2** *The Airport Hotel*, T 462 1191, where some airlines dump you if a missed connection is their fault, is grim and noisy, very depressing after the stress of missing a plane, do not rely on an early morning wake up call although transport to the airport is usually prompt; **A1-A2** *Antigua Mill*, near the airport, T 462 3044, F 462 1500, P O Box 319, 22 rooms, a/c, TV, phone, pool, restaurant.

● **Camping**
Camping is illegal.

FOOD AND DRINK

In addition to a wide selection of imported delicacies served in the larger hotels, local specialities, found in smaller restaurants in St John's, often very reasonable, should never be missed: saltfish (traditionally eaten at breakfast in a tomato and onion sauce), pepper-pot with fungi (a kind of cornmeal dumpling), goat water (hot goat stew), shellfish (in reality the local name for trunk fish), conch stew and the local staple, chicken and rice. Ducana is made from grated sweet potato and coconut, mixed with pumpkin, sugar and spices and boiled in a banana leaf. Oranges are green, while the native pineapple is black. Tropical fruits and vegetables found on other Caribbean islands are also found here: breadfruit, cristophine, dasheen, eddo, mango, guava and pawpaw (papaya). Locally made Sunshine ice cream, American style, is available in most supermarkets. Imported wines and spirits are reasonably priced but local drinks (fruit and sugar cane juice, coconut milk, and Antiguan rum punches and swizzles, ice cold) must be experienced. The local Cavalier rum is a light golden colour, usually used for mixes. Beer costs US$2-2.50 in bars, although street bars in the market are cheaper. cases of beer can be bought at good prices from Wadadli Brewery on Crabbs peninsula. There are no licensing restrictions. Tap water is safe all over the island. Most luxury hotels provide rain water.

● **Places to eat**
If you are planning to eat out in hotels, you need to allow at least US$300 pp per week, but it is possible to eat much more cheaply in the local restaurants in St John's. A 7¾% tax on all meals and drinks is added to your bill. Restaurants tend to move, close down or change names frequently. In St John's, *Sugar House* Lower Church Street, local food, light lunches and salads, popular, T 462 0016, open for 3 meals. *Pizzas on the Quay* (Big Banana Holding Co), at Redcliffe Quay, very popular at lunch time, salads and sandwiches as well as pizzas, rec, T 462 2621, open Mon-Sat 0830-2300; *Julian's* on Church and Corn Alley, lovely courtyard setting of an old home, English chef provides delicious lunch and dinner, T 462 4766; *Chutneys* on Fort Road serves good Indian food (Indian chef), T 462 2977; *La Dolce Vita* makes own pasta, 4-course dinner EC$110, service and wine extra, open daily 1100-2400, T 462 2016; *Redcliffe Tavern*, good lunch, EC$17-35, evening main course EC$25-40, open Mon-Sat 0800-2330, T 461 4557; *Hemingway's*, drink, lunch or dinner West Indian style upstairs on cool veranda overlooking Lower Mary St at entrance to Heritage Quay, open Mon-Sat from 0830, main course EC$24-60, T 462 2763; *Home*, Gambles Terrace, T 461 7651, 20-min walk from tourist area but worth it, Caribbean haute cuisine, Italian pasta dishes, exotic desserts, about EC$80-100 pp, very elegant but no stiff formality, friendly atmosphere, service excellent, welcoming to families, run by Antiguan Carl Thomas and his German wife Kita, rec, open from 1500, last orders 2230; *Lemon Tree*, on Long Street, also rec but management reported to be rude, T 462 1969, closed Sun; *The Hub*, Long St and Soul Alley, opp the Museum, open daily from 0730 until 2200 for drinks and meals, live jazz on Sat night, slow service, local cuisine, pleasant atmosphere T 462 0616; *Talk of the Town*, Lower Redcliffe Street, opp Benjie's Store, lively but good place for a cheap filling lunch, EC$15-20, local dishes only, popular with working Antiguans, open Mon-Sat 0700-2300, no credit cards, T 462 0535; *Calypso Café*, Redcliffe Street, West Indian, seafood, EC$20-30, best pumpkin soup anywhere, strong Italian coffee, open Mon-Sat 1030-1700, T 462 1965; *Smoking Joe's*, opp the cricket ground, for barbecued ribs, chicken, etc, Joe is a local calypsonian; *Fisherman's Wharf* at Heritage Quay, good sandwiches, burgers and pizzas, pleasant setting, cheap, EC$40 for dinner for 2 takeaway and delivery available, open Mon-Sat from 1100, Sun from 1800, happy hour 1800-1900, T 462 2248; *O'Grady's*, Nevis Street, good for pub grub, darts and pool. For fast food lovers there is *Kentucky Fried Chicken* on High and Thames Streets, and a second branch on Fort Road, T 462 1973; *Pizza Hut* also on Fort Road.

For cheap (EC$8), good set meals, go to the restaurant by the fishing boat harbour. By the gas station at the start of the airport road is the well thought of *Best Health* vegetarian restaurant, T 462 1933. In the Hodges Bay area, near the airport, *Le Bistro*, excellent French food, dinner only, closed Mon (T 462 3881); *The Vienna Inn*, see **Accommodation**, creole seafood, Austrian food, special Austrian desserts, rec. Near St James' Club, *Alberto's*, choice dining spot frequented by ex-pat 'locals' plus celebritites like Eric Clapton, Timothy Dalton, Italian run, open air tropical setting, fresh seafood and pasta always available, rec, T 460 3007, reservations essential. At Jolly Harbour marine complex there is an Italian *trattoria*, *Al Porto*, pasta, pizzas, seafood in al fresco setting, poor service, meals from US$10, open daily lunch and dinner, closed 1500-1900, T 462 7695; *Peter's* next door, excellent, barbecued fresh fish and lobster, prices from EC$15, rec.

At English Harbour, there is a restaurant and bar on Shirley Heights, steel band and barbecue every Sun afternoon (See **Excursions**). *Admiral's Inn*, Nelson's Dockyard, breakfast (slow service but good value, rec), lunch and dinner (limited selection but good, slightly overpriced) every day, yachtsman's dinner EC$40, (T 460 1027, closed Sept). *The Copper and Lumber Store* is overpriced, you pay for the 'atmosphere', which is not to everybody's taste and the portions are small although the food is excellent. At *Galleon Beach Club*, English Harbour, *Colombo's* Italian restaurant, rec for good food but expensive, open 1200-1500, 1900-2230, reggae band Wed (T 460 1452). *Abracadabra* just outside Nelson's Dockyard, lively video bar, live music some evenings, Italian and Continental dishes, open every evening, closed Sept-Oct, T 460 1732; *Mario's Pizzeria*, delicious pizza baked in stone ovens, also famous for fresh bread, T 460 1318; *Cathrine's Café* at the Antigua Slipway in Nelson's Dockyard, French chef, divine crêpes, quiches, assorted salads, lovely setting right on water, open daily, breakfast and lunch only, highly rec; *Southern Cross*, expensive Italian restaurant upstairs on newly constructed jetty off Antigua Yacht Club, closed in summer; *Dougie's*, on main road in English Harbour, popular, casual restaurant on open air balcony overlooking Falmouth Harbour, bar, pool hall, 3 tables, chicken wings, Mexican, burgers, daily specials from US$6,

open from 1830 daily, from 1200 Sat, Sun with Sun brunch and roast dinner special, T 460 1231. Between English and Falmouth Harbours, *Le Cap Horn*, pizzeria, Argentine Churrasco steak, lobster, some French dishes, great food, open 1830-2300, T 460 1194. At Falmouth Harbour *G & T's* at the Antigua Yacht Club provides a moderately priced dinner on most nights of the week, though it is livelier at weekends, barbecued burgers, EC$20, T 460 3278.

In the E, *Harmony Hall* (see **Excursions** above), T 460 4120, VHF channel 68, superb setting, food imaginative and good, rec, lunch and snacks 1200-1600, open 1000-1800, lobster, shellfish, Sun barbecue; *Claude's* at *Brown Bay Villas* near Harmony Hall, offers reasonably priced dinner, slow service, special Sun lunch, T 460 4176; *Eastern Parkway*, also known as *Harry's Bar* is at Half Moon Bay Beach, open air covered beach bar, snacks, cold drinks, burgers and local specialities like bread and saltfish, very casual dining on premises or take away, open daily, local entertainment Sun pm, T 460 4402. If you are stuck at the airport, there is a restaurant which serves simple meals but gets very full when planes are severely delayed, often closed Sun and holidays.

GETTING AROUND

LAND TRANSPORT

● **Motoring**

A local driving licence, US$20, valid for 3 months, must be purchased on presentation of a foreign licence.

Remember to drive on the left. There is a 24-hr petrol station on Old Parham Road outside St John's. Other filling stations are marked on the road map distributed by the Tourist Office, updated annually. Petrol costs US$2.25/gallon everywhere. Traffic lights were installed in St John's in 1989, but these are the only ones on the island. Be careful with one way streets in St John's. In rural areas watch out for potholes; the roads are very narrow in places. At night people do not always dim their headlights, beware also of cows straying across the road in the dark.

● **Car hire**

Rental companies are in St John's and some at airport, most will pick you up: Hertz, T 462 4114/5; Avis, T 462 2840, Dollar Rental, T 462 0362 (Nevis Street); National, T 462 2113; at Oakland Rent-A-Car you can negotiate good rates, contact Ann Edwards, T 462 3021. Rates are from US$40 a day, US$225 a week (no mileage charge), inc insurance charges, in summer, more in winter.

Renting a car or motorcycle is probably the best way to see the island's sights if you have only a short time to spend, as the bus service is inadequate.

● **Bicycles**

Ivor's at English Harbour rents motorcycles at US$20/day (plus US$20 driving licence), bikes not in good condition. Also at English Harbour, Rent a Motor Scooter rents Honda C90 scooters for US$30/day, free delivery anywhere, T 460 2711/1762 or VHF 68 SHIPWRECK. Bicycle hire from Cycle Krazy on St Mary's Street, T 462 9253. Sun Cycles in Hodges Bay has good bicycles, also mountain bikes, US$15/day, will deliver and pick up at your hotel, T 461 0324.

● **Buses**

Minivans (shared taxis) go to some parts of the island (eg Old Road) from the West End bus terminal by the market in St John's. Buses, which are banned from the tourist area (N of the line from the airport to St John's), run frequently between St John's and English Harbour, EC$2.50. There are also buses from the E terminal by the war memorial to Willikies, whence a 20 min walk to Long Bay beach and to Parham. There are no buses to the airport (although if you have not much luggage you can walk about 45 mins to the junction with the main road, by the gas station, and get a bus from there) and very few to beaches though 2 good swimming beaches on the way to Old Road can be reached by bus. Bus frequency can be variable, and there are very few buses after dark or on Sun. Buses to Old Road are half-hourly on average, though more frequent around 0800 and 1600. There are no publicly displayed timetables, you'll have to ask for one. Buses usually go when they are full; ask the driver where he is going.

● **Taxis**

Taxis have H registration plates. In St John's there is a taxi rank on St Mary Street, or outside Bryson's supermarket. They are not metered and frequently try to overcharge, so agree a price first, they should have a EC$ price list so ask to see it. There is a list of government approved taxi rates posted in EC$ and US$ at the airport just after customs. From St John's to Runaway Bay, 10 mins, is US$6; to the airport, US$7 or EC$20/car, from the airport

to town EC$20 pp. If going to the airport early in the morning, book a taxi the night before as there are not many around. For excursions a knowledgeable and rec taxi driver is Mr Graham at the *Barrymore Hotel*. A day tour normally costs about US$63 for 2 people, US$10 for each extra person. Taxi excursions advertised in the hotels are generally overpriced. Hitchhiking is easy in daylight but at night you might fall prey to a taxi driver.

COMMUNICATIONS

● **Postal services**

Post office at the end of Long Street, St John's, opposite the supermarkets, open Mon-Thur, 0815-1200, 1300-1600, until 1700 on Fri; also a Post Office at the airport and at English Harbour. A postcard to the USA costs EC$0.45. Federal Express is on Church Street. DHL is in the Vernon Edwards building on Thames Street.

● **Telecommunications**

Cable and Wireless Ltd, 42-44 St Mary's Street, St John's, and at English Harbour. Antigua's international phone code is due to change from 809 to 268.

ENTERTAINMENT

● **Nightlife**

The largest hotels provide dancing, calypso, steel bands, limbo dancers and moonlight barbecues. There are cinemas, nightclubs, discothèques and casinos. *Ribbit Club*, near Deep Water Harbour; *The House*, on the airport road; *Shooters* on High Street; the *Safari Club* at *Parl's Pizza* in *Tradewinds*; *The Web* on old Parham Road is popular with locals. There is also a seedy casino in the King's Building at Heritage Quay. Casinos at *Flamingo*, *Royal Antiguan* and *St James's Club* hotels and Colonna Park in Hodges Bay. At *Dubarry's* bar there is jazz on Sun night, rum punch party on Tues, barbecue on Thur, take swimsuit, parties tend to end up in, not just by, the pool. *Miller's*, at Fort James serves lunch, dinner, or just drinks, often has live music, eg reggae bands, especially on Sun after Shirley Heights, owned by a local jazz hero. Laurie Stevens, British, provides nightly, musical entertainment around the island: Mon, *Columbos* in English Harbour; Tues *Halycon Hotel*; Wed, *O' Grady's irish Pub* on Nevis Street; Fri, *Royal Antiguan*; enquire about other evenings. His wife, Lisette, is a palmist, so ask about a reading if you want to see into the future. A free newspaper, *It's Happening, You're Welcome*, contains lots of information on forthcoming events.

TOURIST INFORMATION

● **Local tourist office**
Antigua Tourist Office on Thames Street, between Long Street and High Street. Postal address: PO Box 363, St John's, Antigua, West Indies. T 462 0480, F 462 2483. Open 0830-1600 (Mon-Fri) and 0830-1200 (Sat). Gives list of official taxi charges and hotel information. Also has an office at airport, will help book accommodation principally at the more expensive resorts.

● **Tourist offices overseas**
Canada: 60 St Clair Avenue East, Suite 304, Toronto, Ontario, M4T IN5, T (416) 961-3085, F 961 7218.

Germany: Thomas Str 11, D-61348, Bad Homburg, T 49-617221504, F 49-617221513.

Italy: Via Madonnina 9, I-20120 Milan, T 39 2 877 983, F 39 2 877 983.

UK: Antigua House, 15 Thayer Street, London W1M 5LD, T 0171-486 7073/5, F 0171-486 9970.

USA: 610 Fifth Avenue, Suite 311, New York, N Y 10020, T (212) 541-4117, F 757 1607.

● **Tour operators**
Mac's Tracks, run by Brian MacMillan, PO Box 107, St John's, T 462 0132 (home T 462 7376), F 461 8774, 2-4 hr tours at weekends or on special request, from US$10 pp, exploring the countryside, lunch and transport to start of hike can be arranged, to Boggy Peak, Mount McNish, Monterose Hill, Signal Hill and Green Castle Hill. **Tropikelly Trails**, run by Kelly Scales, PO Box 1738, St John's, T 461 0383, US$55 pp, Mon-Fri tours inc drinks, lunch, hotel pick-up, 5-6 hr tours, 6 people max, to Body Pond, Monks Hill, the pineapple farm at Claremont Estate, Boggy Peak and the silk cotton tree at Cades Bay, where 10 people can stand inside the hollow trunk.

● **Acknowledgements**
This chapter has been updated with the most welcome help of Martha Watkins Gilkes, who unfortunately gained first hand experience of Hurricane Luis in 1995 when her home took a direct hit. Additional material was received from Kathy Irwin, on board her yacht, which was safely moored in Trinidad at the time.

St Kitts & Nevis

THE ISLAND OF ST KITTS (officially named St Christopher) and NEVIS are in the N part of the Leeward Islands in the Eastern Caribbean. St Kitts has an area of 68 square miles, made up of three groups of rugged volcanic peaks split by deep ravines, and a low lying peninsula in the SE where there are salt ponds and fine beaches. Nevis, separated by a two-mile channel to the S, has an area of 36 square miles. It is almost circular, rising to a peak of 3,232 feet and surrounded by beaches of coral sand. Wherever you go on these two small islands there are breathtaking, panoramic views of the sea, mountains, cultivated fields and small villages. Each island is fully aware of its heritage and cares for its historical buildings; owing to the early colonization, many are of stone and are in interesting contrast with those of wood. While one federation, the sister islands are quite different. St Kitts is the larger, more cosmopolitan, livelier place, while Nevis is quieter and more sedate. Of the total population, 78% live on St. Kitts and 22% on Nevis; 95% are black, the rest are mixed, white or Indo-Pakistani.

HISTORY

Before Columbus's arrival in 1493, there were Amerindians living on both islands, whose relics can still be seen in some areas. As in most of the other islands, however, they were slaughtered by European immigrants, although the Caribs fought off the British and the French for many years and their battle scenes are celebrated locally. St Kitts became the first British settlement in the West Indies in 1623 and soon became an important colony for its sugar industry, with the importation of large numbers of African slaves. In April 1690 a severe earthquake struck, causing heavy damage to St Kitts,

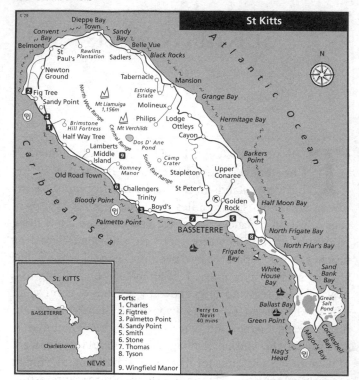

St Kitts

Forts:
1. Charles
2. Figtree
3. Palmetto Point
4. Sandy Point
5. Smith
6. Stone
7. Thomas
8. Tyson
9. Wingfield Manor

Nevis and Redonda. It was followed by a tidal wave which compounded the damage and, it is believed, destroyed Nevis' first capital, Jamestown.

For a time St Kitts was shared by France and England; partition was ended by the Peace of Utrecht in 1713 and it finally became a British colony in 1783. From 1816, St Christopher, Nevis, Anguilla and the British Virgin Islands were administered as a single colony until the Leeward Islands Federation was formed in 1871. (For a detailed history of Nevis during this period, read *Swords, Ships and Sugar—A History of Nevis to 1900*, by Vincent Hubbard, available in St Kitts and Nevis bookshops.)

From 1958, St Kitts-Nevis and Anguilla belonged to the West Indies Federation until its dissolution in 1962. In 1967 their constitutional status was changed from Crown Colony to a state in voluntary association with Britain, in a first step towards self-government. Robert L Bradshaw was the first Premier of the Associated States. Local councils were set up in Anguilla and Nevis to give those islands more authority over local affairs. Anguilla broke away from the group and was reestablished as a Crown Colony in 1971. During the 1970s independence was a burning issue but Nevis' local council was keen to follow Anguilla's lead rather than become independent with St Kitts. Negotiations were stalled because of British opposition to Nevis becoming a Crown Colony. Eventually, on 19 September 1983, St

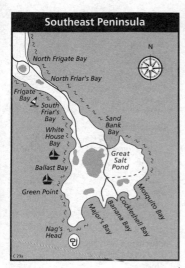

Southeast Peninsula

North Frigate Bay
North Friar's Bay
Frigate Bay
South Friar's Bay
White House Bay
Sand Bank Bay
Ballast Bay
Green Point
Great Salt Pond
Mosquito Bay
Cockleshell Bay
Banana Bay
Major's Bay
Nag's Head

Hurricane Luis

St Kitts and Nevis were in the group of islands badly hit by the winds of Hurricane Luis on 4 September 1995, followed by the rains of Hurricane Marilyn on 12 September. Damage was estimated at EC$200mn to industry and infrastructure, EC$10mn to homes and EC$30mn to hotels. Business was back to normal by mid-1996.

joined the local police force for a week. Negotiations between Dr Denzil Douglas, the SKNLP leader, and Dr Simmonds, for a caretaker government for six months followed by fresh elections, failed. More clashes greeted the budget presentation in February 1994 with the SKNLP boycotting parliament (except to take the oath of allegiance in May) in support of fresh elections.

Also during 1994, St Kitts was rocked by a corruption scandal linked to senior political officials involving drugs trafficking, murder and prison riots. It was alleged that traffickers were exploiting St Kitts and Nevis and avoiding the better monitored, traditional routes. The Deputy Prime Minister, Sydney Morris, resigned after the arrest of two of his sons and the murder of a third. The crisis pushed the Government into calling a forum for national unity, at which it was decided that a general election should be held, three years ahead of schedule. In the meantime, all parties in the National Assembly participated in decisions on matters such as foreign investment and a code of conduct to regulate political activity. A Commonwealth observer team monitored the elections to prevent a recurrence of the 1993 disturbances.

In the months leading up to the 3 July elections, St Kitts suffered a crime wave including arson attacks, and British police officers were brought in to assist the local police force. An advisor from Trinidad also arrived to help administer the

Kitts and Nevis became independent as a single nation.

The main political parties are the People's Action Movement (PAM), the St Kitts and Nevis Labour Party (SKNLP), the Nevis Reformation Party (NRP) and the Concerned Citizens Movement (CCM). Dr Kennedy Simmonds (PAM) was elected Prime Minister in 1980 and held office until July 1995.

Elections in November 1993 were highly controversial when the PAM and the SKNLP each won four seats, the CCM two and the NRP one. The CCM declined to join in a coalition government to form a majority with either major party. The Governor then asked Dr Kennedy Simmonds to form a minority government with the support of the NRP, the PAM's previous coalition partner. This move was highly unpopular, given that the Labour Party had won 54.4% of votes cast in St Kitts compared with 41.7% for the PAM. A state of emergency was declared for 10 days in December because of rioting and other disturbances, a curfew was imposed for five days and a detachment of soldiers from the Regional Security System prison after two prisoners escaped and several prison officers were suspended. The campaign itself was marred by political party rivalry which was often violent, but the result was an overwhelming victory for the SKNLP, which won seven seats. The PAM was reduced to one, while the CCM and the NRP continue to hold two seats and one seat respectively. Dr Denzil Douglas is the new Prime Minister.

GOVERNMENT

St Christopher and Nevis is a constitutional monarchy within the Commonwealth. The British monarch is Head of State and is represented locally by a Governor General. The National Assembly has eleven seats, of which three are from Nevis constituencies and eight from St Kitts. There are also four nominated Senators. Under the Federal system, Nevis also has a separate legislature and may secede from the Government of the Federation. In 1992 Mr Simeon Daniel, the Premier of Nevis for 21 years, lost his assembly seat in elections which saw Mr Vance Amory (CCM) become the new leader. Mr Amory is in favour of the secession of Nevis from the federal state and legislation was being prepared in 1996.

THE ECONOMY

Sugar, the traditional base of economic production, nowadays accounts for only about 2% of gdp, although it still occupies a dominant role within the agricultural sector and generates about a third of export revenues. Production has been in the hands of the Government since 1975, but with low prices for sugar in the world markets, hurricane damage and recent droughts, the industry runs at a loss. Low wages deter locals from seeking jobs on the plantations and labour is imported from St Vincent and Guyana. World Bank consultants recommended policy changes, which included allowing private investment in the industry and production incentives for cane cutters.

St Kitts and Nevis: fact file

Geographic

Land area	269.4 sq km
St Kitts	176.2
Nevis	93.2
forested	17.0%
pastures	3.0%
cultivated	39.0%

Demographic

Population (1995)	39,400
annual growth rate (1990-95)	-1.2%
urban	42.9%
rural	57.1%
density	146 per sq km
Religious affiliation	
Protestant	76.4%
Birth rate per 1,000 (1994)	24.0
	(world av 25.0)

Education and Health

Life expectancy at birth,	
male	63 years
female	69 years
Infant mortality rate	
per 1,000 live births (1994)	20
Physicians (1992)	1 per 1,052 persons
Hospital beds (1995)	1 per 142 persons
Calorie intake as %	
of FAO requirement	101%
Population age 25 and over	
with no formal schooling	1.1%
Literacy (over 15)	90.0%

Economic

GNP (1993 market prices)	US$185mn
GNP per capita	US$4,560
Public external debt (1993)	
	US$39.5mn
Tourism receipts (1993)	US$69.4mn
Inflation (annual av 1989-94)	3.2%
Radio	1 per 1.5 persons
Television	1 per 4.2 persons
Telephone	1 per 3.3 persons

Employment

Population economically active (1980)	
	17,125
Unemployment rate	na
% of labour force in agriculture	29.6
manufacturing	14.7
construction	2.7
Paramilitary police unit	50

Source *Encyclopaedia Britannica*

Initially, management of the state-owned Sugar Manufacturing Company was contracted to Booker Tate, of the UK, for 1991-93, with financial assistance from the World Bank. Sugar production rose by 28% in 1991 to 19,392 tonnes, to 20,159 tonnes in 1992, and again to 21,288 tonnes in 1993, but drought and cane fires cut output to 19,980 tonnes in 1994 and 19,961 in 1995. In 1994 it was announced that the company was to be divested, with the Government having a minority shareholding.

The Government has been encouraged to diversify away from sugar dependence and reduce food imports. More vegetables, sweet potatoes and yams are now being grown, while on Nevis, Sea Island cotton and coconuts are more common on smallholdings. Livestock farming and manufacturing are developing industries. There are enclave industries, such as data processing and garment manufacturing (now over a quarter of total exports), which export to the USA and Caricom trading partners, while sales of sugar-based products such as pure cane spirit go mainly outside the region.

Tourism has become an important foreign exchange earner, and now contributes about 10% of gdp. The construction industry has benefited from the expansion of tourist infrastructure. In 1988 69,608 tourists arriving by air and 53,645 cruise ship passengers spent nearly US$54mn. By 1994, visitors arriving by air had risen to 96,410 while yacht and cruise ship passengers rose to 112,903. Visitor expenditure in 1994 was an estimated US$75mn. Numbers and earnings were expected to be down in 1995 because of the hurricane but pick up again in 1996. The Government plans to increase cruise ship arrivals with a port improvement project (to be completed by 1997) to enable four cruise liners to berth at the same time, while stopover arrivals will be encouraged by the large resort development projects on the SE peninsula of St Kitts, and airport improvements. The number of hotel beds in St Kitts-Nevis is forecast to rise from 1,593 in 1995 to 2,200, giving the islands a potential annual capacity of up to 200,000 visitors.

As a result of economic growth and improvements in tax collection the fiscal accounts are healthy; a budget surplus was recorded in 1993-94 and also forecast for 1995-6. However, growth has slowed, from 4.5% in 1993 to 3.2% in 1994 and 2.0% in 1995, as a result of political uncertainties and hurricane damage. 1996 was likely to be boosted by the construction sector, with hotel expansion as well as repairs, infrastructure and plans for a new hospital and 1,000 new homes.

FAUNA AND FLORA

Both islands are home to the green vervet monkey, introduced by the French some 300 years ago, now dwelling on the forested areas in the mountains. They can be seen in many areas including Brimstone Hill. Scientists have been studying these attractive little creatures and many have been exported; being relatively free of disease they are used for medical research. The monkey is the same animal as on Barbados but the Kittitians used to eat them. Another animal, the mongoose, imported by colonists to kill rats in the sugar estates and snakes never achieved its original purpose (rats being nocturnal whereas the mongoose is active by day) and survives in considerable numbers. It has contributed to the extinction of many species of lizard, ground nesting birds, green iguanas, brown snakes and red-legged tortoises. There are also some wild deer on the SE peninsula, imported originally from Puerto Rico by Philip Todd in the 1930s. In common with other West Indian islands, there are highly vocal frogs, lots of lizards (the anole is the most common), fruit bats, insect bats and butterflies, although nothing particularly rare. St Kitts and Nevis have the earliest documented evidence of honey bees in the Caribbean. Birds are typical of the region, with lots of sea fowl like brown pelicans and frigate birds to be seen, as well as three species of hummingbirds. Fish abound in local waters (rays, barracuda, king fish and brilliantly-coloured smaller species) and the increasingly rare black coral tree can be sighted in the reef of the same name.

The forests (of which a small percentage are rain forests) on the sister islands are restricted in scale but St Kitts is one of the few areas of the world where the forest is expanding. It provides a habitat for wild orchids, candlewoods and exotic vines. Fruits and flowers, both wild and cultivated, are in abundance, particularly in the gorgeous gardens of Nevis. Trees include several varieties of the stately royal palm, the spiny-trunked sandbox tree, silk cotton, and the turpentine or gum tree. Visitors can explore the rainforests on foot with guides and gentle hikes through trails and estates also reap many rewards in terms of plant-gazing. Several trails are clear and do not need a guide, although it should be noted that there are no marked trails; care should be taken and advice sought. Comparatively clear trails include Old Road to Philips, the old British military road, which connected the British settlements on the NE and SW coasts of St Kitts without going through French territory when the island was partitioned. There are also trails from Belmont to the crater of Mount Liamuiga, from Saddlers to the Peak, from Lamberts or the top of Wingfield Heights to Dos d'Ane lake (know locally as Dos d'Ane pond). St Kitts and Nevis are small islands, yet have a wide variety of habitats, with rainforest, dry woodland, wetland, grassland and salt ponds.

DIVING AND MARINE LIFE

There is very good snorkelling and scuba diving. Most dive sites are on the Caribbean side of the islands, where the reef starts in shallow water and falls off to 100 feet or more. Between the two islands there is a shelf in only 25 feet of water which attracts lots of fish, including angelfish, to the corals, sea fans and sponges. There is black coral off the SE peninsula, coral caves, reefs and wrecks with abundant fish and other sea creatures of all sizes and colours. Off St Kitts good reefs to dive include Turtle Reef (off Shitten Bay) which is good for beginners and snorkelling, Coconut Reef in Basseterre Bay and Pump Bay by Sandy Point. There are good wrecks including *MV Talata* in Basseterre Bay and *River Taw* in Frigate Bay. Much of the diving is suitable for novices and few of the major sites are deeper than 70 feet. Several wrecks and some other sites are actually shallow enough for very rewarding snorkelling although the very best snorkelling around St Kitts is only accessible by boat.

Kenneth's Dive Centre based in Basseterre (Bay Road, and also at Timothy Beach, T 465 7043/2670/1950); Kenneth Samuel (friendly, helpful) is a PADI-certified Dive Master offering courses, dive packages (US$70 2-tank dive, 4-day package US$250) and all equipment and he uses catamarans, *Lady Peggy* and *Lady Madonna,* or a 32-foot motor launch, *Lady Majesta.* Pro-Divers gives PADI instruction, T 465 3223, 469 9086, F 465 1057, dive gear available for rent, dive packages available, single tank dive US$40, 2 tank dive US$60, resort course US$75, 3-day PADI Open Water certification US$260, 3-hr snorkelling US$35. Ocean kayaks available for hire.

Snorkelling off Oualie Beach, Nevis, is excellent and also good at Nisbett Beach and Tamarind Bay. Scuba Safaris, run by Ellis Chaderton, is based at Oualie Beach, T 469 9518: diving (US$45 for a single tank dive, US$80 for 2 tanks), PADI and NAUI instruction and equipment rental. Dive Nevis, T 469 9395, offers a 4-dive package, US$165, or 7 dives US$265.

BEACHES AND WATERSPORTS

St Kitts Most of the beaches are of black, volcanic sand but the beaches known as Frigate Bay and Salt Pond fringing the S peninsula have white sand. Swimming is very good in the Frigate Bay area where all water sports are available. The SE peninsula itself also has white sand beaches. Banana Bay, Cockleshell Bay and Mosquito Bay all have sandy beaches, calm water and picturesque views of Nevis just across the straits. There has been little development here so far, but there is the *Turtle Beach Bar and Grill* at Mosquito Bay with a complete range of watersports on offer. Villas are planned here and hotels on other peninsular beaches.

Leeward Island Charters' *Caona II*, a 47-foot catamaran, 67-foot *Eagle*, or *Spirit of St Kitts*, a 70-foot catamaran, T 465 7474, office next to the *Ballahoo* restaurant above the Circus for bookings and private charters, take visitors on a sail, snorkel and beach barbecue. *Celica III* is a catamaran used for day trips with beach barbecue lunch and open bar, US$50, run by Tropical Water Sports, T 465 4039/4167, F 465 6400. Sailing is becoming increasingly popular. The St Kitts-Nevis Boating Club (T 465 8035) organizes sunfish races which are fun, check the bulletin board for details at *PJ's Pizza Bar*, Frigate Bay, the *Ballahoo* in Basseterre or Dougie Brookes who manages the boatyard Caribee Yachts, T 465 8411.

There is a wide range of other water-based activites, such as jet-skis, water skiing, windsurfing etc. Deep sea fishing can be arranged; Oliver Spencer, a fisherman based in Old Road is happy to take visitors, T 465 6314. In summer there is a race for windsurfers and sunfish to Nevis.

Nevis has superb white sandy beaches, particularly on the leeward and N coasts. The beautiful four-mile Pinney's Beach is only a few minutes' walk from Charlestown and is never crowded.

The entire middle stretch of Pinney's Beach has been given over to a 196-room *Four Seasons Hotel*. The sun loungers are for guests only but the public has access to the beach. Watersports facilities are available at *Oualie Beach Club*. Nevis Watersports, at Oualie Beach, T 469 9060/9735, offers water skiing, US$20 pp per pull, US$60 for ½ hour; deep sea fishing US$80/hour (min 3 hrs); snorkelling US$30 half day, jet bikes US$45 ½ hr. Watersports also at Newcastle Bay Marina, T 469 9395 or information from *Mount Nevis Hotel and Beach Club*. On the Atlantic side of Nevis, the beaches tend to be rocky and the swimming treacherous; there is, though, an excellent beach at White Bay in the SW.

OTHER SPORTS

Horse riding, mountain climbing, tennis and golf are available. On St Kitts there is Trinity Stables, T 465 3226, on Nevis at Garners, Ira Dore, T 469 5528, and at the *Hermitage Plantation*, T 469 3477, F 469 2481, where they also have horse-drawn carriage tours, US$50 ½ hr and horseriding US$40 for 1½ hrs. Royal St Kitts Golf Course is an 18-hole international championship golf course at Frigate Bay (T 465 8339) and there is a 9-hole golf course at Golden Rock, St Kitts (T 465 8103), where a fun day is held on the last Sunday of the month. On Nevis, the *Four Seasons* has an 18-hole golf course (T 469 1111). On Nevis horse racing is the second most popular sport after cricket, with races held on the small, stony racetrack at Indian Castle, on national holidays or events, such as New Year's Day, Easter Monday, Labour Day, Whit Monday, August during Culturama, Independence Day and Boxing Day. There is a minimum of five races and horses sometimes come from neighbouring islands. Contact Richard Lupinacci at the Hermitage Inn for details, T 469 3477. Also look out for the more amusing donkey races.

FESTIVALS

St Kitts and Nevis are very proud of their masquerade traditions. The liveliest time to visit St Kitts is for the carnival held over Christmas and the New Year. It gets bigger and better every year with parades, calypso competitions and street dancing. For details, contact the Department of Tourism.

On Nevis, the annual equivalent is Culturama, held in end-July and August, finishing on the first Monday in August. There is a Queen show, calypso competition, local bands and guest bands and many 'street jams'. The Nevis Tourist Office has full details or contact the Department of Culture, T 469 5521 (Mon-Fri) 0800-1600.

ST KITTS

The dormant volcano, Mount Liamuiga (3,792 feet, pronounced Lie-a-mee-ga) occupies the central part of St Kitts. The mountain was previously named Mount Misery by the British, but has now reverted to its Carib name, meaning 'fertile land'. The foothills of the mountains, particularly in the N, are covered with sugar cane plantations and grassland, while the uncultivated lowland slopes are covered with forest and fruit trees.

BASSETERRE

The small port of Basseterre is the capital and largest town, with a population of about 15,000. By West Indian standards, it is quite big and as such has a quite different feel from its close neighbour, Charlestown. It was founded some 70 years later in 1727. Earthquakes, hurricanes and finally a disasterous fire in 1867 destroyed the town. Consequently its buildings are comparatively modern. There is a complete mishmash of architectural styles from elegant Georgian buildings with arcades, verandahs and jalousies, mostly in good condition, to hideous twentieth century concrete block houses. In recent years, the development of tourism has meant a certain amount of redevelopment in the centre. An old warehouse on the waterfront has been converted into the Pelican Mall, a duty-free shopping and recreational complex. It also houses the tourist office and a lounge for guests of the *Four Seasons Hotel* in Nevis awaiting transport. A new deep water cruise ship berth is being built on the waterfront on 25 acres of reclaimed land between Bramble Street and College Street in the heart of Basseterre, capable of accommodating the largest ships afloat, together with a sailing and power boat marina, berthing facilities for the inter-island ferry, the *Caribe Queen*, an expanded shopping area with space for craft vendors and small shops. Work was started in 1994 and should be finished by 1997.

The Circus, styled after London's Piccadilly Circus (but looking nothing like it), is the centre of the town. It is busiest on Fri afternoon and comes alive with locals 'liming' (relaxing). The clock tower is a memorial to Thomas Berkely, former president of the General Legislative Council. South down Fort Street is the imposing façade of the Treasury Building with its dome covering an arched gateway leading directly to the sea front (it is equally impressive from the bay). Next door is the Post Office (open weekdays 0800-1500, 0800-1100 on Thursdays, 0800-1200 on Saturdays). Head N up Fort Street, turn left at the main thoroughfare (Cayon Street) and you will come to **St George's church**, set in its own large garden, with a massive, square buttressed tower. The site was originally a Jesuit church, Notre Dame, which was rased to the ground by the English in 1706. Rebuilt four years later and renamed St George's, it suffered damage from hurricanes and earthquakes on several occasions. It too was a victim of the 1867 fire. It was rebuilt in 1856-69 and contains some nice stained glass windows. There is a fine view of the town from the tower.

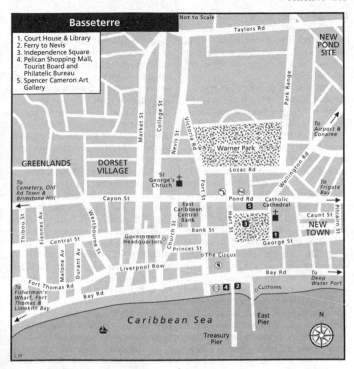

Basseterre

1. Court House & Library
2. Ferry to Nevis
3. Independence Square
4. Pelican Shopping Mall, Tourist Board and Philatelic Bureau
5. Spencer Cameron Art Gallery

Not to Scale

Taylors Rd

NEW POND SITE

Park Range

Market St

College St

Nevis St

Victoria Rd

Warner Park

To Airport & Conaree

GREENLANDS

DORSET VILLAGE

St George's Church

Lozac Rd

Wellington Rd

To Cemetery, Old Rd Town & Brimstone Hill

Cayon St

Fort St

Pond Rd

Catholic Cathedral

To Frigate Bay

Thibou St

Flennes Av

Westbourne St

Central St

Malone Av

Durant Av

East Caribbean Central Bank

Bank St

Hart St

Church St

Government Headquarters

Princes St

George St

Caunt St

Pitcairn St

NEW TOWN

The Circus

Fort Thomas Rd

Liverpool Row

Bay Rd

To Fisherman's Wharf, Fort Thomas & Limekiln Bay

Bay Rd

Customs

To Deep Water Port

Caribbean Sea

Treasury Pier

East Pier

N

Independence Square was built in 1790 and is surrounded now by a low white fence; eight gates let paths converge on a fountain in the middle of the square (it looks like the Union Jack when seen from the air). There are gaily painted muses on top of the fountain. Originally designed for slave auctions and council meetings, it now contains many plants, spacious lawns and lovely old trees. It is surrounded by 18th-century houses and at its E end, the Roman Catholic cathedral with its twin towers. Built in 1927, the Immaculate Conception is surprisingly plain inside. At 10 North Square Street you can visit the very attractive building housing The *Spencer Cameron Art Gallery*. See Rosey Cameron-Smith's paintings and prints of local views and customs as well as an impressive selec-

tion of the work of other artists too, T/F 465 1617. The Bank of Nova Scotia houses some interesting paintings of Brimstone Hill by Lt Lees of the Royal Engineers, circa 1783. St Christopher Heritage Society, Bank Street (off West Independence Square, PO Box 338, Basseterre, T 465 5584) has a small, interesting display of old photographs and artefacts. They work on conservation projects and are grateful for donations. Open Mon-Tues, Thur-Fri 0830-1300, 1400-1600, Wed, Sat, 0830-1300. Basseterre is very quiet on Sundays and most of the restaurants are closed.

EXCURSIONS

A clockwise route round the island will enable you to see most of the historical sites. A cheap way of touring the island is to take a minibus from Basseterre (Bay Road) to Dieppe Bay Town, then walk to Saddlers (there might be a minibus if you are lucky) where you can get another minibus back to Basseterre along the Atlantic coast.

The island is dominated by the SE range of mountains (1,159 feet) and the higher NW range which contains Mount Verchilds (2,931 feet) and the crater of Mount Liamuiga (3,792 feet). There are several good island tours, including excellent hiking tours to the volcano and through the rain forest with Kriss Tours (US$45 full day, overnight camping US$90, T 465 4042) and Greg's Safaris, recommended, pleasant and informative, (US$35-55, T 465 4121, F 465 0707, PO Box 1063). Periwinkle Tours offers guided walks (US$30-35, T 465 6314, F 465 7210. To climb **Mt Liamuiga** independently, get a bus to St Paul's. Just after the village entrance sign there is a track leading through farm buildings which you follow through the canefields. After 20 minutes take a left fork, but don't be shy of asking people working in the fields. At the edge of the forest, the track becomes a path, which is easy to follow and leads through wonderful trees. If you hear something crashing through the upper branches, look up quickly before the monkeys disappear. At 2,600 feet is the crater into which you can climb down, holding on to vines and roots; on the steady climb from the end of the road note the wild orchids in the forest. A full day is required for this climb which is for experienced hikers. To get beyond the crater to the summit you really do need a guide.

You can reach the attractive, but secluded, Dos D'Ane pond near Mount Verchilds from the Wingfield estate, a guide is recommended.

Evidence of sugar cane is everywhere on the comparatively flat, fertile coastal plain. You will drive through large fields of cane and glimpse the narrow gauge railway which is now used to transport it from the fields. Disused sugar mills

are also often seen. Around the island are the Great Houses: Fairview, Romney Manor (destroyed by fire in 1995), Golden Lemon, the White House, Rawlins and perhaps most famous for its colonial splendour, Ottley's. They have nearly all been converted into hotels and have excellent restaurants.

The W coast in particular is historically important. It is guarded by no less than nine forts and the magnificent Brimstone Hill Fortress. Taking the road out of Basseterre, you will pass the sites of seven of them: Fort Thomas, Palmetto Point Fort, Stone Fort, Fort Charles, Charles Fort, Sandy Point Fort and Fig Tree Fort. The remaining two are to the S of Basseterre: Fort Smith and Fort Tyson. Little now remains of any of them. A peaceful spot to admire some of Stone Fort's ruins is a swing for two built by local Rastaman, Jahbalo. At Trinity Church, turn right, up the dirt path. At the well-preserved sugar mill there are some ruins to your right. Climb the small mound to find the swing with a view towards cane fields and the Caribbean (sunset recommended).

Sir Thomas Warner landed at Old Road Bay in 1623 and was joined in 1625 by the crew of a French ship badly mauled by the Spanish. Initially befriended by the local Carib chief Tegreman, as many as 3,000 Caribs, alarmed at the rapid colonization of the island, tried to mount an attack in 1626. 2,000 of them were massacred by the combined French and English forces in the deep ravine at **Bloody Point** (the site of Stone Fort). This is the first point of historic interest and is just before Old Road Town. An amicable settlement meant that the English held the central portion of the island roughly in line from Sandy Point to Saddlers in the N to Bloody Point across to Cayon in the S. French names can be traced in both of their areas of influence (Dieppe Bay Town in the N, the Parishes are called Capisterre and Basseterre in the S). The SE peninsula was neutral. This rapprochement did not last many years as following the colonization of Martinique and Guadeloupe, the French wished to increase their sphere of influence. St Kitts became an obvious target and in 1664 they squeezed the English from the island. For nearly 200 years the coast was defended by troops from one nation or another.

At **Old Road Town** you turn right to visit **Wingfield Estate**. You drive through a deserted sugar mill and the edge of rain forest. Unfortunately Romney Manor was destroyed by fire in 1995 but the beautiful gardens remain with pleasant views over the coast and a giant 350-year old saman tree. The estate is home to Caribelle Batik, open Monday-Friday, 0830-1600, T 465 6253, F 465 3629. Apart from a well-stocked shop you can watch the artists producing the highly colourful and attractive material. A guide will explain the process. Also near here the remains of the island's Amerindian civilization can be seen on large stones with drawings and pictographs.

After a further 1½ miles, at the village of **Middle Island**, you will see on your right and slightly up the hill, the church of St Thomas at the head of an avenue of dead or dying royal palms. Here is buried Sir Thomas Warner who died on 10 March 1648. The raised tomb under a canopy is inscribed "General of y Caribee". There is also a bronze plaque with a copy of the inscription inside the church. Other early tombs are of Captain John Pogson (1656) and Sir Charles Payne, "Major General of Leeward Carribee Islands" who was buried in 1744. The tower, built in 1880, fell during earth tremours in 1974.

Turn right off the coastal road just before *J's Place* (drink and local food, open from 1100, T 465 6264, watch the caged green vervet monkeys: they are very aggressive) for the **Fortress of Brimstone Hill**, one of the 'Gibraltars of the West Indies' (a title it shares with Les Saintes, off Guadeloupe). Sprawled over 38 acres on the slopes of a hill 800 feet above the sea, it commands an incredible view for 70 miles around, of St Kitts and Nevis and on clear days, Anguilla (67 miles) Montserrat (40 miles), Saba (20 miles), St Eustatius (5 miles), St-Barts (40 miles) and St-Martin (45 miles) can be seen. The English mounted the first cannon on Brimstone Hill in 1690 in an attempt to force the French from Fort Charles below. It has been constructed mainly out of local volcanic stones and was designed along classic defensive lines. The five bastions overlook each other and also guard the only road as it zig zags up to the parade ground. The entrance is at the Barrier Redan where payment is made. Pass the Magazine Bastion but stop at the Orillon Bastion which contains the massive ordnance store (165 feet long with walls at least 6 feet thick). The hospital was located here and under the S wall is a small cemetery. You come next to the Prince of Wales Bastion (note the name of J Sutherland, 93rd Highlanders 24 October 1822 carved in the wall next to one of the cannons) from where there are good views over to the parade ground. Park at the parade ground, there is a small café and good gift shop near the warrant officer's quarters with barrels of pork outside it. Stop for a good introduction at the DL Matheson Visitor Centre. A narrow and quite steep path leads to Fort George, the Citadel and the highest defensive position. Restoration is continuing and several areas have been converted to form a most interesting museum. Barrack rooms now hold well-presented and informative displays (pre-columbian, American, English, French and Garrison). Guides are on hand to give more detailed explanations of the fortifications; a video can be seen at the Visitor's Centre. The Fortress was eventually abandoned in 1852 but was inaugurated as a National Park by the Queen in October 1985. Open 0930-1730 daily, entrance EC$13 or US$5 for foreigners, EC$2 for nationals, it is highly recommended both for adults and children (half price). Allow up to 2 hours. The local minibus to Brimstone Hill is EC$2, then walk up to the fortress, less than 30 mins.

To continue the island tour, drive on, looking out for the Plantation Picture House on the right, up a long drive through canefields. A lovely art gallery with stunning views, housing paintings and prints by Kate Spencer, it is open 1100-1700, T 465 7740. Back on the main road, continue N. There is a a black sand beach at Dieppe Bay which is a good place to stop for lunch, either at *Chez Moi*, run by friendly rasta Wingrove Finch, or the more upmarket and excellent *Golden Lemon*. Pass through Saddlers and stop at the **Black Rocks**. Here lava has flowed into the sea providing interesting rock formations. The road continues past Ottley Plantation, through Cayon (turn right uphill to Spooners for a look at the abandoned cotton ginnery) back to Basseterre via the RL Bradshaw Airport. With advance notice, you can tour the sugar factory near the airport, very interesting and informative. Tours are only during harvest season, February-August, T 465 8157.

To visit the SE peninsula, turn off the roundabout at the end of Wellington Road (opp turning to the airport) and at the end of this new road turn left. This leads to the narrow spit of land sandwiched between North and South Frigate Bays. This area is being heavily developed, the natural lagoons providing an additional attraction. A number of establishments have been built, including the *Jack Tar Village* resort with a casino, tennis courts and an 18-hole golf course. The new 6-mile Dr Kennedy A Simmonds Highway runs from Frigate Bay to Major's Bay. After Frigate Bay the peninsula is almost deserted and quite different from the rest of the island. The road climbs along the backbone of the peninsula and overlooks North and South Friars Bays where you may see green vervet monkeys before descending to White House Bay (an abandoned jetty and wreck provides good snorkelling). Skirt the Great Salt Pond. Half way round turn left to reach Sandbank Bay, a lovely secluded bay (unmarked left turn down dirt road opp Great Salt Pond). Continue on the main highway and turn left for Cockleshell Bay and Turtle Beach (good for watersports and stunning views across to Nevis). The main road leads to Major's Bay. At the moment most of the peninsula is isolated and extremely attractive, although tourist development is planned. Despite the road the majority of beaches are difficult to reach. Try to obtain local knowledge if you want to visit them.

Island information – St Kitts
● Accommodation

Price guide

L1	over US$200	**L2**	US$151-200
L3	US$101-150	**A1**	US$81-100
A2	US$61-80	**A3**	US$46-60
B	US$31-45	**C**	US$21-30
D	US$12-20	**E**	US$7-11
F	US$4-6	**G**	up to US$3

There is a wide variety of accommodation ranging from first class hotels to rented cottages, but it is advisable to book well in advance. Large reductions are available in summer. There is a 7% occupancy tax and 10% service charge.

L1-L3 *Ocean Terrace Inn* (*OTI*, Box 65, T 465 2754, F 465-1057) a/c, TV, apartments also available, and **L1-A1** *Fort Thomas Hotel* (Box 407, T 465 2695, F 465 7518), are a few mins walk from Basseterre and have pools, beach shuttles and restaurants. *OTI* also organizes tours and other activities such as scuba diving, evening shows and has a fairly expensive but nice restaurant with views over Basseterre harbour; good service throughout. **L3-A2** *Palms Hotel*, central, on the Circus, pleasant rooms, full range of facilities, 2-bed suites available.

C The *Windsor Guest House*, Cayon Street, opp Wesleyan Church, up steps, no sign, is one of the cheapest w/o private bath but not rec, beds uncomfortable, stuffy, shared toilets (Box 122, T 465 2894). Alternatives to this are the **B-C** *Parkview Inn*, Victoria Road, next to Parkview Amusements (Box 64, T 465 2100), very basic, and **A3-B** *On the Square*, 14 Independence Square (Box 81, T 465 2485), 4 a/c rooms with bathrooms, clean, one larger room with kitchenette and balcony overlooking square, prices include tax, rec. **A3** *Harbour View Guest House*, Bay Road, T 446 6759/60/61, opp buses, newly renovated 10 double rooms, a/c, good restaurant, convenient for central Basseterre; **A3-C** *Glimbaro Guest House*, Cayon Street and Market Street, T 465 2935, F 465 9832, almost opp *Windsor Guest House*, signed 'Guest House, Pest Control, Fumigation...', new rooms, a/c, cable TV, some with bath and patio, cheaper rooms with shared bathrooms, 10% off weekly rates, fans, phone, *Pisces* restaurant with good local food, especially fish.

The **L3-A2** *Fairview Inn* close to Basseterre is a cottage complex (for sale in 1996) situated around an eighteenth century great house, reductions for children under 8, a/c, fans, restaurant, pool, Box 212, T 465 2472, F 465 1056). W of Basseterre, **A3** *Trinity Inn Apartments*, Palmetto Point, T 465 3226/1446, F 465 9460, a/c, pool, restaurant, riding stables, very friendly, excellent value, US$260/week. The highly rec **L1** *Rawlins Plantation*, 16 miles from Basseterre in the NW of the island, is pricey, but beautiful, tranquil and offers grass tennis, swimming pool, horse riding and croquet, no credit cards accepted, 10 cottages, laundry service and afternoon tea included, Box 340, T 465 6221, F 465 4954. **L1** *The White House*, British-run, PO Box 436, T 465 8162, F 465 8275, 8 rooms in the carriage house and other buildings of a plantation great house, swimming pool, courtesy transport to beach 15 mins away, MAP inc afternoon tea and laundry service, elegant and quiet; **L1-A1** *Bird Rock Beach Hotel*, owned/managed by former Director of Tourism, Larkland Richards, T 465 8914, F 465 1675, 38 rooms/suites, a/c, TV, up on the cliffs overlooking the tiny black sand beach and industrial estate, inconvenient suburban location, taxi to Basseterre US$8, pool, tennis, volleyball, watersports, 2 restaurants, 3 bars; 320' above sea level in 35 acres, is the **L1-L3** *Ottleys Plantation Inn*, PO Box 345, T 465 7234, F 465 4760, T 800-772 3039, rooms in the 1832 great house or cottages, a/c, fans, restaurant, pool, nice walks, beach shuttle, tennis/golf shuttle; **L1-L2** *The Golden Lemon Inn and Villas*, Dieppe Bay, T 465 7260, F 465 4019, in the USA T 1-800-633

7411, on black sand beach about 15 miles from Basseterre, has 32 rooms, having built some 1-2 bedroom beachfront cottages with pools next to the original great house building dating from 1610, pool, tennis, watersports, restaurant, each room is tastefully furnished with West Indian antiques, lovely atmosphere, highly rec, no children under 18.

Lots of new hotels and condominiums have now been built in the Frigate Bay area, the main tourist development location: **L1-L3** *Frigate Bay Beach Resort*, PO Box 137, T 465 8935/6, F 465 7050, rooms and suites, a/c, Olympic size pool, restaurant; **A2** *Gateway Inn*, PO Box 64, T 465 7155, F 465 9322, 10 self-catering apartments, a/c, phone, TV, laundry, 10 mins from beach or golf course, US$480/week; **L1-L2** *Island Paradise Beach Village*, PO Box 444, T 465 8035, F 465 8236, 62 condominiums set in 5 acres of woodland on the Atlantic beach, laundry, barbecue, pool, *PJ's Pizza*, store, 1-3 bedrooms, US$895-1,835/week; dominating Frigate Bay with its golf course and casino is the all-inclusive **L1-L2** *Jack Tar Village*, PO Box 406, T 465 8651, F 465 1031, in USA T-800-999-9182, 15-min walk or take shuttle bus to beaches on Atlantic and Caribbean, 244 a/c rooms, some quieter than others, all have balcony or patio, restaurants, watersports, tennis, table tennis, bicycles, lagoon fishing, pedaloes, disco; **L1-L3** *Leeward Cove Condominium*, PO Box 123, T 465 8030, F 465 3476, on Atlantic Beach, 1-2 bedroom self-catering apartments, a/c, free green fees at Golf Club, mini-mart, laundry service, free car per week's stay; **A3** *Rock Haven Bed & Breakfast*, PO Box 821, T/F 465 5503, suite with kitchen facilities, TV, laundry facilities, views of both coasts; **L1-L3** *Sea Lofts on the Beach*, PO Box 813, T 465 1075, F 466 5034, condominiums in 3-acre gardens on Atlantic Beach, 2-3 bedrooms, US$850-1,800/week, pool, 2 tennis courts, barbecue, stores, free green fees; **L1-L2** *Sun 'N Sand Beach Resort*, PO Box 341, T 465 8037/8, F 465 6745, studios or 2-bedroomed cottages on Atlantic Beach, a/c, fans, pool, TV, quite basic but clean, well run, lovely gardens, good food, rec; **L1-L3** *Colony's Timothy Beach Resort*, PO Box 81, T 465 8597, F 465 7723, on Caribbean beach, little shade, studios and suites, watersports, sailing, pool, a/c, TV, café.

● **Places to eat**
The hotels have restaurants, usually serving

local specialities. Most of the Plantation Inns on both islands offer Sunday brunch, usually a 3-course meal and excellent value at around US$25 pp. There are also many places offering snacks, light meals, ice creams and drinks in Basseterre and in the Frigate Bay area. Look out for places selling excellent local patties and fruit juices, *CTM* and *Yellow Bird* rec, both on Fort Street. *Fisherman's Wharf* (T 465 2754) beside *OTI* offers fresh fish, barbecue chicken etc and help yourself to vegetables for US$25-35, conch chowder rec; *Ballahoo* in town, great central meeting place, lovely view of the Circus, excellent local food at reasonable prices, open Mon-Sat 0800-2200, T 465 4197, F 465 7070; also in Basseterre *Circus Grill*, T 465 0143, good well-presented food, a bit more expensive than *Ballahoo*, open Mon-Sat 1130-2200; *Chef's Place*, Church Street, T 465 6176, good breakfasts and West Indian food at reasonable price, 0900-2100 Mon-Sat, no credit cards. *Georgian House*, South Independence Square, T 465 4049, open Tues-Sat 1900-2130, splendid walled garden with exotic plants; *Arlecchino*, Amory Mall, Cayon Street, Italian restaurant, friendly owner, Jasmine makes a delicious coffee shake, T 465 9927, open 0900-1500, 1800-2230; *Stone Walls*, Princess Street, T 465 5248, expensive but excellent food, special theme nights, open Mon-Sat 1700-2300, in pleasant garden; *Vegetarian Plus* in TDC Mall, open Mon-Sat 0800-2300, one of the few places open on Sun 1000-2200, T 465 0709; *Bayembi Cultural Café*, Bank Street, T 466 5280, good snacks, occasional Fri night street parties; *Victor's Hideaway*, Stainforth Street, New Town, Basseterre, T 465 2518, open 0900-1500, 1830-late; *Victoria's Place*, Cayon St, T 465 7741, daily specials, open Mon-Sat 0800-2200; *Coconut Café* in Frigate Bay, *Timothy Beach Resort*, T 465 3020, serves local seafood, burgers, open daily, 0700-2300, good. *The Patio*, Frigate Bay, T 465 8666, open Dec-May, local and international cuisine, complimentary white wine and open bar with dinner, run by Peter and Joan Mallalieu like a private dinner party so reservations essential, entrées US$25-30, dress smartly; *PJ's Pizza*, Frigate Bay, T 465 8373, open from 1000 Tues-Sat. Up at Bird Rock, *Lighthouse*, T 465 0739, open Tues-Sun, serving dinner until 2200, entrées around US$25, go for drinks, open from 1530, to watch glorious sunset over Basseterre Bay. At the end of the peninsula, out at *Turtle Beach Bar and Grill*, excellent barbecue, friendly, T 469 9086, F 466 7771, open Mon-Fri 1000-1800 and for dinner Tues and Thur, reservations required, Sat and Sun from 1000 'till late, go for sunset on Sun evening and stay on for dancing. Small restaurants around the island serving West Indian food, include *Manhattan Gardens*, Old Road, T 465 9121 also bar opp, by the sea, run by Spencer family, serves fresh fish and goat water, busy at weekends; *Chez Moi*, Dieppe Bay, T 465 6113, run by friendly Wingrove Finch, dinner reservations rec.

● **Entertainment**

Flex Fitness Centre on Frigate Bay Road open from 1200 Mon-Sat, pool room and grill open 1800-0300, late night dancing Fri, T 465 7616; *Eclipse* in Canada Estate also fairly smart, open Fri and Sat 2200-0530. *Jack Tar Village*, Frigate Bay offers a night pass which covers all drinks, a light buffet and entertainment. There is also a casino. Steel pan on Fri nights at *OTI*; lively happy hour at *Fort Thomas Hotel*; a good place for a drink in Basseterre is *TOTTs*, opp Post Office on the Bay Road. On Fri night the place to be is *Monkey Bar* at Frigate Bay, open for dancing on the beach, everyone goes but only gets going after midnight. On Sun almost everything closes down in Basseterre.

NEVIS

Across the two-mile Narrows Channel from St Kitts is the beautiful little island of Nevis, with a population of only 9,000. The central peak of the island is usually shrouded in white clouds and mist, which reminded Columbus of Spanish snow-capped mountains and is why he called the island "Las Nieves". (It reminds others, in the wet, of the English Lake District, as does St Kitts.) For the Caribs, it was Oualie, the land of beautiful water. Smaller than St Kitts it is also quieter. The atmosphere is civilized, but low-key and easy-going; all the same, it is an expensive island. Less fertile than St Kitts, the principal crop used to be cotton but only 32 acres were planted in 1995. Nevis was badly affected by Hurricane Hugo but despite considerable damage, nobody was killed and damage has now been repaired.

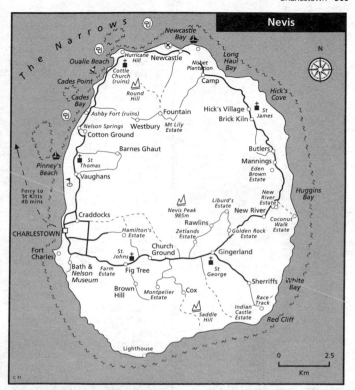

Nevis

CHARLESTOWN

The main town is Charlestown, one of the best preserved old towns in the Caribbean. Situated on Gallows Bay and guarded by Fort Charles to the S and the long sweep of Pinney's Beach to the North, it is a small town with a compact centre. At first sight it would be easy to be disappointed. However there are several interesting buildings dating from the eighteenth century and the excellent Museum of Nevis History.

D R Walwyn's Plaza is dominated by the balconied Customs House built in 1837 on a much older site and housing, the Customs and Agricultural Ministry. Immediately to the N is the Post Office.

Opposite it on the other side of the square is the Tourist Office. Memorial Square is larger and more impressive than D R Walwyn's Plaza, the War Memorial is in a small garden. Explore the Courthouse and library (open Mon-Fri 0900-1800, Sat 0900-1700). It was built in 1825 and used as the Nevis Government Headquarters but largely destroyed by fire in 1873. The curious little square tower was erected in 1909-10. It contains a clock which keeps accurate time with an elaborate pulley and chain system. Visit the library and you can see them together with the weights among the elaborate roof trusses. The courthouse is not open to the public, look in through the open

1. Alexander Hamilton Museum
2. Cotton Ginnery
3. DR Walwyn's Plaza
4. Jewish Cemetery
5. Memorial Square

Charlestown

Gingerland, where it is in a renovated building next to the sugar mill ruins there. On Chapel Street the Wesleyan Holiness Manse built in 1812 is one of the oldest stone buildings surviving on the island while the Methodist Manse (next to the prominent Church) has the oldest wooden structure, the second floor being built in 1802.

The **Alexander Hamilton House Birthplace** and the **Museum of Nevis History** (T 469 5786, open Mon-Fri 0900-1600, Sat 1000-1300, entrance US$2) is next to the sea and set in an attractive garden which contains a representative collection of Nevis plants and trees. The original house was built around 1680 but destroyed in the 1840s probably by an earthquake. This attractive two-storey house was rebuilt in 1983 and dedicated during the Islands' Independence celebration in September of that year. The Nevis House of Assembly meets in the rooms upstairs (again restored after being damaged by Hurricane Hugo), while the museum occupies the ground floor. Alexander Hamilton, Nevis' most famous son, was born in Charlestown on 11 January 1757. He lived on Nevis for only five years before leaving for St Croix with his family. About half of the display is given over to various memorabilia and pictures of his life. There is also an excellent collection of historical documents that you can ask to see. The Museum of Nevis History contains examples of Amerindian pottery, African culture imported by the slaves, cooking implements and recipes, a rum still, and a model of a Nevis lighter. There is also a collection of 17th century clay pipes and the ceremonial clothes of the Warden which were worn on the Queen's birthday and Remembrance Day. A section is devoted to the conservation of reefs, conch and the rain forest. There is a small shop which sells local produce and some interesting books. All proceeds go to the upkeep of the museum.

windows. Along Government Road is the well-preserved Jewish Cemetery dating back to 1679, but locked although entrance is allowed. The key is at Hunkins shop. At the small market a wide range of island produce, including avocados, ginger root, yams and sweet potatoes, is on sale but go early if you want to catch the bustle. Markets are held on Tues, Thurs and Sat mornings, best on Sat. Market Street to the right houses the philatelic bureau, airconditioned and open from 0800-1600 Mon-Fri. The Cotton Ginnery was until 1994 in use during the cotton picking season (Feb-July). In 1995 it was moved out to the New River Estate,

EXCURSIONS

Taking the road S out of Charlestown, you can visit the rather unkempt **Fort Charles**. Fork right at the Shell station and again at the mini roundabout, keep right along the sea shore (rough track), past the wine company building and through gates at the end of the track. The Fort was built before 1690 and altered many times before being completed in 1783-90. Nothing much remains apart from the circular well and a small building (possibly the magazine). The gun emplacements looking across to St Kitts are being badly eroded by the sea, 8 cannon point haphazardly to sea. The Nevis Council surrendered to the French here in 1782 during the seige of Brimstone Hill on St Kitts.

Back on the main road and only about ½ mile outside Charlestown lies the largely ruined **Bath Hotel** and **Spring House**. Built by the Huggins family in 1778, it is reputed to be one of the oldest hotels in the Caribbean. The Spring House lies over a fault which supplies constant hot water at 108°F. Open Mon-Fri 0800-1700, Sat 0800-1200, EC$5 to bathe, EC$1.50 towel rental. Most locals bathe further downstream for free. A new building has been erected here to house the **Nelson Museum** dedicated in 1992 to commemorate the 205th anniversary of the wedding of Admiral Nelson to Fanny Nisbet (open Mon-Fri, 0900-1600, Sat 1000-1300, US$2). Based on a collection donated by Mr Robert Abrahams, an American, the collection contains memorabilia including letters, china, pictures, furniture and books. It is well worth a visit as it contains an interesting insight into the life of Nelson and his connection with Nevis. He was not always popular having come to the island to enforce the Navigation Acts which forbade the newly independent American states trading with British Colonies. Nelson in his ship *HMS Boreas* impounded four American ships and their cargos. The Nevis merchants immediately claimed £40,000 losses against Nelson who had to remain on board his ship for eight weeks to escape being put into gaol. It was only after Prince William, captain of *HMS Pegasus*, arrived in Antigua that Nelson gained social acceptability and married the widow Fanny Woodward Nisbet (reputedly for her uncle's money: this proved a disappointment as her uncle left the island and spent his wealth in London).

More evidence of the Nelson connection is found at the **St John's Fig Tree Anglican Church** about 2 miles on from the Bath House. Originally built in 1680, the church was rebuilt in 1838 and again in 1895. The marriage certificate of Nelson and Fanny Nisbet is displayed here. There are interesting memorials to Fanny's father William Woodward and also to her first husband Dr Josiah Nisbet. Many died of the fever during this period and taxi drivers will delight in lifting the red carpet in the central aisles for you to see old tomb stones, many connected with the then leading family, the Herberts. The graveyard has many examples of tombstones in family groups dating from the 1780s.

Slightly off the main road to the S lies **Montpelier Great House** where the marriage of Nelson and Nesbit actually took place; a plaque is set in the gatepost. The plantation is now a hotel with pleasant gardens. Enormous toads live in the lily ponds formed out of old sugar pans. A very pleasant place for lunch or a drink. Beyond the house lies **Saddle Hill** (1,250 ft). It has the remains of a small fort and it is reputedly where Nelson would look out for illegal shipping. You can follow several goat trails on the hill, giant aloes abound, a track starts at Clay Ghaut, but most trails beyond the fort are dense and overgrown. The *Hermitage* (another of the Great Houses) is signposted left just after the sign for the Montpelier.

The small parish of **Gingerland** is reached after about 3 miles. Its rich soils made it the centre of the islands ginger root production (also cinnamon and nutmeg) but it is noteworthy for the very unusual octagon Methodist Church built in 1830. You turn right here along Hanleys Road to reach **White Bay Beach**. Go all the way down to the bottom and turn left at the Indian Castle experimental farm, past the race course (on Black Bay) and Red Cliff. There is a small shelter but no general shade. Beware, this is the Atlantic coast, the sea can be very rough and dangerous. On quieter days, the surf is fun and provides a welcome change from the quiet Leeward coast at Pinney's. There is a reef further out which is good for fishing (several fishing boats in the bay, one may take you out). There are good views across to Montserrat. On the way back beware of the deep (and hidden) storm drain crossing the road near the church.

After Gingerland the land becomes more barren. Several sugar mills were built here because of the wind, notably **Coconut Walk Estate**, **New River Estate** (fairly intact) and the **Eden Brown Estate**, built around 1740. A duel took place between the groom and best man at the wedding of Julia Huggins. Both men were killed, Julia became a recluse and the great house was abandoned. It has the reputation of being haunted. Although government owned and open to the public, the ruins are in a poor condition and care should be taken.

The island road continues N through Butlers and Brick Kiln (known locally as Brick Lyn), past St James church (Hick's village), Long Haul and Newcastle Bays (with the *Nisbet Plantation Inn*) to the small fishing community of **Newcastle**. You can visit the Newcastle Pottery where distinctive red clay is used to make among other things the traditional Nevis cooking pot. The Newcastle **Redoubt** can be seen from the road. Built in the early 17th century, it was used as a refuge from Carib attack and may have been the site of a Carib attack in 1656. The airport is situated here.

The road continues through an increasingly fertile landscape and there are fine views across the Narrows to the SE peninsula of St Kitts, looking for all the world like the W coast of Scotland. Note **Booby Island** in the middle of the channel, it is mostly inhabited by pelicans (all birds are referred to as boobies by the local population). It offers good diving. The road between here and Charlestown often passes gardens which are a riot of colour. The small hill on your left is **Round Hill** (1,014 ft). It can be reached on the road between Cades Bay and Camps Village (there is supposed to be a soufrière along this road). Turn off the road at Fountain Village by the methodist church. There are good views from the radio station at the top over Charlestown, across to St Kitts and beyond to Antigua. Do not expect to see much wildlife however. There is a small beach at **Mosquito Bay** and some good snorkelling can be had under the cliffs of Hurricane Hill. The *Oualie Beach Hotel* offers a range of watersport facilities including scuba diving and snorkelling equipment. On Sunday afternoons there is often live music and a barbecue at Mosquito Bay. Sailing trips can be negotiated with locals.

Under Round Hill lies **Cottle Chapel** (1824). It was the first Anglican place on Nevis where slaves could be taught and worship with their master. Ruined now, its beautiful little font can be seen in the Museum of Nevis History. Nearby, just off the island road, lies **Fort Ashby**. Nothing remains of the Fort (it is now a restaurant on Cades Bay although the cannons are in their original positions). It protected Jamestown, the original settlement and former capital, which was supposedly destroyed by an earthquake and tidal wave in 1690, and was originally called St James' Fort. Drive past the Nelson springs (where the barrels from *HMS Boreas* were filled) and **St Thomas' Church** (built in 1643, one of the oldest surviving in the Caribbean) to Pinney's Beach. There are many tracks leading down to the beach often

A
journey of
1000 miles
begins with
your first
footprint...

With apologies to
Lao Tzu c.604 - 531 BC

Footprint Handbooks

Win £500-worth of superb quality Rohan travel clothing

Footprint Handbooks
6 Riverside Court
Lower Bristol Road
Bath
BA2 3DZ
England

Affix
Stamp
Here

TEMPERATURE

°C	°F		°C	°F
24	75		50	122
22	72		48	118
20	68		46	115
18	64		44	111
16	61		42	108
14	57		40	104
12	54		38	100
10	50		36	97
8	46		34	93
6	43		32	90
4	39		30	86
2	36		28	82
0	32		26	79

WORLD TIME ZONES

-12
-11
-10
-9
-8
-7
-6
-5
-4
-3
-2
-1
0
+1
+2
+3
+4
+5
+6
+7
+8
+9
+10
+11
+12

South American Handbook
Mexico & Central America Handbook
Caribbean Islands Handbook
Indonesia Handbook
India Handbook
East Africa Handbook
South Africa Handbook
Malaysia & Singapore Handbook

Footprint Handbooks
6 Riverside Court
Lower Bristol Road
Bath BA2 3DZ
T 01225 469141
F 01225 469461
handbooks@footprint.compulink.co.uk

with a small hut or beach bar (eg *Sunshine's*, excellent fish and salads) at the end of them. The *Four Seasons Hotel* lies in the middle of the beach. The sun loungers are reserved for guests only but the beach is public. Behind the resort is the Robert Trent Jones II golf course which straddles the island road. The manicured fairways and greens are in marked contrast with the quiet beauty of the rest of the island but the hotel's considerable efforts at landscaping have lessened its impact.

There are many interesting walks over old sugar plantations and through the rain forest on Mount Nevis. *Sunrise Tours* (T 469 2758) arranges trips to Nevis Peak (4 hrs round trip, US$45 pp), Saddle Hill (1½ hrs, US$20) or the Water Source (3 hrs, US$40). *Heb's Nature Tours* is run by Michael Herbert, Rawlins Village, Gingerland, T 469 2501, offering similar tours: Mt Nevis (5 hrs, US$35-40), Rainforest hike (4 hrs, US$25-30), Saddle Hill hike (3 hrs, US$20-25) and Camp Spring (2½ hrs, US$15-20), price depends on numbers. *Top to Bottom* is run by biologists Jim and Nikki Johnson, who are very flexible and organize walks to suit you, also a night-time, star-gazing walk, mostly 2-3 hrs, US$20 pp, children half price, snacks of fruit and coconut included (T 469 5371). David Rollinson of *Eco-Tours* (T 469 2091) is very knowledgeable; he offers 'eco rambles' three times a week over the eighteenth century Coconut Walk and New River Estates and a Mountravers hike over the old Pinney Estate (US$20 pp) as well as Sun afternoon strolls round historic Charlestown (US$10 pp).

Island information – Nevis
● Accommodation

Price guide

L1	over US$200	L2	US$151-200
L3	US$101-150	A1	US$81-100
A2	US$61-80	A3	US$46-60
B	US$31-45	C	US$21-30
D	US$12-20	E	US$7-11
F	US$4-6	G	up to US$3

Accommodation on Nevis tends to be up-market, in reconstructions of old plantation Great Houses, tastefully decorated in an English style (collectively called *The Inns of Nevis*). Some have reciprocal arrangements whereby you can stay at one and use the facilities of the others. They are well worth a visit. They include the **L1-L3** *Golden Rock Estate*, St George's Parish, PO Box 493, T 469 3346, F 469 2113, 7 cottages, 15 rooms in 18th century plantation house, 2-storey suite in old windmill for honeymooners/families, antique furniture, 4-poster beds, ocean views, family plan available, pool, tennis, beach shuttle, specialist interest tours, principally of ecological content, enjoy afternoon tea and watch the monkeys; **L1** *Hermitage Plantation*, St John's Parish, T 469 3477, F 469 2481, in the UK T 0800-373 742, very friendly, beautiful cottages, 4-poster beds, tennis, pool, horse riding, stunning setting, many guests extend their stay, highly rec; **L1-L2** *Montpelier Plantation Inn*, also St John's, PO Box 474, T 469 3462, F 469 2932, a favourite with British tourists, delightful, friendly and helpful, pool, tennis, beach shuttle, child reductions, 7 cottages (16 rooms). The **L1** *Nisbet Plantation Beach Club*, St James, built on site of 18th century plantation on ½ mile beach, T 469 9325, F 469 9864, 38 rooms in cottages/suites with tennis, swimming pool, croquet, a beach bar and pavilion, good food, huge breakfasts, delicious afternoon tea, excellent dinner, laundry and postage complimentary, highly rec. **L3-A1** *Pinney's Beach Hotel* PO Box 61, T 469 5207, F 469 1088, 46 rooms, 7 cottages, pool, watersports, horse riding, on the beach, dining room has no view, food and service reported poor off season, rooms in need of redecoration. New hotels and resorts are being built all the time. **L1** *Four Seasons Resort*, 196 rooms, on Pinney's Beach, PO Box 565, T 469 1111, F 469 1112, has Robert Trent Jones II 18-hole championship golf course, tennis, pool, watersports inc diving, sailboats, windsurfing and all entertainment inc children's activity programme and live music, particularly in high season; the **L1-L2** *Mount Nevis Hotel and Beach Club*, PO Box 494, T 469 9373, F 469 9375, modern, 32 rooms and studios, a/c, TV, VCR, phone, pool, watersports at beach club 5 mins away inc windsurfing; **L2-L3** *Old Manor Estate and Hotel*, PO Box 70, T 469 3445, F 469 3388, in restored 1690 sugar plantation has 14 rooms inc a cottage 800 feet above sea level, tropical gardens, beach shuttle, pool; **L2-L3** *Oualie Beach Hotel*, on the beach, informal, comfortable, diving and other watersports, 22 rooms, studios, T 469 9735, F 469 9176.

There are also many guest houses, apartments and cottages including **A1** *Yamseed Inn*, T 469 9361, 4 rooms inc delicious breakfast, lovely view of St Kitts, beautiful gardens, excellent value, highly rec, friendly, helpful owner Sybil Siegfried can arrange crossings from St Kitts and car hire; **L1-L3** *Hurricane Cove Bungalows*, T/F 469 9462, on hillside with wonderful sea view, 10 1-3 bedroomed, well-equipped wooden bungalows of Finnish design, swimming pool, path down to stoney beach, good snorkelling, helpful manageress, Brenda, highly rec, sports facilities nearby, 3 night min stay in winter, long term discounts; *Donna's Self-Catering Apartments*, PO Box 503, T 469 3464; **A3** *Sea Spawn Guest House*, PO Box 233, T 469 5239, 5-min walk N of Charlestown, 2 from Pinney's Beach, has 2 fishing boats, car rental and kitchen and dining facilities, quiet.

● **Places To Eat**

The best restaurants are in the hotels and it is usually necessary to reserve a table. The above hotels provide exceptional cuisine as well as barbecues and entertainment on certain nights of the week. There are very few eating places in Charlestown: *Mariner's Wharf*, on the waterfront, serves excellent roti, open Mon-Sat 1000-2200, T 469 0138. *The Courtyard Café*, T 469 5685, minutes from the ferry, good place for breakfast in tranquil courtyard garden, open Mon-Sat 0730-1530, dinner by reservation only, but not necessary on Tues when open for Happy Hour from 1800; *Callaloo* on Main Street serves lunch from US$4 and dinner from US$6, local food, hamburgers, sandwiches, pizzas from 1800, open Mon-Thur 1000-2200, Fri, Sat 1000-2400, no smoking, bring your own wine, friendly service, T 469 5389/5884; *Eddy's* on same street is a tourist favourite for local food, drinks and music with string bands, bush bands or steel bands Sat 2000-2300, Happy Hour Wed 1700-2000; *Miss June's*, Jones Bay, T 469 5330, open three times a week, Caribbean dinner party, preceded by cocktails and *hors d'oeuvres*, wine, dessert, coffee and liqueurs inc in price, numbers strictly limited so reservations essential. The *Oualie Beach Club* does local lunches and dinners, T 469 9735, 0700-2200. Most restaurants only open in the evenings in the off season or even shut completely. *Prinderella's*, on the beach at Tamarind Bay, lunch 1200-1530, dinner 1800-2100, closed Tues, good for Happy Hour on Fri night, substantial snacks (chicken, houmous) are served free with drinks; *Mem's Pizzería*, Prospect Garden, T 469 1390, excellent pizza, seafood rec.

Information for travellers

BEFORE TRAVELLING

● **Documents**

US and Canadian visitors do not require passports but need only produce proof of citizenship to stay up to 6 months. Other nationalities need passports and a return ticket but for up to 6 months visas are not required for Commonwealth and EC countries, Finland, Iceland, Liechtenstein, Norway, San Marino, Sweden, Switzerland, Turkey, Uruguay, Venezuela and nationals of other member countries of the OAS, with the exception of the Dominican Republic and Haiti who do require visas.

● **Climate**

The weather is pleasant all year round but the best time to visit is during the dry months from Nov to May. Locals insist that, with changing weather patterns, May to early Aug can be preferable. The temperature varies between 17°C and 33°C, tempered by sea winds and with an average annual rainfall of 55 ins on St Kitts and 48 ins on Nevis.

● **Health**

Mains water is chlorinated, but bottled water is available if preferred for drinking, particularly outside the main towns. Dairy produce, meat, poultry, seafood, fruit and vegetables are generally considered safe. A yellow fever or cholera vaccination certificate is required if you are arriving from an infected area.

MONEY

● **Currency**

East Caribbean dollar: EC2.70=US$1. US dollars accepted. When prices are quoted in both currencies, eg for departure tax, taxi fares, a notional rate of EC$2.50 = US$1 is used. There are no restrictions on the amount of foreign currency that can be imported or exported, but the amount of local currency exported is limited to the amount you imported and declared.

● **Credit cards**

Check which credit cards are accepted, Visa is the most widely used, Access/Mastercard and Diners Club are not so popular.

GETTING THERE

AIR

The main airport is RL Bradshaw International, St Kitts, 2 miles from Basseterre (2-min walk to road for bus EC$1 to Basseterre, for return catch bus at roundabout NE of Independence Square). Connections to North America and Europe can be made through San Juan (American Eagle and LIAT), St Maarten (LIAT and Winair), Barbados (LIAT) and Antigua (LIAT). There are good connections with other Caribbean Islands (Anguilla, Dominica, Grenada, St Croix, St Eustatius, St Lucia, St Thomas and Tortola) with LIAT and Windward Islands Airways (Winair). Weekly charters inc Canada Air, Royal Air and American Trans Air.

There is also an airport on Nevis, at Newcastle airfield, 7 miles from Charlestown, served by LIAT, Winair, Coastal Air Transport and light charter aircraft from St Kitts, Anguilla, Antigua, St-Barthélémy, St Croix and St Maarten. Expect to have your baggage searched on your way in to the island and likewise expect chaotic scenes on departure. The grander hotels on Nevis will arrange chartered air transfers from Antigua or St Kitts for their guests (for instance, Carib Aviation from Antigua), this is highly rec to avoid the crush.

SEA

28 cruise lines were calling in 1995-96, with a total of 325 calls projected. Basseterre has a deep water port.

● **Ports of entry**

(Own flag). List all anchorage stops on cruising permit at the Port Authority in Basseterre and clear with immigration in Nevis. Charges are EC$20 up to 20 tons, EC$35 up to 30 tons, EC$38 up to 50 tons. Port dues EC$6-25 based on size. There is no additional charge in Nevis once you have cleared in St Kitts.

● **Anchorages**

White House and Ballast Bay are the best on St Kitts, Oualie Beach on Nevis is beautiful. Good groceries, alcoholic drinks, laundry, propane. Can have fuel delivered to dock and buy water by the cubic ton.

ON ARRIVAL

● Airlines

LIAT, TDC Airline Services, PO Box 142, Basseterre, T 465 2511/2286, and Evelyn's Travel, on Main Street, Charlestown, general sales agent for BWIA, LIAT, American Airlines and British Airways, PO Box 211, Charlestown, T 469 5302/5238; BWIA, T 465 2286 on St Kitts, 469 5238 on Nevis; American Eagle, T 465 8490 (St Kitts); Winair, Sprott St, Basseterre, T 465 2186 on St Kitts, 469 5583 on Nevis; Carib Aviation, T 465 3055 (the Circus, Basseterre and Golden Rock airport, St Kitts), F 465 3168, T 469 9295 (Newcastle Airport, Nevis). Air St Kitts Nevis, PO Box 529, Basseterre, T 465 8571, 469 9241, F 469 9018, a charter company specializing in day excursions and other services to neighbouring islands eg Saba, Sint Maarten, Antigua, Guadeloupe, Barbados, USVI. Also air ambulance with medical staff.

● Banks

The Eastern Caribbean Central Bank (ECCB) is based in Basseterre, and is responsible for the issue of currency in Antigua and Barbuda, Dominica, Grenada, Montserrat, St Kitts and Nevis, St Lucia and St Vincent and the Grenadines. There is a local bank on St Kitts: St Kitts-Nevis- Anguilla National Bank (5 branches: on the corner of Central Street and West Independence Square Street; Pelican Mall; Sandy Point, T 465 2204/6331/2701 open 0830-1500 except Thur 0830-1200, Sat 0830-1100, a branch at Saddlers Village, T 465 7362, opens 0830-1300 except Thur 0830-1200 and Sat 0830-1100) and on Nevis, West Square Street, Charlestown, T 469 5244, same hours. In addition, on Nevis, there is the Nevis Co-operative Banking Co Ltd and the Bank of Nevis. Foreign banks on St Kitts: Barclays Bank, Plc (on the Circus, Basseterre, T 465 2519 open Mon-Thur 0800-1500, Fri 0800-1700, the other at Frigate Bay, open Mon-Thur 0800-1300, Fri 0800-1300, 1500-1700, T 465 2264/2510), Royal Bank of Canada (on the Circus, Basseterre, T 465 2519, open Mon-Thur 0800-1500, Fri 0800-1700, T 465 2259/2389), Bank of Nova Scotia (Fort Street, open Mon-Thur 0800-1500, Fri 0800-1700, T 465 4141); on Nevis, Barclays (T 469 5467/5309) and Bank of Nova Scotia (T 469 5411). Open 0800-1500 Mon-Thur, Fri until

1700. Avoid lunchtimes (1200-1300) and after 1500 on Fri as banks are busy with local workers. If you are in a hurry, choose a foreign bank as their queues are often shorter. Visa and MasterCard accepted by all three.

● Embassies and consulates

There is a Venezuelan Embassy on St Kitts and a resident Chargé d'Affaires of the Embassy of the Republic of China. There are also Honorary Consuls of Spain, Germany, Trinidad and Tobago, France and the Netherlands. The acting British High Commissioner is in Antigua.

● Laundry

Warners, Bird Rock Road, Basseterre, inc dry cleaning (allow a week).

● Official time

Atlantic Standard Time, 4 hours behind GMT, 1 ahead of EST.

● Public holidays

New Year's Day (1 Jan), Good Friday, Easter Monday, May Day (first Mon in May), Whit Monday (end of May), the Queen's birthday (June), Aug Bank Holiday Mon (beginning of the month), Independence Day (19 Sept), Christmas Day (25 Dec).

● Security

Note that the penalties for possession of narcotics are very severe and no mercy is shown towards tourists. Theft has increased, do not leave your things unattended in a car or on the beach.

● Shopping

The shopper has plenty of choice and is not swamped by US or British merchandise. Shops are well stocked. Local Sea Island cotton wear and cane and basketwork are attractive and reasonable. Shop opening hours 0800-1600, Mon-Sat. Early closing on Thur and also Sat for some shops. Walls Deluxe Record and Bookshop on Fort Street has a good selection of music and Caribbean books, open Mon-Thur 0800-1700, Fri 0800-1800, Sat 0800-1630.

The Island Hopper Boutique at the Circus, underneath the *Ballahoo* restaurant, stocks the Caribelle Batik range of cotton fashions and also carries clothes from Trinidad, St Lucia, Barbados and Haiti; open 0800-1600 Mon-Fri, 0800-1300 Sat, T 465 1640; also at The Arcade, Charlestown, Nevis, T 469 1491/5426. The Plantation Picture House, at Rawlins Plantation is Kate Spencer's studio and gallery of portraits, still life and landscapes in oils and watercolours, her designs are also on silk, open

1100-1700. She also has a shop in Basseterre, next to Walls Deluxe Record and Bookshop, called Kate, with paintings, prints, silk sarongs, as well as pottery by Carla Astaphan, and another shop in Main Street, Charlestown.

The public markets in Basseterre and Charleston are busiest Sat morning, good for fruit and vegetables, also fish stalls and butchers. Supermarkets in Basseterre include B & K Superfood on the S side of Independence Square and George Street, Horsfords Valumart on Wellington Road, and Rams on Bay Road and at Bird Rock. On Nevis, there are well-stocked supermarkets: Nisbets in Newcastle and Superfood, Parkville Plaza, Charlestown. Several local craft shops in Charlestown. Next to the Tourist Office is Nevis Handicraft Cooperative, rec. On the road to the *Four Seasons Hotel* is an industrial estate with shops selling crafts and a toy shop. In Newcastle there is a pottery with red clay artifacts inc bowls and candleholders. You can watch potters at work. The kilns are fired by burning coconut husks.

There are **philatelic bureaux** on both St Kitts and Nevis which are famous (the latter more so) for their first day covers of the islands' fauna and flora, undersea life, history and carnival. The St Kitts bureau is in Pelican Shopping Mall, the new development for cruise ship arrivals on the wharf, open Mon-Wed, Fri-Sat 0800-1200, 1300-1500, Thur, 0800-1100. The Nevis bureau is open Mon-Fri, 0800-1600.

● **Tipping**
A 10% service charge is added to hotel bills. In restaurants about 10%-15% is expected.

● **Voltage**
230 volts AC/60 cycles (some hotels have 110V).

ON DEPARTURE

● **Departure tax**
There is an airport departure tax of US$10 or EC$27 pp, not payable for stays of less than 24 hrs (or when you leave on the same flight number as you arrived the previous day, ie slightly more than 24 hrs).

● **Airport information**
It is possible to get a bus to the airport and walk the last 5 mins from the main road; some buses might go up to the terminal. If you have not much luggage, it is easy to walk from Basseterre to the airport. There is no currency exchange at the airport. There are duty free and gift shops and a café.

FOOD AND DRINK

Food on the whole is good. Apart from almost every kind of imported food and drink, there is a wide variety of fresh seafood (red snapper, lobster, king fish, blue parrot), and local vegetables. The excellent local spirit is CSR – Cane Spirit Rothschild – produced in St Kitts by Baron de Rothschild (now in a joint venture with Demerara Distillers Ltd of Guyana). It is drunk neat, with ice or water, or with 'Ting', the local grapefruit soft drink (also highly rec). Tours of the CSR factory are possible.

GETTING AROUND

LAND TRANSPORT

● **Motoring**
Drive on the left. The main road on St Kitts is, for the most part, very good and motorists, especially bus drivers, can be very fast. Watch out for corners and be alert at all times. The main road is not as good on Nevis, where storm ditches frequently cross the paved road; drive slowly and carefully. Fuel is US$2/gallon.

Most rental companies will help you obtain the obligatory local driving licence, EC$30, from the Fire Station, Ponds Road or the office opp Government Headquarters in Basseterre.

● **Car hire**
Cars, jeeps, mini mokes can be hired from US$30-35 a day from a variety of agencies on both islands, eg TDC Rentals, West Independence Square, Basseterre, T 465 2991, F 465 1099, or Bay Front, Charlestown, T 469 5960, F 469 1329, also at *Four Seasons*, T 469 1111, if you rent for 3-day min you can arrange for a car on the sister island if you do a day trip to St Kitts or Nevis; Caines Rent-A-Car, Princes Street, Basseterre, T 465 2366, F 465 6172; Sunshine Car Rental, Cayon Street, Basseterre, T 465 2193, Hondas and Korando jeeps. If you are arriving in St Kitts from Nevis, there are several car hire companies on Independence Square, some 3 mins walk from the ferry pier. One of the most convenient is Avis Car Rental, South Independence Square St, T 465 6507, F 465 1042 (Suzuki jeeps, Nissan automatics, efficient). Nisbett Rentals Ltd, 100 yards from Newcastle airport, Minimoke US$40/day, collision damage waiver US$8/day, rec, particularly if you are flying in/out of Nevis, T 469 9211, open 0700-1900. Note that if visiting at Carnival time you should book car hire a long time in advance.

Also on Nevis through Striker's (Hermitage), T 469 2654, Carlton Meade; bicycle rental on Craddock Road, T 469 5235.

Companies insist on you having collision damage waiver, which adds another US$5-10 to quoted rates. There is a 5% tax on car rentals.

● **Buses**

Minibuses do not run on a scheduled basis but follow a set route (more or less), EC$1-3 on most routes, EC$3 from Basseterre to the N of the island, frequent service from market area on the Bay Road from where buses go W to Sandy Point. To catch a bus E, wait off Bakers Corner at the E end of Cayon Street. There are no minibuses on Frigate Bay and the SE peninsula. On Nevis buses start outside Foodworld Cash & Carry supermarket and go to all points, but not on a regular basis, EC$1-3, an island tour is possible, if time consuming. Buses on both islands are a cheap (and speedy) way to get around. Drivers are generally very obliging and, if asked, may even divert their route to accommodate you. Buses run very early in the morning; St Kitts buses run up to 2300, but on Nevis there is a reduced service after 1600 and very few buses after 1800. Buses are identified by their H registration plate.

● **Taxis**

Taxis have a T registration plate. Maximum taxi fares are set, for example: **on St Kitts**, from Golden Rock Airport to Basseterre EC$13-16 (depending on area of town), to the Deep Water Port, EC$22, to Frigate Bay, EC$25, to Old Road, EC$27, to Middle Island, EC$30. From Basseterre to Old Road, EC$24, to Frigate Bay, EC$18, to Middle Island, EC$26, to Sandy Point, EC$30. Taxis within Basseterre cost EC$8, with additional charges for waiting or for more than one piece of luggage. Between 2300-0600 prices rise by 25%. **On Nevis** a taxi from the airport to Charlestown costs EC$30, to *Pinney's Beach Hotel*, EC$30, to *Oualie Beach*, EC$20, to the *Montpelier Inn*, EC$45, to *Hermitage Inn*, EC$40 and to *Nisbet Plantation Inn*, EC$17. Fares from Charlestown are EC$10, EC$23, EC$26, EC$23 and EC$36 respectively. A 50% extra charge is made on Nevis between 2200 and 0600. An island tour of Nevis costs US$50 for about 3 hrs, but you can bargain it down if no cruise ship is in port. *The Traveller* magazine (see below, **Further reading**) has a list of recommended fares. There is also a list at the airports. Complaints have been received that taxis on both islands are poor, do not stick to the regulated fares and are extremely expensive. There is no need to tip.

FERRIES

A passenger ferry, the *Caribe Queen*, operates on a regular schedule between St Kitts (Basseterre deep water port) and Nevis. The crossing takes about 45 mins and costs EC$20 round trip. Departs Basseterre, Mon 0800, 1600; Tues 1300; Wed 0700, 1600, 1900 (good day for day trip); Fri 0830, 1600; Sat 0830, 1500. Departs Charlestown, Mon 0700, 1500; Tues 0730, 1800; Wed 0800, 1800; Fri 0730, 1500; Sat 0730, 1400. Confirm sailing times with Ministry of Communications, T 465 2521, Mon-Fri 0800-1600. Tickets can only be purchased from the quay just prior to departure, so turn up about 1 hr in advance to avoid disappointment. Island tours operate from St Kitts and there is also a water taxi service between the 2 islands: US$25 return, min 4 passengers, 20 mins, operated by Kenneth's Dive Centre, T 465 2670 in advance, or ProDivers, US$20, 10 mins, T 465 3223, 469 9086. The *Four Seasons Hotel* has ferry boats running exclusively for guests' flights. Nevis Express runs a shuttle air service between St Kitts and Nevis, US$20, 6 mins, also charter service.

COMMUNICATIONS

● **Postal services**

Post office in Basseterre is on Bay Road, open Mon-Sat 0800-1500 except Thur when it closes at 1100 and Sat at 1200; in Charlestown on Main Street. Airmail letters to the UK take up to 2 weeks.

● **Telecommunications**

The telephone company, Skantel (part of the Cable & Wireless Group), has digital telecommunications systems for the 2 islands and international direct dialling is available. Telemessages and faxes can be sent from the main office on Cayon Street, Basseterre. Credit card calls T 1-800-877 8000. USA direct public phones available at Skantel office. Phone cards are sold in denominations of EC$10, 20 and 40. Coin boxes take EC quarters minimum and EC dollars. Codes: 809-465/6 (St Kitts), 809-469 (Nevis). The 809 number is due to be replaced by 869 in 1997. Call charges are from US$5 for 3 mins to the USA, Canada or the UK. The Boat Phone Company on the Frigate Bay Road, T/F 465 3003, offers cellular phone service for yachts. Telex and telegram facilities in the main hotels.

MEDIA

● **Newspapers**
Newspapers come out weekly (*The Observer*, *The Democrat*) or twice weekly (*The Labour Spokesman*). There are 2 TV stations: the state run ZIZ and Nevis-based Christian station Trinity Broadcasting. AM/FM ZIZ Radio is on medium wave 555 kHz and 96 FM; Choice FM is on 105FM. VON Radio in Nevis is on 895 kHz medium wave and Radio Paradise is on 825 kHz.

TOURIST INFORMATION

● **Local tourist office**
The St Kitts Department of Tourism (Pelican Mall, PO Box 132, Basseterre, T 465 2620/4040, F 465 8794) and the Nevis Tourist Office (Main Street, Charlestown, T 469 1042, F 469 1066) are both extremely helpful, with plenty of information available, open Mon-Fri 0800-1600, with the Nevis office also open Sat 0900-1200.

● **Tourist offices overseas**
Canada: 11 Yorkville Ave, Suite 508, Toronto M4W 1L3, T 416-921 7717, F 416-921 7997.

Germany: Postfach 2211, D-61293 Bad Homburg 1, T 49 6173 66747, F 49 6173 640969.

UK: 10 Kensington Court, London W8 5DL, T 0171-376 0881, F 0171-937 3611.

USA: at 414 East 75th Street, New York NY 10021, T 212-535 1234, F 212-734 6511.

The St Kitts/Nevis Hotel Association can be reached at PO Box 438, Basseterre, St Kitts, T 465 5304, F 465 7746.

● **Further reading**
Useful publications are *The Traveller* (annual, the official publication of the Tourist Board, available at hotels and the tourist offices. Check the range of books at St Christopher Heritage Society, Basseterre, and Museum of Nevis History, Charlestown. *St Kitts, Cradle of the Caribbean* by Brian Dyde and *Nevis, Queen of the Caribees* by Joyce Gordon are both published by MacMillan.

ACKNOWLEDGEMENTS

The editors are very grateful to Gill Powell, Basseterre, for her very thorough revision of this chapter.

Anguilla

A NGUILLA is a small island, only about 35 miles square, the most N of the Leeward Islands, five miles N of St Martin and 70 miles NW of St Kitts. The island is low lying, the highest point being Crocus Hill at 213 feet above sea level. Unlike its larger sisters it is not volcanic but of coral formation. It is arid, covered with low scrub and has few natural resources. However, it has excellent beaches and superb diving and snorkelling, protected by the coral reefs. The island's name is the Spanish word *anguilla* (eel), a reference to its long, narrow shape. Its Carib name was Malliouhana. The 1992 census put the population at 8,960, predominantly of African descent but with some traces of Irish blood. However, the population has increased since then with Anguillans returning from abroad and foreigners making their home on the island. The administrative centre is *The Valley*, the largest community on the island with a population of 500. The people of Anguilla are very friendly and helpful and it is one of the safest islands in the Caribbean.

To the NW is the uninhabited Dog Island which is excellent for swimming, and beyond that is Sombrero Island, where there is an important lighthouse. Other islets include Scrub Island at the NE tip of Anguilla, Little Scrub Island next to it, Anguillita Island and Blowing Rock at the SW tip and the Prickly Pear Cays and Sail Island to the NW on the way to Dog Island.

HISTORY

The earliest known Amerindian site on Anguilla is at the NE tip of the island, where tools and artefacts made from conch shells have been recovered and dated at around 1300 BC. Saladoid Amerindians settled on the island in the fourth century AD and brought their knowledge of agriculture, ceramics and their religious culture based on the god of cassava (see page 39). By the mid-sixth

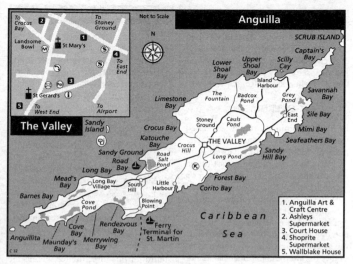

The Valley / Anguilla map. Key:
1. Anguilla Art & Craft Centre
2. Ashleys Supermarket
3. Court House
4. Shoprite Supermarket
5. Wallblake House

century large villages had been built at Rendezvous Bay and Sandy Ground, with smaller ones at Shoal Bay and Island Harbour. Post Saladoid Amerindians from the Greater Antilles arrived in the tenth century, building new villages and setting up a chiefdom with a religious hierarchy. Several ceremonial items have been found and debris related to the manufacture of the three-pointed zemis, or spirit stones, associated with fertility rites. By the 17th century, Amerindians had disappeared from Anguilla: wiped out by enslavement and European diseases.

Anguilla was first mentioned in 1564 when a French expedition passed en route from Dominica to Florida, but it was not until 1650 that it was first colonized by the British. Despite several attempted invasions, by Caribs in 1656 and by the French in 1745 and 1796, it remained a British colony. From 1825 it became more closely associated with St Kitts for administrative purposes and ultimately incorporated in the colony. In 1967 St Kitts-Nevis-Anguilla became a State in Association with the UK and gained internal independence. However, Anguilla opposed this development and almost immediately repudiated government from St Kitts. A breakaway movement was led by Ronald Webster of the People's Progressive Party (PPP). In 1969 British forces invaded the island to install a British Commissioner after negotiations had broken down. The episode is remembered locally for the unusual presence of the London Metropolitan Police, who remained on the island until 1972 when the Anguilla Police Force was established.

The post of Chief Minister alternated for two decades between the rival politicians, Ronald Webster and Emile Gumbs, leader of the Anguilla National Alliance (ANA), the latter holding office in 1977-80 and 1984-94. Mr Gumbs (now Sir Emile) retired from politics at the general elections held in March 1994. These elections proved inconclusive, with the ANA, the Anguilla United Party (AUP) and the Anguilla Democratic Party (ADP) each winning two seats and an Independent, Osbourne Fleming (who was Finance Minister in the ANA government) winning the seventh. A coalition was formed by Hubert

Hughes, leader of the AUP, and Victor Banks, ADP, and the former was sworn in as Chief Minister. Mr Hughes had been a Minister in the 1984 ANA government, but had been dismissed in 1985, subsequently joining the opposition AUP, then led by Ronald Webster.

GOVERNMENT

In 1980, Anguilla formally separated from the State and became a British Dependent Territory with a Governor to represent the Crown. A new constitution was introduced in 1982, providing for a Governor, an Executive Council comprising four elected Ministers and two ex-officio members, and an 11-member legislative House of Assembly presided over by a Speaker. In 1990 the constitution was amended to give the Governor responsibility for international financial affairs. A new post of Deputy Governor was created, to replace the Permanent Secretary for Finance as a member of the Executive Council and House of Assembly.

THE ECONOMY

The main economic activities used to be livestock raising, lobster fishing, salt production and boat building, but tourism is now the major generator of foreign exchange and employment. There are some 800 rooms available in guest houses, villas and apartments and hotels, although the number is steadily rising. However, the hurricane season in 1995 caused havoc to the industry. Total visitor arrivals fell by 14.9% to 107,086, of which stopover visitors were 68,555, a drop of 16.5% from 1994. Gdp declined in 1995 after a growth rate of 8.1% in 1994.

There is also some offshore banking and the Government aims to establish a reputable offshore financial services industry. Thirty out of the 43 offshore banks, who pay an annual licence fee to the Government, had their licences cancelled in 1990 following a review of the sector. At end-1991 the House of Assembly approved legislation to tighten

Operation Dinero

An offshore bank established in 1993 was used by the Governor and the Foreign and Commonwealth Office deliberately to trap drug trafficking and money laundering by the Cali cartel of Colombia. The highly successful 'Operation Dinero', run jointly by the US and British authorities, led to the seizure in 1995 of US$50mn in assets, nine tonnes of cocaine, a shipment of arms for Croatia and the arrest of over 100 people in the USA, Spain and Italy. The Governor, Alan Shave, said that the operation had demonstrated the effectiveness of Anguilla's monitoring system of offshore banking.

control of offshore finance, giving the Governor complete and final authority over the granting of licences. New financial services legislation enacted in late 1994 and a new marketing strategy led to an increase of 23% in the number of registered offshore financial companies that year.

Previously, high levels of unemployment led to migration to other Caribbean islands and further afield, but the unemployment rate has fallen from 26% in 1985 to almost nil and shortages of labour have delayed expansion programmes, as well as putting pressure on prices and wages. Work permits have been granted to more than 1,000 non-Anguillans, but many people have two jobs. Workers' remittances are crucial, particularly since the 1984 suspension of budgetary support in the form of UK grants-in-aid, although the British Government does still provide aid for the development programme, along with other donors such as the EEC and the Caribbean Development Bank. Anguilla is to receive £10.5m in capital aid and technical assistance for 1994-97 under a Country Policy Plan agreed with the UK. The Plan details policy and

Hurricane Luis

Anguilla was one of the islands to be hit by Hurricane Luis in Sept 1995, which caused damage estimated at EC$75mn to housing and hotels. All communications were cut and the airport was closed. However, the island was well-prepared, having had prior warning. On the Friday everything shut down, boats went out to sea, well away from the storm, and tourists left the island. When Luis struck on the Monday the Anguillians were ready. *HMS Southampton* was sent with relief supplies and repairs and reconstruction were soon under way. Despite the proximity to St Maarten, which was devastated, Anguilla came through it all quickly and today the island's resorts, restaurants and tour agencies are operating normally. The message is: business as usual.

programme targets up to 1996/97 and is aimed at promoting 'good government and self-sustainable growth and economic autonomy for Anguilla over the medium to long term'. There is no income tax and the Government gets its revenues from customs duties, bank licences, property and stamps.

FLORA AND FAUNA

The island is low lying, coralline and arid. Although you will see colourful gardens with flowering hibiscus, bougainvillea and other tropical plants, the island is mostly covered with scrub. However, birdwatching is good at Little Bay, Crocus Bay's N point and at ponds and coves, T 2759 for information. It is intended that the wetlands will eventually become sanctuaries. 93 species of birds have been recorded on Anguilla, including the blue faced booby, kingfisher and the great blue heron. The national bird is the turtle dove, which is protected.

DIVING AND MARINE LIFE

The Government is introducing a Marine Parks system, installing permanent moorings in certain areas to eliminate anchor damage. Mooring permits are required. Do not remove any marine life such as coral or shells from underwater. Spear fishing is prohibited.

Scuba diving can be arranged through Tamariain Watersports Ltd, PO Box 247, Sandy Ground, T 2020, F 5125.

Owned and run by Iain Grummit and Thomas Peabody, excellent courses are available at this 5-star PADI training centre, recommended. Retail shop open daily 0800-1600, snorkelling and diving equipment for sale or rent. All dives are guided boat dives; a single tank dive costs US$40, a 2-tank dive US$70, night dives US$50. Anguillian Divers dive the E end of the island and offer PADI courses, T 4750.

There are good dives just off the coast, particularly for novices or for night dives, while the others are generally in a line due W of Sandy Island, NW of Sandy Ground, and along the reef formed by Prickly Pear Cays and Sail Island. Off Sandy Island, there are lots of soft corals and sea-fans, while at Sandy Deep there is a wall which falls from 15 to 60 feet. There are also several wrecks, nine of which have been deliberately sunk as dive sites around the island, the most recent in 1993.

Further W, Paintcan Reef at a depth of 80 feet contains several acres of coral and you can sometimes find large turtles there. Nearby, Authors Deep, at 110 feet has black coral, turtles and a host of small fish, but this dive is more for the experienced diver. On the N side of the Prickly Pear Cays you can find a beautiful underwater canyon with ledges and caves where nurse sharks often go to rest. Most of the reefs around Anguilla have some red coral; be careful not to touch it as it burns.

BEACHES AND WATERSPORTS

There are twelve miles or 45 beaches with fine white coral sand and crystal clear water. Most of them are protected by a ring of coral reefs and offshore islands. The beaches are clean, and many of them are relatively unpopulated, but nude (or topless for women) swimming or sun-bathing is not allowed.

Shoal Bay is the most popular beach and claims to be one of the most beautiful in the Eastern Caribbean. There are hotels, snack bars for lunch, although only one has a toilet. The snorkelling is good, with the closest of two reefs only 10 yards from the shore and you can rent snorkelling equipment. You can also rent beach umbrellas, loungers, rafts and towels.

Mead's Bay is also popular with more expensive bars, hotels and watersports. Road Bay/Sandy Ground has most nightlife and restaurants and is the starting point for most day trips, dive tours and a popular anchorage for visiting yachts. Watersports equipment rentals can be organized here.

Scilly Cay is a small cay off Island Harbour with good snorkelling. A free ferry takes you to the bar on a palm-clad beach where walls are made from conch shells. Live music on Wednesdays, Fridays and Sundays. *Smitty's Bar*, across the water at Island Harbour is less sophisticated, tables made from old cable barrels, TV, popular with the locals. Captain's Bay is rougher but the scenery is dramatic and not many people go there. The dirt road is full of potholes and goats and may be impassable with a low car.

At Crocus Bay the rocks on both sides have nice coral and underwater scenery. There is a bar/restaurant and toilets. At the end of Limestone Bay is a small beach with excellent snorkelling, but be careful, the sea can be rough here. Little Bay is more difficult to reach but eagle rays and turtles can be seen; turn right in front of the old cottage hospital in the Valley, after about half a mile there are

some trails leading down to the water, fishermen have put up a net for the last bit. Glass bottom boats and cruise boats also come here.

Windsurfing and sailing are readily available and some of the hotels offer water skiing, paddle boats, snorkelling, fishing and sunfish sailing. Jet skiing is prohibited. There are glass bottom boats which can be hired for one or two people to operate themselves or crewed for groups. Sport fishing is available, contact Neville Connor, T 5643/6395, F 6234.

Yacht or motorboat charters are offered with beach and snorkelling cruises around the island or trips to St Phillipsburg, St Maarten, charters to Saba, Statia, St Barts on request. Operators change frequently but in 1996 the following were in Anguillan waters: *Bing*, a 37-ft yacht for private charter or trips to Prickly Pear, Sandy Island etc, T 6395/5643, F 6234; *Gotcha!* Garfield's Sea Tours, 30-ft boat for exploring, fishing or island hopping, T 2956; Wildcat Services, T 2665, F 5559, catamaran cruises, sail and powerboat trips, fishing; Chocolat Catamaran Cruises, Captain Rollin Ruan, T 3394, 1000-1600, US$80 pp, 2-12 people inc lunch and drinks, US$50 pp, 2-8 people, 1700-1900 sunset cruise, snacks and drinks, private day charter US$360 or private sunset cruise US$250.

Boat racing is the national sport, the boats being a special class of wooden sloop made in Anguilla. There are frequent races, but the most important are on Anguilla Day (30 May) and during Carnival Week in August.

OTHER SPORTS

Several hotels have tennis courts. The *Malliouhana* has 4 championship courts for guests only; *Cinnamon Reef* has 2 at a cost of US$25 per hour for non-residents, free for guests; *Cap Juluca*, *Casablanca* and *Cove Castles* all have courts for guests' use only, others make a charge for non-guests: *Carimar Beach Club*, US$20/hr;

Coccoloba, US$15/hr; *The Mariners*, US$20/hr; *Masara Resort*, US$10/hr; *Rendezvous Bay*, US$5/hr; *Spindrift Apartments*, US$5-10/hr. For spectator sports, call the Sports Officer, T 2317, for information on fixtures. There is cricket, basketball, soccer, volley ball, soft ball, cycling and track and field. Horse riding, with trail rides or riding lessons, is offered by El Rancho del Blues, T 6164.

FESTIVALS

Carnival is at the beginning of August (the Friday before the first Monday), when the island comes to life with street dancing, Calypso competitions, the Carnival Queen Coronation, the Prince and Princess Show, nightly entertainment in The Valley and beach barbecues.

EXCURSIONS

Near The Valley, **Wallblake House** is a restored, eighteenth-century plantation house where the priest from **St Gerard's Roman Catholic Church** lives. The Church itself is worth a visit to see the unusual ventilation. Several resident artists exhibit their work on Saturday mornings during the winter season in the grounds of Wallblake House. At Sandy Ground Village, you can see the salt pond, around Great Road Pond, although it is not currently in operation.

Northeast of The Valley, by Shoal Village, is **The Fountain** national park. Its focus is in fact a cave which has a source of constant fresh water and a series of Amerindian petroglyphs. Artefacts have been found and it is hoped they will be housed in a museum at the site, but in 1996 the national park was still closed while archaeologists considered policy alternatives and was likely to remain so for a while. Anguilla awaits detailed archaeological investigation, but it is thought that the island had several settlements and a social structure of some importance, judging by the ceremonial items which have been found. Contact the National Trust, T 3041, or the

Anguilla Archaeological and Historical Society for more information; the Society is involved in setting up a national museum (opp the Ronald Webster Park car park) and in several publications including a Review (PO Box 252). There is a very small museum of artefacts found on site at the *Arawak Beach Resort*, together with replicas of furnishings, pottery and baskets, T 4888, F 4498. There is also a mini museum at the *Pumphouse* bar, Sandy Ground. The building was once part of the salt factory and equipment used in the salt making process is on display, T 5154. A local historian, Mr Petty, collects traditional household artefacts, which he has on display at his home at Colville Petty's, Pond Ground, East End. To arrange a visit, T 4440.

Big Spring Cave is an old Amerindian ceremonial centre where you can see petroglyphs. It is near Island Harbour, a fishing village with Irish ancestry. The National Trust has a map of archaeological and historical sites of Anguilla, worth getting if you want to explore caves, Amerindian sites or sugar mill rounds, T 3041, PO Box 1234.

Local deposits of clay have been found and pottery is now made on the island; the work of Barbadian potter and sculptor, Courtney Devonish, and his students, is on display at the **Devonish Cotton Gin Art Gallery** in the Old Factory Plaza opposite the Catholic Church, T 2949. There are sometimes pottery demonstrations on Saturdays.

Day trips can be arranged to some of the neighbouring islands or to the offshore islands and cays. **Sandy Island** is only 15 minutes from Sandy Ground harbour and is a pleasant desert island-type place to swim, snorkel and spend half a day or so. Motorboats or sailboats cross over hourly from 1000, US$8pp. Lunch or drinks available from a beach bar under coconut palms.

There are trips to **Prickly Pear**, six miles from Road Bay, which is well worth a visit, where you can snorkel if you are not a scuba diver, or to some of the other cays where you can fish or just have a picnic. Enchanted Island Cruises have a boat that goes to Prickly Pear daily (except Thursday) leaving 1000 and returning 1600, US$70 including drinks, barbecue lunch and snorkelling equipment, T 3111.

Scrub Island, two miles long and one mile wide, off the NE tip of Anguilla, is an interesting mix of coral, scrub and other vegetation and is worth a visit. It is uninhabited, except by goats, and can only be reached by boat. There is a lovely sandy beach on the W side and ruins of an abandoned tourist resort and airstrip. There can be quite a swell in the anchorage, so anchor well. Boats go from Road Bay, Shoal Bay or Island Harbour.

Chartered yachts and motorboats leave from Road Bay or from Island Harbour for Scilly Cay, privately owned by Eudoxie and Sandra Wallace and also named **Gorgeous Scilly Cay**. They also have their own boat with a free ferry service. Open 1000-1700, lunch only, live music Wed, Fri, Sun, closed Mon.

Information for travellers

BEFORE TRAVELLING

● **Documents**
All visitors need an onward ticket. All must also have a valid passport, except US citizens who need only show proof of identity with a photograph. Visas are not required by anyone. Proof of adequate funds is required if the Immigration Officer feels so inclined.

● **Climate**
The climate is sub-tropical with an average temperature of 27°C (80°F) and a mean annual rainfall of 914 milimetres (36 inches), falling mostly between Sept and December. Any cloud and rain early in the day has usually cleared by mid-morning.

MONEY

● **Currency**
The East Caribbean dollar. US dollars always accepted.

GETTING THERE

AIR

Wallblake airport is just outside The Valley, T 2384. International access points for Anguilla are Antigua, St Maarten or San Juan, Puerto Rico. LIAT has daily flights from Antigua; some flights connect with British Airways from London. Alternatively, charter flights will meet any incoming BA flight and fly you to Anguilla without you having to clear customs in Antigua. LIAT also connects Anguilla with St Kitts and Nevis, St Maarten, San Juan, Dominica, Martinique, Trinidad, St Lucia, Tortola and St Thomas (the LIAT office is at Gumbs Travel Agency, T 2238 and also at T 2748). American Eagle (T 3131/3500) has a twice daily air link with Puerto Rico which connects with their other US flights. Winair (T 2238/2748, F 3351) provides several daily flights from St Maarten (10 mins, about US$15) and has a service to St Barts. Coastal Air Transport (T 2431) flies from St Croix, USVI. Air Anguilla (T 2643) and Tyden Air (T 2719, F 3079, PO Box 107, The Valley) operate charters and air taxi services to the British and US Virgin Islands, St Maarten and St Kitts. In St Maarten, you can get bookings for Anguilla on the spot.

SEA

The principal port is Sandy Ground, T 6403. Ferry between Blowing Point (departure tax EC$5/US$2) and Marigot, Saint-Martin takes at least 20 mins and costs US$10 daytime, US$12 night-time, one way (pay on board). The service starts at about 0730 and continues every 30-40 mins until 1700; (there are also 2 evening ferries in high season at 1900 and 2300 (Marigot to Anguilla) and 1815 and 2215 (Anguilla to Marigot). You pay the US$2 departure tax after putting your name and passport number on the manifest (at booth at head of pier in Marigot or find the ferry clerk in the waiting area near Immigration Office) and before boarding at Marigot but you pay the fare on the boat. The same applies when leaving from Anguilla. Have your passport and tax receipt handy when boarding.

● **Boat documents**

(Own flag). In Road Bay get a cruising permit for other anchorages. Customs and Immigration at Blowing Point and Road Bay at Sandy Ground (Customs at the big wharf near the *Riviera*, Immigration at Police Station next to *Johnno's* on N side, near small pier). Free anchorage in Road Bay and Blowing Point. Fees are based on official tonnage. Charter boats pay additional anchoring fees. Bring your crew lists. There is a departure tax of US$5 pp. Sandy Island, Prickly Pear Cays, Dog Island and Crocus Bay have designated anchoring sites. Boats may not anchor in Rendezvous Bay or Little Bay.

ON ARRIVAL

● **Banks**

In The Valley, Barclays Bank International, T 2301/2304, F 2980, Box 140; Caribbean Commercial Bank, T 2571; National Bank of Anguilla, T 2101, F 3310. At George Hill, Bank of Nova Scotia, T 3333, F 3344.

● **Clothing**

Bathing costumes are not worn in public places. Nude bathing or nude sunbathing is not allowed.

● **Hospital**

There is a new hospital with modern equipment called the Princess Alexandra. Hospital T 2551/2; emergency T 911/999; Doctor T 3792/6522/2882 and T 2632/3233; Pharmacy T 2366/2738; optometrist T 3700. Most people drink bottled water but there is also rainwater or desalinated water for household use.

● **Hours of business**

0800-1200, 1300-1600 Mon to Fri; banks 0800-1300 Mon to Thur, 0800-1200, 1500-1700 on Fri. Gas stations are open in The Valley, Mon to Sat 0700-2100, Sun 0900-1300, and at Blowing Point, Mon to Sun 0700-2400.

● **Official time**

GMT minus 4 hours; EST plus 1 hour.

● **Public holidays**

New Year's Day, Good Friday, Easter Monday, Labour Day, Whit Monday, 30 May (Anguilla Day), the Queen's official birthday in June, the first Mon (August Monday) and the first Thur (August Thursday) and Fri (Constitution Day) in Aug, 19 Dec (Separation Day), Christmas Day, Boxing Day.

● **Shopping**

Mother Weme (Weme Caster) sells originals and limited edition prints of her paintings of local scenes from her home on the Sea Rocks, near Island Harbour, T 4504 for an appointment, prices for prints start from US$75 and for her acrylic and oil paintings from US$300. Ellie's Record Shop sells Caribbean and international music, T 5073, F 5317, open 1000-1800 at Fairplay Commercial Complex. There are lots of places selling T-shirts, beachwear and gifts. Caribbean Fancy boutique and gift shop is at George Hill at the traffic light, T 3133, F 3513.

Bookshop: National Bookstore, in the Social Security Complex next to Cable and Wireless, The Valley, open Mon-Sat 0800-1700, wide selection of novels, magazines, non-fiction, children's books, tourist guides, Caribbean history and literature, managed by Mrs Kelly. A *Dictionary of Anguillian Language* has been published in a 34-page booklet, edited by Ijahnia Christian of the Adult and Continuing Education Unit following the Cultural Educational Fest.

● **Voltage**
110 volts AC, 60 cycles.

● **Weights and measures**
Metric, but some imperial weights and measures are still used.

ON DEPARTURE

● **Departure tax**
There is a departure tax of US$10 at the airport and US$2 at the ferry.

ACCOMMODATION

Anguilla has the reputation of catering for upmarket, independent travellers. This is reflected in the number of relatively small, but expensive hotels and beach clubs. Bargains can be found in the summer months, with discounts of up to 50%. An 8% tax and 10-15% service charge will be added to the bill.

● **Hotels**

Price guide

L1	over US$200	L2	US$151-200
L3	US$101-150	A1	US$81-100
A2	US$61-80	A3	US$46-60
B	US$31-45	C	US$21-30
D	US$12-20	E	US$7-11
F	US$4-6	G	up to US$3

The following (in anti-clockwise direction from Road Bay) have flexible accommodation in rooms, suites, studios or villas, winter-summer prices quoted. **L1-L3 The Mariners**, Sandy Ground, T 2671/2815, F 2901, all-inclusive available, 67 rooms, suites and cottages, on beach, watersports, pool, tennis; **L1 Malliouhana Hotel**, Mead's Bay, T 6111, F 6011, T (800) 835-0796, PO Box 173, 53 rooms, no credit cards, suites up to US$1,185, every luxury, 'sprawlingly sybaritic public areas', very posh, pompous service, on beach, watersports, tennis, 2 pools; **L1-L3 Carimar Beach Club**, Meads Bay, PO Box 327, T 6881, F 6071, T 1-800-235-8667, 23 comfortable 1-3 bedroom apartments, beach, tennis; **L1 Frangipani Beach Club**, new, luxury resort on Mead's Bay beach, 15 units, Spanish style tiled roofs, multilevel, tiled floors, fans, cool, comfortable, T 6442, F 6440; **L1-L2 La Sirena**, Meads Bay, T 6827, F 6829, 36 individually designed rooms, villas up to US$450, beach nearby, pool; **Coccoloba Plantation**, Barnes Bay, T 6871, F 6332, 51 rooms, suites US$225-375, villas US$275-475 inc full breakfast,

beautiful beach, 2 pools, tennis, colourful gardens, gingerbread verandahs round the villas; **L1 Cove Castles Villa Resort**, Shoal Bay West, T 6801, F 6051, T 800 348 4716, PO Box 248, futuristic architecture, 4 3-bedroom villas, 8 2-bedroom beach houses, very expensive, housekeeper, phone, TV, beach, tennis, sunfish, bicycles included, watersports available; **L1 Cap Juluca** at Maundays Bay (T 6666/6779, F 6617), Moorish design, bright white, luxury resort, 98 rooms, every facility here, with 2 beaches, pool, watersports, tennis, also US$1,630-390 suites and US$3,790-1,300 3-5 bedroom villas, CP, full children's activity programmes with watersports and tennis, 179-acre estate; **L1 Casablanca Resort**, on Merrywing Bay, T 6999, F 6899, opulent Moorish style, rooms and villas, all-inclusive rates available, large pool, lots of tennis courts, health club, library, 3 restaurants, 90 unremarkable rooms and still growing; **L1 Pineapple Beach Club**, Rendezvous Bay, T 6061/6621, F 6019, 27 simple rooms, all inclusive, open air restaurant and bar on beach, pool; **L1-L3 Rendezvous Bay Hotel**, T 6549, F 6026, 30 rooms, villas up to US$425, beach, tennis, family run, helpful, rooms with veranda only a few metres from the sea, moderately good snorkelling, lovely beach, run by the Gumbs family, PO Box 31; **L1-L2 Cinnamon Reef**, Little Harbour, T 2727, F 3727, in the USA and Canada T 800-346-7084, F (914) 763-5362, in the UK, T 0800 373 742, 01453-835801, F 01453-835525, 22 rooms, beach sheltered, no surf but good snorkelling and sunfish sailing, pool, tennis, library, spectacular dining room, good food, friendly service, no children under 12 in winter; **L1-L2 Arawak Beach Resort**, PO Box 433, T 4888, F 4898, octagonal villas on the NE coast near Big Spring ceremonial centre, overlooking Scilly Cay, mini museum, health bar and restaurant; **L1-L3 Fountain Beach**, Shoal Bay, T 3491/2, F 3493, 10 rooms, US$245 for a studio, US$365 for 2-bedroom suite in winter, 40% less in summer, EP, beach; **L1-A1 Masara Resort**, Katouche Bay, T 3200, F 2149, 13 rooms, beach nearby, tennis.

There are also villas and apartments to rent, among the cheapest being **A1-A3 Syd Ans Apartments**, Sandy Ground, T 3180, F 5381, one-bedroom apartments, Mexican restaurant, close to Tamariain Watersports; **A1-A3 Sea View**, Sandy Ground, T 2427, 1-3 bedrooms, ceiling fans, kitchen facilities, beach nearby, clean, comfortable, enquire at the house next door for a room; **A2-A3** *La Palma*, Sandy Ground, T 3260, F 5381, on beach, restaurant, ceiling fans; at Lower South Hill, **L3** *Inter Island*, T 6259, F 5381, 14 rooms, apartments, fans, kitchen facilities, restaurant.

Anguilla Connection Ltd at Island Harbour, T 4403, F 4402, has a selection of 1-4 bedroom villas and apartments for rent, with several services on offer, US$80-500. *Select Villas of Anguilla*, Innovation Center, George Hill Road, T 5810, F 5811 has 10 villas of different sizes around the island, cheapest US$500/week in summer, most expensive US$1,100/week in winter, daily rates available.

● **Guesthouses**

Travellers on a lower budget can find accommodation in one of about 10 guesthouses. These include **B-C** *Casa Nadine*, The Valley (T 2358), 11 rooms, EP, with shower, kitchen facilities, basic and sometimes dirty, but very friendly and helpful, price reductions for longer stays, good views over The Valley from the roof; **A3** *Florencia's*, The Valley (T 2319), 5 rooms, MAP, basic, little privacy; at North Side, **B** *Norman B*, T 2242, 11 rooms, closed 1996 for hurricane repairs; and others. **Anguilla under US$100** is an all-inclusive package with some meals, accommodation, ground transfers, car rental, tax and gratuities, for details contact Innovative Marketing Consultants, same company as *Select Villas of Anguilla*, above.

The Anguilla Department of Tourism has a list of all types of accommodation. Inns of Anguilla is an association of over 20 villas or small hotels at moderate prices. A brochure with pictures is available; prices are included in the Department of Tourism Rate Guide. In London there is a free reservation service on 0171-937 7725. In North America, call (800) 553 4939, c/o Medhurst and Associates Inc.

FOOD AND DRINK

● **Restaurants**

Apart from hotel restaurants, where a dinner can cost US$50 and above in a 4-5 star restaurant you can find local cuisine at *Lucy's Harbour View*, Back Street, South Hill, medium prices, on hill, good view, open 1130-1500, 1900-2200, closed Sun, Tel: 6253; *Ship's Galley*, breakfast, lunch and dinner, closed Wed, T 2040, Sandy Ground; *Barrel Stay*, Sandy Ground, T 2831, overpriced because of all the charter boat tourists, fish soup, lobster, steak, open for lunch and dinner. *Le Fish Trap*, Island Harbour, is expensive but one of the best for

seafood, T 4488; *Arlo's Place*, South Hill, Italian, homemade pasta, open 1900-2200, closed Sun, T 6810; *Koalkeel*, The Valley, also expensive, in a restored 18th century Great House, the traditional home of the island's administrator, known as Warden's Place, with 100-year old rock oven, Euro-Caribbean style, T 2930, F 5379, open from 0700; *The Ferry Boat Inn*, Blowing Point, on beach near ferry terminal, view of St Maarten, French and West Indian food, lunch and dinner except Sun, T 6613, also rental apartments, well-equipped, airy, maid service; *Riviera*, French/Caribbean restaurant on beach front in Sandy Ground, some Japanese dishes, delicious Fondant Au Chocolat, quite expensive, T 2833, F 3663, VHF 16; *Tropical Penguin*, beach bar and restaurant, Sandy Ground, Austrian chef, pasta, seafood, salads, T 2253; *La Palma*, Sandy Ground, local food, inexpensive, T 3260; *Beach Terrace*, at *The Mariners*, Sandy Ground, beach terrace restaurant and bar, nice view of harbour, breakfast, lunch and dinner, seafood, hamburgers, salads, special evenings, T 2671; *Ripples*, Sandy Ground, award-winning chef, try his lobster fritters, varied menu inc vegetarian, open daily 1830-2300, T 3380; *Capers*, on Meads Bay Beach is colourful, fish, lobster, US meat, open 1800-2200, closed Mon, T 6369; *Smugglers*, Forest Bay, by jetty, built out over water, lobster cooked in many different ways, also fish and steak, dinner only, closed Sun, T 3728, F 2892; *Roy's Place*, Crocus Bay, beach front, draught beer, fresh seafood, happy hour 1700-1900, Sunday brunch of roast beef and Yorkshire pudding, open 1200-1400, 1800-2100, closed Mon, T 2470; *Paradise Café*, Shoal Bay West, T 6010, imaginative salads with oriental influences as well as burgers and club sandwiches, open 1200-1400, 1900-2100, closed Mon; *Chillies*, Mexican, by roadside in Sandy Ground, beans, *burritos*, try the lobster tacos, veggie *tostadas*, T 3171. Most of the restaurants are small and reservations are needed, particularly in high season.

For those who are self-catering, *Fat Cat*, Main Road, George Hill, T 2307, has meals to go from the freezer, picnic meals, pies and cakes, open 1000-1800, closed Sun. Vista Food Market, South Hill Roundabout, T 2804, good selection, cheeses, meats, pâtés, wines, beer etc, open Mon-Sat 0800-1800. Ashleys Supermarket has a good range inc produce from other islands, eg lime cordial from Montserrat.

GETTING AROUND

LAND TRANSPORT

● **Motoring**

Driving is on the left. Speed limit 30 miles an hour. Fuel costs US$1.84/gallon for regular, US$1.86 unleaded. Watch out for loose goats on the roads. A local driving permit is issued on presentation of a valid driver's licence from your home country and can be bought at car rental offices; US$7 for 3 months. Hitchhiking is very easy.

● **Car hire**

There are several car hire companies, including Apex, The Quarter, T 2642; H and R, The Valley, T 2656/2606; Bennie's (Avis, requires US$100 deposit one month in advance for lowest price), US$180-225/week, Blowing Point, T 5054/6089/4238; Triple K Car Rental (Hertz), on Airport Road, close to Wallblake, PO Box 219, The Quarter, T 2934, free delivery and pick up, jeeps (US$45/day), cars (US$40/day), mini mokes (US$35/day) and small buses; Budget, The Quarter, T 2217, F 5871, free pick up and delivery (to get their low price of US$167/week, reservations must be made direct to Anguilla, not through their US or European offices); Connors, South Hill, T 6433, F 6410; Island Car Rentals, Airport Road, T 2723, F 3723, and many others. Rates are from US$25/day off season, US$35/day high season, plus insurance, jeeps from US$40. You can normally bargain for a good rate if you rent for more than 3 days.

● **Bicycles**

Bicycles can be rented from Happy Trails Mountain Bike Rentals, PO Box 354, George Hill Road, T 5810, F 5811.

● **Taxis**

Taxis are expensive and the driver usually quotes in US dollars, not EC dollars: from Wallblake airport to The Valley costs about US$5; from The Valley to Blowing Point (ferry) US$11. Fares are fixed by the Government but drivers try to overcharge. To hire a taxi for a tour of the island works out at about US$40 for 2 people, US$5 for additional passengers. Dispatchers are at the airport and ferry, there is no central office.

COMMUNICATIONS

● **Postal services**

The main Post Office is in The Valley, T 2528, F 5455, open Mon-Fri 0800-1530. It has a Philatelic Bureau which sells commemorative stamps and other collections.

● **Telecommunications**

Cable and Wireless (T 3100) operates internal and external telephone links (IDD available), telex and fax services. Caribbean phone cards are available throughout the islands. There are 2 AT&T USA direct telephones by Cable and Wireless office in the Valley and by the airport. The international code is 809-497, followed by a 4-digit number.

MEDIA

● **Newspapers**

Chronicle daily, *The Daily Herald*, *The Light*, a local weekly. *What We Do In Anguilla* is an annual tourist magazine and a monthly newspaper, *Anguilla Life* is quarterly.

● **Radio**

Radio Anguilla is on medium wave 1505 kHz and ZJF on FM 105 MHz.

ENTERTAINMENT

Out of season there is not much to do during the week. On Fri the whole island changes, several bars have live music, check the local papers, try *Lucy's Palm Palm*, Sandy Ground, or *Round Rock*, Shoal Bay. On Sat go to *Johnno's Place*, Sandy Ground; on Sun to brunch at *Roy's Place*, Crocus Bay, draught beer, then around 1500 at *Johnno's Place* for a beach party. When the music dies people go to the neighbouring bar, *Ship's Galley* for the night shift. *Uncle Earnie* beach bar on Shoal Bay has a live band playing all day on Sun. *Gorgeous Scilly Cay* has live music on Wed, Fri and Sun, T 5123. At the weekend the *Dragon Disco* opens around midnight. *Mirrors Night Club and Bar*, at Swing High, above Vista Food Market, juke box with music from 1960s to now, happy hour nightly at 1900-2000, live entertainment at weekends. In high season the resort hotels have live music, steel bands etc, check in the tourist *Anguilla Life* magazine. Look for shows with North Sound, Missington Brothers the most popular bands. Dumpa and the Anvibes is led by Pan Man Michael (Dumpa) Martin, who has recorded a CD/cassette of a blend of local music. There is no theatre but plays are sometimes put on at the Ruthwill Auditorium. The Mayoumba Folkloric Theatre puts on a song, dance and drama show at *La Sirena* on Thur nights, T 6827.

TOURIST INFORMATION

● Local tourist office

Anguilla Department of Tourism, The Valley, T 2759/2451, F 3091, open weekdays 0800-1200, 1300-1600. The office at the airport is also closed at lunchtime, but the customs officers will often phone for a hotel reservation for you. No one is keen to give you the numbers of cheaper guest houses. TV Cable Channel 32 shows a 30-min programme called Touring Anguilla, which goes out continuously, giving information on the island.

● Tourist offices overseas

UK: 3 Epirus Road, London, SW6, 7UJ, T 0171-937 7725, F 0171-938 4793. Inns of Anguilla Representative: Mr Erville A Hughes, 30 Griffin Close, Slough, Berkshire, SL1 1DY, T 01753-671819, F 01753-691563.

USA: Medhurst and Associates, The Huntington Atrium, 775 Park Avenue, Huntington, NY 11743, T (800) 553-4939, (516) 425-0900, F (516) 425-0903.

● Local travel agents

Malliouhana Travel and Tours, The Quarter, T 2431/2348, has been rec; Bennie's Travel and Tours, Caribbean Commercial Centre, transfers, car rental, island tours, day trips, T 2788/2360. J N Gumbs' Travel Agency is the local LIAT and Winair agent, T 2238/9, F 3351.

Montserrat

MONTSERRAT, known as 'the Emerald Isle', is pear-shaped and has a land area of 39 square miles. About 11 miles long and seven miles wide, its nearest neighbours are Nevis, Guadeloupe and, 27 miles to the NE, Antigua, from where frequent short-hop flights connect Montserrat with longer-haul aircraft. Three mountain ranges dominate this green-clad island, the highest, the Soufrière Hills, rising to 3,002 feet above sea level at the summit of Mount Chance. Volcanic in origin, the island has active fumaroles and hot mineral springs. Villages, linked by good roads, are situated all round the island on the slopes, but many lie on the W coast of the island at the foot of the hills. The capital, Plymouth, has the best harbour. The second largest village on the island is Harris, which is on the E side, near the airport.

The population of 11,000 has not increased throughout this century, because of emigration and birth control. The vast majority of the people are of African descent, but recent years have seen the influx of white Americans, Canadians and Britons who have purchased retirement homes on the island. In consequence, local amenities like the excellent museum and many of the cultural activities are run by expatriate volunteers with money and time to spare. Montserratians are notable for their easy friendliness to visitors, speaking English flavoured by dialect and the odd Irish expression (see History). The island is quiet all year round but visitors in search of revels should aim for the festive Christmas season, although accommodation rates peak then. The high season, in common with much of the region, is from 15 December to mid-April.

HISTORY

Columbus sighted Montserrat on 11 November 1493, naming it after an abbey of the same name in Spain, where the founder of the Jesuits, Ignacio de Loyola, experienced the vision which led to his forming that famous order of monks. At that time, a few Carib Indians lived on the island but by the middle of the seventeenth century they had disappeared. The Caribs named the island Alliouagana, which means "land of the prickly bush". Montserrat was eventually settled by the British Thomas Warner, who brought English and Irish Catholics from their uneasy base in the Protestant island of St Kitts. Once established as an Irish-Catholic colony, the only one in the Caribbean, Catholic refugees fled there from persecution in Virginia and, following his victory at Drogheda in 1649, Cromwell sent some of his Irish political

Montserrat

Not to Scale

Caribbean Sea

North West Bluff
Thatch Valley
Hell's Gate
Silver Hill
Pinnacle Rock
Yellow Hole
Rendezvous Bay
Little Bay
Marguerita Bay
Carr's Bay
Davy Hill
Gerald's
Blake's Estate
Soldier Ghaut Bay
Brades
Collins River
St John's
Cudjoehead
Statue Rock
Bunkum Bay
St Peter's
Bottomless Ghaut
Trant's Bay
Woodlands Bay
Lawyer's Mountain
Katy Hill
Trant's
Farm Bay
Lime Kiln Bay
CENTRE HILLS
Farm River
Spanish Point
Spanish Point
Olveston
Salem
Old Towne
Waterwork Estate
Farrell's Estate
Harris
Bethel
Old Road Bay
Frith
Windy Hill
Tuitt's
Iles Bay
Belham River
Molyneux
Paradise River
Garibaldi Hill
Fox's Bay
Bird Sanctuary
Cork Hill
Dyer's
Streatham
Bransby Point
St George's Hill
Montserrat Springs
Long Ground
Gages
SOUFRIÈRE HILLS
PLYMOUTH
Gages Estate
Chances Peak
Ghaut Mefraimie
Wapping
Roche's Bluff
Sugar Bay
Kinsale
Spring Estate
Galway's Soufrière
Roche's Estate
Fairfield
White River
SOUTH SOUFRIÈRE HILLS
Landing Bay
Germans Bay
St Patrick's
Great Alps Waterfall
Morris
Shooters Hill
Old Ford Point
Triangle Rock
Shoe Rock
Guadeloupe Passage

C.33

prisoners to Montserrat. By 1648 there were 1,000 Irish families on the island. An Irishman brought some of the first slaves to the island in 1651 and the economy became based on sugar. Slaves quickly outnumbered the original British indentured servants. A slave rebellion in 1768, appropriately enough on St Patrick's Day, led to all the rebels being executed and today they are celebrated as freedom fighters. Montserrat was invaded several times by the French during the seventeenth and eighteenth centuries, sometimes with assistance from the resident Irish, but the island returned to British control under the Treaty of Versailles (1783) and has remained a colony to this day.

The elections held in 1991 resulted in a resounding defeat for the Chief Minister, John Osborne. He failed to hold his seat and only one of the candidates of his People's Liberation Movement was elected and he won by only two votes. The National Development Party, previously considered the main Opposition Party also fared badly with only one candidate elected. One independent also won a seat. Success went to a new party founded by Reuben Theodore Meade called the National Progressive Party, which won four seats. Mr Meade became Chief Minister on 10 October amid general optimism that a new, young and dynamic team would secure improvements for the island. In November 1992 Mr Meade survived a vote of no confidence in the Legislative Assembly following a civil law case concerning the ownership of his car. He was one of seven people who had their cars seized by Scotland Yard detectives investigating the export of stolen cars from Britain to Montserrat.

GOVERNMENT

A British dependent territory, Montserrat has a representative government with a ministerial system. Queen Elizabeth II is Head of State and is represented by a resident Governor (Mr Frank Savage was appointed Governor in 1993). The Government consists of a Legislative and an Executive Council, with elections being

Hurricanes and volcanoes

In 1989, Montserrat was devastated by Hurricane Hugo, the first hurricane to strike the island for 61 years. No part of the island was untouched by the 150 mph winds as 400-year-old trees were uprooted, 95% of the housing stock was damaged or destroyed, agriculture was reduced to below subsistence level and even the 180ft jetty at Plymouth harbour completely disappeared, causing problems for relief supplies. However, within a few months, all public utilities were restored to service and the remaining standing or injured trees were in leaf again.

In 1995 and 1996 the lives of Montserratians were again disrupted, this time by volcanic activity. Three times the residents of Plymouth and villages in the S were evacuated to the N as lava, rocks and ash belched from the Soufrière Hills for the first time since the 1930s. Emergency shelters were erected and schools used as temporary accommodation. The British government and Caricom provided aid and the Government began the development of the N, well away from Chances Peak. Housing construction got underway and a jetty in the N was planned. About 3,000 people left the island but a total evacuation was not needed. By mid-1996, one major hotel, several apartments and many luxury villas were open and operating as usual in the designated safe area. Cruise ships were not calling because the port at Plymouth was closed. For daily scientific updates about the volcanic activity try the Internet at http://www.geo.mtu.edu/volcanoes/west.indies/ soufriere.

held every five years for membership in the former. The head of Government is called the Chief Minister; a Speaker presides over the seven-member Council of Representatives. As executive authority and head of the civil service, the Governor is responsible for defence, internal security and external affairs. A constitutional reform in 1989 added financial services to the Governor's powers and recognized Montserrat's right to self-determination. Montserratians continually discuss the pros and cons of opting for independence, but the official position is that economic independence must precede political independence, so colonial status may remain for many years to come.

THE ECONOMY

Tourism contributes about 30% of gdp, it is the largest supplier of foreign exchange and the Government actively encourages investment in tourism projects. The influx of foreign residents in the 1980s saw a sharp rise in real estate deals and building construction with a parallel dependence on imports of capital and consumer goods. Gross domestic product grew rapidly at the end of the 1980s, expanding by 12.8% in 1988, although a slower rate was recorded in 1989 because of the devastation wreaked by Hurricane Hugo. 95% of the housing stock was totally or partially destroyed; production and exports were disrupted, infrastructure was severely damaged; public sector finances were hit by reduced income and greater expenditure demands; tourism slumped. Similar economic disruption was expected as a result of the volcanic eruption in 1995-96 (see tinted box) when the south had to be evacuated three times to the north. Most ex-pats left the island and tourists stayed away.

In 1990 the reconstruction boom caused gdp to expand by 13.5%, but its end in 1991 brought a contraction. By 1992 the economy was back to normal and gdp growth was a healthy 4.3%. One of the two major hotels, *Montserrat*

Springs, had been fully refurbished and many new villas had been built. Real estate agents mushroomed to handle property sales, rentals and villa management for owners abroad. Work on the new pier was completed in 1993, allowing Plymouth to accommodate small cruise ships as well as cargo ships. Construction activity continues to be one of the motors of growth, helped by a public sector programme of spending on infrastructure. Construction and allied services such as real estate account for about 25% of gdp. A new government headquarters building, a police station and schools have all been built.

In the 1990's the growth in tourism has been spectacular, helped by the new pier. Tourist arrivals increased every year until 1995, with in 1994 stayovers rising by 8.5% to 23,613 and excursionists (including cruise ship passengers) up 21.5% to 12,654. In 1995, stay over visitor's slumped 18.3% to 19,297 and excursionists by 18.6% to 10,297. 1996 was likely to be worse. There are only 116 hotel rooms on the island, but because of the emphasis on self catering, there are 581 apartments and 542 villas for rent. Airport expansion is planned.

Agriculture accounts for only 5% of gdp and much of this is subsistence farming. Small scale commercial farming is being encouraged. An integrated cotton industry had been developing before the hurricane, but the looms used for processing the fine Sea Island cotton were very badly damaged by Hugo. There is a small manufacturing sector (primarily electric and electronic components which has returned to pre-hurricane levels).

In 1978 an offshore banking sector was set up, initially attracting little interest, but by 1987-88 showing rapid growth with the granting of 347 banking licences. However, no bank supervision was introduced and applicants were attracted mainly by the low cost of licences, the speed with which they were granted and the relatively few checks on ownership or accounts. Evidence of fraud on a large scale was investigated by Scotland Yard and the FBI in 1989; most banks were examined and had their licences revoked after it became clear that they had been used for money laundering and fraud. The Government has now reorganized the banking industry and introduced new legislation for the sector to avoid a repetition of previous problems, providing for higher fees and greater supervision to generate foreign confidence.

CULTURE

The Irish influence can still be seen in national emblems. On arrival your passport is stamped with a green shamrock, the island's flag and crest show a woman, Erin of Irish legend, complete with her harp, and a carved shamrock adorns the gable of Government House. There are many Irish names, of both people and places, and the national dish, goat water stew, is supposedly based on a traditional Irish recipe. A popular local folk dance, the Bam-chick-lay, resembles Irish step dances and musical bands may include a fife and a drum similar to the Irish bodhran.

The African heritage dominates, however, whether it be in Caribbean musical forms like calypso (the veteran Arrow is now an international superstar), steel bands or the costumed masqueraders who parade during the Christmas season. Another element in the African cultural heritage are the Jumbie Dancers, who combine dancing and healing. Only those who are intimate with the island and its inhabitants will be able to witness their ceremonies, though. Local choirs, like the long-established Emerald Isle Community Singers, mix calypso with traditional folk songs and spirituals in their repertoire, and the String Bands of the island play the African shak-shak, made from a calabash gourd, as well as the imported Hawaiian ukelele.

There are drama and dance groups in Montserrat, which perform occasionally. The Shamrock, in Plymouth, once a cinema, is now used for dancing and live performances. At the University Centre (the local education wing of the University of the West Indies School of Continuing Studies) poetry readings and writing workshops are held. Paintings by local artists can be seen at the Montserrat Museum (National Trust), a restored sugar mill tower on Richmond Hill (open Wednesday and Sunday, 1430-1700, entrance is free but donations accepted). The museum houses permanent exhibitions on 3 floors of Arawak and Carib artefacts found on the island, a complete collection of the attractive Montserratian stamps, newspaper cuttings, maps and prints. Lots of bits and pieces of geological, anthropological and historical interest. Worth a visit. George Martin's famed recording studios, the Air Studios, used to attract rock megastars such as Elton John, the Rolling Stones and Sting to the island, but the studios were closed after Hurricane Hugo.

Note: On Montserrat a Maroon is not a runaway slave but the local equivalent of 'barn-raising', when everyone helps to build a house, lay a garden, etc.

FLORA AND FAUNA

The island is lushly green, with natural vegetation confined mostly to the summits of hills, where elfin woodlands occur. At lower levels, fern groves are plentiful and lower still, cacti, sage bush and acacias. Flowers and fruit are typical of the Caribbean with many bay trees, from which bay oil (or rum) is distilled, the national tree, the mango and the national flower, *Heliconia caribaea* (a wild banana known locally as 'lobster claw'). Montserrat cannot boast many wild animals, although it shares the terrestrial frog, known as the mountain chicken, only with Dominica. Some 30 species of land birds breed on the island. At sunset many can be seen in the Fox's Bay Bird Sanctuary (see Excursions). Unique to Montserrat is the Montserrat Oriole, *Icterus oberi*, a black and gold oriole named the national bird. Agoutis, bats and lizards, including iguanas which can grow to over four feet in length, can all be found and tree frogs contribute to the island's 'night-music'. The Montserrat National Trust manages the Museum, Woodlands Beach, Galways Plantation and the Fox's Bay Bird Sanctuary. You can become a member or just seek information at the headquarters and gift shop on Parliament Street, Plymouth.

BEACHES AND WATERSPORTS

Montserrat's beaches are volcanic 'black' sand, which in reality means the sand may be a silvery grey or dark golden brown colour. The single white coral beach is at Rendezvous Bay in the N of the island, most easily reached by a boat from Old Road bay. The best beaches are Woodlands (with simple beach hut facilities) where you can safely swim through caves, Fox's Bay (nice beach but pebbly and rocky just offshore, snorkelling worthwhile at N end, shower provided in a tree in the car park), Emerald Isle (near the *Montserrat Springs Hotel*), Old Road (by the *Vue Pointe Hotel*) and Little Bay in the N. Yachting can be organized through the small Yacht Club at Wapping (T 491-2237), outside Plymouth (temporary membership available), where they have sunfish and lasers (Sunday is the official sailing day for members) or at *Vue Pointe*, which also has facilities for snorkelling and windsurfing. Danny's Watersports on Old Road beach, run by Danny Sweeney, offers boat trips (see also below, Rendezvous Bay), fishing trips (US$40/hour, maximum 3 fishermen), waterskiing (US$10), windsurfing (US$10/hour), snorkelling (EC$20/day), pedalos (US$10/hour) etc, T 491-5645. For yacht charters on a trimaran, the *John Willie*, Captain Martin Haxby can be contacted through the *Vue Pointe Hotel*

(US$45 pp with open bar), which can also provide picnics if ordered the previous night. The *Montserrat Springs Hotel* can also arrange yacht charters. There are two whirlpool baths, one with hot mineral spring water, at the *Montserrat Springs Hotel*, just N of Plymouth (T 491-2481).

A regional fishing tournament is held in May, usually on Labour Day. Joel Osborne takes people on fishing tours, deep sea fishing or beach picnics in his 26-ft boat, T 491-6300. Joe Oliver also does fishing charters, T 491-4276 in Harris' Village.

DIVING AND MARINE LIFE

Considerable effort is now being put into promoting Montserrat as a diving destination although the sport is still relatively undeveloped with much virgin diving. Shore diving is good from Lime Kiln Bay, where there are ledges with coral, sponges and lots of fish; Woodlands Bay, where there is a shallow reef at 25-30 feet and at Little Bay. There are toilets, showers and changing rooms at Woodlands Beach. There are some shallow dives from boats, suitable for novices or a second dive, but also deep dives for experienced divers. Pinnacle is a deep dive, dropping from 65 to 300 feet, where you can see brain coral, sponges and lots of fish. O'Garro's is a particularly good dive, a wall with lots of sponge and coral, barracuda and loggerhead turtle. The Government and the Caribbean Conservation Association are building an artificial reef at Fox's Bay, to be made from old vehicles and items damaged by Hurricane Hugo.

Sea Wolf Diving School is on Strand Street, near the Post Office, Box 289, Plymouth, T 491-6859/7807, F 491-3599, open 0900-1400, closed Wednesday and Sunday, courteous and professional, all diving by appointment. Equipment rental, PADI courses and dive packages are available. A beach dive is US$40 including tank, BCD, weights and regulator, boat diving is US$55 for one tank, again including all equipment. They also have kayaks and you can paddle to the dive site, reported great fun. If you want to go off on your own, equipment hire is US$30 for tank, BCD, regulator and weights, and US$10 for mask, fins and snorkel. Aquatic Discoveries, at Old Road Bay, next to the *Vue Pointe Hotel*, T 491-3474/FISH, also do PADI courses, full certification US$280, 2 tank boat dive US$65 on 25-ft boat with shade, whale watching in season, equipment rental, ocean kayaks US$45 ½ day.

OTHER SPORTS

The Belham River Valley **golf** course (T 491-5220, F 491-5016) covers an area of nearly 100 acres and has 11 holes that can be played as two 9-hole courses. Beautiful location edged by flowering trees. Hazards include iguanas who sometimes take the balls mistaking them for eggs. Rates are EC$50/day, EC$250/week, full equipment rental EC$7.50. An enormously popular Annual Open Tournament is held in early March; entries open in October.

Well-maintained floodlit **tennis** courts exist at the *Vue Pointe Hotel*, T 491-5211 and at the *Montserrat Springs Hotel*, T 491-2481. The Golf Club has 2 tennis courts which can be rented for EC$20. The *Vue Pointe* hosts an Open Tennis Tournament in January. **Cricket** is the national sport and played between February and July while football or soccer dominates sporting events during the last half of the year, both at Sturge Park. Basketball is becoming increasingly popular; so, too, volleyball. **Cycling** events are organized, with an around the island road race at Easter and a mountain bike competition in October. A 10-km road **running** race is held on Whit Monday.

FESTIVALS

Not surprisingly in the 'Emerald Isle', St Patrick's Day (a national holiday) is celebrated on 17 March with a fund-raising dinner at St Patrick's Roman Catholic Church in Plymouth, cricket matches are held, and concerts, dances and feasting at St Patrick's village. Another national knees-up is August Monday, connected to Emancipation Day on 1 August, and St Peter's Anglican Fete is held in the village rectory grounds, but the island's main festival is the Christmas season, which starts around 12 December and continues through New Year's Day. Costumed masqueraders parade around the island in small bands, culminating in a Boxing Day competition in Plymouth's Sturge Park, where the finals of the calypso competition are also held. There is a queen show, a whole series of concerts (choirs and bands) and all the night clubs are in full swing. Festival Day starts at dawn on New Year's Eve with jump-ups, and competitions are held in the afternoon in Sturge Park. On New Year's Day there is a parade through Plymouth of all the costumed bands and prize winners, followed by more jump-ups through the night. It's very small-scale and low-key compared with a carnival like Trinidad's, but great fun and visitors are made to feel welcome.

The Montserrat Annual Pilgrimage takes place in August. Started in 1993, this non-religious celebration is designed to attract Montserratians and their friends and relations back to the island. Cultural and sporting activities are organized. For details T 491-8288, F 491-8289 or contact the Tourist Board.

PLYMOUTH

In the capital of **Plymouth** (*pop* 3,500) there are a lot of very attractive old wooden buildings in a variety of ornate styles and colours. You can tour the grounds of the Victorian Government House (week days, except Wednesdays, 1030-1200) and the mansion itself, now restored and open to visitors, which houses a painting collection, antique furniture etc, on a green hill above Wapping Village. St Anthony's Anglican Church is white-walled, airy, with a wooden interior. On Parliament Street is the Lands and Surveys Department and the National Trust. Here you can buy the Ordnance Survey map of Montserrat (1983, EC$15), which is recommended. Also on Parliament Street, in the Empire Building, is the Lloyds Shipping Agency (Llewellyn Wall), which has a notice up of shipping sailings, cargo only; they are also cruise ship agents and tour operator. The arrival of supplies is very important in Montserrat, where so much is imported. The town is well-kept and bustling, by a quiet harbour, and with an adequate range of restaurants, bars and gift shops. The local market is at its liveliest on Friday and Saturday. Outside festive seasons like Christmas there is little nightlife in Plymouth, most of the

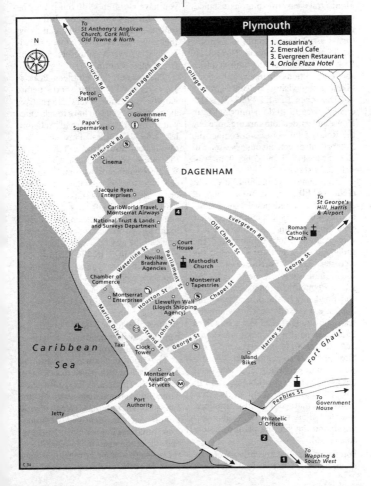

Plymouth

1. Casuarina's
2. Emerald Cafe
3. Evergreen Restaurant
4. Oriole Plaza Hotel

action is in the larger hotels or discos outside town.

NB Plymouth was evacuated in 1996 and at the time of going to press the population of the southern and eastern villages was relocated to the northern section of the island, where many were living in tents and shelters.

EXCURSIONS

Montserrat is easy to explore as distances are short, roads good, and trails well-maintained. For a certified guide contact Cecil Cassell, President of the Montserrat Tour Guide Association, T 491-3160, F 491-2052. Ask at the tourist office about expeditions organized by the local hiking group (visitors welcome). Mole's Bar, Dagenham Road, T 491-2752, is also a good place to find an informal tour. House and garden tours are organized by the Rotary Club, in season contact the Rotary Club direct, but out of season call Gary Swanston, T 491-2998 (home) or 491-2075 (work).

Little remains of the **Old Fort** on **St George's Hill** except some cannons and a recently restored powder magazine, but the site offers a commanding view over Plymouth and environs and it is very pleasant. More cannons and the ruins of a small fort are located at the **Bransby Point Fortification**, from where there are lovely views across the sea to Plymouth in one direction and Old Road Bay in the other (below the Point are two sandy beaches where the sea is a bit rough). The **Fox's Bay Bird Sanctuary** on the SW coast is best visited after 1800, when egrets and other birds return to roost at sunset. This 15-acre mangrove swamp and woodland lies next to an excellent beach, so a full day can happily be spent in the area. Trails are marked but ill-maintained with few signs remaining, trails overgrown and the viewing platform unusable (1996).

Popular excursions and hikes S of Plymouth include Chances Peak, Galway's Plantation, Galway's Soufrière and the Great Alps Waterfall. **NB** Much of this area was prohibited in 1996 because of volcanic eruptions, but our description remains in case things change in 1997.

From St Patrick's onwards, you will be accosted by guides offering their services and insisting that you will get lost without them. If you have a decent map, such as the Ordnance Survey map, you will be fine on your own. However, if you have children with you it may be worth hiring a surefooted, adult guide (check identification), who can assist them over gulleys and rivers, particularly at Galway's Soufrière and the Great Alps Waterfall.

The turn-off for **Chances Peak** is 1½ miles E of Plymouth, shortly before Kinsale. There are several alternatives at the start, so you will have to ask. Once you are on the mountain road itself, fork left after 1½ miles. This takes you through cultivated land and the edge of the forest (sometimes the Cable and Wireless engineers, who make the ascent twice a week, will take you half way up) to where the track starts. It's a steep, hard, hot climb, with over 2,000 steps; one to 2 hours from the end of the road to the top, go on a clear day for brilliant views all the way up. Legend has it that a mermaid lives in the shallow lake (more like a swamp) on top of the mountain. Take plenty of drinking water with you. You need a machete to hack the 50 yards from the lake through the forest to reach the crater rim. It is a stunning 500-feet drop to the bottom but with the rim covered in vegetation it is hard to tell where solid ground ends.

The ruins of **Galway's Plantation** can be reached via a paved road S out of Plymouth, which turns E at St Patrick's. This 18th-century sugar estate is the subject of an ambitious archaeological project which has identified the various stone buildings like the Great House on one side of the road, the tower mill and the boiling house on the other (entrance free). The ruins are in quite a good state of repair and are in a lovely location with the peaks above and sea views below. If you continue up the road you reach **Galway's Soufrière**. From a lookout point where you get a general view, a path leads steeply down to the bubbling, sulphurous, steaming, stinking vents and springs. The path is not difficult, although it can be a bit of a scramble in places, but if you want, a guide will take you for EC$20-30.

Guides will also take you to the **Bamboo Forest** in the S mountains, a 1½ hour walk from the car park at Galway's Soufrière, EC$100 for 1-2 people. The bamboos are about 100 feet tall and there are several species of birds including the Montserrat Oriole. With a guide (Trevor Willock, T 491-6712, rec) you can continue on via the derelict Roche's estate to Long Ground (see map). At Ghaut Mefraimie concrete steps have been built to make the descent into the ravine and the ascent out of it easier. You must be fit to do the whole walk, which takes at least 3-4 hours, and a guide is essential.

Another soufrière, Gages, is no longer accessible; visitors have been prohibited since the path was destroyed in an earthquake.

The Great Alps Waterfall is 70 feet high and reached by a woodland trail that takes about 45 minutes to walk. From St Patrick's, drive along the coast to the White River. Just before the bridge over the river turn left towards a small hut (which sells drinks when open) and a small car park by a tree where guides congregate. Continue on foot on the track out of the car park. Cross the stream, pass a big cashew tree and a little further on is a path going left through thorn scrub, goats etc. It is an easy path to follow, crossing and recrossing the White River (a misnomer, it is yellow ochre from the sulphur in the mountains from which it springs). After a short while you get into a more enclosed, wooded ascent up the river which is cooler and more green and tropical. The waterfall drops down a sheer cliff

into a small pool. Take a sulphurous shower, have a picnic, take your litter home. Guide rates are EC$15 for one person, EC$10 pp for 2, less for more.

Going N from Plymouth along the W side you come to **Carr's Bay** (bus from Plymouth EC$3), from where there is a little road which goes on to **Little Bay**, but it is in very bad condition and it is best to walk round Potato Hill from Carr's Bay. There are plans for a large tourist resort to be built at Little Bay, where there is a nice beach, but at the moment it is completely empty. From Little Bay you can follow a track through a gate at the end of the beach for a stiff hike along a very steep mountainous trail (not suitable for children) to the white sands of **Rendezvous Bay**. Take food and water, it is a long, hot walk. Alternatively, take a boat. Murphy's at the junction in Carr's Bay, offers boat rides to Rendezvous Bay for about EC$50 for 2 people, while Danny's at Old Road Bay by the *Vue Pointe Hotel* charges US$20 pp in a Boston Whaler, returning to pick you up whenever you wish. Two-hour sails are also on offer, but you will not get as far as Rendezvous Bay and back. Rendezvous Bay is the only white sand beach on the island and it is worth making the effort to go there. There is little shade, so take precautions. Also watch out for the spiney sea urchins among the rocks at the N end and avoid the poisonous manchineel trees.

A drive along the dramatic cliffs of the N coast is a must. The road is twisty and steep in places but good on the main route. From the Carr's Bay area you can see Redonda and beyond to Nevis; from the NE you can see Antigua and from the E Guadeloupe is just visible. There is a good view of the airport as you come round the NE coast and you can watch the small planes landing below you. Turning off the road before you get to Harris and continuing S on a paved road you come to Tuitt's, where Mr Greene has a monument garden with spectacular flowering shrubs and concrete statuary

542

(can be illuminated at night), all of which he made himself. Craggy Harris' Lookout behind makes a dramatic backdrop for photographs, T 491-2494 and ask for Mistress Greene for opening hours. The paved road continues to Long Ground but thereafter becomes a trail, impassable for cars. Just the other side of Harris is Farrell's Estate, which used to be the main rum producer and made a 150° proof rum called 'Plastic'. However, the estate was bought some time ago by a US missionary who stopped sugar production and instead reared cattle.

Day excursions are offered by Montserrat Airways (T 491-2713/4) who do charters on request (see below). Charters can also be arranged by Carib Aviation from Antigua throughout the Caribbean T (809) 462-3147, F 462-3125.

The sites of Montserrat can be explored in two or three days, but such speed would force visitors to neglect the gentle charms of the island which can best be appreciated by leisurely strolls and unhurried meals, swimming, and encounters with the delightful local people.

Information for travellers

BEFORE TRAVELLING

● **Documents**
A valid passport is required except for US, Canadian and British visitors, who must only show proof of citizenship for stays of up to 6 months. Visas may be required for visitors from Haiti, Cuba and Eastern bloc countries, which can be obtained from British consulate offices. Those without an onward or return ticket may be required to deposit a sum of money adequate for repatriation.

● **Customs**
200 cigarettes, 50 cigars, 40 ozs of alcoholic beverages, 6 ozs perfume.

● **Climate**
Although tropical, the humidity in Montserrat is low and there is often rain overnight which clears the atmosphere. The average temperature is 26-27°C with little variation from one season to another. The wettest months, according to official statistics, are April and May plus July through Sept, although weather patterns are changing here, as elsewhere.

● **Health**
With its bracing climate and clean, plentiful water, Montserrat is a healthy island. Glendon Hospital in Plymouth (T 491-2552, emergency 911), with 68 beds, also offers a range of services but for specialist treatment patients are sent to larger centres in the region. There is a government health service and also private practitioners. During the rainy season there are mosquitoes and 'no-see-ums', but a good anti-bug repellent should suffice. Rooms that lack air-conditioning often provide mosquito nets for beds. No poisonous snakes or insects.

MONEY

● **Currency**
The currency is the East Caribbean dollar (EC$). The exchange rate is fixed at EC$2.67 = US$1, but there are variations depending on where you change your money (eg Ram's Supermarket gives EC$2.70).

● **Cost of living**
Middle to upmarket prices, generally speaking, so it is not an island for back-packers and the impecunious, although cheap accommodation can be found in private homes and guest houses and eating out can be reasonably priced if you stick to local foods and drink. It is cheap and easy to get around on local minibuses or by hitching.

GETTING THERE

AIR

William H Bramble Airport, on the E coast some 11 miles from Plymouth, has night landing facilities. LIAT (Strand Street, PO Box 257, Plymouth, T 491 2533/2362, at airport T 491-4200/4400) has 4-5 flights daily from Antigua (an 18-min hop), where there are direct connections with international carriers. From Europe many flights connect with the BWIA flight from London Heathrow on Wed and Fri, changing in Antigua, which gets you to Montserrat on a LIAT flight around 1635. From the USA, flights connect with the BWIA flight from Miami daily to Antigua, getting to Montserrat at 1820. Montserrat Airways also have several daily flights from Antigua. There are connections with other islands via LIAT or the charter companies, Carib Aviation (see above) and Montserrat Airways (Box 225, reservations T 491-5342 or airport T 491-6494 or T 491-2713 at Carib World Travel, F 491-6205, or UK T 01279 680453, F 01279 680356). A flight to Montserrat from Antigua costs US$33 one way.

SEA

The Atlantic Lines, Harrison Line and Nedlloyd provide regular services to the port at Plymouth. If you enquire at a shipping agent in Plymouth you may be able to arrange passage on the cargo boat which goes to Guadeloupe, but this is difficult. The jetty was washed away in the 1989 hurricane but a new 75-metre pier with berthing capacity for 2 ships was built and in operation by mid 1993. Small cruise ships can be accommodated here. Regular callers include Windjammer Cruises, Renaissance Cruise Lines and Star Clipper. There is also a tourist information centre and lounge area.

● **Port of entry**
(Own flag) All offices at Plymouth dock. The Customs Department is open Mon, Tues, Thur, Fri 0800-1600, Wed and Sat 0800-1130, but on call 24 hrs on Channel 16 through Montserrat Port Authority. Port fees EC$50, clearance EC$10. Anchorage is rather rolly and uncomfortable.

ON ARRIVAL

● **Banks**
There are 2 international banks: The Royal Bank of Canada on Parliament Street PO Box 222, T 491-2426-8, F 491-3991 (open Mon-Thur 0800-1500, Fri 0800-1700), and Barclays Bank on Church Road PO Box 141, T 491-2501-3, F 491-3801 (open Mon-Thur 0800-1500, Wed 0800-1400, Fri 0800-1700). The Bank of Montserrat on Parliament Street, PO Box 10, T 491-3843, F 491-3163/5470, is open Mon, Tues, Thur 0800 1500, Wed 0800-1300, Fri 0800-1700. Carib World Travel, on Parliament Street is the American Express agent and will cash TCs if they have enough money, T 491-2713/4/2014, F 491-3354.

● **Clothing**
The island is not a formal place, but skimpy clothing on the streets of Plymouth and nude or topless bathing are frowned upon. Informal, lightweight clothes are suitable for virtually every occasion but evenings can be cool and require jackets, wraps or sweaters. There is a laundromat with dry cleaning facilities on Church Road.

● **Hours of business**
Government: 0800-1200; 1300-1600 (Mon-Fri); Business 0800-1200; 1300-1600 except Wed, 0800- 1300, Sat 0800-1200, 1300-1530 (or 0800-1300).

● **Laundry**
Diagonally across from St Anthony's Anglican Church in Plymouth, EC$13 for self-service wash and dry.

● **Official time**
Atlantic Standard Time, 4 hours behind GMT, 1 ahead of EST.

● **Public holidays**
New Year's Day, St Patrick's Day (17 March),

Good Fri, Easter Mon, Labour Day (first Mon in May), Whit Mon (7th Mon after Easter), first Mon in Aug, Christmas Day, Boxing Day (26 Dec) and Festival Day (31 Dec).

● **Shopping**

Wed is half day closing. Sat is market day on the Plymouth waterfront. Sea Island cotton or goods manufactured from this pricey but soft, comfortable fabric; tapestries and wall hangings by local artists; glass and ceramics produced at a studio in Olveston; leather goods from locally-tanned leather; small but delightful range of post cards of naive paintings. The Island House Art Gallery on John St, T 491-3938, Haitian art, Caribbean prints, gifts and pottery. The Paradise Shirt Company Ltd, 3 Church Road, T 491-5949, F 491-3599, hand-decorated, original cotton clothing; Tapestries of Montserrat on Parliament Street, T 491-2520, F 491-3599, sells hand woven items inc rugs and wall hangings. Montserrat T-Shirts has masses of T-shirts in attractive designs for all ages. Jus Looking, on George Street or at the airport, T 491-4076/4040, sells Caribelle Batiks, Haitian lacquered boxes and the Sunny Caribbee range of spices. The Etcetera Shop, John Street, has batiks and Caribbean designs. Sunset Gallery, on the corner of Parliament St and Harney St has original paintings of Montserrat, prints, sculpture and crafts, open Mon, Tues, Thur, Fri, Sat, 0900-1400 or call T 491-5552 for private viewing. Sea Wolf Dive Shop by Post Office sells hand made jewellery and gifts and cards. Montserrat's beautiful stamps can be bought at the Post Office (T 491-2996, F 491-2042) or at the Philatelic Bureau.

Ram's Supermarket in Plymouth near Police Station, probably the best stocked and good for currency exchange (even better than the banks). Supermarkets stock a variety of expensive imported food and drink to cater for the demands of the growing expat population, but the choice is fairly limited (shut Sun). Captain Weekes supermarket on the road out of town going S has a good supply of drink but poor stocks of provisions. Peter & Christina's, a 24-hour bakery on George Street, beyond the Catholic Church on the way to the airport, sells excellent and varied breads and pasties, rec. Just before you get there, on the outskirts of town, a green painted house on your left sells home made ice cream in tropical fruit flavours. The local ginger beer is delicious.

● **Tipping**

10% service charge is usually added to bills. Taxi drivers happily accept a tip but there is no pressure to offer one.

● **Voltage**

Electric current is 220 volts, 60 cycles but newer buildings also carry 110 volts.

ON DEPARTURE

● **Departure tax**

There is a departure tax of EC$25 for all aged 12 and over. No tax is payable for a stay of less than 24 hrs.

ACCOMMODATION

There are only a couple of large hotels and a handful of guesthouses. Most tourism is accommodated in villas and apartments and resort developments have not yet arrived on the island. There is a 7% Government tax on the cheaper hotels, but at the *Vue Pointe*, *Montsarrat Springs* and *Flora Fountain* you pay 10% tax. A 10% service charge is usually added.

● **Hotels**

Price guide			
L1	over US$200	L2	US$151-200
L3	US$101-150	A1	US$81-100
A2	US$61-80	A3	US$46-60
B	US$31-45	C	US$21-30
D	US$12-20	E	US$7-11
F	US$4-6	G	up to US$3

L2-A1 *Vue Pointe* (PO Box 65; T 491-5210, F 491-4813, T 800-235 0709) run for many years by the Osborne family, 28 rondavels (hexagonal cottages) and 12 hotel rooms, children under 12 sharing with adults free in rondavels, fans, restaurant, beach bar, lounge bar, phone, cable TV, entertainment evenings, conference facilities, swimming pool, tennis courts, free transport to Plymouth. **L1-L3** *Montserrat Springs Hotel* (PO Box 259, T 491-2481-2, F 491-4070, T 1-800-253 2134), the other large hotel, was completely refurbished after Hurricane Hugo with 34 a/c rooms and 6 suites to a high standard, cable TV, phone, fans, 2 tennis courts, 70-foot pool, jacuzzi, beach bar, pool bar, restaurant, conference facilities, friendly. **L3-A2** *Woodlands Inn*, (PO Box 252, T 491-5123, F 491-5918) suites with sea view, terraces, bathrooms, breakfast; **A1-A2** *Providence Estate House*, St Peter's T 491-6476, F 491-8476, a restored plantation house on hillside with seaview, pool, TV, gardens, large room with bathroom and kitchenette; **A1-A2** *Flora Fountain* (PO Box 373, T 491-6092/3, F 491-2568) on Lower Dagenham Road, 18 rooms, a/c, private bathrooms and balconies, restaurant; **D** *Niggy's Guest House and Bistro* at Aymers Ghaut, Kinsale, offers simple accommodation, 5 small, spartan rooms, on either side of bar, shared bathrooms, pleasant, friendly, but no peace and quiet, run by Anglo Americans Tony and Niggy Overman, T 491-7489/2690, F 491-3257; **B** *Marie's Guesthouse*, run by Marie and Austin Bramble, PO Box 28, T 491-2745, F 491-3599, close to the road and downwind of the power plant but any noise drowned by frogs at night, 5 bedrooms, double or single beds, bathroom, lots of towels, large, shared kitchen, cable TV, friendly, welcoming, highly rec, car rental can be arranged. *Belham Valley Apartments*, PO Box 409, T 491-5553, F 491-6489, one and 2-bedroomed cottages overlooking Belham River and golf course, beach 5 mins walk, self-catering, kitchens, TV, stereo, phone, maid service available, comfortable but could do with some refurbishment, US$300/week summer, US$575/week, winter, daily rates offered.

● **Apartments and villas**
The Board of Tourism has a complete list of other smaller establishments, apartments and rooms to let, with some 9 agencies renting and selling apartments and villas. Montserrat Enterprises Ltd, PO Box 58, Marine Drive, Plymouth, T 491-2431, F 491-4660, has an extensive list of pleasant villas to rent, average price for one or 2-bedroomed villa with pool, US$400-600 low season, but the same property rents for US$550-1,000 in winter. Jacquie Ryan Real Estate, PO Box 425, Shamrock House, Marine Drive, Plymouth, T 491-2055, F 491-3257, villas available at similar rates. Neville Bradshaw Agencies, PO Box 270, Plymouth, T 491-5270, F 491-5069 has 2-bedroomed properties, highly rec. Villas in Montserrat, PO Box 421, Plymouth, T 491-5513, F 491-7850, have some very grand properties at US$1,650 in summer and US$1,950 in winter for 6 people or less, including private charter from Antigua.

Of the residential developments in Montserrat, **L3-B** Woodsville Condominiums and Town Houses, PO Box 319, T 491-5119, F 491-5230, offer 18 one-three-bedroomed properties with pool on ridge overlooking Belham Valley, to purchase or rent (weekly rates available).

Another residential development Isles Bay Plantation offers rental of 2 of its properties to give potential purchasers a taste of elegant living; prices to purchase start at US$245,000 and rentals US$1,500 low season and US$2,000 high season per week. They all have 40-foot pools, PO Box 64, T 491-4842, F 491-4843, UK: 0171 482 1418, F 0171 482 1071. Agencies usually include maid service most days. *Shamrock Villas*, PO Box 58, T 491-2431-2, F 491-4660, villas on Richmond Hill, 3 mins from beach, 50 one/two-bedroomed units with fans, pool, patio, car rentals available, US$475-600/week in winter, US$375-450 summer. For cheaper self-catering accommodation without maid service, **B** *Lime Court Apartments* in Plymouth, PO Box 250, T 491-3656, F 491-5069, are sometimes vacant, one and 2-bedroomed apartments with balcony overlooking the sea, rather noisy, room dark, weekly, monthly or long term rates available, car hire offered; **A3-B** *Fairways Apartments*, Box 420, T 491-5077, 3938, F 491-3126, overlooks golf course, one bedroom, bathroom, small living room with fridge, kettle and toaster, patio, plunge pool. **A3** *Boston Apartments*, Dagenham, T 491-4672, 2-bedroomed, kitchenette, discount for long stays. Bennette Roach Realty Co, PO Box 306, T 491-3844/5495, F 491-2052, specialize in home rentals as well as real estate sales and car hire; also Caribbee Agencies Ltd, Box 223, T 491-7444, F 491-7426; Dream Home Realtors, Box 28, T 491-2883, F 491-6069; Pauline's Real Estate, Box 171, T 491-3846, F 491-2434; Properties Ltd, Box 495, T/F 491-2986; West Indies Real Estate, PO Box 355, T 491-8666, F 491-8668, Montserrat Company Ltd, PO Box 221, T 491-2431, F 491-4660; Tradewinds Real Estate, Box 365, T 491-2004, F 491-6229; Emmanuel Galloway, PO Box 404, Plymouth, T 491-3318, F 491-4009; Wilston Pickett Johnson Real Estate, PO Box 421, T 491-5513, F 491-7850.

FOOD AND DRINK

A large frog called mountain chicken, indigenous here and in Dominica, is the local delicacy; that and goat water stew are the most commonly found local items on the menu; most other things, like steak and fish are imported. Vegetables are locally grown. The Tourist Board publishes a useful pamphlet, *Eating Out in Montserrat*.

● Restaurants

The *Belham Valley* (PO Box 409, T 491-5553), which also has 4 apartments to rent, quite elegant, reservations required, lunch 1200-1400, Tues-Fri, dinner from 1830, Tues-Sun, Chinese specials Thur. On Wed nights the place to go is the *Vue Pointe Hotel*, T 491-5210, for a barbecue and steel band, food served from 1930, EC$66 set price includes all the salad and sweets you can eat, EC$33 for children if they eat chicken, drinks extra, band from 2100 unimpressive. A Sun lunchtime barbecue is US$35 in summer and US$38.50 in winter, half price for children under 10. Even better for Sun lunchtime is the *Montserrat Springs Hotel*, which does an excellent, all-you-can-eat buffet for EC$40. *The Nest* at Old Road Bay, for sandwiches and salads, excellent menu, quiet, pleasant, 1030-2030 every day except Mon, T 491-5834. Local cuisine can be found in several **Plymouth** restaurants: *Harbour Court*, T 491-2826, Houston Street, Caribbean menu and special ice cream, open for breakfast, lunch and dinner daily from 0800 except Sun 1800-2100; *The Blue Dolphin*, T 491-3263/3388, mountain chicken, lobster, fish and steaks, lunch and dinner, catering service available, overlooks Plymouth harbour; the *Evergreen*, T 491-3514, fast food and pastries, daily specials, ice cream, open weekdays 0700-2200, later at weekends; *La Robe Creole Restaurant and Bar*, Marine Drive, T 491-8974, creole and vegetarian dishes, good, from 0700 daily; *Birds Nest Bar*, Strand St, T 491-8472, fish. *Flora Fountain* (see **Hotels** above) has good, cheap Indian food with vegetarian dishes. Just across the Belham River on the way to Friths, is *Ziggy's*, T 491-8282, new, rec, good food, only open Fri-Mon in low season.

In nearby **Wapping** the *Yacht Club*, T 491-2237, open Tues-Fri for lunch and dinner for non-members, music Fri from 2200, EC$3 cover charge; *Emerald Café*, by the bridge, Wapping, T 491-3821, lobster, fish and meat, Fri night barbecue, meal for 2 with wine US$50, pleasant; the *Oasis*, T 491-2328, Wapping Road, open 1100-1400, 1800-2200, closed Mon, speciality fish and chips. Also in Wapping are bars such as *The Inn on Sugar Bay*, T 491-3336, a restaurant/bar/nightclub with live music twice a week, large TV for sporting events, snacks served at lunch and dinner; *Hang Out Bar*, T 491-3945, chicken and ribs, lunch Mon-Sat, Fri from 1600, specials on Fri and Sat eg goat water; *Late Night Bar*, T 491-7557, Mon-Sat 1900 onwards, Fri night barbecue; *The Green Flash*, T 491-7557, very popular, happy hour 1800-1930, open very late, closed Sun. *The Golden Apple* on the main road through Cork Hill, T 491-2187, serves 3-course meal for EC$35, large quantities of well-cooked vegetables, highly rec, phone the day before to book and order meat/fish course (**NB** mutton means goat, lamb means sheep). *The Hilltop*, St Peter's, T 491-8707, open Fri, Sat 1800-2400, live music and bar, good restaurant, champagne brunch Sun 1000-1400, popular. A must is *Annie Morgan's* at St John's for goat water, open Fri and Sat at lunchtime, other days by arrangement if you can arrange a party of 10 or so, T 491-5419. *Niggy's Bistro* in Kinsale, T 491-7489, bar indoors, restaurant seating on the porch, steak or pasta and salad from EC$15, wine from EC$25 a bottle, food and service highly rec, music (inc by Niggy) and food Tues-Sat, jazz and blues, often drowned out on Fri and Sat by Champion Sound down the road. *Andy's Village Place*, T 491-5202, in the pretty hamlet of Salem is famous for its chicken, prepared in gregarious proprietor Andy's special sauce, lunch by reservation, open evenings daily except Tues. *Gourmets and Gardens*, Salem Village, restaurant and shop, well-stocked with fruit and veg, lovely take away frozen home made meals, cakes and biscuits. A night club with food is the *Nepcoden* in Weekes, which serves excellent rotis.

GETTING AROUND

LAND TRANSPORT

● Motoring

Driving is on the left. Roads are fairly good, but narrow. Drivers travel fast, passing on blind corners with much use of their horns. With a valid driving licence, you can obtain a local 3-month licence (EC$30) at the airport immigration desk or the traffic office in the Treasury Building on Strand Street in Plymouth (open from 0830-1200, 1300-1430 Mon-Fri).

● Car hire

There are several car hire companies (the cars are mostly Japanese). Car hire rates are similar in all agencies: Montserrat Enterprises in Marine Drive, Box 58, T 491-2431, F 491-4660, hires out small cars for US$45/day or US$210/week, US$230/ week with air conditioning, jeeps for US$50/day or US$40 for 2-6 days; NBA car rentals in Lime Court

Building, Parliament Street, Box 270, T 491-2070/5270, F 491-5069; Jefferson's Car Rental, Dagenham, T 491-2126; Ethelyne's Car Rentals, Weekes Road, Box 309, T 491-2855; Fenco Rentals, George Street, PO Box 397, cars, 4WD, trucks, T 491-4901/2169, F 491-3891; Pauline's Car Rental, Church Road, T 491-2345, F 491-2434; Edith's Car Rental, George Street, T 491-6696; Bennette Roach Realty Co, Parliament Street, Box 306, T 491-3844, F 491-2052; Sun Down's Auto Rentals, Parson's Road, Plymouth, T 491-3945, 4WD vehicles; Reliable Car Rental, Marine Drive, Box 442, T 491-6990/2269, F 491-8070, for mokes and pick ups; you can also ask taxi drivers at the airport about car rental, some (eg John Roach, Tuitts Village, T 491-4409) have cars available for US$40/day. You have to pay for half a tank of petrol and usually accept liability up to EC$2,000.

● **Bicycles**

For the fit, hire a mountain bike from Island Bikes of Harney Street, Plymouth, T 491-4696, after hours T 491-5552, F 491-3599, prices start at EC$280/week, EC$54/day or EC$11/hr, guided tours also available.

● **Buses**

The standard fare in minibuses is EC$2-3. Some mini-buses to villages in the N leave from Papa's Supermarket on Church Road, those to the E go from the end of Evergreen Road and those to the S depart from opp the Royal Bank of Canada on George Street. As a general rule, buses run into town in the morning with an immediate return to source, doing the trip about 4 times a day. Outside the fixed times and routes they operate as taxis and journeys can be arranged with drivers for an extra fee. Buses go past the junction with the airport road about 1½ miles from the airport but this can be a bit tricky.

● **Hitchhiking**

Hitching is safe and easy because the local people are so friendly. Similarly, don't be afraid to pick them up when you are driving. Out-of-town hotels like the *Vue Pointe* provide a free bus service into the capital for their staff, phone Carol Osborne at the hotel to see if there is space.

● **Taxis**

Taxis are usually small buses, which can be shared and there is a taxi stand by the Clock Tower War Memorial at the harbour. Fares are set and clearly marked at the airport. The tariff list can be obtained from the tourist office (see address below), eg airport to Plymouth EC$29, Plymouth to *Vue Pointe Hotel* EC$13; a sightseeing tour is EC$30 per hour. Drivers are usually knowledgeable about historical sites and are happy to wait while passengers hike to beauty spots, or return at an appointed time. Fares from Plymouth to the Great Alps Waterfall EC$39 return, to Galway's Soufrière EC$60 return, to St George's Hill EC$22, including waiting and return. Rec is Joseph Murrain, T 491-8150/2222.

COMMUNICATIONS

● **Postal services**

The main Post Office is in Plymouth (open 0815-1555 Mon-Fri) and there is a Philatelic Bureau, also in the capital, selling the attractive Montserrat stamps to collectors. Postcards to the USA EC$1.15.

● **Telecommunications**

Cable and Wireless (West Indies) Ltd (Houston Street, T 491-2112, F 491-3599, open Mon-Thur 0730 1800, Fri 0730-2000, Sat 0730-1800) operates an excellent telecommunications system with a new digital telephone system, international dialling, telegraph, telex, facsimile and data facilities. Phone cards are available, as are credit card service, toll free 800 service and cellular phones. The international code for Montserrat is 1-809, followed by a 7-digit number.

MEDIA

● **Newspapers**

There are 2 weekly newspapers, the *Montserrat News* and the *Montserrat Reporter*.

● **Radio**

Radio Montserrat ZJB relays the BBC World Service news at 0700 daily and the Voice of America news at 0800. Radio Antilles is also on the air, as is Gem Radio, an exclusive outlet for the Associated Press.

● **Television**

Satellite TV Cable is operational in most areas, and stations broadcasting from nearby islands can be received.

TOURIST INFORMATION

● **Local tourist office**

Montserrat Board of Tourism, PO Box 7, Plymouth, T 491-2230, F 491-7430, on Church Road, helpful, plenty of information. On the internet Montserrat's home page is http://www.mrat.com. There is a Tour Guide Association with a membership of trained tour guides, T 491-3160, F 491-2052, contact Cecil Cassell, its President. The Montserrat Chamber of Commerce on Marine Drive (PO Box 384) complements the Tourist Office and offers a business directory, T 491-3640, F 491-4660.

● **Tourist offices overseas**

Canada: New Concepts – Canada, 2455 Cawthra Road, Suite 70, Mississauga, Ontario L5A 3PL, T 905-803-0131, 800-224-4794, F 905-803-0132.

Germany: Montserrat Tourist Board/West India Committee, Lomer Strasse 28, D-22047 Hamburg 70, T 49-40-695-88-46, F 49-40-380-00-51.

UK: Marketing Services (Travel and Tourism) Ltd, Suite 433, High Holborn House, 52-54 High Holborn, London WC1V 6RB, T 0171 242-3131, F 0171 242-2838.

USA: Medhurst & Associates Inc, 1208 Washington Drive, Centerport, NY 11721, T 516-425-0900, 800-646-2002, F 516-425-0903.

● **Local travel agents**

Montserrat Aviation Services Ltd, Lower George Street, Box 257, Plymouth, T 491-2533/2362, F 491-4632, or at airport T 491-4200, sales agent for LIAT and BWIA, day tours on Montserrat and to neighbouring islands. Carib World Travel, Parliament Street, Box 183, T 491-2713-4/2014, F 491-3354, Amex agent and sales agent for Montserrat Airways. Also Runaway Travel Ltd, Marine Drive, Box 54, T 491-2776/2800. Emerald Tours, PO Box 306, Plymouth, T/F 491-3160, does tours to Bamboo Forest, Great Alps Waterfall, Galways Soufrière, Sugar Plantation Ruins, Chances Peak, Bird Sanctuary or an island tour, from US$10-80. Island tours can be arranged through hotels or the Tourist Office too. Ask the Board of Tourism about registered tour guides. They run training courses for guides, issue qualifications and identity passes and fix rates.

● **Further reading**

In the Macmillan series, *Montserrat: Emerald Isle of the Caribbean*, by Howard A Fergus, has been rec, his *History of Montserrat* was published by Macmillan in 1994 and is an interesting and informative work (Dr Fergus is the Resident Tutor at the University Centre, Speaker of the Montserrat Parliament and acting Governor when the British Governor is off-island); also *Alliouagana Folk*, by J A George Irish (Jagpi 1985), as an introduction to Montserratian language, proverbs and traditions.

Netherlands Antilles
the 3 S's

THE '3 S's', Saba, Sint Eustatius (Statia) and Sint Maarten lie 880 km N of the rest of the Netherlands Antilles group lying off the coast of Venezuela, and known as the ABC islands (Aruba, Bonaire and Curaçao). Each has a distinct character and flavour, Statia being the poorest, Saba the smallest and Sint Maarten the most developed and richest.

HORIZONS

Lacking in natural resources, they each depend to a greater or lesser degree on tourism for their foreign exchange revenues, but are developing their potential in different ways. Saba's strength is the richness of the underwater world surrounding the island and is noted for its pristine diving locations. Sint Maarten has the best beaches and resorts, while St Eustatius promotes its historical associations.

Although the '3 S's' precede the ABC islands in this Handbook, the introduction to the Netherlands Antilles group and much of the general Information for travellers is contained in the ABC chapter.

Saba

SABA, pronounced 'Say-bah', is the smallest of this group of islands. Only five miles square, it lies 28 miles S of St Maarten and 17 miles NW of St Eustatius. The island is an extinct volcano which seems to shoot out of the sea, green with lush vegetation but without beaches. In fact there is only one inlet amidst the sheer cliffs where boats can come in to dock. The highest peak of this rugged island is the 2,864-foot Mount Scenery, also known as 'the Mountain', and because of the difficult terrain there were no roads on Saba until 1943, only hand-carved steps in the volcanic rock.

HORIZONS

Although the island was once inhabited by Caribs, relics of whom have been found, there is no trace of their ancestry in the local inhabitants. The population numbers about 1,200, half of them white (descendants of Dutch, English and Scots settlers) and half black. Their physical isolation and the difficult terrain has caused them to develop their ingenuity to enable them to live harmoniously with their environment. Originally farmers and seafarers, the construction in 1963 of the Juancho E Yrausquin Airport on the only flat part of the island, and the serpentine road which connects it tenuously to the rest of the island, brought a new and more lucrative source of income: tourism. However, the island's geographical limitations have meant that tourism has evolved in a small, intimate way. About 28,000 tourists visit each year, most of whom are day trippers. There are only 100 beds available in the eight hotels and guest houses, as well as a few cottages to rent. Those who stay are few enough to get to know the friendliness and hospitality of their hosts, who all speak English, even though Dutch is the official language. In 1993 the Dutch Government stopped 'driver licence tourism'. Previously, driving tests taken in Saba were valid in Holland, where it is more difficult to secure a licence. The system brought Saba an income of about US$300,000 a year. The only other major source of income is the US Medical School, opened in 1993, which attracts about 150 (mainly US) students from overseas. Development is small scale; the island still merits its unofficial title, 'the Unspoiled Queen'. There is no unemployment among the workforce of 600. The island is spotlessly clean; the streets

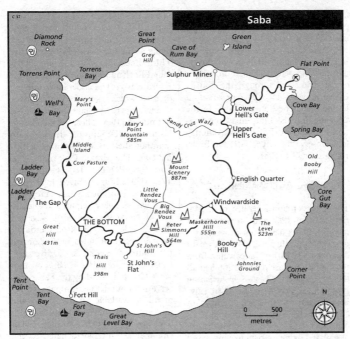

Saba

(Map labels)
Diamond Rock · Great Point · Green Island · Cave of Rum Bay · Grey Hill · Flat Point · Torrens Point · Torrens Bay · Sulphur Mines · Cove Bay · Well's Bay · Mary's Point · Lower Hell's Gate · Spring Bay · Sandy Cruz Walk · Upper Hell's Gate · Mary's Point Mountain 585m · Middle Island · Old Booby Hill · Cow Pasture · Mount Scenery 887m · English Quarter · Ladder Bay · Core Gut Bay · Ladder Pt. · Little Rendez Vous · Windwardside · The Gap · Big Rendez Vous · Great Hill 431m · Maskerhorne Hill 555m · The Level 523m · THE BOTTOM · Peter Simmons Hill 564m · Booby Hill · Thais Hill 398m · St John's Hill · St John's Flat · Johnnies Ground · Corner Point · Tent Point · Fort Hill · Tent Bay · Fort Bay · Great Level Bay

0   500
metres

are swept by hand every day. The main road has concrete barriers, partly to prevent cars driving over the edge and partly because of landslides, which can be frequent after rain.

HISTORY

Saba was first discovered by Columbus on his second voyage in 1493 but not colonized. Sir Francis Drake sighted it in 1595, as did the Dutchmen Pieter Schouten in 1624 and Piet Heyn in 1626. Some shipwrecked Englishmen landed in 1632, finding it uninhabited. In 1635 the French claimed it but in the 1640s the Dutch settled it, building communities at Tent Bay and The Bottom. However, it was not until 1816 that the island became definitively Dutch, the interregnum being marked by 12 changes in sovereignty, with the English, Dutch, French and Spanish all claiming possession.

FAUNA AND FLORA

Vegetation on Saba changes according to altitude and a walk up Mount Scenery reveals many different types of tropical vegetation. At an altitude of 1,600-2,000 feet there is secondary rain forest with trees of between 15 and 30 feet high. Further up there are tree ferns of 13-16 feet, then palm trees, then at 2,700 feet the cloud forest begins (known as Elfin Forest), where you find the mountain mahogany tree (*freziera undulata*). Wildlife on the island is limited to the endemic anole lizard (*anolis sabanus*), iguanas and a harmless racer snake, but over 60 species of birds have been recorded, with many migratory birds coming to nest here. The trembler and the purple-throated hummingbird can be seen in the Elfin forest and the Sandy Cruz rain forest, where you can also find the wood hen (bridled quail dove).

The Saba Conservation Foundation preserves the environment on land and under water, developing protected areas, maintaining trails (with excellent interpretive signboards) and promoting nature conservation. The Foundation can be contacted through the Tourist Office or write to Saba Conservation Foundation, The Bottom, Saba. In the USA the Friends of the Saba Conservation Foundation (FSCF) raises money for conservation, 506 Tiffany Trails, Richardson, Tx 75081.

DIVING AND MARINE LIFE

The waters around Saba became a Marine Park in 1987 and 36 permanent mooring buoys have been provided for dive boats (less than half of which are for big boats). The Park includes waters from the highwater mark down to 200 feet all the way around the island. Spearfishing is prohibited (except by Sabans, free diving in certain areas), as is the removal of coral or shells (Sabans are limited to 20 conch per person a year without the use of scuba). Diving tourism has increased rapidly; scuba divers and snorkellers visit the Marine Park which is noted for its 'virginity'. Saba has no permanent beaches so diving and snorkelling is from boats, mostly along the calmer S and W coasts. The W coast from Tent Bay to Ladder Bay, together with Man of War shoals, Diamond Rock and the sea offshore comprise the main dive sites, where anchoring and fishing are prohibited. From Ladder Bay to Torrens Point is an all-purpose recreational zone which includes Saba's only beach at Well's Bay, a pebbly stretch of coast with shallow water for swimming and areas for diving, fishing, and boat anchorage. The beach comes and goes with the seasons and ocean currents but when it is there it is scenic and good for snorkelling. The concrete road ends here but there are no facilities so take your own refreshments and arrange for a taxi to pick you up later. Another anchorage is W of Fort Bay. East of Fort Bay along the S, E and N coast to Torrens Point is a multiple use zone where fishing and diving are permitted. Some of the most visited dive sites are Third Encounter, Outer Limits, Diamond Rock and Man of War. Tent Reef is also a favourite. Ladder Labyrinth is a dive site which is good for snorkelling.

Dive operators have been granted permits and they collect the mandatory visitor fees (US$2pp per dive) to help maintain the Park which is now self-financing. The Marine Park office is at Fort Bay, PO Box 18, The Bottom, T/F 63295. It is managed by a Scot, Kenny Buchan, and a Saban, Percy Tenhott, who are very helpful and keen to talk about conservation. Percy gives an illustrated lecture at 1830 on Tuesday at *Juliana's*, recommended, or on demand for groups. The guide to the dive sites, *Guide to the Saba Marine Park*, by Tom Van't Hof, published by the Saba Conservation Foundation, is highly recommended, available at dive shops, the museum and souvenir shops, US$15. Saba now has a 5-person recompression chamber at Fort Bay, donated by the Royal Netherlands Navy, which is administered through the Marine Park but operated by volunteers. Summer visibility is 75-100 feet with water temperatures of about 86°F, while winter visibility increases to 125 feet and water temperatures fall to 75°F. Saba's rugged, volcanic terrain is replicated underwater where there are mountains, caves, lava flows, overhangs, reefs, walls, pinnacles and elkhorn coral forests.

Not much fishing is done in these waters, so there is a wide range of sizes and varieties of fish to be seen. Tarpon and barracuda of up to 8 feet are common, as are giant sea turtles. From February to April humpback whales pass by on their migration S, while in the winter dive boats are often accompanied by schools of porpoises. Smaller, tropical fish are not in short supply and together with bright red, orange, yellow and purple giant tube sponges and different coloured coral, are a photographer's delight. Divers are not allowed to feed the fish as it has been proved to alter fish behaviour and encourage the aggressive species.

There are three dive shops on Saba. Saba Deep at Fort bay, near the pier, run by Mike Myers T 63347, F 63397, PO Box 22, has NAUI and PADI instructors and offers a resort course with instruction in the swimming pool at *Captain's Quarters*. They have two 25-foot inflatable boats. Two instructors accompany each party in the water. Boats return to shore between dives so you can spend your surface interval in the a/c bar *In Two Deep*, rather than being tossed about at sea. All your gear is taken care of during your stay or there is well-maintained rental equipment. Avoid days when the ferry *The Edge* comes in (Wed, Fri, Sat) as Saba Deep handles the day divers and groups can be large. A new boat taking 16 passengers was on order for late 1995. A 2-tank dive costs US$80, including equipment, park fees (5% surcharge for credit cards). Sea Saba Dive Centre at Windwardside, T 62246, F 62362, have two larger boats, with shade and sun deck, but limit groups to 10-12 people. Their trips are more of a cruise and recommended if there is a non-diving partner, the surface interval is spent at Well's Bay for sunbathing and snorkelling. Drinks are on board, some people take snacks for the 60-90 minute interval. The atmosphere is relaxed and unrushed, you return to dock after the second dive at about 1430. Thursday is busy with passengers from the Windjammer *Polynesia*. Only one guide goes into the water with divers, the other stays on board, which can affect your underwater experience with a large group. A 2-tank dive costs US$80 including park fee and tax plus US$10 for equipment. Run by Lynn Costenara and John Magar, who are both PADI instructors, they also offer introductory and 5-3day certification courses. Wilson's Dive Shop is opposite the supermarket in Windwardside, PO Box 50, T/F 62541/63334. Owned by Wilson McQueen, one of the pioneers of diving around Saba, the operation is now managed by Phillip and Colette, who have a 36-foot boat and usually take 12 divers maximum. A two-tank dive is US$80 plus US$10 for equipment. The surface interval is usually taken at a calm mooring and there are drinks on board. There are also live-aboard boats: the *Caribbean Explorer*, T 800-322-3577, offers week-long trips for serious divers, usually starting in St Maarten and spending much of their time in Saban waters.

There are many dive sites of 90-100 feet and if you are doing three dives a day you must follow your dive tables and stay within your limit. It is recommended that you take every fourth day off and rest or go hiking. All three dive operations offer *à la carte* diving, and arrange taxi pick-ups from hotels.

WALKING

Before the road was built people got about Saba by donkey or on foot and there are still numerous steep trails and stone steps linking villages which make strenuous, yet satisfying, walking. The Saba Conservation Foundation preserves and marks trails for those who like a challenge and for those who prefer a gentle stroll. All of them are accessible from the road and many can be done without a guide. Named trails include: Tent Point, Booby Hill, The Level, The Boiling House, The Sulphur Mine, The Ladder, Giles Quarter, Rendezvous, Bottom Hill, Crispeen, Mount Scenery, Spring Bay, Troy, Sandy Cruz, Middle Island and Mary's Point.

The most spectacular hike is probably the one from Windwardside up 1,064 steps to the crest of Mount Scenery, best done on a clear day otherwise you end up in the clouds. It is a hard slog, 1 ½ hours each way, but a road goes part of the way up and drinks are available where it ends. The summit has now been cleared (Cable & Wireless have built a telecommunications tower there by helicopter drops) and there is a spectacular view down to Windwardside and the surrounding isles if it is not cloudy. Take a sweater and waterproof jacket, it can be very rough and slippery after rain. There are lots of birds, lizards, snakes and land crabs, and the botanical changes are noticeable as you climb. You can get out of the rain in several shelters on the way up. Buy the T-shirt afterwards: 'I climbed Mt Scenery, 1,064 steps'.

The Ladder is a long path of stone steps from the shore up to The Bottom, up which all provisions used to be hauled from boats before the road was built. There is a picnic place overlooking Ladder Bay. A guide is recommended for the Sulphur Mine track; at Lower Hell's Gate, about halfway up the sharp bends on the way to the airport, a track N of the road leads to the cliffs of the N coast, with splendid scenery, and to the remains of the old sulphur mines. A very nice lookout point is from Booby Hill, up the 66 terraced steps to the Booby Hill Peak.

The Tourist Office has leaflets on the nature trails and hiking on Saba, but in many places a guide is recommended. James Johnson (T 63281 work, T 63307 home), a local man, does guided tours after 1500 weekdays and all day at weekends, US$40-50 per group, maximum eight people. He knows the island intimately and carries a bush knife to hack away obstacles. Although he only knows local plant and animal names, he makes up for his lack of scientific knowledge in stories about past inhabitants (his relatives). Tom Van't Hof (author of the Marine Park guide and Chairman of the Saba Conservation Foundation) is a biologist and also guides walks, so would appeal to more scientific walkers. He lives in The Bottom, by the Art Gallery.

OTHER SPORTS

There is a **tennis** court (concrete) at the Sunny Valley Youth Centre in The Bottom which is open to the public. Basket ball and volley ball matches are held, contact the Tourist Office for a schedule.

EXCURSIONS

There are four picture book villages on Saba, connected by a single spectacular $6\frac{1}{2}$ mile road which begins at the airport and ends at the pier. The road itself is a feat of engineering, designed and built by Josephus Lambert Hassell (1906-83) in the 1940s, who studied road construction by correspondence course after Dutch engineers said it was impossible to build a road on Saba. From the airport, the road rises to Hell's Gate and then on through banana plantations to **Windwardside**, a walk of 20-30 minutes, where most of the hotels and shops are situated. There is a small museum, a bank, post office and the Tourist Office is here. On the first Sunday in each month, a 'happening' is held in the grounds of the Harry L Johnson Museum. Everyone dresses in white (including visitors), plays croquet and drinks mimosas. The museum was a sea captain's house, built in 1840. It is filled with antique furniture and family memorabilia. The kitchen is in its original state. Open 1000-1200, 1300-1530, Monday-Friday, US$2.

The road goes on past Kate's Hill, Peter Simon's Hill and Big Rendezvous to St John's, where the schools are, and which has a wonderful view of St Eustatius, then climbs over the mountain and drops sharply down to **The Bottom**, the island's seat of government, with a population of 350. The Bottom is on a plateau 800 feet above the sea, and gets its name from the Dutch words *de botte*, meaning 'the bowl'. It can be hot, as there is little breeze. Leaving The Bottom, the road makes its final descent to **Fort Bay**, where small cruise ships, yachts and the ferry from St Maarten arrive at the 277-foot pier. Most of the houses on the island are painted white with red roofs and some have green shutters. Heleen Cornet's book, *Saban Cottages*, gives background information on some interesting houses. There are watercolour workshops for those who find the scenery picturesque.

Information for travellers

BEFORE TRAVELLING

● Documents
See main Netherlands Antilles section under Curaçao Information for travellers. Saba is a free port so there are no customs formalities.

● Climate
The average temperature is 78°-82°F during the day but at night it can fall to the low 60°s. The higher up you get, the cooler it will be; so take a jersey, if hiking up the mountain. Average annual rainfall is 42 inches.

MONEY

● Currency
The florin or guilder is the local currency, but US dollars are accepted everywhere. Visa and Mastercard are the only widely accepted credit cards. Hotels and dive shops accept credit cards, but no one else does. You may be charged extra for using credit cards because of the slow processing arrangements.

GETTING THERE

AIR
The landing strip is only 400m long, the shortest commercial runway in the world, so large aircraft cannot yet be accommodated although there are plans to build a longer runway. Planes do not land in bad weather in case they skid off the end. Winair (T 62255), the only scheduled airline, has 4-5 daily 20-seater flights from St Maarten (15 minutes/US$86 return) some of which come via St Eustatius or St Barts. It is essential to reconfirm your return flight.

SEA
A high speed catamaran ferry, *The Edge*, runs Wed, Fri, Sun, 0900 from Pelican Marina,

Simpson Bay, Sint Maarten, US$60 return, 1 hr, T 542640, day trips possible, return to dock by 1700, does not run in rough weather. A deep water pier at Fort Bay allows cruise ships to call.

● **Ports of entry**
(Dutch flag). Go ashore to clear immigration with the Harbourmaster at Fort Bay or with the Police in The Bottom.

● **Anchorages**
Fort Bay has three free moorings but it is rolly with SE winds. The Ladder and Well's Bay moorings (yellow buoys) are available for use by yachts for US$2 pp for anchoring and snorkelling, and US$2 pp for each dive you take on your own. Use a strong line and plenty of scope. Marine patrol will collect fees and explain the rules and regulations. The Marine Park has a leaflet with map of anchorages and dive sites.

ON ARRIVAL

● **Banks**
Barclays Bank, Windwardside, T 62216, open 0830-1230, Mon-Fri.

● **Official time**
Atlantic Standard Time, 4 hours behind GMT, 1 ahead of EST.

● **Public holidays**
New Year's Day, Good Friday, Easter Sunday and Monday, Queen's Coronation Day (30 April), Labour Day (1 May), Ascension Day (Thursday), Saba Days (beginning of December), Christmas Day, Boxing Day. Carnival (Saba Summer Festival) is a week near the end of July and is celebrated with jump-ups, music and costumed dancing, shows, games and contests including the Saba Hill Climb. Saba Days are at the first weekend in December, when donkey races are held, with dancing, steel bands, barbecues and other festivities.

● **Religon**
There are 4 churches: Anglican, Roman Catholic, Wesleyan Holiness and Seventh Day Adventist.

● **Shopping**
Shops open 0900-1200, 1400-1800. Local crafts have been developed by the Saba Artisan Foundation in The Bottom and include dolls, books and silk-screened textiles and clothing. The typical local, drawn-thread work 'Saba Lace' (also known as 'Spanish Work' because

it was learned by a Saban woman in a Spanish convent in Venezuela at the end of the last century) is sold at several shops on the island. Each artisan has his or her own style. Taxi drivers may make unofficial stops at the houses where Saba lace, dolls, pillows etc are made. Boutiques in Windwardside sell a variety of gifts. There are several art galleries in Windwardside where local artists have their studios and sell their watercolours, oil paintings, prints and sculptures. Ask the Tourist Office for a leaflet. Saba Spice is the local rum, very strong (150° proof) and mixed with spices, sugar and orange peel.

● **Useful addresses**
Hospital: T 63288; **Police**: T 63237.

● **Voltage**
110 volts AC, 60 cycles.

ON DEPARTURE

● **Departure tax**
Airport departure tax is US$2 to Netherlands Antilles, US$5 elsewhere.

ACCOMMODATION

● **Hotels**

Price guide

L1	over US$200	L2	US$151-200
L3	US$101-150	A1	US$81-100
A2	US$61-80	A3	US$46-60
B	US$31-45	C	US$21-30
D	US$12-20	E	US$7-11
F	US$4-6		up to US$3

There are no resort hotels yet on Saba and even the most expensive are small and friendly. Dec-April is the busiest season, although divers come throughout the year. July is also busy because of Carnival and students return from foreign universities. Hotels do not usually give you a room key; there is no crime. The four policemen on the island boast that the cells are only used as overspill when the hotels are full! All the hotels offer dive packages with the three dive shops. There is a 5% room tax and usually a 10%-15% service charge.

Windwardside: **L2-L3** *Captain's Quarters*, T 62201, F 62377, best known with 12 rooms in a handsomely decorated restored sea captain's house, some rooms have 4-poster beds, antique furniture, fans, newer block in garden has more contemporary furniture, video lounge, library, restaurant, bar, pool; **L3-A2** *Juliana's*, further up the hill, owned by Juliana and Franklin Johnson, descendants of original settlers, smaller rooms than *Captain's Quarters* but each has kitchenette, some have balcony or patio, *Flossie's Cottage*, same management, charming self-contained apartment next door, garden, kitchen, good views, pool, café, bar, T 62269, F 62389; **A1-A3** *Scout's Place*, T 62205, F 62388, beautiful views, 4 basic but comfortable rooms in former government guest house, 10 rooms with 4 poster beds in new wing, simple, relaxed, slow service, pool, restaurant, music at night, car/jeep hire. **L3** *The Cottage Club*, outside Windwardside, on hill with wonderful views E, owned by Jansen family who also own supermarket, 10 white cottages with red roofs in local style, kitchen, TV, phone, T 62386, F 62434.

On Booby Hill: L1-L2 *Willard's*, luxury or VIP suites in main building or bungalows further up the hill, all with incredible views, tennis, jacuzzi, pool, restaurant, bar/TV, long walk out of town up a slope so steep some taxi drivers refuse to go up it, jeep therefore recommended, good for those who want peace and quiet and are prepared to pay for it, no children under 14, PO Box 515, T 62498, F 62482.

The Bottom: A3 *Cranston's Antique Inn*, T 63203, 130-year old inn, some 4 poster beds, restaurant; **A2** *Caribe Guesthouse*, clean comfortable, no frills, 5 rooms, kitchen available, T/F 63259.

Hell's Gate: A1-A2 *The Gate House*, 6 rooms, all with bath, 2 have kitchens, café for breakfast and dinner, T 62416, F 62415.

The Tourist Office has a list of one-two bedroom cottages and apartments for rent from US$50 a night, which can be let on a weekly or monthly basis, and can also provide hotel rates. They will also make reservations.

FOOD AND DRINK

Many restaurants close by 2130, so eat early. At *Scout's Place*, dinner is at 1930, reservations needed, slow service, good portions; the *Saba Chinese Restaurant*, in fact two restaurants which serve Cantonese food, both in Windwardside, one on the main street more like a bar, the one higher up the hill has an extensive menu, good food, expanding to larger premises, friendly, when the lights are on its open, own generator, useful in power cuts, best bet for a late meal; *Guido's Pizzeria*, open later than other restaurants, popular with students, often runs out of pizza base,

restaurant open Mon-Fri from 1800, lively nightclub Fri, Sat; *Captain's Quarters* for more elegant dining, food good, last orders 2030, reservations rec, good barbecue Fri 1830, get your order in then get a drink, happy hour 1700-1900, popular; *Tropics Café* at *Juliana's* does breakfast, burgers and snacks at lunchtime, full international meals Wed-Sat evenings, go early; *Brigadoon*, in old Saban house close to centre, good reputation with locals, open daily from 1800, international, creole and Caribbean food, fresh seafood. In The Bottom: native specialities at *Queenie's Serving Spoon*, call for reservations T 63225. *Lollipop*, T 63330, is a small restaurant on the mountainside overlooking The Bottom on the way to St John's, free taxi pick-up (waiter is also the driver), excellent 3-course meal for about US$20, fresh lobster, conch melts in the mouth, local cuisine, open breakfast, lunch or dinner, rec for lunch, walk it off afterwards.

GETTING AROUND

LAND TRANSPORT
● **Car hire**
You can hire a jeep or car from Avis, Windwardside, for about US$30-35 a day, T 2279. Doing it through a hotel can cost you US$10 more. Drive on the right. Hitchhiking is safe, very easy and a common means of getting about.

● **Taxis**
There are no buses. There are taxis (minibuses) at the airport and a few others on the island. Wilfred, T 62238; Garvis, T 62358; Billy, T 62262; Evelyn, T 63292; Anthony, T 62378; Manny, T 63328; Wayne, T 62277. Airport to Hell's Gate, US$6; to Windwardside, US$8; to The Bottom, US$12.50. Taxis can be hired for tours round the island (US$40) and the drivers are knowledgeable guides. Some are also fishermen or hotel owners, so they can be valuable contacts.

COMMUNICATIONS

● **Postal services**
Airmail takes about 2 weeks to the USA or Europe. Federal Express is available.

● **Telecommunications**
Most hotels have direct dialling worldwide, otherwise overseas calls can be made from Lands radio phone booths in Windward side or The Bottom. The international code for Saba is 599-4, followed by a 5 digit number.

ENTERTAINMENT

Most of the nightlife takes place at the restaurants. At weekends there are sometimes barbecues, steel bands and dances. Generally, though, the island is quiet at night. In Windward-side, *Guido's* on Fri, Sat, pool room makes way to a disco, popular with all sections of the community, soca, reggae, rap and disco, loud. In The Bottom, there is life in the bar of *Antique Inn*, run by Francesca from the Dominican Republic until about 2300. Later on go to her sister's bar opp *The Inner Circle*, which has merengue music, popular with locals for dancing.

TOURIST INFORMATION

● **Local tourist office**
The Saba Tourist Board (Glenn Holm and Wilma Hassell) is in Windwardside, open 0800-1200, 1300-1700, PO Box 527, T 62231, F 62350, there are plenty of leaflets and maps, and staff are friendly and helpful.

● **Tourist office overseas**
In the **USA**: PO Box 6322, Boca Raton, Florida 33427, T (407) 394-8580, 800-722-2394, F (407) 394-8588.

The Tourist Board's world wide web address is: http://www.turq.com/SABA.

Sint Eustatius

SINT EUSTATIUS, or STATIA, 35 miles S of St Maarten and 17 miles SE of Saba, was originally settled by Caribs and evidence of their occupation dates back to AD300. The name Statia comes from St Anastasia, as it was named by Columbus, but the Dutch later changed it to Sint Eustatius. The island is dominated by the long-extinct volcano called 'The Quill' at the S end, inside which is a lush rainforest where the locals hunt land crabs at night. Visitors are advised, however, to go there only during the day. The N part of the island is hilly and uninhabited except for Statia Terminals, a fuel depot; most people live in the central plain which surrounds the airport.

HORIZONS

Statia is quiet and friendly and the poorest of the three Windward Islands, with only 2,200 people living on the 8 square mile island. A variety of nationalities are represented, the island having changed hands 22 times in the past, but the majority are of black African descent. Everybody speaks English, although Dutch is the official language and is taught in schools. The traditional economic activities of fishing, farming and trading have been augmented by an oil storage and refuelling facility, but the major hope for prosperity is tourism. About 24,000 people visit each year (including returning Statians), of which 14% come from North America and 13% from the Netherlands. About half are on business or combining business with a holiday, while 40% are on holiday and 10% visit friends and relations. Investment in airport expansion and a cruiseship pier is designed to increase capacity. Nevertheless, it remains the sort of place where you will be greeted by passers by and there is no crime.

HISTORY

Statia was sighted by Columbus on his second voyage but never settled by the Spanish. The Dutch first colonized it in 1636 and built Fort Oranje, but the island changed flag 22 times before finally remaining Dutch in 1816. The island reached a peak of prosperity in the 18th century, when the development of commerce brought about 8,000 people to the tiny island, over half of whom were slaves, and the number of ships visiting

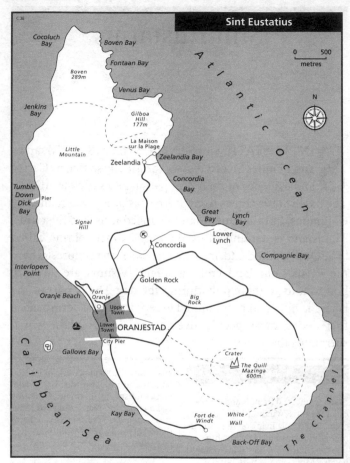

Sint Eustatius

Cocoluch Bay
Boven Bay
Fontaan Bay
Boven 289m
Venus Bay
Jenkins Bay
Gilboa Hill 177m
La Maison sur la Plage
Little Mountain
Zeelandia
Zeelandia Bay
Concordia Bay
Tumble Down Dick Bay
Pier
Signal Hill
Great Bay
Lynch Bay
Concordia
Lower Lynch
Compagnie Bay
Interlopers Point
Golden Rock
Big Rock
Oranje Beach
Fort Oranje
Upper Town
Lower Town
ORANJESTAD
City Pier
Gallows Bay
Crater
The Quill Mazinga 600m
Kay Bay
Fort de Windt
White Wall
Back-Off Bay

Atlantic Ocean

Caribbean Sea

The Channel

0   500 metres

N

the port was around 3,500 a year. Trading in sugar, tobacco and cotton proved more profitable than trying to grow them and the slave trade was particularly lucrative, gaining the island the nickname of 'The Golden Rock'.

The island still celebrates 16 November 1776 when the cannons of Fort Oranje unknowingly fired the first official salute by a foreign nation to the American colours. At that time, Statia was a major trans-shipment point for arms and supplies to George Washington's troops, which were stored in the yellow ballast brick warehouses built all along the Bay and then taken by blockade runners to Boston, New York and Charleston. However, the salute brought retaliatory action from the English and in 1781 the port was taken without a shot being fired by troops under Admiral George Brydges Rodney, who captured 150 merchant ships and £5 million of booty before being ex-

Morning glory

🐛 In 1884, a Dutch botanist, Willem Suringar, visited Statia, and collected a morning glory in fruit on Signal Hill which was described as new to science. Named *Ipomoea sphenophylla* (wedge shaped leafed *Ipomoea*), it was not found by subsequent visiting botanists so the species was put first on the endangered list and then declared extinct. However, in 1994, a vine in the tree tops was found by Edwin Gawlik on the property of Statia Terminals which is believed to be the same pink-flowered morning glory. The area has been closed off and the plant will be protected. The same habitat is also home to a rare iguana and several orchids. Specimens of the plant are being studied in the USA, where it has been noted that the flowers are unusual in having many with free petals, a character not known in *Ipomoea*, while the insects that have been seen to visit and pollinate the flowers on Statia are not those usually associated with tubular flowers.

pelled by the French the following year.

With continuing transfers of power, the economy never recovered, many merchants were banished and the population began a steady decline. The emancipation of slaves in 1863 brought an end to any surviving plantation agriculture and the remaining inhabitants were reduced to subsistence farming and dependency upon remittances from relatives abroad. Prosperity has returned only recently with the advent of tourism and the island is still relatively underdeveloped.

FAUNA AND FLORA

Despite the small size of the island, in the 17th and 18th centuries there were more than 70 plantations, worked intensively by slaves. As a result most of the original forest has disappeared except in the most inhospitable parts of the volcano. Nevertheless there are 17 different kinds of orchid and 58 species of birds, of which 25 are resident and breeding, 21 migrants from North America and 12 seabirds. The harmless racer snake is found here, as on Saba, and there are iguanas, land crabs, tree frogs and lots of butterflies. Unfortunately there are lots of goats too, which eat everything in sight. There are plans to establish a national park which will probably encompass the areas of Boven, Gilboa Hill and Signal Hill. A foundation is being set up

which may also manage The Quill and a proposed marine park. Hikers usually visit The Quill and its crater where you can find huge tree ferns, mahogany, giant elephant ears, begonias, figs, plantains, bromeliads, the balsam tree and many other species in the tropical rain forest. The southern slope of the mountain has not been fully explored by botanists and it is hoped that the proposed foundation will undertake its scientific mapping.

DIVING AND MARINE LIFE

Statia's waters offer a wonderful combination of coral reefs, marine life and historic shipwrecks, of which there are about 200 to explore. Water visibility is over 100 feet and snorkelling is also very good. Diving is excellent, with plenty of corals, sea fans, hydroids and big fish such as groupers and barracudas, as well as rays, turtles and the occasional dolphin but unlike some other Caribbean diving destinations, you will not bump into any other divers underwater. There are 16 charted dive sites, at a depth of 20-130 feet. The Supermarket, half a mile off the coast from Lower Town at a depth of 60 feet, has two shipwrecks 50 feet apart with beautiful coral, red and purple sponges, shoals of fish, sea turtles and the rare flying gurnard. The Garden is another very beautiful reef with hundreds of fish of all kinds from the smallest wrass to large barracudas and extremely tame angel fish. As yet there are few divers on Statia so fish are generally tame and do not swim away. There are no permanent moorings, so boats have to be careful to find a sandy patch to anchor on the reef. A marine park is planned, which would entail the provision of moorings.

Dive Statia is run by Rudy and Rinda Hess T 82435, F 82539, Lower Town, PO Box 158, in USA: 8521 N Georgia, Oklahoma City, OK 73114, F (405) 843-3040. They have a small, rigid inflateable boat for up to 10 divers but six is comfortable. The boat is moored off the beach in front of the dive shop and you have to carry all your equipment down to the sea, wade out and pass it to the guide on the boat. They only take certified divers, although a full range of courses is offered, and do three dives a day with night dives on request. Once in the water the dives are not strictly guided, buddies may go off and explore. Some dives are deep (take care not to get lost) and the operation does not really cater for inexperienced or nervous divers. A two-tank dive is US$72 plus US$12 equipment rental, PADI Open Water 4-day course US$325, snorkel trips US$25 with equipment, photographic and video equipment rental, 3-7 day accommodation and diving packages available with most hotels. In 1996, Connie and Aad, previous managers of Landhuis Daniel, Curaçao, moved to Statia to set up Blue Nature Watersports (PDIC Instructor Trainer Facility), T 82725, F 82756, offering courses, boat dives, shore dives and night dives. A single dive costs US$34 inc tank and weights, Scubapro rental gear and packages available. Very friendly, divers are welcome to hang around for lunch, dinner, happy hour and spontaneous beach barbecues. Another new dive shop, Golden Rock Dive Shop, is opposite the *Blue Bead Restaurant*. Owned by Glen Fairs, who charges US$75 for a 2-tank dive. On leaving Statia Customs officials may give you and your luggage a rigorous search if they discover you are a diver. They are looking for treasure, or artifacts, beware.

BEACHES AND WATERSPORTS

Oranje Beach stretches for a mile along the coast away from Lower Town. The length and width of the beach varies according to the season and the weather, but being on the Leeward side it is safe for swimming and other watersports. On the Windward side are two fine beaches but there is a strong undertow and they are not considered safe for swimming. Zeelandia Beach is 2 miles of off-white sand with heavy surf and interesting beachcombing, particularly after a storm. It is safe to wade and splash about in the surf but not to swim. There is a short dirt road down to the beach just before you get to *Maison Sur La Plage*; do not drive too close to the beach or you will get stuck in the sand. Avoid the rocks at the end of the beach as they are very dangerous. The other beach on the Windward side is Lynch Beach, which is small and a bit safer for swimming as long as you do not go out very far and pay attention to the undertow. Drive past the airport terminal entrance for about 75 yards and turn right on to a dirt road. Go past the Agricultural Experiment Station, keeping right at intersections but staying on the dirt road. Park just beyond the small white house on the left and walk for 6 minutes, not to the beach you can see, which is unsafe for swimming, but down a steep gully and then down a stony path to the smaller beach. It is often empty during the week. Take your litter home with you.

Kings Well Resort, T/F 82538, offers sport fishing and encourages the sailing fraternity. The swimming pool at *Golden Era Hotel* is open for non-guests during the day for US$1.25 an hour.

OTHER SPORTS

There is little to offer on Statia for the sporting enthusiast. At the Community Centre on Rosemary Laan: tennis (US$5), basketball, softball and volleyball; changing rooms are available. Tennis, volleyball and basketball also at Gene's Sports Complex, T 82711, as well as table tennis, dominoes, checkers, open Mon-Sat 1430-2230, Sun 0800-1800. There is also a children's playground. Horseriding lessons, beach or trail rides available with Sabra Pressman at Zeelandia, T 82760.

ORANJESTAD

Oranjestad is the capital, situated on a cliff overlooking the long beach below and divided between Upper Town and Lower Town. The town used to be defended by Fort Oranje (pronounced Orahn'ya) perched on a rocky bluff. Built in 1636 on the site of a 1629 French fortification, the ruins of the fort have been preserved and large black cannons still point out to sea. The administrative buildings of the island's Government are

here. The fort was partly destroyed by a fire in 1990, but has been restored since then. Other places of historical interest include the ruins of the Honen Dalim Synagogue built in 1739 and the nearby cemetery. Statia once had a flourishing Jewish community and was a refuge for Sephardic and Ashkenazic Jews, but with the economic decline after the sacking of Oranjestad by Admiral Rodney, most of the Jewish congregation left. The Dutch Reformed Church, consecrated in 1755, suffered a similar fate when its congregation joined the exodus. The square tower has been restored but the walls are open to the elements. The surrounding graveyard has some interesting tombs. Legend has it that it was here that Admiral Rodney found most of his booty after noticing that there were a surprising number of funerals for such a small population. A coffin, which he ordered to be opened, was found to be full of valuables and

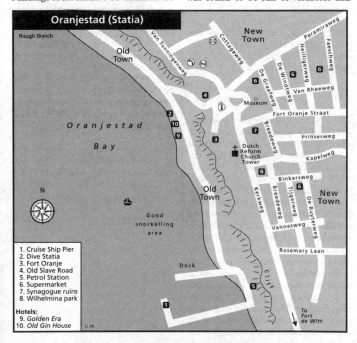

Oranjestad (Statia)

Rough Sketch

Old Town
New Town
Van Tonningenweg
Cottageweg
Paramiraweg
Heiligerweg
Faeschweg
De Graafweg
De Windtweg
Van Rheeweg
Fort Oranje Straat
Museum
Breedeweg
Prinseweg
Oranjestad Bay
Kapelweg
Dutch Reform Church Tower
Binkersweg
New Town
Old Town
Kerkweg
Breedeweg
Tijgerweg
De Ruyterweg
N
Good snorkelling area
Vannesweg
Rosemary Laan
Dock
cliff
To Fort de Witt

1. Cruise Ship Pier
2. Dive Statia
3. Fort Oranje
4. Old Slave Road
5. Petrol Station
6. Supermarket
7. Synagogue ruins
8. Wilhelmina park

Hotels:
9. *Golden Era*
10. *Old Gin House*

further digging revealed much more.

On Wilhelminaweg in the centre, the 18th century Doncker/ De Graaff House, once a private merchant's house and also where Admiral Rodney lived, has been restored by the St Eustatius Historical Foundation and is now a museum. There is a pre-columbian section which includes an Arawak skeleton and a reconstruction of 18th century rooms at the height of Statia's prosperity. Open 0900-1600, Monday-Saturday, 0900-1200 Sundays and holidays, T 82288, admission US$2 or US$1 for children, the curator normally shows you around, explaining the history of the exhibits.

It is possible to walk round the village and see the sights in a morning. The museum or Tourist Office will provide you with a Walking Tour brochure listing the historical sites and other walking tours. In its heyday Lower Town stretched for 2 miles along the bay, with warehouses, taverns and slave markets attracting commercial traffic. Parts are now being restored as hotels or restaurants. If you like beach combing, blue, 5-sided slave beads over 200 years old can be found along the shore at Oranjestad.

EXCURSIONS

Twelve hiking trails using old donkey or farm tracks are marked and numbered. The Tourist Office has a guide leaflet of the trails. There are several paths to the rainforest crater at the top of The Quill, which is remarkable for its contrast with the dry scrub of the rest of the island. The plant life includes mahogany and breadfruit trees, arums, bromeliads, lianas and orchids. The walk to the top is of course steep, but once there you can walk down a path to the centre. The vegetation in the crater is very dense and a local guide is recommended. The highest point, called Mazinga, affords a magnificent view. The Quill was damaged by Hurricane Hugo in 1989 and although it is possible to walk round the rim, the path deteriorates after Mazinga. The crater is the breeding ground for land crabs, which Statians catch at night by blinding them with a flashlight. Charley (brother of Roland Lopes at the Tourist Office) works as a professional hiking guide. He arrives at dawn in full combat uniform and beret like Rambo and tends to go quickly without much explanation, fine for the walk round the Quill crater but better to go alone if birdwatching.

A road, and then a track, leads round the lower slopes of The Quill to the White Wall, a massive slab of limestone which was once pushed out of the sea by volcanic forces and is now clearly visible from miles away across the sea. You can also see it from Fort de Windt, built in 1753, the ruins of which are open to the public, at the end of the road S from Lower Town. St Kitts can also be seen clearly from here. About 14 forts or batteries were built around the island by the end of the 18th century but the ruins of few of them are accessible or even visible nowadays. Another track affording panoramic views is that up Gilboa Hill. If you start from the Venus Bay track, turn E at post 11; you can see all across Statia.

Berkels family museum is on the Lynch Plantation, a domestic museum with a collection of household utensils and antiques on the NE side of the island, T 82338.

Information for travellers

● **Documents**
See main Netherlands Antilles section under Curaçao Information for travellers. There are no customs regulations as Statia is a free port.

● **Climate**
Average temperature is around 27°C in the daytime and 23°C at night time with cooling trade winds from the E. Average rainfall is 45 inches a year. Average water temperature in the sea is 26°C.

● **Health**
The Queen Beatrix Medical Centre is on Prinsesweg, T 82371 for an ambulance, or 82211 for a doctor. Two doctors are on 24-hr call. Outpatient hours are 0800-until finished, Mon, Tues, Thur and Fri, or by appointment. The resident dentist is Dr Herman Gorter, at the Medical Centre Mon-Fri 1400, T 82371/82211 or at home T/F 82750. Hotels serve purified water. Bottled water is sold at groceries. Tap water is usually rain water and not really suitable for drinking.

MONEY
● **Currency**
The currency is the Netherlands Antilles florin or guilder, but US dollars are accepted everywhere. Credit cards are not widely used (Amex hardly every accepted, Visa and Mastercard better), although some shops do now accept them. Check beforehand at hotels and restaurants. US$100 bills are often not accepted.

GETTING THERE

AIR
Winair has several daily 20-minute flights from St Maarten (US$70 return) connecting with flights from the USA, Europe and other islands. It is possible to get to Statia in a day from New York. There are other connecting Winair flights from St Kitts and Saba (10 minutes). Golden Rock Airways has charter flights daily to St Maarten and some other islands, T 82451, F 82572. All flights are in small planes, although the airport has been extended to 5,265 feet to allow larger jets to land. You get an impressive view of The Quill when you come in to land.

SEA
Cruise ships come in at Gallows Bay, where there is a deep-water pier. Statia is on the itineraries of the smaller cruise ships, inc the *Polynesia, Starflyer/Starclipper*.

● **Anchorage**
Oranje Baii is the only anchorage, US$9 for charter boat and US$5 for cruising boats. Groceries, alcoholic drinks and ice available. The long pier accommodates ships with draft not exceeding 14 feet, the short pier has vessels with draft of up to 10 feet. The Harbour Office is open 24 hrs, T 82205, F 82888, VHF Channel 14. The Harbour Master, Murvin Gittens, works Mon-Fri, 0800-1700. Fly an Antillean flag. Marine weather is on VHF 1 or 162.550 MHz continual broadcast.

● **Banks**
Barclays Bank, Wilhelminaweg, T 82392, open Mon-Thur 0830-1530, Fri 0830-1230, 1400-1630, The Post Office Bank, Post Spaarbank, is open Mon-Fri 0730-1600. The Windward Islands Bank is by Mazinga Gift Shop, open Mon-Thur 0830-1200, 1300-1530, Fri 0800-1200, 1400-1630, T 82846, F 82850.

● **Clothing**
No topless bathing anywhere on the island. Men are not allowed to walk without shirts on public streets, even behind the beach.

● **Official time**
Atlantic Standard Time, 4 hours behind GMT, 1 ahead of EST, all year.

● **Public holidays**
New Year's Day (fireworks at midnight), Good Friday, Easter Sunday, Easter Monday, Queensday (30 April), Labour Day (1 May), Ascension Day, Statia Day (16 November), Kingdom Day (15 December), Christmas Day, Boxing Day.

Carnival is 10 days in July-Aug and is celebrated with steel bands, picnics, sports and contests. On Boxing Day actors parade through the streets depicting the social, cultural or political group of the year, stopping at various homes for food and drink.

● **Religion**

Anglican, Apostolic Faith, Methodist, Roman Catholic and Seventh Day Adventist.

● **Shopping**

Lots of shops or businesses are in people's homes with no visible sign of the trade from the outside, but if you ask for help it will be willingly given and you will find the right place. Offices and stores are usually open 0800-1800, although supermarkets stay open until 1900. Mazinga Gift Shop sells local books and a wide range of gifts and duty free liquor, T 82245, F 82230. Duty free shops catering for cruise ship visitors open when there is a demand. The Park Place is an art gallery selling local artists' paintings, ceramics and sculptures, also arts and crafts section, T 82452, F 82805.

● **Voltage**

110 volts A/C 60 cycles.

ON DEPARTURE

● **Departure tax**

Airport departure tax is US$5 for Antilles, US$10 international. Windward Islands Airways (Winair) T 82362/82381, F 82485.

ACCOMMODATION

● **Hotels**

Price guide

L1	over US$200	L2	US$151-200
L3	US$101-150	A1	US$81-100
A2	US$61-80	A3	US$46-60
B	US$31-45	C	US$21-30
D	US$12-20	E	US$7-11
F	US$4-6	G	up to US$3

L3-A2 *The Old Gin House*, Lower Town, T 82319, F 82555, a reconstructed 18th century cotton gin building, using old ballast bricks, closed for renovation 1996; **A1-A2** *La Maison Sur La Plage*, at Zeelandia Bay, T 82256, F 82831, run by Thérèse and Michel Viali (who only speaks French), beautiful location, best view on the island, 10 rooms for those who want seclusion and comfort, pool, boules, particularly noted for its French cuisine,

closed September, the beach is not safe for swimming, car hire rec; **A1** *Golden Era Hotel*, Lower Town, T 82345, F 82445, on the beach, modern, 20 rooms, not much charm but convenient and close to dive shop, manager Roy Hooker is also the cook, friendly but slow service, pool bar lively and snack bar/restaurant good. **A1-A2** *Talk of the Town*, on road to airport a little way out of Oranjestad, 18 rooms and efficiencies, some around pool, TV, phone, a/c which is a must as inland hotels are hotter, no sea breeze, restaurants, bar, popular with oil station contractors, takes credit cards but not US$100 bills; **A1-A3** *Kings Well*, between Upper and Lower Town, N end of beach by Smoke Alley, T/F 82538, run by Win and Laura, popular with divers and sailors, rooms modern and large, ceiling fans, tasteful decor, some waterbeds, health spa planned, some rooms overlook bar, more expensive have sea view, accepts Visa/Mastercard; **A3** Blue Nature Watersports, T 82725, F 82756, offers dive/hotel packages, some with guesthouse accommodation, comfortable, large rooms, clean, private bathrooms, some antique furniture, good food, friendly, family atmosphere; **A3** *Country Inn*, at Concordia near airport, Biesheuvelweg, owned by Mrs Iris Pompier, T/F 82484, 6 guesthouse rooms, noisy a/c but essential, TV, fridge, inc breakfast, other meals on request, hot and cold water, TCs but no credit cards.

● **Guesthouses**

There are several guest houses and apartments for rent which are much cheaper: **B** *Henriquez Apartments*, T 82299, 2 places, one near the airport, basic, no frills, cold water, private bathroom and also in Oranjestad on Prinseswg, near the hospital; also near the airport, *Alvin Courtar Apartments*, T 82218; and **B** *Lens Apartments*, no children; off the road towards The Quill, **B** *Daniel's Guest House*, T 82358, on the Rosemary Laan road, efficiencies, taxi available; **B** *Richardson's Guest House*, T 82378, Union Estate 3; **C** *Sugar Hill Apartments*, T 82305, upper end of Rosemary Laan. On the N side of The Quill, *Harry's Efficiency*, PO Box 82, no phone, good view.

Guest houses, villas and apartments are in the **A3-B** price range, double occupancy. Expect a 7% government tax, 15% service charge and sometimes a 5% surcharge. The Tourist Office also has a list of home rentals, T 82209 or 82213, ext 117.

FOOD AND DRINK

The best restaurants are in the hotels. *La Maison Sur La Plage* serves a high standard of simple French cuisine with excellent French wine, reservations rec; *Talk of the Town*, Golden Rock, T 82236, fairly standard menu and a few Dutch/Indonesian dishes, the bar is a good meeting place. Good creole and international food at the *Golden Era Hotel*, Sun night buffet; *The King's Well*, good lobster, steak, German food, cocktails, friendly atmosphere, owners like to chat and play cards with guests. Cheaper meals at *Chinese Restaurant*, Prinsesweg 9, T 82389, shut Sun, tell cook not to put in msg; *B's Garden*, just by Tourist Office and Governor's House, handy for lunch when exploring the town centre, burgers and snacks OK but meat a bit gristly and fish not rec; *Blue Bead Bar and Restaurant*, right on beach, West Indian, Indonesian and international food, T 82873, open for lunch Mon-Sat 1130-1430, for dinner daily 1800-2100, bar open Mon-Sat 1000-2400, Sun 1500-2400. *Stone Oven*, T 82543, West Indian food. *Cool Corner*, on the square opp Museum, currently the most popular bar on the island, run by Chucky, a friendly Chinese who manages to serve drinks, talk to customers and prepare decent Chinese food when he has time. If you are self-catering and want to buy fresh fish, go to the fish processing plant (Statia Fish Handling) at Lower Town opp short pier, Mon-Fri, usually 0800-1300 depending on the catch, they will clean the fish for you. Grocers sell only frozen fish. Lobster is available fresh Nov-March. Fresh bread is baked daily in outdoor charcoal-fired stone ovens and best bought straight from the oven at "fresh bread time", which varies according to who makes it. Listings of fresh bread times are available. Bake sales are announced by the town crier: open air takeaway meals of local dishes some Fri and Sat, from 1100, usually at Charlie's Place just below Mazinga Gift Shop and Africa Crossroads Park opp Museum.

GETTING AROUND

LAND TRANSPORT

● **Motoring**

Driving is on the right, but some roads are so narrow you have to pass where you can. Cows, donkeys, goats and sheep are a traffic hazard as they roam about freely, but if you drive slowly and carefully they will soon get out of your way.

● **Car hire**

To hire a car you need a driving licence from your own country or an international driver's licence. Companies include Brown's, T 82266, F 82454, US$40-50/day inc tax and insurance, weekend deals; Rainbow, T 82811, F 82586, US$35 inc CDW; Walkers, T 82719, US$30 plus tax and insurance; ARC, T 82595, F 82594, US$35 plus tax and insurance, 1995 cars, near airport; Lady Ama's Services, T 82451, F 82572, US$30-45, 5% surcharge on day rates; Avis, T 32421/82303, F 82285, US$40/day, US$35 second day. CDW is US$7.50/day, US$50/week. The speed limit in the country is 50 km (31 miles) an hour and in residential areas it is 30 km (19 miles) an hour. Mopeds are also available. Try Lopes Car Rental, T 82291, for cars, motor bikes, scooters and donkey carts. Scooters also from Dive Statia (see above).

● **Taxis**

Taxi drivers are well-informed guides and can arrange excursions, although most places are within walking distance if you are energetic. Airport to town is US$3.50, most other trips US$2-4 pp. A round island tour costs US$35 for 4 people, US$5 for every additional passenger.

COMMUNICATIONS

● **Postal services**

The post office is at Cottageweg 4, T 82207, F 82457, open Mon-Fri 0730-1200, 1300-1700 except Fri when it closes at 1645. Airmail letters to the USA, Canada, Holland, US$0.99 first 5 grams, to the Caribbean US$0.85, postcards US$0.51 and US$0.48, aerograms US$0.71. Express mail is available. Limited banking services also available inc currency exchange. There are special stamp issues and First Day Covers for collectors. DHL agent is Peggy van der Horde-Jacobson, Lampeweg 33, T/F 82401, packages to the USA US$22-30 first 2lbs. Lady Ama's Services is agent for Federal Express.

● **Telecommunications**

Fax, telex and cablegrams at Landsradio, Van Tonningenweg, Open Mon-Fri, 0730-1930, Sat, Sun 0900-1200, 1500-1800, pay phone on the wall for local calls, accepts only US quarters (US$0.25). For operator assisted overseas prepaid and collect calls, telegrams, telex and fax pay at counter when you place your call. Telephone cards of US$10 and US$17 can be used at phone booth outside near Police Station and at the corner of Korthalsweg and the road to the airport, for local or international calls. The telephone code number for Statia is 599-3.

ENTERTAINMENT

Statians like partying and every weekend something is always going on. Quite often you will hear a 'road block' from far away: cars stopped with huge stereos blaring and everyone jumping up in the street. Ask anybody what is going on next weekend, or just wait for the music to start in the evening. The only nightclub is *Largo Height Disco* by the cable TV station at Chapel Piece, closed Wed, busy mainly Fri, Sat, run by Pamela Hook, good zouk music and local food.

TOURIST INFORMATION

● **Local tourist offices**

The St Eustatius Tourism Development Foundation, Fort Oranjestraat, Mon-Fri 0800-1700, T/F 82433. Tourism Information booth at the airport, T 82620; at the Harbour Office, T 82205; Dutch Reformed Church and Paper Corner, T 82208. The St Eustatius Historical Foundation, PO Box 171. The town crier (Mr Cyril Lopes) announces events with loudspeakers on his car as he drives around town. Listen for news of jump-ups, sports events, food sales or community events. An excellent booklet, *Get to know St Eustatius 'Statia', A Guide & Directory for Visitors and Residents* is produced by Bill Richter, US$3.

● **Tourist office overseas**

In **Venezuela**: Edificio EXA, Oficina 804, Avda Libertador, Caracas, T 313832.

Sint Maarten

S INT MAARTEN (Dutch) or St-Martin (French – see under French Antilles section) lies 260 km N of Guadeloupe and 310 km E of Puerto Rico, in a cluster of islands on the Anguilla Bank. The island is amicably shared by the Dutch, who have 37 square km and the French, who have 52 square km.

The population of at least 62,000 (33,459 in St Maarten and 28,518 in St-Martin) has mushroomed with the tourist boom: the 1950 St Maarten census gave the total population at 1,484. While many of the residents were formerly ex-patriates who returned to their island, there is a large proportion who have come from other Caribbean islands to seek work. Few people speak Dutch, the official language, although Papiamento has increased with the migration of people from the ABC Dutch islands. Nearly everybody speaks English and there is a large Spanish-speaking contingent of guest workers from the Dominican Republic.

The Dutch side of the island has the main airport and seaport and most of the tourists. The French side is noticeably Gallic and few speak English. There are no border formalities: only a modest monument erected in 1948, which commemorates the division of the island three centuries earlier. The Dutch side occupies the S part of the roughly triangular island. The W part is low-lying and mostly taken up by the Simpson Bay Lagoon, which provides a safe anchorage for small craft. The lagoon is separated from the sea by a narrow strip of land on which the airport has been built. The rest of the Dutch part is hilly and dry and covered with scrub, although it can quickly turn green after rain. The coastline is indented with sandy bays, while just inland are several salt ponds, which first attracted settlers.

HISTORY

The Amerindians who originally settled on the island named it Sualouiga, meaning land of salt. The belief that Columbus discovered the island on his second voyage in 1493 is disputed, with historians now claiming it was Nevis he named St-Martin of Tours, and that later Spanish explorers misinterpreted his maps. Nevertheless, the Spanish were not interested in settling the island and it was not until 1629 that some French colonists arrived in the N, and then in 1631 the Dutch were attracted to the S part by the salt ponds. By this time, there were no Caribs left on the island and the two nationalities lived amicably enough together. Spain then reconsidered and occupied St Maarten from 1633 to 1648, fending off an attack

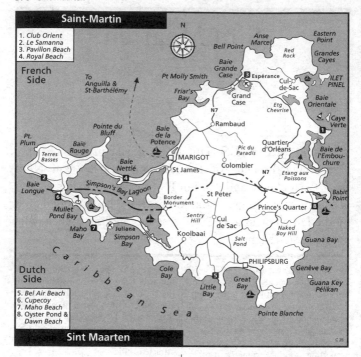

Saint-Martin

1. Club Orient
2. Le Samanna
3. Pavillon Beach
4. Royal Beach

French Side

5. Bel Air Beach
6. Cupecoy
7. Maho Beach
8. Oyster Pond & Dawn Beach

Dutch Side

Sint Maarten

by Peter Stuyvesant in 1644 which cost him his leg.

When the Spanish left, the Dutch and French settlers returned and after a few territorial skirmishes, they divided the island between them with the signing of the 23 March 1648 Treaty of Mount Concordia. Popular legend has it that the division was settled with a race starting from Oyster Pond. The Frenchman went N and the Dutchman went S, but the Frenchman walked faster because he drank only wine while the Dutchman's penchant for Genever (a drink similar to gin) slowed him down. Since 1648, however, St Maarten has changed hands 16 times, including brief occupations by the British, but the Dutch-French accord has been peaceably honoured at least since it was last revised in 1839.

At the height of its colonial period, sugar cane and livestock were the main agricultural activities, although the poor soil and lack of rain meant they were not very profitable. The emancipation of slavery in 1863 broke up the plantation system and the population began to decline as ex-slaves left to look for work elsewhere. Most of the salt produced from the Great Salt Pond behind Philipsburg was exported to the USA and neighbouring islands, but by 1949 this industry had also ended and a further exodus to other islands took place. The remaining population survived on subsistence farming, fishing and remittances from relatives abroad.

However, in 40 years the island has become unrecognizable, hotels and resorts, villas and guest houses now line the shore and there is no bay untouched by tourism. Over 1 million stopover and cruiseship tourists visit St Maarten (and French St-Martin) every year, attracted

Hurricane Luis

St Maarten was one of the islands worst hit by Hurricane Luis in Sept 1995. Six people were killed, damage of US$1bn was reported and at least 2,000 people lost their jobs in the tourist industry when hotels and about 300 yachts were smashed. The shanty towns housing Haitians and Dominicans (many of them illegal immigrants) were flattened and the Government moved quickly to bulldoze the remains, offering jobs and a tent camp for those with papers and deportation for those without. Rebuilding of public buildings, including the hospital, started quickly; cruise ships returned in Oct but the airport was closed to commercial traffic until November. Only a third of private homes were insured, while others (including the *Dawn Beach Resort*) were victims of a crooked insurance broker who disappeared with their premiums. Only half the island's hotel rooms were open for the winter season and several resorts remained closed in 1996. The hurricane highlighted low building standards and dodgy construction practices, particularly with newer houses.

by the duty-free shopping, casinos and a wide range of accommodation, as well as the beaches and watersports. Little of historical interest remains, except the walls of Fort Amsterdam overlooking Philipsburg, and a few other ruined fortifications, but this has not hindered the tourist industry, which is among the most successful in the region. For those who want more than sun, sand and sea, St Maarten's well-developed transport links make it an excellent jumping-off place for visiting other islands. Nearly 250,000 people are usually classified as in transit, making their way to other destinations with only a brief stop over in St Maarten.

Controversy arose in 1992 over the Dutch Government's decision in July to introduce 'higher supervision' of the St Maarten Island Council following an inquiry into its administration. The change meant that expenditure decisions by the island government had to be approved by the Lieutenant-Governor. In February 1993 supervision was tightened further with all major decisions requiring approval. There had been many reports of crime, corruption and financial maladministration and the USA was particularly concerned about suspected widespread drug smuggling through Juliana airport, where there were no customs controls. During 1993 several prominent members of government, including the hugely influential Dr Claude Wathey, leader of the St Maarten Democratic Party and former Prime Minister, his son Al Wathey, formerly the airport board chairman, Ralph Richardson, the former Lieutenant Governor, and Frank Arnell, the airport manager as well as other influential colleagues, came under judicial investigation in connection with irregularities in the airport and Great Bay harbour expansion projects. Investigations were also carried out in France, Italy and other countries. In 1994, the four men were jailed for forgery and perjury, while two Italians were jailed for drugs trafficking. The St Maarten executive council agreed to introduce customs checks at seaports and Juliana airport from January 1994 in an effort to control trafficking in arms, drugs and illegal immigration. The higher supervision order was extended until 1 June 1994 and France and the Netherlands agreed jointly to monitor air and sea traffic around the island.

In 1994 the electorate were asked whether they wished to remain part of the Netherlands Antilles, have separate status within the Kingdom (like Aruba), have complete integration with the

Netherlands, or be independent. At the referendum in October, 59.8% voted for the status quo, while about 30% wanted separate status. This was the lowest vote in favour of remaining in the Federation, compared with 90.6% in St Eustatius, 86.3% in Saba, 88% in Bonaire and 73.6% (in 1993) in Curaçao.

The islands council election in April 1995 gave five seats each to the Democratic Party (DP) and the St Maarten Patriotic Alliance (SPA). The latter had governed since June 1994 in alliance with the Progressive Democratic Party. The Serious Alternative People's Party (SAPP) won the remaining seat on the 11-member council and agreed with the DP to form an alliance which took office in July. The DP won 4,323 of the 9,536 votes cast against 4,177 for the SPA, while the DP's leader, Sarah Westcott-Williams won the highest individual vote with 2,204. However, the coalition government collapsed in Oct 1995 following the resignation of one DP commissioner and 2 from the SAPP.

DIVING AND MARINE LIFE

Water visibility is usually 75-125 feet and the water temperature averages over 70°F, which makes good snorkelling and scuba diving, from beaches or boats. Wreck Alley on Proselyte Reef, has several wrecks which can be explored on one dive. *HMS Proselyte* is a 200-year-old British frigate (mostly broken up and covered in coral, although cannons and anchors are visible), while *The Minnow* and *SS Lucy* are modern ships deliberately sunk as dive sites. Training with NAUI instructors or just equipment rental is offered by Beach Bums and Ocean Explorers at Simpson Bay, Trade Winds Dive Center at Great Bay Marina (T 75176, 249096, ext 14, PADI and SSI certification also offered, US$45 single tank 50-ft dives 0900, 1100, 1300 Mon-Fri, 1000, 1300 Sat, Sun).

BEACHES AND WATERSPORTS

The bays on the S and W shores are excellent for swimming, diving and fishing, and the beaches are of fine white sand. The most popular beach is Mullet Bay, where you can rent umbrellas, beach chairs etc. It can get crowded in season and all weekends. On the E side is Oyster Pond, a land-locked harbour which is difficult to enter because of the outlying reefs, but which is now home to a yacht club and is a centre for bare boat charter. Dawn Beach nearby is popular with body surfers and snorkelling is good because of the reefs just offshore; Guana Bay, next to Dawn Beach, is the bodysurfers best beach. Maho Beach, by the airport, has regular Sunday beach parties with live music competitions; don't forget to duck when planes arrive. The most W beach on the Dutch side of the island is Cupecoy, where rugged sandstone cliffs lead down to a narrow sandy beach, providing morning shade and a natural windbreak.

Every conceivable form of watersports is usually available. Surfing is possible all year round, from different beaches depending on the time of the year.

There are boat charter companies with sailing boats and motor boats, with or without a crew. You find most of them around Bobby's Marina, Philipsburg, from US$200 a day for bare boat. The marinas are open for business after serious hurricane damage in 1995, although boat salvaging is still in progress.

There are around 40 boats offering different trips around the islands, some just going out for snorkelling on the reefs or taking cruise ship passengers around. The *Falcon* (US$50 pp plus tax, 0900-1700, Mon-Sat, T 22167) sails to St-Barts from Great Bay Marina. Also the 75-foot motor catamaran, *White Octopus*, departs 0900, returns 1700, from Bobby's Marina, most days or from Captain Oliver's Marina on Wednesday, T 24096/23170. The trip to St Barts is normally quite rough and unpleasant on the way there but more pleasant on the return journey. Check the weather, the swell and the waves can be up to 12 feet even on a nice day. The *Golden Eagle*, a new wing mast 76-foot catamaran sails to Tintamarre from Great Bay Marina, 4 hours, US$45 pp, breakfast on board, snorkelling gear, T 75828/30068. Most boats offer some snacks, sodas and rum punch. Trips cost from US$50-75, plus departure tax. Check what is available from Marigot too. Some of the time share resorts offer free boat trips with snorkelling, lunch, taxis, (you pay departure tax), if you participate in one of their sales drives.

For fishing there are numerous boats available for a whole (US$500-750) or half (US$280-375) day from Bobby's Marina, Pelican Marina or Great Bay Marina. Arrangements can be made through the hotels. Marlin, barracuda, dolphin (not the mammal) and tuna are the best catches. Game fishing tournaments are held all year round.

The largest annual regatta takes place each February and lasts for three days with a round the island race on the Sunday. A race to Nevis and back is held in mid-June with a day for resting/parties. Other regattas held are for catamarans, match racing with charter boats, windsurfing etc. For more information check with St Martin Yacht Club or ask Robbie Ferron at Budget Marina in Philipsburg. A popular half day excursion is match racing on *Canada II*, *True North*, *True North IV* or *Stars and Stripes*, boats from the Americas Cup, US$60, races Wednesday 1315, 3 hours (T 43354, Bobby's Marina).

OTHER SPORTS

All the large hotels have **tennis** courts, many of which are lit for night play, but check availability, most were out of action in 1996. There is an 18-hole championship **golf** course at *Mullet Bay Resort*, which stretches along the shores of Mullet Pond and Simpson Bay Lagoon. **Running** is organized by the Road Runners Club, St Maarten, with a fun run of 5-10 km every Wednesday at 1730 and Sunday at 1830, starting from the *Pelican Resort & Casino* car park. On Sundays at 0700 there are two 20-km runs. There are monthly races with prizes and an annual relay race around the island to relive the legendary race between the Dutch and the French when they divided the island. Contact Dr Fritz Bus at the Back Street Clinic or Malcolm Maidwell of *El Tigre*, T 44309/22167. Crazy Acres Riding Centre takes groups **horseriding** every weekday morning at 0900 from the Wathey Estate, Cole Bay, to Cay Bay, where horses and riders can swim, T 42793. Make reservations two days in advance. Beach riding is also available on the French side.

CARNIVAL

Carnival starts in mid-April and lasts for three weeks, culminating in the burning of King Moui-Moui. It is one of the biggest in the area, with up to 100,000 people taking part. Most events are held at the Carnival Village, next to the University.

PHILIPSBURG

Philipsburg, the capital of Dutch St Maarten, is built on a narrow strip of sandy land between the sea and a shallow lake which was once a salt pond. It has two main streets, Front and Back, and a ringroad built on land reclaimed from the salt pond, which all run parallel to Great Bay Beach, perhaps the safest and cleanest city beach anywhere. Front Street is full of shops offering duty-free goods. Back Street contains low cost clothes shops and low budget Chinese restaurants.

The Simartn Museum at Museum Arcade on 119 Front Street is open 1000-1600 Mon-Fri, 0900-1200 Sat, closed Sun. In a restored 19th century house, the museum exhibits the history and culture of the island. There is a museum shop. The historic Courthouse dating from 1793, on De Ruyterplein, better

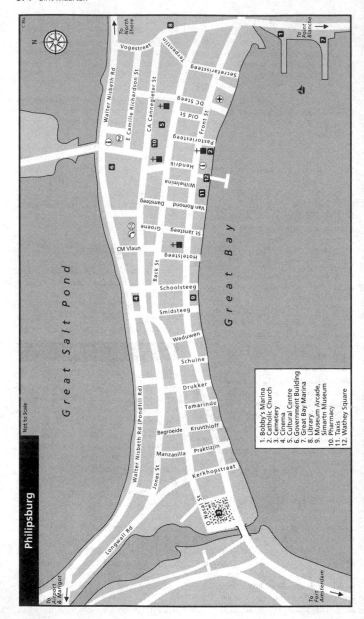

Philipsburg

Not to Scale

To Airport & Marigot

To Fort Amsterdam

To Point Blanche

To North Shore

N

Great Salt Pond

Great Bay

Walter Nisbeth Rd

Vogestreet

E Camille Richardson St

CA Cannegieter St

Old St

Front St

Terpentijn

Secretarissteeg

DC steeg

Pastorlesteeg

Hendrik

Wilhelmina

Van Romond

Damsteeg

Groene

St Jansteeg

Hotelsteeg

CM Vlaun

Back St

Schoolsteeg

Smidsteeg

Weduwen

Schuine

Drukker

Tamarinde

Kruvthioff

Begroeide

Praktizjin

Manzanilla

Jones St

Kerkhopstraat

Walter Nisbeth Rd (Pondfill Rd)

Longwall Rd

Nisaal St

1. Bobby's Marina
2. Catholic Church
3. Cemetery
4. Cinema
5. Cultural Centre
6. Government Building
7. Great Bay Marina
8. Library
9. Museum Arcade, Simartn Museum
10. Pharmacy
11. Taxis
12. Wathey Square

known as Wathey Square, faces the pier. In the past it has been used as a Council Hall, a weigh station, jail and until 1992, a Post Office. Now renovated, it is used exclusively as a courthouse.

The harbour is frequented by cruise ships and a host of smaller craft and the town gets very crowded when up to eight cruise ships are in port. For information on outdoor concerts, choirs, theatre and art exhibitions, ask at the Cultural Center of Philipsburg on Back Street (T 22056).

There is a zoo, opened 1991, on Arch Road in Madam Estate, close to New Amsterdam shopping centre, with a small exhibition of the fauna and flora from the islands, open weekdays 0900-1700, weekends 1000-1800, entrance US$4, children US$2, T 32030.

There are several ruined fortresses, but not a lot remains of them. Fort Amsterdam was the first Dutch fort in the Caribbean, built in 1631 but captured by the Spanish in 1633 and partly pulled down before they left the island in 1648. It was still used for military purposes until the 19th century and as a signalling and communications station until the 1950s. Fort Willem has a television transmitting tower and there is a good view from the top. Construction was started by the British, who called it Fort Trigge, at the beginning of the 19th century, but the Dutch renamed it in 1816. Fort Bel-Air and Sint Peter's Battery gave way to modern development although a few ruins are still visible near Great Bay Marina.

EXCURSIONS

You can take a day trip round the island, visiting the ruined Fort Amsterdam overlooking Philipsburg and the French part of the island. It is well worth having lunch in one of the many French restaurants in Grand Case or the other French villages. Generally, however, there is not much of either historical or natural interest to see on the island, and most excursions are day trips to neighbouring islands: Anguilla, St-Barthélémy, Saba, St Eustatius, St Kitts or Nevis, either by boat (see **Beaches and watersports**) or by plane.

Information for travellers

BEFORE TRAVELLING

● **Documents**
See main Netherlands Antilles section, under Curaçao Information for travellers. In addition, under a 1994 Franco-Dutch immigration accord, visitors to Dutch Sint Maarten have to meet French immigration criteria, even if not visiting the French side. Therefore, many nationalities now have to obtain a French visa before embarking on a shopping trip to Philipsburg. The local immigration officials are particularly concerned that you fill in your tourist card with a hotel address, even if you do not know whether you will be staying there.

● **Climate**
Average temperature is 80°F and average annual rainfall is 45 inches.

● **Health**
There is a new hospital on Cay Hill with 60 beds, all basic specialism, a haemodialyse department and 24-hour emergency services, T 31111, F 30116. A helicopter airlift to Puerto Rico is available for extreme medical emergencies. Drinking water in the hotels is purified. Be careful of the sun.

MONEY

● **Currency**
Netherlands Antilles guilders or florins are the official currency, but the most common currency is the US dollar, which one need never change at all. You will get a poor exchange rate for French francs. It is often difficult to get change from payments in any currency other than US dollars. Supermarkets price their goods in local currency. Credit cards widely accepted.

GETTING THERE

AIR

From Europe: Air France 4 times a week, Air Liberté once a week and AOM French Airlines twice a week from Paris, KLM twice a week from Amsterdam in a joint operation with ALM.

From the USA: Direct flights from New York (American Airlines, Continental), Baltimore (US Air, American Airlines), Boston (American Airlines), Pittsburgh (US Air) and Miami (American Airlines) with connecting flights from several other US cities. American Airlines flights from US cities mostly make their connections in San Juan, Puerto Rico. Aerolíneas Argentinas flies from Buenos Aires via Miami.

Other Caribbean islands: There are lots of flights from other Caribbean islands: Anguilla, Antigua, Barbados, Curaçao, Dominica, Martinique, Dominican Republic, Grenada, Haiti, Nevis, Guadeloupe, Trinidad and Tobago, Saba, St Barthélémy, USVI (St Croix and St Thomas), St Eustatius, St Kitts, St Vincent, Puerto Rico, St Lucia, Jamaica, and the British Virgin Islands (Tortola), with a variety of regional and international carriers. ALM also flies from Caracas via Curaçao and Viasa flies direct.

SEA

There are no long distance sea communications except cruise ships which usually stay 5-9 hours. A catamaran, *The Edge*, runs from Pelican Marina, Simpson Bay, to Saba, Wed, Fri, Sun, US$60 return, and to St Barths, Mon, Tues, Thur, Sat, US$50 return, plus US$5 port surcharge, T 42640. Boats to Anguilla leave from the French side. See **Beaches and watersports** for boats to St Barths.

● **Ports of entry**
(Dutch/French flag) Philipsburg and Marigot.

● **Boat documents**
Clear in with Immigration at Police station in town at weekends or after hours in Philipsburg. No charge, just a long form to fill in. To clear out, go to the Port Authority and Harbourmaster S-S 0730-1200, 1300-1600, US$2 and another copy of the same form. At Marigot you pay US$10 at the ferry dock.

● **Marinas**
No fee yet for Simpson Lagoon bridge. Dutch bridge openings 0600, 1100, 1600, 1800, outbound boats first. Good groceries and

laundry in Lagoon. Radio net VHF 78 at 0730. Send mail with someone flying out or Federal Express. Duty free Caribbean headquarters for boat parts, outboard motors, beer. Anchorages: Great Bay, Orient Beach, Oyster Bay, Marigot, Simpson Bay, Simpson Bay Lagoon Marinas: Great Bay Marina, Bobby's Marina, in Simpson Bay Lagoon: Simpson Bay Yacht Club, Island Water World, Port de Plaisance Marina, Palapa Marina. Mail/fax/phone: Dockside Management and The Mailbox. Charter fleets include Jet Sea, Moorings, Nautor Swan, Sunsail, Stardust ATM, Sun Yachts.

ON ARRIVAL

● Airlines
Airline offices at the airport: ALM, T 54240/54210; Air Guadeloupe, T 54212; KLM, T 52120; LIAT, T 54203; American Airlines, T 52040; Air France, T 54212; Air St Barthélemy, T 53151; BWIA/Ogden Aviation, T 54234; Continental, Northwest and USAir, T 54344; Lufthansa, T 52040; Winair, T 54230/54237.

Airport flight information, T 52161.

● Banks
Scotiabank, Back Street, T 22262, 1% commission on TCs; Windward Islands Bank, T 23485, charges US$5 per traveller's cheque cashed; Barclays Bank, 19 Front Street, T 22491; Chase Manhattan Bank, Mullet Bay, T 44204; Algemene Bank Nederland, main office at Front Street, T 23505; Citco Bank Antilles, 16 Front Street, T 23471, 3 other offices on the island as well; Nederlandse Credietbank, T 22933. Open 0830-1500, Mon-Thur, 0830-1500, 1600-1700, Fri.

● Official time
Atlantic Standard Time, 4 hours behind GMT, 1 ahead of EST.

● Public holidays
New Year's Day, Carnival Monday (April), Good Friday, Easter Monday, 30 April, Labour Day (1 May), Ascension Day, St Maarten Day (11 November), Christmas Day, Boxing Day.

● Religion
Many denominations are represented. Seventh Day Adventist, Anglican, Baptist, Jehovah's Witness, Methodist, Roman Catholic, Church of Christ, Baha'i, The New Testament Church of God. Look in *Today* (see below) for details of services.

● Security
Crime has increased on St Maarten and there have been armed robberies on the roads in the Lowland area, although the police have now clamped down with considerable force.

● Shopping
Duty-free shopping is a tourist attraction, but it helps if you have an idea of prices at home to compare, and shop around as prices vary. In the electronics and camera shops many outdated models are on display. European visitors planning to take home hi-fi or domestic appliances should make sure that they can be switched to 220 volts. Check your duty-free allowance when returning home. Most of the shops are along Front Street. Open 0800-1200, 1400-1800.

● Useful addresses
Police: T 22222. **Fire**: T 22222. **Ambulance**: T 22111. **Hospital**: T 31111.

● Voltage
110 volts AC. Note that it is 220 volts on the French side.

ON DEPARTURE

● Departure tax
US$5 when leaving for the Netherlands Antilles, US$10 for other destinations at Juliana Airport except for French visitors returning to Guadeloupe or France. Travel agents ask for US$3 to confirm flights.

● Airport information
Allow plenty of time on departure from Juliana airport at busy times as it can get very chaotic with several flights departing at once. If waiting for a plane, rather than wait in the airport there is a waterfront bar and café across the main road from the arrivals area.

ACCOMMODATION

● Hotels

Price guide			
L1	over US$200	L2	US$151-200
L3	US$101-150	A1	US$81-100
A2	US$61-80	A3	US$46-60
B	US$31-45	C	US$21-30
D	US$12-20	E	US$7-11
F	US$4-6	G	up to US$3

There is a 5% Government tax on all hotel bills and a 10-15% service charge. Some add an energy surcharge. Prices are high, package deals in summer can be good value if you are prepared to shop around. In 1996 several hotels were still closed or partly open after hurricane repairs. Check for availability of sports and other facilities. The largest resort hotels are **L1-L2** *Mullet Bay Resort & Casino*, closed 1996, hurricane damage, T 52801, F 54281, 600 rooms-suites; **L1-A1** *Great Bay Beach Hotel & Casino*, convenient for Philipsburg, all resort facilities, caters to all-inclusive tourism, activities organized, games around the pool, barbecue buffet Mon, T 22446, F 23859, 150 of the 285 rooms-suites open in 1996; **L1** *Cupecoy* perched on a cliff above Cupecoy beach, pool, tennis, casino, T 52309 F 52312, rooms-suites; **L1-A1** *Dawn Beach* on Dawn Beach at Oyster Pond, closed 1996, hurricane damage, T 22929, F 24421; **L1-L3** *Maho Beach Hotel & Casino*, 400 of the 600 rooms/suites open in 1996, T 52115, F 53018, another all-inclusive, right by airport; **L1-L3** *Pelican Resort & Casino*, pool, tennis etc, T/F 42503, F 42133, on Simpson Bay, huge, but only partly open 1996; **L1-L3** *Divi Little Bay Beach Resort & Casino*, reopened late-1996 after hurricane repairs, tennis, pool, watersports, T 22333, F 23911, 220 rooms; **L1-L2** *The Towers At Mullet Bay*, watersports, disco, casino closed for repairs 1996, close to airport, 5 miles from Philipsburg, T 53069, F 52147, 81 units, a/c, kitchenettes, TV, VCR etc.

Middle-sized hotels and resorts include **L1-L2** *Bel Air Beach Hotel*, at Little Bay, T 23366, F 25295, 72 suites; **L1-A1** *La Vista*, near Pelican, 24 suites and cottages, tennis, pool, horse riding, T 43005, F 43010; **A1-A3** *Seaview Beach Hotel*, 45 rooms on Great Bay Beach, Philipsburg, casino, a/c, TV, children under 12 free, T 22324, F 24356; **L1** *ITT Sheraton Port de Plaisance*, on Simpson Bay, due to reopen late-1996, hurricane damage, T 45222, F 42428, 88 units; also on Simpson Bay, **L3-A2** *White Sands Beach Club*, PO Box 3043, T/F 54370, 1-2 bedroom suites, chalets, villas, special deals for cash customers, all beach front units, no restaurant but several nearby, car hire, rec, airport runway runs parallel to this part of Simpson Bay. **L1-L3** *Oyster Pond Hotel*, near Dawn Beach, 40 rooms, marina, fishing and water sports, tennis, pool, beach, T 22206, F 25695, no children under 10.

Small hotels include **L2-A2** *Pasanggrahan*, in Philipsburg, rec, formerly the Governor's home, the oldest inn, 30 rooms, PO Box 151, T 23588, F 22885, pool, no children under 12, nice atmosphere; **A3-B** *Bute*, Illidge Road 2, Philipsburg, on Great Bay Pond, 13 rooms, a/c available, T 22400; **A1** *Mary's Boon*, on Simpson Bay beach, 12 studios with kitchenettes, pets welcome but no children under 16, no credit cards, T 44235; **A2** *Midtown Motel*, 42 Back Street, T 26838/9, built end-1995, clean, modern, very friendly, near shops, casinos etc, rec.

Guesthouses on Front Street: **B-C** *Marcus*, 7 rooms, T 22419, **C** *Seaside*, 5 rooms, PO Box 72; on Back Street: **A3-B** *Lucy's*, 9 rooms, clean and adequate, no children under 6, PO Box 171, T 22995; **B-C** *Jose's*, prepay for 6 nights, get 7th free, 11 rooms, very basic, mosquitoes T 22231; **A1-B** *Joshua Rose*, 7 Backstreet, slightly better, a/c but still mosquitoes, 14 rooms, T 24317, F 30080.

At Simpson Bay: **A1** *The Horny Toad*, 8 studios, no children under 7, right on beach, not seriously troubled by aircraft noise, well cared for, pretty patio gardens, no credit cards, T 54323, F 53316; **L2-A2** *Calypso*, 8 efficiency apartments, Simpson Bay, PO Box 65, T 44233.

At Pointe Blanche: **A1-A2** *Great Bay Marina*, 10 rooms, fridge, a/c, TV, grocery, pier facilities, PO Box 277, T 22167; **L3-A2** *Tamarind* 45 apartments with kitchenettes, swimming pool, deli, T 24359, F 25391.

At Cole Bay: **A3** *Ernest*, 9 rooms in Cay Hill, 16 on Bush Road, swimming pool, a/c, TV, T 22003; **A3-B** *George's*, 10 rooms in Cole Bay, 10 rooms in Philipsburg, a/c, kitchen, T 45363 or 22126.

● **Apartments**

The Tourist Office has a list of apartments, villas and houses to rent weekly or monthly. The best way of finding an apartment is to look in the newspaper. There are several apartments for rent on Back Street, look for signs on the houses. A studio will cost about US$400-500/week in a good location. Apartments at Simpson Bay Beach cost US$350-500/week.

● **Camping**

Camping is safe but you must seek permission from the landowner.

FOOD AND DRINK

● **Restaurants**

All the major hotels have restaurants with international cuisine. Pick up a free tourist guide to choose from the myriad restaurants now open on St Maarten with food from all over the world. At *Mullet Bay Resort*: **The Frigate**, serves excellent charcoal-broiled steaks and lobster; *Bamboo Garden* offers some of the best Chinese dining, T 52801 for both restaurants. In Philipsburg: *Le Bec Fin*, French, highly rec, elegant, favoured by the Dutch Royal Family and winner of awards, T 22976 for reservations. Front Street is full of good restaurants and even a *Burger King*. *Da Livio*, W end, high class Italian restaurant on waterfront, run by Livio Bergamasco and his British wife, excellent seafood and pasta, not cheap, pastas from US$9, main courses from US$24, T 22690. **San Marco**, is an Italian restaurant, nice location overlooking sea, good for a break from shopping, T 22166. *Callaloo*, a pleasant bar/restaurant, steaks, hamburgers and pizzas are served at reasonable prices, no credit cards, very popular, T 73641. Indonesian rijsttafel at the hotels. For the budget minded try Back Street where you mostly find Chinese and *roti* places such as *Hong Kong*, *ABC Restaurant* and *Kings Fastfood* where you can eat for US$5. *Admiral's Quarters*, 7 Front St, interesting menu, international with Caribbean touches; *Shiv Sagar*, tor Indian food, large portions, Tandoori specialities; *Grill and Ribs*, the best ribs on the island at Old St and also Simpson Bay, all you can eat for US$12.95, reservations essential; Americanized French at *L'Escargot*, Front Street, T 22 483. In the Simpson Bay area: **Turtle Pier Bar and Restaurant** is reasonably priced at US$10 maximum per dish with an interesting setting in a mini zoo with parrots, monkeys, turtles etc, live music 2 or 3 times a week, T 52562; *Lynette's* is a local restaurant with good seafood quite close to airport US$40 pp inc wine and tip and upstairs is *Clayton's* sport bar, where you can see most major sporting events on a big screen TV; *Don Carlos*, tasty Mexican food, US$10-15 pp for dinner, open daily 0730-2230, Mexican buffet Thur, US$12.95, all you can eat, T 53112; *Ma Chance Shrimphouse* at Simpson Bay Yacht Club specializes in seafood, try the tiger shrimps; *Boat House* for drinks and food, live music several times a week, rec, reservations essential; **The Greenhouse Bar and Restaurant**, next to Bobby's Marina at Great Bay, view over yachts, menu includes hamburgers, steak and local fish, disc jockey, dancing, Tues night 2 drinks for the price of one, T 22941; *The News Music Café*, a '60s and '70s type of *Hard Rock Café* for late night meals, dancing, drinks, food overpriced and tasteless, 344 Airport Road on Simpson Bay,

open daily from 2200; at the end of Front St near the *Pasanggrahan Hotel* is a nice pastry shop, with fresh French pastries and juices; *Rembrandt Café* at New Amsterdam shopping centre, a Dutch coffee shop/café, very popular for late drinks, best after 2100-2200. The most popular bars with nice sunsets are **Greenhouse** and **Chesterfield**, where you can find yachtsmen if you want to hitchhike by boat. Also *Paradise Café* (*Maho Resort*), *The Boat House* (*Simpson Bay*), *News Café* (*Simpson Bay*), *Turtle Pier Bar* (airport).

● **Drink**

The traditional local liqueur is *guavaberry*, made from rum and the local berries, whose botanical name is *Eugenia Floribunda*. They are not related to guavas. The berries are found on the hills and ripen just before Christmas. Used nowadays mostly in cocktails.

GETTING AROUND

LAND TRANSPORT

● **Motoring**

Foreign and international driver's licences are accepted. Drive on the right. The speed limit is 40 kmph in urban areas, 60 kmph outside town, unless there are other signs. The roads on both sides of the island are very busy and full of pot holes, making them rather unsafe for mopeds or walking, particularly at night. **Hitchhiking**: is possible but allow half an hour waiting time; it is not rec for women.

● **Car hire**

There can be a shortage of cars or jeeps for hire in high season, although there are now 15 rental companies, and it is advisable to request one from your hotel when you book the room. Many have offices at the airport or in the hotels; free pick up and delivery are standard and you can leave the car at the airport on departure. Prices range from US$25-55 a day. Car hire companies include: Risdon's Car Rentals, Front Street, T 23578; Avis, Cole Bay, T 42322; Hertz, Juliana Airport, T 44314; Budget, Philipsburg, T 44038, Cannegie Car Rental, Front Street, T 22397; Opel Car Rental, Airport, T 44324; Speedy Car Rental, Airport, T 23893; Roy Roger's, Airport, T 42701, US$30 plus US$10 CDW.

● **Bicycles**

Two-wheeled transport hire from Super Honda, Bush Road Cul-de-Sac, T 25712; Moped Cruising, Front Street, T 22330; OK

580

Scooter Rental, at *Maho Beach Hotel* and *Cupecoy Resort*, T 42115, 44334. Mountain bike hire from Tri-Sport Rent a Bike, Airport Road, T 54384, US$15/day, delivery and pickup available, guided tours.

● **Buses**
Mini-vans or tour **buses** also offer tours and are generally cheaper than taxis. Island tours from US$15; for more information ask at the Tourist Office on the square. There is a fairly regular bus service from 0600 until 2400 to Marigot (US$1.50 Philipsburg-Marigot), French Quarters and St Peters, and from Marigot to Grand Case on the French side. After 2000 there are few buses. The best place to catch a bus is on Back Street. Buses run along Back Street and Pondfill and only stop at bus stops. Outside towns, however, just wave to stop a bus. Fare price is usually US$0.80 in town, US$1 for short trips, US$1.50 for long trips. There is no regular bus service between Philipsburg and the airport although the route to *Mullet Bay Resort* passes the airport. Buses on this route run mostly at the beginning and the end of the working day (although there are a few during the day) and drivers may refuse to take you, or charge extra, if you have a lot of luggage.

● **Taxis**
There are plenty of **taxis**, which are not metered so check the fare first, which is fixed according to your destination. Trips to other beaches or tours of the island can be arranged with taxi drivers: island tour US$35 plus US$2 for each additional passenger; hourly rate US$10 plus US$2.50 each additional 15 minutes. From Philipsburg to Juliana airport US$10, Dawn Beach US$18, Marigot US$10, Mullet Bay US$5, Pelican Resort US$8, all for 2 passengers, additional passengers US$2 each. Night tariffs are an extra 30% 2200-2400, an extra 50% 0001-0600. Pick up taxi at the square in Philipsburg (T 22359) or Juliana airport (T 54317).

COMMUNICATIONS

● **Postal services**
Two safe places for holding mail are *Bobby's Marina*, PO Box 383, Philipsburg and *Island Water World*, PO Box 234, Cole Bay. It is not possible to send a parcel by sea, only airmail which is expensive.

● **Telecommunications**
At Landsradio telecommunications office in Cannegieter Street, open until midnight. This is where you can buy telephone cards for the Dutch side of the island, open from 0700. You can also buy telephone cards at Landsradio's offices at Simpson Bay, Cole Bay and St Peter's. Note that card phones at Juliana airport, although marked as 'téléphone' and displaying instructions in French, do not work with French phone cards.

MEDIA

● **Newspapers**
Local events are noted in the free weekly newspaper, *Today*, published in English weekly and distributed in hotels, retail stores and other outlets on Sint Maarten, Anguilla and St Barthélémy as well as on regional airlines. *The Chronicle*, *The Herald Caribbean* and *The Guardian* come out 6 times a week and *Newsday* twice a week. After 1500 in the shops on Front Street or at the airport you can find US newspapers (*New York Times*, *Miami Herald* and *San Juan Star*). American magazines (30%-40% more expensive than the USA) are especially good at Paiper Garden, Front Street.

● **Radio**
PJD2 Radio is on medium wave 1300 kHz and FM 102.7 mHz.

ENTERTAINMENT

Nearly all the resorts have casinos, which are a major attraction, the most popular being the casino at *ITT Sheraton Port de Plaisance*, *Pelican Casino* (*Pelican Resort*) and *Casino Royale* (*Maho/Mullet Bay*). The *Studio 7* discothèque at Grand Casino, Mullet Bay, is the most visited, entrance US$10 including one drink, can be higher if they have a special show, all drinks US$6, the disco starts late, rec to pass the time in *Cherry's* bar, a 5-min walk away, when people leave there most head for the disco. *Coconut Comedy Club* have stand up comedians Tues-Sun, 2130 and 2330, US$10 cover charge, most comedians from HBO or Carsons, well worth the price. *Caribbean Revue*, at *Mullet Bay Resort*, has a Caribbean show with Calypsonians and Limbo dancers, keep an eye open for King Bo Bo, the King of Calypso. Most resorts have live entertainment, such as limbo dancing, fire eating or live music, both local and international. In Philipsburg, *The Movies*, on Pondfill, has newly released films, US$5. *The News* is good for dancing, with live music every other night, extremely popular. Look out for Jack (Irish folk songs etc), G-Strings (pop-rock 1950s-70s), King Bo-Bo, the most popular bands of the last few years, whose music fills all the bars.

TOURIST INFORMATION

● **Local tourist office**
Imperial building, 23 Walter Nisbeth Road, 3rd floor, T 22337, F 22734. Well supplied with brochures and guides to St Maarten, and the monthly *St Maarten Holiday*. Sightseeing tours available by bus or by car.

● **Tourist offices overseas**
In **Holland**: Minister Plenipotentiary of the Netherlands Antilles, Badhuisweg 173-175, 2597JP, S-Gravenhage, T (070) 351-2811, F (070) 351-2722.

In **Canada**: 243 Ellerslie Ave, Willowdale, Toronto, Ontario, M2N 1Y5 T 416-223 3501, F 416-223 6887; 1682 Victoria Park Avenue, Scarborough, Ontario, M1R 1P7, T 416-755 5247, F 416-755 8697.

In the **USA**: St Maarten Tourist Bureau, 675 Third Avenue, New York, NY 10017, T 1-800-786 2278.

In **Venezuela**: Edificio EXA, oficina 804, Avda Libertador, Caracas, T 31 38 32, F 416-223 6887.

French Antilles

THE FRENCH CARIBBEAN ISLANDS form two Départements d'Outremer: one comprises Martinique, and the other Guadeloupe with its offshore group, Marie-Galante, Les Saintes, La Désirade, and two more distant islands: Saint-Barthélémy and the French part of Saint-Martin (shared with the Dutch). Geographically, the main islands form the N group of the Windward Islands, with the ex-British island of Dominica in the centre of them. Saint-Barthélémy and Saint-Martin are in the Leeward group.

HORIZONS

While aware of the fact that we are breaking the geographical sequence of the book, we shall deal with the French Antilles as a single entity. As the islands are politically Departments of France they have the same status as any Department in European France. Each Department sends two senators and three deputies to the National Assembly in Paris. The inhabitants are French citizens. The currency is the French franc (F). The people speak French. Visitors are often surprised by how French the islands are. The connection with France confers many benefits on the islands, which enjoy French standards of social legislation etc, but it also drives up the cost of living, which is rather higher than elsewhere in the Caribbean. There is an independence movement, whose more extremist members have been responsible for violent protests against high unemployment.

Both the main islands were sighted by Columbus on his second voyage in 1493, but no colonies were established by the Spanish because the islands were inhabited by the Caribs (who are now virtually extinct); it was not until 1635 that French settlers arrived.

Because of their wealth from sugar, the islands became a bone of contention between Britain and France; other French islands, Dominica, St Lucia, Tobago, were lost by France in the Napoleonic wars. The important dates in the later history of the islands are 1848, when the slaves were freed under the influence of the French 'Wilberforce', Victor Schoelcher; 1946, when the islands ceased to be colonies and became Departments; and 1974, when they became Regions.

CULTURE

The cultural, social and educational systems of France are used and the official language is French. However, Créole is widely spoken on Guadeloupe and Martinique; it has West African grammatical structures and uses a mainly French-derived vocabulary. Although still not officially recognized, it is the everyday language of the Guadeloupean and Martiniquan people. English is not widely spoken, although it is becoming more common in hotels and particularly on St Barts, where it is understood nearly everywhere and on St-Martin, where it is the common language. A knowledge of French is therefore a great advantage.

Another feature common to the two main islands is the pre-Lenten Carnival, said to be more spontaneous and less touristy than most. There are also picturesque Ash Wednesday ceremonies (especially in Martinique), when the population dresses in black and white, and processions take place that combine the seriousness of the first day of the Christian Lent with the funeral of the Carnival King (Vaval).

Also shared are the African dances: the *calinda, laghia, bel-air, haut-taille, gragé* and others, still performed in remote villages. The famous biguine is a more sophisticated dance from these islands, and the mazurka can also be heard. French Antillean music is, like most other Caribbean styles, hybrid, a mixture of African (particularly percussion), European, Latin and, latterly, US and other Caribbean musical forms. Currently very popular, on the islands and in mainland France, is zouk, a hi-tech music which overlays electronics on more traditional rhythms.

Traditional costume is commonly seen in the form of brightly-coloured, chequered Madras cotton made into elegant Parisian-style outfits. It is the mixture of French and Créole language and culture that gives Martinique and Guadcloupe an ambience quite different from that of the rest of the Caribbean. An extra dimension is added by the Hindu traditions and festivals celebrated by the descendants of the 19th century indentured labourers.

The spectacles of cockfighting and mongoose versus snake are popular throughout the French Islands. Betting shops are full of atmosphere (they are usually attached to a bar). Horseracing is held on Martinique, but not Guadeloupe, but on both islands gambling on all types of mainland France track events is very keen.

The dominance of French educational and social regimes on its colonial possessions led, in the 1930s and 1940s, to a literary movement which had a profound influence on black writing the world over. This was *négritude*, which grew up in Paris among black students from the Caribbean and Africa. Drawing particularly on Haitian nationalism (1915-30), the *négritude* writers sought to restore black pride which had been completely denied by French education. The leaders in the field were Aimé Césaire of Martinique, Léopold Senghor of Senegal and Léon Damas of Guyane.

Césaire's first affirmation of this ideology was *Cahier d'un retour au pays natal* (1939); in subsequent works and in political life (he was mayor of Fort-de-France) he maintained his attack on the "white man's superiority complex" and worked, in common with another Martiniquan writer, Frantz Fanon, towards "the creation of a new system of essentially humane values" (Mazisi Kunene in his introduction to the Penguin edition of *Return to My Native Land*, 1969).

Information for travellers

BEFORE TRAVELLING

● Documents
The regulations are the same as for France. In most cases the only document required for entry is a passport, the exceptions being citizens of Australia, South Africa, Bolivia, Dominica, St Lucia, Barbados, Jamaica, Trinidad, Haiti, Honduras, El Salvador, Dominican Republic, Turkey, when a visa is required. However, any non-EC citizen planning to stay longer than 3 months will need an extended visa. Citizens of the United States and Canada intending a stay of less than 3 months will not need a passport, although some form of identification is required. A valid passport is highly recommended, however, to avoid unnecessary problems and delays. An onward ticket is necessary but not always asked for.

● Customs
With the abolition of EC frontiers, Europeans are able to bring back 100 litres of rum etc. However you could run into problems if returning via Antigua, with a long, uncomfortable wait in transit. Take a direct flight if buying in bulk.

● Health
Vaccination certificates are not required if you are French, American or Canadian, but if you come from South America or some of the Caribbean Islands an international certificate for small pox and yellow fever vaccinations is compulsory.

MONEY

● Currency
Banking hours are given under the various islands, as are the names of banks. There are money-changing offices in the big hotels and at airports. The French franc is the legal tender, but US$ are preferred in Saint-Martin and are widely accepted elsewhere. There is no limit to

travellers' cheques and letters of credit being imported, but a declaration of foreign banknotes in excess of 3,500F must be made.

GETTING THERE

AIR

Transport to each island is given separately. Note: French Saint-Martin has only a small airport; the international flights arrive and depart from Juliana International Airport on the Dutch side.

SEA

Contact Continental Shipping and Travel, 179 Piccadilly, London W1V 9DB, T 071-491 4968, for help in arranging passage from France to the French Antilles (see also **Introduction and Hints**).

ON ARRIVAL

● **Official time**
4 hours behind GMT, 1 ahead of EST in all cases.

● **Public holidays**
New Year's Day; Carnival at the beginning of February; 8 March Victory Day; Good Friday; Easter Monday; Labour Day on 1 May; Ascension Day at the beginning of May; Whit Monday in May; National Day on 14 July; Schoelcher Day on 21 July; Assumption Day in August; All Saints Day on 1 November; Armistice Day on 11 November and Christmas Day.

● **Tipping**
Check if your bill says 'Service Compris', in which case no tip is necessary.

ACCOMMODATION

● **Hotels**
Addresses for the local *gîtes* associations are also under the individual islands. In France, contact Gîtes de France, 35 Rue Godot de Mauroy, 75009 Paris, T 4742 2543. Restaurants divide fairly neatly into generally very expensive French cuisine or the more moderate créole. There is not much evidence of the *plat du jour* as there would be in France. Children may find créole food rather spicey. Fast food hamburger bars are not common.

FOOD AND DRINK

● **Food**
A delightful blend of French, African, and Indian influences is found in Créole dishes, and the cuisine is quite distinctive. Basic traditional French and African recipes using fresh local ingredients; seafood, tropical fruits and vegetables are combined with exotic seasonings to give original results rich in colour and flavour. Here are a few local specialties not to be missed:

Ti-boudin, a soft well-seasoned sausage; *court bouillon de poisson* or *blaff* is conch (*lambis*), red snapper or sea urchin cooked with lime, white wine and onions; *ragout*, a spicy stew often made with squid (*chatrous*), or conch, or with meat; *colombo*, a recipe introduced by Hindu immigrants in the last century, is goat, chicken, pork or lamb in a thick curry sauce; *poulet au coco*, chicken prepared with onions, hot peppers (*piment*) and coconut; chunks of steakfish (usually tuna, salmon, or red snapper) marinaded and grilled; *morue* (salt cod) made into sauces and *accras* (hot fishy fritters from Africa) or grilled (*chiquetaille*), or used in *ferocc d'avocat*, a pulp of avocados, peppers and manioc flour; lobster (*langouste*), crab (*Crabe*), crayfish (*écrevisses*, *ouassous*, *z'habitants*), prawns (*gambas*) and snapper (*vivaneau*) are often fricaséed, grilled or barbecued with hot pepper sauce. Also popular are stuffed crab (*crabe farci*) and stuffed urchin (*oursin farci*).

Main dishes are usually accompanied by white rice, breadfruit, yams or sweet potatoes (*patate douce*) with plantains and red beans or lentils. *Christophine au gratin*; a large knobbly pear-shaped vegetable grilled with grated cheese and breadcrumbs, or a plate of fresh *crudités* are delicious, lighter side dishes.

Exotic fresh fruit often ends the meal; pineapples, papayas, soursops and bananas can be found all year round and mangos, mandarin oranges, guavas and sugar apples in season. Ice cream (*glace*) is also a favourite dessert.

● **Drink**
As in other Caribbean islands the main alcoholic drink is rum. Martiniquan rum has a distinctive flavour and is famous for its strength. There are 2 main types: white rum (*blanc*) and dark rum (*vieux*) which has been aged in oak vats and is usually more expensive. *Ti punch* is rum mixed with cane syrup or sugar and a slice of lime and is a popular drink at any time of the day. *Shrub* is a delicious Christmas liqueur made from rum and orange peel.

Planteur is a rum and fruit juice punch. There is a huge choice of Martiniquan rum, recommended brands being Trois Rivières, Mauny, Neisson and St Clément. There are different brands on Guadeloupe. French wines are available, although even red wine is usually served as a cool drink with ice. The local beer is Lorraine, a clean-tasting beer which claims to be 'brewed for the tropics'. Corsaire, made in Guadeloupe, is bitter tasting and insipid. Locally-brewed Guinness, at 7% alcohol, stronger than its Irish counterpart, is thick and rich. Malta, a non-alcoholic beverage similar to malt beer, is produced by most breweries and said to be full of minerals and vitamins. Thirst quenching non-alcoholic drinks to look out for are the fresh fruit juices served in most snackbars and cafés. Guava, soursop, passionfruit, mandarin, and sugar cane juice are commonly seen. Tap water is drinkable.

TOURIST INFORMATION

● **Local tourist office**
Addresses of the French Tourist Offices on the individual islands are given separately.

● **Tourist offices overseas**
Office Inter-Régional du Tourisme des Antilles Françaises, 2 Rue des Moulins, 75001 Paris, T 44 77 86 00, F 49 26 03 63.

Service Official Français du Tourisme:

Belgium: 21 Ave de la Toison d'Or, 1060 Brussels, T 25130762, F 25143375.

Canada: 1981 Ave MacGill College, Suite 480, Montréal PQH 3A 2W9, T 514 844 8566, F 844 8901; 30 St Patrick St, Suite 700, Toronto, M ST 3A3, T 416 593 4723, F 979 7587.

Germany: Französisches Fremdenverkehrsamt, Post Fach 150465, 1000 Berlin 15, T 30218 2064, F 30214 1738.

Italy: 5 Via San Andrea 20121, Milan, T 2 76000268, F 278 4582.

Spain: Administration: Gran Via, 59-28013 Madrid, T 541 8808, F 541 2412.

Switzerland: Löwenstrasse 59, Postfach 7226, 8023 Zurich, T 12 21 35 78, F 12 12 16 44.

UK: 178 Piccadilly, London, T 0171-629 2869, F 0171 493 6594.

USA: 610 Fifth Avenue, New York, NY 10020, T 212 757 0218, F 212 247 6468; 645 North Michigan Ave, Suite 630, Chicago, Illinois 60611, T 312 751 7800.

● **Further reading**
Les Antilles, produced by Nouvelles Frontières (Les Éditions JA, 2nd edition, Paris, 1987), contains both practical information and very interesting background information on geography, local customs and architecture, and the French Antilles' place in the Caribbean and in relation to France.

Guadeloupe

GUADELOUPE is surrounded by the islands La Désirade, Marie-Galante and Les Saintes, all of which can easily be visited from the main island, with each one offering something different. Including the two more distant islands of Saint-Barthélémy and Saint-Martin in the Leewards, the total area of the Department is 1,780 square km.

Guadeloupe (1,510 square km) is really two islands, separated by the narrow bridged strait of the Rivière Salée. To the W is mountainous egg-shaped Basse-Terre, with the volcano Grande Soufrière (1,484 metres) at its centre. It has an area of 848 sq km, a total of 150,000 inhabitants, and the administrative capital of the same name on its SW coast. The commercial capital of Guadeloupe is Pointe-à-Pitre, situated in the flat half of the island, Grande-Terre. Grande-Terre, triangular in shape and 590 sq km, has a total population of 177,570. The names of the two parts shows a most un-Gallic disregard of logic as Basse-Terre is the higher and Grande-Terre is the smaller; possibly they were named by sailors, who found the winds lower on the Basse-Terre and greater on the Grande-Terre side.

Guadeloupe was badly hit by Hurricane Hugo in 1989. Much of the structural damage has been repaired or replaced with aid from the French Government, and the island's flora has recovered.

HISTORY

Christopher Columbus discovered Guadeloupe in 1493 and named it after the Virgin of Guadalupe, of Extremadura, Spain. The Caribs, who had inhabited the island, called it Karukera, meaning 'island of beautiful waters'. As in most of the Caribbean, the Spanish never settled, and Guadeloupe's history closely resembles that of Martinique, beginning with French colonization in 1635. The first slaves had been brought to the island by 1650. In the first half of the seventeenth century, Guadeloupe did not enjoy the same levels of prosperity, defence or peace as Martinique. After four years of English occupation, Louis XV in 1763 handed over Canada to Britain to secure his hold on these West Indian islands with the Treaty of Paris. The French Revolution brought a period of uncertainty, including a brief reign of terror under Victor Hugues. Those landowners who were not guillotined fled; slavery was abolished, only to be restored in 1802. Up to 1848, when the slaves were finally freed by Victor Schoelcher, the

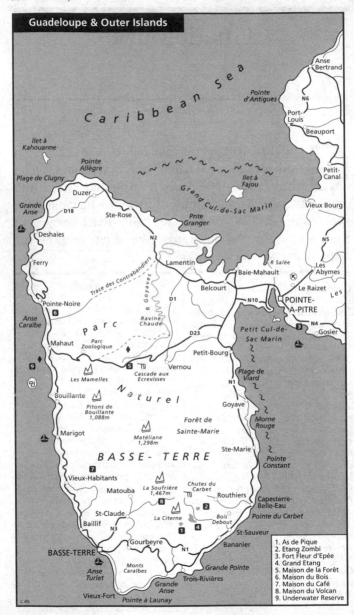

Guadeloupe & Outer Islands

Caribbean Sea

Anse Bertrand

Pointe d'Antigues

N6

Port-Louis

Beauport

Petit-Canal

Ilet à Kahouanne

Pointe Allègre

Plage de Clugny

Grand Cul-de-Sac Marin

Ilet à Fajou

Vieux Bourg

Duzer

Grande Anse

D18

Ste-Rose

Pnte Granger

N5

Deshaies

Les Abymes

N2

Ferry

Lamentin

R Salée

Baie-Mahault

Le Raizet

Trace des Contrabandiers

Belcourt

N10

POINTE-A-PITRE

Pointe-Noire

D1

N4

Anse Caraïbe

Ravine Chaude

D23

Petit Cul-de-Sac Marin

Gosier

Les

Mahaut

Parc Zoologique

Petit-Bourg

Vernou

Plage de Viard

Parc

Les Mamelles

Cascade aux Ecrevisses

N1

Bouillante

Pitons de Bouillante 1,088m

Naturel

Forêt de Sainte-Marie

Goyave

Morne Rouge

Marigot

Matéliane 1,298m

Ste-Marie

BASSE-TERRE

Pointe Constant

Vieux-Habitants

La Soufrière 1,467m

Chutes du Carbet

Routhiers

Capesterre-Belle-Eau

Matouba

Bois Debout

Pointe du Carbet

St-Claude

La Citerne

St-Sauveur

Baillif

N3

Gourbeyre

Bananier

BASSE-TERRE

N1

Monts Caraïbes

Grande Pointe

Anse Turlet

Grande Anse

Trois-Rivières

Vieux-Fort

Pointe à Launay

R Goyaves

Pnte

C 40k

1. As de Pique
2. Etang Zombi
3. Fort Fleur d'Epée
4. Grand Etang
5. Maison de la Forêt
6. Maison du Bois
7. Maison du Café
8. Maison du Volcan
9. Underwater Reserve

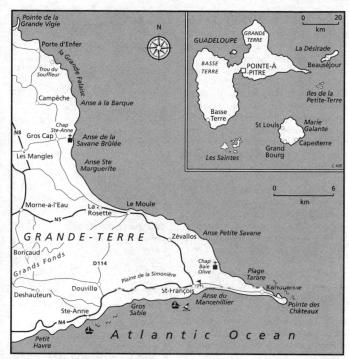

island's economy was inhibited by sugar crises and imperial wars (French and English). After 1848, the sugar plantations suffered from a lack of manpower, although indentured labour was brought in from East India.

Despite having equal status with Martinique, first as a Department then as a Region, Guadeloupe's image as the less-sophisticated, poor relation persists. In common with Martinique, though, its main political voice is radical (unlike the more conservative Saint-Barthélémy and Saint-Martin), often marked by a more violent pro-independence movement.

In the presidential elections of 1995, Guadeloupe gave 38.2% of the vote in the first round to Jacques Chirac and 35.1% to the Socialist candidate, Lionel Jospin. However, in the second round, M Jospin won 55.1% compared with 44.9% for M Chirac, although the turn-out was even lower than in 1988, with an abstention rate of over 50%.

GOVERNMENT

Guadeloupe is administered by a prefect, appointed by the French Ministry of the Interior. The local legislature consists of a 43-seat general council, elected by popular vote, which sits for 6 years, and a 41-seat regional council made up of the locally-elected councillors and the two senators and four deputies elected to the French parliament. Guadeloupe also sends two councillors to the Economic and Social Council in Paris. Political parties include the Socialist Party, the Communist Party, Union for French Democracy, Union for the Liberation of Guadeloupe and Rally for the Republic.

THE ECONOMY

Agriculture and, increasingly since the 1970s, tourism are the principal activities. Bananas have displaced sugar as the single most important export earner. In 1994 Guadeloupe suffered its worst drought for 30 years and was declared a disaster zone in August as livestock, fisheries, vegetables, bananas and sugar were severely affected. Later on, further damage was caused by Tropical Storm Debbie, which swept through the island causing shortfalls in banana production. Export quotas were made up by imports from Latin American producers for reexport to the EU. Sugar and its by-products (rum and molasses) generate about 35% of exports. A 6-year plan was announced in 1994 to increase the annual harvest from 550,000 to 800,000 tonnes a year. The Gardel factory will be modernized and will carry out all sugar manufacturing on the island. A coal and bagasse electric power plant will be attached to the plant. Melons and tropical flowers have been promoted for sale abroad, while many other fruits, vegetables and coffee are grown mainly for the domestic market.

Wages and conditions similar to those in metropolitan France force the price of local products to levels viable only on the parent market; 75% of all exports go to France and 13% to Martinique (61% of exports are agricultural products). At the same time, the high rate of imports raises local prices above those of the island's non-French neighbours. Consequently there has been little move towards industrialization to satisfy a wider market and unemployment is high, although declining.

Investment in the tourism industry raised the number of hotel rooms on Guadeloupe from 3,037 in 1980 to an estimated 4,500. Nearly 90% of stopover visitors come from Europe, mostly from France. Although the North American market has been growing strongly it is only about 8% of the total of about

Département de Guadeloupe: fact file

Geographic

Land area	1,780 sq km
forested	39.1%
pastures	13.6%
cultivated	17.7%

Demographic

Population (1995)	434,000
annual growth rate (1990-95)	2.2%
urban	48.4%
rural	51.6%
density	243.8 per sq km
Religious affiliation	
Roman Catholic	85.9%
Birth rate per 1,000 (1994)	17.4
	(world av 25.0)

Education and Health

Life expectancy at birth,	
male	71.1 years
female	78 years
Infant mortality rate	
per 1,000 live births (1994)	7.9
Physicians (1991)	1 per 680 persons
Hospital beds	1 per 122 persons
Calorie intake as %	
of FAO requirement	111%
Population age 25 and over	
with no formal schooling	10.7%
Literate males (over 15)	89.7%
Literate females (over 15)	90.5%

Economic

GNP (1990 market prices)	
	US$1,160mn
GNP per capita	US$2,970
Public external debt (1990)	US$58mn
Tourism receipts (1993)	US$370mn
Inflation (annual av 1989-94)	2.4
Radio	1 per 4.2 persons
Television	1 per 2.8 persons
Telephone	1 per 2.7 persons

Employment

Population economically active (1992)	
	181,000
Unemployment rate (1993)	26.1%
% of labour force in agriculture	5.2
mining and manufacturing	5.9
construction	8.9
Military forces	535

Source *Encyclopaedia Britannica*

160,000 a year. Cruise ship passengers have shown spectacular growth in the 1990s, reaching over 75,000 a year.

CULTURE

See the general introduction to the French Antilles above.

FLORA AND FAUNA

Guadeloupe is in some ways reminiscent of Normandy or Poitou, especially the farms, built in those regional styles. The comparatively low-lying Grande-Terre is mainly given over to sugar cane and livestock-raising. Mostly a limestone plateau, it does have a hilly region, Les Grands-Fonds, and a marshy, mangrove coast extending as far N as Port-Louis on its W flank.

The island's National Park (7th French National Park) includes 30,000 hectares of forest land in the centre of Basse-Terre (known as the Natural Park), which is by far the more scenic part. As the island is volcanic there are a number of related places to visit. The Park has no gates, no opening hours and no admission fee. Do not pick flowers, fish, hunt, drop litter, play music or wash anything in the rivers. Trails have been marked out all over the Park, including to the dome of Soufrière volcano with its fumaroles, cauldrons and sulphur fields (see below). The National Park includes 3 protected land and sea reserves, open to the public: **Les Réserves Naturelles des Pitons du Nord et de Beaugendre, La Réserve Naturelle du Grand Cul-de-Sac Marin** and **La Réserve Naturelle de Pigeon**, or **Réserve Cousteau** (see below). The waters after which the Caribs named the island come hot (as at the Ravine Chaude springs on the Rivière à Goyaves), tumbling (the waterfalls of the Carbet river and the Cascade aux Écrevisses on the Corossol), and tranquil (the lakes of Grand Étang, As de Pique and Étang Zombi). One traveller has described the island as "idyllic – were it not for the noise of motorcycles".

A **Maison du Volcan** at Saint-Claude (open Tues-Sun 0900-1300, 1400-1600) and a **Maison de la Fôret** (1000-1700) on the Route de la Traversée give information on the volcano and its surrounding forest. From the Maison de la Forêt there are 10, 20 and 60-minute forest walks which will take you deep among the towering trees. The **Cascade aux Ecrevisses**, a waterfall and small pool, is about 2 km from the Maison (clearly marked) and is a good place to swim and spend the day; popular with the locals. Also on the Route de la Traversée is the **Parc Zoologique et Botanique** above Mahaut, which allows you to see many of the species which exist in the Natural Park, unfortunately in very small cages (entrance 25F, children 15F, open 0900-1650). It is worth a visit for the fine panoramic views from the café (free drink included in entrance ticket) and the restaurant is simple but excellent.

The National Park's emblem is the racoon (*raton laveur*) which, although protected, is very rare. You are much more likely to see birds and insects in the Park. On La Désirade a few agoutis survive, as well as iguana, which can also be found on Les Saintes. Much of the island's indigenous wildlife has vanished.

The vegetation of Basse-Terre ranges from tropical forest (40% of the land is forested: trees such as the mahogany and gommier, climbing plants, wild orchids) to the cultivated coasts: sugar cane on the windward side, bananas in the S and coffee and vanilla on the leeward. As well as sugar cane on Grande-Terre, there is an abundance of fruit trees (mango, coconut, papaya, guava, etc). On both parts the flowers are a delight, especially the anthuriums and hibiscus.

BEACHES

Guadeloupe has excellent beaches for swimming, mostly between Gosier and St-François on Grande Terre. Petit Havre is popular with its small coves and reefs offshore. Here are mostly fishermen and locals and a small shed selling fish meals and beer. The best is at Ste-Anne where the fine white sand and crystal clear water of a constant depth of 1.5 metres far from shore make idyllic bathing; the Plage du Bourg in town is ideal for young children, the Plage de la Caravelle is excellent with access only through the *Club Med*. About 2 km from the town is the Plage de Bois Jolan, reached down a track, where the water is shallow enough to walk to the protecting reef. Further E are good beaches at St-François and the 11-km road to Pointe des Colibris skirts the Anse Kahouanne with lots of tracks going down to the sea; sand is limited but there are snorkelling possibilities.

On the N coast of the peninsula is Plage Tarare, the island's only nude bathing beach where there is a good restaurant by the car park. It is not a good place for women to arrive unaccompanied. Plage de l'Anse à la Gourde has good sand and is popular with campers at weekends. More deserted beaches can be found on the NE of Grande Terre.

On the leeward coast of Basse-Terre are some good beaches. South of Pointe Noire on the W coast is Plage Caraïbe, which is clean, calm and beautiful, with restaurant *Le Reflet* (helpful owners), picnic facilities, toilets and a shower. A small, black sand beach, La Grand Anse, just W of Trois Rivières, has a barbecue and drinks (expensive) on the beach and a shower and toilets (which do not always work). In the NW, La Grande Anse, 30 mins walk N of Deshaies, is superb and undeveloped with no hotels, golden sand but no snorkelling except round a large rock where the current is quite strong. Body surfing is good when the waves are big. Camping sites in the area and a beach restaurant at the S end with charcoal-grilled chicken and rice. There are several snack bars half way along the beach, serving sandwiches and drinks. On Sundays local people sell hot créole food quite cheaply. The beaches on the N coast of Basse-Terre can be very dangerous and

at Plage de Clugny there are warning signs not to swim as there have been several drownings.

MARINE LIFE AND WATERSPORTS

On the Leeward Coast (Côte-Sous-le-Vent, or the Golden Corniche), is the **Underwater Reserve** developed by Jacques Cousteau. *Nautilus*, from Malendure beach, S of Mahaut, black sand, T 98 89 08, F 98 85 66, is a glass-bottom boat which takes you round the marine park, departs 1030, 1200, 1430 and 1600, 80F adults, 40F children 5-12 years. The boat anchors for about 15 minutes off **Ilet Pigeon** for snorkelling, but it is rather deep to see much. In wet weather the water becomes too murky to see anything. The boat is often booked solid by cruise ship visitors. There is a créole restaurant on the beach where you can eat while waiting for the boat. Diving trips can be arranged at Les Heures Saines (T 98 86 63) at Rocher de Malendure, or Chez Guy (T 98 81 72, friendly, recommended for beginners' confidence, 140F for one dive, everything included), at Pigeon, Bouillante. Both also offer fishing trips as do Fishing Club Antilles, T 84 15 00, Le Rocher de Malendure, T 98 73 25, and Nautilus Club near Bouillante, all around 4,000-4,500 F per boat for a full day. Caraïbes Peche at Marina Bas du Fort, offers deep sea fishing or day trips with barbecues and fishing along the way, T 90 97 51, 95 67 26.

Papyrus, Marina Bas-du-Fort, Pointe-à-Pitre, T 90 92 98, is a glass-bottom boat which runs excursions through the Rivière Salée and the mangroves of Grand Cul de Sac Marin, to l'Ilet Caret and coral reef off the NE coast of Basse-Terre. The *Paoka* also does this trip through the mangroves from Lamentin at the Ginature centre at La Boucan, T 25-74-78. Alternatively, contact the National Forests Office who have an information centre behind Le Raizet airport at Abymes. Most of the hotels on the seaboard offer windsurfing for guests and visitors, and some arrange water skiing and diving courses.

Sailing boats can be chartered for any length of time from Captain Lemaire, Carénage A, Route du Gosier, 97110 Pointe-à-Pitre. With a crew of 3 the cost works out at about US$75-100 pp per day, excluding food, or US$250-300 per boat. There are two marinas between Pointe-à-Pitre and Gosier, and good, shallow- draught anchorage at Gosier. Windsurfers gather at the UCPA Hotel Club in Saint François.

OTHER SPORTS

Hiking in the Natural Park (contact the Organisation des Guides de Montagne de la Caraïbe (OGMC), Maison Forestière, 97120 Matouba, T 80 05 79, a guided hike to La Soufrière will cost around 300 F, make sure the guide speaks a language you understand, approximate hiking times, mileage and description of terrain and flora are included in the booklet *Promenades et Randonnées*); **horseriding** (Le Criolo, Saint-Félix, 97190 Gosier, T 84 04 86, La Martingale, La Jaille, T 26 28 39, Ranch Caraïbes, T 82 11 54); **tennis**, with lighting for night games, at several hotels, including *Auberge de la Vieille Tour, PLM Arawak, Salako, Creole Beach, Novotel*, and *Village Viva* (also squash, T 90 87 66), all at Gosier, *Méridien, Hamak, Trois-Mâts* at Saint-François. There is one 18-hole, municipal **golf course** at Saint-François (T 88 41 87). The *Hotel Golf Marine Club* at Saint-François, T 88 60 60, has an 18-hole course designed by Robert Trent Jones, green fees 220F/day or 1,000F/week.

Bullock cart racing is popular on the W coast of Grand-Terre and draws large crowds. They race along the flat, then turn sharply and charge up a steep hill. The wheels are then chocked and they have to see how far they can get, zig zag fashion, with about 10 minutes of very hard work. Much shouting, plenty of beer, food tents and an overloud PA system.

FESTIVALS

Carnival starts on Epiphany and runs through Ash Wednesday with different events each Sunday, the main ones on the last weekend. The Festival of the Sea is in mid-August with beach parties, boat races, crab races, etc. La Fête des Cuisinières (Cooks' Festival) in the middle of August is a lot of fun with parades in créole costumes and music.

GRANDE-TERRE

Pointe-à-Pitre, on Grande-Terre at the S end of the Rivière Salée, is the chief commercial centre, near the airport of Le Raizet and the port of entry for shipping (population is 80,000). The city lies to the S of the Route Nacional N1 (the ring road) and any of the intercepts will take you to the city centre, which is quite compact, lying to the S of Boulevard Chanzy (a short stretch of dual carriageway). It is a functional city, variously described as characterless, or colourful and bustling. Its early colonial buildings were largely destroyed by an earthquake in 1843; nowadays it is an odd mixture of parts which could have been transplanted from provincial France and parts which are Caribbean, surrounded by low-cost housing blocks.

The central **Place de la Victoire** was once the site of a guillotine, and the streets adjacent to it contain the oldest buildings. Having been refurbished in 1989 it lost several of its large trees in Hurricane Hugo but there are still some flame trees at the N end and pleasant gardens. In the middle is a statue to Félix Eboue (1884-1944), a Governor General. There is a bandstand and lots of cafés surrounding the park with tables outside, very pleasant but crowded with office workers at lunch time. The buildings around the park are a mixture of coloured tin roofs and concrete. At its S end is La Darse, where the inter-island ferries tie up. When the boats arrive/depart there is plenty of activity and chaotic scenes with buses and taxis fighting for space. At the SW corner of the Place is a war memorial dedicated to *La Guadeloupe et ses enfants, morts pour La France 1914-18,* flanked by two First World War guns. Behind it is the Tour-ist Office (quite helpful, some English spoken). On the E side of the Square is the Renaissance Cinema.

The **Place de l'Eglise** lies NW of the Place de la Victoire behind the *Hotel Normandie* and contains the ochre-col-

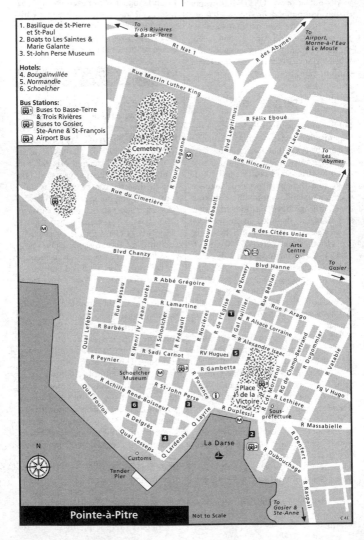

1. Basilique de St-Pierre et St-Paul
2. Boats to Les Saintes & Marie Galante
3. St-John Perse Museum

Hotels:
4. *Bougainvillée*
5. *Normandie*
6. *Schoelcher*

Bus Stations:
1. Buses to Basse-Terre & Trois Rivières
2. Buses to Gosier, Ste-Anne & St-François
3. Airport Bus

Pointe-à-Pitre   Not to Scale

oured **Basilique de St Pierre et St Paul**, a high modern structure held up by unusual metal columns supporting a gallery running around the top of the church with some elaborate gingerbread-style metal work. Outside there is a bubbling fountain and a statue of Admiral Gourbeyre who helped the people of Pointe-à-Pitre after the huge 1843 earthquake (see Fort Louis Delgrès, Basse-Terre). The square is flanked by the hideous Palais de Justice but looks quite attractive with florists on the street.

The colourful red-roofed central market place (between rues Peynier, Fréboult, St-John Perse and Schoelcher) is indeed bustling, with the nearest thing to local hustlers, women (some wearing the traditional Madras cotton hats) who try to sell you spices, fruit, vegetables or hats. There are other markets on the dockside in Place de la Victoire, between Blvd Chanzy and the docks and between Blvd Légitimus and the cemetery. Local handicrafts, particularly Madras cotton (from which the traditional costumes of the *doudous*, or local women, are made), are good buys. Such items are in great contrast to the French fashions, wines and perfumes available at normal French domestic prices in the shops.

There are two museums: **Musée Schoelcher**, 24 rue Peynier, which celebrates the liberator of the slaves (open Mon-Tues 0900-1230, 1400-1730, Thur-Fri 0900-1230, 1400-1830, Sat 0900-1230, entry 10 F), and **Musée Saint-John Perse**, in a lovely colonial-style house, rues Nozières et A R Boisneuf, dedicated to the poet and diplomat who was awarded the Nobel Prize for literature in 1960 (open 0900-1700, closed Sundays, entry 10F, children half price). On AR Boisneuf is the old town hall, being restored. It has a stone/brick ground floor and a fine wooden first floor with an intricately carved gutter.

Just outside Pointe-à-Pitre on the N4 towards Gosier is **Bas du Fort**, the site of the large new marina, said to be the biggest in the Caribbean. The aquarium is also here, at Place Créole, T 90 92 38, open daily 0900-1900 (entrance 35F, children under 12 20F). At the next turning off the main road to Gosier (follow the signs to the CORA hypermarket) are the ruins of the 18th-century fortress, **Fort Fleur d'Epée** (open daily 0800-1800, free) which once guarded the E approaches to Pointe-à-Pitre. There are now pleasant, shady gardens within the ramparts. Art exhibitions are regularly held either in the officers' quarters or in the underground rooms. Also note the pre-war graffiti with pictures of old sailing ships. Excellent views of Pointe-à-Pitre and across Petit Cul-de-Sac Marin towards the mountains of Basse-Terre.

Gosier itself is the holiday centre of Guadeloupe, with hotels, restaurants, night clubs. There has been lots of building in this area, even up into the hills above the coast road. Nevertheless, Gosier is a pleasant place with a marvellous picnic spot overlooking a small beach (Plage de l'Anse Canot), a little island about 100m offshore (Ilet du Gosier) and lighthouse. You could swim to it, there is a channel marked by buoys, but watch out for speed boats. There are a few old wooden houses up the hill from the church, where one or two are restaurants. The modern resort with the large hotels has been built on reclaimed mangrove marshes but the beach is nice with the usual watersports facilities. Gosier is quite sleepy but wakes up at night when the restaurants open.

The S coast between Gosier and **Sainte-Anne** is hilly with cliffs, making it particularly suited to development and on most headlands there are huge condominium developments looking across the sea to Marie-Galante as well as to the S tip of Basse-Terre. Sainte-Anne is a small, pleasant town and has a small church with a slightly crooked spire overlooking the square. Here you will find the **Plage de la Caravelle**, rated by some as the best on the island. The land gradually subsides towards **St-François**, originally a fishing village but now home to *Méridien, Hamak, La Cocoteraie* and *Plantation Ste-Marthe* which are all luxury hotels. There is a light aircraft landing strip and eighteen hole par 71 golf course designed by Robert Trent Jones. You can catch the ferry to La Désirade from here. Watersports equipment can be hired from several companies at the marina.

The rugged **Pointe des Châteaux** at the easternmost tip of the island is part of the national park. From the car park, there is a small, self-guided walk to the cross (**Pointe des Colibris**) erected in 1951, on the point where there are two 'compass' tables showing distances to various landmarks. The limestone outcrop is quite steep in places but the view over the inshore island of **La Roche** (housing a colony of sooty terns, *sterna fuscata*) to La Désirade in the distance, is spectacular especially on a windy day when the sea whips over the rocks. It is worth taking the slightly longer return path around the headland as you get good views of the completely flat **Petite Terre** with its lighthouse and on clear days Marie-Galante (30 km), Les Saintes (60 km) and Dominica (75 km). Note the **Grandes Salines** (salt lagoons) where flamingoes were once common. There are signs on the walk pointing out particular plants and describing features. There is a restaurant selling welcome cold drinks and exotic icecream. **NB** the beach between the two points is dangerous.

Between Saint-François and **Le Moule**, a colonial mansion at **Zévallos** can be visited. Le Moule was the original capital of Guadeloupe and there are still some cannon from the fortifications against English attack. A precolumbian Arawak village, called Morel, has recently been uncovered on the beautiful sandy beaches N of the town; the **Musée d'Archéologie Précolombienne Edgar Clerc** is at La Rosette (open Mon-Tues 0900-1230, 1400-1700, Thur-Sat 0900-1230, 1400-1800, free). On the Abymes road (D101) from Le Moule is the **Distillerie Bellevue**, makers of Rhum Damoiseau, which can be toured Monday-Friday 0800-1400. From Le Moule you can either return to Point-à-Pitre through **Les Grands Fonds**, or continue up the rugged, rough Atlantic coast to **Pointe de la Grande Vigie** in the extreme N. Take a good map as it is easy to get lost on the little roads in the sugar cane fields. After travelling through the small towns of La Rosette, Gros Cap and Campèche (small restaurant/bar), the countryside becomes more barren. At **Porte d'Enfer** (Hell's Gate) there are a number of barbecue places and little huts at the mouth of an inlet. You can camp here. There is not much sand and the sea can be dangerous, do not go too far out. The coastline from here is very rocky with cliffs and spectacular views.

Grande-Terre's leeward coast has beaches at Port-Louis and Petit-Canal which are the usual concrete towns with restaurant and filling station. North of Anse Bertrand there is a fine clean, sandy beach, Anse Laborde, which has plenty of shade, a restaurant, and a reef close to the beach, good for snorkelling. Inland, at **Morne-à-l'Eau**, there is a remarkable terraced cemetery built around a natural amphitheatre, very attractive on All Saints Day when lit by thousands of candles. Beware of large crowds.

BASSE-TERRE

Basse-Terre, on the other wing of the island, is the administrative capital of Guadeloupe and the entire Department, with a population of 20,000. There can be found in the city some very pretty and authentic old buildings of the colonial period. It is a charming port town of narrow streets and well-laid-out squares with palm and tamarind trees, in a lovely setting between the sea and the great volcano La Soufrière. Market day is Saturday. There is an interesting 17th-century cathedral, and nearby are the ruins of **Fort Louis Delgrès**, well-preserved and full of interesting ramparts and bastions (original building 1667, considerably enlarged in the 18th century; open daily 0900-1200, 1400-1700, free). The British occupied the fort in 1759-1763 and again in 1810-1816 when it was known as Fort Mathilde. It was fought over and renamed many times, being given its present name in 1989 in memory of the man who escaped the forces of Bonaparte after the reimposition of slavery in 1802. The **Grande Caverne**, formerly the billet of the non-commissioned officers, is now a cultural museum, with an exhibition of clothes and photographs

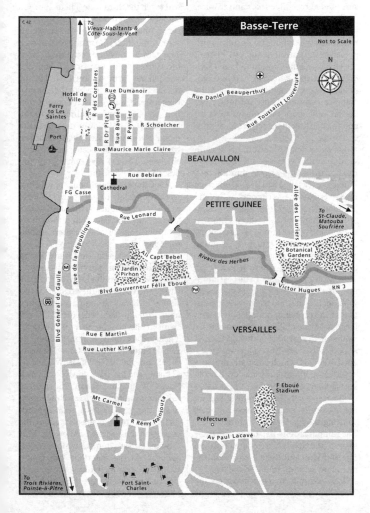

Basse-Terre

Not to Scale

N

To Vieux-Habitants & Côte-Sous-le-Vent

Rue Dumanoir

Hotel de Ville

R des Corsaires

Ferry to Les Saintes

Port

R Dr Pitat

Rue Baudet

R Peynier

R Schoelcher

Rue Daniel Beauperthuy

Rue Toussaint Louverture

Rue Maurice Marie Claire

BEAUVALLON

FG Casse

Rue Bebian

Cathedral

PETITE GUINEE

Allée des Lauriers

To St-Claude, Matouba Soufrière

Rue Leonard

Rue de la République

Blvd Général de Gaulle

Capt Bebel

Jardin Pirhon

Rivaux des Herbes

Botanical Gardens

Blvd Gouverneur Félix Eboué

Pol

Rue Victor Hugues

RN 3

Rue E Martini

Rue Luther King

VERSAILLES

F Eboué Stadium

Mt Carmel

R Rémy Nainsouta

Préfecture

Av Paul Lacavé

To Trois Rivières, Pointe-à-Pitre

Fort Saint-Charles

of the area. In the cemetery is the tomb of Admiral Gourbeyre. The date of his tomb is not that of his death (he disappeared in 1845) but of 8 February 1843 when there was a huge earthquake; the Admiral was instrumental in disaster relief.

Saint-Claude, a wealthy suburb and summer resort 6 km into the hills, is surrounded by coffee trees and tropical gardens. **Matouba**, above Saint-Claude, is an East Indian village in lovely surroundings (waterfall and springs) with a good restaurant. On the outskirts of the village is a monument to Louis Delgrès on the spot where he and his companions were caught and killed by Napoléon's troops. There are hot springs a good walk above the village (1,281 m) and the bottling plant for the local mineral water.

On Basse-Terre island one of the main sights is the volcano **La Soufrière**, reached through a primeval rain forest. A narrow, twisty road leads up from Basse-Terre town to a car park at **Savane à Mulets** (1,142 m) from where the crater, 300m higher, is a 1½-hour climb up the Chemin des Dames, a fascinating trail with changing flora, but becoming eroded through overuse. Buses go to Saint-Claude from where it is a 6 km walk to Savane à Mulets. (The best clothing for the climb is the least; jackets worn against the dampness merely compound the problem; but take a sweater, it can get quite chilly. Leave some spare clothes in the car.) From the top there is a spectacular view (if you are not enveloped in clouds, which is usually the case, observe the mountain for a few days to see whether early morning or mid-day is clearest, above the lush jungle foliage on the E slopes and sulphurous fumes spurting over yellow and orange rock. The summit is quite flat; the main vent is to the S (the view is more interesting than the Soufrière) and there are discs in the ground to help you find it in the fog.

It is possible to come down on the Trace Micael, along a forest path, to the **Chutes de Carbet** waterfalls where the water becomes cool and clear. Carry on down, past more waterfalls, until you get to a car park (often full, parking can be a problem).

If starting from the bottom, take a bus from Capesterre to Routhiers, 10F, then walk along the D3 road until it ends. Follow a trail and within 50 minutes you will reach the third waterfall of 20m. Go back 100m and follow the trail upwards again until you reach the 110-metre, second waterfall, 711m above sea level. The path is stony and you have to cross the Carbet on a rope bridge. You can swim in the warm, sulphuric pool below the fall but if you visit when there is rain higher up, beware of flash floods. From here you can continue climbing to the first waterfall, at 125m, or turn SE to the picnic place, Aire d'Arrivée, 15 minutes, where there are barbecue stalls (good chicken). The D4 road starts here and descends to St-Sauveur.

La Citerne, a neighbouring volcano, has a completely round crater. There is a trail but part requires climbing ladders straight up the wall. There are more leisurely trails to other craters, fumaroles and lakes.

Also on this side are **Grand Etang** and **Etang Zombi**. You can drive, hitch-hike or walk down the D4 road from the Chutes de Carbet to the edge of Grand Etang and walk around it, about one hour through lush vegetation. Do not swim in the lake because of bilharzia. There are also marked trails to **Etang de l'As de Pique**, high above Grand Etang to the S on the slope of la Madeleine (2 hours) and the Trace de Moscou which leads SW to the Plateau du Palmiste (2½ hours), from where a road leads down to Gourbeyre. Walk down to St-Sauveur for fine views over banana plantations, the coast and Les Saintes. Allow at least 5 hours to walk from Capesterre to St-Sauveur via the waterfalls and Grand Etang and wear good hiking shoes.

You can walk the Trace Victor Hugues, along the main ridge of Basse-

Terre (a 29-km hike), and a number of other Traces. The River Quiock trail has been recommended but take the Serie Bleu map; despite being well-marked originally, storm damage has made it difficult to find all the markers. It can be very muddy, wear good boots. You can start from the car park at the Cascade des Ecrevisses (see above) on the D23. Walk 300m along the road and take a path to the right (follow the sign to the Pathfinders camp) to Piolet, near the entrance to the Bras-David-Tropical-Parc on the other side of the road. The trail leads down to where the River Quiock meets the larger River Bras-David, carefully cross the river, then the trail heads W along the Quiock until returning to the D23. Hitchhike back to your car (if you have one). The walk will take you 3-4 hours depending on the state of the trail. Other features of the Natural Park are described under **Flora and Fauna**, above.

Besides the Maisons du Volcan and de la Fôret (see above), there are on Basse-Terre **Maisons du Café** at La Grivelière, Vieux Habitants (T 98 48 42), **du Bois** at Bourg, Pointe Noire (a cabinet-making and woodworking centre with a permanent exhibition of household implements, furniture and other things made of wood, daily hours 0915-1700, 5F) and a **Centre de Broderie**, Fort l'Olive, Vieux-Fort (daily 0830-1800). Vieux-Fort is on the island's SW tip, the other side of the Monts Caraïbes from the main Basse-Terre to Pointe-à-Pitre road. There are nice gardens surrounding the lighthouse, with good views. One or two cannon can be seen from the old battery. Good créole restaurant with dance hall attached.

Also visit the ancient Amerindian rock carvings dating from around 300-400 AD, at the **Parc Archéologique des Roches Gravées**, near Trois Rivières, on Basse-Terre's S coast; the most important is a drawing of the head of a Carib chief inside a cave where he is presumably buried. The site is now in a garden setting, with wardens (it's a good idea to consult the leaflet which comes with the 4F entry fee, children free, because some of the engravings on the stones are hard to decipher; many are badly eroded; the pamphlet also explains the garden's trees). The Parc is a 10-minute walk down from the church in Trois Rivières where the buses stop. Five minutes further down the hill is the boat dock for Les Saintes (paying car park).

Capesterre-Belle-Eau (*pop* 18,000) is the third largest town and is an important agricultural centre with lots of shops, restaurants and a market. Above the town is the garden of Paul Lacavé, which can be visited. North of the town is the **Allée de Flamboyants**, a spectacular avenue of flame trees which flower May-September. South of the town is the **Allée Dunmanoir**, a magnificent 1-km avenue of royal palms.

At **Sainte-Marie**, a statue erected in 1916 commemorates the site of Columbus' landing in 1493. It has now been defaced by nationalists. South of Sainte-Marie, near Carangaise, there is a Hindu temple, built in 1974 by René Komla, richly decorated with statues of Vishnu and Ganesh outside.

Between Basse-Terre town and the Route de la Traversée on the W coast are **Vieux-Habitants**, with a restored 17th-century church, and the underwater reserve (see **Marine Life** above). Contact the Syndicat d'Initiative de Bouillante, T 98 73 48, for information on the Bouillante area, which considers itself the capital of diving, including gîtes, restaurants and dive operators.

A good hike is the Trace des Contrebandiers, 3 hours, from the Maison du Bois, Pointe Noire. A long but beautiful road takes you to the Trace. When you leave the trail on the other side you need to hitch-hike because there are no buses.

North of the Traversée, on the Côte-Sous-Le-Vent, are the calm, clean beaches at Ferry and Grand-Anse and the rougher ones at Deshaies. **Deshaies** is attractive, strung out along the beach with cliffs at each end; there are hotels, restaurants (*Le Madras* and the more expensive *Le Mouillage*, offering local food such as fish, créole chicken), basketball and tennis courts. There is an information (unmanned) centre at **Batterie de Deshaies** overlooking the town, with information on the vegetation of the area. All that remains of the old fort are some rusty cannons and the outline of various buildings but it is a popular, shady picnic spot and there are barbecue places. Round the N of Basse-Terre is the town of **Sainte-Rose** where you can visit the rum museum, Distillerie Reimonencq, Bellevue Ste-Rose (T 28 70 04, F 28 82 55, open 0900-1700 Mon-Sat, 1000-1300, 1500-1700 Sun); the road continues S to Lamentin (visit the Domaine de Séverin distillery at La Boucan, still using a paddle wheel, T 28 91 96, F 28 36 66, open 0800-1300, 1400-1800, Sun 0900-1200, with restaurant open for lunch Tues-Sun, and dinner Thur, Fri, Sat; also the Grosse-Montagne distillery for guided tours and tastings) and the hot springs at Ravine Chaude (Thermal Station T 25 78 29).

OUTER ISLANDS OF GUADELOUPE

The outer islands of Guadeloupe are among the least visited of the West Indian islands; they can easily be reached by air or boat from Guadeloupe. One can still get on a trading schooner between the islands if patient.

LES SAINTES

On **Les Saintes** (a string of small islands named Los Santos by Columbus: only Terre-de-Haut and Terre-de-Bas are inhabited) the people are descendants of Breton fisherfolk who have survived among themselves with little intermarriage with the dominant West Indian races. Some still wear the same round hats, the salako, that Breton fisherfolk used to wear, and fishing is still the main occupation on the islands. They are a popular excursion from Guadeloupe now, but are not too spoilt, and with a good, natural harbour, many small cruise ships spend the day here. Nevertheless, to get a better idea of the islanders' traditional way of life, staying overnight is recommended so that you can appreciate it once the day trippers leave at 1600. Public holidays are particularly heavy days with hundreds of day trippers.

Terre-de-Haut is the main island visited by tourists: irregularly shaped and surprisingly barren, it is about 6 km long and 2 km wide at its widest point. Most of the 1,500 inhabitants live around the Anse Mire, looking across the **Ilet à Cabrit**. There are some excellent beaches including that of Pont Pierre, also known as Pompierre, where snorkelling is good and camping is possible, Marigot, L'Anse du Figuier (good diving, no shade), L'Anse Crawen (nudist) and Grand'Anse (white sand, rougher waters, swimming not allowed). The UCPA sailing school at Petit Anse offers half or full day sailing or windsurfing courses. Walking on the islands is good, either from the town to the beaches, or to the top of Le Chameau (TV mast on top) on Terre-de-Haut's W end (spectacular views of Les Saintes, Marie-Galante, Guadeloupe and Dominica).

An easy trail, Trace des Crétes, starts at Terre-de-Haut. Turn right at the pier, follow the main street about 100m, turn left at the chapel and follow the road up to Le Marigot (look out for the *sentier du morne morel* sign behind the restaurant on the S side of the bay) and on to the beach of Baie de Pont Pierre, a lovely golden beach with rocks, Roches Percées, in the bay. Boats and diving equipment can be rented at the landing stage. Goats can be a nuisance if you decide to picnic here. At the end of the beach the trail leads up the hill where you have a good view of the islands, if you keep left, one branch of the trail leads to Grand'Anse beach. The 'white' cemetery, **La Cimétière Rose**, worth visiting, pretty, with paths bordered by shells, is close to the beach and from here you can walk back to Terre-de-Haut, about 1½ hours in total. Alternatively, you can walk along Grand'Anse and on to Pointe Rodriguez and the small cove Anse Rodriguez below it.

There are beautiful views also from **Fort Napoléon**, high up above the town on Pointe à l'Eau, open 0900-1230 except 1 Jan, 1 May, 15-16 Aug and 25 Dec (20F to enter, children 6 to 12 half price). The views demonstrate the strategic importance of Les Saintes (the Gibraltar of the

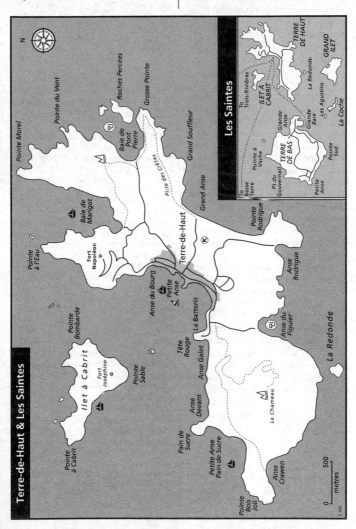

Terre-de-Haut & Les Saintes

Caribbean), and the museum in Fort Napoléon gives the French view of the decisive sea battle of Les Saintes (1782 – the English Admiral Rodney defeated and scattered the fleet of France's Commander de Grasse, who was preparing to attack Jamaica). The fort itself is rather disappointing but the exhibitions are good with interesting models of the ships and battles. A guide will give you a 30-minute tour (in French) of the main building. If not historically-minded, just sit and watch the weather. There are exhibits also of local fishing (including a *saintois*, a local fishing boat, originally with blue and white striped sail, but now diesel-powered) and crafts, a bookshop and drinks on sale. Around the ramparts is the **Jardin Exotique** which specializes in growing succulents and includes a wild area where plants native to Les Saintes are grown. On the Ilet à Cabrit are the ruins of **Fort Joséphine**.

Terre-de-Bas is home to about 1,500 people, mostly fishermen. There is a pottery which also gives some employment, but many have left for work in France.

Boats land at **Grande Baie** which is a small inlet guarded by a fort and two small statues. You get good views of La Coche and Grand Ilet (two of the uninhabited islands) on the way across. There is a good little information centre at the dock. Buses will meet the ferry and you can go to the main settlement at Petite Anse where there is a new fishing port as well as the secondary school for the islands and a pretty little church with a red roof (tour approx 40 mins 30F). The beach at Grand Anse is very pleasant and there are a few bars and restaurants nearby (*A La Belle Etoile* is actually on the beach). There is a track which runs from Petite Anse to Grand Anse which is a good walk. It is very quiet compared with Terre-de-Haut. Salakos and wood carvings are made by local inhabitants.

Island information – Les Saintes
● **Accommodation**

Price guide			
L1	over US$200	**L2**	US$151-200
L3	US$101-150	**A1**	US$81-100
A2	US$61-80	**A3**	US$46-60
B	US$31-45	**C**	US$21-30
D	US$12-20	**E**	US$7-11
F	US$4-6	**G**	up to US$3

On Terre-de-Haut: **L1-A1** *Bois Joli*, reached by 10-min boat ride from town, at the W end of the island on hillside, hotel van transport to town or airport, 21 rooms, 8 bungalows, MAP, most have a/c, phones, pool, bar, restaurant, 2 beaches, one clothes optional, watersports, scooters, T 99 50 38, F 99 55 05, T 800 322 2223 in USA; **L3** *Kanaoa*, Anse Marie, T 99 51 36, F 99 55 04, a/c, but rather basic, fair restaurant used by tour groups, beautiful waterfront setting 10 mins' walk from landing jetty, very quiet; **L1-A1** *Le Village Créole*, Pointe Coquelot, T 99 53 83, F 99 55 55, T 800 322 2223, multilingual helpful owner, Ghyslain Laps, who acts as unofficial tourist chief for the island (contact him to book villas), 22 suites, 1-4 people, 2 bedrooms, 2-storey duplex, a/c, mosquito nets, collection from harbour, private beach, no restaurant but will provide bread etc for breakfast, yacht charter, boats to rent, bike and scooter rental all arranged; **A2** *La Saintoise*, T 99 52 50, in town, *Auberge Les Petits Saints aux Anacardiers*, La Savanne, T 99 50 99, F 99 54 51, T 800-322-2223, former mayor's house overlooking town and bay, furnished with French antiques, attractive, intimate, clean, pool, sauna, art gallery, good restaurant, rec and **A2** *Jeanne d'Arc*, good, T 99 50 41, at Fond de Curé village on S coast, all with 10 rooms. On Terre-de-Bas there is one hotel, *Le Poisson Volant*, 9 rooms, T 99 81 47. On both Terre-de-Haut and Terre-de-Bas there are rooms and houses to rent; tourist office has list of phone numbers. Rec are Mme Bonbon, T 90 50 52, on the road to the airfield, who has several rooms; Mme Bernadette Cassin, T 99 54 22, clean studio under her house on road to cemetery, less without kitchen facilities, if she is full she has family and friends who offer rooms; and Mme Maisonneuve, T 99 53 38, on the same road as the *Mairie*. Reservations are generally rec in peak season, especially Christmas and New Year. The Mairie and the Gendarmerie are reported as very unhelpful regarding accommodation and will not tell you where the hotels are situated. The telephone at the jetty only takes phone cards. Not good for first impressions but otherwise idyllic. There is a shortage of water on the island.

● **Places to eat**
Plenty of **restaurants** around the island, specializing in seafood and offering *menus* for about 60F, but try the *tourment d'amour* coconut sweet. Home made coconut rum punches are also rec, particularly in the little bar on the right hand side of the *gendarmerie* in front of the jetty. Check beer prices before ordering, cheapest 15F. *Le Mouillage* restaurant has been rec, T 99 50 57. *Le Genois*, excellent and cheap pizza house on water's edge by harbour square, highly rec, but book, also does takeaways, T 99 53 01. *La Saladerie*, at top of steps on road to Fort Napoléon, popular, rec, not always open out of season. *Galerie de la Baie*, first floor overlooking harbour, snacks and very expensive ice cream. The *boulangerie* next to the *Mairie* is open from 0530, good. The supermarkets are expensive, double French prices. There are a couple of markets every morning on the road towards the Post Office, good for fresh produce.

● **Transport**
Buses Minibuses take day trippers all over Terre-de-Haut; tour of the island 52F, bus up to Fort Napoléon, 10F (or 25 mins' walk). No transport after dark.

Bike hire There are few cars, unlike on Guadeloupe. Scooter rental, 200F/day, also bicycles, several central locations, 80F/day. It is not necessary to hire a scooter for the whole day, as you can walk to most places, but it may be nice to have one in the afternoon to go to the beach at Pompierre or Figuier. Scooters are banned from the town 0900-1200, 1400-1600 and have to be pushed. At the Mairie you can get some very basic information and a poor map.

Ferries There are daily boats from Trois Rivières (Guadeloupe) to Terre-de-Haut via Terre-de-Bas (40F one way, 30 mins, 70F return: depart Trois Rivières between 0800 and 0900, and 1500 and 1645, different each day; depart Terre-de-Haut 0545-0630, 1500-1615, T 92 90 30/99 53 79) and from Pointe-à-Pitre (80F one way, 160F return, children 85F, about 1 hour, daily 0800, return 1600, Trans Antilles Express from La Darse, T 83 12 45). Boat from Basse-Terre Mon, Wed, Thur and Sat 1200 and

1205, 45 mins, 50F one way (buses from Pointe Noire on W coast drop you at ferry dock). It can be a rough crossing, not suitable for those prone to seasickness. Daily flight except Sun from Pointe-à-Pitre, 180F one way, 0800, 1700, 15 mins, return 0830, 1725, Air Guadeloupe (address above); or Air Sport, Le Raizet, T 82 25 80. The ferry between Terre-de-Haut and Terre-de-Bas runs about 5 times a day (0800, 0930, 1330, 1500 and 1600, 25F, 15F for children, return) passing the pain de sucre and stopping briefly at the *Bois Joli* (except 0800 and 1500 boats).

MARIE-GALANTE

Marie-Galante, a small round island of 153 square km, is simple and old-fashioned but surprisingly sophisticated when it comes to food and drink. It was named by Christopher Columbus after his own ship, the *Santa María La Galante*, and has three settlements. The largest is **Grand-Bourg** (rather run down) in the SW with a population of around 8,000; **Capesterre** is in the SE and **Saint-Louis** (sugar factory, see the bullock carts delivering cane during the cutting season) in the NW. By Grand-Bourg plage try the *batterie de sirop*, selling a treacle-like sugar cane syrup mixed with rum and lime or with water. The beaches, so far almost completely untouched by the tourist flood, are superb. By Capesterre, the Plage de la Feuillère has fine sand beaches and is protected by the coral reef offshore. Follow the path N to Les Galeries, which are large cliffs eroded by the sea to make a covered walkway over 15m above sea level.

There is a pleasant beach at **Anse de Vieux Fort**, the site of the first settlement on the island in 1648 and of a series of fierce skirmishes between the French and the Amerindians. The **Trou à Diable** (off the D202) is a massive cave which runs deep into the earth. To visit it, it is essential to have strong shoes, a torch with extra batteries, and a guide. It is a very remote spot and there is no organized tourism. The descent requires ropes and should not be attempted unassisted. The walk from the road is striking.

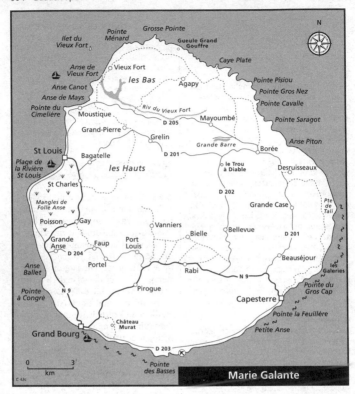

Marie Galante

The D202 road meets the D201 at La Grande Barre, from where there are good views of the N end of the island and to Guadeloupe. On the coast there are limestone cliffs over 30m high which have been eroded in places to form spectacular arches with the sea splashing through them. One is at Gueule Grand Gouffre (cold drinks on sale) and another, less good example, further E at Caye Plate.

In the nineteenth century the island boasted over 100 sugar mills; a few have been restored and may be visited: Basses, Grand-Pierre, Agapy and Murat. Some are still operating. The former plantation houses of **Château Murat** (museum open Mon to Thur 0900-1300, 1500-1800, Sat and Sun 0900-1200, free)

and **Brille** are interesting. Murat gives a good impression of the great 18th century sugar plantations; below the sweeping lawn lies the old sugar mill with cane crushing machinery still intact. Behind the house is a walled herb garden.

The Bellevue rum distillery on the D202 is a cottage industry. The rum (clear and branded as *'agricole'*) is very powerful and you will be invited to taste and buy. You may also be offered bags of brown sugar and dessicated coconut, a surprisingly nice combination. At the Distillerie Bielle you can taste and buy rum as well as ceramic rum flasks made at the pottery *atelier*, open mornings, T 97 93 62. The Distillerie Poisson in the W on the N9 makes the Père Labat rum and is open for visits (also small museum) with tastings, 0930-1200, T 97 03 79. There is a cinema in Grand-Bourg, El Rancho, which has movies dubbed into French.

Island information – Marie-Galante
● **Accommodation**
There are no deluxe hotels on Marie-Galante, prices in **A3-B** range. At Grand-Bourg: *L'Auberge de l'Arbre à Pain* (T 97 73 69), 7 rooms, restaurant; *Le Salut* (clean) is S of the pier at St-Louis, T 97 02 67, 15 rooms, restaurant; *Chez Hajo* at Capesterre, 6 rooms, restaurant, T 97 32 76; *Le Soleil Levant*, on hill overlooking Capesterre and sea, 10 rooms, tiny pool, kitchenettes, T 97 31 55, F 97 41 65; *Le Touloulou*, 2 km from Capesterre on the Grand Bourg road, clean, well-equipped bungalows backing directly on to the sea, discothèque and restaurant nearby, T 97 32 63, F 97 33 59. There are rooms to let, **C** (enquire at the tourist board), and contact Gîtes de France Guadeloupe, BP759, 97110 Pointe-à-Pitre, T 91 64 33, F 91 45 40. For accommodation, 24-hour advance booking is necessary.

● **Transport**
To get to the island there are regular flights (20 mins) from Pointe-à-Pitre, which is only 43 km away (Air Guadeloupe, as above).

Buses On the island there are buses and taxis.

Car hire Self-drive cars can be hired from the airport or in the towns, eg M Seytor, rue Beaurenom, Grand-Bourg. Rates for a full day 240F, for part of a day 190F (2,000F deposit); scooters 150F (1,000F deposit).

Sea There are ferries between Pointe-à-Pitre and Grand-Bourg and it is possible to do a day trip (85F one way, 160F return, children 85F, 1-1½ hours, times are posted on the booth at the dockside): *Tropic* and *Regina* sail at least 3 times a day (T 90 04 48), Trans Antilles Express 0800, 1230, 1700 Mon-Sat, 0800, 1700, 1900 Sun, returning from Grand-Bourg 0600, 0900, 1545 Mon-Sat, 0600, 1545 1800 Sun. The latter also runs a service from Saint-François to Saint-Louis, (depart Tues and Thur 0800). *Amanda Galante*, a car ferry, crosses from Pointe-à-Pitre to Saint-Louis in 1½ hrs, 560F car and driver return, 50F for each passenger, takes 22 cars and 156 passengers. Trans Antilles offer full and half-day tours to Marie-Galante from Pointe-à-Pitre, including boat trip, visits to beaches, the towns, sugar factories, rum distillery (plus tasting) and other sites (0800-1630 daily, except 0730 weekends, 230F, or 180F for half day, meals 75F extra). Generally you are better off hiring a car or scooter and doing it independently. The *Mistral* also does a Thur tour to Marie-Galante from Saint-François (210F, 0800-1600, T 88 48 74 or 88 48 63).

LA DÉSIRADE

La Désirade is an attractive but rather arid island with 1,600 inhabitants, who occupy themselves in fishing, sheep-rearing and cultivating cotton and maize. A road 10 km long runs along the S coast to the E end of the island, where a giant cactus plantation can be seen. Also at the E end of the island is Pointe du Mombin where there is an outstanding view of the coastline. There are excellent beaches, such as at Souffleur. Perhaps the nicest is in the E at a village called Baie-Mahault, enhanced by a good restaurant/bar, *Chez Céce*, where you can sample dozens of different rum punches.

Columbus named the island La Desiderada as it was the first land he saw on his second voyage in 1493. Archaeological research has shown evidence of Amerindian settlement but it was uninhabited when Columbus passed by.

La Désirade was occupied by the French for the first time in 1725, when all the lepers on Guadeloupe were deported there during an epidemic. In 1930 a leper hospital was built, but it was closed in 1954.

The lack of fresh water has always hampered economic activity. In 1991, however, La Désirade was linked to Grande-Terre underwater with a fresh water supply.

Island information – La Désirade
● **Accommodation & places to eat**
B *L'Oasis du Désert*, Quartier Désert Saline, T 20 02 12, 8 rooms, restaurant, reservations advisable; *Le Mirage*, 7 rooms, T 20 01 08, F 20 07 45, restaurant. *Le Kilibibi*, local specialities, T 20 00 97; *La Payotte*, seafood, T 20 01 94; *Chez Marraine*, créole, T 20 00 93.

● **Transport**

Air There are air services from Guadeloupe several times a week (Air Guadeloupe).

Sea Boat services from St-François, Guadeloupe (depart 0800, return 1600, 2 hours), to La Désirade. The *Mistral* (as above) runs excursions from Saint-François to La Désirade daily, except Tues and Thur, 0830-1530 (1630 Sat, 1600 Sun), including minibus tour of the island and lunch, 180F. Minibuses normally meet incoming flights and boats. There are bicycles and scooters for hire.

Information for travellers

BEFORE TRAVELLING

● **Climate**
The temperature on the coasts varies between 22° and 30°C, but is about 3° lower in the interior. Jan to April is the dry season (called *carême*), July to Nov the wet season (*l'hivernage*), with most rain falling from Sept to Nov. Trade winds moderate temperatures the year round.

MONEY

● **Exchange**
Hotels give the worst rates, then banks (but their rates vary so shop around), post offices change dollars (but not all makes of travellers' cheque, slow service), and the best rates can be found in Edouard Saingolet, Bureau de Change, rues Nozières et Barbès, Pointe-à-Pitre (T 90 34 63), open daily (am only Sat and Sun). There is one exchange facility at the airport and it is closed all day Mon. There is a 24-hour automatic teller at Bas-du-Fort marina which accepts most European currencies, US, EC and Canadian dollars and yen. It can be difficult to change EC dollars.

GETTING THERE

AIR

From Europe: Like Martinique, Guadeloupe is on Air France's direct route from Paris (about 8 hrs) with other flights from Cayenne, Miami, Caracas, Fort-de-France, Port-au-Prince and Santo Domingo; for more details, see under Martinique for Air France's services from France and elsewhere. Other airlines with services to Guadeloupe include AOM French Airlines (from Paris), Air Liberté (Bordeaux, Lyon, Nantes, Paris, Toulouse).

From North America: Air Canada has direct flights from Montréal; American Eagle has flights from San Juan, with connections from the USA.

From the Caribbean: LIAT offers inter-Caribbean connections to Dominica, Antigua, St Vincent, Barbados and St Lucia. Air Guadeloupe connects Pointe-à-Pitre with Cayenne, Port-au-Prince, Dominica, Fort-de-France, La Désirade, Marie-Galante, St Barts, Sint-Maarten, St Martin, San Juan, Santo Domingo and Terre-de-Haut. Air Martinique from Fort-de-France and Sint Maarten, Cubana from Havana, Air St Barthélémy from St Barts, Air Caraïbe Exploitations from St Barts, St Martin, and Air St Martin from St Martin.

SEA

Numerous cruise lines sail from US and French ports. *Atlantica* and *Caribbean Express* operate a fast, scheduled ferry service between Pointe-à-Pitre, Dominica and Martinique (see **Dominica** for details). Agents include T-Maritimes Brudey Frères, Centre St-John Perse, 97110 Pointe-à-Pitre, T 91 60 87. You can get a small motor-sail vessel to Dominica from Pointe-à-Pitre for not much less than the flight. The boat leaves at 1300, 3 days a week, takes 2 hours, is not very comfortable and sea sickness is a distinct possibility.

● **Ports of entry**
(French flag) Deshaies, Basse-Terre and Pointe-à-Pitre are ports of entry but Iles des Saintes is not. No charge for EC or US citizens. French forms to fill in.

● **Anchorages**
Pointe-à-Pitre has good groceries, marine supplies, fuel, water, free 220 electricity, bus to town from marina. Free dinghy dock in marina. Duty free fuel when you clear out of the country. Charter companies include Moorings, Jet Sea, Stardust ATM.

ON ARRIVAL

● **Airports**
Le Raizet airport is large, modern and efficient with plenty of shops, a café and restaurant as well as an exchange. There is also a cash point machine which accepts credit cards with a PIN. Luggage lockers (*consigné*) are outside the terminal building in the car park, 10F for most lockers, 5F coins needed. Bus into Point-à-Pitre leaves from other side of car park, over roundabout and outside Cora (Mamouth) supermarket, 5.70F to Place de la Victoire. No buses Sat pm or Sun.

● **Airlines**
Air France, Blvd Légitimus, Pointe-à-Pitre, T 82 50 00/82 30 00, or Le Raizet airport, T 82 30 20; all others are at Le Raizet: American, T 83 62 62; Air Canada, T 83 62 49; LIAT, T 82 12 26/82 00 84. Nouvelles Frontières for charter flights, T 90 36 36, Pointe-à-Pitre. Air Guadeloupe, Le Raizet, T 82 28 35, or 10 rue Sadi Carnot, Pointe-à-Pitre, T 90 12 25.

● **Banks**
Banque Nationale de Paris (good for Visa cash advances), Banque Française Commerciale, Banque des Antilles Françaises, BRED, Crédit Agricole all have branches throughout the island. Banks charge 1% commission and 4% *dessier* (filing fee). No commission charged on French traveller's cheques. Exchange is handled up to midday so go early to avoid the late morning pandemonium. American Express is at Petreluzzi Travel, 2 rue Henri IV, English spoken, helpful. Credit cards are widely accepted, including at the hypermarkets.

● **Embassies and consulates**
Most diplomatic representation in the French Antilles is in Martinique; however, the Netherlands has a consulate at 5 rue de Nozières, Pointe-à-Pitre, T 82 01 16, and the Dominican Republic at rues St-John Perse et Frébault, Pointe-à-Pitre, T 82 01 87.

● **Hours of business**
0800-1200, 1430-1700 weekdays, morning only on Sat; government offices open 0730-1300, 1500-1630 Mon and Fri, 0730-1300 Tues-Thur. Banking hours: 0800-1200, 1400-1600 Mon to Fri.

● **Shopping**
An unusual fruit, the *carambole*, can be bought in Pointe-à-Pitre. The location of the markets is given above. Good Mamouth Supermarket near Le Raizet airport 3.50F by bus from Pointe-à-Pitre. There are lots of hypermarkets just like in France, stocked with excellent cheese counters and massive wine departments (both French only, of course). They also sell chemist sundries, toys, electrical equipment, film, cameras etc. Most have film processing facilities where prints will be ready in 24 hours or less. Generally open Mon-Sat 0800-2030. Expensive, everything imported from France. In Gosier there is a supermarket on the road to Plage de l'Anse Canot, open on Sun, otherwise hypermarkets are better value and cleaner.

● **Useful addresses**

Police assistance: T 82 00 05 in Pointe-à-Pitre, 81 11 55 in Basse-Terre; **Nautical assistance:** T 82 91 08; **Medical centre:** T 82 98 80/82 88 88.

ON DEPARTURE

● **Departure tax**
No departure tax.

● **Airport information**
If waiting for a flight remember that food and drinks at Cora are half the price of the airport, good for sandwiches and beer, only 2 mins walk.

ACCOMMODATION

● **Hotels**

Price guide

L1	over US$200	L2	US$151-200
L3	US$101-150	A1	US$81-100
A2	US$61-80	A3	US$46-60
B	US$31-45	C	US$21-30
D	US$12-20	E	US$7-11
F	US$4-6	G	up to US$3

On **Grande-Terre**: At **Pointe-à-Pitre**: top of the range is **A1-A2** *La Bougainvillée*, 9 rue Frébault, T 90 14 14, F 91 36 82, which is comfortable, a/c, plumbing could be better, good expensive restaurant; **A1** *Anchorage Hôtel Saint John*, rue Quai Lesseps, T 82 51 57, F 82 52 61, a/c, TV, balcony, comfortable, very good; **A2-A3** *Normandie*, 14 Place de la Victoire, T 82 37 15, with shower and a/c, cheaper without bath, popular, best to book in advance, restaurant is good; **A3-B** *Schoelcher*, rue Schoelcher, not very clean, reasonably-priced restaurant; **A3** *Relais des Antilles*, corner of rue Massabielle and rue Vatable, just off the Place de la Victoire, basic, noisy but friendly and cheap, with toilet; **B** *Karukera*, 15 rue Alsace-Lorraine, with bath, no fan, not good; **B** *Pension Mme Rilsy*, T 91 81 71, 90 39 18, 34 Bis Rue Pegnier, rooms inc breakfast, very friendly, rec.

There are a great many hotels in the **Bas du Fort Bay/Gosier** tourist area; the Tourist Board publishes full descriptions and price lists for the majority. We include a small selection: **L1** *Auberge de la Vieille Tour*, Montauban, 97190 Gosier, T 84 23 23, F 84 33 43, 800-322-2223, named after an 18th-century sugar tower incorporated into the main building, is on a bluff over the sea, beach, pool, tennis, 3 2-room bungalows and 8 rooms in French colonial style, gourmet restaurant, like a number of others this is a member of PLM-Azur group; another is **L1-L2** *Marissol Bas-du-Fort*, 15 mins from Pointe-à-Pitre, 200 rooms and bungalows, restaurants, discothèque, tennis, beach with watersports and a spa/gym with instructors and physiotherapist, T 90 84 44, F 90 83 32; **L1-A1** *Canella Beach*, Pointe de la Verdure, BP 73, 97190 Gosier, T 90 44 00, F 90 44 44, 800-322-2223, 150 studios and suites on waterfront, a/c, TV, phone, showers, kitchens, balconies, pool, children's pool, tennis, beach, multilingual staff, excursions and watersports arranged, 11 km from airport, beachside restaurant; **L1-L3** *La Créole Beach*, Pointe de la Verdure, BP 61, 97190 Gosier, T 90 46 46, F 90 46 66, 800-322-2223, 156 rooms, a/c, showers, TV, phone, minibar, good sized rooms, pool, bar and restaurant, watersports arranged, tennis, volley ball and putting green available; also under same management are **L1-A1** *Les Résidences Yucca*, 100 studios and **L1-L3** *Hôtel Mahogany*, 64 rooms and suites, which share facilites of *La Créole Beach*. **L3** *Arawak*, T 84 24 24, F 84 38 45, nice beach, pool, a/c, buses 400 m away, modern, used by tour groups, comfortable rooms but poor food, not very friendly service; **L1-L3** *Callinago* 143 rooms, beach, pool, T 84 25 25, F 84 24 90, also apartments at *Callinago Village*; **A3** *Serge's Guest House*, on seafront, T 84 10 25, F 84 39 49, very basic, not very clean, convenient for buses and beach, has nice garden and swimming pool. In the same area, **A2** *Les Flamboyants*, is clean, a/c, T 84 14 11, F 84 53 56, pool, sea view, some kitchenettes, friendly. A smaller establishment is the **A3** *Hotel Corossol*, Mathurin, 97190 Gosier, T 84 39 89, 8 rooms, no towels, friendly, good meals, 20 mins walk to Gosier. Many places advertise rooms to let.

Near **Sainte-Anne** are **L3** *Relais du Moulin*, 40 a/c bungalows, rec restaurant, pool (T 88 23 96, F 88 03 92); **L3** *Motel Sainte-Anne*, T 88 22 40, 10 rooms, a/c, **L3** *Auberge le Grand Large*, neither grand nor large, but friendly and with good restaurant on the beach, T 85 48 28, F 88 16 69; and **L3** *Mini Beach*, 1 km from town, also on the beach, relaxed, good location, many restaurants nearby, T 88 21 13, F 88 19 29, can fall to half price in summer, good restaurant, excellent fish soup, a meal in itself. Between Gosier and Sainte-Anne, at La Marie-Gaillarde, is **A2-A3** *Marie-Gaillarde*, T 85 84 29, over-looking Les Grands Fonds, 2 km from Petit Havre beach, 9 rooms can fit 3-4 people, with restaurant and bar. **L1-L3** *La Toubana*, BP63, 97180 Ste-Anne, T 88 25 78, F 88 38 90, T 800-322 2223, 32 cottages, a/c, kitchenettes, phones, terraces, pool, private beach, tennis, pocket billiards, views of nearby Caravelle beach, *Club Med* and islands, *Toubana* is Arawak for little house, restaurant serves French and Créole cuisine. At **Saint-François**: **L1** *Méridien*, T 88 51 00, F 88 40 71, modern and conventional seaside complex, 265 rooms, beach, pool, golf, tennis, flying school, dock, discothèque, and casino; **L1-L2** *Plantation Ste-Marthe* (Euro Dom Hotels), T 93 11 11, 88 43 58, F 88 72 47, 120 magnificent rooms of 42 or 65 sq m with large terrace, a/c, restaurant, bars, 900 sq m swimming pool, close to golf course, 7-acre property; among other luxury places: **L1** *Hamak*, T 88 59 99, F 88 41 92, 56 bungalows, private beach, marina, landing strip, sports. **A2** *Chez Honoré*, Place du Marché, T 88 40 61, F 88 60 73, clean, simple, friendly, noisy because of the disco next door but still one of the cheapest in the French West Indies. At **Pointe du Château**: **L1** *Iguana Bay Villas*, T 88 48 80, F 88 67 19, T 800-322-2223, 17 villas, 2-3 bedrooms, private pools, overlooking La Désinade, pretty beach, private. At **Le Moule**: **L1-L3** *Tropical Club Hotel*, BP 121, 97160 Le Moule, T 93 97 97, F 93 97 00, T 800-322 2223, 72 rooms, 1-4 people, a/c, TV, kitchenctte, phone, terrace, fan, pool, volley ball, ping pong, restaurant, snack bar, in coconut grove on beach, watersports, tennis and golf available nearby.

Club Méditerranée has a hotel-village on the island: *La Caravelle* at Sainte-Anne is on a spectacular white sand beach, perhaps the best on Guadeloupe, surrounded by a 13-hectare reserve; atmosphere strictly informal (nude bathing), all sports equipment available, deep sea fishing and golf at extra cost, children's clubs, circus school, 329 rooms, some with 3 beds, some singles, T 85 49 50, F 85 49 70.

On **Basse-Terre**: accommodation is neither plentiful nor high class in **Basse-Terre city**: **C** *Hotel Basse-Terre-Charley*, 52 rue Maurice Marie Claire, T 81 19 78, central, basic, clean and cheap, good oriental restaurant next door; also central is **B** *Le Drouant*, 26 rue Dr Cabre; **A3** *Hotel Higuera*, on main square opp *Hotel de Ville*, T 81 11 92. At **Saint-Claude**: **A1-A2** *Relais de la Grand*

Soufrière, an elegant but rather poorly-converted old plantation mansion, a/c, attractive surroundings, old wooden furniture, friendly staff, T 80 01 27, F 80 18 40, regular bus service to Basse-Terre, including Sun. At **Bouillante**: **L1-A1** *Domaine de Malendure*, T 98 92 12, F 98 92 10, T 800-322 2223, 44 loft suites with views of Ilet Pigeon, on hillside, 400m from sea, a/c, TV, phone, mini-bar, good location for diving or walking, pool, restaurant, car rental, shuttle to Malendure beach or Grand Anse beach, car rental in advance rec. **L2** *Fort Royal* at Deshaies: T 25 50 00, F 25 50 01, used to belong to *Club Med*, now Touring Hotel Club, dramatically situated on a promontory between 2 beautiful but rather rough beaches; **A2** *La Vigie*, overlooking Deshaies bay, small studios with kitchenette, bathroom, terrace, fan, cleaned daily, T 28 42 52; rooms *chez M Eric Bernier*, T 28 40 04 or 28 42 70, about **B** on waterfront, opp *Le Mouillage* restaurant more rooms are available; an apartment **C** *chez Jean Memorin*, T 28 40 90, just outside town on hill in direction of Grand Anse beach, 1 bedroom, TV. **L3-A2** *Auberge de la Distillerie*, Route de Versailles, Tabanon, 97170 Petit Bourg, T 94 25 91, F 94 11 91, T 800-322 2223, 16 rooms, a/c, TV, phone, mini-bar, pool, jacuzzi, pocket billiards, country inn at entrance to Parc Naturel surrounded by pineapple fields, créole restaurant, *Le Bitaco* and small pizza café, the owner also designed **L3-A1** *Créol'Inn*, Bel'Air Desrozières, T 94 22 56, F 94 19 28, T 800-322 2223, 20 cabins in wooded area, a/c, fans, phone, kitchenette, hammocks, pool, barbecue, snack bar. At **Trois Rivières**: are *Le Joyeux*, a 3F bus ride from the centre of the town (bus stop right outside) or short walk, in Le Faubourg, 100m above the sea, T 92 74 78, F 92 77 07, 6 simple rooms, kitchenettes, Créole restaurant, bar, disco, closed Mon except for reservations, rec, good views to Les Saintes, very friendly, Monsieur will drive you to the boat dock for nothing, the family also run a small supermarket and the Serie Bleu maps are sold there; **L1-L3** *Le Jardin Malanga*, T 90 46 46, F 90 46 99, T 800 322 2223, beautifully renovated 1927 Créole house and bungalows, hillside setting in banana plantation, lovely views, a/c, TV, terraces, mini-bar, bath tubs, huge beds, pool, car rental in advance rec; **L3** *Grand'Anse*, T 92 90 47, F 92 93 69, bungalows, also has Créole restaurant and views; *Les Gîtes de l'Habitation Cardonnet*, T 92 70 55, 5 self-contained cottages.

The Tourist Board has current price lists (they run an information desk at Raizet airport but do not make reservations).

● **Gîtes**

Throughout the island there are a large number of gîtes for rent on a daily, weekly or monthly basis. Weekly rates range from 700F to 3,000F, but most are in the 1,000-1,500F bracket. The tourist offices in both Pointe-à-Pitre and Basse-Terre have lists of the properties available and should be consulted in the first instance. Gîtes are arranged by the local Syndicats d'Initiative who have an office next to the Tourist Office on rue Provence. For example, the Syndicat d'Initiative de Deshaies, T 28 49 70, lists 14 local people who let gîtes. Some gîtes are quite isolated, so choose one that is conveniently located. The Syndicats charge a 5% rental fee.

The tourist offices also have lists of villas for rent (there are a number in Saint-François, for instance); prices vary between 1,500F and 4,500F depending on number of occupants, size of villa and season.

● **Camping**

Compared with metropolitan France, camping is not well organized and the Tourist Office does not have much information. 7 km E of Ste-Anne is *Camping du Voyageur*, T/F 88 36 74, Chateaubrun 97180 Ste-Anne, cooking facilities but no washing machine, **E** for 2 people, tent rental, gîtes, clean, beach 10 mins walk. A small campsite is *Sable d'Or*, near Deshaies, Basse-Terre, T 81 39 10. **D** per tent for 2 people. Also small bungalows, **B-C**, cooking facilities, pool. There are buses from Pointe-à-Pitre. *Camping Traversée* is near Mahait on Basse-Terre, not suitable for tents after heavy rain, they float away. Otherwise ask mayors if you may camp on municipal land, or owners on private property. Camper vans can be arranged through Découverts et Loisirs Créoles in Abymes, T 20 55 65.

FOOD AND DRINK

● **Restaurants**

Apart from the hotel restaurants mentioned above, there are a large number of restaurants, cafés and patisseries to choose from. Many are closed in the evening. In **Pointe-à-Pitre**: *Oasis*, rues Nozières et A R Boisneuf (French), T 82 02 70; *Relais des Antilles* (cheaper, but good Créole cooking), near the *Auberge Henri IV*, in a private house, good, cheap meals (ask Valentin at the *Auberge* for directions); *Krishna*,

47 rue A R Boisneuf, Indian; *Le Moundélé*, rue Juan Jaurès, T 91 04 30, African. At Le Raizet airport: *Oiseau des Iles* (French), and *Godire*, self-service. On the Grande-Terre holiday coast: *La Case Créole*, Route de la Rivière; *Chez Rosette*, Av Général de Gaulle, both Créole at Gosier; *Le Boukarou*, rue Montauban, T 84 10 37, good Italian, pizza made on charcoal grill, moderately priced; lots of small restaurants in Gosier: pizzas, Vietnamese, Chinese and of course French. The local pizza house is near the park, rec, good for takeaways. The *pâtisserie* is good for an early morning coffee while collecting the *baguettes*; *Chez Gina*, in a little village cafétière, 2½ km inland from Les Sables d'Or campsite, up the hill, excellent food, order in advance in the morning for an evening meal, 4 courses and apéritif, served in a sort of garage with flowers, friendly, don't be put off by the untidy surroundings; *Côté Jardin*, at Bas du Fort marina, French; *La Plantation*, same location, same cuisine. In Sainte-Anne, *Chez Yvette* is budget-priced; *La Toubana*, perched high above village overlooking *Club Med*, nice but expensive French cuisine, take swimming gear, pool and sun deck, rec; the *Relais du Moulin* has an excellent French-Créole menu, rec; and in Saint-François, *Madame Jerco* has good food in a small creaking house. At Campêche there is a small restaurant in the middle of the village, cheap and welcome relief if travelling in this area. **On Basse-Terre**: *Chez Paul* in Matouba has been rec for Créole and East Indian cuisine. At Bouillante, *Chez Loulouse*, Plage de Malendure, T 98 70 34, beach restaurant, créole fair; *Restaurant de la Phare*, Vieux Fort, good créole cooking, excellent fresh fish, reasonable prices, dance hall attached. **In Deshaies**: several reasonably priced restaurants inc *Le Madras* and *Le Mouillage*, serving créole food; for breakfast try the *boulangerie* opp *Le Mouillage* for *croissants*, *pain au chocolat*, coffee, juice. The *Relais de la Grande Soufrière*, at Saint-Claude, highly rec créole meals at reasonable prices, T 80 01 27. For a description of local cuisine, see page 585.

GETTING AROUND

LAND TRANSPORT

● **Motoring**

Pointe-à-Pitre has a dual carriage ring road which runs from Gosier across the Rivière Salée to the industrial centre at Baie-Mahault and

S towards Petit-Bourg. It is well used and the driving is very French with dead animals on the road quickly covered with lime. There can be major traffic holdups in the rush hour; expect to find slow moving traffic on the major routes for up to 20 km out of Pointe-à-Pitre. Bottlenecks include the roundabout at the university at Bas-du-Fort, the turning to Le Raizet and beyond to Abymes and the turnoff to Baie-Mahualt. In the city, parking is a nightmare in the daytime. There are no car parks, just meters. There are 2 zones, green (about 5F for max 8 hrs) and orange (cheaper). The system does not operate 1230-1400. Most traffic is one way.

● **Car hire**

Self-drive hire cars are available mainly at the airport, which is inconvenient for those not arriving by air. A small, old Peugeot will cost about 350F per day. In Pointe-à-Pitre, there is a small office above an icecream parlour on Av V Hugues, just off Place de la Victoire, which has a small selection. Rental can also be arranged through the major hotels. International and local agencies are represented. At Trois Rivières, Rosan Martin, Location de Voitures, is close to the dock, T 92 94 24, 262F a day, unlimited mileage, for a Renault B571, deposit 3,000F or credit card. Tropic-Car, 25 rue Schoelcher, 97110 Pointe-á-Pitre, T 91 84 37, F 91 31 94, evenings and weekends T 84 07 25, has a variety of models for hire. There are also mopeds for hire in Pointe-à-Pitre, Gosier, Saint-François, or through hotels. Mokes and scooters can be rented at Sainte-Anne. If you don't have a credit card you normally have to deposit up to 5,000F for a car; 2,000F for a scooter; and 1,000F for moped or bicycle.

● **Bicycles**

Bicycle rental from Velo-Vert, Pointe-à-Pitre, T 83 15 74, Le Relais du Moulin, near Sainte-Anne, T 88 23 96, Rent-a-Bike, *Meridien Hotel* Saint-François, T 84 51 00, around 50F a day.

● **Buses**

In Pointe-à-Pitre there are 3 main bus terminals: from La Darse (by Place de la Victoire), buses run to Gosier (5F), Sainte-Anne (15F), Saint-François (15F); for N Grande-Terre destinations, buses leave from the Mortenol station. From Blvd Chanzy (near the cemetery) they go to Trois Rivières (27F) and Basse-Terre (30F, 2 hrs). Pointe-à-Pitre to La Grande Anse, 20F, 1 hr 45 mins. Buses from Pointe-à-Pitre to Deshaies leave from Gare Routière, 1 hr 15

mins, 25F. Basse-Terre to Trois Rivières, 20 mins. The terminal in Basse-Terre is on Blvd Général de Gaulle, between the market and the sea. Buses run between 0530 and 1800, leaving for the main destinations every 15 mins or so, or when full. The airport bus leaves from 0800 from outside Renaissance Cinema, Place de la Victoire, 5.70F. It is possible to cover the whole island by bus in a day – cheap, interesting and easy, but exhausting. You can just stop the bus at the side of the road or wait at the bus stations in the villages. Buses are crowded and play zouk music at top volume (exhilarating or deafening, depending on your mood); have your money ready when you get off.

Organized bus tours and boat excursions are available but expensive, about 330-400F in a bus for about 40 people. Check with Tourist Office, Petrelluzzi Travel Agency (American Express Agents), 2 rue Henri IV, Pointe-à-Pitre, and other agencies.

● **Hitchhiking**

Hitchhiking is no problem and if you speak French it is a rec way of meeting local people, who are very friendly. However, a bus will often come before you have been waiting long.

● **Taxis**

Taxis are rather expensive; some are metered; some routes have fixed fares. All fares double at night. Taxi from the airport to Place de la Victoire costs about 50F but it may be only 45F to the airport from Place de la Victoire.

COMMUNICATIONS

● **Postal services**

Post office and telephones building in Pointe-à-Pitre is on Blvd Hanne, crowded, sweltering. Post and phones in Basse-Terre is on rue Dr Pitat, between Dumanoir and Ciceron, smaller but a bit more comfortable than the Pointe-à-Pitre office. Parcel post is a problem and you can usually send parcels of up to 2 kg only. In Pointe-à-Pitre there is an office near the stadium where you can mail parcels of up to 7 kg by air but it is unreliable; one correspondent sent a tent but received a cake wrapped in the same paper. Unlike in France, stamps are not sold in bars and tobacconists, go to Post Offices in small towns to avoid the crush of the main offices.

● **Telecommunications**

For local calls you must buy phone cards (*télécartes*, 40F or 96F, from a *tabac*), fairly essential when phoning ahead to book accommodation; to call abroad, you must hand over identification at the desk (calls to the USA 12.85F/minute, Europe 18.50F/minute, Australia 23.10F/minute; hotels charge twice as much). You can not make a credit card or collect call abroad from a pay phone. You can not have a call returned to a pay phone either.

TOURIST INFORMATION

● **Local tourist offices**
Tourist offices in Guadeloupe: 5 Square de la Banque, BP 1099, 97181, Pointe-à-Pitre, T 82 09 30, F 83 89 22 (the Gîtes office next door is helpful); Maison du Port, Cours Nolivos, Basse-Terre, T 81 24 83; Av de l'Europe, Saint-François, T 88 48 74, and at airport. The tourist office publishes a booklet called *Bonjour Guadeloupe*, which contains descriptive and practical information; a broadsheet, *Pratique*, which gives details on concerts and exhibitions, flights, shipping, emergency numbers and all-night chemists and doctors; *Living in Guadeloupe* is a useful, free, bimonthly magazine written in English and French.

● **Maps**
The Serie Bleu maps (1:25,000, 7 maps of Guadeloupe, No 4601G-4607G) issued by the Institut Geógraphique National, Paris, which include all hiking trails, are available at the bigger book stores in the rue Frébault in Pointe-à-Pitre, and at *Le Joyeux* hotel in Trois Rivières/Le Faubourg for 52F. National Park: Parc National de la Guadeloupe, Habitation Beausoleil, Montéran, BP13-97120, Saint-Claude, T 80 24 25, F 80 05 46.

Saint-Martin

S AINT-MARTIN, the largest of Guadeloupe's outer islands, at 52 sq km, is divided between France and the Netherlands. See Netherlands Antilles section for general description and information. The French part (population 28,518) used to be a sleepy place, but has become very Americanized since the building of the yacht marina and lots of luxury hotels. There is no restriction on travel between the two halves of the island.

GOVERNMENT AND ECONOMY

The French side is a sub-prefecture of Guadeloupe, with the sub-prefect appointed in Paris. There is an elected town council, led by a mayor. The economy is entirely dependent upon tourism, with the twin attractions of duty-free shopping and the sea (for bathers and sailors).

FESTIVALS

Carnival is held pre-Lent and most of the events are on the waterfront in Marigot. It is not as big and grandiose as on the Dutch side, where carnival is held a few weeks later, but there are calypso and beauty contests and a Grand Parade. Bastille Day (14 July) has live music, jump-ups and boat races; the celebrations move to Grand Case the weekend after (more fun). In Grand Case on New Year's Day there is a small parade with live music, while at Easter another parade is held with a lot of dancing.

MARIGOT

Marigot, the capital of French Saint-Martin, lies between Simpson Bay Lagoon and the Caribbean sea. ('Marigot' is a French West Indian word meaning a spot from which rain water does not drain off, and forms marshy pools.) Shopping is good. Boutiques offer French *prêt-à-porter* fashions and St Barts batiks, and gift shops sell liqueurs, perfumes, and cosmetics at better duty-free prices than the Dutch side. At the *Marina Port La Royale* complex there are chic shops, cafés and bistros where you can sit and watch the boats. Rue de la République and Rue de la Liberté also have good shopping with fashion names at prices below those of Europe or the USA. A fruit market is held every morning in the market place next to Marigot harbour. It is best on Wednesdays and Saturdays. On the right hand side of the market place is the Tourist Office and taxi rank; also the only public toilet on the French side. From here it is a 10-minute walk to **Fort**

Saint-Martin

1. Club Orient
2. Le Samanna
3. Pavillon Beach
4. Royal Beach

French Side

Sint Maarten

Dutch Side

5. Bel Air Beach
6. Cupecoy
7. Maho Beach
8. Oyster Pond & Dawn Beach

St Louis (restored 1994) overlooking Marigot Bay and Marigot. Follow the signs from the Tourist Office.

On the waterfront the historical and archaeological **Museum 'On the trail of the Arawaks'** open 0900-1300, 1500-1900, Monday-Saturday, T 29 22 84, may open longer during high season, has a well-presented exhibition from the first settlers of Saint-Martin around 3500 BC to 1960. Entrance US$5 (US$2 children).

EXCURSIONS

Grand Case, 13 km from the capital, is anything but grand: a quaint town between an old salt pond (which has been partially filled in to provide the Espérance airstrip) and a long sandy and secluded beach. At the far NE end is another beach, Petite Plage, delightfully *petite* in a calm bay. Every other Saturday

all year round there are sailing races of old fishing boats between Anguilla and St-Martin, mostly to Grand Case. Ask for information at the *Ranch Bar* at the beach (live music every Sunday). From Grande Case pier a semi-submarine leaves daily, for a 1½-hour tour. You sit in the bottom of the boat, 2m under water, but the view is better than on a glass-bottomed boat, adults US$30, children US$20, call the Dutch side, T 24078, F 24079, for bookings, reservations essential.

Anse Marcel, N of Grand Case, is a shallow beach, ideal for small children. Inland, **Pic Paradise** (424m) is a good lookout point from where, on a fine day, you can see Anguilla, Saba, St Eustatius, St Kitts, Nevis and St-Barts. By car, take a turn off at Rambaud on the Marigot-Grand Case road. There are also footpaths from **Colombier** (1½ km) and **Orléans** (1 km). Colombier is a small,

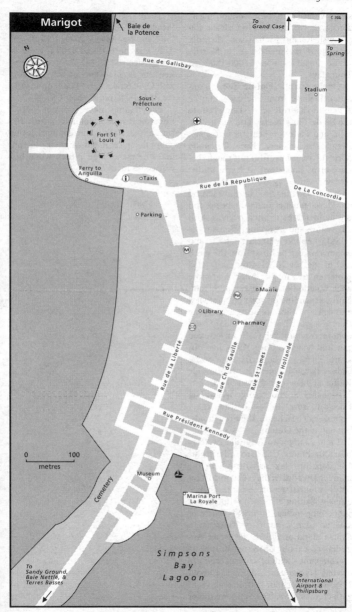

Marigot

To Grand Case

To Spring

Baie de la Potence

N

Rue de Galisbay

Stadium

Sous - Préfecture

Fort St Louis

Ferry to Anguilla

Taxis

Rue de la République

De La Concordia

Parking

M

Muirie

Pol

Library

Pharmacy

Rue de la Liberté

Rue Ch de Gaulle

Rue St James

Rue de Hollande

Rue Président Kennedy

0   100
metres

Museum

Marina Port La Royale

Cemetery

Simpsons Bay Lagoon

To Sandy Ground, Baie Nettlé, & Terres Basses

To International Airport & Philipsburg

sleepy village with some wonderful gardens, well worth a visit. In Orléans you can visit Roland Richardson, the only well-known native artist on St-Martin, whose home is open 1000-1800 on Thursdays.

On the Atlantic, **Cul-de-Sac**, is a traditional village, from where you may be able to hitch a ride on a fishing boat to the **Île de Tintamarre**. The sea here is calm and there are boat trips to Pinel Island just offshore. **Baie Orientale** (Orient Bay) is beautiful but rough (beware of its undertow); it has a nudist section which is considerably less crowded than the rest. There are several new developments along the beach and the naturist area is often overrun with day visitors and shrinking. Windsurfers (US$15/hr plus credit card deposit) and catamarans can be hired from the south end of the beach, friendly staff, good protected area for beginners and more open waters. For the intrepid, or foolhardy, depending on your point of view and courage, there is bungee jumping from a parasail at 100m, US$85, not done on very windy days. From here you can find boats to Caye Verte, just offshore. There is a butterfly farm on Le Galion Beach Rd next to the Bayside Riding Stables, open 0900-1700, T 87 31 21. Further S, snorkelling is good at Coconut Grove. Topless bathing is accepted at all beaches on the French side, but not on the Dutch.

From Marigot to Anguilla by ferry boat (20 minutes) US$20 round trip plus 10F departure tax, or with one of the many charter boats; they tend to do it for only one tourist season, so names change quickly. Sailing trips with lunch and snorkelling to beaches on St-Martin or smaller islands such as Tintamarre, Sandy Island or Prickly Pear (see Anguilla), cost about US$65pp. Boat charter companies, with or without crew, are around *Marina Port La Royale*, about US$360/day for four people on a yacht with crew, or US$200-1,500 for a motor boat.

There are 2 squash courts at Le Privilège (T 87 37 37). Horse riding at Caïd and Isa, Anse Marcel, T 87 45 70, daily rides at 0900 and 1500 if there is enough demand, US$45, 2½ hrs, reservations one day in advance. Beach rides also with OK-Corral, Oyster Pond, up to Orient Bay, US$50 pp, 2½ hrs, T 87 40 72.

For nature hikes, contact Serge L'homme if you can get hold of him. He runs a spice stall in Marigot market (he wraps the spices in red gingham) and on hikes he makes fruit punch while his wife cooks lunch.

Information for travellers

● **Exchange**
The US dollar is as widely used as the franc, but watch the rate. Credit card transactions are usually in US$. It is sometimes difficult to get change from payments in francs. Dollars are preferred. The best place for exchange is the Post Office in Marigot where they will change all currencies and traveller's cheques, but normally only into francs. There are several exchange houses for changing from francs to dollars, one in Rue du Kennedy and one in the *Marina Royale* complex. Two banks, both on rue de la République, Marigot, Banque des Antilles Françaises and Banque Française Commerciale.

AIR
International flights arrive at the Juliana airport on the Dutch side. On the French side is the Espèrance airport which can only take light planes. Air Guadeloupe (address under Guadeloupe above) has scheduled services to Espérance from Pointe-à-Pitre, Port-au-Prince and Saint-Barthélémy. Air St Barthélémy flies from Basse-Terre, Point-à-Pitre and St Barts. Air Caraïbes Exploitations also flies from Pointe-à-Pitre and St Barts. Air St Martin flies to Espérance from Pointe-à-Pitre. A 5-seater helicopter run by Héli-inter, T 87 35 88, runs day tours to St-Barts, US$700, and Anguilla, US$645, from Anse Marcel every day. Charters also available. Trans Helico Caraïbes offers helicopter tours of St-Martin; US$170 for 10 mins for 4 people, US$370 for 25 mins, T 27 40 68.

SEA
Besides the excursions to Anguilla (see above), connections can be made with Saint-Barthélémy; St Barts Express, twice daily except Sun and holidays, departs Gustavia 0715, 1530, departs Marigot market place 0900, 1715 (see St Barts **Information for travellers** for more details). *Voyager I*, a high speed ferry St Martin-St Barts departs Marigot waterfront 0845 Mon-Sat, 1½ hrs, departs Gustavia 1600, US$50 return plus US$6 port fees, T 87 10 68. See also Sint Maarten chapter for connections with neighbouring islands. Try putting a notice up at the Capiteneri Marina Port La Royale for hitching a lift to other islands.

● **Ports of entry**
(French flag) Marigot. For information on marinas and cruising fees see chapter on Sint Maarten.

● **Hours of business**
Shops open around 0900 and close between 1800-1900 with normally a 2-hour lunch break between 1200-1500, depending on the shop. Banks open 0800-1300; both slightly different from the Dutch side.

● **Voltage**
220 volts, 60 cycles (compared with 110 volts on the Dutch side).

● **Useful addresses**
Hospital: T 87 50 07; **Ambulance**: T 87 74 14; **Gendarmerie**: T 87 50 10; **Police**: T 87 50 04; **Fire**: T 87 50 08.

● **Departure tax**
There is a US$10 departure tax on St-Maarten, payable only at Juliana airport, or US$5 to the Netherlands Antilles.

● **Hotels**

Price guide			
L1	over US$200	L2	US$151-200
L3	US$101-150	A1	US$81-100
A2	US$61-80	A3	US$46-60
B	US$31-45	C	US$21-30
D	US$12-20	E	US$7-11
F	US$4-6	G	up to US$3

There are a number of luxury resorts dotted around the coast, lesser establishments and guest houses and a building boom has raised the total number of hotel rooms to 3,000. We list here only a very small selection; non-inclusion does not mean non-recommendation. The tourist office lists only those in the upper range, guest houses in Grand Case are rented from US$350-450/week, but for low budget accommodation would be better in the Dutch half. **L1** *La Samanna*, Baie Longue, T 87 64 00, F 87 87 86, in USA T (800) 854-2252, part of Rosewood chain of luxury hotels, one of the most exclusive resorts in the Caribbean, reopened Mar 1996 following renovation and repairs, excellent dining, 2 and 3 bedroomed villas also available, up to US$1,800, tennis, water skiing, windsurfing, sunfish sailing. **L2-L3** *Le Pirate*, Marigot, a favourite with island-hoppers, studio or duplex, T 87 78 37, F 87 95 67; **A3** *Beauséjour*, T 87 52 18, Rue de la République in centre of Marigot; **A2** *Rosely's*, 39 studios, 7 duplex, Concordia, T 87 70 17, F 87 70 20, pool in garden, kitchenette, a/c, very nice; **A3** *Malibu*, also in Concordia, a few blocks from the centre of Marigot, 43 rooms, modern, kitchens, fridge, T 87 98 98, F 87 92 34; **B** *Fleming's*, in St-James end of Marigot, T 87 70 25, 8 rooms, some with marina view, a/c, fan, kitchenettes, clean, comfortable, nicely furnished; **L3-A1** *Royal Beach*, on Nettlé Bay, modern, a/c, beachfront but not all rooms have sea view, pool, bar, restaurant, watersports nearby, T/F 87 89 89. In Grand Case, **L3-A2** *Hévèa*, T 87 56 85, F 87 83 88, small colonial-style hotel, 2 rooms, 3 studios, 3 apartments with kitchenettes, gourmet restaurant, beach across the street; **L3-A1** *Grand Case Beach Club*, 76 rooms and apartments, watersports, tennis, on the beach, T 87 51 87, F 87 59 93; **L3** *Chez Martine*, T 87 51 59, F 87 87 30, 5 rooms, 1 suite, excellent restaurant, overlooks Grand Case Bay. **L1-A1** *Pavillon Beach*, RN 7, Grand Case 97150, T 87 96 46, F 87 71 04, in the USA T 800-322 2223, new, elegant hotel on lagoon, walking distance from Grand Case, 6 studios, 10 suites and 1 honeymoon suite, a/c, fans, TV, kitchenettes, phones, beach, watersports and land sports can be arranged. **L1** *Club Orient* (naturist), is Baie Orientale, tennis, volleyball, watersports, massage, rooms or chalets for 3-4 people, T 87 33 85, F 87 33 76.

FOOD AND DRINK

● Restaurants

French cuisine in all hotel restaurants on the French side is quite good but expensive. Picturesque gourmet dining places on the seashore are the islanders' favourites. The likelihood of finding a cheap meal is rare. Many restaurants close in Sept-October. **In Marigot**: the *Mini-Club* with its bar and dining arbour, serves a Caribbean buffet Wed and Sat, closed August and September. Traditional French in centre of Marigot is *La Calanque*. *David's Pub and Restaurant*, near the Post Office, good food, not expensive, fun bar, rec. For travellers on a small budget try the snackbars and cafés on Rue de Hollande. *La Maison sur le Port*, (T 87 56 38), *L'Aventure* (T 87 13 85) and *Le Poisson d'Or* (on the harbour, part art gallery, closed Sept-Oct, T 87 72 45) offer excellent French cuisine and seafood. *Le Bar de la Mer*, (T 87 81 79) serves lunch and dinner, good place to go before a disco; many bars on the water front next to the tourist office serving barbecue lunch and dinner. There are also lots of restaurants overlooking the boats at Marina Port la Royale, many with open air dining. *Brasserie de la Gare*, a brasserie and pizzeria, open daily 1130-2230, T 87 20 64; more upmarket and expensive is *Jean Dupont*, T 87 71 13, French gourmet with some Vietnamese and Thai specialities, open 1130-1530 (except Sun in low season), 1730-2300. Browse around, see what takes your fancy.

Grand Case has a reputation of having more restaurants than inhabitants. Most are on the street next to the beach but these are generally more expensive than those on the other side of the boulevard and not recommendable on a windy night. *Fish Pot*, overlooking the sea, sea food, T 87 50 88, F 87 20 37, open 1130-1500 in high season, dinner 1800-2230; *L'Alabama*, across the street offers excellent cuisine and thoughtful service. *Chá Chá Chá*, 61 Blvd de Grand Case, has Brazilian and Créole food, OK but expensive, T 87 53 63, open Mon-Sat 1800-2300, closes June and mid-Sept-mid-October. At the small snackbars near the little pier you can find barbecue fish, ribs and lobster as well as other local snacks, very popular at weekends and holidays, rec; *Jimbo's* has Mexican food, run by an American. At weekends there is usually live music in one of the bars/restaurants along the beach.

Mark's Place, Cul de Sac, T 87 34 50, open daily in season 1230-1430, 1800-2130, closed Sept-Oct, popular with locals and tourists, Créole and continental dishes, moderate prices; *Hoa Mai*, Cul de Sac, T 87 32 52, indoor or outdoor dining, French Créole and Vietnamese dishes, assortment of 6 Vietnamese dishes US$34 for 2 people, open 1830-2200. At Orient Baie, *Bikini Beach* for Spanish *tapas*, *paella* and *sangria*, helped along with Brazilian music some nights, T 87 43 25.

GETTING AROUND

LAND TRANSPORT
● **Car hire**
Car hire from several agencies, eg L C Fleming, Marigot, T 87 50 01 (also travel agency); Sunrise, St-James, Marigot, T 87 51 91, Saint-Martin Auto, Grand Case, T 87 50 86, or Marigot T 87 54 72; Avis, Port La Royale, Marigot, T 87 54 36; many others. Scooter rental from US$20/day inc helmets and insurance from Concordia Services Scoot Rental, T 87 70 84.

● **Buses**
Buses run from Grand Case to Marigot (US$1) and from Marigot, French Quarters and St Peters to Philipsburg, normally from 0600-2200, US$1.50. Traffic jams on Sat evening cause serious delays.

● **Taxis**
There are plenty of taxis, with controlled fares. You find them next to the Tourist Office in Marigot, T 87 56 54. From Juliana airport to Marigot about US$10, Marigot to Grand Case US$10, Marigot to Oyster Pond, US$24, 2½ hr island tour US$50, add 25% 2200-2400 and 50% 2400-0600. It is easy to hitchhike.

COMMUNICATIONS

● **Postal services**
The Post Office will hold mail, but only for 2 weeks. Letters sent c/o Capiteneri Marina Port La Royale, Marigot, will be kept 4-6 weeks.

● **Telecommunications**
There are several telephone booths on the French side but they only take telephone cards. 120 units for 90F, sold at the Post Office and at the bookshop opposite. There are 8 telephones on the square in Marigot and 2 in

Grand Case in front of the little pier. To call the Dutch side use the code 19-599-5. To call the French side from the Dutch side use the code 06. All Dutch side numbers have 5 digits while French side numbers have 6. The international code for St-Martin is 590. Calls from one side of the island to the other are expensive. To call France from the French side dial 16 and the number.

MEDIA

● **Newspapers**
Le Monde, *France Soir* and *Le Figaro* from France are available 1-3 days after publication. *France Antilles*, same day. A few German and Italian magazines are sold at Maison de la Presse (opposite Post Office) and other locations.

ENTERTAINMENT

L'Atmosphere is a disco for 'chic' French people, at Marina Port La Royale, very little English spoken, drinks US$6. *Le Bar de la Mer* at the waterfront is a popular meeting place for French-speaking young travellers, with live music once a week. *La Fiesta*, Marigot waterfront, South American music, Brazilian house band, popular bar for locals. Grand Case normally has live music Fri-Sun in high season with beach party style entertainment in one of the many bars. *Surf Club South*, Grand Case, a New Jersey-type bar, has beach parties every other Sun, all food and drinks US$1, with mainly 60s and 70s music, great fun. *Circus* bar in Nettlé Bay in the newly built resort area is a popular night bar, live music once in a while. *Le Privilège Disco* at Anse Marcel, T 87 46 17, US$10 entrance, one drink included, one of the best but taxis expensive to get there, open from 2300, closed Mon, in Sept only opens Thur, Fri, Sat. Every full moon there is a beach party at Friar's Bay starting around 2100-2200, barbecues on the beach every Fri and Sat.

TOURIST INFORMATION

● **Local tourist office**
Port de Marigot, 97150 Saint-Martin, T 87 57 21/23, F 87 56 43.

Saint-Barthélémy

SAINT-BARTHÉLÉMY (St Barts or St Barth's), also in the Leewards, is 230 km N of Guadeloupe, 240 km E of the Virgin Islands, and 35 km SE of Saint-Martin. Its 21 square km are inhabited by a population of 5,043, mostly people of Breton, Norman, and Poitevin descent who live in quiet harmony with the small percentage of blacks. Thirty-two splendid white sandy beaches, most of which are protected by both cliff and reef, are surrounded by lush volcanic hillsides. The Norman dialect is still widely spoken while most of the islanders also speak English. A few elderly women still wear traditional costumes (with their characteristic starched white bonnets called *kichnottes*); they cultivate sweet potato patches and weave palm fronds into hats and purses which they sell in the village of Corossol. The men traditionally smuggled rum among neighbouring islands and now import liqueurs and perfumes, raise cattle, and fish for lobsters offshore. The people are generally known for their courtesy and honesty. St Barts has become a very 'chic' and expensive holiday destination; the Rockefellers, Fords, and Rothschilds own property on the island, while the rich, royal and famous stay in the luxury villas dotted around the island.

HISTORY

Although called Ouanalao by the Caribs, the island was renamed after Christopher Columbus' brother, Saint-Barthélémy when discovered in November 1496. It was first settled by French colonists from Dieppe in 1645. After a brief possession by the Order of the Knights of Malta, and ravaging by the Caribs, it was bought by the Compagnie des Iles and added to the French royal domain in 1672. In 1784, France ceded the island to Sweden in exchange for trading rights in the port of Göteborg.

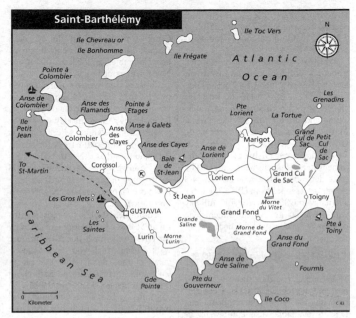

In 1801, St Barts was attacked by the British, but for most of this period it was peaceful and commercially successful. The island was handed back to France after a referendum in 1878.

GOVERNMENT AND ECONOMY

St Barts is administered by the sub-prefect in Saint-Martin and is a dependency of Guadeloupe. The island has its own elected mayor, who holds office for 7 years. Much the same as Saint-Martin, St Barts relies on its free port status and its anchorages and beaches for the bulk of its revenue. It is popular with both French and North American visitors and, despite the limitations of its airstrip, it is claimed that twice as many tourists as the island's population pass through each month.

DIVING AND MARINE LIFE

There is excellent diving all round St Barts, especially out round the offshore rocks, like the Groupers, and islands like Ile Fourche. Sometimes in May the migrating sperm whales pass close by. From April to August female sea turtles come to Colombier, Flamands and Corossol to lay their eggs.

Dive shops are Plongée La Bulle, rue Centenaire, Gustavia, T 27 68 93, 27 62 25 at Océan Must (run by Jean-Luc and Angela, no more than 5 divers per group); West Indian Dive, Stardust Marina Quay, Gustavia (run by Lawrence and Erik, PADI and CMAS instructors), T 27 91 79, 27 31 29 (boat), F 27 91 80, VHF Channel 79; Marine Service, rue Jeanne d'Arc, Gustavia, T 27 70 34; St Barth Plongée, Quai de la République, Gustavia, T 27 43 33, F 27 67 95. A single dive costs about US$50, or there are packages of 5 or 10 dives for US$220 or US$400. PADI open water certification costs US$480.

A submersible, l'Aquascope, offers trips to the reefs around Gustavia, descending to no more than 10 feet. Tickets from Marine Service. US$32 adults, children 5-12 US$16, Quai du Yacht Club, Gustavia, T 27 70 34.

Deep sea fishing for marlin, tuna, wahoo and dolphin can be arranged with Océan Must Marina at La Pointe, Gustavia, T/F 27 62 25, VHF 10, who also charter boats for cruising, diving, water-skiing and offer a full service marina. Marine Service at Quai du Yacht Club, Gustavia, T 27 70 34, F 27 70 36, VHF 74, also do deep sea fishing trips and the same watersports and boat rentals. The price depends on the type of boat (4-8 people) and ranges from US$470-640 for a half day to US$780-1,100 for a full day with open bar and picnic lunch. The catch is the property of the boat.

BEACHES AND WATERSPORTS

St Barts is a popular mid-way staging post on the yachting route between Antigua and the Virgin Islands. Boat charters are available, also courses in, or facilities for, windsurfing (Toiny is the windsurfers' favourite beach), snorkelling (very good, particularly at Marigot), water-skiing and sailing. Surfboard rental (not windsurfing) at Hookipa, T 27 71 31. Sailing and snorkelling cruises are offered by several catamarans: *Kachina*, T 27 66 98, 27 85 25, *Ne me quitte pas*, Marine Service, T 27 70 34, *Ttoko Ttoko*, Océan Must, T 27 62 25. They go to Colombier beach, Fourchue Island, Tintamarre, Anguilla or St Martin. Half day cruises cost US$55-60, whole day with lunch US$90-95, sunset cruises US$46, or with dinner, US$70-80.

Some beaches are more accessible than others, most uncrowded. The main resort area is Baie de Saint-Jean, which is two beaches divided by Eden Rock, the most visited beach with several bars and restaurants open for lunch or a snack, watersports, but no waterskiing, small boats, snorkelling rentals, ideal for families, good windsurfing, safe swimming, some snorkelling. Motorized watersports are only allowed 150 m off the beach. Others are Lorient, Marigot, Grand Cul de Sac on the N coast, Grande Saline, Gouverneur on the S, and Colombier and Flamands at the NW tip, to name but a few.

To get to **Gouverneur** from Gustavia take the road to Lurin. A sign will direct you to the dirt road leading down to the beach, lovely panoramic view over to the neighbouring islands, where there is white sand with palm trees on the beach. A legend says that the 17th century pirate, Montbars the Exterminator, hid his treasures in a cove here and they have never been found. Also a very good spot for snorkelling.

Colombier beach is the most beautiful on St Barts. It can not be reached by car but is well worth the 20-30 minute walk during which you have majestic views of the island. Park the car at Colombier, there are several trails going down to the beach. There are also several day tours by boat from Gustavia. **Flamands** beach is of very clean white sand, bordered with Latania palm trees. The surf can be rough, watersports available. In **Corossol** is the **Inter Oceans Museum**, a private collection of sea shells open for visitors daily 1000-1600. Petite Anse de Galet, in Gustavia, 3-5 minute walk from Fort Karl, is also known as Shell beach because it is covered in shells, not sand. Trees give shade and swimming is safe, shelling is of course extremely good.

OTHER SPORTS

Tennis at several hotels, guests take priority: *St Barth Beach Hotel, Taïwana, Manapany, Flamboyant Restaurant, Isle de France, Guanahani*. Also at ASCCO in Colombier, 2 lit courts, T 27 61 07, AJOE in Lorient, one lit court, T 27 67 63. Some opportunities for hiking. Horse riding at Flamands, Laure Nicolas, T 27 80 72. Body building at *St Barth Beach Hotel*, open 0730-2130, 100F, instructor on duty all the time. In the first week of December the Swedish

Marathon Race is held, a traditional annual race of 2, 10 and 15 km for men, women and children from anywhere.

FESTIVALS

Carnival is held before Lent, on Mardi Gras and Ash Wednesday. The Festival of Gustavia is 20 August, with dragnet fishing contests, dances and parties, while 24 August is the day of the island's patron saint, St-Barthélémy, when the church bells ring, boats are blessed and there are regattas, fireworks and a public ball. On 25 August the Feast of St Louis is celebrated in the village of Corossol, with a fishing festival, *petanque, belote,* dancing and fireworks. In the last week

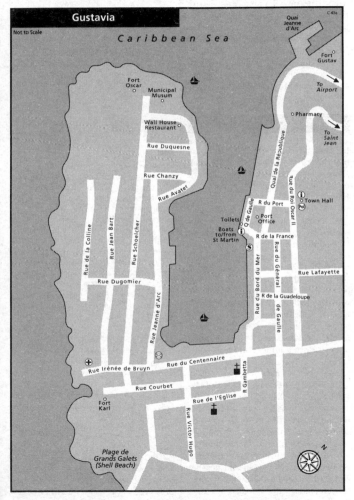

Gustavia

Not to Scale

Caribbean Sea

Quai Jeanne d'Arc

Fort Gustav

To Airport

Fort Oscar
Municipal Musum

Wall House Restaurant

Rue Duquesne

Pharmacy

To Saint Jean

Rue Chanzy

Rue Avate

Quai de la République

Rue du Roi Oskar II

R du Port

Town Hall

Rue de la Colline

Rue Jean Bart

Rue Schoelcher

Q de Gaulle

Toilets

Port Office

Boats to/from St Martin

R de la France

Rue du Général

de Gaulle

Rue Lafayette

Rue Dugomier

Rue du Bord du Mer

R de la Guadeloupe

Rue Jeanne d'Arc

Rue Irénée de Bruyn

Rue du Centenaire

R Gambetta

Rue Courbet

Rue de l'Eglise

Fort Karl

Rue Victor Hugo

Plage de Grands Galets (Shell Beach)

of July the northern villages hold special events. Fête du Vent is held in Lorient on 26-27 August with dragnet fishing contests, dancing, lottery and fireworks.

The St Barts regatta in February is the main event for sailors. Other regattas should be checked at Lou Lou's Marine Shop, Gustavia, because none is fixed annually. The local traditional sailboats participate on all public events with their own regattas like Bastille Day, Gustavia Day and one regatta a month.

A music festival is held annually in January with two weeks of classical, folk, jazz music and ballet performed by both local school children and guest artistes and musicians from abroad in Gustavia and Lorient churches.

GUSTAVIA

In **Gustavia**, the capital, there are branches of several well-known French shops (such as Cartier). The small crowd of *habitués* is mostly young, chic, and French. The food, wine, and aromas are equally Gallic. The harbour or Carénage was renamed Gustavia after the eighteenth-century Swedish king, Gustavus III, and became a free port, marking the beginning of the island's greatest prosperity. In 1852 a fire severely damaged the capital, although the Swedish influence is still evidenced in the city hall, the belfries, the Forts (Karl, Oscar and Gustave), the streetnames and the trim stone houses which line the harbour. **St Barts Municipal Museum** with an exhibition of the history, traditions and local crafts of the island, is at La Pointe, near the *Wall House*, open Monday-Thursday 0800-1200, 1330-1730, Friday 0800-1200, 1330-1700, Saturday 0830-1200, entrance 10F.

From Gustavia, you can head N to the fishing village of Corossol (see above), continuing to Colombier and the NW beaches; S over Les Castelets and the hills of Morne Lurin to Anse du Gouverneur; or to Saint-Jean and beaches and settlements on the E end. A hired car can manage all the roads.

Information for travellers

BEFORE TRAVELLING

● **Currency**
As on Saint-Martin, dollars are widely accepted but shops, restaurants will give a bad rate of exchange.

GETTING THERE

AIR
Scheduled flights from St Maarten with Air Guadeloupe (Juliana and Espérance airport), Air Caraïbes Exploitations (Espérance), Air St Barthélémy (Espérance) and Winair (Juliana airport); from Pointe-à-Pitre with Air Guadeloupe, Air Caraïbes Exploitations and Air St Barthélémy and from Basse-Terre with Air St Barthélémy; from St Thomas with Air St Thomas. San Juan, Puerto Rico, is served by Air St Thomas and Air Guadeloupe and Saint Croix by Coastal Air Transport, Anguilla by Winair and Coastal Air Transport and Saba by Winair. Charters available locally. Air Guadeloupe T 27 61 90, Winair T 27 61 01, Air Caraïbes (charter) T 27 99 41.

SEA
Enquire locally for **boat** services between St Barts and the French and Dutch sides of Saint-Martin/Sint Maarten. Gustavia Express goes to St Martin, Mon-Sat, departs Gustavia 0715, 1530, departs Marigot market place 0900, 1715, adults one way US$36 inc US$6 tax, round trip US$56, children up to 12 US$26 and US$31, cheaper for residents, ID required, T 27 54 10, 27 77 24, F 27 77 23 in Gustavia, T 87 99 03, F 87 73 03 in St-Martin. In December 1994 *Voyager I* began a 125-passenger ferry service between St Barts and St Martin, contact St Barth Ship Service for details, Quai de la République, T 27 77 38, F 27 67 95.

Several catamarans go to Sint Maarten, but you leave in the afternoon and return in the morning so a day trip is not possible. There are no other regular boats to other islands.

● **Anchorages**
(French flag) Outside the inner harbour of Gustavia, daily anchorage fee of US$2.50-5, depending on location. Inside the main harbour, stern to or on double moorings, fees are based on length of boat. Water, waste disposal, showers and toilets are available at the dock. Other anchorages around the island are free. Provisioning and some marine supplies.

ON ARRIVAL

● **Banks**
Banque Nationale de Paris (0745-1200, 1405-1530) with an automatic bankteller that is supposed to work 24 hrs with US and European credit cards, Visa, Mastercard and Eurocard, but is reported to work only with the French 'carte bleue', T 27 63 70, F 27 85 70; Banque Française Commerciale (0745-1215, 1400-1630, Mon, Tues, Thur, Fri), withdrawals at counter with Visa, Mastercard and Eurocard, T 27 62 62, F 27 87 75, both in Gustavia. BFC head office is at Saint-Jean, Galeries du Commerce (open Tues-Fri 0815-1215, 1400-1700, Sat 0800-1300) where there is an automatic teller open 24 hrs for withdrawals in US$ or F, T 27 65 88, 27 89 19, F 27 81 48. Crédit Martiniquais, at Le Carré d'Or in the centre of Gustavia (open Mon-Fri 0815-1215, 1400-1615), T 27 86 57, F 27 82 79. Crédit Agricole, rue Bord de Mer, Gustavia, automatic cash machine accepts nearly all cards inc eurocheque cards (cheaper than cash advance with credit card), also automatic bank note exchange machine (open Tues-Fri 0800-1300, 1430-1700, Sat 0800-1300), T 27 89 90, F 27 64 61. Crédit Lyonnais West Indies, rue Auguste Nyman, Gustavia (open Mon-Fri 0900-1200, 1400-1700), T 27 92 00, F 27 91 91.

● **Hours of business**
0800-1200, 1430-1700, morning only on Wed and Sat.

● **Shopping**
Wide range of goods available from T shirts to duty free luxury goods and fine wines. There are 5 small shopping centres in Saint-Jean: La Savane, Les Galeries du Commerce, La Villa Créole, Centre Commercial de Sain-Jean and Centre Commercial de Neptune. Gustavia also has lots of shops.

● **Useful addresses**
Gendarmerie: T 27 60 12; **Police**: T 27 66 66; **Fire**: T 27 62 31; **Sub Prefect**: T 27 63 28; **Radio St Barts**: T 27 74 74, broadcasting on FM 98 mHz; **Hospital**: T 27 60 85; **Doctor on call**: T 27 73 04.

ACCOMMODATION

● **Hotels**

Price guide

L1	over US$200	L2	US$151-200
L3	US$101-150	A1	US$81-100
A2	US$61-80	A3	US$46-60
B	US$31-45	C	US$21-30
D	US$12-20	E	US$7-11
F	US$4-6	G	up to US$3

In Gustavia: **A2** *La Presqu'île*, 10 rooms, T 27 64 60, F 27 72 30, restaurant specializes in French and Créole cooking (closed September- October); **L1** *Carl Gustaf*, Rue des Normands, Gustavia 97133, overlooking harbour, T 27 82 83, F 27 82 37, in the USA T 800-322 2223, in the UK T 800-373 742, 14 one or 2-bedroom suites, luxury, with high prices to match, breakfast and airport transfers, a/c, TV, kitchenette, private mini pool and sun deck, fax, stereos, gym-sauna, pool side restaurant, short walk to beach.

In hills: **L1-L3** *Les Castelets*, high in the hills, good views, a/c, fans, pool, terrace, antique furniture in rooms and suites, good but expensive restaurant, T 27 61 73, F 27 85 27.

Along the N coast: **L3** *Auberge de la Petite Anse*, T 27 64 60, F 27 72 30, 16 bungalows, pool, no restaurant, no credit cards, receptionist only there when you check in or out, picturesque but difficult path to Colombiers Beach starts here; at Colombier, overlooking Flamands beach is **L1** *François Plantation*, elegant plantation style hotel with 12 bungalows, pool, good restaurant, a/c, fan, telephone, satellite TV, T 27 78 82, F 27 61 26; **L1-L2** *Hotel Baie des Flamands*, modern, near Anse Rockefeller, 24 rooms on beach, triples available, excellent restaurant with fine wine list, closed Sept-mid Oct, T 27 64 85, F 27 83 98; **L1** *St Barth Isle de France*, BP 612, Baie de Flamands 97098, T 27 61 81, F 27 86 83, in USA 800-322 2223, luxury hotel, 33 rooms, bungalows and suites, tennis, 2 pools, squash, fitness centre, open air restaurant, marble bathrooms, can arrange watersports and horse riding; the luxury, 4-star **L1** *Manapany Cottages*, T 27 66

55, F 27 75 28, 32 cottages with 52 suites and rooms on hillside, descending to beach, 2 gourmet restaurants, can be booked through Mondotels in New York, T 212-719 5750 or 800-847 4249 or in Canada 800-255 3393; **L1-L2** *Emeraude Plage*, 28 bungalows, kitchenette, T 27 64 78, F 27 83 08; **L1** *Filao Beach*, 30 units, on beach, poolside bar and restaurant, T 27 64 84, F 27 62 24; **L1-L2** *Tropical*, 20 units, pool, short walk to beach, T 27 64 87, F 27 81 74; **L1-L2** *Le Tom Beach Hotel*, Plage de St-Jean, T 27 53 13, F 27 53 15, T 800-322 2223, 12 rooms on beach, luxury 4-poster beds, a/c, fans, private terraces, popular restaurant with good view and fresh lobster specialities; **L1-L3** *Village St-Jean*, 21 1-2 bedroom cottages with kitchenettes, 4 rooms **L3-A1** with mini-fridge, special packages available, a/c, fans, phones, pool, jacuzzi, Italian restaurant, short walk to beach, managed by Charneau family (T 27 61 39, F 27 77 96, in the USA T 800-322 2223), watersports facilities; a few hundred yards from Lorient beach is **L1** *La Banane*, owned by Jean-Marie Rivière, who owns 2 nightclubs in Paris, pastel painted bungalows, all different, beautifully furnished and decorated, 2 pools, lots of bananas, highly rec if you can afford it, fine dining, T 27 68 25, F 27 68 44; in the hills above Lorient, **L2-L3** *Les Islets Fleuris*, Hauts de Lorient 97133, T 27 64 22, F 27 69 72, 7 studios, pool, kitchenettes, lovely views over coastline, maid service, car rental available with room package; **L1** *The Christopher Hotel*, Pointe Milou, 40 rooms, a/c with sitting room and bathroom, terrace, balcony or patio, 3 rooms with facilities for the disabled, managed by Sofitel, shuttle service to beaches, large pool, Total Fitness Club, watersports arranged, closed in September, T 800-322-2223, T 27 63 63, F 27 92 92; **L1-L3** *El Sereno*, T 27 64 80, F 27 75 47, in USA T 800-322 2223, 16 cottages on edge of lagoon, 6 deluxe suites, a/c, TV, telephone, fridge, large pool, superb restaurant, gardens, hammocks, private beach, the hotel also manages **L1-L3** *El Sereno Beach Villas*, 9 villas on hillside, a/c, TV, phones, fans, kitchen, use of hotel facilities; **L1** *St Barths Beach Hotel*, 36 rooms and 16 bungalows, pool, gym, tennis, windsurfing school, built on strip of land between sea and lagoon, T 27 60 70, F 27 75 57; in the E, at Anse de Toiny, **L1** *Le Toiny*, T 27 88 88, F 27 89 30, 12 villa suites with a/c, fans, TV, phone, fax, plunge pools, restaurant, bar, room service, high luxury, closed Sept-October.

The above is just a selection. **Apartments and villas** may also be rented. In the USA contact French Caribbean International, T 800-322 2223 for their list of over 50 villas and apartments. On St Barts contact the following agencies: Sibarth Real Estate, BP 55, Gustavia, T 27 62 38, F 27 60 52; New Agency, Quai de la République, Gustavia, T 27 81 14, F 27 87 67; Claudine Mora Immobilier (CMI), Galeries du Commerce, Saint-Jean, T 27 80 88, F 27 80 85; Saint-Barth Immobilier, Rue Auguste Nyman, Gustavia, T 27 82 94, F 27 64 74; Jean Yves Robert Immobilier, Saint-Jean, T 27 60 65, F 27 60 56; Ici et Là, Quai de la République, T 27 78 78, F 27 78 28.

FOOD AND DRINK

● **Restaurants**

Food in St Barts is expensive, there are few bargains, expect to pay minimum US$25 for dinner (per person). There are many excellent restaurants all over the island, mostly French but some Créole and Italian. Very few vegetarian options, nearly all restaurants serve seafood. Several good ones on Saint-Jean beach; the hotel restaurants are generally good. In Gustavia: *Wall House*, T 27 71 83 for reservations, for good French cuisine on the waterfront with harbour view but overpriced wine; *Au Port* also offers fine dining overlooking the harbour, better value for money, rec, T 27 62 36 for reservations, one of the most expensive restaurants on the island; *Le Repaire* is a good restaurant at the *Yacht Club*, overlooking the harbour open 0600-0100, on rue de la République, offers few but well-prepared French dishes (also has a few rooms to let, T 27 72 48); *Côté Jardin* (T 27 70 47) for Italian food and ice creams. *Bar Le Select* is a central meeting spot, an informal bar for lunch with hamburger menu, but also one of the most popular night-time bars and sort of general store, only a few tables in a small garden. *L'Escale*, across the harbour, a pizza, pasta place with low prices for St Bart's but still expensive, T 27 81 06. Two local places serving Créole food are *Eddy's Ghetto* and *Les Lauriers*, T 27 64 12. For early starters try the bakery on Rue du Roi Oscar II, they open 0600 every day except Mon (closed). *La Crêperie* on the same street is open 0700-2230 and does American and Continental breakfast as well as sweet and savoury *crêpes*, salads and ice creams. On St-Jean beach, *Chez Martine* is nice and family-friendly; *Le Restaurant* next door offers gourmet food at reasonable prices, duck when planes take off, you are just a few metres from the airstrip.

GETTING AROUND

LAND TRANSPORT
● **Car hire**
Many agencies at the airport. Hertz T 27 71 14, Avis T 27 71 43, Budget T 27 66 30, Turbe T 27 71 42, Gumbs Rental T 27 61 93, Questel T 27 73 22, Aubin Mathieu T 27 73 03, Europcar T 27 73 33, Soleil Caraïbes T 27 67 18, Island Car Rental T 27 70 01. It is not easy to hire a car for only one day: ask your hotel to obtain a car if required. Scooters can be rented from Honda-Duffau T 27 70 59, Chez Beranger T 27 89 00, Ounalao Moto T 27 88 74, Saint Barth Moto Bike T 27 67 89. There are 2 gas stations, one near the airport terminal, open Mon-Sat 0730-1200, 1400-1700, the other in Lorient open Mon-Wed, Fri 0730-1700, Sat am. There is self service with payment to the cashier, or automatic service machine open 24 hrs using Visa card, maximum allowance F600.

● **Buses and taxis**
Taxi stand at the airport T 27 75 81, and in Gustavia T 27 66 31. Minibuses (and ordinary taxis) do island tours, 2½-3 hours, US$45 for 2 people, dropping you off at Baie de Saint-Jean and collecting you later for the boat if you are on a day trip.

COMMUNICATIONS

● **Postal services**
Three offices, in Gustavia: open 0800-1500 Mon, Tues, Thur, Fri, 0800-1400 Wed, Sat, T 27 62 00, F 27 82 03; in Saint-Jean: open 0800-1400 Mon, Tues, Thur, Fri, 0700-1100 Wed, Sat, T 27 64 02; in Lorient: open 0700-1100 Mon-Fri, 0800-1000 Sat, T 27 61 35.

● **Telecommunications**
The SiBarth agency on General de Gaulle in Gustavia, T 27 62 38, has a fax service and a mail holding service. There are phone booths on the Quai de Gaulle, at the airport, Galeries du Commerce and Flamands, among other places. There are some phones which take coins but most take phone cards. There is a USA Direct phone at the airport; you can phone the USA using a phone card and have the recipient return the call to the payphone.

ENTERTAINMENT

● **Nightlife**
Most of the nightlife starts around the bars at Bay Saint Jean. In Gustavia at *Bar Le Select* (closed Sun). In Lurin try *Why Not?* (open from 2100, disco, billiards, T 27 88 67) or in Lorient for a dinner show try *Club La Banane*.

Contact the Tourist Office for details of concerts and ballets held in the January music festival, see above.

TOURIST INFORMATION

● **Local tourist office**
Quai de Gaulle, Gustavia, T 27 87 27, F 27 74 47. Open Mon-Thur 0830-1230, 1400-1700, Fri 0830-1230, 1400-1600..

Martinique

THE ISLAND OF MARTINIQUE is 65 km long and 31 km wide. It lies at 14°40 North and 61° West and belongs to the Lesser Antilles. The Caribbean Sea is to the W, the Atlantic Ocean to the E. Martinique's neighbouring islands are Dominica to the N and St Lucia to the S, both separated from it by channels of approximately 40 km.

Martinique is volcanic in origin and one active volcano still exists, Mount Pelée (1,397m), situated to the NW, which had its last major eruption in 1902. The rest of the island is also very mountainous; the Pitons de Carbet (1,207m) are in the centre of the island and Montagne du Vauclin is in the S. Small hills or *mornes* link these mountains and there is a central plain, Lamentin, where the airport is situated. An extensive tropical rainforest covers parts of the N of the island, as well as pineapple and banana plantations, with the rest of the island mainly used for the cultivation of sugar cane. The coastline is varied: steep cliffs and volcanic, black sand coves in the N and on the rugged Atlantic coast, and calmer seas with large white or grey sand beaches in the S and on the Caribbean coast.

The population of the island is about 388,000 of which half live in the capital, Fort-de-France. This is the main settlement located on the Baie des Flamands on the W coast, with the burgeoning town of Lamentin, slightly inland, the second largest. The rest of Martinique is fairly evenly scattered with the small towns or *communes*.

HISTORY

When Christopher Columbus discovered Martinique either in 1493 or in 1502 (the date is disputed), it was inhabited by the Carib Indians who had exterminated the Arawaks, the previous settlers of the Lesser Antilles. Columbus named the island Martinica in honour of St Martin; the Caribs called it Madinina, or island of flowers.

The Spanish abandoned the island for richer pickings in Peru and Mexico and because of their constant troubles with the Caribs. In 1635 Martinique was settled by the French under the leadership of Pierre Belain d'Esnambuc. The cultivation of sugar cane and the importation of slaves from West Africa commenced. Fierce battles continued between the Caribs and the French until 1660 when a treaty was signed under which the Caribs agreed to occupy only the Atlantic side of the island. Peace was shortlived, however, and the Indians were soon completely exterminated.

During the seventeenth and eighteenth centuries England and France fought over their colonial possessions and in 1762 England occupied Martinique, only to return it to the French in exchange for Canada,

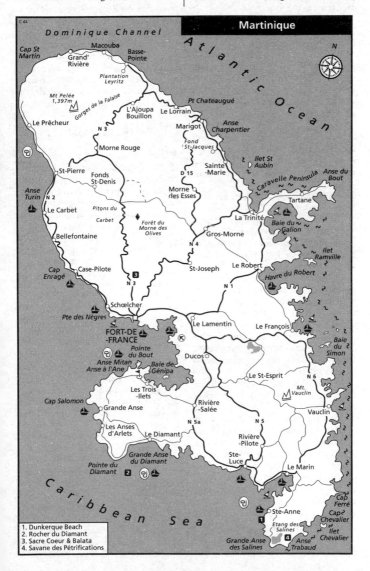

Martinique

Dominique Channel

Atlantic Ocean

Cap St Martin
Macouba
Grand' Rivière
Basse-Pointe
Plantation Leyritz
Mt Pelée 1,397m
Gorges de la Falaise
L'Ajoupa Bouillon
Le Lorrain
Pt Chateaugué
Le Prêcheur
N 3
Marigot
Anse Charpentier
Morne Rouge
Fond St-Jacques
Ilet St Aubin
St-Pierre
Fonds St-Denis
Sainte-Marie
D 15
Caravelle Peninsula
Anse du Bout
Anse Turin
N 2
Le Carbet
Pitons du Carbet
Morne des Esses
Tartane
Baie du Galion
Forêt du Morne des Olives
La Trinité
Bellefontaine
Gros-Morne
Ilet Ramville
Cap Enragé
Case-Pilote
N 3
St-Joseph
N 4
Le Robert
Havre du Robert
Schœlcher
Pte des Nègres
Le Lamentin
N 1
Le François
FORT-DE-FRANCE
Pointe du Bout
Anse Mitan
Anse à l'Ane
Baie de Génipa
Ducos
Baie du Simon
Cap Salomon
Les Trois-Ilets
Grande Anse
Rivière-Salée
Le St-Esprit
N 6
Mt. Vauclin
Les Anses d'Arlets
Le Diamant
N 5a
N 5
Vauclin
Rivière-Pilote
Pointe du Diamant
Grande Anse du Diamant
Ste-Luce
Le Marin
Cap Ferré
Cap Chevalier
Ilet Chevalier
Ste-Anne
Etang des Salines
Grande Anse des Salines
Anse Trabaud

Caribbean Sea

1. Dunkerque Beach
2. Rocher du Diamant
3. Sacre Coeur & Balata
4. Savane des Pétrifications

Senegal, the Grenadines, St Vincent, and Tobago. France was content to retain Martinique and Guadeloupe because of the importance of the sugar cane trade at the time.

More unrest followed in the French Caribbean colonies when in 1789 the French Revolution encouraged slaves to fight for their emancipation. Martinique was occupied by the English again from 1794 to 1802, at the request of the plantation owners of the island who wanted to preserve the status quo and avoid slave revolts.

Slavery was finally abolished in 1848 by the French and in the late nineteenth century tens of thousands of immigrant workers from India came to Martinique to replace the slave workforce on the plantations.

In 1946 Martinique became a French Department, and in 1974 a Region.

Political parties include the Progressive Party of Martinique, Socialists Communists, Union for French Democracy, Rally for the Republic and several small left-wing parties. A small independence movement exists but most people prefer greater autonomy without total independence from France. In the October 1990 elections, pro-independence groups entered the Regional Council for the first time, winning nine of the 41 seats. The ruling Progressive Party lost its majority but remained in power with 14 seats.

In 1988 Martinique voted for the Socialist François Mitterand for president and in the 1995 elections the island remained socialist. In the first round the socialist candidate, Lionel Jospin received 36.4% of the vote compared with 29.1% for Jacques Chirac, while in the second round M Jospin won 59.9%. However, the turnout was low at only 48.8% of the electorate in the second round and of those, 5-6% cast spoilt papers.

GOVERNMENT

Martiniquans are French citizens and Martinique is officially and administratively part of France. The President of the French Republic is Head of State and the island is administered by a Prefect, appointed by the French Government. It is represented by three Deputies to the National Assembly in Paris, by two Senators in the Senate and by one representative on the Economic and Social Council. The Legislative Council of Martinique has 36 members elected for six years, who sit on the Regional Council which includes the locally elected Deputies and Senators.

THE ECONOMY

Martinique is dependent upon France for government spending equivalent to about 70% of gnp, without which there would be no public services or social welfare. Even so, unemployment is high at over a quarter of the labour force, the economy is stagnant and the balance of payments deficit expands continuously. The economy is primarily agricultural, about 5% of the economically active population is engaged in farming and fishing, and the main export crops are bananas, sugar, rum and pineapples, while aubergines, avocados, limes and flowers are being developed. Crops grown mainly for domestic consumption include yams, sweet potatoes, Caribbean cabbages, manioc, breadfruit, plantains, tomatoes and green beans. Fishing contributes to the local food supply but most of the domestic market is met by imports. Most manufactured goods are imported, making the cost of living very high. There is some light industry and the major industrial plants are an oil refinery, rum distilleries and a cement works, while there is also fruit canning, soft drinks manufacturing and polyethylene and fertilizer plants.

Tourism is the greatest area of economic expansion. In 1988 hotel and villa capacity was 3,274 rooms and the island received 280,372 visitors arriving by air and 385,513 cruise ship visitors, all of whom spent US$230mn. In the 5 years to 1993, stopover visitors rose by 31% to 366,353, while cruise ship passenger arrivals grew more slowly, by 11%, to 428,695. Of the total stopover visitors, 71% come from France and 4% from the USA, while of the total cruise ship visitors, 83% come from the USA and only 5% from the whole of Europe. Tourism income is now around US$300mn a year; cruise ship passengers spend an average of US$42 per person.

CULTURE

See the general introduction to the French Antilles.

FESTIVALS

Martinique has more than its fair share of festivals. The main carnival, **Mardi Gras**, takes place in February when the whole of Martinique takes to the streets in fantastic costume. On Ash Wednesday, black and white clad 'devils' parade the streets lamenting loudly over the death of Vaval. At Eastertime, the children fly coloured kites which once had razors attached to their tails for kite fights in the wind. At *Toussaint* in November, the towns are lit by candlelight processions making their way to the cemeteries to sit with the dead.

Every village celebrates its Saint's Day with games, shows and folk dancing, usually over the nearest weekend. The town of Saint-Marie holds a cultural festival in July, and Ajoupa-Bouillon has a festival of the crayfish, while in August the town of Marin holds its cultural festival.

Among the many other festivities there is the Martinique Food Show, in April, a culinary fair with lots of competitions; the May of St-Pierre, in May, which commemorates the eruption of the volcano Mt Pelée; the biennial International Jazz Festival, or World Crossroads of the Guitar, in December (see also **Information for travellers, Entertainment**).

Martinique : fact file

Geographic

Land area	1,128 sq km
forested	44.3%
pastures	17.0%
cultivated	16.0%

Demographic

Population (1995)	388,000
annual growth rate (1990-95)	1.5%
urban	80.5%
rural	19.5%
density	344 per sq km
Religious affiliation	
Roman Catholic	84.6%
Birth rate per 1,000 (1994)	14.9
	(world av 25.0)

Education and Health

Life expectancy at birth,	
male	74.7 years
female	81.0 years
Infant mortality rate	
per 1,000 live births (1993)	4.0
Physicians (1991)	1 per 584 persons
Hospital beds	1 per 97 persons
Calorie intake as %	
of FAO requirement	117%
Population age 25 and over	
with no formal schooling	9.8%
Literate males (over 15)	91.8%
Literate females (over 15)	93.2%

Economic

GNP (1991 market prices)	
	US$3,375mn
GNP per capita	US$9,210
Public external debt (1994)	
	US$186.7mn
Tourism receipts (1993)	US$332mn
Inflation (annual av 1989-94)	3.3%
Radio	1 per 5.4 persons
Television	1 per 5.8 persons
Telephone	1 per 2.5 persons

Employment

Population economically active (1990)	
	164,870
Unemployment rate (1994)	26.2%
% of labour force in	
agriculture	5.2
mining and manufacturing	6.0
construction	5.7
Military forces (French troops)	1,542

Source *Encyclopaedia Britannica*

WATERSPORTS

Sailing and windsurfing at Club de la Voile de Fort-de-France, Pointe de la Vièrge, T 61 49 69, and Pointe des Carrières, T 63 31 37; Club Nautique de Marin, Bassin la Tortue, Pointe du Marin, T 74 92 48; Club Nautique du François, Route de la Jetée, T 54 31 00; Club Nautique du Vauclin, Pointe Faula, T 74 50 58; Yacht Club de la Martinique, Fort de France, T 70 23 60; Base de Plein Air et de Loisirs, Anse Spoutourne, Tartane, T 58 24 32. There are glass bottom boats, motor boats, sailing boats for excursions and lots of craft for hire. Windsurfing is available on hotel beaches where there are board rentals. Jet skiing, sea scooters and water skiing at Pointe du Bout hotel beaches, Marouba Club (Carbet) and Pointe Marin beach in Ste-Anne. Many hotels like Bambou, La Dunette, Diamant-les-Bains organize fishing trips with local fishermen for their guests. Deep sea fishing can be arranged at Bathy's Club (*Meridien*), T 66 00 00 or Rayon Vert, T 78 80 56, for around 4,000F per boat.

Gommier races (huge rectangular sailing boats with coloured sails and teams of oarsmen) are an amazing sight at festivals all over the island from July to January. In Fort-de-France races take place in November and December from the little beach next to Desnambuc quay. Other major sailing occasions include the Schoelcher International Nautical Week in February, with sailing and windsurfing competitions; International Sailing Week in March (Yacht Club of Fort-de-France); the Aqua Festival, the Great Nautical Celebration at Robert in April; the Round Yawl Regatta Tour of Martinique in July or August, when over a period of 8 days about 20 round yawls set off for a colourful race.

Diving is especially good along the coral reef between St-Pierre and Le Prêcheur, over the wrecks off St-Pierre and along the S coast. A medical certificate is required unless you are a qualified diver, in which case you need your certification card. There are lots of dive operators, most of which are based at the large hotels, we list a few here: Cressma, BP 574 Anse Madame, 97233 Schoelcher; Méridien Plongée, *Hotel Méridien*, T 66 00 00 ext 225; Oxygene Bleue, *Hôtel Bakoua*, T 66 02 02; Tropic Alizes, *Hôtel La Batelière*, T 61 49 49; Histoire d'Eau, BP1-97 227 Ste-Anne, T 76 92 98; Carib Scuba Club, BP3, 97250 St-Pierre, T 55 59 84; Club Nautique du Marin, Pointe du Marin, T 74 92 48; Club Bleu Marine Evasion, *Marine Hôtel*, Pointe la Chéry, T 76 46 00; Planete Bleue, Marina Pointe du Bout, T 66 08 79/66 06 22; Sub Diamant Rock, *Hôtel Novotel*, T 76 42 42, F 76 22 87.

For those who do not dive, there is the *Seaquarium* glass-bottomed boat at Marina Pointe du Bout, Trois Ilets, T 66 05 50, F 66 05 52. To get even further under the water, there are two semi-submersibles: *Aquascope Seadom Explorer*, Marina Pointe du Bout, T 68 36 09 and *Zemis Aquascope*, rue de Caritan, Ponton de la Mairie, T 74 87 41.

SPORTS

Tennis: courts are at many large hotels; *Bakoua*; *Club Méditerranée*; *Plantation Leyritz*; *PLM Azur Carayou*; *Novotel*; *Meridien*, *Hôtel Casino la Batelière* and others where visitors can play at night as well as during the day. There are also about 40 clubs round the island where you can play by obtaining temporary membership. For more information contact *La Ligue Regional de Tennis*, Petit Manoir, Lamentin, T 51 08 00.

Golf: At Trois-Ilets is a magnificent, 18-hole championship golf course with various facilities including two tennis courts, shops, snackbar, lessons and equipment hire. Green fees in high season are US$46 and in low season US$39, or you can book for a week (US$285, US$227) or a month (US$960, US$900). Electric carts and other equipment is available for rent. Contact *Golf Country Club de la Martinique*, 97229 Trois-Ilets,

T 68 32 81, F 68 38 97. Two mini-golf courses are at Madinina Plage à Schoelcher and Anse l'Etang à Tartane.

Riding is a good way to see Martinique's superb countryside; Ranch Jack, Anse d'Arlets, Galochas, T 68 37 69; Black Horse, La Pagerie, Trois-Ilets, T 66 00 04; La Cavae, Diamant, T 76 20 23; and others offering schooling, hacking and other facilities. At *Plantation Leyritz* there are 2 horses for guests' use.

Cycling. Touring the island by bike is one of the activities offered by the Parc Naturel Régional. For information T 73 19 30. VT Tilt, Anse Mitan, Trois-Ilets, offers excursions by bike and cycle rallies, T 66 01 01, F 51 14 00.

Spectator Sports: Mongoose and snake fights and cockfights are widespread from December to the beginning of August at Pitt Ducos, Quartier Bac, T 56 05 60; Pitt Marceny (the most popular), Le Lamentin, T 51 28 47, Pitt Cléry, Rivière-Pilote, T 62 61 69 and many others. Horse racing is at the Carère racetrack at Lamentin, T 51 25 09.

FORT-DE-FRANCE

Fort-de-France was originally built around the Fort St Louis in the seventeenth century. It became the capital of the island in 1902 when the former capital, St-Pierre, was completely obliterated by the eruption of Mount Pelée. The city of today consists of a bustling, crowded centre bordered by the waterfront and the sprawling suburbs which extend into the surrounding hills and plateaux. The bars, restaurants, and shops give a French atmosphere quite unlike that of other Caribbean cities. The port of Fort-de-France is situated to the E of the town centre, where cargo ships and luxury cruise liners are moored side by side.

The impressive **Fort St-Louis** still functions as a military base. Built in Vauban style, it dominates the waterfront. It is sometimes open to the public for exhibitions but once inside beware the low ceiling arches said to have been designed to foil the invading English who were generally taller than the French at that time. Adjacent to the fort is **La Savane**, a park of 5 hectares planted with palms, tamarinds, and other tropical trees and shrubs. The park contains statues of two famous figures from the island's past: a bronze statue of Pierre Belain d'Esnambuc, the leader of the first French settlers on Martinique; and a white marble statue of the Empress Josephine (now beheaded), first wife of Napoléon Bonaparte, who was born on the island.

The **Bibliothèque Schoelcher** is situated on the corner of Rue Victor Sévère and Rue de la Liberté, just across the road from the Savane. This magnificent baroque library was constructed out of iron in 1889 in Paris by Henri Pick, also the architect of the Eiffel Tower. The following year it was dismantled, shipped and reassembled in Fort-de-France where it received the extensive collections of books donated by Victor Schoelcher (responsible for the abolition of slavery in Martinique). Today it still functions as a library and regularly holds exhibitions (open Mon-Fri 0830-1200, 1400-1600, Sat 0830-1200, T 70 26 67).

Just along the Rue de la Liberté towards the seafront is the **Musée Départemental de la Martinique**, also called **Musée d'Archéologie et de Prehistoire**. It contains relics of the Arawak and Carib Indians: pottery, statuettes, bones, reconstructions of villages, maps, etc. Open 0900-1700 Monday-Friday, 0900-1200 Saturday, T 71 57 05. Price of admission 12F, children 3F. Worth a visit.

In the centre of town, in the Square of Père Labat, rue Schoelcher, there is a second chance to see the baroque architecture of Henri Pick with the **Cathedral of St Louis** which towers above the Fort-de-France skyline. The interior is very beautiful, there is a magnificent organ and stained glass windows depicting the life of St Louis.

The **Parc Floral et Culturel** (also called **Galerie de Géologie et de Botanie** or **Exotarium**) is a shady park containing two galleries, one of which concentrates on the geology of the island, the other on the flora. Almost 2,800 species of plants have been identified in Martinique and the Parc Floral has a very good selection. Open Tuesday-Saturday, 0900-1200, closed Sunday, Monday, T 70 66 25. Admission 5F. The Aquarium, on Boulevard de la Marne, has 250 species, open daily 0900-1900, 38F adults, 25F children, T 73 02 20, rather overpriced for its size.

Next to the Parc Floral are a feature

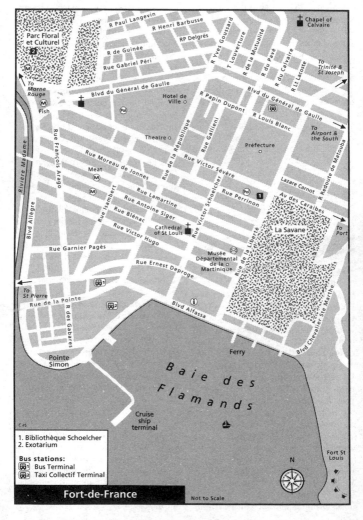

1. Bibliothèque Schoelcher
2. Exotarium

Bus stations:
🚌1 Bus Terminal
🚌2 Taxi Collectif Terminal

Fort-de-France

Not to Scale

of Fort-de-France not to be missed, the markets. The fishmarket is by the Madame river, where the fishermen unload from their small boats or *gommiers*. Close by is one of several markets selling fruit, vegetables and flowers as well as exotic spices. The markets are always humming with activity from 0500 to sunset, but are best on Friday and Saturday. A fresh green coconut picked from a huge pile by the seller and hacked open with a machete, makes a refreshing drink for about 4F.

NORTH MARTINIQUE AND THE EAST COAST

The coastal road heading N from Fort-de-France passes through several fishing villages and is flanked by beaches that gradually become blacker with volcanic sand. At the popular beach of Anse Turin just N of **Le Carbet**, is the small **Gauguin Museum**. The artist stayed at Anse Turin during 1887 before he went to Tahiti. Open from 0930 every day. Admission 15F, T 78 22 66. The museum has letters, sketches and some reproductions of the artist's work as well as some pieces by local artists and examples of traditional costume.

Carbet also has a small zoo containing seventy species of animal including monkeys, lions, and ocelots, mainly from the Amazon region. Open every day 0900-1800. Admission 15F, children 10F, T 78 00 64.

To the N of Carbet is the famous **St-Pierre**. The modern village is built on the ruins of the former capital of Martinique, which was destroyed by a cloud of molten volcanic ash when Mount Pelée erupted in May 1902. As the cultural and economic capital, the town was known as the 'Petit Paris' of the West Indies. Out of 26,000 inhabitants there was only one survivor, named Cylbaris, a drunkard who had been thrown into a cell for the night. Today his small cell is one of the ruins that visitors can still see. It is hidden away behind

the remains of the once splendid and celebrated theatre of St-Pierre. The ruined church, originally built in the Fort of St-Pierre, also survives. In the **Musée de Saint-Pierre, Museum of Vulcanology** (open every day, 0900-1700, T 78 15 16, admission 10F) is an interesting collection of objects and documents evoking life before 1902 and remains from the disaster: household metal and glass objects charred and deformed by the extreme heat, photographs and volcanology displays. Guided tours of the Museum are available. The town of St-Pierre is well worth a visit and is an eerie reminder of destructive natural forces that dominate life in the Caribbean. For a guided tour in English or French ask at *La Guinguette* restaurant; tours about 40 minutes, Monday-Friday 0930-1300, 1430-1730, around 15F per person. You can even go in a submersible down to 100m to visit the wrecks in the bay, recommended, T 78 18 18, F 78 20 84, Compagnie de la Baie de St-Pierre.

The next village on the coastal road is the picturesque fishing village of **Le Prêcheur**. The road then continues towards the spectacular beach of Anse Ceron where the sand seems to be at its blackest. A rock called the Pearl juts out from the sea which is roughish on this beach but safe for swimming. It is a wild and beautiful beach, a pleasant change from the calm, white sand tourist beaches in the S. The coastal road ends a mile or two further on at another beach, Anse Couleuvre.

At the extreme N of the island is another small fishing village, **Grande Rivière**. There is no direct road linking Grande Rivière and Le Prêcheur but there is a coastal track through the rain forest which is a lovely 6-hour walk crossing several rivers (see **Tourist Agencies**, Island Information). The first 20 minutes on a concrete road are discouraging, but once in the forest the path is cooler and the views beautiful. Grande Rivière itself is set in breathtaking scenery characteristic of this part of the island; plunging cliffs covered with the lush vegetation of the rainforest. The island of Dominica faces the village from across the sea. Winding roads lead through the mountains to the next village, Macouba, perched on top of a cliff.

The area of **Basse-Pointe** is the pineapple cultivation area of the island, where huge fields of spikey pineapple tops cover the easternmost flanks of Mount Pelée. Inland from here is **Plantation Leyritz**, one of several former plantation houses (mostly in ruin). The restored eighteenth century building is now a hotel and restaurant (recommended) and anyone can stroll around the extensive grounds. There is a tiny exhibition of dolls made from plants and vegetables, exploiting the colours and textures of tropical leaves, which is open every day from 1000-1830, T 78 53 92.

From the road along the NE coast of the island tempting beaches with crashing waves are visible, but the Atlantic Coast is too dangerous for swimming. However, there is a safe beach at Anse Azérot, just S of **Ste-Marie**. To the N is the ancient monastery of **Fond St-Jacques**, built in 1658, where a restored chapel, a mill and aqueduct can be seen.

The **Père Labat Museum** in Ste-Marie presents the life story of the famous Dominican friar who lived in Martinique at the turn of the eighteenth century. Also, the history of the island is interestingly summarized using documents and photographs. Open 0900-1800 every day. There is a plan to transfer the museum to the slavery museum (Musée de l'Esclavage) in Fort-de-France.

Nearby, in the St James Distillery, is the **Rum Museum**. The free guided tour includes an explanation of the process of rum production and its history, and rum tasting. There is a collection of engraved spoons. The grounds are also very attractive. Rum is sold here but it is cheaper at the airport at the duty free shops. Open Monday to Friday, 0900-1700 and Saturday and Sunday 0900-

1300, T 69 30 02, admission free. A little inland is **Morne des Esses** which has a good view of Trinité and the Caravelle peninsula. There is an exhibition of Carib-style handicrafts: pottery, baskets, rugs and bags; and artisans can be seen at work.

The sea front at **La Trinité** looks out onto the Caravelle Peninsula, where the vegetation is scrubby but the scenery is gently interesting. The peninsula has beaches at Tartane (the only village on the Caravelle), Anse l'Etang (the best) and Anse du Bout. It is an area protected by the **Parc Naturel of Martinique**; several well-marked paths criss-cross the peninsula so that visitors can enjoy the varied flora and fauna. It is also possible to visit the historic ruins of the **Château Dubuc** and various buildings that belonged to a Monsieur Dubuc, a smuggler and pirate who lived in the area. Open Monday-Friday 0800-1200, admission 5F, children 2F.

The southernmost village on the Atlantic Coast is **Vauclin** where the main activity is fishing. Pointe Faula is a very safe beach here, with dazzling white sand and shallow water. To the S of Vauclin a road leads to Anse Macabou, a group of impressive white sand beaches.

THE TROPICAL RAINFOREST AND MOUNT PELEE

La Route de la Trace winds through the tropical rainforest from Fort-de-France to Morne Rouge, Ajoupa-Bouillon and Mount Pelée. The forest itself is truly magnificent, covering the sides of the steep, inland mountains (Les Pitons de Carbet and Pelée) with a bewildering array of lush, green vegetation that stretches for miles. Giant bamboo, mountain palms, chestnut and mahogany trees, over a thousand species of fern and many climbing and hanging parasitic plants and orchids are examples of rainforest vegetation. The forest is protected as part of Martinique's Parc Naturel and makes interesting walking country (see **Tourist Agencies**).

At **Balata**, not far from the capital along the Route de la Trace is the bizarre building of **Sacré Coeur**, a close replica of the Parisian Cathedral, perched high up in the forest. A little further along the road is the **Botanical Garden of Balata** with superb views across to the capital. The gardens have a marvellous setting, though are slightly disappointing, depending on the season, when compared with the pictures in the official brochure. They are normally good in November-December. However, the gardens are well planted and the display of anthuriums, ranging from dark maroon, crimson and pink to white, is impressive. Look out for the numerous hummingbirds and brilliant green lizards. Umbrellas are provided if it is raining and the foliage gleams impressively when wet. Open 0900-1700 every day, T 64 48 73. Admission 30F, children aged 7-15, 10F. All signs are in French.

As the Route de la Trace winds its way through the rainforest, the flanks of the surrounding mountains are clearly visible, covered with cultivated tropical flowers such as anthuriums and ginger lilies. The **MacIntosh plantation**, a 5 km steep climb from Morne Rouge, has a tourist route through its extensive fields of waxy blooms. Open Monday-Friday, 0900-1630, adults 20F, children 8F, T 50 34 21.

Mount Pelée is reached via a track branching off the Route de la Trace, between Morne Rouge and Ajoupa-Bouillon. From the car park at the foot of the volcano there is a view of the Atlantic Coast, Morne Rouge and the bay of St-Pierre. The mountain air is deliciously fresh and cool even at the foot of the volcano. Not far away are **Les Gorges de la Falaise**, the dramatic waterfalls of the Falaise river, wonderful for swimming in, accessible only by following the course of the river on foot. Much of the walk is actually in the water and you clamber over waterfalls, making the carrying of cameras impractical.

The local Syndicat d'Initiative in Ajoupa-Bouillon organizes guided tours up the river, T 53 77 35.

At Ajoupa-Bouillon you can visit a botanical garden, **Les Ombrages** T 53 31 90, entrance 15F, children 5F) and a butterfly garden (open daily 0900-1600, 25F, T 59 35 46).

SOUTH MARTINIQUE

The small village of **Les Trois-Ilets** across the bay from Fort-de-France has a charming main square and is surrounded by tourist attractions. At the Museum of La Pagerie, where Empress Josephine was born, it is possible to walk among the ruins of the old plantation house and the sugar processing plant. There is a collection of furniture, letters, and portraits which belonged to the Empress. Also on display are local works of art both contemporary and dating from the precolumbian era. Open Tuesday-Friday 0900-1730, Saturday-Sunday 0900-1300, 1430-1730, entrance 20F, children 5F, T 68 34 55, 68 38 34, F 68 38 41. Close by is the sugar cane museum (**Musée de la Canne**) which uses documents, machinery and superb models of sugar processing plant to illustrate the history of the Martiniquan sugar industry. Guided tours are available. Open 0900-1700 every day except Monday, entrance 10F, children 5F, T 68 32 04. The pottery at Trois-Ilets has an exhibition room where traditional pottery is on sale.

A short bus ride from Trois-Ilets is the tourist complex of **Pointe du Bout**, directly opposite Fort-de-France, and linked by regular ferries. There is a marina, shops, discothèques, cafés, restaurants, sport facilities and a conglomeration of luxury hotels. The first beach after stepping off the ferry is a crowded strip of sand in front of the *Hotel Meridien*, almost completely covered with deckchairs for hire. Perhaps preferable is the beach at **Anse Mitan**, a 5-minute walk away, where there are numerous reasonably priced restaurants and bars. There is a direct ferry from the capital to **Anse à l'Ane**, a little way along the coast to the W. This beach is quieter than Anse Mitan and Pointe du Bout and has a pleasant atmosphere. Nearby, in the **Musée des Coquillages** (seashell museum), local scenes are depicted using seashells. Open 1000-1200 and 1500-1700 every day. Admission 15F, children 5F, T 68 34 97.

At Grande Anse is a magnificent beach, less frequented by tourists than the beaches at Pointe du Bout, although it does get more crowded at weekends. The pretty village of **Anse d'Arlets** is nearby.

Just S of Anse d'Arlets and around the **Pointe du Diamant** is Diamant beach. This is an idyllic beach stretching for 2½ miles along the S coast and dominated by the famous **Rocher du Diamant** (Diamond Rock). This huge rock, of volcanic origin, is about a mile out to sea and was occupied by the English at the beginning of the eighteenth century. They stationed cannons and about 200 soldiers there before the French reconquered it a year and a half later in 1605. British ships passing it still salute "Her Majesty's Ship Diamond Rock". The beach itself is secluded and bordered by groves of coconut palms and almond trees. The area is pleasantly unspoiled by the tourist industry. The sand is splendid but there are strong currents and it is advisable not to swim out too far, or indeed at all in rough conditions.

Inland and to the E of Diamant is the town of **Rivière-Pilote**, the largest settlement in the S of the island. The Mauny Rum distillery is located here, where free guided tours are available, Monday-Friday 1000, 1100, 1230, 1400 and 1530, T 62 62 08. The famous Cléry cock-fighting pit stages regular mongoose-snake fights. These take place on Sunday afternoon, T 62 61 69. From the town of **Le Marin**, southwards are long white sand beaches lined with palm groves, and calm clear sea which epitomize the classic image of the Caribbean. Marin itself boasts a very fine eighteenth

century Jesuit church.

At **Ste-Anne** is the extensive Club Méditerrannée complex. It has its own private beach adjacent to the long public beach, which has a spectacular view along the SW coast, including Rocher du Diamant. Ste-Anne beach is picturesque and shady with trees that overhang the sea in some places. There is a wide selection of lively bars and restaurants, some selling snacks or *menu du jour*, others more expensive. You can rent all types of watersports equipment: windsurfers, catamarans, seedoos, kayaks, sunfish, or take a sea plane ride. The swimming area is marked off with yellow buoys.

The road heading E from Marin leads to the beach at Cap Chevalier, a popular family beach at weekends. Among others along the barrier reef, the islet of Chevalier is visible from here.

At the southernmost tip of the island is the famous Grande Anse des Salines and the beaches of Dunkerque, Baham and Anse Trabaud, all of which are remarkably attractive. Inland from Anse Trabaud lies the salt marsh and the forest petrified by former lava flow. The forest is now sadly diminished thanks to the efforts of museums and souvenir hunters.

Information for travellers

BEFORE TRAVELLING

● **Documents**
See French Antilles, page 584.

● **Climate**
The lushness of Martinique's vegetation is evidence that it has a far higher rainfall than many of the islands, due to its mountainous relief. The wet season lasts from June to late November and the frequency of sudden heavy showers make an umbrella or raincoat an essential piece of equipment. The cooler dry season lasts from December to May and the year round average temperature is 26°C although the highlands and Mount Pelée are quite cool.

● **Cost of living**
Remember that the standard of living is high and expect to pay French prices or higher, which means expensive. Small beers or cokes cost around 15F, petrol 52F/litre, a nice meal at a medium priced restaurant will be at least 350F for 2.

GETTING THERE

AIR

From Europe: Scheduled direct flights from Europe are with Air France, which has flights from Paris; Air Liberté flies from Bordeaux, Lyon, Nantes, Paris and Toulouse; AOM French Airlines from Paris. Air France also has direct flights from Cayenne, Caracas, Miami, Pointe-à-Pitre, Port-au-Prince and Santo Domingo. Ask Air France for youth fares if you are under 26, or for seasonal prices, as they vary. Nouvelles Frontières has charter flights from France.

From North America: Air Canada flies from Montréal via Barbados. American Eagle flies from San Juan, with connections from the USA.

From the Caribbean: Local airlines include SNAM (Société Nouvelle Air Martinique), which flies to Guadeloupe (884F), St Lucia (800F), Sint Maarten, St Vincent, Canouan and Union Island, Air Guadeloupe, which flies to Pointe-à-Pitre, Cubana from Havana, while LIAT flies to Anguilla, Antigua, Barbados, Dominica, St Lucia, St Vincent, San Juan, Tortola and Trinidad.

There are connecting flights from the UK via San Juan, Antigua or Barbados, and from the USA via Miami, linked with most major North and South American airports.

SEA

Caribbean Express ferry service to Dominica and Pointe-à-Pitre, Guadeloupe, runs only at weekends, see **Dominica** for details. Terminal Inter Iles 97200 Fort-de-France, T 63 12 11, F 63 34 47, for timetable and fares. Overnight packages available with several hotels, also car hire.

Agents for the more frequent *Atlantica* ferry to Dominica and Guadeloupe are Brudey Frères, 108 rue Victor Hugo, 97200 Fort-de-France, T 70 08 50 (or T 91 60 87/97 77 82/90 04 48 for timetable information. Martinique is on the route of most Caribbean cruises. Information on travelling by cargo boat can be obtained from the travel agency next door to the CGM office at the harbour, but if going to South America it is cheaper to fly. CGM has a trans-Atlantic cargo ship from Le Havre/Dunkerque to Fort-de-France and Pointe-à-Pitre, T 55 32 00/46 25 70 00, F 46 25 78 05, cars can be brought as accompanied baggage, single or double cabins, a/c, bathroom, swimming pool, sports room (see **Introduction and Hints**).

● **Ports of entry**
(French Flag) Fort-de-France, St-Pierre, Le Marin. No fees or visas for EC or US citizens. French forms to clear in and clear out.

Customs in Fort-de-France open 0800-1100, 1300-1700 daily, inc holidays, no overtime fees charged; at Le Marin from 0730 until lunchtime, at St Pierre on Wed am.

● **Anchorages**
The facilities are among the best in the Caribbean. Anchorages at St-Pierre, Fort-de-France, Anse Mitan, Les Trois-Ilets, Anse Noir, Grand and Petit Anse d'Arlets, Ste-Anne, Cul-de-Sac Marin. Marinas at Fort-de-France, Les Trois-Ilets, Le Marin. The marina at Pointe du Bout

is reported safe, but congested and hot. Major charter companies inc Moorings Antilles at Club Nautique du Marin (T 74 75 39, F 74 76 44), Sun Sail (Soleil et Voile, Capitainerie Marina Pointo du Bout, T 66 09 14), and Stardust (Port de Plaisance du Marin, T 74 98 17, F 74 98 12). Many other smaller companies. Excellent provisioning, stock up on French wines.

For those looking to hitch on a boat, consult the noticeboards at the Yacht Clubs, especially the bar at the Public Jetty and refuelling at the W end of Boulevard Alfassa on the Baie des Flamands.

ON ARRIVAL

● Airports

Lamentin Airport, T 59 81 81. There is a Tourist Office for hotel reservations and information, T 51 28 55, Crédit Agricole and Change Caraïbes for foreign currency exchange (see below), car rental offices and ground tour operators. To get to the airport at Lamentin, either take a taxi, which presents no difficulties but is expensive, or take a bus marked 'Ducos' and ask to be set down on the highway near the airport. It is then a 100 metres' walk. On arrival at Lamentin, walk to near Budget office, about 300m, and wait for the minibus. The fare is 10F and the buses take reasonable-sized luggage.

● Airlines

Air France, T 55 33 00; Air Liberté, T 59 81 81; AOM French Airlines, T 70 09 16/51 74 85; Air Martinique T 51 08 09/60 00 23; Nouvelles Frontières-Corsair, T 70 59 70; American Airlines, T 51 12 29; LIAT, T 51 10 00/51 21 11. Charter companies inc Air Foyal, T 51 11 54; Air Caraïbe, T 51 17 27; Air St-Martin, T 51 57 03; Jet Aviation Service, T 51 57 03; Antilles Aero Service, T 51 66 88; Envol, T 68 45 49 (sight seeing trips round the island).

● Banks

Change Caraïbes, Airport, open 0730-2100, daily, T 51 57 91, Rue Ernest Deproge, 97200, Fort-de-France, open 0730-1800 Mon-Fri, 0800-1230 Sat, T 60 28 40; Crédit Agricole also has an office at the airport for currency exchange, open 0730-1230, 1430-1800 Tues-Fri, 0800-1130 Sat, T 51 25 99, also at rue Ernest Deproge, T 73 17 06, closed Mon, open Sat am. Banque Française Commerciale, 6/10 rue Ernest Deproge, T 63 82 57. Banque des Antilles Françaises, 34 rue Lamartine, T 73 93 44, Société Générale de Banque aux Antilles, 19 rue de la Liberté, T 71 69 83. Crédit Martiniquais, 17 rue de las Liberté, T 59 93 00. BRED, Place de Père Labat, T 63 22 67, 63 77 63. Martinique Change, 37 rue Victor Hugo, T 63 80 33 and in Trois-Ilets T 66 04 44. Banque National de Paris, 72 Avenue des Caraïbes, T 59 46 00 (the best for cash advances on Visa, no commission). Banks and exchange houses charge 5% commission on travellers' cheques. Not all banks accept US dollar TCs. Some banks charge 15-30F for any size transaction, so change as much as you think you're going to need. Always go to the bank early; by mid-morning they are very crowded. Do not change US dollars at the Post Office in Fort-de-France, you lose about 15% because of the poor exchange rate and commission. American Express at Roger Albert Voyages, 10 rue Victor Hugo, upstairs, efficient.

● Embassies and consulates

France has responsibility for diplomatic representation; other countries with a consular service in Fort-de-France are: Belgium, Denmark, Italy, Netherlands, Norway, Spain, Sweden, Switzerland, UK (Honorary Consul Mme Jane-Alison Ernoult, T 61 56 30), Venezuela, Mexico and Germany.

● Hours of business

Shops are open from 0900-1800 (banks from around 0730) and until 1300 on Sat. Nearly everything closes from 1200-1500 and on Sun.

● Hospitals

There are 18 hospitals and clinics which are well-equipped and well-staffed. In an emergency: SAMU, Pierre Zobda Quitmann Hospital, 97232 Le Lamentin, T 55 20 00. Ambulance service T 71 59 48. The Sea Water Therapy Centre is at Grand Anse, 97221 Carbet, T 78 08 78.

● Laundry

There are several launderettes in Fort-de-France; Laverie Automatique, Galerie des Filibustiers, rue E Deproge; Lavexpress, 61 rue Jules-Monnerot; Laverie Self-Service, Lavematic, 85 rue Jules-Monnerot, Terres Sainville, T 63 70 43. Laundry service behind Pointe du Bout marina, also at Bakou Marina dock.

● Religion

Although the majority of the population is Catholic there are other churches represented including the Seventh Day Adventists, Baptists, the Evangelical Awakening Assembly, the Full Evangelical Mission and the Evangelical

Christian Mission. There is a synagogue, Maison Grambin, Plateau Fofo.

● Shopping

Fort-de-France has ample scope for shoppers, with an abundance of boutiques selling the latest Paris fashions, as well as items by local designers, and numerous street markets where local handicrafts are on sale. Seekers of clothing and perfume should head for Rue Victor Hugo and its 2 galleries (malls). Jewellery shops are mostly in Rue Isambert and Rue Lamartine, selling crystal, china and silverware, and unique gold jewellery. At markets in the Savane and near the cathedral bamboo goods, wickerwork, shells, leather goods, T-shirts, silk scarves and the like are sold. Wines and spirits imported from France and local liqueurs made from exotic fruits are readily available, and Martiniquan rum is an excellent buy. There are large shopping centres at Cluny, Dillon, and Bellevue. Annette supermarket at Fort-de-France and Le Marin has a free shuttle service from the Marina. St Anne has several small groceries open daily, catering to the tourist trade. American and Canadian dollars are accepted nearly everywhere and many tourist shops offer a 20% discount on goods bought with a credit card or foreign traveller's cheques.

● Useful addresses

Fire department: T 18; Police: T 17; Gendarmerie, rue Victor Sévère, 97200 Fort-de-France, T 63 51 51, Hôtel de Police: T 55 30 00; Sea rescue: T 63 92 05, 63 20 88; radio phone (international), T 10; Radio taxi: T 63 63 62.

● Voltage

The electric current is 220 volts AC.

● Weights and measures

The metric system is in use.

ACCOMMODATION

● Hotels

Price guide

L1	over US$200	L2	US$151-200
L3	US$101-150	A1	US$81-100
A2	US$61-80	A3	US$46-60
B	US$31-45	C	US$21-30
D	US$12-20	E	US$7-11
F	US$4-6	G	up to US$3

Martinique offers a wide range of accommodation from the modest family-run auberges scattered over the remote and spectacular N, to the huge 5 star complexes of Pointe du Bout

and Trois Ilets, the main tourist area, in the S. 20 hotels with over 60 rooms are classed as Grand Hôtellerie. About 100 smaller places are grouped as Relais Créoles. The Sucrier Créole is awarded to hotels with a high quality of service and hospitality. Gîtes, furnished holiday apartments and bungalows are widely available, some connected to hotels. Information and reservations can be made through Centrale de Réservation, BP823-97200 Fort-de-France Cédex, T 71 56 11, F 63 11 64. The tourist office at the airport is helpful and will telephone round the hotels to get you a room for your first night if you have not booked beforehand. Alternatively, for gîtes and country guesthouses, contact the Association Martiniquaise Pour le Tourisme en Espace Rural (Amater), Maison du Tourisme Vert, 9 Boulevard du Géneral de Gaulle, BP 1122, 97248 Fort-de-France Cédex, T 73 67 92, F 63 55 92. Generally, prices are high and some hotels add 10% service charge and/or 5% government tax to the bill.

Pointe du Bout and Les Trois-Ilets are the main tourist centres, well equipped with shops, night clubs, casinos, a marina, facilities for golf, watersports and tennis as well as several beaches. Trois-Ilets: benefits from the facilities of Pointe du Bout and the pleasant beaches of Anse Mitan and Anse à l'Ane, a 20-min ferry ride from Fort-de-France. The main hotels are L1 Meridien, 97229 Trois-Ilets, T 66 00 00, F 66 00 74, where the staff show a lack of interest at this huge modern complex with 295 rooms and traditional bungalows in landscaped grounds, the swimming is superb and it is fun to walk through the marina village (take a picnic lunch because food and drink is expensive); L1-L3 Sofitel Bakoua (named after traditional Martiniquan straw hats) with 139 apartments and rooms, T 66 02 02, F 66 00 41, T 800-322-2223, a/c, TV, phone, minibar, 2 restaurants, tennis, fitness centre, pool, on beach. L2-L3 Hôtel la Pagerie, PLM Azur, pool, T 66 05 30, F 66 00 99; A1 Auberge de l'Anse Mitan, T 66 01 12, F 66 01 05, a friendly, family-run hotel with apartments and rooms; A3 Le Nid Tropical, rents studios and has a lively beach bar and restaurant, T 68 31 30, F 68 47 43, also camping, see below. A2 La Bonne Auberge Chez André, T 66 01 55, F 66 04 50, again basic but clean, offering underwater fishing and watersports.

Medium to low priced hotels in Fort-de-France include L3-A2 Impératrice, T 63 06 82, F 72 60 30, rue de la Liberté, 1950s décor and architecture, apparently unchanged since it was built in 1957, friendly, and **A2-A3** *La Malmaison*, good and clean, spacious, rec for price range but some rooms smell of cigarettes, T 63 90 85, F 60 03 93, higher prices during Carnival, also in Rue de la Liberté opp the Savane and both with lively bars and restaurants frequented by a young crowd; the **A2** *Balisier* on 21 Rue Victor Hugo is also very centrally located with a view over the port, T/F 71 46 54, good value. On Rue Lazare Carnot is **A2-A3** *Un Coin de Paris*, T 70 08 52, F 63 09 51, small, friendly and cheap. **A2-A3** *Le Gommier*, 3 Rue Jacques Cazotte, T 71 88 55, F 73 06 96, one of the oldest buildings in town, highly rec, has clean spacious rooms and good continental breakfasts, friendly management. **L3** *Squash Hotel*, 3 Boulevard de la Marne, T 63 00 01, F 63 00 74, 108 modern rooms, TV, minibar, pool, 3 squash courts, gym, dancing room, saunas, jacuzzi, billards, conference facilities. In the elegant suburbs of Didier is the **A1** *Victoria*, Route de Didier, 97200 Fort-de-France, T 60 56 78, F 60 00 24, in the USA 800-322 2223, on hillside overlooking bay, popular with businessmen as well as holiday makers, 36 rooms, good restaurant, a/c, TV, phone, fridge, buses into town every few mins, pool. At Schoelcher, on the outskirts of Fort-de-France, is **L1-L2** *La Batelière* with pool, tennis courts and casino, very fine hotel, rec, T 61 49 49, F 61 70 57.

The hotels at **Diamant** on the S coast benefit from miles of superb, uncrowded beach with magnificent views of coastal mountains and, of course, Diamant Rock. **L1-L3** *Novotel* has excellent facilities, lovely pool, tennis courts, watersports, disco and it rents apartments and rooms, T 76 42 42, F 76 22 87, T 800-322-2223. **L3** *Diamant les Bains*, rec, fine views over swimming pool and sea, T 76 40 14, F 76 27 00, and **L3** *Le Village du Diamant*, T 76 41 89, F 63 53 32, has 59 basic, beachside bungalows, rooms or apartments for rent.

At **Ste-Luce A2** *Aux Delices de la Mer* offers fishing amongst other activities, T 62 50 12, only 5 rooms.

Outside **Ste-Anne**, to the N, is the *Club Med Village Les Boucaniers*, T 76 74 52, F 76 72 02, lots of tennis and land based sports, waterskiing, windsurfing, sailing, diving and golf at extra cost, no children under 12, 313 rooms, a/c; just S of the Ste-Anne on sandy beach is **L1-L3** *Hôtel Anse Caritan*, BP 24, 97227 Sainte-Anne, T 76 74 12, F 76 72 59,

in USA 800-322 2223, 96 rooms with views across to Diamond Rock, a/c, terraces, kitchenettes, phone, pool, restaurant, watersports and excursions arranged.

On the rugged **Atlantic coast**: **A3** *Chez Julot*, T 74 40 93, a modest but pleasant hotel, one street back from foreshore road, a/c, rec, restaurant, rue Gabriel Perí, Vauclin. **A2** *Les Brisants*, T 54 32 57, F 54 69 13, at François provides good Créole cuisine. On the old NI, near Trinité, within easy reach of the Caravelle peninsula, **L3-A1** *St Aubin* is a magnificent colonial-style hotel, splendid location, views and exterior, but interior badly damaged by 1960s refurbishment, T 69 34 77, F 69 41 14, and **L3** *Le Village de Tartane* is near the pretty fishing village of Tartane, T 58 06 33, F 63 53 32. In Tartane, **A2** *Madras*, hotel and restaurant, on the beach, spotless rooms, sea view or road view, T 58 33 95, F 58 33 63. **L1-L3** *Hôtel Primerêve*, Anse Azérot, just S of Sainte Marie, T 69 40 40, F 69 09 37, T 800-322 2223, 20 rooms, 80 suites, new hotel on hillside, elegant, 5-min walk to superb beach, secluded cove, pool, good restaurant, tennis, snorkelling, easy access to rainforest.

Moving N through dramatic scenery at **Basse Pointe**, rather difficult to find, **L2-L3** *Plantation de Leyritz*, T 78 53 92, F 78 92 44, is a former plantation house set in beautiful grounds with a lot of insects because of all the fruit trees and water, glamorous accommodation, excellent restaurant serving local specialities, efficient and friendly service, pool, tennis courts, health spa, discothèque. In the remote, Northern- most commune, Grand-Rivière, a small fishing village surrounded by rainforest and close to several idyllic black sand coves, **B** *Chanteur Vacances* is a simple, clean hotel with only 7 rooms, shared facilities, restaurant, T 55 73 73.

One of the few hotels within easy reach of the ruined town of St-Pierre: is **A3** *La Nouvelle Vague*, 5 rooms only (doubles), T 78 14 84, rooms over bar, overlooks beach.

On **Carbet's** enormous black sand beach are **A3** *Le Cristophe Colomb*, good value, T 78 08 53, and the more upmarket **L1-L2** *Marouba Club* which has apartments and bungalows, pool, disco, T 78 00 21, F 78 05 65, MAP rates.

Finally, convenient for the airport, at **Ducos**: in the plain of Lamentin, **A3** *Airport*, 6 rooms, basic a/c, hot water, no restaurant, T 56 01 83.

● **Youth hostels**

Fédération des Oeuvres Laiques (FOL) has a hostel, **D** pp, along the Route de Didier, Rue de Prof Raymond Gardens, T 64 04 10, 64 00 17, head office at 31 Rue Perrinon, Fort de France, T 63 50 22, F 63 83 67. The hostel is several miles from the town centre and difficult to find, only one small FOL sign. No public transport in evenings, taxis can make staying here expensive. Rooms sleep 4 with shower and toilet, basic, renovated 1994.

● **Camping**

The most convenient campsite for Fort-de-France is at Anse à l'Ane where the *Courbaril Camping* is situated, with kitchenette and washing facilities. They also have small bungalows, studios and chalets to rent, **A3** T 68 32 30, F 68 32 21. Right next to it is *Le Nid Tropical* campsite, 70F for 2 people if you have your own tent, 100F, if you rent one, T 68 31 30. A small bakery/restaurant on the beach serves cheap meals, bread and pastries. On the S coast, Ste-Luce has a good campsite with adequate facilities in the VVF Hotel, but the beach is not nice. There are no tents for hire. T 62 52 84. *Camping Municipal* at Ste-Anne is a popular campsite with a pleasant situation in a shady grove right on the beach, but rather overgrown and dirty, 40F, cheap food available, water sometimes shut off. Next to the *Club Med*, it is on the cleanest and nicest beach. You can rent tents from Chanteur Vacances, 65 rue Perrinon, Fort-de-France, T 71 66 19, around 35F/day.

FOOD AND DRINK

Sampling the French and Créole cuisine is one of the great pleasures of visiting Martinique. There is an abundance of restaurants, cafés, and snack bars to be found everywhere. The quality is generally very high so it is worth being adventurous and trying the various dishes and eating places. The main meal of the day is at midday and many restaurants and cafés offer very reasonable fixed price *menus du jour* ranging from 30-60F. Some worth seeking out are as follows:

Le Blenac, 3 rue Blenac, T 70 18 41, closed Sun evening; *King Creol*, 56 Av des Caraïbes, T 70 19 18, closed Sat midday and Sun; *El Chico Chico*, 29 rue Garnier Pagès, T 72 48 92, open Mon-Sat lunch only; for crêpes and salads try *La Crêperie*, 4 rue Garnier Pagès, T 60 62 09, closed Sat midday, Sun; *Espace Créole*, 8 rue Voltaire, T 70 05 95, open Mon-Sat 1100-2200; *Le Victor Hugo*, 69 rue V Hugo, T 63 61 08, closed Sun midday; *Marie Sainte*, 160 rue V Hugo, T 70 00 30, open daily except Sun. For vegetarians, *Le Second Soufflé*, 27 rue Blenac, T 63 44 11, open Mon-Fri lunchtime. In the market at Fort-de-France are small kiosks selling créole *menu du jour* for 50F inc dessert and drink, other meals also served, with tableclothes and flowers on table, Miriam enthusiastically greets customers at *Chez Louise* and explains menu in English.

For an Italian atmosphere try *Le Vieux Milan*, 60 Avenue des Caraïbes, T 60 35 31, excellent pizza for US$7-11, closed Sat, Sun. There are several restaurants serving Vietnamese and Chinese food, inc *Le Cantonnais*, Marina Pointe du Bout, T 66 02 33, open daily; *Le Chinatown*, 20 rue Victor Hugo, T 71 82 62, Mon-Fri lunch; *Indo*, Vietnamese, 105 route de la Folie, T 71 63 25, closed Sun evening and Mon; *Le Jardin de Jade*, Anse Colas, T 61 15 50, closed Sun evening; *Le Kiwany's*, 2 rue Kernay, Trinité, T 58 42 44, closed Sun evening, Mon; *Le Lotus d'Asie*, Vietnamese, 24 Bd de la Marne, T 71 62 96, closed Sun lunch, *Le Xuandre*, Vietnamese, Voie No 2 Pointe des Nègres, T 61 54 70, evenings only, closed Mon. Other nationalities are also well represented: *Le Couscousser*, 1 rue Perrinon, looking out on to Bibliothèque Schoelcher, is excellent with choice of sauces and meats to accompany *couscous*, reasonably priced, interesting, rather young Algerian red wine goes well with the food, open Mon-Fri 1200-1500, 1900-2300, Sat 1900-2300, T 60 06 42; *Les Cèdres*, Lebanese, in rue Redoute de Matouba, excellent humous, kebabs and other Lebanese meze, owner speaks English, all major credit cards accepted; *Le Salambo*, Tunisian, Patio de Cluny, T 60 47 70, closed Sun, Mon, Tues; *Le Beyrouth*, Lebanese, 9 rue Redoute de Matouba, T 60 67 45, lunch menu from 80F; *Le Méchoui*, Moroccan, Pte Simon, behind Bricogite, reservations preferred, takeaway service, T 71 58 12, open 1200-1600, 1900-2400, closed Sun; *Las Tapas de Sevillas*, Spanish, 7 rue Garnier Pagès, T 63 71 23.

Amongst the many restaurants across the Baie des Flamands at Anse Mitan is the charming *L'Amphore* where the fresh lobster is delicious, T 66 03 09, closed Mon-Tues, lunchtime. *Bambou* is a little further along the beach, specializes in fresh fish and offers an excellent *menu du jour*. *Chez Jojo* on the beach at Anse à l'Ane, T 68 37 43, has a varied seafood menu. Two-star restaurants include *Auberge de l'Anse Mitan*, T 66 01 12, open every evening, reservations required; *Hemingway's* off Anse Mitan beach, flat fee for créole buffet, small or large plate, opens 1900, arrive early for first sitting, soon fills up; *La Bonne Auberge*, Chez André, T 66 01 55; *La Langouste*, T 66 04 99, open daily; *La Villa Créole*, T 66 05 53, closed Sun-Mon lunch. At Diamant, *La Case Créole*, Place de l'Église, T 76 10 14, French and Créole, seafood and other specialities, open daily 1100-1600, 1900-2330; *Hotel Diamant Les Bains* has a reasonable and well-situated restaurant specializing in seafood, T 76 40 14, shut Wed. There are several other restaurants in the town which front directly on to the beach, mostly offering créole cooking and seafood. In Pointe du Bout marina, *La Marine Bar and Restaurant*, good pizza, drink wine, not beer, good seafood platter; *l'Embarquerie* snack bar by ferry dock has happy hour 3 times a day, 1030-1130, 1430-1530, 1700-1800, buy a local Corsaire beer, get one free; *Pizzeria* and ice cream snack bar at innermost corner of Pointe du Bout marina sells beer for 10F. *Hibiscus Restaurant* has reasonably priced salads and *menu du jour*, with use of hotel pool for pm; *Bakou Hotel* dock bar is a great place to meet yachties and watch the sunset.

At Carbet the *Grain d'Or*, a spacious airy restaurant, is another good spot to sample Martinique's seafood specialities, T 78 06 91, open daily, and *La Guinguette* on the beach near St-Pierre is also rec. On the coast, N of St-Pierre is *Chez Ginette*, good food but overpriced, T 52 90 28, closed Thur.

The restaurant at *Plantation Leyritz* near Basse Pointe is in the restored plantation house and has waterfalls trickling down the walls giving a cool, peaceful feel to the place, elegant dining, good food and service, open daily, T 78 53 92. At Grand' Rivière, *Chez Tante Arlette* serves excellent créole food in cool, pleasant surroundings, finished off with home made liqueurs, rue Louis de Lucy de Fossarieu, T 55 75 75.

At Ste-Anne, dine in style at the *Manoir de Beauregard* or at *Les Filets Bleus*, right on the beach and lighter on the pocket, T 76 73 42, closed Sun evening, Mon. *Anthor* on front street and *L'Ouire Mer* serve reasonable créole meals and pizza; *Les Tameriniers* chef decorates expensive dishes with flowers, closed Tues evenings, Wed; *Poi et Virginie*, overlooks bay with good seafood, closed Mon.

At Cap Chevalier, *Chez Gracieuse* is a good créole restaurant, choose the terrace and order the catch of the day, not too expensive, T 76 72 31, 76 93 10, open daily.

For travellers on a smaller budget wishing to eat out in the capital there are plenty of good snackbars and cafés serving various substantial sandwiches and *menus du jour*. The area around Place Clemenceau has lots of scope; *Le Clemenceau* is very good value and extremely friendly – try the *accras* or a fresh *crudité* salad; *Le Lem* on Boulevard Général-de-Gaulle has superior fast food at low prices and a young crowd. It also stays open later than many restaurants that close in the evenings and on Sun. Behind the Parc Floral on Rue de Royan is the *Kowossol*, a tiny vegetarian café which serves a cheap and healthy *menu du jour*. The pizzas are rec and the fruit juice is especially delicious – try *gingembre* (ginger) or *ananas* (pineapple). On François Arago *Los Amigos* and *Le Coq d'Or* are particularly good for substantial sandwiches for around 12F. Try *poisson* (steak fish) or *poulet* (chicken). *Le Renouveau* on Boulevard Allegre offers delicious, filling *menus du jour* for 40F, again with a warm welcome.

The place to head for in the evening when all of these eateries close (except *Le Lem* which stays open until 2100), is the Boulevard Chevalier de Ste-Marthe next to the Savane. Here every evening until late, vans and caravans serve delicious meals to take away, or to eat at tables under canvas awnings accompanied by loud Zouk music. The scene is bustling and lively, in contrast to the rest of the city at nighttime, and the air is filled with wonderful aromas. Try *lambis* (conch) in a sandwich (15F) or on a *brochette* (like a kebab) with rice and salad (30F). Paella and *Colombo* are good buys (40F) and the crêpes whether sweet or savoury are delicious. For a description of local food see page 585.

GETTING AROUND

LAND TRANSPORT

● **Car hire**

There are numerous car hire firms at the airport and around town; *Europcar Interent*, Aéroport Lamentin, T 51 20 33, F 51 81 15, Fort-de-France T 73 33 13 and several hotels; *Hertz*, 24 Rue Ernest-Deproge, Fort-de-France, T 60 64 64. Airport, T 51 28 22; *Avis*, 4 Rue Ernest-Deproge, Fort-de-France, T 70 11 60, Airport,

T 51 26 86. Prices start from 200F a day for a Citroën AX or Renault 5. It will normally be cheaper to have unlimited mileage. You can get a discount if you book your car from abroad at least 48 hours in advance. An international driver's licence is required for those staying over twenty days. Car hire companies in Fort de France close at weekends. If you want to return a car you have to go to the airport, you can't even drop off the key in town.

Caravans and camper vans can be rented from ETC, 13 cité la Martienne, le François, T 54 59 04; West Indies Tours, Beauregard, Le François, T 54 50 71; Tropicamp, A9 Gros Raisin, 97228 Ste Luce, T 62 49 66; Aligator Vacances, Place d'Armes Bat AGS – 97232 Le Lamentin, T 57 10 10, F 51 89 30.

One look at Fort-de-France's congested streets will tell you it's well worth avoiding driving in the city centre. Parking in central Fort-de-France is only legal with a season ticket and the capital's traffic wardens are very efficient; cars may be towed away.

● Hitchhiking
Hitching is a common way of getting around, and very easy, recommended.

● Motorcycles
Mopeds can be hired at Funny, in Fort-de-France, T 63 33 05; Moppet, 3 rue Jules Monnerot Terres Sainville, Fort de France, T 71 51 60, 60 40 62; Discount, Trois-Ilets, T 66 04 37; and Grabin's Car Rental, Morne Calebasse, T 60 02 88. Motorcycles of 80cc and over need a licence, those of 50cc do not. Rental for all is about 170F/day. A bicycle can be hired for 50F/day, 250F/week, 350F/fortnight, from Funny, T 63 33 05; Discount, T 66 04 37; TS Location Sarl, T 63 42 82, all in Fort-de-France.

● Buses
There are plenty of buses running between Fort-de-France and the suburbs which can be caught at Pointe-Simon on the seafront and from Boulevard Général-de-Gaulle. The buses are all privately owned and leave when they're full and not before. Short journeys cost around 5F and the buses run from 0500-2000 approximately. To request a stop shout "arrêt"!

● Taxis
To go further afield the taxi collectif (estate cars or minibuses) are the best bet. 'Taxicos', or TCs, run until about 1800 and leave Pointe Simon for all the communes; Ste-Anne 39F, Diamant 19F, St-Pierre 18F. It is worth noting that there are no buses to the airport, although the Ste-Anne buses go close, and a private taxi is the only way of getting into town from the airport, around 70F. There is a 40% surcharge on taxi fares between 1900 and 0600 and on Sun. Private taxi stands are at the Savane, along Boulevard Général-de-Gaulle and Place Clemenceau.

FERRIES

There are ferries running between Desnambuc quay on the sea front and Pointe du Bout, Anse Mitan and Anse à l'Ane. These run until about 2300 to Pointe du Bout and 1830 to Anse Mitan and Anse à l'Ane and apart from a few taxis are about the only form of transport on a Sun or after 2000. Make sure you get on the right one. The 20-min ferry from Fort de France to Trois-Ilets costs 30F return, is punctual, pleasurable and saves a 45-min drive by road. To the *Méridien* there is only one boat each hour (don't believe boatmen who say they go near, they drop you at Anse à l'Ane which is a long hot walk away). For information about ferry timetables call 73 05 53 for Somatour and 63 06 46 for Madinina.

COMMUNICATIONS

● Postal services
Post offices are open from 0700-1800 and Sat mornings. The main post office is on Rue de la Liberté and always has long queues. Post card to USA 3.70F

● Telecommunications
Nearly all public telephones are cardphones except a few in bars and hotels which take coins. At the PTT office in Rue Antoine Siger, just off the Savane, there are numerous card and coin phones and *Télécartes* (phone cards) are sold. These can also be bought in most newsagents, cafés, and some shops for 36.50F upwards. A 50-unit card (about US$8) lasts nearly 4 mins when phoning North America; a 120-unit card costs about US$16. Don't get caught out on arrival at the airport where there are only cardphones. Try the tourist office where they are very helpful and will phone round endless hotels to find the unprepared new arrival a room. You can not have a call returned to a payphone. Directory enquiries, T 12. To make a long distance credit card or collect phone call from a pay phone: buy the smallest card possible and insert in phone, dial 19 00 11 to get USA direct English speaking operator for credit card or collect or dial USA

DIRECT calls. Other lines available for Sprint and MCI. To use phone card dial 19 00 plus 10 digit number. Check in the phone book for other numbers. To dial non-French islands in Caribbean dial 191 plus 3-figure code and local number.

ENTERTAINMENT

For those whose visit does not coincide with any festivals, there is plenty of other entertainment. The *Ballet Martiniquais* (T 63 43 88) is one of the world's most prestigious traditional ballet companies. Representing everyday scenes in their dance, they wear colourful local costume and are accompanied by traditional rhythms. Information about performances and venues, usually one of the large hotels (*Novotel, Caritan, Carayou, Méridien, Bakoua* and *Batelière*) can be obtained from the tourist office. Every year in July, SERMAC (Parc Floral et Culturel and at the Théâtre Municipal) organizes a two-week arts festival in Fort-de-France with local and foreign artistes performing plays and dance, T 71 66 25. CMAC (Centre Martiniquais d'Action Culturelle, Avenue Franz Fanon, Fort-de-France, T 61 76 76) organizes plays, concerts, the showing of films and documentaries all year round and an annual festival in December.

● **Cinemas**
There are several comfortable, air-conditioned cinemas in Fort-de-France and the various communes. No film is in English; tickets cost 30F. The 2 main theatres are the *Théâtre Municipal* in the lovely old Hôtel de Ville building and *Théâtre de la Soif Nouvelle* in the Place Clemenceau.

● **Nightclubs**
Nightclubs abound and tend to be very expensive (70F to get in and the same price for a drink, whether orange juice or a large whisky). Night clubs include *Le New Hippo*, 24 Blvd Allègre, Fort-de-France, T 60 20 22; *La Vesou* at Hotel *Carayou, Zipp's Club*, Dumaine, Francois, T 54 65 45. Casinos charge 60F entrance fee if you are not staying at the hotel, take passport or identification card. There are several bars (*piano bar* or *café théâtre*) where you can listen to various types of music. At *Coco Loco*, rue Ernest Déproge in Fort-de-France, regular jazz sessions are held, T 63 63 77. Others include *Chez Gaston*, rue Felix Eboué, *La Carafe*, rue Lamartine, *Le Pagayo*, Rond Point du Vietnam Héroïque, *Le Blue Cup*, 7 rue

Lamartine, all in Fort-de-France. Most large hotels lay on Caribbean-style evening entertainment for tourists; limbo dancers, steelbands, etc. Hôtel Meridien has the island's main casino 2300-0300, proof of identity is required for entry. *Hotel La Batelière* also has a casino. *Choubouloute*, the local entertainments guide, is sold in most newsagents, priced 5F.

TOURIST INFORMATION

● **Local tourist office**
Lamentin Airport, T 51 28 55; Bord de la Mer, Fort-de-France, T 63 79 60, F 73 66 93. Postal address: Office Départemental du Tourisme de la Martinique, BP 520, 97206 Fort-de-France Cédex. There are local information bureaux (Syndicat d'initiative) all round the island, many of which can be found through the town hall (mairie).

● **Tourist offices overseas**
Abroad there are the Office Départemental du Tourisme de la Martinique, 2 rue des Moulins, 75001, Paris, T 44 77 86 22, 77 86 22, F 49 26 03 63; the Commercial Representative Office Nordic Countries, PO Box 717 Frettvägen 14, S 1818 07 Lidingo, Sweden, T 468 765 58 65, F 765 93 60; Office due Tourisme de la Martinique au Canada, 1981 Av MacGill College, Ste 480, Montréal PQH 3A 2W9, T (514) 844 8566, F 844 8901; The Martinique Promotion and Development Bureau, 610 Fifth Av, New York, NY 10020, T (212) 757 0218, F 247 6468; La Martinique Reisen GMBH, Adel mannstrasse, 2-D 8000 Munich 82, Germany, T (089) 430 2966, F 430 7224.

● **Local travel agents**
Guided tours: of the island by bus, trips on sailing boats and cruise ships around Martinique and to neighbouring islands, and excursions on glass-bottom boats are organized by the following companies: *STT Voyages*, 23 Rue Blénac, Fort-de-France, T 71 68 12; *Carib Jet*, Lamentin Airport, T 51 90 00; *Madinina Tours*, 89 rue Blénac, 97200 Fort-de-France, T 70 65 25, F 73 09 53; *Caribtours*, Marina Pointe du Bout, 97229 Trois-Ilets, T 66 02 56, F 66 09 66; *Colibri Tours*, Hôtel La Batelière, 97233 Schoelcher, T 61 66 74, F 61 66 69; AVS Angle des rues F Arago et E Deproge, Fort-de-France, T 65 55 55; M Vacances, 97290 Le Marin, T 74 85 61, F 74 71 07; Biguine Voyages, 51 rue Victor Hugo, Fort-de-France, T 71 87 87, F 60 55 96.

Touring on foot: contact the *Parc Naturel Régional*, 9 Boulevard Général- de-Gaulle, T 73 19 30, for well-organized walks in the island's beauty spots such as the rainforest and the Caravelle Peninsula. The charge is 60-80F per person and includes the coach fare to the walk's starting point. Guides can be found through the tourist office, or at Morne Rouge for climbing Mount Pelée and at Ajoupa-Bouillon for the Gorge de la Falaise walk.

Windward Islands

Dominica

DOMINICA (pronounced Domin*ee*ca) is the largest and most mountainous of the anglophone Windward Islands. The official title, Commonwealth of Dominica, should always be used in addresses to avoid confusion with the Dominican Republic. It is 29 miles long and 16 miles wide, with an area of 290 square miles. The highest peak, Morne Diablotin, rises to 4,747 feet and is often covered in mist.

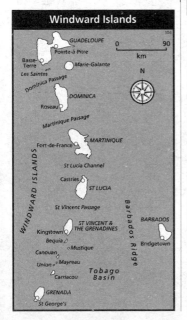

Windward Islands

HORIZONS

Materially, it is one of the poorest islands in the Caribbean, but the people are some of the friendliest; many of them are small farmers: the island's mountainous terrain discourages the creation of large estates. In Dominica, over 2,000 descendants of the original inhabitants of the Caribbean, the once warlike Caribs, live in the Carib Territory, a 3,700-acre 'reservation' established in 1903 in the NE, near Melville Hall airport. There are no surviving speakers of the Carib language on the island. The total population, which is otherwise almost entirely of African descent, is around 72,000, of whom about 29% live in the parish of St George, around Roseau, the capital, on the Caribbean coast. Other parishes are much more sparsely populated. The parish of St John, in which Portsmouth (the second largest town) is situated contains only about 5,000 people, or 7% of the population.

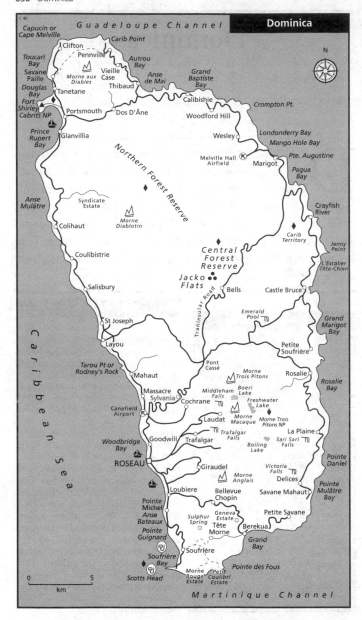

Dominica

C 46

Guadeloupe Channel

Capucin or
Cape Melville
Clifton
Carib Point
Pennville
Toucari
Bay
Autrou
Bay
Savane
Paille
Morne aux
Diables
Vieille
Case
Anse
de Mai
Grand
Baptiste
Bay
Douglas
Bay
Thibaud
Fort
Shirley
Cabrits NP
Tanetane
Calibishie
Prince
Rupert
Bay
Portsmouth
Dos D'Âne
Crompton Pt.
Woodford Hill
Glanvillia
Wesley
Londonderry Bay
Mango Hole Bay
Melville Hall
Airfield
Pte. Augustine
Anse
Mulâtre
Northern Forest Reserve
Marigot
Pagua
Bay
Syndicate
Estate
Colihaut
Morne
Diablotin
Carib
Territory
Crayfish
River
Coulibistrie
Central
Forest
Reserve
Jenny
Point
L'Escalier
Tête-Chien
Salisbury
Jacko
Flats
Bells
Castle Bruce
Transinsular Road
Emerald
Pool
Grand
Marigot
Bay
St Joseph
Layou
Petite
Souffrière
Rosalie
Tarou Pt or
Rodney's Rock
Mahaut
Pont
Cassé
Morne
Trois Pitons
Rosalie
Bay
Massacre
Sylvania
Middleham
Falls
Boeri
Lake
Cochrane
Freshwater
Lake
Canefield
Airport
Laudat
Morne
Macaque
Morne Trois
Pitons NP
La Plaine
Woodbridge
Bay
Goodwill
Trafalgar
Falls
Trafalgar
Boiling
Lake
Sari Sari
Falls
Pointe
Daniel
ROSEAU
Giraudel
Victoria
Falls
Morne
Anglais
Delices
Pointe
Mulâtre
Bay
Loubiere
Bellevue
Chopin
Savane Mahaut
Pointe
Michel
Anse
Bateaux
Sulphur
Spring
Geneva
Estate
Petite Savane
Pointe
Guignard
Tête
Morne
Berekua
Soufrière
Grand
Bay
Souffrière
Bay
Scotts Head
Morne
Rouge
Estate
Petit
Coulibri
Estate
Pointe des Fous

Caribbean Sea

N

0   5
km

Martinique Channel

Hurricanes

In 1979 the island was devastated by Hurricane David; 37 people were killed and 60,000 were left homeless. Much of what David left standing was felled by Hurricane Allen the next year. In 1995 Dominica was hit by three storms in August and September. Storm Iris damaged roads and spoilt some crops; Hurricane Luis destroyed many roads, sea fronts and coastal properties and devastated the banana crop; finally Hurricane Marilyn finished off the job that Luis started, causing great damage in the NE where the eye passed over. One person was killed and another seriously injured, but the biggest problem was the loss of banana income.

Like St Lucia, Dominica was once a French possession; although English is the official tongue, most of the inhabitants also speak créole French (French-based patois). In the Marigot/Wesley area a type of English called 'cocoy' is used; the original settlers of the area, freed slaves, came from Antigua and are mostly Methodists. Catholicism predominates, though there are some Protestant denominations and an increasing number of fundamentalist sects, imported from the USA.

HISTORY

The Caribs, who supplanted the Arawaks on Dominica, called the island Waitikubuli ("tall is her body"). Columbus sighted it on 3 November, 1493, a Sunday (hence the modern name), but the Spanish took no interest in the island. It was not until 1805 that possession was finally settled. Until then it had been fought over by the French, British and Caribs. In 1660, the two European powers agreed to leave Dominica to the Caribs, but the arrangement lasted very few years; in 1686, the island was declared neutral, again with little success. As France and England renewed hostilities, the Caribs were divided between the opposed forces and suffered the heaviest losses in consequence. In 1763, Dominica was ceded to Britain, and between then and 1805, it remained British. Nevertheless, its position between the French colonies of Guadeloupe and Martinique, and the strong French presence over the years, ensured that despite English institutions and language the French influence was never eliminated.

During the 19th century, Dominica was largely neglected and underdevelopment provoked social unrest. Henry Hesketh Bell, the colonial administrator from 1899 to 1905, made great improvements to infrastructure and the economy, but by the late 1930s the British Government's Moyne Commission discovered a return to a high level of poverty on the island. Assistance to the island was increased with some emphasis put on road building to open up the interior. This, together with agricultural expansion, house building and use of the abundant hydro resources for power, contributed to development in the 1950s and 1960s.

In 1939, Dominica was transferred from the Leeward to the Windward Islands Federation; it gained separate status and a new constitution in 1960, and full internal autonomy in 1967. The Commonwealth of Dominica became an independent republic within the Commonwealth in 1978. The Dominica Labour Party dominated island politics after 1961, ushering in all the constitutional changes. Following independence, however, internal divisions and public dissatisfaction with the administration led to its defeat by the Dominica Freedom Party in the 1980 elections. The DFP Prime Minister, Miss (now Dame) Mary Eugenia Charles, adopted a pro-business, pro-United States line to lessen the island's dependence on limited crops and markets. She was re-elected in 1985 and again in 1990, having survived an earlier attempted invasion by supporters of former DLP premier, Patrick John. (For a thorough history of the island, see *The Dominica Story*, by Lennox Honychurch, The Dominica Institute, 1984, revised and republished 1995, ISBN 0-333-62776-8.)

In the general election of 1990 the Dominica Freedom Party (DFP) retained its majority by a single seat, winning 11 of the 21 seats. The official opposition was the recently-formed (1988) United Workers Party (UWP) led by Edison James with six seats, while the former official opposition party, the Dominica Labour Party (DLP) won four seats. A by-election in 1993 increased the UWP's representation to seven seats while the DLP lost one.

In 1995 Dame Eugenia retired at age 76, having led her party since 1968, and the DFP campaigned for the June general elections under the leadership of Brian Alleyne, External Affairs minister in her government. However, the contest was won by the UWP, with 11 seats, while the DFP and the DLP won five each. Mr Edison James was sworn in as Prime Minister. Mr Alleyne and Mr Rosie Douglas, leader of the DLP, were to share the position of Leader of the Opposition, taking the post a year at a time. In 1996, Mr Alleyne resigned and was replaced as leader of the DFP by Charles Savarin, who was elected unopposed.

GOVERNMENT

Dominica is a fully independent member of the British Commonwealth. The single chamber House of Assembly has 31 members: 21 elected by the constituencies, nine Senators who are appointed by the President on the advice of the Prime Minister and Leader of the Opposition, and the Attorney-General. The Prime Minister and Leader of the Opposition also nominate the President, currently Crispin Sorhaindo, who holds office for five years.

THE ECONOMY

Owing to the difficulty of the terrain, only about a quarter of the island is cultivated. Nevertheless, it is self-sufficient in fruit and vegetables and agriculture contributes about 17.5% to gross domestic product. The main products are bananas (the principal export), coconuts (most of which are used in soap and cooking oil production), grapefruit, limes and other citrus fruits. Bananas were badly hit by Hurricane Hugo in 1989 when over 70% of the crop was damaged and by Hurricane Luis in 1995 when 95% of the crop was lost. The opening up of the European market in 1992 affected Dominica's banana industry. Together with the other Windward Islands producers it had to compete with the large exporters from the US dollar areas, mainly in Latin America. Prices paid to local farmers fell while they were unable to match the economies of scale found in Latin America. Other crops are under development, such as coffee, cocoa, mango, citrus and root crops such as dasheen, which are being promoted to diversify away from bananas. There is a very successful aqua culture project, prawn farming.

Manufacturing industry is small, but can take advantage of locally-generated hydroelectricity. Under pressure to purchase Caribbean products for their cruise ships, Royal Caribbean Cruise Lines buys 3mn bars of soap a year from Dominica Coconut Products (DCP), Dominica's largest business. In 1995, Colgate Palmolive, the US transnational company, acquired a controlling interest in DCP. Labour intensive electronic assembly plants and clothing manufacturing are being encouraged for their foreign exchange earnings potential, while data processing is also growing. There is a large pool of labour for garment production which attracts manufacturers, but they often move on to other areas when their duty free concessions expire, usually after 10 years.

Dominica: fact file

Geographic

Land area	750 sq km
forested	67.0%
pastures	3.0%
cultivated	23.0%

Demographic

Population (1995)	72,100
annual growth rate (1990-95)	0.1%
density	96.1 per sq km
Religious affiliation	
Roman Catholic	70.1%
Protestant groups	17.2%
Birth rate per 1,000 (1994)	20.5
	(world av 25.0)

Education and Health

Life expectancy at birth,	
male	74.1 years
female	79.9 years
Infant mortality rate	
per 1,000 live births (1994)	10.3
Physicians (1994)	1 per 3,130 persons
Hospital beds	1 per 231 persons
Calorie intake as %	
of FAO requirement	115%
Population age 25 and over	
with no formal schooling	4.2%
Literacy (over 15)	90.0%

Economic

GNP (1993 market prices)	US$193mn
GNP per capita	US$2,680
Public external debt (1993)	US$85.5mn
Tourism receipts (1994)	US$34.8mn
Inflation	
(annual av 1989-94)	3.4%
Radio	1 per 1.6 persons
Television	1 per 14 persons
Telephone	1 per 4.6 persons

Employment

Population economically active (1991)	
	26,364
Unemployment rate (1994)	23.0%
% of labour force in	
agriculture	30.8
mining and manufacturing	8.5
construction	11.8
trade, hotels, restaurants	15.4
Military forces	none

Source *Encyclopaedia Britannica*

Tourism is being promoted with the emphasis officially on nature tourism. After a sluggish start in the early 1990s because of the world slowdown, arrivals jumped by 10.6% in 1993, 8.8% in 1994 and 7.0% in 1995 to reach a total of 60,471 in that year. Visitors from the French West Indies make up 29% of the total and Americans 18%. The introduction of American Eagle direct flights from Puerto Rico was expected to increase that percentage in 1996. The authorities claim they do not wish to jeopardize the 'Nature Island' image, but concern has been expressed by conservationists over damage to the environment. Meanwhile, the island's hotel capacity continues to expand while more hotels are planned; construction of the large *Shangrila Hotel*, with Taiwanese investment under the economic citizenship programme, is due for completion in 1997 opposite the *Layou River Hotel*, now also owned by Taiwanese. A jetty for cruise ships, with related facilities, has been built at Prince Rupert Bay and in 1995, 267 cruise ship calls were made, compared with 40 in 1990, having shown steady growth each year. In Phase Two of the Roseau Seawall and Bay Front Development Project, a dedicated cruise ship berth was finished in 1995, which will further increase passenger numbers. A jetty for the high speed ferries between Dominica, Martinique and Guadeloupe (French funding) was built in 1995, damaged by the hurricane and since repaired. Also to be completed in 1996 on the bayfront is a fish landing and processing plant (Japanese funding).

There is controversy over the Government's decision in 1992 to grant economic citizenship to investors; up to 1,200 economic citizens, plus their dependents, are to be accepted and the first to be granted passports all came from Taiwan. By end-1994 615 people had been granted economic citizenship; they paid US$7.1mn into an escrow account, of which US$5.4mn had been withdrawn to buy shares in a linked hotel company.

The mining industry also became a controversial issue in 1996, when the House of Assembly passed a bill vesting all mineral rights in the government, whether on public or privately owned land. Soon afterwards, BHP Minerals International of Australia, began drilling in NE Dominica to establish the extent of copper deposits there. The Dominica Conservation Association demanded an environmental impact study before any commercial mining took place.

In 1995 gdp grew by 2% despite the devastation to the banana industry by storms. Good performances by tourism, manufacturing and other agriculture offset the loss of earnings. The Government approached the IMF for help in dealing with its economic problems, including debt, which would be impossible to reschedule without an IMF programme. Plans were announced for the sale of 4 state enterprises: the Dominica Electricity Co (Domlec), the Agricultural, Industrial and Development Bank, the Dominica Export-Import Agency and the port of Roseau.

CULTURE

The best known of Dominica's writers are the novelists Jean Rhys and Phyllis Shand Allfrey. Rhys (1894-1979), who spent much of her life in Europe, wrote mainly about that continent; only flashback scenes in *Voyage in the Dark* (1934), her superb last novel, *Wide Sargasso Sea* (1966), which was made into a film in 1991, her uncompleted autobiography, *Smile Please* and resonances in some of her short stories draw on her West Indian experiences. Allfrey published only one novel, *The Orchid House* (1953); *In the Cabinet* was left unfinished at her death in 1986. Allfrey was one of the founder members of the Dominica Labour Party, became a cabinet minister in the short-lived West Indian Federation, and was later editor of the *Dominica Herald* and *Dominica Star* newspapers. *The Orchid House* was filmed by Channel 4 (UK) in 1990 for international transmission as a 4-part series.

Popular culture reflects the mixture of native and immigrant peoples. While most places on Dominica have a Carib, a French or an English name, the indigenous Carib traditions and way of life have been localized in the NE, giving way to a dominant amalgam of Créole (French and African) tradition. Dominicans are proud of their local language, which is increasingly being used in print. A dictionary was published in 1991 by the Konmité pou Etid Kwéyol (Committee for Créole Studies). You can get hold of this at the Cultural Division, 30 Queen Mary Street on the corner of King George V Street in Roseau. Opposite is the cultural centre for the Carib community, Kalinago, which contains lots of general information about the Carib Reserve and its people and has a selection of Carib goods for sale. There has recently been a great increase in the awareness of the arts and crafts. Both at Caribana, the craft and art gallery (see below, **Shopping**), the Alliance Française French cultural centre, and in the media, the poets, writers and artists of Dominica have been reading or exhibiting their work. Ask at Caribana, T 448-7340, when the next poetry workshop or exhibition, is to be held, or wander the side streets of Roseau to find small shops and galleries. Dance and choral artists are active mostly around Christmas, when there are diverse concerts given by church choirs and Dominica's National Chorale.

FLORA AND FAUNA

Dominica is rightly known as the Nature Island of the Caribbean. Much of the S part of the island (17,000 acres) has since 1975 been designated the **Morne Trois Pitons National Park**. Its principal attractions include the **Boiling Lake** (92° C), which may be the largest of its kind in the world (the other contender is in

New Zealand) and reached after a six-mile, three or four-hour challenging climb. You have to return on the same path as an alternative trail is no longer maintained. An experienced guide is recommended as the trail can be treacherous, but it is easy to follow once you are on it (guides charge about EC$100 per couple, EC$180 for 2 couples; Lambert Charles, T 448-3365, strong and knowledgeable; Kenrich Johnson, friendly, informative; Edison and Loftus Joseph, Wotten Waven, T 448-9192 at a telephone box, cheaper than organized tours, the brothers are shoe makers).

In the valley below the Boiling Lake is a region known as the **Valley of Desolation**, where the forest has been destroyed by sulphuric emissions. At the beginning of the trail to the Boiling Lake is the Titou Gorge, now considerably damaged by rock fall from the hydroelectric development in the area, where a hot and a cold stream mingle. A new track, the Kent Gilbert Trail, has been cut; it starts in La Plaine and is about 4½ miles long. It affords views of the Sari Sari and Bolive Falls, but avoids the spectacular Valley of Desolation. While this makes it a less strenuous route, it also renders it less impressive.

Also in the Park is the **Freshwater Lake**; it is to the E of **Morne Macaque** at 2,500 feet above sea level, and can be reached by road (two miles from Laudat). Do not swim here, it is the drinking water reservoir for Roseau. A trail leads in ¾ hour on foot (follow the road where the river joins the lake about ½ mile to the pipeline, take the path to the left through the dense forest) to the highest lake in the island, Boeri, situated between Morne Macaque and **Morne Trois Pitons**. Work on a hydroelectric project in this area was completed in 1991. There have been lasting consequences for both the Trafalgar Falls (a diminished flow of water) and the Freshwater Lake (a raised water level).

The National Park Service has built a series of paths, the Middleham Trails,

through the rain forest on the NW border of the Park. The Trails are accessible from Sylvania on the Transinsular Road, or Cochrane, although the signs from Sylvania are not very clear. The road to Cochrane is by the Old Mill Cultural Centre in Canefield, once through the village the trail is marked. About 1½-2 hours walk from Cochrane are the **Middleham Falls**, about 250 feet high, falling into a beautiful blue pool in the middle of the forest. Once past the Middleham Falls the trail emerges on the Laudat road.

North of the Transinsular road are the **Central Forest Reserve** and **Northern Forest Reserve**. In the latter is **Morne Diablotin**; about 3 hours steep walking and climbing up and 2½ hours down, not for the faint hearted, you must take a guide. At the highest levels on the island is elfin woodland, characterized by dense vegetation and low-growing plants. Elfin woodland and high montane thicket give way to rainforest at altitudes between 1,000 and 2,500 feet, extending over about 60% of the island. Despite the large area of forest, its protection is essential, against cutting for farm land and other economic pressures, as a water source, and as a unique facility for scientific research. It is hoped, moreover, that tourism can coexist with conservation, since any losses, for whatever reason, would be irreversible.

The Cabrits Peninsula in the NW is also since 1986 a National Park of 1,313 acres, its twin hills covered by dry forest, separated from the island proper by marshland (a pier and cruise ship reception centre have been built) which is a nesting place for herons and doves and hosts a variety of migrant bird species. A walk through the woods and around the buildings of **Fort Shirley** (abandoned in 1854) will reveal much flora and wildlife (easiest to see are the scuttling hermit- or soldier- and black crabs, ground lizard – abòlò – and tree lizard).

Dominica is a botanist's paradise. In addition to the huge variety of trees, many of which flower in March and April, there are orchids and wild gardens of strange plant life in the valleys. Bwa Kwaib or Carib wood (*Sabinea carinalis*) was declared the national flower in 1978; it can be found mostly growing along parts of the W coast. It is a birdwatcher's paradise, too. Indigenous to the island are the Imperial parrot, or Sisserou (*amazona imperialis*), which is critically endangered, and its marginally less threatened relative, the Red-necked parrot, or Jacquot (*amazona arausiaca*). The Sisserou has been declared the national bird. They can be seen in the Syndicate area in the NW which is now a protected reserve and the site of a future information and research centre for visitors and scientists. There is a nature trail but signs are difficult to spot. The parrots are most evident during their courting season, in April and early May. To get the best from a parrot-watching trip, it is worth taking a guide. Bertrand Jno Baptiste, of the Forestry Division (T 448-2401) is highly recommended and charges EC$80 a group. While there are other rare species, such as the Forest Thrush and the Blue-headed hummingbird, there are a great many others which are easily spotted (the Purple-throated Carib and Antillean-crested hummingbirds, for instance), or heard (the Siffleur Montagne). Waterfowl can be seen on the lakes, waders on the coastal wetlands (many are migrants). There are various bat caves, most particularly at Thiband on the NE coast.

There are fewer species of mammal (agouti, manicou-opossum, wild pig and bats), but there is a wealth of insect life (for example, over 55 species of butterfly) and reptiles. Besides those mentioned above, there is the rare iguana, the crapaud (a large frog, eaten under the name of mountain chicken) and five snakes, none poisonous (including the boa constrictor, or tête-chien). Certain parts of the coast are used as nesting grounds by sea turtles (hawksbill, leatherback and green).

The Forestry Division in the Botanical Gardens, Roseau, has a wide range of publications, trail maps, park guides, posters and leaflets (some free) on Dominica's wildlife and National Parks, T 448-2401, F 448-7999.

DIVING AND MARINE LIFE

Dominica is highly regarded as a diving destination and has been featured in most diving magazines as 'undiscovered'. Features include wall dives, drop-offs, reefs, hot, freshwater springs under the sea, sponges, black coral, pinnacles and wrecks, all in unpolluted water. Frequent rainfall and many rivers have led to some very dramatic seascapes with beautiful hard and soft coral; because of the steep drops the sediment falls away and visibility is excellent, at up to 30m depending on the weather. Many drop-offs are close to the beaches but access is poor and boats are essential. There is a marine park conservation area in Toucari Bay and part of Douglas Bay, N of the Cabrits, but the most popular scuba sites are S of Roseau, at Pointe Guignard, Soufrière Bay and Scotts Head. An unusual site is Champagne, with underwater hot springs where you swim through bubbles, fascinating for a night dive, lots of life here. This area in the SE, Soufriére-Scotts Head, is now a marine park without moorings so that all diving is drift diving and boats pick up divers where they surface. Areas may be designated for diving and other areas for fishing. Along the S and SE coast there are more dive sites but because of the Atlantic currents these are for experienced, adventurous divers only. Note that the taking of conch, coral, lobster, sponge, turtle eggs etc is forbidden and you may not put down anchor in coral and on reefs; use the designated moorings.

Whale watching is extremely popular, although the success rate is relatively low. The World Wildlife Fund and many marine conservation groups have used Dominica as a base for documentaries and conferences, so much is known about the local population. It appears that female whales and their calves are in the Caribbean waters for much of the year, with only the mature males leaving the area to feed for any length of time. If your trip is successful, you could be treated to the sight of mothers and their young swimming close to the boat, or young males making enormous jumps before diving below the waves. Dolphin are abundant too, particularly in the Soufrière Bay area and even if you miss the whales your boat is accompanied by a school of playful dolphin. Several different types of whales have been spotted not far from the W shore where the deep, calm waters are ideal for these mammals. Sperm whales are regularly seen, especially during the winter months, as are large numbers of spinner and spotted dolphins. You can also sometimes see pilot whales, pseudorcas, pygmy sperm whales, bottlenose dolphins, Risso's dolphins and melon-headed whales. Whale watching trips can be arranged with the *Anchorage Hotel*, Dive Dominica or Game Fishing Dominica and cost around US$40 pp.

Scuba diving is permitted only through one of the island's registered dive operators or with written permission from the Fisheries Division. All certification courses are PADI and are around US$350. Single tank dives are from US$45 and 2-tank dives are from US$65. Snorkelling trips are around US$25, particularly recommended for the Champagne area. Dive Dominica Ltd, at the *Castle Comfort Guest House* (PO Box 2253, Roseau, T 448-2188, F 448-6088), offers full diving and accommodation packages, courses, single or multiple day dives, night dives and equipment rental. Owned by Derek Perryman, this company is one of the most friendly and experienced operations, recommended for its professional service. Anchorage Dives (T 448-2638, F 448-5680, US$80 2-tank dive inc weights and belt) is based at the *Anchorage Hotel*, Castle Comfort, with a sister operation at the *Portsmouth Beach Hotel*. This is another long established operation with a good reputation, owned by Andrew Armour. Other dive companies are Dive Castaways at the *Castaways Beach Hotel* (T 449-6244, F 449-6246, US$40 one dive, US$55 with full equipment, which covers the northern dive sites; East Carib Dive at Salisbury (T 449-6602, F 449-6603) is based at the *Lauro Club*, contact Gunther Glatz; and Nature Island Dive at Soufrière (T 449-8181, F 449-8182, also kayaking and mountain biking), run by a team of divers from around the world, courses on the bayside recommended. Ask them about accommodation and dive packages, they have a bayside wooden cottage on stilts with porch for up to 4 divers, *Gallette*.

BEACHES AND WATERSPORTS

Compared with other Caribbean islands, Dominica has few good beaches, but does have excellent river bathing. Following the storm of 1995 the Caribbean side of Dominica lost all its sand. Subsequent swells and storms are slowly bringing it back but the black coral sandy areas are few and far between. A small one exists just off Scotts Head but further N you must travel to Mero beach or *Castaways Beach Hotel*. Macousheri Bay and Coconut Beach near Portsmouth are probably the best areas for Caribbean bathing. Don't be tempted to swim anywhere near Roseau or the larger villages because of effluent. For some really beautiful, unspoilt, white sandy beaches, hire a 4WD and investigate the bays of the NE coast. Turtle Beach, Pointe Baptiste, Hampstead and Woodford Hill are all beautiful but on the Atlantic coast terrific underswells and freak waves make swimming dangerous. Look at the sea and swim in the rivers is the safest advice.

Very few watersports are on offer. Gusty winds coming down from the hills making sailing difficult and unreliable; conditions are rarely suitable for the beginner. Game fishing Dominica is a new operation run by Paul Wren (T 448-7285, F 448 7817) with charters at US$400 ½ day or US$600 full day. Sea kayaks can be hired from Nature Island Dive, life jackets and instruction in Soufrière Bay provided.

The best harbour for yachts is Portsmouth (Prince Rupert Bay), but there are no facilities and you should guard your possessions. Stealing from yachts is quite common. The new jetty in Roseau (see below) is designed for small craft, such as yachts, clearing for port entry. Both the *Reigate Waterfront* and *Anchorage Hotels* have moorings and a pier, and yachtsmen and women are invited to use the hotels' facilities.

OTHER SPORTS

Football and cricket are among the most popular national sports; watch cricket in the beautiful setting of the Botanical Gardens. Basketball and netball are also enthusiastically played. There are hard tennis courts at the privately-owned Dominica Club (T 448-2995), *Reigate Hall* and *Castaways*, rental for minimal fee, bring your own racket. *Anchorage Hotel* and *Dominica Club* have squash courts. Cycling is growing in popularity and the island's roads, although twisty, are good. Mountain bikes can be hired from Nature Island Dive at Soufrière (T 449-8181), where there are marked off-road trails. Hiking in the mountains is excellent, and hotels and tour companies arrange this type of excursion. Mountain climbing can be organized through the Forestry Division in the Botanical Gardens, Roseau, T 448-2401. Guides are necessary for any forays into the mountains or forests, some areas of which are still uncharted.

FESTIVALS

The main one is Carnival, on the Monday and Tuesday before Ash Wednesday; it is not as commercialized as many in the Americas as it lacks the sponsorship of a carnival like Trinidad's, but it is one of the most spontaneous and friendly. Sensay costume has returned to the streets: layer upon layer of banana or cloth is used for the costume, a scary mask is worn over the face, usually with horns, and large platform clog boots finish the effect. Large quantities of beer are required for anyone who can wear this costume and dance the streets for several hours in the midday sun. During Carnival, laws of libel and slander are suspended. Independence celebrations (3/4 November) feature local folk dances, music and crafts. On Créole Day, the last Friday in October, the vast majority of girls and women wear the national dress, 'la wobe douillete', to work and school and most shop, bank clerks etc speak only Créole to the public. Domfesta, The Festival of the Arts, takes place during July and August and includes exhibitions by local artists (notably Kelo Royer, Earl Etienne, Arnold Toulon), concerts and theatre performances, (see local papers, *The New Chronicle* or *The Tropical Star*, for details or ask at hotel.)

ROSEAU

Roseau (pronounced *Rose-oh*) is small, ramshackle and friendly, with a surprising number of pretty old buildings still intact. Quite a lot of redevelopment has taken place over the last few years, improving access and making the waterfront more attractive. The Old Market Plaza has been made into a pedestrian area, with shops in the middle. Between the Plaza and the sea is the old Post Office, now housing the **Dominican Museum**, which is well worth a visit. There are public toilets here. The Post Office is on the Bay Front at the bottom of Hillsborough St. It has a colourful mural depicting the development of Dominica's postal service, and a Philately Counter. The market, at the N end of Bay St, is a fascinating sight on Saturday mornings from about 0600-1000; it is also lively on Friday morning, closed

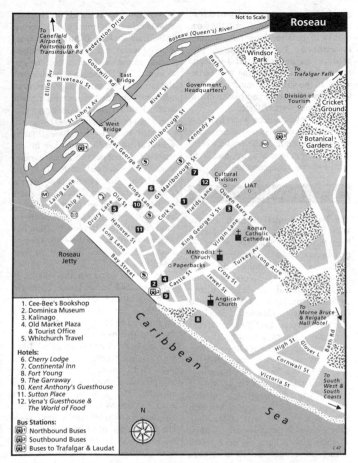

Roseau

Not to Scale

To Canefield Airport, Portsmouth & Transinsular Rd

Federation Drive

Roseau (Queen's) River

Windsor Park

To Trafalgar Falls

Goodwill Rd

East Bridge

Piveteau St

Elliot Av

Bath Rd

Government Headquarters

Division of Tourism

Cricket Ground

River St

St John's Av

West Bridge

Hillsborough St

Kennedy Av

Botanical Gardens

Great George St

Pol

Kings Lane

Gt Marlborough St

7

12

Cultural Division

LIAT

6

Old St

10

1

Fields Lane

3

Drury Lane

11

Cork St

King George V St

Queen Mary St

Virgin Lane

Roman Catholic Cathedral

Laing Lane

Ship St

Hanover St

Long Lane

Turkey Av

Long Acre

Roseau Jetty

Bay Street

Methodist Chruch

Paperbacks

Cross St

2

4

Castle St

Jewel St

9

8

Anglican Church

To Morne Bruce & Reigate Hall Hotel

Caribbean

High St

Glover L

Cornwall St

Bath Rd

To South West & South Coasts

Victoria St

Sea

N

C 42

1. Cee-Bee's Bookshop
2. Dominica Museum
3. Kalinago
4. Old Market Plaza & Tourist Office
5. Whitchurch Travel

Hotels:
6. Cherry Lodge
7. Continental Inn
8. Fort Young
9. The Garraway
10. Kent Anthony's Guesthouse
11. Sutton Place
12. Vena's Guesthouse & The World of Food

Bus Stations:
1 Northbound Buses
2 Southbound Buses
3 Buses to Trafalgar & Laudat

Sundays. The sea wall was completed in late 1993, which has greatly improved the waterfront area of town, known as the Bay Front. The Roseau jetty, destroyed by Hurricane David in 1979, was rebuilt in the Seawall and Bay Front Development Project for the use of yachts and other small craft. A promenade with trees and benches, a road from the Old Jetty to Victoria St, and parking bays take up most of the space. A new T-shaped cruise ship jetty was completed in 1995

and for several weeks in the winter season ships tower above the town pouring forth tourists into 16-seater taxis for tours around the island. Although small, you may need to ask for directions around Roseau. Streets have been given signs but it is still tricky to find your way around.

The 40-acre **Botanical Gardens** are principally an arboretum, although seriously damaged by Hurricane David in 1979; they have a collection of plant species, including an orchid house.

Several Jacquot and Sisserou parrots can be seen in the bird sanctuary in the park, thanks in part to the Jersey Wildlife Preservation Trust. Breeding programmes are underway and it is hoped that some of the offspring will be released to the wild. In honour of its centenary in 1990, trees and plants lost in the hurricane were replaced.

The town has no deep-water harbour; this is at Woodbridge Bay over a mile away, where most of the island's commercial shipping is handled, and some tourist vessels are accommodated.

EXCURSIONS

The **Trafalgar waterfalls** in the Roseau Valley, five miles from the capital, have been the most popular tourist site for many years. Hot and cold water flowed in two spectacular cascades in the forest, but unfortunately the volume of the hot fall was sharply diminished by a hydroelectric scheme higher up (see **Flora and fauna**) and a landslide after the Sept 1995 hurricanes covered both the hot and cold water pools. The path to the falls is easy to follow, but if you want to go further than the viewing point, take a guide because there is a lot of scrambling over rocks and the way can be difficult at times. There are always lots of guides, you will probably be approached well before reaching the start of the trail. Some guides can be abusive if you insist on going alone. Agree the price before setting out, around EC$10 for two or more people in a group. Some guides are official and wear badges. Trying to cross over the falls at the top is very hazardous; bathing should be confined to pools in the river beneath the falls. The Trafalgar Falls are crowded because they are close to the road (bus EC$5 from Roseau). A natural sulphur pool has been set up at *Papillote* restaurant by the falls, set in lovely gardens and great to relax in by moonlight with a rum punch. There is also a one-hour trail from the sulphur springs of the tiny settlement of Wotten

Waven through forest and banana plantations across the Trois Pitons River up to the Trafalgar Falls. **D'Auchamps Gardens** is about a mile out of Trafalgar Village on the way back to Roseau. The designer, Sara Honychurch has laid out the family estate with a huge variety of wild and cultivated plants with a citrus orchard and a traditional Caribbean garden. For a guided tour, T 448-3346.

South and inland of Roseau (turn inland at *Sisserou Hotel* and then immediately right behind the Texaco garage) a steep road leads 2½ miles up to Giraudel. From here a trail goes up **Morne Anglais** (3,683 feet). This is the easiest of the high mountains to climb and you get some lovely views of the whole island. The trail is fairly easy to follow but someone will need to show you where it begins. Ask in the village or go with Dominica Tours.

In the far south are the villages of **Soufrière** and **Scotts Head**. There are plenty of buses (EC$3) to Scotts Head, over the mountain with excellent views all the way to Martinique. Ask around the fishing huts if you are hungry, and you will be directed to various buildings without signs where you can eat chicken pilau for EC$6 and watch dominoes being played. There is a new, clean and friendly café, *Gachettes*, on the main road just across from the most active fishing area (this boasts the only lavatories for the use of visitors). Better still walk along to the *Seabird Café* between Soufrière and Scotts Head which has a spectacular view of the whole bay (see **Places to eat**).

On the S coast is **Grand Bay**, where there is a large beach (dangerous for swimming), the 10-foot high Belle Croix and the **Geneva Estate**, founded in the 18th century by the Martinican Jesuit, Father Antoine La Valette, and at one time the home of the novelist Jean Rhys. From Grand Bay, it is a two-hour walk over the hill, past Sulphur Spring to Soufrière.

The Leeward coastal road, N from Roseau, comes first to **Canefield**, passing the turning for the twisting Imperial Rd to the centre of the island, and then the small airport. The coast road passes through **Massacre**, reputed to be the settlement where 80 Caribs were killed by British troops in 1674. Among those who died was Indian Warner, Deputy Governor of Dominica, illegitimate son of Sir Thomas Warner (Governor of St Kitts) and half-brother of the commander of the British troops, Colonel Philip Warner. From the church perched above the village there are good views of the coast.

The road continues to **Portsmouth**, the second town. Nearby are the ruins of the 18th-century **Fort Shirley** on the Cabrits, which has a museum in one of the restored buildings (entry free). Clearly marked paths lead to the Commander's Quarters, Douglas Battery and other outlying areas. The colonial fortifications, apart from the main buildings which have been cleared, are strangled by ficus roots, and cannon which used to point out to sea now aim at the forest.

From the bridge just S of Portsmouth, boats make regular, one-hourly trips up the **Indian River** (EC$25 pp), a peaceful 40-min trip, through a tunnel of vegetation as long as you are not accompanied by boatloads of other tourists. Competition for passengers is keen. Negotiate with the local boatmen about price and insist they use oars rather than a motor, so as not to disturb the birds and crabs. There is a bar open at the final landing place on this lovely river which accommodates large numbers of cruise ship passengers and serves them the very potent spiced rum, aptly named Dynamite. You can then continue on foot through fields and forest to the edge of a marsh where migrating birds come in the winter months. The river and the swamps and marshes are being considered for inclusion in the national parks system.

From Portsmouth, one road carries on to the **Cabrits National Park** and the island's N tip at Cape Melville. An unpaved road leads off this at Savanne Paille; impassable except on foot, it is a beautiful route over the mountain, through a valley with sulphur springs, to Penville on the N coast, from where you can pick up the road heading S. Allow several hours. Another road from Portsmouth heads E, winding up and down to the bays and extensive coconut palm plantations of the NW coast, Calibishie, Melville Hall airport and Marigot. **Calibishie** is a charming fishing village looking out towards Guadeloupe. There are hiking trails to the forest and wide, sandy beaches nearby (some lost in the 1995 storms); local guides are available. Transport to most areas in the northern part of the island is good, as is accommodation in and around the village.

The shortest route from Roseau to Marigot and Melville Hall is via the

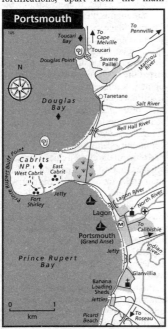

Portsmouth

Transinsular Rd, which climbs steeply and with many bends from Canefield. Along this road you will see coconut and cocoa groves; look out for the land crabs' holes, the orange juveniles come out in the daytime, the white adults at night. There are banana plants all along the gorge, together with dasheen, tannia, oranges and grapefruit. At Pont Cassé, the road divides three ways at one of the island's few roundabouts. One branch turns left, down the Layou Valley, to join the Leeward coast at Layou; the Transinsular Rd goes straight on, through Bells, to Marigot; the third branch goes E (the path up the Trois Pitons is signed on the right just after the roundabout, 3 hrs to the summit), either to Rosalie and La Plaine on the SE Windward coast, or to Castle Bruce and the Carib Territory.

Heading W from Pont Cassé the road affords some spectacular views. Layou River has some good spots for bathing, two of which are particularly good. Just over 4 miles from the roundabout there is a track to the right signposted suspension bridge, which descends to the river; bathe by the bridge. A mile further on along the road look for a narrow foot path on the right, immediately before a sizeable road bridge. It passes through a banana field to the riverside. On the opposite bank a concrete bath has been built around a hot spring to create an open air hot tub with room for 4-5 good friends.

At Bells there is a fascinating and beautiful walk to **Jacko Flats**. Here a group of maroons (escaped slaves) led by Jacko had their encampment in the late 17th and early 18th centuries. Carved into the cliffs of the Layou River gorge, a flight of giant steps rises 300 feet up to a plateau on which the maroons had their camp. Ask at the *Paradise Bar* in Bells for a guide and dress for river walking since much of the trail is in the river itself.

The **Emerald Pool** is a small, but pretty waterfall in a grotto in the forest, 15 mins by path from the Pont Cassé-Castle Bruce road. Avoid the area on days when cruise ships have docked, as hundreds of passengers are taken to visit the Pool, with resulting damage to its delicate ecology. There is a picnic area, and toilet facilities are being built. There are no buses from Roseau but you can catch a minibus to Canefield and wait at the junction for a bus going to Castle Bruce.

The Atlantic coast is much more rugged than the Caribbean, with smaller trees, sandy or pebbly bays, palms and dramatic cliffs. Castle Bruce is a lovely bay and there are good views all around. After Castle Bruce the road enters the **Carib Territory**, although there is only a very small sign to indicate this. At the N end there is another sign, but it would still be easy to drive through the Territory without seeing anything of note except a few small souvenir shops selling basket work. In fact, there is much to see; to appreciate it fully, a guide is essential. Horseback Ridge affords views of the sea, mountains, the Concord Valley and Bataka village. At Crayfish River, a waterfall tumbles directly into the sea by a beach of large stones.

The Save the Children Fund has assisted the Waitikubuli Karifuna Development Committee to construct two traditional buildings near **Salybia**: a large oval *carbet* (the nucleus of the extended Carib family group), and an A-frame *mouina*. The former is a community centre, the latter a library and office of the elected chief. The Carib chief is elected for five years and his main tasks are to organize the distribution of land and the preservation of Carib culture. In 1994, Hilary Frederick was re-elected to the post after serving in 1979-84, defeating Irvince Auguiste, who had been chief since 1984. The dilapidated Church of the Immaculate Conception at Salybia is being restored as a Carib Museum (opening date uncertain; it has been replaced by the new church of St Marie of the Caribs, which opened in May 1991), its design is based on the traditional *mouina* and has a canoe for its altar, murals about Carib history both inside and out. Outside is a cemetery and a three-stone monument to the first three Carib chiefs after colonization: Jolly John, Auguiste and Corriett.

L'Escalier Tête-Chien, at Jenny Point in Sineku is a line of rock climbing out of the sea and up the headland. It is most obvious in the sea and shore, but on the point each rock bears the imprint of a scale, circle or line, like the markings on a snake. It is said that the Caribs used to follow the snake staircase (which was made by the Master Tête-Chien) up to its head in the mountains, thus gaining special powers. However, there are more prosaic, geological explanations.

Taking the road from Pont Cassé to the SE part of the island, you come to Rosalie. Cross the River Rosalie and go S to Pointe Daniel and Délices, passing through La Plaine. At La Plaine a fairly easy trail can be followed to the **Sari Sari Falls** (about 150 feet high). At Délices, you can see the **Victoria Falls** from the road. The Forestry Division plans to improve the rugged trail to the Falls. Be sure to take an experienced guide if you attempt the steep hike to these Falls (or the Sari Sari Falls) and avoid it in the rainy season. The White River falls in to the Atlantic at **Savane Mahaut**, reached by a steep road from Victoria Laroche down to the sea. There are delightful places to picnic, rest or swim in the river. At the weekend local families picnic and wash their cars here. If it has not rained much the previous day you can follow the river up, jumping from one to another of the big stones in the river bed. Be wary of flash floods and do not attempt to cross the river if there has been heavy rainfall as you might not be able to get back. Sea bathing here is very dangerous.

Information for travellers

BEFORE TRAVELLING

● **Documents**

All visitors entering Dominica must be in possession of an outward ticket and a valid passport. Proof of citizenship with photo only is required for US and Canadian citizens. A *Carte identité* allows French nationals to visit for up to 2 weeks. Visas are required by nationals of communist countries: they can be obtained from the Ministry of Home Affairs, Government Headquarters, Roseau. Immigration will normally grant you a stay of 21 days on arrival; extensions can be applied for but you will need a return or onward ticket.

● **Warning**

The police are strict in their enforcement of anti-narcotic laws. The present Government takes a strong stand on "moral" issues.

● **Climate**

Daytime temperatures average between 70° F and 85° F, though the nights are much cooler, especially in the mountains. The rainy season is from July to October though showers occur all through the year. Note that the mountains are much wetter and cooler than the coast, Roseau receives about 85 inches of rain a year, while the mountains get over 340 inches.

● **Currency**

East Caribbean dollar.

GETTING THERE

AIR

There are no direct flights from Europe or North America to Dominica. Connections must be made in Puerto Rico, St Maarten, Antigua, St Lucia or the French Leewards. LIAT flies from Antigua, Anguilla, Martinique, Guadeloupe, Port of Spain, St Lucia, St Maarten, San Juan and Tortola, BVI; Air Guadeloupe from Guadeloupe. Cardinal Airlines flies daily from Antigua and St Maarten and Mon-Fri from Barbados. American Eagle flies daily from San Juan; Helenair has 3 flights a day from St Lucia into Canefield, it is also a charter service, good for making tight connections.

SEA

Two ferry services operate between Dominica and the French islands. The *Caribbean Express* runs only at weekends, EC$243 to Martinique and EC$246 to Guadeloupe. The Caribbean Express agency office is upstairs in the Whitchurch Centre, T 448-2181, F 448-5787. The *Atlantica* is a 350-passenger ferry running every day except Tues and Thur, EC$263 to Martinique and EC$214 to Guadeloupe; the agent is Trois Pitons Travel, 5 Great Marlborough Street, T 448-6977. The channel where the Atlantic meets the Caribbean can be very rough sometimes so this crossing is not for the faint-hearted.

● **Ports of entry**

(Own flag) Roseau and Portsmouth. Obtain coast-wide permit. EC$1 to clear in. Permits are required for sports fishing or scuba diving. Customs main office is at the deep water harbour at Woodbridge Bay where all the large ships come in (T 448-4462). Other offices are at Anse de Mai, Portsmouth and at both airports. When the bayfront jetties are finished in Roseau there will be customs offices there too.

● **Anchorages**

Anchorages at Salisbury, *Castaways Beach Hotel*, Layou River. Do not anchor in Scotts Head/Soufrière Bay or Douglas Bay or where fishing activities are underway. In Roseau tie up to trees, using boat boys. Waste disposal at the commercial docks in Portsmouth and Roseau.

ON ARRIVAL

● **Airports**

Dominica has 2 airports, the older **Melville Hall (DOM)** in the NE, which handles larger planes, and **Canefield (DCF)** near Roseau, which takes smaller aircraft. Check which your flight will be using. Variable winds and short landing strips mean that planes do not land before 0600 or after 1800 in the dark. Melville Hall is 36 miles from Roseau; taxis cost EC$42 on the Transinsular Rd, but they can go via the East Coast Rd or the West Coast Rd and charge

more. From Melville Hall to Portsmouth by taxi is EC$30. These rates are per seat; find someone to share with, or it will be assumed you want the vehicle to yourself, which is much more expensive. Canefield is only a 10-mins' drive from Roseau; taxi fare to town is EC$20, per car of up to 4 passengers. Minibus (public transport) fare from Canefield to Roseau is EC$1.50. (You must flag one down on the highway passing the airport, frequent service weekdays, very few on Sun.)

● **Airlines**

LIAT, King George V St, Roseau, T 448-2421/2, Canefield airport T 449-1421, Melville Hall T 445-7242. Agent for Air Guadeloupe and American Eagle is Whitchurch Travel, Old St, Roseau, T 448-2181, or Canefield Airport, T 449-1060. Cardinal Airlines, T 449-0322/8922, F 449-8923. Mussons Travel, also for flight bookings, T 448-2550.

● **Banks**

Royal Bank of Canada, Bay St, Roseau, T 448-2771; Barclays Bank Plc, 2 Old St, T 448-2571 (branch in Portsmouth, T 445-5271); National Commercial Bank of Dominica, 64 Hillsborough St, T 448-4401 (opens lunchtime, branch at Portsmouth, T 445-5430); Banque Française Commerciale, Queen Mary St, T 448-4040; Scotia Bank, 28 Hillsborough St, T 448-5800. American Express agent is Whitchurch Travel, T 448-2181, efficient and helpful for emergency cheque cashing. Visa and Mastercard well accepted with cash advances from all banks.

● **Clothing**

Clothing is informal, though swimsuits are not worn on the streets. A sweater is rec for the evenings. When hiking take a raincoat and/or a pullover; a dry T-shirt is also a good idea. Take good walking shoes.

● **Hours of business**

Government offices: Mon, 0800-1300, 1400-1700, Tues to Fri, close one hour earlier in the afternoon; the only government offices open on Sat are the tourist kiosk in Old Market Plaza, and the tourist office at Canefield airport (open daily 0615-1115, 1415-1730 – or last flight); the Melville Hall tourist office is only open at flight arrival times. Shops: 0800-1300, 1400-1600, Mon-Fri, 0800-1300 Sat. Some of the larger supermarkets in Roseau stay open until 2000 and tiny, local shops may still be open at 2200 even on Sun. Banks: 0800-1500 Mon-Thur, 0800-1700 Fri.

● **Laundry**
Mr Clean Laundry, Federation Drive, Roseau,
EC$16 for big load, they wash it for you.

● **Official time**
Atlantic Standard Time, 4 hours behind GMT,
1 ahead of EST.

● **Public Holidays**
1 January; Carnival; Good Friday and Easter
Monday; 1st Monday in May; Whit Monday;
1st Monday in August; 3/4 November (Independence); Christmas Day and Boxing Day.
2 January is a merchant's holiday, when all
shops and restaurants are closed, although
banks and hotels remain open; Government
offices will in most cases not be open.

● **Representation overseas**
The **British** Honorary Consul is Mr Robert
Duckworth, general manager of Cable & Wire-
less in Dominica.

● **Security**
Crime is rising and there have been mugging
cases on beaches at Castle Bruce in the E and
Hampstead on the NE coast. Robberies from
the *Red Rock Haven* and *Pointe Baptiste* cottages are fairly common; the former now
employs a night security guard. Theft is normally non violent and is of cash and easily saleable
items (eg jewellery) rather than credit cards.
Always report theft to the police, they generally
have a shrewd idea of where to look for stolen
goods and jewellery is often recovered.

● **Shopping**
Straw goods are among the best and cheapest
in the Caribbean; they can be bought in the
Carib Territory and in Roseau. Best shops for
crafts in Roseau are the Caribana, 31 Cork St
and, for the famous vetiver-grass mats, Tropi-
crafts, Queen Mary St, where you can see the
women making the mats. It takes 4 weeks to
complete a 10-foot mat. Note 4% extra
charged on VISA. Portsmouth has a sizeable
craft shop at the Cruise Ship Berth on the
Cabrits but prices are much higher than in
Roseau, eg a bar of coconut soap was 4 times
the price. Other good buys are local Bay rum
(aftershave and body rub), soap, tea, coffee,
marmalade, hand cream, shampoo, spices,
chocolate and candles. Bello 'Special' or 'Classic' pepper sauce is a good souvenir. The public
market is lively and friendly. Try a jelly coconut.
Cee-Bee's Bookshop, 20 Cork St and Paperbacks at 6 King George V St, for Caribbean
and other English books and magazines. Front

Line Cooperative Services Ltd, 78 Queen Mary
St, T 448-8664, has books, CDs, cassettes,
stationery, photography etc. Dominica Pottery
has a showroom on corner of Bayfront and
Kennedy Avenue with plenty of original pieces
made by inmates of the prison. Batiks are made
locally and available from Cotton House Batik,
8 Kings Lane. Many local crafts available at the
NDFD Small Business Complex, 9 Great
Marlborough St.

● **Useful addresses**
T 999 for Police, Fire and Ambulance.

● **Voltage**
220/240 volts AC, 50 cycles. There is electricity
throughout the island, but many places lack
running water, especially in the villages between Marigot and La Plaine.

ON DEPARTURE

● **Departure tax**
Departure tax was raised in the 1996/97
budget but details were unavailable at the time
of going to press. In 1995/96 there was a
departure tax of EC$20 and a security service
charge of EC$5, or US$10 if you paid in dollars.
Day trippers pay EC$5; under 12s are free.

ACCOMMODATION

● **Hotels and guesthouses**

Price guide

L1	over US$200	L2	US$151-200
L3	US$101-150	A1	US$81-100
A2	US$61-80	A3	US$46-60
B	US$31-45	C	US$21-30
D	US$12-20	E	US$7-11
F	US$4-6	G	up to US$3

There are a number of small, informal hotels,
guest houses and apartment facilities on the
island. Always verify whether tax (5%) and
service (10%) are included in the quoted rate.
The are 2 large hotels in the centre of **Roseau:**
L2-L3 *Fort Young Hotel*, within the old fort
(P O Box 519, T 448-5000, F 448-5006), has
33 rooms of an excellent standard and full
conference facilities for the business traveller,
service brusque, food adequate, pool, the atmosphere is more relaxed on weekends, special events like concerts and barbecues and a
popular Happy Hour every Fri, 1800-1900;
also the **L2-L3** *Garraway*, Place Heritage, 1
Bay Front, PO Box 789, T 449-8800, F 449-
8807, 31 rooms, again of a good standard,

conference facilities, restaurant, cocktail bar, weekend deals available to encourage tourists. **L3-A1** *Sutton Place Hotel*, 25 Old St, PO Box 2333, T 449-8700, F 448-3045, one of the newest hotels on the island, 8 rooms, beautiful decor, excellent service, self-catering suites available. Otherwise, lodging in town is in guesthouses: **A3** *Continental Inn*, 37 Queen Mary St, T 448-2214/6, F 448-7022, 13 rooms, a/c, fans, TV, bar, restaurant, entertainment, used by travelling salesmen and visiting sailors, good food; **C** *Kent Anthony Guesthouse*, 3 Great Marlborough St, T 448-2730, 18 rooms, with fan and bath, cheaper rooms without, good food, rooms of varying standard, lack of maintenance, brusque landlady; **C** *Vena's Guesthouse*, 15 rooms, prices higher during carnival, 48 Cork St, T 448-3286, Jean Rhys' birth place, interesting, rather inefficient, rooms small and grim, rooms without bath more spacious and comfortable but noisy as on the corner of the 2 main streets, *The World of Food* restaurant is next door; **D** *Wykies Guesthouse*, 51 Old St, T 448-8015, F 448-7665, 6 rooms, shared shower, no fan, clean, friendly owner, very popular bar to the front so do not plan an early night. **B** *Cherry Lodge Guesthouse*, 20 Kennedy Ave, T 448-2366, historic and quaint, some rooms with bath, rooms can be noisy and mosquitoes abundant, coils provided but no fans, good value meals available to order; **B-C** *Bon Marché Guest House*, 11 Old St, PO Box 449, T 448-2083/4194, 6 rooms, fans, bar, souvenir shop and boutique on site; **B-C** *Ma Bass Central Guest House*, 44 Fields Lane, T 448-2999, 7 rooms, fans, food available. Apartments are available to rent in and around Roseau, check at the Tourist Office, look in the *New Chronicle*, *Tropical Star* or ask a taxi driver. **A3** *Honychurch apartment*, 5 Cross St, T 448-3346, PO Box 1889, very central, discounts for a week, even nicer to stay at their *D'Auchamps Apartments* up in the Trafalgar Valley and hire a car, see below. **A2-A3** *Itassi Cottages*, self-catering, on Morne Bruce, spectacular view of S coast, one studio, 2 cottages, attractively furnished, phone, TV, contact Mrs U Harris, PO Box 2333, T 448-4313, F 448-3045.

Outside Roseau, up a steep and windy hill (King's Hill), is **A1-A3** *Reigate Hall*, with a splendid location but laid back management, rec for sunset rum punch to watch the Green Flash, T 448-4031/2/3, F 448-4034, 15 rooms and suites, fans, service in restaurant sloppy and slow, pricey, bar, swimming pool, tennis courts, dive packages with Dive Dominica. Further up the Roseau Valley are **L1-A3** *Roseau Valley Hotel*, T 449-8176, 11 rooms and suites, also cottages for longer term rental, and nearby **A3-C** *End of Eden Guest House*, Copthall, Roseau Valley, c/o 2 Princess Lane, Goodwill, T/F 448-8272, fans, some with shared bathroom. A short distance S of Roseau, at Castle Comfort on the way to Soufrière, are: **L3-A2** *Anchorage*, on seafront, T 448-2638/9, F 448-5680, waterfront restaurant, some rooms rather tatty, bar, friendly service, food nothing special, swimming pool and diving facilities, a 7-night, 10-dive package available, squash court with rather low ceiling; a friendly and delightful place to stay, family-run, with good restaurant and excellent service is **L3-A1** *Evergreen*, P O Box 309, T 448-3288/448-3276, F 448-6800, 16 rooms, with breakfast, a/c, TV, bar; **A2-A3** *Reigate Waterfront*, P O Box 134, T 448-3111, F 448-3500, restaurant with well-known barbecue Wed night, 24 rooms, recently refurbished; **L3** *Castle Comfort Lodge*, highly rec, very friendly, professional, excellent local food, good service, P O Box 2253, T 448-2188, F 448-6088, a 7-night 10-dive package available inc transfers, unlimited shore diving, tax and service, (see above under **Diving and marine life**).

Also close to Roseau is **A2** *Ambassador*, within walking distance of Canefield airport, PO Box 2413, T 449-1501/2, F 449-2304, reasonable restaurant, comfortable, but can be noisy, good for business visitors; **L3-A2** *The Hummingbird Inn*, Morne Daniel, PO Box 1907, Roseau, T/F 449-1042, rooms or a suite, run by Mrs Finucane who is very knowledgeable on Dominica, peaceful, simple, comfortable, good food, stunning views down the hill over the sea, 5 mins N of Roseau, on bus route, rec; **L3** *The Wesleean Apartel*, PO Box 1764, T 449-0419, F 449-2473, towers over 8th Street in Canefield, 11 very tastefully decorated apartments for daily or longer rental.

Near the Trafalgar Falls (15 mins' walk) is **A2** *Papillote Wilderness Retreat*, PO Box 2287, T 448-2287, F 448-2285, 10 bedrooms or cottage in beautiful gardens landscaped by owner Anne Jean Baptiste, with hot mineral pool and geese, food good but slightly limited for long stay; new restaurant for non-residents now open near road, lunch and dinner, food well prepared and nicely presented, closed Sun (avoid days when cruise ship passengers invade, reservations required). Good road from the nearby village of Trafalgar all the way to the Falls car park, spectacular setting; on the road to Trafalgar and Papillote, the Honychurch family rents a 4-room apartment on their lovely estate, **B** *D'Auchamps*, PO Box 1889, T 448-3346. **A2-B** *Roxy's Mountain Lodge* in Laudat, PO Box 265, T/F 448-4845, good breakfast and hearty supper, friendly owners, basic rooms, good beds, hot showers, also apartment, 4-6 people, convenient for visiting Boiling Lake, Boeri Lake, Middleham Falls, Trafalgar Falls and Freshwater Lake, all within walking distance, guides arranged if required, transport into Roseau 0700 except Sun, returning 1615, EC$3. Also in Laudat, **A2-A3** *Symeszee Villa*, PO Box 1728, T 448-2494/3337, F 448-4476, 16 rooms. **A2** *Springfield Plantation*, in the interior but only 6 miles N from Roseau, PO Box 456, T 449-1401, F 449-2160, has a magnificent setting 1,200 feet above sea level, overlooking a lush valley, lovely rooms, apartments, suites, cottages, modernized and enlarged wooden plantation house, but now also an agricultural research centre so periodically overrun by students, erratic management, but food can be good. **L3** *Exotica Enterprises*, PO Box 109, T 448-7895, F 448-3855, nestled under the peaks of Morne Anglais close to Giraudel, new ecotourism centre, run by Athie Martin, president of the Dominica Conservation Society, 8 wooden cottages, sympathetic design, good base for hiking, self-catering, with advance notice the *Sugar Apple Café* will prepare meals.

On the extreme S coast E of Scotts Head, reached from Soufrière, are **L1-A1** *Petit Coulibri Guest Cottages*, PO Box 331, Roseau, T 446-3150, F 449-8182, on the Petit Coulibri Estate which used to grow sugar, cacao, and until recently aloe vera, but still grows citrus. The 3 cottages have 2 bedrooms, pool, maid service, built 1,000 feet above sea, overlooking Martinique, isolated setting, described by some as one of the most beautiful places in the world, solar powered, home grown food and locally caught fish, run by Barney and Loye Barnard. In Scotts Head **A2-B** *Gachette's Seaside Lodge*, Bay St, T 448-4551, F 449-8000, 12 rooms, fans, a/c, TV, fish restaurant, watersports, diving, fishing arranged. Other self-catering apartments include **A3** *Castille Apartment*, Scotts Head, T 448-2926; **L3-A1** *Hilfrance Cottage*, Scotts Head, PO Box 133 (Roseau), T 448-8777, F 449-8544; *Ocean View Apartments*, T 449-8266,

owned by the very hospitable Frank and Caroline Charles, 1 or 2 bedroom apartment, nicely furnished, large secluded garden with fruit trees, mosquito nets, also 2 rooms in main house, maid and laundry service offered and transport to airport, rec.

A1 *Castaways*, Mero, PO Box 5, T 449-6244, F 449-6246, in USA T 800-322-2223, just N of St Joseph, convenient with hired car for visiting all parts of the island, on black sand beach, restaurant, beach barbecue on Sun, popular, watch out for beach cricket balls, staff slow but friendly, reasonable rooms all with balcony and sea view but in need of redecoration, ask for fan and mosquito net, good tennis court, sailing sometimes available, dive shop attached, German spoken, dive package available. **L2-L3** *Lauro Club*, Grand Savanne, PO Box 483, Roseau, T 449-6602, F 449-6603, opened 1992, self-contained bungalows sleep 1-4, half-way between Roseau and Portsmouth, multi-lingual Swiss owners, pool, bowls, small shops and snack bar in central building, built on cliff top overlooking sea, access to sea but no beach.

In **Portsmouth** are **B** *Casa Ropa*, on Bay St, T 445-5492, F 445-5277, rooms or apartments with bath, single downstairs, friendly, clean, rec; **C** *Douglas Guest House*, Bay St, T 445-5253, single, double or triple rooms, ask for fan, clean, next to noisy disco and cinema; **B** *Mamie's On The Beach*, Prince Rupert's Bay, T/F 445-3099, has pleasant, modern rooms, fans, bathroom, no mosquito screens, adjoining restaurant. Ask around for low budget rooms/huts to let. **Southern Prince Rupert Bay**, **A3** *Portsmouth Beach Hotel* is primarily used by students at the nearby Ross Medical School (PO Box 34, T 445-5142, F 445-5599), half price for children, there is a pool, restaurant, diving packages available. On the beach is a sister establishment, **L3-A2** *Picard Beach Cottage Resort* (also PO Box 34, T 445-5131, F 445-5599) which has an attractive open-sided restaurant and bar, self-catering cottages which, at a pinch, can sleep 4, good sea bathing with coral reef, 7-night, 10-dive, package available. Further apartments are being built on the beach. **A3** *Sango's Sea Lodge*, Prince Rupert's Bay, beach bar, fresh fish and 6 apartments set in lovely gardens, spacious, self-contained, insect nets, 2 double beds, bathroom, run by Willie (who catches the fish) and Harta (German) Sango, T 445-5211, rec, yachts can moor in the bay, sandy outside beach bar.

On the N coast near the charming fishing village of **Calibishie**, **L2** *Pointe Baptiste* estate rents out the Main House, sleeping 6, inc cook and maid, US$960-1,050 a week, spectacular view from the airy verandah, house built in 1932, wooden, perfect for children, cot, also smaller house **A2** sleeping 3, self-catering, reduced weekly rates, book locally through the housekeeper Geraldine Edwards, T 445-7322. A more luxurious option next door are 3 new self-catering villas **L1-L3** *Red Rock Haven*, call Rose Aird, T 448-2181, F 448-5787, tastefully decorated, sleep up to 6, maid service can be arranged, share beach, 10-min walk below with guests from *Pointe Baptiste*, go down at sunset and red rocks glow against white sand, also safe cove for children's bathing, wonderful to have the place to yourself. In the village, **A3** *Veranda View*, run by Mrs Teddy Lawrence, facing beach, beautiful view of Guadeloupe, clean, bright and large rooms, light cooking facilities, hot showers, meals US$5-8, rec; **L3** *Eden Estate House* is also available for rent, 3 bedrooms, in middle of coconut and fruit plantation, only 3 miles from Melville Hall airport, maid service can be provided.

In **Marigot**, **B** *Thomas's Guest House*, W end of main street, T 445-5591, clean, basic, near Melville Hall airport (check in advance if it is open); **B** *Paul Carlton's Guest House*, E end of main street, 6 clean, basic rooms, cooking facilities, cheaper for longer than 1 night, Paul also runs taxi service.

Away from the Leeward Coast: **A1** *Layou River*, PO Box 8, T 449-6281, F 449-6713, nice location, pool, restaurant, bar, river bathing, may be noise from construction of neighbouring *Shangrila* hotel; **A1** *Layou Valley Inn*, 5 rooms, rather bossy landlady at times but very comfortable, excellent cuisine, high in the hills with superb views, need a car to get there, T 449-6203, F 448-5212, PO Box 196. **A2** *Floral Gardens*, Concord Village, at the edge of the Carib Territory, T/F 445-7636, comfortable rooms, with breakfast, apartments, **A1**, 10% discount for stays of 5 days and over, dinner, excellent food but expensive and service very slow, lovely gardens by the Pagua River where you can swim, 15 mins away from beaches of Woodford Hill, electrics basic, ask for a mosquito coil for your room, many minibuses in the morning, easy to get a pick-up, bus to Roseau EC$9, 1 hour, bus to airport and Woodford Hill Beach, lovely walks in the area, either into the Carib territory or around Atkinson further N, rec. Charles Williams and his wife, Margaret, run the **B** *Carib Territory Guest House*, Crayfish River, on the main road, T 445-7256, she cooks if meals are ordered in advance but there are no restaurants nearby as an alternative and you may go hungry, water intermittent, he also does island-wide tours but is better on his own patch. About a mile away, **E** *Olive's Guest House* at Atkinson, slightly set back off the road, has been rec, bamboo huts, comfortable, friendly, meals extra, T 445-7521.

● **Camping**
Camping is not encouraged and, in the National Parks, it is forbidden. Designated sites may be introduced in the future.

FOOD AND DRINK

(Not including hotels, where a sales tax of 3% may be added to meal charges.) In Roseau, *La Robe Créole*, Victoria St, créole and European, good but expensive, service inattentive; with same ownership is the *Mouse-Hole Café*, underneath, which is excellent for little pies and local pasties; *Pearl's Cuisine*, 19 Castle St, good local food and service, reasonable prices, also mobile wagon in town centre catering for lunchtime takeaway trade; *Restaurant Paiho*, Castle St, T 448-8999, good Chinese food, delicious fruit punch, uncrowded, slightly pricey, open Mon-Fri 1100-2200, Sat-Sun 1800-2200; *Flibuste*, Great Marlborough St, French chef, pricey but lunch time specials available, daily salad bar, steaks and fish grilled to order; *The Blue Max Café*, Hanover St, rec, cappuccino, foreign beers, deli-style food, Egyptian owner Morad Zakha is an archaeologist and pilot, lively conversation at the bar; *The World of Food*, next to *Vena's Guesthouse*, local dishes but unexciting, good breakfast about EC$10, lunch and dinners EC$20-30, drink your beer under a huge mango tree which belonged to writer Jean Rhys's family garden. *Guiyave*, 15 Cork St, for midday snacks and juices, patisserie and salad bar, popular, crowded after 1300. *Cartwheel Café*, Bay St (next to Royal Bank of Canada), clean, on waterfront, good place to stop for a coffee; the smell of *Baylime's* spit roasted chickens waft across the bayfront at night, grab a cold beer to go with it, on Fri and Sat their customers line the bayfront listening to music and chilling out; *Creole Kitchen Ltd*, in Woodstone Shopping Mall on corner of

George St and Cork St, fried or barbecued chicken, sandwiches, burgers, cold drinks, open Mon-Thur 0800-2300, Fri-Sat 0800-1200, Sun 1500-2300; *Green Parrot*, King George V St, small, family-run, good value creole food, daily specials for US$4-5; *Cottage Restaurant*, Hillsborough St, friendly, fish, rice, salad and provisions for EC$10; *Orchard*, corner of Great George and King George V Streets (friendly yet slow service, but food OK, good *callaloo*). Lots of 'snackettes', eg *Hope Café*, 17 Steber St, good local dishes and snacks, lively, open till late; *Celia's Snack*, EC$1.50 for delicious bread and codfish, good local ice cream, fruit juice, on Great Marlborough St; *Margherita's Pizzeria*, opp the Old Market Plaza, nice pizza but be prepared to wait a long time, also pasta, open also on Sun 1300-2200; *Erick's Bakery* has a small patisserie on Old St for 'tasty island treats'. *Wykie's*, 51 Old St, cheap and plentiful food, Fri nights often has a Jing Ping band playing on the verandah, casual, relaxed atmosphere. On Wed night *The Anchorage* has a good value buffet and reggae band. If staying in town there are 2 places worth taking a taxi to eat: *Papillote* (see above, **Accommodation**), book before 1600, take swimming costume and towel for bathe in sulphur pool under the stars; *Reigate Hotel* (also see above), book ahead, slow service but ask to eat out on balcony overlooking valley of Roseau, catch the sunset for spectacular view.

E George Chicken Shack, on roadside between Emerald Pool and Pont Cassé, small bar, cold beer and great fried chicken. *La Flambeau Restaurant* at Picard Cottage, near Portsmouth, is comfortable, has an attractive beachside setting and a varied menu. *The Almond Beach Bar and Restaurant* at Calibishie on the N coast has been rec, it has very good food and fresh fish; *Teddy's Guest House* also does meals, US$5-8; *New Stop Café and Bar*, close to Trafalgar Falls, overlooking river, just down the road from *Papillotte*, tiny, outdoors, seats 10-15 people, delicious food, contact the proprietors in the morning (c/o Mayfield Denis) to arrange menu, also good for beer, conversation and reggae, rec. *Seabird Café*, between Soufrière and Scotts Head, spectacular view of whole bay, adventurous menu, best to book, especially for Sat night barbecue, T 448-7725; *Roger's Fish Shack and Bar*, Scotts Head good food and service.

On weekdays in the capital the lunch hour begins at 1300 and places fill up quickly. Do minicans eat their main meal at lunch time and

it is often hard to get anything other than takeaways after 1600 or on Sun except at hotels. If you have a car, try different hotel restaurants on different nights and check when the barbecue specials etc are being held. Generally, Dominicans eat in restaurants at lunchtime and in hotels at night.

There is little in the way of international or fast food on the island, but a **Kentucky Fried Chicken** was to open in 1996. Fried chicken, bakes (a fried dough patty filled with tuna, codfish or corned beef) and rotis (pancake like parcel of curried chicken and veg) are the most popular snacks available in most bakeries. There is plenty of local fruit and vegetables, fish and 'mountain chicken' (crapaud, or frog) in season. Try the seedless golden grapefruit, US$1 for 6 in the market. The term 'provisions' on a menu refers to root vegetables: dasheen, yams, sweet potatoes, tannia, pumpkins, etc. To buy fresh fish listen for the fishermen blowing their conch shells in the street; there is no fish shop but fish can be bought in the market on Fri and Sat, get there early, usually EC$7/lb. Try the sea-moss drink, rather like a vanilla milk shake (with a reputation as an aphrodisiac), also drunk on Grenada, see page 759.

GETTING AROUND

LAND TRANSPORT

● **Motoring**

Driving is on the left. The steering wheel may be on either side. You must purchase a local driving permit, valid for one month, for EC$50, for which a valid international or home driving licence is required; the permit may be bought from the police at airports, or at the Traffic Dept, High St, Roseau or Bay St, Portsmouth (Mon to Fri). Main roads are fairly good; the Portsmouth-Marigot road built in 1987 is excellent, but in towns and S of Roseau, roads are very narrow and in poor condition. There are few road signs, but with a good map finding your way is not difficult. The Tourism Office in the Old Market, Roseau, sells Ordnance Survey maps.

You have nothing to fear if you offer local people a lift and men, women and children are unfailingly courteous; the carrying of machetes is not an indication of likely violence, the bearer is probably just on his way home from his banana field.

● **Car hire**
Rates are about US$60 per day for a small

Hyundai, inc collision damage waiver and US$70 for a jeep; unlimited mileage for hiring for 3 days or more. A car rental phone can be found at the airport and several of the companies will pick you up from there and help to arrange the licence. It may be preferable to rent a car or jeep as the taxi service is expensive and buses take a lot of planning. Failing that, get a scooter from Francis Scooter Rental, 5 Cross St, T 448-5295, US$25/day. On either hand, Dominicans drive fast in the middle of the road and many visitors prefer to take a taxi so that they can enjoy the views. Companies: ACE Car Rentals, 8 Castle St, T 448-4444, jeeps, some with bikini tops, free pick up and delivery; Anselm's, 3 Great Marlborough St, T 448-2730, F 448-7559; Budget, Canefield Industrial Estate, T 449-2080, F 449-2694, rec as cheaper, more reliable and informative than some other companies, cars in good condition; Wide Range Car Rentals, 81 Bath Rd, T 448-2198, F 448-3600 rents out old Lada cars for US$30 a day, not rec for smaller roads, also Suzuki jeeps, US$60 a day including 80 miles and collision protection free; Valley, PO Box 3, T 448-3233, on Goodwill Rd, next to Dominican Banana Marketing Corporation, or in Portsmouth, T 445-5252, free delivery to Canefield and within 2 miles of Roseau or Portsmouth offices, cars in need of maintenance but in the cheaper category; also on Goodwill Rd, S T L, US$387/10 days inc EC$20 licence and insurance, PO Box 21, T 448-2340, free deliveries as for Valley, but only in Roseau area. It is extremely difficult to hire a vehicle between Christmas and New Year without prior reservation.

● **Bicycles**
Mountain bikes can be rented from Nature Island Dive, T 449-8181, F 449-8182, US$11/hr, US$21 half day, US$32/day. Biking excursions also arranged, US$55-84pp with guide.

● **Buses**
Minibuses run from point to point. Those from Roseau to the NW and NE leave from between the East and West bridges near the modern market; to Trafalgar and Laudat from Valley Rd, near the Police Headquarters; for the S and Petite Savane from Old Market Plaza. They are difficult to get on in the early morning unless you can get on a 0630 bus out to the villages to pick up schoolchildren and return in similar fashion. Apart from the Soufrière/Scotts Head route, it is difficult to get anywhere on the island by public transport, and return to

Roseau, in one day. This is because buses leave Marigot, or wherever, to arrive in Roseau around 0700, then return at about 1300. It is just possible to get to Portsmouth and return in one day, the first bus is at 1000, returning at 1600. Many buses pass the hotels S of Roseau (eg *Anchorage*). Fares are fixed by the Government. Roseau to Salisbury is EC$3.50, to Portsmouth EC$7.50, to Woodford Hill EC$9, to Marigot EC$9, to Castle Bruce EC$7, Canefield EC$1.50, Laudat EC$3, Trafalgar EC$2.25.

Hitchhiking rides in the back of the ubiquitous pick-up trucks is possible. It is often difficult at weekends.

● **Taxis**
A sightseeing tour by taxi will cost EC$45 per hour, per car (4 people), but it is wise to use experienced local tour operators for sightseeing, particularly if hiking is involved. Fares on set routes are fixed by the Government (see above for rates to the airports). Ask at your hotel for a taxi; in Roseau, Mally's Taxi Service, 64 Cork St, T 448-3360/3114 (if planning a day trip out of town on public transport, you can sometimes arrange to be picked up and returned to Roseau by their airport taxi service), Eddie, 8 Hillsborough St, T 448-6003, and others.

COMMUNICATIONS

● **Language**
English is the official language but patois is spoken widely. It is very similar to that spoken on St Lucia and to the créole of Martinique and Haiti but people tend to speak more slowly (see **Culture,** above).

● **Postal services**
Hillsborough St and Bay St, Roseau, 0800-1600 Mon to Fri. A mural depicts the development of the postal service in Dominica. This Post Office opened in 1993; it has a list of other stamp sellers around the island. Paperbacks on Cork St and other stationers or gift shops. A postcard to Europe costs EC$0.55. Parcels go airmail only. Post your mail at the main Post Office if possible, post boxes around the country are not all in operation and there is no indication of which ones have been taken out of service. DHL is in the Whitchurch Centre, represented by Whitchurch Travel Agency, T 448-2181, F 448-5787.

● **Telecommunications**
Telephone, fax and telex services at Telecommunications of Dominica (TOD), Mercury

House, Hanover St, Roseau, open 0700-2000, Mon-Sat. Phone cards are available for EC$10, 20 and 40 from Cable and Wireless and some shops. The international telephone code for Dominica is 809.

MEDIA

● **Radio**
DBS broadcasts on AM 595 kHz and FM 88.1, 88.6, 89.5, 103.2 and 103.6 MHz. Kairi Fm is the most listened to radio station with a more lively presentation style than the state-owned DBS. It is on FM 93.1, 107.9 MHz. Vol is on AM 1060 KHz, FM 102.1, 90.6 MHz. There are 2 religious radio stations (one Protestant and one Catholic) as well as a repeater for St Lucian Radio Caribbean International on FM 98.1 MHz.

ENTERTAINMENT

Mid-week entertainment at *Anchorage* and *Reigate Waterfront* hotels. Weekends at *Fort Young Hotel*, Fri night happy hour 1800-1900, live music, popular with ex-pats, tourists and locals alike, night club open Fri and Sat. On the bayfront, the *Bayline* is a popular spot on Wed (live music) and at weekends, great fried chicken. *Symes-Zee* on King George V St is the spot to be on Thur night with live jazz and friendly atmosphere. Discos at Canefield: *Warehouse* on Sat, in converted sugar mill by the airport, gets going after 2300, rec; *Club Coconuts* on Fri. *Good Times*, an old house next to the *Warehouse Disco*, opens periodically for live shows featuring local bands. For lovers of zouk music, try *WCK, Midnight Grooves* or *First Serenade*. A cinema has opened in Roseau at the Prevo Cinemall, Old St and Kennedy Avenue.

TOURIST INFORMATION

● **Local tourist office**
The Dominica Division of Tourism has its headquarters in the National Development Corporation, in a converted Rose's Lime Juice factory, Valley Rd, Roseau (PO Box 293, T 448-2045, F 448-5840). There is a Dominica Information Desk in the arrival section of VC Bird International Airport, Antigua, open daily. A useful brochure is *Discover Dominica* available free from the tourist offices at both airports or in the Old Market Square (open Mon-Fri 0800-1600, Sat 0900-1300). Other useful guides and booklets are produced by the Forestry

Division and are available from their offices in the Botanical Gardens, priced from EC$0.25-EC$15.

● **Tourist offices overseas**
Canada: OECS Mission in Canada, Suite 1050, 112 Kent St, Ottawa, Ontario KIP 5P2, T 613-236-8952, F 613-236-3042.

UK: Dominica High Commission, 1 Collingham Gardens, Earls Court, London SW5 0HW, T 0171 835 1937, F 0171 373 8743, or the Caribbean Tourism Organization, Suite 3.15, Vigilant House, 120 Wilton Rd, Victoria, London SW1V 1JZ, T 0171 233 8382. F 0171 873 8551.

USA: In New York information can be obtained from the Caribbean Tourism Association, 20 East 46th St, New York, NY 10017-2452, T 212-682 0435, F 212-697 4258, or the Dominica Consulate Office, Suite 900, 820 2nd Avenue, New York, NY 10017, T 212-599 8478, F 212-808 4975.

● **Local travel agents**
Island tours can be arranged through many of the hotels, for instance Dominica Tours at the *Anchorage Hotel*, T 448-2638, F 448-5680, PO Box 34 (an 8-day, 7 night package including accommodation, all meals, transfers, plus a photo safari, hiking, birdwatching, boating and sailing, costs about US$1,000 pp). The most knowledgeable operators are Antours (Anison's Tour and Taxi Service), 10 Woodstore Shopping Mall, Roseau. T 448-6460, F 448-6780, Ken's Hinterland Adventure Tours and Taxi Service, Ken and Clem rec, 62 Hillsborough St, Roseau, PO Box 447, T 448-4850, F 448-8486 and Lambert Charles, strong on conservation and hiking, no office but T 448-3365. Other operators include Paradise Tours, 4 Steber St, Pottersville, Roseau, T 448-5999/448-4712, F 448-4134; Alfred Rolle's Unique Tour Services, Trafalgar Village, T 448-7198/2287, or through *Papillote*, Alfred is rec as competent, responsible, knowledgeable and charming. Check beforehand which tours are offered on a daily basis or once or twice a week. You may have to wait for the tour you want or be offered an alternative. German, French, Spanish and English are offered at different agencies. The Whitchurch Travel Agency, PO Box 771, Old St, Roseau, T 448-2181, F 448-5787, handles local tours as well as foreign travel and represents American Express Travel Related Services, several airlines and Caribbean Express. Fun, Sun Inc at 21 Hanover St, T 448-6371, F 448-1606.

● **Maps**

The Ordnance Survey, Romsey Rd, Southampton, SO9 49H, UK, T 01703 792792, publishes a 1:50,000 colourful map of Dominica, with a 1:10,000 street map insert of Roseau, including roads, footpaths, contours, forests, reserves and National Parks. This can be bought at the Old Market tourist office in Roseau.

ACKNOWLEDGEMENTS

Thanks go to Karen Peirson, resident in Dominica, for her extensive review of this chapter.

St Lucia

S T LUCIA is the second largest of the Windwards, lying between St Vincent and Martinique with an area of 238 square miles. St Lucia (pronounced 'Loosha') has become a popular tourist destination, with sporting facilities, splendid beaches, a clear, warm sea and sunshine. (The island was the scene of the films *Dr Doolittle*, *Water*, and *Superman Two*.) It also has some of the finest mountain scenery in the West Indies.

The highest peak is Morne Gimie (3,118 feet), but the most spectacular are the Gros Piton (2,619 feet) and the Petit Piton (2,461 feet) which are old volcanic forest-clad plugs rising sheer out of the sea near the town of Soufrière on the W coast. A few miles away is one of the world's most accessible volcanoes. Here you can see *soufrières*: vents in the volcano which exude hydrogen sulphide, steam and other gases and deposit sulphur and other compounds. There are also pools of boiling water. The mountains are intersected by numerous short rivers; in places, these rivers debouch into broad, fertile and well-cultivated valleys. If you are staying in one of these valleys on the W coast (eg Marigot Bay) expect to be hot, they are well-sheltered from the breeze.

The scenery is of outstanding beauty, and in the neighbourhood of the Pitons it has an element of grandeur. Evidence of volcanic upheaval can be found in the layers of limestone and even sea shells in the perpendicular cliffs on the W coast and which occur at about 100 to 150 feet just N of Petit Piton above Malgretout and in other areas. An uplift of from 50-100 feet is supposed to have occurred comparatively recently and is thought to explain the flat plain of Vieux Fort district in the S and the raised beaches of the N Gros Islet district.

HISTORY

Even though some St Lucians have claimed that their island was discovered by Columbus on St Lucy's day (13 December, the national holiday) in 1502, neither the date of discovery nor the discoverer are in fact known, for according to the evidence of Columbus' log, he appears to have missed the island and was not even in the area on St Lucy's Day. A Vatican globe of 1520 marks the island as Santa Lucía, suggesting that it was at least claimed by Spain. In 1605, 67 Englishmen en route to Guiana touched at St Lucia and made an unsuccessful effort to settle though a Dutch expedition may have discovered the island first. The island at the time was peopled by Caribs.

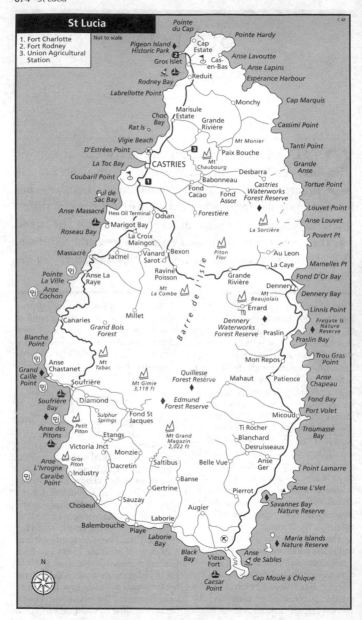

St Lucia

C 48

1. Fort Charlotte
2. Fort Rodney
3. Union Agricultural Station

Not to scale

Pointe du Cap
Pointe Hardy
Cap Estate
Pigeon Island Historic Park
2
Anse Lavoutte
Gros Islet
Cas-en-Bas
Anse Lapins
Reduit
Espérance Harbour
Rodney Bay
Labrellotte Point
Monchy
Cap Marquis
Marisule Estate
Choc Bay
Grande Rivière
Cassimi Point
Rat Is
Mt Monier
Tanti Point
Vigie Beach
Paix Bouche
D'Estrées Point
3
Grande Anse
La Toc Bay
Mt Chaubourg
CASTRIES
Desbarra
Coubaril Point
1
Babonneau
Tortue Point
Cul de Sac Bay
Fond Cacao
Fond Assor
Castries Waterworks Forest Reserve
Anse Massacré
Hess Oil Terminal
Odsan
Forestiére
Louvet Point
Marigot Bay
La Sorcière
Anse Louvet
Roseau Bay
Povert Pt
La Croix Maingot
Massacré
Vanard
Bexon
Au Leon
Jacmel
Sarot
La Caye
Mamelles Pt
Pointe La Ville
Anse La Raye
Ravine Poisson
Piton Flor
Fond D'Or Bay
Anse Cochon
Mt La Combe
Grande Rivière
Dennery
Millet
Mt Beaujolais
Dennery Bay
Canaries
Errard
Linnis Point
Grand Bois Forest
Denney Waterworks Forest Reserve
Praslin
Fregate Is Nature Reserve
Blanche Point
Barre de l'Isle
Praslin Bay
Anse Chastanet
Mt Tabac
Quillesse Forest Reserve
Mon Repos
Trou Gras Point
Grand Caille Point
Soufrière
Mt Gimie 3,118 ft
Mahaut
Patience
Anse Chapeau
Diamond
Edmund Forest Reserve
Micoud
Fond Bay
Sulphur Springs
Fond St Jacques
Port Volet
Soufrière Bay
Petit Piton
Ti Rocher
Troumassé Bay
Anse des Pitons
Etangs
Mt Grand Magazin 2,022 ft
Blanchard
Victoria Jnct
Monzie
Desruisseaux
Gros Piton
Dacretin
Saltibus
Belle Vue
Anse Ger
Anse L'Ivrogne
Industry
Point Lamarre
Caraibe Point
Banse
Anse L'slet
Choiseul
Sauzay
Gertrine
Pierrot
Savannes Bay Nature Reserve
Augier
Balembouche
Laborie
Maria Islands Nature Reserve
Piaye
Laborie Bay
Black Bay
Vieux Fort
Anse de Sables
Cap Moule à Chique
Caesar Point

N

Deluged by Debbie ...

On 10 September 1994, St Lucia was hit by Tropical Storm Debbie, which dumped 26 inches of rain on the island in seven hours. Four people were killed and 24 injured, while the fertile valleys became a sea of mud and the damage was worse than that caused by Hurricane Allen in 1980. The valleys in the W were under a foot of silt and in some cases depths of three to four feet were recorded, the Roseau Valley being worst hit. The Winban laboratory building in the Roseau Valley was swept out to sea while Winban's offices were flooded and its computers and records destroyed. Castries was flooded, Hewanorra airport was closed for three days, most water supply systems packed up and the Roseau hydroelectric dam was damaged as miles of drains and roads were blocked by mud. The banana crop was devastated, with 70,000 tonnes of bananas destroyed, about 68% of the crop.

... And Iris, Luis and Marilyn ...

In 1995 St Lucia was again hit by bad weather. In August and September Tropical Storm Iris left one dead and 17% of the fragile banana crop destroyed. Hurricanes Iris and Luis which followed it eroded all the coastal beaches but then Hurricane Marilyn brought back the sand.

There are Amerindian sites and artefacts on the island, some of which are of Arawak origin, suggesting that the Caribs had already driven them out by the time the Europeans arrived, as no trace of the Arawaks was found by them. The Indians called their island Iouanalao, which may have meant: where the iguana is found. The name was later changed to Hiwanarau and then evolved to Hewanorra. In 1638 the first recorded settlement was made by English from Bermuda and St Kitts, but the colonists were killed by the Caribs about three years later.

In 1642 the King of France, claiming sovereignty over the island, ceded it to the French West India Company, who in 1650 sold it to MM Houel and Du Parquet. There were repeated attempts by the Caribs to expel the French and several governors were murdered. From 1660, the British began to renew their claim to the island and fighting for possession began in earnest. The settlers were mostly French, who developed a plantation economy based on slave labour. In all, St Lucia changed hands 14 times before it became a British Crown

Colony in 1814 by the Treaty of Paris (more historical details can be found in the text below).

From 1838, the island was included in a Windward Islands Government, with a Governor resident first in Barbados and then Grenada. Universal adult suffrage was introduced in 1951. The St Lucia Labour Party (SLP) won the elections in that year and retained power until 1964. The United Workers' Party (UWP) then governed from 1964-79 and from 1982 onwards. In 1958 St Lucia joined the West Indies Federation, but it was short-lived following the withdrawal of Jamaica in 1961-62 (see Jamaica, **History**). In 1967, St Lucia gained full internal self-government, becoming a State in voluntary association with Britain, and in 1979 it gained full independence.

From 1964 until 1996 the UWP was led by Mr John Compton, who held power in 1964-79 and subsequently won elections in 1982, 1987 and 1992. The UWP holds an 11-6 seat majority in the 17-member House of Assembly. In 1996 Mr Compton retired as leader of the UWP and was replaced as Prime Minister and leader of the party by Dr Vaughan Lewis, former Director General of the Organization of Eastern Caribbean States (OECS), who will lead the party into the 1997 elections. The leader of the SLP, Julian Hunte, resigned after his party's poor performance in the by-election which brought Dr Lewis into parliament. He was replaced by Dr Kenny Anthony.

GOVERNMENT

St Lucia is an independent member of the Commonwealth and the British monarch is the Head of State, represented by a Governor General. The 17-member House of Assembly is elected every five years, while the 11 members of the Senate are appointed by the Governor General, six on the advice of the Prime Minister, three on the advice of the Leader of the Opposition and two of his own choice.

THE ECONOMY

St Lucia's economy has historically been based on agriculture, originally sugar, but since the 1920s particularly on bananas and also cocoa and coconuts. It has the largest banana crop in the Windward Islands. Banana exports rose from 99,000 tonnes in 1991 to 135,000 tonnes in 1992 but fell back to 108,830 tonnes in 1993, were drastically cut by storm damage in 1994 (see box) and recovered to 105,400 tonnes in 1995. The industry has suffered because of low prices; strikes by farmers have caused further damage, and in 1994 the St Lucia Banana Growers Association was put into receivership with debts of EC$44 mn. Greater competition in the European banana market, particularly after EC unification in 1992, is leading to diversification away from bananas; dairy farming, flowers and fisheries are being encouraged.

There is also some industry, with data processing and a diversified manufacturing sector producing clothing, toys, sportswear and diving gear, and 14% of the workforce is now

Saint Lucia: fact file	
Geographic	
Land area	617 sq km
forested	13.0%
pastures	5.0%
cultivated	30.0%
Demographic	
Population (1995)	143,000
annual growth rate (1990-95)	1.3%
urban	48.1%
rural	51.9%
density	231.8 per sq km
Religious affiliation	
Roman Catholic	79.0%
Birth rate per 1,000 (1994)	23.0
	(world av 25.0)
Education and Health	
Life expectancy at birth,	
male	67.0 years
female	72.0 years
Infant mortality rate	
per 1,000 live births (1994)	19.0
Physicians (1992)	1 per 2,235 persons
Hospital beds	1 per 318 persons
Calorie intake as %	
of FAO requirement	107%
Population age 25 and over	
with no formal schooling	17.5%
Literacy (over 15)	80.0%
Economic	
GNP (1993 market prices)	US$480mn
GNP per capita	US$3,040
Public external debt (1993)	
	US$96.8mn
Tourism receipts (1993)	US$221mn
Inflation	
(annual av 1988-93)	4.1%
Radio	1 per 1.4 persons
Television	1 per 5.7 persons
Telephone	1 per 5.8 persons
Employment	
Population economically active (1992)	
	57,797
Unemployment rate (1994)	25.0%
% of labour force in	
agriculture	8.9
manufacturing	13.8
construction	6.9
trade, restaurants	27.5
Paramilitary police unit	80
Source Encyclopaedia Britannica	

engaged in manufacturing. However, unemployment in the manufacturing sector rose sharply in 1996 with the closure of three foreign-owned garment factories, which had been operating for nearly 10 years, the period during which tax-free concessions are granted. The island is promoted as a location for industrial development within the US Caribbean Basin Initiative. An oil trans-shipment terminal has been built and the Government has set up several industrial estates. There are plans to establish a free zone at Vieux Fort, where a new deep water container port was opened in 1993. Public sector investment in large scale infrastructure projects includes electricity expansion and road construction.

Tourism is now a major foreign exchange earner, and in 1995 232,000 visitors stayed on the island, an increase of 6.3% over 1994. St Lucia is one of the few Caribbean islands to show consistent growth in tourism, particularly from Europeans, who stay longer than Americans. In 1994 the US market picked up, taking the largest share with 77,928 arrivals compared with 76,983 from Europe, of which 46,763 came from the UK. There are over 3,000 hotel rooms, of which the eight all-inclusive resorts of the 12 major hotels account for almost half. Further expansion is taking place with new hotels being built in the N of the island and a 350-room hotel and marina to be built by the Jamaican Superclubs chain, is planned for the S, near Hewanorra airport. Small hotels and restaurants have suffered a reported 75% drop in business since the growth of all-inclusives. The Atlantic Rally for Cruisers was changed from Barbados, its original venue, to Rodney Bay, St Lucia in 1990 and this brings revenue of about US$2mn to the tourist industry. Tourists are estimated to have spent over US$209mn in the island in 1992.

Cruise ship passengers have also shown steady increases. Although the number of calls has fallen, larger ships accounted for the rise.

CULTURE

There is a good deal of French influence: most of the islanders, who are predominantly of African descent (though a few black Caribs are still to be found in certain areas), speak a French patois, and in rural areas many people, particularly the older generation, have great difficulty with English. There is a French provincial style of architecture; most place names are French; about 79% of the population are Roman Catholics. The French Caribbean also has an influence on music, you can hear zouk and cadance played as much as calypso and reggae. The Folk Research Centre (see box) has recorded several cassettes and CDs of local music. *Musical Traditions of St Lucia* is an album of 32 selections representing all the musical genres, with information on the background of the various styles. *Lucian Kaiso* is an annual publication giving pictures and information on each season of St Lucian calypso. In the pre-Christmas period, small drum groups play in rural bars which sometimes are no bigger than a banana shed. Traditionally, singers improvise a few lines about people and events in the community and the public joins in. The singing is exclusively in patois, wicked and full of sexual allusions. The dance moves also differ from what you see at other events. It is difficult to find out where and when the drums are playing, seek local knowledge. Some announcements are made on Radio St Lucia in the patois programme (Thur and Fri evening for the weekend).

One of the Caribbean's most renowned poets and playwrights in the English language, **Derek Walcott**, was born in St Lucia in 1930. He has published many collections of poems, an autobiography in verse (*Another Life*), critical works, and plays such as *Dream on Monkey Mountain*. Walcott uses English poetic traditions, with a close

Patois for beginners

For people interested in learning a few phrases of patois, or Kweyol, there is a booklet, *Visitors Guide to St Lucia Patois*, available for EC$10 at the book shop next to the Tourist Office. For the more ambitious reader there are traditional story booklets which explain a lot about country life. Short stories are written in a style a child can understand with an English translation at the back. Examples are *Mwen Vín Wakonte Sa Ba'w*, (I am going to explain it to you), which has a tale for every letter of the alphabet about an animal starting with the same letter, or *Se'kon Sa I Fèt* (know how it is done), a book about farm life. These books are not available in shops. Contact the Summer Institute of Linguistics, Box 321, Vieux Fort, price around EC$10. Until recently, patois was not a written language but it has been developed to facilitate teaching. The Folk Research Centre (PO Box 514, Mount Pleasant, Castries, T 452 2279, F 451 7444, open Mon-Fri 0830-1630) preserves and documents the local culture and folklore and has published several books, cassettes and CDs. *A Handbook for Writing Creole* gives the main points and features, while a *Dictionary of St Lucian Creole* and *Annou Di-Y an Kweyol*, a collection of folk tales and expressions in Creole and English, accompany it well.

With thanks to Ulrike Krauss.

understanding of the inner magic of the language (Robert Graves), to expose the historical and cultural facets of the Caribbean. His books are highly recommended, including his latest work, the narrative poem *Omeros*, which contributed to him winning the 1992 Nobel Prize for Literature. Another St Lucian writer worth reading is the novelist **Garth St Omer** (for instance *The Lights on the Hill*).

St Lucia has also produced painters of international renown. **Dunstan St Omer** was born in St Lucia in 1927 into a Catholic family and is best known for his religious paintings. He created the altarpiece for the Jacmel church near Marigot Bay, where he painted his first black Christ, and reworked Castries Cathedral in 11 weeks in 1985 prior to the Pope's visit. St Omer and his four sons have also painted other countryside churches and a quarter of a mile of sea wall in Anse La Raye. **Llewellyn Xavier** was born in Choiseul in 1945 but moved to Barbados in 1961, where he discovered painting. He moved to England in 1968, where he created Mail Art, a new concept in modern art involving many well-known personalities around the world. Galleries in North America and Europe have exhibited his work and his paintings are in many permanent collections. Xavier returned to St Lucia in 1987, where he was shocked by the environmental damage. He has since campaigned vigorously for the environment through his art. *The Global Council for Restoration of the Earth's Environment* is a work created from recycled materials including prints, postage stamps and seals and logos of preservation societies. It is on permanent display at the artists studio, T 450 9155 for an appointment.

FAUNA AND FLORA

The fauna and flora of St Lucia is very similar to that on Dominica, the Windwards chain of islands having been colonized by plants and animals originally from South and Central America, with endemic species such as sisserou and jacquot. Rainforest would have covered most of the island prior to European colonization but the most dramatic loss has been in the last 20 years. Much of the remaining forest is protected, mainly for water supply, but also specifically for wildlife in places. There are many orchids and anthurium growing wild in the rain forests, while tropical flowers and flowering trees are found everywhere. To date, 1,179 different species of flowering plants have been documented. There are several endemic reptile species including St Lucia tree lizard, pygmy gecko, Maria Island ground lizard and Maria Island grass snake. The only snake which is dangerous is the Fer de Lance which is restricted to dry scrub woodland on the E coast near Grande Anse and Louvet and also near Anse La Raye and Canaries in the W. The agouti and the manicou are present throughout the island, but rarely seen.

The national bird is the colourful St Lucian parrot (*Amazona versicolor*), which can be seen in the dense rain forest around Quillesse and Barre de l'Isle. A successful conservation programme established in 1978 probably saved the species from extinction and allowed numbers to rise from 150 birds in 1978 to over 400 by 1994. However, Tropical Storm Debbie blew over the hollow trees they nest in and most St Lucian parrots moved N. Other endemic birds are the St Lucia oriole, Semper's warbler and the St Lucia black finch. Several other species such as the white breasted thrasher are rare and endangered. Measures are being taken to protect these birds and their habitats. The transinsular rainforest walk from Mahaut to Soufrière is good for birdwatching. You need a permit from the Forestry Department. Organized tours are available but are often noisy and scare the parrots higher into the mountains. There is a good chance of seeing the St Lucian parrot on the Barre de L'Isle rainforest walk, for which a permit is also needed. Only the lower half of the trail is visited by groups, because the upper part has not yet been protected against human erosion. However, it is possible to climb all the way up to Mount La Combe on a path which is not too difficult for hikers. The bird enthusiast is advised to get a permit (EC$25) and organize a private trip in a small party.

In the N of the island, Pigeon Island, Pointe du Cap and Cap Hardy are worth visiting for their landscapes, seabird colonies and interesting xerophytic vegetation, including cactus, thorn scrub etc. Union is the site of the Forestry Department headquarters, where there is a nature trail, open to the public, a medicinal garden and a small, well-organized zoo (free, but donations welcome). The Forestry Department also organizes a strenuous seven-mile trek across the island (franchized to several local tour operators and booked only through them, twice a week, with pickup from your hotel) through rainforest and mature mahogany, Caribbean pine and blue mahoe plantations which will give you the best chance of seeing the St Lucia parrot, as well as other rainforest birds: thrashers, vireos, hummingbirds, flycatchers etc. Wear good shoes and expect to get wet and muddy.

The isolated E coast beaches are rarely visited and have exceptional wildlife. Leatherbacks and other turtles nest at Grand Anse and Anse Louvet and the Fisheries Department/Naturalists Society organize nocturnal vigils to count nesting females and discourage poachers (see below). This area is also the main stronghold of the white-breasted thrasher and St Lucia wren; there are also iguanas (although you will be lucky to see one) and unfortunately the fer de lance snake, although attacks are extremely rare. The bite is not always fatal but requires hospitalization (it is extremely painful). Avoid walking through the bush, especially at night, and wear shoes or boots and long trousers.

La Sorcière and Piton Flor are densely forested mountains in the N with excellent rainforest vegetation. Piton Flor can be walked up in 40 mins although it is a strenuous climb and you will need to ask how to get to the top, from where there are spectacular views. It is the last recorded location of Sempers warbler, an endemic bird now probably extinct.

In the S, Cap Moule à Chique has spectacular views and good bird populations. The **Maria Islands**, just offshore, are home to two endemic reptiles, a colourful lizard and small, rare, harmless snake, the Kouwes snake (see page 44). The National Trust (T 452 5005/453 2479) and Eastern Caribbean Natural Areas Management Programme (EC-NAMP) run day trips with a licensed guide. All participants must be capable swimmers. Interpretive facilities are on the mainland at Anse de Sables, where you can arrange boat transport. Unauthorized access is not allowed. Good beach, excellent snorkelling. From 15 May to 31 July public access is not permitted while the birds are nesting. However, you can visit the **Fregate Islands Nature Reserve**, handed over to the National Trust by the Government in 1989. Frigate birds nest here and the dry forest also harbours the trembler, the St Lucian oriole and the ramier. The reserve includes a section of mangrove and is the natural habitat of the boa constrictor (tête chien). There is a major SE coast conservation programme being coordinated by ECNAMP.

Some of these areas are very isolated and you are recommended to get in touch with the relevant organizations before attempting to visit them.

The St Lucia Naturalists' Society meets every month at the Castries Library, Derek Walcott Square and often has interesting talks and slide shows on St Lucia. Visitors welcomed. Details in local press or from Library. The National Trust (T 452 5005) and the Naturalists' Society (T 452 2611, ask for Lunita) offer excursions involving participation in conservation. The (irregular) trips start on weekends around 0700 in front of the Library and cost EC$10. They include visits to waterfalls, beaches, rain and mangrove forests, where you are not allowed entry without a guide or permission from the National Trust or relevant Ministry. Bird watching trips start at 0500. Turtle watching is

organized during March-September when Green, Hawksbill and Leatherback turtles come ashore to lay eggs (Saturdays, 1700, EC$10, return around 0600, take food, torch, warm clothing, tents supplied, children welcome, contact Jim Sparks, T 452 8900).

DIVING AND MARINE LIFE

There is some very good diving off the W coast, although this is somewhat dependent on the weather, as heavy rain tends to create high sediment loads in the rivers and sea. Diving on the E coast is not so good and can be risky unless you are a competent diver. Several companies offer scuba diving with professional instructors, catering for the experienced or the novice diver. One of the best beach entry dives in the Caribbean is directly off Anse Chastanet, where an underwater shelf drops off from about 10 feet down to about 60 feet and there is a good dive over Turtle Reef in the bay, where there are over 25 different types of coral. Below the Petit Piton are impressive sponge and coral communities on a drop to 200 feet of spectacular wall. There are gorgonians, black coral trees, huge barrel sponges and plenty of other beautiful reef life. The area in front of the *Anse Chastanet Hotel* is a Marine Reserve, stretching from the W point at Grand Caille N to Chamin Cove. The area is buoyed off and only the hotel boats and local fishermen's canoes are allowed in. Other popular dive sites include Anse L'Ivrogne, Anse La Raye Point and the Pinnacles (an impressive site where four pinnacles rise to within 10 feet of the surface), not forgetting the wrecks, such as the *Volga* (in 20 feet of water N of Castries harbour, well broken up, subject to swell, requires caution), the *Waiwinette* (several miles S of Vieux Fort, strong currents, competent divers only), and the 165-foot *Lesleen M* (deliberately sunk in 1986 off Anse Cochon Bay in 60 feet of water).

Scuba St Lucia (PADI 5 star, BSAC, SSI and DAN) operates from Anse

Chastanet, PO Box 7000, Soufrière, T 459 7000, F 459 7700, three dive boats with oxygen on each one, photographic hire and film processing, video filming and courses, day and night dives, resort courses and full PADI certification, multilingual staff; Buddies Scuba at Vigie Marina, T 452 5288/7044, two-tank day dives, one tank night dives, camera rental, open water certification or resort course, dive packages available; Rosemund's Trench Divers at *Marigot Beach Club*, Marigot Bay, T 451 4974, F 451 4973, day and night dives, equipment rental, certification courses. The St Lucia Tourist Board can give help and advice on sites and the dive companies. A single tank dive costs around US$45-55, introductory resort courses are about US$65, a 10-dive package US$265 and open water certification courses US$390-400.

The Fisheries Department is pursuing an active marine protection programme; divers should avoid taking any coral or undersized shellfish. Corals and sponges should not even be touched. It is also illegal to buy or sell coral products on St Lucia. The Soufrière Marine Management Association coordinates problems between local fishing boats, divers and yachts and preserves the environment between Anse Chastanet and Anse L'Ivrogne to the south. Collection of marine mammals (dead or alive) is prohibited, spearguns are illegal and anchoring is prohibited. Yacht moorings are EC$40 for 1-2 nights and EC$57 for up to a week. Rangers come by at night to collect the fee and explain the programme. Dive moorings have been installed and are being financed with Marine Reserve Fees, EC$8 daily, EC$27 a year. Visitors must dive with a local company.

BEACHES AND WATERSPORTS

All the W coast beaches have good swimming but many are dominated by resort hotels. The Atlantic E coast has heavy surf and is dangerous but with very spectacular and isolated beaches (difficult to get to without local knowledge or the Ordnance Survey map and 4-wheel drive) which make a pleasant change from the W coast. Many are important habitats and nesting places for the island's wildlife (see **Fauna and flora**, above). Cas en Bas Beach can be reached from Gros Islet (45-mins' walk, or arrange taxi T 450 0806), it is sheltered, shady and a bit dirty but challenging for experienced windsurfers. There is a bar and basic facilities. Donkey Beach can be reached from there by taking a track to the N (20-mins' walk), the scenery is wild and open and it is windy. To the S of Cas en Bas Beach are Anse Lavoutte, Anse Comerette and Anse Lapins, follow the rocks, it is a 30-mins' walk to the first and an hour to the last. Access is also possible from Monchy. They are deserted, wind-swept beaches and headlands. Grande Anse, further S, is a long windy beach, reached from Desbarras. A hotel is planned here. If the road is all right you can drive, or walk (1 hour down, 1½ hours back).

Anse Louvet is a sheltered beach in a stunning setting, reached from Desbarra (3 hours' walk but no longer drivable) or Au Leon (2 hours' walk or drive if possible, but track is steep, washed out and impassable on a wet day). Ask locally about the state of the roads, which change frequently. Walking takes as long as driving; if you walk take lots of water. Louvet has a special, spooky atmosphere; La Sorcière mountain forms a long wall which seems to separate Louvet from the rest of the world. Rugged cliffs are beaten by waves and there is a blow hole. A high waterfall in the forest can be reached by following the river from the ford in the main valley (little water flow). Vanilla grows wild in the sheltered valley.

The beaches on the W coast N of Castries can be reached by bus, with a short walk down to the sea. Vigie (1½ miles from Castries) is a lovely strip of sand with plenty of shade and popular, but rather littered and neglected. Its only drawback is that it runs parallel to the airport runway. Choc Bay (Palm Beach) has good sand and shade (get off the bus after *Sandals Halcyon*). Marisule is a small beach, but popular with the locals. Labrellotte Bay is also popular and you can get lunch at *East Winds* or *Windjammer Landing*. Bois d' Orange is a deserted bay (except on public holidays), best reached on foot or 4-wheel drive. Rodney Bay has another excellent beach at Reduit, dominated by the *Rex St Lucian* (parasailing) and *Royal St Lucian* hotels, where you can use their bars and sports hire facilities but it is crowded with their guests. The northern part of the bay is cut off by the marina and it is now a 45-mins' walk or 5-10 mins' bus ride into Gros Islet, but there is no resort near the beach. There are more beaches on the way to Pigeon Island, with ample shade, where snorkelling equipment can be hired for EC$10 for 2 hrs, and two small beaches on Pigeon Island itself.

Heading S from Castries there are beaches at all the small towns but they are not generally used by tourists and you may feel an oddity. Marigot Bay is a popular tourist spot. Anse Chastanet is well used and claims to have the best snorkelling on the island, see above, **Diving and marine life**. Anse Cochon is also popular, visited by boats doing day trips, being accessible only by sea with no facilities. The smell of motor boats can be unpleasant. The trade winds blow in to the S shore and the sandy beach of Anse de Sables near Vieux Fort offers ideal windsurfing. Many hotels hire out hobbycats, dinghies, windsurfing equipment, jet bikes and small speedboats.

At Marigot Bay and Rodney Bay you can hire any size of craft, the larger ones coming complete with crew if you want. Many of these yachts sail down to the Grenadines. Rodney Bay has been developed to accommodate 1,000 yachts (with 232 berths in a full-service boatyard) and hosts the annual Atlantic Rally for Cruisers race, with over 150 yachts arriving there each December. Charters can be arranged to sail to neighbouring islands. At Rodney Bay Marina is: Trade Winds Yachts, T 452 8424, F 452 8442, an extensive range of services on offer, bareboat or crewed charters, liveaboard sailing school, trips to Martinique or St Vincent (one-way available); Sunsail Stevens Yachts, T 452 8648, bareboat or crewed charters, one-way cruises to the Grenadines. At Marigot Bay: The Moorings, T 451 4357/4246, bareboat fleet of 38-50-ft Beneteaus and crewed fleet of 50-60-ft yachts, 45-room hotel for accommodation prior to departure or on return, watersports, diving, windsurfing. There is a yacht basin at Gros Islet. Soufrière has a good anchorage, but as the water is deep it is necessary to anchor close in. There is a pier for short term tie-ups. Fishing trips for barracuda, mackerel, king fish and other varieties can also be arranged. Several sport fishing boats sail from Rodney Bay Marina. There is an annual billfish tournament, at which in 1993 a 549-lb blue marlin was landed, breaking the record.

As some of the best views are from the sea, it is recommended to take at least one boat trip. There are several boats which sail down the W coast to Soufrière, where you stop to visit the volcano, Diamond Falls and the Botanical Gardens, followed by lunch and return sail with a stop somewhere for swimming and snorkelling. The price usually includes all transport, lunch, drinks and snorkelling gear; the *Unicorn*, a 140-foot replica of a 19th century brig which started life in 1947 as a Baltic trader (used in the filming of *Roots*) sails on Tuesday, Thursday and Friday in low season, more often in high season, and has been recommended, US$70 pp, children 2-11 half price, including lunch and the inevitable rum punch, can only be booked through Sunlink International, T 452 0842 (*Unicorn* is based at Vigie Marina, T 452

6811). Other excursions on catamarans (*Endless Summer*, rec) and private yachts can be booked with tour operators in Castries or through the hotels. At the swimming stop on the return journey local divers may try to sell you coral. Don't buy it, it is illegal, and what is more, a reef dies if you do. The catamarans are usually very overcrowded and devoid of character but cost the same as the *Unicorn*. An alternative to the brig is to charter a yacht with skipper and mate (Stirrup Yachts at Rodney Bay Marina, Capt Richard Lubin, T 452 8000, 451 7403 at home or 484 9245 boat phone); a 40-foot Beneteau for up to 6 people (8 if some children) costs around US$350/day and will take you wherever you want including drinks and meals. Motor boats can also be chartered for customized trips including fishing and snorkelling, eg *Duke* (T 450 0284). Only local companies are allowed to operate day charters.

OTHER SPORTS

There is a **golf** course at Cap Estate (green fee US$49.50 inc 18 holes of golf, power cart and club rentals, T 450 8523) and a private course for guests at La Toc. The larger hotels usually have **tennis** courts, or there is the St Lucia Tennis Club. *Club St Lucia* has nine floodlit tennis courts, T 450 0551 for bookings. The *St Lucian Hotel* also has courts available for public use and lessons can be arranged, T 452 8351. **Squash** is available at St Lucia golf clubhouse at Cap Estate and the St Lucia Yacht Club (2 courts, a/c, wooden floored, glass backed, open 0800-1600, racquets for hire, balls for sale, T 452 8350). The St Lucia Raquet Club at *Club St Lucia* also has a court and optional instruction, T 450 0551.

Horses for hire at Trim's Stables, Casen-Bas (PO Box 1159, Castries, T 452 8273), riding for beginners or advanced; also offers lessons and picnic trips to the Atlantic, US$45. Country Saddles, T 453 1231, highly rec for a ride through the countryside and the seashore, good horses, guides are encouraging with beginners but still manage to give the more experienced lots of fun. The International Riding Stables in Gros Ilet also does trail rides and caters for all levels of rides, T 452 8139, choice of English or Western style.

Laborde's Gym, Hospital Rd, exercise equipment and body building, open Monday-Friday 0600-2000, T 452 2788, no credit cards. Body Inc at Gablewoods Mall has weight training, aerobics and a cardio centre, T 451 9744. Jazzercise Fitness Centre at Vide Bouteille offers fitness classes, step, stretch and weights on a walk-in basis, T 451 6853. *Hotel Le Sport* specializes in health and fitness, with tennis, cycling, weight training, volley ball etc, all inclusive packages. Jogging is organized by The Roadbusters, who meet outside JQ's Supermarket, La Clery, on Tuesdays and Thursdays at 1700 and on Sundays at 0800, call Jimmie James for details, T 452 5112 daytime, T 452 4790 evenings. Cricket and football are the main spectator sports.

FESTIVALS

Carnival is held in the days leading up to Shrove Tuesday and Ash Wednesday and is a high point in the island's cultural activities, when colourful bands and costumed revellers make up processions through the streets. On the Saturday are the calypso finals, on Sunday the King and Queen of the band followed by J'ouvert at 0400 until 0800 or 0900. On Monday and Tuesday the official parades of the bands take place. Most official activities take place at Marchand Ground but warming-up parties and concerts are held all over the place. Tuesday night there is another street party.

22 February is Independence Day. The annual St Lucia Jazz Festival in May is now an internationally recognized event, drawing large crowds every year. On 29 June St Peter's Day is celebrated as the

Fisherman's Feast, in which all the fishing boats are decorated. St parades are held for the Feast of the Rose of Lima (La Rose), on 30 August, and for the Feast of St Margaret Mary Alacoque (La Marguerite), on 17 October, which are big rival flower festivals.

Another very interesting festival is *Jounen Kweyol* (Creole Day), on the last Sun in October. Four rural communities are selected for the celebration. There is local food, craft, music and different cultural shows. Expect traffic jams everywhere that day because people like to visit all the venues across the island. On the first Sun in Oct, the different groups give a sample of their show in Pigeon Point Park. A lot is in patois, but even without basic language skills you will have a good time and a chance to sample local food.

22 November is St Cecilia's Day, also known as Musician's Day (St Cecilia is the patron saint of music). The most important day, however, is 13 December, St Lucy's Day, or the National Day, on which cultural and sporting activities are held throughout the island. This used to be called Discovery Day, but as Columbus' log shows he was not in the area at that time, it was renamed (see **History**). St Lucy, the patron saint of light, is honoured by a procession of lanterns accompanied by traditional music and mouth watering local foods. For details contact Castries City Council, T 452 2611 ext 7071. Some processions start around 0400 and are all over by midday.

CASTRIES

The capital, **Castries**, (*pop* 60,000) is splendidly set on a natural harbour against a background of mountains. The town was originally situated by Vigie and known as Carenage (the dock to the W of Pointe Seraphine is still referred to as Petit Carenage). An area of disease and defensively vulnerable, it was moved in 1768 and renamed Castries after the Minister of the French Navy and the Colonies, Marechal de Castries. It was guarded by the great fortress of **Morne Fortune** (Fort Charlotte and Derrière Fort). There is a spectacular view from the road just below Morne Fortune where the town appears as a kaleidoscope of red, blues, white and green: it promises much. However it can be a disappointment as, close to, the town is thoroughly modern but this is more than compensated by the bustle of its safe streets. The city centre is very crowded when cruise ships come in and it is best to stay away if you can. Castries is twinned with Taipei, in China, who have provided all of the town's litter bins (most of which are not used, full, or destroyed).

Largely rebuilt after being destroyed by four major fires, the last in 1948, the commercial centre and government offices are built of concrete. Only the buildings to the S of Derek Walcott Square and behind Brazil St were saved. Here you will see late 19th and early 20th century wooden buildings built in French style with three storeys, their gingerbread fretwork balconies overhanging the pavement. *Chez Paul* restaurant, 1885, is a fine example as is Marshalls pharmacy further along the street. The other area which survived was the market on the N side of Jeremie St. Built entirely of iron in 1894, it was conceived by Mr Augier, member of the Town Board, to enhance the appearance of the town and also provide a sheltered place where fruit and produce could be sold hygienically. Covered with rather flaky red paint, the fine old clock has been repaired and now tells the exact time. A new market has been built next door to house the many fruit sellers and their huge selection on the ground floor, while on the first floor and in an arcade opposite are vendors of T-shirts, crafts, spices, basket work, leeches and hot pepper sauce who have been relocated from the streets outside.

Derek Walcott Square was the site of the Place D'Armes in 1768 when the town transferred from Vigie. Renamed Promenade Square, it then became Columbus Square in 1893. In 1993 it was renamed Derek Walcott Square in honour of Derek Walcott, the poet (see above, **Culture**). It was the original site of the Courthouse and the market. The library is on its W side. The giant Saman tree is about 400 years old. On its E side lies the Cathedral which, though sombre outside, bursts into colour inside. Suffused with yellow light, the side altars are often covered with flowers while votive candles placed in red, green and yellow jars give an almost fairy tale effect. The ceiling, supported by delicate iron arches and braces is decorated with large panelled portraits of the apostles. Above the central altar with its four carved screens, the apse ceiling has

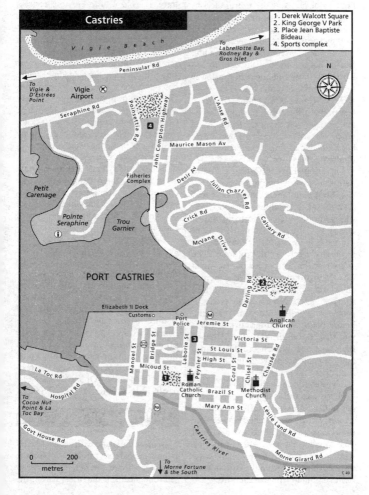

Castries

1. Derek Walcott Square
2. King George V Park
3. Place Jean Baptiste Bideau
4. Sports complex

paintings of five female saints with St Lucy in the centre. The walls have murals of the work of the church around the island painted by Dunstan St Omer, probably the most famous of St Lucia's artists (see above, **Culture**).

As you wander around the town, note the **Place Jean Bapiste Bideau** (a sea captain who dedicated his life to freedom and heroically saved the life of Simón Bolívar) and the mural on Manoel St by the St Lucia Banana Growers Association building. It was painted in 1991 by Dunstan St Omer and two of his sons and depicts scenes of St Lucian life: banana boats, tourism, 18th century sea battles, the king and queen of the flower festivals and Carib indians.

Most Ministries have moved into new Government Buildings on John Compton Highway on the waterfront. Some offices are still scattered all over town, but a fourth building is under construction for them.

On the outskirts of Castries is **Pointe Seraphine**, a duty-free complex (see below, **Shopping**), near the port. From Castries take the John Compton Highway N towards Vigie airport and branch off just past the new fish market. All of the goods are priced in US dollars and it consists largely of chic boutiques. The Tourist Board head office is here, open 0800-1630 Monday-Friday, and there is an information desk serving the cruise ship passengers. **NB** There are plenty of people who will 'mind your car' here. Ignore them. The rather curious pyramid-shaped building is the Alliance Française, the French cultural centre built in conjunction with the St Lucia Ministry of Education.

If you continue on the John Compton Highway past the sports complex and at the traffic lights turn left to go to the airport, you are sandwiched between the runway on your left and the beautiful Vigie beach on your right. There is a small war cemetery here mostly commemorating those from the British West Indies regiment who lost their lives. You can drive around Vigie point, there is much evidence of the colonial past. The St Lucia National Trust has its headquarters here in an old barrack.

Just S of Castries you can walk (unfortunately only on the main road, allow about one hour each way) or drive to the Governor's Mansion with its curious metalwork crown, at the top of Mount Morne. From here carry on to **Fort Charlotte**, the old Morne Fortune fortress (now Sir Arthur Community College). You will pass the Apostles' battery (1888) and Provost's redoubt (1782). Each has spectacular views, but the best is from the Inniskilling Monument at the far side of the college (the old Combermere barracks) where you get an excellent view of the town, coast, mountains and Martinique. It was here in 1796 that General Moore launched an attack on the French. The steep slopes give some idea of how fierce the two days of fighting must have been. As a rare honour, the 27th Inniskillings Regiment were allowed to fly their regimental flag for one hour after they took the fortress before the Union Jack was raised. The college is in good condition having been carefully restored in 1968.

On returning to Castries, branch left at the Governor's mansion to visit La Toc point with its luxury *Sandals* hotel. Take the road to the hotel through its beautiful gardens and take the path to the the right of the security gate if you want to visit the beach. Further on is the road leading to Bagshaws studio. Down a long leafy drive, you can buy attractive prints and visit the printshop to watch the screen printing process. Max, a blue green Guyanese Macau, has been in residence for decades. Open Monday-Friday 0830-1600, Saturday 0830-1200.

NORTH TO POINTE DU CAP

The part of the island to the N of Castries is the principal resort area, it contains the best beaches and the hotels are largely self contained. It is the driest part of the

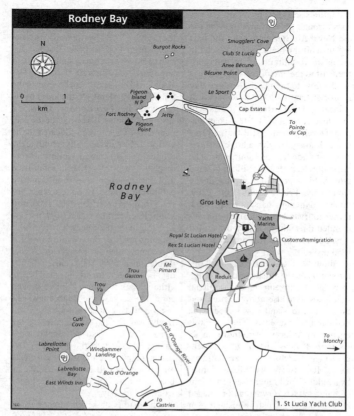

Rodney Bay

N

0   1
km

Burgot Rocks

Smugglers' Cove
Club St Lucia
Anse Bécune
Bécune Point

Pigeon
Island
N P

Le Sport

Fort Rodney   Jetty

Cap Estate

Pigeon Point

To
Pointe
du Cap

*Rodney
Bay*

Gros Islet

Yacht
Marina

Royal St Lucian Hotel
Rex St Lucian Hotel

Customs/Immigration

Trou
Gascon

Mt
Pimard

Trou
Ya

Reduit

Cuti
Cove

Labrellotte
Point

Windjammer
Landing

Bois d'Orange River

To
Monchy

Labrellotte
Bay

Bois d'Orange

East Winds Inn

To
Castries

1. St Lucia Yacht Club

island with little evidence of the banana plantations or rain forest. The John Compton highway leaves Castries past Vigie airport and follows the curves of Vigie Beach and Choc Bay. Where the road leaves the bay and just before it crosses the Choc river, a right turn to Babonneau will take you past the **Union Agricultural station** (about one mile) where there is a nature trail and interpretive centre. A mini zoo boasts a pair of St Lucian parrots. The trail goes through a nursery and herbal garden before going through Caribbean pine trees, latanier palms and cinnamon and bay trees. It takes about 20 mins.

Back on the main highway, the road passes the turning to **Labrellotte Bay** (dominated by the *Windjammer Hotel*) before reaching Rodney Bay and the town of Gros Islet. Here is the site of the US Naval Air Station of **Reduit**. Built in February 1941, the swamps were reclaimed and the bay dredged. It was the first of a chain of bases established to protect the Panama Canal. Acting as a communications centre (code name 'Peter Item'), it supported a squadron of sea planes. The base was eventually closed in 1947. The whole area now supports a mass of tourist facilities including the *Rex St Lucian* and *Royal St Lucian* hotels, restaurants and sport facilities. You can pass through the entrance gates of the old Naval Air Station or take the next left turn off the main road to reach the hotels and restaurants. If you drive past them all to the end of the road there is good access to the beach. **Rodney Bay** is an excellent base for watersports; it is ideal for windsurfing. At the back of the development is a 1,000-boat marina. Development is still taking place and at Rodney Heights a huge area has been set aside for condominiums. The normally sleepy fishing village of **Gros Islet** holds a popular jump-up in the street each Friday night, from 2200, music, dancing, bars, cheap food, rather touristy but still highly recommended for night owls. Try the grilled conch from one of the booths selling local dishes.

About ¾ mile after Elliot's Shell filling station on the outskirts of Gros Islet, turn left to **Pigeon Island** National Landmark (see also above, **Fauna and flora**), once an island, now joined to the mainland by causeway. The park was opened by Princess Alexandra on 23 February 1979 as part of St Lucia's Independence celebrations (Park entrance EC$5). It has two peaks which are joined by a saddle. The higher rises to a height of about 360 feet. Owned and managed by the National Trust, the island is of considerable archaeological and historical interest. Amerindian remains have been found, the French pirate François Leclerc (known as Jamb de Bois for his wooden leg) used the large cave on the N shore and the Duke of Montagu tried to colonize it in 1722 (but abandoned it after one afternoon). From here, Admiral Rodney set sail in 1782 to meet the French navy at the Battle of Les Saintes (see under Guadeloupe). It was captured by the Brigands (French slaves freed by the leaders of the French revolution) in 1795 but retaken in 1798 by the English. Used as a quarantine centre from 1842 it was abandoned in 1904 but became an US observation post during World War

II. The island finally became the home of Josset Agnes Huchinson, a member of the D'Oyly Carte Theatre who leased the island from 1937 to 1976. The bay became a busy yacht haven and 'Joss' held large parties to entertain the crews. Her abandoned house can still be seen on the S shore of the island. On the lower of the two peaks lies **Fort Rodney**. There is a steep climb but well worth it for the 360° panorama. The museum (located in the Officers' Mess and recently rebuilt to the original design) contains an interesting display of the work of the National Trust as well as a comprehensive interpretive exhibition. There is an entrance fee (EC$10, open every day 0900-1800; museum closed Sundays). *The Captain's Cellar* bar is in the basement. The park also contains *Jambe de Bois* restaurant which is recommended for snacks and a cool drink (open 0900-1600, closed Saturdays). You can swim off the small beach, although sandy, it has a lot of broken coral. The park is a good place for watching sea birds. Four peacocks also roam freely over the park. Offshore are the remains of the Castries telephone exchange, donated to the Fisheries Department by Cable and Wireless to make an artificial reef. It is also accessible by boat and there is a regular ferry service from Rodney Bay.

The road N passes through the Cap estate (golf course and the *Club St Lucia*) to **Pointe du Cap**, a viewpoint some 470 feet high with a splendid panorama along the coast. If you wish to explore further the N part of the island contact Safari Adventures Ltd (T 452 8778) who run all terrain vehicles to Cas-en-Bas beach. A good circular walk from Gros Islet can be done to Cas-en-Bas taking the road past *La Panache Guesthouse* (ask the owner, Henry Augustin for directions if necessary, he is always willing to help) down to the beach (sheltered, shady, a bit dirty), then following tracks N until you reach the golf course, from where you return along the W coast to Gros Islet. You will see cacti, wild scenery, Martinique and no tourists. The sea is too rough to swim. If exploring the Atlantic beaches by vehicle, make sure it is 4-wheel drive, check your spare tyre and tools, take OS map and water, be prepared to park and walk, and if possible take a local person with you. Always take local advice on the state of the roads, which change quickly. For more details, see above, **Beaches and watersports**.

The road to Monchy from Gros Islet is a pleasant drive inland through several small villages. You gradually leave the dry N part of the island and climb into forest. The ridge between Mount Monier and Mount Chaubourg gives particularly impressive views over the E coast. You will also pass through Paix Bouche where it is thought that Napoleon's empress Josephine was born. There are no road signs. Watch out for the names on schools and if in doubt at junctions bear W. At the larger village of Babonneau, you can turn right to follow the river down to the coast at Choc Bay or go straight on to Fond Cacao where a W turn will take you back to Castries. The road to Forestière is the access point for the climb to Piton Flor (1,871 feet).

EAST COAST TO VIEUX FORT

The transinsular highway from Castries to Vieux Fort has been completely repaved for most of the 33 miles to the S. Leaving Castries, one gets an increasingly good view of the town and harbour as the road climbs to the 'top of the morne', over a thousand feet. (Construction was due to start in mid-1996 on a new road from Castries to the Cul de Sac valley, which would involve the construction of two tunnels in the Morne Fortune area and cost US$19.7mn.) A detour to Calypso Ridge is worthwhile as it offers some of the most spectacular views of the island. Branch off into Sarot from the main Cul de Sac highway in Bexon. As you approach the summit, a paved road branches off to your right (note the flat V-shaped drain separating it from the main road Sarot-Vanard). The ridge road ends at a T-junction where you can turn left for La Croix/Maingot or right for Odsan in the Cul de Sac valley.

The transinsular road goes through extensive banana plantations with the occasional packaging plant through the village of Ravine Poisson before climbing steeply over the **Barre de l'Isle**, the mountain barrier that divides the island. There is a short, self-guided trail at the high point on the road between Castries and Dennery, which takes about 10 mins and affords good views of the rainforest and down the Roseau valley. There is a small picnic shelter. It is neglected and can be slippery after rain. The experience is rather spoilt by the noise of traffic. A longer walk to **Mount La Combe** can also be undertaken from this point although it is overgrown and easy to get lost. The Forestry Department may provide guides for the day for a fee. Unfortunately there have been incidents of tourists being robbed here, so caution is advised.

The road descends through Grande Rivière to **Dennery** where the vegetation is mostly xerophytic scrub. Dennery is set in a sheltered bay with Dennery Island guarding its entrance and dominated by the Roman Catholic church. Here you can see the distinctive St Lucia fishing boats pulled up on the beach. Carved out of single tree trunks, the bows are straight and pointed rather than curved and are all named with phrases such as 'God help me'. A US$6mn fishing port has been built with improved moorings, cold storage and other facilities, with Japanese assistance. There are lots of small bars but no other facilities. You can follow the Dennery River inland towards Mount Beaujolais. At Errard there is a photogenic waterfall. Permission should be obtained from the estate office before attempting this trip. A plantation tour with lunch and hotel transfers costs US$50. You will be driven around the estate by the owner whoexplainshow cocoa is processed and points out different fruits.

Fregate Island Nature Reserve, on the N side of Praslin Bay has a small but interesting visitor centre. The two small islands provide nesting sites for the frigate bird and the N promentory of Praslin bay gives a good vantage point. The reserve is closed from May-July during the breeding season. At other times call the National Trust, T 452 5005 for a guide. The area is also of some historical interest as there was an Amerindian lookout point in the reserve. It was also the site of a battle between the English and the Brigands. It used to be known as Trois Islet and the nearby Praslin River is still marked as Trois Islet river on maps today.

Praslin is noted as a fishing community with traditional boat building. The road leaves the coast here and goes through banana plantations and the villages of Mon Repos and Patience. Mon Repos is a good area to witness the flower festivals of La Rose and La Marguerite. The coast is regained at **Micoud**. There are one or two restaurants (including *Palm*, simple and clean), a department store, post office and a branch of Barclays bank. It is also the centre of St Lucia's wine industry: banana, guava, pineapple and sugar cane brewed and bottled under 'Helen Brand'.

Mangrove swamps can be seen at **Savannes Bay Nature Reserve**. The bay is protected by a living reef and is a very active fishing area. The shallow bay is excellent for the cultivation of sea moss, an ideal breeding ground for conch and sea eggs. Scorpion island lies in the bay and to the N are more archaeological sites on Saltibus Point and Pointe de Caille (the latter excavated by the University of Vienna in 1983 and 1988).

After about three miles you reach **Vieux Fort** (population 14,000), the island's industrial centre, where the Hewanorra international airport is situated. It is a bustling town with a good Saturday market, a lot of traditional housing and gaily-painted trucks for transport, although they are gradually being replaced by the ubiquitous Toyota vans. The area is markedly less sophisticated than the N of the island. The town boasts lots of supermarkets. The post office is on Theodore St which with the police station is right in the middle of the town. Fishing boats are pulled up on the small beach but there is no proper beach here. On Clarke St you will pass the square with a war memorial and band stand. The bus terminal is being relocated to a site at the end of Clarke St near the airport. Vieux Fort makes a good base for exploring the S of the island. Helen Brand, the local wine producer, is just outside Vieux Fort. You can try the different wines (rather like a heavy port) and take an unusual souvenir home. Ask your taxi driver to stop there on the way to the airport.

The perimeter road skirts Anse de Sables beach (no shade), the base for *Club Med* watersports and looks across to the **Maria Islands** (see above, **Fauna and flora**). The interpretive centre on the beach is not always open. If you want to visit **Cap Moule à Chique**, turn left at the T junction and follow the road to the banana loading jetty (you will pass truck after truck waiting to be weighed). Bear left and go up a badly maintained track. Finally go left again through the Cable and Wireless site up to the lighthouse. The duty officer will be glad to point out the views including the Pitons, Morne Gomier (1,028 ft) with Morne Grand Magazin (2,022 ft) behind it. Unfortunately Morne Gimie ((3,118 ft) is largely obscured. Further to the E is Piton St Esprit (1,919 ft) and Morne Durocher (1,055 ft) near Praslin. The lighthouse itself is 730 feet above sea level and also has good views over the Maria islands and SW to St Vincent.

THE WEST COAST TO SOUFRIERE AND THE PITONS

The West Coast Road was opened in 1995 and is in excellent condition with good signposting and many viewpoints. It is a very curvy, but spectacular, drive down to Soufrière.

Take the transinsular highway out of Castries and instead of branching left at Cul de Sac bay carry straight on. The road quickly rises to La Croix Maingot where you get good views of the Roseau banana plantation.

On reaching the Roseau valley, one of the main banana growing areas, take the signposted road to **Marigot Bay** (plenty of 'guides' waiting to pounce). A good place to stop for a drink, the *Marigot Bay Resort* dominates both sides of the valley. In between is a beautiful inlet which is a natural harbour and provided the setting for *Dr Doolittle*. It supports a large marina and not surprisingly a large number of yachts in transit berth here to restock with supplies from the supermarket and chandler. You will notice a small strip of land jutting out into the bay. This has a small beach (not particularly good for swimming) and can be reached by the *gingerbread express* (a small water taxi, EC$2 return, refundable at *Doolittle's* if you eat or drink there) either from the hotel or the customs post. It is a good place for arranging watersports and the staff of the resort are most helpful. There is a police station and immigration post here. High above the bay are *JJ's* and *Albert's* bars, popular alternatives to Gros Islet on Friday nights. You can also eat well at *JJ's*, a much cheaper alternative to the expensive restaurants at Marigot Bay.

At the bottom of the Roseau Valley, the road to Vanard and Millet branches off to the left (signposted). Millet is high up in the mountains and offers a good view of the rainforest. The road ends there. An interesting detour is Jacmel (take first right hand turn off Vanard road). If you take the first left turn in the village you reach the church, which was painted by Dunstan St Omer (see **Culture**).

The main road continues to Soufrière and passes through the fishing villages of **Anse La Raye** and **Canaries** (no fa-

cilities). A narrow, steep, bad road branches off to the right and leads to a restaurant run by Chef Harry from the *Green Parrot* (no regular service, used for private functions). Half way along this road, before it gets really steep, you can park and climb down the hill towards Canaries. There is a man-made cave and oven used by escaped slaves. Difficult to find (as intended), you need a knowledgeable local to show you where it is. There are also many waterfalls in the vacinity of Canaries, some of which are visited by organized tours. If you go independently you need a 4WD and a guide. The closest is right at the end of the road into the rainforest, others are $1/2$-$2^{1}/2$ walk away. It is safe to swim.

After Canaries the road goes inland and skirts Mount Tabac (2,224 ft) before descending into **Soufrière** (*pop* 9,000). This is the most picturesque and interesting part of the island, with marvellous old wooden buildings at the foot of the spectacular Pitons, surrounded by thick vegetation and towering rock formations looming out of the sea. Note that Petit Piton is dangerous to climb (several people have fallen off in recent years) and also that it is restricted Crown Lands. This does not stop local guides offering to show visitors up, though, for about EC$80. Because of its location, the town is a must for tourists although it is not geared for people wanting to stay there and nobody seems bothered about visitors. It can help to have an hotel guide or dayboat skipper with you. In any event it is not cheap, expect to be charged for everything (see warnings under **Information for travellers**). A stay in this town within view of the majestic Pitons is well worth while. Indeed, it is essential if you have no transport of your own and want to see the volcano and the Pitons, as there are no buses back to Castries after midday unless you make a roundabout journey via Vieux Fort. To do this, leave Castries at 0800, the ride can take 2 hrs. After visiting Soufrière, wait at the corner opposite the church and ask as many people as possible if they know of anyone going to Vieux Fort; you will get a lift before you get a bus. It is important to get off at Vieux Fort 'crossroads', where there are many buses returning to Castries by another route, 1¼ hrs. Buses to Castries leave from the market area. If you arrive by boat head for the N end of the bay, you will find plenty of help to tie up your yacht (EC$5) and taxis will appear from nowhere. It is a much cheaper alternative to tying up at the jetty. Organized tours are available from the hotels further N, by sea or road, from around US$65-70 including lunch, drinks, transfers and a trip to Soufrière, Diamond Gardens and the Sulphur Springs (see below).

Soufrière is a charming old West Indian town dating back to 1713 when Louis XIV of France granted the lands around Soufrière to the Devaux family. The estate subsequently produced cotton, tobacco, coffee and cocoa. During the French Revolution, the guillotine was raised in the square by the Brigands but the Devaux family were protected by loyal slaves and escaped. It is situated on a very picturesque bay totally dominated by the pitons. The water here is extremely deep and reaches 200 feet only a few yards from the shore, which is why boats moor close in. To reach Anse Chastanet from here take the rough track at the N end of the beach (past the yacht club) about one mile. This is an absolute must if you enjoy snorkelling (the S end near the jetty is superb but keep within the roped off area). The hotel has a good and inexpensive restaurant (although if you are on a budget you may prefer to take a picnic) and the dive shop is extremely helpful, they will hire out equipment by the hour. The *Unicorn* and day boats often stop here for a brief swim in the afternoon on their return to Castries.

Most visitors come to the town to see the Diamond Gardens and Waterfall and the Sulphur springs. There are no road signs in Soufrière and locating these two places can be difficult (or expensive if forced to ask). From the square take the road E past the church (Sir Arthur Lewis St) and look for a right hand turning to reach the **Diamond Gardens**. These were developed in 1784 after Baron de Laborie sent samples taken from sulphur springs near the Diamond river to Paris for analysis. They found minerals present which were equivalent to those found in the spa town of Aix-la-Chapelle and were said to be effective against rheumatism and other complaints. The French King ordered baths to be built. Despite being destroyed in the French Revolution, they were eventually rebuilt and can be used by members of the public for about EC$6.50. The gardens are well maintained and many native plants can be seen. Only official guides are allowed in, do not accept offers from those at the gates. Entrance EC$6 (children EC$3), open daily 1000-1700, T 452 4759. All the car parks are free, no matter what some people may tell you.

To get to the **Sulphur Springs** take the Vieux Fort road between wooden houses about half way along the S side of Soufrière square. Follow the road for about two miles (stopping off on the way to visit the Morne Coubaril Estate, an open-air farm museum, guided tour EC$15, nicely done but not a lot to see) and you will see a sign on the left. You will also be able to smell the springs. Originally a huge volcano about eight miles in diameter, it collapsed some 40,000 years ago leaving the W part of the rim empty (where you drive in). The sign welcomes you to the world's only drive-in volcano, although actually you have to stop at a car park. The sulphur spring is the only one still active, although there are seven cones within the old crater as well as the pitons which are thought to be volcanic plugs. Tradition has it that the Arawak deity *Yokahu* slept here and it was therefore the site of human sacrifices. The Caribs were less superstitious but still named it *Qualibou*, the place of death. There is a small village of about 40 inhabitants located inside the rim of the volcano. Water is heated to 180°F and in some springs to 275°F. It quickly cools to about 87°F below the bridge at the entrance. There has been much geothermal research here since 1974. From the main viewing platform, you can see over a moonscape of bubbling, mineral rich, grey mud. It is extremely dangerous to stray onto the grey area. The most famous 'crater' was formed a few years ago when a local person fell into a mud pocket. He received third degree burns. There are good, informative guides (apparently compulsory) on the site but you must be prepared to walk over uneven ground. Allow approximately ½ hour. Entrance EC$3, open every day 0900-1700.

South of Soufrière, in the valley between Petit Piton and Gros Piton, a luxury all inclusive resort, *Jalousie Plantation*, has been built despite complaints from ecological groups and evidence from archaeologists that it is located on a major Amerindian site. An important burial ground is believed to be under the tennis courts and there have been many finds of petroglyphs and pottery. Take the turning opposite the Morne Coubaril Estate on the unsigned concrete road. Half way along the drive to *Jalousie* you will see a little sign to a small, warm waterfall on your left. A Rastaman will collect about US$2 for access. You can relax in the warm waters after the hassle of visiting Soufrière.

The road from Soufrière to Vieux Fort takes about 40 mins by car. The branch of the road through Fond St Jacques runs through lush rain forest and a track takes you to the W end of the rain forest trail. In a few miles the road rapidly descends from Victoria Junction (1,200 ft) to the coastal plain at **Choiseul**. Choiseul is a quaint old West Indian village, there is a fish market and church on the beach. You can visit Caraibe Point from here: the last place on St Lucia where Caribs still survive, living in simple thatched houses. On the S side of Choiseul is the Art and Craft development centre sponsored by China. Experts from Taiwan are teaching St Lucians skills in bamboo handicrafts and you can buy pottery and carvings, as well as baskets. Bigger pieces of furniture are made from mahogany in the workshops at the back of the complex. There is a snack bar.

SE of Choiseul, there are Arawak petroglyphs on rocks in the Balembouche River. You will probably need somebody to show you the way from Balembouche or Saltibus.

Information for travellers

BEFORE TRAVELLING

● **Documents**

Citizens of the UK, USA and Canada may enter with adequate proof of identity, as long as they do not intend to stay longer than 6 months. A British Visitors Passport is valid. Citizens of the Organization of Eastern Caribbean States (OECS) may enter with only a driving licence or identity card. Visas are not required by nationals of all Commonwealth countries, all EC countries except Eire and Portugal, all Scandinavian countries, Switzerland, Liechtenstein, Turkey, Tunisia, Uruguay and Venezuela. Anyone else needs a visa; check requirements, duration of validity, cost, etc at an embassy or high commission. Without exception, visitors need a return ticket. You also need an address for where you are staying.

On arrival you will be given a 42-day stamp in your passport. The immigration office at the central police station in Castries is very bureaucratic about extensions; they cost EC$40 per period and it is worth getting one up to the date of your return ticket.

Work permits are very difficult to get and cost about US$2,500 a year. If you work for a volunteer or international organization you can obtain an exemption of work permit which is free.

● **Climate**

There is a dry season roughly from January to April, and a rainy season starting in May, lasting almost to the end of the year. The island lies in latitudes where the NE trade winds are an almost constant, cooling influence. The mean annual temperature is about 26°C. Rainfall varies (according to altitude) in different parts of the island from 60 to 138 inches.

● **Health**

Despite the breeze, the sun is strong. Take precautions, wear a hat and use high factor sun tan lotion (Banana Boat is a local range) or sun screens. Take particular care with children, who are often seen terribly burned, keep them in T shirts. There is a doctor's surgery on Manoel St, Castries, Mon-Thur 0800-1330, 1715-1815, Fri 0800-1330. Dr King at Gablewoods Mall holds a morning surgery, appointments cost about EC$50, T 451 8688. Most villages have health centres. For emergency T 999; Victoria Hospital, Castries, T 452 2421/453 7059; St Jude's , Vieux Fort, T 454 6041, Soufrière Casualty, T 459 7258, Dennery, T 453 3310. Larger hotels have resident doctors or doctors 'on call', visits cost about EC$50. If given a prescription, ask at the Pharmacy whether the medication is available 'over the counter', as this may be cheaper. The AIDS hotline is T 452 7170. As on most Caribbean islands, there is dengue fever (see **Health information**), carried by the mosquito, *Aedes egyptii*. Take anti-mosquito repellent.

● **Water**

Drinking water is safe in most towns and villages. Many rivers, however, cannot be described as clean and it is not recommended that you swim or paddle in them unless you are far upstream. There is bilharzia (see **Health i nformation**). If there has been very heavy rain there is often no water supply. This is because the intake pumps at the rivers clog up with silt and the Water Authority has to shut off all the pumps and clean them out before they can start pumping again. Hotels usually provide bottled water for drinking when this happens.

MONEY

● **Currency**

East Caribbean dollar.

● **Exchange**

It is better to change currency at a bank than in a hotel where you can get 5-10% less on the exchange. There is no rate quoted for many currencies, such as Deutsch Marks; if you insist, Canadian banks will convert them first into Canadian dollars and then into EC dollars, but you get a poor rate. The Thomas Cook representative is on Brazil St.

GETTING THERE

AIR

From Europe: The only direct scheduled services from Europe are with BWIA or British

Airways from London, Condor or BWIA from Frankfurt and BWIA from Zurich. Flights from Europe usually come via Antigua or Barbados, and Air France has a connection with Air Martinique via Fort-de-France.

From North America BWIA has direct flights from New York, and Miami. American Airlines has flights from Miami and Philadelphia and connects with other US cities through San Juan, Puerto Rico, from where there are daily American Eagle flights. Air Canada flies from Toronto.

LIAT flies from Caracas.

There are excellent connections with other **Caribbean islands**: from Anguilla (LIAT), Antigua (LIAT, BWIA), Barbados (LIAT, BWIA, Helenair and British Airways), Bequia (Helenair), Carriacou (LIAT), Dominica (LIAT, Helenair), Grenada (LIAT), Guadeloupe (LIAT), Martinique (LIAT, Air Martinique), San Juan (LIAT, American Airlines), Tortola, BVI (LIAT); St Vincent (LIAT, Helenair), Trinidad and Tobago (BWIA and LIAT) and Union Island (LIAT, Helenair).

SEA

The island is served by several shipping lines, including cargo vessels and local trading schooners. Windward Lines Ltd operate a weekly passenger and cargo ferry service linking Venezuela (Guiria or Pampatar, Margarita), Trinidad, St Vincent, Barbados and St Lucia, arriving St Lucia 0800 Sat, departing Sun, fare St Lucia to Trinidad US$62 one way, US$95 return, rate does not include port taxes, embarcation fees, transfers or food; child reductions, restaurant on board, rec for good way to see several islands at reasonable price. For information contact Windward Lines Ltd, Mendes Shipping, Valco Building, Cadette St, Castries, T 452 1364, or Global Steamship Agencies Ltd, Mariner's Club, Wrightson Road, PO Box 966, Port of Spain, Trinidad, T 809-624 2279, F 627 5091. *Caribbean Express*, or *Express Des Iles*, does a day-trip (shopping trip) to Martinique on Sat, EC$172 round trip, leaving 0700, arriving Fort-de-France 0820, return 1700 arrive 1820, tax inc, reservations Cox & Co Ltd, William Peter Boulevard, T 452 2211/3, F 453 1868, or travel agents. Continues to Guadeloupe, Les Saintes and Dominica.

Many cruise lines call. There is a US$10 pp tax on cruise ship passengers.

Captain Artes of the S/H *Krios*, Rodney Bay Harbour, runs a boat taxi (sailing) service: to Martinique, 3 days, US$220 plus customs

charges, Customs officers will contact his boat for you. Highly rec, even for the seasick.

● **Ports of entry**
(Own flag) Rodney Bay (Customs open 0800-1800 but overtime charges from 1600), Marigot, Castries, Soufrière (clear in at police station) and Vieux Fort. Pratique EC$10 up to 100 tons. Clearance EC$5 for under 40', EC$15 for over 40'. Navigational aids EC$15. EC$25 for a 24-hr permit to visit the Pitons at Soufrière. Charter boats pay additional fees. Permission is granted to stay up to 2 months, extensions cost extra.

● **Anchorages**
Halifax Harbour, Happy Hill, Grand Mall, Rodney Bay, Castries, Marigot Bay (managed by Moorings), Soufrière (see **Diving and marine life**), *Jalousie Plantation* (moorings US$15/night), Vieux Fort. Marinas at Rodney Bay, Marigot and Castries Yacht Centre. *Jalousie* has fuel and water. Charter fleets include Sunsail (T 452 8648/8848), Tradewinds (T 452 8424), Moorings (T 451 4357).

ON ARRIVAL

● **Airports**
St Lucia has 2 airports: Vigie Airport (T 452 1156), for inter-island flights only (2 miles from Castries, taxi for EC$12, no exchange facilities), and Hewanorra International Airport (T 454 6355) in the Vieux Fort district, where international flights land; there is an air shuttle to Vigie by helicopter, 12 mins, US$90. Alternatively a taxi to Castries costs EC$120 (though, out of season, you can negotiate a cheaper rate) and it will take you 1½-2 hrs to reach the resorts N of Castries. This can seem a very long journey after a transatlantic flight. If you are travelling light you can walk to the main road and catch the minibus or route taxi to Castries, or if you are staying in Vieux Fort you can walk there. No baggage storage yet available at Hewanorra. Try to arrange it with one of the Vieux Fort hotels. Porters expect a tip of EC$0.50 at Vigie and EC$0.75 at Hewanorra.

● **Airlines**
The following airlines have offices on Brazil St, Castries: LIAT (T 452 3051, or at Hewanorra airport T 454 6341, or Vigie airport T 452 2348, F 453 6584), Air Canada (T 452 3051, at Hewanorra T 454 6249) and BWIA (T 452 3778/3789 and at Hewanorra T 454 6249, F 454 5223); British Airways is at Cox and Co

Building, William Peter Boulevard (T 452 3951, F 452 2900 and at Hewanorra T 454 6172); Air Martinique, Vigie Airport (T 452 2463); American Airlines, Hewanorra Airport (T 454 6777, 454 6779, 454 6795, F 454 5953). Eagle Air Services, at Vigie, T 452 1900. Helenair, at Vigie, T 452 7196, F 452 7112.

● **Banks**
Bank of Nova Scotia (T 452 2292), Royal Bank of Canada (T 452 2245), Canadian Imperial Bank of Commerce (T 452 3751), all on William Peter Boulevard, Castries; Barclays Bank (T 452 3306), and the St Lucia Cooperative Bank (T 452 2881), on Bridge St, National Commercial Bank, Waterfront (T 452 3562), Castries. All have branches in Vieux Fort, and Barclays and National Commercial Bank in Soufrière; Barclays and Royal Bank of Canada (T 452 9921) at Rodney Bay marina. Royal Bank of Canada is reported better than Barclays for cash advances on credit cards.

Banks opening hours vary, but most are open 0800-1500 Mon-Thur, 0800-1700 Fri. Barclays Bank and Royal Bank of Canada at Rodney Bay open Sat until 1200, as does the National Commercial Bank in Castries.

● **Clothing**
Lightweight clothing all year; a summer sweater may be needed on cooler evenings. Short shorts and swimming costumes are not worn in town. An umbrella or light mac may be handy in the wet season.

● **Embassies and consulates**
Danish Consulate, Cap Estate, PO Box 328, Castries, T 450 8522/3, F 450 8317. **Embassy of the Republic of China**, Cap Estate, Gros Islet, T 450 0643. **French** Embassy, Clarke Av, Vigie, T 452 2462/5877, F 452 7899, open Mon-Fri 0800-1230, 1330-1600. **German** Consul, 6 Manoel St, Castries, T 452 2511/3671, open Mon-Fri 0800-1230, 1330-1630. **Italian** Vice Consul, Reduit, PO Box GM 848, T 452 0865, open Mon-Fri 1300-1600. **Netherlands** Consulate, M & C Building, Bridge St, PO Box 1020, Castries, T 452 3592, F 452 3623. **Norwegian** Consulate, Barnard Sons Bldg, Bridge St, Box 169, Castries, T 452 2216, F 453 1394. **Organization of American States**, Vigie, T 452 4330. **Organization of Eastern Caribbean States**, Morne Fortune, T 452 2537. **UK**: British High Commission, 24 Micoud St, Derek Walcott Square, PO Box 227, Castries, T 452 2484, F 453 1543, open Mon-Fri 0830-1230. **Venezuelan** Embassy, Casa Vigie, PO Box 494, Castries, T 452 4033.

● **Hours of business**
Shops: 0800-1230, 1330-1700 Mon-Fri (shops close at 1200 on Sat); banks: 0800-1300 Mon-Thur, although some are open until 1400-1500, plus 1500-1700 on Fri; government offices: 0830-1230, 1330-1600 Mon-Fri.

● **Laundry**
There are no self-service launderettes on St Lucia, but there are dry cleaners at Rodney Bay, Gros Islet and Gablewoods Mall in the N of the island. Sparkle, in Gros Islet, will collect and deliver laundry to a boat or marina.

● **Official time**
Atlantic Standard Time, 4 hours behind GMT, 1 ahead of EST.

● **Public holidays**
New Year's Day, Carnival, Independence Day on 22 February, Good Friday, Easter Monday, Labour Day on 1 May, Whit Monday, Corpus Christi, Emancipation Day in August, Thanksgiving Day, National Day on 13 December, Christmas Day and Boxing Day.

● **Shopping**
Pointe Seraphine, next to the main port in Castries, is a designer-built, duty-free shopping centre (same opening hours as other shops, so closed Sat pm), with many tourist-oriented outlets, restaurants, entertainment and tour operators. Goods bought here can be delivered directly to the airport. Cruise ships can tie up at the complex's own berths. Batik fabrics and cotton clothing from Caribelle Batik on Old Victoria Rd, The Morne and Bridge St; Bagshaw's silk screening workshops at La Toc, T 452 2139, are very popular, studio open Mon-Fri 0830-1630, Sat 0830-1200, also shops at *Marigot* and *Windjammer*; souvenirs from Noah's Arkade, Jeremie St, Castries, T 452 2523 and other branches at Rodney Bay opp *St Lucian Hotel*, Pointe Seraphine, Hewanorra duty free and Soufrière; local crafts and paintings from Artsibit, corner of Brazil and Mongiraud Streets, open Mon-Fri 0900-1700, Sat 0930-1300. Eudovics Art Studio, T 452 2747, in Goodlands, coming down from the Morne heading N, sells local handicraft and beautiful large wood carvings. Perfume from Caribbean Perfumes, by *Green Parrot*, T 453 7249. Sunshine Bookshop, Gablewoods Mall, books, foreign newspapers and magazines, open Mon-Fri 0830-1630, Sat half day; Book Salon, Jeremie St on corner of Laborie St, good selection of paperbacks, several books on St Lucia, also stationery. Rodney Bay Shipping

Services runs a book exchange, 2 for one, mostly spy thrillers and light novels, not a huge selection, but useful.

Market day in Castries is Sat, very picturesque (much quieter on other days, speakers of Patois pay less than those who do not). A new public market has been built on the Castries waterfront, with the old market building renovated and turned into a craft market. Buy a coal-pot (native barbecue) for EC$12 and bring it home on your lap. Buy a cocoa stick or 10 for US$5 for chocoholics. There is a new Fisherman's Cooperative Market on the John Compton Highway at the entrance to Pointe Seraphine. Many fishermen still sell their catch wherever they can. Fish is cheap and fresh. JQ's supermarket at the traffic lights at the end of the Vigie runway, open Mon-Fri 0800-1900, Sat 0800-1600, bank next door, fair range of goods, also supermarket on Jeremie St opp the Fire Station and on the William Peter Boulevard. Wholesale meat from Chicken Galore behind Shell station on Manoel St. Gablewoods shopping Mall opened in 1992 between Rodney Bay and Castries with a selection of boutiques, gift shops, book shop, Post Office, pharmacy, deli, open air eating places and Julie N's Supermarket, open Mon-Thur until 2000, Fri, Sat until 2100. Next door is a delicatessen with a choice of frozen and defrosted foods. Rodney Bay Marina has a variety of shops: Pieces of Eight has a good choice of gifts, although few are made in St Lucia; Le Marché de France Supermarket is one of the few to open on Sun morning; the Bread Basket sells excellent fresh loaves, sandwiches and cakes. Soufrière has a market on the waterfront. At Choiseul, on the SW coast, there is an art and craft centre, T 459 3226. In Castries cold drinks are sold on street corners, EC$1 for a coke, drink it and return the bottle. Snokone ice cream vendors roam the beach and streets, a cup of ice cream should cost EC$2.

● **Voltage**
220v, 50 cycles.

● **Warnings**
When visiting the waterfalls and sulphur springs on Soufrière note that 'guides' might expect large payments for their services. Be prepared to say no firmly, they are persistent and bothersome. Even children try to squeeze money out of the tourists offering to dive for a dollar in the harbour. Visiting with a hired car (H reg) can be a hassle and beach bums will even follow you into the church. Readers' letters tell us of some harassment and hostility towards tourists but these are few in number and not on the scale of Jamaica. People staying at well-protected resorts and using organized tours generally have no problem. Be careful taking photographs, although everybody seems to be accustomed to cameras in the market. The use and sale of narcotics is illegal and penalties are severe. Most readily available is marijuana, or 'wacky backy', which is frequently offered to tourists, but hard drugs are a problem.

● **Weights and measures**
Most often imperial, though metric measurements are gradually being introduced.

ON DEPARURE

● **Departure tax**
At both airports there is a departure tax of EC$37.

● **Airport information**
If leaving the country temporarily with electronic equipment such as computers, register the goods at the airport to avoid problems on return.

ACCOMMODATION

● **Hotels**

Price guide

L1	over US$200	L2	US$151-200
L3	US$101-150	A1	US$81-100
A2	US$61-80	A3	US$46-60
B	US$31-45	C	US$21-30
D	US$12-20	E	US$7-11
F	US$4-6	G	up to US$3

Many of the hotels are resorts, providing everything their guests need. Apart from those around Rodney Bay they are remote and you will have to arrange car hire or expensive taxis to get around the island or go to restaurants. All-inclusive resorts are usually, but not always booked from abroad. There is a 10-15% service charge and a 8% government tax on all hotel bills.

Working roughly N to S down the W coast, hotels include: **L1** *Club St Lucia*, T 450 0551, F 450 0281/450 9544, with 372 rooms, making it the island's largest hotel, rooms and family suites, simply furnished but comfortable and clean, an all-inclusive family resort including free membership of the St Lucia Racquet

Club on site, 7 tennis courts, gymnasium, squash court and 3 swimming pools, 2 beaches, lots of watersports, food served buffet style, eat and drink as much as you like, golf costs about US$60/week, diving US$60/day, entertainment for families with theme evenings, stay at home if you don't like steel bands, all-inclusive day passes for visitors EC$150, half-day EC$95; **L1** *Le Sport*, in the N at Cap Estate, T 450 8551, F 450 0368, is for health and fitness lovers, lots of sporting facilities, massage, beauty salon, all-inclusive, rec; **L1** *Wyndham Morgan Bay Hotel*, T 450 2511, F 450 1050, all-inclusive, 240 rooms N of Castries on the beach, pool, watersports, tennis; **L1-L3** *Rex St Lucian* (Reduit Beach, T 452 8351, F 452 8331), on the beach, 260 a/c rooms, in need of renovation, 6 miles from Castries, diving, watersports, tennis, discotheque, restaurants, very poor lunch reported; the **L1** *Royal St Lucian*, its sister property, next door, T 452 9999, F 452 9639, 98 luxury suites, interconnecting pools, swim up bar and waterfalls, restaurants, use of sports facilities at *Rex*, bit inconvenient, breakfast chaotic, lunch poor quality, facilities for wheelchair users at both hotels. **L3** *Islander Hotel*, T 452 0255, F 452 0958, short walk to Reduit beach, or complimentary bus, 60 rooms or apartments, no watersports offered, but close to all Rodney Bay facilities, friendly and efficient staff; **L1-L2** *Harmony Marina Suites*, on Rodney Bay lagoon, close to beach, T 452 8756, 800-452 8094, F 452 8677, recently modernized studios and apartments, restaurant, bar, pool, mini-mart, watersports inc canoeing; **L3-A3** *Bay Gardens Hotel*, Rodney Bay, T 452 2211, new, 53 rooms, pool, restaurant, a/c, TV; **L1** *East Winds Inn* (Labrellotte, T 452 8212, F 452 9941), 26 hexagonal bungalow rooms, in tropical gardens close to the beach, all-inclusive; **L1-L2** *Windjammer Landing*, Labrellotte Bay, (PO Box 1504, T 452 0913, F 452 0907, in the UK T 0800-373 742), a beautiful resort in a lovely setting, but isolated, probably the best villa complex with hotel facilities, 1-bedroomed suites clustered together, 2/4-bedroomed villas more spread out with own plunge pool, luxury resort, tennis and all watersports available, on the beach, honeymoon, family, diving packages available, rec, 30 mins walk to a bus route or EC$20 taxi to Rodney Bay; **L1** *Sandals Halcyon*, Choc Beach, T 453 0222, F 451 8435, all-inclusive, opened 1994, 170 rooms, couples only, all facilities interchangeable with *La Toc*, transport between 2 sites; **L1** *Rendezvous* (Vigie Beach, T 452 4211, F 452 7419), couples only, all inclusive, has some self-catering cottages, many facilities, tennis, gym, jacuzzi, sauna, scuba, yacht cruises, lots of sports equipment, noise of aircraft landing and taking off; **L3-A1** *Morne Fortune Apartments*, Morne Fortune, T 452 3603/2531, F 453 1433, 1-2 bedrooms for 1-5 people, very friendly, spectacular view, catering on arrival arranged by request, no credit cards, discounts given on car rental, pool; **A1-A3** *Auberge Seraphine*, Vigie Marina, T 452 3712, new, rec, 22 rooms, pool, restaurant, a/c, TV; **A1-A2** *Caribees*, La Pensée, overlooking Castries, new, PO Box 1720, T 452 4767, 453 1210, 60 rooms, pool, tennis, a/c, TV, restaurant, rec; **L1** *Sandals St Lucia La Toc*, T 452 3081/9, F 452 1012, luxuriously appointed, couples only, all-inclusive, tennis courts, golf course, watersports, facilities for wheelchair users. Nine miles S of Castries is **L3-A1** *Marigot Bay Resort* (T 451 4357/451 4246, F 451 4353), a Club Mariner resort, dive shop, sailing, yacht chartering and watersports, there is a pleasant beach 300 yds away by ferry; across the bay is *Marigot Beach Club* (PO Box 101 Castries, T 451 4974, F 451 4973), renovated under new ownership 1995, waterfront restaurant and bar, *Café Paradis* open from 0800, sailing, kayaking, PADI dive shop run by Rosemond Clery, pool, sundeck, beach, studios with kitchenett, fans, bathrooms and patio or villas with 1-3 bedrooms on hillside; **L3-A2** *Seahorse Inn* (PO Box 1825 Main Post Office, Castries, T 451 4436, F 451 4872, in Canada T (403) 244-2730, F (403) 262-8786), N side of Marigot Bay, 8 bedrooms, more planned, waterside cottage with own dock US$600-950/week, beach short walk, pool, restaurants inc *Doolittle's* within walking distance, watersports arranged; **L1-L2** *Anse Chastanet Hotel* (PO Box 7000, Soufrière, T 459 7000, 800-223-1108, F 459 7700), 36 hillside and 12 beachside rooms, the best scuba diving on the island, consistently highly rated dive operation, diving packages available, watersports, tennis, lovely beach setting, isolated; **L1-L3** *Humming Bird Beach Resort*, T 459 7232, F 459 7033 only 10 rooms and a hillside cottage, nice gardens, pool, beach, MAP rates, near Soufrière; **L1** *Jalousie Plantation*, Soufrière T 459 7666, F 459 7677, all inclusive, 115-room luxury resort built in 1991 amid much controversy over its location at the foot of the Pitons but very popular with guests, very good food, programmes include massage, sauna, jacuzzi and most sports, diving also available at extra cost, all-inclusive packages available for day visitors, US$100 half day 1000-1600 or 1600-close, US$130 full day and evening, children under 6 free, 6-15 half price, in 1996 *Jalousie* was closed for several months for renovation while its financial problems were sorted out, the Government is to take a 50% shareholding in a rescue package with Hilton (25%) and the Iranian Mahvi family (25%), who previously owned it; **L1** *Ladera Resort* (PO Box 225, Soufrière, T 459 7323, F 459 5156), in spectacular setting between Gros Piton and Petit Piton, 1,000 ft up, 1-3 bedroomed villas and suites, an interesting design feature is the lack of a W wall in each unit to take maximum advantage of the wonderful view, every luxury here, plunge pools, swimming pools, maximum 50 guests, used to film *Superman II*, good restaurant; There is also a *Club Méditerranée* at Vieux Fort, T 454 6547, F 454 6017, PO Box 246, 256 rooms, children's clubs, pool, lots of windsurfing, sailing, tennis, pitch and putt, diving and horseriding (dressage and show jumping lessons available) at extra cost.

Several other apartment hotels and villas for rent. Full details from tourist offices. **A3** *Cloud's Nest Apartments* (Vieux Fort, T 454 6711), 1-3 bedroom apartments; *Villa Beach Cottage* (Choc Beach, T 450 2884/452 2691), no credit cards.

● **Guesthouses**
Castries: **C** *Damascus*, 20 Victoria St, shared bathroom and toilets, unfriendly; **C** *Lee's*, Chauseé Rd, T 452 4285, noisy and no fan, with bath; **C** *Chateau Blanc*, on Morne du Don Rd 300m away, 7 rooms with fan and bathroom, basic but good central location, food available, T 452 1851, F 452 7967; **C** *Thelma's Guesthouse*, near Courts Store on Morne du Don Rd, T 452 7313, pay cash in advance, TCs not accepted, fan, TV in rooms, private bathroom, kitchen, laundry, popular, clean and central, hot and noisy, recognizable by its bright red awnings; **A3-C** *Chesterfield*, southern end of Bridge St, T 452 1295, central, 16 rooms, tropical garden, some rooms with balcony, great view, a/c, kitchen, excellent value.

Above the town on Morne Fortune are: **B-C** *Dubois Guesthouse*, T 452 2201, F 452 7967, 4 rooms, a long way from anything but on bus route, wins prizes for cleanliness; **B** *Hotel Bon Appetit*, nearby, T 452 2757, F 452 7967, beautiful view, clean, friendly, cable TV, restaurant, inc breakfast, rec, book early for evening meal, popular.

A2 *Tapion Reef Apartment Hotel*, just off La Toc Rd, T 452 7470, pool, nothing

special, not on beach; **A3** *Tropical Haven*, La Toc, 10 mins by car from town, T 452 3505, F 452 5476, 10 rooms and 2 apartments (negotiable), no credit cards, more than adequate, excellent food.

A3-C *Sunset Lodge Guesthouse*, near Vigie Airport T 452 2639, John Compton Highway, convenient, a/c, TV, restaurant, bar, nothing special, ask for a room away from the road; **D** *Summersdale Hideaway*, 20 mins walk N of Vigie airport, off the main road and bus route, T 452 1142 for directions, cheap restaurant.

Vide Bouteille (just outside Castries): **A1-A2** *Beach Haven*, Vide Bouteille, 10 rooms, clean, comfortable, a/c, TV, 100m to sandy beach, restaurant with expensive food and breakfast, inexpensive fast food, public phone inside hotel, T 453 0065, F 453 6891; **A2-B** *E's Serenity Lodge*, 3 miles from Castries overlooking Choc Bay, T 452 1987, F 451 8600, 11 rooms, few facilities but good; **B-D** *Modern Inn*, on the main road N of Castries, 3 km from Vide Bouteille, T 452 4001, friendly, good rooms, very clean and pleasant, breakfast available. In the hills at **Marisule**, a 15 mins' walk from Labrellotte Bay, the Zephirin family has cottages to let, self-catering, highly rec.

At **Gablewoods Mall**, **B-C** *Sundale Guest House*, T 452 4120 is very popular, inc breakfast, own bathroom, fan, TV in lobby, check availability; nearby the **A3** *Friendship Inn*, T 452 4201, F 453 2635, has rooms with kitchenette and baby sitting services, small pool, restaurant; further N, on highway to Gros Islet, **B** *The Golden Arrow*, T 451 1832, 15 clean, pleasant rooms, 10 with private bathroom, no single rooms, walking distance from beach and bus, friendly host, breakfast and dinner available; recently renovated, the **A1-A3** *Orange Grove Hotel*, T 452 8213/0021, F 452 8094, is set in the hills of Bois d 'Orange, very comfortable, pool, complimentary bus to beach; **B** *Parrots Hideaway*, T 452 0726, 7 rooms, 3 suites, 1 apartment, discounts for long stays, bar, restaurant, creole menu, charming hostess.

At **Gros Islet**: **B** *Alexander Guesthouse*, T 450 8610, a new building on Mary Thérèse St, 1 min from beach, rec, clean, safe, friendly, helpful, kitchen, credit cards accepted; **B** *Bay*, mini guest house, Bay St, on village beach, T 450 8956, min stay 2 nights, spacious rooms, fan, kitchen, fridge, bathroom, run by Klaus Koef; **A1-A2** *Glencastle Resort*, Massade, on hillside overlooking Rodney Bay, PO Box 143 Castries, T 450 0833, F 450 0837, new, luxurious, good value for money, a/c, pool, 17 rooms, restaurant, rec, only snag is that it is opp small, temporary detention centre, but does not matter really; **B-C** *La Panache*, PO Box 2074, T 450 0765, F 450 0453, on Cas-en-Bas Rd, run by Henry Augustin, helpful and friendly, who can give information on Atlantic beaches and coastal walking, bird watching tours, inc tax and service, own bathroom, hot water, insect screens, clean, fans, good meals, breakfast US$3-8, créole dinners US$11 or dinners can be ordered from outside, snacks during day, bar with excellent alcoholic and non-alcoholic cocktails, lunch EC$10 per load, no food Fri nights when everyone goes to *Jump-up*, highly rec; **B-C** *Nelson's Furnished Apartments* on Cas-en-Bas Rd, T 450 8275; opp Reduit beach; **A1-A2** *Tuxedo Villas*, popular location, T 452 8553. Others include **A3-C** *B&B Guesthouse*, on Gros Islet highway, T 452 8689, F 452 1971, walking distance of Marina, beaches and Pigeon Island causeway, pizza restaurant attached; **B-C** *Daphil's*, Marie Thérèse St, T 450 9318, basic, fan, very noisy, Fri nights, close to 'jump-up'; **C** *Scott's Café/Bar*, friendly but noisy location. At Cap Estate, **L3-A3** *Royall B & B*, run by Lorraine Royall, T/F 450 0264, best room on top floor with 30-ft verandah, close to golf course, good views, rec.

Soufrière: there is a lack of good accommodation for the budget traveller, all guesthouses appear to charge about US$30d for a basic room without private facilities; **B** *Soufrière Sailing Club Guest House*, T 459 7194, 4 rooms, meals available, no credit cards; **B-C** *Home Guesthouse*, T 459 7318, on the main square, clean, pay cash, TCs not accepted; **B-C** *Tropical Palm Inn*, near hospital, it is possible to bargain cheaper rates for longer stays, friendly, basic, helpful, T 459 7487; *Claudina's*, very basic rooms with shower and toilet in courtyard of boutique of same name, kitchen facilities, cheaper than some. Mrs Mathurin, 18 Church St, Soufrière, has rooms to rent, **D** for bed and cooking facilities, reduction for long stay. *The Still Plantation*, T 459 7261, apartments, studios or beachfront rooms, popular, pool, restaurant, spectacular view of Pitons; **A2-C** *Khayere Pann B+B*, T 459 7441, walking distance from shops and beach, inc breakfast and airport transfers, quiet, friendly, great views, wonderful atmosphere, library, cheaper in loft without bath, rec. Peter Jackson rents an apartment in his house on the edge of Soufrière, new, basic but good, 3 rooms, 3 beds, full

cooking facilities, Peter is friendly and helpful, US$160/week, US$280/2 weeks, PO Box 274, T 459 7269.

On the E coast: **A2** *Foxgrove Inn*, 12-bedroomed guest house, on hillside with view of Praslin Bay and Fregate Islands, beach 1 mile, pool, tennis, riding stables, good food, owned by Mr and Mrs Louis-Fernand, T 454 0271.

Vieux Fort: *St Martin*, on main street, clean, friendly, cooking and washing facilities, rec; **B** *Kimatrai Hotel* (Vieux Fort, 5 mins from Hewanorra, T 454 6328), also has self-catering apartments; **A1** *Sky Way Inn*, T 454 7111, 2 restaurants, night club, pool, shuttle service to airport and beach; **A3** *Il Pirata*, clean, welcoming motel, 5 mins from airport, restaurant, good breakfast, on beach.

● **Villas**

Villa rentals for short or long terms can be arranged, usually with maid service and car hire: *Barnard Sons & Co*, Bridge St, Castries, T 452 2216, F 453 1394, PO Box 169; *Property Shop*, Rodney Bay, T 450 8288, F 450 0318; *Tropical Villas*, Cap Estate, Box 189, Castries, T 450 8240, F 450 8089; *Marlin Quay*, on the waterfront in Rodney Bay, is a villa resort offering rentals or purchases with a 37' yacht for combination holidays, luxurious, restaurant attached, pool, T 452 0393, F 452 0383, PO Box 2204 Gros Islet.

● **Camping**

Not rec, not encouraged, particularly on beaches, no facilities, lots of sandflies and very strong land crabs which could break into your tent. There are no official campsites.

FOOD AND DRINK

All the large hotels have a selection of restaurants and there are snack bars and restaurants all along the W coast. Most places add on a 10% service charge, the menu usually specifies and it is rarely left to your discretion.

In **Castries** *Kimlans*, Derek Walcott Square, upstairs café and bar with verandah, cheap, serves local food, open 0700-2300 Mon-Sat, T 452 1136; on the opp side of the square on Bridge St is *Chez Paul*, in a lovely old wooden mansion, pleasant balcony for lunchtime refreshment, open for breakfast, lunch and dinner, T 452 3022; vegetarian and health foods are available from *The Natural Café* on Chauseé Rd, T 452 6421, open 0830-1800 Mon-Fri and 0900-1400 on Sat; there are several roti houses on Chauseé Rd, especially at S end, rec.

South of Castries on The Top of the Morne, *Bon Appetit*, is rec for its daily specials and spectacular views, but is not cheap, meals from EC$35, T 452 2757; also on the Morne, *San Antoine*, is a plantation great house, lovely gardens, elegant dining room, open for lunch and dinner except Sun, expensive, voted most elegant restaurant by St Lucia Hotel Association, T 452 4660, reservations requested; in the same area *The Green Parrot*, T 452 3399, 4-course dinner EC$95, serves excellent lunches daily, lots of Caribbean specialities and good selection of tropical vegetables, have a cocktail in the lounge before dinner, the chairs are worth it alone, shows Wed, Sat, ladies' night Mon.

North of Castries is *D's Restaurant*, on Vide Bouteille, indoor or on patio, special 3-course set menu at EC$25, rec, T 453 7931; *Jimmie's*, tucked away at Vigie Cove, great views of harbour at sunset, but standards dropped 1996, T 452 5142; *Coal Pot*, one junction beyond *Jimmie's*, S of Vigie airport, badly signposted, bear left after the two left hand turns off the highway, food similar to *Jimmie's*; *Vigie Beach Bar*, beside *Rendezvous Hotel* serves good rotis and inexpensive cold beers; in Gablewoods Mall there are a selection of fast food outlets open from 0800-2100 daily: Mexican, SE Asian, pizza, crêpes, ice cream. You can expect to pay just EC$30 for 2 people at *Chungs* Chinese restaurant at Choc Bay, service is often poor, but the food is delicious, closed from about 2100 and on Sun, T 452 4795.

Further N in the **Rodney Bay** area, *The Lime* serves good meals and snacks at moderate prices, friendly, highly rec, open from 1100 till late, closed Tues, T 452 0761; *The Ginger Lily* nearby is rec for its Chinese food, open 1130-1430 and 1830-2330, special lunch menu at EC$20, Tues-Sat, T 452 8303; *Razmataz*, on way to marina, Indian, good, friendly, T/F 452 9800; *Mortar and Pestle*, waterfront bar and restaurant, mini-mart, dinghy dock, T 452 8756, F 452 8677; *A Pub*, on waterfront, 2 happy hours, 1730-1830, 2030-2130, pool tables, Mon live jam session; *Planet Mexico*, excellent Mexican food; *Capone's*, is a restaurant in the speakeasy style of the 1920s, open for dinner only and quite expensive, but attached to a *pizzeria*, open from 1100, both closed Mon, with prices starting at EC$12, T 452 0284. Further along the road and directly on the beach at Reduit is *Spinnakers*, T 452 8491, breakfast, lunch and dinner daily, with full English breakfast EC$26, happy hour 1800-1900, excellent location, though food and service suffer when it is busy, good too for coffee and desserts, they also hire out loungers for EC$5 a day. In the marina complex at Rodney Bay is *Key Largo*, T 452 0282, delicious, authentic, huge Italian pizzas, reasonably priced, if you like hot food ask for the hot sauce; call in also to *The Bread Basket* for breakfast or lunch, open Mon-Sat 0730-1700, Sun 0730-1200. *Charthouse*, T 452-8115, closed Sun, known for its steak, seafood and spare ribs, rib steak highly rec; *Miss Saigon*, T 452 0580, southeast Asian cuisine, open daily, rec; *Snooty Agouti*, night place with jazz/blues, gourmet coffee, cocktails, food, gooey desserts, breakfast waffles, art gallery, boutique, book swap, backgammon, Internet; *The Bistro*, close to marina, seafood a speciality, also English pub grub and daily specials, sunset/early bird 20% off meals 1730-1830, happy hour drinks, nice setting on waterfront, open daily from 1700, T 452 9494. Good selection of reasonably priced local food in the market complex.

In the far N **Cap Estate** is *The Great House Restaurant*, traditional tea from 1430-1730 is worthwhile for watching the sunset, and affordable, dinner is extravagantly priced, T 450 0450; *Portias* on the road to Corinth is a fairly new restaurant with a large selection of affordable meals.

South of Castries, **Marigot Bay** has several hotels for lunch and dinner, but *JJ's Restaurant and Bar* on the road down to the bay is a cheaper alternative, specializes in fresh local dishes and seafood, open from 1000 till late, Wed night rec, reasonably priced crayfish, crab and lobster (in season), T 451 4076, Fri night jam session.

In **Soufrière**, *The Still* specializes in authentic St Lucian dishes, open daily 0800-1700 it is not cheap but serves local vegetables grown on site, T 459 7224; *Spotlight* near *Home Guesthouse* and Barclays Bank, good local food, tuna and kingfish rec, lunches and dinners EC$16-25; *Jacquot*, on Church St, try the Jacquot Special cocktail; *The Humming Bird* is a good place to eat and take a swim, French, Créole and seafood, daily specials, reasonable food but reported overpriced, good views, open from 0700, T 459 7232; *Dasheene*, at *Ladera Resort*, good food, Austrian chef cooks with local produce, T 459 7850, wonderful views, rec, worth coming here even if only for a drink just for the views; The *Purity Bakery* near the church in the main square serves breakfast with good coffee, rolls and cakes; *Le Haut Plantation* on the W coast road changed management in 1996 and is reported overpriced, you won't get shown a menu and no prices are displayed; at Étangs Soufrière, on the road to Vieux Fort, is *The Barbican* restaurant and bar, T 459 7888, run by the very welcoming Mr and Mrs Smith, local food at local prices, good home cooking, not sophisticated, but clean, popular, rec.

Vieux Fort, *Il Pirata* is rec, Italian restaurant on the beach, prices from EC$25, attached to a motel, open Tues-Sun 0700-2130, T 454 6610; close to Hewanorra airport is the *Chak Chak Café*, open from 0900 to midnight, T 454 6260.

GETTING AROUND

LAND TRANSPORT
● Motoring
Drive on the left. Signposting has been greatly improved so that renting a car and exploring by yourself is now much easier. Although there are about 500 miles of roads on the island only 281 are paved so be prepared for some rough driving. Local drivers are fairly rough too, steer clear of them if possible. The new road from Castries to Soufrière has cut the journey time to about 1 hr. Filling stations are open Mon-Sat 0630-2000, selected garages open Sun and holidays 1400-1800. Leaded fuel costs EC$6, unleaded EC$6.50.

● Car hire
Hire in advance if possible. It is cheaper and more certain. Cars and Suzuki jeeps can be rented. They are more expensive than on some islands because of all the extras which are included. Car hire starts at about US$40-50 a day, jeep rental is US$60 a day, US$295-390 a week; if you hire for 8 days you will be charged for one week and one day. It is often cheaper to book from abroad. Insurance is another US$15-20 a day. A 5% tax is added to everything. A temporary licence costs EC$30. If arriving at Vigie airport, get your international licence endorsed at the immigration desk (closed 1300-1500) after going through Customs. Car hire companies can usually arrange a licence. You can only hire a car if you are aged 25 or over.

Car rental agencies include Avis, Vide Bouteille (T 452 2700, F 453 1536) and lots of other locations; Hertz headquarters at Rodney Bay (T 452 0680); National, Gros Islet Highway (T 450 8721, F 450 8577); also at Pointe Seraphine (T 453 0085), *Le Sport* (T 450 9406), Vigie airport (T 452 3050), Hewanorra airport (T 454 6699) and *Club Med*, Vieux Fort (T 454 6547); Royal (T 452 8833/452 0117); Budget, Marisule T 452 0233/452 8021, F 452 9362. Most have offices at the hotels, airports and in Castries. *Morne Fortune Apartments* have the best rates for residents, Sunset Motors at Choc are the next cheapest, will deliver/pick up at airport. Check for charges for pick-up and delivery. If dropping off a car at Vigie airport you can sometimes leave the keys with the Tourist desk if there is no office for your car hire company.

Water taxis and speedboats can be rented. Waynes Motorcycle Centre, Vide Bouteille, rents bikes; make sure you wear a helmet and have adequate insurance, potholes are everywhere.

● Buses
It is much cheaper to go by bus. The service has been described as tiresome by some, but as reliable by others. St Lucia's buses are usually privately-owned minibuses and have no fixed timetable. The N is better served than the S and buses around Castries and Gros Islet run until 2200, or later for the Fri night Jump-up at Gros Islet. There are several bus stands in Castries: those going to Gros Islet and Rodney Bay leave from behind the market on Darling Rd; to Dennery from the Customs shed on Jeremie St; to Jacmal, Marigot (be prepared to walk over steep hill as few buses turn off into the bay), Bois D'Inde and Roseau Valley from Victoria St; to Vieux Fort from Jno Baptiste St off Darling Rd. From Castries to Vieux Fort, EC$7; to Choc Beach, EC$1; to Soufrière, EC$6; to Dennery EC$2.25; to Gros Islet EC$1.50; to Morne Fortune EC$0.75. Ask the driver to tell you when your stop comes up, they are usually cooperative.

● Ferry
The *Gingerbread* express in Marigot Bay costs EC$2 return, but is refunded by *Doolittle's Restaurant* if you eat or drink there and present your tickets.

● Taxis
Fares are supposedly set by the Government, but the EC$95 Castries-Soufrière fare doubles as unlucky tourists discover that there are no buses for the return journey. *Club St Lucia*, in

the extreme N, to Castries, about 10 miles away, costs EC$40 one way. Fare to or from Gros Islet (for Fri evening street party), EC$30; to Pigeon Island National Park, EC$35 one way; to Vigie airport, EC$12; to Hewannora airport, EC$120; Vigie airport to Rodney Bay EC$40; Marigot Bay to Hewanorra airport EC$120, to Vigie airport EC$60, to Castries EC$50 (30 mins). Always agree the fare before you get in. There is no extra charge to have the a/c switched on. If in doubt about the amount charged, check with the tourist office or hotel reception. You can see a copy of the fixed fares at the airport. Courtesy Taxi Service, T 452 3555 can be rec. At rush hour it is almost impossible to get a taxi so allow plenty of time, the traffic jams are amazing for such a small place.

A trip round the island by taxi, about US$20 per hour for 1-4 people, can be arranged.

COMMUNICATIONS

● **Postal services**
Main Post Office is on Bridge St, Castries, open Mon-Fri, 0815-1230, 1330-1530, Sat, 0800-1200, poste restante at the rear. Fax and photocopying facilities upstairs. Postcards to Europe EC$0.45, to the USA EC$0.45; letters to Europe EC$0.95, to the USA EC$0.85-0.90. The DHL office is on Bridge St.

● **Telecommunications**
The island has an adequate telephone system, with international direct dialling, operated by Cable and Wireless, Bridge St, Castries. There is a sub-office on New Dock Rd, Vieux Fort. Telex and Fax facilities at both offices. Hotels do not generally allow direct dialling, you will have to go through the operator, which can be slow and costly. Intra-island calls are EC$0.25, no limit if on the same exchange, EC$0.25 for 90 seconds to another exchange. Pay phones use EC$0.25 and EC$1 coins. Cable and Wireless phone cards are sold for EC$10, EC$20, EC$40 or EC$53; with these you can phone abroad. There is a credit card phone at Vigie airport operated via the boat phone network, open daily 0800-2200. The International code for St Lucia is 1809, but a new number, 1758, will be phased in to replace it in 1996-97. Call USA T 1-800-674 7000; Sprint Express T 1-800-277 7468; BT Direct T 1-800-342 5284; Canada Direct T 1-800-744 2580; USA Direct phone at Rodney Bay Marina, or T 1-800-872 2881. If you want to dial a toll-free US number, replace the 800 with 400. You will be charged a local call. St Lucia

has access to the Internet and Snooty Agouti (Rodney Bay) is the first 'cyber café' with one terminal (EC$20/30 mins) for the seriously addicted.

MEDIA

● **Newspapers**
The Voice is a twice-weekly paper (Tues, Thur), and *The Mirror, The Weekend Voice, One Caribbean, The Crusader* and *The Star* appear weekly.

● **Radio**
There is a commercial radio station, Radio Caribbean, which broadcasts daily in Patois and English, and a government-owned station, Radio St Lucia. Most programmes have been taken over by Radio Caribbean International in Castries.

● **Television**
A commercial television service operates in English only. There is lots of cable TV.

ENTERTAINMENT

Most of St Lucia's night life revolves around the hotels, while some restaurants host live bands. The choice varies from steel bands, jazz groups, folk dancing, crab racing, fire eating and limbo dancers. The hotels welcome guests from outside and advertize the month's activities in *The Tropical Traveller*. In May, nightlife is dominated by the annual jazz festival with lots of outdoor concerts. *Splash Disco* at the *St Lucian Hotel* is the only European style disco on the island. At other places, but particularly around Rodney Bay, venues like *The Lime* and *The A Pub* are popular places for those who just want to hang out. *Indies* is a nightclub and disco next to the *Bay Gardens Hotel*, Rodney Bay, a good selection of Caribbean and international music can be heard, depending on the night, look out for specials, Wed ladies night (first 75 free), EC$20 cover charge Fri, Sat, free shuttle bus from major hotels, late night happy hour 2200-2400. *Shack Shack* in Vieux Fort has live bands regularly. *JJ's*, Marigot, casual, good mixture of locals and tourists, Caribbean music in simple disco, Fri can be very busy, Sat pleasantly so, frequent shows, live bands, karaoke, taxi service can be arranged, T 451 4076. The highlight of the week, for locals and visitors however, is Friday night's jump up at Gros Islet, where it is hard to resist getting involved (see above, **Gros Islet**). For a more cultural evening,

704

tours are available to La Sikwi, patois for sugar mill, at Anse La Raye. There is a visit to the 150 year-old mill, followed by a full costume play reliving life in the village on a stage set into the hills with jazz bands and local acts. There is no cinema on the island.

There are (irregular) shows: concerts, drama, dance, comedy, at the National Cultural Centre (Castries), the Light House Theatre (Tapion) and the Great House Theatre (Cap Estate). They can give you a better taste of St Lucian culture than hotel shows which are adapted to international taste. Contact the Department of Culture for programmes as shows are often poorly advertised. Tickets available at the Department of Culture and Sunshine Bookstore (Gablewoods Mall).

TOURIST INFORMATION

● **Local tourist office**
St Lucia Tourist Board, Pointe Seraphine, PO Box 221, Castries, St Lucia, T 452 5968, Telex 6380 LC, F (809) 453 1121. There are Tourist Board information centres at the Pointe Seraphine Duty Free Complex; Vigie Airport (most helpful but closed for lunch 1300-1500), T 452 2596; Hewanorra Airport (very helpful, particularly with hotel reservations, only open when flights are due or leave), T 454 6644 and Soufrière (very helpful, local phone calls free), T 459 7419.

● **Tourist offices overseas**
France: ANI, 53 Rue François Ler, 7th floor, Paris 75008, T 47-20-3966, F 47-23-0965.

Germany: Postfach 2304, D-61293 Bad Homberg 1, T (06172) 30-44-31, F (06172) 30-50-72.

UK: 421a Finchley Rd, London NW3 6HJ, T 0171 431 3675, F 0171 431 7920.

USA and Canada: 9th Floor, 820 2nd Avenue, New York, NY 10017, T 800-456-3984.

● **Local travel agents**
Most hotels will arrange tours (US$40-80) to the island's principal attractions either by road, boat or helicopter. Coach tours are cheaper and are usually daily in high season, falling to once or twice a week off season. Alternatives are to go by boat (easy between Castries and Soufrière, some hotels have their own boats: *Anse Chastanet, Jalousie Plantation, Windjammer Landing* and *Sandals*) or by helicopter (rec for a spectacular view of the sulphur springs). From Pointe Seraphine a N island helicopter tour costs US$40, 10 mins; S island US$80, 20

mins; a heli-hike with tour of Atlantic beaches and Cactus Valley US$65, T 450 0806; helicopters can also be hired for airport transfers, US$85 from Pointe Seraphine to Hewanorra, also pick-up from some hotels, St Lucia Helicopters, PO Box 2047, Gros Islet, T 453 6950 and Eastern Caribbean Helicopters, PO Box 1742, Castries, T 453 6952 at Vigie airport.

Tours can also be arranged to coconut oil and other craft shops, fabric manufacturers, and so on. Local tour operators offer highly rec plantation tours; Errard, Marquis and Balembouche offer fascinating insights into colonial history and local environments. A tour of a working banana plantation, US$50, is rec, you see a lot of the country and see and taste a lot of native fruit and vegetables. You can take a carriage ride through the N of the island, or spend an evening cruising into the sunset with as much champagne as you can drink. There are also day trips to neighbouring islands: Dominica US$215, Grenadines inc sail, US$199, Barbados US$225 and others. Contact St Lucia Reps, Sunlink Tours, T 452 8232/0842, F 452 0459, PO Box 389. Trailblazer, T 452 9292, offers a very worthwhile land and sea tour. The National Trust runs excursions to Maria Island (T 454 5014) and Fregate Island Reserve (T 452 5005, 453 1495). Many other companies, eg Jungle Tours and Sunshine Tours (Castries), have posters in most major hotels and are listed in the phone book.

● **Maps**
Maps of the island may be obtained from the Land Survey in the last government building. At 1:50,000 they are the best but not 100% accurate. Ordnance Survey, Romsey Rd, Southampton, UK (T 01703 792792), produce a map of St Lucia in their World Maps series which includes tourist information such as hotels, beaches, climbing and climate. The Tourist Board map is free.

● **Further reading**
The Tropical Traveller is distributed free to hotels, shops, restaurants etc every month and contains some extremely useful information. *Visions of St Lucia*, a quarterly magazine produced by the St Lucia Hotel and Tourism Association is also of a high standard and widely available.

ACKNOWLEDGEMENTS

Thanks go to Ulrike Krauss for a great deal of helpful and interesting information on St Lucia.

St Vincent

S T VINCENT, and its 32 sister islands and cays which make up the Grenadines, were, until fairly recently, almost unknown to tourists except yachtsmen and divers, and are still uncrowded. St Vincent is very picturesque, with its fishing villages, coconut groves, banana plantations and fields of arrowroot, of which the island is the world's largest producer. It is a green and fertile volcanic island, with lush valleys, rugged cliffs on the leeward and windward coasts and beaches of both golden and black volcanic sand. The highest peak on the island is La Soufrière, an active volcano in the N rising to about 4,000 feet. It last erupted in 1979, but careful monitoring enabled successful evacuation before it blew. The steep mountain range of Morne Garu rises to 3,500 feet and runs southward with spurs to the E and W coasts. Most of the central mountain range and the steep hills are forested. St Vincent is roughly 18 miles long and 11 miles wide and has an area of 133 square miles, while the Grenadines contribute another 17 square miles all together.

About a quarter of the people live in the capital, **Kingstown** and its suburbs. 8% live on the Grenadines. 66% of the population is classed as black and 19% as mixed, while 2% are Amerindian/black, 6% East Indian, 4% white and the remainder are 'others'.

HISTORY

By the time Columbus discovered St Vincent on his third voyage in 1498, the Caribs were occupying the island, which they called Hairoun. They had overpowered the Arawaks, killing the men but interbreeding with the women. The Caribs aggressively prevented European settlement until the 18th century but were more welcoming to Africans. In 1675 a passing Dutch ship laden with settlers and their slaves was shipwrecked between St Vincent and Bequia. Only the slaves survived and these settled and mixed with the native population and their descendants still live in Sandy Bay and a few places in the NW. Escaped slaves from St Lucia and Grenada later also sought refuge on St Vincent and interbred with the Caribs. As they multiplied they became known as 'Black Caribs'. There was tension between the Caribs and the Black Caribs and in 1700 there was civil war.

In 1722 the British attempted to colonize St Vincent but French settlers had already arrived and were living peaceably

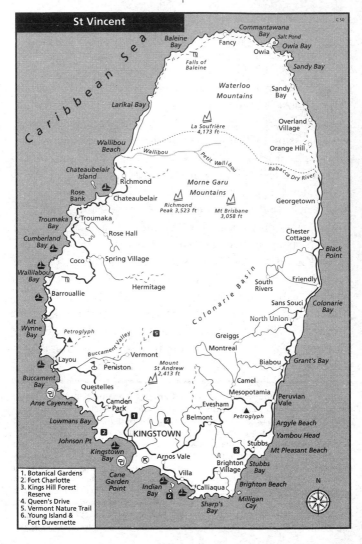

St Vincent

C 50

Caribbean Sea

Commantawana Bay
Salt Pond
Baleine Bay
Fancy
Owia Bay
Owia
Falls of Baleine
Sandy Bay
Waterloo Mountains
Sandy Bay
Larikai Bay
La Soufrière 4,173 ft
Overland Village
Wallibou Beach
Wallibou
Petit Wallibou
Orange Hill
Rabacca Dry River
Chateaubelair Island
Richmond
Morne Garu Mountains
Rose Bank
Chateaubelair
Richmond Peak 3,523 ft
Mt Brisbane 3,058 ft
Georgetown
Troumaka Bay
Troumaka
Rose Hall
Chester Cottage
Cumberland Bay
Coco
Spring Village
Black Point
Wallilabou Bay
Hermitage
South Rivers
Friendly
Barrouallie
Colonarie Basin
Sans Souci
Colonarie Bay
Mt Wynne Bay
Petroglyph
North Union
Buccament Valley
5
Greiggs
Layou
Vermont
Montreal
Peniston
Mount St Andrew 2,413 ft
Biabou
Grant's Bay
Buccament Bay
Questelles
Camel
Anse Cayenne
Camden Park
Evesham
Mesopotamia
Peruvian Vale
Lowmans Bay
1
Belmont
Petroglyph
Johnson Pt
2
4
Argyle Beach
KINGSTOWN
Stubbs
Yambou Head
Kingstown Bay
Arnos Vale
3
Mt Pleasant Beach
Cane Garden Point
Brighton Village
Stubbs Bay
Villa
Calliaqua
Brighton Beach
Indian Bay
6
Sharp's Bay
Milligan Cay
N

1. Botanical Gardens
2. Fort Charlotte
3. Kings Hill Forest Reserve
4. Queen's Drive
5. Vermont Nature Trail
6. Young Island & Fort Duvernette

with the Caribs growing tobacco, indigo, cotton and sugar. Possession was hotly disputed until 1763 when it was ceded to Britain. It was lost to the French again in 1778 but regained under the Treaty of Versailles in 1783. However, this did not bring peace with the Black Caribs, who repeatedly tried to oust the British in what became known as the Carib Wars. A treaty with them in 1773 was soon violated by both sides. Peace came only at the end of the century when in 1796 General Abercrombie crushed a revolt fomented the previous year by the French radical Victor Hugues. In 1797, over 5,000 Black Caribs were deported to Roatán, an island at that time in British hands off the coast of Honduras. The violence ceased although racial tension took much longer to eradicate. In the late 19th century, a St Vincentian poet, Horatio Nelson Huggins wrote an epic poem about the 1795 Carib revolt and deportation to Roatán, called *Hiroona*, which was published in the 1930s. Nelcia Robinson, above Cyrus Tailor shop on Grenville Street, is an authority on Black Caribs/Garifuna and is the coordinator of the Caribbean Organization of Indigenous People on St Vincent.

In the 19th century labour shortages on the plantations brought Portuguese immigrants in the 1840s and East Indians in the 1860s, and the population today is largely a mixture of these and the African slaves. Slavery was abolished in 1832 but social and economic conditions remained harsh for the majority non-white population. In 1902, La Soufrière erupted, killing 2,000 people, just two days before Mont Pelée erupted on Martinique, killing 30,000. Much of the farming land was seriously damaged and economic conditions deteriorated further. In 1925 a Legislative Council was inaugurated but it was not until 1951 that universal adult suffrage was introduced.

St Vincent and the Grenadines belonged to the Windward Islands Federation until 1959 and the West Indies Federation between 1958 and 1962. In 1969 the country became a British Associated State with complete internal self-government. Government during the 1970s was mostly coalition government between the St Vincent Labour Party (SVLP) and the People's Political Party. In 1979 St Vincent and the Grenadines gained full independence, but the year was also remembered for the eruption of La Soufrière on Good Friday, 13 April. Fortunately no one was killed as thousands were evacuated, but there was considerable agricultural damage. In 1980 Hurricane Allen caused further devastation to the plantations and it has taken years for production of crops such as coconuts and bananas to recover. Hurricane Emily destroyed an estimated 70% of the banana crop in 1987.

The general elections held in February 1994 were won for the third successive time by the National Democratic party (NDP), which has held power under Prime Minister James Mitchell (Sir James after receiving a knighthood in the 1995 New Year Honours list) since 1984. The NDP won 12 of the 15 seats in the House of Assembly, compared with all 15 previously, and its share of the vote fell. The three remaining seats were won by an alliance of the opposition SVLP, led by Stanley John, and the Movement for National Unity (MNU), led by Ralph Gonsalves. Stanley John failed to win a seat, but a former SVLP leader, Vincent Beache did and was subsequently endorsed as parliamentary opposition leader. The two parties agreed on the alliance only shortly before the elections, having previously disagreed over the leadership of such an alliance. It was later decided to merge the MNU and the SVLP. The new party is called the United Labour Party (ULP). Vincent Beache was elected leader, unopposed, at the inaugural convention in October.

The Prime Minister appointed a largely unchanged cabinet but for the first time named a deputy prime minister,

Parnel Campbell, who is also the Attorney General and Minister of Justice, Information and Ecclesiastical Affairs. The Government survived an opposition motion of no confidence in August when the opposition accused it of failing to tackle economic problems, particularly in the banana industry, and of failing to deal with drug trafficking and health and education issues. US officials believe that offshore banks in St Vincent are being used to launder drugs money and that the southern Grenadines are a transshipment point.

GOVERNMENT

St Vincent and the Grenadines is a constitutional monarchy within the Commonwealth. The Queen is represented by a Governor General. There is a House of Assembly with 15 elected representatives and six senators.

THE ECONOMY

The St Vincent economy is largely based on agriculture and tourism, with a small manufacturing industry which is mostly for export. The main export is bananas, the fortunes of which fluctuate according to the severity of the hurricane season; in 1990 the volume rose to 79,586 tonnes, the highest ever, but in 1991-93 the crop was reduced because of drought. Drought again affected the 1994 crop which was then hit by Tropical Storm Debbie and exports fell to 30,933 tonnes. The sector used to contribute about 60% of export revenues and the fall in prices brought about by the new European banana policy has hit hard. The Banana Growers Association is in debt and has been attempting to cut costs, but has launched a EC$50 mn programme to rehabilitate and improve 3,200 acres of banana land by 1997. Nevertheless, the Government is encouraging farmers to diversify and reduce dependence on bananas with incentives and land reform. About 7,000 acres of state-owned land is being split up into 1,500 small holdings.

St Vincent and the Grenadines: fact file

Geographic
Land area	389.3 sq km
forested	36.0%
pastures	5.0%
cultivated	28.0%

Demographic
Population (1995)	112,000
annual growth rate (1990-95)	1.3%
urban	24.6%
rural	75.4%
density	287.7 per sq km
Religious affiliation	
Protestant	76.0%
Roman Catholic	10.0%
Birth rate per 1,000 (1992)	24.8
	(world av 25.0)

Education and Health
Life expectancy at birth,	
male	71 years
female	74 years
Infant mortality rate	
per 1,000 live births (1992)	17.1
Physicians (1992)	1 per 2,708 persons
Hospital beds	1 per 209 persons
Calorie intake as %	
of FAO requirement	97%
Population age 25 and over	
with no formal schooling	2.4%
Literacy (over 15)	96.0%

Economic
GNP (1993 market prices)	US$233mn
GNP per capita	US$2,130
Public external debt (1993)	
	US$62.4mn
Tourism receipts (1993)	US$55mn
Inflation (annual av 1989-94)	4.4%
Radio	1 per 1.5 persons
Television	1 per 6.3 persons
Telephone	1 per 6.6 persons

Employment
Population economically active (1991)	
	41,682
Unemployment rate (1994)	30-40%
% of labour force in agriculture	20.1
mining	0.2
manufacturing	6.8
construction	8.5
Paramilitary police unit	80

Source *Encyclopaedia Britannica*

Arrowroot starch is the second largest export crop, of which St Vincent is the world's largest producer; the Government plans to increase production by raising the area sown from 140 acres in 1990 to 1,200 acres by 1996. Arrowroot is now used as a fine dressing for computer paper as well as the traditional use as a thickening agent in cooking. Other exports include coconuts and coconut oil, copra, sweet potatoes, tannias and eddoes. Over half of all exports are sold to the UK.

Fishing has received government promotion and substantial aid from Japan, which in 1994 looked unsuccessfully to St Vincent for support in the dispute over whaling. In 1996 Japan gave the island a grant of EC$12mn for construction of jetties and fish refrigeration facilities in St Vincent, Canouan and Bequia, having previously granted 72mn yen (about US$7mn) for a coastal fisheries development project and 916mn yen for the national fisheries development plan.

St Vincent emerged as the largest flag of convenience in the Caribbean, with 521 ships on its register in 1990. In 1991 about 100 more were added as a direct result of the Yugoslav conflict, most of which came from Croatia and Slovenia. However, ships carrying the Vincentian flag have a poor record for safety, second only to Romania. Between 1990-92, 16.5% were detained by European port officials for unseaworthiness.

Tourism has grown steadily in St Vincent and the Grenadines and is important as a major employer and source of foreign exchange. Expansion is limited by the size of the airport and the Government has encouraged upmarket, often yacht-based tourism. Around 55,000 stopover tourists come each year, of which over 30% come from Europe and 27% from the USA. Visitor expenditure is about US$50mn a year. Plans to expand tourist capacity include the construction of a US$100mn resort on Union Island, including a hotel, 300-berth marina, golf course and villas. A US$75mn shipyard and marina is being built near Kingstown, St Vincent with Italian investment and expertise, but in 1996 construction was halted because of financial difficulties and legal disputes.

Healthy economic growth was recorded in the 1980s: government receipts grew faster than spending, investment in infrastructural development was promoted and social development projects such as schools and hospitals received foreign concessionary financing. In the 1990s growth slowed as the banana industry faced considerable difficulties but remained positive. The large tourism development project on Union Island, was expected to boost the rate of economic growth, as well as the construction of a new cruise ship terminal and new ferry facilities in Kingstown. Construction of the cruise ship berths (one for a 1,000 passenger liner and one for a 300-passenger ship) was expected to start in 1996.

FLORA AND FAUNA

St Vincent has a wide variety of tropical plants, most of which can be seen in the Botanical Gardens, where conservation of rare species has been practised since they were founded in 1765. There you can see the mangosteen fruit tree and one of the few examples of *spachea perforata*, a tree once thought to be found only in St Vincent but now found in other parts of the world, as well as the famous third generation sucker of the original breadfruit tree brought by Captain Bligh of the *Bounty* in 1793 from Tahiti. Other conservation work taking place in the gardens involves the endangered St Vincent parrot, *Amazona guildingii*, which has been adopted as the national bird. An aviary, originally containing birds confiscated from illegal captors, now holds 12 parrots. In 1988 the first parrot was hatched in captivity and it was hoped that this was the first step towards increasing the number on the island, estimated at down to only 500. This mostly golden brown parrot with a green, violet, blue and yellow-flecked tail, spectacular in flight, is found in the humid forests in the lower and middle hills on the island. The main colonies are around Buccament, Cumberland-Wallilabou, Linley-Richmond and Locust Valley-Colonarie Valley. Their main enemy is man, who has encroached into the forest for new farming land and exploited the bird's rarity in the illegal pet trade, but they have also suffered severely from hurricanes and volcanic eruptions such as in 1979. They are protected now by the Wildlife Protection Act, which covers the majority of the island's birds, animals and reptiles and carries stiff penalties for infringements. A parrot reserve is being established in the upper Buccament Valley.

Another protected bird unique to St Vincent is the whistling warbler, and this, as well as the black hawk, the cocoa thrush, the crested hummingbird, the red-capped green tanager, green heron and other species can be seen, or at least heard, in the Buccament Valley. There are nature trails starting near the top of the Valley, passing through tropical forest, and it is possible to picnic. The Vermont Nature Trail can be reached by bus, from the market square in Kingstown to the road junction in Peniston near the *Emerald Valley Hotel and Casino*; the sign for the trail is clearly marked. If travelling by car, look for the Vermont Nature Trail sign about one mile past Questelles. The car park, at 975 feet, is close to the Vermont Nature Centre. Get a trail map from the information hut on the right. There is a rest stop on the trail, at 1,350 feet, and a Parrot Lookout Platform at 1,450 feet. It is a beautiful trail, through thick forest and is probably the best place to see the St Vincent parrot. Be prepared for rain, mosquitoes and chiggars, use insect repellent. Anyone interested in nature trails should visit the Forestry Department (in the same building as the Land and Survey Department),

who have prepared official trail plans, published in conjunction with the Tourism Department. A pamphlet details the Vermont Nature Trails, Wallilabou Falls, Richmond Beach, Trinity Falls, Falls of Baleine, Owia Salt Pond and La Soufrière Volcano Trails. The Tourist Office may also have a supply of pamphlets.

DIVING AND MARINE LIFE

The underwater wildlife around St Vincent and the Grenadines is varied and beautiful, with a riot of fish of all shapes and sizes. There are many types and colours of coral, including black coral at a depth of only 30 feet in places. On the New Guinea Reef (Petit Byahaut) you can find three types of black coral in six different colours. The coral is protected so do not remove any. There are 10 marine protected areas including the NE coast and the Devil's Table in Bequia, Isle de Quatre, all Mustique, the E coast of Canouan, all of Mayreau, the Tobago Cays, the whole of Palm Island, Petit St Vincent and the surrounding reefs. Spearfishing is strictly forbidden to visitors and no one is allowed to spear a lobster. Buying lobster out of season (1 May-30 Sept) is illegal as is buying a female lobster with eggs. Fishing for your own consumption is allowed outside the protected areas. Contact the Fisheries Department for more information on rules and regulations, T 456-2738.

There are facilities for scuba diving, snorkelling, deep sea fishing, windsurfing and water ski-ing, with experienced instructors for novices. There is reef diving, wall diving, drift diving and wrecks to explore. The St Vincent reefs are fairly deep, at between 55 to 90 feet, so scuba diving is more rewarding than snorkelling. Dive sites include Bottle Reef, the Forest, the Garden, New Guinea Reef and the Wall. In Kingstown Harbour there are three wrecks at one site, the *Semistrand*, another cargo freighter and an ancient wreck stirred up by Hurricane Hugo, as well as two cannons, a large anchor and several bathtubs from the old wreck.

Bequia is also considered excellent, with a leeward wall and 30 dive sites around the island and nearby, reached by boat within 15 minutes. The Devil's Table is good for snorkelling as well as diving; other dive sites are *M/S Lirero*, the Wall off West Cay, the Bullet, the Boulders and Manhole. The best snorkelling is found in the Tobago Cays and Palm Island. There is snorkelling and diving around most of the other islands with at least one dive shop on each inhabited island. As well as the specialist companies, many of the hotels offer equipment and services for their guests and others.

There is a network of dive shops: Dive St Vincent (Bill Tewes) at Young Island Dock, PO Box 864, T 457-4714/457-4928, F 457-4948 NAUI, PADI and CMAS certification courses, camera rental, trips to Bequia and the Falls of Baleine; also on St Vincent are St Vincent Dive Experience at the Lagoon marina, NAUI instruction, also waterskiing with instruction and trips to Bequia and Baleine Falls, T 456-9741, F 457-2768, and there is diving at Petit Byahaut Bay organized by the hotel there, T/F 457-7008, VHF68.

On the other islands are: Dive Bequia, a full service PADI/NAUI/CMAS dive shop at the *Plantation House Hotel*, near Port Elizabeth, PO Box 16, Bequia, T 458-3504, F 458-3886; Sunsports at the *Gingerbread* complex has PADI/NAUI diving, sunfish and tennis (T 458-3577, F 457-3031). Dive Paradise, *Friendship Bay Hotel*, Bequia, T/F 458-3563, 3 dive boats, waterskiing, German and English speaking staff, no credit cards; Paradise Windsurfing has five different locations and offers different levels of instruction, call Basil Cumberland, T 458-3425; Bequia Dive Resort at *Bequia Beach Club*, Friendship Bay, can accommodate up to 16 people on the boat but groups are normally smaller, PADI/NAUI instruction, German and English spoken,

T 458-3248, F 458-3689; Dive Anchorage at Anchorage Yacht Club on Union Island, T 458-8221; Grenadines Dive (Glenroy Adams), at *Sunny Grenadines Hotel*, Clifton, Union Island, T 458-8138/8122, F 458-8122, VHF 16/68, rendezvous service in Tobago Cays and surrounding islands; Dive Canouan, at *Canouan Beach Hotel* and *Tamarind Beach Hotel*, instruction, rentals, boat trips and rendezvous service, T 458-8648, F 458-8875. You can organize packages of 10 dives with or without certification course, combining Dive St Vincent on Young Island, Dive Canouan and Grenadines Dive, Union Island, a good way of diving throughout the islands. Some dive operations offer discounts to 'yachties'.

BEACHES AND WATERSPORTS

St Vincent has splendid, safe beaches on the leeward side, most of which have volcanic black sand. The windward coast is more rocky with rolling surf and strong currents. All beaches are public. Some are difficult to reach by road, but boat trips can be arranged to the inaccessible beauty spots. Sea urchins are a hazard, as in many other islands, especially among rocks on the less frequented beaches. Nearly all the inhabited islands of the Grenadines have at least one beach, and often many more, some fringed with palm trees, others without any sun protection. As elsewhere in the Caribbean, the windward side is too rough for swimming, with heavy surf, while the leeward side of the islands has calm water, excellent for swimming, snorkelling or windsurfing.

Sailing is excellent, indeed it was yachtsmen who first popularized the Grenadines and it is one of the best ways to see the islands. You can take day charter boats, easily arranged through hotels, or charter your own boat. There is a variety of boats for skippered day charters. Talk to the operators about size and predicted wind conditions if you are inclined towards seasickness. The large catamarans are usually quite stable so that you will hardly know you are on a boat, but they take quite large groups. Check with the *Beachcomber Hotel* on St Vincent, T 458-4283. On Bequia the *Friendship Rose* schooner, T 458-3202 (0800-1700), 458-3090 (1700-2000); *Getaway* at *Friendship Bay Hotel*, T 458-3222; the 60-foot catamaran, *Passion*, highly recommended, US$50 for day trip to Mustique via Moonhole, Petit Nevis, snorkelling stop at the *Cotton House* and *Basil's Bar* for lunch, departs 1100 from the Gingerbread House, all drinks and excellent rum punch included, T 458-3884; *Pelangi* at *Hotel Frangipani*, T 458-3255; the *Quest* at the *Plantation House*, T 458-3425; Wind and Sea in Clifton on Union Island offers day cruises aboard the *Jet Set*, a 65-foot catamaran, visiting Palm Island, Mayreau and the Tobago Cays with snorkelling and drinks included, T 458-8647. On Bequia, Captain Danny with his 43-foot yacht, *Prospect of Whitby*, has been recommended for tailor-made charters. A 2-day sail to the Tobago Cays via Mayreau costs about US$50 pp, food US$15 extra, contact through Frangipani Yacht Services, T 458-3244, F 458-3824, or on VHF 68 'Prospect'.

Bareboat and crewed yachts are available through Stardust Yacht Charters at the Anchorage Yacht Club, Union Island, T 458-8221; Barefoot Yacht Charters (Blue Lagoon), T 456-9526, 800-677-3195, F 693-7245; Lagoon Yacht Charters (Lagoon Marina), T 458-4308, F 457-4716; Nicholson Yacht Charters for crewed yachts, T 460-1530/1059, in USA T 617-225-0555; Tradewind Yachts (Lagoon Marina) T 456-9736, 800-825-7245, F 456-9737. Moorings charter boats from bases in St Lucia or Grenada also cruise the Grenadines.

Yacht races include the Bequia Easter Regatta, in which there are races for all sizes and types of craft, even coconut boats chased by their swimming child owners or model sailing yachts chased by rowing boats. Everyone is welcome and there are crewing opportunities; you may find yourself crewing alongside the Prime Minister. There are other contests on shore and the nights are filled with events such as dancing, beauty shows and fashion shows. The centre of activities is the *Frangipani Hotel*, which fronts directly on to Admiralty Bay. The Canouan Yacht Race is in August.

OTHER SPORTS

Many of the more expensive hotels have tennis courts but there are others at the Kingstown Tennis Club and the Prospect Racquet Club. On Bequia, tennis is offered at four hotels: *Friendship Bay*, *Spring*, *Plantation House* and *Frangipani*. Squash courts can be found at the Cecil Cyrus Squash Complex (St James Place, Kingston, reservations T 456-1805), the *Grand View Beach Hotel* and the Prospect Racquet Club. Horse riding can be arranged at the *Cotton House Hotel*, Mustique. Spectator sports include

Cricket Grenadine style

Cricket is played throughout the Grenadines on any scrap of ground or on the beach. In Bequia, instead of the usual three stumps at the crease, there are four, while furthermore, bowlers are permitted to bend their elbows and hurl fearsome deliveries at the batsmen. This clearly favours the fielding side but batsmen are brought up to face this pace attack from an early age and cope with the bowling with complete nonchalance. Matches are held regularly, usually on Sundays, and sometimes internationals are staged. In Lower Bay v England, which Lower Bay usually wins, the visitors' team is recruited from cricket lovers staying in the area. Ask at *De Reef*, it is best to bat at number 10 or 11.

cricket (Test Match cricket ground at Arnos Vale, near the airport), soccer, netball, volleyball and basketball. Pick up games of basket ball are played on St Vincent after 1700, or after the heat has subsided, at the Sports Complex behind the airport. Everyone is welcome, although it can get very crowded and there is only one court, arrive early. There is also a court in Calliaqua (same times), but it is right on the street. Players beware, fouls are rarely called, although travelling violations are. No one is deliberately rough but overall the game is unpolished, unschooled but spirited.

FESTIVALS

St Vincent's carnival, called Vincy Mas, is held in the last week of June and the first week of July for 10 days. Mas is short for masquerade, and the three main elements of the carnival are the costume bands, the steel bands and the calypso. During the day there is J'Ouverte, ole mas, children's carnival and steel bands through Kingstown's streets. At night calypsonians perform in 'tents', there is the King and Queen of the bands show, the steel bands competition and Careval, a beauty competition with contestants from other Caribbean countries (consisting of a talent contest, a beauty contest and local historical dress). Thousands of visitors come to take part, many of whom come from Trinidad.

From 16 December, for nine mornings, people parade through Kingstown and dances are held from 0100. At Easter on Union Island there are sports, cultural shows and a calypso competition. Also on Union Island, in May, is the Big Drum Festival, an event which marks the end of the dry season, culminating in the Big Drum Dance, derived from African and French traditions. It is also performed on other occasions, for weddings or launching boats and even in times of disaster.

KINGSTOWN

The capital, **Kingstown**, stands on a sheltered bay where scores of craft laden with fruit and vegetables add their touch of colour and noisy gaiety to the town. However, much land has been reclaimed and continuing dock works shield the small craft from sight, except at the N end of the bay.

The market square in front of the Court House is the hub of activity. Market day is Friday and Saturday and very colourful with all the produce spread out on sacks or on makeshift tables. The shopping and business area is no more than two blocks wide, running between Upper Bay Street and Halifax Street/Lower Bay Street and Grenville Street. There are quite a lot of new buildings, none of them tall. A Fish Market, built with Japanese aid, was opened in 1990 near the Police Headquarters. This complex, known as Little Tokyo, has car parking facilities and is the point of departure for minibuses to all parts of the island. Looking inland from the bay, the city is surrounded on all sides by steep, green hills, with houses perched all the way up.

Kingstown has two cathedrals, St George's (Anglican) and St Mary's (Catholic). St George's, parts of which date from 1820, has an airy nave and a pale blue gallery running around the N, W and S sides. There is an interesting floor plaque in the nave, commemorating a general who died fighting the Caribs. St Mary's is of far less sober construction, with different styles, all in dark grey stone, crowded together on the church, presbytery and school. Building was carried out throughout the 19th century, with renovation in the 1940s. The exterior of the church is highly decorated but the interior is dull in comparison. The Methodist church, dating from 1841, also has a fine interior, with a circular balcony.

At the jetty where the boats for the Grenadines berth, you can see island

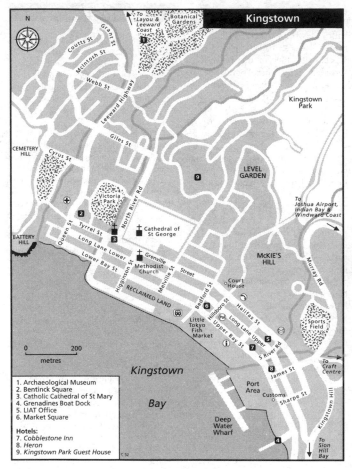

Kingstown

1. Archaeological Museum
2. Bentinck Square
3. Catholic Cathedral of St Mary
4. Grenadines Boat Dock
5. LIAT Office
6. Market Square

Hotels:
7. Cobblestone Inn
8. Heron
9. Kingstown Park Guest House

schooners loading and unloading, all of which is done by hand. The men throw crates from one to the other in a human chain; the whole business is accompanied by much shouting and laughter. When the banana boat is in dock, the farmers queue in their pick-ups to unload their boxes of bananas, and the food and drink stalls on the road to the Reception Depot do good business.

In Kingstown the **Botanical Gardens** just below Government House and the Prime Minister's residence are well worth a visit (for a description see above under **Fauna and flora**). Established in 1765, they are the oldest in the Western Hemisphere. In the Gardens, there is a very interesting **Archaeological Museum** of Amerindian artefacts, some of which date from about 4,000 BC. The most spectacular exhibit is the bat effigy.

Outside is a collection of shrubs which may have been planted in a Carib garden. Anyone interested in St Vincent history, flora or fauna should talk to the curator, Dr Earle Kirby (Doc); he is very knowledgeable and friendly. Unfortunately, the museum is only open Wednesday morning 0900-1200 and Saturday afternoon 1500-1800. Dr Kirby is elderly and not always at the museum. Occasionally he will open the museum and give a personal tour for especially interested visitors. The Gardens themselves are open 0600-1800 daily. They are about a 20-minute walk from the market square: go along Grenville Street, past the cathedrals, turn right into Bentinck Square, right again and continue uphill to the gate. Or take a bus, EC$1 from the terminal. You will be approached by guides who can explain which plant is which. There are notices specifying the official tour rates, so make sure you agree a price beforehand. Some guides can be persistent and bothersome, and have been known to get aggressive and demand payment for unrendered services. You do not have to have a guide.

Fort Charlotte (completed 1805) is on the promontory on the N side of Kingstown Bay, 636 feet above sea level, 15 minutes' drive out of town (EC$1.50 from bus terminal to village below, if you ask the driver he might take you into the fort for EC$1-2, worth it if it is hot). The views of Kingstown and surroundings are spectacular, and on a clear day the Grenadines and even Grenada are visible. Although the fort was designed to fend off attacks from the sea, the main threat was the Black Caribs and many of its 34 guns (some of which are still in place) therefore faced inland. In the old barrack rooms, a series of paintings shows the early history of St Vincent. There is also a coast guard lookout which controls the comings and goings of ships entering the port. Below, the ruins of a military hospital can be seen, as well as a bathing pool at sea level on the end of the point, used when the fort housed people suffering from yaws. The National Trust and the Caribbean Conservation Association (CCA) are proposing to develop Fort Charlotte as part of an Eastern Caribbean plan for historic military sites, with an Interpretive Centre, gift shop and museum. The National Trust of St Vincent and the Grenadines, PO Box 752, T 456-2591, has further information.

EXCURSIONS

The highest peak on the island, **La Soufrière** volcano, rises to about 4,000 feet. In 1970 an island reared itself up out of the lake in the crater: it smokes and the water round it is very warm. Hiking to the volcano is very popular, but you must leave very early in the morning and allow a full day for the trip. About two miles N of Georgetown (van from Kingstown to Georgetown EC$4) on the Windward side you cross the Dry River, then take a left fork and walk/drive through banana plantations to where the trail begins. A local guide is recommended, although not essential, always useful for carrying food and water as well as ensuring you do not get lost. It takes about three hours to reach the crater edge and it is a strenuous hike along a marked trail, the first three miles are through the Rabacca plantation, then up, along Bamboo Ridge and all the way to the crater's magnificent edge; the top can be cloudy, windy, cold and rainy, take adequate clothing and footwear. There is an alternative, unmarked and even more challenging route from the Leeward side starting from the end of the road after Richmond, but you will need a guide. After crossing a river delta, turn right into a ravine and climb; it will take about four hours. Guided tours usually on Tuesdays and Thursdays, about US$20-35, guides provide and carry drinks. If you want to avoid organized tours, a guide can be obtained in Georgetown. One such is Benjamin Hudson, who lives opposite Sadoo's

Grocery. Leave an extra set of clothes in the van in case you get wet through. Take water and insect repellent.

An easier climb is up **Mount St Andrew**, near Kingstown. A tarmac track runs up to the radio mast on the summit of the peak, at 2,413 feet, passing first through banana and vegetable gardens and then through forest. There are no parrots but otherwise virtually all the species of birds which can be found on the Vermont Nature Trail. It is particularly good for the Antillean crested hummingbird and black hawks. The view from the summit covers the Grenadines and the Vermont and Mesopotamia valleys. To reach the track either take a van running along the Leeward Highway and ask to be put down at the junction with the Mt St Andrew road, or start your walk in Kingstown.

There are few good roads, but cars, including self-drive, can be hired and most of the beauty spots are accessible by road. The Leeward Highway is a dramatic drive, passing through Questelles and Layou. Much of this road is in very poor condition N of Barrouallie (pronounced Barrelly), a small whaling village. This drive along the W coast towards La Soufrière should not be missed; it has been described as a 'tropical corniche'. There are lush valleys and magnificent sea views.

On the Leeward coast 14 miles N of Kingstown and two miles N of Barrouallie, are the **Wallilabou Falls** (Wally-la-boo), 15-20 feet high with a pool at the bottom which you can bathe in. There are changing rooms, toilets and a picnic site. On the opposite side of the road is a nutmeg plantation. You can get there by car or by bus from Little Tokyo Fish Market to Barrouallie and walk from there. Another set of falls, also on the Leeward side, is 20 miles N of Kingstown; **Petit Wallibou Falls** are a double waterfall in a very remote region and you can bathe at the bottom of the second waterfall. To get there, go through Richmond and turn right up the side road

beside the Richmond Vale Academy; follow this road for one mile, it then turns into a track for two miles. At the river the top of the waterfall is on your left. There is a steep climb on the left hand side of the waterfall to reach the pool where you can swim. **Trinity Falls** are 45 minutes' walk from Richmond in the Wallibou Valley, set deep in a canyon in the rainforest. The only known hot springs are in the canyon, having appeared since the last volcanic eruption.

A boat trip to the falls of **Baleine** (on the NW coast) is recommended. Wading ashore and for a few minutes up a river which originates on Soufrière, you come to the falls. At their base are natural swimming pools. It is possible to reach the falls on foot, but the easiest way is to take an excursion by motor boat (eg with Dive St Vincent, or Grenadine Tours), which includes a stop for snorkelling, and a picnic lunch, for US$35-40. Sea Breeze Boat Service uses a 36-foot auxiliary sloop, not recommended if you get seasick, otherwise nice, includes snorkelling stop, rum punch but no lunch, for US$25 pp, Captain Al is an authority on the bottle-nosed dolphin and may find a school of them to watch, recommended, T 458-4969.

The Queens Drive takes you into the hills S of Kingstown and gives splendid views all around. The Marriaqua Valley with its numerous streams is particularly beautiful. In the Valley, beyond Mesopotamia (commonly known as Mespo), the lush, tropical gardens of Montreal are worth a visit; anthuriums are grown commercially there. The drive along the Windward coast to Georgetown offers good views of rocks, black sand beaches and rolling breakers. The road to **Sandy Bay** (beyond Georgetown), where St Vincent's remaining Black Caribs live, is now good, however you have to cross the Dry River, which sometimes is not dry and therefore not passable. Sandy Bay is poor but beyond it is an even poorer village along a rough dirt road, **Owia**. Here is **Salt Pond**, a natural area of tidal pools filled with small marine life. The rough Atlantic crashes around the huge boulders and lava formations and is very picturesque. The villagers have planted flowers and made steps down to the Salt Pond area. There is also an arrowroot processing factory which can be visited. Past Owia is **Fancy**, the poorest village on the island, also Black Carib and very isolated, reached by a rough jeep track which makes a pleasant walk. A project to bring electricity to the northern villages is under way with French financial assistance. Baleine Falls (see above) are a two-mile hike from here around the tip of the island, rugged and not recommended for the unadventurous. Fishing boats can be hired in Fancy to collect you (do not pay in advance).

The SE of the island is drier and has different vegetation and birdlife. Take a van running to Stubbs and alight at the Post Office by the Brighton road junction. Walk into Brighton village and find a guide who can lead you to see, among others, the mangrove cuckoo, smooth-billed ani, broad-winged hawk and green heron. When tidal conditions are right it is possible to cross to Milligan Cay. To see seabirds in the bay visit early morning or late afternoon.

There are some interesting petroglyphs and rock carvings dating back to the Siboney, Arawak and Carib eras. The best known are just N of Layou, carved on a huge boulder next to a stream. They can only be visited on payment of US$2 for the owner, Mr Victor Hendrickson to open the gate to the fenced off area. Ask the local children to show you his house and then the petroglyphs for a tip, well worth a visit.

YOUNG ISLAND

A tiny, privately-owned islet, 200 yards off St Vincent. Pick up the phone at the crossing to see if you will be allowed over. **Fort Duvernette**, on a 195-foot high rock just off Young Island, was built at the beginning of the 19th century to defend Calliaqua Bay. To visit it, arrangements must be made with the hotel or ask around the dock for a boat to take you out: approximately EC$20 to be dropped off there and picked up later; wonderful view, inspires imagination, recommended. There is a lovely lagoon swimming pool, surrounded by tropical flowers. **L1** *Young Island Resort*, P O Box 211, T 458-4826, F 457-4567, in UK T 0800-373742; all accommodation in cottages, (MAP), yachts are US$500-650 a day, no children 15 January – 15 March, part sailing and honeymoon packages available. The Thursday noon buffet for US$12 is highly rec. A 3-course meal costs about US$40 in the evening. Sunset cocktail parties with *hors d'oeuvres* are held on Fort Duvernette behind the resort. The 100 steps up the hill are lit by flaming torches and a string band plays. Reservations are necessary for non-guests, about US$15. On Saturday night there is a jump-up to a steel band.

Island information – St Vincent
● Accommodation

Price guide

L1	over US$200	L2	US$151-200
L3	US$101-150	A1	US$81-100
A2	US$61-80	A3	US$46-60
B	US$31-45	C	US$21-30
D	US$12-20	E	US$7-11
F	US$4-6	G	up to US$3

In **Kingstown**: on Upper Bay Street, **A2** *Cobblestone Inn* (PO Box 867, T 456-1937, F 456-1938), upstairs in a building which used to be a sugar and arrowroot warehouse, a/c, very quiet, rooms good, rec; nearby, at junction with South River Road, is **A3** *Heron* (PO Box 226, T 457-1631, F 456-2726, 457-1189), also once above a warehouse (now above a screenprinting shop and bookshop), popular with business visitors, but has recently lost a lot of its class, set-menu food in restaurant, a/c, TV lounge, the place for a well-earned bacon and egg breakfast after crossing from Bequia on the early boat; **A3** *Haddon*, Grenville Street (PO Box 144, T 456-1897, F 456-2726) good food, helpful, a/c, tennis courts nearby, car hire available. **C-D** *Kingstown*

Park (PO Box 41, T 456-1532, F 457-4174), the oldest guest house on the island with a certain old-fashioned colonial ambience (originally the governor-general's residence), but being refurbished in 1996 and likely to reopen with higher prices and less ambience. **A2** *Kingstown Park Inn*, PO Box 765, T 457-2964, F 457-2505, new bed and breakfast, 8 rooms, fans, a/c in one room, bar and restaurant, car rental. **C** *Bella Vista Inn*, behind *Kingstown Park*, 7 rooms, 3 with private bath, fans, run by Nzinga Miguel and her daughter Cleopatra, friendly, homely atmosphere, breakfast EC$10, dinner on request EC$15.

At **Villa Point** and Beach, and **Indian Bay**, 3 miles from town, **L1-L3** *Grand View Beach*, Villa Point (PO Box 173, T 458-4811, F 457-4174), refurbished 1993/94, 19 rooms, first class, pool, tennis, squash, fully-equipped gym, snorkelling, excursions arranged, restaurant; **L3** *Villa Lodge*, Villa Point (PO Box 1191, T 458-4641, F 457-4468), 10 rooms overlooking Indian Bay, a/c, fans, TV, pool, restaurant, bar, 10 mins from airport, rec; **L3-A1** *Brownes*, on the water in Villa, 24 a/c rooms, phone, TV, restaurant, free shuttle to Kingstown, T 457-4000, F 457-4040; **A3** *Umbrella Beach* (P O Box 530, T 458-4651, F 457-4930), 9 double rooms with kitchen, bath, balcony, nice, simple, opp Young Island, 13 rooms face sea. Also at Villa Beach is **L3** *Sunset Shores*, PO Box 849, T 458-4411, F 457-4800, 32 rooms, a/c, TV, sunfish, snorkelling gear, pool, table tennis, dining room, bar; **A3** *TranQuillity Beach Apartment Hotel*, Indian Bay (PO Box 71, T/F 458-4021), excellent view, kitchen facilities, fans, TV, laundry service, clean, friendly, rec, very helpful owners, Mr and Mrs Providence, delicious meals if given a few hours' notice; **A2** *Beachcombers Hotel*, T 458-4283, F 458-4385, PO Box 126, small, family-run, inc breakfast, laundry service, restaurant and bar; **A3** *Belleville Apartment Hotel*, T 458-4776, F 456-2344, PO Box 746, 8 self-contained apartments or 2-bedroomed suite A2; **B** *Ocean View Inn*, PO Box 176, T 457-4332, 5 rooms in villa, laundry service, fans, meals on request; **A1** *Breezeville Apartments*, PO Box 222, T 458-4004, F 457-4468, 8 one-bedroomed studios, kitchens, a/c, pool, restaurant, bar; **A2-A3** *Paradise Inn*, PO Box 1286, T 457-4795, F 457-4221, rooms or apartments, beach, restaurant, bar, laundry service, a/c or fans, helpful and friendly staff, view of Young Island, on bus route to Villa, special rates for

senior citizens and church groups; **A2** *Coconut Beach Inn*, nice, clean, comfortable rooms, beautiful seaview, rec, T 457-4900, good restaurant (see below); **A2** *Indian Bay Beach Hotels and Apartments* (PO Box 538, T 458-4001, F 457-4777) hotel on beach, nice verandah, good snorkelling just outside the hotel, daily or weekly rates, 2 bedroomed apartments available, sleep 3-4, a/c, kitchenettes, restaurant, watersports nearby. **L3-A1** *The Lagoon Marina and Hotel*, Blue Lagoon, (PO Box 133, T/F 458-4308), 19 rooms with lovely view, run by Vincentians, Richard and Nancy Joachim, also 1-bedroom and 3-bedroom apartments, yacht charter US$275-400/day, US$1,400-2,800/week, full service marina, bar, restaurant, pools, scuba diving, windsurfing. Other guest houses: **C** *Sea Breeze Guest House*, Arnos Vale, near airport (T 458-4969), cooking facilities, 6 rooms with bath, no credit cards, noisy, friendly, helpful, bus to town or airport from the door. At Ratho Mill: *Ridgeview Terrace Apartments*, PO Box 176, T 456-1615, F 457-2874, 200 yds from Blue Lagoon Beach, 5 apartments overlooking yacht basin and Grenadines, a/c, kitchens, balconies, daily maid service, US$175-290/week.

On the Leeward coast, **L1-L3** *Petit Byahaut*, set in a 50-acre valley, no TV or phones, 10 x 13-ft tents with floors, queen-sized bed, shower and hammock in each tent, inc all meals, snorkelling, sail and row boats, water taxi transfer on stays of 3 days and over, scuba packages available, you can hire the whole resort for 14 people for US$1,500/day, T/F 457-7008, VHF 68, access only by boat, diving and snorkelling good in the bay, ecological and conservation emphasis, solar powered. In the Peniston Valley: **A2** *Emerald Valley Resort & Casino*, PO Box 1081, T 456-7140, F 456-7145, extensively renovated, 12 cottages, a/c, kitchenettes, 9-hole golf course, poolside restaurant, tennis. On the Windward coast: **A1-A2** *Argyle Nature Resort*, PO Box 1639, T 458-0992, F 457-2432, 10 rooms, fans, TV, phone, restaurant, pool, natural jacuzzi, horse riding, short walk to beach or petroglyphs.

● **Where To Eat**
There is a shortage of good restaurants in Kingstown, the better ones, eg the *French Restaurant*, are in the beach area several miles E. *Vee-Jay's* restaurant on Lower Bay Street is friendly and offers local food; open Mon-Sat

1000-1900, Fri until late, also *Vee-Jay's Rooftop Diner & Pub* on Upper Bay St, T 457-2845/1395, above Roger's Photo Studios, open Mon-Sat from 0900, sandwiches, rotis etc for lunch, good local juices, dinner by reservation only, cocktail bar, entrés EC$12-45, great steel band. For genuine West Indian food and local company *Aggie's Bar and Restaurant* on Grenville St, T 456-2110, is superb; *Sid's Pub* is a great bargain, good native food, main course from EC$10, friendly, clean, good service, sports on satellite TV, open Mon-Sat from 1100, Sun from 1900, T 456-2315. *Basil's Bar and Restaurant* (see below) has a branch underneath the *Cobblestone Inn*, in Upper Bay Street, buffet 1200-1400 for hungry people, open from 1000, rather overrated, T 457-2713. *Cobblestone Roof Top Restaurant*, belonging to the *Cobblestone Inn*, T 456-1937, West Indian lunches and hamburgers, open Mon-Sat 0730-1500, good place for breakfast, as is the *Heron Hotel* (see above).

At the bus station (Little Tokyo) you can buy freshly grilled chicken and corn cobs, good value and tasty. Cafés on the jetty by ferry boats serve excellent, cheap, local food, eg salt cod rolls with hot pepper sauce. On market days fruit is plentiful and cheap, great bananas. Take away food from *Pizza Party*, T 456-4932/9, in Arnos Vale by the airport, delivery and takeaway until 2300, no credit cards; *Chung Wua*, Upper Bay Street, T 457-2566, open Mon-Sat 1100-2230, Sun 1700-2200, Chinese eat in or take away, no credit cards, from EC$10.

In the **Villa** area, *The French Restaurant*, T 458-4972, VHF Channel 68, open daily for lunch and dinner, very good food, lobster from the tank, rec, superb service and lovely beach view, the place for a treat. The *Lime'n' Pub* on the waterfront at Villa has a casual menu and a dinner menu, reasonable prices, T 458-4227, open 1000-2400; *Beachcombers* on Villa Beach has light fare and drinks, very casual, or à la carte menu, open air, food 1000-2200, bar open later, happy hour 1700-1830, T 458-4283; *Dolphins*, T 457-4337,

VHF68, moderate prices, building decorated with artwork of owner and other local artists; *Stilly's Aquatic Club* has weekend and holiday evening action; *Paradise Inn*, T 457-4795, offers local food and occasional Fri night barbecues with live music; the adventurous should try *Papa Spoon's Rasta Ranch* on the Callaquia playing field for inexpensive local, all natural food served in calabash bowls. The *Coconut Beach Inn* on Indian Bay has a good restaurant and rooms to let (see above), West Indian specialities, sandwiches, fish and chips etc, open daily from 1000, dinner by reservation only before 1500, entrées, EC$10-45. *Villa Lodge Hotel* is a good place to eat, not cheap but wonderful piña colada. *Sugar Reef*, at the *Lagoon Marina and Hotel*, Blue Lagoon, T 456-9847, run by Americans, Janet and Neil Becker, breakfast, lunch and dinner with daily specials, pleasant for happy hour watching the sunset, reasonable prices.

Stephens Hideout, Cumberland Bay, T 458-2325, West Indian and seafood, restaurant on Leeward Highway, Beach Bar on the bay, call ahead for meals or picnic on beach, open 0900-2230, no credit cards, tours arranged; *Wallilabou Anchorage*, T 458-7270, caters mainly to yachties, mooring facilities, West Indian specialities.

● **Entertainment**

Several hotels have live music some evenings. *Emerald Valley Casino*, T 456-7140, call for transport, closed Tues. *Young Island* hosts sunset cocktail parties (see above). *Basils Too*, T 458-4205, offers lunch, dinner and dancing on Villa Beach by Young Island. Check for happy hours at bars for lower-priced drinks, snacks and often entertainment. In Kingstown, *Touch Entertainment Centre* opened its dance hall in 1993, run by the Vincentian band, *Touch*, T 457-1825. *The Attic*, T 457-2558, at the corner of Melville and Grenville Streets, nightly live entertainment, jazz, karaoke, dancing, large screen video, music bar open 1200 till late, restaurant open Mon-Sat for lunch 1100-1430.

The Grenadines

THE GRENADINES, divided politically between St Vincent and Grenada, are a string of 100 tiny, rocky islands and cays stretching across some 35 miles of sea between the two. They are still very much off the beaten track as far as tourists are concerned, but are popular with yachtsmen and the 'international set'.

BEQUIA

Named the island of the clouds by the Caribs, (pronounced Bek-*way*) this is the largest of the St Vincent dependencies with a population of 4,874 (1991 census). Nine miles S of St Vincent and about seven miles square, Bequia attracts quite a number of tourists, chiefly yachtsmen but also the smaller cruise ships and, increasingly, land-based tourists. The island is quite hilly and well-forested with a great variety of fruit and nut trees. Its main village is **Port Elizabeth** and here Admiralty Bay offers a safe anchorage. Boat building and repair work are the main industry. Experienced sailors can sometimes get a job crewing on boats sailing on from here to Panama and other destinations. For maps and charts (and books) go to Iain Gale's Bequia Bookshop, which is very well stocked. The nearest beach to Port Elizabeth is the pleasant Princess Margaret beach which shelves quickly into the clear sea. There are no beach bars to spoil this tree-lined stretch of soft sand. At its S end there is a small headland, around which you can snorkel to Lower Bay, where swimming is excellent and the beach is one of the best on the island. Local boys race their homemade, finely finished sailing yachts round the bay. In the village is *Kennedy's Bar*, a good place to watch the sunset with a rum punch. Further along is *De Reef*, whose bar and restaurant are the hub of much local activity.

Away from Port Elizabeth the beaches are empty. Take a taxi through coconut groves past an old sugar mill to Industry Bay, a nice beach surrounded by palms with a brilliant view across to Bullet Island, Battowia and Balliceaux where the Black Caribs were held before being deported to Roatán. Some luxury homes have been built at the N end of the bay. Food and drink available at the *Industry Beach Bar*. A short walk along the track leads to Spring Bay, to the S, where there is a beach bar (may be closed). Both beaches are narrow with shallow bays and a lot of weed, making them less good for swimming and snorkelling.

The walk up Mount Pleasant from Port Elizabeth is worthwhile (go by taxi if it is too hot), the shady road is overhung with fruit trees and the view of

St Vincent and the Grenadines

Waterloo Mountains

Georgetown

Barrouallie

KINGSTOWN

ST VINCENT

N

PORT ELIZABETH *Bequia*

Isle à Quatre Petit Nevis Battowia
Baliceaux

The Pillories

LOVELL VILLAGE

Mustique

Petit Mustique

Petit Canouan Savan Is

Canouan

CHARLESTOWN

Catholic Is

Union Island *Mayreau*

Tobago Cays

CLIFTON Palm (Prune) Is

The GRENADINES

Petit St Vincent

0   10
km

current, take care. Friendship Bay is particularly pleasant, there is some coral but also quite a lot of weed, a taxi costs EC$15, or you can take a dollar bus (infrequent) in the direction of Paget Farm, get out at Mr Stowe's Store (EC$1.50) and walk down to the bay (you may have to ring for a taxi at one of the hotels to get back, though).

The Tourist Office by the jetty (very helpful) can help you arrange a visit to the cliffside dwellings of Moon Hole at the S end of the island, where a rocky arch frames the stone dwelling and the water comes up the front yard. At Paget Farm, whale harpooning is still practised from February to May by a few elderly fishermen who use two 26-foot long cedar boats, powered by oars and sails. They do not catch much. If you can arrange a trip to **Petit Nevis**, to the S, you can see the whaling station and find out more about Bequia's whaling tradition.

Island information – Bequia
● **Accommodation**
L3 *The Old Fort*, on Mount Pleasant, a 17th century French built fortified farmhouse, probably oldest building on Bequia, magnificent views, idyllic restaurant (dinner only, must book), animals in spacious grounds inc donkeys, kittens, peacocks, talking parrot, 4 apartments and a cottage, T 458 3440, F 458-3340, excursions, diving, boat trips arranged, highly rec, German run; **L2** *Friendship Bay* (PO Box 9, T 458-3222, F 458-3840), lovely location, boat excursions, water and other sports facilities, friendly, jump-up at beach bar, Sat night; **A1-A2** *Blue Tropic Hotel*, Friendship Bay, T 458-3573, F 457-3074, newly built, 10 rooms, view of bay, restaurant, bar, free bikes, beach mats and sun chairs; **L3** *Bequia Beach Club*, Friendship Bay, T 458-3248, F 458-3689, 10 rooms, restaurant, bar, diving, windsurfing, tennis nearby, day sails, weekly barbecues; **L2-A1** *Spring on Bequia* (T 458-3414), on a bay

Admiralty Bay is ever more spectacular. There is a settlement of airy homes at the top, from where you can see most of the Grenadines. By following the road downhill and S of the viewpoint you can get to Hope Bay, an isolated and usually deserted sweep of white sand and one of the best beaches. At the last house (where you can arrange for a taxi to meet you afterwards), the road becomes a rough track, after ½ mile turn off right down an ill-defined path through cedar trees to an open field, cross the fence on the left, go through a coconut grove and you reach the beach. The sea is usually gentle but sometimes there is powerful surf, a strong undertow and offshore

Price guide			
L1	over US$200	L2	US$151-200
L3	US$101-150	A1	US$81-100
A2	US$61-80	A3	US$46-60
B	US$31-45	C	US$21-30
D	US$12-20	E	US$7-11
F	US$4-6	G	up to US$3

Bequia

Man Point

L'Anse Chemin
East End

0   750
metres

Brute Point

Industry

Cinnamon Garden

Northwest Point

Spring Bay

Hamilton

Anse la Coite

C a r i b b e a n   S e a

PORT ELIZABETH

Admiralty Bay

Hope Bay

Princess Margaret Beach

Ships Stern

Lower Bay

Mt Pleasant

Moon Hole

Paget Farm

Ravine Bay

N

West Cay

Adams Bay

Derrick

Friendship Bay

C Stb

to the NE of Port Elizabeth, part of a 200-yr old working plantation, 10 rooms, pool, tennis, bar, restaurant, beach bar. In Port Elizabeth itself, **L3-A1** *Frangipani* (PO Box 1, T 458-3255, F 458-3824), cheaper rooms share bathroom, on beach, pleasant, bar, terrible sandflies and mosquitoes in wet season, mosquito net provided; **L3-A2** *Gingerbread Apartments* , PO Box 1, T 458-3800, F 458-3907, one-bedroomed with kitchen and bathroom, no children, restaurant and bar upstairs, café downstairs, dive shop, tennis, water skiing, international phone calls 0700-1900 in upstairs office of restaurant, attractive, friendly, rec, run by Mrs Mitchell, Canadian, ex-wife of Prime Minister; **D** *Mitchells*, overlooking harbour (above Bookshop, go round the back and seek out the owner), inc morning coffee, but 10% more if you are staying only one night, cooking facilities available, good, cheap, basic; **A3** *Julie's Guest House*, 19 rooms with bath and shower, turn right by the police station, T 458-3304, F 458-3812, mosquito nets in rooms, rec, good local food, good cocktails in noisy bar downstairs, meeting place for travellers to form boat charter groups; **L1-L2** *Plantation House Hotel*, rebuilt after 1988 fire, on beach at Admiralty Bay, tennis, swimming pool, watersports, Dive Bequia dive shop, cottages or rooms, all MAP, PO Box 16, T 458-3425, F 458-

3612, entertainment at weekends; **C** *The Old Fig Tree*, PO Box 14, T 458-3201, restaurant with basic rooms, shared or private bath, meals extra (good), friendly, on extremely narrow beach. **A2** *Keegan's Guesthouse*, T 458-3254, lovely position, 11 rooms, also 2-bedroom apartment US$340/week, and **A3** *Creole Garden Hotel* at Lower Bay above Corner Bay and Lower Bay beach, new, MAP, bath, porch, refrigerator, T/F 458-3154.

There are also apartments to rent: **A2-B** *The Village Apartments* in Belmont, overlooking Admiralty Bay, studio, one or 2-bedroomed apartments, T 456-4960, F 456-2344, PO Box 1621, Kingstown; *Fairmont Apartments*, Admiralty Bay, T 457-1121, F 456-2333, studios, 1-2 bedrooms, some with pools, maid service, from US$175-700/week; **A3-C** *Hybiscus Apartments*, Union Vale, T 458-3316, F 458-3210, 4 units, kitchenettes, laundry service, scooters and bike hire; *Roberts Apartments*, Friendship Bay, T 458-4363/3462, 456-1511, 457-1967, 2 bedrooms, US$550-600/week, use of watersports at *Bequia Beach Club; De Reef Apartments*, Lower Bay, US$200-280/week, 1 bedroom; **A2-A3** *Kingsville Apartments*, Lower Bay, T 458-3404, F 458-3000, 1-2 bedrooms; *Friendship Bay Villa Rentals*, T 458-3222, F 458-3840.

● **Places to eat**

Apart from hotel restaurants, *Mac's Pizza* on Belmont Beach, is rec, very popular, get there early or reserve in advance, even in low season, also takeaways, T 458-3474; *Le Petit Jardin*, Back Street, T 458-3318, French and international, open daily 1130-1400, 1830-2130, reservations preferred, EC$30-85 for entrées; *La Mezzaluna*, closed Tues, dinner to 2330, live entertainment, T 458-3080; *Harpoon Saloon*, happy hour 1700-1800, wide ranging menu, moderate prices, managed by Vincentian, Noel Frazer, steel band some nights, T 458-3272; *Whaleboner*, food fresh from their own farm, EC$5-65, open Mon-Sat 0800-2200, Sun 1400-2200, T 458-3233; *Daphne's*, just off the main street, cooks excellent créole meals to eat in or take away, T 458-3271, no credit cards; *Dawn's Créole Tea Garden*, Lower Bay, at the far end, open from 0900, breakfast, lunch and dinner, good home cooked food, fairly expensive, must book, T 458-3154; the *Gingerbread House* has sandwiches and snacks all day, also *Gingerbread BBQ*, outdoors on bayside 1200-1500; *Green Boley* on the beach a bit S, local fast food to EC$20, T 458-3247, *Maranne's* at the *Green Boley Bar* for ice cream and other frozen desserts EC$2-10; *The Old Fig Tree*, fish and chips, rotis, pizza, fresh food, T 458-3201; *Schooners* own jetty, happy hour 1730-1830, fresh or frozen dinners for yachties; *De Reef*, Lower Bay, if you rent a locker note that all keys fit all locks, lovely position, popular with yachties, set meals and bar snacks, the place for Sun lunch; the *Frangipani* has sandwiches and snacks all day, slow service but friendly and you have a good view to look at.

There are small supermarkets in Port Elizabeth (limited choice of meat), S & W, Knights, Shoreline and 2 deli-type shops, with improving selection of groceries and beverages; fish is sometimes on sale in the centre by the jetty although a new fish market is being built, fruit and vegetable stalls by the jetty daily, frozen food and homemade bread from *Doris's*, also *Daphne's* for homemade bread. Fresh bakeries also from *Mac's Pizzeria*, *Harpoon Saloon*, *Gingerbread Coffee Shop* and *Whaleboner*.

● **Entertainment**

Jump ups on Tues at *Plantation House*, Thurs at *Frangipani* with barbecue and steel band, Tues and Sat at *Harpoon Saloon* with steel band, occasionally at *De Reef*, sometimes Sat night at *Friendship Bay*, string band several nights a week at *Gingerbread*. Check bars for happy hours. There is something going on most nights either at Admiralty Bay or Friendship Bay, check locally. Bands play reggae music in the gardens of several hotels, popular with residents and tourists.

● **Tour agencies**

Chris and Jazelle Patterson of Dolphin Tours (Ebony and Ivory Ltd) have been rec for giving comprehensive tours of Bequia and St Vincent, PO Box 1, Bequia, T 458 3345, 457 3205.

● **Transport**

An airport named the J F Mitchell Airport, after the Prime Minister, has been built on reclaimed land with a 3,200-foot runway, a terminal and night landing facilities, at the island's SW tip. Residents view it as a mixed blessing, some not wanting the island's peace and tranquility disturbed by an influx of visitors. The island's infrastructure and hotel accommodation is inadequate to handle greater numbers of tourists.

For about US$45, you can take a taxi around the island. You can also rent Honda scooters (and bicycles) from an agency between the bookstore and the National Commercial Bank for US$10/hour or US$30/day, but you need to get the police to verify your licence. Water taxis scoot about in Admiralty Bay for the benefit of the many yachts and people on the beach, whistle or wave to attract their attention, fare EC$10 per trip. There are day charters to other islands (see above, **Beaches and Watersports**). Bart has trips to the Tobago Cays and one other island with snorkelling, swimming, breakfast, lunch and all drinks on the *Island Queen*, US$75 pp, attentive, friendly service, hotel pick-up, beautiful scenery, rec. For those arriving on yachts, there are anchorages all round either side of the channel in Admiralty Bay, Princess Margaret Beach, Lower Bay, Friendship Bay and off Petit Nevis by the old whaling station. Bequia Slipway has dockage, some moorings are available.

MUSTIQUE

Lying 18 miles S of St Vincent, Mustique is three miles long and less than two miles wide. In the 1960s, Mustique was acquired by a single proprietor who developed the island as his private resort where he could entertain the rich and

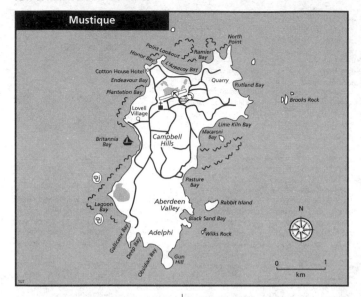

Mustique

famous. It is a beautiful island, with fertile valleys, steep hills and twelve miles of white sandy beach, but described by some as 'manicured'. It is no longer owned by one person and is more accessible to tourists, although privacy and quiet is prized by those who can afford to live there. There is no intention to commercialize the island; it has no supermarkets and only one petrol pump for the few cars (people use mopeds or golf carts to get around). Apart from the private homes, there is one hotel, one beach bar, a few boutiques, shops, a small village and a fishing camp. All house rentals are handled by the Mustique Company, which organizes activities such as picnics and sports, especially at Easter and Christmas. Radio is the principal means of communication, and the airstrip, being in the centre of the island is clearly visible, so check-in time is five minutes before take off (ie after you've seen your plane land).

There is sailing, diving, snorkelling, and good swimming (very little water-skiing), while riding can also be arranged or you can hire a moped to tour the island. The main anchorage is Brittania Bay, where there are 18 moorings for medium sized yachts with waste disposal and phones. Take a picnic lunch to Macaroni Beach on the Atlantic side. This gorgeous, white sand beach is lined with small palm-thatched pavilions and a well-kept park/picnic area. It is isolated and wonderful. Swimming and snorkelling is also good at Lagoon Bay, Gallicaux Bay, Brittania Bay and Endeavour Bay, all on the leeward side.

Basil's Bar and Restaurant is *the* congregating spot for yachtsmen and the jet set. From it there is a well-beaten path to the *Cotton House Hotel*, which is the other congregating point. There is an honour system to pay for moorings at *Basil's Bar*, EC\$40 a night, EC\$20 second night. Johanna Morris has a group of shops: *The Pink House, The Purple House, Johanna's Banana, Treasure Fashion, Basil's Boutique* and *Across Forever*.

Since the island has no fresh water, it is shipped in on Mustique Boats *Robert Junior* (T 457-1918) and the *Geronimo*. Both take passengers and excursions on Sunday (EC\$10, 2 hrs trip).

Island information – Mustique

● Accommodation

Mustique hotels: **L1** *Cotton House*, a 20-room refurbished 18th century cotton plantation house built of rock and coral, is the only hotel and is expensive, pool, tennis, windsurfers, sailfish, snorkelling, all complimentary, horseriding and scuba diving available, sailing packages tailor made, T 456-4777, F 456-5887, in Europe T 0-453-835-801, in USA T 800-447-7462; smaller, less expensive **L3-A1** *Firefly House*, T 458-4621 (all rooms with view overlooking the bay), bed and breakfast. 43 of the private residences are available for rent, with staff, from US$2,800/week in summer for a 2-bedroomed villa to US$13,000/week in winter for a villa sleeping 10. Contact Pauline Wilkins of Mustique Villa Rentals, Chartam House, 16a College Avenue, Maidenhead, Berkshire, SL6 6AX, UK, T 01628 75544, F 01628 21033, or the Mustique Company Renters Office by the airstrip on Mustique, mailing address PO Box 349, T 458-4621, F 456-4565, or Resorts Management Inc, The Carriage House, 201½ East 29th Street, New York, NY 10016, T (212) 696-4566, (800) 225-4255, F (212) 689-1598.

● Places to eat

Basil's Bar and The Raft, for seafood and night life, T 458-4621 for reservations, open from 0800, entrées EC$10-75. Locals' night on Mon with buffet for EC$35 excluding drinks and dancing, Wed is good, on Sat go to the *Cotton House*. Up the hill from *Basil's* is the local *Piccadilly* pub, where rotis and beer are sold, and pool is played; foreigners are welcome, but it is best to go in a group and girls should not go on their own. You can buy fresh fish, conch (lambi) and lobster from local fishermen. There is a good, small grocery.

UNION ISLAND

40 miles from St Vincent and the most S of the islands, it is three miles long and one mile wide with two dramatic peaks, Mount Olympus and Mount Parnassus, the latter being 900 feet high. Arrival by air is spectacular as the planes fly over the hill and descend steeply to the landing strip. The runway and airport building were completed in 1993. The road from the airport to Clifton passes a mangrove swamp which is being used as a dump prior to filling it in to get rid of mosquitoes and enable building to take place. A walk around the interior of the island (about two hours Clifton-Ashton-Richmond Bay-Clifton) is worth the effort, with fine views of the sea, neighbouring islands, pelicans and Union itself. It has two settlements, **Clifton** and **Ashton** (minibus between the two, EC$2), and the former serves as the S point of entry clearance for yachts. The immigration office and customs are at the airport. For visiting yachts there are anchorages at Clifton, Frigate Island and Chatham Bay, while the *Anchorage Yacht Club* marina has some moorings. The *Anchorage Yacht Club* seems to be full of French people. The barmen are slow and sometimes rude. Phone calls can be made from here, the airport or Clifton; credit card calls or operator assisted calls can be made.

A good reason to visit Union Island is to arrange day trips to other islands or to find a ride on a yacht to Venezuela towards the end of the season (May-June). Day trip boats leave around 1000 and are all about the same price, EC$100, including lunch. Ask at the *Anchorage Yacht Club* or Park East, across the airport runway, about boats going to the **Tobago Cays** (see below), you may be able to join a group quite cheaply. A large catamaran, *Typhoon*, runs a charter service, well worth while. An old sailing vessel, *Scaramouch*, also sails to the Tobago Cays, stopping additionally at Mayreau and Palm Island. The *Clifton Beach Hotel* arranges tours of Palm Island, Petit St Vincent and other small islands.

The beach at **Chatham Bay** is beautiful and deserted (very good mangoes grow there), but not particularly good for swimming as there is a coral ledge just off the beach. Snorkelling and diving are good though. It is one of the last undeveloped anchorages in the Grenadines. An area at the N end of the bay has been cleared for a hotel development and a road has been cut over the mountain from Ashton to Chatham Bay.

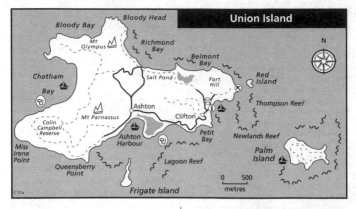

Union Island

A large tourist development is planned for Union Island, with a luxury hotel, 300-berth marina, golf course and villas. Work began in 1994 on the US$108mn project, with investment from Europe and the Middle East. The Government has a 14% shareholding.

Island information – Union Island

● Accommodation

L2-A1 *Anchorage Yacht Club*, Clifton, full marina service, French restaurant, room, cabana or bungalow, T 458-8221, F 458-8365; **B-C** *Clifton Beach Hotel and Guest House* (T/F 458-8235), a bit run down; **A1** *Sunny Grenadines* (T 458-8327, F 458-8398), reductions sometimes offered if business is slack, 5 mins' walk from airport, adequate rooms, laundry service, bar quite lively, food very good, boats can tie up at jetty; **C** *Lambis Guest House*, Clifton, T 458-8549, F 458-8395, 14 rooms; **A1-A3** *The Cays Apartments*, PO Box 748, Richmond Bay, T 456-2221, F 457-4266, 5 studio apartments, self-contained, maid service.

● Places to eat

Food is expensive; *Clifton Beach* and *Sunny Grenadines* hotels both have good restaurants and bars. The *Anchorage* restaurant has been criticized for serving bland, overpriced food, the occupants of the shark pool are given food rejected by customers. *Eagle's Nest Entertainment Center*, has a bar with light snacks; *Lambis Restaurant*, casual downstairs, more formal upstairs; *T & N*, upstairs bar, light meals, good rotis; *Sydney's Bar & Restaurant*, owned by Sydney, who handpaints T-shirts for

sale in Tobago Cays, and run by Marin from Munich, local meals, snacks, seafood crêpes, pasta, happy hour 1800-1900, two for one; *Jennifer's Restaurant*, West Indian food at reasonable prices, music at weekends.

CANOUAN

A quiet, peaceful, crescent-shaped island 25 miles S of St Vincent, with very few tourists and excellent reef-protected beaches. The beach at the *Canouan Beach Hotel* is splendid with white sand and views of numerous islands to the S. There are no restaurants outside the hotels and only basic shops. The main anchorage is Charlestown, Grand Bay, with Corbec and Rameau Bays as possibilities. In settled weather, South Glossy and Friendship Bays make possible anchorages, with excellent snorkelling. Diving and snorkelling are good at all these anchorages and on the reefs on the windward side. A recommended day trip is to the Tobago Cays, Mayreau or Petit St Vincent, depending on the weather and conditions, on the *Canouan Beach Hotel* 35-foot catamaran, EC$100 with lunch and drinks, non-hotel guests are permitted to make up numbers if the boat is not fully booked. There is an airstrip. A Swiss company, Canouan Resorts Development Ltd, has leased 1,200 of the island's 1,866 acres in a US$100mn development plan.

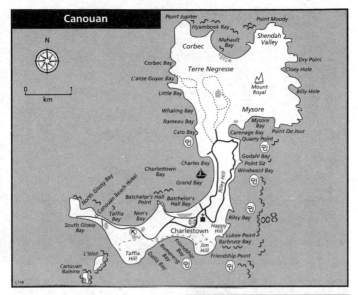

Canouan

Point Jupiter
Hyambook Bay
Point Moody
Corbec
Mahault Bay
Shendah Valley
Dry Point
Corbec Bay
Cloey Hole
Terre Negresse
L'anse Guyac Bay
Little Bay
Mount Royal
Billy Hole
Whaling Bay
Mysore
Rameau Bay
Mysore Bay
Cato Bay
Carenage Bay
Point De Jour
Quarry Point
Charles Bay
Godahl Bay
Point Siz
Charlestown Bay
Windward Bay
Grand Bay
Riley Hill
North Glossy Bay
Canouan Beach Hotel
Batchelor's Hall Point
Batchelor's Hall Bay
Riley Bay
Taffia Bay
Nen's Bay
Happy Hill
South Glossy Bay
Charlestown
Lukee Point
Barbruce Bay
L'Islot
Taffia Hill
Jim Hill
Friendship Bay
Rameau Bay
Dalls Bay
Friendship Point
Canouan Baleine

Island information – Canouan

● **Accommodation**

L1 *Canouan Beach Hotel* has developed the S part of the island with de luxe bungalows as well as the main building, nudist beach, (T 458-8888, F 458-8875, PO Box 530); **L3** *Villa le Bijou* (Mme Michelle de Roche, T 458-8025), MAP, on hill overlooking town, superb views, friendly, helpful, showers, water and ice for yacht visitors, no credit cards; George and Yvonne at the **A1** *Anchor Inn Guest House* in Grand Bay, T 458-8568, offer clean and basic accommodation, for double rooms, MAP, packed lunches available, no credit cards; also possible to rent houses. **L1** *Tamarind Beach Hotel and Yacht Club*, opened 1995 with 48 rooms, FAP, T 458-8044, F 458-8851, two restaurants, watersports, scuba diving at extra charge, golf course, long dock for dinghies, yachties welcome to use bar and restaurant, excellent conch creole appetizers, moorings rather rolly, more comfortable sleeping to anchor in N corner of bay. You are recommended to phone in advance to book rooms.

MAYREAU

A small privately-owned island with deserted beaches and only one hotel, **L1** *Salt Whistle Bay Club* (contact by radio, VHF Ch 16, boatphone 493 9609, T 613-634 7108, in UK T 0800-373742, 10 rooms, MAP, yacht charters and picnics on nearby islands), and one guest house, **A2-A3** *Dennis' Hideaway*, (3 rooms), though there is a plan to develop tourism. You can reach it only by boat. Once a week, however, the island springs to life with the arrival of a cruise ship which anchors in the bay and sends its passengers ashore for a barbecue and sunburn. In preparation for this, local women sweep the beach and the manchineel trees (poisonous) are banded with red.

Good food and drinks at reasonable prices can be found at *Dennis' Hideaway*. *J & C Bar and Restaurant*, has the best view of the harbour with soft music, boutique, room for a large group, good lobster, fish and lambi, for parties of 4 and over the captain's dinner is free;

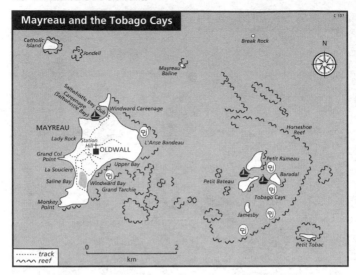

Mayreau and the Tobago Cays

C 107

Catholic Island

Jondell

Break Rock

N

Mayreau Baline

Saltwhistle Bay Club
Careenage (Saltwhistle Bay)

Windward Careenage

MAYREAU

Horseshoe Reef

Lady Rock

Station Hill

OLDWALL

L'Anse Bandeau

Grand Col Point

La Souciere

Upper Bay

Petit Rameau

Baradal

Saline Bay

Windward Bay
Grand Tarchie

Petit Bateau

Tobago Cays

Monkey Point

Jamesby

Petit Tobac

------- track
∼∼∼ reef

0   2
km

Island Paradise, everything is prepared fresh, good lobster, fish and curried conch, half price happy hour 1800-1900, barbecue Fridays with local band, free ride up the hill, skipper's meal free with more than three for dinner. There is a payphone in the village with an overseas operator for credit card calls.

TOBAGO CAYS

The **Tobago Cays** are a small collection of islets just off Mayreau, protected by a horseshoe reef and surrounded by beautifully clear water. The beaches are some of the most beautiful in the Caribbean and there is diving and snorkelling on Horseshoe reef and wall. Unfortunately their popularity has caused considerable destruction. There are day charters out of St Vincent, Bequia and Union Island. Anchor damage, together with over-fishing and removal of black coral has led to the death of some of the reef; hard coral lies broken on the bottom. The cays have now been declared a wildlife reserve and visitors are asked to take care not to damage marine resources. Although the

Tobago Cays are crowded with charter boats, liveaboard boats or day charter catamarans, the reef is slowly coming back to life. Mooring buoys have been put in to prevent anchoring on the reef. Parrot fish, grouper, trunkfish, snapper and other reef fish, including a 6-foot nurse shark, can now be seen again. There are free moorings inside Horseshoe reef for day charter boats or dinghies, and anchorages W of Petit Rameau in the cut between Petit Rameau and Petit Bateau, or to the S of Baradal. You can shop at your boat or on the beach. Ice, fresh fish, lambi, lobster, T-shirts, even French designer clothes.

PETIT ST VINCENT

Locally referred to as PSV, this is a beautiful, privately-owned, 113-acre island with one of the Caribbean's best resorts, the *Petit St Vincent* (rates vary during the year from US$450d to US$710d, FAP, inc room service and all facilities, plus 10% service and 7% tax, closed Sept/Oct, no credit cards). The island is owned and managed by Hazen Richardson, with help from his wife, Lynn, a staff of 80 (for 44 guests) and 7 labradors (who seem to be in charge of entertainment). Accommodation is in 22 secluded cottages, there is a tennis court, fitness track and a wide range of watersports (sunfish, hobie cats, windsurfers, yacht day sails, snorkelling) is available, T 458-8801, F 458-8428. You can have room service (especially nice for breakfast) or eat in the central building. Once a week dinner is moved to the beach with music from a local band. Communication with the administration is done with coloured flags hoisted outside your cottage. Picnics can be arranged on the tiny islet Petit St Richardson. US reservations: PSV, PO Box 12506, Cincinnatti, Ohio 45212; T (513) 242-1333 or 800-654-9326, F (513) 242-6951. The island can be reached by the resort's launch from Union Island. The resort will charter a flight from Barbados to Union Island for US$113 pp one way, children half price. The one anchorage is off the bar and restaurant, protected by a reef. The bar is open to visiting yachties or charter boats and reservations can be made for dinner if space is available. You can snorkel and dive off the Mopion and Punaise sandbar islands to the NW, where moorings are available.

PALM ISLAND

Also known as **Prune Island**, is another privately-owned resort, about a mile from Union Island, with coral reefs on three sides. The island was developed by John and Mary Caldwell, after they had made several ocean voyages. John is the author of *Desperate Voyage*, a book describing his first ocean crossing; he sailed from the USA to Australia to meet Mary, with virtually no experience. The boat was demasted, wrecked on a reef and John was stranded on an island and forced to eat slime off the bottom of the boat until he was rescued. The Caldwells later arranged to lease this swampy island from the St Vincent government and their family still runs the resort.

There are four beaches, of which the one on the W coast, Casuarina, is the most beautiful. **L1-L3** *Palm Island Beach Club*, apartments and individual bungalows, T 458-8824, F 458-8804 (full board, no credit cards). The *Sunset Bar* is a casual bar and restaurant open to yachties and passengers of small cruise ships. Water purchase is possible for yachts, moorings available. Sailing, windsurfing, scuba diving, snorkelling, fishing, tennis, health club all available for guests; a dive master is also available to accompany yacht visitors, snorkelling and diving is usually on the Mopion and Punaise sandbar islands. There is a 10-minute launch service from Union Island. Shared charter flights can be arranged on Mustique Airways from Barbados to Union Island, where you will be met.

Information for travellers

BEFORE TRAVELLING

● **Documents**

All visitors must have a passport and an onward, or return, ticket. Nationals of the UK, USA and Canada may enter for up to 6 months on proof of citizenship only. As well as the 3 countries already mentioned, citizens of the following countries do not need a visa: all Commonwealth countries, all the EC countries (except Eire and Portugal), Chile, Finland, Iceland, Liechtenstein, Norway, Switzerland, Sweden, Turkey, Uruguay, Venezuela. You will be asked where you will be staying on the island and will need a reservation, which can be done through the Tourist Office at the airport, before going through immigration. If you are only given entry of a few days and want to stay longer, extensions are easily obtained for EC$20.

● **Customs**

200 cigarettes, or 50 cigars, or 250 grams of tobacco, and 40 fluid ounces of alcoholic beverage may be imported duty free.

● **Climate**

Temperatures the year round average between 77°F and 81°F (25-7°C), moderated by the trade winds; average rainfall is 60 inches on the coast, 150 inches in the interior, with the wettest months May to November. Best months to visit are therefore December to May. You can expect a shower most days, though. Low season is June to mid-December.

MONEY

● **Currency**

The East Caribbean dollar, EC$.

GETTING THERE

AIR

There are no direct services from Europe or North America but same day connecting flights with BWIA, British Airways, Air France, Air Canada, American Airlines are available through Antigua, Barbados and Puerto Rico. The only carriers with scheduled services are LIAT, which connects **St Vincent** with Antigua, Barbados, Carriacou, Dominica, Guadeloupe, Martinique, Trinidad, St Lucia, St Maarten, Puerto Rico, Tortola, Grenada and Union Island; Helenair from Bequia, St Lucia and Union Island; Mustique Airways from Mustique, Union Island, Canouan and Bequia and Air Martinique, with flights to Canouan, Union Island, St Lucia and Martinique (linking with Air France to Paris). **Bequia** has scheduled service connections with Carriacou, Grenada, St Vincent, Canouan, St Lucia and Union Island, using Airlines of Carriacou, Region Air, Helenair and Mustique Airways. **Union Island** is reached by LIAT, Helenair, Mustique Airways, Airlines of Carriacou, Region Air and/or Air Martinique from Canouan, Carriacou, Fort de France, Grenada, Bequia, St Lucia, St Vincent and Tobago. **Mustique** is served by Mustique Airways from St Vincent. Prices from St Vincent to Bequia are US$17 one way, US$30 undated return, US$26 day return; from St Vincent to Mustique US$21 one way, US$42 return; from Bequia to Mustique, US$17 one way, US$34 return. Inter island charters are also operated by SVGAIR, Mustique Airways and Aero Services, may be economical for a group.

SEA

Windward Lines Ltd operates a passenger and cargo ferry service on the *MV Windward* from Trinidad on Thur pm, arriving St Vincent Fri 0730, departing 1000 for Barbados-St Lucia-Barbados arriving back in St Vincent Mon 0700 and leaving for Trinidad 1600 (occasional visit to Bequia) with a following service to Guiria, Venezuela or Pampatar, Margarita, round trip fare from St Vincent to Trinidad US$90, one way fare US$60. For information contact Global Steamship Agencies Ltd, Mariner's Club, Wrightson Road, PO Box 966, Port of Spain, Trinidad, T 809-624-2279, 625-2547, F 627-5091. Several flour ships ply between St Vincent and St Kitts via Montserrat, and it is possible to hitch a lift on these, T 457-1918. There is a regular boat service to Grenada and the Grenadines (see below).

● **Ports of entry**
(Own flag) Wallilabou, on the NW coast, Kingstown, Bequia (police station), Mustique and Union Island (airport). Yachtsmen often anchor at Blue Lagoon or Young island and bus/taxi to Kingstown to complete customs and immigration formalities. Fees are EC$10/US$4 pp (EC$20 on Sat on Union Island) and charter yachts are charged US$2 per foot per month. For an exit stamp, go to the airport customs and immigration one day before departure.

● **Anchorages**
On Bequia the local businesses cater to the boating community, delivering water, fuel, laundry, beer and groceries. Men and boys meet yachts in the northern St Vincent anchorages and ask to assist in tying stern line to a tree or offer other services. EC$7 is the current fee for tying up; other services negotiable. Others meet boats in Bequia, Union and the Tobago Cays, offering to supply bread, ice, vegetables, fruit, lobster, or conch (lambi) as well as selling T shirts and jewelry. They can take 'no' for an answer, but will return if you say 'maybe tomorrow'. Marinas at Ottley Hall, Caribbean Charter Yacht Yard, Lagoon Marina, Bequia Slipway, Anchorage Yacht Club on Union Island. Anchorages at Wallilabou, Young Island, Petit Byahaut, Blue Lagoon, Bequia, Palm (Prune) Island, Mustique, Canouan, Mayreau (Salt Whistle Bay and 2 others), Tobago Cays, Union Island (Clifton, Frigate Island, Chatham Bay), Petit St Vincent. Moorings at Young Island, Blue Lagoon, Friendship Bay, Union Island, Palm Island, Petit Byahaut (US$10 fee is deducted if you have dinner), Mustique (pay at *Basil's Bar*, EC$40). For possibilities of crewing on yachts, check the notice board at the Frangipani Yacht Services, Bequia.

ON ARRIVAL

● **Airports**
ET Joshua 2 miles from Kingstown. Taxi fare to town EC$20 (with other fares ranging from EC$15-40 for nearer or more distant hotels set by government); minibus to Kingstown EC$1.50, 10 mins. In the Grenadines there is a new airport on Bequia, built along the waterside; a new airport on Union Island, built by connecting a small island to the mainland; a private airport on Mustique and a small, private airport on Canouan.

● **Airlines**
LIAT, Halifax Street, Kingstown, T 457-1821 for reservations, airport office T 458-4841, on Union Island T 458-8230; Air Martinique T 458-4528, F 458-4187, or T 458-8328 on Union Island; Mustique Airways, PO Box 1232, T 458-4380, F 456-4586; SVGAIR, PO Box 39, Blue Lagoon, St Vincent, T 456-5610, F 458-4697; British Airways, T 457-1821; Airlines of Carriacou, Point Salines Airport, Grenada, T 444-2898/4101 ext 2005/2035.

● **Banks**
Barclays Bank plc, Scotia Bank, Canadian Imperial Bank of Commerce, National Commercial Bank of St Vincent, all on Halifax Street, Caribbean Banking Corporation, 81 South River Road, Kingstown, and at Port Elizabeth, Bequia. Barclays Bank has a branch on Bequia; National Commercial Bank has branches at ET Joshua airport, on Bequia and Union Island. There is no bank on Canouan, but the National Commercial Bank at Grand Bay opens every alternate Wed from 1000-1400. When you cash traveller's cheques you can take half in US dollars and half in EC dollars if you wish.

● **Clothing**
Wear light, informal clothes, but do not wear bathing costumes or short shorts in shops or on Kingstown's streets.

● **Embassies and consulates**
UK British High Commission, Grenville St, Box 132, Kingstown, T 457-1701 (after hours T 458-4381), F 456-2750; **Netherlands** Consulate, in the East Caribbean Group of Companies building in Campden Park, T 457 1918; **China**, Murray Road, T 456-2431; **Venezuela**, Granby St, T 456-1374; **France**, Middle St, Box 364, Kingstown, T 456-1615; **Italy**, Queen's Drive, T 456-4774.

● **Hospitals**
Kingston General Hospital, T 456-1185. Emergency T 999. Bequia Casualty Hospital, Port Elizabeth, T 458-3294.

● **Hours of business**
Shops: 0800-1200, 1300-1600 Mon-Fri (0800-1200 only, Sat); government offices: 0800-1200, 1300-1615 Mon-Fri; banks: 0800-1200 or 1300 Mon-Fri, plus 1400/1500-1700 on Fri. The bank at the Airport is open Mon-Sat 0700-1700.

● **Official time**
Atlantic Standard Time, 4 hours behind GMT, 1 hour ahead of EST.

● Public holidays

1 January, St Vincent and the Grenadines Day (22 January), Good Friday and Easter Monday, Labour Day in May, Whit Monday, Caricom Day and Carnival Tuesday (first or second Monday and Tuesday in July), August Bank Holiday first Monday in August, Independence Day (27 October), Christmas Day and Boxing Day.

● Security

The S end of the waterfront in Kingstown should be avoided at night as there are no lights and is an area frequented by drugs users.

● Shopping

Kingstown market and Bequia have excellent fresh vegetables and supermarkets. Mustique has a good, small grocery. Union Island has several supermarkets with the basics. The St Vincent Philatelic Society on Bay Street, between Higginson Street and River Road, sells stamps in every colour, size and amount for the novice and collector alike. Service is helpful but slow in this second floor warehouse, complete with guard. The St Vincent Craftsmen's Centre is on a road to the right off James Street, heading towards the airport; all local handicraft items are on display here. *Crab Hole* on Bequia, overlooking Admiralty Bay is a boutique where silk screened fabrics are made downstairs and sewn into clothes upstairs, open 0800-1700 Mon-Sat in season, closing earlier out of season, T 458-3290. Bequia has lots of boutiques: *Solana's, Almond Tree, Island Things, Local Color, Melinda's, Sprotties, the Garden, Whalebones, Green Boley,* and numerous T-shirt stands by the waterfront. Also don't miss Mauvin's and Sargeant's model boat shops, where craftsmen turn out replicas of traditional craft and visiting yachts. For handicrafts, resort wear and books, Noah's Arkade, Blue Caribbean Building, Kingstown (T 457-1513, F 456-9305), and at the *Frangipani* and *Plantation House* Boutique on Bequia (T 458-3424). Other bookshops: Wayfarer, beneath the Heron Hotel, and the Bequia Bookshop in Port Elizabeth, run by Iain Gale, who keeps an excellent stock of books, maps and charts, T 458-3905. There are several marine stores and fishing tackle shops on Bequia.

● Tipping

10% of the bill if not already included.

● Voltage

220/240 v, 50 cycles, except Petit St Vincent and Palm Island, which have 110 v, 60 cycles.

ON DEPARTURE

● Departure tax

There is a departure tax of EC$20.

WHERE TO STAY

● Hotels

All prices quoted in the text above are for a double room, 1995 rates. There is a government tax of 7% on hotel rooms, and most add a 10% service charge. Air conditioning is not generally available. If there is no fan in your room, it is often worth asking for one.

● Camping

Camping is not encouraged and there are no organized camp sites. Exceptions are made for groups such as Boy Scouts or Girl Guides.

FOOD AND DRINK

The national dish is fried jackfish and breadfruit. The island's rum is called Captain Bligh, and the local beers are Hairoun and EKU.

GETTING AROUND

AIR TRANSPORT

Flights within the Grenadines are cheap but prices rise if travelling to or from another country, eg Carriacou or St Lucia. If economizing it is worth considering a boat to travel internationally, eg from Union Island to Carriacou. Inter-island flights operated by Air Martinique are erratic and sometimes leave early, while LIAT often fails to appear at all, but do not expect the ferry to be any different. Check in for flights a good hour before departure. LIAT Explorer allows you to visit any 3 islands and return to St Vincent for US$199. They also offer day return flights to Martinique (US$155), Barbados (US$102) and St Lucia (US$94).

LAND TRANSPORT

● Motoring

Driving is on the left. A local driving licence, costing EC$40, must be purchased at the airport, the police station in Bay Street, or the Licensing Authority on Halifax Street, on presentation of your home licence. However, there is no need to pay if you have an International Driving Permit and get it stamped at the central police station. There are limited road signs on St Vincent.

● **Car hire**

If you do want to travel round St Vincent, it is better to rent a car, or hire a taxi with driver for EC$40 per hour. Note that the use of cars on the island is limited, so that only jeeps may be used to go right up Soufrière or beyond Georgetown on the E coast. Charges at Kim's (T 456-1884) for example are: EC$100/day for a car, with restrictions on where you drive in the N, EC$125 for a jeep, 60 miles free a day, EC$1/mile thereafter, weekly rental gives one day free, EC$1,000 excess deposit in advance, delivery or collection anywhere on the island, phone from airport for collection to save taxi hassle, credit cards accepted. Among other agencies (all offering similar rates and terms) are Ben's T 456 2907, David's T 456 4026, Lucky Car T 457 1913, 456 1215, Star Garage T 456 1743, Sunshine T 456 5380, UNICO T 456 5744, Valley T 458 5331.

● **Bicycles**

Bicycles from Sailors Cycle Centre, T 457-1712. On Bequia, Lighthouse, T 458 3084. Dennis Murray rents motor bikes on Bequia, T 457 2776/9113.

● **Buses**

Minibuses from Kingstown leave from the new Little Tokyo Fish Market terminal to all parts of the island, including a frequent service to Indian Bay, the main hotel area; they stop on demand rather than at bus stops. At the terminal they crowd round the entrance competing for customers rather than park in the bays provided. They are a popular means of transport because they are inexpensive and give an opportunity to see local life. No service on Sun or holidays. Fares start at EC$1, rising to EC$2 (Layou), EC$4 (Georgetown on the Windward coast), to EC$5 to the Black Carib settlement at Sandy Bay in the NE (this is a difficult route, though, because buses leave Sandy Bay early in the morning for Kingstown, and return in the afternoon). The number of vans starting in Kingstown and running to Owia or Fancy in the N is limited. The best way is to take the early bus to Georgetown and try to catch one of the 2 vans running between Georgetown and Fancy (EC$10). To get to Richmond in the NW take a bus to Barrouallie and seek onward transport from there. It is worthwhile to make a day trip to Mesopotamia (Mespo) by bus (EC$2.50). On Bequia, buses leave from the jetty at Port Elizabeth and will stop anywhere to pick you up, a cheap and reliable service.

● **Taxis**

Taxi fares are fixed by the Government but drivers are rarely prepared to make a journey at the official price and you may have to pay double the rates quoted here: Kingstown to Airport EC$20, Indian Bay EC$25, Mesopotamia EC$40, Layou EC$40, Orange Hill EC$80, Blue Lagoon EC$35, airport to Young Island EC$20, airport to Blue Lagoon EC$25. Hourly hire EC$40 per hour. On Bequia, taxis are pick-up trucks with benches in the back, brightly coloured with names like 'Messenjah', call them by phone or VHF radio. Young Island Taxi Association can be reached through Young Island on VHF 68. Chevi Taxi is rec.

FERRIES

From Kingstown to Bequia, MV *Admiral 1* sails at 0900 and 1900 Mon-Fri, returning 0730 and 1700; 0700 returning 1700 on Sat, 1 hour; MV *Admiral II* (passengers and cars) sails at 1030 and 1630 Mon-Fri (1230 on Sat), returning 0630 and 1400 (0630 on Sat), 1 hour journey, EC$10, EC$12 at night and weekends (both vessels run by Admiralty Transport Co Ltd, T 458-3348 for information); if you travel under sail, be prepared to get wet from the spray as the crossing is often rough, *Friendship Rose* (a mailboat until 1992, now passengers only) and *Maxann O* (island schooner) sail at 1230, returning 0630 Mon-Fri, 1¼ hrs.

MV *Barracuda* sails on Mon and Thur from Bequia (0600) for Kingstown, then returns (1030) to Bequia, continuing (1145) to Canouan, Mayreau, arriving in Union Island at 1545; on Tues and Fri she returns to St Vincent via Mayreau, Canouan and Bequia, leaving Union Island at 0530, arriving St Vincent 1200. On Sat she departs St Vincent at 1030 for Canouan, arriving 1400, then sails via Mayreau to Union Island, returning to St Vincent at 2230. All times are approximate, depending on the amount of goods to be loaded. There are 3-4 cabins, 2 of which are used by the crew but you can negotiate for one quite cheaply if you need it. The *Barracuda* is the islands' main regular transport and carries everything, families and their goods, goats and generators; she rolls through the sea and is very cheap, eg Bequia-Union EC$15, Union-Canouan EC$12, Canouan-Mayreau EC$8; the trip can be highly entertaining but note that the timetable is highly unreliable.

MV *Obedient* sails twice a week (Mon and Thur) between Union Island, departs 0745 approximately, and Carriacou, arriving 1300.

Two fishing boats sail Carriacou-Union Island from Hillsborough Pier, Mon 1300, 1 hour, EC$10. Frequent boat trips are organized, ask at hotels, take your passport even though not strictly necessary. For other services, check at the Grenadines dock in Kingstown. There are often excursions from Kingstown to Bequia and Mustique on Sun. Fares from Kingstown to Bequia EC$10, EC$12 at night and weekends, Canouan EC$13, Mayreau EC$15 and Union Island EC$20. From Bequia you can take a boat trip to Mustique for US$40 pp by speedboat from Friendship Bay or by catamaran from Port Elizabeth, ask at Sunsports at *Gingerbread*. Throughout the Grenadines local power boats can be arranged to take small groups of passengers almost any distance. If possible try to ensure that the boat is operated by someone known to you or your hotel to ensure reliability. Prices are flexible. Do not expect a dry or comfortable ride if the sea is rough.

COMMUNICATIONS

● **Postal services**
Halifax Street, open 0830-1500 (0830-1130 on Sat, closed Sun). St Vincent Philatelic Services Ltd, General Post Office, T 457-1911, F 456-2383; for old and new issues, World of Stamps, Bay 43 Building, Lower Bay Street, Kingstown.

● **Telecommunications**
Operated by Cable and Wireless, on Halifax Street; there is a 5% tax on international phone calls. Phone cards, fax, telex and telegraph available. Portable phones can be rented through Boatphone or you can register your own cellular phone with them upon arrival, T 456-2800. The international code for St Vincent is 809, followed by a 7-digit local number beginning with 45. From many cardphones you can reach USA Direct by dialling 1-800-872-2881.

MEDIA

● **Newspapers**
Two newspapers, *The Vincentian* and *The News*, are both published every Friday.

● **Radio**
NBC Radio is on 705 kHz. Radio Antilles can sometimes be picked up on 930 AM. Weather can be heard on SSB weather net 4001 at 0800, 8104 at 0830.

TOURIST INFORMATION

● **Local tourist office**
St Vincent and the Grenadines Department of Tourism, Finance Complex, Bay Street, PO Box 834, Kingstown, T 457-1502, F 456-2610 open Mon-Fri 0800-1200, 1300-1615; helpful desk at ET Joshua airport, T 458-4685, hotel reservation EC$1; on Bequia (at the landward end of the jetty), T 458-3286, open Sun-Fri 0900-1230, 1330-1600, Sat morning only; on Union Island, T 458-8350, open daily 0800-1200, 1300-1600.

There is a desk in the arrivals hall at the Grantley Adams airport on Barbados, open daily from 1300 until 2000 or the last flight to St Vincent (T 428-0961). This is useful for transfers to LIAT after an international flight.

● **Tourist offices overseas**
UK: 10 Kensington Court, London W8 5DL, T 0171-937 6570, F 0171-937 3611. **USA**: 801 2nd Avenue, 21st floor, New York, NY 10017, T (212) 687-4981, 800-729-1726, F (212) 949-5946 and 6505 Cove Creek Place, Dallas, Texas, 75240, T (214) 239 6451, 800-235-3029, F (214) 239 1002. **Canada**: 32 Park Road, Toronto, Ontario N4W 2N4, T (416) 924-5796, F (416) 924-5844. **Germany**: Bruno Fink, Wurmbersstrasse 26, D-7032, Sindelfingen, T 49-7031 801033, F 49-7031 805012.

● **Maps**
A map of St Vincent, 1:50,000 (and Kingstown, 1:10,000), EC$15, is available from the Ministry of Agriculture, Lands and Survey Department, Murray Road (on the road to Indian Bay, or if walking, go through the alleyway at the General Post Office and turn right at the Grammar School). In 1992 the Ordnance Survey (Southampton, UK) brought out a new tourist map of St Vincent, 1:50,000, with insert of Kingstown, 1:10,000, double sided with Grenadines on the reverse, with text panels giving information, walks etc.

● **Further reading**
The Tourist Office and the Hotel Association publish *Escape*, a good magazine on the islands giving details of accommodation, restaurants and shopping as well as articles of interest. Bequia publishes its own brochure, *Holiday Bequia*, and Mustique Airways also has a magazine.

Grenada

GRENADA, the most southerly of the Windwards, is described as a spice island, for it produces large quantities of cloves and mace and about a third of the world's nutmeg. It also grows cacao, sugar, bananas and a wide variety of other fruit and vegetables. Some of its beaches, specially Grand Anse, a dazzling two-mile stretch of white sand, are very fine. The majority of the tourist facilities are on the island's SW tip, but the rest of the island is beautiful, rising from a generally rugged coast to a spectacular mountainous interior. The highest point is Mount St Catherine, at 2,757 feet. The island seems to tilt on a NE-SW axis: if a line is drawn through ancient craters of Lake Antoine in the NE, the Grand Étang in the central mountains and the Lagoon at St George's, it will be straight. NW of that line, the land rises and the coast is high; SE it descends to a low coastline of rias (drowned valleys). The island is green, well forested and cultivated and is blessed with plenty of rain in the wet season.

Grenada (pronounced "Grenayda") has two dependencies in the Grenadines chain, Carriacou and Petit (often spelt Petite) Martinique. They, and a number of smaller islets, lie N of the main island. The group's total area is 133 square miles. Grenada itself is 21 miles long and 12 miles wide.

The population of some 92,000 (of which 4,600 live on Carriacou and 720 on Petit Martinique) is largely of African (85%) or mixed (11%) descent. In contrast to other Windward Islands which have had a similar history of disputed ownership between the French and English, the French cultural influence in Grenada has completely died out. Nevertheless, it is a predominantly Catholic island, though there are Protestant churches of various denominations, and a Baha'i Centre. Many people who emigrated from Grenada to the UK are returning to the island and are building smart houses for their retirement which are in stark contrast to the tiny, corrugated iron shacks which are home to many of their countrymen. The population is very young; 36% are under 15 years old and nearly 29% are in the 15-29 years' age bracket.

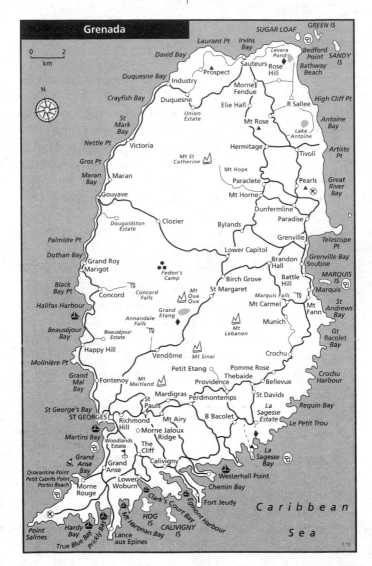

HISTORY

When Columbus discovered the island on his third voyage in 1498, it was inhabited by Caribs, who had migrated from the South American mainland, killing or enslaving the peaceful Arawaks who were already living there. The Amerindians called their island Camerhogue, but Columbus renamed it Concepción, a name which was not to last long, for shortly afterwards it was referred to as Mayo on maps and later Spaniards called it Granada, after the Spanish city. The French then called it La Grenade and by the 18th century it was known as Grenada. Aggressive defence of the island by the Caribs prevented settlement by Europeans until the 17th century. In 1609 some Englishmen tried and failed, followed by a group of Frenchmen in 1638, but it was not until 1650 that a French expedition from Martinique landed and made initial friendly contact with the inhabitants. When relations soured, the French brought reinforcements and exterminated the Amerindian population. Sauteurs, or Morne des Sauteurs, on the N coast, is named after this episode when numerous Caribs apparently jumped to their death in the sea rather than surrender to the French.

The island remained French for about one hundred years, although possession was disputed by Britain, and it was a period of economic expansion and population growth, as colonists and slaves arrived to grow tobacco and sugar at first, followed by cotton, cocoa and coffee. It was during the Seven Years' War in the 18th century that Grenada fell into British hands and was ceded by France to Britain as part of a land settlement in the 1763 Treaty of Paris. Although the French regained control in 1779, their occupation was brief and the island was returned to Britain in 1783 under the Treaty of Versailles. The British introduced nutmeg in the 1780s, after natural disasters wiped out the sugar industry. Nutmeg and cocoa became the main crops and encouraged the development of smaller land holdings. A major slave revolt took place in 1795, led by a free coloured Grenadian called Julian Fedon (see **Around the Island**), but slavery was not abolished until 1834, as in the rest of the British Empire.

In 1833, Grenada was incorporated into the Windward Islands Administration which survived until 1958 when it was dissolved and Grenada joined the Federation of the West Indies. The Federation collapsed in 1962 and in 1967 Grenada became an associated state, with full autonomy over internal affairs, but with Britain retaining responsibility for defence and foreign relations. Grenada was the first of the associated states to seek full independence, which was granted in 1974.

Political leadership since the 1950s had alternated between Eric (later Sir Eric) Gairy's Grenada United Labour Party (GULP) and Herbert Blaize's Grenada National Party. At the time of independence, Sir Eric Gairy was Prime Minister, but his style of government was widely viewed as authoritarian and corrupt, becoming increasingly resented by a large proportion of the population. In 1979 he was ousted in a bloodless coup by the Marxist-Leninist New Jewel (Joint Endeavour for Welfare, Education and Liberation) Movement, founded in 1973, which formed a government headed by Prime Minister Maurice Bishop. Reforms were introduced and the country moved closer to Cuba and other Communist countries, who provided aid and technical assistance. In 1983, a power struggle within the government led to Bishop being deposed and he and many of his followers were murdered by a rival faction shortly afterwards. In the chaos that followed a joint US-Caribbean force invaded the island to restore order. They imprisoned Bishop's murderers and expelled Cubans and other socialist nationalities who had been engaged in building a new airport and other development projects.

An interim government was set up until elections could be held in 1984, which were won by the coalition New National Party, headed by Herbert Blaize. Since the intervention, Grenada has moved closer to the USA which maintains a large embassy near the airport.

Further reading on this era of Grenada's history includes: *Grenada: Whose Freedom?* by Fitzroy Ambursley and James Dunkerley, Latin America Bureau, London, 1984; *Grenada Revolution in Reverse* by James Ferguson, Latin America Bureau, London, 1990; *Grenada: Revolution, Invasion and Aftermath* by Hugh O'Shaughessy, Sphere Books, London, 1984; *Grenada: Revolution and Invasion* by Anthony Payne, Paul Sutton and Tony Thorndike, London, Croom Helm, 1984; *Grenada: Politics, Economics and Society*, by Tony Thorndike, Frances Pinter, London 1984, and many others.

After the New National Party (NNP) coalition's victory at the polls, with an overwhelming majority, Herbert Blaize became Prime Minister. The NNP won 14 of the 15 seats in the legislature while GULP, led by Sir Eric Gairy, won one. In 1987, the formation of a new opposition party, the National Democratic Congress, led to parliamentary changes. Defections reduced the NNP's representation to 9 seats while the NDC gained 6. Further divisions within the NNP preceded Mr Blaize's death in December 1989; his faction, led by Ben Jones, became the National Party, while the New National Party name was retained by Keith Mitchell's faction.

In general elections held on 13 March 1990, each of these parties won 2 seats while the NDC, led by Nicholas Brathwaite (formerly head of the interim administration), won 7. The GULP gained 4 seats, but one of its members joined the Government of Mr Brathwaite in a gesture of solidarity after the fire on the Carenage in April 1990 (see below, under **St George's**), another subsequently joined the NDC and a third left GULP to become an Independent. The fourth

was expelled from the party in 1992. By mid-1991 the NDC Government could count on the support of 10 of the 15 MPs. Another opposition party, the left wing Maurice Bishop Patriotic Movement (MBPM), led by Terry Marryshow, failed to win a seat in the elections.

In 1991 the Government decided to commute to life imprisonment the death sentences on 14 people convicted of murdering Maurice Bishop after world wide appeals for clemency. The decision set an important precedent in the region, where the death penalty is still practised. Soon afterwards, Grenada was readmitted to the OECS court system, which it had left in 1979, and which allows for final recourse to the Privy Council. Amnesty International and other organizations have appealed for the release of Mrs Phyllis Coard, one of the 14 convicted, on grounds of ill-health following years of solitary confinement, but so far the Government has refused.

In February 1995 Mr Brathwaite retired and was succeeded by George Brizan, previously Minister of Agriculture, Trade, Energy and Industry, who took on Mr Brathwaite's portfolios of External Affairs and National Security in addition to his own. General elections were held in June 1995. The NDC campaigned on its economic stabilization policies, which helped to achieve rising rates of gdp growth, but faced keen opposition from the NNP, led by Keith Mitchell, and GULP, led by Sir Eric Gairy. The NNP won 8 seats, compared with 5 for the NDC and 2 for GULP, so Keith Mitchell became Prime Minister. Sir Eric Gairy failed to win a seat. In Dec 1995, Grenada's eighth political party, the Democratic Labour Party (DLP), was launched by Francis Alexis, former deputy leader of the NDC.

GOVERNMENT

Grenada is an independent state within the Commonwealth, with the British monarch as Head of State represented by a Governor General. There are two legislative houses, the House of Representatives with 15 members. and the Senate with 13 members. The Government is elected for a five year term.

THE ECONOMY

Structure of production

Agriculture accounts for about 14% of gdp and employs about 6,000 people. The major export crops are nutmeg, bananas and cocoa; nutmeg and mace together account for about 14% of all exports and Grenada is a leading world producer of this spice. However, prices tumbled following the collapse of the minimum price agreement with Indonesia. At end-1993 prices had fallen to US$0.30/lb, compared with US$1.50/lb four years before. Stocks of nutmeg have been burnt in both Grenada and Indonesia. There are now signs of an improvement in the industry and an informal agreement on price stability has been reached with Indonesia; new projects are coming on stream (eg a nutmeg oil distillation plant began operations in 1994 which will produce 30 tons a year from 300 tons of defective nutmeg) and sales are growing.

Banana exports have been falling because of labour shortages and inconsistent quality and quantity but account for about 11% of exports. Cocoa exports (15% of the total) fluctuate according to the volume of rainfall but the fine flavour of Grenadian cocoa allows it to command a premium over the world price. Nevertheless, both cocoa and nutmeg growers receive funds from the European Community commodity price funds (Stabex). There is also some cotton grown on Carriacou and limes are grown on both Carriacou and Grenada. Sugar cane is grown in the S of Grenada but efficiency is not high. Most of the rest of farming land is devoted to fruit and vegetables for export as well as domestic consumption, such as yams,

Grenada: fact file

Geographic

Land area	344 sq km
forested	9.0%
pastures	3.0%
cultivated	32.0%

Demographic

Population (1995)	92,000
annual growth rate (1990-95)	0.2%
urban	32.2%
rural	67.8%
density	267.4 per sq km
Religious affiliation	
Roman Catholic	53.0%
Anglican	14.0%
Birth rate per 1,000 (1994)	30.0
	(world av 25.0)

Education and Health

Life expectancy at birth,	
male	68.0 years
female	73.0 years
Infant mortality rate	
per 1,000 live births (1994)	12.0
Physicians (1991)	1 per 1,445 persons
Hospital beds (1992)	
	1 per 228 persons
Calorie intake as %	
of FAO requirement	99%
Population age 25 and over	
with no formal schooling	2.2%
Literacy (over 15)	85.0%

Economic

GNP (1993 market prices)	US$219mn
GNP per capita	US$2,410
Public external debt (1993)	
	US$96.2mn
Tourism receipts (1994)	US$58.7mn
Inflation (annual av 1988-93)	3.5%
Radio	1 per 1.7 persons
Television	1 per 3.1 persons
Telephone	1 per 4.6 persons

Employment

Population economically active (1988)	
	38,920
Unemployment rate (1994)	16.7%
% of labour force in	
agriculture	14.3
quarrying	0.3
manufacturing	7.3
construction	9.1
trade, restaurants	13.9
Police inc paramilitary unit	650

Source *Encyclopaedia Britannica*

eddoe, sweet potatoes, tannia, pumpkin, cassava, pigeon peas and maize.

Manufacturing is also mostly processing of agricultural produce, making items such as chocolate, sugar, rum, jams, coconut oil, honey and lime juice. There is also a large brewery (now majority owned by Guinness following the sale of the Government's shares in 1994) and a rice mill. There are 10,000 acres of forest, of which three-quarters are owned by the Government which is undertaking a reafforestation programme to repair hurricane damage. Fishing is a growing industry, involving about 1,500 people. Japan financed the construction of fishing centres in Gouyave and Grenville in 1991 and is providing a grant of US$3mn for a jetty and fish processing plant near St George's.

Recent trends

The economy suffered from the uncertainties surrounding the Bishop murder and the US invasion, but confidence has gradually returned and investment has picked up. The main area of expansion has been tourism, which has benefited from the airport expansion started with Cuban assistance by the Bishop administration. Air arrivals grew every year in the decade 1983-93 by an annual average of 10%. An even greater rise was recorded in 1994 following the opening, in late 1993, of two large new hotels on the S coast, the *Rex Grenadian* and *La Source*, which between them raised room capacity by 28% to 1,428 rooms, and a second weekly flight by British Airways in October. A record 109,000 visitors stayed on Grenada in 1994 and in 1995.

The yacht charter business has expanded considerably, attracting 7,070 and 7,561 arriving by air in 1993 and 1994 respectively, compared with under 5,900 in 1992. The number of yachts calling at Grenadian harbours fluctuates annually, but in 1994 rose to 5,413 from 3,373 in 1992.

The greatest increase, however, has been in cruise ship visitors, although they are low spending and do not generate so much foreign exchange, with the number of passengers rising from 34,166 in 1984 to 280,000 in 1995.

Despite bouyant tourism, Grenada has considerable financial imbalances and unemployment is a problem. Imports are five times the value of exports and tourism revenues are insufficient to cover the trade deficit. Income tax was abolished in 1985/86 but there were problems in collecting the value added tax which replaced it; a 10% levy introduced on higher incomes to help service public sector debt was criticized as reintroducing a form of income tax. Poverty increased because of the worldwide recession, the high cost of imported goods and the introduction of indirect taxation. The World Bank called for direct taxation to be reintroduced. A five-year economic programme announced in 1991, called for fiscal balance to be achieved in 1993. It envisaged selective debt rescheduling, a reduction in the number of public employees, the sale of certain state assets and an overhaul of the tax system. The IMF approved a structural adjustment programme to allow Grenada to seek credits from other multilateral agencies. Economic output declined in 1992 but grew slightly by 0.7% in 1993. In the 1994 budget income tax was reintroduced and VAT was downgraded to a consumption tax. The fiscal position had improved, allowing the Government to consider greater capital spending. After three years of structural adjustment the Government announced a new economic programme aimed at producing annual growth of 3% in 1994-96. Fiscal policy was to remain tight, but public sector investment would rise. Positive results were recorded in 1994 and 1995, with a 2.3% and 3.0% rise in gdp, led by tourism, which also helped to produce a current account surplus.

In 1996 the NNP Government announced its intention to abolish income tax again and reintroduce VAT, but implementation was delayed while ways were sought to curb potential smuggling to evade VAT.

FLORA AND FAUNA

A system of national parks and protected areas is being developed. Information is available from the Forestry Department, Ministry of Agriculture, Archibald Avenue, St George's. The focal point of the system is the **Grand Étang National Park**, eight miles from the capital in the central mountain range. It is on the transinsular road from St George's to Grenville. The Grand Étang is a crater lake surrounded by lush tropical forest. A series of trails has been blazed which are well worth the effort for the beautiful forest and views, but can be muddy and slippery after rain. The Morne Labaye nature trail is only 15 mins' long, return same route; the shoreline trail around the lake takes $1\frac{1}{2}$ hrs and is moderately easy; much further, $1\frac{1}{2}$ hrs walk, is Mount Qua Qua. The trail then continues for an arduous three hours to Concord Falls, with an extra $\frac{1}{2}$ hour spur to Fedon's Camp (see page 748) if you wish. From Concord Falls it is 25 mins' walk to the road to get a bus to St George's. These are hard walks (Mount Qua Qua, Fedon's Camp, Concord): wet, muddy, it rains a lot and you will get dirty. Take food and water. A guide is not necessary.

An interpretation centre overlooking the lake has videos, exhibitions and explanations of the medicinal plants in the forest. Leaflets about the trails can be bought here for EC$2 each. There is a bar, a shop and some amusing monkeys and parrots. The Park is open 0830-1600, entrance US$2, closed Sat but there are some stalls open selling spices and souvenirs. There is overnight accommodation at Lake House, T 442-7425 or enquire at forest centre, also for camping.

The high forest receives over 150 inches of rain a year. Epiphytes and mosses cling to the tree trunks and many species of fern and grasses provide a thick undergrowth. The trees include the gommier, bois canot, Caribbean pine and blue mahoe. At the summit, the vegetation is an example of elfin woodland, the trees stunted by the wind, the leaves adapted with drip tips to cope with the excess moisture.

Apart from the highest areas, the island is heavily cultivated. On tours around the country look for nutmeg trees and the secondary product, mace, cloves, cinammon, allspice, bay, tumeric and ginger. In addition there are calabash gourds, cocoa, coffee, breadfruit, mango, paw paw (papaya), avocado, and more common crops, bananas and coconuts. Sugar cane is used to make rum at 3 distilleries. Many of the spices can be seen at the Douglaston Estate or the Nutmeg Cooperatives in Gouyave or Grenville. Laura's Spice and Herb Garden, near Perdmontemps in St David's, has samples of herbs and spices grown in their natural habitat.

In the NE, 450 acres around **Levera Pond** was opened as a National Park in 1994 (US$1 entrance). As well as having a bird sanctuary and sites of historic interest, Levera is one of the island's largest mangrove swamps; the coastal region has coconut palms, cactus and scrub, providing habitat for iguana and land crabs. There are white beaches where turtles lay their eggs (leatherbacks come ashore April, May and June) and, offshore, coral reefs and the Sugar Loaf, Green and Sandy islands (boat trip to the last named on Sunday, see **Ferries**). You can swim at Bathway but currents are strong at other beaches. The coast between Levera Beach and Bedford Point is eroding rapidly, at a rate of several feet a year. South of Levera is Lake Antoine, another crater lake, but sunken to only about 20 feet above sea level; it has been designated a Natural Landmark.

On the S coast is **La Sagesse Protected Seascape**, a peaceful refuge which includes beaches, a mangrove estuary, a salt pond and coral reefs. In the coastal woodland are remains of sugar milling and rum distilleries. To get there turn S off the main road opposite an old sugar mill, then take the left fork of a dirt road through a banana plantation. Close to the pink plantation house (accommodation available), a few feet from a superb sandy beach, is *La Sagesse* bar and restaurant, good food, nutmeg shells on the ground outside. Walk to the other end of the beach to where a path leads around a mangrove pond to another beach, usually deserted apart from the occasional angler, fringed with palms, good snorkelling and swimming, reef just offshore.

Marquis Island, off the E coast, can be visited; at one time it was part of the mainland and now has eel grass marine environments and coral reefs. Nearby is La Baye Rock, which is a nesting ground for brown boobies, habitat for large iguanas and has dry thorn scrub forest. It too is surrounded by coral reefs.

To see a good selection of Grenada's flowers and trees, visit the Bay Gardens at Morne Delice (turn off the Eastern Main Road at St Paul's police station, the gardens are on your left as you go down). It's a pleasant place with a friendly owner; the paths are made of nutmeg shells. In the capital are the rather run down Botanic Gardens.

Grenada is quite good for birdwatching. The only endemic bird is the Grenada Dove, which inhabits scrubby woodland in some W areas. In the rainforest you can see the emerald-throated hummingbird, yellow-billed cuckoo, red-necked pigeon, ruddy quail-dove, cocoa thrush and other species, while wading and shore birds can be spotted at both Levera and in the S and SW. The endangered hookbilled kite (a large hawk) is found in the Levera National Park and nowhere else in the world. It uses its beak to pluck tree snails (its only food) out of their shells. A pile of shells with holes in them is evidence that a kite ate there. Watch also for the chicken hawk. Yellow-breasted bananaquits are very common.

There is little remarkable animal life: frogs and lizards, of course, and iguana, armadillo (tatoo) and manicou (possum), all of these are hunted for the pot. One oddity, though, is a troop of Mona monkeys, imported from Africa over 300 years ago, which lives in the treetops in the vicinity of the Grand Étang. Another import is the mongoose.

DIVING AND MARINE LIFE

The reefs around Grenada provide excellent sites for **diving**. A popular dive is to the wreck of the Italian cruise liner, *Bianca C* which went down in 1961. Other dive sites include Boss Reef, the Hole, Valley of Whales, Forests of Dean, Grand Mal Point (wall dive), Dragon Bay (wall dive) ends at Molinière, Happy Valley (drift with current to Dragon Bay); 3 wrecks from cargo ships off Quarantine Point, St George's, are in strong currents; Molinière reef for beginners to advanced has a sunken sailboat, the *Buccaneer*; Whibble Reef is a slopey sand wall (advanced drift dive); Channel reef is a shallow reef at the entrance to St George's with many rusted ships' anchors; Spice Island reef is for resort dives and beginners as well as the wrecks *Red Buoy*, *Veronica L* and *Quarter Wreck*. Dive sites around Carriacou include Kick Em Jenny, Isle de Ronde, Sandy Island, Sister Rocks (to 100 ft), Twin Sisters (walls to 180 ft and strong currents), Mabouya Island, Saline Island (drift dive).

Dive companies change locations and resort affiliations rapidly, but there is usually one at any of the larger resorts. Dive Grenada is at *Cot Bam* on Grand Anse beach and *Calabash Hotel*, Lance aux Épines, T 444-1092, 444-5875 (evenings), F 440-6699, PADI courses, wreck dives for experienced divers, night dives, snorkelling. Grand Anse Aquatics at *Coyaba Beach Resort*, in Grand Anse, offers PADI courses, snorkelling, kayak and sunfish instruction, T 444-4129. Sanvics Watersports, *Renaissance Grenada Resort*, is an all-inclusive operation with trips to islands, T 444-4371, ext 638, F 444-5227. Scuba Express at *True Blue Inn*, has a custom designed dive boat with groups limited to 10 and a fully equipped dive shop with all new equipment, T 444-2133. Scuba World at the *Rex Grenadian* and *Secret Harbour*/The Moorings, T 444-3333, ext 584, F 444-1111. On Carriacou both dive operations are German speaking: Tanki's Watersport Paradise, at Paradise Beach, Carriacou, T 443-8406, and Silver Beach Diving at Main St, Hillsborough, T 443-7882.

A basic scuba dive costs about US$40 pp, a 2-tank dive is US$60, resort course US$50, snorkelling trips US$16; dive packages and open water certification are available. Several charter boats doing day trip sailing excursions also offer scuba equipment.

Snorkelling equipment hire costs about US$12 for 3 hrs, sometimes for a day; again, there are plenty of opportunities for this. Glass-bottomed boats make tours of the reefs.

Humpback whales can be seen off Grenada and Carriacou during their migrations in Dec-Apr. Contact Mosden Cumberbatch (see below) for whale watching tours. Pilot whales and dolphins are also found in Grenadian waters (see **Whale and Dolphin Watching** by Erich Hoyt at the beginning of this *Handbook*).

BEACHES AND WATERSPORTS

There are 45 beaches on Grenada. The best are in the SW, particularly Grand Anse, a lovely stretch of white sand which looks N to St George's. It can get crowded with cruise passengers, but there's usually plenty of room for everyone. Watch your bags, petty theft has been reported and vendors can be bothersome. Morne Rouge, the next beach going SW, is more private, has good snorkelling and no vendors. There are other nice, smaller beaches around Lance aux Épines. The beaches at Levera and Bathway in the NE

are also good, and since the construction of a new road are much easier to get to.

Windsurfing, waterskiing and parasailing all take place off Grand Anse beach. Windsurf board rental about US$7 for ½ hour, waterskiing, US$15 per run, parasailing US$25. The Moorings' Club Mariner Watersports Centre at *Secret Harbour*, T 444-4439, F 444-4819, has small sail boats, sunfish, windsurfing, waterskiing, speedboat trips to Hog Island including snorkelling. Inshore sailing on sunfish, sailfish and hobiecats is offered by Grand Anse and Lance aux Épines hotels and operators. Rates are about US$10 for ½ hour for sunfish rental. If you want someone else to do all the work, take a booze cruise on the *Rhum Runner* (T 440-2198/3422), daytime or evening.

Sailing in the waters around Grenada and through the Grenadines, via Carriacou, is very good; sheltered harbours, such as Halifax Bay on the Leeward coast, can be found and there are marinas on the S coast. Starwind Enterprises has 39-ft and 43-ft sailing yachts for all types of charters, day, overnight, sunset, maximum 14 passengers, call Mosden Cumberbatch, T 440-3678, US$50 pp day sail, snorkelling included, US$15 sunset cruise. The Moorings Club Mariner Watersports Centre has skippered charters at US$25 pp half day, US$40 pp whole day, minimum 4 people, T 444-4439. Trips go to Carriacou, Sandy Island, Calivigny Island and Hog Island, or up the coast, stopping at beaches for barbecues or reefs for snorkelling. Seabreeze Yacht Charters at Spice Island Marine Centre offers day and weekly charters on sailing or power yachts, bareboat or skippered, T 444-4924. On Carriacou the *Silver Beach Resort* has a catamaran, *Afoxe*, for day sails, US$50 including lunch.

On the first weekend in August the Carriacou Regatta is held, which has developed into a full-scale festival, with land as well as watersports and jump-ups at night. On Grenada yacht races are held at New Year and Easter (another big regatta). In 1994 the First Sailing Festival was held in what has become an annual event, held at the end of January or beginning of February, with feeder races from Trinidad, Barbados and Bequia, Match Racing and other races and on-shore activities. In October an end-of-hurricane-season yacht regatta sponsored by Carib Beer is timed to coincide with Beach Fest, a weekend of beach parties and watersports.

Deep-sea fishing can be arranged through Grenada Yacht Services. Fishermen with charter boats include *Bezo*, a 31-ft Bower Pirogue, call Graham or Ian, T 443-5477/5021/5161, Evans Chartering Services (T 444-4422) and Tropix (T 440-4961). At the end of January each year, Grenada hosts The Spice Island Game Fishing Tournament, which had its 25th anniversary in 1994.

OTHER SPORTS

Cricket, the island's main land sport, is played from January to June. There is a large stadium at Queen's Park, just outside St George's, but the locals play on any piece of fairly flat ground or on the beaches. **Soccer** is also played. Hotels have **tennis** courts and public courts are found at Grand Anse and Tanteen, St George's. A recommended tennis pro is Richard Hughes, an ex-Davis Cup player who teaches at Richmond Hills and goes round the hotels giving basic tuition and advanced level sessions, contact him through the *Grenada*, T 444-4371. There is a 9-hole **golf** course at the Grenada Golf and Country Club, Woodlands, above Grand Anse; the club is open daily 0800 to sunset, but only till 1200 on Sunday (T 444-4128). **Volleyball** can be played at the Aquarium Beach Club after snorkelling on the reef. It is a fun spot on a secluded beach just below Point Salines off the airport road, T 444-1410. **Hiking** is excellent, if muddy, in the Grand Étang National Park (see above, **Flora and Fauna** and below, **Around the Island**).

An annual **triathlon** is held in January, with a 1 km swim along the Grand Anse beach to the *Grenada Renaissance*, a 25-km bicycle race to the airport, St George's and back to the hotel, then a 5-km run to the Carib brewery and back. The next day a 3-person relay is held, with a 1½ km swim, a 40-km cycle and 10-km run; one of the competitors in each team must be female and the combined ages of all three must exceed 100. For information, contact Paul Slinger, PO Box 44, St. George's, T 444-3343. **Horseriding** can be arranged with The Horseman, St Paul's, St George's, for lessons or trail riding, T 440-5368.

FESTIVALS

Carnival takes place over the second weekend in August, although some preliminary events and competitions are held from the last week in July, with calypsos, steelbands, dancing, competitions, shows and plenty of drink. The Sunday night celebrations, Dimanche Gras, continue into Monday, J'Ouvert; Djab Djab Molassi, who represent devils, smear themselves and anyone else (especially the smartly dressed) with black grease. On Monday a carnival pageant is held on the stage at Queen's Park and on Tuesday the bands parade through the streets of St George's to the Market Square and a giant party ensues. For information on playing Mas with a band contact Derrick Clouden (T 440-2551) or Wilbur Thomas (T 440-3545) of the Grenada Band Leaders Association.

Also in August, over the first weekend, are the Carriacou Regatta (see above) and the Rainbow City cultural festival in Grenville which goes on for about a week. Carriacou celebrates its carnival at the traditional Lenten time, unlike Grenada. It is not spectacular but it is fun and there is a good atmosphere.

Throughout the island, but especially at Gouyave, the Fisherman's Birthday is celebrated at the end of June (the feast of Saints Peter and Paul); it involves the blessing of nets and boats, followed by dancing, feasting and boat races. Independence Day is 7 February.

During Carnival it is difficult to find anywhere to stay and impossible to hire a car unless booked well in advance.

ST GEORGE'S

The island's capital, **St George's**, with its terraces of pale, colour-washed houses and cheerful red roofs, was established in 1705 by French settlers, who called it Fort Royale. Much of its present-day charm comes from the blend of two colonial cultures: typical 18th century French provincial houses intermingle with fine examples of English Georgian architecture. Unlike many Caribbean ports, which are built around bays on coastal plains, St George's straddles a promontory. It therefore has steep hills with long flights of steps and sharp bends, with police on point duty to prevent chaos at the blind junctions. At every turn is a different view or angle of the town, the harbour or the coast. The tourist board publishes a booklet, *Historic Walking Tour of St George's*, which is recommended.

St George's is one of the Caribbean's most beautiful harbour cities. The town stands on an almost landlocked sparkling blue harbour against a background of green and hazy blue hills. **The Carenage** runs around the inner harbour, connected with the Esplanade on the seaward side of Fort George Point by the **Sendall Tunnel**, built in 1895. There is always plenty of dockside activity on the Carenage, with food, drinks and other goods being loaded and unloaded from wooden schooners. It is planned to redevelop St George's harbour, moving the cruise liner dock from the mouth of the Carenage to a point further down the SW coast. The Carenage would then be left to small shipping and all the shopping would be duty-free. So far, a small promenade and shelter have been built.

The small **National Museum**, in the cells of a former barracks, in the centre of town (corner of Young and Monckton Streets) is worth a visit; it includes some items from West Africa, exhibits from the sugar and spice industries and of local shells and fauna (entry US$1, open Mon-Fri 0900-1600, Sat 1030-1300). **Fort George** (1705) on the headland is now the police headquarters, but public viewpoints have been erected from which to see the coast and harbour. Photographs are not allowed everywhere. Some old cannons are still in their positions; tremendous views all round. Just down from the Fort is St Andrew's Presbyterian Kirk (1830) also known as Scot's Kirk. On Church Street are a number of important buildings: St George's Anglican Church (1825), the Roman Catholic Cathedral (tower 1818, church 1884) and the Supreme Court and Parliament buildings (late 18th, early 19th century). St George's oldest religious building is the Methodist Church (1820) on Green Street.

The Public Library is an old government building on the Carenage which has been renovated and stocked with foreign assistance. In this part of the city are many brick and stone warehouses, roofed with red, fish tail tiles brought from Europe as ballast. A serious fire on 27 April 1990 damaged six government buildings on the Carenage, including the Treasury, the Government Printery, the Storeroom and the Post Office. Restoration work is taking place. Also on the Carenage is a monument to the Christi Degli Abbissi, moved from the entrance to the harbour, which commemorates "the hospitality extended to the crew and passengers of the ill-fated liner", *Bianca C* (see **Diving and marine life** above). It stands on the walkway beside Wharf Road. The Market Square, off Halifax Street (one of the main streets, also steep block from the Esplanade), is always busy. It is the terminus for many minibus routes and on Saturday holds the weekly market.

Just N of the city is **Queen's Park**, which is used for all the main sporting activities, carnival shows and political events. It is surrounded by a turquoise palisade. From **Richmond Hill** there are good views (and photo opportunities) of both St George's and the mountains of the interior. On the hill are Forts Matthew (built by the French, 1779), Frederick (1791) and Adolphus (built in a higher position than Fort George to house new batteries of more powerful, longer range cannon), and the prison in which are held those convicted of murdering Maurice Bishop.

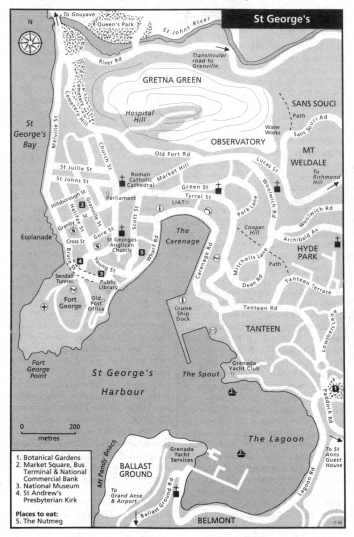

St George's

1. Botanical Gardens
2. Market Square, Bus Terminal & National Commercial Bank
3. National Museum
4. St Andrew's Presbyterian Kirk

Places to eat:
5. The Nutmeg

From the Carenage, you can take a road which goes round the Lagoon, another sunken volcanic crater, now a yacht anchorage. It is overlooked by the ruins of the *Santa Maria Hotel*, which was taken over by the revolutionary government and subsequently destroyed in the intervention. Several plans have been submitted for the rehabilitation of the hotel.

Carrying on to the SW tip you come to **Grand Anse**, Grenada's most famous beach. Along its length are many hotels, but none dominates the scene since, by law, no development may be taller than a coconut palm. A side road leads round to the very pleasant bay and beach at Morne Rouge, which is away from the glitz of Grande Anse. There is a good view across Grande Anse to St George's from the little headland of **Quarantine Point**. From Grand Anse the road crosses the peninsula to the Point Salines airport and the Lance aux Épines headland. The road to Portici and Parc à Boeuf beaches leads to the right, off the airport road; follow the signs to *Groomes* beach bar on Parc à Boeuf (food and drink available). Portici beach is virtually deserted, with good swimming despite a steeply shelving beach and excellent snorkelling around Petit Cabrits point at its NE end. On **Prickly Bay** (the W side of Lance aux Épines) are hotels, the Spice Island Marina and other yachting and watersports facilities. Luxury homes take up much of Lance aux Épines down to Prickly Point. There is a glorious stretch of fine white sand, the lawns of the *Calabash Hotel* run down to the beach, very nice bar and restaurant open to non-residents, steel bands often play there.

From the Point Salines/Lance aux Épines crossroads you can head E along a road which snakes around the S coast. At **Lower Woburn**, a small fishing community (which can be reached by bus from St George's), you can see vast piles of conch shells in the sea, forming jetties and islets where they have been discarded by generations of lambie divers. Stop at *Island View Restaurant* or a local establishment, *Nimrod and Sons Rum Shop*. Yachtsmen visit this spot to sign the infamous guest register and to be initiated with a shot of Jack Iron rum (beware, it is potent!). Past Lower Woburn is the **Clarks Court Rum Distillery** (tours available with rum sales, tip the guide). It is a steam driven operation, unlike the River Antoine water wheel system. Any number of turn-offs, tracks and paths, go inland to join the Eastern Main Road, or run along the rias and headlands, such as Calivigny (which is being developed, together with neighbouring Calivigny and Hog Islands, into a resort), Fort Jeudy, Westerhall Point or La Sagesse with its nature reserve (see above). Many of Grenada's most interesting and isolated bays are in the SE, accessible only by jeep or on foot; taxi drivers can drop you off at the start of a path and you can arrange to be picked up later. The East Coast road from Westerhall to Grenville is being upgraded from a dirt to a concrete road, which makes driving difficult in parts.

AROUND THE ISLAND

The W coast road from St George's has been rebuilt with funds from the government, the Caribbean Development Bank, the EEC and USAID. It is good all the way to Industry. Only the section from Industry to Sauteurs has particularly rough patches but it is fine in an ordinary car with care.

Beauséjour Estate, once the island's largest, is now in ruins (except for the estate Great House). On its land are a Cuban-built radio station, a half-completed stadium and squatters; the owners and the government cannot agree on the estate's future. Beyond Beauséjour is Halifax Bay, a beautiful, sheltered harbour.

At Concord, a road runs up the valley to the First **Concord Falls** (45 mins hot walk from the main road or go by car, driving slowly, children and vendors everywhere), where you can pay US$1 to go to a balcony above the small cascade. There are changing rooms for bathers. The Second Concord Falls are a 30-mins' walk (each way), with a river to cross seven times; a guide will charge EC$20 but there is no need for one, the path has been improved and security at the lower falls has stopped occasional thefts. Three hours further uphill is **Fedon's Camp**, at 2,509 feet, where Julian Fedon (see **History** above) fortified a hilltop in 1795 to await reinforcements from Martinique to assist his rebellion against the British. After bloody fighting, the camp was captured; today it is a Historical Landmark. It is possible to hike from Concord to Grand Étang in five hours, a hard walk, wet and muddy but rewarding (see **Flora and fauna**). The trail is hard to spot where it leaves the path to the upper falls about two thirds of the way up on the left across the river. There is no problem following the trails in the opposite direction.

North of Concord, just before Gouyave, is a turn-off to **Dougaldston Estate**. Before the revolution 200 people were employed here in cultivating spices and other crops. Now there are only about 20 workers, the place is run down, the buildings in disrepair, the vehicles wrecked. Still, you can go into a shed where bats fly overhead and someone will explain all the spices to you. Samples cost EC$3 for a bag of cinammon or cloves, EC$2 for nutmeg, or there are mixed bags; give the guide a tip.

Gouyave, 'the town that never sleeps', is a fishing port, nutmeg collecting point and capital of St John's parish. At the Nutmeg Processing Station, you can see all the stages of drying, grading, separating the nutmeg and mace and packing (give a tip here too). The husks are used for fuel or mulch and the fruit is made into nutmeg jelly (a good alternative to breakfast marmalade), syrup or liquor. The Station is a great wooden

building by the sea, with a very powerful smell. A tour for US$1 is highly recommended. Gouyave is the principal place to go to for the Fisherman's Birthday festival (see above).

Just outside Victoria, another fishing port and capital of St Mark's Parish, is a rock in the sea with Amerindian petroglyphs on it (best to know where to look over the parapet). The road continues around the NW coast, turning inland before returning to the sea at **Sauteurs**, the capital of St Patrick's parish, on the N coast. The town is renowned as the site of the mass suicide of Grenada's last 40 Caribs, who jumped off a cliff rather than surrender to the French (see **History** above). Behind Sauteurs is McDonald College from whose gate there are marvellous views out to sea, with the Grenadines beyond the town's two church towers, and inland to cloud-covered mountains. In March Sauteurs celebrates St Patrick's Day with a week of events, exhibits of arts and crafts and a mini-street festival.

From Sauteurs a road approaches **Levera Bay** (see above) from its W side. Turn left at *Chez Norah's* bar, a two-storey, green, corrugated iron building (snacks available); the track rapidly becomes quite rough and the final descent to Levera is very steep, suitable only for 4-wheel drive. A better way to Levera approaches from the S. The road forks left about two miles S of Morne Fendue, passes through River Sallee and past Bathway Beach. The River Sallee Boiling Springs are an area of spiritual importance; visitors are inspired to throw coins into the fountain while they make a wish. Swimming is good at the beautiful Levera Beach and there is surf in certain conditions. Do not swim far out as there is a current in the narrows between the beach and the privately-owned Sugar Loaf Island. Further out are Green and Sandy Islands; you may be able to arrange a trip there with a fisherman who keeps his boat on Levera Beach.

Morne Fendue plantation house offers accommodation and serves lunch for EC$40, including drinks; good local food and all you can drink, T 442-9330, reservations essential. The house, owned by Betty Mascoll MBE, is full of atmosphere (although some of the plaster and stucco work is in poor shape), and the driveway ends in a flowerbed full of poinsettias. St Patrick's is an agricultural region, comparatively poor and marginal.

On the E side of the island, Amerindian remains can be seen on rock carvings near Hermitage (look for a sign on the road) and at an archaeological dig near the old Pearls airport. Apparently it's so unprotected that lots of artefacts have been stolen. An excursion can be made to Lake Antoine (see above) with, nearby, the **River Antoine Rum Distillery**, driven by a water mill, the oldest in the Caribbean (guided tours, T 442 7109). The only modern equipment is the lock for government control. Try the 151° proof rum, they sell all by the bottle.

Grenville is the main town on the E coast and capital of St Andrew's Parish, the largest parish in Grenada with a population of about 25,000. It is a collection point for bananas, nutmeg and cocoa, and also a fishing port. You can tour the Nutmeg Cooperative Processing Station, US$1, with samples of nutmeg and mace (tip the guide). There are some well-preserved old buildings, including the Court House, Anglican Church, police station and Post Office. Saturday is market day, worth seeing. Weavers turn palm fronds into hats, baskets and place mats.

The Rainbow City Festival is held here at the beginning of August, with arts and crafts displays, street fairs, cultural shows and a 10 km road race. Funds are being raised to restore and convert the old Roman Catholic church into a library, museum, art gallery and cultural centre. Construction of the church began in 1841 and was used as a church until 1915, when mosquitoes finally triumphed over worshippers. From 1923-1972 it was used as a school, but then abandoned.

Two miles S of Grenville are the **Marquis Falls**, also called Mt Carmel Falls, the highest in Grenada. Trails are being improved, with sign posts and picnic areas. Marquis village was the capital of St Andrew's in the 17th and 18th centuries. Nowadays it is the centre of the wild pine handicraft industry. Historical sites nearby are Battle Hill and Fort Royal. From here boats go to Marquis Island (see above).

Mount St Catherine can be climbed quite easily, contrary to popular opinion, although in places it is a climb rather than a walk. There are several routes, the easiest reported to be from the village of Mt Hope (minibuses go there from Grenville), from where a 4-wheel drive can take you to within an hour of the summit or you can walk along the track, 30 mins. A guide is not essential but you will need someone to point out the route. Do not go alone and do not go if you suffer from vertigo. Do not take chances with daylight. For information on this and anything else, contact Mr and Mrs Benjamin at Benjamin's Variety Store, Victoria Street, Grenville. If they do not know the answer they will know someone who does. Mrs Benjamin is on the Tourist Board. Telfer Bedeau, from Soubise, is the walking expert, and can be contacted on T 442-6200.

The transinsular, or hill road, from Grenville to St George's used to be the route from the Pearls airport to the capital, which all new arrivals had to take. Now it is well-surfaced, but twisty and narrow. The minibus drivers on it are generally regarded as 'maniacs'. To give an idea of the conditions, one bend is called 'Hit Me Easy'. The road rises up to the rain forest, often entering the clouds. If driving yourself, allow up to 1½ hours from Levera to St George's and avoid the mountain roads around Grand Étang in the dark, although the night time sounds of the dense jungle are fascinating. Shortly before reaching the Grand Étang (full details above), there is a side road to the St Margaret, or **Seven Sisters Falls**. They are only a ½-hour walk from the main road, but a guide is essential, or else get very good directions. After Grand Étang, there is a viewpoint at 1,910 feet overlooking St George's. A bit further down the hill is a detour to the **Annandale Falls** which plunge about 40 feet into a pool where the locals dive and swim. Tourists are pestered for money here, for diving, singing, information, whether requested or not. If coming from St George's on Grenville Road, fork left at the Methodist Church about half way to Grand Étang.

The peaks in the SE part of the Grand Étang Forest Reserve can be walked as day trips from St George's. **Mount Maitland** (1,712 feet), for instance, is a pleasant morning out. Take a bus from the Market Place to Mardigras, or if there is none, get off at the junction at St Paul's and walk up. At the Pentecostal (IPA) church, turn left and immediately right. The paths are reasonably clear and not too muddy, but shorts are not recommended and long sleeves are preferable. The walk takes less than an hour each way and there are good views from the top over both sides, with some hummingbirds.

Mt Sinai (2,306 feet) is not as spectacular as Mt St Catherine, nor as beautiful as Mt Qua Qua, but is not as muddy either. Take a bus from St George's to Providence, then walk up (two hours) the particularly lovely (and friendly) road to Petit Étang and beyond, where the road turns into a track in the banana fields. The path up the mountain is hard to spot; it begins behind a banana storage shed and must be closely watched. The terrain is a bit tricky near the top. There is a path down the other side to Grand Étang. Local opinions differ over how badly you would get lost without a guide as the paths are no longer maintained.

The highest point in the SE is known on the Ordnance Survey map as **South East Mountain** (2,348 feet), but to locals as Mount Plima (Plymouth?). You can get up to the ridge, from where there are fine views, but both this summit and the nearby Mount Lebanon are inaccessible without a guide and machete. Here too it used to be possible to descend to Grand Étang but it is difficult now. For this area take a bus from St George's to the junction for Pomme Rose and walk up through the village. Mayhe Hazard lives near the top of the village and is the local expert on the trails (traces). He is good company and may be prepared to guide in the area; he will certainly show you the trail to the ridge, which you could never find alone.

CARRIACOU

Carriacou (pronounced *Carr*-yacoo) is an attractive island of green hills descending to sandy beaches. It is much less mountainous than Grenada, which means that any cloudy or rainy weather clears much quicker. With an area of 13 square miles, it is the largest of the Grenadines. It lies 23 miles NE of Grenada; 2½ miles further NE is Petit Martinique, which is separated by a narrow channel from Petit St Vincent, the southernmost of St Vincent's Grenadine dependencies. Efforts are being made by the Government to curb contraband and drug smuggling in Carriacou. An opposition proposal has been put forward to make the island a free trade zone, or to allow it to secede from Grenada.

Carriacou's population is under 5,000, less than 600 of whom live in the capital, **Hillsborough**. On the one hand, the islanders display a strong adherence to their African origins in that the annual Big Drum Dances, which take place around Easter, are almost purely West African. The Tombstone Feasts are unique. On the other hand, French traditions are still evident at L'Esterre and there is a vigorous Scottish heritage,

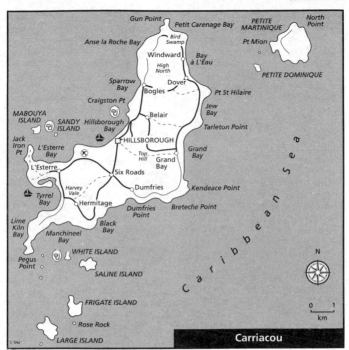

Carriacou

especially at **Windward**, where the people are much lighter skinned than elsewhere on the island as a result of their Scottish forebears. Windward used to be the centre for the craft of hand-built schooners but in recent years the boat builders have moved to Tyrrel Bay. Begun by a shipbuilder from Glasgow, the techniques are unchanged, but the white cedar used for the vessels now has to be imported from Grenada or elsewhere. The sturdy sailing vessels are built and repaired without the use of power tools in the shade of the coconut palms at the edge of the sea. To demonstrate the qualities of these local boats, the Carriacou Regatta was initiated in 1965. It has grown into the major festival described above.

The local painter, Canute Calliste, has his studio at L'Esterre. His naive style captures the scenes of Carriacou (kite flying, launching schooners, festivals); a collection of his paintings have been published in a book by MacMillan, he is also an accomplished violinist and performs the quadrille, a dance which is part of the island's cultural heritage.

The **Carriacou Historical Society Museum** on Paterson Street in Hillsborough has exhibits from Amerindian settlements in the island and from later periods in its history; the woman who runs it is the daughter of Canute Calliste, and can tell you about the Arawak ruins on the island, open Monday-Friday, 0930-1600, Sat 1000-1600. There are also ruined plantations. On Hospital Hill, Belair, NE of Hillsborough, there is an overgrown old sugar Mill, stunning views. There is good walking on the back roads and the woods are teeming with wildlife such as iguanas.

There are interesting underwater reefs and sandy islets with a few palms on them, ideal for snorkelling and picnicking. **Sandy Island** is a tiny, low-lying atoll in Hillsborough Bay off Lauriston Point, with a few palm trees for shade, safe and excellent swimming and snorkelling, take food, drink and plenty of suntan lotion. Boat from Hillsborough EC$60, 30 mins each way, pick a day when the islet is not swamped with boat loads of cruise ship visitors. Alternatively try **White Island**, a similar islet in Manchineel Bay off the S coast, ask for boats at *Cassada Bay Hotel*. Visitors should see the oyster beds at **Tyrrel Bay** where 'tree-oysters' grow on mangrove roots. Tyrrel Bay is a favourite anchorage for the many yachts which visit the island.

A beautiful beach is **Anse La Roche**, which faces W and has a spectacular view across the strait to the mountains of rugged Union Island. Snorkelling is good, particularly among the rocks at the side. Walk from Bogles along the dirt road heading northwards, past the *Caribbee Inn* and forking right at Honey Hill House; after about 30 mins the road starts to rise, turn left at the large tree which overhangs the track and follow a narrow path through the woods to a ruined farmhouse. The path leads to the right, through bushes; keep to the downhill side of the open slope, bear right down a steep slope leading through more trees to the beach. Take food and drink, there are no facilities and few people, about 45-min walk each way. We have received reports that it is very easy to get lost finding Anse La Roche beach and it might be easier to take a water taxi there. Very peaceful, watch the yachts rounding the headland on their way to anchorage; at night turtles swim ashore to lay their eggs.

Instead of turning off the track to Anse La Roche, carry on walking northwards; the well-shaded, grassy road

rounds Gun Point with lovely views of the Grenadines. A path leads down (opposite a mauve-painted house) to the beach at **Petit Carenage Bay**, which has coarse, coral sand, good swimming and modest surf in some conditions. Returning to the road, Windward is a few mins walk further on, a few shops and local bars.

It is advisable to use insect repellent on the beaches, especially in the rainy season. At night it is best to use a mosquito net.

Island information – Carriacou
● **Hotels**
L2-L3 *Silver Beach Resort*, MAP also available room or apartment, simple but attractive, though for a longer stay a cheaper rate can be negotiated with the owner, good, helpful, child-friendly, T 443-7337, F 443-7165, scuba diving on site; **A1** *Cassada Bay Resort*, reopened 1996 after extensive refit, 9 cabins, 16 double rooms, use of private island, fitness room, use of watersports equipment, mini-cinema room, T 443-7494, F 443-7672; **L2-L3** *Caribbee Inn*, Prospect, T 443-7380, F 443-8142, lovely but isolated setting, pricey for small room, also suites, villa, refurbished 1994 with lots of white, expensive food, snorkelling off stoney beach, 40-mins walk to excellent beach, out of town.

● **Guesthouses**
C *Peace Haven Guest House*, S of pier, Main Street, Hillsborough, T 443-7475, basic, small but good rooms, share small kitchen and bathroom, contact Lucille Atkins, very friendly and helpful, on the sea front a few hundred yards S of the jetty, also apartments **B-C**, sometimes water shortages, more rooms being built; **A3-C** *Ade's Dream*, T 443-7317, F 443-8435, N of pier, Main Street, Hillsborough, newly extended with 16 rooms or apartments, own kitchenette or share large kitchen, very clean, run by hard-working and friendly Mrs Mills (good reports), supermarket downstairs open daily; **B-C** *Millies Guest Rooms & Apartments*, Main Street, Hillsborough, T/F 443-7310, room or one-, 2-, or 3-bedroomed apartments with kitchen, bathroom/shower, fans, a/c, ocean view; **B-C** *The Sand*, T 443-7100, between Hillsborough and the airport, quiet, basic but clean, across the road is a nice beach, 9 rooms, with or without shared kitchen and bathroom, or apartment; **C** *Scraper's*, Tyrrel Bay, T 443-7403, local

restaurant and 7 rooms, 2-bedroomed cottages available, close to bay, cheaper for locals; **B-D** *Constant Spring*, T 443-7396, overlooks Tyrrel Bay, 3 double rooms with shared bathroom and kitchen, comfortable, attractive; **A3** *Bogles Round House*, T/F 443-7841, 3 cottages built by long-term travellers Kim and Sue Russell around their round house, self-contained, sleep 2-3, no service or tax, discounts available, located away from the main tourist areas.

For villas and apartments try *Alexis Luxury Apartment Hotel*, Tyrrel Bay, T 443-7179, F 443-8435; *Bayview Holiday Apartments*, Tyrrel Bay, T 443-7403; *Down Island Ltd*, Villa Rental Agents, T 443-8182, F 443-7086, weekly rentals from US$395-1,350; *Grammas Apartments*, Hillsborough, T 443-8406, F 443-8619; and others, ask at tourist office.

● **Places to eat**
There are some basic local bar/restaurants but they often run out of food quite early or close in the evenings, check during the day if they will be open for dinner; finding meals is particularly difficult at weekends. Several small bars and restaurants in Tyrrel Bay which do takeaways and other services for visiting yachts. *Scraper's*, Tyrrel Bay, very good lunch, Mr Scraper and his family are very hospitable; *Roof Garden*, misleading name, near Market Hall, Hillsborough, T 443-7204, clean and friendly but limited choice; *Hillsborough Bar*, Main Street, attractive place for a drink, Eddie uses fresh fruit juices in his cocktails (strong) and won't serve rum punches if he hasn't any fresh limes, meals can be ordered the day before; *Kayak*, Main St, good food, cheap, limited menu, live guitar music from friendly owner; *Callaloo*, Hillsborough, T 443-8004, entrées EC$12-50, plenty of choice, highly rec, open Mon-Sat 1000-1400, 1800-2200, closed Sept; *Talk of the Town*, in Hillsborough, cheap and good; *Turtle Dove* snack bar in Hermitage, T 443-7194; try the full moon barbecue at *Paradise Inn*, Paradise Beach; *Cassada Bay Resort* in the SE is good for a meal or drink, good food and wonderful sunset view, friendly, open 0800-2200 for food, bar from 1000 until late. The *Caribbee Inn* at Prospect, N of Hillsborough, T 443-7380, candlelit dining in country house hotel, creole cooking, home made bakeries, set dinner EC$65 at 1900, reservations only. The *Silver Beach Resort* is good for breakfast, snacks and lunch, quiet out of season, slow service in evenings, dinner EC$40-60, transport (and showers) available for yachtsmen from Tyrrel Bay. *The Old Fort*, Grand

Bay, T 443-8629 (443-8436 after hours reservations), live music Sat from 2130.

● **Local services**
Barclays Bank and National Commercial Bank have branches on Carriacou. These, the government and customs offices, post office and the commercial centre are around the pier in Hillsborough. The market is here too; it comes alive on Monday when the produce is brought in. Food is limited in variety, especially fresh vegetables, but according to season you can get onions, tomatoes, potatoes, cucumbers etc from Grenada. 'Jack Iron' rum (180° proof) is a local hazard, it is so strong that ice sinks in it. It is distilled in Barbados but bottled in Carriacou; it costs around EC$10 per bottle and is liberally dispensed on all high days and holidays (fairly liberally on other days too).

● **Transport**
Buses go from Hillsborough to Bogles, Windward (EC$2) and to Tyrrel Bay. A bus also goes from the airport to Windward (EC$1.50). The normally excellent service goes to pieces if it is wet. There are also plenty of taxis, or you can hire a car. Water taxis to beaches cost EC$60-100 depending on the length of the journey. Alternatively, just walk around. Fishing and sailing trips from Hillsborough pier or ask at hotels. Yachts can be hired by the day from Tanki's diving base near the airport; ask for Captain Dennis. Out of season the island is quiet, and not all the hotels are open.

PETIT MARTINIQUE

Petit Martinique is the only offshore island from Carriacou on which people live (about 600 of them). Its area is 486 acres, rising to a pointed peak. The principal occupations are boatbuilding and fishing. There is a dock with fuel, water, ice and other yachting supplies. Water taxis are available from Windward on Carriacou. Accommodation at **B** *Sea Side View Holiday Cottages*, T 443-9210, T/F 443-9113, one 2-bedroomed and two 1-bedroomed, self-contained cottages near beach, supermarket and boutique. *Palm Beach Restaurant and Bar*, menu emphasizes sea food, free water taxi service for those anchored in Petit St Vincent, Mon-Sat 1000-2200, Sun 1400-2200, T 443-9103, VHF 16.

754

Information for travellers

BEFORE TRAVELLING

● **Documents**
Citizens of the UK, USA and Canada need only provide proof of identity (with photograph) and an onward ticket (but note that if you go to Grenada via Trinidad, a passport *has* to be presented in Trinidad). For all others a passport and onward ticket are essential, though a ticket from Barbados to the USA (for example) is accepted. Departure by boat is not accepted by the immigration authorities. Citizens of certain other countries (not the Commonwealth, Caribbean – except Cuba—, South Korea, Japan and most European countries) must obtain a visa to visit Grenada. Check before leaving home. When you arrive in Grenada expect to have your luggage examined very thoroughly. It may take you at least 45 mins to get through passport control and customs. You must be able to give an accommodation address when you arrive.

● **Climate**
The average temperature is 26°C. December and January are the coolest months. The rainy season runs from June to November. Winter (high) season prices come into effect from 16 December to 15 April. The tourist season is at its height between December and March, although visitor numbers also pick up in July and August.

MONEY

● **Currency**
The currency is the East Caribbean dollar: EC$2.70 = US$1.

GETTING THERE

AIR

From Europe Scheduled flights from London, Gatwick, twice a week with British Airways, or connections with BWIA's flights from Heathrow via Antigua, Barbados or Trinidad with LIAT. BWIA also has a weekly flight from Frankfurt.

From the USA BWIA flies from Miami and New York. American Airlines fly daily from Orlando and Tampa/St Petersburg, Florida, via San Juan, Puerto Rico.

From the Caribbean BWIA connects Grenada with Antigua, Trinidad and St Lucia. LIAT flies to Grenada from Antigua, Barbados, Beguia, Trinidad, St Lucia, St Vincent and Tobago. LIATS Region Air and Airlines of Carriacou connect Grenada with Carriacou, flying 6 or 7 times a day from 0700 to 1745. Region Air and/or Airlines of Carriacou also fly to Bequia, St Vincent, Tobago and Union Island.

Several companies operate charters to Grenada from Europe, the Caribbean and North America. Martin Air has a weekly charter service from Amsterdam.

SEA

A large number of North American cruise lines call, including Chandris American Line and Royal Caribbean Cruise Line. Cargo boats to Trinidad include *Little Desrine, Edna David* and *Winnified*, Tues 1900, return Fri 0800. The *Eastward* sails about once a month to Isla de Margarita, Venezuela, US$60 one way but you have to buy a return to satisfy Venezuelan entry requirements (the captain will refund your return fare, less 10%, on arrival).

● **Ports of entry**
(Own flag) Hillsborough on Carriacou, Grenada Yacht Services at St George's, Spice Island Marina, Prickly Bay. No port fees for clearing in or out of Prickly Bay or St George's during normal working hours, Mon-Thurs 0800-1145, 1300-1600, Fri until 1700, overtime charges will apply outside those hours. On Carriacou, anchor in Tyrrel Bay and take bus, EC$2, to Hillsborough, charges EC$15 port fees during most times. Three crew and/or passenger lists, ships stores and health declaration, port clearance from the last country and valid passports. Mon-Thur 0800-1145, 1300-1600, Fri until 1700. To clear out of the country take the boat to Prickly Bay (where they can see the boat), and 3 copies of the crew list. Firearms must be declared. Seal in a proper locker on board or take to an official locker on shore to be returned on departure.

● **Anchorages**

Halifax Harbour (may have smoke from garbage burning), St George's Lagoon (security problems noted), True Blue Bay, Prickly Bay, Mt Hartman Bay, Clark's Court Bay, Port Egmont, Calivigny Harbour, Westhall Bay. Hog Island can be used as a day anchorage; government and coast guard uncertain about overnight use; occasionally clear out all boats but then don't come back for a while. Can dinghy to Lower Woburn from Mt Hartman or Hog Island to catch bus, EC$2, to St George's, otherwise taxi from Secret Harbour. Prohibited anchorages include Grand Anse Bay, Prickly Bay close to shore, Pingouin (Pink Gin) Beach, Point Salines, Tyrrel Bay (Carriacou), Mangrove Lagoon, the entire inner Lagoon. The outer Lagoon is prohibited to yachts and other liveaboard vessels. The Mangrove Lagoon may only be entered to shelter from a hurricane. Marine weather for Grenada and the Windward Islands on VHF Ch 6 at 1000. Secret Harbour cruising community has morning VHF net.

● **Marinas**

Grenada Yacht Services in St George's Lagoon (T 440-2508) is dilapidated and run down, but still in use, frequent rumours of multi-million dollar renovation. Spice Island Marina in Prickly Bay (Lance aux Épines), T 444-4267/4342, F 444-2816, has a small boatyard with bar, restaurant, ship's store, laundry and mini-market, where boats can be stored or repaired on land as well as stern-to-dock, fuel and water. The Moorings Secret Harbour base in Mt Hartman has stern-to-docks, fuel and water, a mini-mart with basic food and drink, *Rum Squall* bar, will hold message/fax and mail for yachties, T 440-4546/4439, F 444-4819. Day charter services, bareboat or with captain, from the marina.

ON ARRIVALS

● **Airports**

The Point Salines airport is 5 miles from St George's: taxis only, fixed rates as advertised to St George's, US$12, 15 mins; US$10 to Grand Anse and Lance aux Épines. Journeys within a one-mile radius of the airport US$2.75. Add 33.3% to fares between 1800 and 0600. However, if you start walking down the road towards St George's, you will find that the taxi changes into a bus and will pick you up for much less (only feasible with light luggage). If you are energetic, it takes an hour to walk to Grand Anse, longer to St George's.

Carriacou's airport is Lauriston, a US$4 taxi ride from Hillsborough, US$10 from Mt Pleasant. Disconcertingly, the main road goes straight across the runway. A fire engine drives out from Hillsborough to meet incoming flights, bringing the Immigration Officer, who clings to a platform at the back in Keystone Cops fashion.

● **Airlines**

LIAT, The Carenage, St George's, T 440-2796/7 (444-4121/2 Point Salines, 443-7362 Carriacou); British Airways T 440-2796; BWIA, The Carenage, St George's, T 440-3818/9 (T 444-4134 at airport); American Airlines, T 444-2222; Aereotuy, T 444-4732/6, F 444-4818; Airlines of Carriacou, T 440-2898; Helen Air, T 444-2266/4101, on Carriacou T 443-8260.

● **Banks**

Barclays Bank (branches in St George's-Halifax Street, Grand Anse, Grenville and Carriacou), T 440-3232; National Commercial Bank of Grenada, (Halifax Street and Hillsborough Street, St George's, Grand Anse, Grenville, Gouyave, St David's, Carriacou), T 440-3566; Scotiabank (Halifax Street, St George's), T 440 3274, branch at Grand Anse; Grenada Bank of Commerce (Halifax and Cross St, St George's, and Grand Anse), T 440-4919; Grenada Co-operative Bank (Church St, St George's, Grenville and Sauteurs), T 440-2111. They do not exchange European currencies other than sterling.

● **Clothing**

Dress is casual, with lightweight summer clothes suitable all year. Bathing costumes are not accepted in hotel dining rooms, shops or on the streets.

● **Embassies and consulates**

The **British** High Commission is at 14 Church St, St George's, T 440-3222/3536, F 440-4939. The **Venezuelan** Embassy is at Archibald Avenue, St George's, T 440-1721/2. **USA**, Point Salines, T 444-1173/1179; **Republic of Taiwan**, Archibald Avenue, T 440-3054; **Netherlands**, Grand Etang Road, St George's, T 440-2031; **Guyana**, Gore Street, St George's, T 440-2189; **Sweden**, T 440-1832; **France**, Honorary Consul, 7 Lucas Street, T 440-2547; **European Community**, Archibald Avenue, T 440-3561; **Spain**, Honorary Consul, T 440-2087; **Turkey**, Honorary Consul, T 440-2018.

● **Hospitals**
St George's has a general hospital, there is a smaller one in Mirabeau, on the E coast and clinics all round the island. For an ambulance, T 434 in St George's, T 724 in St Andrew's and T 774 on Carriacou.

● **Hours of business**
Banks: 0800-1200 or 1400 Mon- Thur; 0800-1200 or 1300, 1430- 1700 Fri. Shops: 0800-1145, 1300-1545 Mon-Fri, 0800-1145 Sat; government offices the same, but closed all day Sat.

● **Laundry**
Tangie's Laundry & Dry Cleaning Service, Sugar Mill Roundabout, St George's, T 444-4747, next to the *Sugar Mill Night Club*, pick up and delivery service. Also Super Kleen, T 440-8499, Henry's Safari Tours, T 444-5313 (will pick up and deliver even if you change hotels or anchorages), and Spice Island Marina, T 444-4257.

● **Official time**
Atlantic Standard Time, 4 hours behind GMT, 1 ahead of EST.

● **Public holidays**
New Year's Day (1 January), Independence Day (7 February), Good Fri and Easter Mon, Labour Day (1 May), Whit Mon (in May/June), Corpus Christi (June), August holidays (first Mon and Tues in August) and Carnival (second weekend in August), Thanksgiving (25 October), 25 and 26 December.

● **Religion**
Roman Catholic, Anglican, Presbyterian, Methodist, Scots Kirk, Seventh Day Adventist, Jehovah's Witnesses, Islam, Salvation Army, First Church of Christian Scientists, Church of Christ and Baha'i.

● **Security**
On the Carenage in St George's, you may be pestered for money, particularly after dark, but it is no more than a nuisance. Lagoon Road, however, does appear to be unsafe at times. Unemployment and drug abuse are serious problems; more than three quarters of the prison population have been sentenced for drug related crimes. Night police patrols have been introduced in hotels and beach areas. In the countryside people are extremely helpful and friendly and there is no need anywhere for anything other than normal precautions against theft. If visiting St George's it is best to pick a day when there are no cruise ships in port, to avoid hassle from vendors and touts.

● **Shopping**
The Yellow Poui Art Gallery sells Grenadian paintings and is worth a visit, above Noah's Arkade souvenir shop on Cross Street. Spice Island Perfumes on the Carenage sells perfumes and pots pourris made from the island's spices, as well as batiks, T-shirts, etc. Arawak Island factory and retail outlet on the Upper Belmont Road between Grand Anse and St George's, T 440-4577, open Mon-Fri 0830-1630, perfumes, body oils, spices, syrups, cocoa bars etc. Batik Art Factory on Young Street, see batik being made by deaf and handicapped women, sign language greatly appreciated if you know how. White Cane Industries on the Carenage adjacent to the Ministry of Health, featuring a wide variety of arts and crafts made by skillful blind Grenadians. Blind People's Work Shop at Delicious Landing, and others. You can purchase straw and palm wares, and items in wood. Spices are cheaper in the supermarket than on the street or in the market. There is duty-free shopping at the airport and on the Carenage for cruise ship passengers. Yachties are advised to buy alcoholic drinks and French wines here at near duty free prices before going N or S. Trinidad rum and gin are cheaper in Grenada than in Trinidad.

St George's Bookshop is on Halifax Street; The Sea Change Book and Gift Shop is on the Carenage, beneath the *Nutmeg* bar, it has *USA Today* when cruise ships come in. Good supermarkets include Foodland, on Lagoon with dinghy dock; Food Fair in St George's with dinghy tie up; Food Fair in Grand Anse; Matheson's Supermarket, open daily from 0800, will deliver to yachts.

● **Voltage**
220/240 volts, 50 cycles AC.

ON DEPARTURE

● **Departure tax**
For stays of over 24 hrs, departure tax is EC$35 (EC$17.50 for children aged 5 to 12) and a security supplement is EC$10 (EC$5 for children 5 to 11). Children under 5 pay nothing. There is a EC$5 tax on airline tickets purchased in Grenada. No tax payable on flights from Grenada to Carriacou.

● **Airport information**
Returning to the airport you can take a bus from St George's market to Calliste (EC$1.50) then walk, 20 mins downhill. Another route is by bus to the 'Sugarman', EC$1, then catch

another minibus or collective taxi to the airport, EC$5. Alternatively, when reconfirming your ticket with LIAT ask about taxis, they offer a reliable taxi service for EC$25 if paid in advance. There are no exchange facilities at the airport.

ACCOMMODATION

Hotel rooms are subject to a 10% service charge and an 8% tax on accommodation, food and beverages. Rates quoted here are 1995/96 winter-summer. The majority of hotels are in the Grand Anse area, with several around Lance aux Épines. In St George's there are more guesthouses than hotels.

● Hotels

Price guide

L1	over US$200	L2	US$151-200
L3	US$101-150	A1	US$81-100
A2	US$61-80	A3	US$46-60
B	US$31-45	C	US$21-30
D	US$12-20	E	US$7-11
F	US$4-6	G	up to US$3

St George's: **A3** *Tropicana Inn*, Lagoon Rd, T 440-1586, F 440-9797, 20 double rooms, bath, some with patio, cater to business as well as vacation traveller, family run, overlooks marina, on bus route.

On Grand Anse: **L2-L3** *Coyaba*, PO Box 336, St George's, T 444-4129, in North America T 800-223 9815, F 444-4808, popular with package tours, but very comfortable, lots of facilities, 70 rooms on 5½ acres, 3 are wheelchair accessible, large pool with swim-up bar; **L1-L3** *Grenada Renaissance*, PO Box 441, St George's, T 444-4371, F 444-4800, 186 rooms and suites, a/c, garden view, or beachfront, suites or rooms, many facilities, restaurant pricey, open 0700-2300; **L1** *Spice Island Inn*, PO Box 6, St George's, T 444-4258, F 444-4807, garden view, beach suite or pool suite, no children under 12 in pool suites, no children under 5 in winter, all inclusive available on request, lots of sports and other facilities on offer; **A2** *Hibiscus*, PO Box 279, St George's, T 444-4233, F 444-2873, car hire available; **L2-L3** *Blue Horizons Cottage Hotel*, PO Box 41, St George's, T 444-4316, F 444-2815, its *La Belle Créole* restaurant is one of the island's best, shared amenities with *Spice Island*. **L1-A2** *The Flamboyant*, PO Box 214, St George's, T 444-4247, F 444-1234, 39 units in rooms, suites and cottages, EP, TV, phone,

pool, free snorkelling equipment, at the end of Grand Anse, lovely views, steep walk down to beach, rec but food nothing special, quite a walk to bus stop; **A2-B** *South Winds Holiday Cottages and Apartments*, Grand Anse, PO Box 118, St George's, T 444-4310, F 444-4404, monthly rates on request, a/c or fan, cable TV, radio, electric mosquito killer, large kitchen, terrace or balcony, simple but clean, good restaurant, friendly staff and dogs, 5-10-min walk from beach, good view, rec (also car hire).

At **Morne Rouge**: **L3-A2** *Gem Holiday Beach Resort*, PO Box 58, T 444-4224, F 444-1189, rooms vary in quality, one or 2-bedroomed apartments, lovely beach, good position but hot, a/c nice and cool, enjoyable beachside lounge also popular with locals, restaurant limited. **L2-A2** *True Blue Inn*, P O Box 308, St George's, T 444-2000, F 444-1247, between Grand Anse and Point Salines airport, small and friendly, owner-managed cottages and apartments, kitchenettes, pool, dock facilities, boat charter available, restaurant and bar. **L1-L3** *Rex Grenadian*, Point Salines, PO Box 893, St George's, T 444-3333, F 444-1111, opened 1993, 212 rooms, the largest on the island, a/c, fans, gym, pool, tennis, 2 beaches, watersports, scuba diving, 4 restaurants and bars, conference facilities, 5 rooms for handicapped guests, labour disputes with unions 1994/95; also at Point Salines, **L1** *La Source*, PO Box 852, T 444-2556, F 444-2561, opened 1993, 100 rooms, all-inclusive, pool, 9-hole golf course, health and leisure facilities.

Lance aux Épines: **L1** *Calabash*, PO Box 382, St George's, T 444-4334, 800-223 1108, F 444-5050, winner of a prestigious Golden Fork award for quality of food and hospitality, probably the poshest hotel on Grenada, 30 suites, 8 with private pool, 22 with whirlpool, expensive, MAP inc breakfast in suite, afternoon tea and dinner, on beach, nice grounds, tennis, games room; **L1-L3** *Twelve Degrees North*, PO Box 241, St George's, T/F 444-4580, T 800-322-1753, 8 apartments with maid/cook, laundry, no children under 15, very private, tennis, pool, snorkelling, windsurfing, sunfish all included; **L1-L3** *Secret Harbour*, PO Box 11, St George's, T 444-4439, F 444-4819, 20 luxury rooms, chalets built into the rock face overlooking the harbour, private, wonderful views, pool, friendly, steel band at times, no children under 12 accepted, this is a Club Mariner Resort and bareboat or crewed yacht charters are available from the marina; **L2-A2** *Horse Shoe Beach*, PO Box 174, St George's, T 444-4410, F 444-4844, rooms, suites or villas, children under 12 free if sharing with parents, wheelchair ramp to dining room; **A2** *Villamar Holiday Resort*, PO Box 546, St George's, T 444-4716, F 444--1341, 20 rooms near Grand Anse and Prickly Bay, a/c, kitchenette, TV, phone, patio, 1 and 2 bedroom suites for families, business or single travellers, children under 12 sharing free, monthly/group rates on request; *Holiday Haven*, above a cove on Prickly Point, 2-3 bedroomed villas US$500-600/week in summer, US$600-700 in winter, 1-2 bedroomed apartments also available, contact Dr John Watts, T 440-2606, 444-4325.

On the S coast: **L3-A2** *Petit Bacaye*, on bay of same name, PO Box 655, St George's, T/F 443-2902, T 443-2902, thatched self-catering cottages, one or 2-bedroom, inc tax and service, breakfast and snacks at beach bar, fisherman call daily, catch can be cooked to order, reef and own Islet 200m offshore, jeep and guide hire arranged, sandy beach round the bluff; **A1-A3** *La Sagesse Nature Centre* (see **Flora and fauna** above), St David's, PO Box 44, St George's, T/F 444-6458, 4 rooms, small, excellent, perfect setting, an old plantation house on a secluded, sandy bay (the sea may be polluted in the rainy season, seek the hotel's advice), child-friendly, good restaurant, excursions, highly rec.

On the E coast: near Grenville, *St Martins Catholic Retreat Centre*, Mount St Ervans, PO Box 11, Grenville, T 442-7348, spectacular views, lovely surroundings, good spot for lunch, open to non-residents.

● **Guesthouses**

St George's: **B** *Mitchell's Guest House*, Tyrrel Street, T 440-2803, central, downstairs rooms dark and not very private, no towels, town noises, ability to sleep through cock crowing essential; **C** *Simeons*, Green Street, T 440-2537, 9 rooms, inc breakfast, central, clean, friendly, rec, view over Carenage; **B** *St Ann's Guest House*, Paddock, beyond Botanic Gardens (some distance from centre), T 440-2717, inc excellent breakfast, friendly, entrance forbidden to 'prostitutes and natty dreds', meals (communal), EC$20, good value, a bit difficult to sleep because of dogs and roosters, take ear plugs; **B-D** *Yacht's View*, Lagoon Road, T 440-3607, cheap but noisy and frequently without water or fans; **B-D** *Mamma's Lodge*, PO Box 248, Lagoon

Road, T 440-1623, F 440-7788, good value, double and single rooms, pleasant, friendly, very clean, nice view, inc breakfast, no credit cards, now managed by a daughter after Mama's death in 1991; **E** *Lakeside*, at the end of Lagoon Road going towards Grand Anse, T 440-2365 (Mrs Ruth Haynes), view over yacht marina, helpful, cooking facilities, drinks available, mixed reports. **C** *Skyline*, Belmont, between St George's and Grand Anse Beach, T 444-4461, mixed reports.

At **Grand Anse**: **A1-B** *Roydon's*, T 444-4476, EP or MAP, helpful staff, fans, very nice even if a bit overpriced, rec but next to a busy street, good restaurant, 10 mins' walk from beach, access through *Grenada Renaissance*;

Grenville: **B** *Rainbow Inn*, PO Box 923, T 442-5332, 15 rooms, buses stop outside, studios and apartments for US$350-400/week.

There are also many furnished villas and apartments available for rent from various agents, with prices for daily or weekly rental. **B-C** *RSR Apartments* on Lagoon Road, Springs PO, St George's, T 440-3381, has been rec for good value, one or 3 bedroom apartment, kitchen, living room, bathroom, veranda, guard at night, also cockroaches, bus into town; **A3** *Windward Sands Inn*, PO Box 199, T 444-4238, apartments US$250-370/week, friendly, helpful, tours arranged, nice place, walk to the beach, good cooking, laundry service.

● **Camping**

Camping is not encouraged as there are no facilities, but it is permitted in the Grand Etang National Park and in schools and church grounds on Carriacou.

FOOD AND DRINK

● **Food**

To repeat, Grenada's West Indian cooking is generally very good. Lambi (conch) is very popular, as is callaloo soup (made with dasheen leaves), souse (a sauce made from pig's feet), pepper pot and pumpkin pie. There is a wide choice of seafood, and of vegetables. Goat and wild meat (armadillo, iguana, manicou) can be sampled. Nutmeg features in many local dishes, try nutmeg jelly for breakfast, ground nutmeg comes on top of rum punches. Of the many fruits and fruit dishes, try stewed golden apple, or soursop ice cream. There is limited food or choice on Carriacou.

● **Drink**

Rum punches are excellent, and be sure to try the local sea-moss drink (a mixture of vanilla, algae and milk). There are 3 makes of rum, whose superiority is disputed by the islanders, Clarke's Court, River Antoine and Westerhall Plantation Rum, made by Westerhall Distilleries. Several readers have endorsed Westerhall Plantation Rum for its distinct flavour and aroma. The term 'grog', for rum, is supposed to originate in Grenada: taking the first letters of 'Georgius Rex Old Grenada', which was stamped on the casks of rum sent back to England. Grenada Breweries brew Carib Lager, Guinness and non-alcoholic malt beers.

● **Restaurants**

There is quite a wide choice of restaurants, apart from the hotels mentioned above, and you are recommended to eat the local dishes, which are very good. Tax of 8% and service of 10% is usually added to the bill. Unless stated otherwise, restaurants below are in **St George's**. *Nutmeg*, on the Carenage above the Sea Change Book Store (T 440-2539), delicious local dishes and its own famous rum punch, very popular, but avoid if you do not want to see turtle on the menu, open Mon-Sat 0900-2100, Sun 1700-2100; *Rudolph's*, also on the Carenage, (T 440-2241), entrées EC$18-50, but good, local and international food, in friendly pub atmosphere, excellent rum punch, open Mon-Sat 1000-2400; *Sand Pebble*, T 440-2688, the Carenage too, cheap and clean, good rotis EC$5, excellent sea moss, take away or eat in, bar snacks only, also taxi service; *Portofino*, on the Carenage, Italian, about US$20 for meal and drink, nice place, witty proprietor, T 440-3986; *Delicious Landing*, on the Carenage, local and international food, good; *Tropicana*, on the Lagoon, T 440-1586, popular, Chinese and local food, good, entrées from EC$10-45, excellent egg rolls, rec, seating inside or out on covered patio, barbecues, open 0730-2400, reservations rec in high season, also take away rotis and Chinese; *Mamma's*, Lagoon Road, try multifarious local foods (famous for wild meat dishes when in season but you don't always know what you are getting, you may not be told until you've finished that there is no wild game that night), need to book, T 440-1459, full dinner EC$45 1930-2100, bar open until 2400; *Ebony*, Victoria St, unique local dishes in relaxed setting, snacks and entrées, no credit cards, T 442-8246; *Bobby's Health Stop*, Gore Street, daytimes, also at Morne Rouge shopping centre, vegetable rotis; also *Snug Corner* near the Market Square; on Melville Street, near waterfront taxi stand, *Deyna's*, new, modern, good local food at local prices, and lots of it, rotis, excellent coffee, open daily 0730-2200, crowded at lunch, T 440-6795, rec; *Pitch Pine Bar*, fun place on the sea for a drink.

At the St George's end of Grand Anse is *Coconut Beach, The French Creole Restaurant*, T 444-4644, with excellent food and fruit juices and punches, barbecues and live music Wed, Fri, Sun evenings in high season, open 1000-2200. *The Bird's Nest* at Grand Anse has good Chinese food, very reasonable, slow service, confusing menu with $1/4$, $1/2$ and full portions all quoted, opp *Grenada Renaissance*, T 444-4264; *Fish 'n' Chick*, at roundabout, barbecue and grilled fish and chicken, local fast food and takeaway; *Joe's Steakhouse*, seafood restaurant and bar, Le Marquis complex, King Cuts of USDA steaks, marinated and grilled with Caribbean touch, T 444-4020; *Beachside Terrace*, owned and run by Grenadian Lawrence Lambert, big buffet and steel band Wed in season, good, very cheap Sun barbecue lunch, geared towards families; the *Cot Bam Beach Bar* on Grand Anse in front of *Coyaba* (approach by road at night) has good food, cheap, limited menu, locals drink here from morning onwards and are keen conversationalists; *Kentucky Fried Chicken* and *Pizza Hut* outlets were being built in this area in 1996; *Canboulay*, Morne Rouge, T 444-4401, rec, upmarket and very good but not cheap, vegetarian menu, seafood specials on Wed, entrées from EC$14, full dinner EC$70-90, open Mon-Fri for lunch 1130-1430, Mon-Sat for supper from 1830. *Tabanca*, near *The Flamboyant*, excellent food, a mixture of Grenadian and international, run by an Austrian, her coffee is superb, open 1100-2300, live music weekly after 2100, closed Tues, T 444-1300. *La Boulangerie* at Le Marquis Mall, Grand Anse, T 444-1131, French bakery and coffee shop with baguettes, croissants, sandwiches, pizza and roast chicken, good picnic food. *Indigo* at True Blue Inn, transport on request, Thur night barbecue, call for daily specials, dinghy dock; Knap's *South Winds*, Grand Anse, T 444-1299, 500m from beach, free transport within hotel belt, German spoken, entertainment room with bar, darts, burgers, bar snacks 1100-2300, daily lunch specials EC$19-22, dinner reservations requested, happy hour Fri

1730-1830; *Bas Ass Café*, Le Marquis Complex, Grand Anse, Mexican, burgers, baked potatoes, sandwiches, salad bar. *Aquarium Beach Club and Restaurant*, T 444-1410, Balls Beach, run by Ollie and Rebecca, rec, bar open from 1000, kitchen 1200-2200, happy hour 1730-1900, Sat volleyball, Sun lobster barbecue, showers, toilets, snorkelling offshore, good food, lobster, fish, steak, sandwiches, live music and buffet from 1900 first Sat in month, dinner reservations requested. *Cicely's*, Lance aux Épines, T 444-4334, reservations required, dinner 1900-2300, award winning restaurant overlooks Prickly Bay, entrées EC$40-60; *Red Crab*, Lance aux Épines, T 444-4424, excellent local seafood and international, entrées from EC$25, fabulous steak dinner EC$60, live music Mon, Fri in season, darts Wed nights; *Choolight*, next door, Chinese, good service, food and prices, also takeaway; *Island View Seafood Restaurant*, Clark's Court Bay, Woburn, T 443-2054, VHF 16, open 1000-2300, casual games room with pub food, pool tables, pinball machine etc, dinghy dock, boat outings arranged with food and drinks; *Petit Bacaye*, on bay of same name, fresh fish, fishermen's catch cooked to order.

See above for *Morne Fendue* plantation house restaurant, good local food and drinks, lunch EC$40, reservations essential, T 442-9330. *La Sagesse* (see above, **Accommodation** and **Flora and fauna**) rec for lunch, fresh lobster, grilled tuna, outdoor restaurant, beautiful location, walk it off afterwards, good hiking over the mountain, T 444-6458 for reservations which are rec, especially for dinner, US$28 for return transport, lunch, guided nature walk with exotic fruit tasting, dinner packages available, entrées EC$15-50; *Mount Rodney Estate*, St Patrick's, open for lunch 1200-1400 Mon-Fri, reservations essential, EC$40 set price, T 442-9420.

● **Bars**

Happy hours at marinas: *Boatyard Bar* at Prickly Bay Marina, 1730-1830, TV and live music several times a week in season; *Rum Squall Bar* at Secret Harbour Marina, inexpensive weekly barbecue and daily happy hour 1600-1700; *Grenada Yacht Club* in St George's has happy hour Wed, Fri, Sat 1800-1900, yachtsmen and others welcome, great place to sit and watch the boats entering the lagoon (and see if they are paying attention to the channel markers or run aground).

GETTING AROUND

AIR TRANSPORT

Every day LIAT, Region Air and Airlines of Carriacou fly frequently between Grenada and Carriacou: US$62 return, half that one way (flying time is 12 mins).

LAND TRANSPORT

● **Motoring**

Driving is on the left. When driving, be prepared for no road signs, no indication which way the traffic flow goes (just watch the other cars), and few street names. Maps are often not accurate, so navigation becomes particularly difficult. Also be careful of the deep storm drains along the edges of the narrow roads.

● **Car hire**

Cars can be rented from a number of companies for about US$55 or EC$150 a day, plus US$2,500 excess liability and 5% tax (payable by credit card). You must purchase a local permit, on presentation of your national driving licence, for EC$30/US$12; a local permit is not required if you hold an international driving licence.

Companies in St George's include Spice Island Rentals (Avis), Paddock and Lagoon Road, T 440-3936; Dollar Rent-a-Car, airport, T 444-4786, F 444-4788; David's, at the airport, the *Grenada Renaissance*, the *Rex Grenadian* and the Limes in Grand Anse, T 440-2399; Mc Intyre, True Blue, cars and jeeps, T 440-2044; Maitland's (who also rent motorcycles), Market Hill, T 444-4022, also an office at the airport which is often open for late arrivals when others are closed; Rent-a-Moke (Lance aux Épines), T 444-4431, F 440-4195; C Thomas and Sons, cars, minibuses, jeeps, T 444-4384, mixed reports. On Carriacou: Barba Gabriel, T 443-7454; Leo Cromwell, T 443-7333; Martin Bullen, T 443-7204; *Silver Beach Resort*, T 443-7337. Jeep hire is available for EC$100/day or less for a week.

We have received reports that daily rates quoted over the phone are not always honoured when you pick up the car; check that the company does not operate a 3-day minimum hire if you want a rate for one day only, this often applies in high season.

● **Bicycles**

Bike rentals can be arranged with Ride Grenada, T 444-1157.

● **Buses**

Buses run to all parts of the island from the Market Square and the Esplanade in St George's; on the Esplanade look for the signs, in the Square, ask around. Fares are EC$1 within St George's, EC$3 to Grand Étang, and EC$4.50 to Grenville and EC$5 to Sauteurs. There is also a regular bus service between Grenville and Sauteurs. The last buses tend to be in mid-afternoon and there are very few on Sun. On Carriacou, buses cost EC$1 for 1 mile, EC$2 for more than that.

● **Taxis**

Fares are set by the Tourist Board. On Grenada, taxis charge EC$4 for the first 10 miles outside St George's, then EC$3 per mile thereafter (an additional 33% charge is made after 1800 and before 0600). From St George's Pier it is US$3 to the city or Botanical Gardens, US$12 to L'Anse aux Épines. A taxi tour of Grenada costs about US$40-55 pp for a full day or US$15 pp per hour. Island tours of Carriacou cost the same as on Grenada. A rec driver is Leroy Wilson (VHF 16/68, T 443-1171, 444-3640, pager 441-7089), good local history, driving and hiking tours (Seven Falls, Hot Springs); also Christopher Greenidge, T 444-7334.

Taxis and buses are heavily 'personalized' by the drivers with brightly coloured decorations and names like 'Rusher with Love' or 'Danny Boy', while large speakers blast out steel bands or reggae music; taxi drivers will adjust the volume on request. A water taxi service runs from in front of the *Nutmeg* restaurant, St George's to the Grand Anse beach. Hitchhiking is quite easy though the roads are not very good.

FERRIES

On Wed and Sat at 0930 the trading schooners *Alexia II* and *Adelaide B* sail from The Carenage, St George's to Carriacou (4 hrs, EC$20 one way, EC$30 return), returning on Thur and Mon at 1000. *Alexia III* departs Tues 0930, Fri 1100 and Sun 0700, returning Wed 1300, Sat 1300 and Sun 0830, same fares. In heavy seas you may be better opting for a schooner, which despite being smaller, ride the waves better than the larger boats which may make you seasick. Be prepared for incredibly loud reggae/rap music. The *MV Edna David* sails on Sun 0700, arriving Carriacou 1030, returning 1700, arriving in St George's 2030, EC$35. Times are subject to change and you must check. There are also unscheduled schooner

services between these islands; by asking around you might be able to get a passage on one. *Eagle Quest* sails from Grenada to Sandy Island and back on Sun, departing 0930, return 1700.

Carriacou is one hour by schooner from Union Island; scheduled service by MV *Obedient* twice a week. Two small fishing boats sail Mon 1300 from Hillsborough pier, one hour, EC$10.

COMMUNICATIONS

● **Postal services**

The General Post Office in St George's is on Lagoon Road, S of the Carenage, open 0800-1530 Mon to Thur, and 1630 on Fri, only postage stamps are sold during the lunch hour, 1200-1300. Villages have sub-post offices.

● **Telecommunications**

Grenada Telephone Company (Grentel, a joint venture with Cable and Wireless), T 440-1000, with offices on the Carenage, St George's, operates telephone services, including USA Direct and calls to USA on Visa card, etc, at a fee, facsimile, telex, telegraph and cellular phones. Payphones take coins or phone cards issued by Grentel, available at outlets near payphones. Home Direct Service can be made from any phone, if you have a credit or telephone charge card, and is available to the UK through BT Direct and to Canada through Teleglobe. Credit card holders and Visaphone card holders' access number is 1-800-877-8000 for domestic and international calls. If you dail 1-800-872-2881 at any public phone (no coin required), you get through to AT and T. A call to the UK costs approximately EC$37.50 for 5 mins. The international code for Grenada is 809. Grentel Boatphone provides mobile cellular phone service.

MEDIA

● **Newspapers**

There are no daily papers, only weeklies, including *Grenadian Voice*, *Indies Times*, *Grenada Guardian*, *The National*, and *The Informer*.

● **Radio**

There are 4 radio stations, on AM 535 kHz, AM 1440 kHz, FM 90 kHz and FM 101.7 kHz.

● **Television**

There are 2 television stations but many hotels have satellite reception. Cable TV is being installed.

ENTERTAINMENT

The resort hotels provide evening entertainment, including dancing, steelband and calypso music, limbo, etc. There are not a great many discothèques and night clubs outside the hotels and low season can be very quiet. *The Boatyard* at the marina on L'Anse Aux Epines Beach has bands playing Wed and Fri nights with dancing; *Dynamite Disco* at the Limes on Grand Anse Beach has weekend parties; *Fantazia 2001 Disco* on Morne Rouge Beach from 2130 Fri and Sat dancing and Cultural Cabaret, cover charge, Golden Oldies Wed; *Le Sucrier*, in the Sugar Mill at Grand Anse roundabout, Wed-Sat 2100-0300, DJs or live music. On Carriacou there is a good jump-up every Fri after mass at *Liz' Refreshment*, Tyrrel Bay, with excellent DJ. The Regal Cinema is off Lagoon Road, next to *Tropicana*, movies nightly at 2030, EC$5 for double feature. The Marryshow Folk Theatre in the University of the West Indies building on Tyrrel Street, has concerts, plays and special events.

TOURIST INFORMATION

● **Local tourist office**
Grenada Board of Tourism, the Carenage, St George's (PO Box 293), T 440-2279/ 2001/ 3377/ 2872, F 440-6637/2123. Its hours are 0800-1600 and it is very helpful. There is also a cruise ship office and tourist office at the airport, helpful, hotel reservation service, T 444-4140.

● **Tourist offices overseas**
In the USA: Grenada Board of Tourism, 820 2nd Avenue, Suite 900D, New York, NY 10017, T (212) 687-9554, (800) 927 9554, F (212) 573 9731; in Canada: Grenada Board of Tourism, Suite 820, 439 University Avenue, Toronto, Ontario M5G 1Y8, T (416) 595-1339, F (416) 595 8278; in the UK: 1 Collingham Gardens, London SW5 0HW, T (0171) 370 5164/5, F (0171) 370 7040, 244-0177; in Germany: Grenada Tourism Office, Johanna-Melber-Weg 12, D 60599 Frankfurt/Main, T 069-611 178, F 069-629 264.

● **Local travel agents**
All in St George's: Grenada International Travel Service, of Church Street (American Express representative), T 440-2945; Huggins Travel Service, the Carenage, T 440-2514 and many others. For guided hikes contact Telfer Bedeau

in the village of Soubise on the E coast; you must ask around for him (or T 442-6200 or see if the Tourism Department can put you in touch). Edwin Frank, from the Tourism Bureau, T 443-5143, does guided tours at weekends, US$20 pp island tour, very knowledgeable on history, politics, geography, people, fauna, hiking etc, rec and much better than an untrained taxi driver. Henry, of Henry's Safari Tours (T 444-5313) conducts tours of the island and is very well informed on all aspects of Grenada. Arnold's Tours, Archibald Avenue, T 440-0531, F 440-4118, offers similar services to Henry's, also rec, but in German as well. Clinton 'Guava' George, of Clinton's Taxi Service, T 444-4095, 441-9648, knows a lot about Grenadian geography, politics and biology and gives a well-informed, fun tour of the island. Sunsation Tours is very knowledgeable and rec, bilingual guides are available for half or full day tours, PO Box 856, St George's, T 444-1656, 444-1594, F 444-2836. Mrs Pat Walcott, of Bamboo Tours, T 444-1785, uses 3 old, open-sided buses with wooden seats, rec. Organized tours usually take in St George's and/or most of the island including plantation tours, Concord waterfall, the Nutmeg Processing Station, National Parks, the River Antoine Rum Distillery, Lake Antoine and the Marquis Waterfall. Most tour agencies are happy to tailor a tour to suit you.

● **Maps**
Grenada National Parks publishes a series of map and trail guides, worth having for the Grand Étang National Park and related walks. The Overseas Surveys Directorate, Ordnance Survey **map** of Grenada, published for the Grenada Government in 1985, scale 1:50,000, is available from the Tourist Office, from the Lands and Surveys Department in the Ministry of Agriculture (at the Botanic Gardens) and from shops for EC$10.50-15 (it is not wholly accurate). Also available from Ordnance Survey, Southampton, are 2 separate sheets, North (1979) and South (1988) at 1:25,000 scale.

ACKNOWLEDGEMENTS

This chapter has been revised with the welcome help of Kathy Irwin, aboard *Scheel Delight*.

Barbados

BARBADOS is 21 miles long and 14 miles wide, lying E of the main chain of the Leeward and Windward islands. It is flatter, drier, and more prosperous and tourists who come here looking for the 'untouched' Caribbean are in for a disappointment. There are no volcanoes or rain forests, and hardly any rivers, but there are plenty of white sand beaches and lots of pleasantly rolling countryside with fields of sugar cane, brightly painted villages, flowering trees and open pastures. The island is probably better equipped with infrastructure and reliable tourist services than anywhere else to the S of Miami on this side of the Atlantic.

HORIZONS

Most of the island is covered by a cap of coral limestone, up to 600,000 years old. Several steep inland cliffs or ridges run parallel to the coast. These are the remains of old shorelines, which formed as the island gradually emerged from the sea. There are no rivers in this part of the island, although there are steep-sided gullies down which water runs in wet weather. Rainwater runs through caves in the limestone, one of which, Harrison's Cave, has been developed as a tourist attraction. The island's water supply is pumped up from the limestone. In the Scotland District in the NE, the coral limestone has been eroded and older, softer rocks are exposed. There are rivers here, which have cut deep, steep-sided valleys. Landslides make agriculture and construction hazardous and often destroy roads.

Barbados has a population of 265,000. This is more than any of the Windwards or Leewards, and is considered enough to make the island one of

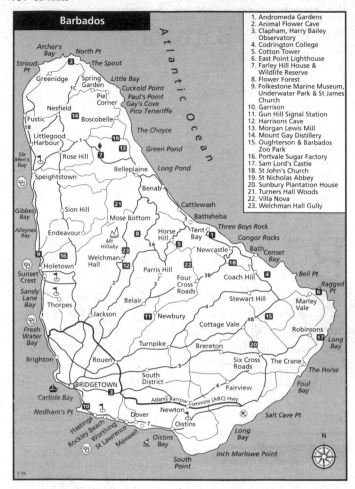

Barbados

1. Andromeda Gardens
2. Animal Flower Cave
3. Clapham, Harry Bailey Observatory
4. Codrington College
5. Cotton Tower
6. East Point Lighthouse
7. Farley Hill House & Wildlife Reserve
8. Flower Forest
9. Folkestone Marine Museum, Underwater Park & St James Church
10. Garrison
11. Gun Hill Signal Station
12. Harrisons Cave
13. Morgan Lewis Mill
14. Mount Gay Distillery
15. Oughterson & Barbados Zoo Park
16. Portvale Sugar Factory
17. Sam Lord's Castle
18. St John's Church
19. St Nicholas Abbey
20. Sunbury Plantation House
21. Turners Hall Woods
22. Villa Nova
23. Welchman Hall Gully

the 'big four' in the Caribbean Community. With population density of 1,595 per square mile in 1995, Barbados is one of the most crowded countries in the world.

HISTORY

There were Amerindians on Barbados for upwards of a thousand years. The first Europeans to find the island were the Portuguese, who named it 'Os Barbados' after the Bearded Fig trees which grew on the beaches, and left behind some wild pigs. These bred successfully and provided meat for the first English settlers, who arrived in 1627 and found an island which was otherwise uninhabited. It is not clear why the Amerindians abandoned the island, although several theories exist.

King Charles I gave the Earl of Carlisle permission to colonize the island and it was his appointed Governor, Henry Hawley, who in 1639 founded the House of Assembly. Within a few years, there were upwards of 40,000 white settlers, mostly small farmers, and equivalent in number to about 1% of the total population of England at this period. After the 'sugar revolution' of the 1650s most of the white population left. For the rest of the colonial period sugar was king, and the island was dominated by a small group of whites who owned the estates, the 'plantocracy'. The majority of the population today is descended from African slaves who were brought in to work on the plantations; but there is a substantial mixed-race population, and there has always been a small number of poor whites, particularly in the E part of the island. Many of these are descended from 100 prisoners transported in 1686 after the failed Monmouth rebellion and Judge Jeffrey's 'Bloody Assizes'.

The two principal political parties are the Barbados Labour Party (BLP) and the Democratic Labour Party (DLP). A third party is the National Democratic Party (NDP). The Democratic Labour Party won office in 1986, and was re-elected in 1991, when it won 18 seats in a general election. The Prime Minister was Mr Erskine Sandiford. The BLP is led by Mr Owen Arthur, previously its economic affairs spokesman, who took over the leadership in 1993 from Mr Henry Forde, when he resigned on health grounds. Economic difficulties in the 1990's eroded support for the DLP and by 1994 the Government's popularity was low. Mr Sandiford was criticized for his autocratic style and the resignation of three ministers was seen as damaging the party's hopes for the general election, due by January 1996. In June he lost a vote of no-confidence by 14-12 votes and soon afterwards called a general election for 6 September 1994.

Mr Sandiford resigned as leader of the party and was replaced by the Finance Minister, David Thompson, who was unable to restore the party's popularity in such a short time. The BLP won the elections with 19 seats, compared with 8 for the DLP and one for the NDP. Mr Owen Arther, 44, an economist, became Prime Minister and took on the portfolios of Finance and Economic Affairs. For the first time, the deputy Prime Minister is a woman, Ms Billie Miller, who is also Minister for Foreign Affairs, Trade and International Business, Tourism and International Transport.

GOVERNMENT

Barbados has been an independent member of the Commonwealth since November 1966. The British Monarch is the Head of State, represented by a Governor General. There is a strong parliamentary and democratic tradition. The House of Assembly is the third oldest parliament in the Western Hemisphere and celebrated its 350th anniversary in 1989, although voting was limited to property owners until 1950. There are 21 senators appointed by the Governor General, of whom 12 are on the advice of the Prime Minister, two on the advice of the Leader of the Opposition and seven at his own discretion to reflect religious, economic and social interests. 28 single-member constituencies elect the House of Assembly.

THE ECONOMY

Structure of production

There are few natural resources and sugar is still the main crop. The sugar industry has been in the hands of the receivers since 1992 and many producers have abandoned the land, while trying to get planning permission for golf courses or housing developments. The industry is under the management of Booker Tate, through the Barbados Agricultural Management Co established in 1993. Under a restructuring plan production is to be restored to 75,000 tonnes by 1999. Production was over 100,000 tonnes a year in the early 1980s

Barbados: fact file

Geographic

Land area	430 sq km
forested	11.6%
pastures	4.7%
cultivated	37.2%

Demographic

Population (1995)	265,000
annual growth rate (1990-95)	0.4%
urban	37.9%
rural	62.1%
density	616 per sq km
Religious affiliation	
Anglican	39.7%
Other protestant	25.6%
Birth rate per 1,000 (1994)	13.4
(world av 25.0)	

Education and Health

Life expectancy at birth (1989-91)	
male	72.9 years
female	77.4 years
Infant mortality rate	
per 1,000 live births (1994)	8.5
Physicians (1992)	1 per 842 persons
Hospital beds	1 per 134 persons
Calorie intake as %	
of FAO requirement	133%
Population age 25 and over	
with no formal schooling	0.8%
Literacy (over 15)	98.0%

Economic

GNP (1993 market prices)	
	US$1,620mn
GNP per capita	US$6,240
Public external debt (1993)	
	US$346.5mn
Tourism receipts (1993)	US$502mn
Inflation (annual av 1990-94)	3.3%
Radio	1 per 1.2 persons
Television	1 per 3.8 persons
Telephone	1 per 2.4 persons

Employment

Population economically active (1994)	
	129,000
Unemployment rate	21.9%
% of labour force in	
agriculture	4.6
trade and restaurants	19.9
manufacturing	7.7
construction	6.0
Military forces	154

Source *Encyclopaedia Britannica*

but the 1994/95 was hit by drought and only reached 38,000 tonnes, earning US$22mn, and the country was unable to meet its 54,000-tonne EC quota in 1995. All sugar is exported under the Lomé Convention. Domestic consumption is Guatemalan or Guyanese sugar.

There is some export-oriented manufacturing and an expanding off-shore financial sector. At the end of 1995 there were 1,834 international business companies, 1,501 foreign sales corporations, 230 captive insurance companies and 34 off-shore banks, all showing steady growth. There is a well-established service sector, and a wide range of light industries which produce mainly for the local, regional, and North American markets. Manufacturing is the second largest foreign exchange earner, employing 10,300 people in 1996.

By far the main foreign exchange earner is now tourism, which accounts for 14% of gdp and employs 10,300 people. In 1995, 442,107 tourists, 29% of whom came from the UK, the single largest market, stayed in Barbados and 484,670 cruise ship passengers also visited, spending about US$550 mn. In 1994 there were 5,685 rooms available in hotels, guest houses and apartments, a decline of 15% since 1980.

Recent trends

The slowdown in the USA and other industrialized countries at the beginning of the 1990s had a negative affect on the Barbadian economy. Stopover arrivals declined by over 7% in 1990, nearly 9% in 1991 and a further 2.2% in 1992, while construction and agriculture also declined, leading to an overall gdp contraction of 4.2% in 1991 and 4.0% in 1992. The Government's budget deficit rose to 8.9% of gdp in 1990, while foreign reserves declined and unemployment rose to 14.7%. The 1991 budget sought to close the gap by raising taxes and the deficit fell to 2.9% of gdp but at the cost of rising unemployment with 20% of the labour force out of work.

In 1992 the IMF approved a loan package of US$65mn over 15 months; inflation was 6.5% and unemployment rose to 25% but results for 1993 were more positive with public finances and the external accounts showing improvement. The economy grew by 1.0% after 3 years of decline and then by 4% in 1994. Tourism, distribution and construction were the leading growth sectors and unemployment began to decline. A tight budget was set for 1994 and 1995 as both Governments continued austerity policies, although some tax cuts were made.

A small fiscal surplus was recorded in 1995, principally because of increased tax collections as employment rose. However, a deficit was forecast for the 1996/97 fiscal year, based on an estimated 3.5% gdp growth and 2% inflation. Revenues were expected to fall because of a reorganization of the tax system with the introduction of a 15% VAT to replace 11 existing taxes on 1 January 1997. New projects were announced which were expected to boost growth: an expansion of the offshore financial sector, which earned US$150 mn in 1995; a regeneration of Bridgetown, with port expansion, construction of a marina, pedestrian streets, multistorey car parks and market improvements; a renovation and expansion of the state-owned *Hilton Hotel* with the transfer of majority ownership to the private sector. Also started in 1996 was the construction of a marina at Heywoods, near Speightstown, called Port St Charles, with 140 yacht berths and 145 housing untis.

CULTURE

Because Barbados lies upwind from the main island arc, it was hard to attack from the sea, so it never changed hands in the colonial wars of the 17th and 18th centuries. There is no French, Dutch, or Spanish influence to speak of in the language, cooking or culture. People from other islands have often referred to Barbados as Little England, and have not always intended a compliment. Today, the more obvious outside influences on the Barbadian way of life are North American. Most contemporary Barbadians stress their Afro-Caribbean heritage and aspects of the culture which are distinctively 'Bajan'. There are extremes of poverty and wealth, but these are not nearly so noticeable as elsewhere in the Caribbean. This makes the social atmosphere relatively relaxed. However, there is a history of deep racial division. Although there is a very substantial black middle class and the social situation has changed radically since the 1940s and 50s, there is still more racial intolerance on all sides than is apparent at first glance.

Two Barbadian writers whose work has had great influence throughout the Caribbean are the novelist George Lamming and the poet Edward Kamau Brathwaite. Lamming's first novel, *In The Castle Of My Skin* (1953), a part-autobiographical story of growing up in colonial Barbados, deals with one of the major concerns of anglophone writers: how to define one's values within a system and ideology imposed by someone else. Lamming's treatment of the boy's changing awareness in a time of change in the West Indies is both poetic and highly imaginative. His other books include *Natives Of My Person*, *Season Of Adventure* and *The Pleasures Of Exile*.

Brathwaite too is sensitive to the colonial influence on black West Indian culture. Like Derek Walcott (see under St Lucia) and others he is also keenly aware of the African traditions at the heart of that culture. The questions addressed by all these writers are: who is Caribbean man, and what are his faiths, his language, his ancestors? The experience of teaching in Ghana for some time helped to clarify Brathwaite's response. African religions, motifs and songs mix with West Indian speech rhythms in a style which is often strident, frequently using very short verses. His collections include *Islands*, *Masks* and *Rights Of Passage*.

Heinemann Caribbean publish the *A to Z of Barbadian Heritage* which is worth reading. Macmillan publish *Treasures of Barbados*, an attractive guide to Barbadian architecture.

DIVING AND MARINE LIFE

Scuba diving to the reefs or the wrecks around the coast can be arranged with Underwater Barbados, *Coconut Court Hotel*, Hastings, or Carlisle Bay Centre, Bay St, St Michael, T/F 426 0655. West Side Scuba Centre at *Sunset Crest Beach Club*, Holetown, T/F 432 2558; Hightide Watersports, T/F 432 0931, and several others. These companies also offer PADI diving courses, equipment rental and other facilities such as snorkelling. The only BSAC accredited school (also PADI and NAUI courses) is Coral Isle Divers on the Careenage in Bridgetown, T 431 9068, who use a 40-ft catamaran dive boat. The BSAC meets at 0800 on Saturday and Sunday at the *Boatyard Pub* on the waterfront on Bay Street, Bridgetown. They do not hire out equipment but if you have your own they are most welcoming to members from other branches. One of their groups dives for old bottles on a reef just offshore where ships have anchored for some 350 years. There is a recompression chamber at St Anne's Fort, T 427 8819, or tell the operator if there is an emergency.

For those who want to see the underwater world without getting wet, the Atlantis Submarine near the Careenage in Bridgetown (1st floor, Horizon House, McGregor Street), T 436 8929, has day and night dives at US$70, children aged 4-12 half price. The tour starts with a short video and then you go by bus to the deep water port or join the launch at the Careenage. The boat takes about 10 minutes to get to the submarine, sit at the front to be first on the sub, an advantage as then you can see out of the driver's window as well as out of your own porthole. Two divers on underwater scooters join the submarine for the last 15 minutes, putting on a dive show. Booking is necessary, check in half an hour before dive time, whole tour takes 1½ hrs. The Atlantis Seatrec is a reef observation craft with large windows below deck giving you a snorkeller's view of the reefs. There are also video monitors to watch as a diver films the reef.

BEACHES AND WATERSPORTS

There are beaches along most of the S and W coasts. Although some hotels make it hard to cross their property to reach the sand, there are no private beaches in Barbados. The W coast beaches are very calm, and quite narrow, beach erosion is a serious worry and the Government's Coastal Conservation Unit is trying to sort it out. A swell can wash up lots of broken coral making it unpleasant underfoot. The S coast can be quite choppy. The SE, between the airport and East Point, has steep limestone cliffs with a series of small sandy coves with coconut trees, and waves which are big enough for surfing. Be careful on the E side of the island, currents and undertow are strong in places. Don't swim where there are warning signs, or where there are no other bathers, even on a calm day. Bathsheba, on the E coast, is quite spectacular, with wonderful views. Some hotels sell day passes, eg *Hilton*, US$10 pp, for the use of their facilities: pool, showers, deck chairs, etc.

Beach vendors now have a licence, plastic stalls, and a blue and yellow uniform shirt. Unscrupulous cocaine and sex vendors still operate but are more subtle in their approach than in the past.

There are a large number of motor and sailing boats available for charter by the day or for shorter periods. These include *Irish Mist*, T 436 9201, lunchtime or dinner cuisine, US$50, *Station Break*, T 436 9502, *Tiami* and *Spirit of Barbados* catamarans, T 427

7245, F 431 0538, *La Paloma*, T 427 5588, *Cap'n Jack*, T 427 5800, *Calypso Charters*, T 426 7166, *Secret Love*, T 432 1972, lunch and snorkelling US$49 pp, sunset snorkelling cruise US$37.50, *Jolly Jumper*, T 432 7090. *Limbo Lady* has been highly recommended, Patrick and Yvonne Gonsalves take no more than 8 people on their 48-ft yacht and give you a really good day/evening out, with snorkelling, fishing, sunset cruise with delicious canapés, Cava and singing by Yvonne, who plays the guitar, T 420 5418, F 420 3254. Others are moored in the Careenage in Bridgetown, with a telephone number displayed. Most are equipped for fishing and snorkelling, and will serve a good meal on board. Rates and services offered vary widely.

Deep sea fishing can be arranged with *Blue Jay* Charters, T 422 2098 (competitive prices, discounts offered) or *Honey Bea III*, T 428 5344.

Glass-bottomed boats can be hired from several private operators along the W coast. In December, the Mount Gay International Christmas Regatta for yachts is held.

The S coast is good for windsurfing and the International Funboard Challenge is held in March. The best surfing is on the E coast and the Barbados International Surfing Championship is held at the Soup Bowl, Bathsheba, in early November. Contact the Barbados Windsurfing Association at the *Silver Rock Hotel*, Silver Sands, or the Barbados Surfing Association at the *Coconut Court Hotel*, Hastings. Skyrider Parasail, T 435 0570 for parasailing.

SPORTS

Ask the Tourist Office for the Sports and Cultural Calendar, which has lots of information about what is on and who to contact in all possible areas of sport. Contact the National Sports Council, Blenheim, St Michael, T 436 6127, for information on any sport not mentioned below.

Cricket Lots of village cricket all over the island at weekends. A match here is nothing if not a social occasion. For information about the bigger matches at Kensington Oval phone the Barbados Cricket Association, T 436 1397.

Horseracing At the Garrison on Saturdays for most of the year. Again, this is something of a social occasion. The Cockspur Gold Cup Race, held in March, features horses from neighbouring islands. For information on race meetings phone Barbados Turf Club, T 426 3980.

Golf There are four courses, the best and most prestigious of which has traditionally been Sandy Lane, 18 holes, 9 more planned, T 432 2946/432 1311/432 1145. However, a new course at Royal Westmoreland Golf and Country Club, St James, T 422 4653, associated with the *Royal Pavilion* and *Glitter Bay Hotels*, has opened and this will soon have 27 holes spread over 480 acres on a hilly site in St James with views over the W coast. To play here you must be staying at a hotel with an access agreement. Members can use the hotels' beach club facilities 5 minutes' drive away. There are plans to build 350 villas around one of the 9-hole loops, three club houses, a swimming pool and five tennis courts. *Rockley* has no clubhouse and is not highly rated, 9 holes, T 435 7880. *Almond Beach Village*, 9 holes, T 422 4900. The Barbados Open Golf Championship is held in December.

Polo Barbados Polo Club near Holetown, St James, T 432 1802. National and international matches are played at Holders Hill between Sept and March.

Water Polo is played at the Barbados Aquatic Centre, where visitors are welcome to join in practice sessions with the team, which is sponsored by the local beer company, Banks. Confirm practice times, T 429 7946.

Squash *Rockley Resort* has two courts, T 435 7880, Barbados Squash Club, Hastings, 3 courts, T 427 7193, *Casuarina Hotel*, T 428 3600, *Marine House* has three courts.

Tennis The best courts are at *Paradise Beach Hotel*; they are also good at *Royal Pavilion* and *Glitter Bay*. *Paragon*, T 427 2054, *Hilton*, T 426 0200, *Rockley Resort*, T 435 7880, *Sam Lord's*, T 423 7350, *Crane Hotel*, T 432 6220.

Athletics In November 1992 a multi-purpose gymnasium was opened as part of the Sir Garfield Sobers Sports Complex at Wildey, St Michael, T 437 6016. It has facilities for badminton, body-building, boxing, basketball, gymnastics, handball, judo, karate, netball, table tennis, volleyball and weightlifting, with plenty of changing rooms and showers. There are also sauna and massage rooms, a medical room and warm-up/practice area. Adjacent to the complex is the Aquatic Centre, with an Olympic-size swimming pool and tennis courts and there are plans for hockey, football and cricket pitches outside, T 436 2272. The Universal Gym in Hastings is good, with reasonable equipment, aerobic classes and weights at moderate prices.

Motor racing on the circuit in St Philip.

Riding There are 8 riding schools offering beach and/or country rides. Some do not give instruction and cater for pleasure riding only. Congo Road Riding Stables, T 423 6180, one hour ride including lift to and from hotel is US$25, beginners or advanced; also Brighton Stables on W coast, T 425 9381; Beau Geste Stables, St George, T 429 0139, Tony's Riding School, St Peter, T 422 1549, Caribbean International Riding Stables, St Joseph, T 433 1453, Trevena Riding Stables, St James, T 432 6404 and Big C Riding Stables, Christ Church, T 437 4056.

Running The Run Barbados Series is held in December and is comprised of a 10 km race and a marathon. 1993 was the 10th anniversary of the race.

Walking The most beautiful part of the islands is the Scotland District on the E coast. There is also some fine country along the St Lucy coast in the N

and on the SE coast. Walking is straightforward. There is a good 1:50,000 map available from the Public Buildings in Bridgetown, from the museum, in the airport and from some bookstores in town. The Ordnance Survey, Southampton, UK, produces a map of Barbados in its tourist map series, 1:50,000 scale with 1:10,000 inset of Bridgetown. There is a particularly good route along the old railway track, from Bath to Bathsheba and on to Cattlewash. The National Trust, together with the Duke of Edinburgh Award Scheme, T 426 2421, organizes walks at 0600 on a Sunday morning and sometimes at 1530 or 1730 (depending on season) on Sunday afternoon. Details are usually printed in the *Visitor* magazine. Their walk to Chalky Mount in the Scotland District has been recommended.

FESTIVALS

Cropover is the main festival, with parades and calypso competitions over the weekend leading up to Kadooment Day (the first Monday in August), and calypso 'tents' (mostly indoors though) for several weeks beforehand. The celebrations begin with the ceremonial delivery of the last canes on a brightly-coloured dray cart pulled by mules, which are blessed. There is a toast to the sugar workers and the crowning of the King and Queen of the crop (the champion cutter-pilers). The bands and costumes are a pale imitation of what Trinidad has to offer but even Trinidadians now take Barbadian calypso seriously. The big crowd is on the Spring Garden Highway outside Bridgetown Monday afternoon. Baxters Road Mall runs for a couple of weekends beforehand; the road is closed off for fried fish, music and beer. Some related activities take place in July.

The Holetown Festival in February, commemorating the first settlers' landing in February 1627, and the Oistins Fish Festival at Easter, celebrating the signing of the Charter of Barbados and the history of this fishing town, are much less elaborate. There are competitions and a big street party with music goes on until late at night. Many villages will also hold a 'street fair' from time to time.

NIFCA, the National Independence Festival of Creative Arts, is a more serious affair, with plays, concerts and exhibitions in the weeks before Independence on 30 November. The Holders Season, held around Easter, is a fairly new festival started in 1992 with a season of opera, Shakespeare, cabaret and sporting events such as cricket, golf and polo. Performances are staged outdoors at Holders, an old plantation house. Some events are free, such as in 1995 the cricket match between the Holders Hill XI against the John Paul Getty XI, on a tiny pitch where bowlers had to cross a road to run up to the wicket. Pavarotti is scheduled for a 1997 appearance.

BRIDGETOWN

The capital, **Bridgetown**, is on the SW corner of the island. The city itself covers a fairly small area. It is busy, and full of life. There are no really large buildings except the central bank. The suburbs sprawl most of the way along the S and W coasts, and quite a long way inland. It is houses and hotels almost all the way along the coastal strip between Speightstown in the N and the airport in the SE, but many of the suburban areas are very pleasant, full of flowering trees and 19th century coral stone gingerbread villas. There are two interesting areas, downtown Bridgetown with Trafalgar Square on the N side of the Careenage and the historic area at Garrison.

Trafalgar Square has a statue of Lord Nelson, sculpted by Sir Richard Westmacott and predating its London equivalent by 36 years. It has recently been the subject of some controversy as it was thought to link Barbados too closely with its colonial past. There were plans to remove it but instead Nelson was turned through 180° and now no longer looks down Broad Street, the main shopping area. There is a memorial to the Barbadian war dead and the fountain commemorates the piping of water to Bridgetown in 1861. To the N is the Parliament Building. Built in 1872, the legislature is an imposing grey building with red roof and green shutters. Built in gothic style, the clock tower is more reminiscent of a church. You can walk between the buildings (providing you are correctly dressed).

Take the NE exit out of Trafalgar Square along St Michael's Row to reach the 18th century **St Michael's Cathedral**. It has a fine set of inscriptions and a single-hand clock. The first building was consecrated in 1665 but destroyed by a hurricane in 1780. The present cathedral is long and broad, with a balcony. It has a fine vaulted ceiling and some tombs (1675) have been built into the porch. Completed in 1789, it suffered hurricane damage in 1831. If you contine W, you reach **Queen's Park**, a pleasant, restful park just outside the city centre. **Queen's Park House** is now a small theatre and art gallery. There is a small restaurant and bar, which does a good lunch and a buffet on Fridays.

The **Synagogue** is an early 19th century building on the site of a 17th century one, one of the two earliest in the W hemisphere. Built in the late 1660s by Jews fleeing Recife, Brazil, who heard that Oliver Cromwell had granted freedom of worship for Jews and gained permission to settle in Barbados. The tomb of Benjamin Massiah, the famous circumciser of 1782 lies on the left hand side of the graveyard, just inside the entrance. The original synagogue was destroyed in 1831, the present one was dedicated in 1838. Recently painstakingly restored, it is now used for religious services again although some work still needs to be done on the ceiling and cemetery. It is supported by only 16 families now.

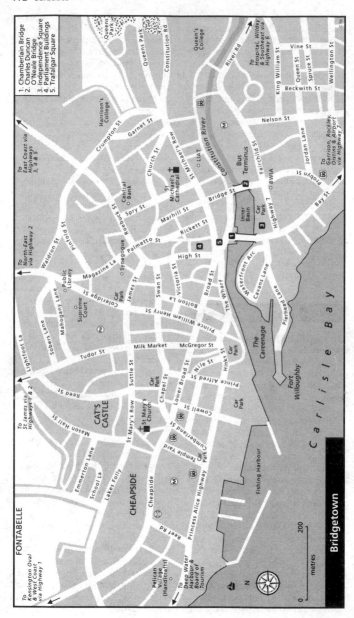

Bridgetown

1. Chamberlain Bridge
2. Charles Duncan O'Neale Bridge
3. Independence Square
4. Parliament Buildings
5. Trafalgar Square

FONTABELLE

To Kensington Oval & West Coast via Highway 1

To St James via Highways 1 & 2

To North-East via Highway 2

To East Coast via Highways 3, 4 & 5

Queen's Park

Constitution Rd

Queen's College

River Rd

To Hospital, Wildey & Southeast via Highway 5

Vine St
Queen St
Spruce St
Wellington St
King William St
Beckwith St

Nelson St

To Garrison, Rockley, Oistins & Airport via Highway 7

Jordan Lane

Harrison's College

Crumpton St

Garnet St

Church St

St Michael's Row

Bus Terminus

Fairchild St

LIAT

Bridge St

Probyn St

Bay St

Central Bank

St Michael's Cathedral

Highway 7

BWIA

Spry St

Roebuck St

Marhill St

Rickett St

Inner Basin

Car Park

Waldron St

Pinfold St

Palmetto St

Synagogue

High St

Magazine La

Public Library

James St

Coleridge St

Car Park

Swan St

Victoria St

Bolton La

Broad St

The Wharf

Waterfront Arc

Cavans Lane

Pierhead Lane

Sobers Lane

Mahogany Lane

Supreme Court

Prince William Henry St

Lightfoot La

Tudor St

Milk Market

McGregor St

Suttle St

Chapel St

Nile St

Hinks St

Car Park

The Careenage

Reed St

Mason Hall St

CAT'S CASTLE

St Mary's Row

St Mary's Church

Temple Yard

Cumberland St

Cowell St

Lower Broad St

Prince Alfred St

Car Park

Car Park

Fort Willoughby

Emmerton Lane

School La

Lakes Folly

CHEAPSIDE

Cheapside

Reef Rd

Princess Alice Highway

Fishing Harbour

Carlisle Bay

Pelican Village (Handicrafts)

To Deep Water Harbour & Board of Tourism

metres
0   200

N

Constitution River

The National Trust

The National Trust runs an Open House programme of visits to interesting private houses on Wed afternoons from Jan to April every year. A National Trust Heritage passport is US$35, which admits you to all 15 National Trust properties and several privately-owned places like Sunbury Plantation House. Mini passports entitle you to entry to 5 sites, US$18. National Trust properties admit children under 12 free if accompanied by a passport holder. You can buy passports from many hotels or from the National Trust Headquarters at Ronald Tree House, 10th Avenue, Belleville, St Michael (T 426 2421/436 9033). The Duke of Edinburgh Award Scheme (Bridge House, Cavans Lane, Bridgetown, T 436 9763) and National Trust joint scheme also arrange early Sunday morning walks to places of historical and natural interest.

The area S of James Street is good for street markets. A whole range of goods can be bought along Swan Street and Boulton Lane, good fruit and vegetables as well as leather goods. Street music is sometimes performed. This is in marked contrast to the large shopping malls and department stores on Broad Street. Here you will find a whole range of sophisticated shops catering for tourists (see **Shopping** below). The Government plans to ban traffic from Broad St as part of a plan to regenerate the city centre. More developments are planned along by the Careenage where old warehouses are being converted into restaurants, discos, smart shops. Multi-storey car parks, a marina and port expansion are also part of the US$25mn project.

Further out, to the S of the Constitution river is **Ronald Tree House** on Tenth Avenue, Belleville (T 426 2421), the headquarters of the Barbados National Trust. Nineteenth century suburban house with furniture, photographs and objets d'art. Useful source of information on historical and natural sites.

The **Harry Bailey Observatory** in Clapham (T 426 1317/422 2394) is open Friday nights 2030-2230. It is in Wildey, not far from Banks Brewery. A chance for northern visitors to look at the Southern hemisphere stars.

The **Mount Gay Visitor Centre** at Brandons, St Michael, does a very good 30-minute tour of the blending and bottling plant, 0900-1600 Mon-Fri, B$10, or a special luncheon tour (T 425 8757), with an exhibition of rum, rum tasting and shop. For their distillery tour, see page 776. *Where the Rum Comes From*, is a guided tour of the **Cockspur West India Rum Refinery** near the deep water port in Bridgetown on the Spring Garden Highway, with rum tasting and steel band entertainment every Wed, US$10, or US$25 with transport and US$40 with transport and traditional food such as coconut bread, plantain and other buffet delicacies.

THE GARRISON AREA

Cross the Careenage by the Charles Duncan O'Neale Bridge (one of the bus terminals and market area are just to the W) and follow Bay Street around the curve of Carlisle Bay. You will pass St Patrick's Cathedral (Roman Catholic), the main government offices with St Michael's Hospital behind it before reaching the historic Garrison area. From here you can visit **Fort Charles** on Needham Point (turn right at the Pepsi plant). The Fort was the largest of the many which guarded the S and W coasts. It now forms part of the gardens of the *Hilton Hotel*. Only the ramparts remain but there are a number of 24 pounder cannons dating from 1824. There is a military cemetery here and the Mobil oil refinery was the site of the naval dockyard. Built in 1805, it was subsequently moved to English Harbour, Antigua. The buildings were then used as barracks before being destroyed in the 1831 hurricane.

Carry on up the hill to the **Garrison Historical Area**, which contains many interesting 19th century military buildings, grouped around the Garrison Savannah. There are numerous buildings surrounding the parade ground, now the 6 furlong race course. These were built out of brick brought as ballast on ships from England. They are built on traditional colonial lines, the design can be seen throughout the Caribbean but also in India. Painted bright colours, some now contain government offices. There are several memorials around the oval shaped race course, for instance in the SW corner, the 'awful' hurricane which killed 14 men and one married woman and caused the destruction of the barracks and hospital on 18 August 1831 and outside the Barbados Museum in the NE corner to the men of the Royal York Rangers who fell in action against the French in Martinique, Les Saintes and Guadeloupe in the 1809/10 campaign.

Across the road is **St Anne's Fort** which is still used by the Barbados defence force. You cannot enter but look for the crenellated signal tower with its flag pole on top. It formed the high command of a chain of signal posts, the most complete of which is at Gun Hill (see below). The long, thin building is the old drill hall. **The Main Guard**, overlooking the savannah, has a nice old clock tower and a fine wide verandah. It has been turned into an information centre and houses exhibits about the West Indian Regiment. The Garrison Secretary of the Regiment, Major Michael Hartland, T 426 0982, is here. Outside is the **National Cannon Collection** which he created, an impressive array of about 30 cannon, some are mounted on metal 'garrison' gun carriages (replaced with wooden ones during action as they were prone to shatter). There are also a number of newer howitzers, dating from 1878. Major Hartland welcomes visitors but he is still creating a Regimental museum, so make an appointment first.

The **Barbados Museum** (T 427 0201/436 1956; Mon-Sat 0900-1700, B$10 for adults, B$5 for children) is housed in the old military prison on the NE corner of the savannah. Based on a collection left by Rev N B Watson (late rector of St Lucy Parish), it is well set out through a series of 10 galleries. It displays natural history, local history (in search of *Bim*), a fine map gallery including the earliest map of Barbados by Richard Ligon (1657), colonial furniture (Plantation House Rooms), military history (including a reconstruction of a prisoners cell), prints and paintings which depict social life in the West Indies, decorative and domestic arts (17-19th century glass, china and silver), African artefacts, a children's gallery and one to house temporary exhibits. The museum shop has a good selection of craft items, books, prints, and cards. Library available for research purposes. The *Cafe Musée* under the trees in the museum courtyard is a delightful place for a drink or for lunch.

Nearby there are stables for the race course. The Barbados Turf Club holds meetings on Saturdays during three seasons (January to March, May to October and November to December). The biggest one being the Cockspur Gold cup held in March. Races go clockwise. A good place to watch is from the Main Guard. At other times, it is used as a jogging course for people in the mornings, when you can see the horses being exercised, or on weekday evenings. There is also rugby, basketball, etc, played informally in the Savannah, go and see what is going on on Sunday afternoons. There is a small children's playground in one corner. Later, at night, prostitutes parade here.

EXCURSIONS

Being the most easterly island and extremely difficult to attack, there are few defensive forts on Barbados. Instead the great houses of the sugar growing plantocracy give the island its historic perspective and most of its tourist attractions. Many parish churches are also impressive buildings. The island is not large but it is easy to get lost when driving. There are deep gullies cut in the coral limestone which is the surface rock over most of the island. These are often full of wildlife and plants but make travelling around very confusing. It sometimes helps to remember that the island is divided into 11 parishes named after 11 saints. A good map is essential. The bus service is cheap and efficient and recommended even for families with small children.

THE WEST COAST

The mass development of the W coast was carried out only recently. The beaches are easily eroded and can be covered with broken coral after storms. Pre-war, the area was regarded by the local Bajans as unhealthy. They preferred to go for their holidays to the E coast. Nowadays, the road N of Bridgetown on Highway 1 is wall to wall hotels. Highway 2a runs parallel inland and goes through the sugar cane heartland, with small villages and pleasant views.

Holetown today is a thoroughly modern town but was the place where the earliest settlers landed on 17 February 1627. The Holetown monument commemorates Captain John Powell claiming the island for England. Initially named Jamestown, it was renamed Holetown because of a tidal hole near the beach. It was quite heavily defended until after the Napoleonic Wars. Little trace of the forts can be seen now. Well worth visiting is **St James Church**. Originally built of wood in 1628, it was replaced by a stone structure in 1680. This building was extended 20 feet W in 1874 when columns and arches were added and the nave roof raised. You can see the original baptismal font (1684) under the belfry and in the N porch is the original bell of 1696. Many of the

original settlers are buried here (although the oldest tombstone of William Balston who died in 1659 is in the Barbados Museum). Church documents dating to 1693 have been removed to the Department of Archives. It was beautifully restored between 1983-86.

On the beach at the back of the church is the post office and also the **Folkestone Marine Museum** and **Underwater Park**. Here you can snorkel in a large area enclosed by buoys. The reef is not in very good condition but there are some fish. The small museum is open Mon-Fri 1000-1700. Slide shows are held about every hour. Entrance B$1. Snorkelling equipment (eg mask and snorkel B$5) for hire as are glass bottomed boats which will take you over the reef to two small wrecks further down the coast opposite the *Gold Palm Hotel*. A diving platform about 100 yards offshore allows you to snorkel over the wrecks. Expect to pay B$20 pp (children B$10) but be prepared to bargain. There are toilets and a shower here.

The **Portvale Sugar Factory** (best in the crop season, February to May) and **Sugar Machinery Museum** inland has an exhibition on the story of sugar and its products. Open 0900-1700, Mon-Sat, US$2.50, children half price, T 432 1100 to check.

Follow the coast road and glimpse the sea at Gibbes and Mullins Bays to reach **Speightstown** where William Speight once owned the land. An important trading port in the early days, when it was known as Little Bristol. Speightstown (pronounced Spitestown, or Spikestong in broad dialect) is now the main shopping centre for the N of the island. There are several interesting old buildings and many two-storey shops with Georgian balconies and overhanging galleries (although sadly many have been knocked down by passing lorries). The Lions Club building (Arlington) is 17th century, built very much on the lines of an English late mediaeval town house. No longer occupied, it is rapidly becoming derelict, but well worth a look. In 1989, the Barbados National Trust launched an appeal for funds to help restore the town.

In 1996 construction started on a new marina at Heywoods Beach just N of Speightstown, to be known as Port St Charles. The US$60mn project will include 145 residential units, restaurants, a yacht club and watersports as well as have a capacity for 9 mega-yachts and 140 yachts on completion in 4 years.

ST LUCY

The road N of Speightstown is mercifully free of buildings and there is a good sandy beach on **Six Men's Bay**. Go through Littlegood Harbour and notice the boat building on the beach. The jetty you can see is at Harrison Point. You are now entering the almost unspoilt (apart from the Arawak Cement Plant) parish of St Lucy. Almost any of the roads off Highway 1b will take you to the N coast, at first green and lush around Stroud Point but becoming more desolate as you approach North Point. The NW coast, being slightly sheltered from the Atlantic swells, has many sandy coves (for example Archers Bay). The cliffs are quiet and easy to walk. You may spot turtles swimming in the sea.

The **Animal Flower Cave** at **North Point** is a series of caverns at sea level which have been eroded by the sea. The animals are sea anemones. There are various 'shapes' in the rock which are pointed out to you. The main cave can be closed due to dangerous seas, so T 439-8797 around 0930 to enquire. Entrance B$3 (B$2 if you cannot see full cave). The floor of the cave is very stony and can be slippery. Following the rocky coast, turn into the semi-abandoned *North Point Surf Resort* (park outside the wall to avoid being charged for parking, the buildings are half ruined now, and there is an enormous empty swimming pool) where you can walk around the Spout, which has lots of blow holes and a small, rather dangerous beach.

Good walks along the cliffs can be enjoyed, for instance from River Bay to Little Bay along the Antilles Flat, but beware as there is no shade and there are shooting parties during the season. If driving, several back roads go through the attractive communities of Spring Garden and St Clements. At Pie Corner you can rejoin the coast and visit **Little Bay**. This is particularly impressive during the winter months with the swell breaking over the coral outcrops; lots of blowholes. Note the completely circular hole on the N edge of the Bay. If you climb through this natural archway in the cliff, there is a big, calm pool, just deep enough to swim, between the cliffs and a line of rock on which the enormous waves break and send up a wall of spray. Wear shoes to stop your feet getting cut to pieces on the sharp rock.

At Paul's Point is a popular picnic area. If the ground looks wet park at the millwall by the Cove Stud Farm as it is easy to get bogged down. You will get a good view of Gay's Cove with its shingle beach (safe to swim in the pools at low tide) and beyond it the 240-feet high Pico Teneriffe, a large rock (almost in the shape of Barbados and named by sailors who thought it looked like the mountain on Teneriffe in the Canaries) on top of a steeply sloping cliff. The white cliffs are oceanic rocks consisting of myriad tiny white shells or microscopic sea creatures. The whole of the coast to Bathsheba is visible and it is easy to see the erosion taking place in Corben's Bay. Indeed you get an excellent impression of the Scotland District, where the coral limestone has been eroded. The whole of this coast between North and Ragged Points has been zoned, no further development will be allowed along the seafront.

The **Mount Gay Rum Distillery** is reached off the road between the St Lucy church junction and Alexandra. There are tours Monday-Friday at 1100 and 1400. They also have a visitor's centre in St Michael (see page 773). This makes an alternative to Cockspur's West Indian Rum Refinery.

THE SCOTLAND DISTRICT

Heading S, you get excellent views from Cherry Tree Hill. Just to the NW is **St Nicholas Abbey** which is approached down a long and impressive avenue of mahogany trees. Dating from around 1660, it is one of the oldest domestic buildings in the English-speaking Americas (Drax Hall, St George, open once a year under the National Trust Open House programme, is probably even older). Three storied, it has a façade with three ogee-shaped gables. It was never an abbey, some have supposed that the 'St' and 'Abbey' were added to impress, there being lots of 'Halls' in the S of the island. Visitors are given an interesting tour of the ground floor and a fascinating film show in the stables behind the 400-year-old sand box tree. Narrated by Stephen Cave, the present owner and son of the film maker, its shows life on a sugar plantation in the 1930s. You will see the millwall in action and the many skilled workers from wheelwrights to coopers who made the plantation work. The importance of wind is emphasized. If the millwall stopped the whole harvest came to a halt as the cane which had been cut would quickly dry out if it was not crushed straight away. The waste was used to fuel the boilers just as it is today in sugar factories. There is a collection of toy buses and lorries in the stables.

Going back down the steep Cherry Tree Hill you come to the National Trust-owned **Morgan Lewis Mill**, a restored millwall with original machinery. You can climb to the top of it. Note the 100-foot tail, this enabled the operators to position the mill to maximize the effect of the wind. It is on a working farm. Open Monday-Friday 0800-1600, entrance B$2. On the flat savannah at the bottom of the hill is a cricket pitch, a pleasant place to watch the game at weekends.

The **Barbados Wildlife Reserve**, established with Canadian help in 1985, is set in 4 acres of mature mahogany off Highway 2. It is an excellent place to see lots of Barbados green monkeys close up. Most of the animals are not caged, you are warned to be careful as you wander around the shady paths as the monkeys can bite. They have a collection of the large red-footed Barbados tortoise. Also (non-Barbadian) toucans, parrots and tropical birds, hares, otters, opossums, agoutis, wallabies, porcupines, and iguanas. You can observe pelicans and there is a spectacled caiman (alligator) in the pond. The primate research centre helps to provide farmers with advice on how to control the green monkeys who are regarded as a pest. The animals are fed near it at about 1600. Café and shop. Open daily 1000-1700. Admission B$10, children half price. T 422-8826. Can be reached by bus from Bridgetown, Holetown, Speightstown or Bathsheba. The centre has also developed a nature trail in the neighbouring Grenade Hall Forest, ask for further details. An early 19th century signal station next to Grenade Hall Forest has been restored and is open for visitors, daily 1000-1700, admission B$10, children half price. The wonderful panoramic view gives you a good idea of its original role in the communications network.

Farley Hill House, St Peter (T 422 3555), is a 19th century fire-damaged plantation house; a spectacular ruin on the other side of the road from the Wildlife Reserve, set in a pleasant park with views over the Scotland District. There is a large number of imported and native tree species planted over 30 acres of woodland. Open daily 0830-1800. US$1 per vehicle.

From Farley Hill it is possible to walk more or less along the top of the island as far as Mt Hillaby, through woods and then canefields. However, it helps to know where you are going as the paths have a mind of their own and losing them can be uncomfortable. You will see plenty of monkeys on the way and good views.

THE ATLANTIC PARISHES

The five-mile East Coast Road, opened by Queen Elizabeth on 15 February 1966 affords fine views. From Belleplaine, where the railway ended, it skirts Walker's Savannah to the coast at Long Pond and heads SE to Benab, where there is **Barclays Park**, a good place to stop for a picnic under the shady casuarina trees. A walk up Chalky Mount has been recommended for the magnificent views of the E coast, easily reached at the end of the bus line from Bridgetown. If you ask locally for the exact path you are likely to be given several different routes. Walk down through the meadows to Barclays Park for a drink when you come down. There is no paved road. Staff in the café will know times of buses to either Bathsheba or Speightstown, only one a day. The East Coast Road continues through Cattlewash, so named because Bajans brought their animals here to wash them in the sea, to Bathsheba.

The tiny hamlet of **Bathsheba** has an excellent surfing beach (see **Watersports** above). Guarded by two rows of giant boulders, the bay seems to be almost white as the surf trails out behind the Atlantic rollers. Surfing championships are often held here. A railway was built in 1883 (but closed in 1937) between Bridgetown and Bathsheba. Originally conceived as going to Speightstown, it actually went up the E coast to a terminus at Belleplaine, St Andrew. The cutting at My Lady's Hole, near Conset Bay in St John is spectacular, with a gradient of 1:31, which is supposed to have been the steepest in the world except for rack and pinion and other special types of line. The railway suffered from landslides, wave erosion, mismanagment and underfunding so that the 37 miles of track was in places in very bad condition. The crew would sprinkle sand on the track, the first class passengers remained seated, the second class walked and the third class pushed.

Above the bay at Hillcrest (excellent view) are the **Andromeda Gardens**. Owned by the Barbados National Trust, the gardens contain plants from all over Barbados as well as species from other parts of the world. There are many varieties of orchid, hibiscus and flowering trees. Open every day. Admission B$10. The *Hibiscus Café* at the entrance is a useful place to stop for refreshment. The *Atlantis Hotel* is a good place for lunch especially on Sunday (1300 sharp) when an excellent buffet meal containing several Bajan dishes is served. Almost an institution and extremely popular with Bajans, so book ahead.

From Bathsheba you can head inland to **Cotton Tower signal station** (also National Trust owned but not so interesting as Gun Hill). Then head S to Wilson Hill where you find Mount Tabor Church and **Villa Nova**, another plantation Great House (1834), which has furniture made of Barbadian mahogany and beautiful gardens. It was owned by the former British Prime Minister, Sir Anthony Eden, and until 1994 was part of the National Trust's heritage trail. However, it has now been bought by Swiss investors who are converting it into a 5-star country resort hotel, due to open winter 1996, T 436 1710, F 436 1715. You can continue from here via Malvern along the scenic **Hackleton's Cliff** (allegedly named after Hackleton who committed suicide by riding his horse at full gallop over the cliff) or via Sherbourne (**D** *Coconut Inn*, 2-room guest house run by Geoff and Terry Browne, who also do excellent Bajan lunches) to Pothouse, where **St John's Church** stands with excellent views over the Scotland District. Built in 1660 it was another victim of the great hurricane of 1835. There is an interesting pulpit made from six different kinds of wood. You will also find the curious grave of Fernando Paleologus "descendant of ye imperial line of ye last Christian emperors of Greece". The full story is in Leigh Fermor's *The Traveller's Tree*.

At the satellite tracking station turn off to **Bath**. Here you will find a safe beach, popular with Barbadians and a recreation park for children. It makes a good spot for a beach barbecue and a swim.

Codrington College is one of the most famous landmarks on the island and can be seen from Highway 4b down an avenue of Cabbage Palm trees. It is steeped in history as the first Codrington landed in Barbados in 1628. His son acted as Governor for three years but was dismissed for liberal views. Instead he stood for parliament and was elected speaker for nine years. He was involved in several wars against the French and became probably the wealthiest man in the West Indies. The third Codrington succeeded his father as Governor-General of the Leeward islands, attempted to stamp out the considerable corruption of the time and distinguished himself in campaigns (especially in taking St Kitts). He died in 1710, a batchelor aged 42, and left his Barbadian properties to the Society for the Propagation of the Gospel in Foreign Parts. It was not until 1830 that Codrington College, where candidates could study for the Anglican priesthood, was established. From 1875 to 1955 it was associated with Durham University, England. Apart from its beautiful grounds with a fine avenue of Royal Palms, a huge lily pond (flowers close up in the middle of the day) and impressive façade, there is a chapel containing a plaque to Sir Christopher Codrington and a library. There are plans to develop it as a conference centre. You can follow the track which drops down 360 feet to the sea at the beautiful Conset Bay. You can take the Sargeant Street bus as far as Codrington College, then walk 7 miles back along the Atlantic Coast to Bathsheba.

At **Ragged Point** is the automatic East Point lighthouse standing among the ruined houses of the former lighthouse keepers. There are good views N towards Conset Point, the small

Culpepper island, and the S coast. Note the erosion to the 80-foot cliffs caused by the Atlantic sweeping into the coves.

THE CENTRE

NE of Holetown and reached from St Simon's Church are **Turners Hall Woods**, a good vantage point. Some think that the wood would have been very similar to the one covering the island before the English arrived. This 50-acre patch of tropical mesophytic forest has never been clear-felled (although individual trees were often taken out). You can walk over the steep paths here and see many species, ranging from the sandbox tree to Jack-in-the-box and the 100-foot locust trees supported by massive buttresses. The island's first natural gas field was here and the main path through the wood is the remains of the old road.

On Highway 2, take the Melvin Hill road just after the agricultural station and follow the signs to the **Flower Forest**, a 50-acre, landscaped plantation, opened in 1983 with beautifully laid out gardens. Dropping downhill, the well-maintained paths afford excellent views over the valley to the E coast. To the W you can see Mount Hillaby, at 1,116 feet the island's highest point (see above for walking from Farley Hill). It too contains species not only from Barbados but also from all over the world, they are beautifully arranged with plenty of colour all year round. There is a *Best of Barbados* shop, cafeteria and toilets. Good information sheet. Open daily 0900-1700, entrance B$12, children half price, T 433 8152.

Roads in this area are often closed by landslides and circuitous routing may be necessary.

Close by and to the S on Highway 2 is **Welchman Hall Gully**, a fascinating walk through one of the deep ravines so characteristic of this part of Barbados. You are at the edge of the limestone cap which covers most of the island to a depth of about 300 feet. There is a small car park opposite the entrance (despite the sign to the contrary). Maintained by the National Trust, a good path leads for about half a mile through six sections, each with a slightly different theme. The first section has a devil tree, a stand of bamboo and a judas tree. Next you will go through jungle, lots of creepers, the 'pop-a-gun' tree and bearded fig clinging to the cliff (note the stalactites and stalagmites); a section devoted to palms and ferns: golden, silver, macarthur and cohune palms, nutmegs and wild chestnuts; to open areas with tall leafy mahogany trees, rock balsam and mango trees. At the end of the walk are ponds with lots of frogs and toads. Best of all though is the wonderful view to the coast. On the left are some steps leading to a gazebo, at the same level as the tops of the cabbage palms. Open daily, 0900-1700, B\$5, children B\$2.50.

Harrison's Cave nearby has an impressive visitors' centre which has a restaurant (fair), shop and a small display of local geology and Amerindian artefacts. You are taken into the cave on an electric 'train'. The visit takes about 20 minutes and you will see some superbly-lit stalactites and stalagmites, waterfalls and large underground lakes. There is a guide to point out the interesting formations and two stops for photo-opportunities. Interesting as it is, it is all rather overdone, you even have to wear hard hats and serviettes on your head despite claims that the caves are totally stable. Open daily 0900-1600, admission B\$15,

children half price, T 438 6640. The bus from Bridgetown to Chalky Mount stops near Harrison's Cave and the Flower Forest.

If you take Highway 2 heading to Bridgetown you will pass Jack-in-the-Box gully, part of the same complex of Welchman Hall Gully and Harrison's Cave. Coles Cave (an 'undeveloped' cave nearby, which can easily be explored with a waterproof torch or flashlight) lies at its N end.

At **Gun Hill** is a fully restored signal tower. The approach is by Fusilier road and you will pass the Lion carved by British soldiers in 1868. The road was built by Royal Scot Fusiliers between September 1862 and February 1863 when they were stationed at Gun Hill to avoid yellow fever. The signal station itself had its origins in the slave uprising of 1816. It was decided that a military presence would be maintained outside Bridgetown in case of further slave uprisings. It was also intended for advance warning of attack from the sea. The chain of six signal stations was intended to give very rapid communications with the rest of the island. The hexagonal tower had two small barrack rooms attached and would have been surrounded by a pallisade. They quickly lost importance as military installations but provided useful information about shipping movements. Informative guides will explain the workings of the signal station and point out interesting features of the surrounding countryside.

The Easter Rebellion

The 1816 Easter Rebellion was an uprising by slaves who thought (incorrectly) that William Wilberforce had introduced a bill in the English parliament granting slaves their freedom. It was thought by the slaves that the Barbados plantation owners were denying them this freedom. Despite destroying a large acreage of cane fields, no owners or their families were killed and the uprising was quickly crushed by the West Indian Regiment. Several hundred slaves were killed in battle or hanged afterwards, including the best-known leader, an African called Bussa, and Washington Francklyn, a free man of mixed race who was thought, probably erroneously, to have planned the rebellion. 123 slaves were exiled to Sierra Leone.

You will not necessarily get the same story from all the guides. Entrance B$5 (children B$2.50), guide book B$2.

THE SOUTH COAST

The area around Six Cross Roads was where the Easter Rebellion of 1816 took place (see box). You can visit two of the great houses. Turn N at Six Cross Roads for **Sunbury Plantation**. Some 300 years old, the house is elegantly furnished in Georgian style, much of it with mahogany furniture, and you can roam all over it as, unusually, there is access to the upstairs private rooms. In the cellars, you can see the domestic quarters. There is a good collection of carriages. Open 1030-1630 every day. There is a restaurant in the courtyard.

Take the road to Harrow and Bushy Park to reach **Oughterson Plantation House** and the **Barbados Zoo Park**. Although not as extensive as Sunbury, the entrance to the Wildlife Park takes you through the ground floor of the house which is quite interesting. There is a self-guided nature trail. The zoo is very small but has expanded from a bird garden and more animals have slowly been added. Vikki, a small monkey, is a great favourite with children as she will stroke their hands. You are given bread and encouraged to feed the ducks.

Sam Lord's Castle on the SE coast is the site of the *Marriott Hotel*. It is high on the list of tourist attractions because of the reputation of Sam Lord who reputedly lured ships onto Cobbler's Reef where they were shipwrecked. There is supposed to be a tunnel from the beach to the castle's cellars to facilitate his operation. The proceeds made him a wealthy man although the castle was supposed to have been financed from his marriage to a wealthy heiress. The castle is not particularly old or castle-like, being in fact a regency building. Unfortunately the rooms are poorly lit making it difficult to appreciate the fine mahogany furniture or the paintings. Note the

superb staircase, you are not allowed upstairs. Wander down to the cove where there is a good example of a turtlecrawl, a salt water pond enclosed by a wall. Here turtles were kept alive until wanted for the kitchen. Today the *Marriott Hotel*, in conjunction with the Barbados Wildlife park, keeps a few hawksbill turtles, a shark and a congor eel. There is a B$7 entrance charge (children free) even though the hotel reception forms part of the two rooms open to the public.

Crane Bay, SW of Sam Lord's Castle, is worth a detour. It is a pleasant cove overlooked by 80-foot cliffs.

Information for travellers

BEFORE TRAVELLING

● **Documents**

Visitors from North America, Western Europe, Commonwealth African countries, Argentina, Venezuela, Colombia, and Brazil need a passport but no visas. Visitors from most other countries are usually granted a short stay on arrival, and tourist visas are not necessary. Officially, you must have a ticket back to your country of origin as well as an onward ticket to be allowed in. Immigration officers do check.

State the maximum period you intend to stay on arrival. Overstaying is not rec if you wish to re-enter Barbados at a later date. Extending the period of stay is possible at the Immigration Office, Careenage House on the Wharf in Bridgetown (T 426 011 9912) but costs US$12.50 and is fairly time consuming. When visiting the Immigration Office, which is open from 0830-1630, you will need to take your passport and return ticket. Tickets are inspected quite carefully.

You will need an accommodation address on arrival, they do not check your reservation but if you say you do not know where you will be staying, you will be sent to the back of the queue and 'helped' to select a hotel (which may be more expensive than you wanted) at least for one night.

Work permits are extremely difficult to obtain and the regulations are strictly enforced.

MONEY

● **Currency**

The currency unit is the Barbados dollar, which is pegged at B$2.00 for US$1.00. Banks will of course charge a small commission on this rate. Many tourist establishments quote prices in US dollars, if you are not careful a hotel room may end up costing twice as much as you bargained for. Rates offered by the banks for currencies other than the US dollar, sterling, and Deutschmark are not good. Credit cards are accepted in the large resorts, but their use is not widespread.

GETTING THERE

AIR

From North America: BWIA and American Airlines fly from New York and Miami daily, American Airlines also flies daily from Philadelphia, San Juan and Puerto Rico; Air Canada flies from Toronto and Montreal.

From Europe: British Airways and BWIA have several flights a week from London (including Concorde on Sat, 4 hrs flight time, leaves Heathrow 0930, arrives Barbados 0945). BWIA and Condor have weekly flights from Frankfurt, BWIA flies weekly from Zurich, Martinair flies from Amsterdam and LTU from Dusseldorf. There are also lots of charter flights which are usually cheaper and rec if you are staying only on Barbados.

From South America: Liat, BWIA and Surinam Airways from Georgetown, Guyana; Surinam Airways from Paramaribo, Suriname. There is no longer a direct flight from Venezuela, but there is a daily BWIA connecting flight through Port of Spain.

From Caribbean Islands: Connections with Caribbean islands are good, from Antigua (Liat, British Airways, BWIA), Dominica (Liat, Cardinal Airlines), Fort-de-France, Martinique (Liat), Grenada (Liat), Kingston, Jamaica (BWIA, with connecting flight from Havana with Cubana), Pointe-à-Pitre, Guadeloupe (Liat), Port of Spain, Trinidad (BWIA, Liat, Surinam Airways), St Lucia (Liat, British Airways, Helenair), St Maarten (Liat, BWIA), St Vincent (Liat), San Juan, Puerto Rico (Liat, American Airlines), Tobago (Liat, BWIA) and Tortola, BVI (Liat).

Check different airlines for inter-island travel, the Trinidad route is particularly competitive, British Airways often has good offers between Barbados, Antigua, St Lùcia and Trinidad and a comfortable plane. Air tickets bought in Barbados, and tickets bought elsewhere for journeys starting in Barbados, have VAT added. It is usually worth organizing ticketing at the start of your journey so that Barbados appears as a stopover rather than as the origin for any side trips you make. Note that flights to Barbados are heavily booked at Christmas and for Cropover.

SEA

Windward Lines Limited run a weekly passenger/car/cargo ferry service: Trinidad – St Vincent – Barbados – St Lucia – Barbados – St Vincent – Trinidad – Guiria (or every other week to Pampatar, Margarita), arriving Fri 1900 from St Vincent, departing 2230, coming back from St Lucia on Sun or Mon and leaving again for St Vincent Sun or Mon. Information from Windward Agencies, T 431 0449, or in Trinidad, Global Steamship Agencies Ltd, Mariner's Club, Wrightson Road, PO Box 966, Port of Spain, T (809) 624-2279, F 627-5091. To Venezuela is especially good value as you see several islands and have somewhere to sleep on the way. Restaurant on board. Fare Barbados-Trinidad round trip US$90, one way US$60.

Barbados is not well served by small inter-island schooners. Information and tickets from the shipping agents, Eric Hassell & Son, 2nd floor, Citibank building, Bridgetown (T 436 6102). If you buy a one-way ticket, you will need to show passport and onward ticket when paying for your passage. You may be able to get a passage to another island on a yacht, ask at the harbour or at the *Boatyard* on Carlisle Bay. There is no marina yet in Barbados. All boat needs are met by the *Boatyard*. Mooring facilities are available at the Shallow Draft next to the Deep Water Harbour, or there are calm anchorages in Carlisle Bay.

There are several companies running mini-cruises based on Barbados. Caribbean Safari Tours (T 427 5100, F 429 5446), organize day trips to St Lucia, Dominica, Grenada, Martinique and the Grenadines; they also do 2 and 3 night packages to these islands and to Trinidad, Tobago, St Vincent and Caracas. Some of these are quite competitively priced. The cruise ship passenger tax is to be raised.

ON ARRIVAL

● Airports
The airport is modern and well equipped. Clearing immigration can be a problem and it can take an hour to clear a 747. If three 747s arrive together expect delays. There is a Liat connection desk before immigration. There is a helpful Tourism Authority office, Barbados National Bank (very slow), (bureau de change in the arrivals and departure areas is open from 0800-2200), a post office, car hire agencies and quite a wide range of shops (good for stocking up on film or alcohol even if just going on a day trip) including an Inbound Duty Free Shop (very useful, saves carrying heavy bottles on the plane). *The Voyager* restaurant is fairly expensive. Taxis stop just outside customs, and there is a bus stop just across the car park, with buses running along the S coast to Bridgetown, or (over the road) to the *Crane* and *Sam Lord's Castle*. But you may have a long wait for a bus, and they often pass full in the rush hour.

● Airlines
The Liat office is at St Michael's Plaza, St Michael's Row (T 436 6224). BWIA (T 426 2111); British Airways (T 436 6413), are all on Fairchild Street. American (T 428 4170) and Cubana (T 428 0060) have offices at the airport.

● Banks
Barclays Bank, the Royal Bank of Canada, Canadian Imperial Bank of Commerce, Scotiabank, Caribbean Commercial Bank, Barbados Mutual Bank and Barbados National Bank all have offices in Bridgetown. The first 5 also have branches in the main S and W coast tourist centres. Opening hours for banks are 0800-1500 Mon to Thur, and 0800-1200 and 1500-1700 on Fri. Caribbean Commercial Bank in Hastings and Sunset Crest is also open on Sat from 0900 to 1200. The Barbados National Bank has a branch and a bureau de change at the airport; the latter is open from 0800-2200, but inaccessible unless you are actually arriving or departing. Barclays Bank and Royal Bank of Canada in Bridgetown both have cash machines which you can use with a credit card after hours.

● Embassies and consulates
British High Commission, Lower Collymore Rock, St Michael, PO Box 676, T 436 6694, F 436 5398. Canadian High Commission, Bishop Court Hill, St Michael, T 428 3550. Germany, Banyan Court, Bay Street, St Michael, T 427 1876; USA, Consular Section, Alico Building, Cheapside, Bridgetown, T 436 4950; Brazilian Embassy, 3rd floor, Sunjet House, Fairchild Street, T 427 1735; Venezuelan Embassy, El Sueño, Hastings, Christ Church, T 435 7619; France, Hastings, Christ Church, T 435 6847.

● Official time
Atlantic Standard Time, 4 hrs behind GMT, 1 ahead of EST.

● Public holidays
New Year's Day, 21 January (Errol Barrow Day), Good Friday, Easter Monday, 1 May, Whit Monday, Kadooment Day (first Monday in August), United Nations Day (first Monday in October), Independence Day (30 November), Christmas Day; Boxing Day.

● Religion
Barbadians are a religious people and although the main church is Anglican, there are over 140 different faiths and sects, including Baptists, Christian Scientists, Jews, Methodists, Moravians and Roman Catholics. Times of services can be found in the *Visitor*.

● Security
Bridgetown is still much safer than some other Caribbean cities but crime rates have increased. Local people are now more cautious about where they go after dark and many no longer go to Nelson Street or some other run-down areas. Baxters Road, however, is generally quite safe although the former attracts prostitutes while the latter attracts cocaine addicts (paros). Unlike Jamaica, where crime is concentrated mainly in Kingston, crime has become prevalent in Barbados where tourists congregate, particularly at night. Care should be taken not to go for romantic walks along deserted beaches and to watch out for pickpockets and bag snatchers in tourist areas. Families with small children care for at night rarely notice any crime and have commented on how secure they felt on Barbados. If hiring a car, watch out for people who wash the vehicle unasked and then demand US$5. Police have patrols on beaches and plain clothes officers around some rural tourist attractions.

● Shopping
Prices are generally high, but the range of goods available is excellent. Travellers who are going on to other islands may find it useful to do some shopping here. If coming from another Caribbean island you can bring fresh fruit and vegetables, but no mangoes from St Lucia, Dominica or Martinique, no fruit from Latin America, no soft fruit from Guyana or Trinidad (you can bring pineapples and citrus), no bananas or plantains from Grenada.

The best stocked supermarket is JB's Mastermart in Wildey. Big B in Worthing and Supercentre in Oistins and Holetown are also good, and are easier to reach by public transport. Food is not cheap but generally most things are available and good quality except items like tinned pâté or good quality salami, which you might like to bring with you. Supermarkets shut on Sun. Big B Supermarket in Worthing is open 0800-1900 Mon-Tues, 0800-2000 Wed-Sat, photocopying available.

Duty-free shopping is well advertised. Visitors who produce passport and air ticket can take most duty-free goods away from the store for use in the island before they leave, but not camera film or alcohol. Clothing for example is significantly cheaper duty-free, so don't go shopping without ticket and passport. But cameras and electrical goods may be much cheaper to buy in an ordinary discount store in the USA or Europe than duty free in Barbados. A new duty-free shopping centre for cruise ship passengers opened in Bridgetown in 1994.

The *Best of Barbados* shops (plus Walkers' Caribbean World, Mount Gay Visitor Centre Shop and Great Gifts) sell high quality items made or designed in Barbados, including paintings and designs by Jill Walker, pottery, basketwork, island music and dolls. Locations include *Sandpiper Inn*, *Sam Lord's Castle*, Mall 34, Broad Street, St Lawrence Gap, Flower Forest, Andromeda Gardens, Quayside Centre, Rockley. Other good displays of craft items are at Pelican Village on the Princess Alice Highway near the harbour, where you can watch artisans at work. Origins on the Careenage in Bridgetown is a gallery with well-designed but expensive clothing, jewellery and ceramics. There is also a street market in Temple Yard where Rastafarians sell leather and other goods.

Street vendors are very persistent but generally friendly even when you refuse their wares.

Bookshops are much better stocked than on other islands. The Cloister on the Wharf probably has the largest stock. The Book Place on Probyn Street specializes in Caribbean material and has a good secondhand section. Brydens and Cave Shepherd also have a good selection. Also Roberts Stationery, The Book Shop, The Bookstop.

Camera repairs Skeetes Repair Service on Milkmarket is a small workshop which repairs most brands of camera. Louis Bailey in Broad Street is well-equipped but more expensive. Professional Camera Repair, Bolton Lane, Bridgetown, T 426 7174.

Film processing Graphic Photo Lab in Worthing is quick and efficient. Rec for slides and enlargements. Be prepared to wait a day or 2 for slides wherever you go.

● **Voltage**
120 volts (American standard) and 50 cycles per second (British standard). Some houses and hotels also have 240-volt sockets for use with British equipment.

ON DEPARTURE

● **Departure tax**
There is a departure tax of B$25, not payable if your stay is for less than 24 hrs.

ACCOMMODATION

● **Hotels**

Price guide

L1	over US$200	L2	US$151-200
L3	US$101-150	A1	US$81-100
A2	US$61-80	A3	US$46-60
B	US$31-45	C	US$21-30
D	US$12-20	E	US$7-11
F	US$4-6	G	up to US$3

Most of the accommodation offered is very pleasant to stay in, if not particularly cheap. VAT of 7.5% is levied on hotel accommodation.

Super Luxury Most of these are on the W coast. The newest development is the 288-room *Almond Beach Village*, on the old *Heywoods Resort* site, with its sister resort, *Almond Beach Club* 4 miles away. Rebuilt at a cost of US$15mn, the two all-inclusive resorts cost US$410-530d in winter and US$315-450 in summer. The *Almond Beach Village* is on 30 acres of land with a 9-hole golf course, 1 mile of beach, 9 pools, 4 restaurants, shops, watersports centre, nightclub and children's play areas, families or couples welcome, T 422 4900, F 422 0617. *Sandy Lane*, US$545-950 summer, rises in winter to US$720-2,000 MAP, is Trust House Forte, extensively renovated in 1991 and quite nice of its type. Has a golf course. Watch out for extras on top of the astronomical room rate, golf, honeymoon packages available (T 432-1311, F 432 2954). *Glitter Bay*, US$365-525 winter, US$195-345 summer EP, (T 422 5555, F 422 3940), and *Royal Pavilion*, US$475-520 winter, US$485 summer EP (T 422 5555, F 422 3940), are newer and just as smart, next to each other and under the same Pemberton management. One is 'Spanish Colonial Style', the other a pink palace. Perhaps better value to stay elsewhere

and visit for a drink or afternoon tea, but well worth looking at, the guests as spectacular in some cases as the (faultless) interior design and landscaping. Guests here are offered special green fees and preferred tee-off times, at the Royal Westmoreland Golf Club (see **Sports** above). St James Beach Hotels has 4 beachfront properties within 5 miles, guests may use the facilities of all 4 and there is a free water taxi between them: *Colony Club*, 98 colonial-style rooms and suites, US$325-475d winter, US$260-330d summer, MAP, in 7 acres of palms, ponds and free form pool with swim up bar, T 422 2335, F 422 0667; *Crystal Cove*, 88 rooms and suites, US$305-455d winter, US$240-315 summer, MAP, also with pools and gardens, swim up bar through waterfall, T 432 2683, F 432 8290; *Tamarind Cove*, 168 rooms each with 2 beds, US$345-535d winter, US$270-350d summer, MAP T 432 1332, F 432 6317; *Coconut Creek*, 53 rooms with 2 beds, US$295-345d winter, US$220-255d summer, MAP, pool, tennis. *Settlers Beach*, St James, T 422 3062, F 422 1937, US$550-600d winter, US$240-260d summer EP, no children in Feb, pool, on beach, and *Treasure Beach*, Paynes Bay, T 432 1346, F 432 1094, US$325-750 winter, US$135-300 summer EP, both Unique Hotels, in UK T 0800-373742. *Coral Reef Club*, St James (T 422 2372, F 422 1776), US$310-1065 winter MAP, US$180-620 summer EP, member of Elegant Resorts of Barbados and Prestige Hotels, London, very highly regarded; also in St James, under same management, *Sandpiper Inn*, T 422 2251, F 422 1776, US$460-820 winter, US$280-430 summer EP, family-run, with award-winning restaurant. Also on the W coast, good but not as luxurious, **L1-L3** *Kings Beach Hotel*, at Mullins Bay, T 422 1690, F 422 1691 or 0932 849 462 in the UK or 800 223 1588 in the USA, facilities for children and the handicapped.

Convenient for Bridgetown L1-L3 *Barbados Hilton*, good location on a nice beach with gentle surf, good pool, concrete structure showing its age but due to undergo a 2-year US$8mn refurbishment, expansion and privatization, good buffet breakfast and lunch, (T 426 0200, F 436 8946); **L1-L3** *Grand Barbados*, EP rooms and suites (T 426 0890, F 436 9823); an all-inclusive **L1** *Sandals Royal Barbados Resort*, Paradise Beach, is due to open mid-1997 with 310 rooms, 5 restaurants, all facilities inc state of the art fitness centre; **L3-A3** *Blue Horizon*, Rockley, large hotel with pool, bar, restaurant, 100 yards from beach across main road, EP with kitchenette, 10 mins from Bridgetown, T 435 8916, F 435 8153; **L2-A2** *Ocean View Hotel*, S coast, the island's oldest hotel, designated of historic interest by the National Trust, very old fashioned, with mahogany furniture and a dining terrace overlooking the sea but no beach (T 427 7821, F 427 7826), mediocre food.

Near the Airport A3-B *Shonlan Inn Airport Hotel*, T 428 0039, F 428 0160, 16 rooms, 11 bathrooms, some rooms with kitchenette, very mixed reports, noisy, nowhere near a beach, but only a mile from the terminal, although the taxi fare makes it no cheaper than a guest house further away. **L1-L3** *Crane Beach*, fairly near the airport, but definitely a taxi ride away, spectacular cliff top setting, good beach, and good pool, tennis, luxury prices and usually fairly quiet with only 18 rooms, but they are planning an extra 250 units (T 423 6220, F 423 5343); **L3-A3** *Silver Sands Resort*, Christ Church, (T 428 6001, F 428 3758), 20 mins drive from airport, on the sea at South Point, rooms spacious and well-equipped, good service, food dull, good beach but take care swimming, waves strong and high, good for surfing but children and weak swimmers should use the pool.

Good value, rec are **L2-A3** *Sandridge*, 1 mile from Speightstown, good-sized rooms or family apartments with cooking facilities, N-facing balconies overlook pool, friendly staff and management, watersports free for guests, good value barbecue evenings, excellent for families, T 422 2361, F 422 1965. **A3-B** *Travellers Palm*, 265 Palm Ave, Sunset Crest, St James (T 432 6666/7722), 1-bedroom apartment with kitchen, roomy apartments, pool, 10 mins walk to the beach, close to the underwater sea park. N of Bridgetown in Prospect is **A3-A2** *Chrizel's Guest House*, 2 min walk to beach, friendly, helpful, rec, run by Hazel Rice-Harper, T 438 0207, and in the USA Christine Harden, T (718) 712-9567, rooms with private bath or apartments. **A1-B** *Tower* in Paradise Village, Black Rock, N of Bridgetown on Princess Alice Highway, 1-bedroom apartment, or 2 bedrooms, a/c, fridge, very pleasant (T 424 3256). **A2-B** *The Nook Apartments*, Dayrells Road in Rockley has 4 excellent 2-bedroom apartments with pool, maid service, clean, secure, convenient for shops and restaurants, highly rec, discounts for airline staff and Caricom residents (T 427 6502). **B** *Tree Haven*,

Rockley, a short bus ride from the centre of town, excellent studio apartments opp the beach, very clean, helpful and friendly owner, T 435 6673. **B** *Bona Vista*, on a side road off Golf Club Road, rec, T 435 6680. Along the S coast are **L3-A3** *Woodville Apartments*, Worthing, T 435 6694, F 435 9211, studio apartment, 1-bedroom or, 2-bedroom. **L3-A3** *Worthing Court Apartment Hotel*, Worthing, T 435 7910, F 435 7374, studios or 1-bedroom connecting apartments, very pleasant, discounts for airline staff, food not so good. **B-C** *Summer Place on Sea*, run by George de Mattos, Rydal Water, Worthing (T 435 7424), rooms basic but clean, 2 rooms with cooking facilities available, very pleasant and good value, right on the beach, friendly, bus to/from airport, get off at Star Discount Supermarket, but both always seem to be booked up well in advance. Ring ahead. Lots of pubs, nightlife and other small hotels in the area. **B-C** *Rydal Waters Guest House*, 3rd Ave in Worthing, repeatedly rec but reported burnt down 1996 (T 435 7433), Chinese restaurant next door, quite good but expensive. **L2-B** *Chateau Blanc Apartments*, T 435 7518, F 435 7414, 50m from *Rydal Waters*, good value studios, well-equipped but old kitchen facilities, friendly management, also has 1/2 bedroomed apartments on beach front. **B-C** *Shells Guest House*, First Avenue, Worthing, T 435 7253, with breakfast, 6 rooms with fan, 5 bathrooms, TV room, excellent food in restaurant, rec. **D** *Set Set's Guest House*, on corner of 4th Ave, Worthing, small, friendly, family atmosphere, shared bathroom, use of kitchen, clean, rec, T 435 7334, Tony Vanderpool; **L1-A1** *Casuarina Beach Club*, Dover, T 428 3600, F 428 1970, on beach, pool, tennis. **A3-C** *Fred La Rose Bonanza*, Dover, studio, one or 2 bedrooms, helpful, quite convenient but not too clean, T/F 428 9097. There are several other cheap places to stay in this area, all within walking distance of each other. **A3-B** *Meridian Inn*, Dover, T 428 4051/2, F 420 6495, studios, kitchenettes, balconies, daily maid service, beach, credit cards. All these are well served by the S coast bus routes. **C** *Pegwell Inn*, Oistins (T 428 6150), good for shops and airport buses, not brilliant for beaches. **A3-B** *Miami Beach Apartments*, Enterprise Drive, Christ Church, T/F 428 5387, kitchen, 1-2 bedroom, living room, veranda, TV, phone, 2 min from small, clean beach, 3 min to main road and minibus route. **A2-B** *Romans Beach Apartments*,

Enterprise, studios, T 428 7635, friendly, comfortable, on beautiful beach.

Away from the main tourist areas A2-B *Atlantis*, Bathsheba, MAP, T 433 9445, and **L3-A1** *Kingsley Club*, Cattlewash, T 433 9422, F 433 9226, both on the E coast, with a spectacular setting. Both do good food, pleasant, family-run hotels but the former is a little run down, owned by Enid Maxwell, who started the hotel with her late father in the 1940s. **L1-A3** *Edgewater Hotel*, Bathsheba, T 433 9900, F 433 9902, pool overlooking sea, quiet and out of the way, popular with Venezuelans. **L1-L3** *Sam Lord's Castle*, Marriott's fun-factory (T 423 7350, F 423 5918). Lots of new stuff round a cliff-top plantation house with some fairly spurious pirate legends attached. Good Sun buffet, 3 swimming pools, and outdoor bars where they serve the drinks in plastic cups.

● **Villa rental**

Agents and property managers include Realtors Limited, Riverside House, River Road, St Michael, T 426 4900, F 426 6419; Bajan Services Ltd, Seascape Cottage, Gibbs, St Peter, T 422 2618, F 422 5366. Weekly rates for a small villa on the beach start at US$800 in the summer but can be twice the price in the winter, plus 8% tax. If staying for a while, try the small ads in the *Advocate* and *Nation*. Ordinary apartments to let can be rented furnished for about US$400 a month which could work out cheaper even if you do not stay that long. If possible get a Bajan who knows the island well to help you.

● **Youth hostel**

The YMCA has a **D-E** hostel at Pinfold St, Bridgetown, T 426 3910/1240 which can accommodate 24 people, dormitory beds or single rooms, breakfast B$6.50, lunch B$7.50.

FOOD AND DRINK

● **Food**

Fresh fish is excellent. The main fish season is December to May, when there is less risk of stormy weather at sea. Flying fish are a speciality and the national emblem, 2 or 3 to a plate. Dolphin (dorado, not a mammal in spite of its name) and kingfish are larger *steak-fish*. Snapper is excellent. *Sea eggs* are the roe of the white sea urchin, and are delicious but not often available. Fresh fish is sold at the fish markets in Oistins, Bridgetown and elsewhere in the late afternoon and evening, when the fishermen come in with their catch.

Cou-cou is a filling starchy dish made from breadfruit or corn meal. *Jug-jug* is a Christmas speciality made from guinea corn and supposedly descended from the haggis of the poor white settlers. Pudding and souse is a huge dish of pickled breadfruit, black pudding, and pork.

● **Drink**

Barbados rum is probably the best in the English-speaking Caribbean, unless of course you come from Jamaica, or Guyana or ... It is worth paying a bit extra for a good brand such as VSOP or Old Gold, or for Sugar Cane Brandy, unless you are about to drown it in Coca Cola, in which case anything will do. A rum and cream liqueur, Crisma, has now been introduced, popular in cocktails or on the rocks. Malibu, the rum and coconut drink, also comes from Barbados. *Falernum* is sweet, slightly alcoholic, with a hint of vanilla. *Corn and oil* is rum and falernum. *Mauby* is bitter, and made from tree bark. It can be refreshing. *Sorrel* is a bright red Christmas drink made with hibiscus sepals and spices; it is very good with white rum. Water is of excellent quality, it comes from inland springs.

● **Restaurants**

Barbados has a very wide range of places to eat. There is a good listing in the *Visitor*. Good places include:

Low prices fast food from Chefette chain, Pizza House chain or Del's chain. *Chicken Barn*, Broad Street and Rockley (big portions if you're hungry), *China Garden* (Bay Street). For those who like that sort of thing there are several *Kentucky Fried Chickens*, although for vegetarians the salad bars here and at the *Chefettes* have been rec. In St Lawrence Gap is the *Duke of Edinburgh Pub*. In Worthing on the main road opp the Plantation supermarket, the *Roti Hut* is cheap but nasty, nothing like rotis on Trinidad. *Granny's* in Oistins is more traditional and good value. *The Hotel School* in Marine House (T 427 5420) does an excellent lunch at certain times of year, and a smarter evening meal on Tues. Also drinks and snacks in the evening when they are running courses for bar staff. You could also try the canteens in the Light and Power Company on Bay Street and at Spring Gardens which are open to the public and do a huge traditional lunch. Good reports about *Kingsley Inn*, Cattlewash and *Little Edge*, Bathsheba (T 433 9900), for breakfast and lunch. *Mangoes*,

Holetown, on balcony overlooking beach, view spoilt by enormous satellite dish, better bet is small beach bar next door, delicious flying fish and good club sandwiches. There is a good cheap café in Mall 34, just behind Atlantis Submarine office in Bridgetown. The *Pirate's Bar* at the Animal Flower Caves has the best value coke on the island, B$1.75 for 1/2 litre. Most sightseeing attractions have some kind of food available, eg Harrison Cave, fair snacks.

Middle price range *Waterfront Café* on the Careenage, interesting food, plenty to look at and a good social centre in the evenings. *39 Steps*, T 427 0715, on the coast road near the Garrison is well run and lively, lunchtimes and evenings, imaginative blackboard menu and choice of indoors or balcony, opened by Josef, previously of restaurant of that name, see below, popular, so book at weekends. There are some good beach bars, which do light meals and sometimes have a lively atmosphere; *Carib Beach Bar* at Worthing, near *Rydal Waters Guest House*, has inexpensive meals and drinks, barbecue and music twice a week, excellent rum punches, happy hour 1700-1800 Mon-Fri, great fun even if you are not eating; even better is the Fri night barbecue at *Stowaways Beach Bar* at the *Sheringham Hotel* in Maxwell; *Sandy Banks* in Rockley; *The Boatyard* in Bay Street, full of divers and friends at weekends, food unimportant. In Holetown, *Rumours Beach Bar* is a nice place to sit and drink, but do not bother to eat there; *Garden Grill* has an imaginative menu and is good value; *Coach House*, Paynes Bay, good value meals and bar snacks, sometimes have live bands in the evenings. *Nico's* wine bar, partially washed away by hurricane but rebuilt in 1996 by *Tamarind Cove*, who now own it; *Café Calamari*, Sunset Crest, St James, good but does not accept Amex despite notice; the *Beach Club*, Sunset Crest, on some nights has set price meal, entertainment and unlimited drinks, worth visiting. *Mango Café* in Speightstown is good value; *Mullins Beach Bar* just S of Speightstown has good menu (very good pepperpot and jerk chicken) and worth a visit to see the *trompe l'oeil* monkey murals. *The Ship/Captain's Carvery*, St Lawrence, has a good lunchtime buffet; in the evening there is usually a big crowd in the bar and often a live band. *Boomers* in St Lawrence Gap has quite good fast-food type dishes in a restaurant-type setting. *Sam's Lantern* and the *Pot and Barrel*, good inexpensive pizzas, just outside *Sam Lord's Castle* are worth a try. *Barclays Park*

Beach Bar on the E coast does light meals (closed after 1900).

More expensive *The Treasure Beach Hotel* has the best food on the island, but at US$50 a head. *Kokos* (T 424 4557) has an interesting menu and a waterfront setting on the W coast. They will also do a good vegetarian meal if they have advance warning. *Brown Sugar* (T 426 7684), Aquatic Gap, Bay Street, St Michael, buffet lunch B$22, dinner, regional specialities, rather overrated; *Reid's* (T 432 7623) on the W coast (quite capable of producing an already-opened bottle of wine at the table). *Josef's* (T 435 6541/428 3379) on St Lawrence Gap, small, delightful, is well used by Barbadians, you need to book well ahead, arrive early and have pre-dinner drinks on the lawn with the sea lapping the wall a few feet below you. *Pisces* (T 428 6564), much larger, also on St Lawrence Gap, has some excellent and original fish dishes, an excellent vegetarian platter and a perfect waterfront setting; *David's*, also on waterfront, in Worthing, very good with better service and friendlier, reasonable prices. *Ile de France* in Worthing is French managed and very good. Another fish restaurant is *Fisherman's Wharf* (T 436 7788), upstairs, 'the best shrimp roti ever', get there early or wait hours for a table, on the Careenage in Bridgetown. *Da Luciano's* (T 427 5518) is a good Italian restaurant. *Luigi's*, Dover Woods, Christ Church, T 428 9218, run by Miles and Lisa Needham, Italian cuisine, reservations preferred. In Prospect, N of Bridgetown, *The Rose & Crown* has been rec, seafood, lobster, Bajan cuisine, T 425 1074. Also good: *La Cage aux Folles*, St James, but expensive and rather pretentious; *Carambola*, St James; *Schooner* and *Golden Shell* in *Grand Barbados*. *Putters on the Green*, Sandy Lane Golf Club, T 432 2694, delicious local 'Bajan platter', good value, lovely outlook onto greens, rec; *The Fathoms*, Paynes Bay, St James, T 432 2568, always good, especially the oriental lobster stirfry, good value, beautiful at night in gardens overlooking beach under shade of large mahogany tree, open all day every day; *La Maison*, Holetown, T 432 1156, award winning restaurant in beautiful setting on beach, gourmet but rather pretentious, US$20-40 main course for dinner; *The Mews*, 2nd St, Holetown, T 432 1122, quite expensive but superb food, Austrian chef cooks mix of local and French dishes, very pretty house, tables on balcony or interior patio, rec; *The Cliff*, Derricks, St James, T 432 1922, worth the prices for a glimpse of the décor, stunning desserts, attractive and delightful meal.

Generally, eating out in Barbados is not cheap. Buffets are good value. Unlimited food for a fixed price, usually lunchtime only, certain days only. Try *Hilton, Colony Club* (buffet by the beach on Sun B$25) or **Sam Lord's**. *Atlantis Hotel* in Bathsheba has an enormous Sun buffet, which is the place to try for traditional Barbadian cooking at its best (filling). Get up early and do a National Trust Sun morning walk to work up an appetite.

GETTING AROUND

AIR TRANSPORT
● **Helicopters**
For those who want to make a lot of noise buzzing round the island, Bajan Helicopters do tours from US$65/20 mins, US$115/30 mins right round the coastline. The heliport is near the deep water harbour at Bridgetown, T 431 0069.

LAND TRANSPORT
● **Motoring**
The island is fairly small (just over 21 miles from N to S) but it can take a surprisingly long time to travel from A to B as the rural roads are narrow and winding. Note that a new Adams Barrow Cummins highway has been built from the airport to a point between Brighton and Prospect, N of Bridgetown. This road (called the ABC, or industrial access highway) skirts the E edge of the capital, giving access by various roads into the city.

Drivers need a visitor's driving permit from Hastings, Worthing, or Holetown police stations (cost US$5). You will need this even if you have an International Driving Licence. Car hire companies usually sort it out for you. Petrol costs B$1.64 per litre. The speed limit is 55mph.

● **Car hire**
Car hire is efficient and generally reliable. There is a car hire company stand at the airport outside Arrivals, but they are often fully booked. Costs range upwards from B$100 per day for an open Mini Moke (not rec in the rainy season). Small cars are often cheaper. Weekly rates work out lower. Sunny Isle Motors, Dayton, Worthing, T 435 7979, car hire B$147/day or B$522/week, collision damage waiver B$20/day, B$70/week. Stoutes Car Rentals (T 435 4456/7, F 435 4435) are particularly helpful, and will arrange to meet you at the

airport if you telephone in advance, minimokes B$100/day, B$435/week, small car B$110/day, B$530/week, Suzuki B$150/day, CDW B$15/day, B$70/week. L E Williams (T 427 1043) has slightly lower rates for some vehicles. Regency Renta-a-Car, 77 Regency Park, Christ Church, T 427 5663/0909, F 429 7735, B$80-125/day, B$400-560/week, free pick up and delivery. Other companies are listed in the Yellow Pages. There are often discounts available and tourist magazines frequently contain 10% vouchers.

● **Bicycles and motorcycles**
It is also possible to hire a light motorcycle or a bicycle. Fun Seekers, Rockley Main Road, T 435 8206, have motor scooters B$58/day, B$298/week, bicycles B$17/day, B$63/week. Deposit B$200 on scooter, B$100 on bicycle.

● **Buses**
Buses are cheap and frequent, but also crowded and unreliable. Prices were raised in mid-1995 but no details were available as we went to press. There is a flat fare which will take you anywhere on the island. Around Bridgetown, there are plenty of small yellow privately-owned minibuses and route taxis with ZR numberplates; elsewhere, the big blue buses (exact fare required or tokens sold at the bus terminal) belong to the Transport Board. Private companies tend to stick to urban areas while the public buses run half empty in rural areas. Almost all the routes radiate in and out of Bridgetown, so cross-country journeys are time-consuming if you are staying outside the city centre. The main Fairchild Street bus terminal, serving the S coast, is clean and modern. Other terminals at Lower Green and Princess Alice Highway serve the N and centre of the island. During the rush hour, all these terminals are chaotic, particularly during school term. Terminals for minibuses and route taxis are close to the bus terminals (River Road for S coast, Cheapside for W, others by Treasury building on Careenage). Don't rely on a bus to the airport (Route 12 to *Sam Lord's Castle*) if you have a plane to catch as this route is notorious, although reportedly better than it used to be. On most routes, the last bus leaves at midnight and the first bus at 0500.

However, travelling by bus can be fun. There are some circuits which work quite well; for example:
1. Any S coast bus to Oistins, then cross country College Savannah bus to the E coast, then direct bus back to Bridgetown.

2. Any W coast bus to Speightstown, then bus back to Bathsheba on the E coast, then direct bus back to Bridgetown.

Out of town bus stops are marked simply 'To City' or 'Out of City'. For the S coast ask for Silver Sands route.

● **Taxis**

Taxis are expensive. There are plenty at the airport, the main hotels, and in Bridgetown. There are standard fares (which were raised mid-1995, no details as we went to press) These are displayed just outside "arrivals" at the airport, and are also listed in the *Visitor* and the *Sunseeker*. Fares are quoted also by mile or kilometre (the latter slightly cheaper) but there are no taxi meters. Up to 5 people can travel for one fare. You may have to bargain hard for tours by taxi but always agree a fare in advance. Vehicles which look like route taxis but with ZM numberplates, are taxis plying for individual hire, and will charge accordingly. **VIP limo services** (T 429 4617) hire a vehicle with driver for a whole-day tour at a cost of US$150 for up to 4 persons.

COMMUNICATIONS

● **Postal services**

The General Post Office Headquarters is in Cheapside, Bridgetown and there are District Post Offices in every parish. Collections from red post boxes on roadsides. Local postal rates are B$0.35. Airmail rates to North America B$0.90, to Europe B$1.10 and the West Indies B$0.70. There is an express delivery service of 48 hrs to London and New York. A Philatelic Bureau issues first-day covers 4 times a year.

● **Telecommunications**

The international code, 809, is to be phased out by 15 January 1997 and replaced by 246, which came into use in July 1996. Calls from a pay phone cost 25 cents for 3 mins. Otherwise local calls are free. Many business places will allow you to use their telephone for local calls. International calls can be made from most hotels or (more cheaply) from Barbados External Telecommunications (Wildey). Telexes and Faxes can also be sent from and received by BET's office by members of the public. BET has a public office on the Wharf in Bridgetown for international calls, and telex. Phone cards are available for B$10, 20, 40, 60 from phone company offices, Cave Shepherd or Super Centre supermarkets; a cheaper way of making overseas calls than using hotel services,

and can be used on most English-speaking islands except Trinidad, Jamaica, Guyana, Bahamas.

MEDIA

● **Newspapers**

The Advocate, which also publishes *The Sunday Advocate* and *Sunseeker* tourist magazine; *The Nation* (publisher also of *Sun on Saturday*, *Sunday Sun* and *The Visitor* tourist weekly); *Caribbean Contact*, irregularly published by the Caribbean Conference of Churches. *Caribbean Week*, a newspaper covering the whole of the Caribbean, is published in Barbados, rec.

● **Radio**

CBC Radio, medium wave 900 kHz; Voice of Barbados, medium wave 790 kHz; BBS, FM 90.7 MHz; Yess-Ten 4, FM 104.1 MHz; Radio Liberty, FM 98.1 MHz; FAITH 102 FM and Rediffusion Star Radio (Cable).

ENTERTAINMENT

● **Cinemas**

There are 2 cinemas in Bridgetown and a drive-in not far from the S coast. Fairly second-rate selection of features.

● **Dances**

For something less glossy and more Bajan, it might be worth trying one of the dances which are advertized in the *Nation* newspaper on Fri. People hire a dance hall, charge admission (usually B$5), provide a disco, and keep the profits. There are very few foreigners, but the atmosphere is friendly, and the drinks a lot cheaper than in the smarter nightclubs. Unfortunately, there have been a few fights at 'Dub' fêtes and they are no longer as relaxed as they were.

● **Rumshops**

Baxters Road in Bridgetown is the place to try. The one-roomed, ramshackle, rumshops are open all night (literally), and there's a lot of street life after midnight, although you might get pestered by cocaine addicts. Some of the rumshops sell fried chicken (the *Pink Star* is rec, it has a large indoor area where you can eat in peace and the place also has clean lavatories) and there are women in the street selling fish, seasoned and fried in coconut oil over an open fire. Especially rec if you are hungry after midnight. The Government plans to upgrade Baxters Road as a tourist attraction.

If you drink in a rumshop, rum and other drinks are bought by the bottle. The smallest size is a mini, then a flask, then a full bottle. The shop will supply ice and glasses, you buy a mixer, and serve yourself. The same system operates in dances, though prices are higher; night clubs, of course, serve drinks by the glass like anywhere else. Wine, in a rumshop, usually means sweet British sherry. If you are not careful, it is drunk with ice and beer.

● **Nightclubs**
There are quite a selection. Most charge US$10 for entry. It's worth phoning in advance to find out what is on offer. There are live bands on certain nights in some clubs, and on other nights drinks may be included in the cover charge. Most do not get lively until almost midnight, and close around 0400. Some have a complicated set of dress codes or admission rules, which is another reason for phoning ahead.

After Dark, St Lawrence Gap, recently redecorated, huge selection at the bar, very lively. *Frontline* on Cavans Lane in Bridgetown is another but lacks adequate fire exits and attracts a rough crowd. *The Warehouse*, across the road has reopened after a fire and has a pleasant open air balcony to cool off, it gets overcrowded, particularly Mon when entry covers drinks, and Thur. Others are *Harbour Lights* (lots of tourists and expats, open air on the beach, local and disco music, crowded on Wed, entry covers drinks, Fri, Sat) and *Septembers* on Bay Street (lots of Barbadians). *The Boatyard* is the sailor's pub in front of the anchorage at Carlisle Bay, Bay Street. *The Ship Inn* in St Lawrence has a big outdoor area and is often packed, especially at weekends and when there is a live band. The beach bars can be lively (see listings above), but pick your night. Cheap bars in St Lawrence Gap are *Harry's* and *Colonnade*. At *Shakey's Pizza Parlour* in Rockley they have a Karaoke sing-along machine nightly from 2100.

● **Party cruises**
The *Jolly Roger* and *Bajan Queen* (T 436 6424) run 4-hour daytime and evening cruises along the W coast to Holetown, near the Folkestone Underwater Park (where the fun and games take place) from the deepwater harbour. The drinks are unlimited (very). There is also a meal, music, dancing, etc, US$52.50 for the dinner cruise. On daytime cruises, there is swimming and snorkelling.

● **Shows**
The *Visitor* has a fairly full listing. Some of the better ones are: *The Off Off Off Broadway Revue*, Ocean View Hotel. Hollywood music with a twist. *Barbados By Night*, cabaret dinner show with energetic dancing at the *Plantation Restaurant and Garden Theatre*, Wed-Fri, with fire eating and limbo dancers. *1627 And All That*, Sherbourne Conference Centre, Thur, 1830, colourful show, bar, hors d'oeuvres, buffet dinner, tour of 17th century market place and cultural village, steel band, complimentary transport, T 428 1627, 429 6016 to book. At the museum, *Now Museum, Now You Don't* and on Thur, *Trouble in Paradise*, a murder mystery at St Ann's Garrison.

● **Theatres**
There are several good semi-professional theatre companies. Performances are advertized in the press. It is usually wise to buy tickets in advance. Most people dress quite formally for these performances.

TOURIST INFORMATION

● **Local tourist office**
The Barbados Tourism Authority has its main office in Harbour Road, Bridgetown (PO Box 242, T 427 2623/4, F 426 4080). There are also offices at the deepwater harbour (T 426 1718) and the airport (T 428 0937). The BTA publishes a useful annual Sports and Cultural Calendar, which gives information on what to see throughout the year and the addresses of sporting organizations. Two good sources of information are *Visitor* and the *Sunseeker*, published weekly and distributed free by Barbados's 2 daily newspapers. *Ins and Outs of Barbados*, also free, is published annually, a glossy magazine with lots of advertising and distributed by hotels. *Exploring Historical Barbados*, by Maurice Bateman Hutt, is quite good but perhaps slightly out of date as it was published in 1981.

● **Tourist offices overseas**
UK: 263 Tottenham Court Road, London W1P 0LA, T 0171-636 9448/9, F 637 1496. **USA**: 800 Second Avenue, New York, NY 10017, T 212-986 6516/8 or toll-free 800-221 9831, F 212-573 9850; 3440 Wilshire Boulevard, Suite 1215, Los Angeles, CA 90010, T 213-380 2198/9, toll free 800-221 9831, F 213-384 2763. **Canada**: 5160 Yonge Street, Suite 1800, North York, Ontario M2N GL9, T 416-512 6569-71 or toll free 800-268 9122, F 416-512 6581. **Germany**: Neue Mainzer Strasse 22, D-60311 Frankfurt/Main, T 069 23 23 66, F 069 23 00 77. **Sweden**: Target Marketing

of Scandinavia, Kammakargatan 41, 11124 Stockholm, T (8) 11 3613, F (8) 20 6317. **France**: c/o Caraibes 102, 102 Ave des Champs- Élysées, 75008 Paris, T 45 62 62 62, F 40 74 07 01.

The Barbados Embassy in Caracas (Quinta Chapaleta, 9a Transversal, Entre 2 y 3 Avenidas, Altamira, T 582-39 1471, F 32 3393) can also provide tourist information.

● **Local travel agents**

Bus tours L E Williams (T 427 1043, has a sign up in the bus: 'no 10% service charge is paid with the tour price', heavy pressure selling of tapes, drinks limited from bar), Bartic tours (T 428 5980), Sunflower Tours (T 429 8941), International Tour Services (T 428 4803), Bajan Tours (T/F 437 9389, cheaper and better value than some, no pressure on tipping) and Blue Line (T 423 9268) do round-the-island tours for US$25-55, including entrance fees to sites visited. Longer tours generally include lunch at the *Atlantic Hotel* in Bathsheba. A criticism of the tours with some companies is that it can take 1½ hrs to pick up everyone from hotels, depending on who has booked, and those further north do not get the full tour through Bridgetown and Holetown. If there are more than 4 of you, it is cheaper and more flexible to take VIP tours in a limousine with Shelly Fern.

● **Maps**

Ordnance Survey Tourist Maps include Barbados in the series, 1:50,000 scale with inset of Bridgetown 1:10,000.

Trinidad and Tobago

TRINIDAD, the most S of the Caribbean islands, lying only seven miles off the Venezuelan coast, is one of the most colourful of the West Indian islands. It is an island of 1,864 square miles, traversed by two ranges of hills, the N and S ranges, running roughly E and W, and a third, the central range, running diagonally across the island. Apart from small areas in the northern, forested range which plunges into the sea on the N coast, of which the main peaks are Cerro del Aripo (3,083 feet) and El Tucuche (3,072 feet), all the land is below 1,000 feet. The flatlands in central Trinidad are used for growing sugar cane. There are large areas of swamp on the E and W coasts. About half the population lives in the urban E-W corridor, stretching from Chaguaramas in the W through Port of Spain to Arima in the E. Trinidad is separated from the mainland of South America by the Boca del Dragón strait in the NW (Dragon's Mouth) and Boca del Serpiente in the SW (Serpent's Mouth, both named by Columbus).

HORIZONS

Tobago (116 square miles) is only 21 miles by sea to the NE. It is 26 miles long and only nine miles wide, shaped like a cigar with a central 18-mile ridge of hills in the N (the Main Ridge, highest point 1,890 feet) running parallel with the coast. These NE hills are of volcanic origin; the SW is flat or undulating and coralline. The coast itself is broken by any number of inlets and sheltered beaches.

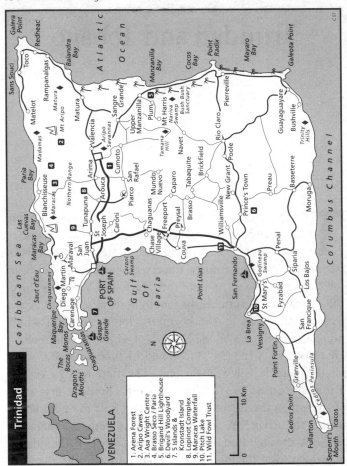

Trinidad

VENEZUELA

Caribbean Sea

Atlantic Ocean

Gulf of Paria

Columbus Channel

Galera Point
Redhead
Sans Souci
Toco
Balandra Bay
Rampanalgas
Matelot
Madamas
Mt Aripo
Matura
Matura Bay
Manzanilla Bay
Point Radix
Cocos Bay
Mayaro Bay
Galeota Point
Paria Bay
Northern Range
Blanchisseuse
Maracas
Valencia
Sangre Grande
Manzanilla
Upper Manzanilla
Mt Harris
Bush Bush Sanctuary
Nariva Swamp
Pierreville
Las Cuevas Bay
Maracas Bay
Arima
Arouca
San Rafael
Aripo Savannas
Cumuto
Tamana Hill
Navet
Rio Claro
Guayaguayare
Bushville
Trinity Hills
St Joseph
Tunapuna
Piarco
Mundo Nuevo
Caparo
Tabaquite
Brickfield
Poole
Preau
Basseterre
Maraval
San Juan
Caroni
Chaguanas
Chase Village
Freeport
Pleysal
Brasso
New Grant
Prince's Town
Moruga
PORT OF SPAIN
Caroni Swamp
Couva
Williamsville
Penal
Diego Martin
Carenage
Point Lisas
San Fernando
Godineau Swamp
Siparia
Chaguaramas
Gaspar Grande
The Bocas
Monos
Dragon's Mouths
Maqueripe Bay
Saut d'Eau
La Brea
Vessigny
St Mary's
Fyzabad
Los Bajos
San Francique
Point Fortin
Granville
Cedros Point
Fullarton
Icacos
Serpent's Mouth
Cedros Peninsula

1. Arena Forest
2. Aripo Caves
3. Asa Wright Centre
4. Brasso Seco / Paria
5. Brigand Hill Lighthouse
6. Devil's Woodyard
7. 5 Islands &
   Kronstadt Island
8. Lopinot Complex
9. Maracas Waterfall
10. Pitch Lake
11. Wild Fowl Trust

10 Km
0

The population is concentrated in the W part of the island around Scarborough. There are small farms, but the main ridge is forested and quite wild. The climate is generally cooler and drier, particularly in the SW, than most parts of Trinidad.

Trinidad has one of the world's most cosmopolitan populations. The emancipation of the slaves in 1834 and the adoption of free trade by Britain in 1846 resulted in far-reaching social and economic changes.

To meet labour shortages over 150,000 immigrants were encouraged to settle from India, China and Madeira. Of today's population of approximately 1,265,000, about 40% are black and 40% East Indian. The rest are mixed race, white, Syrian or Chinese. French and Spanish influences dominated for a long time (Catholicism is still strong) but gradually the English language and institutions prevailed and today the great variety of peoples has become a fairly harmonious entity, despite some political tension between blacks and those of East Indian descent. Spanish is still spoken in small pockets in the N mountains and French patois here and there. Catholics are still the largest religious group but Hindus are catching up fast. The Anglican Church and Methodists are also influential. There are many evangelical groups. Spiritual Baptists blend African and Christian beliefs; the women wear white robes and head ties on religious occasions. They can be seen performing the sea ceremony on the coast to the W of Port of Spain late on Sunday nights. Most East Indians are Hindu, some are Muslim, others have converted to Christianity, particularly Presbyterianism (Canadian Presbyterian missionaries were the first to try converting the Indian population). Unlike most other Caribbean islands tourism plays a small role in Trinidad's economy. In the 1960s and 1970s the official policy was to discourage tourism, and although this has now changed, visitors are still a rarity in some parts of the island, big hotels are set up for business visitors and some tourist services may be lacking. Nevertheless, Trinidadians are genuinely welcoming to strangers.

Tobago's population, mainly black, numbers about 51,000. The crime rate is much lower than on Trinidad and the people are noticeably helpful and friendly. Tourism is a major source of income here and considerable investment has gone into hotels and infrastructure in the last few years.

HISTORY

Trinidad was discovered by Columbus and claimed for Spain on his third voyage in 1498. Whether he named the island after the day of the Holy Trinity, or after a group of three hills that he spied from the sea is in dispute. At that time there were at least seven tribes of Indians living on the island: the Arawaks, Chaimas,

Tamanaques, Salives, Chaguanes, Quaquas and Caribs, the last being divided into four sub-groupings, the Nepoios, Yaios, Carinepagotos and Cumanagotos. The peaceful Arawaks were the majority and lived in the S part of the island, having originally come from the upper regions of the Orinoco river. The N part was populated by Indians of the Carib strain from the Amazon area who were aggressive and warlike. It was their hostility which prevented successful colonization until the end of the 17th century when Catalan Capuchin missionaries arrived. However, European diseases and the rigours of slavery took their toll of the Indian population; by 1824 there were only 893 Indians left on Trinidad and today there are none.

The first Spanish governor was Don Antonio Sedeño who arrived in 1530, but failed to establish a permanent settlement because of Indian attacks. In 1592 the governor, Don Antonio de Berrio y Oruna, founded the town of San José de Oruna (now St Joseph), but it was destroyed by Sir Walter Raleigh in 1595 and not rebuilt until 1606. In 1783 a deliberate policy to encourage immigration of Roman Catholics was introduced, known as the Royal Cedula of Population, and it was from this date that organized settlement began with an influx of mostly French-speaking immigrants, particularly after the French Revolution. Many also came from St Lucia and Dominica when these islands were ceded to Britain in 1784, others came with their slaves from the French Caribbean when slavery was abolished and from Saint Domingue after the war of independence there (eg the Compte de Lopinot, whose house in Lopinot has been restored, see page 813).

British rule in Trinidad began in 1797 when an expedition led by Sir Ralph Abercromby captured the island. It was later ceded to Britain by Spain in 1802 under the Treaty of Amiens. (VS Naipaul's *The Loss of El Dorado* is a fascinating, if pessimistic, account of the early

Spanish settlement, Sir Walter Raleigh's raid, and the early years of British rule). At this time large numbers of African slaves were imported to work in the sugar fields introduced by the French until the slave trade was abolished in 1807. After the abolition of slavery in 1834, labour became scarce and the colonists looked for alternative sources of workers. Several thousands of immigrants from neighbouring islands came in 1834-48, many Americans from Baltimore and Pennsylvania came in 1841, Madeirans came seeking employment and religious freedom and were joined by European immigrants, namely the British, Scots, Irish, French, Germans and Swiss. There was also immigration of free West Africans in the 1840s, but by 1848 this had ceased as conditions improved in their own countries. In 1844 the British Government gave approval for the import of East Indian labour and the first indentured labourers arrived in 1845 (Indian Arrival Day, 30 May, is now a public holiday). By 1917, when Indian immigration ceased, 141,615 Indians had arrived for an indentured period of five years, and although many returned to India afterwards, the majority settled. The first Chinese arrived in 1849 during a lull in Indian immigration. Initially these were men only and this naturally encouraged intermarriage, but later arrivals included women. In 1866 the Chinese Government insisted on a return passage being paid, and this put an end to Chinese immigration. Persistent labour shortages led to higher wages in Trinidad than in many other islands and from emancipation until the 1960s there was also migration from Barbados, Grenada and St Vincent.

Tobago is thought to have been discovered by Columbus in 1498, when it was occupied by Caribs. He is said to have called the island 'Bella Forma'; the present name is a corruption of tobacco, which the Caribs used to grow there. In 1641 James, Duke of Courland (in the Baltic), obtained a grant of the island from Charles I and in 1642 a number of Courlanders settled on the N side. In 1658 the Courlanders were overpowered by the Dutch, who remained in possession of the island until 1662. In this year Cornelius Lampsius procured Letters Patent from Louis XIV creating him the Baron of Tobago under the Crown of France. After being occupied for short periods by the Dutch and the French, Tobago was ceded by France to Britain in 1763 under the Treaty of Paris. But it was not until 1802, after further invasions by the French and subsequent recapture by the British, that it was finally ceded to Britain, becoming a Crown Colony in 1877 and in 1888 being amalgamated politically with Trinidad. By some reckonings Tobago changed hands as many as 29 times because of its strategic importance and for this reason there are a large number of forts.

The first political organizations in Trinidad and Tobago developed in the 1930s, when economic depression spurred the formation of labour movements. Full adult suffrage was introduced in 1946 and political parties began to develop. In 1956, the People's National Movement (PNM) was founded by the hugely influential Dr Eric Williams, who dominated local politics until his death in 1981. The party won control of the new Legislative Council, under the new constitutional arrangements which provided for self-government, and Dr Williams became the first Chief Minister. In 1958, Trinidad and Tobago became a member of the new Federation of the West Indies, but after the withdrawal of Jamaica in 1961 the colony was unwilling to support the poorer members of the Federation and Dr Williams sought the same rights for Trinidad and Tobago. The country became an independent member of the Commonwealth on 31 August, 1962 and became a republic within the Commonwealth on 1 August, 1976. Dr Williams remained Prime Minister, his party drawing on the support of the majority

African elements of the population, while the opposition parties were supported mainly by the Indian minority.

In 1986, the National Alliance for Reconstruction (NAR) ended 30 years' rule by the PNM which had been hit by corruption scandals, winning 33 of the 36 parliamentary seats in the general election. Six NAR members defected in 1989 to form the United National Congress (UNC), led by former Deputy Prime Minister, Basdeo Panday. The popularity of the Prime Minister, A N R Robinson, was extremely low and he was seen as heading an uncaring administration which alienated voters by its economic policies of cutting the public sector and other costs.

General elections were held on 16 December 1991, bringing another about turn in political loyalties. Patrick Manning, of the PNM, led his party to victory, winning 21 seats, while the UNC won 13 and the NAR was left in the cold with only the two Tobago seats. Elections for Tobago's House of Assembly, in Dec 1992, gave the NAR 11 seats and the PNM one seat, the same as in the previous assembly. By mid-term the Government was suffering from unpopularity and lack of confidence. Its economic policies were blamed for higher unemployment, lack of growth and rising crime. However, the opposition was not strengthened by the formation of three new parties, which were likely to split any anti-Government vote. The National Development Party (NDP) was launched in 1993 by Carson Charles, former leader of the NAR, after he failed in a second bid for the party's leadership. The Republic Party (RP) was formed by the late Nello Mitchell, a former general secretary of the PNM, after he was expelled from the PNM for gross disrespect of the party. Third, Yasin Abu Bakr, leader of the Jamaat-al-Muslimeen, formed the National Vision Party in 1994. Two PNM MPs and one UNC MP died, causing by-elections to be held in 1994. One seat was won by the

PNM, the two others by the UNC. The UNC, NAR and NDP announced a joint platform in July 1994, which led to the resignation of the leader of the NAR, Selby Wilson. At the end of 1994 another new party, the Movement for Unity and Progress, was set up by a former UNC MP, Hulsie Bhaggan.

In 1995 the economy began to improve and the Prime Minister took a gamble in calling early general elections to increase his majority. His tactic failed, however, when the UNC and the PNM both won 17 seats. Although the PNM received 48.8% of the vote compared with 45.8% for the UNC, Basdeo Panday formed an alliance with the NAR, who again won the two Tobago seats, and he was sworn in as Prime Minister on 9 November 1995. A lawyer and trade union leader, he was the first head of government of Indian descent. Greater autonomy for Tobago was anticipated as a result of the coalition with the NAR.

GOVERNMENT

Trinidad and Tobago became a republic within the Commonwealth on 1 August 1976 under a new constitution which provides for a President and a bicameral Parliament comprising a 31-seat Senate and a 36-seat House of Representatives. Noor Mohammed Hassanali took office as President in Mar 1987. Tobago has its own 12-seat House of Assembly, which runs many local services.

THE ECONOMY

Structure of production

Petroleum and petroleum products dominate the economy, providing about a quarter of gdp, one third of government current revenue and two thirds of foreign exchange earnings. Three quarters of oil production comes from marine fields. Production is around 131,000 barrels a day but proven reserves are enough to last only 11 years. There is one refinery, at Pointe-a-Pierre, the other at Point Fortin having been mothballed. The island has

Trinidad and Tobago: fact file

Geographic

Land area	5,128 sq km
forested	45.8%
pastures	2.2%
cultivated	23.7%

Demographic

Population (1995)	1,265,000
annual growth rate (1990-95)	0.6%
urban	71.3%
rural	28.7%
density	246.7 per sq km
Religious affiliation	
Roman Catholic	29.4%
Hindu	23.7%
Anglican	10.9%
Moslem	5.9%
Birth rate per 1,000 (1993)	17.4
	(world av 25.0)

Education and Health

Life expectancy at birth, male	68.0 years
female	73.2 years
Infant mortality rate	
per 1,000 live births (1994)	17.0
Physicians (1993)	1 per 1,191 persons
Hospital beds	1 per 297 persons
Calorie intake as %	
of FAO requirement	107%
Population age 25 and over	
with no formal schooling	4.5%
Literacy (over 15)	96.9%

Economic

GNP (1994 market prices)	US$4,351mn
GNP per capita	US$3,626
Public external debt (1995)	US$1,905mn
Tourism receipts (1993)	US$80mn
Inflation (annual av 1989-94)	8.1%
Radio	1 per 1.8 persons
Television	1 per 5.0 persons
Telephone	1 per 6.5 persons

Employment

Population economically active (1995)	523,500
Unemployment rate (1995)	17.8%
% of labour force in agriculture	12.9
petroleum and gas	3.7
manufacturing	10.0
construction	12.0
Military forces	2,600

Source *Encyclopaedia Britannica* and Trinidad and Tobago Central Bank

substantial proven reserves of natural gas of 10 trillion cubic feet (tcf), producing 700mn cubic feet daily in 1996. These are used as a basic raw material for the production of petrochemicals such as methanol and ammonia and the provision of electric power in the Point Lisas industrial estate. New methanol plants will raise annual capacity to 1.06mn tonnes by end-1996.

Trinidad is rich in mineral deposits including asphalt from the pitch lake at La Brea on the SW coast, gypsum, limestone, sand, gravel, argillite and fluorspar, but apart from the asphalt, which is used for road surfacing, they are not well developed.

The soil in Trinidad is remarkably rich and the first settlers had no difficulty in raising a variety of crops, with tobacco, sugar and cocoa being the major exports. Today, however, agriculture contributes 2.4% of gross domestic product and employs only 10.4% of the labour force. Agricultural exports have been broadened to include citrus fruits, coconut oils and flowers, and diversification of the traditionally sugar-based agriculture of the Caroni area with rice, pawpaw, other fruit and vegetables has led to improvements in supplies for the domestic market. Sugar production and exports grew in the early 1990s, exceeding targets and enabling Trinidad to meet its export quotas to the EU and USA.

Recent trends

Dependence on oil has led to wide fluctuations in the rate of economic growth, with the 1970s a period of rapid expansion and rising real incomes as oil prices soared, and the 1980s a decade of declining output and falling wages as the oil market retrenched. The recession in the oil industry exposed structural imbalances in the rest of the economy and the inability of agriculture, manufacturing or services to counter its effects.

Assistance was sought from the IMF in the context of debt rescheduling agreements with the Paris Club of creditor governments and with commercial banks. The Government also turned to the World Bank, the Inter American Development Bank and Japan for the new lending to support structural adjustment of the economy. Proceeds from the sale of state enterprises were to be used to reduce the outstanding external debt of US$2.4bn. The second standby agreement expired on 31 March 1991 and the Government did not seek a third IMF programme.

From 1990 the economy did begin to grow slowly after seven consecutive annual declines in gdp but it contracted again in 1992 and 1993. A liberalization of some foreign exchange controls in 1992 led to an easing of liquidity constraints and a return of some capital held overseas. In April 1993 the TT dollar was floated, with an initial depreciation of 26% to TT$5.75 = US$1, and a consequent rise in the rate of inflation, but then stabilized and by mid-1996 had not crossed the TT$6=US$1 threshold. The economy was also liberalized in other ways, for example by lowering import tariffs, abandoning quotas, progressively reducing the tax rate and selling state companies to private investors. Foreign investment began to increase in 1995-96, led by inflows from the USA. Gdp was expected to increase by 2.8% in 1996 after a growth of 5.1% in 1994 and 1.9% in 1995.

Unemployment is most acute in the 15-19 age group, where about 43% are out of work. The crime rate has increased noticeably since the 1970s, particularly serious crimes and murders, many of which were related to drugs and gang killings.

A concerted attempt is being made to diversify the economy and lessen the dependence on petroleum. Tourism is becoming an important source of foreign exchange and the Government is actively promoting both islands abroad. Expenditure by Trinidadians abroad still exceeds earnings from incoming tourism but only by a narrow margin, thanks to a recession-induced slowdown in holidays abroad and increased visitor revenues. Stayover arrivals rose by 7.1% in 1994 to 265,618, of which North American visitors made up 48% and Europeans 23%. Tobago now has 1,050 hotel rooms available, following an expansion in construction and more are planned, notably a 250-room Hilton hotel. The Government aims to construct 5,400 new hotel rooms in Trinidad (1,200 at present) and 1,750 in Tobago by 2005, at a cost of US$700mn, a target which the press has described as 'an exercise in fantasy'. A new cruise ship complex was opened in Aug 1989 at Port of Spain. A similar terminal has been constructed in Tobago as part of the Scarborough harbour re-development project. Cruise ship passenger arrivals increased by nearly 2% in 1992 to 26,948, but then by 21% in 1993 to 32,572 visitors.

CULTURE

The most exciting introduction to the vivid, cosmopolitan culture of this Republic is, of course, Carnival, or 'De Mas', as locals refer to the annual 'celebration of the senses'. Background reading is a help for a visit at any time of the year. It is sensible to purchase books before departure, as prices are much higher in Trinidadian shops, even for locally produced reading matter. Some authors to investigate are C L R James, Samuel Selvon, Shiva Naipaul, all now deceased, as well as Shiva's more famous brother, V S Naipaul. Also, the historian and past prime minister Dr Eric Williams, Earl Lovelace and newcomer Valerie Belgrave (whose *Ti Marie* has been described as the Caribbean *Gone with the Wind*). Although the tradition of performance poetry is not as strong here as in, say, Jamaica (calypso fulfils some of its role), the monologues of Paul Keens-Douglas (not so active nowadays), some of which are on album or cassette, are richly entertaining and a great introduction to the local dialect or patois.

Alongside a strong oral/literary tradition goes a highly developed visual culture, reflecting the islands' racial melange. The most obvious examples are the inventive designs for the carnival bands, which often draw on craft skills like wire bending, copper beating, and the expressive use of fibreglass moulds. Fine painters and sculptors abound, too, although the only good galleries are small and commercial and located primarily in Port of Spain. Michel Jean Cazabon, born 1813, was the first great local artist (an illustrated biography by Aquarela Gallery owner Geoffrey MacLean is widely available). Contemporary work to look out for, often on the walls of the more enlightened hotels, restaurants and banks, includes paintings by Emheyo Bahabba, Pat Bishop, Isaiah Boodhoo, Francisco Cabral, LeRoy Clarke, Kenwyn Crichlow, Boscoe Holder and the fabled, controversial Mas' designer Peter Minshall, who designed the opening ceremony for the 1992 Barcelona Olympic Games (thousands twirled silk squares in one sequence) and the Atlanta Games in 1996.

Jewellery and fashion designers also figure strongly in the life of these islands, with exceptionally high standards of work demonstrated by jewellers like Barbara Jardine, Gillian Bishop and Rachel Ross. The doyenne of the fashion business is the gifted Meiling, but attractive original clothing by a growing number of native fashionmakers can be found in boutiques and shopping centres.

Carnival   This extraordinary fête (see **Festivals** for dates and details) is considered by many to be safer, more welcoming to visitors and artistically more stimulating than its nearest rival in Rio de Janeiro. Commercialization is undermining many of the greatest Mas' traditions, but some of the historical characters like the Midnight Robber and the Moko Jumbies can be glimpsed at the Viey La Cou old time Carnival street theatre at Queens Hall a week before Carnival and often at J'Ouverte (pronounced joo-vay) on Carnival Monday morning and in small, independent bands of players. But it's a great party, enlivened by hundreds of thousands of costumed masqueraders and the homegrown music, calypso and steelband (usually referred to as 'pan').

Calypsonians (or kaisonians, as the more historically-minded call them) are the commentators, champions and sometime conscience of the people. This unique musical form, a mixture of African, French and, eventually, British, Spanish and even East Indian influences dates back to Trinidad's first 'shantwell', Gros Jean, late in the 18th century. Since then it has evolved into a popular, potent force, with both men and women (also children, of late) battling for the Calypso Monarch's crown, in a fierce competition that climaxes on Dimanche Gras, the Sunday immediately before the official beginning of Carnival. Calypsonians band together to perform in 'tents' (performing halls) in the weeks leading up to the competition and are judged in semi-finals, which hones down the list to six final contenders. The season's calypso songs blast from radio stations and sound systems all over the islands and visitors should ask locals to interpret the sometimes witty and often scurrilous lyrics, for they are a fascinating introduction to the state of the nation. Currently, party soca tunes dominate although some of the commentary calypsonians, like Sugar Aloes, are still heard on the radio. There is also a new breed of 'Rapso' artistes, fusing calypso and rap music. Chutney, an Indian version of calypso, is also becoming increasingly popular, especially since the advent of radio stations devoted only to Indian music. Chutney is also being fused with soca, to create 'chutney soca'.

Pan music has a shorter history, developing this century from the tamboo-bamboo bands which made creative use of tins, dustbins and pans plus lengths of bamboo for percussion instruments. By the end of World War II (during which Carnival was banned) some ingenious souls discovered that huge oil drums could be converted into expressive instruments, their top surfaces tuned to all ranges and depths (eg the ping pong, or soprano pan embraces 28 to 32 notes, including both the diatonic and chromatic scales). Aside from the varied pans, steelbands also include a rhythm section dominated by the steel, or iron men. For Carnival, the steelbands compete in the grand Panorama, playing calypsoes which are also voted on for the Road March of the Year. Biennally, the World Steelband Festival highlights the versatility of this music, for each of the major bands must play a work by a classical composer as well as a calypso of choice. On alternate years the National Schools Steelband Festival is held, similarly in late Oct/early November. A pan jazz festival is held annually in Nov, with solos, ensembles and orchestras all emphasizing the versatility of the steel drum.

Other musical forms in this music-mad nation include **parang** (pre-Christmas). Part of the islands' Spanish heritage, parang is sung in Castillian and accompanied by guitar, cuatro, mandoline and tambourine. For the Hindi and Muslim festivals, there are East Indian drumming and vocal styles like chowtal, which is particularly associated with Puagwa in early March.

Throughout the year, there are regular performances of plays and musicals, often by Caribbean dramatists, and concerts by fine choirs like the Marionettes Chorale, sometimes accompanied by steelbands. There is a lot of comedy but some serious plays too, see press for details. Theatres include the Little Carib Theatre (T 622-4644), Space Theatre (T 623-0732), the Central Bank Auditorium (T 623-0845) and Queen's Hall (624-1284).

In short, Trinidad and Tobago boast some of the most impressive artists to be found anywhere in the region, and visitors can enjoy that art throughout the year, although many of the now internationally recognized performers tour abroad during the summer months.

FAUNA AND FLORA

The rainforests of the Northern Range running along the N coast and the wetlands on the E and W coast are more extensive, more dense and display a greater diversity of fauna and flora than any other ecosystems in the Caribbean. Trinidad combines the species of the Caribbean chain from Jamaica to Grenada with the species of the continental rainforests of South America. The Forestry Division of the Ministry of Agriculture, Land and Marine Resources (Long Circular Road, St James, Port of Spain, T 622-7476, contact them for information on guided tours and hikes) has designated many parts of Trinidad and Tobago as national parks, wildlife reserves and protected areas. On Trinidad, the national parks are the Caroni and Nariva Swamps, Chaguaramas, and Madamas, Maracas and Matura in the N range of hills.

Wetlands

Trinidad's wetlands are unparalleled by any other Caribbean island. There are mangrove swamps, fresh swamps, grassy fresh water marshes, palm marshes and water-logged savannah land, covering 7,000 acres of the Central Plain. A permit from the Forestry Division is necessary for trips into restricted areas such as the Nariva Swamp and Bush Bush Island in the Aripo Scientific Reserve; 72 hrs notice is required, best to visit with a guide who can arrange it for you.

The **Nariva Swamp**, the largest freshwater swamp in Trinidad is a Wetland of International Importance under the Ramsar Convention. It contains hardwood forest and is home to red howler monkeys and the weeping capuchin as well as 55 other species of mammal of which 32 are bats. Birds include the savannah hawk and the red-breasted blackbird. A tour by kayak is recommended (T 624-7281 or 629-2680) as it permits the sighting of wildlife not possible on a motor boat. You paddle silently across fields of giant water lilies, through channels in thick forest of mangroves and towering silk cotton trees with monkeys and parrots chattering overhead and exotic butterflies fluttering around you. Catch the dawn for seeing most birds and other wildlife. The **Caroni Swamp** is usually visited in the late afternoon as it is the roosting place of scarlet ibis and egrets. You go out through mangroves into a lagoon where the boat's engine is turned off so that you can quietly watch the birds. No permit is necessary, see below, **Excursions**.

Rainforests

The slopes of the Northern Range are covered with forest giants like the silk cotton trees, which carry creepers and vines and the thick forest canopy of mahogany, balata, palms and flowering trees like the poui and immortelle which provide cover and maintain a cool, damp environment no matter the heat of the day. There are organized bus tours to places like Chaguaramas National Park or the Asa Wright Nature Reserve (where in turn there are further tours for ornithologists,) or you can find a guide for a day's hike tailored to your interest in ecology or adventure.

The **Northern Range Sanctuary**, Maracas, or El Tucuche Reserve, is a forest on the second highest peak, at 3,072 feet, covering 2,313 acres. It contains some interesting flora, such as giant bromeliad and orchids, as well as fauna, including the golden tree frog and the orange-billed nightingale-thrush. There are several hiking trails, the most popular of which is from Ortinola estate; guides can be hired. The 11 km trek to the peak takes 5 hrs through dense forest; the views from the top are spectacular; for information contact the Field Naturalists' Club (see below). Walking alone is not recommended in the N hills, join a group or at least walk with someone who knows the (often badly defined) trails well.

There are seven natural landmarks, three of which are described below (Blue Basin, the Pitch Lake and the Devil's Woodyard) and others include Tamana Hill in the central range, and Galera Point in the NE. Twelve areas are scientific reserves (eg Trinity Hills, Galeota Point and the Aripo Savannas); twelve are nature conservation reserves: the Asa Wright Centre is described below, but also Cedros Peninsula and Godineau Swamp in the SW, Manzanilla in the E and Valencia. The **Trinity Hills Wildlife Sanctuary** lies W of Guayaguayare and was founded in 1934. Its forests are home to a large variety of birds, monkeys, armadillos and opossums. Permission to visit must be obtained from the Petroleum Company of Trinidad and Tobago (Petrotrin) in Pointe-a-Pierre.

The **Valencia Wildlife Sanctuary** covers 6,881 acres and contains at least 50 species of birds including antbirds and tanagers. Several mammals live here: deer, wild pig, agouti, tatoo. Near Valencia is the Arena Forest, one of ten recreation parks, while five areas have been designated scenic landscapes (Blanchisseuse, Maracas and Toco-Matelot on the N coast, Cocos Bay on the Atlantic, and Mount Harris on the Southern Road, S of Sangre Grande). Permission to visit certain forests and watershed areas must be obtained from the Water and Sewerage Authority (WASA), Farm Road, Valsayn, St Joseph. Their ponds often serve as home to caymans and a variety of waterbirds and are easily accessible off the main highway E of Port of Spain. Although about 46% of the island remains forested, there is much concern about the loss of wildlife habitats.

On Tobago, apart from two national parks (Buccoo Reef and the virgin and secondary forests of E Tobago), there are the Goldsborough natural landmark, the Kilgwyn scientific reserve, the Grafton nature conservation area, the Parlatuvier-Roxborough scenic landscape, and three recreation parks (including Mount Irvine). Many of the small islands off the coasts of the two larger ones are reserves for wildlife and are important breeding grounds for red-billed tropic birds, frigate birds, man-o-war and other sea birds (for instance Saut d'Eau, Kronstadt Island and Soldado Rock off Trinidad, and Little Tobago, see below, St Giles and Marble Islands off Tobago).

Many flowering trees can be seen: pink and yellow poui, frangipani, cassia, pride of India, immortelle, flamboyant, jacaranda. Among the many types of flower are hibiscus, poinsettia, chaconia (wild poinsettia – the national flower), ixora, bougainvillea, orchid, ginger lily and heliconia. The Horticultural Society of Trinidad and Tobago (PO Box 252) has its office on Lady Chancellor Road, Port of Spain, T 622-6423.

The islands boast 60 types of bat, and other mammals include the Trinidad capuchin and red howler monkeys, brown forest brocket (deer), collared peccary (quenk), manicou (opossum), agouti, rare ocelot and armadillo. A small group of manatee is being protected in a reserve in the Nariva Swamp. Caymans live in the swamps. Other reptiles include iguanas and 47 species of snakes, of which few are poisonous: the fer-de-lance, bushmaster and two coral snakes.

Trinidad and Tobago together have more species of birds than any other Caribbean island, although the variety is South American, not West Indian. No species is endemic, but Tobago has 13 species of breeding birds not found on Trinidad. Most estimates say that there are 433 species of bird, including 41 hummingbirds (the aboriginal name for the island of Trinidad was Ieri, the land of the hummingbird), parrots, macaws, the rare red-breasted blackbird, the nightingale thrush and the mot mot. There are also 622 recorded species of butterfly. The most accessible bird-watching sites are the Caroni Bird Sanctuary, the Asa Wright Centre, the Caurita Plantation and the Wild Fowl Trust, all described elsewhere in this chapter.

Recommended is *A Guide to the Birds of Trinidad and Tobago*, by Richard ffrench (Macmillan Caribbean), with introductory information on rainfall, the environment and vegetation as well as birds. *Birds of Trinidad and Tobago*, also by Richard ffrench (M Caribbean Pocket Natural History Series) is a shorter guide with colour photos of 83 of the more common species. *Birds of Trinidad and Tobago – A Photographic Atlas*, by Russell Barrow (MEP Trinidad, 1994) is the most recent bird book.

Those interested can also contact the Trinidad Field Naturalists Club, 1 Errol Park Road, St Anns, Port of Spain (T 624-3321 evenings or weekends, walks on Sundays). *The Trinidad and Tobago Field Naturalists' Club Trail Guide*, by Paul Comeau, Louis Guy, Ewoud Heesterman and Clayton Hull, was published in 1992, 288 pages on 48 trails, difficult to obtain. French and Bacon's *Nature Trails of Trinidad*, first published in 1982 has been revised by Dr Victor Quesnel and reissued by SM Publications Ltd under the auspices of the Asa Wright Nature Centre. Each Oct Trinidad and Tobago hold Natural History Festivals to foster understanding of the islands' flora and fauna.

BEACHES AND WATERSPORTS

The best beaches are on the N coast and the views from the coastal road are spectacular as you drive through forest and look down on sandy bays and rocky promontories. Close to Port of Spain **Maqueripe Bay** has a sheltered beach. **Maracas Bay**, 10 miles/16 km from the capital, has a sheltered sandy beach fringed with coconut palms; despite small waves there can be a dangerous undertow here and at other beaches and drownings have occurred, do not swim far out and watch the markers. Lifeguards are on duty until 1800 at weekends and holidays and new beach facilities were built in 1995 with changing rooms, showers etc, car parking and cabanas for beach vendors. Try 'shark-and-bake', shark meat in a heavy fried dough, a Maracas speciality, or the 'shark and bread,' a roll with shark meat in it, very tasty, especially after a drinking session at 0300, sold all along the beach. Maracas Bay Village is scheduled for development. At present a few people rent out basic rooms in the village, ask at the small shop. There are buses to Maracas Bay running every 4 hours (but they can be irregular) from the bus terminal. Difficulties in catching the bus have led travellers to recommend car hire or taxis: from Port of Spain costs US$25 or there is a pick-up 'route taxi' service from the centre of town, TT$10. Another method is maxi-taxi to Maraval then 4-wheel drive jeep to Maracas, irregular, get back in good time. The jeep may go right into Port of Spain but do not rely on it.

Next to Maracas Bay is **Tyrico Bay** (surfing, lifeguard, another horseshoe-shaped beach with a dangerous undertow and sandflies). **Las Cuevas**, also on the N coast (like Maracas Bay there are changing rooms, showers, lifeguards, surfing is good here but beware of the sandflies in the wet season), is a picturesque bay with fishing boats moored at one end. It can get crowded at weekends but is empty during the week. **Blanchisseuse** beach has a sweet water lagoon where the river runs into the sea and the place is kept clean by the owners of *Cocos Hut* restaurant who are establishing a 28-acre nature reserve on the banks of the river. Leatherback turtles come on to Blanchisseuse beach in the nesting season. At the NE end, near Toco, are a number of bays, including **Balandra** for good bathing. For Toco, get an express bus or highway maxi to Arima, then route taxi to Sangre Grande, then taxi to Toco.

Further down, the Atlantic coast from Matura to Mayaro is divided into three huge sweeping bays, with palm trees growing as high as 200 feet in some places. Of these bays **Mayaro** and **Manzanilla** both have beautiful sandy beaches, but be careful of the Atlantic currents, swimming can be dangerous. There are several beach houses to rent at Mayaro, heavily booked in peak holiday periods, some are poor, check beforehand. Manzanilla has new public facilities and a hotel development is planned. From nearby Brigand Hill Lighthouse, a TSTT signal station, you can get a wonderful view of the E coast, the Nariva Swamp and much of Trinidad. Light patches of green are rice fields encroaching on the swamp. In the SW, near La Brea and the Pitch Lake is the resort of Vessigny. The SW, or Cedros, peninsula is a 3-hour car trip from Port of Spain along often atrocious roads, but is worth it for the unspoilt beaches and miles of coconut palm plantations. Generally, the beaches are difficult to get to except by taxi or hired car.

For boat trips to the islands N and W of Port of Spain T 622-8974, Elton Pouchet, US$75 for 1-3 people.

Tobago is noted for its beaches, two of the best being only minutes from the airport: **Store Bay**, popular with locals, lots of vendors, food stalls and glass bottom boats; and **Pigeon Point**, a picture postcard beach fringed with palms with calm, shallow water protected by **Buccoo Reef**. You have to pay to use the beach (TT$10), but you get changing facilities, umbrellas and beach bars. Here also there are lots of glass bottom boats going out to Buccoo Reef and a catamaran for coastal tours and swimming in the **Nylon Pool**, a shallow area offshore. Other good beaches on the leeward side of the island are **Stone Haven Bay, Mount Irvine Bay** and **Courland Bay**, one of the longest. All have resort hotels and watersports. **Englishman's Bay** is another lovely bay, with the forest coming down to the beach and a river running into the sea. Hotel development is planned. The E coast is more rugged and windswept, with cliffs and coves carved out by the Atlantic Ocean. **Hillsborough Bay**, just outside Scarborough, has a glorious long beach with overhanging palms, but the sea is dangerous because of rip tides. Do not swim there. **Big Bacolet Bay**, also known as Minister Bay, is great for surfing, body surfing and boogie boarding, but watch out for the currents. In the NE, **King's Bay** has a beach bar, toilets and huts for shade. There is a signpost to the beach, almost opposite the track to King's Bay Waterfall. **Speyside** and **Charlotteville** both have protected bays, from the former you can take glass bottom boat trips to **Little Tobago** with birdwatching, walking and snorkelling included (about US$12.50) and from the latter you can walk to Pirate's Bay through the forest. Snorkelling is good on the reef here.

Yachting has become big business in Trinidad and there are now several marinas attracting custom from other islands more at risk from hurricanes. Provisioning is excellent and there are boat repair and maintenance facilities; local teak costs a fraction of US prices, workmen are highly skilled, services are tax free and spare parts can be imported duty free. Marinas have both dry storage and stern-to docks (see **Information for travellers, Marinas**). Facilities have been built at Courland Bay, Tobago, to attract the yachting crowd.

Every July/Aug, there is a power boat race from the Trinidad and Tobago Yacht Club (TTYC), Trinidad to Store Bay, Tobago. The Trinidad and Tobago Yachting Association (TTYA) sponsors Carnival Fun Race and a weekly racing programme in winter and spring. Each year Tobago has a sailing week in May, sponsored by Angostura and Yachting World Magazine; many crewing possibilities, lots of parties.

The annual International Game Fishing Classic is held in Feb/March. **Fishing** charters can be arranged, for deep sea fish such as blue marlin, sailfish, tuna, wahoo offshore, king fish, barracuda, Spanish mackerel, African pompano, grouper, snapper in coastal waters or bonefish and tarpon in the mangroves and flats. Prices for deep sea fishing are around US$250/4 hrs, US$400/8 hrs, maximum six people and for bonefishing US$150/4 hrs, maximum three people. On Tobago contact Capt Gerard 'Frothy' De Silva, Friendship Estate, Canaan, T 639-7108.

For **surfing** or **windsurfing**, contact the Surfing Association of Trinidad and Tobago, T 637-4533, and the Windsurfing Association of Trinidad and Tobago, T 659-2457.

Kayaking (including tuition) is available at many hotels on Tobago or at the Chaguaramas Kayak Centre run by Merryl See Tai, ½ km after the Alcoa dock, just before Pier One. You can hire kayaks for use in the bay or go on excursions along the coast, up rivers or to the Bush Bush Sanctuary in the Nariva Swamp. Walking tours and overnight expeditions also arranged, T 633-7871, 680-3480, 629-2680 (home).

DIVING AND MARINE LIFE

The waters around Tobago are becoming known as an unspoilt diving destination and several dive shops have started operations in the last few years. Coral reefs flourish almost all round the island. Every known species of hard coral and lots of soft corals can be found, and there is a huge brain coral, believed to be one of the world's largest, off Little Tobago which you can see on a glass bottom boat tour. The Guyana current flows round the S and E shores of Tobago and supports a large variety of marine life. Dive sites are numerous and varied, there are walls, caves, canyons, coral gardens and lots of fish. There is exciting drift diving, not recommended for novices although they will teach you (Aquamarine Dive rec, very safety conscious, good record). The only thing better than racing past dancing sea fans at 3 knots is to do it again at 5 knots. You are swept along the coral reef while, high above, manta rays flap lazily to remain stationary in the current as they sieve out the plankton. Snorkelling is also excellent almost everywhere, with good visibility. Some of the most popular sites are Arnos Vale, Pirate's Bay, Store Bay, Man O'War Bay and Batteaux Bay.

Tobago Dive Experience (Sean Robinson) at the *Grafton Beach Resort*, T 639-0191, F 639-0030 (also at *Manta Lodge*, T/F 660-5268, and *Ocean Point*). Aquamarine Dive Ltd (Keith Darwent) is at *Blue Waters Inn*, Speyside, T 660-4341, F 639-4416. *(Blue Waters Inn* tends to be full throughout the year so book early.)* This is a 5-star PADI facility, dives are around Little Tobago and all escorted by at least two dive masters because of the currents. Full range of courses available. *Man Friday Diving*, Charlotteville, T/F 660-4676, covers the area from Charlotteville to Speyside. Other dive operators include Dive Tobago Ltd (Jimmy Young), Pigeon Point, PO Box 53 (Scarborough), T 639-0202, F 639-2727 and Ron's Watersports, Main Road, Charlotteville, T 622-0459. There are several more people involved in diving, fishing and other watersports, who are not listed here. A single tank dive costs on average US$35, night dives US$45, rental of BCD and regulator US$6-7, mask, fins and snorkel US$8-10.

The only really safe place for diving off Trinidad is in the channels called the Bocas, between the islands off the NW peninsula (The Dragon's Mouth). However, the currents are cold, so protective gear is essential. Contact the Diving Association of Trinidad, or Twin-Island Dives, Maraval.

The leatherback turtle nests Mar-July on several beaches on Trinidad (Matura, Fishing Pond on E coast, Paria, Tacaribe and Grand Riviere on N coast) and Tobago (Great Courland Bay known as Turtle Beach, Stonehaven Bay, Bloody Bay and Parlatuvier), up to 8 times a season, laying 75-120 eggs each time about 10 days apart. Incubation is 60 days. Turtle watching tours are organized by the Asa Wright Nature Centre and others.

OTHER SPORTS

Cricket is very popular. Test matches are played at Queen's Park Oval, W of Queen's Park Savannah, Port of Spain; take a cushion, sunhat/umbrella, whistle (!) and drinks if sitting in the cheap seats. It is a private club but a friendly gate guard might let you in for a look around. For information, ring Queen's Park Cricket Club, T 622-2295/3787. Hockey and soccer are also played at the Oval (Football Association T 624-5183/7661). Also played are rugby, basketball, cycling and marathon running.

There is **horse-racing** at Santa Rosa Park, Arima, about 15 km outside Port of Spain. Horse-hire near Fort George.

Swimming at the *Hilton Hotel*, US$4 (US$2 children), *Valley Vue Hotel* (chutes and waterslides, very busy at weekends and holidays) or *La Joya* at St Joseph, check first for availability, T 662-1184; see below for swimming and **golf** at St Andrews (Moka) Golf Club (T 629-2314); there are 5 other golf clubs on Trinidad, including a 9-hole public course at Chaguaramas (T 634-4349); squash, Long Circular Mall, T 622-1245, 0600-2200 (0900-1700 Saturday), US$3 for 40 minutes, advance booking essential.

Tennis: Trinidad Country Club Maraval, T 622-3470/2111/2113, temporary membership, advance booking necessary, also at *Hilton Hotel*, Tranquility Square Lawn Tennis Club (T 625-4182) and public tennis courts at Princes Building Grounds, Upper Frederick Street (T 623-1121). The *Valley Vue Hotel*, Ariapita Road, St Ann's has 2 **squash** courts with seating for 100 spectators per court, tennis courts, sauna and gym with lots of equipment and facilities, open for non-members, 0600-2100 Mon-Fri, 0900-1700 Sat, T 623-3511. Squash also at Pelican Squash Club, *Pelican Inn*, Cascade, T 637-4888, equipment for hire, and at Body Works Squash Courts, Long Circular Mall, T 622-1215.

On Tobago, golf and lawn tennis at Mount Irvine Bay, T 639-8871: green fee US$20/day, tennis US$3 in day, US$6 at night. Squash at Grafton Beach Resort, 0800-2200, US$9.50 for 45 minutes including court, ball and racket rental. Black Rock has a basketball league in late Aug, early Sept; you can play before or after the games. At the Turtle Beach Hotel it is possible to play volleyball. For hiking, bird-watching on- and off-shore, contact the very knowledgeable naturalist, David Rooks, PO Box 58, Scarborough, T 639-9408.

FESTIVALS

Carnival (see also above, **Culture**) takes place officially each year on the two days before Ash Wednesday which marks the beginning of the Christian season of Lent. In practice, the festivities start well in advance, with the Mas' camps abustle, the calypsonians performing most nights of the week and the impressive Panorama finals taking place with the competing steelbands at the Queen's Park Savannah stadium the week before Mas' proper. Band launching parties, where band leaders show off their costume designs, are held before Christmas. Calypso 'tents', where calypsoes are played, start in January. Try SWWUT Hall on Wrighton Road, NUGFW Hall on Henry Street, Spektakula on Henry Street. Panyards start practising even earlier; visiting one is usually no problem. Amoco Renegades are at 17a Oxford Street, Port of Spain; Exodus is at St John's Village on Eastern Main Road, St Augustine; Witco Desperadoes is at Laventille Road, Port of Spain. There are parties most of the time from then on. The biggest public fetes at Spectrum, previously Soca Village near the National Stadium, may have a crowd of 20,000 or more. Getting a ticket in advance or arriving early (eg 2130) saves a struggle at the door; most go on until 0400-0500.

Panorama steel band finals are at the Savannah on Carnival Saturday night. Parties on Sunday start early; then there is the Dimanche Gras show, also at the Savannah. There are two main Carnival shows for children: the Red Cross Kiddies Carnival one week before Carnival proper, and the school-based children's Carnival the following Saturday. On Carnival Monday, the festivities start with 'J'Ouverte' at 0200, which involves dressing up in the cheapest and most outlandish disguises available ('old mas'), including mud, which will inevitably be transferred to the spectators. In the afternoon is the Parade of Bands at the Savannah, featuring the very large and colourful bands, portraying a wide sweep of historical and cultural events. Though the Savannah is the main venue, on both Carnival Monday and Tuesday the bands are required to appear before the judges at other locations, including Independence Square and Victoria Square.

Tickets for all National Carnival Commission shows (about US$3.50 for most events) are sold at the Queen's Park Savannah, where the shows are held. You can join one of the Mas' camps by looking in the newspaper for the times and locations of the camps. If you are early enough you can get a costume which will allow you to participate in one of the 'tramps' through town. The Tourist Office (see **Information for travellers**) has a list of names and addresses of the bands to whom you can write in advance to organize a costume. Fair-skinned visitors should avoid the skimpy costumes. You will be two full days in the hot sun and sun block lasts about five minutes. There is a lot of alcohol consumed during the road marches but there are no drunken brawls. Police are much in evidence on the streets. Note that it is illegal to sell tapes of carnival artists but 'bootleg' tapes are inevitably sold on the streets. If you have the strength, don't forget Last Lap, which means jumping up with a steel band around Port of Spain to squeeze the last ounce out of the festival, prior to its official end at midnight on Tuesday.

The Hosay, or Hosein Festival, commemorating the murder of two Moslem princes, starts ten days after the first appearance of the new moon in the Moharrun month of the Moslem calendar. Colourful processions, hauling 10-to 30-foot-high miniature temples of wood, paper and tinsel, start the next day, heralded by moon dancers and accompanied by drum-beating. The main celebrations are in St James, W of Port of Spain. There is also a Hosay celebration in Cedros in S Trinidad. Many strict Muslims disapprove; lots of beer and rum is consumed. Also celebrated is the Moslem festival of Eid-ul-Fitr, to mark the end of Ramadan. Two principal Hindu festivals are Puagwa, or Holi, the colour, or spring, festival on the day of the full moon in the month of Phagun (Feb/Mar), and Divali, the festival of lights, usually in the last quarter of the year. At Puagwa everyone gets squirted with brightly coloured dyes (abeer); strict Hindus have their doubts about some of the dancing styles. Divali is more of a family affair and involves a lot of rather good food in Indian homes. On 29 Aug in Arima the feast of St Rose of Lima is celebrated; the parish church is dedicated to her. Descendants of the original Amerindians come from all over the island to walk in solemn procession round the church (see below, *Arima*).

On Tobago there is a carnival, but it is very quiet compared with Trinidad's. On Easter Monday and Tuesday, there are crab, goat and donkey races at Buccoo Village. The Tobago Heritage Festival lasts for the second fortnight of July, with historical re-enactments, variety shows and parades.

TRINIDAD

PORT OF SPAIN

With a population of 51,000 (350,000 including suburbs), Port of Spain lies on a gently sloping plain between the Gulf of Paria and the foothills of the Northern Range. The city has a pleasant atmosphere, but the streets and buildings are not well maintained. It is also full of life and an exciting city to spend time in. The streets are mostly at right-angles to one another; the buildings are a mixture of fretwork wooden architecture and modern concrete, interspersed with office towers and empty lots. Within easy reach of the port (King's Wharf and its extension) are many of the main buildings of interest. On the S side of Woodford Square, named after the former governor, Sir Ralph Woodford, is the fine Anglican Cathedral Church of the Holy Trinity (consecrated 1823), with an elaborate hammer-beam roof festooned with carvings. It was built during Woodford's governorship (1813-28) and contains a very fine monument to him. The Red House (completed 1907) contains the House of Representatives, the Senate and various government departments. It was the scene of an attempted overthrow of the Robinson Government by armed black Muslim rebels in July 1990. The rebels held the Prime Minister and several of his Cabinet captive for five days before surrendering to the Army (see box, page 809). On the W side of the Red House, at the corner of St Vincent and Sackville Streets, can still be seen the skeletal remains of the former Police Headquarters, which the rebels firebombed before launching their assault on the Red House. The first Red House on this site was, ironically, destroyed by fire in 1903 during riots over an increase in water rates. On the opposite side of the Square to the Cathedral are the modern Hall of Justice (completed 1985), Central Library and City Hall (1961), with a fine relief sculpture on the front. The Square is Trinidad's equivalent to Speaker's Corner in London's Hyde Park.

On Independence Square (2 blocks S of Woodford Square) are the Roman Catholic Cathedral of the Immaculate Conception, built on the shore-line in 1832 but since pushed back by land reclamation, and the Salvatori building at the junction with Frederick Street. The central area of Independence Square, from the cruise ship complex to the Cathedral, has been made into an attractive pedestrian area, known as Lara Promenade in honour of the Trinidadian cricketer, Brian Lara. Behind the Cathedral is Columbus Square, with a small, brightly-painted statue of the island's European discoverer. South of Independence Square, between Edward and St Vincent Streets is the financial complex, two tall towers and Eric Williams Plaza, housing the Central Bank and Ministry of Finance. Also, a little to the S of the square is the old neo-classical railway station, now known as City Gate, a transport hub for taxis and buses travelling between Port of Spain and eastern Trinidad.

To the N of the city is Queen's Park Savannah, a large open space with many playing fields and a favourite haunt of joggers. It was the site of Trinidad's main racecourse for decades, until racing was centralized in Arima. In the middle of the Savannah is the Peschier cemetery, still owned and used by the family who used to own the Savannah. Below the level of the Savannah are the Rock Gardens, with lily ponds and flowers. Opposite are the Botanic Gardens, founded in 1818 by Sir Ralph Woodford. There is an amazing variety of tropical and subtropical plants from SE Asia and South America, as well as indigenous trees and shrubs.

Adjoining the Gardens is the small Emperor Valley Zoo, dating from 1952, which specializes in animals living wild on the island. It has a number of reptiles, including iguanas, four species of boas and the spectacled caiman. (Open 0930-1800, no tickets after 1730, adults US$0.50, children 3-12, US$0.25). Also next to the Gardens is the presidential residence: a colonial style building in an 'L' shape in honour of Governor James Robert Longden (1870-74). Just off the

Jamaat-Al-Muslimeen

On 27 July 1990 Trinidad was shaken by an attempted overthrow of the Government by a Muslim fundamentalist group, the Jamaat-al-Muslimeen, led by the Imam Yasin Abu Bakr. The rebels held the Prime Minister, A N R Robinson, eight of his Cabinet and other hostages, until their unconditional surrender on 1 August. A total of 23 people were killed in the disturbances and about 500 were injured (including the Prime Minister) during the bombing of the police headquarters, the takeover of the parliament building and TV station and subsequent rioting. Despite a promise of an amnesty 114 Jamaat members were arrested and charged with a number of offences, including murder and treason. After taking their case to the courts their appeal was heard in 1992 and the amnesty was reinstated, leading to the release of prisoners. The Government's appeal against the decision was turned down by the High Court in 1993. It then turned to the Privy Council, which heard its case in 1994. The Judicial Committee of the Privy Council ruled that the amnesty was not valid, because the Muslimeen breached its conditions when they continued to hold hostages and make demands for four days after the amnesty was granted instead of ending their insurrection immediately. The Muslimeen will therefore receive no compensation for wrongful imprisonment but neither can they be rearrested and charged for offences committed during their rebellion.

Port of Spain

Not to Scale

Serpentine Rd

Serpentine Pl

Flood St

Mary St

19

8

King George V Park

Elizabeth St

Alexandra St

Hayes St

Maraval Rd

16

St Clair Av

Sweet Briar Rd

Queen's Park Oval

Gray St

Picton St

Alcazar St

Marli St

Rust St

Woodford St

Herbert St

Warner St

Luis St

Alfredo St

Carlos St

Tragarete Rd

Cipriani Blvd

Queens Park West

Stanmore Av

Albion St

Dere St

23

Circular Rd

Rock Gardens

Emperor Valley Zoo

Botanical Gardens

24

Coblen Av

14

15

St Anns Rd

Lady Young Rd

21

Queen's Park Savannah

Circular Rd

12

11

Keate St

Roberts St

Kitchener St

Baden Powell St

Ariapita Av

Fitt St

Murray St

Cornelio St

French St

Methuen St

Gatacre St

Buller St

McDonald St

Wrightson Rd

1

Tranquility St

Melville L

Fitzgerald L

Gordon St

New St

10

Oxford St

Victoria Av

Borde St

Dundonald St

Philip St

Lapeyrouse Cemetery

St Vincent St

Abercromby St

Pembroke St

Frederick St

9

Park St

Flament St

Stone St

Scott-Bushe St

Shine St

Melbourne St

18

Richmond St

Edward St

Duke St

7

Knox St

Charles St

4

Sackville St

17

20

Prince St

London St

Hart St

Chacon St

3

Queen St

Henry St

Charlotte St

George St

Dock Rd

22

2

Independence

Independence

Square North

Square South

5

6

South Quay

13

To Airport & Eastern Rd

N

Observatory St

1. Adam Smith Square
2. Air Caribbean
3. Anglican Cathedral
4. BWIA Office
5. Catholic Cathedral
6. Financial Complex
7. Hall of Justice
8. Jackson Square
9. LIAT Office
10. Lord Harris Square
11. Memorial Park
12. National Museum
13. Port Authority / Boats to Tobago
14. President's Residence
15. Queen's Hall
16. Queen's Royal College
17. Red House
18. Victoria Square
19. White Hall
20. Woodford Square

Hotels:
21. Hilton
22. Holiday Inn
23. Kapok
24. Normandie

C58

Savannah (on St Ann's Road) is Queen's Hall, where concerts and other entertainments are given.

There are several other Edwardian-colonial mansions along the W side of Queen's Park Savannah, built in 1904-10 and known as the Magnificent Seven (after the film of the same name). From S to N, they are Queen's Royal College; Hayes Court, the residence of the Anglican Bishop; Prada's House, or Mille Fleurs; Ambard's House, or Roomor; the Roman Catholic Archbishop's residence; White Hall, formerly the Prime Minister's office, now under repair; and Killarney, Mr Stollmeyer's residence (now owned by the Government). Apart from Hayes Court, which was built in 1910, all were built in 1904. A walk along the N and W sides of the Savannah can be made late in the early morning (before it gets too hot), arriving outside Queen's Royal College as the students are arriving and the coconut sellers are turning up outside. The Anglican Church of All Saints at 13 Queen's Park West is also worth a visit; its stained glass windows are recently restored. Knowsley, another 1904 building, and the now closed *Queen's Park Hotel* (1895), both on the S side of the Savannah, are interesting buildings too. For a history of Port of Spain buildings, with illustrations, read *Voices In The Street*, by Olga J Marrogordato (Inprint Caribbean Ltd 1977).

Just off the Savannah, at the corner of Frederick and Keate Streets, is the small National Museum, in the former Royal Victoria Institute. It has sections on petroleum and other industries, Trinidad and Tobago's natural history, geology, archaeology and history, carnival costumes and photographs of kings and queens, and art exhibitions (including a permanent exhibition of the work of the 19th-century landscape artist, M J Cazabon, see **Culture** above). Entry free.

Away from the city centre, to the W of Port of Spain, is the suburb of St James where in Ethel Street is a large new Hindu temple, the Port of Spain Mandir. On the waterfront is the San Andres Fort built about 1785 to protect the harbour.

EXCURSIONS

There are pleasant drives in the hills around with attractive views of city, sea, and mountain: up Lady Young Road about two miles from Savannah to a look-out 563 feet above sea level (not on a taxi route, but some cars take this route from the airport); by Lady Chancellor Road to a look-out 600 feet above sea level (not always safe, even by car) and to the Laventille Hills to see the view from the tower of the shrine of Our Lady of Laventille. From **Fort George**, a former signal station at 1,100 feet, there are also excellent views; to reach it take the St James route taxi from Woodford Square and ask to get off at Fort George Road; from there it is about one hour's walk uphill passing through some fairly tough residential territory. The Fort was begun in 1804 and

formerly called La Vigie. Although it was never used to defend the island, in times of danger people from Port of Spain brought their valuables up here for safe keeping. From Fort George you can also continue on foot on a rough road up to the telecommunications masts at the top of the hill, from where there are views down to Port of Spain, over to Venezuela and across the N hills.

CHAGUARAMAS

Midway along the Western Main Road to Chaguaramas a road runs off to the N, through the residential area of Diego Martin. The **Blue Basin** waterfall and natural landmark, on the Diego Martin river, is off this road, about a five-minute walk along a path from the town. (If you do leave your car to visit the fall, leave nothing of value in it. Also, you are advised to visit the falls in a group of five or six people if possible to avoid being robbed.) At River Estate, by Diego Martin, is a waterwheel which was once the source of power for a sugar plantation.

The Western Main Road, with many pretty views, especially of the Five Islands, runs on past West Mall in Westmoorings, where there is a large new residential development and the Chamber of Commerce on the waterfront, to Carenage, where there is a remarkable little church, St Peter's Chapel, on the waterside. From here the road continues along the coast past the Trinidad and Tobago Yacht Club (TTYC) (opposite Goodwood Park where the rich live) and the Alcoa transhipment facility, past Point Gourde, where a new Yachting Centre was opened in 1996, to Chaguaramas, on the bay of the same name. This area used to belong to the US navy 1945-64 but is now being developed by the yachting industry. Pier One is a small marina with restaurant and entertainment facilities, popular at weekends, just at the entrance to Chaguaramas.

Further along the coast road, the **Chaguaramas Military History and Aviation Museum** (PO Box 3126, Carenage, T 634-4391) has exhibitions of VE Day and Trinidad's role in both world wars with intricate models as well as relics. Entry through military checkpoint, TT$10 adults, TT$5 children, T 634-4391, knowledgeable staff. Next you come to the Yachting Association, Power Boats, Peake's and Industrial Marine Services (IMS), all offering services to the yachting clientele and the area is packed with boats stacked on land or in the water. From Chaguaramas you can sometimes get a launch (known locally as a *pirogue*) to Gaspar Grande, one of the islands offshore, on which are the Gasparee Caves (entrance TT$5). Monos Island, at the W tip of Trinidad, has many deep caves of white sandy beaches, popular with more affluent Trinidadians. Buses from Port of Spain to Chaguaramas run about every 30 mins, TT$2.

THE NORTH COAST

North of Port of Spain is **Maraval**, just beyond which is the 18-hole St Andrews golf course at Moka (there is also a swimming pool, US$3 for non-members). The North Coast Road branches off Saddle Road (which runs through Maraval back over the hills to meet the Eastern Main Road at San Juan), leading to Maracas Bay, Las Cuevas and Blanchisseuse (see **Beaches** page 804). There is a lookout point on the road to Maracas Bay at the *Hot Bamboo Hut*, where a track goes steeply down to *Timberline* (see **Accommodation**). The stall-holder can call the toucans in the forest, take binoculars to see them fly close and answer him. The Northern Range locations for hiking are best reached from the coastal villages, where there are small hotels, guesthouses and restaurants.

EAST OF PORT OF SPAIN

The E corridor from Port of Spain is a

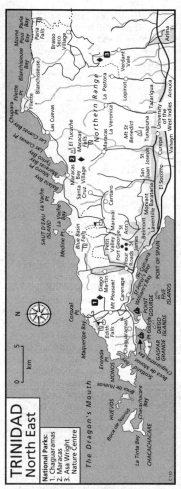

TRINIDAD North East

National Parks:
1. Chaguaramas
2. Maracas
3. Asa Wright Nature Centre

Further E, high on a hill, is Mount St Benedict monastery, reached through St Johns Rd in St Augustine. Although the monastery was founded by a Belgian, the first Benedictine monks came from Bahia, Brazil, in 1912, making this the oldest Benedictine complex in the Caribbean. It started with a tapia hut but construction of the main building on Mt Tabor began in 1918. The monastery has a retreat, lots of educational facilities, a drug rehabilitation centre, a farm and a guest house and is popular with birdwatchers and walkers. There are marvellous views over the Caroni Plain to the sea. A minibus from Port of Spain to St Augustine takes at least 40 minutes, TT$5. There are several good, cheap Chinese restaurants in Tunapuna, the next town after St Augustine, and a wide variety of fruits in the market.

A little further along the Eastern Main Road, the Golden Grove Road branches S to Piarco international airport. If you turn N at this point (Arouca) a road winds 10 km up into the forested mountains to the Lopinot Complex, an estate built by the Comte de Lopinot (see page 795) at the turn of the 19th century. Originally called La Reconnaissance, it is now a popular picnic spot and destination for school trips; there is a small museum. Bar across the road, open 'anyday, anytime'.

High on a ridge in the Maracas Valley are the only known Amerindian rock drawings (petroglyphs) in Trinidad, known as the Caurita drawings. They are probably Arawak and show a series of faces with curving lines indicating limbs. To get there it is a stiff climb of 1-1½ hours in the valley, with access from the main cross roads between San Juan and Tunapuna.

ARIMA

Arima is the third largest city, 16 miles/25 km E of Port of Spain, reached by bus or route taxi, population 26,000. It has a small but interesting Amerindian

dual carriageway and a priority bus route through the industrial and residential suburbs. At **St Joseph**, which was once the seat of government, is the imposing Jinnah Memorial Mosque. North of St Joseph is the Maracas Valley (nothing to do with Maracas Bay), which has a 300-foot waterfall about two miles from the road. Get a Maracas Valley taxi from St Joseph and ask where to get off.

museum at the Cleaver Woods Recreation Centre, on the W side of town housed in a reproduction Amerindian long house, entrance free but donations welcome. In Arima there is a group of people who regard themselves as descendants of the original Amerindians of the area, although there are none left of pure blood. They have a figure head Carib queen and call themselves the Santa Rosa Carib Community, although it is not clear whether they are of Carib, Arawak or other Amerindian descent. West of the church in the centre of town is the Santa Rosa Carib Community Crafts Centre selling traditional crafts: cassava squeezers, serving trays, carvings etc. The Catholic church has good stained glass windows. At the end of Aug there is an annual religious procession where the image of Santa Rosa de Lima is carried from the church and paraded through the streets, very picturesque and interesting.

From Arima the road runs either to Toco at Trinidad's NE tip (which is well worth a visit though its rocky shore defies bathing) or, branching off at Valencia, to the E coast.

The **Hollis Reservoir** can be visited with a permit from WASA (see **Fauna and Flora**). There are a number of short, well-marked trails through beautiful forest and birdwatching is rewarding. From the Valencia junction (avoid the road to Sangre Grande) drive about 1½ km and turn left after a small church into Quarrie Road. Continue N until you reach a WASA pump house, where the guard on duty inspects permits. You can park here or drive along the Quarrie River to the dam where parking is also available.

At **Galera Point**, reached off the road which goes to Toco, over a rickety wooden bridge, there is a small, pretty lighthouse. If you arrive before 1530 it is often open and you can climb to the top for a breathtaking view from the ramp.

The **Salibea Waterfall** is also near Toco. At the Toco 14-mile post, cross the bridge and turn left immediately after the 14¼-mile post into the Salibea/Matura Trace. Follow a 20-min, rather rough drive and park in front of two houses. Walk 15 mins along the trail, turn left at the junction, continue about 10 mins to a second junction where the path narrows on the right going slightly uphill into Mora Forest. Keep on the trail, crossing first a small stream and then a larger river. Ten minutes later at another junction you may bear right over a small hill or walk upstream. Either will get you to Salibea Waterfall and pool in 10 mins. The pool is 6m deep and recommended for good swimmers. There is a picnic area or continue by car to the *Grande Rivière Hotel*, on a wide, sandy beach, where lunches are served at midday.

About eight miles N of Arima, off the Blanchisseuse Road, you can get (by car or taxi, US$7, the driver should wait for you, or warm 2½-hour walk up hill through lovely forests) to the **Asa Wright Nature Centre**, an old plantation house overlooking a wooded valley and a must for bird-lovers. The Nature Centre now owns 700 acres of forest and the annual Christmas bird count usually numbers 161-186 (1990-94) species. There is swimming in a beautiful man-made pool, a network of trails and guided tours (US$6 pp tour and coffee/tea, US$10.50 including buffet Sun lunch, US$6.50 including weekday lunch, see below for accommodation). Sit on the verandah and watch the hummingbirds. The rare oil-birds in Dunstan Cave (also called Diablotin Cave) can only be seen if you stay more than 3 nights; their numbers had dwindled but 138 were counted on 1994 bird count day. Field trips for guests are also organized to the Caroni Swamp, Nariva Swamp, Aripo Savannah, Arena Forest and Blanchisseuse, while turtle watching tours are also offered to the E and W coasts during leatherback nesting season Mar-August. The centre is open daily 0900-1700 (PO Box 4710, Arima, T 667-4655, F 667-0493 for booking, or in the USA, Caligo Ventures, 156 Bedford Rd, Armonk, NY 10504, T 914-273 6333, 800-426 7781, F 914-273 6370). It is wise to give 48 hours notice of your visit. The Centre publishes a newsletter, *The Bellbird*.

This road carries on to Blanchisseuse. A 9-mile (14 km) walk from the road are the **Aripo Caves** (the longest system in Trinidad) with spectacular stalagmites and stalactites (in the wet season, June to Dec, a river runs through the caves). Oilbirds can be seen at the entrance. Only fully equipped spelunkers should venture beyond the entrance. To get there, turn at Aripo Road off the Eastern Main Road, turn right at the 4-mile post, over the bridge into Aripo village. Keep left, continuing uphill to a wide bend to the left where you may park off the road and begin the walk uphill. After a couple of minutes turn left at the small house. After a further 10 mins take the trail to the right of the junction and to the left at the next junction, continuing uphill along the river. At a shelf of rock there is a well-cleared trail away from the river. Keep to this trail heading N until the top of the hill. Go downhill 5 mins to the stream which leads into the cave. Do not enter without a flashlight, rope and other equipment. A knowledgeable guide is recommended.

Blanchisseuse was named after the washerwomen who did their laundry in the Marianne River. The population of about 3,000 is divided between the Upper Village and Lower Village, with the Arima road being the dividing line. There is a Post Office, Health Centre, RC Church, government offices and Police Station in Lower Village, while Upper Village has the school, recreation field and several wood and leather artisans. All this part of the coast is very beautiful with the forest coming down to the sea.

From Arima you can take a (rare) bus, or hitchhike, to Brasso Seco and Paria (though the latter does not appear on some maps). From here the trail runs to **Paria Bay**, which is possibly the best beach on the island, about 8 miles/13 km, ask directions, or see the Tourism and Industrial Development Co (TIDCO) *Sites (trail guide)* book for the route. There is a primitive shelter on the beach but no other facilities so take provisions with you. At the beach, turn right to get to the bridge over the Paria River, from where it is a five-minute walk inland to the spectacular Paria waterfall. Another path from the beach leads W to Blanchisseuse (7 miles/11 km), where the track forks; take the fork closer to the shore if you want to continue along the coast to Las Cuevas (see **Beaches and watersports**).

SOUTH OF THE CAPITAL

Driving S from Port of Spain you see Indians in the rice fields, herds of water buffalo, buffalypso (bigger animals, selectively bred for meat), Hindu temples and Moslem mosques. There are boat trips to the **Caroni Bird Sanctuary**, the home of scarlet ibis, whose numbers are dwindling as the swamp in which they live is encroached upon. The boats leave around 1600 so as to see the ibis returning to their roost at sunset. A spectacular sight, recommended even for those who do not consider themselves bird watchers. Egrets, herons and plovers can also be seen. Bus or route taxi from Port of Spain or San Fernando to Bamboo Grove Settlement no 1, on the Uriah Butler Highway, from where the boats leave, TT$2.50 or TT$5 respectively. Maxi taxi (green bands) from Independence Square. Ask to be dropped off at the Caroni Bird Sanctuary. Arrange return transport in advance, it is impossible to hail a bus in the dark. The only boat operator in the swamp is Winston Nanan (T 645-1305), US$10, group rates available, although a visitors' centre is under construction and an entrance fee may be imposed. Nanan rarely guides now and not all his boatmen are informative; enquire at the Asa Wright Centre for more detailed tours. Tour operators in Port of Spain offer tours, usually on Nanan's boats. Take mosquito repellent and if possible a cold bag with drinks, repellent is essential when you get off the boat at the end of your trip.

SAN FERNANDO

San Fernando on the SW coast is a busy, hot city (population 60,000), as yet not spoilt by tourism but spoilt by just about everything else and not especially attractive. An expressway connects Port of Spain with San Fernando, making it a half hour drive (one hour by taxi). In its neighbourhood are the principal industrial-development area of **Point Lisas** and the **Pointe-a-Pierre** oil refinery. Within the oil refinery is the 26-hectare **Wild Fowl Trust**, a conservation area with two lakes and breeding grounds for many endangered species. Many birds bred in captivity are later released into the wild. There is a Learning Centre with a small archaeological exhibition and shell collection, open 1000-1700, closed Saturday, T 637-5145, Ms Molly Gaskin or Mrs K Shepard on T 662-4040, you must call 48 hours in advance to get permission to enter the compound (there are many entrances, it can be confusing).

A famous phenomenon to visit on the SW coast near San Fernando is **Pitch Lake**, about 47 hectares of smooth surface resembling caked mud but which really is hot black tar; it is 41m deep. It has been described by disappointed tourists, expecting something more dramatic, as looking like a parking lot, although others have pointed out that it is parking lots that look like the Pitch Lake. If care is taken it is possible to walk on it, watching out for air holes bubbling up from the pressure under the ooze. In the wet season, however, most of the area is covered with shallow fresh water. The legend is that long ago the gods interred an entire tribe of Chaima Indians for daring to eat sacred hummingbirds containing the souls of their ancestors. In the place where the entire village sank

into the ground there erupted a sluggish flow of black pitch gradually becoming an ever-refilling large pool. It provides a healthy, though recently decreasing, item in Trinidad's export figures. It can be reached by taking a bus from Port of Spain to San Fernando (US$1 by air-conditioned express, by route taxi it costs US$1.75) and then another from there to La Brea (US$0.75). Insist on a professional guide as locals who pose as guides harass tourists for large tips. Agree on a price in advance as there are no fixed rates. Sometimes there are crowds of guides who are difficult to avoid, but on the other hand it is difficult to understand the lake without explanation.

East of San Fernando, near Princes Town, is the **Devil's Woodyard**, one of 18 mud volcanoes on Trinidad, this one considered a holy site by some Hindus (it is also a natural landmark). It last erupted in 1852 and the bubbling mud is cool, not hot.

On the S coast is the fishing village of **Moruga**, which is reached by a fascinating drive through the Trinidad countryside. Every year around the middle of July they have an unusual celebration of Columbus' 1498 landing on the beach. Fishing boats are decked out as caravels, complete with red Maltese cross. Columbus, a priest and soldiers are met by Amerindians (local boys, mostly of East Indian and African extraction); after the meeting everyone retires to the church compound where the revelry continues late into the night.

The **Karamat Mud Volcano** is a comparatively easy walk through forest in Moruga. There is not at present volcanic activity although major vents are located a short distance away. From Penal Rock Road proceed W to the 8 mile post. On the right head down Haggard Trace driving S until the Moruga West oil field gate. Enter on the road and continue left for 1.7 km. Pass a series of tank batteries, no. 7, on the left, and continue to an oil pump on the right. Take the side road for 400m. Park near the oil pump at a well-head. Do not take the side track into the forest road. Continue up hill.

It is quite difficult to get beyond Arima and San Fernando by bus, but there are route taxis, privately-operated maxi taxis, or you can hire a car or motorcycle.

Island information – Trinidad
● Accommodation

Price guide

L1	over US$200	L2	US$151-200
L3	US$101-150	A1	US$81-100
A2	US$61-80	A3	US$46-60
B	US$31-45	C	US$21-30
D	US$12-20	E	US$7-11
F	US$4-6	G	up to US$3

If you intend to stay in Trinidad for Carnival, when prices rise steeply, you must book a hotel well in advance. Some are booked a year ahead. If arriving without accommodation arranged at Carnival time, the tourist office at the airport may help to find you a room with a local family, though this like hotels will be expensive. You will be lucky to find anything. VAT of 15% will be added to your bill.

Hotels in the upper bracket in the **Port of Spain** area include: **A1-A2** *Bel Air Piarco*, by the airport, T 664-4771/3, F add ext 15, small room, overpriced, typical airport hotel, swimming pool, good bar and restaurant but noise from planes; **L3** *Holiday Inn*, Wrightson Rd (PO Box 1017), T 625-3361, F 625-4166, in the business centre, all facilities very nice, friendly but poor breakfast service; **L1-A1** *Hilton*, on a rise at the corner of Lady Young and St Ann's Rds, NE Queen's Park Savannah (PO Box 442), T 624-3211, F ext 6133, public areas and pool deck are on top and 394 rooms and 25 suites on lower levels, view and breeze from pool level excellent, all facilities, restaurants, bars, eating by the pool is not expensive, non-residents can eat/swim there, conference centre, ballroom, executive suite, frequent entertainment; off St Ann's Rd, at the end of Nook Av (No 10) is **A1-A2** *Normandie* (PO Box 851), T 624-1181/4, 52 standard, superior and loft rooms, a/c, reduced rates for businessmen, swimming pool, in a complex with craft and fashion shops, art gallery and restaurants, comfortable, nice furnishings, wooden floors, good restaurant, outdoor theatre and *Breakfast Shed* for lunch; **L3-A1** *Kapok*, a Golden Tulip hotel, 16-18 Cotton Hill, St Clair (NW

Queen's Park Savannah, T 622-6441, F 622 9677, in USA T 800-74 CHARMS, in UK T 0800-951000), 71 rooms, a/c, TV, phone etc, good, friendly, comfortable, light, big windows, some studios with kitchenette, prices to get room on upper floors for good view and away from traffic noise, restaurants with Chinese and Polynesian cuisine, small pool, facilities for meetings, computer room, shopping arcade; **L1-A2** *Valley Vue*, 67 Ariapita Road, St Ann's, T 623-3511/13, F 627-8046, up in the hills, 68 rooms, children under 12 free, redecorated 1995-96, rooms and suites vary, nice pool, chutes and waterslide (TT$25 for non-guests to use pool), sports facilities inc squash, tennis, gym, sauna, conference facilities, *Coconuts Club* disco, restaurant, bar, busy at weekends; **L3-A3** *Royal Palm Hotel*, 7 Saddle Rd, Maraval, T 628-6042, kitchenette, pool; **A1-A2** *Chaconia Inn*, 106 Saddle Rd, Maraval, under new management 1995, T 628-8603/5, F 628-3214; **A3** *Tropical Hotel*, 6 Rookery Nook Road, Maraval, T 622-5815/4249, F 628-3174, a/c, pool, maid service, bar and restaurant attached, short walk from the Savannah, friendly, helpful, rec. **A1-A2** *Hosanna Hotel*, 2 Santa Margarita Circular Rd, St Augustine, T 662-5449, F 662-5451, pool, all credit cards; **B** *The Cove*, PO Box 3123, Carenage, T 634-4319, the only seaside resort in Chaguaramas, pool, seaside bathing, maid and laundry, kitchenette, access to golf, one 3-bedroom apartment **A2**, breakfast US$6, lunch/dinner US$10.

Guesthouses below US$20 a night are few and far between in the capital. Several of these listed here are not recommended by TIDCO. The **D** *Hillcrest Haven Guesthouse*, 7A Hillcrest Rd, Cascade, T 624-1344 prices rise to **C** during Carnival, minimum stay 6 nights, use of kitchen facilities, mixed reports. **A3** *Zollna House*, 12 Ramlogan Development, La Seiva, Maraval, T 628 3731, F 628-3737, owned by Gottfried (Fred) and Barbara Zollna, small guest house, food varied with local flavour, special diets catered for, breakfast and dinner US$6 and US$12 pp respectively; **B-C** *Copper Kettle Hotel*, 66-68 Edward Street, T 625-4381, central, good, clean but hot and dingy rooms with shower, price depends on whether you have a/c, friendly and helpful staff, good restaurant; **C** *Schultzi's Guest House and Pub*, 35 Fitt Street, Woodbrook, T 622-7521, inc breakfast, kitchen, hot shower, good; **A3-B** *Five Star Guesthouse*, 7 French St, Woodbrook, kitchenette, T 623-4006; **B** *Pelican*

Inn, 2-4 Coblentz Avenue, Cascade, T 627-6271; **B** *Halyconia Inn*, 7 First Avenue, Cascade, T 623-0003, 624-6481; **C** *Scott's Guest House*, 5 Pomme Rose Avenue, Cascade, T 624-4105, friendly, safe area, can be booked from airport; **B-C** *La Calypso Guest House*, 46 French Street, Woodbrook, T 622-4077, ask for room at back or high up for less noise, clean, safe, efficient, kitchen, helpful, car hire available, breakfast US$3, pool at their other guest house; **A3** *Alicia's Guest House*, 7 Coblentz Gardens, St Ann's, T 623-2802, F 623-8560, 17 rooms, expansion planned, all different, some dark, some cheap, all a/c, fan, TV, phone, fridge, family rooms, suites, small pool, jacuzzi, exercise machine, meals available, excursions organized; **C** *Trini House*, 5A Lucknow Street, St James, T/F 638-7550, 4 rooms, inc breakfast, English, German, Italian and French spoken by owners Michael Figuera and Margrit Lambrigger; **B** *Valsayn Villa*, 34 Gilwell Road, Valsayn North, T/F 645-1193, very large, modern, private house with beautifully furnished rooms and lovely garden, in one of the safest residential areas, close to university, 15 mins from airport, 20 mins by bus from down town Port of Spain, excellent home-cooked Indian meals available, rec; **A3-C** *Par-May-La's Inn*, 53 Picton St, T 628-2008, F 628-4707, rec, convenient for carnival and cricket, double or triple rooms with bathroom, a/c, TV, phone, some cheap singles, some shared bathrooms, family run by Bob and Pamela Gopee, friendly, helpful, redecorating 1996, parking, gates locked at night, full American breakfast, or local cuisine with roti, tax and service inc, evening meals on request, credit cards accepted, nearby the same family has some apartments, sleep 6, a/c, US$200/week; **A3-C** *The Abercromby Inn*, 101 Abercromby Street, T 623-5259, F 627-

6658, 18 rooms, a/c, TV, phone, laundry facilities, some large and some very small economy rooms, clean, no food, have to order from outside, 5 mins walk to Queen's Park Savannah, karaoke lounge; **C** *Kitty Peters*, 26 Warren Street, breakfast extra, immaculately clean, hot water showers, fans, quiet area, friendly; **D** *Mardi Gras Guest House*, 134A Frederick Street, T 627-2319, price rises in carnival week, with private bath, dining room, bar; **D** *The New City Cabs Guesthouse*, 33 St Ann's Road, St Ann's, T 623-6443, cheap; **D** *Pearl's Guest House*, 3-4 Victoria Square East, T 625-2158, access to kitchen, can prepare own meals, laundry room, very friendly, family home from home, excellent location for Carnival; **E** *Royal Guest House*, 109 Charlotte Street, T 623 1042, in front of gas station, coffee shop next door owned by same family, shared bathroom, good beds, friendly, safe, but do not walk down Charlotte Street towards the harbour area which is dangerous; *Bullet Guest House*, 6 Park Street, central, clean and safe, does not raise prices during carnival; **C** pp *YWCA*, 8a Cipriani Blvd, women only, rooms with 2 beds, fan, breakfast inc. **A3** *Monique's Guest House*, 114-116 Saddle Road, Maraval, T 628-3334/2351/5511, F 622-3232, on way to golf course and N coast beaches, easy access from city, maxi taxi US$0.50, 10 rooms in main house, 10 more over the hill, large rooms, different sizes sleep 4/5, a/c, TV, phone, some kitchenettes, good food in restaurant, clean, attractive, facilities for the disabled, Monica and Michael Charbonné are helpful and hospitable. **A3-B** *Carnetta's House*, 28 Scotland Terrace, Andalusia, Maraval, just off Saddle Road, T 628-2732, F 628-7717, children under 12 free, **L3** during carnival, a/c, all rooms different sizes, some fridges, some kitchenettes, TV, phone, ironing board, carpets, family room, laundry, nice gardens, grow some produce, meals on request, parking, family atmosphere, videos for TV, lots of repeat business, maxi taxi will drop you at gate for extra US$0.50, run by Carnetta and Winston Borrell; **B** *Jireh's Guesthouse*, 109 Long Circular Road, Maraval, kitchenette, T 628-2337; **B** *Naden's Court Guesthouse*, 32 St Augustine Circular Road, Tunapuna, T 645-2937 (15-30 minutes to Port of Spain by bus on the priority route), with bath, a/c, **C** without, friendly, comfortable, safe and clean, laundry facilities, breakfast room where you can also get sandwiches in the evening, highly rec; **A2** *Pax Guesthouse*, Mt St Benedict, Tunapuna, T 662-4084, built 1932, original furniture made by monks, popular with birdwatchers, 147 species of bird on estate, donkey trails into forest, rooms have high ceilings, no a/c necessary, one family room, most share showers, renovation underway 1995-96, prices MAP, simple but wholesome food, lovely view of central Trinidad as well as of occasional monk. Halfway between the airport and Port of Spain near the St John's Road bus stop in the Saint Augustine district on East Main Road is the **C** *Scarlet Ibis Hotel*, T 662-2251, without shower, once upmarket, restaurant, pool, but now run down with mostly short stay visitors although rec for its cleanliness. **A3** *Sadila House*, run by Savitri and Dinesh Bhola, Waterpipe Road, Five Rivers, Arouca, T 640-3659, F 640-1376, close to airport, breakfast inc, credit cards accepted, weekly and group rates available, a/c, TV; **B** *Airport View Guesthouse*, St Helena Junction, Piarco airport 1.5 km, convenient, a/c, hot water, double rooms have 2 double beds, breakfast US$5, restaurant nearby serving American style food. At Longdenville, near Chaguanas, is the **D** *Unique Hotel*, corner of

Dam Road and Nelson Street, good service, with bathroom, excellent meals, ask for the local Indian food, even at breakfast, rec.

L3-A1 pp *Asa Wright Nature Centre*, PO Box 4710, Arima, T/F 667-4655 or in USA, Caligo Ventures, 156 Bedford Rd, Armonk, NY 10504, T (914) 273-6333, 800-426 7781, F (914) 273-6370, price inc all meals, rum punch, tax and service, 2 main house rooms colonial style, high ceilings, wooden furniture and floors, fan, bathroom, 24 standard rooms and bungalow in gardens, all designed to be private and secluded, verandahs for birdwatching, 80% of guests in high season are birdwatching groups.

At milepost 23 on the Toco Main Road, N of **Balandra Bay** is Mr Hugh Lee Pow's **D** *Green Acres Guest House*, on a farm backed by the ocean, 3 good meals a day inc, very kind and restful.

On the N coast, **L3** *Timberline*, inc breakfast, dinner, tax and service, T 638-2263 for reservations, 2 large rooms in former manager's house on old cocoa plantation, a few cabins, very basic, rustic, mainly used by religious groups on peninsula, fantastic sea views, track down to secluded beach, peaceful, isolated, vegetarians catered for.

At **Blanchisseuse** at Paradise Hill, Upper Village, Mrs Cooper offers bed and breakfast, not cheap but very good. **A3** *Second Spring*, PO Box 3342, Maraval, T 664-3909, 623-8827, T/F 623-4328, cottage or 3 studios inc breakfast and service, at milepost 67¾, rustic, comfortable, in gardens on clifftop with wooden walkway, spectacular views of coast, beaches in walking distance, restaurant 5 mins' walk, owned by Ginette Holder who is friendly and hospitable, excellent value, rec; **A3** *Surf's Country Inn*, in the same village, is a good restaurant on hill above coast road, 3 rooms inc breakfast, owners plan 6 cabanas to sleep 4, nice furnishings, picturesque, small beach below, T 669-2475; **A3** *Laguna Mar Nature Lodge*, at milepost 65½ just before suspension bridge over Marianne River, *Cocos Hut* restaurant attached, opened 1994 by Fred Zollna, close to beach and lagoon, see **Beaches**, rooms with 2 double beds, bathroom, write c/o Zollna House, 12 Ramlogan Development, La Seiva, Maraval, or T 628-3731, F 628-3737, 627-0856. It can be hard to get a hotel room on the N coast in the low season when many places shut; self-catering may be difficult with few shops, no bank, no car rental. **A1** *Grand Riviere*, on bay of same name on N coast, Italian run, fan, friendly, good food, price inc breakfast and dinner, T 670-8381, T/F 680-4553.

In **San Fernando**, not a lot of choice, **A1-A2** *Royal Hotel*, 46-54 Royal Road, T 652-4881, F 652-3924, a/c, kitchenette, lovely hilltop garden; **L3** *Farrell House Hotel*, Southern Main Road, Claxton Bay, near San Fernando, T 659-2230, F 659 2204, a/c, swimming pool, kitchenette, restaurant, good view of the Gulf of Paria, popular with visiting oil men. **B** *Mikanne Hotel and Restaurant*, Railway Avenue, Plaisance Village, Pointe-a-Pierre, T/F 659-2584, a/c, private bath, meal plans, TV on request, pleasant, convenient for oil business and Wild Fowl Trust. At La Brea near the pitch lake is a hotel called *The Hideaway*, some rooms a/c, OK but not for the faint hearted, rooms available for 3, 12 or 24 hours.

At **Mayaro** on the SE coast there are beach houses to rent but check their condition, some are unacceptable; the **C** *Queen's Beach Hotel* is pleasant, friendly, rec, meals around US$10. Inland, the Victoria Regia Research Station, La Gloria Rd, Talparo, Mundo Nuevo, central Trinidad, T 662-7113 or 662-5678, for all-inclusive accommodation and airport transfers, **B** pp, or 7-night package inc 5 guided tours, US$595 pp.

The Bed and Breakfast Cooperative of Trinidad and Tobago, Cruise Ship Complex, Wrightson Road, Port of Spain, T 627-2337, lists a number of establishments in Port of Spain, the suburbs, Carenage, Tunapuna, Arima and Blanchisseuse. It has a desk at the airport before immigration, very helpful.

If arriving by boat, the Seaman's Mission, opp the immigration office, has been helpful in finding hotel rooms.

● **Places to eat**

In **Port of Spain**: at the main hotels where you can expect to pay US$15 in a nice setting with imaginative menus, eg *Tiki Village* in the *Kapok Hotel*, T 622-6441, serves good Polynesian and Chinese food, nice Chinese lunchtime buffet; The *Hilton* Sun brunch buffet is good value at TT$66 plus 15% VAT and 10% service and use of pool, the food here is of an international standard but breakfast is uninspiring often with stale bakeries despite popularity as business meeting place; *Rafters*, 6 Warner Street, Newtown, T 628-9258, pasta, burgers, salads or more elaborate local and seafood, good, bar and restaurant have different menus, rec; in the *Normandie* complex, Nook Av, *La Fantasie*, for fine dining, T 624-1181, and *Café Trinidad*, lovely baking smell, good for breakfast or tea, both pricey; also outside, *The Breakfast Shed*, see below, women come from the main location to serve lunch. *Michael's*, 143 Long Circular Road, T 628-0445, Italian. Smart, but good value restaurants include *Monsoon*, 72 Tragarete Road, at corner with Picton St, T 628-7684, serving Indian dishes and roti, rec, good selection, large meal for about US$3, take away or eat in, very popular at lunchtime, open 1100-2200 Mon-Sat; *Woodford Café*, 62 Tragarete Road, open 1100-2200, Mon-Sat, Creole fare, US$4-6, T 622-2233; *Wazo Dayzeel*, T 623-0115, the name is a corruption of the French word for bird, perched on steep hill above St Ann's, spectacular views over city lights, ask for a table on edge of verandah, food is simple and cheap, nice place for late meal and a drink, closed Wed; *Veni Mangé*, 67 Ariapita Avenue, T 622-7533, small, friendly, good food inc vegetarian dishes, rec, open Mon-Fri 1130-1430, dinner Wed only 1930-2230; at 6 Nook Av is *Solimar*, T 624-6267, international, reasonable prices, good service, outdoor dining, excellent food, reservations advisable and essential at weekends; *Ali Baba*, T 622 5557, on first floor level in Royal Palm Plaza shopping mall on Saddle Road, Maraval, open air dining with a roof, Arabic and other dishes, US$10 and upwards, excellent service, popular, run by a Lebanese, Joe; *Gourmet Club*, upstairs at Ellerslie Plaza, Maraval, T 628-5113, Italian, expensive but good, nice decor, open 1100-2300 weekdays, Sat 1800-2300; *Café Gordon*, 39A Gordon Street, T 627-5514, breakfast 0730-1100, lunch 1100-1500, small, pleasant, Indian-owned, different lunch menu every day with choice of 2 dishes, usually

TT$10; *Une Cachette*, Dheine's Bay, Carenage, T 637-5954, Caribbean-style food, US$3-17 lunch and dinner. If you've a yen for the best pepper shrimps in the Caribbean, the Chinese *Hong Kong City Restaurant*, 86A Tragarete Road, is the place, good food but rather snooty service.

Fast food outlets include *Mario's Pizza Place*, Tragarete Rd and other outlets, average to awful; *Joe's Pizza*, St James, good, also other Italian dishes; *Pizza Burger Boys*, Frederick St, and Ellerslie Plaza, Boissiere Village, Maraval (for take away T 628-2697, best of its type, will deliver to boatyards and marinas). The first *Pizza Hut* opened in Curepe but the largest one in the world is *Pizza Hut Roxy*, which used to be a cinema, central. *Kentucky Fried Chicken* in most cities and towns, better than you might expect; *Royal Castle*, 49 Frederick St and other locations throughout Trinidad, chicken and chips with a local flavour. All along Western Main Road in St James there are lots of cafes, snack bars and restaurants, all reasonably priced, lots of choice. The *Pelican Inn*, Coblenz Av, Cascade, serves food, but is mainly a pub, hugely popular (late arrivals at the weekend have to park 600 m away); *New Shay Shay Tien*, 81 Cipriani Blvd, T 627-8089, rec; *De Backyard*, 84 Picton Street, local dishes; *Golden Palace*, 212 Southern Main Road, Marabella, T 658-6557, also Chinese, very good. *Imperial Garden*, Highland Plaza, Glencoe, T 663-6430, 'authentic' Chinese food. Also *China Palace II*, Ellerslie Plaza, Maraval, T 622-5866. For Chinese food in San Fernando, try *Soongs Great Wall*, 97 Circular Rd, T 652-2583, round the corner from the *Royal Hotel*, very good, the distinctive, Trinidadian version of Chinese food. At the cruise ship harbour, *Coconut Village*, good food, cheap; *Breakfast Shed*, opp *Holiday Inn* and sometimes called *Holiday Out*, a big hall with several kitchens where locals eat, US$2.50 for very substantial lunch with juice; *Hot Shoppe* has by far the best rotis, see *Food*; next to the Maraval Road branch, the jerk chicken/jerk pork places have good, spicey Jamaican-style food; the Town Centre Mall and Voyager Mall on Frederick Street have indoor halls with a varied and good selection of stands selling food, seating in the middle. Colsort Mall is similar but not so good. *Willie's Ice Cream*, branches in Arima, Montrose, Mid Centre Mall, Coffee St, Marabella and Tunapuna, and franchises in other places, tropical fruit flavours.

At *Chaguaramas Pier One*, T 634-4472/4426, F 634-4556, like country club, restaurant, conference facilities, family club, marina, seafood, live entertainment at weekends, open 1100-2300, popular at weekends, pool, kayaks, dinghies, fishing area; *Anchorage*, Point Gourde Road, T 634-4334, for seafood, open 1100-2400 Mon-Sat, dancing, live entertainment some evenings, popular with yachties. *Pisces*, TTYC, moderately priced local food and special nights, call for reservations; *Windjammers*, TTYA, fast food and inexpensive local dishes after sailing with TTYA members; *The Bight*, Peake's, bar and restaurant with outdoor dining overlooking the Chaguaramas anchorage.

Timberline, T 638-2263, off the coast road to Maracas, renovated cocoa house on promontory, down very steep track, gourmet local food, grow own herbs and some fruit and vegetables, path down to small beach, very peaceful, lovely view, lots of wildlife, accommodation available. At Blanchisseuse, *Surf's Country Inn*, North Coast Road, T 669-2475, good value, delicious meals, beautiful setting, changing rooms available; *Cocos Hut*, also on coast road at Mile 65½ by Marianne River, small, friendly, both these restaurants offer rooms. For afternoon tea (and other meals by reservation) *Pax Guesthouse* on Mt St Benedict, above Tunapuna, where tea is a tradition and all the bread, cakes, jam, honey etc are handmade by the monks, wholesome and tasty, lovely views of Trinidad from patio.

Tobago

Tobago is not as bustling as Trinidad but tourism is booming. The end of the oil boom in Trinidad and the growth of tourism in Tobago has narrowed the gap in living standards between the two islands. Nevertheless, it is ideal for those in search of relaxation. The tourist area is concentrated on the SW end, near the airport, and about six miles from the capital, **Scarborough**. There are small hotels and guest houses scattered around the island, however, offering peace and quiet in beautiful surroundings. The forest on the central hills provides a spectacular backdrop for the many horseshoe bays around the coast and there is good walking, sailing and diving.

SCARBOROUGH

Above the town is Fort King George (1770), which is well-maintained and has good views along the coast. At the Barrack Guard House is the Tobago museum, with an excellent display of early Tobago history including Amerindian pottery, shells, military relics, maps and documents from the slave era. Open Mon-Fri, 0900-1700, adults US$0.50, children US$0.15. At the same location is a hospital. In Scarborough itself there are interesting Botanic Gardens on the hill behind the Mall. The town is pleasant but perhaps not worth an extended visit. There are some interesting buildings, such as the House of Assembly on James Park (built in 1825), and Gun bridge, with its rifle-barrel railings, but there is plenty of new development with a new deep water harbour and cruise ship terminal. Scarborough Mall is modern, concrete and rather tatty but most activity is around here: the Tourist Office, Post Office, Library and bus station as well as the market, where you can find local varieties of fruit and vegetables, clothing, meat and fresh coconut water. There are banks on Main Street. Just off Main Street, George Leacock has turned his home into a museum, quite interesting.

EXCURSIONS

If you are driving around Tobago, the 1:50,000 map, usually available from the tourist office in Scarborough, at US$3.50, is adequate, although note that many of the minor roads are only suitable for 4-wheel drive. If you are hiking, get the three 1:25,000 sheets, not currently available in Tobago but you can get them from the Lands and Survey Division, Richmond Street, Port of Spain, or a good map shop abroad. You can walk anywhere as long as you can get there. There is a book of trails.

East from Scarborough, on the Windward coast, is Bacolet Bay. Off the coastal road you can go to the Forest Reserve by taking a bus from Scarborough to **Mount St George** and then walking or hitching to **Hillsborough Dam** (access TT$4, payable on site, the lake is the drinking water supply for the island, no swimming, you may find a man to take you on the lake in a rowing boat, lovely forest setting); from there continue NE through the forest to **Castara** or **Mason Hall** on an unpaved, rough road. A guide is not necessary, but directions, compass and supplies, including water, are essential. Birdwatching is excellent (oropendulas, mot-mots, jacamans, herons) and there are cayman in the lake, but look out for snakes (none of them poisonous). Alternatively, take a taxi to Mason Hall and walk to Mount St George via Hillsborough Dam, which is easier walking as the track is on the level or

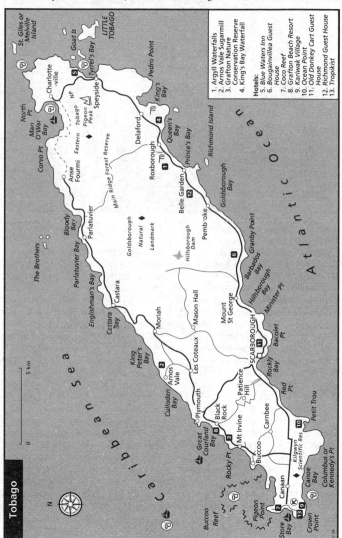

Hotels:
1. Argyll Waterfalls
2. Arnos Vale Sugarmill
3. Grafton Nature Conservation Reserve
4. King's Bay Waterfall
5. Blue Waters Inn
6. Bougainvillea Guest House
7. Coco Reef
8. Grafton Beach Resort
9. Kariwak Village
10. Ocean Point
11. Old Donkey Cart Guest House
12. Richmond Guest House
13. Tropikist

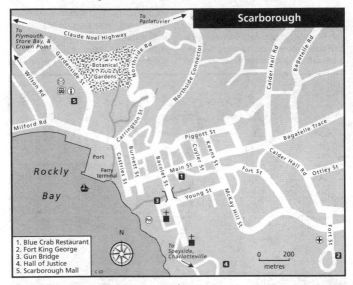

Scarborough

1. Blue Crab Restaurant
2. Fort King George
3. Gun Bridge
4. Hall of Justice
5. Scarborough Mall

downhill, about 7 miles. By Mount St George (Tobago's first, short-lived principal town, then called George Town) is **Studley Park House** and **Fort Granby** which guards Barbados Bay.

The road continues through **Pembroke** and **Belle Garden**, near where is **Richmond Great House**, now a hotel. **Roxborough**, the island's second town, also on the Windward coast, is worth a visit. The **Argyll River** waterfalls near Roxborough comprise four beautiful falls with a big green pool at the bottom, a 10-minute walk upstream from the road which can be very muddy. You can't miss them because of all the rather overpriced and pushy guides standing in the road.

A good walk is the road from Roxborough to Parlatuvier and Bloody Bay through the Main Ridge Forest Reserve. There is hardly any traffic and you go through singing forests with masses of birds (best walked early morning or late afternoon for maximum birds, including cocricos, collared trogon, mot-mots, jacamans, humming birds). After the

5-mile marker is a semi-circular trail in the forest called Gilpin's Trace. Great views from the hut at the top of the road. Beyond Roxborough is **King's Bay**, with waterfalls near the road in which you can swim.

From the fishing village of **Speyside** you can visit **Little Tobago**, a forested islet off the NE coast, and sanctuary for birds. There are wild fowl and 58 species of other birds, including the red-billed tropic bird found here in the largest nesting colony in the N Atlantic. Boats across cost US$12.50 (includes a guided tour of the islet and snorkelling). Go early in the morning to see the birds. If you want to camp, you are supposed to have prior permission from the Forestry Division at Studley Park, T 639-4468. They also have a rudimentary camp on the main ridge by the Roxborough-Parlatuvier road, which can be used by arrangement. At Speyside, you can sling a hammock near the government centre on the beachfront: well-lit, a nightguard may keep your belongings under lock, but it may be windy.

From Speyside you can climb **Pigeon Peak**, at about 1,900 ft the highest point on the island. A guide is essential and Lebeque Jack has been recommended. There are two routes up the hill through the forest, the shorter one is steeper than the longer, so both take about 3 hrs. From the top you can see over the N and S coasts and the offshore islets.

A trip to **Charlotteville** in the NE (route taxi: from Scarborough, TT$9, 3 a day but not on Saturdays, when the Adventist drivers do not work, for the return journey you can arrange to be picked up) is recommended; there are magnificent views on the way and the village itself is on a fine horse-shoe bay with a good beach; swimming and snorkelling. From Charlotteville, it is a 15-min walk to **Pirate's Bay**, which is magnificent and unspoilt and is good for snorkelling. Also adjacent is **Man O'War Bay**. **Campbellton Bay** is a 30-40-min walk from Charlotteville (ask locally for directions) through dense forest to a secluded beach, mostly used only by fishermen. It is fairly easy to hitch a ride from Charlotteville to Speyside.

The road between Charlotteville and Plymouth along the Caribbean coast has been improved but 4-wheel drive is needed for part of the way even in summer. The stretch between L'Anse Fourmi and Charlotteville is usually impassable to normal traffic and a notice says you travel at your own risk. A motorbike is recommended. The views are worth the trouble with lots of lovely bays beneath you. It is not advisable to drive this road when it is raining. Alternatively get a taxi to L'Anse Fourmi and walk (comfortable 4 hrs) along the track to Corvo Point, Hermitage (bush rum for sale), Man O'War Bay and Charlotteville. It is undulating, with no very steep hills. Bird life is plentiful, including parrots, and you can see iguanas. Take water. The stretch of road between Anse Fourmi and Moriah is smooth, traffic is light and it is very picturesque.

At the SW/tourist end of the island, many hotels and resorts are within walking distance of the airport. At **Store Bay** are the ruins of small **Milford Fort**, and brown pelicans frequent the beautiful but crowded beach, which is a good place to watch the sunset. **Pigeon Point** has the island's most beautiful beach, clean and with calm water, though US$2 is charged for adults and US$0.50 for children for admission as the land is private; a wall has been built to stop you walking along the foreshore and groynes built by the owners have caused beach erosion. There are huts, tables and benches, lockers, bars, shopping, boat hire and water sports. It is another good place to watch the sunset.

From **Mount Irvine Bay** (further N on the Caribbean coast), where there is an attractive, palm-fringed championship golf course (the hotel of the same name has a good beach – surfing) you can walk up to **Bethel** (about 2 miles), the island's highest village, for excellent views across the island. Another beach which is well worth a visit is **Turtle Bay**.

The main town on this coast is **Plymouth**, with **Fort James** overlooking **Great Courland Bay** (site of the Courlander settlement in the 17th century). A much-quoted attraction in Plymouth is the enigmatic tombstone of Betty Stevens (25 November, 1783), which reads: "She was a mother without knowing it, and a wife, without letting her husband know, except by her kind indulgences to him."

Hidden in the forest some miles from **Arnos Vale** is the **Arnos Vale Sugarmill**, dating from 1880; a recommended excursion, it is possible to hitchhike. It is difficult to continue along this coast by public transport, Plymouth to Parlatuvier is not a recognized route. You have to go instead via Roxborough, with a lovely journey from there through the forest. Check that there is transport back in the afternoon as there is nowhere to stay in Parlatuvier.

The small village of **Castara** on the coast can be seen in 10 mins but is a pleasant place to visit. There is a small bay with a sandy beach and a snorkelling reef, or a 10-min walk inland will take you to an easily accessible waterfall. Eating places are readily available and there is accommodation.

Buccoo Reef Glass-bottomed boats for visiting this undersea garden leave from Pigeon Point, Store Bay and the larger hotels nearby. Boats may be cheaper if hired from Buccoo Village. The charge is US$6 for 2-2½ hours, with shoes and snorkel provided; wear swimming costume and a hat. Longer trips with barbecue cost around US$20, worth it if you eat and drink plenty. The dragging of anchors and greed of divers have tarnished the glory of this once marvellous reef, though, and you may prefer to make the trip to Speyside where there are also glass bottomed boat trips over a pristine reef. Elkhorn and other corals have been badly damaged by snorkellers and divers walking on them. The reef is now protected by law; it is forbidden to remove or destroy the corals or other marine life. Boat trips also include the **Nylon Pool**, an emerald-green pool in the Caribbean. Boats leave between 0900 and 1430, depending on the tide. Be selective in choosing which boat – and captain – you take for the trip; some are less than satisfactory (Selwyn's *Pleasure Girl* has been recommended, so has Archie and Mala's *Come to Starcheck*, others include Hew's Tours, Hewlett Hazel, T 639-9058, F 639-7984, Kenneth Christmas, Buccoo Reef Cooperative, Buccoo Point, T 639-8582, or after 1900, T 639-8746). From Scarborough to Buccoo by bus is TT$2. Taxis also go to Buccoo.

Island information – Tobago

● Accommodation

In the vicinity of **Crown Point**: **L1-L2** *Coco Reef*, PO Box 434, T 639-8571, F 639-8574, in N America T 800-221 1294, F 305-639 2717, opened 1995 on site of old *Crown Reef* hotel, modelled on Bermudan hotel, peach and white walls, red roof, 96 rooms, 20 suites, 17 garden villa suites, 3 villas, on man made

Price guide

L1	over US$200	L2	US$151-200
L3	US$101-150	A1	US$81-100
A2	US$61-80	A3	US$46-60
B	US$31-45	C	US$21-30
D	US$12-20	E	US$7-11
F	US$4-6	G	up to US$3

beach, pretty view of Pigeon Point, height of luxury, several restaurants, small pool, conference facilities, spa, gym, tennis, shops, dive shop, sail boats, close to airport and in main hotel area, go and talk to the old blue macaw at the rear of the complex, he used to live at the *Crown Reef* in a prominent site, but now he's isolated and lonely; **A1-A2** *Tropikist*, T 639-8512, F 645-0341, 33 a/c rooms with balcony, pool, loungers, large lawn, swings, restaurant overlooks sea, small beach but not suitable for swimming, painted white with lots of bougainvillea, right by airport; **L3-A1** *Sandy Point Village*, T 639-8533, F 639-8496, 48 large rooms and suites, some split level, TV, kitchenette, balcony, quiet a/c, in pleasant gardens, pool, beach rooms under renovation open on to sea, poor beach, most people go to Store Bay, airless disco in basement, *The Deep*, music goes on until early hours; **A2-A3** *Crown Point Beach Hotel*, PO Box 223, (T 639-8781/3, F 639-8731), studios and cabins, pool; **A2-A3** *Arthur's On-Sea*, Crown Point, T 639-0196, F 639-4122, kind and helpful, a/c, pool, 4 mins' walk from safe beach, rec; **A2** *Jimmy's Holiday Resort*, Store Bay, T 639-8292, F 639-3100, apartment, bars, eating places, shops nearby. If you turn right out of the airport, and take the first right, you come to **B-C** *Store Bay Holiday Resort*, T/F 639-8810, 5 mins' walk, do not be fooled by taxi drivers who will charge US$5 for the ride, about the cheapest in this area, but self-catering only, 16 apartments, clean, well-furnished, kitchen, gardens, night time security guard, small pool, friendly, good value, rec; next door is **A2** *Kariwak Village*, very nice, compact rooms in cabins, restaurant with excellent food, no beach, small pool, no radios or TV, expansion for 1996 with more rooms and meeting facilities, owners involved in the arts, exhibitions held here, yoga and therapy, retreats, PO Box 27 (T 639-8545/8442, F 639-8441); also close by is **A2-A3** *Toucan Inn*, PO Box 452, T 639-7173, F 639-8933, inc tax and service, African style huts, good food and entertainment, highly rec; **C** *Jetway Holiday Resort*, 100m from airport terminal, can be noisy until after 2200, pleasant self-contained units with cooking facilities, friendly, helpful, a few mins' walk to Pigeon Point and Store Bay, T 639-8504; a bit further from the main road is **A3-B** *Golden Thistle*, T 639-8521, F 639-7060, quiet location, 36 rooms around pool, lawn or neither, single storey, a/c, TV, phone, bath tub and shower, functional but dark, no atmosphere; **A3-B** *James Holiday Resort*, Crown Point, T/F 639-8084, standard room or apartment, **L2** 3-bedroom apartment max 12 people, car and jeep rental, credit cards accepted, 2 mins' walk from airport, a/c, shower, TV, patio or balcony, restaurant; **C-D** *Surf Side Holiday Homes*, Crown Point, T 639-3521/2418, 35 rooms and suites, kitchenettes, a/c, walking distance to beaches; **A3** *Conrado Beach Resort*, Milford Extension Rd, between Store Bay and Pigeon Point, T 639-0145, beach front, standard or superior rooms, some small, some with balconies, TV, phone, some roadside view, priced accordingly, restaurant on beach for breakfast, inside for night-time, good snorkelling offshore on small reef, fishing boats moored outside, family owned, excellent service, highly rec; **D** *Plaza 2*, Milford Road, Canaan, no kitchen facilities, away from the beach but buses stop outside; **E** *Balgobin & Dorris Guest House*, and taxi service, John Gorman Trace, Milford Road, Crown Point, T 639-7328, 5 mins walk from airport and beach, nice, clean rooms with bathroom and cooking facilities, mosquito nets on windows, fan, quiet and safe, friendly owners. There are lots of guesthouses and small hotels along the road between the airport and Pigeon Point. **D** *Anjo's Villa*, PO Box 148, Crown Point, T 639-7963, 15 mins' walk from airport, use of kitchen; **D** *Lewis Villa*, T 639-8022, small units with kitchen, good value; **D** *Classic Resort Guest House*, turn left out of airport and walk along track, double room with kitchen and lounge with TV, friendly; **C** *Spence's Terrace*, Crown Point, T 639-8082, room, kitchenette, bathroom, balcony, new and fresh, rec, near beach and airport, Spence is helpful, car rental available. Beyond Pigeon Point is **L3** *Lagoon Lodge*, Bon Accord, T 639-8555, F 639-0957, approached down poor track, isolated, split level cabins sleep 2 adults and 2 children, fully equipped, TV, music, phone, fan, a/c, airy, comfortable, ideal for self-catering, owner provides fruit, eggs, milk, maid/cook available, set in 4 acres of gardens with chickens, peacocks, rhea, boardwalk through mangroves to sea lagoon, jetty with hammock,

kayak and sailboat, very private, tranquil, rec, mosquitoes in wet season.

In the **Lowlands** area, **L3-A3** *Ocean Point*, Milford Road, Lowlands, T/F 639-0973, studios sleep 3, suites fit 5, dive packages available, a/c, TV, pool, sundeck, restaurant serves East Indian specialities, 2 min walk from sea, transport needed, family-run, friendly, rec, in USA T 800-692 4094, UK T 0181-741 4894; on the same road, **A2-B** *Hampden Inn Guest House*, Lowlands Post Office, Milford Road LP 171, T/F 639-7522, bed and breakfast, German spoken, standard or superior rooms all on ground floor, hammocks, large bathrooms, restaurant/bar, bike hire, dive packages, no pool; **A2** *Coral Reef*, T 639-2536, F 639-0770, PO Box 316, 17 rooms, 18 apartments, 30 years old and showing it, basic, dark corridor, no view, hard beds, old carpets, pool, a/c; **L1-L2** *Palm Tree Village*, Little Rockly Bay, Milford Road, T 639-4180, F 623-5776, a/c, 2-, 4-bedroom villas or rooms in villas, kitchenettes, pool, small beach, quite smart but lacking atmosphere, nightclub attached, tennis, fitness centre, conference room for 60, horse.

Accommodation in **Scarborough** is mostly in guesthouses or bed and breakfast (contact the *Association* c/o *Federal Villa*, 1-3 Crooks River, Scarborough, T 639-3926/8836, F 639 3566, or the Tourism Development Authority on Tobago; the brochure lists 14 properties, mostly in the SW or near Scarborough, about US$20d). Highly rec is *Glenco Guest House*, Glen Road, Scarborough (rates negotiable according to length of stay), clean, basic, mosquitoes, no fans, breakfast, T 639 2912. **C** *Jacob's Guesthouse*, Scarborough, in a bad area for drugs, no longer rec, T 639-2271; **C** *Hope Cottage*, Fort Street, b&b; several others, eg **B** *Della Mira Guest House*, Windward Rd, T 639-2531, on outskirts of town, below road, sea view; **B** *Miriam's Bed and Breakfast*, or *Federal Villa*, Crooks River, T 639-3926, 6 rooms, shared bath, fan, modest but clean and comfortable, 7 mins' walk to harbour, run by friendly and helpful Miriam Edwards, secretary of the Bed and Breakfast Association. **C** *Sea Breeze Motel*, Milford Road, Scarborough, T 639-6404, spotlessly clean, bathroom, TV, on seafront W of the port, rec as base for touring. About ½ mile S of Scarborough is the **L3-A1** *Old Donkey Cart House Restaurant and Apartment Suites*, run by Gloria Jones-Knapp, 2 mins from beach on hillside with sea view, inc breakfast, tax and service, charming rooms in old house or in new building, restaurant, good food, T 639-3551, F 639-6124, Bacolet Street 73, Scarborough. Ten mins' drive from Scarborough is **A3** *Ocean View*, John Dial, T 639-6796, rec; under same management is **A3** *Windy Edge*, Concordia, 12 minutes drive from the harbour, 600 feet above sea level overlooking the Atlantic and the Caribbean, spacious grounds, quiet, highly rec, inc breakfast, evening meals by arrangement US$25-30, route taxis pass by, T 639-5062.

On the **Windward coast**, **A3-C** *Bougainvillea Guest House*, by Fort Granby, Studley Park, T 660-2075, F 622-5674, inc breakfast and airport transfer, owned by Hilton McFarlane who also lectures in medicine at UWI, beautiful location on hillside overlooking bay, lots of birds, fruit trees, stress free, all rooms different, some small, some family rooms, some shared bathrooms, new rooms being built 1995-96, beach 3 mins' walk, small pool; **L2-A2** *Richmond Great House*, T/F 660-4467 (see page 824), overlooking Richmond Bay, lovely, airy, quiet, colonial elegance, polished wood floors, suites in main house or newer rooms downstairs, pool, owned by Professor of African history; one **E** guest house in Roxborough, ask for Mrs Carter, Police Station Road, 2 rooms, kitchen, shower, quiet, friendly; **A1-A2** *The Speyside Inn*, Windward Road, Speyside, T/F 660-4852, 6 rooms, 1 studio, lovely airy rooms, nicely furnished, excellent value, tax and large breakfast inc with home made breads, dinner by reservation only, small beach across road, view of Little Tobago, close to *Jemma's* restaurant; **L2-A2** *Manta Lodge*, Windward Road, Speyside, PO Box 433, Scarborough, T 660-5268, F 660-5030, 22 standard, superior or loft rooms, new, rather sterile, loft has no view, a/c essential as hot under roof, superior rooms, though cheaper are better, with balcony, view and more air, small pool, bar, restaurant, caters mainly to divers, packages available with Tobago Dive Experience; **L1-A1** *Blue Waters Inn*, Batteaux Bay, Speyside, T 660-4341, F 660-5195, an isolated and delightfully unsophisticated hotel, 28 rooms, 1-2 bedroom bungalows and self-catering units, caters for people who want to sit on the beach, bird watchers and divers, inc tax and service, dive packages with Aquamarine Dive on site, very pretty bay, no other development, view of Little Tobago.

At **Charlotteville** are **L3-A3** *Man O'War Bay Cottages*, T 660-4327, F 660-4328, cottages sleep 4, minimum 2 nights, spacious, well-equipped kitchen, right on beach with tropical gardens behind, barbecue facilities, expensive shop with limited range, check your shopping bill carefully; **D** *Cholson's Chalet* has 1-3 bedroomed apartments separated from the beach by the road, contact Hewitt Nicholson (T 639-2847) or Pat Nicholson (T 639-8553), the price sometimes rises after you have moved in. **D** *Alyne*, very friendly, clean, comfortable. Ask around for private accommodation, it is available, eg Mrs McCannon's house in Bellaire Road, not luxury but OK; for rooms or small houses to rent try asking in *Phebe's Ville View* restaurant, see below.

At **Castara**, **C** *Blue Mango*, T 639-2060, owned by friendly Colin Ramdeholl, simple but charming, good walking and swimming nearby, eating places in the village.

At **Arnos Vale**, **L2** *Arnos Vale Hotel*, PO Box 208, T 639-2881, F 639-4629, Italian run and 90% Italian guests, 30 rooms, beautiful surroundings in tropical forest, great birdwatching, many birds come to be fed at 1630, including the blue crowned mot mot, hospitable, dive shop, new 30-room complex being built at site of old water wheel.

At **Plymouth**, **B** *Cocrico Inn*, T 639-2961, F 639-6565, swimming pool; **L3-A2** *Turtle Beach Hotel*, PO Box 201, Plymouth, T 639-2851, F 639-1495, 125 rooms, pool, on beach, tennis, a/c, refurbished 1995, service and management good, Sun West Indian buffet highly rec, especially the curried crab; **L1-L2** *Mount Irvine Bay Hotel and Golf Course* (see page 807), PO Box 222, T 639-8871, F 639-8800), rooms, suites or garden cottage, luxury furnishings, TV, phone, pool, beach, mediocre food at *Sugar Mill* restaurant, tennis, gardens of 16 acres; **L1-L2** *Grafton Beach Resort*, PO Box 25, Black Rock, T 639-0191/9444, F 639 0030, luxury, highly rec, a/c, pool, TV, friendly and efficient service, good food at restaurants, breakfast rec, excellent beach front location in Stonehaven Bay, *Le Grand Courlan* is a new wing, opened 1995-96, T 639-9667, F 639-9292, 78 luxury rooms, 10 1-bedroom suites, 8 garden rooms with jacuzzis, all have phone, fan, a/c, hairdryers, minibar, handsome furnishings, shops, pools, restaurants, business centre, health spa, very upmarket compared with other hotels on Tobago; next door is **L1** *Plantation Beach Villas*, Stonehaven Bay Road, Black Rock T/F 639-0455, 6 villas each with 3 bedrooms, verandah, maid service, pool; **L1** *Sanctuary Resort*, PO Box 424, T 639-9556, F 639-0019, just inland, luxury villa development, hotel planned, fantastic views across island to Pigeon Point and Buccoo Reef from hill, bordered by 260-acre bird sanctuary; **A2** *La Belle Creole*, Mt Irvine, PO Box 372, T 639-0908, run by Mrs Gerhild Oliver, English, German, French and Italian spoken, right by golf course, 5 mins' walk from beach, bed and breakfast, dinner on request, queen sized beds; *Massiah's Cottage*, Mt Irvine, reasonable rates, T 639-4444 after 1600, owner works for Liat; **B** *Old Grange Inn*, PO Box 297, Buccoo, Mt Irvine, T/F 639-0275, a/c, in Buccoo on Battery St, **D** *Aunty Flo's*, T 639-9192, nice, friendly, run by Mrs Flora Howie; **B** *Golf View Apartments*, Buccoo Junction, Mt Irvine, T 639-0979, 7 apartments, 5 rooms, kitchenette; **A3-B** *Blue Horizon*, Jacamas Drive, Mt Irvine, T 639-0432/3, kitchenette, pool; **D-E** *Rolita Tea Hut*, Old Grange Road, Mt Irvine, opp *Blue Horizon*, small guest house run by Roy and Pat Cousins, rooms with shower and WC, pool, meals available 0700-2100 daily, also lunch boxes, 20 mins' walk from beach, highly rec, T 639-7970; **C** *Green Acres*, Daniel Trace, Carnbee, T 639-8287, clean rooms with shower, safe, some with kitchens, inc breakfast, delicious local food, friendly family, US$4-5 taxi service, highly rec; **D** *Michael Baker's* apartments, Daniel Trace, Carnbee, T 639-8243, owner is chief of lifeguards and singer.

There are many cheap guesthouses throughout Tobago and many people take in visitors: ask at any village store (prices for room only).

● **Places to eat**

At Store Bay there are a number of restaurants, many have tables outside near the beach. The *Beach Bar* has music all day on Sat, and a barbecue from 2000-2400, for US$17 per head for drinks and small portions of fish and chicken, poor value unless you drink a lot; rec is *Miss Jean's*, US$2 and less for all kind of 'ting', a full meal with drinks for 2 costs less than US$10, crab and dumplings are a speciality but the crabs are woefully small because of overfishing, also most of the food here and at other huts is reheated, not freshly cooked; *Dillon's Seafood Restaurant*, Crown Point, T 639-8765, open daily from 1800 except Mon, food and service have deteriorated; the restaurant at the *Kariwak Village* has interesting, excellent food and drinks, well served; nearby is *Golden Spoon* (junction of roads to Scarborough and Pigeon Point, T 639-8078, open for breakfast, lunch and dinner, local

dishes) and *Columbus Snackette* (at the crossroads). *Joy's*, in Buccoo, small, friendly, good local food for US$3.50, barbecue on Wed for US$2.50; *La Tartaruga*, Buccoo Bay, T 639-0940, Italian restaurant café-bar, PO Box 179, excellent Italian food, limited menu, expensive, reservations essential.

The *Black Rock Café* on Black Rock main road, T 639-7625, rec for very good food, slow service, very busy; *Under the Mango Tree*, Black Rock, very tasty local food, US$17 for full meal; *The Seahorse Inn*, next to *Grafton Beach Resort*, excellent dinners, extensive menu. *Peacock Mill*, Friendship Estate, Canaan, T 639-0503, restaurant and bar in old sugar mill with lots of peacocks wandering around and coming to be fed at around 1700, their squawks accompany the jazz sometimes featured outdoors under the trees. *Phebe's Ville View*, Charlotteville, nice view of the bay, very good and cheap meals, try the prawns if available, dumplings and curried crab also rec, very friendly, rooms and apartments for rent at reasonable prices, Phebe also has a laundry and special prices for people on yachts.

Jemma's Sea View, Speyside, T 660-4066, on a tree top platform by the beach, good, filling lunch or dinner, TT$40, slow service, nice atmosphere, highly rec, closed Sat (Adventists), you can get hassled here for boat trips.

The *Blue Crab*, at the corner of Main Street with Fort Street, Scarborough, T 639-2737, specializes in local food, very good lunch but terribly slow service, reasonable prices, nice view over harbour; *Rouselles*, Bacolet Street, T 639-4738, one of the best, seafood, short but excellent menu, very busy Sat; *Old Donkey Cart*, Bacolet, T 639-3551, good food, European wines, closed Wed except Dec-April. *De Bamboo Bar & Restaurant*, Milford Road, Scarborough, next to *Sea Breeze Motel*, rec, lobster good value, 3-course meal US$20; *Buddies Café* in the Mall, Scarborough, is reasonable, T 639-3355; *The Cabin Pub*, opposite the Customs House near the port in Scarborough, a favourite 'liming' spot for locals and yachties, owned by Gus, a Tobagonian who is full of stories, open from 0900, lots of happy people, rec; *Patinos*, Shirvan Road, run by Kenneth and Marcia Patino with their son as chef, excellent food, grilled red snapper with ginger sauce rec, delicious West Indian platter at lunchtime, evening steel band once a week, reservations needed; *The Starting Gate*, Shirvan Road, good food, pool and table football.

Information for travellers

BEFORE TRAVELLING

● **Documents**

Visas are not required for visits of under 3 months by nationals of most Commonwealth countries, West European countries, Brazil, Colombia, Israel, South Korea and Turkey; holders of OAS passports; for US citizens for visits up to 2 months; and for Venezuelans for stays of up to 14 days. Some Commonwealth citizens do need visas, however; these include Australia, New Zealand, India, Sri Lanka, Nigeria, South Africa, Uganda, Tanzania, and Papua New Guinea. A visa normally requires 48 hours' notice. A waiver for those with no visa can be obtained at the airport, but it costs TT$50. Passports are required by all visitors. Entry permits for 1-3 months are given on arrival; a 1 month permit can be extended at the immigration office in Port of Spain (at 67 Frederick Street) for TT$5. This is a time-consuming process, so try and get a 3-month entry permit if planning a long stay.

Even though you may not get asked for it all travellers need a return ticket to their country of origin, dated, not open-ended, proof that they can support themselves during their stay, an address at which they will be staying in Trinidad (the tourist office at the airport can help in this respect). A ferry ticket to Venezuela has often satisfied immigration officials instead of a full return ticket to your own country. Only those coming from an infected area need a yellow fever inoculation certificate. People going to Venezuela can obtain a tourist card (free of charge) at the BWIA office; this means buying a return ticket but this can be refunded or changed if an alternative ticket out of Venezuela is later purchased.

● **Customs**

Duty-free imports: 200 cigarettes or 50 cigars or 250g tobacco, 1 litre wine or spirits, and US$100 worth of gifts. Perfume may not be imported free of duty, but may be deposited with Customs until departure. Passengers in transit, or on short visits, can deposit goods such as liquor with Customs at the airport and retrieve it later free of charge.

● **Climate**

The climate on the islands is tropical, but, thanks to the trade winds, rarely excessively hot. Temperatures vary between 21° and 37°C, the coolest time being from Dec to April. There is a dry season from Jan to mid-May and a wet season from June to Nov, with a short break in September. It can rain for days at a stretch but usually falls in heavy showers. Humidity is fairly high.

MONEY

● **Currency**

The Trinidad and Tobago dollar, TT$. Notes are for TT$1, 5, 10, 20 and 100. Coins are for 1, 5, 10, 25 and 50 cents.

● **Exchange**

The Trinidad and Tobago dollar, fixed at TT$2.40 = US$1 since 1976, was devalued to TT$3.60 = US$1 in Dec, 1985, then to TT$4.25 = US$1 in Aug, 1988 and finally floated in April 1993. The rate moved initially to TT$5.75, a depreciation of 26%, but then stabilized at around TT$5.99.

Travellers' cheques and major credit cards are accepted almost everywhere on Trinidad. On Tobago there are no banks outside Scarborough; TCs are changed by large hotels but if you are travelling to the northern end of the island make sure you have enough TT$ as not everyone accepts US$.

All banks charge a fee for cashing travellers' cheques, some more than others, so check first. Banks generally will not change Venezuelan or other South American currencies.

GETTING THERE

AIR

Canada: Air Canada and BWIA from Toronto to Port of Spain.

Europe: BWIA (from Frankfurt to Port of Spain and/or Tobago, London, to Port of Spain via St Lucia, Antigua or Barbados). Several charters, including Air Caledonian to Tobago.

Guyana: BWIA, Suriname Airways, daily flights from Georgetown to Port of Spain.

Suriname: Suriname Airways from Paramaribo to Port of Spain.

USA: BWIA to Trinidad or Tobago (Miami, New York); American Airlines (New York via Miami to Port of Spain).

Venezuela: BWIA has a daily service to Port of Spain; Air France handles BWIA at Caracas airport and as they are not linked by computer to Trinidad they do not know until the last moment if the plane is fully booked, line up at the counter and insist; you can pay by credit card, price to Trinidad is about US$15 less than to Tobago, round trip about US$185.

Caribbean: BWIA, Liat, ALM and Region Air connect Trinidad with other Caribbean islands including Anguilla, Antigua, Barbados, Curaçao, Dominica, Grenada, Jamaica (Kingston), Martinique, St Lucia, St Maarten, St Vincent, San Juan, Puerto Rico and Tortola (BVI). There are flights to Tobago (Crown Point Airport) with BWIA, Liat or Region Air from Antigua, Barbados, Grenada and Union Island. BWIA (and possibly other airlines) are reluctant to let you leave unless you have an onward ticket from your immediate destination to the next one.

SEA

A weekly 250-passenger and cargo ferry service run by Windward Lines Limited sails from Trinidad to Güiria, Venezuela on Tues, returning from Güiria on Wed, arriving Trinidad Thur. This service alternates with a ferry to Margarita (Pampatar), every other week, with 12 hours in Margarita. On Thur it sets off for St Vincent, Barbados and St Lucia, arriving there Sat 0800, returning Sun, getting back to Trinidad Tues. Check in 2 hours before departure in Trinidad (1 hour in other ports). The schedule is printed in 2 daily newspapers, times vary depending on the Güiria or Margarita crossing, occasionally there is a stop in Bequia, everything stops for Carnival in Trinidad. For information and tickets contact Global Steamship Agencies Ltd, Mariner's Club, Wrightson Road, PO Box 966, Port of Spain, T 624-2279, 625-2547, F 627-5091. For a round trip to St Lucia the fare is US$95 (one-way US$62), return fare to Barbados US$90 (US$60), to St Vincent US$90 (US$60) and to Güiria US$60 (US$40), to Margarita add US$10. Cabins, aircraft seats and convertible berths are available.

Every Fri morning a boat carrying racing pigeons leaves for Güiria, Venezuela. Contact Francis Sagones, T 632-0040; or talk to Siciliano Bottini in the Agencia Naviera in Güiria for sea transport in the other direction. Fishing boats and trading vessels ply this route frequently and can often be persuaded to take passengers. Be careful to get your passport stamped at both ends of the journey. A Trinidadian, Adrian Winter Roach, travels at least once a week with his boat *El Cuchillo*, and charges US$60 one way, US$100 return, he can be contacted in Venezuela through the Distribuidora Beirut, Calle Valdez 37, Güiria, T/F 81677. Lots of shipping lines have a service going N, go to Queen's Wharf and ask to speak to the captains. For Guyana, try Abraham Shipping Company Ltd, 10 Abercromby Street, T 624-1138/1131, they handle 90% of the Guyana and Suriname trade.

● **Ports of entry**

Chaguaramas, Trinidad, and Scarborough, Tobago. In Chaguaramas, take the boat to the Customs dock (open 24 hrs) to clear on arrival in Trinidad and fill in combined Customs and Immigration form. Crew will be admitted for 90 days; a 90-day extension costs US$30 pp. **Departure by sea**: clear out with Customs and Immigration. Pay port fees of US$6 for each month that the boat was in Trinidad and Tobago waters. To go from one island to the other clear out with Immigration and in on the new island. Clear Customs only when making final departure from the country. New arrivals must be signed aboard the vessel as crew by Immigration in Chaguaramas. **Departure by air**: boats can be left in storage; yacht yards will help with paperwork, present it to Customs and clear with Immigration within 24 hrs of departure for exemption from departure tax. When returning to Trinidad by air, go to third party line at airport to get paperwork to take with baggage to Chaguaramas Customs to clear. Arriving outside office hours leave boat parts for weekday review. Arriving guests should have return ticket and letter to Trinidad Immigration stating vessel name and official number.

● **Marinas**

The Trinidad marinas are all W of Port of Spain along the coast to Chaguaramas. Trinidad and Tobago Yacht Club (TTYC), Bayshore, T/F 637-4260, a private club, leases members' slips to visiting yachts when available, 60 in-water berths, security, restaurant, bar, laundry. Point Gourde Yachting Centre, T 627-5680, F 625-4083, opened 1996, 65 in-water berths, full service marina. Trinidad and Tobago Yachting

Association (TTYA), Chaguaramas, PO Box 3140, Carenage, T/F 634-4376/4210/ 4519, a private members' association with moorings and anchorage available to visiting yachts, full service haul out yard, 15-ton marine hoist, moorings, repair shed, bar, laundry. Power Boats Mutual Facilities, Chaguaramas, PO Box 3163, Carenage, T 634-4303, F 634-4327, haul-out and storage, 50-ton marine hoist, 23 in-water berths, boat storage, marine supplies, fibreglass repairs, welding, woodworking, apartments, grocery, restaurant, laundry. Peake Yacht Services, Chaguaramas, T 634-4423, F 634-4387, full service marina, 150-ton marine hoist, capable of beams to 31 ft, 21 in-water berths, boat storage, 10-room hotel, restaurant, laundry, skilled maintenance, rec. Industrial Marine Services (IMS), Chaguaramas, T 634-4337, F 634-4437, full service haul-out and storage yard, 70-ton marine hoist, paint shop, chandlery, sail maker, fibreglass repair, welding, woodworking, sandblasting, restaurant, laundry. All locations charge a fee to anchored boats for use of shoreside facilities.

ON ARRIVAL

● **Airport**

Piarco International, 16 miles SE of Port of Spain. The taxi fare to Arouca is US$7 and to the centre of Port of Spain is US$20, to Maraval US$24, Diego Martin US$27, San Fernando US$31 (50% more after 2200). Taxi despatchers find taxis for new arrivals, ask to see the rate card for taxi fares to different places. Unlicensed taxis outside the main parking area charge less, depending on the volume of business. If you are not loaded with luggage public transport is much cheaper. To get to Port of Spain walk out of the airport and cross the road to catch a route taxi (see **Information for travellers, Taxis**), destination Main Road, or, rather better if slower, go a bit further to Arouca (US$0.30). Then take a route taxi or maxi taxi from the junction into Port of Spain (US$0.90). Coming back to the airport do the same in reverse. People are very helpful if you need to ask. There is a direct bus, US$0.30, 45 mins-1 hour, from the airport to Port of Spain bus station, which departs from the terminal building at 1600 and 1700. From the central bus terminal at the old railway station you will have to walk to Independence or Woodford Square for a route taxi for your ultimate destination. This is not advisable at night, especially

if carrying luggage (ie take a taxi from the airport at night).

Tobago's Crown Point airport is within walking distance of the hotels in the SW.

● **Airlines**

BWIA is at 30 Edward Street (T 625-2470, 625-5866/8, F 625-2139), opens for reservations at 0800; be prepared for a long wait, particularly for international tickets. BWIA at Piarco airport, T 669-3000 (open later than Edward Street office); also at Carlton Centre, San Fernando, T 657-9712/6485, and at Crown Point airport, Tobago, T 639-8741/2. Air Caribbean for flights between the two islands, 1 Richmond Street, T 623-2500, F 623-8182. American Airlines, 90 Independence Square (T 623-5008, F 669-0261, Piarco, T 664-4838/4731-2); Air Canada is at 88 Independence Square (T 625-2195, F 627-304, at Piarco T 664-4065). LIAT, CIC Building, 122-124 Frederick Street, T 623-1837/ 4480, F 624-8211, at Piarco airport T 664-5458, on Tobago at Crown Point airport, T 639-0484. Suriname Airways, Cruise Ship Complex, Wrightson Road, T 627-4747; Carib Express, Cruise Ship Complex, T 625-1719, F 624-3051. There is a 15% VAT on airline tickets purchased in Trinidad and Tobago.

● **Banks**

In Port of Spain: Republic Bank Ltd (formerly Barclays, gives cash on Visa card), 11-17 Park St, T 625-4411, F 623-0371, also at airport, very slow, open 0800-1100, 1200-1400, on Fri 0800-1200, 1500-1700; Royal Bank of Trinidad and Tobago, 3B Chancery Lane, T 623-4291; Bank of Commerce, 72 Independence Square, T 627-9325-8; Bank of Nova Scotia, Park and Richmond Streets, T 625-3566; Citibank, Queens Park East, T 625-1040; Citicorp Merchant Bank, same address, T 623-3344. In 1993 3 banks which had been brought under Central Bank control were merged; the Trinidad Cooperative Bank, the National Commercial Bank of Trinidad and Tobago, and the Workers' Bank merged to become the First Citizens Bank. Western Union Money Transfer, Uptown Mall, Edward Street, Port of Spain, T 623-6000, and 10 other locations in Trinidad and Tobago. Banks in the West and Long Circular Malls are open until 1800. Peake's Yacht Yard has a branch with a 24-hr cash machine and a teller from 0900-1400.

● **Clothing**

Beachwear should be kept for the beach. In

Information for travellers 833

the evening people dress more smartly but are less formal than, for example, the Bahamians.

● **Embassies and consulates**
(Port of Spain) **Canadian** High Commission, Huggins Building, 72 South Quay, (T 623-7254, F 624-4016); **US** Embassy, 15 Queen's Park West (T 622-6371/6, F 628-5462), 0700-1700; **British** High Commission, 19 St Clair Avenue, St Clair, T 622-2748, F 622-4555, a very smart, modern building, its upper floors have an excellent view over Queen's Park Oval; **Dutch** Embassy, Life of Barbados Building, 69 Edward Street, PO Box 870, T 625-1210/1722, F 625-1704; **Jamaican** High Commission, 2 Newbold Street, St Clair, T 622-4995/7, F 628-9180; **Japanese** Embassy, 5 Hayes Street, St Clair, T 622-6105/5838, F 622-0858; **Guayanese** Consulate, 3rd floor, Park Plaza, Corner of Park and St Vincent Streets, T 627-1692, F 623-3881; **German** Embassy, 7-9 Marli St, PO Box 828 (T 628-1630/2, F 628-5278); **French** Embassy, 6th floor, Tatil Bldg, Maraval Rd, T 622-7446/7, F 628-2632; **Danish** Consulate, 20-22 Tragarete Road, T 625-1156, F 623-8693; **Brazilian** Embassy, 18 Sweet Briar Rd, St Clair (T 622-5779/5771, F 622-4323); **Venezuelan** Embassy, 16 Victoria Av (T 627-9823/4), 0900-1300, 1400-1600, Consulate at same address, T 627-9773/4, visa section only open mornings. Changes of address, and other representatives, can be checked at the Ministry of External Affairs, T 623-4116/60.

● **Hospitals**
There are hospitals in Port of Spain, San Fernando, Scarborough (T 639-2551) and Mount Hope, as well as several district hospitals and community health centres. The Port of Spain General Hospital is at 169 Charlotte Street, T 623-2951. Rec doctors are Dr Harry N Singh, Main Road, Kelly Village, Caroni, T 669-1854 and Dr Pham Van Cong, 195c Western Main Road, Cocorite, T 622-8972.

● **Hours of business**
Government offices 0800-1600, Mon-Fri. Banks: 0900-1400, Mon-Thur, 0900-1200, 1500-1700, Fri. Some banks have extended hours until 1800. Businesses and shops: 0800-1600/ 1630, Mon-Fri (shops 0800-1200 on Sat). Shopping malls usually stay open until about 2000, Mon-Sat.

● **Official time**
Atlantic Standard Time, 4 hours behind GMT, 1 hour ahead of EST.

● **Public holidays**
New Year's Day, Carnival Monday and Tuesday, before Ash Wednesday (not officially holidays but everyone regards them as such), Spiritual Shouter Baptist Liberation Day (30 Mar), Good Friday, Easter Monday, 30 May, Indian Arrival Day celebrating the arrival of Indian labourers in 1845, Corpus Christi, Eid ul-Fitr (changes according to religious calendar), Labour or Butler's Day (19 June), Emancipation Day (1 Aug), Independence Day (31 Aug), Divali (depends on religious calendar), Christmas Day, Boxing Day.

Special events: All Souls' Day (2 Nov) is not a holiday, but is celebrated. The Hindu festival of Divali is a holiday, but Puagwa (Feb/Mar) is not. Similarly, of the Moslem festivals, Eid ul-Fitr is a public holiday, but Eid ul-Azha and Yaum um-Nabi are not (all fall 10-11 days earlier each year).

● **Security**
The people of both islands are, as a rule, very friendly but several areas are no longer safe at night, especially for women. To the E of Charlotte Street, Port of Spain becomes increasingly unsafe. Laventille and East Dry River are to be avoided. Central Port of Spain is fairly safe, even at night, as there are plenty of police patrols. Care must be taken everywhere at night and walking on the beach is not safe. Stick to main roads and look as if you know where you are going. The incidence of theft has risen sharply. Avoid the area around the port or bus terminal except when making a journey. A favourite local saying is 'Tobago is Paradise, Trinidad is New York'. Take care accordingly but do not underestimate crime in Tobago. We have received reports of theft and muggings on the Pigeon Point road and parts of Scarborough are known to have crack houses. Do not walk in the Turtle Beach area after dark. Soft top jeeps are at risk of theft. Leave nothing in them. If there is no safe where you are staying take your valuables (passport, tickets etc) to a bank in Scarborough; the Royal Bank charges US$12 for 2 weeks. Women alone report feeling 'uncomfortable', particularly if they look like a tourist. There is constant pestering, especially on the beach.

● **Shopping**
Bargains can be found in fabrics, carvings, leather and ceramics. Most shops take US dollars at a reasonable exchange rate. The main Port of Spain shopping area is in Frederick Street, Queen Street, Henry Street

andCharlotte Street (fruit and vegetables), less exciting but pleasanter are Long Circular Mall at the junction of Long Circular Rd and Patna Street, St James, West Mall, Cocorite, Port of Spain, Ellerslie Plaza on the way to Maraval, close to Savannah. Purchases can be made at in-bond shops in Port of Spain and at the airport. There is a huge selection of duty-free shops, accessible to both arriving and departing passengers, selling everything, including computers. Markets offer wide varieties of fruit. Handicrafts can also be purchased at markets. In Port of Spain there is a craft market in Independence Square with leather, hand painted T-shirts etc. There are also street vendors on Frederick Street and elsewhere. Crafts also at East Mall on Charlotte Street and at the cruise ship complex. There are several kilns in the Freeport area, turn off the Uriah Butler Highway before the Hindu temple for Chase Village where most of the pottery is unpainted; the potters sell it on to others for decoration and glazing. Good quality local pottery in a variety of designs is available from Ajoupa Pottery, owned by Rory and Bunty O'Connor. You can get it in Port of Spain but a wider selection can be viewed at their kiln at Freeport, central Trinidad; T 622-5597 at Port of Spain shop at Ellerslie Plaza, or T 673-0604 at kiln/factory. Batik can be bought at many places including the Ajoupa pottery shop at Ellerslie Plaza. Althea Bastien, a designer and batik maker, has a shop at her house, 43 Sydenham Ave, T 624-3274, difficult to find. The Central Market is on the Beetham Highway. Do not purchase turtle shell, black coral, or other protected, shell items. For music, try Crosby's Music Centre, 54 Western Main Road, St James, or Rhyner's, 54 Prince Street, Port of Spain. Production costs are a problem and despite being the main music outlets in this island of music they frequently have no stock.

On Tobago, you can get excellent handicrafts at the Cotton House, Bacolet Street, just outside Scarborough (taxi US$2.50), batik studio, high standard, pictures and clothes at reasonable prices. Francis Supermarket at Crown Point is not particularly well stocked but is open Mon-Sat 0800-1800, Sun and holidays 1000-1400.

Bookshops Metropolitan Books, Colsort Mall, good selection; R I K Services Ltd, Queen Street, Port of Spain, and 104 High Street, San Fernando, mostly school books; St Aubyns Book Services, Palm Plaza, Maraval. There are second hand bookshops in Town Centre Mall

and various side streets. Generally the selection is poor, particularly for Caribbean novels which is disappointing in a country with such a long literary tradition.

● **Tipping**
If no service charge on bill, 10% for hotel staff and restaurant waiters; taxi drivers, 10% of fare, minimum of 25 cents (but no tip in route taxis); dock-side and airport porters, say 25 cents for each piece carried; hairdressers (in all leading hotels), 50 cents.

● **Voltage**
110 or 220 volts, 60 cycles AC.

● **Weights and measures**
Trinidad and Tobago has gone metric, so road signs are given in kilometres, but people still refer to miles.

ON DEPARTURE

See also **Ports of entry** above for **Departure by sea**.

● **Departure tax**
There is a TT$75 exit tax payable in local currency, or US$15, plus a TT$10 security fee. Passengers in transit do not have to pay, but are required to obtain an 'exempt' ticket from the departure tax window before being allowed through to the immigration officers on the way to the departure lounge. Visitors leaving by sea pay the departure tax to the shipping agent. Your immigration card must be presented on departure.

● **Airport information**
If intending to take the bus to Piarco airport, Trinidad, allow plenty of time to ensure arriving in time for checking in. Try to avoid overnight connections at Piarco airport. Airline schedules ensure that it is possible to arrive at Piarco after the check-in counters have closed until next morning, so you cannot go through to the departure lounge. Sky cap has 24-hr left luggage service. There is a restaurant upstairs open 24 hrs. There is seating under 3 covered areas but it is not comfortable for an overnight wait. If you are in transit always check that your bags have not been off-loaded at Piarco, most are not checked through despite assurances. To eat at the airport, there is the *Pizza Boys* restaurant upstairs in the terminal building and a variety of fast food outlets downstairs, including *KFC*. Indian delicacies, like 'doubles' or roti, can be had at informal food stalls to the right as you exit the terminal.

Crown Point airport is also uncomfortable for a long wait, often with no food available after you have been through immigration control. There are a few shops, snack bars and a bank outside the terminal building but only a small duty free inside.

ACCOMMODATION

● **Hotels**
There are many hotels on the islands and the better known ones are expensive, but there are very good guest houses and smaller hotels which are reasonable. Information about accommodation can be obtained from the Tourism and Industrial Development Co (TIDCO). Their office at Piarco airport is helpful. A 15% value added tax is charged at all hotels and in most a 10% service charge is added to the bill. Some, like the *Hilton*, add a 2% surcharge. See **Island information** sections for details of hotels. For bed and breakfast in private homes contact Trinidad and Tobago Bed and Breakfast Co-operative Society, PO Box 3231 Diego Martin, T/F 627-BEDS.

● **Camping**
Camping on Trinidad is unsafe and is not rec. Try the Boca Islands to the W. On Tobago, it is possible near the Mt Irvine beach. Ask the taxi drivers for advice on where to camp.

FOOD AND DRINK

● **Food**
A wide variety of European, American and traditional West Indian dishes (these include pork souse, black pudding, roast sucking pig, sancoche and callaloo stews, and many others) is served at hotels and guest houses. Some also specialize in Créole cooking. There is also, of course, a strong East Indian influence in the local cuisine and also lots of Chinese restaurants. Seafood, particularly crab, is excellent. The many tropical fruits and vegetables grown locally include the usual tropical fruits, and sapodillas, eddoes and yam tanias. The variety of juices and ice creams made from the fruit is endless. Coconut water is refreshing, usually sold around the Savannah, Port of Spain. For those economizing, the *roti*, a chapatti pancake which comes in various forms, filled with peppery stew, shrimp or vegetable curries, is very good. The best place for *roti* is *Patraj* at 159 Tragarete Road, Port of Spain. *Buss up shut* (shut means shirt) is a paratha, or Indian bread accompaniment to curries. *Pelau*, savoury peas

and rice and meat cooked with coconut and pepper, is also good, but when offered pepper sauce, refuse unless you are accustomed to the hottest of curries or *chili* dishes. Try also *saheena*, deep-fried patties of spinach, dasheen, split peas and mango sauce. *Pholouri* are fritters made with split peas. *Buljol* is a salt fish with onions, tomatoes, avocado and pepper. *Callaloo* is a thick soup based on dasheen leaves. *Doubles* are curried chick peas (channa) in two pieces of fried bara bread. *Pastelles*, eaten at Christmas, are maize flour parcels stuffed with minced meat, olives, capers and raisins, steamed in a banana leaf (known as *hallacas* in Venezuela). A hops is a crusty bread roll. If you go to Maracas Bay, have shark-and-bake, a spicy fried bread sandwich of fried shark with a variety of sauces such as tamarind, garlic, *chadon beni*. Dumplings are a must on Tobago, particularly good with crab. The shopping malls offer a variety of places to eat, including Créole, Indian, Chinese, etc. On Tobago there are lots of small eating places, clean and nice, where you can get a freshly cooked meal and a beer for US$3-4pp.

● **Drink**
A local drink is mauby, like ginger beer, and the rum punches are rec. Fresh lime juice is also rec; it is sometimes served with a dash of Angostura bitters. Local beers are Carib ("each bottle tastes different") and Stag ("the recession fighter"), both owned by the same company which also brews Heineken and Guinness. A nice place to drink Guinness is the *Cricket Wicket*, in Tragarete Road, opp the Queen's Park Oval. There are lots of rums to try, many of which deserve better than to be swamped with punch or coke.

GETTING AROUND

AIR TRANSPORT

A new airline, Air Caribbean, took over the Trinidad-Tobago route in 1993 offering 7-8 daily flights; the crossing takes 20 mins and costs US$40 return, adults, cheaper for children under 12. Departures, however, are often heavily booked at weekends and holidays, particularly Christmas and afterwards (at other times tickets can be bought the day before, even standby).

LAND TRANSPORT

● **Motoring**
Driving is on the left and the roads are narrow

and winding. On Trinidad the Uriah Butler Highway and Solomon Mocmoy Highway are good dual carriageways from Port of Spain S to San Fernando, but other roads are not of such a high standard. On Tobago the roads are good in the S but badly maintained further N. There are lots of pot holes in Scarborough and traffic weaves about all over the place to avoid them. The road between Charlotteville and Bloody Bay is for 4-wheel drive vehicles only and then only in the dry season. Mountain bikes are fine on these roads if you can stand the hills and the heat. International and most foreign driving licences are accepted for up to 90 days, after that the visitor must apply for a Trinidad and Tobago licence and take a test. Visitors must always carry their driving document with them. Do not leave anything in your car, theft is frequent. Be careful where you park in Port of Spain, police are diligent and will tow the car away. It costs US$17 to retrieve it.

● **Car hire**

Car rental can be difficult on Trinidad, particularly at weekends, because of heavy demand. Best to make reservations in advance. Several companies do not accept credit cards, but require a considerable cash deposit. Small cars can be rented from US$30 a day upwards, unlimited mileage, check tyres before driving off. Deposit varies from company to company, as does method of payment, book in advance. Insurance costs US$1. Many car rental companies have offices at the airport. Car rental firms are numerous and include Auto Rentals Ltd, Uptown Mall, Edward Street, Port of Spain (623-3063), Piarco (T 669-2277), and at Cruise Ship Complex, 1 D Wrighton Road (T 624-8687); Bacchus Taxi and Car Rental, 37 Tragarete Rd (622-5588); Lord Calloo, 100 la Paille Village, Caroni (T/F 645-5182), helpful, check tyres; Singh's, 7-9 Wrightson Rd (625-4247) and at airport (T 645-5417, F 664-3860); Southern Sales and Service Co Ltd, rec, main office at Victoria Village, San Fernando, also have office at Piarco, T 669-2424, friendly and helpful. Also on Tobago: Auto Rentals Ltd, Crown Point Airport (T 639-0644, F 639-0313); Banana Rentals at *Kariwak Village*, cars and jeeps, US$21/day, scooters US$10/day (deposit US$60), bicycles US$4/day (T 639-8441/8545); Suzuki Jeep Rental (and small cars), and Cherry Scooter Rental at *Sandy Point Beach Club* (scooters and deposit cheaper than Banana); Tobago Travel, P O Box 163, Store Bay Road, Crown Point (639-8778/8105, F 639-

8786), Baird's, Lower Sangster Hill Road (639-2528) and other agencies. Some companies only rent for a minimum of 3 days.

● **Buses**

In Trinidad, the word 'taxi' includes most forms of public transport. The word 'travelling' means going by bus or taxi rather than by private car. **Buses** are run by the PTSC. They are big and cheap, also slow, irregular and dirty. However, the PTSC also has newer air-conditioned buses on main routes from Independence Square to Arima, Chaguanas and San Fernando. These are not quite so cheap, faster and more comfortable, US$1 to San Fernando. On all routes, you must purchase your ticket at the kiosk before boarding the bus; you may have to tender the exact fare. At the PTSC office in the old railway station on South Quay, you can get information showing how to reach the various sights by bus.

On Tobago (as on Trinidad), buy **bus** tickets in advance as drivers will not accept money. All buses originate in Scarborough. Schedules are changed or cancelled frequently. Buses every 1/2 hour between Crown Point (airport) and Scarborough, TT$2. Buy tickets from the grey hut outside the airport building where timetable is posted. Also an express bus to Scarborough, TT$2, ticket from souvenir shop, not hut as for the other bus. On Tobago, route taxis charge TT$4. The Crown Point Airport route is the best, every 15-30 mins, 0530-1830; Black Rock route is fair, every 30 mins Mon-Fri 0530-2030, every 60-75 minutes Sat and Sun until 2000. The route taxi system is difficult for the foreigner, being based on everyone knowing every car and therefore where it is going. They leave from Republic Bank in Scarborough.

● **Taxis**

Look for **cars with first letter H** on licence plates (no other markings). Agree on a price before the journey and determine whether the price is in TT or US dollars. On Tobago, taxi fares are clearly displayed as you leave the airport: to Crown Point US$5, Pigeon Point US$6, Scarborough US$9, Mt Irvine, Roxborough US$30, Speyside US$36, Charlotteville US$40. Taxis are expensive, although **route taxis** (similar to colectivos) are very cheap. These cannot be distinguished from ordinary taxis, so ask the driver. They travel along fixed routes, like buses, but have no set stops, so you can hail them and be dropped anywhere along the route. During rush hour it is not easy to hail them, however, and in general it takes time to master how they work. Be warned that route taxis are not covered by insurance so you cannot claim against the driver if you are involved in an accident. There are also 'pirate' taxis with the P registration of a private car, which cost the same as the ordinary taxis, although you can sometimes bargain with the drivers. 'Ghost' taxis accept fares and drive off with your luggage as well – be warned. Be careful if hitching on Tobago as the cars that stop often prove to be pirate taxis.

● **Route taxis**

In Port of Spain most sedan taxis (saloon cars, often rather beat up) set off from Chacon St, but those for St Ann's and St James leave from Woodford Square, for Carenage from St Vincent and Park Streets, for the Diego Martin area from South Quay, and for Maraval, Belmont and Morvant from Duke and Charlotte Streets. Fares in town US$0.50, further out US$0.75. If you are in a hurry you can pay for any remaining empty seats and ask the driver to go. They will also go off-route for a little extra but going off route to the *Hilton* costs US$7. They are the only means of transport on some suburban routes, such as to St Ann's, and in rural areas away from main roads. Travelling to remote areas may involve 3 or more taxis, not really a problem, just ask where the next one stops. Major routes run all night and are amazingly frequent during the day, others become infrequent or stop late at night. St Christopher's taxis or airport taxis are taxis as understood in most countries. Some are smarter and more comfortable than route taxis. St Christopher's operates from the main hotels. Take a taxi if you have a complicated journey, or you have heavy baggage, or it is raining. At night it can be a lot cheaper than getting robbed.

● **Maxi-taxis**

Maxi-taxis are minibuses which cover longer distances than route taxis; they are frequent and go as fast as the traffic will allow, often a bit faster. They are colour coded (yellow for Diego Martin and W, red for E, green for San Fernando, brown or black for maxis which start in San Fernando and travel S from there) and they set off mostly from South Quay except the Carenage and Chaguaramas maxis, which start from Green corner on St Vincent and Park Streets (Globe cinema) and Maraval maxis, which start from Oxford and Charlotte Streets. Check exact route before starting, eg E taxis are either 'San Juan' or 'all the way up' the

Eastern Main Road to Arima, or 'highway', which is faster and runs closer to the airport but misses places like Tunapuna and Curepe. Fares start at US$0.30 and run to Arima, US$1; to Chaguanas, US$1; to San Fernando, US$1.75. If you are worried about being overcharged, pay with TT$10 and look as though you know how much change to expect, but drivers are usually very helpful and friendly.

SEA TRANSPORT

● **Ferry**

Boats from Port of Spain to Tobago go once a day at 1400 Mon-Fri and 1100 on Sun and public holidays, no crossings on Sat; return crossings from Scarborough at 2300 Mon-Fri and Sun. The crossing is supposedly 5 hours. Hammocks can be slung at night. The trip can be rough. There are 2 vessels: M/F *Tobago*, and M/V *Panorama*. Tickets are sold at the Port Authority (T 625-3055, 639-2417) on the docks, US$8-10 return, cabin for 2 US$13 when available, children under 12 half price, under 3 free, office hours Mon-Fri 0700-1500, 1600-1800, 1900-2200 (buy passage in advance, everyone will recommend you to queue at 0800, but 1000 is usually early enough). You need a boarding pass and not just a ticket before you can board. Taking the ferry is a very time consuming operation; it is a lot less hassle to fly.

ENTERTAINMENT

Trinidad abounds in evening entertainment. Monday's local song and dance at the *Hilton* is less authentic in atmosphere than the steel band concerts on Fri at the same venue. Entrance US$2. For those wishing to visit the places where the local, rather than tourist, population go, anyone in the street will give directions. Though the atmosphere will be natural and hospitality generous, it will not be luxurious and the local rum is likely to flow. *Chaconia* on Saddle Rd has live music on Fri and Sat. *Moon Over Bourbon Street*, West Mall, has a cocktail lounge and live local entertainment at weekends. The *Bel Air* near the airport has live entertainment on Sat night. Other discos and clubs include the *Upper Level Club*, West Mall, Westmoorings; *Ramparts*; *The Attic Pub*, Shoppes of Maraval, Saddle Road; *Club Coconuts* in Valley Vue Hotel, St Ann's; *The Pickle House*, Abercromby St, orange building, different types of music on different nights, New Orleans jazz, rhythm and blues, local music, Latin American and panang in the run up to Christmas; *Genesis* in Diego Martin; *The Tunnel*, 89 Union Road, Marabella near San Fernando and in Chaguanas. For spicier entertainment, go to the *International* (Wrightson Rd). *Mas Camp Pub* in Woodbrook has nightly entertainment inc calypso and steel band, the best place to see live calypso out of season (cover charge usually US$2). *007 Club* nearby is good, open late (but lots of prostitutes who can be ignored). The Silver Stars Steel Orchestra (formed in the 1950s) can occasionally be seen in rehearsal (check beforehand) at the Panyard, 56 Tragarete Road, Newtown, Woodbrook, Port of Spain. Silver Stars plays at local parties, cruise ships or on the beach, workshops for individuals or groups can be arranged, contact Michael Figuera, T/F 628-7550. For late drinking and music, *Pelican* (down hill from Hilton), Coblentz Avenue, Cascade, is lively; so are *Smokey and Bunty's* in St James, an area which is normally livelier at night than Port of Spain.

Theatres: Queen's Hall, 1-3 St Ann's Rd; Little Carib, White and Roberts Streets; Central Bank Auditorium, Eric Williams Plaza, Edward St. In San Fernando, Naparima Bowl reopened after a lengthy period of renovation; the folk theatre of the South National Institute of Performing Arts (T 653-5355). See press for details of performances.

Cinemas: 3 cinemas are grouped near Park Plaza on Park Street and Tragarete Road. They are very cheap and occasionally show something good. Audiences are audibly enthusiastic, particularly for sex and violence. The cinema in Scarborough is good value, US$1.10 for two films, but the audience can be a bit noisy. On a quieter level, the Public Library in Charlotteville is stocked with all the literature in the English language you ever wanted to read and some German books too.

Though not as lively as Trinidad, Tobago offers dancing in its hotels. The Buccoo Folk Theatre gives an attractive show of dancing and calypso every Thur at 2100. There is a Tobago Folk Performing Company. In Scarborough, *El Tropical* is a club frequented mostly by locals; it has a live show every Sat night at about 2330. Also *JG's Disco*, nightly. *Michael's Bar*, Black Rock, rec for friendly evening entertainment. The *Starting Gate Pub*, Shirvan Road, is rec. Don't miss Sunday School on Buccoo Beach, a big party starting early every Sun evening with live music, followed at about 2300 by a DJ playing until

earlyinthemorning.Entertainmentisavailable every night of Tobago Race Week, mostly at Crown Point but also at *Grafton Beach* or *Grand Courlan* hotels.

COMMUNICATIONS

● **Postal services**
The main Post Office is on Wrightson Road, Port of Spain, and is open 0700-1700, Mon-Fri. Stamps for Europe TT$3 upwards.

● **Telecommunications**
The main Telecommunications Services of Trinidad and Tobago Ltd (TSTT) office on Frederick St operates international telephone, cable, telex and fax. There is a TSTT telephone office in Scarborough, Tobago. The service for international calls has improved greatly, with direct dialling to all countries. The fax, telex and telegraph service shuts from 2300 Sat to 2300 Sun and on public holidays except for 'life or death' messages. This means no faxes for 3 days over Carnival. Phone cards are available for TT$15, 30, 60, or 100 plus 15% VAT, from TSTT offices, banks, airport, cruise ship complex etc. Home Direct Service for AT&T, Sprint and MCI available frOM TSTT, Cruise Shop Complex in Port of Spain, TTYC, TTYA and Peake's Yacht Yard. In Tobago, at airport and TSTT office.

MEDIA

● **Newspapers**
The main daily papers are the *Trinidad and Tobago Express*, the *Trinidad Guardian* and *Newsday*. The *Mirror* on Fri and Sun has interesting investigative journalism. *Trinidad and Tobago Review* is a serious monthly. *Tobago News* is weekly. There are several racier weekly papers which appear on Fri or Sat. *Punch*, *Bomb*, *Heat* and *Blast* are sensational tabloids, not to be missed by the visitor who wants the gossip.

● **Radio**
ICN Radio (610 AM), Radio Trinidad (730 AM), Music Radio (97 FM), RadiYo (98.9 FM), WABC (103 FM), ICN Radio (100 FM), Radio 95 FM, Radio Tempo (105 FM), Radio 96.1 FM, Rhythm (Radio 95.1 FM), Radio 1CN (91.1 FM), Sangeet (106.1 FM).

TOURIST INFORMATION

● **Local tourist office**
The Tourism and Industrial Development Company of Trinidad and Tobago Ltd (TIDCO), 10-14 Phillips Street, 3rd Floor, Port of Spain, T 623-1932/4, 623-INFO, F 623-3848 (PO Box 222) is the sole tourism agency. Lists of hotels, restaurants, tour operators, monthly schedule of events, maps for sale etc. Piarco Tourist Bureau (at the airport), T 664-5196, helpful with hotel or guest house reservations for your first night. You can also buy maps of Trinidad and Port of Spain here. In Tobago the Division of Tourism is in Scarborough, NIB Mall, there is a kiosk, and the head office is on the third level, next to *Buddy's Restaurant* (T 639-2125/3566, F 639-3566), or at Crown Point airport, T 639-0509. TIDCO Tobago is at Unit 12 IDC Mall, Sangster's Hill, Scarborough, T 639-4333, F 639-4514. The National Carnival Commission is at 82-84 Frederick Street, Port of Spain, T 623 8867/9.

Internet TIDCO's internet address is http//www.tidco.co.tt.

● **Tourist offices overseas**
Overseas offices all have up-to-date hotel lists: **USA**: 7000 Blvd East, Guttenberg, New Jersey, 07093, T (201) 662 3403/3408, 800-595-ITNT, F (201) 869 7628. **UK**: International House, 47 Chase Side, Enfield, Middlesex, EN2 6NB, T 0181 367 3752/5449, F 0181 367 9949. **Germany**: Berger Strasse 17-D-60316, Frankfurt/Main, T 69 9433 5811, F 69 9433 5820. **Canada**: Taurus House, 512 Duplex Ave, Toronto, M4R 2E3, T (416) 485 8724, F (416) 485 8256.

● **Local travel agents**
The Travel Centre Limited, Level 2, Uptown Mall, Edward Street, Port of Spain, T 625-1636/4266, F 623-5101 (P O Box 1254) is an American Express Travel Service Representative. The Davemar Reservations Agency, 2 Aylce Glen, Petit Valley, T 637-7583, run by Marjorie Cowie, can arrange accommodation

in hotels, guesthouses or self-catering and organize sightseeing tours. Walking tours, cave exploration, horse riding in the Northern Range, kayaking expeditions and other trips off the beaten track can be arranged with Caribbean Discovery Tours Ltd, 9B Fondes Amandes Road, St Ann's, T 624-7281 run by Stephen Broadbridge together with Merryl See Tai of the Kayak Centre, T 629-2680 (see **Beaches and Watersports**), camping (in basic-luxury tents or cabins) or lodging in guesthouses arranged for longer trips, highly rec for tailor-made tours. Roger Neckles, a local bird photographer, runs specialist minibus tours for birdwatchers. On Tobago, AJM Tours at the airport, T 639-0610, F 639-8918, day trips on Tobago and to Margarita, Angel Falls, Grenada and the Grenadines. Peter Gremli is a rec tour guide, friendly, knowledgeable and popular. Taxi drivers have set rates for sightseeing tours and can be more flexible than an organized tour. A day tour on Trinidad can include the Asa Wright Centre and the Caroni Swamp with sightseeing along the way.

FURTHER READING

The official visitor's guide, *Discover Trinidad and Tobago* is published twice a year and distributed free to all visitors by TIDCO and through hotels. There are 3 book-length guides including *Trinidad and Tobago, An Introduction and Guide*, by Jeremy Taylor (Macmillan 1991).

ACKNOWLEDGEMENTS

Sarah Cameron is very grateful to the staff of TIDCO for assistance during a recent research visit to Trinidad and Tobago, to Stephen Broadbridge and Merryl See Tai for kayaking tuition and adventure and, not least, to David Renwick, of Port of Spain, for reading and revising this chapter.

The Guianas

L IKE the West Indians, the people of the three Guianas, Guyana (formerly British Guiana), Suriname (formerly Dutch Guiana) and French Guyane, are not regarded as belonging to Latin America. The explanation of these three non-Iberian countries on the South American continent goes back to the early days of the Spanish conquest of the New World. There was no gold or any other apparent source of wealth to attract the attention of the Spanish discoverers. This part of the coast, which Columbus had first sighted in 1498, seemed to them not only barren but scantily populated and seemingly uninhabitable. The English, the French and the Dutch, anxious to establish a foothold in this part of the world, were not so fastidious.

HORIZONS

All three countries are geographically very similar: along the coast runs a belt of narrow, flat marshy land, at its widest in Suriname. This coastland carries almost all the crops and most of the population. Behind lies a belt of crystalline upland, heavily gouged and weathered. The bauxite, gold and diamonds are in this area. Behind this again is the massif of the Guiana Highlands. They reach a height of 3,000 feet (915m) in the Tumuc-Humac range, the divide

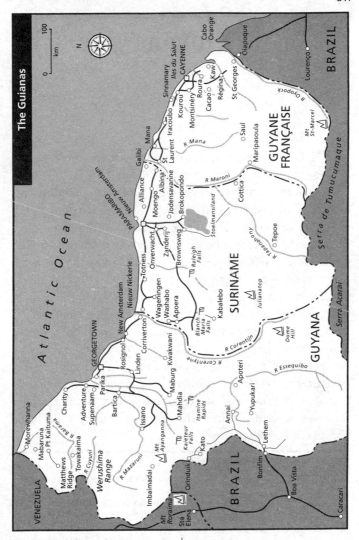

The Guianas

between French Guyane, Suriname and Brazil, and 9,219 feet (2,810m) at flat-topped Mount Roraima, where Guyana, Venezuela and Brazil all meet.

NB Flights through the Guianas are solidly booked; be certain to confirm and reconfirm your flights (in person for BWIA).

Guyana

G UYANA has an area of 83,044 square miles, nearly the size of Britain, but only about 2.5% (or 1,328,000 acres) is cultivated. About 90% of the population lives on the narrow coastal plain, either in Georgetown, the capital, or in villages along the main road running from Charity in the W to the Suriname border. Most of the plain is below sea level. Large wooden houses stand on stilts above ground level. A sea wall keeps out the Atlantic and the fertile clay soil is drained by a system of dykes; sluice gates, *kokers* are opened to let out water at low tide. Separate irrigation channels are used to bring water back to the fields in dry weather. In several places fresh water is supplied by reservoirs, known as conservancies. Most of the western third of the coastal plain is undrained and uninhabited. The strange cultural mix: Dutch place names and drainage techniques, Hindu temples, mosques, coconut palms and calypso music, reflect the chequered history of the country.

HORIZONS

Four major rivers cross the coastal plain, (from W to E) the Essequibo, the Demerara, the Berbice, and the Corentyne (which forms the frontier with Suriname). Only the Demerara is crossed by bridges. Elsewhere ferries must be used. At the mouth of the Essequibo river, 21 miles wide, are islands the size of Barbados. The lower reaches of these rivers are navigable (75 miles up the Demerara to Linden and 45 miles up the Essequibo to the mouth of the Cuyuni River); but waterfalls and rapids prevent them being used by large boats to reach the interior.

Inland from the coastal plain most of the country is covered by thick rain forest, although in the E there is a large area of grassland. Some timber has been extracted, but the main economic activity is mining: principally bauxite, but gold and diamonds are sifted from the river beds by miners using mercury (at considerable environmental cost). The largest goldmine in the western

Guyana

VENEZUELA

Atlantic Ocean

Morawhanna
Mabaruna
Pt Kaituma
Matthews Ridge
Towakaima
Charity
Anna Regina
Adventure
Supenaam
Parika
GEORGETOWN
R Barama
R Cuyuni
Werushima Range
R Mazaruni
Kyk-over-al
Bartica
Rockstone
Rosignol
New Amsterdam
Linden
Corriverton / Springlands
Issano
Ituni
R Demerara
R Berbice
Kwakwani
Mt Roraima
Imbaimadai
Mt Ayanganna
Kaieteur National Park
Pakaraima Mts
Kangaruma
Mahdia
Mabura Hill
Kaieteur Falls
Sta Elena
Orinduik
Itamine Rapids
Kurupukari
Kato
R Corentyne
SURINAME
Surama
Annai
Apoteri
BRAZIL
Yupukari
R Essequibo
Bonfim
Lethem
Moco-Moco Falls
Kanuku Mountains
Dome Hill
Boa Vista
Rupununi Savanna
Aishalton

0   100
Km

Caracarai

N

hemisphere has been opened by Omai Gold Mines of Canada on the W bank of the Essequibo river. It is located in a fairly remote area and is planned to produce 250,000 ozs of gold for 10 years. In 1994 the government issued 12 new mineral prospecting licences, covering some 240 square miles. Large areas of rain forest are still undisturbed and even the more accessible areas have varied and spectacular wildlife, including brightly-plumaged birds. The timber industry has been based primarily on Greenhart, a wood renowned for its resistance to sea water. It is used in piers and piles around the world and, until the introduction of carbon fibre fishing rods, was a favourite with fishermen and women. When the Duke of Edinburgh visited Guyana in 1992 he was presented with two Greenhart rods. Also in 1992, however, a tract of land totalling between 7 and 8% of Guyana's land area was granted to a Korean/Malaysian consortium, Barama, for logging (in 1994 Barama was meeting international standards for felling). At any event, general timber exports are increasing, although Guyana's loggers practise selective, as opposed to clear felling in an effort to foster a sustainable timber industry. Towards the Venezuelan border the rain forest rises in a series of steep escarpments, with spectacular waterfalls, the highest and best-known of which are the Kaieteur Falls on the Potaro river. In the southwest of the country is the Rupununi Savanna, an area of open grassland more easily reached from Brazil than from Georgetown.

The area W of the Essequibo river, about 70% of the national territory, is claimed by Venezuela. In the SE, the border with Suriname is in dispute, the contentious issue being whether high or low water is the boundary (in the area of the Koeroeni and New rivers).

Until the 1920s there was little natural increase in population, but the eradication of malaria and other diseases has since led to a rapid growth in population, particularly among the East Indians (Asian), who, according to most estimates comprise about 50% of the population. The 1980 census showed the following ethnic distribution (1992-93 estimates in brackets): East Indian 51.4% (49.4%); black 30.5% (35.6%); mixed 11% (7.1%); Amerindian 5.3% (Carib 3.7%, Arawak 1.4%) (6.8%); Chinese 0.2% (0.4%); white (mostly Portuguese) 0.1% (0.7%); other 1.5%. Descendants of the original Amerindian inhabitants are divided into nine ethnic groups, including the Akawaio, Makuxi and Pemon. Some have lost their isolation and moved to the urban areas, others keenly maintain aspects of their traditional culture and identity.

HISTORY

The country was first partially settled between 1616 and 1621 by the Dutch West India Company, who erected a fort and depot at Fort Kyk-over-al (County of Essequibo). The first English attempt at settlement was made by Captain Leigh on the Oiapoque River (now French Guyane) in 1604, but he failed to establish a permanent settlement. Lord Willoughby, famous in the early history of Barbados, founded a settlement in 1663 at Suriname, which was captured by the Dutch in 1667 and ceded to them at the Peace of Breda in exchange for New York. The Dutch held the three colonies till 1796 when they were captured by a British fleet. The territory was restored to the Dutch in 1802, but in the following year was retaken by Great Britain, which finally gained it in 1814, when the three counties of Essequibo, Berbice and Demerara were merged to form British Guiana.

During the 17th century the Dutch and English settlers established posts up-river, in the hills, mostly as trading points with the Amerindian natives. Plantations were laid out and worked by slaves from Africa. Poor soil defeated this venture, and the settlers retreated with their slaves to the coastal area in mid-18th century: the old plantation sites can still be detected from the air. Coffee and cotton were the main crops up to the end of the 18th century, but sugar had become the dominant crop by 1820. In 1834 slavery was abolished. Many of the slaves scattered as small landholders, and the plantation owners had to look for another source of labour. It was found in indentured workers from India, a few Chinese, and some Portuguese labourers from the Azores and

Madeira. At the end of their indentures many settled in Guyana.

The end of the colonial period was politically turbulent, with rioting between the mainly Indo-Guyanese People's Progressive Party (PPP), led by Dr Cheddi Jagan, and the mainly Afro-Guyanese People's National Congress (PNC), under Mr Forbes Burnham. The PNC, favoured over the PPP by the colonial authorities, formed a government in 1964 and retained office until 1992. Guyana is one of the few countries in the Caribbean where political parties have used race as an election issue. As a result, tension between the main ethnic groups has manifested itself mainly at election time.

On 26 May 1966 Guyana gained independence, and on 23 February 1970 it became a cooperative republic within the Commonwealth, adopting a new constitution. Another new constitution was adopted in 1980; this declared Guyana to be in transition from capitalism to socialism. Many industries, including bauxite and sugar, were nationalized in the 1970s and close relations with the USSR and Eastern Europe were developed. Following the death of President Forbes Burnham in Aug 1985, Mr Desmond Hoyte became President. Since then, overseas investors have been invited back and relations with the United States have improved.

Elections to the National Assembly and to the Presidency have been held regularly since independence, but have been widely criticized as fraudulent. The main opposition parties were the PPP, still led by Dr Jagan, and the Working People's Alliance, which attracts support from both East Indian and African communities. Having been delayed since May 1991, national assembly and presidential elections were finally held on 5 October 1992. The polling was monitored by both the Carter Center and a team from the Commonwealth, who declared the elections free and fair even though the campaign was not free of incidents. The PPP/Civic party, led by Dr Jagan, won power after 28 years in opposition, and the installation of a government by democratic means was greeted with optimism. The result also prompted foreign investors to study potential opportunities in Guyana. Recovery has to some extent begun, with several years of positive gdp growth recorded. Nevertheless, the economic recovery programme, part of an IMF Enhanced Structural Adjustment Facility, which aided economic improvement, has also seriously eroded workers' real income and hit the middle classes very hard.

GOVERNMENT

A Prime Minister and cabinet are responsible to the National Assembly, which has 65 members elected for a maximum term of 5 years. The President is Head of State. The country is divided into 10 administrative regions.

THE ECONOMY

Structure of production The agriculture, fishing and forestry sector of the economy makes up 37% of gdp and is a major exporter. Most agriculture is concentrated on the coastal plain, where sugar is the main crop. Many sugar plantations are below sea level, necessitating an extensive system of dams, dykes, canals and pumps to prevent inundation. Production of sugar has risen steadily since the British company, Booker Tate, was awarded a management contract for the industry in 1991. From a low of 129,920 tonnes in 1990 output rose to 249,840 tonnes in 1995, with a target of 287,189 tonnes for 1996. Most of Guyana's sugar exports go to Europe under the EU quota system. The state-owned Guyana Sugar Corporation was put on the list for privatization in 1993, but no sale has yet been made. Output of rice has also grown in the 1990s, following a decade of decline. A target of 340,000 tonnes of rice was set for 1996, up from

93,443 tonnes in 1990, because of greater investment in machinery and different varieties of rice with higher yields. Other farm products are coffee, cocoa, cotton, coconut, copra, fruit, vegetables and tobacco. Dairy herds are kept mostly on the coast and beef herds on the savannah inland. Fishing is mostly small scale, but both fish and shrimp are exported. Forestry is a booming area of growth with significant foreign investment, much of it from Malaysia, South Korea and Singapore. In 1991 the Government began leasing millions of acres of forest in the NW and Mazaruni districts for 'sustainable logging'. The largest company, Barama, leases 4,125,000 acres and is investing US$154mn in 1992-2001 in its forestry complex, which produces plywood for export. Most industrial production is processing of agricultural products (sugar, rice, timber, coconuts).

The area of greatest growth in the mining sector is gold, which is now the leading export earner. A new pricing system was introduced in 1990, which resulted in more of the gold produced being officially declared, but it was the development of the Omai gold mine, one of the largest open pit mines in South America, which pushed growth and it now produces 70% of total output. Expansion plans were announced in 1995, but were dashed by a tailings pond dam collapse and cyanide spill into the Omai River, which forced the closure of the mine for several months. A commission of inquiry called on the Government to prepare environment protection legislation and establish a regulatory agency to monitor compliance with environmental regulations. The mine was reopened in 1996 following concern about the loss of earnings of the 900-strong workforce. Reserves at the mine are 3.6 million ozs after the discovery in 1995 of a further 9 million tonnes of gold bearing ore representing 446,000 ozs of gold. Total gold production in 1996 was forecast to reach 360,000 ozs.

Guyana: fact file

Geographic

Land area	215,083 sq km
forested	83.8%
pastures	6.3%
cultivated	2.5%

Demographic

Population (1995)	770,000
annual growth rate (1990-95)	0.4%
urban	31.0%
rural	69.0%
density	3.9 per sq km
Religious affiliation	
Christian	52.0%
Hindu	34.0%
Muslim	9.0%
Birth rate per 1,000 (1994)	20.0
	(world av 25.0)

Education and Health

Life expectancy at birth,	
male	62 years
female	68 years
Infant mortality rate	
per 1,000 live births (1994)	49.0
Physicians (1992)	1 per 5,314 persons
Hospital beds (1989)	1 per 300 persons
Calorie intake as %	
of FAO requirement	105%
Population age 25 and over	
with no formal schooling	8.1%
Literate males (over 15)	98.1%
Literate females (over 15)	97.5%

Economic

GNP (1993 market prices)	US$285mn
GNP per capita	US$350
Public external debt (1993)	
	US$1,727mn
Tourism receipts (1993)	US$36mn
Inflation (annual av 1989-94)	22.0%
Radio	1 per 1.9 persons
Television	1 per 49 persons
Telephone	1 per 18 persons

Employment

Population economically active (1987)	
	270,074
Unemployment rate (1992)	12.9%
% of labour force in agriculture	20.4
mining	3.9
manufacturing	11.8
construction	2.8
Military forces	1,600

Source *Encyclopaedia Britannica*

Guyana was the world's largest producer of calcined bauxite, the highest grade of the mineral, but has lost its dominance to China. Nationalized in 1971, bauxite and alumina were traditionally the biggest foreign exchange earners but the industry collapsed in the 1980s. In 1992 the heavily indebted state company, Guymine, was dissolved and replaced by two new entities, Linden Mining Enterprises (Linmine) on the Demerara River and Berbice Mining Enterprises (Bermine) at Kwakwani. A bauxite rehabilitation project was started, with the help of a World Bank loan. Production in 1996 was expected to be 2.2 million tonnes, up from a low of 1.3 million in 1988. No alumina has been exported since 1982 when the Linden refinery closed.

Other mineral deposits include copper, molybdenum, tungsten, iron, nickel and quartz. Diamonds are mined, granite is being quarried to reconstruct sea defences and the coastal road system and oil is being sought offshore and onshore.

Recent trends Guyana's economy was in almost permanent recession between 1970 and 1990, apart from temporary prosperity brought about by a brief non-oil commodities boom in the mid-1970s. Venezuela's long standing claim to the Essequibo region discouraged exploitation of the natural resources in that area but the overall investment climate was damaged by inefficient management in the dominant state sector which undermined both domestic and foreign savings. During the 1980s the Government struggled to come to terms with the IMF, which declared Guyana ineligible for further lending in 1985 because of the accumulation of arrears. It was only in 1990 that the Bank for International Settlements and a group of other donors provided funds to clear the arrears to the IMF and other creditors. This opened the way for new loans from a variety of sources as well as debt rescheduling or cancellation agreements and the resumption of foreign aid.

The 1990s have seen a dramatic turnaround with gdp growth averaging 10.8% in 1990-94. The economy slowed to 5.1% in 1995 as a result of the closure of the Omai gold mine, but was expected to record a growth of about 6.6% in 1996, with continued gains in production of sugar, rice, gold and bauxite. Under an IMF-approved Economic Recovery Programme (1990-93), a number of state companies were privatized. Others are earmarked for divestment but progress has slowed. A second, 3-year Enhanced Structural Adjustment Facility was agreed with the IMF in 1994 and the Government has succeeded in meeting its targets. Tax reform and improved collection methods have greatly increased fiscal revenue. Following the passage of the Financial Institutions Act and other legislation the InterAmerican Development Bank granted loans for strengthening and reform of the financial system, including privatization of state banks. The World Bank provided finance for several sectoral adjustment projects together with a Social Impact Amelioration Programme aimed at easing the hardship inflicted on lower income groups by economic restructuring. The Government is committed to poverty eradication and makes annual budget allocations. Debt remains a problem but the burden is becoming less as the economy grows. The debt: gdp ratio fell from 511% in 1990 to 434% in 1994, while the debt service ratio declined from 118% to 20% in the same period.

● Guyana has suffered from serious economic problems for over 15 years. Wages are very low and many people depend on overseas remittances or 'parallel market' activities to survive. The country is basically self-sufficient for its food supply. Many foreign goods are readily available. The country's infrastructure is seriously run down. Electricity blackouts occur and last anywhere from 10 mins to days on end. New equipment, aimed to improve supply, is scheduled for early 1997. Outside Georgetown, facilities are much more basic.

GEORGETOWN

Georgetown, the capital, and the chief town and port, is on the right bank of the River Demerara, at its mouth. Its population is roughly 200,000. The climate is tropical, with a mean temperature of 27°C, but the trade winds provide welcome relief. The city is built on a grid plan, with wide tree-lined streets and drainage canals following the layout of the old sugar estates. Despite being located on the Atlantic coast, Georgetown is known as the 'Garden City of the Caribbean'. Parts of the city are very attractive, with white-painted wooden 19th century houses raised on stilts and a profusion of flowering trees. In the evening the sea wall is crowded with strollers and at Easter it is a mass of colourful paper kites. Although part of the old city centre was destroyed by fire in 1945, there are some fine 19th century buildings, particularly on or near the Avenue of the Republic (eg on Brickdam). The Gothic-style **City Hall** dates from 1887; its interior has been recently restored and may be viewed. **St George's Anglican Cathedral**, which dates from 1889 (consecrated 1894), is 44m (143 feet) high and is reputed to be the tallest wooden building in the world (it was designed by Sir Arthur Blomfield). Above the altar is a chandelier given by Queen Victoria. The **Public Buildings**, on Brickdam, which house Parliament, are an impressive neoclassical structure built in 1839. Opposite, is **St Andrew's Kirk** (18th century). **State House** on Main Street is the residence of the president. Much of the city centre is dominated by the imposing tower above **Stabroek market** (1880). At the head of Brickdam, one of the main streets, is an aluminium arch commemorating independence. Nearby is a monument to the 1763 slave rebellion, surmounted by an impressive statue of Cuffy, its best-known leader. Near the *Guyana Pegasus Hotel* on Seawall Road is the **Umana Yana**, a conical thatched structure built by a group of Wai Wai Amerindians using traditional techniques for the 1972 conference of the Non-Aligned Movement.

The **National Museum**, opposite the post office, houses an idiosyncratic collection of exhibits from Guyana and elsewhere, including a model of Georgetown before the 1945 fire and a good natural history section on the top floor (free, 0900-1700 Mon-Fri, 0900-1200 Sat). The **Walter Roth Museum of Anthropology**, opposite *Park Hotel* on Main Street, has a collection of Amerindian artefacts (closed until early 1997).

The **Botanical Gardens** (20 mins' walk from Anglican Cathedral, entry free), covering 50 hectares, have Victorian bridges and pavilions, palms and lily-ponds (run-down, but undergoing continual improvements). Be alert in the Gardens at all times. Near the SW corner is the former residence of the President, Castellani House, which now houses the **National Art Collection** (Tues-Sun 1000-1700), and there is also a large mausoleum containing the remains of the former president, Forbes Burnham, which is decorated with reliefs depicting scenes from his political career. Look out for the rare cannonball tree (Couroupita Guianensis), named after the appearance of its poisonous fruit. The **zoo** (being upgraded) has a collection of local animals and the manatees in the ponds will eat grass from your hand. The zoo also boasts a breeding centre for endangered birds which are released into the wild. The zoo is open 0800-1800, US$0.30 for adults, half-price for children; to use personal video US$14.50. There are also beautiful tropical plants in the **Promenade Gardens** (frequently locked) on Middle Street and in the **National Park** on Carifesta Avenue. The National Park has a good public running track.

The **Georgetown Cricket Club** at Bourda has one of the finest cricket grounds in the tropics. Near the SE corner of the Botanic Gardens is a well-equipped **National Sports Centre**.

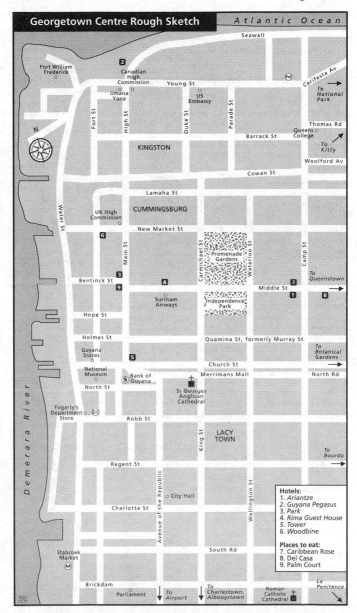

Georgetown Centre Rough Sketch

Atlantic Ocean

Seawall

Fort William Frederick

Canadian High Commission

Umana Yana

Young St

US Embassy

Carifesta Av

To National Park

Fort St

High St

Duke St

Parade St

Thomas Rd

Queens College

Barrack St

To Kitty

KINGSTON

Woolford Av

Cowan St

Lamaha St

CUMMINGSBURG

UK High Commission

New Market St

Water St

Main St

Carmichael St

Promenade Gardens

Waterloo St

Camp St

To Queenstown

Bentinck St

Middle St

To Queenstown

Surinam Airways

Independence Park

Hope St

Holmes St

Guyana Stores

Quamina St, formerly Murray St

To Botanical Gardens

Church St

National Museum

Bank of Guyana

Merrimans Mall

North Rd

North St

St Georges Anglican Cathedral

Fogarty's Department Store

Robb St

King St

LACY TOWN

To Bourda

Regent St

Avenue of the Republic

City Hall

Wellington St

Charlotte St

Stabroek Market

South Rd

Brickdam

Parliament

To Airport

To Charlestown, Albouystown

Roman Catholic Cathedral

La Penitence

Demerara River

Hotels:
1. *Ariantze*
2. *Guyana Pegasus*
3. *Park*
4. *Rima Guest House*
5. *Tower*
6. *Woodbine*

Places to eat:
7. Caribbean Rose
8. Del Casa
9. Palm Court

Nearby is the **Cultural Centre**, an impressive air-conditioned theatre with a large stage. Performances are also given at the **Playhouse Theatre** in Parade Street.

Local Information – Georgetown

● **NB**

Despite the delights of this beautiful city, normal security precautions should be taken. Don't walk the streets at night. Check where it is safe to go with your hotel and in particular avoid Albouystown (S of the centre) and the Tiger Bay area, 1 block W of Main St. Leave your valuables in your hotel.

● **Accommodation**

Price guide

L1	over US$200	L2	US$151-200
L3	US$101-150	A1	US$81-100
A2	US$61-80	A3	US$46-60
B	US$31-45	C	US$21-30
D	US$12-20	E	US$7-11
F	US$4-6	G	up to US$3

L2-L3 *Guyana Pegasus*, Seawall Rd, PO Box 101147, T 52853-9, F 60532, recently renovated and extended with new Kingston wing, very safe, a/c, comfortable, fridge, cable TV, lovely swimming pool, poolside barbecue every night, 2 bars, 2 restaurants, gym, tennis, business centre, has a shoeshine boy between 0700 and 1000, 24-hrs back up electricity, organizes tours to *Timberhead*; **L3-A2** *The Embassy Club*, Pere St, Kitty, T 50811, F 50808, lovely surroundings, self-contained apartments, tennis, gym, playground, good pool, sauna, massage, laundry, secretarial and computer facilities; **L3-A1** *Cara Lodge*, 294 Quamina St, T 55301, F 55310, a Heritage House hotel, 150-year-old converted mansion, 14 rooms, clean, good service, restaurant, bar, taxi service, laundry; **L3-A1** *Cara Suites*, 176 Middle St, T 61612/5, F 61541, luxurious, secure, clean, self-contained rooms with kitchen, Irish Bar serving Guinness and Irish and Scotch whiskies, grocery, shoeshine, laundry, no restaurant; **L2-A2** *Tower*, 74-75 Main St, T 72011-5, F 56021, a/c, lively bar, excellent restaurant, *The Cazabon*, 24-hrs restaurant, good breakfasts, *Main Street Café*, nightly buffets, swimming pool (membership for non-residents takes 4-5 days to process), gym, business centre, boutique, beauty salon, in-house tour company (see below), 24-hrs electricity back up; **L3-A2** *Ocean View*, Liliendaal,

Rupert Craig Highway, 2 miles E of Georgetown, T 022-5429, pool, bar, dining room; **A2-B** *Park*, 37-38 Main St, T 54914-16/70312-3, F 60351, a/c, secure, beautiful Victorian ballroom (worth a visit), beautiful restaurant too (vegetarian), but food could be better (average meal US$5.50); **L3-A3** *Woodbine*, 41-42 New Market St, T 59430-4, F 58406, just off Main St, a/c or fan, bar, restaurant, health club, overpriced; **L3-A2** *Queenstown Inn*, 65 Anira St, Queenstown, T 61416, F 61411, 6 self-contained rooms with a/c, inc gourmet breakfast, US-style, family-run, clean friendly, safe, afternoon tea, laundry, non-alcoholic drinks; **A3-B** *Ariantze*, 176 Middle St, T 65363/70115, simple, clean, fans, or a/c in deluxe rooms and suites, inc breakfast, dining room with TV and a/c, rec; **A3-C** *Friends*, 82 Robb St, T 72383, renovated with a/c, safe, fan, shower, mosquito net, bar, restaurant, travel agency; **A3-B** *Campala*, Camp St, T 52951, 61920/51620, very clean, modern, a/c, near prison (other meals: lunch US$4, dinner US$6); **A3-B** *Waterchris*, Waterloo St, between Murray and Church sts, T 71980, a/c (E pp with fan), good restaurant, friendly.

There are also many smaller, cheaper hotels. Recommended are: **B-C** *Hotel Glow*, 23 Queen St, clean, fan, 24-hrs restaurant; *Florentine's*, North and Waterloo sts, clean but hot and noisy; **C-D** *Demico*, near Stabroek Market, T 56372, with a/c, E without, no breakfast, lunch US$5; **C-D** *Rima Guest House*, 92 Middle St, T 57401, good area, modernized, well-run, good value, central, clean, safe, mosquito nets, restaurant (breakfast US$3.55, lunch and dinner US$5); **F** *Van Ross*, North Rd and Camp St, same management, very basic. Others include: **D** *Belvedere*, Camp St, on the same block as the hospital and thereby benefitting from constant electricity, unhelpful, breakfast available, ice cream parlour next door; opposite is **E** pp *Alpha Guest House*, 203 Camp St, T 54324, all rooms with double beds, shower, fan and mosquito nets, bar downstairs and noisy *Blue Note* nightclub next door; **D-F** *Trio La Chalet*, corner of Camp St and Hadfield St, T 56628 (D in self-contained a/c unit), popular with locals but not very hospitable, 24-hrs bar (breakfast US$1.30, other meals US$1.60); **G** *Dal-Jean's Guest House*, Albert St, Queenstown, noisy but friendly; **E-F** *German's*, 81 Robb St, T 53972, with bath, no fan; **F** *Tropical*, Waterloo and Middle sts, very basic. Many small hotels and guest houses are full of long-stay residents, while some are rented by the hour. Try to book in advance. If in doubt, go to a larger hotel for first night and look around next day in daylight.

Apartments: *N and R*, 246 Anaida Ave, Eccles, East Bank Demerara, T 60921 (reservations through N and R Apartment Rentals, 301 Church and Thomas sts, Georgetown, T 58079/664040), US$45 a day, 1 bedroom, a/c, TV, maid service, washer, dryer, guard service, generator; *Blue Wave*, 3 locations, office at 8-9 North Rd, Bourda, T 64295, fully-furnished, kitchenette, TV, a/c, hot water, 24-hrs electricity and security, US$45-75. Mrs Lee has 3 flats on Middle St, 2 bedrooms, bathroom, kitchen, US$400/month, contact her at *Polly's Hairdressers*, Middle St, next to *Caribbean Rose*.

● **Places to eat**

Eating out is very cheap at present because of the favourable exchange rate. 10% service may be added to bill. Many restaurants are closed on public holidays. Prices given below are for an average main course. At Hotels: *Pegasus*, *El Dorado*, good atmosphere, Caribbean, Continental and European, flambé menu US$9, *Browne's Old Cafe*, lunch special US$4.70, main course from menu US$6, good breakfasts US$4; *Tower*, *Cazabon*, very good food, US$7.50-9.20, also *Main Street Café*, very good breakfast US$6, open 24 hrs; *Bottle Bar and Restaurant* at *Cara Lodge*, good, pleasant surroundings, must book, from US$6; very good breakfast from US$4 at *Waterchris*, lunch/dinner from US$5. Best in town are *Del Casa* (good food and atmosphere – no shorts, from US$12), *Tahli*, in same building, good Indian food, expensive; *Caribbean Rose*, opp *Ariantze* (US$4-12, slow service, mixed reports, up 4 flights of stairs and on the roof, the open sides will cool you down, credit cards not accepted but will take US$ or Guyanese dollars); *Return to Eden*, opp hospital, rec, cheap and vegetarian, all on Middle St (US$7.50-9.20); also rec are *Palm Court*, Main St (many Chinese dishes US$3-10, good food, fair service), and *Arawak Steak House*, in roof garden above *Demico Hotel* (casual atmosphere, busy in pm, good value, average price US$5, closes 2200). *Ranch*, Vlissengen Rd, T 66311, good food, western decor, breeze at night. Good lunches for around US$4-5 at the *Rice Bowl* in Robb St, the *Coalpot* in New Town (no shorts allowed, cheaper cafeteria) and *Hack's*

Hallal; *Country Pride* in Robb St, serves lunch and dinner, US$4-5. Fresh daily baking at *Jerries*, 228 Camp St, and wild meats and seafood at *Anchor*, 136 Waterloo St. Good Chinese: *Yue Yuan*, Robb St, *Hing Loon*, Main St, *New Thriving*, Regent St, also in Alexander St, all good. Many Chinese restaurants (all pretty rough), inc *Double Dragon*, Av of the Republic; and *Diamond Food House*, 9 Camp St. For late night eating there are several Chinese restaurants on Sheriff St inc *Double Happiness*. For fast food, try *Quality Fast Food*, Hincks St; *Creole Hot Pot*, 37C Cummings St, exclusively Guyanese dishes; *Red Rooster*, Regent St; *Arapaima*, Main St; *Idaho*, Brickdam; *Forest Hills*, Camp St; *Calypso*, Regent St; *Demico House*, Stabroek Market, convenient, but poor service. *KFC* at Stabroek Market and on Vlissengen Rd. Cheap counter lunches at *Guyana Stores*, Main St. Haagan-Daz ice cream sold at *Shaynors*, Ave of the Republic, US$2.50. Ice cream at *Igloo*, Camp and Middle sts; *Brown Betty's*, nr Stabroek. Excellent fruit juices at *Organic Juices*, Croal St, Bourda. *Juice Power*, Middle St, past the hospital, also sells drinking water. Beacon Foundation, 3 branches in Georgetown (ask a local for directions) is a charitable organization to feed the homeless and care for the terminally ill; it has good food at reasonable prices.

● **Entertainment**

Nightlife: Georgetown is surprisingly lively at night, mainly with gold miners, traders and overseas Guyanese throwing US$ around. Take care walking home at night. Liveliest disco is *Planet Hollywood*, Camp St, corner of Regent St (entrance US$3.50, expensive); *The Library*, Camp St, very popular Wed night (ladies free), barbecue, beer garden, dance floor, bar (entrance US$2.50); *Blue Note*, Camp St, disco and beer garden, entry US$3.50; also on Camp St *Rumour Bar* and *The Spectrum*. *Palm Court*, Main St, popular bar/café (French style), very lively Fri pm (entry US$3.50) and holidays, no entrance fee on other days; *Jazz Club* in *Ariantze Hotel*, Middle St, temporarily closed 1996; *Trump Card*, Church St, near St George's, sometimes has a live band. Near the Kitty Market are *Jazzy Jacks*, Alexander St (open till 0400 at weekends), and *Wee Place*, Lamaha St, but this area is unsafe unless you go with locals. Sheriff St is some way from the centre but is 'the street that never sleeps' full of late night Chinese restaurants and has some good bars inc *Tennessee Lounge*, *Burns Beat* and *Sheriff* (live band). Most nightclubs sell imported, as well as local Banks beer; many sell drinks by the bottle rather than shot, this works out cheaper. You can visit the steel pan yards and watch practice sessions. There are 2 theatres in Georgetown. **Cinemas**: *Astor*, Waterloo and Church sts; *Strand*, Charlotte St; one on Main St; all worth a visit, US$0.75 for a double bill (protect against mosquitoes).

● **Shopping**
Normal shopping hours are 0830-1600, Mon-Thur, 0830-1700 Fri, 0830-1200 Sat. Market hours 0800-1600, Mon-Sat, except Wed 0900-1200, Sun 0800-1000. The main shopping area is Regent St. The two main department stores are **Guyana Stores** in Church St, and *Fogarty's*, but neither has a wide range of goods. Most Guyanese do their regular shopping at the four big markets: Stabroek (don't take valuables), Bourda, La Penitence and Kitty. Craft items are a good buy; Amerindian basketwork, hammocks, wood carvings, pottery, and small figures made out of Balata, a rubbery substance tapped from trees in the interior. *Houseproud*, 6 Avenue of the Republic, has a good selection of expensive craftwork, but there are many other craft shops including *Creations Craft*, Water St. Also *Hibiscus Craft Plaza*, outside General Post Office; others are advertised in the papers. Good T-shirts are sold at Guyana Stores and in the markets. Gold is also sold widely, often at good prices but make sure you know what you are buying. Do not buy it on the street. Films over ASA400 are normally not available; bring your own stock. 24-hr developing is available at *Risans* on Main St (top end) and Ave of the Republic recommended as efficient, sells slide film (photocopying, too), also *Guyana Stores* and a 1-hr photo print service in Quamina St, near Main St.

Bookshops: some interesting books in *Houseproud*. Try also *GNTC* on Water St, *Argosy* and *Kharg* both on Regent St, *Dimension* on Cummings St, as well as *Guyana Stores* and *Fogarty's*, *Universal Bookstore* on Water St, nr *Fogarty's*, has a good selection of books and greetings cards. Hughes and Thorne Publishing House, 61 Hadfield and Cross sts, copies of *Guyana Tourist Guide*, US$2.50, and *El Dorado*, inflight magazine of Guyana Airways. *Newsweek* sold at *Hotel Tower*.

● **Vehicle rental**
Car hire is available through numerous companies (page 18 of Guyana Telephone Book gives details). Prices range from US$35/day to US$65/day for a new Nissan Sentra. Better is **N and R Rentals**, 301 Church and Thomas sts, T 58079/66404, Toyota Camry and Corolla, Nissan Station Wagon. Scooters can be hired from Addis Scooter Enterprise Ltd, 38 Sussex St, Charlestown, T 66789, from US$14/day. A permit is needed from local police; rental agencies can advise. Bicycle hire: Roshan Ali at *Fullwork Cycles*, Robb St and Light St, US$25/week plus deposit.

● **Local Transport**
Minibuses run regularly to most parts of the city, mostly from Stabroek market or Avenue of the Republic, standard fare US$0.20, very crowded. It is difficult to get a seat during rush hours. **Taxis** charge US$1.20 for short journeys, US$2.20 for longer runs, with higher rates at night (a safe option) and outside the city limits. Normal collective taxis ply set routes at a fixed fare; they stop at any point on request. Certain hand signals are used on some routes to indicate the final destination (ask). Special taxis at hotels and airports, marked 'special' on the windscreen, charge US$1.25 around town, stops and waiting time extra, or you can negotiate a 'by the hour' deal, usually US$6.

● **Exchange**
National Bank of Industry and Commerce; Guyana Bank of Trade and Industry; Bank of Baroda; Bank of Nova Scotia will give cash advance on Visa card. Bank hours are 0800-1230 Mon-Fri, plus 1500-1700 on Fri. **Exchange houses** (*cambios*) in shops may be open longer hours. A good, safe *cambio* is *Joe Chin Travel* on Main St. The *cambio* opp the *Tower Hotel* accepts Thomas Cook travellers' cheques, but not at the best rates. There is a *cambio* next to *Rima Guest House*, Middle St. Roving *cambios* at entrance to Stabroek Market, take care.

● **Laundry**
Car Wash Laundromat, Camp St, past the prison, going S; ask taxi drivers to take you to a laundry.

● **Post & telecommunications**
Post Office: main one on North St.

● **Places of worship**
Anglican: St George's Cathedral, Christ

Church, Waterloo Street; St Andrew's (Presbyterian), Avenue of the Republic; Roman Catholic Cathedral, Brickdam; Pentecostal, Full
Gospel Fellowship, South Rd corner of Albert
Rd, welcoming.

● **Sports**
The national indoor sport is dominoes. There
are sports clubs for cricket, tennis, football,
rugby, hockey, riding, swimming, cycling, athletics, badminton, volley ball, netball, snooker,
pool, golf, boxing, ballroom dancing and rifle
shooting. At Easter there are kite flying competitions.

● **Bus Services**
There are regular services by minibuses and
collective taxis to most coastal towns from the
Stabroek Market. To **Rosignol** (for New Am-
sterdam, Springlands and Suriname), 2 hrs,
US$3; to **Parika** US$1.50; to **Linden** US$3.
Ask other passengers what the fare should be.

● **Travel agents**
Try Mr Mendoza at *Frandec Travel Service*,
Main St, repeatedly rec (no tours to the interior); *Wieting and Richter*, Middle and Camp
sts, very helpful, ask for Onassis Stanley; *H and
R Ramdehol*, 215 South Rd, Lacytown,
T 70639/73183/73486; *Joe Chin Travel*, rec
(see **Exchange**, above). For **Tour Operators**,
see below.

● **Tour Operators**
The tourism sector is promoting ecotourism in
the form of environmentally friendly resorts and
camps on Guyana's rivers and in the rainforest.
There is much tropical wildlife to be seen.
    Wilderness Explorers, 61 Hadfield and
Cross sts, 1st floor, Hadfield Foundation Bldg,
Georgetown, T/F 62085, T 77698, after hours
T 54929, offer ready-made itineraries and spe-
cialize in custom-designed, personal itineraries

for any group size. Tours available to all of
Guyana's interior resorts, day and overland
tours to Kaieteur Falls, horse trekking, hiking
and general tours in the Rupununi and rain-
forest. Specialists in nature, adventure and
bird-watching tours. Free tourism information,
booklet and advice available. *Wonderland
Tours*, 65 Main St, Georgetown, T 65991,
T/F 59795, day trips to Kaieteur and Orinduik
Falls, Santa Mission, Essequibo and Mazaruni
Rivers (developing own camp on the Mazaruni
river), city tours; special arrangements for overnight stays available. *Torong Guyana*, 56
Coralita Ave, Bel Air Park, Georgetown,
T 50876/65298, F 50749, trips to Kaieteur and
Orinduik Falls and 3-day Rupununi Safaris, inc
Kaieteur (US$450). *Discover Tours*, Hotel
Tower, 74-75 Main St, Georgetown, T 72011-
5/58001, F 65691/56021, custom-designed
itineraries to inland resorts, day and overland
trips to Kaieteur Falls and other locations, rates
fully inclusive, 4-14 day tours US$450-2,000
pp, group sizes 8-15. *Cattleya Rainforest
Tours*, 228 South Rd, Georgetown, T 76590,
F 70944, overland trips to Kaieteur. *Shell
Beach Adventures*, T 52853/9, trips to Almond Beach in NW Guyana to see 4 species
of nesting turtles in season and scalet ibis
roosting, 2-day trip US$250 pp using light
aircraft and camping on beach. *Rainbow
River Safari Ltd*, c/o Allison, Guyenterprise
Agency, 234 Almond St, F 2-56959 or phone
Allison 2-69874, can provide tours into the
interior, to its campsite on the Mazaruni River
(see below), arranges overland tours to
Kaieteur Falls, director Miss I Prowell, resident
at the campsite (London office, Mrs Sabat,
T 0181-671 1414, F 0171-703 5500). *Green-
heart Tours*, 36 Craig St, Campbellville, Georgetown, T/F 58219, itineraries for any group
size, tours of Georgetown City (US$25), to

Santa Mission (US$50 pp), Essequibo/Mazaruni Rivers (US$100 pp), Kaieteur/Orinduick Falls (US$180 pp), Ituni Savannahs (US$150 pp). *Cortour*, 1651 Crabwood Creek, Corentyne, Berbice, T 41746, tours to the Corentyne, river and land. *Evergreen Adventures*, 185 Shribasant St, Prashad Nagar, Georgetown, T 51048, tours on the Essequibo River to Baganara Island. *White Water Adventure Tours*, T/F 65225, daytrips to Barakara Island on the Mazaruni River from US$58; trips to Marshall Falls (rapids) available. *Roraima Airways*, 101 Cummings St, Bourda, T 59648, F 59646.

● **Resorts**

Timberhead, operated by *Pegasus Hotel* in the Santa Amerindian Reserve, situated on a sandy hill overlooking Savannah and the Pokerero Creek, 3 beautifully appointed native lodges with bath and kitchen facilities, well-run, good food, lovely trip up the Kamuni River to get there, much wildlife to be seen, 212 species of bird have been recorded, activities include swimming, fishing, jungle treks, visit to Santa Mission Amerindian village, volley ball, US$90 pp for a day trip, US$145 pp for 1 night and 2 days, plus US$110 per night from second night on (includes all transport, meals, bar, guide, accommodation), highly rec. *Shanklands*, contact Joanne Jardim, PO Box 10194, Residence No 4, Thirst Park, Georgetown, T/F 51586 (or through *Wilderness Explorers*), on a cliff overlooking the Essequibo, 3 colonial style cottages with verandah and kitchen, activities include swimming, walking, bird watching, croquet, fishing, watersports, first class, overnight rate US$125-155. *The Gazebo*, contact Bibi Zackeryah, Willems Timber Trading Co Ltd, PO Box 10443, Georgetown, T 72046/7, 69252, F 60983, the country home of the Willems family on 136-acre Kaow Island in the Essequibo River, facilities include a jungle walk, tennis, swimming, watersports, trekking, bird watching, room rates US$240d, US$155s full board, most activities included, transport from Georgetown not included (air, 30 mins, US$200; minibus and boat via Parika, 2 hrs, US$125 or US$275, latter in cabin cruiser; day trips for US$95). *Double 'B' Exotic Gardens*, 58 Lamaha Gardens, Georgetown, T 52023, F 60997, contact Boyo Ramsaroop, near Timehri Airport, good birdwatching, gardens specializing in heliconias, day tours US$35. *Emerald Tower Rainforest Lodge*, Madewini on the Demerara River,

rain forest lodges, T 72011, F 56021, reached by minibus from Georgetown, 8 private tree-level cabins, activities include swimming, bicycle and nature trails, croquet, putting green, sauna, birdwatching, archery, all inclusive rates US$265d, 175s; organizes custom itineraries, including other interior resorts, Kaieteur and Orinduik Falls. *Barakara Resort*, beautifully designed resort on an island in the Mazaruni River, 10 mins by boat from Bartika, T/F 65225, from US$120 overnight. For *Rock View Ecotourism Resort*, *Karanambu Ranch* and *Dadanawa Ranch*, see under Rupununi, below.

● **Camps**

Rainbow River Safari, a 17,000 acre conservation site on the Mazaruni River, dormitory style accommodation in 3 large tented camps (chalets planned), pit latrines, washing in river, cooking over wood fire, US$60-90 pp all inclusive, day trips with 3 different jungle trails US$3.75, swimming, whitewater rafting, wildlife walking, birdwatching, hill climbing, gold panning, no music unless requested, no caged animals; 12 further camps are planned. Day trippers pay a landing fee of G$500. See above for contact addresses, which should be approached for all latest details. Agent in Bartica, Bell Boats, Monty Bell, T 05-2405, or Stephen Bell, T 05-2414, or Attack, T 05-2484.

A new camp is being built at Saxacalli Mission between Parika and Bartica on a beach on the Essequibo.

● **NB**

For visiting many parts of the interior, particularly Amerindian districts, permits are required in advance from the Ministry of Home Affairs and/or the Public Works, Communications and Regional Development in Georgetown. If venturing out of Georgetown on your own, you must check beforehand whether you need a permit for where you intend to visit.

SOUTHEAST TO SURINAME

Linden (*pop* 60,000), the second-largest town in Guyana, is a bauxite mining town 70 miles/112 km S of Georgetown on the Demerara river. A good road connects the two towns; the police checks are to stop drug and gun running. On the W bank of the river Linden is a company mining town. The opencast mine is 200-300 ft deep and is said to have the world's longest boom walking dragline. Across the river (bridge or ferry, G$5) are the poorer suburbs of Wismar and Christianburg. The town is dominated by a disused alumina plant and scarred by old bauxite pits. **Accommodation** is scarce: in town *Crescent* and *Chez Docs*, cheap basic; *Hotel Star Bonnett*, three-quarters of a mile out of town on Georgetown road, clean, good lunches; nearby **E** *Summit Hotel*.

From Linden rough roads suitable for four-wheel drive vehicles run S to the bauxite mining towns of Ituni and Kwakwani. The road S to the logging centre at Mabura Hill is in excellent condition; it continues to Kurupukari (this stretch is being upgraded). A good road goes W from Linden to Rockstone ferry on the Essequibo river. From Rockstone very bad roads run N to Bartica and SW to Issano.

New Amsterdam (*pop* 25,000) is 65 miles S-E of Georgetown on the E bank of the Berbice river, near its mouth. From Georgetown, take a minibus (44, or express No 50) or collective taxi to Rosignol (**G** *Hotel Hollywood*, 'dubious') on the W bank of the Berbice, then cross the river by the ferry, 15 mins (US$0.30; also takes vehicles) or by launch to Blairmont, 1 mile past Rosignol. The town is picturesque.

● **Hotels** **C-D** *Church View Guest House*, 3 Main and King sts, T (03) 2880, F 3927, inc breakfast, clean, rec; **C-D** *Parkway*, 4 Main St, T (03) 3928, clean, friendly, safe, with bath, rec but food poor; *Hotel Embassy*, at Rose Hall. **C-D** *Astor*, 7 Strand, T (03)3578, verandah with lounge chairs, breakfast from US$3, rec.

● **Places to eat** *Circle C*, Main and Charlotte sts, Créole; *Brown Derby*, Main and Church sts, Créole; both US$3-6 per meal, various Chinese on Main St; *Oik Banks Est*, Main St, nice, slow.

From New Amsterdam, it is sometimes possible to get a lift on a bauxite barge up the Berbice river to the small mining town of Kwakwani (there is a guesthouse, reasonable, check for vacancies at Guymine in Georgetown).

The road continues E from New Amsterdam (minibus, US$1), to **Springlands** and Skeldon at the mouth of the Corentyne river. The two towns are officially known as **Corriverton** (Corentyne River Town, *pop* about 31,000). Springlands is 2 km long, so you need to know where you want to get off the bus.

● **Hotels in Springlands**: *Ambassador*, near point for ferry to Nieuw Nickerie; **D-F** *Swiss Guest House*, T (039) 2329, Pakistani run, rough but helpful. In Skeldon: **E** *Parapak*, no fan, no mosquito net, poor value; **F** *Mahogony*, fan, clean, friendly, rec; **G** *Arawak*, rough, avoid. Several good Chinese restaurants within a few blocks of Springlands town centre. Good Indian food at *Mansoor*, Skeldon.

● **Exchange** National Bank of Industry and Commerce; Guyana National Commercial Bank. *Cambio* (National Bank of Industry and Commerce) at Skeldon for arriving ferry passengers. Suriname guilders can officially be changed into Guyanese dollars.

CROSSING TO SURINAME

Before you leave Georgetown, check with the Suriname embassy whether you need a visa (without one, if required, you may be imprisoned before being sent back to Georgetown). See **Documents**, Suriname, **Information for travellers**. From Springlands there is a daily ferry (not Sun or national holidays of either country) to Nieuw Nickerie (foot passengers only). Queue at the booking office near the jetty from 0700, office opens 0800, booking fee US$0.25, all passports must be presented when booking, tickets are sold later on the ferry, Sf65 one way, payable in Suriname guilders only. Immigration and customs formalities (very slow and thorough) take place from 0900, ferry sails in the afternoon depending on tides and weather, crossing time normally 2 hrs.

WEST FROM GEORGETOWN: ROUTES TO VENEZUELA

Travelling W from Georgetown, the road crosses the $1\frac{1}{4}$-mile long floating Demerara bridge (opens often for shipping, US$0.20 toll, pedestrians free) and continues to **Parika**, a small town on the E bank of the Essequibo river (minibus US$1). Speedboats cross the river from Stabroek market, US$0.30. If you need accommodation, there are two small guesthouses where you can stay fairly safely. From here ferries cross the river to **Adventure** on the W bank at 1700 daily and 0830 Wed and Fri, returning at 0300 daily and 1330 Wed and Fri; alternatively take a speedboat US$2.40. (See *Three Singles to Adventure* by Gerald Durrell.) There are also three ferries a day to Leguan Island (30 mins, US$0.25); accommodation available at the *Hotel President*.

The NW coastal area is mainly accessible by boat only. Speedboats cross from Parika to Supenaam, US$2.80, a very wet crossing. From Supenaam minibuses or taxis (US$3.50 pp) go to Charity. From Adventure a road runs N through Anna Regina. Nearby is Lake Mainstay, a small resort, reached by taxi; it is also known as the hot and cold lake because it varies in temperature from one place to another. The road goes on to **Charity**, a pleasant little town with two small hotels (**E** *Purple Heart*, cheaper than *Xenon*) and a lively market on Mon (quiet at other times).

Near the border with Venezuela are the small ports of **Morawhanna** (Morajuana to the Venezuelans) and **Mabaruma**. Mabaruma has replaced Morawhanna as capital of the region since it is less at risk from flooding. **D** *Kumaka Tourist Resort*, Maburama, contact *Somwaru Travel Agency*, Georgetown, T (02) 59276, meals (excellent, huge helpings), pool (filled if requested in advance), bath, balcony, hammocks, rec, owner Lincoln Broomes; offers trips to Hosororo Falls, Babarima Amerindian settlement, rainforest, early examples of Amerindian art.

- **Transport** GAC flies from Georgetown Mon and Fri, US$72.50 return. An unreliable ferry from Georgetown (US$6.50) goes to Mabaruma. The journey is surprisingly rough and 'you will have to fight for hammock space and watch your possessions like a hawk'. From Mabaruma boats sail up the river to Port Kaituma, 40 miles/ 64 km inland, from where a small passenger railway connects with the isolated settlement of Matthews Ridge (more easily reached by chartered aircraft from Georgetown). The site of the Jonestown mass-suicide is nearby.

The Venezuelan border can be crossed at the River Cuyuni (at least from Venezuela into Guyana). On the Venezuelan side is San Martín, from which a narrow road goes to El Dorado on the road S to Brazil. It is possible to reach this border by boat from Georgetown (very infrequent), or by military plane, about 4 or 5 times a week, no schedule, US$60.

SOUTHWEST FROM GEORGETOWN: TO BRAZIL

From Parika there is a ferry up the Essequibo river to Bartica on Mon, Thur and Sat, returning next day, US$1.50 one way. The 36 mile/58 km journey takes 6 hrs, stopping at Fort Island; small boats come out from riverside settlements to load up with fruit. On Fort Island is a Dutch fort (built 1743, restored by Raleigh International in 1991) and the Dutch Court of Policy, built at the same time. There is also a small village; the rest of the island is dairy farms. Local people generally prefer to take a speedboat, US$4.35 pp, 1-2 hrs, depending on horsepower.

Bartica, at the junction of the Essequibo and Mazaruni rivers, is the 'take-off' town for the gold and diamond fields, Kaieteur Falls, and the interior generally. Here an Amazon-like mass of waters meets, but with an effect vastly more beautiful, for they are coloured the 'glossy copper' of all Guyanese rivers and not the dull mud-brown of most of the Amazon. Swimming very good. The *stelling* (wharf) and market are very colourful. Bars flank the main street;

Crystal Crest has a huge sound system and will play requests. Easter regatta.

• **Accommodation D-E** *Main Hotel*, 19 Second Ave, T (05) 2243, meals available (breakfast US$3.20, lunch and dinner US$6.40); **E** *Harbour Cove*, very nice, eat elsewhere; **E** *The Nest* on Fifth Ave, unsafe, very noisy, meals to be had from disco after 1730, or 'Robbie's'. **F** *Modern*, nr ferry, 2 luxury rooms, others basic, with bath and fan, rec, good food; **F** *Pink House* (Mrs Phil's), Second Ave, cheaper, clean, without bath, basic, secure, family-run, quiet. Book ahead if possible. Mrs Payne, near Hospital, basic, clean. *Sea View*, condominium-style resort, under construction. *Riverview Beach Bar*, nr Bartica, popular hotel and bar, disco, videos, nice beach, safe swimming.

The Essequibo is navigable to large boats for some miles above Bartica. The Cuyuni flows into the Mazaruni 3 miles above Bartica, and above this confluence the Mazaruni is impeded for 120 miles by thousands of islands, rapids and waterfalls. To avoid this stretch of treacherous river a road has been built from Bartica to Issano, where boats can be taken up the more tranquil upper Mazaruni.

At the confluence of the Mazaruni and Cuyuni Rivers are the ruins of the Dutch stronghold Kyk-over-al, once the seat of government for the Dutch county of Essequibo. Nearby are the Marshall Falls (35 mins by boat from Bartica, US$38 per boat, return) where you can swim in the falls themselves ('a natural jacuzzi'), or the nearby bay, part of the Rainbow River Safari conservation area, GS$500 landing fee.

The **Kaieteur Falls**, on the Potaro river, rank with the Niagara, Victoria, and Iguazú Falls in majesty and beauty, but have the added attraction of being surrounded by unspoilt forest. The Falls, nearly five times the height of Niagara, with a sheer drop of 228m (741 ft), are nearly 100m wide. They are unspoilt because of their isolation.

The Kaieteur Falls lie within the **Kaieteur National Park**, where there is a variety of wildlife: tapirs, ocelots, monkeys, armadillos, anteaters, and jungle and river birds. At the Falls themselves, one can see the magnificent silver fox, often near the rest house, the cock-of-the-rock and the Kaieteur swift, which lives behind the falls. At dusk the swifts swoop in and out of the gorge before passing through the deluge to roost behind the water. Permission to enter the national park must be obtained from the National Parks Commission in Georgetown, T 59142. In the dry months, April and Oct, the flow of the falls is reduced; in Jan and June/July the flow is fullest, but in June, the height of the wet season, the overland route is impassable.

A trip to the Kaieteur Falls costs US$145 (eg with GAC, T 52002, from Timehri airport, no regular schedule, inc lunch, drinks and guide, also goes to Orinduik Falls; see below, sit on left for best views, take swimming gear). Most agencies include the Orinduik Falls as well, US$170, including ground and air transport, meal, drinks, US$5 national park entrance fee and guide. Trips depend on the charter plane being filled; there is normally at least one flight per week. Cancellations only occur in bad weather or if there are insufficient passengers. Operators offering this service are *Wilderness Explorers* (T 62085), trips to both falls by light aircraft, *Discover Tours* at Hotel Tower (T 72011-5), US$175, *Wonderland Tours* (T 65991, Richard Ousman), and *Torang Guyana*, Mrs Chan-A-Sue in Georgetown, T 65298. You may get very little time at the Falls. To charter a plane privately costs US$1,000 to Kaieteur and Orinduik. *Wilderness Explorers*, *Discover Tours* and *Cattleya Rainforest Tours*, all in Georgetown offer overland trips, as does *Rainbow River Safari* (7-10 days, not including rest days).

To go independently overland to Kaieteur involves much boating and some tough walking. The route starts at Kangaruma village (reached by truck from Bartica to Kangaruma junction, if the road is passable), then to Tukeit via Amatok falls and Waratok falls. From

Tukeit you walk to Kaieteur in about 2 hrs in the dry season; not rec in the rainy season. In the dry season it is possible to walk from Kangaruma to Kaieteur. The whole route is very hard going and it would seem that there is much more chance of being near people if you go by boat.

Once at Kaieteur, you can walk to the top of the falls, at least 2 hrs, but worth it to watch the blue, white and brown water tumbling into the stupendous gorge.

● **Precautions** If going on your own, detailed planning and a guide are essential. Take adequate supplies of food and drink, a sleeping bag, a sheet and blanket, a mosquito net, and kerosene for Tilley lamps.

● **Accommodation** The rest house at the top of the Falls was not open in mid-1996, enquire first at the National Parks Commission, Georgetown, T 59142 (if planning to stay overnight, you must be self-sufficient, whether the guesthouse is open or not; take your own food and a hammock, it can be cold and damp at night). It is nearly impossible to get down the gorge below the falls; the path is completely overgrown, a guide is essential and it takes a full day.

The Pakaraima Mountains stretch from Kaieteur westwards to include the highest peak in Guyana, Mount Roraima, the possible inspiration for Conan Doyle's *Lost World*. Roraima is very difficult to climb from the Guyanese side.

There are several other spectacular waterfalls in the interior, including Imbaimadai and Orinduik, but none is very easy to reach. **Orinduik Falls** are on the Ireng River, which forms the border with Brazil; the river pours over steps and terraces of jasper, with a backdrop of the grass-covered Pakaraima Mountains. There is good swimming at the falls. Vincent and Rose Cheong run a tourist shelter and are full of information about the area and about routes to Brazil from Orinduik (take hammock, food and fuel for outboard motors). It is a 3-hr walk from Orinduik to Urimutang, on the Brazilian side of the Ireng River (essential to get detailed description or a guide

for the correct place to cross the river – no bridge); public transport runs from Urimutang to Boa Vista, 5 hrs. *Wilderness Explorers*, T 62085, offer 4 trips per year from Orinduik N on Ireng River in dugout canoes with Amerindian guides.

The **Rupununi Savanna** in the SW is an extensive area of dry grassland with scattered trees, termite mounds and wooded hills. The freshwater creeks, lined with Ite palms, are good for swimming. The region is scattered with occasional Amerindian villages and a few large cattle ranches which date from the late 19th century: the descendants of some of the Scots settlers still live here. Links with Brazil are much closer than with the Guyanese coast; many people speak Portuguese and most trade, both legal and illegal, is with Brazil.

Avoid visiting the Rupununi in the wet season (mid-May to Aug) as much of the Savanna is flooded and malaria mosquitoes widespread. The best time is Oct to April. River bathing is good, but watch out for the dangerous stingrays. Wild animals are shy, largely nocturnal and seldom seen. Among a wide variety of birds, look out for macaws, toucan, parrots, parakeets, hawks and jabiru storks. Note that a permit from the Ministry of Home Affairs is usually required to visit Rupununi, unless you are going with a tour operator. Check in advance if your passport is sufficient. A separate permit to visit Amerindian villages is needed from the Ministry of Public Works, Communications and Regional Development in Georgetown.

Lethem, a small but scattered town on the Brazilian frontier, is the service centre for the Rupununi and for trade with Brazil. There are a few stores, a small hospital, a police station and government offices which have radio telephone links with Georgetown. A big event at Easter is the rodeo, visited by cowboys from all over the Rupununi. Prices are about twice as high as in Georgetown. About 1½ miles/ 2½ km S of town at St Ignatius there is a Jesuit mission dating from 1911. In the nearby mountains there is good birdwatching and there are waterfalls to visit.

● **Accommodation** A number of places take guests, full board, organize tours and transport. **Accommodation** in Lethem at **F** pp *Takutu Guest House*, clean, basic, poor water supply, Claire cooks food on request (has information on trucks to Georgetown); *Casique Guest House*, OK, and *Regional Guest House*. The *Manari Ranch Hotel*, 7 miles N of Lethem, US$60/day, also *Pirara Ranch*, 15 miles further N, US$50/day, both on creeks for swimming. Duane and Sandy de Freitas at the *Dadanawa Ranch*, 60 miles S of Lethem, one of the world's largest ranches, US$95 pp/day. They can organize trekking and horse riding trips (contact *Wilderness Explorers*, T 62085). Dianne McTurk at *Karanambo Ranch*, 60 miles NE of Lethem, on the Rupununi River, US$120/day (unique old home with cottages for visitors, fishing, excellent birdwatching and boat rides). The owner rears and rehabilitates orphaned giant river otters. Can be booked through *Wilderness Explorers*, T 62085. At the village of Annai on the road to Georgetown, some 70 miles from Lethem *The Rock View Ecotourism Resort* has 4 rooms and cheaper rooms in the main ranch house, several bars, zoo; it is located in the Pakaraima foothills, where the savannah meets the Iwokrama rainforest project; T 64210, F 57211, can also be booked through *Wilderness Explorers*, T 62805; pony treks to nearby foothills, nature tours with opportunities for painting, photography and fishing, regional Amerindian and other local cooking, US$115/day full board, rec. All can be contacted at the Airport Shop in Lethem, where Don and Shirley Melville provide the most comprehensive information and assistance service in the Rupununi (accommodation due to open in 1997). In Georgetown contact Wendella Jackson, T 53750 (for *Karanambo*), or Tony Thorne at *Wilderness Explorers*, T 62085.

● **Places to eat** *Foo Foods*; *Savannah Inn* (accommodation under construction; the Airport Shop.

● **Transport** At *Foo Foods* bicycles can be hired for US$8/day; also available at the Airport Shop, as are horses for US$8/hr. The Airport Shop can arrange landrovers and trucks at US$3 per mile. For birdwatching trips and transport contact Loris Franklin through the

Airport Shop. The best time to ask for hiring a vehicle (always with driver), bicycle or horse is when the plane arrives, the only time when lots of people are around. Car hire is expensive and there are fuel shortages.

Transport around the Rupununi is difficult; there are a few four-wheel drive vehicles, but ox-carts and bicycles are more common on the rough roads. From Lethem transport can be hired for day-trips to the Moco-Moco Falls and the Kamu Falls and to the Kanuku Mountains (four-wheel drive and driver to Moco-Moco US$72.50, long, rough ride and walk, but worth it). Trucks may also be hired to visit Aishalton, 70 miles/110 km S along a very bad road, 6-hr journey, US$300; and to Annai, 60 miles/96 km NE along a better road, 3-hrs' journey, US$200. All trucks leaving town must check with the police so the police know all trucks that are departing.

A road link between Georgetown and Lethem via Mabura Hill and Kurupakari was opened in early 1991. Once completed it will provide a through route from Georgetown to Boa Vista (Brazil), which will have a major impact on Guyana. The funding for the final section has not been found, and it remains virtually impassable. The present route is: good road to Linden, and good for 50 miles beyond, then rapid deterioration for 100 miles to the Essequibo river. Creeks are often bridged by just 2 logs. It is either very dusty or very muddy, challenging, uncomfortable, and a great experience. The road is better in the dry season, but in the rains the worst sections are bypassed with boats.

Truck Georgetown-Lethem: contact Ministry of Regional Development, Georgetown; Eddie Singh, 137 Herstelling, nr Providence police station, 5 miles S of Georgetown, T (065) 2672; Ng-a-fook, on Church St, between Camp St and Waterloo St. Trip takes 2-3 days, can take 7, US$28 pp one-way, no seat but share truck with load, take food, lots of water and hammock. (Care is needed on this route, but it is exciting, through savannah and rainforest.) Guyana Airways Corporation flies from Georgetown to Lethem and back Tues, Wed, Fri and Sat 0515, US$53 one-way (diversions available to Annai and Karanambu Ranch for extra US$90 per flight); book well in advance at the GAC office on Main St, Georgetown. Regular charter planes link the town with Georgetown, about US$200 return.

Annai is a remote Amerindian village in the southern plains. It is possible to trek over the plains to the Rupununi River, or through dense jungle to the mountains. 1 hr on foot is Kwatamang village where Raleigh International built a Health Centre in 1995.

FRONTIER WITH BRAZIL

The Takutu River separates Lethem from Bonfim in Brazil. The crossing is about 1 mile N of Lethem (taxis, or pick-ups, US$2.15) and 2½ km/1½ miles from Bonfim. Small boats ferry foot passengers (US$0.35); vehicles cross by pontoon, or can drive across in the dry season. Formalities are generally lax on both sides of the border, but it is important to observe them as people not having the correct papers may have problems further into either country.

● **Guyanese immigration & customs**
All procedures for exit and entry are carried out at the police station, on the left as you approach the crossing. There is also immigration at Lethem airport.

For accommodation, exchange, transport, etc, see above under Lethem. **Buses** from Bonfim to Boa Vista (Brazil) daily at 0600, 2 hrs, US$5; colectivos charge US$18.

Information for travellers

BEFORE TRAVELLING

● **Documents**
Visa requirements have been relaxed; as of 15 February 1993, the following countries do not need a visa to visit Guyana: USA, Canada, Belgium, Denmark, France, Germany, Greece, Ireland, Italy, Luxembourg, the Netherlands, Portugal, Spain, UK, Norway, Finland, Sweden, Australia, New Zealand, Japan, Korea, and the Commonwealth countries. Visitors are advised to check with the nearest Embassy, Consulate or travel agent for further changes. All visitors require passports and all nationalities, apart from those above, require visas. To obtain a visa, two photos, an onward ticket and yellow fever certificate are required. Visas are charged strictly on a reciprocal basis, equivalent to the cost charged to a Guyanese visitor to the country concerned. Visitors from those countries where they are required arriving without visas are refused entry. To fly in to Guyana, an exit ticket is required, at land borders an onward ticket is usually not asked for. For **Tourist Information** see page 881 below.

● **Customs**
Baggage examination can be very thorough. Duties are high on goods imported in commercial quantities.

● **Climate**
Athough hot, is not unhealthy. Mean shade temperature throughout the year is 27°C; the mean maximum is about 31°C and the mean minimum 24°C. The heat is greatly tempered by cooling breezes from the sea and is most felt from Aug to October. There are two wet seasons, from May to June, and from Dec to the end of Jan, although they may extend into the months either side. Rainfall averages 2,300mm a year in Georgetown.

● **Health**

There is a high risk of both types of malaria in the interior, especially in the wet season. Recommended prophylaxis is chloroquine 500 mg weekly plus paludrine 200 mg daily. Reports of chloroquine-resistant malaria in the interior (seek advice before going). If travelling to the interior for long periods carry drugs for treatment as these may not be available. Sleep under a mosquito net. Although there are plenty of mosquitoes on the coast, they are not malarial.

There is some risk of typhoid and waterborne diseases (eg cholera) owing to low water pressure. Purification is a good idea. Tapwater is usually brown and contains sediment. It is not for drinking; bottled water (Tropical Mist) should be bought for drinking. In the interior, use purification. The Georgetown Hospital is run down, understaffed and lacking equipment, but there are a number of well-equipped private hospitals, including St Joseph's on Parade St, Kingston; Prasad's on Thomas St, doctor on call at weekends; and the Davis Memorial Hospital on Lodge Backlands. Charges are US$2 to US$8 per day and medical consultations cost US$2 to US$4. If admitted to hospital you are expected to provide your own sheets and food (St Joseph's and Davis provides all these). Rec doctor, Dr Clarence Charles, 254 Thomas St, surgery hours 1200-1400.

In the interior, travellers should examine shower pipes, bedding, shoes and clothing for snakes and spiders. Also, in most towns there is neither a hospital nor police. If travelling independently, you are on your own. Besides protecting against mosquitoes, take iodine to treat wounds and prevent infection (can also be used for water purification), a hammock with rope for securing it, and a machete, especially if in the jungle. Remember to drink plenty of water.

MONEY

● **Currency**

The unit is the Guyanese dollar. There are notes for 1, 5, 10, 20, 100 and 500 dollars, though devaluation and inflation mean that even the largest of these is worth very little. Coins for amounts under a dollar exist but are of little practical use.

● **Exchange**

The devaluation of the Guyanese dollar in Feb 1991 aligned the official exchange rate with that offered by licensed exchange houses (known as *cambios*). Since that date the exchange rate was to be adjusted weekly in line with the market rate. On 30 May 1996, this stood at G$138 = US$1. At present *cambios* only buy US or Canadian dollars and pounds sterling. Most *cambios* accept drafts (subject to verification), travellers' cheques and telegraphic transfers, but not credit cards. Rates vary slightly between *cambios* and from day to day and some *cambios* offer better rates for changing over US$100. Rates for changing travellers' cheques are good in *cambios* or on the black market. A few banks accept Thomas Cook travellers' cheques. Note that to sell Guyanese dollars on leaving the country, you will need to produce your *cambio* receipt. The illegal black market on America St ('Wall Street') in Georgetown still operates, but the rates offered are not significantly better than the *cambio* rate and there is a strong risk of being robbed or cheated. The black market also operates in Springlands, the entry point from Suriname. If you arrive when *cambios* are closed and you need to change on the black market, go by taxi and ask someone to negotiate for you.

● **Cost of living**

The devaluation to the *cambio* rate means that, for foreigners, prices for food and drink are low at present. Even imported goods may be cheaper than elsewhere and locally produced goods such as fruit are very cheap. Hotels, tours and services in the interior are subject to electricity and fuel surcharges, which make them less cheap.

GETTING THERE

AIR

There are no direct flights to Guyana from Europe, but BWIA's flights from London, Frankfurt and Zurich to Antigua or Port of Spain connect; from North America BWIA flies daily from New York and Miami, and 3 times a week from Toronto; most BWIA flights involve a change of planes in Port of Spain. Guyana Airways fly daily from New York and once from Miami, most direct. BWIA flies to Guyana from Trinidad 12 times a week (Surinam Airways 4 a week). LIAT and BWIA fly daily from Barbados (Surinam Airways twice a week); BWIA flies daily from Antigua. LIAT have connecting flights with British Airways in Barbados to/from London and Air Canada from Toronto. Surinam

Airways flies 4 times a week from Paramaribo, but these flights are difficult to book from outside the Guianas and are subject to cancellation at short notice. Guyana Airways twice a week from Curaçao. There are no direct flights to Caracas, Venezuela, which can be reached via Port of Spain with an overnight stop.

Flights are often booked weeks in advance, especially at Christmas and in Aug when overseas Guyanese return to visit relatives. Flights are frequently overbooked, so it is essential to reconfirm your outward flight, which can take some time, and difficult to change your travel plans at the last minute. A number of travel agents are now computerized, making reservations and reconfirmations easier. Foreigners must pay for airline tickets in US$ (most airlines do not accept US$100 bills), or other specified currencies. Luggage should be securely locked as theft from checked-in baggage is common.

ON ARRIVAL

● **Airports**
The international airport is at Timehri, 25 miles/40 km S of Georgetown. Check in 2 hrs before most flights, listen to the local radio the day before your flight to hear if it has been delayed, or even brought forward. Minibus No 42 to Georgetown US$1 (from Georgetown leaves from next to Parliament building); for a small charge they will take you to your hotel (similarly for groups going to the airport). Taxi US$14-18 (drivers charge double at night; if arriving on internal flights at night, ask a local to book minibus seats for you). There are two duty-free shops, one selling local and imported spirits (more expensive than downtown), the other local handicrafts and jewellery. There is also an exchange house, open usual banking hours; if closed, plenty of parallel traders outside (signboard in the exchange house says what the rate is). It is difficult to pay for flight tickets at the airport with credit cards or TCs. The exchange desk will change TCs for flight ticket purchases. Internal flights go from Ogle airport; minibus from Market to Ogle US$0.20.

● **Embassies and consulates**
There is a large number of embassies in Georgetown, including: **British High Commission** (44 Main St, PO Box 10849, T 592-2-65881/4); **Canadian High Commission** (Young St) and the Embassies of the **United States** (Young St, Kingston, near *Guyana Pegasus Hotel*), Honorary **French** Consul (7 Sherriff St, T 65238), **Venezuela** (Thomas St), **Brazil** (308 Church

St, Queenstown, T 57970, visa issued next day, 90 days, 1 photo, US$12.75), **Cuba** (Main St) and **Suriname** (304 Church St, T 56995; 2 passport photos, passport, US$20 and 5 days minimum needed).

● **Official time**
4 hrs behind GMT; 1 hr ahead of EST.

● **Public holidays**
1 Jan, New Years' Day; 23 Feb, Republic Day and Mashramani festival; Good Friday, Easter Monday; Labour Day, 1 May; Independence Day, 26 May (instigated in 1996); Caricom Day, first Mon in July; Freedom Day, first Mon in Aug; Christmas Day, 25 Dec, and Boxing Day, 26 December.

The following public holidays are for Hindu and Muslim festivals; they follow a lunar calender, and dates should be checked as required: Phagwah, usually Mar; Eid el Fitr, end of Ramadan; Eid el Azah; Youm un Nabi; Deepavali, usually November.

Note that the Republic Day celebrations last about a week: during this time hotels in Georgetown are very full.

● **Things to take**
A good torch/flashlight and batteries (for the electricity cuts) is essential. Small gift items (eg imported cigarettes, batteries, good quality toiletries) may be appreciated in the interior (they are readily available in Georgetown).

● **Voltage**
100 v in Georgetown; 220 v in most other places, including some Georgetown suburbs.

● **Weights and measures**
Although Guyana went metric in 1982, imperial measures are still widely used.

ON DEPARTURE

● **Departure tax**
There is an exit tax of G$1,500, payable in Guyanese dollars, or US dollars at US$12. It can be paid when reconfirming your ticket at least 3 days before expected departure, in Georgetown, or at the airport after check-in. There is also a 15% tax on international airline tickets for all flights leaving Guyana even if bought abroad.

ACCOMMODATION

The largest hotels in Georgetown have their own emergency electricity generators and water pumps to deal with the frequent interruptions in supply. Other hotels usually provide a bucket of water in your room, fill this up when water is available. When booking an air-conditioned room, make sure it also has natural ventilation. A room tax applies to hotels with more than 16 rooms.

FOOD AND DRINK

● **Food**

The blend of different national influences – Indian, African, Chinese, Creole, English, Portuguese, Amerindian, North American – gives a distinctive flavour to Guyanese cuisine. One well-known dish, traditional at Christmas, is pepper-pot, meat cooked in bitter cassava (casareep) juice with peppers and herbs. Seafood is plentiful and varied, as is the wide variety of tropical fruits and vegetables. The staple food is rice. The food shortages and import ban of the early 1980s had the positive effect of encouraging experimentation with local ingredients, sometimes with interesting results. In the interior wild meat is often available – try wild cow, or else labba (a small rodent).

● **Drink**

Rum is the most popular drink. There is a wide variety of brands, all cheap, including the best which are very good and cost less than US$2 a bottle. Demerara Distillers' 12-year-old *King of Diamonds* premium rum won the *Caribbean Week* (Barbados) Caribbean rum tasting for 2 years running (1992, 1993); its 15-year old *El Dorado* won in 1994. High wine is a strong local rum. There is also local brandy and whisky (Diamond Club), which are worth trying. The local beer, Banks, made partly from rice is good and cheap. There is a wide variety of fruit juices. A new drink, D'Aguiar's Cream Liqueur, produced and bottled by Banks DIH Ltd, is excellent (and strong).

GETTING AROUND

AIR TRANSPORT

Guyana Airways has scheduled flights between Georgetown and Lethem (see text above). There are several charter companies, including the best Mazaharally, Trans Guyana Airways (158-9 Charlotte St, T 73010) and Kayman Sankar; US$320/hr. Ask the charter companies at Ogle airport for seats on cargo flights to any destination, they will help you to get in touch with the charterer. Prices vary, up to US$0.80

per pound. Returning to Ogle can be cheaper, even, if you are lucky, free.

LAND TRANSPORT

Most coastal towns are linked by a good 185 mile road from Springlands in the E to Charity in the W; the Berbice and Essequibo rivers are crossed by ferries, the Demerara by a toll bridge, which, besides closing at high tide for ships to pass through (2-3 hrs) is subject to frequent closures (when an alternative ferry service runs). Apart from a good road connecting Timehri and Linden, continuing as good dirt to Mabura Hill, most other roads in the interior are very poor. Car hire is available from several firms, see under Georgetown. There are shortages of car spares. Gasoline costs about US$1.90 a gallon. Traffic drives on the left. Minibuses and collective taxis, an H on their number plate, run between Georgetown and the entire coast from Charity to Corriverton; also to Linden. All taxis also have an H on the number plate.

RIVER TRANSPORT

There are over 600 miles of navigable river, which provide an important means of communication. Ferries and river boats are referred to in the text, but for further details contact the Transport and Harbours Department, Water St, Georgetown. 6-seater river boats are called *ballahoos*, 3-4 seaters *corials*; they provide the transport in the forest. Note that there is no vehicle ferry across the Courantyne to Suriname.

COMMUNICATIONS

● **Postal services**

Overseas postal and telephone charges are very low. Letters to N and S America US$0.21, to Europe US$0.25, to rest of world US$0.42; post cards US$0.15; aerogrammes US$0.18. Parcels sent abroad have to be weighed and checked by customs before sealing. Take all materials and passport; choose between ordinary and registered service.

● **Telecommunications**

Telecommunications are rapidly improving. It is possible to dial direct to any country in the world. Blue public telephones in Georgetown only allow collect calls overseas; phone booths have overseas, 3-digit codes printed inside. Yellow phones are for free calls to local areas. Some businesses and hotels may allow you to use their phone for local calls if you are buying something – usual charge about US$0.05. Overseas calls can be made from the Guyana Telephone and Telegraph Company office behind the Bank of Guyana building; open daily till 2000 (arrive early and be prepared for a long wait), or from the *Tower Hotel* (more expensive but more comfortable). Calls are subject to 10% tax. Travel agencies may allow you to make overseas collect calls when buying tickets. Hotels add high extra charges to phone bills. Canada Direct, dial 0161; UK direct 169. Fax rates to Europe are economical, under US$1 per page. Most hotels have fax service.

MEDIA

● **Newspapers**
The Chronicle, daily; *The Mirror*, weekly PPP-run; *The Stabroek News*, daily, independent; *The Catholic Standard*, weekly, well-respected and widely read. Street vendors charge more than the cover price, this is normal and helps them make a living.

● **Radio**
GBC Radio is government-run and is often difficult to receive.

● **Television**
There are six TV channels, mainly broadcasting programmes from US satellite television. Local content is increasing.

TOURIST INFORMATION

● **Local tourist office**
The combination of incentives, the stabilization of the economy and government recog-

nition of the foreign exchange earning potential of tourism has led to many new ventures since 1990. The Ministry of Trade, Tourism and Industry has a Tourism Department which can provide information through its office on South Rd near Camp St, Georgetown, T 62505/63182, F 02-544310. The Ministry has a booth (often closed) at Timehri Airport. Substantial private sector growth has led to the formation of the Tourism Association of Guyana (TAG – office and information desk at 157 Waterloo St, T 50807, F 50817), which covers all areas of tourism (hotels, airlines, restaurants, tour operators, etc). The TAG produces a 40-page, full-colour booklet on Guyana; the *Tourist Guide* may be obtained by writing to the Association at PO Box 101147, Georgetown, or by phoning the above number.

● **Maps**
Maps of country and Georgetown (US$6) from Department of Lands and Surveys, Homestreet Ave, Durban Backland (take a taxi). T 60524-9 in advance, poor stock. Rivers and islands change frequently according to water levels, so maps can only give you a general direction. A local guide can be more reliable. City and country maps are sold at *Pegasus* and *Tower* hotels. City maps also from *Guyana Store*, Water St, next to the ice house (take a taxi). Maps of Georgetown and Guyana in 1996 *Guyana Tourist Guide*.

ACKNOWLEDGEMENTS

We are grateful to Tony Thorne (Georgetown) for an update of the Guyana chapter, also, for his assistance, to Greg Thorne.

Suriname

S URINAME has a coastline on the Atlantic to the N; it is bounded on the W by Guyana and on the E by French Guyane; Brazil is to the S. The principal rivers in the country are the Marowijne in the E, the Corantijn in the W, and the Suriname, Commewijne (with its tributary, the Cottica), Coppename, Saramacca and Nickerie. The country is divided into topographically quite diverse natural regions: the northern part of the country consists of lowland, with a width in the E of 25 km, and in the W of about 80 km. The soil (clay) is covered with swamps with a layer of humus under them. Marks of the old seashores can be seen in the shell and sand ridges, overgrown with tall trees. There follows a region, 5-6 km wide, of a loamy and very white sandy soil, then a slightly undulating region, about 30 km wide. It is mainly savannah, mostly covered with quartz sand, and overgrown with grass and shrubs. South of this lies the interior highland, almost entirely overgrown with dense tropical forest and intersected by streams. At the southern boundary with Brazil there are again savannahs. These, however, differ in soil and vegetation from the northern ones. A large area in the SW is in dispute between Guyana and Suriname. There is a less serious border dispute with Guyane in the SE.

HORIZONS

The 1980 census showed that the population had declined to 352,041, because of heavy emigration to the Netherlands. By 1995 it was estimated to have grown to 430,000. The 1991 population consisted of Indo-Pakistanis (known locally as Hindustanis), 33%; Creoles (European-African and other descent), 35%; Javanese, 16%; Bush Negroes,

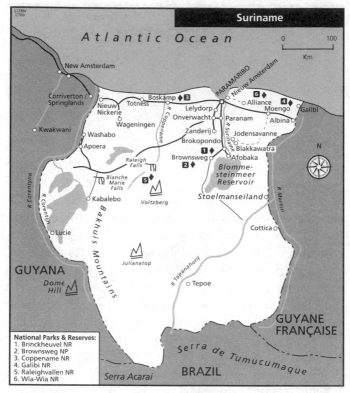

Suriname

Atlantic Ocean

National Parks & Reserves:
1. Brinckheuvel NR
2. Brownsweg NP
3. Coppename NR
4. Galibi NR
5. Raleighvallen NR
6. Wia-Wia NR

called locally 'bosnegers' (retribalized descendants of slaves who escaped in the 17th century, living on the upper Saramacca, Suriname and Marowijne rivers), 10%; Europeans, Chinese and others, 3%; Amerindians, 3% (some sources say only 1%). About 90% of the existing population live in or around Paramaribo or in the coastal towns; the remainder, mostly Carib and Arawak Indians and bosnegers, are widely scattered.

The Asian people originally entered the country as contracted estate labourers, and settled in agriculture or commerce after completion of their term. They dominate the countryside, whereas Paramaribo is racially very mixed. Although some degree of racial

tension exists between all the different groups, Creole-Hindustani rivalry is not as fundamental an issue as in Guyana, for example. Many Surinamese, of all backgrounds, pride themselves on their ability to get along with one another in such a heterogeneous country.

The official language is Dutch. The native language, called Sranan Tongo, originally the speech of the Creoles, is now a *lingua franca* understood by all groups, and standard English is widely spoken and understood. The Asians still speak their own languages among themselves.

HISTORY

Although Amsterdam merchants had

been trading with the 'wild coast' of Guiana as early as 1613 (the name Parmurbo-Paramaribo was already known) it was not until 1630 that 60 English settlers came to Suriname under Captain Marshall and planted tobacco. The real founder of the colony was Lord Willoughby of Parham, governor of Barbados, who sent an expedition to Suriname in 1651 under Anthony Rowse to find a suitable place for settlement. Willoughbyland became an agricultural colony with 500 little sugar plantations, 1,000 white inhabitants and 2,000 African slaves. Jews from Holland and Italy joined them, as well as Dutch Jews ejected from Brazil after 1654. On 27 February 1667, Admiral Crynssen conquered the colony for the states of Zeeland and Willoughbyfort became the present Fort Zeelandia. By the Peace of Breda, 31 July 1667, it was agreed that Suriname should remain with the Netherlands, while Nieuw Amsterdam (New York) should be given to England. The colony was conquered by the British in 1799, and not until the Treaty of Paris in 1814 was it finally restored to the Netherlands. Slavery was forbidden in 1818 and formally abolished in 1863. Indentured labour from China and the East Indies took its place.

On 25 November 1975, the country became an independent republic, which signed a treaty with the Netherlands for an economic aid programme worth US$1.5bn until 1985. A military coup on 25 February 1980 overthrew the elected government. A state of emergency was declared, with censorship of the press, radio and TV. The military leader, Colonel Desi Bouterse, and his associates came under pressure from the Dutch and the USA as a result of dictatorial tendencies. After the execution of 15 opposition leaders on 8 December 1982, the Netherlands broke off relations and suspended its aid programme, although bridging finance was restored in 1988.

The ban on political parties was lifted in late 1985 and a new constitution was drafted. In 1986 guerrilla rebels (the Jungle Commando), led by a former bodyguard of Col Bouterse, Ronny Brunswijk, mounted a campaign to overthrow the government, disrupting both plans for political change and the economy. Nevertheless, elections for the National Assembly were held in Nov 1987. A three-party coalition (the Front for Democracy and Development) gained a landslide victory over the military, winning 40 of the 51 seats but conflicts between Assembly President Ramsewak Shankar and Col Bouterse led to the deposition of the government in a bloodless coup on 24 December 1990 (the 'telephone coup'). A military-backed government under the presidency of Johan Kraag was installed and elections for a new national assembly were held on 25 May 1991. The New Front of four traditional parties won 30 National Assembly seats. Twelve went to the army-backed National Democratic Party (led by Col Bouterse) and nine to the Democratic Alternative, which favours closer links with The Netherlands. Ronald Venetiaan of the New Front was elected president on 6 September 1991. Meetings between Suriname and the Netherlands ministers after the 1991 elections led to the renewal of aid in the second half of 1992. In Aug 1992, a peace treaty was eventually signed between the government and the Jungle Commando in Aug 1992, but the different factions retained control of their respective areas in the interior and violence breaks out occasionally.

By 1993, the New Front's popularity had slumped as its handling of the economy failed to reap any benefit from the 1992 Structural Adjustment Programme and corruption scandals undermined its claim to introduce 'clean politics'. The wide ideological differences between opposition parties meant that no concerted campaign was mounted against the New Front until the 23 May 1996 general election. Until then, much greater impetus was given to popular discontent by the economic decline, which reached catastrophic proportions by 1995. For most Surinamese, their standard of living was said to be almost as low as that of Haiti. Although Bouterse promised to reverse many of Venetiaan's economic reforms, he did not win a majority in the National Assembly. New Front gained 24 seats to the NDP's 16. Venetiaan rejected Bouterse's offer of forming a coalition, preferring to bolster his majority through alignments with smaller parties.

GOVERNMENT

There is one legislative house, the National Assembly, which has 51 members. The President is both head of state and government. Suriname is divided into ten districts, of which the capital is one.

THE ECONOMY

Structure of production Suriname has rich and varied natural resources, yet political upheavals and inconsistent economic management have damaged the country's prosperity. From 1980 gdp per capita declined every year by an average of 3% to only US$703 in 1994.

Agriculture is restricted to some districts of the alluvial coastal zone, covering about 0.8 million ha. At least two thirds of permanent crop and arable land is under irrigation. Farming (including fishing and forestry) accounts for 13% of gdp. The main crops are rice (the staple) and bananas which are exported to Europe, along with small quantities of sugar, citrus fruits, vegetables and coffee. The fishing subsector is predominantly of shrimp for export and processing facilities have expanded. Suriname has vast forestry potential but development has been hampered by civil war. In 1994 the Indonesian group, Musa, was granted a 150,000 ha concession to extract tropical hardwood for export. It also has plans to expand into wood processing.

Suriname: fact file

Geographic

Land area	163,820 sq km
forested	96.2%
pastures	0.1%
cultivated	0.4%

Demographic

Population (1995)	430,000
annual growth rate (1990-95)	1.3%
urban	49.0%
rural	51.0%
density	2.6 per sq km
Religious affiliation	
Hindu	26.0%
Roman Catholic	21.6%
Muslim	18.6%
Protestant	18.0%
Birth rate per 1,000 (1993)	31.0
	(world av 25.0)

Education and Health

Life expectancy at birth,	
male	66.6 years
female	71.8 years
Infant mortality rate	
per 1,000 live births (1993)	36.5
Physicians (1990)	1 per 1,348 persons
Hospital beds	1 per 212 persons
Calorie intake as %	
of FAO requirement	113%
Literate males (over 15)	95.1%
Literate females (over 15)	94.7%

Economic

GNP (1993)	US$488mn
GDP per capita	US$1,210
Public external debt (1990)	US$138mn
Tourism receipts (1992)	US$11mn
Inflation (annual av 1988-93)	40.2%
Radio	1 per 1.4 persons
Television	1 per 7.0 persons
Telephone	1 per 8.9 persons

Employment

Population economically active (1992)	
	138,000
Unemployment rate	13.4%
% of labour force in	
agriculture	21.0
mining	1.6
manufacturing	5.9
construction	3.6
Military forces	1,800

Source *Encyclopaedia Britannica*

The manufacturing sector is small, at only 12% of gdp, and includes beverages, edible oils, tobacco and some construction materials. Production is severely constrained by shortages of foreign exchange.

Mining accounts for only 4% of gdp, but its growth in 1990-94 reached an average of nearly 8% a year, one of the few sectors of the economy to register any growth at all. Suriname has traditionally been a major producer of bauxite, with reserves estimated at nearly 2% of the world's total. However, fluctuations in world prices and the closure of the Moengo mines in the mid-1980s because of the civil war badly disrupted output of alumina, the country's major export. Two companies are involved in the bauxite/aluminium industry, the Suriname Aluminium Company (Suralco), a subsidiary of Alcoa, and Billiton Maatschappij, part of Royal Dutch Shell.

A joint operation between the state mining company, Grasalco, and the Canadian companies, Golden Star Resources and Cambior, is preparing a feasibility study for development of a gold mine in the Gross Rosebel area. About 2,000 local gold miners were evicted from the area in 1995 and given the right to dig further S in another gold-bearing region.

Staatsolie, the state oil company, has about 129 wells producing some 6,300b/d, much of which comes from the Tambaredjo heavy oil deposit. Its refinery produces heavy fuel oil, asphalt, liquefied petroleum gas and diesel.

Recent trends After 5 years of decline and a fall in gdp of 8.1% in 1987 alone, the economy began to recover, helped by resumption of activity in the bauxite industry, the attenuation of the domestic insurgency and the resumption of aid from the Dutch Government. Consistent improvement was not maintained and international creditors urged Suriname to unify the exchange rates, reduce state involvement in the economy and cut the huge budget deficit to attract overseas investment. It was only after the 1990 coup and a 25% fall in the price of alumina in 1991 that these issues began to be addressed. In 1992 a Structural Adjustment Programme (SAP) was drawn up as a forerunner to a 1994-98 Multi-Year Development Programme. A complex system of exchange rates was replaced with a unified floating rate in 1994, but apart from that the Government made little progress in complying with the SAP. Monetization of Central Bank losses and purchases of gold led to a rapid increase in the money supply, which in turn caused souring inflation (to an average of 370% in 1994) and a rapid depreciation of the parallel exchange rate, thereby cutting real incomes. Despite substantial inflows of remittances from Surinamese living in the Netherlands, consumption fell in real terms.

In 1995 inflation dropped sharply to 37%, partly because of a massive appreciation of the parallel exchange rate for the US dollar from 750 to 400 guilders because of Central Bank intervention in the market. The fiscal position improved as the Government campaigned against tax evasion and raised income tax for high earners to 60%. The proportion of taxpayers making returns grew from 10% to 70% and tax revenue rose from 11.5 billion guilders in 1994 to 58 billion in 1995. Subsidies on basic consumer goods were eliminated, interest rates were raised and the salaries of 40,000 public employees were increased.

NATURE RESERVES

Stinasu, the Foundation for Nature Preservation in Suriname, Jongbawstraat 14, T 75845/71856, PO Box 436, Paramaribo, offers reasonably priced accommodation and provides tour guides on the extensive nature reserves throughout the country. One can see 'true wilderness and wildlife' with them, recommended. See also *NV Mets* under **Tourist Agencies**, below.

Many reserves were badly damaged during the civil war. At present only **Brownsweg** has any organized infrastructure. Located atop hills overlooking the van Blommesteinmeer reservoir, it features good walking and three impressive waterfalls. There are all-inclusive tours from Paramaribo with Stinasu (1- and 3-day tours, price includes transport, accommodations, food, and guide). One can also make an independent visit. Buses for Brownsweg leave Paramaribo daily at approx 0830 from Saramacastraat by BEM shop, trucks at the same time. Go to Stinasu at least 24 hrs in advance of your visit to reserve and pay for accommodation in their guest houses and to arrange for a vehicle to pick you up in Brownsweg. Take your own food.

Raleighvallen/Voltzberg Nature Reserve (57,000 ha) is rainforest park, including Foengoe Island and Voltzberg peak; climbing the mountain at sunrise is unforgettable. The **Coppename Estuary** is also a national park, protecting many bird colonies.

Two reserves are located on the NE coast of Suriname. Known primarily as a major nesting site for sea turtles (five species including the huge leatherback turtle come ashore to lay their eggs), **Wia-Wia Nature Reserve** (36,000 ha) also has nesting grounds for some magnificent birds. The nesting activity of sea turtles is best observed April-July (July is a good month to visit as you can see adults coming ashore to lay eggs and hatchlings rushing to the sea at high tide). Since the beaches and consequently the turtles have shifted westwards out of the reserve, accommodation is now at **Matapica** beach, not in the reserve itself. (After a visit to the reserves please send any comments to Stinasu. Your support is needed to keep the reserve functioning.) There may also be mosquitoes and sandflies, depending on the season. The SMS riverboat from Paramaribo stops at Alliance on its journey up the Commewijne

River. You then transfer to a Stinasu motorboat for a one-hour ride to Matapica. The motorboat costs US$50 for 4 people, round trip. Suitable waterproof clothing should be worn. Fishermen make the crossing for US$3-4. The beach hut accommodates 18 people in 4 rooms, and costs US$4 pp. Take your own bedding/food. Cooking facilities provided. Book the hut and boat through Stinasu and keep your receipts or you will be refused entry. Early booking is essential as the closure of the other reserves has made Matapica very popular.

The **Galibi Nature Reserve**, where there are more turtle-nesting places, is near the mouth of the Marowijne River. There are Carib Indian villages. From Albina it is a 3-hour (including ½ hour on the open sea) boat trip to Galibi.

PARAMARIBO

Paramaribo, the capital and chief port, lies on the Suriname river, 12 km from the sea. It has a population of about 192,000. There are many attractive colonial buildings.

The **Governor's Mansion** (now the Presidential Palace) is on Onafhanke-lijkheidsplein (also called Eenheidsplein and, originally, Oranjeplein). Many beautiful 18th and 19th century buildings in Dutch (neo-Normanic) style are in the same area. A few have been restored but much of the old city is sadly decaying. **Fort Zeelandia** houses the Suriname Museum, restored to this purpose after being repossessed by the military. The whole complex has been opened to the public again and its historic buildings can be visited. The fort itself now belongs to the Stichting (foundation) Surinaams Museum, but it needs to be restored. Very few exhibits remain in the old museum in the residential suburb of Zorg-en-Hoop, Commewijnestraat, 0700-1300. Look for Mr FHB Lim-A-Po-straat if you wish to see what Paramaribo looked like only a comparatively short time ago. The

19th century **Roman Catholic Peter and Paul Cathedral** (1885), built entirely of wood, is said to be the largest wooden building in the Americas, and is well worth a visit (closed indefinitely for repairs since 1993). Much of the old town, dating from the nineteenth century, and the churches have been restored. Other things to see are the colourful **market** and the waterfront, **Hindu temples** in Koningstraat and Gravenstraat 31, one of the Caribbean's largest **mosques** at Keizerstraat (magnificent photos of it can be taken at sunset). There are two synagogues: one next to the mosque at Keizerstraat 88, the other (1854) on the corner of Klipstenstraat and Heerenstraat (services on Sat morning, alternating monthly between the two – to visit when closed T 498944 and ask for Dennis Kopinsky). A new harbour has been constructed about 1½ km upstream. Two pleasant parks are the **Palmentuin**, with a stage for concerts, and the **Cultuurtuin** (with well-kept zoo, US$1.20, busy on Sunday), the latter is a 20-mins walk from the centre. National dress is normally only worn by the Asians on national holidays and at wedding parties, but some Javanese women still go about in sarong and klambi. A university was opened in 1968. There is one public swimming pool at Weidestraat, US$0.60 pp. There is an exotic Asian flavour to the market and nearby streets. Cinemas show US, Indian and Chinese movies, with subtitles.

An interesting custom practised throughout Suriname is the birdsong competitions. These are held in parks and public plazas on Sundays and holidays. People carrying their songbird (usually a small black tua-tua) in a cage are a frequent sight on the streets of Paramaribo at any time; on their way to and from work, off to a "training session", or simply taking their pet for a stroll!

Local information – Paramaribo
● Accommodation

Price guide

L1	over US$200	L2	US$151-200
L3	US$101-150	A1	US$81-100
A2	US$61-80	A3	US$46-60
B	US$31-45	C	US$21-30
D	US$12-20	E	US$7-11
F	US$4-6	G	up to US$3

Service charge at hotels is 10-15%. **L3-A2** *Torarica*, T 471500, F 411682, PO Box 1514, best in town, very pleasant, book ahead, swimming pool, casino, nightclub, tropical gardens, a/c, central, 3 restaurants (bar, poolside buffet, and very good French restaurant), superb breakfast; **A3** *Krasnapolsky* Domineestraat 39, T 475050, F 420139, a/c, central, good breakfast and buffet, shops, launderette, takes Amex, bank (see **Exchange** below), swimming pool; **A3-B** *Ambassador*, Dr Sophie Redmondstraat 66-68, T 477555, F 477688, a/c, inc breakfast, good 24-hr restaurant, rec; **A3** *Era Fit*, Cornelis Prinsstraat 87, T 493284, 5 km from centre, good report; **A1-A3** *Stardust*, at Leonsberg (8 km from city), T 451544/453065/450854, F 452992, a/c, nightclub, small restaurant, swimming pool, golf course, tennis courts, sauna, fitness room; **A2-B** *ABC-plus*, Mahonylaan, central, new, with bath, a/c, TV; **A3-B** *Mets Residence Inn*, 10A Rode Kruislaan, T 431990/490739, F 432630, with bath, a/c, TV, minibar, laundry, incl breakfast, credit cards accepted, new, 3-star, in a residential area.

C *Guesthouse Flair*, Kleine Waterstraat 7, T 422455/474794, opp *Torarica*, a/c, clean, safe, helpful; **D** *Lambada*, Keizerstraat 162, T 411073, F 420603. For budget travellers, best is **E** *YWCA Guesthouse* at Heerenstraat 14-16, T 476981, cheaper weekly rates, clean, full of permanent residents, essential to book in advance (office open 0800-1400); if it's full try the **E** *Graaf Van Zinzendorff-Herberg* at Gravenstraat 100, T 471607, large rooms, TV lounge, advance booking advisable; **C** *Doble R*, Kleine Waterstraat opp *Torarica*, T 473592, a/c, clean, good value, but noisy bar downstairs, restaurant, often full, the Suriname Museum in Zorg-en-Hoop now has a good guest house; book in advance. Otherwise, try **E-G** *Fanna*, Princessestraat 31, T 476789, from a/c with bath to basic, breakfast extra, safe, clean, friendly, family run, English spoken, rec, can book in advance; *La Vida* on the way in from the airport is 'cheap but nice'; **E** *Mivimost*, Anamoestraat 23, 3 km from centre, T 451002, a/c, cheaper with fan, toilet, clean, safe, friendly, rec; *Mrs Robles' Guesthouse*, Roseveltkade 20, T 474770, family run, organizes tours; *Balden*, Kwattaweg 183, 2 km from centre on the road to Nickerie is probably the cheapest available accommodation; its Chinese restaurant serves cheap meals. Beware: many cheap hotels not listed above are 'hot pillow' establishments. A religious organization, Stadszending, Burenstraat 17-19,

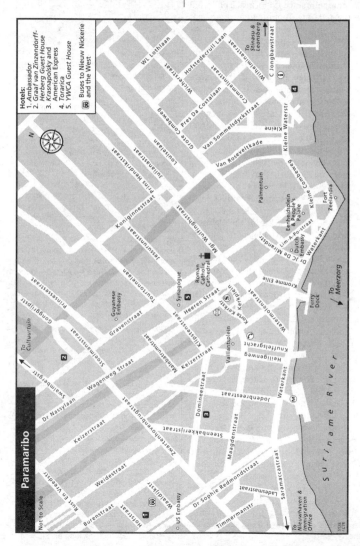

Paramaribo

Hotels:
1. Ambassador
2. Graf van Zinzendorff-Herberg Guest House
3. Krasnapolsky and American Express
4. Torarica
5. YWCA Guest House

Ⓑ Buses to Nieuw Nickerie and the West

Not to Scale

T 47307, **G**, good location, clean, friendly, best to reserve. The *Salvation Army*, Saramaccastraat, will give the hard up a bed for a minimal price. Mrs Rudia Shair-Ali, Toenalaan 29, 20 mins walk from centre, not a hotel but a large private house: Mrs Shair-Ali charges US$1-2 a night if she has a free room, free use of fridge and kitchen equipment.

● **Places to eat**
There are some good restaurants, mainly Indonesian and Chinese dishes. Try a *rijsttafel* in an Indonesian restaurant, eg *Sarinah* (open-air dining), Verlengde Gemenelandsweg 187; *Bali*, Ma Retraiteweg 3, T 422325, very good food, service and atmosphere. *La Bastille*, Kleine Waterstraat, opp *Torarica*, good, T 473991; also opp *Torarica*, *Restaurant 'T VAT'*; *Golden Dragon*, Anamoestraat 22, *Golden Crown*, David Simmonstraat; *Roja's*, corner of Mahonylaan and Grote Combeweg, and *New China*, Verlengde Gemenelandsweg; *Fa Tai*, Maagdenstraat 64, a/c. *Oriental Foods*, Gravenstraat 118, for well-prepared Chinese food, rec. Many other Chinese restaurants. Cheap lunches and light meals at *Chindy's*, Keizerstraat opp TeleSur, lunch only, try *pom*, also ice cream; *Hofje*, Wagenwegstraat, and *Chalet Swiss*, Heerenstraat (more Chinese than Swiss). *Natura*, Rust-en-Vredestraat between Keizerstraat and Weidestraat, whole-grain bread and natural foods. Meat and noodles from stalls in the market are very cheap. Javanese foodstalls on Waterkant are excellent and varied, lit at night by candles. Try *bami* (spicy noodles) and *petjil* (vegetables). Especially recommended on Sun when the area is busiest. In restaurants a dish to try is *gadogado*, an Indonesian vegetable and peanut concoction. Good places for lunch include *Hola's Terrace*, Domineestraat. For breakfast, try *Klein Maar Fijn*, Watermolenstraat. The local beer is called Parbo; imported Heineken is more expensive.

● **Nightclubs**
Discothèques: *Touche*, Waaldijk/Dr Sophie Redmonstraat 60, Fri and Sat only 2300, small restaurant and the best disco; *Crush* (take a taxi); *Cartousj*, nr *Krasnapolsky*, on 1st floor. There are many Brazilian girls seeking European husbands and several nightclubs cater for this trade. A good one where it is not blatant is *El Condor*, Zwartenhovenbrugstraat 158, not far from *Ambassador Hotel*, a/c, clean, restaurant, soft music, often full. Many other clubs.

● **Shopping**
Crafts of Amerindian and Bush Negro origin. *Arts & Crafts*, Neumanpad 13a. Amerindian goods, batik prints, carvings, basket work, drums are attractive. *Cultuurwinkel*, Anton de Kom Straat, bosneger carvings, also available at *Hotel Torarica*. Carvings are better value at the workshops on Nieuwe Dominee Straat and the Neumanpad. *Peet* woodworks have been rec for hardwood pieces. Local ceramics are sold on the road between the airport and Paranam, but they are rather brittle. *Disco Amigo* sells local and international music on cassette (no CDs of national music, which is heavily influenced by Caribbean styles). Old Dutch bottles are sold. **Bookshops** The two main bookshops are *Vaco* (opp *Krasnapolsky*) and *Kersten*, both on Domineestraat, and both sell English-language books. Also *Hoeksteen* (Gravenstraat 17) and the kiosk in *Krasnapolsky Hotel*. *Boekhandel Univers NV*, Gravenstraat 61, is rec for nature, linguistic and scholarly books on Suriname. Second hand books, English and Dutch, are bought and sold in the market. Maps are hard to find, but try *Vaco*.

● **Local Transport**
There are very few regular buses; the few services that are left leave from Waterkant or Dr Sophie Redmondstraat. There are privately run 'wild buses', also known as 'numbered buses' which run on fixed routes around the city; they are minivans and are severely overcrowded. **Taxis**: generally have no meters. The price should be agreed on beforehand to avoid trouble. Rec is *Ally's Taxi* service, T 479434, English spoken. If hiring a taxi for touring, beware of overcharging.

● **Long Distance Transport**
To **Nickerie** from Dr Sophie Redmondstraat, nr *Hotel Ambassador*, minibuses leave when full between 0500 and 1000; there are also buses after 1200, but the price then depends on the driver, 4-5 hrs (depending on ferry crossing), extra for large bag. Taxis from the same area are slightly faster. To **Albina** from near ferry dock or from Meerzorg, 2-3 hrs, Sf1,500, large bag extra (take an APB or PBA bus, which has a plainclothes policeman on board). Taxis are available, but dishonest (usually). There are irregular bus services to other towns. For full details ask drivers or enquire at the tourist office. Verify all fares in advance and beware of overcharging. There is much jostling in the queues and pure mayhem

whenboarding vehicles. They are all minivans and have no luggage space. Try to accommodate baggage under your seat or you will have to hold it in your lap.

● **Exchange**

Algemene Bank Nederland (Kerkplein 1), **AMRO Bank**, **Surinaamsche Bank** (near the cathedral) and **Hakrin Bank**, 0700-1400 (closed Sat). Surinaamsche branch in *Hotel Krasnapolsky* open 0700-1430; 0800-1200 Sat, charges commission on each TC exchanged. Amex agent is C Kersten and Co, NV, in *Hotel Krasnapolsky*, T 477148. Black market changers congregate outside the *Hotel Krasnapolsky* and they are the best bet when banks are closed. Be very wary of money changers in the market and on the street, who approach you calling 'wissel' (exchange). Many visitors have been robbed or cheated and, as the black market is illegal, you have no recourse. Many shop keepers will change cash at parallel rates and this is a much safer option. Ask around for best rates.

● **Places of worship**

The Anglican Church is St Bridget's, Hoogestraat 44 (Sunday 0900 service in English). Roman Catholic Cathedral on Gravenstraat. Dutch Reformed Church and many other denominations.

● **Tourist Agencies**

NV Mets (Movement for Eco-Tourism in Suriname), PO Box 9080, 5 Rudielaan, Paramaribo, T 492892/497180, F 497062, the national tour operator (sales office Dr J F Nassylaan 2, T/F 477088, e-mail mets@sr.net; also in Cayenne, 15 rue Louis Blanc, T 317298, F 305786, and Georgetown, Surinam Airways, 91 Middle St, T 254894, F 252679), organizes trips to the interior at reasonable rates. Tours offered are City Tour, US$20 pp, Rivercruise, US$45 pp, Santigron, US$50 (all day trips); Matapica Beach, US$120 pp (2 days); 4/5 day trips to Tukunari Island, US$250 pp; 4/5-day trips to Palumeu (see below) or to Gran Rio (Bosneger area) for US$375 pp staying in lodges; 8-day trip to Mount Kasikasima in remote southern Suriname, US$625 pp (all transport, food and guides included). Mrs W J Robles-Cornelissen, *Independent Tours*, Rosenveltkade 20, T 474770, and *Suriname Safari Tours*, Waterkant 54, T 471624, organize excursions to the interior. Trips take 3-5 days and cost about US$120 (parallel exchange), all inclusive. *CHTM Travel*, Sophie Redmondstraat, opp

Hakrin Bank building, 0730-1600, helpful. *Ram's Tours*, Neumanpad 30 Ben, T 476011/476223. *Does Travel Service*, Domineestraat. *Amadine's Tours and Travel*, Alice Kasan, *Hotel Torarica* Arcade, T/F 477268, helpful. *Saramaccan Jungle Safaris* (John Ligeon), PO Box 676, Zwartenhovenbrugstraat 19, Paramaribo, for visits by canoe to Saramaccan Bush Black villages and wildlife tours.

NB If intending to take a tour to the jungle and either Amerindian or Bush Black villages, check how much time is spent in the jungle itself and on the conditions in the villages. One such trip is to Palumeu, an Amerindian village (Trio, Wajana and Akurio peoples) due S of Paramaribo, not far from the Brazilian border. A 4-day, 3-night trip costs US$250, including flights, food, accommodation, jungle hikes and boat trips.

EXCURSIONS

Accaribo resort, about 1 hr by car from the capital on the Suriname River, near the villages of La Vigilantia and Accaribo: 7 rooms with bath, visit Amerindian settlement, pottery making, swimming in the river, Creole and Javanese cultures; details from NV-Mets. **Powaka**, about 90 mins outside the capital, is a primitive village of thatched huts but with electric light and a small church. In the surrounding forest one can pick mangoes and other exotic fruit. An interesting half, or full day excursion is to take minibus 4, or taxi, to **Leonsberg** on the Suriname river (restaurant *Rusty Pelikan* on waterfront; at *Leonsberg* restaurant try *saoto* soup and other Javanese specialities, overlooking the river), then ferry to **Nieuw Amsterdam**, the capital of the predominantly Javanese district of Commewijne. There is an open-air museum inside the old fortress which guarded the confluence of the Suriname and Commewijne rivers (badly rundown, open only in mornings except Friday, 1700-1900, Sf20). There are some old plantation mansions left in the Commewijne district which are of interest; **Mariënburg** is the last sugar estate in operation in Suriname. The return trip can be made by bus to Meerzorg on the river, taking the vehicle ferry back to Paramaribo.

Braamspunt is a peninsula at the mouth of the Suriname River, about 10 km from Paramaribo. Nice beaches. Hire a boat at the Leonsberg scaffold for a trip up the river.

By private car to **Jodensavanne** (Jews' Savanna, established 1639), S of Paramaribo on the opposite bank of the Suriname River, where a cemetery and the foundations of one of the oldest synagogues in the Western Hemisphere has been restored. There is no public transport and taxis won't go because of the bad road. It is still only 1½ hrs with a suitable vehicle. There is a bridge across the Suriname River to Jodensavanne. Mrs Robles, T 474770, organizes tours if there are enough people. **Blakawatra** is said to be one of the most beautiful spots in all Suriname (shame about the amount of rubbish strewn around). This was the scene of much fighting in the civil war. A full day trip to Jodensavanne and Blakawatra, returning to Paramaribo via Moengo, has been recommended if one can arrange the transport. Some 5 km from the International Airport there is a resort called **Colakreek**, so named for the colour of the water, but good swimming (busy at weekends), lifeguards, water bicycles, children's village, restaurant, bar, tents or huts for overnight stay, entre Sf500 (children under 12 half price).

Approximately 30 km SW of Paramaribo, via **Lelydorp** (*Hotel De Lely*, Sastrodisomoweg 41), is the Bush Negro village of **Santigron**, on the E bank of the Saramaca River. Mini-buses leave from Saramacastraat in front of BEM store at approx 0700 and 1030, Mon-Sat, one afternoon bus on Sat, 1 hr, crowded. They return as soon as they drop off passengers in the village, so make sure you will have a bus to return on, no accommodation in Santigron. Nearby is the Amerindian village of **Pikin Poika**. The two make a good independent day trip. Tour agencies also visit the area about twice month, including canoe rides on the Saramaca River and a Bush Negro dance performance.

By bus or car to **Afobakka**, where there is a large hydro-electric dam on the Suriname River. There is a government guesthouse (price includes 3 meals a day) in nearby **Brokopondo**. Victoria is an oil-palm plantation in the same area. The Brownsberg National Park is one hour by car from here.

Tukunari Island, in Professor Van Blommesteinmeer lake, is about 3 hrs drive from Paramaribo to Brokopondo then a 2-hr canoe ride. The island is near the village of Lebi Doti, where Aucaners Maroons live. Tours with NV Mets include fishing, visits to villages to see Maroon culture, jungle treks and visits to rapids.

Stoelmanseiland, on the Lawa River (guest house with full board) in the interior, and the *bosneger* villages and rapids in the area can be visited on excursions organized by tour operators. Price US$170 pp for 3 days (5 persons, minimum). They are, however, more easily reached by river from St-Laurent du Maroni and Maripasoula in Guyane.

WEST OF PARAMARIBO

Leaving Paramaribo, a narrow but well paved road leads through the citrus and vegetable growing districts of **Wanica** and **Saramaca**, connected by a bridge over the Saramaca River. At **Boskamp** (90 km from Paramaribo) the Coppename River is reached. Daytime only ferry to **Jenny** on the W bank takes about 20 mins.

A further 50 km is **Totness**, where there was once a Scottish settlement. It is the largest village in the Coronie district, along the coast between Paramaribo and Nieuw Nickerie on the Guyanese border. There is a good government guesthouse. The road (bad, liable to flooding) leads through an extensive forest of coconut palms. Bus to Paramaribo at 0600. 40 km further W, 5 km S of the main road is **Wageningen**, a modern little town, the centre of the Suriname rice-growing area. The road from Nickerie has recently been renewed. One of the largest fully mechanized rice farms in the world is found here (*Hotel de Wereld*). The **Bigi-Pan** area of mangroves is a bird-watchers' paradise; boats may be hired from local fishermen.

Nieuw Nickerie, on the S bank of the Nickerie River 5 km from its mouth, opposite Guyana is the main town and port of the Nickerie district and is distinguished for its ricefields and for the number and voraciousness of its mosquitoes. The town has a population of more than 8,000, the district of 35,000, mostly East Indian. Paramaribo is 237 km away by road. For bus services, see under Paramaribo. Sit on the left-hand side of the bus to get the best views of the bird-life in the swamps. The coastal ferry service has been discontinued, but once a week the SMS company makes an interesting water trip, using inland waterways, to Nieuw Nickerie taking 36 hrs; it leaves Paramaribo on Mondays at 0800, departs Nieuw Nickerie 1200 Wednesday (times subject to 2 hrs variation due to tides), no cabins, only slatted seats, but there is hammock space; take food and drink; lots of mosquitoes.

- **Accommodation** E *Moksie Patoe*, Gouverneurstraat 115, T 232219, restaurant, owner rents a 2-bedroom house (3 beds) next door; E *De-Vesting*, similar quality, Balatastraat 6, T 031265; E *Americali*, a/c, good, clean, friendly; F *De President*, Gouverneurstraat, with bath, cheaper without, a/c, good value, friendly; F *Luxor*, Jozefstraat 22, T 231365, private bath, friendly; G *Diamond*, Balatastraat 29, T 232210, some rooms with bath, close to ferry, basic; G *Tropical*, Gouverneurstraat 114, T 231796, noisy bar downstairs.

- **Places to eat** *Jean Amar*, Gouverneurstraat 115, run by Dr Jacques Durauchelle, provides European and Indian dishes with items rarely found elsewhere in friendly atmosphere, slow service; *Incognito*, Gouverneurstraat 44, Indonesian; *Pak-Hap*, Gouverneurstraat 101, Chinese (mice in the dining room). Many others on same street.

- **Exchange** The bank at the immigration office is reported to close at 1500 Mon-Fri, whether or not the ferry has arrived.

- **Air** Surinam Airways to/from Paramaribo, twice weekly, US$29 (booked up weeks in advance), office on main square on river, helpful, can book international flights, no credit cards, open till 1600.

FERRY TO SPRINGLANDS, GUYANA

Normally operates Mon to Sat (except public holidays of either country), foot passengers only, Sf65 one way, heavy luggage extra. Booking office at Landenstraat 26, open Mon-Sat, 0630-0645, 0900-1200, 1600-1700, essential to book the day before travelling, booking fee Sf2.50, must show passport.

All immigration and customs formalities take place at the ferry dock. Queue up at gate at 0600, expect about 3 hrs of waiting before sailing. The trip takes at least 2 hrs, Guyanese immigration and customs forms handed out on board, cold drinks are sometimes sold. There may be up to another 3 hrs of queuing for Guyanese formalities. Visa requirements have been relaxed (see Guyana, **Documents**) and a return ticket is not always asked for. Ferry returns to Nickerie the same afternoon (bookings in the am).

The entire journey from Paramaribo to Georgetown takes 2 days including overnight in Nickerie (Nickerie-Georgetown takes 10-12 hrs).

Vast reserves of bauxite were discovered in the Bakhuis Mountains, S of Nickerie District in the NW of Sipaliwini District. A road once ran as far as Lucie on the Corantijn River, but it is now mostly overgrown. The infrastructure developed for the bauxite industry in the 1970s was subsequently abandoned or destroyed. **Apoera** on the Corantijn can be reached by sea-going vessels. **Blanche Marie Falls**, 320 km from Paramaribo on the Apoera road, is a popular destination. There is a guesthouse, B *Dubois*, contact Eldoradolaan 22, Paramaribo T 476904/2. There is a good guesthouse at Apoera (**C** with 3 meals, advance booking from

Paramaribo advisable). **Washabo** near Apoera, which has an airstrip, is an Amerindian village. There is no public transport from Paramaribo to the Apoera-Bakhuis area, but there are frequent charter flights to the Washabo airstrip. Irregular small boats go from Apoera to Nieuw Nickerie and to Springlands (Guyana). Try to rent a canoe to visit the Amerindian settlement of Orealla in Guyana or Kaboeri creek, 12 km downstream, where giant river otters may possibly be seen in October or March.

EAST OF PARAMARIBO TO GUYANE

Eastern Suriname was the area most severely damaged during the civil war, and its effects are still evident. A paved road connects Meerzorg (vehicle ferry from Paramaribo, every 30 min, passengers Sf1) with Albina, passing through the districts of Commewijne and Marowijne. There is little population or agriculture left here. **Moengo**, 160 km up the Cottica River from Paramaribo, is a bauxite mining and loading centre for Suralco (*Government Guesthouse*). Paranam, another loading centre, is on the left bank of the Suriname River. It can be reached by medium draught ships and by cars. Near Paranam is Smalkalden, where bauxite is loaded by the Billiton company on the road to Paramaribo.

East of Moengo, the scars of war are most obvious. Temporary wooden bridges replace those that were blown up, shell craters dot the road, and many abandoned or destroyed houses are seen. **Albina** is on the Marowijne River, the frontier with Guyane. Once a thriving, pleasant town, it is today a bombed-out wreck. No services are available here.

FRONTIER WITH GUYANE

Customs and immigration on both sides close at 1900, but in Albina staff usually leave by 1700. Be wary of local information on exchange rates and transport (both the ferry and buses to Paramaribo).

● **Exchange**
Changing money on the Suriname side of the border is illegal; see **Currency**, below. Money can be changed on the Guyane side.

● **Transport**
A passenger and vehicle ferry leaves Albina for St Laurent du Maroni Mon, Thur, 0800, 1000, 1500, 1700, Tues, Wed, Sat, 0800, 1000, Sun 1630, 1700, 30 mins voyage; the fare is US$4 pp, which is the same charged by *pirogues*, US$20 for cars.

Information for travellers

irrelevant). If you stay more than 2 weeks, you should return to Immigration at that time, to collect your blue card which you can carry instead of your passport (it is prudent to carry both). You must also return here for any further extensions and for an exit authorization stamp (called 'stamp out') 2 days before you leave the country. The final exit stamp is again given by the military police at the airport or land border.

Despite suggestions that these procedures be simplified, they remain law and failure to comply can result in very serious consequences. They are not usually explained to visitors on arrival.

BEFORE TRAVELLING

● **Documents**

Visitors must have a valid passport (one issued by the Hong Kong government, and a few others, will not be accepted), a visa, or tourist card. Visas must be obtained in advance by citizens of all countries except Great Britain, Japan, Israel, The Gambia, South Korea, Denmark, Finland, Sweden, Switzerland, Netherlands Antilles, Brazil, Ecuador, Canada, Chile and Guyana (these require a tourist card, obtainable at the airport, US$14). To obtain a visa in advance, write to the Ministry of External Affairs, Department for Consular Matters, Paramaribo, sending 1 passport photo; cost is US$50. Visas issued at the consulate in Cayenne normally take 15 days and cost F150 (US$28), but may be obtained the same day (an extra charge for this is sometimes made). Take photocopy of exit ticket out of South America. In Georgetown a visa takes 5 days minimum and costs US$20. On entry to Suriname (by land or air) your passport will be stamped by the military police indicating a brief period (usually 7-10 days) for which you can remain in the country, regardless of the length of stay authorized by your visa. If you are considering a longer visit, you should go as soon as possible to the Immigration Office in Paramaribo to get a second stamp in your passport and to apply for a 'blue card' (foreigner registration card): Immigration Office, van't Hogerhuystraat, Nieuwe Haven, Paramaribo. To get this you need a receipt for Sf10 from the Commissariat Combé, Van Sommelsdijkstraat, opposite *Torarica Hotel*, take passport and two passport photos, allow a week to get it. Mon-Fri, 0700-1430. The procedure is relatively quick and painless and you will generally be authorized a 3 month stay (once again the length of your entry visa seems

● **Representation overseas**

USA: Embassy, Van Ness Center, 4301 Connecticut, NW Suite 108, Washington DC, 20008, T 202-244-7488, F 202-244-5878; Consulate, 7235 NW 19th St, Suite A, Miami, FLA 33125, T 305-593-2163. **Belgium**, Avenue Louise 379, 1050 Brussels, T 640-11-72; **Netherlands**: Embassy, Alexander Gogelweg 2, 2517 JH Den Haag, T 65-08-44; Consulate, De Cuserstraat 11, 1081 CK Amsterdam, T 642-61-37; **Brazil**, SCS Quadra 2 Lotes 20/21, Edif, OK, 2e Andar, 70457 Brasília, T 244-1824; **Venezuela**, 4a Av de Altamira 41, entre 7 y 8a Transversal, Altamira, Caracas 1060A, PO Box 61140, Chacao, T 261-2095; **Guyana**, 304 Church St, Georgetown, PO Box 338, T 56995; **Guyane**, 38 TER, Rue Christoph Colomb, Cayenne, T 30-04-61.

For **Tourist information**, see page 881, below.

● **Customs**

Duty-free imports include 400 cigarettes or 100 cigars or ½ kg of tobacco, 2 litres of spirits and 4 litres of wine, 50 grams of perfume and 1 litre of toilet water, 8 rolls of still film and 60m of cinefilm, 100m of recording tape, and other goods up to a value of Sf40. Personal baggage is free of duty. Customs examination of baggage can be very thorough.

● **Climate**

Tropical and moist, but not very hot, since the NE trade wind makes itself felt during the whole year. In the coastal area the temperature varies on an average from 23° to 31°C, during the day; the annual mean is 27°C, and the monthly mean ranges from 26° to 28°C. The mean annual rainfall is about 2,340mm for Paramaribo and 1,930mm for the western division. The seasons are: minor rainy season, Nov-Feb; minor dry season, Feb-April; main rainy season, April-Aug; main dry season, Aug-November. None of these seasons is, however, usually either very dry or very wet. The degree of cloudiness is fairly high and the average humidity is 82%. The climate of the interior is similar but with higher rainfall.

● **Health**

No information has been made available about the incidence of cholera in Suriname. Since the disease is almost certainly present, take the approrpriate precautions. Boil or purify water, even in the capital. Otherwise, no special precautions necessary except for a trip to the malarial interior; for free malaria prophylaxis contact the Public Health Department (BOG, 15 Rode Kruislaan), but better to take your own. METS and Suriname Safari Tours provide malaria prophylaxis on their package tours. Chloroquine-resistant malaria in the interior. Mosquito nets should be used at night over beds in rooms not air-conditioned or screened. In some coastal districts there is a risk of bilharzia (schistosomiasis). Ask before bathing in lakes and rivers. Vaccinations: yellow fever and tetanus advisable, typhoid only for trips into the interior. Swim only in running water because of poisonous fish. There is good swimming on the Marowijne river and at Matapica beach and on the Coppename river. There are five hospitals in Paramaribo, best is St Vincentius.

MONEY

● **Currency**

The unit of currency is the Suriname guilder (Sf) divided into 100 cents. There are notes for 5, 10, 25, 100 and 500 guilders. Coins are for 1 guilder and 5, 10, 25 (the 25-cent coin is usually known as a *kwartje*) and 50 cents.

● **Exchange**

In July 1994 all exchange rates were unified and a floating rate was established at Sf183 = US$1. By the end of 1995 the floating rate was around Sf500 = US$1. The street rate for the dollar was Sf550. Dutch guilders and French francs are readily exchanged in banks and on the black market, cash only in the latter case. It is, however, illegal to change money on the black market; police pretend to be black marketeers.

On arrival, change a little money at the airport (where rates are poorer than in the city), then go to the main banks for further exchange. Officially visitors must declare their foreign currency on arrival. When arriving by land, visitors' funds are rarely checked, but you should be prepared for it.

GETTING THERE

AIR

AOM flies from Paris once a week. Surinam Airways flies 3 times a week from Amsterdam (joint operation wtih KLM), Belém (4 times a week), Port of Spain (5 times), Barbados (twice), Aruba (4 times), Curaçao (twice), Cayenne (5 times a week), and Georgetown (4 times a week). ALM flies from Curaçao 4 times a week. There is a weekly connecting flight from Miami via Curaçao with ALM. Many people go to Cayenne to take advantage of cheap Air France tickets to Europe as well as increased seat availability. Internal services are maintained by SLM and two small air charter firms.

SEA

Fyffes banana boats sail from Portsmouth, UK, and Flushing, Holland, to Paramaribo on 13-14 day schedule. Occasionally they call at Georgetown. The 35-38 day roundtrip costs £1,980 pp.

ON ARRIVAL

● **Airports**

The Johan Pengel International Airport (formerly Zanderij), is 47 km S of Paramaribo. Minibus to town costs Sf2,000 (eg De Paarl, T 479610); taxi costs Sf10,000/US$20 (Ashruf, T 450102), but negotiate. Surinam Airways, T 473939/477153, F 491213. (At Pengel Airport T 0325-181, F 0325-292.) Money exchange facilities, Central Bank of Suriname between Customs and Immigration (closed Sun). There is a guest house near the airport. Internal flights leave from Zorg-en-Hoop airfield in a suburb of Paramaribo (take minibus 8 or 9 from Steenbakkerijstraat).

● **Clothing**

Except for official meetings, informal tropical clothing is worn, but not shorts. An umbrella or plastic raincoat is very useful.

● **Embassies**

USA (Dr Sophie Redmondstraat 129, PO Box 1821, T 477881), Netherlands, Belgium, Brazil, Cuba, France, Mexico, Venezuela, India, Indonesia, Guyana, India, Japan, China (People's Republic).

● **Consulates**

There are consuls-general, vice-consuls or consular agents for Canada, Denmark, Dominican Republic, Ecuador, Finland, Germany, Haiti, UK, Mexico, Norway, Spain, and Sweden – all in Paramaribo. British Honorary Consul, Mr James Healy, T 472870 office/474764 house, is very helpful.

● **Hours of business**
Shops and businesses: Mon-Fri 0900-1630, Sat 0900-1300. Government departments: Mon-Thur 0700-1500, Fri 0700-1430. Banks are open Mon-Fri 0900-1400. The airport bank is open at flight arrival and departure times.

● **Official time**
3 hrs behind GMT.

● **Public holidays**
1 Jan, New Year; Holi Phagwa (Hindu festival, date varies each year, generally in Mar, very interesting but watch out for throwing of water, paint, talc and coloured powder); Good Friday; Easter (2 days); 1 May (Labour Day); 1 July (National Unity); 25 Nov (Independence Day); Christmas (2 days). For Moslem holidays see note under Guyana.

● **Security**
Photography is now generally permitted. Only military installations remain off limits. When in doubt, ask first. Those travelling to the interior should inquire in the capital about the public safety situation in the areas they plan to visit. The presence of rival armed factions in some places remains a hazard and the government is not fully in control of the entire country. Street crime in Paramaribo is rising: take the usual precautions with cameras, watches, etc. Downtown and near the market should be avoided at night unless accompanied by a local.

● **Voltage**
127 volts AC, 60 cycles. Plug fittings are usually 2-pin round (European continental type). Lamp fittings are screw type.

● **Weights and measures**
The metric system is in general use.

ON DEPARTURE

● **Departure tax**
There is an exit tax of US$5.

WHERE TO STAY

Hotels and restaurants are rare outside the capital, and you usually have to supply your own hammock and mosquito net, and food. A tent is less useful in this climate. Travelling is cheap if you change cash dollars on the black market; taking your own hammock and food will reduce costs.

FOOD AND DRINK

Surinamese cuisine is as rich and varied as the country's ethnic makeup. Rice is the main staple and of very high quality. Cassava, sweet potatoes, plantain, and hot red peppers are widely used. *Pom* is a puree of the tayer root (a relative of cassava) tastily spiced and served with *kip* (chicken). *Moksie Alesie* is rice mixed with meat, chicken, white beans, tomatoes, peppers and spices. *Pinda soep* (peanut soup with plantain dumplings) and *oker soep met tayerblad* (gumbo and cassava soup) are both worth a try. Well known Indonesian dishes include *bami* (fried noodles) and *nassie goreng* (fried rice), both spicy with a slightly sweet taste. Among the Hindustani dishes are *roti* (a crêpe wrapped around curried potatoes, vegetables and chicken), *somosa* (fried pastry filled with spicy potatoes and vegetables), and *phulawri* (fried chick-pea balls). Among the many tropical fruits of Suriname, palm nuts such as the orange coloured awarra and the cone shaped brown maripa are most popular.

GETTING AROUND

AIR TRANSPORT
E-W, Paramaribo-Nieuw Nickerie twice a week. N-S: the interior is currently open. Bush flights are operated by Gum-Air and Gonini to several Amerindian and bosneger villages. Most settlements have an airstrip, but internal air services are limited. These flights are on demand. Gum-Air (T 498760) also flies to St-Laurent du Maroni in Guyane, US$250 to charter 5-seater plane.

LAND TRANSPORT
● **Motoring**
There are 2,500 km of main roads, of which 850 km are paved. East-west roads: From Albina to Paramaribo to Nieuw Nickerie is open; buses and taxis are available (details in the text above). North-south: the road Paramaribo - Paranam - Afobaka - Pokigron is open. **Self-Drive Cars** City Taxi, Purperhart, Kariem, Intercar, U-Drive Car rental, T 490803, and other agencies. All driving licences accepted, but you need a stamp from the local police and a deposit. Gasoline/petrol is sold as 'regular', or 'extra' (more expensive). **Bicycles**

Can be bought from A Seymonson, Rijwielher-steller, Rust en Vredestraat. Rec rides from Paramaribo include to Nieuw Amsterdam, Marienburg, Alkmaar and back via Tamanredjo in the Javanese Commewijne district or from Rust en Werk to Spieringshoek to Reijnsdorp (3½ hrs) and return to Leonsberg via ferry, whence it is a 30 mins ride to Paramaribo. Driving is on the left, but many vehicles have left-hand drive.

FERRIES

The three ferries across the main rivers operate only in daytime (the Paramaribo-Meerzorg ferry until 2200). The Suriname Navigation Co (SMS) has a daily service, leaving 0700, on the Commewijne river (a nice four-hour trip; one can get off at *De Nieuwe Grond*, a plantation owned by an English couple, and stay over-night). SMS also has infrequent services on other rivers (Wayombo and Cottica), and makes an interesting water trip, using inland waterways, to Nieuw Nickerie (see text above).

● **Note**
It is advisable to check the weather conditions and probabilities of returning on schedule be-fore you set out on a trip to the interior. Heavy rains can make it impossible for planes to land in some jungle areas; little or no provision is made for such delays and it can be a long and hungry wait for better conditions.

COMMUNICATIONS

● **Postal services**
The postal service is remarkably quick and reliable. Letters must be franked at the post office and posted the same day (no stamps sold). Both postal and telecommunications charges are very low at the black market exchange rate. **NB** Postcard rate for postcards means only 5 words.

● **Telecommunications**
Overseas phone calls must be booked any-where between 30 mins to several days in advance, specifying the exact duration of the call. Rates are higher if you request more than 5 mins. Calls can be booked up to 2200, Mon-Sat, no operator assisted calls on Sun.

Overseas calls can also be direct dialled from some public phones using tokens, but there are only 4 such phones (just outside TeleSur, often broken) and the queues get very long. USA direct available at both *Torarica* and *Krasnapolsky* Hotels, as well as from private phones. The public fax number from overseas is +597-410-555, good service.

MEDIA

● **Newspapers**
Newspapers are in Dutch, *De Ware Tijd* (morn-ing) and *DeWest* (evening).

● **Television**
There are several stations in Paramaribo and in the districts, broadcasting in Dutch, Hindi, Negro English and Javanese. There is also one state-controlled television station called Suri-naamse Televisie Stichting (STVS), transmitting for 4 hrs daily in colour on channel 8 (in Dutch), and a second channel, ATV.

TOURIST INFORMATION

Information about Suriname can be had from: Suriname representatives abroad (see above), the Suriname Tourism Foundation at Cornelius Jongbawstraat 2, T 471163, F 420425, Telex 118 ALBUZA SN, Paramaribo, or Stinasu or NV Mets, address of both above.

The *Surinam Planatlas* is out of print, but can be consulted at the National Planning office on Dr Sophie Redmondstraat; maps with natural environment and economic develop-ment topics, each with commentary in Dutch and English.

Points of interest are: some colonial archi-tecture, especially in and around Paramaribo; and the tropical flora and fauna in this very sparsely populated country. There are no beaches to speak of; the sea and the rivers in the coastal area are muddy, and mosquitoes can be a worry in places. Hitchhiking is not common, but it is possible. The **high seasons**, when everything is more expensive, are 15 Mar-15 May, July-Sept and 15 Dec-15 Jan.

Guyane

GUYANE, an Overseas Department of France, has its eastern frontier with Brazil formed partly by the River Oiapoque (Oyapock in French) and its southern, also with Brazil, formed by the Tumuc-Humac mountains (the only range of importance). The western frontier with Suriname is along the River Maroni-Litani. To the N is the Atlantic coastline of 320 km. The area is estimated at between 83,900 and 86,504 square km, or one-sixth that of France. The land rises gradually from a coastal strip some 15-40 km wide to the higher slopes and plains or savannahs, about 80 km inland. Forests cover some 8 million hectares of the hills and valleys of the interior, and timber production is increasing rapidly. The territory is well watered, for over twenty rivers run to the Atlantic.

HORIZONS

There are widely divergent estimates for the ethnic composition of the population. Calculations vary according to the number included of illegal immigrants, attracted by social benefits and the high living standards. (The prefect stated in 1994 that Guyane had 30,000 illegal residents.) By some measures, over 40% of the population are Créoles, with correspondingly low figures for Europeans, Asians and Brazilians (around 17% in total). Other estimates put the Créole proportion at 36%, with Haitians 26%, Europeans 10% (of whom about 95% are from France), Brazilians 8%. Asians 4.7% (3.2% from Hong Kong, 1.5% from Laos), about 4% from Suriname and 2.5% from Guyana. The Amerindian population is put at 3.6% (over 4% by some estimates). The main groups are Galibis (1,700), Arawak (400), Wayanas (600), Palikours (500), Wayampis-Oyampis (600) and Emerillons (300). There are also bush negroes (Bonis, Saramacas, Djukas), who live mostly in the Maroni area, and others (Dominicans, St Lucians, etc) at 0.7%. The language is French, with officials not usually speaking anything else. Créole is also widely spoken. The religion is predominantly Roman Catholic.

● **Note** The Amerindian villages in the

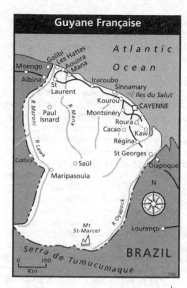

Guyane Française

Atlantic Ocean

Moengo · Galibi · Les Hattes · Aouara · Mana
Albina · St Laurent · Iracoubo · Sinnamary
Kourou · Iles du Salut
Paul Isnard · Montsinéry · CAYENNE
R Maroni · R Mana · Roura · Kaw
Cacao · Régina
R Lawa · St Georges
Cottica · Saül · Oiapoque
Maripasoula · N
Mt St-Marcel · R Oyapock · Lourenço
Serra de Tumucumaque · BRAZIL
0 · 100 · Km · 126L

Haut-Maroni and Haut-Oyapock areas may only be visited with permission from the Préfecture in Cayenne *before* arrival in Guyane.

HISTORY

Several French and Dutch expeditions attempted to settle along the coast in the early 17th century, but were driven off by the native population. The French finally established a settlement at Sinnamary in the early 1660s but this was destroyed by the Dutch in 1665 and seized by the British two years later. Under the Treaty of Breda, 1667, Guyane was returned to France. Apart from a brief occupation by the Dutch in 1676, it remained in French hands until 1809 when a combined Anglo-Portuguese naval force captured the colony and handed it over to the Portuguese (Brazilians). Though the land was restored to France by the Treaty of Paris in 1814, the Portuguese remained until 1817. Gold was discovered in 1853, and disputes arose about the frontiers of the colony with Suriname and Brazil. These were settled by arbitration in 1891, 1899, and 1915. By the law of 19 March, 1946, the Colony of Cayenne, or Guyane Française, became the Department of Guyane, with the same laws, regulations, and administration as a department in metropolitan France. The seat of the Prefect and of the principal courts is at Cayenne. The colony was used as a prison for French convicts with camps scattered throughout the country; Saint-Laurent was the port of entry. After serving prison terms convicts spent an equal number of years in exile and were usually unable to earn their return passage to France. Those interested should read *Papillon* by Henri Charrière. Majority opinion seems to be in favour of greater autonomy: about 5% of the population are thought to favour independence. 1995 and 1996 were marked by indictments of many prominent people, notably Gérard Holder, mayor of Cayenne, on charges of corruption and diversion of funds.

● *Rhum*, by the French Guyanese writer Blaise Cendras, is worth reading for its descriptions of the country's unique customs and traditions.

GOVERNMENT

The head of state is the President of France; the local heads of government are a Commissioner of the Republic, for France, and the Presidents of the local General and Regional Councils. The General Council (19 seats) and the Regional Council (31 seats) are the two legislative houses. In regional council elections in March 1992, the Parti Socialiste Guyanais won 16 seats, while the other major party, the Front Democratique Guyanais, won 10. Guyane is divided into two *arrondissements*, Cayenne and St-Laurent du Maroni.

THE ECONOMY

Structure of production Most of the population lives in the coastal strip and it is here that farming is concentrated.

The main crops are sugar cane, rice, maize and bananas; sugar is processed into rum, much of which is exported. Some market gardening is undertaken by Laotian Hmong immigrants, near Cacao, who produce fresh vegetables. The cattle farms on the coast are not large enough to meet domestic demand. Fishing is mainly for shrimp, with most of the 2,000-3,000 tonne annual catch exported to the USA or Japan. Guyane has renewable natural riches in its forests (about 75,000 sq km) and development of the timber industry is underway. Apart from the export of hardwood, trees are also used for the extraction of essence of rosewood and gum products.

There are deposits of gold, several of which have attracted Brazilian *garimpeiros* and consequent ecological damage through the silting of rivers and indiscriminate use of mercury. Officiallly gold production has risen from 330 kg in 1986 to 2.5 tonnes in 1995, largely as a result of increased declaration. An estimated 42 million tonnes of extractable bauxite have been located in the Kaw mountains to the SE of Cayenne, but development has not yet been started. Other minerals include sulphide of mercury, iron and clay; some 40 million tonnes of kaolin have been located at St-Laurent du Maroni.

Electricity is generated by three thermal power stations at Cayenne, Kourou and St-Laurent, but these may be replaced by the construction of a 120-MW hydroelectric scheme at Petit Sant on the Sinnamarie River. An estimated 1 million animals and 1.5 million birds lost their habitat when the area was flooded, but a French government-funded project rescued some of them and relocated them in Guyane's first nature reserve. More nature reserves are being created as a result of investment by the French government.

Recent trends Guyane is overwhelmingly dependent upon France for finance of about US$1.2bn a year, which is principally directed to providing social services and improving infrastructure. Most foodstuffs, consumer goods and manufactured products are imported from France or the French Caribbean and prices are consequently very high. Much of the country remains sparsely populated and underdeveloped despite French aid but the department is known internationally for its space station at Kourou, home to the European Ariane space programme, where economic activity and investment is concentrated. The site has been used to launch over half the world's commercial satellites and over 20,000 foreigners are employed there. Tourism is slowly being developed, but the lack of good beaches and the proximity of the Amazon which muddies the water has deterred many. About 10,000 tourists visit annually, mainly for adventure trips into the forests, but their numbers are dwarfed by the 60,000 other visitors, businessmen and those who work in the space programme.

CAYENNE

Cayenne, the capital and the chief port, is on the island of Cayenne at the mouth of the Cayenne River. It is 645 km from Georgetown (Guyana) and 420 km from Paramaribo (Suriname) by sea. Population estimated between 52,000 and 60,000. There is an interesting museum, the **Musée Departemental**, in rue de Remire, near the Place de Palmistes (Mon and Wed 0900-1330, Tues and Fri 0900-1330, 1630-1830, Sat 0900-1200; US$2, students US$1). It contains quite a mixture of exhibits, from pickled snakes to the trunk of the 'late beloved twin-trunked palm' of the Place de Palmistes; there is a good entomological collection and excellent paintings of convict life. Next door is the municipal library. The **Musée de L'Or**, Impasse Buzaré (Mon-Fri 0800-1200) has been restored. **L'Orstom** (scientific research institute), Route de Montabo, Mon and Fri 0700-1330, 1500-1800, Tues-Thur 0700-1300, has a research library and permanent

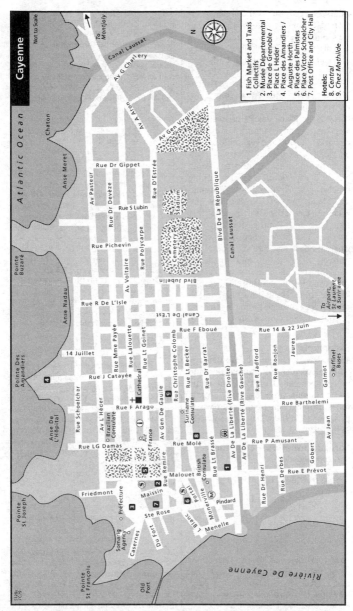

Cayenne

Not to Scale

Atlantic Ocean

To Montjoly

Canal Laussat

Av G Charlery

Chaton

Anse Meret

N

1. Fish Market and Taxis
   Collectifs
2. Musée Départemental
3. Place de Grenoble /
   Place L Héder
4. Place des Amandiers /
   Auguste Horth
5. Place des Palmistes
6. Place Victor Schoelcher
7. Post Office and City Hall

Hotels:
8. Central
9. Chez Mathilde

Av N Aron

Av Gen Virgile

Rue Dr Gippet

Rue D'Estrée

Rue Dr Devèze

Av Pasteur

Rue S Lubin

Pointe Buzaré

Rue Pichevin

Rue Polycarpe

Blvd De La République

Stadium

Cemetery

Blvd Jubelin

Canal Laussat

Anse Nadau

Rue R De L'Isle

Av Voltaire

Canal De L'Est

To Airport,
St Laurent
& Surinam

Rue F Eboué

Rue 14 & 22 Juin

Pointe Des Amandiers

14 Juillet

Rue Mme Payée

Rue Lalouette

Rue Lt Goinet

Rue J Catayée

Cathedral

Rue Christophe Colomb

Rue Lt Becker

Rue Dr Barrat

Rue R Radford

Rue Ronjon

Jaurès

O Ruffinel
Buses

Galmot

Rue Barthelemi

Rue Schoelcher

Av L Héder

Rue F Arago

Brazilian
Consulate

Air
France

Suriname
Consulate

Av Gen De Gaulle

Av De La Liberté (Rive Droite)

Av De La Liberté (Rive Gauche)

Rue P Amusant

Av Jean

Anse De L'Hôpital

Rue LG Damas

Rue Molé

Gobert

Rue Derbes

Rue E Prévot

Friedmont

Maissin

Rue Remire

Malouet

British
Consulate

Rue Lt Brassé

Rue Dr Henri

Préfecture

Portail

Moneyville

Pindard

Ste Rose

J Menelle

Somaig
Agency

Du Fort

L Blanc

Casernes

Pointe St Joseph

Pointe St François

Old Port

Rivière De Cayenne

exhibits on ecosystems and archaeological finds in Guyane. Also worth a visit are **La Crique**, the colourful but dangerous area around the Canal Laussat (built by Malouet in 1777); the Jesuit-built residence (circa 1890) of the Prefect (**L'Hôtel-de-Ville**) in the Place de Grenoble; the **Place des Amandiers** (also known as the Place Auguste-Horth) by the sea; the **Place des Palmistes**, with assorted palms; a swimming pool and five cinemas. The **fruit and vegetable market** on Monday, Wednesday, Friday and Saturday mornings has a Caribbean flavour, but it is expensive. There are bathing beaches (water rather muddy) around the island, the best is **Montjoly**, but watch out for sharks. Minibuses run from terminal to Rémire-Montjoly for beaches. They leave when full – check when the last one returns. There is a walking trail called '**Rorota**' which follows the coastline and can be reached from Montjoly or the Gosselin beaches. Another trail, '**Habitation Vidal**' in Remire, passes through former sugar cane plantations. Remains of sugar mills can be seen on the way.

Excursions

43 km SW of Cayenne is **Montsinéry**, with a zoo featuring Amazonian flora and fauna (open daily 1000-1900), an orchid and a walking trail, 'Bagne des Annamites', through remains of a camp where prisoners from Indochina were interned in the 1930s.

Local information – Cayenne
● Accommodation

Price guide

L1	over US$200	L2	US$151-200
L3	US$101-150	A1	US$81-100
A2	US$61-80	A3	US$46-60
B	US$31-45	C	US$21-30
D	US$12-20	E	US$7-11
F	US$4-6	G	up to US$3

L3 *Novotel Cayenne*, Chemin Hilaire-route de Montabo, T 30-38-88, F 31-78-98, not central, on beach, restaurant, a/c, very good; **A2** *Hotel des Amandiers*, Place Auguste Horth, T 30-26-00, F 30-74-84, a/c, excellent restaurant; **A2** *Phigarita Studios*, 47 bis, rue F Arago, T 30-66-00, F 30-77-49, spacious apartments with kitchenette, a/c, rec, friendly, helpful, breakfast; **A2** *Amazonia*, 26 Av Gen de Gaulle, good, friendly, a/c, luggage stored, central location, T 31-00-00, F 31-94-41; **A3** *Central Hotel*, corner rue Molé and rue Becker, T 31-30-00, F 31-12-96, downtown, a/c; **A3** *Le Grillardin*, PK6 Route Matoury, 4 km from airport, T 35-63-90, a/c, restaurant; **A3** *Ket-Tai*, Ave de la Libertie corner Blvd Jubelin, T 30-11-00, new, clean, modern; **A2** *Guyane Studios*, 16 rue Molé, T 30-25-11, a/c, kitchenette; **B** *Le Baduel*, Route de Baduel, T 30-51-58, F 30-77-76, a/c, TV, cooking facilities; **B** *Ajoupa*, T 30-33-08, F 30-12-82, Route Camp de Tigre, 2 km from town, helpful; **B-C** *Chez Mathilde/Hotel du Palais*, 42 Av Gen de Gaulle, T 30-25-13, cheaper with fan and without bath, hammock space, friendly, clean, noisy, not safe for left luggage, always full; **B** *Madeleine*, T 30-17-36, a/c, basic, clean, breakfast, will book Raffinel bus to St-Laurent, 1 km out of town, friendly (good Surinamese snackbar nearby); **B** *Neptima*, rue F Eboué 21, T 30-11-15, F 37-98-60 (15 rooms), best value, a/c, clean, friendly. Cheapest in town is **D** *Foyer Paul VI*, rue des Mangues, 10-15 mins walk from centre, T 30-04-16, cheaper rooms without water, cheap meals.

About 10 km from Cayenne is the **A2** *Beauregard*, route de Rémire, T 35-41-00, F 35-44-05, rec for business visitors, pool, tennis, squash, sauna, restaurant *Cric-Crac*; also *Hotel M*, a motel with a/c rooms and a small swimming pool; the owner hires out small cars, rec for business visitors, breakfast, T 35-41-00, Telex 010 310, and **A1** *Motel du Lac*, T 38-08-00, F 38-10-34, Chemin Poupon, Montjoly, 10 km from centre, pool, bar, restaurant, good business hotel. *Hotel-restaurant Le Polygone*, between airport and Cayenne, T 35-14-00, F 35-21-64, rooms, suites, bungalows, pool.

The best value is to rent an apartment for a week or more: **C** *Mme Romieu*, PK 5.5 Route de Montabo, T 31-06-55; *Mme Mirta*, 35 Lot Alexandre, T 31-48-78, US$576/month; *M Roques*, 2 Lot Amarillys, T 38-18-20, US$230/week, a/c; **C** *Mme Stanistlas*, Villa Sonia PK 0.4 Rte de Rémire, T 38-22-13; *Mme Anastase*, 59 Av de Gaulle, T 35-17-70, US$203/week, a/c; **B** *Mme Castor*, 4 rue du Dr Gippet, T 31-27-38, F 31-66-13, a/c; **B** *Mme de Chadirac*, Route de Montjoly PK

6, T 38-23-01; **B M Firmin**, Cité Thémire, 28 rue René Maran, T 80-46-56; **B Mme Girard**, Route de Montabo PK3.5, T 30-61-28; **B M Benoit**, 117 rue Ch Colomb, T 31-42-81. Most hotels do not add tax and service to their bill, but stick to prices posted outside or at the desk. Hotel rooms are expensive—it is hard to find a room under 200F a night double. Bed and breakfast accommodation (gîte) is available for about 150F a night (breakfast is usually at extra cost)—contact the tourist office for details. Ask the Catholic Fathers at Cité Messaih, nr *Hotel Madeleine*, about sleeping possibilities. Amex cards often not accepted but Visa OK.

● **Places to eat**
Main hotels. *Hostellerie 'Les Amandiers'*, Place Auguste-Horth, excellent, the most famous French, expensive (US$38); *Au Vieux Genois*, 89 rue Christophe Colomb, very good, French with local products, fish specialities, good business lunches; *La Caravelle*, 21 rue Christophe Colomb; *Le Vesuvio*, route Montabo, very good, clean; *Armand Ti A Hing*, Place des Palmistes, French, excellent, 180F pp; *Cap St Jacques*, rue Docteur E Gippet, excellent Vietnamese food, reasonable; also *Thang-Long Vietnamese*, 1 rue Mentel; *Maxim'um*, Av Estrée; *La Croix du Sud*, 80, Av de Gaulle; *Tournesol*, rue Lt Goinet, real French food, fine wines, expensive, highly rec; *Porto Verde*, 58 rue Lt Goinet, Brazilian menu, mostly under 50F, rec; *Le Grillardin* (see **Hotels**), very good Créole; *Paris-Cayenne*, 59 rue Lallouette, French, very good, nice décor; *La Belle Epoque*, French, expensive; *Cric-Crac* (at *Hotel Beauregard*), Créole cooking, lovely atmosphere; *Le Snack Créole*, 17 rue Eboué; *Mille Pâtes*, 16 rue Felix Eboué; *Palmiste*, Place des Palmistes (downtown), good daily menu, US$17, breakfast US$4, central and spacious; *Frégate*, Av de Gaulle; *Le Traiteur de la Fôret*, Blvd Jubelin, friendly, good; *Marveen Snack Bar*, rue Ch Colombe, near Canal de L'Est, food and staff pleasant, the patrons are very helpful regarding air travel and excursions (the elder of the two is a pilot for the Guyane Flying Club); *Ko Fei*, 18 rue Lalouette, T 312888, good Chinese; *Apsara*, 95 rue Colombe, Chinese, good value; *La Rose d'Asie*, 20 rue Samuel Lubin, very good Vietnamese; *Hindu-Creol*, rue J Catayee, Indian, good. Along the Canal Laussant there are Javanese snack bars; try *bami* (spicy noodles) or *saté* (barbequed meat in a spicy peanut

sauce). Also along the canal are small, cheap Créole restaurants, not very clean. Vans around Place des Palmistes in evenings sell cheap, filling sandwiches. *Delifrance*, Av de Gaulle at rue Catayée, hot chocolate and croissants; *Epi D'or*, Av Jubelin, good sweets and cakes, rec. Food is about 38% more expensive than Metropolitan France: it is hard to find a meal for under 50F (small Chinese restaurants charge 50-80F for a full meal).

● **Bars**
Bar Cayenne Palace, 45 Av de Gaulle, disco 80F with first drink.

● **Bookshops**
Librairie AJC, 31 Boulevard Jubelin, has some stock in English. Also old maps and prints. Current map sold at *Librairie Alain Pion*, Av de Gaulle and in most bookshops.

● **Exchange**
Banque Nacional de Paris-Guyane, 2 Place Schoelcher; no exchange facilities on Sat. **Banque Française Commerciale**, 2 Place des Palmistes (best bank exchange rates); **Crédit Populaire Guyanais**, 93 rue Lalouette. Most banks have ATMs for cash withdrawals on Visa, sometimes Mastercard, never Amex. *Cambio Caraïbe*, Av Gen de Gaulle near Catayée (best rates for US$); *Guyane Change*, Av Gen de Gaulle near rue F Eboué. The Post Office exchanges cash and TCs at good rates, but complicated and time-consuming. There are no exchange facilities at the airport; if in extreme need on Sat you may be able to change money at Air France office in Place des Palmistes. Central drugstore may help when banks closed. Almost impossible to change dollars outside Cayenne or Kourou. Buy francs before arrival if possible.

● **Laundromat**
Corner of rue Lalouette and rue Eboué, US$5 load all in; *Ros'in*, 87 Av Liberté, T 31-73-13.

● **Main Post Office**
Route de Baduel, 2 km out from town (15F by taxi or 20 mins on foot). Poste Restante letters are only kept for 2 weeks maximum. Also Poste Cayenne Cépéron, place L Heder.

● **Tourist offices**
Agence Régionale de Développement du Tourisme et des Loisirs de la Guyane (ARDTLG), 12 rue Lalouette (T 30-09-00), 0800-1200, 1500-1800. Free map and tourist guide (Guyane Poche). At the airport, **Chambre de Commerce et d'industrie de Guyane**, has

plenty of hotel and tour information and map. The SLM manager is reported to be very helpful with advice.

● **Travel Agents**
Takari Tour, Colline du Montabo, T 31-19-60 (BP 513) and at *Novotel*, rec for inland tours. *Guyane Excursions*, Centre Commercial Simarouba, Kourou, T 32-05-41, specializes in inland tours, particularly to the Maroni river, highly rec, US$700 for 5-6 days, but a wide variety of options. Also *JAL Voyages*, 1 ave des Plages, Montjoly, T 31-68-20, for a wide range of tours. *Somarig*, place L Héder, T 30-29-80, is reported to be good for South American and European airline tickets. It also sells boat tickets to Ile Royale as well as meal tickets for the Auberge which are rec. *Agence Sainte-Claire*, 8 rue de Remire, T 30-00-38, for travel outside Guyane (inc charters to Caracas and Cuba); *Havas*, 2 place du Marché, T 31-26-22/31-27-26 (also 26 ave de l'Opéra, 75001 Paris, T 40-41-80-00).

● **Transport**
Bus terminal at corner of rue Molé and Av de la Liberté. Regular urban services. The only westbound bus is run by Raffinel & Cie, 8 Av Galmot, T 31-26-66 (Kourou US$12, St Laurent US$25) leaves 0530 (not Sun). Minibuses to St-Laurent du Maroni leave when full from the terminal, 0400-1200, 3 hrs, US$25. Service to *Mana* Mon and Thur only. To Kaw, Wed. Otherwise transport is by shared taxis (collectifs), which leave from Av de la Liberté, near the fish market early in the morning (Kourou US$12, St Laurent US$30-38).

WEST TO SURINAME

Kourou, 56 km W of Cayenne, where the main French space centre (Centre Spatial Guyanais), used for the European Space Agency's Ariane programme, is located, is referred to by the Guyanais as 'white city' because of the number of metropolitan French families living there; its population is about 20,000. Tourist attractions include bathing, fishing, sporting and aero club, and a variety of organized excursions. The space centre occupies an area of about 4 km deep along some 30 km of coast, bisected by the Kourou river. Public guided tours are given Mon-Fri 0745-1130 and 1300-1630 (Fri am only). Write to Centre Spatial Guyanais, Jupiter 2, Acceuil Visite, 97310, Kourou, or T 33-44-82. The tour includes the new museum, which can be visited without reservation, open Mon-Fri 1000-1800, Sat 1400-1800, US$7.70. No public transport, take a taxi or hitch. Visits are free. To watch a launch you must write to M Le directeur du Centre Spatial Guyanais, BP726, 97387 Kourou Cedex, or F 33-50-55, saying you want to attend; fax, or T 33-44-82 to find out when launches take place. Supply full names and ID; ask for your invitation from Centre d'acceuil du CSG, or Syndicat d'Initiative de Cayenne, 7 ave G Monnerville, 97300 Cayenne (312919). Invitations must be collected 2-3 days before the launch; if you hear nothing, it's probably full, but you can try wait-listing (arrive early). There are five viewing sites: Toucan (for VIPs, but wait-listing, or enquiries, possible), Kikiwi, Colibri (both good), Agami (OK) and Ibis (not rec). Alternatively, you can watch the launch for free, from 10 km, at Montagne Carapa at Pariacabo.

Local Information – Kourou
● **Accommodation**
All hotels are overbooked and raise their prices when there is an Ariane rocket launch (about once a month).

L3 *Relais de Guyane (Hotel des Roches)*, Avenues des Roches, T 32-00-66, F 32-03-28, not too good, a/c, incl breakfast, pool, beach, good restaurants; **A1** *Atlantis*, T 32-13-00, F 32-40-12, nr Lac Bois Diable, a/c, modern, pool, good restaurant, best value for business visitors; also at Lac Bois Diable, **L2** *Mercure*, T 32-07-00; **L3** *La Corissante*, 23 rue des Alizés, T 33-11-00, F 33-11-60, studios with 2-5 rooms, cooking facilities; **A2** *Studios Le Gros Bec*, T 32-91-91, 52 rue Dr Floch, cooking facilities; **A2** *Les Jardins D'Hermes*, 56 rue Duchesne, T 32-01-83, F 32-09-17, in heart of old Kourou, a/c, modern, good; **A3** *Ballahou*, 1 rue Armet Martial, T 32-42-06, F 32-52-08, a/c, TV, nice, modern, friendly, good restaurant; **A** *Mme Moutton*, rue Séraphin 56, T 31-21-45, studios with or without kitchen, friendly; **A3** *Auberge des Iles du Salut*, T 32-11-00, F 32-42-23, see below.

E Centre d'Acceuil, T 32-25-40/32-26-33, various sizes of room, clean, good value. Cheap hotels and rooms for 100F on Av de Gaulle.

20 km S of Kourou on the road to Saramaca is **Les Maripas**, tourist camp, T 32-05-41, F 32-28-47, river and overland excursions available, D for tent, book at Guyane Excursion, 7 quartier Simarouba, nr *Restaurant Saramaca*.

● **Places to eat**
Many, especially on de Gaulle, offer 60F menu (Creole or Chinese) inc *Le Catouri*, *Cachiri Combo* (No 3, T 32-44-64, 100-150F, also has basic rooms, C), *Vieux Montmartre*. *La Grillade*, Av Berlioz; *L'Enfer Vert*, Av G Monnerville; *Le Paradisier* in Hotel des Roches (see above); *L'Hydromel*, rue Raymond Cresson, good pancakes; *Le Provence*, 11 passage G Monnerville, best French, expensive; *Ballahou* (see **Hotels**), best for fish and seafood (try *Guyabaisse*); pizza at *Le Valentino*, 4 place Galilé, pizzas, seafood Fri; *Le Saramaca*, place du Marché. *La Pirogue*, Quartier de l'Europe, 20m from post office, at 60F good value; in same area, *Le Citron Vert*, *Le Moaï*, *Le Roc*, *Le Gourbi*, *Viet Nam*, *Le Colibri* (good chicken) and *Bar des Sports* (beside Post Office, 50F). Many cheap Chinese (also takeaway): *Le Chinatown*, rue Duchesne, rec; *Kong Loong*, rue du Levant; many vans sell sandwiches filled with Créole food, good. *Le Glacier des 2 Lacs*, 68 ave des 2 Lacs, ice cream, cakes, teas, very good.

● **Bars**
La Nouvelle Dimension (Créole and European style); *American Bar* in Hotel des Roches (see **Hotels**); *Le Forban*, rue Dreyfus, district 205, worth seeing the murals (also for the lonely, many young Brazilian women).

● **Entertainment**
Nightclubs: *3ème Dimension* (Créole style), *Le Vieux Montmartre*, both on de Gaulle; *Clibertown*, quartier de l'Anse, very good.

● **Exchange**
Banque National de Paris Guyane, Place Newton; Banque Française Commerciale, Place Jeanne d'Arc; **Crédit Populaire Guyanais**, Simarouba; **Crédit Martiniqueis**, ave G Monnerville.

● **Post Office**
Avenue des Frères Kennedy.

● **Travel Agency**
Guyane Excursions, T 32-05-41 (see under Cayenne); *Agence Sainte Claire*, T 32-36-98, F 32-50-40; *Air France*, place Newton, T 32-10-50; *Amazonie Détente*, 18 rue A Renoir, T 32-82-52.

● **Tourist offices**
Quartier de l'Europe, T 32-48-840.

● **Transport**
Taxi in town US$10, Lopez T 320560, Gilles T 320307, Kourou T 321444. To Cayenne, bus leaves from Shell service station, corner Av de France, Av Vermont Polycarpe; bus to St-Laurent du Maroni from same place, 2 between 0600 and 0700, US$30; *taxis collectifs*, 0600, 0630, 0700, 1330, US$12 to Cayenne. Taxi to Cayenne or airport, US$60 (US$85 at night); to St-Laurent du Maroni US$25 by *taxi collectif* (irregular) or by minibus from Shell Station.

The **Iles du Salut** (many visitors at weekends), opposite Kourou, include the Ile Royale, the Ile Saint-Joseph, and the Ile du Diable. They were the scene of the notorious convict settlement built in 1852; the last prisoners left in 1953. The Ile du Diable ("Devil's Island"), a rocky palm-covered islet almost inaccessible from the sea, was where political prisoners, including Alfred Dreyfus, were held. There is a 60-bed hotel on Ile Royale, **A3** *Auberge Iles du Salut* (address Sothis, 97310 Kourou, T 32-11-00, F 32-42-23), also hammock space US$20 pp; former guard's bungalow, main meals (excellent), minimum US$36, breakfast US$8 (ex-mess hall for warders, with good food; bottled water sold); gift shop with high prices (especially when a cruise ship is in), good English guide book for sale. Camping is possible, but suitable sites are limited, the stronghearted may try the old prison barracks; take food and water (you can also sling a hammock in the open, take a plastic sheet to protect yourself from morning mist); bread and water (check bottle is sealed) can be bought from the hotel stall. You can see agoutis, turtles, humming birds and macaws, and there are many un-owned coconut palms. Beware the many open wells. Take a torch for visiting the ruins. Paintings of prison life are on show in the tiny church. Points of interest include the children's graveyard, hospital, mental asylum and death cells. These, and the church, are not always open. Little is being done to prevent the deterioration of the buildings. Boat from Kourou's port at the end of Av General de Gaulle, 4 km from old centre US$37 return (children under 12 half price), leaves 0830 and 1030 daily, returns from island at 1600 and 1800 (check, T 32-09-95) additional sailing Sat 1600, 1 hour each way. Tickets may be obtained from Somarig Voyages, address under Cayenne **Travel Agents**; Air Guyane Voyages, 2 rue Lallouette, T 31-72-00; in Kourou from au Carbet des Roches, cash only. There are no regular boats from Ile Royale to Ile Saint-Joseph, which is wilder and more beautiful, with a small beach (this island had solitary-confinement cells and the warders' graveyard). It may be possible to hire a private boat at the ferry dock, or ask for James on the Kourou-Ile Royale ferry. Surfing and swimming are possible between Ile Royale and Ile du Diable; strong currents at high tide. Boat owners are very reluctant to visit Ile du Diable except around July-August when the sea is calmer.

Between Kourou and Iracoubo, on the road W to St-Laurent, is **Sinnamary** (103 km from Cayenne), a pleasant town where Galibi Indians at a mission make artifical flowers from feathers, for sale to tourists. Scarlet ibis can be seen in numbers on the Sinnamary estuary at Iracoubo. Also at Iracoubo is a pretty church in the woods with paintings by convicts.

St-Laurent du Maroni, population 20,000, formerly a penal transportation camp, is now a quiet colonial town 250 km from Cayenne on the River Maroni, bordering Suriname. It can be visited as a day tour from Cayenne if you hire a car. There are no gîtes in St-Laurent; those on a tight budget wanting a room or hammock space can try to make advance arrangements in Cayenne with:

Fedération d'Oeuvres Laïques, Centre d'Hebergement de Saint-Louis, T 34-11-40; CAS EDF, centre d'Hebergement, T 34-12-96/34-23-03; or Le Carbet du Balat, Mme Emille Lamtoukai, T 34-10-35.

The old Camp de Transportation (the original penal centre) can be wandered round at will (an absolute must if visiting the country); closed Mon. Next door is the new tourist office. Guided tours of Les Bagnes (prison camps) daily 0830-1230, 1500-1800, chilling. The Charbonière refugee camp, next to the ferry pier housed Surinamese Bush Negro refugees during that country's civil war. A few have remained and more have returned. (Nearby is St-Jean du Maroni, an Indian village.)

Local Information
● Accommodation
Sinnamary: **A3** *Sinnarive Motel*, T 34-55-55; **A3** *Eldo Grill*, T 34-51-41, F 34-50-90, a/c, TV, coffee, breakfast extra, rec; **A1** *Hotel du Fleuve*, T 34-54-00, F 34-53-03, expensive. *Restaurant Madras*, good Creole; ask for *Gaya Baru*, Indonesian restaurant in an Indonesian village. Wood carvings and jewellery are on sale here and the workshops can be visited. There are 3 to 5 day excursions up the Sinnamarie river.

St-Laurent: **A1-A3** *Hotel La Tentiaire*, 12 Av Franklin Roosevelt, T 34-26-00, F 34-15-09, a/c, the best, breakfast extra; **B** *Hotel Toucan*, Boulevard Republique, T 34-12-59, F 34-17-06, a/c, dirty, TV, poor value; **B** *Star Hotel*, rue Thiers, T 34-10-84, a/c, pool, cheap restaurant, friendly, rec; **A3** *Chez Julienne*, Route des Malgaches, T 34-11-53, a/c, TV, shower, good.

In the countryside not far from St-Laurent are 2 *Auberge de brousse*, which are good places to stay for walking, or for trips to see turtles at Les Hattes (see below): **C** *Auberge Bois Diable*, PK8 Acarouany, T 34-19-35, 1 bedroom, hammock space, US$6, meals, US$16, breakfast US$4, good food, hospitable, tours arranged; **C** *Relais d'Acarouany*, T 34-17-20, 6 rooms, meals US$18, breakfast US$4.

● Places to eat
St-Laurent: *Restaurant La Saramaca*, Av Felix Eboué, the best (also has rooms to rent at

the back); *Restaurants Vietnam*, *La Goelette* (French/Brazilian, closed Wed), and *Le Point d'Intérrogation*, have been rec, also *Loe*, nr hospital, Créole, excellent; many cheap Chinese.

● **Bars**

Jean Solis, opp Catholic church, rec.

● **Exchange**

BNP opp *Restaurant Le Saramaca* will change US$ TCs. **Cambio COP**, 19 rue Montravel, nr BNP, T 34-38-23, changes Dutch and Suriname guilders, dollars

● **Transport**

Minibuses to Cayenne meet the ferry from Suriname, leaving when full, 3 hrs, US$25. Bus to Cayenne, US$30, same price to Kourou, but no regular service; *taxis collectifs* to and from Cayenne, US$25 a head, 3½-hour trip. Freight *pirogues* sometimes take passengers inland along the Maroni River; alternatively a group can hire a *pirogue* at about US$200 a day. Avis has a car rental office in St-Laurent.

FRONTIER WITH SURINAME

Make sure you obtain proper entry stamps from immigration, not the police, to avoid problems when leaving. Customs and immigration close at 1900.

● **Exchange**

Many aggressive touts on the St-Laurent and Albina piers. It is best to change money in the Village Chinois in St-Laurent; although rates are lower than in Paramaribo, it is illegal to change money in Albina. Beware theft at St-Laurent's black market.

● **Transport**

Ferry for vehicles and passengers to Albina Mon, Thur, 0700, 0900, 1400, 1600, Tues, Wed, Sat 0700, 0900, Sun, 1530, 1600, ½ hr. Passengers US$4 one way, car US$20 one way. Minibuses and taxis for Paramaribo meet the Albina ferry. GUM airways have charters between St-Laurent and Paramaribo domestic airport for US$250 (5 seats; enquire in Paramaribo).

EXCURSIONS

About 3 km from St-Laurent, along the Paul Isnard Road, is Saint-Maurice, where the rum distillery of the same name can be visited, Mon-Thur 0630-1430, Fri 0630-1330. At Km 70 on the same dirt road is access to **Voltaire Falls**, 1½ hrs walk from the road (**A3** *Auberge des Chutes Voltaires*, T 34-27-16). 7 km S of St-Laurent on the road to St-Jean is the Amerindian village of **Terre Rouge**; canoes can be hired for day trips up the Maroni River (see Maripasoula below). These can be arranged with *Youkaliba (Maroni) Expeditions*, 3 rue Simon, T 34-16-45/31-23-98 and *Guyane Adventure*, T 34-21-28/34-13-78: eg 1-night trip to Apatou, US$140; to Saut Anana on Mana River, 10 days, US$655.

40 km N of St-Laurent du Maroni is **Mana**, a delightful town with rustic architecture near the coast (**E** pp *Gite d'Etape*, rooms OK, filthy kitchen, mosquitoes, disco next door; nuns next to the church rent beds and hammocks, clean and simple, T 34-17-29, Communauté des Soeurs de St-Joseph de Cluny, 1 rue Bourguignon; Mme Hidair, T 34-80-62, has rooms, **C**; restaurants *Le Bufalo* and *Le Manoa del Dorado*). 20 km W of Mana following the river along a single track access road is **Les Hattes**, or Awala-Yalimapo (**B** *Gite Rureau*, clean; restaurant *Au Paradis des Acajous*; Indian restaurant near beach) an Amerindian village (ask M Daniel for permission to stay in the church); 4 km further on is Les Hattes beach where leatherback-turtles lay their eggs at night; season April-Aug with its peak in May-June. No public transport to Les Hattes and its beach, but hitching possible at weekends; take food and water and mosquito repellent. In spite of the dryish climate Mana is a malaria region. The fresh water of the Maroni and Mana rivers makes sea bathing very pleasant. Very quiet during the week.

Aouara, an Amerindian village with hammock places, is a few kilometres S E of Les Hattes. It also has a beach where the leatherback turtles lay their eggs; they take about three hours over it. Take mosquito nets, hammock and insect repellent.

CENTRAL MASSIF

There are daily flights from Cayenne to **Maripasoula**; details in **Air transport**, page 895 (**C** *Auberge Chez Dedè*, Av Leonard, T 37-20-05, US$4 per extra person; **A1** *Campement Touristique de Sant Sonnelle*, T 31-49-45, full board) up the Maroni from St-Laurent (2-4 day journey up river in *pirogue*). There may be freight canoes which take passengers (US$40) or private boats (US$150) which leave from St-Laurent; 5-6 day tours and other options with Guyane-Excursions or with Takari Tour (see under Cayenne **Travel Agents**). Maripasoula has 5,000 inhabitants in town and its surroundings. Many bush negros live here. 20 mins by canoe from Maripasoula is **A2** *Campement Touristique Lassort*, T 31-49-45.

Saül, a remote gold-mining settlement in the 'massif central' is the geographical centre of Guyane. The main attractions are for the nature-loving tourist. Beautiful undisturbed tropical forests are accessible by a very well-maintained system of 90 km of marked trails, including several circular routes. The place has running water, a radiotelephone, and electricity. Ten-day expeditions are run by Christian Ball, 'Vie Sauvage', 97314 Saül, US$86 (30% in advance) per day with meals, maps of local trails provided, own hammock and bedding useful but not essential. It can be cold at night. Another fascinating overland route goes from Roura (see below) up the Comte River to Belizon, followed by a 14 to 16-day trek through the jungle to Saül, visiting many villages en route, guide recommended. 7 km N of Saül is *Eden des Eaux Claires*, tourist camp, T 30-91-11, **A2** full board, **C** in hammock including breakfast and dinner (drinks extra).

● **Transport** Air service with Air Guyane from Cayenne or via Maripasoula (see **Air transport**, below); try at airport even if flight said to be full. By *pirogue* from Mana up Mana River, 9-12 days, then one day's walk to Saül, or from St-Laurent via Maripasoula along Moroni and Inini Rivers, 15 days and one day's walk to Saül, both routes expensive.

SOUTHEAST TO BRAZIL

30 km S of Cayenne at Carrefour de Gallion, the intersection of RN2 and CD5, is **B** *Emerald Jungle Village*, a tropical nature centre with a small botanical and zoological collection. Eco-tours can be taken into the forests by boat or canoe with expedition gear. Meals and drinks extra, airport transportation US$18, mountain bike hire US$10/day, canoes for hire. Owned by Joep Moonen and his wife, who both speak English, German and Dutch F 30-06-82; or write to CDS-PK0.5, 97356 Montsinéry.

28 km SE of Cayenne is the small town of **Roura** (**B** *Hotel-restaurant Amazone River*, T 31-91-13, a/c, good restaurant, good views of the river; **B** *Auberge des Orpailleurs*, PK62 route de l'Est, T 37-62-97, hammock space US$5, breakfast and dinner available; rooms to rent from Mme Luap, **C**, T 31-54-84), which has an interesting church; an excursion may be made to the Fourgassier Falls several km away (*L'Auberge des Cascades*, excellent restaurant). From Cayenne the road now crosses a new bridge over the River Comte. Excursions can be arranged along the Comte River. For information about the area contact the Syndicat D'Initiative de Roura, T 31-11-04. Nearby is Dacca, a Laotian village. 27 km from Roura is **C** *Auberge du Camp Caïman* (tourist camp, F to hang hammock), T 37-60-34, tours arranged to watch caiman in the swamps.

From Roura an unpaved road runs SE towards the village of Kaw. At Km 36 from Cayenne is the **C** *Hotel Relais de Patawa* (T 28-03-95), or sling your hammock for US$4, cheaper rates for longer stays, highly recommended. The owners, M and Mme Baloup, who are entomologists, will show you their collection, take you on guided tours of local sights and introduce you to their pet anaconda and boa constrictors. At Km 59 on the road to Régina is the turn-off to **Cacao** (a further 13 km), a small, quiet village, where Hmong refugees from Laos are settled; they are farmers and produce fine traditional handicrafts. (Accommodation: C *Restaurant La Lan*, one room, good value, good food; E *Quimbe-Kio*, hammock camp, breakfast US$3; M Levessier, T 30-51-22, has hammocks, E; best restaurant is *Chez By et David*, Laotian food; also good is *Degrad Cacao*). Minibus from Cayenne, Monday 1200; Friday 1800, return Mon 0730, Fri 1400. Halfway along the side road is the *Belle Vue* restaurant, which lives up to its name, because of the superb view over the tropical forest; the restaurant is open at weekends. SW of Cacao is the tourist camp **A2** *Carbet La Source*, with full board, T 31-96-64. **Kaw**, at Km 83, is on an island amid swamps which are home to much rare wildlife including caymans. The village is reached by dugout either from the Cayenne road or from Régina, or by road from Roura (50 km dirt road through the mountains with the last 2 km by dugout). Basic accommodation available (Mme Musron, T 31-88-15; *Jacana Tour*, T 38-07-95, excursions by day or night on the river), take insect repellent. Southwest of Kaw on the River Approuague is **Régina**, linked with Cayenne by a mostly paved road. A good trip is on the river to Athanase with G Frétique, T 30-45-51.

A trail has been cut by the French army from the road-head at Régina to St-Georges de l'Oyapock, along which a road is currently under construction (planned for completion 1998). It is 4 to 5 days of hard trekking with many rivers to be forded, impassable during the rainy season.

FRONTIER WITH BRAZIL

St-Georges de l'Oyapock is 15 mins down river from Oiapoque (Brazil) US$4 pp by motorized canoe, bargain for a return fare. The **Saut Maripa** rapids (not very impressive with high water) are located about 30 mins upstream along the

Oiapock River, past the Brazilian towns of Oiapoque and Clevelândia do Norte. Hire a motorized *pirogue* (canoe) to take you to a landing downstream from the rapids. Then walk along the remains of a narrow gauge railway line (one of only two in Guyane, formerly used for gold mining) for 20 mins through the jungle, to reach a small tourist complex with restaurant, bar, and guest houses by the rapids. A pleasant day trip. There are more rapids further upstream.

● **Immigration**
Immigration (*gendarmerie*) for entry/exit stamps at E end of town, follow signs, open daily 0700-1200, 1500-1800 (sometimes not open after early morning on Sun, in which case try the police at the airport); French and Portuguese spoken.

● **Accommodation & services**
B *Hotel Modestine*, T 37-00-13, restaurant, rooms to rent from M Carème; D unnamed hotel to left of supermarket opposite town hall, a dump, no fan, no window; also *Theofila*, lunch US$3, other restaurants and a night club. Two supermarkets with French specialities. Post Office; public telephone which takes phone card.

● **Exchange**
One of the Livre Service supermarkets and *Hotel Modestine* will sometimes change dollars cash into francs at very poor rates; if entering the country here, change money before arriving in St-Georges. Note that nowhere in town accepts Visa cards.

● **Transport**
For Air Guyane flights to Cayenne see below, **Air transport**. Air Guyane office at airport open 0700-0730, 1400-1430 for check in, open 0800-1100 for reservations. Flights are fully-booked several days in advance; you must check in at stated times. Extra flights are sometimes added. The police check that those boarding flights who have arrived from Brazil have obtained their entry stamp; also thorough baggage search.

Shipping A small vessel, the *Sao Pedro*, normally runs a shipping service to Cayenne, deck passengers US$30, but check it is not under repair. A cargo ship, the *Normelia*, calls at St-Georges about twice a month and will sometimes take passengers to Cayenne, 12-14 hrs, US$30 inc meals. Speak directly to the captain. The Elf petrol station has details on ship arrivals.

Information for travellers

BEFORE TRAVELLING

● **Documents**

Passports are not required by nationals of France and most French-speaking African countries carrying identity cards. For EC visitors, documents are the same as for Metropolitan France (ie no visa, no exit ticket required – check with a consulate in advance). No visa (45F) required for most nationalities (except for those of Guyana, Australia, some Eastern European countries, and Asian – not Japan – and other African countries) for a stay of up to 3 months, but an exit ticket out of the country is essential (a ticket out of one of the other Guianas is not sufficient); a deposit is required otherwise. If one stays more than 3 months, income tax clearance is required before leaving the country. Inoculation against yellow-fever is officially required only for those staying in Guyane longer than 2 weeks, but advisable for all. Travel to certain Amerindian villages is restricted. For **Tourist information** see page 896 below.

● **Climate**

Tropical with a very heavy rainfall. Average temperature at sea-level is 27°C, and fairly constant at that. Night and day temperatures vary more in the highlands. The rainy season is from November to July, with (sometimes) a short dry interruption in February and March. The great rains begin in May.

● **When to go**

The best months to visit are between Aug and Nov, which are the usual months for trips to the jungle.

● **Health**

Tropical diseases, dysentery, malaria, etc, occur, but the country is fairly healthy. Malaria pro-phylaxis recommended.

Recommended specialist in tropical diseases, Dr P Chesneau, Place Europe, T 32-11-05, Kourou. Dentists: R Fournier, 115 Lot Moucayou, Matoury, T 35-64-99; J-P Brugerie, Impasse France Equinociale, Kourou, T 32-12-58.

MONEY

● **Currency**

The currency is the French franc (5.20F = US$1 June 1996). These are bank rates; *cambios* offer rates for cash. Try to take francs with you as the exchange rate for dollars is low, many banks do not offer exchange facilities and most places demand cash. A better rate can be obtained by using Visa cards to withdraw cash from all the banks in Cayenne, Kourou and St-Laurent du Maroni.

GETTING THERE

AIR

Air France flies daily direct to Guyane from Paris, 10 times a week from Pointe-à-Pitre (Guadeloupe), Fort-de-France (Martinique), and once a week from Santo Domingo, once a week from Miami and once a week from Port-au-Prince. AOM French Airlines fly 5 times a week direct from Paris (continuing twice a week to Quito and Lima) and are reported to be the cheapest from Europe (Paris T 40-74-00-04). Corsair flies once a week from Paris (T Paris 41-41-58-58). Surinam Airways flies to Belém and Paramaribo 4 and 5 times a week; Surinam Airways sells tickets for Cayenne-Paramaribo-Georgetown-Port of Spain.

SEA

The Compagnie Général Maritime runs a passenger service to France once a month via Martinique and a freight service every 3 months. To Brazil from St-Georges to Oiapoque, see text above.

ON ARRIVAL

● **Airports**

Cayenne-Rochambeau (T 29-97-00) is 16 km from Cayenne, 20 mins by taxi, and 67 km from Kourou (US$60-80). No exchange facilities. No public transport; only taxis (US$25 daytime, US$30 night, but you can probably bargain or share). The cheapest route to town is taxi to Matoury US$10, then bus to centre US$2. Cheapest method of return to airport is by collective taxi from corner of Av de la Liberté and rue Malouet to Matoury (10 km) for US$2.40, then hitch or walk.

● **Airline offices**
Air France, 13, rue L G Damas, Place des Palmistes, T 37-98-99; Air Guyane, 2 rue Lalouette, T 31-72-00/35-65-55; Surinam Airways, 2 place Schoelcher, T 31-72-98.

● **Embassies & consulates**
British (Honorary), 16 Av Monnerville (BP 664, Cayenne 97300, T 31-10-34/30-42-42, F 30-40-94); Brazilian, 12 rue L Héder, at corner of Place des Palmistes, nr Air France offices (closed Sats T 30-04-67); Dutch (Honorary), Batiment Sogudem, Port de Dégrad des Cannes, BP139, Cayenne 97323, T 35-49-31, F 35-46-71; Suriname, 38 rue Christophe Colomb (T 30-04-61), Mon-Fri 0900-1200, visa 150F, two photos needed, takes 15 days (may be obtained same day, at extra cost).

● **Hours of business**
Hours vary widely between different offices, shops and even between different branches of the same bank or supermarket. There seem to be different business hours for every day of the week, but they are usually posted.

● **Official time**
3 hrs behind GMT.

● **Public holidays**
Public holidays are the same as in Metropolitan France, with the addition of Slavery Day, 10 June.

Carnaval (Feb or Mar) Although not as famous as those of its neighbours in Brazil or the Caribbean, Guyane's Carnaval is joyous and interesting. It is principally a Créole event, but there is some participation by all the different cultural groups in the department (best known are the contributions of the Brazilian and Haitian communities). Celebrations begin in Jan, with festivities every weekend, and culminate in colourful parades, music, and dance during the 4 days preceding Ash Wednesday. Each day has its own motif and the costumes are very elaborate. On Sat night, a dance called 'Chez Nana – Au Soleil Levant' is held, for which the women disguise themselves beyond recognition as 'Touloulous', and ask the men to dance. They are not allowed to refuse. On Sun there are parades in downtown Cayenne. Lundi Gras (Fat Monday) is the day to ridicule the institution of marriage, with mock wedding parties featuring men dressed as brides and women as grooms. 'Vaval', the devil and soul of Carnaval, appears on Mardi Gras (Fat Tuesday) with dancers sporting red costumes, horns, tails, pitch-forks, etc. He is burnt that night (in the form of a straw doll) on a large bonfire in the Place des Palmistes. Ash Wednesday is a time of sorrow, with participants in the final parades dressed in black and white.

● **Shopping**
The best buys are handicrafts in wood in the Saramaca village (Kourou) and in the prison at St-Laurent du Maroni and white rum.

● **Weights and measures**
The metric system is in use.

WHERE TO STAY

Details of hotels are given in the text. For information on *Gîtes* and *Chambres chez l'habitant* write to Agence Régionale de Développement du Tourisme et des Loisirs de la Guyane (ARDTLG), 12 rue Lalouette, 97338, Cayenne Cedex, T 30-09-00, Telex 910364 FG; also, for *Gîtes*, Association pour le Tourisme Vert en Guyane, 27 rue Justin Cataye, 97300 Cayenne, T 31-10-11.

FOOD AND DRINK

Most food is imported, except seafood; it is of very high quality but expensive.

GETTING AROUND

AIR TRANSPORT

Internal air services are by Air Guyane. These flights are always heavily booked, so be prepared to wait or write or telephone Air Guyane, address above. There are regular connections with Maripasoula, daily at 0930, 474F; Saül on Mon, Wed and Fri, at 0930, 364F; St-Georges, daily at 0745 and usually one early pm, 30 mins, 350F one-way; Régina, Mon, Wed and Fri at 0745, 165F. Baggage allowance 10 kg; 6.45F per kg excess. No services on Sun. Locals are given preference on internal flights; reservations cannot be made other than at the office in Cayenne, with cash.

LAND TRANSPORT

● **Motoring**
There are no railways, and about 1,000 km of road. The main road, narrow but now paved, runs for 130 km from Pointe Macouris, on the

roadstead of Cayenne, to Iracoubo. Another 117 km takes it to Mana and St-Laurent.

● **Car hire**

Car hire can be a great convenience (there are 15 agencies in Cayenne; those at the airport open only for flight arrivals). All types of car available, from economy to luxury to pick-ups and jeeps. Cheapest rates are US$57 a day, US$385/week. Check insurance details carefully; the excess is very high. Gasoline/petrol costs 5.32F a litre; diesel 3.64F a litre.

● **Bus**

There is a lack of public transport.

● **Hitchhiking**

Hitching is reported to be easy and widespread.

FERRIES

One- to three-ton boats which can be hauled over the rapids are used by the gold-seekers, the forest workers, and the rosewood establishments. There is a twice-a-month shipping service which calls at nearly all the coastal towns of Guyane. Ferries are free. Trips by motor-canoe (*pirogue*) up-river from Cayenne into the jungle can be arranged.

COMMUNICATIONS

● **Language**

French, with officials not usually speaking anything else.

● **Telecommunications**

International calls can be made direct to any country from any phone: dial 19 + country code. Public telephones are widely installed and used. They take phonecards of 50 or 120 units (35F or 80F), which can be bought at tobacconists, bookshops or supermarkets. How to use the phone is displayed in each phone booth in French, English, Italian and Spanish. To call the USA, 1 unit buys 3.6 secs, to EC 2.5 secs; discounts at weekends and

between 1700 and 0700. The system is totally interconnected with the French system. International code for Guyane is 594.

MEDIA

● **Newspapers**

La Presse de la Guyane is the daily paper (circ 1,500). *France-Guyane-Antilles* is a weekly newspaper with a good information page for the tourist.

TOURIST INFORMATION

The French Government tourist offices generally have leaflets on Guyane; good sources of information are **La Maison de La France**, 8 ave de l'Opéra, 75001 Paris, T 42-96-10-23, and **Ministere des Départements et Territoires D'Outre-Mer**, 27 rue Oudinot, 75007 Paris, T 47-83-01-23. The latter publishes a comprehensive directory, *CAP'97*, in six European languages. Two specialist travel agents in Paris are **Havas Voyages** (also in Cayenne, see above), 26 ave de l'Opéra, 75001 Paris, T 40-41-80-00, and **Fleuves de Monde**, 122 rue d'Assac, 75006 Paris, T 42-04-25-92. The Cayenne tourism offices are at 12 rue Lalouette, Cayenne (Tx 910356, T 300900); Délégation Régionale, 10, rue L-Heder, 97307 Cayenne, T 31-84-91; Syndicat d'initiative de Cayenne, Jardin Botanique, PO Box 702, 97338 Cayenne, T 31-29-19; Syndicat d'Initiative Rémire-Montjoly, Mairie de Rémire, 97305 Rémire, T 35-41-10.

ACKNOWLEDGEMENTS

We are most grateful to Rachel Rogers for updating the Guianas section, to Gérald Lorin (Kourou, Guyane) for a most helpful contribution on Suriname and Guyane, to Jerry R A-Kum of NV METS, Paramaribo, and to the travellers listed at the beginning of the book.

The Venezuelan Islands

V ENEZUELA has 2,800 km of coastline on the Caribbean Sea. The country's total area is 912,050 square km, and its population exceeds 20,227,000. It was given its name, 'Little Venice', by the Spanish navigators, who saw in the Indian pile dwellings on Lake Maracaibo a dim reminder of the buildings along Venetian waterways.

When the Spaniards landed in E Venezuela in 1498, in the course of Columbus' third voyage, they found a poor country sparsely populated by Indians who had created no distinctive culture. Four hundred years later it was still poor, almost exclusively agrarian, exporting little, importing less. The miracle year which changed all that was 1914, when oil was discovered near Maracaibo. Today, Venezuela is said to be the richest country in Latin America and is one of the largest producers and exporters of oil in the world.

In the 1980s, the country faced economic difficulties resulting from a combination of falling oil prices and a large external debt. In consequence, the government has reappraised the potential of tourism as one of a number of means of earning foreign exchange. There is still much scope for improving every facet of tourist infrastructure.

Venezuela has 72 island possessions in the Caribbean, of which the largest and the most visited is Isla de Margarita. This island, and two close neighbours, Coche and Cubagua, form the state of Nueva Esparta. Most of the other islands are Federal Dependencies (whose capital is Los Roques) stretching in small groups of keys to the E of Bonaire. Two other sets of islands are incorporated in the national parks of Morrocoy (W of the country's capital, Caracas) and Mochima, E of Caracas.

ISLA DE MARGARITA

Isla de Margarita is in fact one island whose two sections are tenuously linked by the 18 km sandspit which separates the sea from the Restinga lagoon. At its largest, Margarita is about 32 km from N to S and 67 km from E to W. Most of its people live in the developed E part, which has some wooded areas and fertile valleys. The W part, the Peninsula de

Macanao, is hotter and more barren, with scrub, sand dunes and marshes. Wild deer, goats and hares roam the interior, but 4-wheel drive vehicles are needed to penetrate it. The entrance to the Peninsula de Macanao is a pair of hills known as Las Tetas de María Guevara, a national monument covering 1,670 ha.

The climate is exceptionally good, but rain is scant. Water is piped from the mainland. The roads are good, and a bridge connects the two parts. Nueva

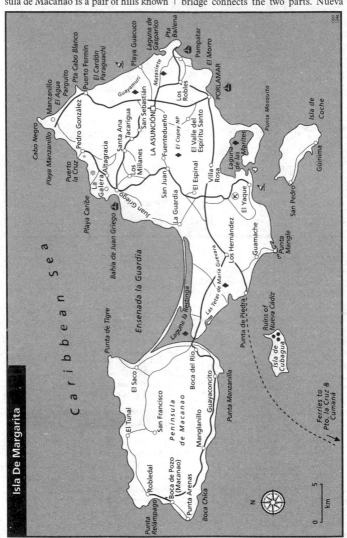

Isla De Margarita

Esparta's population is over 200,000, of whom about 68,000 live in the main city, Porlamar (which is not the capital, that is La Asunción).

HISTORY

Christopher Columbus made landfall on the nearby Paria Peninsula in Aug 1498. Two years later, a settlement had been established at Santiago de Cubagua (later called Nueva Cádiz) to exploit the pearls which grew in its waters. Cubagua became a centre for pearling and for slavery, as the local Indians were used, under appalling duress, to dive into the oyster beds. By 1541, when Santiago was destroyed by an earthquake and tidal wave, the pearl beds had been almost exhausted, but the Greek word for pearl, *margarita*, was retained for the main island of the group.

Margarita, and the nearest town on the mainland, Cumaná, were strongholds of the forces for the independence of South America from Spain. Between 1810 and 1817, the island was the scene of revolts and harsh Spanish reprisals. The liberator Simón Bolívar declared the Third Republic, and was himself declared Commander in Chief of the Liberating Army, at Villa del Norte (now Santa Ana) in 1816. After the war, the name of Nueva Esparta (maintaining the Greek allusion) was conferred in recognition of the bravery of Margarita in the struggle. Subsequent events have been nothing like so heroic, with life revolving around fishing and small agriculture. After a regeneration of the the pearl industry at the end of the 19th century, it has gone into decline, the oyster beds having all but disappeared through disease.

THE ECONOMY

The island has enjoyed a boom since 1983, largely as a result of the fall in the value of the bolívar and the consequent tendency of Venezuelans to spend their holidays at home. Margarita's status as a

Venezuela: fact file

Geographic	
Land area	912,050 sq km
forested	34.0%
pastures	20.2%
cultivated	4.4%
Demographic	
Population (1995)	21,844,000
annual growth rate (1989-94)	2.3%
urban	84.6%
rural	15.4%
density	24.0 per sq km
Religious affiliation	
Roman Catholic	92.1%
Birth rate per 1,000 (1994)	25.7
	(world av 25.0)
Education and Health	
Life expectancy at birth,	
male	70.1 years
female	76.0 years
Infant mortality rate	
per 1,000 live births (1994)	27.7
Physicians (1989)	1 per 576 persons
Hospital beds	1 per 382 persons
Calorie intake as %	
of FAO requirement	106%
Population age 25 and over	
with no formal schooling	23.5%
Literate males (over 15)	93.5%
Literate females (over 15)	91.1%
Economic	
GNP (1993 market prices)	
	US$58,916mn
GNP per capita	US$2,840
Public external debt (1993)	
	US$26,856mn
Tourism receipts (1992)	US$432mn
Inflation (annual av 1989-94)	40.7%
Radio	1 per 2.6 persons
Television	1 per 5.7 persons
Telephone	1 per 10 persons
Employment	
Population economically active (1993)	
	7,546,200
Unemployment rate	6.3%
% of labour force in	
agriculture	9.9
mining and petroleum	0.9
manufacturing	14.3
construction	8.7
Military forces	79,000
Source *Encyclopaedia Britannica*	

duty-free zone also helps. Venezuelan shoppers go in droves for clothing, electronic goods and other consumer items. Gold and gems are good value, but many things are not. There has been extensive building in Porlamar, with new shopping areas and Miami-style hotels going up. A number of beaches are also being developed. The island's popularity means that various packages are on offer, sometimes at good value, especially off-season.

Local industries are fishing and fibre work, such as hammocks and straw hats. Weaving, pottery and sweets are being pushed as handicraft items for the tourists. An exhibition centre has been opened at El Cercado, near Santa Ana, on Calle Principal, near the church.

FLORA AND FAUNA

Despite the property boom and frenetic building on much of the coast and in Porlamar, much of the island has been given over to natural parks. Of these the most striking is the Laguna La Restinga. Launches provide lengthy runs around the mangrove swamps, but they create a lot of wash and noise. The mangroves are fascinating, with shellfish clinging to the roots. The launch will leave you on a shingle and shell beach (don't forget to arrange with your boatman to collect you), and you can rummage for shellfish in the shallows (protection against the sun essential). Flamingoes live in the lagoon.

There are mangroves also in the Laguna de las Marites Natural Monument, W of Porlamar. Other parks are Las Tetas de María Guevara, Cerro el Copey, 7,130 ha, and Cerro Matasiete y Guayamurí, 1,672 ha (both reached from La Asunción). Details of Inparques, the National Parks office, are given in the **Information for travellers**.

By boat from Porlamar you can go to the Isla de los Pájaros, or Morro Blanco, for both bird-spotting and underwater fishing. In Boca del Río there is a Museum of the Sea.

BEACHES AND WATERSPORTS

Apart from the shopping, what attracts the holidaymakers from Venezuela and abroad are the beaches: long white stretches of sand bordered by palms, but rather hot, with little shade (sunscreen essential). Topless bathing is not seen, but the tanga (*hilo dental* – dental floss) is fairly common.

In Porlamar, the main beach suffers from its popularity: calm shallow water, pedalos for hire, windsurf classes; but that by the *Bella Vista*, although crowded with foreign tourists, is kept clean. Playa Morena is a long, barren strip of sand serving the expanding hotel zone to the E of the city (renamed Playa Caracola). For a more Venezuelan atmosphere go NE to Pampatar, which is set around a bay favoured by foreign yachtsmen as a summer anchorage; jet skis for hire on a clean and pretty beach. A scale model of Columbus' *Santa María* is used for taking tourists on trips. A fishing boat can be hired for US$12 for 2½ hrs, 4-6 passengers; shop around for best price, good fun and fishing.

The beaches on the eastern side are divided into ocean and calm beaches, according to their location in relation to the open sea. The former tend to be rougher (good surfing and windsurfing) and colder. Water is uniformly clear and unpolluted. It is still possible, even in high season, to find practically deserted beaches. Restaurants, *churuatas* (bars built like Indian huts), sunshades and deckchairs are becoming widespread. (Hire charges are about US$1.50 per item.)

FESTIVALS

6-13 Jan at Altagracia; 20-27 Jan at Tacarigua (San Sebastian); 16-26 Mar at Paraguachí (*Feria de San José*); 3-10 May at Los Robles; 24-30 May at La Guardia; 6 June at Tacarigua (Sagrado Corazón de Jesús); 25-26 July at Santa Ana; 27 July at Punta de Piedra; 31 July (Batalla de Matasiete) and 14-15 Aug (Asunción de la Virgen) at La Asunción; 30 Aug-8 Sept at Villa Rosa; 8-15 Sept at El Valle; 11-12 (Fiesta del Virgen del Pilar) and 28 Oct (San Juan Tadeo) at Los Robles; 4-11 Nov at Boca del Río, 4-30 Nov at Boca del Pozo; 5-6 Dec at Porlamar; 15 Dec at San Francisco de Macanao; 27 Dec-3 Jan at Juan Griego. See map for locations.

PORLAMAR

Most of the hotels are at **Porlamar**, 20 km from the airport and about 28 km from **Punta de Piedra**, where most of the ferries dock. It has a magnificent cathedral. At Igualdad y Díaz is the Museo de Arte Francisco Narváez. The main, and most expensive, shopping area is Avenida Santiago Mariño; better bargains and a wider range of shops are to be found on Gómez and Guevara. The centre of the city is crowded with cars and shoppers, while to the E there is continuing, apparently chaotic development of big holiday hotels and condominiums, separated by vast areas of waste ground and construction sites. Costa Azul is the main *urbanización*, served by a long strip of featureless sand known as Playa Moreno. At night everything closes by 2300; women alone should avoid the centre after dark. Porlamar has many casinos, all of which lack legal status. Note that in Porlamar there is a Calle Mariño and an Avenida Santiago Mariño in the centre.

Ferries go to the Isla de Coche (11 km by 6), which has over 5,000 inhabitants and one of the richest salt mines in the country. They also go, on hire only, to Isla de Cubagua, which is totally deserted, but you can visit the ruins of Nueva Cádiz (which have been excavated).

EXCURSIONS

The capital, **la asunción** (*pop* 16,660), is a few km inland from Porlamar. It has several colonial buildings, a cathedral, and the fort of Santa Rosa, with a famous bottle dungeon (open Mon 0800-1500, other days 0800-1800). There is a museum in the Casa Capitular, and a local market, good for handicrafts. On Plaza Bolívar, as well as the statue of Simón Bolívar, there is a statue of Luisa Cáceres de Arismendi, heroine of the Liberation and second wife of Gen Arismendi. Nearby are the Cerro Matasiete historical site, where the defeat of the Spanish on 31 July 1817 led to their evacuation of the island, and the Félix Gómez look out in the Sierra Copuy.

Between La Asunción and Porlamar are the Parque Francisco Fajardo, beside the Universidad de Oriente, and **El Valle del Espíritu Santo**. Here is the church of the Virgen del Valle, a picturesque building with twin towers, painted white and pink. The Madonna is richly dressed (one dress has pearls, the other diamonds); the adjoining museum opens at 1400, it displays costumes and presents for the Virgin, including the "milagro de la pierna de perla", a leg-shaped pearl. A pilgrimage is held in early September. Proper dress is requested to enter the church.

Throughout the island, the churches are attractive: fairly small, with baroque towers and adornments and, in many cases, painted pink.

Pampatar (*pop* 10,590) has the island's largest fort, San Carlos Borromeo, and the smaller La Caranta, where the cannon show signs of having been spiked. Visit also the church of Cristo del Buen Viaje, the Library/Museum and the customs house (Aduana, now the offices of Fondene, the local development agency, can be visited during office hours, helpful and friendly tourist office on 1st floor, good maps and leaflets, open Mon-Fri 0800-1200, 1300-1630, T 095-622494). New hotels are being put up along this stretch. There is an amusement park to the SW of Pampatar, called Isla Aventura, with ferris wheel, roller coaster, water slide, dodgems etc, open Fri and Sat, 1800-2400, Sun, 1700-2400, and more frequently in peak holiday season. Entrance in peak season is US$5 adults, US$3.35 children, inc all rides; in low

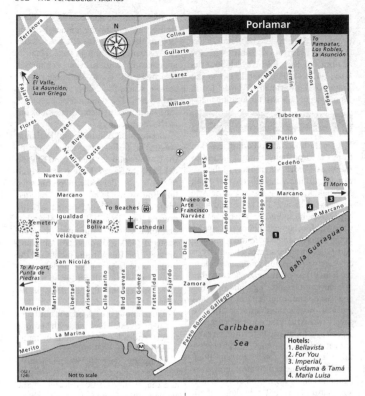

Porlamar

To Pampatar, Los Robles, La Asunción

To El Valle, La Asunción, Juan Griego

Terranova
Colina
Guilarte
Larez
Milano
Fajardo
Flores
Paez
Av Rivas
Oeste
Av Miranda
Nueva
Marcano
Igualdad
Cemetery
Meneses
Velázquez
San Nicolás
To Airport, Punta de Piedras
Maneiro
Martinez
Libertad
Arismendi
Calle Mariño
Blvd Guevara
Blvd Gómez
Fraternidad
Calle Fajardo
La Marina
Merito

Av 4 de Mayo
Fermín
Campos
Ortega
Tubores
Patiño
Cedeño
San Rafael
Amador Hernández
Narváez
Av Santiago Mariño
Marcano
To El Morro
P. Marcano
Plaza Bolívar
Cathedral
Museo de Arte Francisco Narváez
To Beaches
Díaz
Zamora
Paseo Rómulo Gallegos
Bahía Guaraguao

Caribbean Sea

Hotels:
1. Bellavista
2. For You
3. Imperial, Evdama & Tamá
4. María Luisa

Not to scale

season entrance is US$0.50 and each ride US$0.30-0.60.

On the eastern coast are **Playa Guacuco**, reached from La Asunción by a road through the Guayamurí reserve: a lot of surf, fairly shallow, palm trees, restaurant and parking lot; excellent horseriding here or up into the hills, US$30 for 2 hrs, contact Harry Padrón at the ranch in Agua de Vaca, or phone travel agent on 611311. Liquor shop at La Sabana sells ice by the bucket, cheap, 1 km before the beach. Parguito: long and open, best for surfing; Paraguachí: some *churuatas*.

Playa El Agua 45 mins by bus from Porlamar (US$0.45) is 4 km of stone-free white sand with many *kioskos*, which

have palm-leaf shade areas. 2 sun chairs under one of these cost US$2-3 (umbrella US$1 extra). The sea is very rough for children, but fairly shallow (beware the cross current when you are about waist deep, it gets very strong and can quickly carry you out to sea). This is the most popular beach on the island and at Venezuelan holiday times it is overcrowded. At other times it is ideal for sunbathing and walking; the fashionable part is at the southern end; the northern end is popular with younger people, is less touristy, has fewer facilities, and less shade. It is possible to see the island by Ultralight from here at weekends. Contact Omar Contreras, T 095-617632 or José-Antonio Fernández 095-623519, English spoken,

US$35 per flight. (Also possible from the old airport at Porlamar.)

Manzanillo (*pop* 2,000): water gets deep rather suddenly, fishing huts, fish sold on beach, apartments, expensive restaurant, Playa Escondida at the far end; **Puerto Fermín**/El Tirano (Lope de Aguirre, the infamous conquistador, landed here in 1561 on his flight from Peru), El Caserío handicrafts museum is nearby; Punta Cabo Blanco: attractive limestone outcrop; **El Cardón**.

The coast road is interesting, with glimpses of the sea and beaches to one side, inland vistas on the other. There are a number of clifftop look-out points. The road improves radically beyond Manzanillo, winding from one beach to the next. Playa Puerto la Cruz adjoins **Pedro González** (*pop* 3,700), with a broad sweeping beach, running from a promontory (easy to climb) to scrub and brush that reach down almost to the water's edge (ask for Antonietta Luciani at *Restaurant Pedrogonzález*, she has an apartment to rent, US$40 per day, sleeps 6, well-equipped, rec as is her restaurant). The next bay is accessible by scrambling over rocks (major building here). There are a lot of pelicans and sea urchins (harmless).

Further W is **Juan Griego** bay and town (pop 8,300), a small, sleepy town whose picturesque bay is full of fishing boats, drawn up on the narrow beach or moored offshore. The little fort of La Galera is on a promontory at the northern side, beyond which is a bay of the same name with a narrow strip of beach, more fishing boats and many seafront restaurants. Playas Caribe (the best deserted beach) and Galera are less spoilt. (**D** *Posada del Sol*, bedroom, bath, kitchen, sitting area, clean, fan, fridge.)

South of Juan Griego, the road goes inland to San Juan Bautista (a pleasant colonial town ringed by hills; *por puesto* from Juan Griego), then to Punta de Piedra, the ferry dock, see below (a pleasant stretch through cultivated land and farms at regular intervals; *por puesto*

Juan Griego to ferry). Due S of San Juan is El Yaque, near the airport and the mouth of the Laguna de las Marites. This is said to be the best place for windsurfing. Surf boards can be hired at the *Club El Mistral*, good service, very helpful and friendly, ½ day costs US$30. It is being rapidly developed with small hotels, but it suffers from aircraft noise and lacks public transport (taxi from Porlamar, US$5). The hinterland around El Yaque is very bleak.

Near San Juan is Fuentedueño park which has special walks. A branch goes NW to La Guardia at the eastern end of La Restinga. The dyke of broken sea-shells stretches to the Peninsula de Macanao: on its right a spotlessly clean beach, on its left the lagoon. At the far end are many little restaurants and a cluster of fishermen's huts with landing stages from which the launches make trips into the labyrinth of canals in the lagoon (US$14 per boat taking 5 passengers; bus from Porlamar harbourfront US$1, ask driver to drop you off).

The **Peninsula de Macanao** is quite underdeveloped, although it is hardly an untouched paradise. Construction companies are extracting large amounts of ballast for the building boom in Porlamar, while urban waste is simply being dumped in large quantities along the roadside. Some of the beaches, however, are highly regarded: Manzanilla, Guayaconcito, Boca de Pozo, Macanao, Punta Arenas and Manglanillo. Harbour at Chacachacare.

Island Information – Isla de Margarita
● **Accommodation**

Price guide

L1	over US$200	L2	US$151-200
L3	US$101-150	A1	US$81-100
A2	US$61-80	A3	US$46-60
B	US$31-45	C	US$21-30
D	US$12-20	E	US$7-11
F	US$4-6	G	up to US$3

Hotels La Asunción B-C *Ciudad Colonial*, C La Margarita, upmarket, looks nice; **E** pp *de* *la Asunción*, C Unión, 2 blocks from Plaza Bolívar, with bath, a/c, TV, fridge (rooms with balcony cost more but face noisy road, rooms without window cost less).

Pampatar A2 pp *Flamingo Beach*, T (095) 624822, F 620271, 5-star, all-inclusive, food, drinks, entertainment, service, taxes, casino, good value; *Hippocampus Beach*, next door, T 623090, F 623510, 4-star, package holidays, gaudy; **D** *Residencial Don Juan*, with bath and fan; apartments sleeping 6 are available, bargain over price; beach restaurant *Antonio's*, rec; also *Trimar*, good value. **A1** *Lagunamar*, a few km N of Pampatar, T 620711, F 621445, occupies a vast spread of flat coastland, beach, 9 pools and 6 restaurants. *Tamarindo Guaycuco Playa*, is a new 4-star hotel at the northern end of Playa Guacuco in a rustic Mediterranean style, T/F 422727. **F** pp guesthouse of David Hart (Windward Lines agent), Av Principal 12, T 095-623527, next to supermarket, with bath, fan, welcoming, dark rooms, mosquitoes.

Porlamar L3-A1 *Hilton* (+13% tax), T (095) 624111, F 620810, sailing dinghies for hire; other top class establishments; **A1** *Bella Vista*, Av Santiago, T 617222, F 612557, swimming pool, beach; **A2** *Dynasty*, T 621252, F 625101, opp *Hilton*, nice restaurant, pool; **A3** *Stauffer*, T 613222, F 618708, large rooms, excellent service and restaurant, bar on roof, casino being added; **A3-B** *Marbella Mar*, Av Principal y Calle Chipichipi, clean rooms, friendly, especially with children, free bus service to the beach, highly rec. **B** *Aguila Inn*, Narváez, 500m N of centre, T 616322, F 616909, clean, swimming pool, restaurant, rec; **B** *Colibrí*, Av Santiago Mariño, T 616346, new rooms, **D** in older rooms, both with bath, a/c, TV, rec; **B** *Imperial*, Av Raúl Leoni, Vía El Morro, T 095-616420, F 615056, best rooms in front have balcony, clean, comfortable, safe, a/c, good showers, triple rooms available, English spoken, rec; **B** *La Perla*, Calle Los Pinos, pool, bar, restaurant, TV, laundry, shops in lobby inc travel agency Latsa, rec; **B** *Venus*, T (095) 23722, Calle Milano y San Rafael, clean, a/c, safe; **C** *Contemporáneo*, Calle Mariño entre Igualdad y Velásquez, modern, a/c, TV, clean, bar, restaurant; **C** *Italia*, San Nicolás, with bath, cold water, a/c, clean, safe, rec, but district is a bit rough; **D** *Marocco*, Mariño between Zamora y San Nicolás, a/c, TV, fridge, bath, but dark, windowless rooms; **D** *Porlamar*, Igualdad y Fajardo, clean, good restaurant and video bar La Punta, a/c or fan,

hot water, friendly; **E** *Brasilia*, San Nicolás, quiet, clean, nice new rooms at back; nearby **E** *Boston*, very clean, fan, private bath; **E** *Domino*, La Libertad 7-40, with fan or a/c, basic, friendly; **E** *España*, Mariño 6-35, T 095-612479, cold shower, very clean, friendly, good breakfast, fan, highly rec; **E** *La Viña*, La Marina, No 14-24, T 635723, very friendly, clean, bath, a/c, bar, restaurant, laundry; **E** *Malecón*, Marina y Arismendi, T 635723, seaview from front rooms, the Mexican owner, Luis and his wife are very helpful and generous, rec; **E** *Palermo*, Calle Igualdad, opp cathedral, friendly, clean, best rooms on top floor with views of plaza; **E** *Robaldar*, Igualdad, near Libertad, shower, a/c, TV, friendly, rec. Many others round Plaza Bolívar (eg **F** *San Miguel*, clean, good value). Cheaper places on Maneiro; **E** *Tamá*, next to *Imperial*, gringo place with basic rooms, OK, excellent restaurant and atmosphere, bar is German-run, lots of languages spoken; **E** *Torino*, Mariño on right coming from Plaza Bolívar between Zamora and Maneiro, T 610734, with bath, a/c, TV, friendly.

Playa El Agua C *Residencias Miramar*, Av 31 de Julio-Carretera Manzanillo, esq calle Miragua, 3 mins from beach, 1 min from supermarket, family-run, self-catering apartments, comfortable, barbecue, clean, rec; **B** the small *Casa Trudel*, T/F 589-548735, 4 rooms with bath, bed and breakfast, homely atmosphere, with bath (Dutch/Canadian owners), no young children, evening food service, barbecue once a week, 5-min walk from beach; **B** *Trudel's Garden Vacation Home*, Calle Miragua, T/F 095-48735, 6 large, 2-bedroom houses set in a beautiful garden, 200m from beach, fresh towels daily, fully-equiped kitchens, for reservations by post write to Dan and Trudy O'Brien, Apdo 106, Isla Margarita, 6301, Parlamar, Venezuela. **E** *Hostería El Agua*, Av 31 de Julio vía Manzanillo, T 48935, contact Sarah Studer, English, French, German and Italian spoken, clean bathroom, good beds, fan, fridge, laundry facilities, 4 mins walk from beach; **B** *Pelican Village*, northern end, small group of bungalows, satellite TV, pool, restaurant, bar, German run, quiet. An unnamed chalet park next to the *Miragua Club Resort*, self-catering, all facilities, very welcoming, highly rec (no price but "usually cheaper than *Miramar*").

El Cardón B *Hotel Karibek*, overlooks the sea, wonderful view, quiet rooms, extremely clean, balcony, bath, fan, swimming pool, bar and restaurant adjacent, breakfast provided, evening meals not great but there are a couple of good restaurants down on the beach, easy taxi ride to other beaches, rec; **C** *Pahayda Vilas*, nice apartments, large rooms, 2 baths for 4 people, sign at main road; 100m further on towards Playa Azul, beach house with rooms to let and German-owned restaurant, good food. Between Manzanillo and Pedro González, each on its own stretch of beach, are two new luxury hotels. **A1** *Isla Bonita*, T (095) 657111, F 657211, Playa Puerto Cruz, a monstrous edifice of reflective glass, 18-hole golf course, business centre, posh restaurants; **A3** *Dunes*, Playa Puerto Cruz, T 631333, F 632910, a more modest option, all-inclusive resort of low rise, tiled buildings in pinks and creams, activities, sports, fun and games.

Juan Griego B *El Yare*, T 55835, one block from beach, some suites with kitchen, owner speaks English, highly rec; *Hotel La Galera*, rec; **D-E** *Aparthotel y Res El Apureno*, C La Marina y C El Fuerte, T 530901, friendly, English speaking manager, 2-bedroom apartments with bath, hot water, a/c, but no utensils or towels (because of theft); **D** *Gran Sol*, La Marina, entrance in shopping arcade, T 55736, a/c, bath, TV; **E** *Residencia Carmencita*, Calle Guevara 20, T 55561, a/c, private bath, rec; **E** *Fortín*, a/c, cold water, opp beach, most rooms have good views, good restaurant and tables on the beach; **E** *La Posada de Clary*, C Los Mártires, T 530037, rec; several others; also cabins for 5 with cooking facilities US$20.

San Juan Bautista E apartments of Rosa Hernández, C La Vega, on left leaving town, past cemetery, fan, a/c, cold water.

El Yaque C *California*, T (014) 951907, F 950908, 46 rooms, small pool; *Casarita*, T (016) 950290 (cellular number), resort, pleasant building in neo-colonial style, bed and breakfast, 400m from beach.

● **Places to eat**
La Gran Pirámide, Calle Malave y JM Patiño, superb food, very good service, cocktails worth trying, very good value, highly rec; *Doña Martha*, Velázquez near Hernández, Colombian food, good, inexpensive; *El Punto Criollo*, Igualdad near *Hotel Porlamar*, good; *El Peñero*, Vía El Morro, service slow but good food; *Vecchia Marina*, Vía El Morro, good but more expensive; *Bahía* bar-restaurant, Av Raúl Leoni y Vía El Morro, excellent value, live music;

excellent pizzas at *París Croissant* on Blvd Santiago Mariño; *Los 3 Delfines*, Cedeño 26-9, seafood, rec; *Guanaguanare*, pedestrian boulevard by sea, good food and service, reasonable prices. *La Isla*, Mariño y Cedeño, 8 fast food counters ranging from hamburgers to sausages from around the world. *Dino's Grill*, Igualdad y Martínez, T 642366, open 0700-1400, buffet lunch, indoor/outdoor seating, grill, homemade sausages, wood-fired pizza oven, cheap, friendly, good service, rec; *Bella China*, Igualdad, good; *La Tapa Tasca*, Marcano entre Narváez y Mariño, good seafood and atmosphere, expensive; *La Pilarica*, Ortega y Marcano, good service; *Pizzería Pida Pasta II*, *Da Giovanni*, 4 de Mayo near Calle Carnevali, popular.

Playa El Agua: *Restaurant El Paradiso*, southern end, rents out cabins, US$12, small but comfortable; *Kiosko El Agua*, helpful, English spoken; *Posada Shangri-Lá*, rec, *Casa Vieja*, seafood, *La Dorada*, French owned by Gérard and Hilda, with good beach view, rec as good value. Since the opening of the large *Playa El Agua Beach Resort* (L2) and the *Miragua Club Resort* (A3), many beach restaurants stay open till 2200. Rec are *Moisés* (Venezuelan-owned), *Sueño Tropical*, Italian owned, also own *Jardín Tropical* further down beach, spacious, serving pasta, traditional seafood dishes; *Tinajón del Agua* (on main road near beach entrance, small, popular, good).

Juan Griego *Restaurant Mi Isla* is rec, also the Lebanese restaurant on the beach; *Viña del Mar*, opp *Hotel Fortín*, a/c, attractive, excellent food; *Juan Griego Steak House*, same building as *Hotel El Yare*, good value, rec; also rec, *El Buho*; *Viejo Muelle*, next door, good restaurant, live music, outside beach bar.

● **Shopping**
Besides all duty-free shops, *Del Bellorín*, Cedeño, near Santiago Mariño, is good for handicrafts. Good selection of jewellery at *Sonia Gems*, on Cedeño; *Ivan Joyería* and *Inter Gold*, both on 4 de Mayo (latter is between *Ivan* and *Hotel Flamingo*); many other places on the main street are overpriced. When purchasing jewellery, bargain hard, don't pay by credit card (surcharges are imposed), get a detailed guarantee of the item. Designer clothes are cheap in many places, especially on Blvd Guevara, Blvd Gómez, Calles Igualdad and Velázquez; cosmetics and perfumes also good value.

● Entertainment

Mosquito Coast Club, behind *Hotel Bella Vista*, disco with genuine Venezuelan feel, good *merengue* and rock music, bar outside; also does excellent Mexican meals (beware of overcharging on simple items like water). Discothèque for singles, *Village Club*, Av Santiago Mariño, rec for good music with a variety of styles but expensive drinks, cover charge. *Doce 34*, Av 4 de Mayo, entrance US$3, 2 dance floors, highly rec. Nightlife is generally good, but at European prices.

● Exchange

Banco Mercantil for changing TCs; Banco Consolidado, Guevara y San Nicolás; banks generally slow with poor rates; best at Banco Construcción, Guevara or at *Hotel Contemporáneo* next to Banco Consolidado. *Casa de cambio* at Igualdad y Av Santiago Mariño; also *Cambio La Precisa*, Maneiro entre Mariño y Blvd Guevara, good rates. Amex office closed on Mon. Banks are open 0830-1130, 1400-1630. There are often long queues. Most shops accept credit cards.

● Tourist Information

Fondene the group for the development of Nueva Esparta, runs tourist information offices at the airport (see above) and on the first floor of the restored Aduana (customs) building on the little square at Pampatar (see under Pampatar). **NB** Fondene is to be restructured, so these details may alter. An outspoken and well-informed English-language newspaper, *Mira*, is published on the island; the editor/publisher acts also as an inexpensive tour guide; Av Santiago Mariño, Ed Carcaleo Suites, Apartamento 2-A, Porlamar (T 095-61-3351). The best map is available from Corpoven.

● Travel Agents

Supertours, Calle Larez, Quinta Thaid, T 61-8781, F 61-7061, tours of the island and elsewhere; *Zuluoga Tours*, Calle San Nicolás entre Arismendi y Mariño No 16-40, helpful. Ask travel agents about excursions on the sailing catamaran, *Catatumbo*, rec.

● Transport

Air General Santiago Mariño, between Porlamar and Punta de Piedra; comfortable and modern, has the international and national terminals at either end. Two tourist desks at the former extremity, one at the latter. Bus from Plaza Bolívar, US$0.70, taxi US$7. There are up to 12 flights a day from **Caracas**, with Avensa, Servivensa, Viasa, Zuliana and Aserca, 50 mins flight; tickets are much cheaper if purchased

in Venezuela in local currency. Reservations made from outside Venezuela are not always honoured. Daily Servivensa flight to **Ciudad Guyana**, also Aserca. Daily flights from **Cumaná**, **Carúpano**, Barcelona, Valencia. Aerotuy flies Parlamar-Canaima and back daily. Once a week with Viasa from Frankfurt, Rome, Milan, twice a week from Miami. Viasa, Av 4 de Mayo, Edif Banco Royal, Porlamar (T 32273, airport 691137); Avensa on Calle Fajardo, Porlamar, T 617111, airport 691021.

Sea Ferries (very busy at weekends and Mon; in good condition, punctual): from **Puerto La Cruz**, to Margarita (**Punta de Piedra**): Conferries, Los Cocos terminal, T 677221, and *Meliá Hotel*, Pto La Cruz, T 653001, to Margarita, 4 a day between 0700 and 2400 each way (extras at 0400 and 1600 at busy times), 4 hrs, passengers US$8-9 return 1st class, US$4-5 2nd (in enclosed middle deck with limited views), children and pensioners half price, cars, US$16-17. From **Cumaná**, Conferry Terminal, Cumaná Puerto Sucre, T 311462, ferries at 0700 and 1600 to Margarita, returning 1100 and 2000, US$4 one way for passengers. A ferry from Punta de Piedra to Coche sails Mon-Fri, 1600, returns 1730, Sat and Sun, 0800 and 1730, returns 0530 and 1730.

A ferry sails from Mercado Viejo to Chacopata on the mainland at 1000 and 1200, also takes cars.

Windward Lines (Global Steamship Agencies Ltd, Mariner's Club, Wrightson Road, PO Box 966, Port of Spain, Trinidad, T 809-624-2279) sails to Pampatar, Isla Margarita every other week (Tues) from Trinidad, leaving again on Wed at 2300, arriving in Port of Spain on Thur and continuing to St Vincent, Barbados and St Lucia. Return fares: from Trinidad US$70 (a return ticket satisfies onward ticket requirements for Trinidad), St Lucia, St Vincent or Barbados US$155. TCs can be changed on board at good rates. Contact David Hart, Windward Lines agent, Calle José María Vargas, frente Monederos, Pampatar, T 623527, efficient, speaks English, ensure immigration/customs goes smoothly.

By Road Several bus companies in Caracas sell through tickets from Caracas to Porlamar, arriving about midday. Buses return from Porlamar from terminal at Centro Comercial Bella Vista, at bottom end of Calle San Rafael. By car from Caracas to the ferry terminal, it takes about 4 hrs.

NB Aug and Sept are the vacation months when flights and hotels are fully booked.

● **Public Transport**

Por Puestos serve most of the island, leaving mainly from the corners of Plaza Bolívar in Porlamar. Fares: to Punta de Piedra (from 4 blocks from Plaza Bolívar, towards sea-front), US$0.50, to the ferry terminal US$0.70; to La Asunción, US$0.25, from Calle Fajardo, half a block from Igualdad; to Pampatar, US$0.20; to La Restinga (from La Marina y Mariño), US$0.70, El Agua (from corner of Guevara and Marcano), US$0.40; Juan Griego, US$0.40. **Taxi** fares are published by the magazine *Mira* but are not uniformly applied by drivers. If you want to hire a taxi for a day you will be charged US$7-10 per hr. Always establish the fare before you get in the car. There is a 30% surcharge after 2100.

● **Car Hire**

An economic proposition for any number above one and a good way of getting around the island, from US$16 to US$50 per day depending on the make of car. To the cheapest rate add US$0.20-0.50/km and US$3.25-9.70 for each hour after the first day. With 250 km free rates are from US$32 to US$100, plus US$6.45-19.50 for each extra hour over the first day (Hertz rates). Several offices at the airport (*Beach* have been rec as cheap and reliable) also at *Hotel Bella Vista* (inc Hertz, reliable, Avis, and Lizmar, cheapest, but watch insurance excess), others on Av Santiago Mariño. In all cases check the brakes. Scooters can also be hired from, among others, Maruba Motor Rentals, La Mariña (English spoken, good maps, highly rec, US$16 bike for 2, US$13 bike for 1). Motor cycles may not be ridden between 2000 and 0500; although this (apparently) should not apply to tourists, police officers have been known to confiscate tourists' machines and impose heavy fines. **NB** remember to keep an eye on the fuel gauge; there are service stations in towns, but a/c is heavy on fuel. Always check the gauge on the fuel pump carefully: overcharging is common.

Driving on Isla Margarita: the roads are generally good and most are paved. Sign posts are often poorly-positioned (behind bushes, round corners), which adds to the nighttime hazard of vehicles with badly adjusted lights. It is best not to drive outside Porlamar after dark. Also beware of robbery of hired vehicles, several incidents reported. Check conditions and terms of hire very carefully for your liability.

ISLAS LOS ROQUES

Islas Los Roques lie 150 km due N of Caracas; the atoll, of about 340 islets and reefs, constitutes one of Venezuela's loveliest National Parks (225, 241 ha). There are long stretches of white beaches (little shade), miles of coral reef with crystal-clear water ideal for snorkelling (best at Francisqui – Cayo Francés – and Cayo Agua) and many bird nesting sites (eg the huge gull colonies on Francisqui and the pelicans, boobies and frigates on Selenqui). Small lizards, chameleons and iguanas, and cactus vegetation on some islets also add to the atoll's variety. Many of the islands' names are contractions of earlier names: eg 'Sarky' comes from Sister Key, 'Dos Mosquices' from Domus Key, where there are sea turtles and a Marine Biology Centre researching the coral reef and its ecology. For more information write to La Fundación Científica Los Roques, Apartado No 1, Av Carmelitas, Caracas 1010, T 32-6771.

Gran Roque is the main and only inhabited island; here flights land near the scattered fishing village (*pop* 900) which is Park Headquarters; average temp 27°C with coolish nights. Nordisqui is very isolated while Madrisqui has many summer houses. Cayo Francés is two islands joined by a sandspit, with calm lagoon waters on the S and rolling surf on the N; May is nesting time at the gull colonies here. For solitude, Los Roques are a 'must' midweek: Venezuelans swarm here on long weekends and at school holidays.

You can negotiate with local fishermen for transport to other islands: you will need to take your own tent, food and (especially) water.

Watersports

Eola is a yacht, fully equipped, with cabins, chartered for US$100 per day, all inclusive, highly recommended as a worthwhile way of getting some shade on the treeless beaches. Run by Italians Gianni and Jaqueline, book direct by phone, T (99) 216735. *Sesto Continente Dive Resort*, on the edge of the village, ask for Saul and Marianne, very kind people, two dives cost US$60, the boat is comfortable, rec.

Island Information – Los Roques
● **Accommodation**

Gran Roque Private accommodation is available, eg small *pensión* run by Sra Carmen Zambrano; *Posada Vora La Mar*, run by Marta Agusti, US$30 full board, T Caracas 238-5408; **C** *Posada Margot*, very clean, breakfast and dinner included, often has water and electricity problems; rooms rented by Maria, fiancée of Silvestre, cheap and friendly with excellent seafood, and others.

Cayo Francés has an abandoned house and enough vegetation to provide shaded hammock sites, and accommodation at US$30 pp, full board inc drinks, good food, friendly staff, nice beach, snorkelling gear, water and light 24 hrs, bargaining possible if you stay for several days. The *Pelicano Club* has accommodation and organizes excursions, boat trips, dives, recommended. Warning to would-be campers: leave nothing out on the ground, the crabs eat everything!

Tiny but irritating biting insects in the calmer months can make camping miserable. Marta Agusti at *Posada Vora La Mar* can put you in touch with fisherman Andrés Ibarra, who can negotiate for transport to other islands; reasonable prices. If you are looking for solitude, ask Andrés to take you to Nordisqui or Isla Larga.

● **Transport**

To get to Los Roques, take a flight with Chapi Air to Gran Roque from Maiquetía at 0800, returning at 1600, US$100. Aereotuy (T 02-262-1966/71-6231) fly to Gran Roque from Maiquetía 3 times a day: 3-day package (return flight, accommodation, meals, drinks, catamaran excursion with snorkelling and diving equipment), US$400 pp, 1 and 2-day packages available.

OTHER VENEZUELAN ISLANDS

Also worth mentioning are the **Archipelago of Las Aves**, W of Los Roques, where fishing and diving are good. **La Tortuga** is Venezuela's second largest island, lying W of Margarita. Further out are **La Blanquilla** and **La Orchila**, both with coral reefs. About 500 km N of Margarita, at the same latitude as Dominica, is **Isla de Aves**, 65 sq km of seabirds (sooty and brown noddy tern, frigate birds, gulls) surrounded by crystal clear water. The island is also a nesting site of the endangered green turtle. There is a Venezuelan coast guard station. For a full description of the island see *Audubon*, the magazine of the US National Audubon Society, Jan 1991, pages 72-81.

Much closer to the mainland are two areas of reefs and islands which have been designated national parks. There is no way to get to them other than by spending time in Venezuela itself.

PARQUE NACIONAL MORROCOY

The **National Park of Morrocoy** comprises hundreds of coral reefs, palm-studded islets, small cosy beaches and calm water for water-skiing, snorkelling, and skin-diving. The Park is reached from Tucacas in the S and Chichiriviche in the N. With appropriate footwear it is possible to walk between some of the islands. The largest, cleanest and most popular of the islands is **Cayo Sombrero** (very busy at weekends); even so it has some deserted beaches, with trees to sling a hammock. **Playuela** is beautiful and better for snorkelling (beware of mosquitoes in the mangrove swamps), while **Playa del Sol** has no good beach and no palm trees. **Bocaseca** is more exposed to the open sea than other islands and thus has fewer mosquitoes. **Cayo Borracho** is one of the nicest islands.

Adjoining the park to the N is a vast nesting area for scarlet ibis, flamingoes and herons, the **Cuare Wildlife Sanctuary**. Most of the flamingoes are in and around the estuary next to Chichiriviche, which is too shallow for boats but you can walk there or take a taxi. Birds are best watched early morning or late afternoon.

● **Camping** You may camp on the islands, but there are no facilities or fresh water (three islands have beach restaurants serving simple fish dishes, clean, good). At weekends it is very crowded and, at holiday seasons, litter-strewn. You may require a permit from Inparques (National Parks). Take precautions against rats.

ACCESS From Tucacas: boats are for hire: US$10-20 return to Cayo Sombrero, per boat, US$5.25 to nearer islands; ticket office to the left of the car entrance to the Park, they will pick you up for the return journey; Orlando is reliable and one of the cheaper boatmen, Pepe has been recommended. **From Chichiriviche**: prices posted onboard or on the jetty are per boat, not pp, and vary according to distance, starting at about US$10 (take a snorkel, no hire facilities; snorkel and mask can be bought from a shop near *Hotel Capri*). All day cruises, stopping at 3 islands, cost US$50/boat. Prices are fixed, but bargaining may be possible on Paseo por la Bahía.

TUCACAS

Tucacas (*pop* 15,100) is a hot, busy, dirty and expensive town, 30 mins from Morón, with lots of new building in progress, where bananas and other fruit are loaded for Curaçao and Aruba.

● **Accommodation** The only accommodation within the park is **A1** pp *Villa Mangrovia* on the Lizardo Spit between Tucacas and Chichiriviche, 3 rooms, good service, reservations through Last Frontiers, UK, T 01844-208405. **B** *Hotel Manaure-Tucacas*, Av Silva, a/c, hot water, clean, good restaurant. **D** *La Suerte* on main street, very clean, fan, with small shop. **E** *Carlos*, basic, with fan, kitchen and laundry facilities, cheap and cheerful, helpful, friendly, rec, organizes boat trips to islands; **E** *Palma*, without shower, fan, owner organizes boat trips. Cheap accommodation is difficult to find, especially in high season and at weekends, hotels are generally more expensive than elsewhere in Venezuela.

Camping: gas available in Tucacas or Puerto Cabello for camping in the Park.

● **Places to eat** *Restaurant Fruti Mar*, very good; *Cervezería Tito*, good food; many good bakeries.

● **Banks & money changers** Banco Unión for exchange, Visa card and TCs accepted.

● **Sports Diving**: scuba diving equipment can be hired from nr the harbour, but the diving is reported not very interesting. Try American-owned *Submatur*, C Ayacucho 6, T 042-84082, 2 dives, lunch and gear US$65, for scuba diving and trips. *Mike Osbourne's* dive shop, situated on the left hand of the street that leads into Morrocoy National Park, his shop was the first ever opened in Venezuela and you can buy or rent what you need for snorkelling, he and his staff are very helpful and will tell you where it is best to go, diving courses are also available, André Nahon rec.

Bicycles: can be hired in town.

● **Tour companies & travel agents** *Guili*, C Sucre y C Silva, No 1, T 84661, organizes trips to any of the islands; Freddy speaks English, French and Spanish, Valentine speaks German and Russian, if you want to spend several days they will come and check on you every 2 days. Also tours to Los Roques, Coro desert and Yaracuy river trips.

● **Transport** Frequent *por puesto* from Valencia, US$3, bus US$1.40. Coro, US$3.

CHICHIRIVICHE

A few kilometres beyond, towards Coro, is the favourite, and hence expensive, beach resort of **Chichiriviche** (*pop* 4,700); the town is filthy and crowded at holidays and long weekends.

● **Accommodation & places to eat A2** *La Garza*, Av Principal, attractive, pool, restaurant, full board, cheaper without, comfortable, popular, rec; **C** *La Puerta*, out of town, next to the port, very clean, nice bar and restaurant, helpful owners, rec; **C** *Náutico*, T 99-35866, friendly, clean, good meals (breakfast and dinner inc in price), fans but no a/c, transport to nearest islands inc, popular; **D** *Capri*, nr docks, shower, fan or a/c, clean, pleasant Italian owned, good restaurant and supermarket; bakery opp has tiny rooms, fan, shared bathroom; **D** *Gregoria*, with bath, clean, fan, laundry facilities, very friendly, Spanish run, highly rec; **D** *Posada La Perrera*, C Riera, nr centre, 150 km from bus stop, quiet, fan, clean, laundry facilities, patio, hammocks, friendly Italian owner, tours arranged; **E** pp *Parador Manaure*, T 86236/86121/86452, sharing apartments for 5, clean, small pool, bad restaurant; **E** *Residencial Linda*, 1 block from docks, Italian owners, friendly, helpful, use of kitchen, rec; **E** pp *Villa Marina*, aparthotel, good, clean, safe, pool, rec, friendly; **E** Sra Delia Lavala, C Mariño 30, behind hotel

Puerto la Cruz

Caribbean Sea

To Ferry Dock

† Catholic Church

To Barcelona, airport & El Morro

To Cumaná & Parque Nacional Mochima

To Caracas & Barcelona

1. Plaza Bolívar

Hotels:
2. Caribbean Inn
3. Gaeta
4. Meliá
5. Neptuno, Monte Carlo & Margelina
6. Riviera

Places to eat:
7. El Parador
8. Guatacarauzo

Don Pepe, T 86089, 4 double rooms, shared bath, clean, free coffee, very friendly. Good fish at *Restaurant Veracruz*.

● **Banks & money changers** Exchange at banks on main street.

● **Sports Diving**: *Subma Tur*, on main street; *Centro de Buceo Caribe*, Playa Sur; *Aqua-Fun Diving*, Casa El Monte, C El Sol, Virgen del Valle, T 042 86265, run by Pierre and Monika who speak German, English, French and Spanish, high quality dive equipment, PADI courses from beginner to pro level, excursions for divers with certification card (US$40 pp inc full rental), accommodation available, 2 plain double rooms with fan.

● **Transport Buses** To Puerto Cabello, 2 hrs; frequent *por puestos*, US$2; 3 hrs to Barquisimeto; 9 hrs to Valera. Direct buses from Valencia to Chichiriviche turnoff.

MOCHIMA

Venezuela's second Caribbean coastal National Park is **Mochima**, 55 km from the port of Puerto la Cruz. This city is 320 km, 5 hrs E of Caracas. It is the main commercial centre in this part of the country, especially for oil, but is also a popular holiday centre with good watersports and yachting facilities. The park itself also includes the mainland coast between Los Altos and Cumaná. The beaches and vistas of this stretch of the coast are beautiful (although see the note about litter, below). Since both Puerto La Cruz and Cumaná are ferry terminals for Margarita, Mochima can easily be incorporated into a visit to this part of Venezuela.

The easiest island to reach is **Isla de la Plata**, yet another supposed lair of the pirate Henry Morgan. It has a white sand beach, and clear waters which are ideal for snorkelling. There are food and drink stalls, but take drinking water as there is none on the island. Also take a hat and sunscreen. It's about 10 mins by boat to the island, and the fare is about US$4 pp return. Further away, and larger, are the **Chimana islands** with

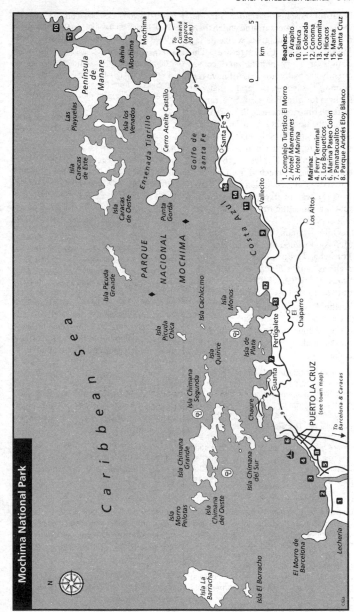

Mochima National Park

Beaches:
9. Arapito
10. Blanca
11. Colorada
12. Conoma
13. Conomita
14. Hicacos
15. Marita
16. Santa Cruz

1. Complejo Turístico El Morro
2. Hotel Maremares
3. Hotel Marina

Marina:
4. Ferry Terminal
5. Los Boqueticos
6. Marina Paseo Colón
7. Pamatacualito
8. Parque Andrés Eloy Blanco

To Cumaná (approx 20 km)

Mochima

Bahía Mochima

Península de Manare

Las Playuelas

Isla los Venados

Isla Caracas de Este

Isla Caracas de Oeste

Ensenada Tigrillo

Cerro Aceite Castillo

Golfo de Santa Fe

Santa Fe

Punta Gorda

PARQUE NACIONAL MOCHIMA

Vallecito

Isla Picuda Grande

Isla Cachicamo

Isla Monos

Costa Azul

Los Altos

Isla Picuda Chica

Isla de Plata

El Chaparro

Pertigalete

Isla Quirice

Guanta

Isla Chimana Segunda

Chaure

Caribbean Sea

Isla Chimana Grande

Isla Chimana del Sur

PUERTO LA CRUZ (see town map)

To Barcelona & Caracas

Isla Morro Pelotas

Isla Chimana del Oeste

El Morro de Barcelona

Lechería

Isla La Barracha

Isla El Borracho

N

km
0   5

beautiful beaches (Grande, Sur, del Oeste), in the waters around which there is snorkelling and good scuba diving (boat ride about US$14 return). The islands are very popular and consequently are badly littered. All have restaurants, snack-bars and thatched shelters for hire. Boats can be arranged through Embarcadero de Peñeros, Paseo Colón (behind *Tejas* restaurant), Puerto La Cruz; departures throughout the morning to a dozen points along the coast (about US$15); return 1630. Several small jetties reached from the central part of Paseo Colón offer island trips. Prices are fixed, payable in advance, arrange the time of return, reliable service.

Other islands in the vicinity are Monos (also good for scuba diving), **La Borracha**, **El Borracho** and **Los Borrachitos**, and **Caracas de Oeste** and **Caracas del Este**. All are in sheltered waters and are easy to explore by boat.

Further E from Puerto La Cruz is **Santa Fe**, a good place to relax, but there is plenty of loud music, a golf course on the dark red, sandy beach, and a market on Sat.

- **Accommodation** D *Hotel Cochaima*, difficult to find, take road parallel to main road, on the left hand side, and follow it to the end of the beach, run by Margot, clean, friendly, noisy, popular, close to beach, fan, bath, meals available, rec; **D-E** *Siete Delfines*, on beach, near market, safe, friendly, bath, fan, café and terrace where you can cook, excellent food available, bar, very popular, many parties, warmly rec; ask here for tours or information about the area, tours organized for US$4-10, ask Ricardo about transport and any kind of watersports. D *Café El Mar*, Playa Cochaima, owner Matias (German), nice, new rooms with or without, restaurant, bar, very good food, a/c. Two hotels on beach; private houses let rooms; accommodation at Señor Julio's home, a bit further down the beach from *Restaurant Cochaima*, sign 'Rooms for Rent', US$3 pp, cooking facilities, clean, safe, very friendly and helpful, rec. *Salón de Juegos Chomena* has one basic, cheap room for real budget travellers, owner changes TCs. The *pizzería* on the

beach has good food and room to let, owner, José, is friendly and will let you stay in his house if hotel is full, but no locks on doors.

- **Transport** Gasoline is available; *por puesto* at 0600 and bus to Cumaná (US$1), and Puerto La Cruz (US$0.80). It is sometimes difficult to get the bus from Puerto La Cruz to stop at Santa Fe, *por puesto* may be a better bet, US$1.10, 1 hr.10, or taxi, US$13.30 inc wait. Jeep, boat or diving tours available. Francisco is rec for boat trips, he can be found a few houses to the W of the *Cochaima*. Beware of the fishermen, they offer similar trips but their prices are extortionate. Boat trips to Playas Colorada or Blanca cost US$10pp; better to hire your own boat for half the price, or hitch down the road to Colorada. Ask for Thomas, he has a boat and will take you wherever.

- **Diving** Scuba diving is possible at Explosub, reported unhelpful. Better is *Lolo's Dive Centre*, Guanta Marina, Bahía de Guanta, T 683052, F 682885, cel 014-801543, experienced, English spoken, all types of course offered, 1/2-day beginners course US$80. There are many other agencies, all charging about the same. Hotels and travel agents organize trips. The nearest recompression chamber is on Isla Margarita.

The sleepy and friendly village of **Mochima**, beyond Santa Fe, is 4 km off the main road, hitching difficult. The sea is dirty near the town, but if you do swim, beware of the rusty ladder at the end of the pier. There is a lot of construction going on in town. Boats to nearby beaches, such as Playa Marita and Playa Blanca, and around the islands, fares negotiable, about US$10 to one island, US$12 for a 2-hr trip round the islands (up to 6 people).

- **Accommodation** *Hotel Mochima*, good restaurant, cheap, good beer, they will allow you to stay on the terrace if there are no more rooms; Sras Cellita Día, Gaby, Mama Inés and Doña María let out rooms, **E**, Señor Padriño, private room, **F**, basic but safe, they will store luggage when you go to the nearby beaches by boat, the house has no sign but it is just a few houses before Gaby's *pensión*; houses to rent with kitchens and fans from US$12 per day depending on length of stay. Eat at *Los Mochimeros*, good and friendly (try the *empanadas* with ice cold coconut milk), or *Don Quijote*, Av Bermúdez, very good.

• **Transport** The restaurants and few shops are often closed. From Puerto La Cruz, the trip can be organized by taxi, US$30 inc the journey home. Buses do not travel between Santa Fe and Mochima, *por puestos* can be taken, bargain hard on the price, US$10-12 is reasonable. Once in Mochima it is very difficult to find a taxi, you should arrange to be picked up again by the same driver if just staying for 1 day. Bus to Cumaná, 1400, US$0.80.

NB At holiday times this coast is very busy and, has become littered and polluted, especially at Santa Fe and on the islands. Repeated warnings about broken glass on the beaches. Beware of fishermen robbing campers on the islands; it is only advised to go to islands with guards (during the day) and where people live.

Information for travellers

BEFORE TRAVELLING

● **Documents**

Entry is by passport and visa, or by passport and tourist card. Tourist cards (*tarjetas de ingreso*) are valid only for those entering by air and are issued by most airlines to visitors from: Andorra, Antigua and Barbuda, Argentina, Australia, Austria, Barbados, Belgium, Brazil, Canada, Chile, Costa Rica, Dominica, Denmark, Finland, France, Germany, Ireland, Italy, Iceland, Japan, Liechtenstein, Luxembourg, Lithuania, Mexico, Monaco, Norway, Netherlands, Netherlands Antilles, New Zealand, Paraguay, Portugal, St Kitts/Nevis, St Lucia, San Marino, St Vincent, Spain, Sweden, Switzerland, Taiwan, Trinidad and Tobago, UK, Uruguay and USA. They are valid for 90 days with, theoretically, 2 extensions of 60 days each permissible, at a cost of US$25 each (alternatively leave the country and re-enter). Overstaying your 90 days without an extension can lead to arrest and a fine when you try to depart. DIEX offices in many cities do not offer extensions – best to go to DIEX, Av Baralt on Plaza Miranda in Caracas, T 483 2744, take passport, tourist card and return ticket; opens 0800, passport with extension returned at the end of the day.

If you enter the country overland, it is safest to obtain a multiple entry visa in advance. In theory, this may not be necessary, but in practice you may well be asked for it. Apply to a Venezuela consulate prior to arrival. For a Tourist Visa, you need 1 passport photo, passport valid for 6 months, references from bank and employer, onward or return ticket, completed and signed application form. The fee in the UK is £22 (costs vary from country to country). Transit visas, valid for 72 hrs are also available, mostly the same requirements and cost (inward and onward tickets needed). DIEX in Caracas will not exchange a transit for a tourist visa. It appears that you cannot get a visa in advance in the USA (although a 1 yr, multiple-entry visa is available in advance from 455 Market St, San Francisco, open Mon-Fri, 0900-1300, with US$ cash and letters of reference from your bank and employer), or Canada, so to apply for an overland visa in Colombia or Brazil you need: passport, one photo and an onward ticket. In Manaus you also need a yellow fever inoculation certificate. A tourist card issued by Viasa in Bogotá is only valid for arriving in Caracas by air from Bogotá, not if you travel overland. To extend a visa for 1 month, in any city, costs about US$25 (passport photo needed). Consuls may give a 1-year visa if a valid reason can be given. To change a tourist visa to a business visa, to obtain or to extend the latter, costs £42 in UK. Visas to work in Venezuela also cost £42 and require authorization from the Dirección Gen Sectorial de Identificación y Control de Extranjeros in Caracas. Student visas require a letter of acceptance from the Venezuelan institution, proof of means of support, medical certificate, passport photo, passport and £42. It generally takes 2 days to issue any visa. Tourist visas are multiple entry within their specified period.

NB Carry your passport with you all the time you are in Venezuela as the police mount frequent spot checks and anyone found without identification is immediately detained (carrying a certified copy for greater safety is permissible, though not always accepted by officials). A press card as identification is reported to work wonders. Border searches are very thorough and there are many military checkpoints in military areas, at which all transport is stopped. Have your documents ready and make sure you know what entry permits you need; soldiers may be unfamiliar with regulations for foreigners. Do not lose the carbon copy of your visa as this has to be surrendered when leaving the country.

Information for business visitors is given in *Hints to Exporters: Venezuela*, issued by the DTI Export Publications, PO Box 55, Stratford-upon-Avon, Warwickshire, CV37 9GE. Businessmen on short visits are strongly advised to enter the country as tourists, otherwise they will have to obtain a tax clearance certificate (*solvencia*) before they can leave.

● **Customs**
You may bring into Venezuela, free of duty, 25 cigars and 200 cigarettes, 2 litres of alcoholic drinks, 4 small bottles of perfume, and gifts at the inspector's discretion. New items to the value of US$1,000 may be brought in.

● **Climate**
Tropical, with little change between season.

● **Health**
Water in all main towns is heavily chlorinated, so safe to drink, although most people drink bottled water. Medical attention is good. State health care is free and said to be good (the Clínica Metropolitana in Caracas has been recommended). A doctor's consultation costs about US$10. On the coast from Cumaná E precautions against vampire bat bite are warranted since they can be rabies-carriers. Lights over hatches and windows are used by local fishermen to deter bats from entering boats and shore cabins. If bitten seek medical advice. Some rivers are infected with bilharzia and in some areas there are warning signs; check before bathing.

MONEY

● **Currency**
The unit of currency is the bolívar, which is divided into 100 céntimos. There are nickel alloy coins for 25 and 50 céntimos and 1, 2 and 5 bolívares, and notes for 5, 10, 20, 50, 100, 500, 1,000, 2,000 and 5,000 bolívares. There is a shortage of small coinage: many shops round up prices unless you have small change and bars may refuse to serve you unless you produce the correct change.

Popular names for coins: Fuerte, Bs 5; Real, Bs 0.50; Medio, 0.25; Puya or Centavo, 0.05. The brown Bs 100 note is sometimes referred to as a *marrón*, or a *papel*, the Bs 500 note as an *orquidea*, because of its picture.

● **Exchange**
In response to the political and economic crisis of mid-1994, which saw the collapse of 10 banks, stringent exchange controls were introduced which, for the traveller, mean: to convert unused bolívares back into dollars upon leaving, you must present the original exchange receipt (up to 30% of original amount charged); only banks and authorized *casas de cambio* can legally sell bolívares. In Dec 1995 the exchange rate was set at Bs290 = US$1, before being allowed to float in April 1996. In July 1996 the rate was Bs470 = US$1. The black market is illegal. If caught by the authorities, the money may be confiscated. *Casas de cambio* may be reluctant to change TCs; they

always insist on seeing a passport and may also insist on proof of purchase. Ital Cambio seems to be the most fastidious; they may even take your photo. Visa and Mastercard transactions offer good rates. Banco Consolidado is affiliated with American Express, no commission, some branches cash personal cheques from abroad on an Amex card; Banco Unión and Banco Mercantil (not all branches) handle Visa and ATM transactions, including cash advances and Banco Mercantil handles Mastercard. Thomas Cook Mastercard refund assistance point, Edif Cavendes, piso 7, of 706, Av Fco de Mirando, Los Palos Grandes, 1060 Caracas, T 284-3866/3255. When changing dollars cash in banks, it is best to go in the morning, queues can be very long. If changing money in hotels, do not take sterling or any other European currencies. Have money sent to you by telex and not by post, which can take weeks. Rates of exchange in hotels are generally poor.

NB It is quite common for tour companies not to accept credit cards, other than for flights, so you will need cash or travellers' cheques for buying tours.

GETTING THERE

AIR

From Europe: British Airways and Viasa fly from London to Simón Bolívar, the international airport for Caracas, the former twice a week direct, the latter out via Paris, back direct. Viasa also serves Frankfurt, Lisbon, Madrid, Milan, Porto, Rome, Santiago de Compostela and Zurich. There are also services from Europe by Air France, KLM, Iberia, Alitalia, TAP and Lufthansa. There is a weekly flight from Amsterdam to Porlamar by Viasa.

From North America: direct flights with American Airlines (New York, Orlando, Miami, Chicago), United Airlines (New York, Miami, Los Angeles, Chicago), Viasa (Miami) and Servivensa (Miami, New York).

Within the Caribbean: BWIA have services from Port of Spain (daily to Caracas). LIAT flies twice a week from St Lucia. Air France flies from Guadeloupe once a week. Viasa flies 6 days a week to Havana, Cubana once. Ideal Tours, Centro Capriles, Plaza Venezuela, Caracas, T 267-3812, 4 days, 3 nights US$649, inc flight, hotel, half-board, city tour. *The Tour Hunters*, T 91-2511, offers 5-day 4 night tours for US$286, 6 days, 5 nights US$340, inc everything except the airfare.

From The Netherlands Antilles: from Aruba to Caracas: Servivensa and ALM daily, Aserca 3 a week, Air Aruba 6; from Las Piedras/Punto Fijo on the Paranaguá Peninsula, Servivensa and Avia daily, US$190 return. From Curaçao to Caracas: ALM and Servivensa daily; to Las Piedras, Servivensa daily (if you have no onward ticket from Curaçao, you must buy a return). Private flights to Coro airport from Curaçao cost US$70 one-way.

ON ARRIVAL

● **Airports**
28 km from Caracas, near the port of La Guaira: Maiquetía, for national flights, Simón Bolívar for international flights, adjacent to each other (5 mins' walk – taxis take a circular route, fare US$2.25; airport authorities run a shuttle bus between the two every 10 mins from 0700). Flight enquiries T (031) 522 222; passenger assistance T 55-2424; police T 55-2498. Many facilities close 1 Jan, including duty and money exchangers. 3 *casas de cambio* open 24 hrs (Italcambio, good rates, outside duty-free area; also Banco Industrial, branch in International terminal and another, less crowded, in baggage reclaim area). If changing TCs, you may be asked for your purchase receipt; commission 2.5%. There are cash machines for Visa, Amex and Mastercard. Pharmacy, bookshops, basement café (good value meals and snacks, open 0500-2400, hard to find; cafes and bars on 1st floor viewing terrace also good value); no seating in main terminal until you pass through security and check in. No official left luggage; ask for Paulo at the mini bar on the 1st floor of international terminal. Look after your belongings in both terminals. Direct dial phone calls to USA only, from AT&T booth in international departure lounge. CANTV at gates 15 and 24, open 0700-2100, long-distance, international and fax services, inc receipt of faxes. At Simón Bolívar, airline offices are in the basement, hard to find: Viasa information and ticket desk open 0500-2400 daily, others at flight times. A Viasa lounge on the 1st floor of the International departure lounge, near to the viewing gallery, is open to transit passengers, serving free tea, coffee and soft drinks. If it is closed, transit facilities are poor.

When several flights arrive close together there are long queues for immigration. Taxi fares from airport to Caracas cost US$14 minimum, depending on the quality of the taxi, the part of city, or on the number of stars of your hotel, regardless of distance; overcharging is rife. Fares are supposedly controlled, but it is essential to negotiate with the drivers; find out what the official fare is first. After 2200 and at weekends a surcharge of 20% may be added, you may get charged up to US$40. Drivers may only surcharge you for luggage (US$0.50 per large bag). If you think the taxi driver is overcharging you, make a complaint to Corporturismo or tell him you will report him to the Departamento de Protección del Consumidor. The airport shuttle bus (blue and white with "Aeropuerto Internacional" on the side) leaves from E end of terminal, left out of exit (in the city, under the flyover at Bolívar and Av Sur 17, 250m from Bellas Artes metro, poorly lit at night, not rec to wait here in the dark), regular service from 0400 to 0030, bus leaves when there are enough passengers; fare to international terminal US$1.50. The bus is usually crowded so first time visitors may find a taxi advisable.

● **Hours of business**
Banks are open from 0830 to 1130 and 1400 to 1630, Mon to Fri only. Government office hours vary, but 0800-1200 are usual morning hours. Government officials have fixed hours, usually 0900-1000 or 1500-1600, for receiving visitors. Business firms generally start work about 0800, and some continue until about 1800 with a midday break. Shops, 0900-1300, 1500-1900, Mon to Sat. Generally speaking, Venezuelans start work early, and by 0700 everything is in full swing. Most firms and offices close on Sat.

● **Official time**
Atlantic Standard Time, 4 hrs behind GMT, 1 hr ahead of EST.

● **Public holidays**
There are 2 sorts of holidays, those enjoyed by everybody and those taken by employees of banks and insurance companies. Holidays applying to all businesses include: 1 Jan, Carnival on the Mon and Tues before Ash Wednesday (everything shuts down Sat-Tues; make sure accommodation is booked in advance), Thur-Sat of Holy Week, 19 April, 1 May, 24 June (24 June is the feast day of San Juan Bautista, a particularly popular festival celebrated along the central coast where there were once large concentrations of plantation slaves who considered San Juan their special Saint. Some of the best-known events are in villages between Puerto Cabello and Chuspa, to the E, such as Chuao, Cata and Ocumane de la Costa), 5, 24 July, 12 Oct, 25 December. Holidays for banks and insurance companies include all the above and also: 19 Mar and the nearest Mon to 6 Jan, Ascension Day, 29 June, 15 Aug, 1 Nov and 8 December. There are also holidays applying to certain occupations such as Doctor's Day or Traffic Policeman's Day. From 24 Dec-1 Jan, most restaurants are closed and there is no long-distance public transport. On New Year's Eve, everything closes and does not open for a least a day. Queues for tickets, and traffic jams, are long. Business travellers should not visit during Holy week or Carnival.

Local: La Guaira: 10 March Maracaibo: 24 Oct, 18 November.

● **Security**
Cameras and other valuables should not be exposed prominently. The police may confiscate pocket knives as 'concealed weapons' if they find them, although they are sold legally in the shops. In Caracas, carry handbags, cameras etc on the side away from the street as motor-cycle purse-snatchers are notorious. Hotel thefts are becoming more frequent.

● **Tipping**
Taxi drivers are tipped if the taxi has a meter (hardly anywhere), but not if you have agreed the fare in advance. Usherettes are not tipped. Hotel porters, Bs 200; airport porters Bs 200 per piece of baggage. Restaurants, between 5% and 10% of bill.

● **Voltage**
110 volts, 60 cycles, throughout the country.

● **Weights and measures**
are metric.

ON DEPARTURE

● **Departure tax**
All tourists and diplomats leaving the country, except transit passengers, must pay US$3.80 approx, Bs 1,800 at the airport or port of embarkation, payable in bolívares or dollars. At Caracas airport this procedure is split between 2 desks; the form, or parts of it, may be required for up to 3 separate checks. Minors under twelve years of age do not pay the exit tax. Venezuelans, resident foreigners and holders of a *visa transeunte* have to pay Bs 1,200 on departure. There is also an airport tax of Bs 60 for those passengers on internal flights.

● Airport information

If you travel with Viasa or any other airline for which Viasa is agent, it is possible to check in the day before flying out of Caracas by taking baggage, ticket and passport to their office at Centro Comercial Tamanaco, Nivel C2, 'Prede-spacho', between 1500 and 2100 (cost US$0.40); take bus from Chacaíto. To avoid overbooking the Government now obliges airlines to post a passenger list, but it is important to obtain clear instructions from the travel agent regarding confirmation of your flight and checking-in time. Passengers leaving Caracas on international flights must reconfirm their reservations not less than 72 hrs in advance, it is safer to do so in person than by telephone; not less than 24 hrs for national flights (if you fail to do this, you lose all rights to free accommodation, food, transport, etc if your flight is cancelled and you may lose your seat if the plane is fully booked). Beware of counterfeit tickets; buy only from agencies. If told by an agent that a flight is fully booked, try at the airport anyway. International passengers must check in 2 hrs before departure or they may lose their seat to someone on a waiting list. Viasa flights to Miami are often heavily overbooked. Venezuelans are prepared for this and check in during the morning before an evening flight. Read carefully any notice you see posted with the relevant instructions. Handling charge for your luggage US$0.50.

Always allow plenty of time when going to the airport, whatever means of transport you are using: the route can be very congested (2 hrs in daytime, but only 30 mins at 0430). Allow at least 2 hrs checking-in time before your flight, especially if flying Viasa. From city to airport at night, to obtain unsafe shuttle departure point, take local La Guaira bus from right hand side of exit from Nuevo Circo bus terminal to highway by airport. *Por puesto* airport – Caracas US$1.35; leave airport from upper level and climb concrete steps to main road above (not safe after dark). From Caracas they are marked "Caracas Litoral", asked to be dropped off. Airport bus or *por puesto* to airport can be caught at Gato Negro metro station. When checking in, keep 10 bolívar bills handy to pay departure tax levied at most large airports.

ACCOMMODATION

● Hotels

Fairmont International, Torre Capriles, Planta Baja, Plaza Venezuela, Caracas, T 782 8433, Telex 21232 SNRHO, F 782 4407, will book hotel rooms both in Caracas and in other towns, where they have 102 hotels on their books. All, except luxury class hotels charge officially controlled prices.

● Camping

Camping in Venezuela is a popular recreation, for spending a weekend at the beach, on the islands, in the *llanos* and in the mountains. Camping, with or without a vehicle, is not possible at the roadside. If camping on the beach, for the sake of security, pitch your tent close to others, even though they play their radios loud.

FOOD AND DRINK

● Food

There is excellent local fish (*pargo* or red snapper), crayfish, small oysters and prawns. Of true Venezuelan food there is *sancocho* (a stew of vegetables, especially yuca, with meat, chicken or fish); *arepas*, a kind of white maize bread, very bland in flavour; toasted *arepas* served with a wide selection of relishes, fillings or the local somewhat salty white cheese are cheap, filling and nutritious; *cachapas*, a maize pancake (soft, not hard like Mexican *tortillas*) wrapped around white cheese; *pabellón*, made of shredded meat, beans, rice and fried plantains vegetarian versions available); and *empanadas*, maize-flour pies containing cheese, meat or fish. At Christmas only there are *hallacas*, maize pancakes stuffed with chicken, pork, olives, etc boiled in a plantain leaf (but don't eat the leaf). A *muchacho* (boy) on the menu is a cut of beef. *Ganso* is also not goose but beef. *Solomo* and *lomito* are other cuts of beef. *Hervido* is chicken or beef with vegetables. *Contorno* with a meat or fish dish is a choice of chips, boiled potatoes, rice or yuca. *Caraotas* are beans; *cachitos* are croissants of bread. *Pasticho* is what the Venezuelans call Italian *lasagne*. The main fruits are bananas, oranges, grapefruit, mangoes, pineapple and papaya. **NB** Some Venezuelan variants of names for fruit: *lechosa* is papaya, *patilla* is water melon, *parchita* passion fruit, and *cambur* a small banana. A delicious sweet is *huevos chimbos* – egg yolk boiled and bottled in sugar syrup. Venezuelans dine late.

● Drink

Venezuelan rum is very good; recommended brands are Cacique, Pampero and Santa Teresa. There are 4 good local beers: Polar (the most popular), Regional (with a strong flavour of hops), Cardenal and Nacional (a *lisa* is a glass of keg beer; for a bottle of beer ask for a *tercio*); Brahma beer (lighter than Polar), is imported from Brazil. There are also mineral waters and gin. Now there is a good, local wine in Venezuela. The Polar brewery has joined with Martell (France) and built a winery in Carora. Wines produced are 'Viña Altagracia' and 'Bodegar Pomar'. 'Bodegar Pomar' also produces a sparkling wine in the traditional champagne style. Liqueurs are cheap, try the local *ponche crema*. The coffee is very good (*café con leche* has a lot of milk, *café marrón* much less, *cafe negro* for black coffee, which, though obvious, is not common in the rest of Latin America); visitors should also try a *merengada*, a delicious drink made from fruit pulp, ice, milk and sugar; a *batido* is the same but with water and a little milk; *jugo* is the same but with water. A *plus-café* is an after-dinner liqueur. Water is free in all restaurants even if no food is bought. Bottled water in *cervecerías* is often from the tap; no deception is intended, bottles are simply used as convenient jugs. Insist on seeing the bottle opened if you want mineral water. *Chicha de arroz* is a sweet drink made of milk, rice starch, sugar and vanilla; fruit juices are very good.

GETTING AROUND

AIR TRANSPORT

Most places of importance are served by Avensa and/or Servivensa. Some internal flights are also operated by Viasa, while Aerotuy, Zuliana and Aserca (rec for good service) fly to a variety of destinations. Internal airlines offer special family discounts and student discounts, but this practice is variable (photocopies of ISTC card are useful as this allows officials to staple one to the ticket). Sometimes there is little difference between 1st class and tourist class fares. Beware of overbooking during holiday time, especially at Caracas airport; it is recommended that you check in 2 hrs before departure, particularly at Easter.

Avensa/Servivensa operate an airpass, which must be bought outside Latin America or the Caribbean. It is valid for 45 days and passengers must buy a minimum of 4 coupons. No route may be flown twice in the same direction. Economy class only; children pay 66% and infants 10% of the adult fare. Prices are by

Zone: Caracas to Aruba, Bonaire or Curaçao US$50; Caracas-Miami (but not Barquisimeto or Maracaibo-Miami), Caracas-Bogotá, Bogotá-Quito, or Quito-Lima US$70; Caracas-Lima US$180; Caracas-Mexico City US$200; any internal Venezuelan flight US$40.

LAND TRANSPORT

● **Motoring**

All visitors to Venezuela can drive if they are over 18 and have a valid driving licence from their own country; an international driving licence is preferred. If you have an accident and someone is injured, you will be detained as a matter of routine, even if you are not at fault. Do not drive at night if you can help it (if you do have to, do not drive fast). Carry insect spray if you do; if you stop and get out, the car will fill with biting insects. Self-drive tours, and fly-drive are now being marketed, the latter through National Car Rental, which has a wide network of offices. Car rental rates are given under Porlamar.

There are 5 grades of gasoline: 'normal', 83 octane; 87 octane; 89 octane; 91 octane; and 'alta', 95 octane. Gasoline costs on average 50-60/US$0.10-0.12 a litre; diesel costs Bs48/US$0.10 a litre. Service stations are open 0500-2100, Mon-Sat, except those on highways which are open longer hours. Only those designated to handle emergencies are open on Sun. In the event of breakdown, Venezuelans are usually very helpful. There are many garages, even in rural areas; service charges are not high, nor are tyres, oil or accessories expensive, but being able to speak Spanish will greatly assist in sorting out problems. Carry spare battery water, fan belts, an obligatory breakdown triangle, a jack and spanners. Some cars have a security device to prevent the engine being started and this is recommended. The best road map is published by Lagoven, available from most service stations (not just Lagoven's), latest edition 1989. **Warning** There is an automatic US$20 fine for running out of fuel.

● **Buses**

There are excellent (but slow) bus services between the major cities, but the colectivo taxis and minibuses, known in Venezuela as *por puesto*, seem to monopolize transport to and from smaller towns and villages. Outside Caracas, town taxis are relatively expensive.

COMMUNICATIONS

● **Postal services**

The postal service can be extremely slow and unreliable. For a letter up to 20 grams to the Americas, the cost is US$0.30; to the rest of world US$0.35. Air mail letters to the USA or Europe can take from one to 4 weeks and registered mail is no quicker. Important mail should be sent by air courier to a Venezuelan address. Internal mail also travels slowly, especially if there is no PO Box number. As in other countries, removing stamps from letters occurs; insist on seeing your letters franked, saying that you are a collector. Avoid the mail boxes in pharmacies as some no longer have collections. A private parcel delivery company, such as DHL, will charge around US$60 for parcels of up to 500g to Europe.

● **Telecommunications**

All international and long distance calls are operated by CANTV in Caracas at Centro Plaza, first floor, on Francisco Miranda near US Embassy in E Caracas (corner of Andrés Bello between metros Parque del Este and Altamira), open Mon-Sat 0800-1945, I 284-7932, phone cards (*tarjetas* – see below) sold here. Most major cities are now linked by direct dialling (*Discado Directo*), with a 3-figure prefix for each town in Venezuela. Otherwise CANTV offices deal with most long-distance and international calls in the cities outside Caracas. Collect calls are possible to some countries, at least from Caracas, though staff in offices may not be sure of this. Calls out of Venezuela are more expensive than calls into it and are subject to long delays. Local calls are troublesome and the connection is often cut in the middle of your conversation; calls are best made from hotels or CANTV offices, rather than from booths (of which there are few). Most public phones on prepaid CANTV cards in denominations of 500, 1,000 and 2,000 bolívares. Buy them from CANTV or numerous small shops bearing the CANTV logo, or a scrap of card reading "Si! hay tarjetas!" They are also sold by street vendors. Make sure they are still in their clear plastic wrapper with an unbroken red seal. Many small shops impose a 25% handling charge and *tarjetas* may be out of stock. International calls are cheaper with a *tarjeta*, minimum needed Bs2,000, but you get little more than a minute to Europe. To make an international call, dial 00 plus country code, etc. Canada direct: 800-11100. For UK, BT Direct, 800-11440 (BT chargecard works from

any phone). International calls are charged by a series of bands, ranging from about US$1/min to USA and Canada, to US$2 to UK, to US$2.15. There are various reduced and economy rates according to band. Fax rates are as for phones.

TOURIST INFORMATION

● **Local tourist office**

Corpoturismo, Apartado 50.200, Caracas, main office for information is on floors 35-37, Torre Oeste, Parque Central, T 507-8607. The Tourist Office at the international airport has good maps, helpful; some English spoken, open 0700-2400, T 55-1060; tourist office at national terminal open 0700-2100, T 55-1191. When manned both offices are useful, will book hotels, reconfirm flights, English spoken, better service than the Corpoturismo office in the city.

● **Further reading**

GAM, the monthly *Guía Aérea y Marítima de Venezuela*, gives details of all flights into and within the country, but also of hotels, travel agents, car hire, etc. *Guía Progreso*, published by Seguros Progreso SA, available at the company offices and elsewhere, is very detailed. The *Guide to Venezuela* (925 pages, updated and expanded 1989), by Janice Bauman, Leni Young and others, in English (freely available in Caracas) is a mine of information and maps, US$11.

For sailors, *A Sailor's Guide to a Venezuelan Cruise*, by Chris Doyle, is recommended, US$10 from Frances Punnett, PO Box 17, St Vincent, T (809) 458 4246; it gives information on all the small islands as well as Margarita.

For information on the **National Parks** system, and to obtain necessary permits to stay in the parks, go to Instituto Nacional de Parques (Inparques), Avenida Rómulo Gallegos, Parque del Este (exit Parque del Este metro opp park, turn left, office is a few hundred metres further on up a slight incline), T 284-1956, Caracas, or to the local office of the *guardaparques* for each park. Further information can be had from the Ministerio del Ambiente y de los Recursos Naturales Renovables (MARNR) in Caracas. The book: *Guía de los Parques Nacionales y Monumentos Naturales de Venezuela*, is obtainable in Audubon headquarters (open 0900-1230, 1430-1800), Las Mercedes shopping centre, Las Mercedes, Caracas, in the La Cuadra sector next to the car parking area (it is difficult to find), T 91-3813. It is also available at Librería Noctúa, Villa Mediterránea, in the Centro Plaza Shopping Centre. The society will plan itineraries and make reservations.

ACKNOWLEDGEMENTS

We are grateful to travellers who wrote to *The South American Handbook* with material on the islands.

Netherlands Antilles and Aruba the ABCs

THE NETHERLANDS ANTILLES consist of the islands of (Aruba – autonomous, see below, Government) Bonaire and Curaçao (popularly known as the ABCs) 60-80 km off the coast of Venezuela, outside the hurricane belt; 880 km further N (in the hurricane belt) are the '3 S's': Sint Eustatius (Statia), Saba, and the S part of Sint Maarten (St-Martin) in what are generally known as the Leeward Islands. Because of the distance separating the N islands from the other Dutch possessions, the 3 S's are described in a separate section earlier in the Handbook. There is some confusion regarding which islands are Leeward and which Windward: locals refer to the ABCs as 'Leeward Islands', and the other 3 as 'Windward', a distinction adopted from the Spaniards, who still speak of the *Islas de Sotavento* and *de Barlovento* with reference to the trade winds. Each island is different from the others in size, physical features, the structure of the economy and the level of development and prosperity.

HORIZONS

HISTORY

The first known settlers of the islands were the Caiquetios, a tribe of peaceful Arawak Indians, who lived in small communities under a chieftain or a priest. They survived principally on fish and shellfish and collected salt from the Charoma saltpan to barter with their mainland neighbours for supplements to their diet. There are remains of Indian villages on Curaçao at Westpunt, San Juan, de Savaan and Santa Barbara, and on Aruba near Hooiberg. On each of the ABC islands there are cave and rock drawings. The Arawaks in this area had escaped attack by the Caribs but soon after the arrival of the Spaniards most were forcibly transported from Curaçao to work on Hispaniola. Although some were later repatriated, more fled when the Dutch arrived. The remainder were absorbed into the black or white population, so that by 1795, only 5 full-blooded Indians were to be found on Curaçao. On Aruba and Bonaire the Indians maintained their identity until about the end of the 19th century, but there were no full-blooded Indians left by the 20th century.

The islands were discovered in 1499 by a Spaniard, Alonso de Ojeda, accompanied by the Italian, Amerigo Vespucci and the Spanish cartographer Juan de la Cosa. The Spanish retained control over the islands throughout the 16th century, but because there was no gold, they were declared 'useless islands'. After 1621, the Dutch became frequent visitors looking for wood and salt and later for a military foothold. Curaçao's strategic position between Pernambuco and New Amsterdam within the Caribbean setting made it a prime target. In 1634, a Dutch fleet took Curaçao, then in 1636 they took Bonaire, which was inhabited by a few cattle and 6 Indians, and Aruba which the Spanish and Indians evacuated. Curaçao became important as a

Papiamento glossary

Bon bini	Welcome
Con ta bai	How are you?
Mi ta bon	I am well
Bon dia	Good morning
Bon tardi	Good afternoon
Bon nochi	Good evening
Cuanti?	How much?
Danki	Thank you
Te aworo	See you later
A yo	Goodbye

trading post and as a base for excursions against the Spanish. After 1654, Dutch refugees from Brazil brought sugar technology, but the crop was abandoned by 1688 because of the very dry climate. About this time citrus fruits were introduced, and salt remained a valuable commodity. Much of Curaçao's wealth came from the slave trade. From 1639-1778 thousands of slaves were brought to Willemstad, fed with funchi and sold to the mainland and other colonies. The Dutch brought nearly half a million slaves to the Caribbean, most of which went through Curaçao.

Wars between England and the Netherlands in the second half of the 17th century led to skirmishes and conquests in the Caribbean. The Peace of Nijmegen in 1678 gave the Dutch Aruba, Curaçao, Bonaire and the 3 smaller islands in the Leeward group, St Eustatius, Saba and half of St Martin. Further conflicts in Europe and the Americas in the 18th century led to Curaçao becoming a commercial meeting place for pirates, American rebels, Dutch merchants, Spaniards and créoles from the mainland. In 1800 the English took Curaçao but withdrew in 1803. They occupied it again from 1807 until 1816, when Dutch rule was restored, during when it was declared a free port. From 1828 to 1845, all Dutch West Indian colonies were governed from Surinam. In 1845 the Dutch Leeward Islands were joined to Willemstad in one colonial unit called Curaçao and Dependencies. The economy was still largely based on

Papiamento – the Netherlands Antilles' ABC

Dutch is the official language, and many islanders also speak English or Spanish, but the *lingua franca* of the ABC islands is Papiamento (also spelt Papiamentu), which originated with the Portuguese spoken by Jewish emigrants from Portugal, who were the most numerous settlers in the 17th century. Since then it has developed into a mixture of Portuguese, Dutch, Spanish, English, and some African and Indian dialects. Papiamento has been in existence since at least the early 18th century, but has no fixed spelling, though there is a committee seeking to establish a standard orthography. It is spoken by all social classes and is becoming prized as a symbol of cultural identity. The Aruban parliament now conducts its debates in Papiamento; poetry, plays and novels have been published in it; Curaçao has 3 Dutch-language newspapers but 8 in Papiamento. There are differences of accent and vocabulary between Aruba, Bonaire and Curaçao but speakers from the different islands have no difficulty understanding one another. There is more of a Dutch influence in Curaçao's Papiamentu and more of a Spanish influence in Aruba's Papiamento. There is a useful *Papiamentu Textbook* by E R Goilo (6th edition, published by De Wit Stores nv, Oranjestad, Aruba, also Dutch and Spanish versions). The most comprehensive dictionary by Sidney Joubert is available only in Papiamento/Dutch, 2 others in Papiamento/English are by Jossy M Mansur (published by Edicionnan Clasico Diario, Oranjestad, Aruba) and Betty Ratzlaff (TWR Dictionary Foundation, Bonaire).

commerce, much of it with Venezuela, and there was a ship building industry, some phosphate mining and the salt pans, although the latter declined after the abolition of slavery in 1863.

In the 20th century the economy prospered with the discovery of oil in Venczuela and the subsequent decision by the Dutch-British Shell Oil Company to set up a refinery on Curaçao because of its political stability, its good port facilities and its better climate than around Lake Maracaibo. In 1924 another refinery was built on Aruba, which brought unprecedented wealth to that island and the population rose. The Second World War was another turning point as demand for oil soared and British, French and later US forces were stationed on the islands. The German invasion of Holland encouraged Dutch companies to transfer their assets to the Netherlands Antilles leading to the birth of the offshore financial centre. After the War, demands for autonomy from Holland began to grow.

GOVERNMENT

The organization of political parties began in 1936 and by 1948 there were four parties on Curaçao and others on Aruba and the other islands, most of whom endorsed autonomy. In 1948, the Dutch constitution was revised to allow for the transition to complete autonomy of the islands. In 1954 they were granted full autonomy in domestic affairs and became an integral part of the Kingdom of the Netherlands. The Crown continued to appoint the Governor, although since the 1960s this has gone to a native-born Antillian. Nevertheless, a strong separatist movement developed on Aruba and the island finally withdrew from the Netherlands Antilles in 1986, becoming an autonomous member of the Kingdom of the Netherlands, the same status as the whole of the Netherlands Antilles.

The Netherlands Antilles now form two autonomous parts of the Kingdom of the Netherlands. The main part, comprising all the islands except Aruba, is a parliamentary federal democracy, the seat of which is in Willemstad, Curaçao, and each island has its own Legislative and Executive Council. Parliament (Staten) is elected in principle every four years, with 14 members from Curaçao, three from Bonaire, three from Sint Maarten and one each from Saba and St Eustatius.

Ms Maria Liberia-Peters became Prime Minister of the five-island federation for the second time in 1990, as head of a coalition led by the National People's Party (Partido Nashonal di Pueblo-PNP) with 10 of the Curaçao seats and the support of the five from Bonaire, Saba and St Eustatius in the 22-seat Parliament.

Mr Nelson Oduber became Prime Minister of Aruba in 1989, as head of a coalition led by the People's Electoral Movement with 12 seats in the 21-seat Parliament. The coalition remained in office following the Jan 1993 elections even though the MEP won fewer votes than the opposition Arubaanse Volkspartij (AVP). Both parties won nine seats and the three smaller parties of the coalition won one seat each. Mr Oduber initially governed with the support of the minority parties but when two of them left his coalition in April 1994 he was unable to reach agreement with the AVP on a new coalition and the government fell. A new general election was held on 29 July 1994. The AVP won 10 of the 21 seats and formed a new government led by Prime Minister Heny Eman. The MEP won 9 seats. The Organisashon pa Liberashon de Aruba (OLA) won two seats and joined in a coalition with the AVP.

Separate status for some or all of the islands has been a political issue with a breakaway movement in Curaçao and St Maarten. The Netherlands Government's previous policy of encouraging independence has been reversed. The Hague has been trying to draw up a new constitution governing relations between the Netherlands, the Antilles Federation and Aruba. A round-table conference was held in 1993 to establish the basis for future relations including financial support but ended without any decision on Aruba's desire to cancel proposals for independence in 1996, Curaçao's demand for *status aparte* and future relations of the islands with the Netherlands if the Federation collapses.

In Nov 1993 a referendum was held in Curaçao on its future status within the Federation. The Government was soundly defeated when the electorate unexpectedly voted to continue the island's present status as a member of the Antillean federation (73.6%), rejecting the other options of separate status (11.9%), incorporation in the Netherlands (8.0%) and independence (0.5%). Ms Liberia-Peters resigned and the Antillean Justice Minister, Suzy Romer, took over until late Dec, when Professor Alejandro Paula was sworn in pending elections.

General elections were held on 25 February 1994. A new party formed after the referendum, the Partido Antiya Restruktura (PAR - Antillean Restructuring Party), of Curaçao, won eight of the 22 seats. The PNP won only three of Curaçao's 14 seats, the Movimiento Antiyano Nobo (MAN- New Antillean Movement) won two and the Democratic Party (DP) one. In St Maarten, the St Maarten People's Alliance (SPA) won two seats and the third was won by the Progressive Democratic Party (PDP). In Bonaire the DP won two seats and the Union Patriotico Bonairiano (UPB) the third. The DP also won St Eustatius' single seat and the Windward Islands People's Movement retained its seat for Saba. On 31 March, Miguel Pourier, a former Prime Minister and leader of the PAR, was sworn in as federal Prime Minister, leading a coalition government. Mr Pourier advocates greater autonomy for the Antilles within the federation and has the support of 16 members of the Staten.

The new cabinet agreed that the other islands, Saba, Statia, St Maarten and

Bonaire, should also hold referenda, with the aim of restructuring the Antilles in a new form to go into effect in 1996. The vote in October 1994 was overwhelmingly in favour of the status quo, with 90.6% support in Statia, 86.3% in Saba, 88.0% in Bonaire and 59.8% in Sint Maarten. The position of the Netherlands has yet to be clarified, particularly over higher financial supervision for those islands which choose to remain part of the Federation but desire greater autonomy. The issues of good government, drugs trafficking and illegal immigration are high on the agenda.

Island governments seemed particularly unstable in 1994 as alliances collapsed. In Curaçao, the island government resigned on 1 June after three of the ten PNP island councillors resigned over education policy differences and the MAN declined an offer to join a new coalition. In St Maarten the leader of the governing PDP joined forces with the opposition SPA to vote through a motion of no confidence in the executive on 3 June. Two of the four commissioners on the executive council resigned, but the other two refused and had to face individual no-confidence motions. The SPA and PDP signed a coalition agreement on 20 June, their first since 1991 when a similar alliance collapsed after two months.

Island council elections were held in April 1995 in Sint Maarten and Bonaire, and in May in Curaçao, Saba and Statia. In Sint Maarten, the PDP and the SPA won 5 seats each and the SAPP won the eleventh. The PDP and the SAPP formed a coalition led by Sarah Westcott-Williams, who recorded the highest individual vote for the PDP. The coalition collapsed in October following 3 resignations and the PDP held talks with the SPA on a new coalition. In Bonaire the DP, led by Jopie Abraham, won 5 seats, the UPB two and the Paboso Party two. In Curaçao, the PAR, led by federal Prime Minister Miguel Pourier, won 8 of the 21 seats and the MAN 6.

Netherlands Antilles: fact file

Geographic

Land area	800 sq km
Bonaire	288
Curaçao	444
Saba	13
Statia	21
Sint-Maarten	34

Demographic

Population (1995)	201,000
annual growth rate (1990-95)	1.4%
urban	92.4%
density	251.3 per sq km
Religious affiliation	
Roman Catholic	74%
Birth rate per 1,000 (1991)	18.3
	(world av 26.4)

Education and Health

Life expectancy at birth, male	
	71.1 years
female	75.8 years
Infant mortality rate	
per 1,000 live births (1989)	6.3
Physicians (1994)	1 per 677 persons
Hospital beds	1 per 137 persons
Calorie intake as %	
of FAO requirement	107%
Literacy	93.8%

Economic

GDP (1993 market prices)	
	US$1,800mn
GDP per capita	US$9,700
Total external debt (1995)	
	US$1,100mn
Tourism receipts (1993)	US$721mn
Radio	1 per 1.0 persons
Television	1 per 5.7 persons
Telephone	1 per 3.9 persons

Employment

Population economically active (1992)	
	87,800
% of labour force in	
agriculture and mining	0.6
manufacturing and public utilities	
	9.6
construction	7.4
trade, hotels, restaurants	23.8

Source *Encyclopaedia Britannica*

They formed a coalition to govern the island as they were already federal coalition partners. The PNP won 4 seats and the DP one seat while the Frente Obrero di Liberashon (FOL) won two. The PAR's seats were later reduced to 6 as a result of the 'internal opposition' of 2 PAR union leaders who were expelled from the party. In Saba the Saba Democratic Labour Movement (SDLM) won 3 of the 5 seats, ousting the Windward Islands People's Movement (WIPM) and reducing their seats from 4 to two. The SDLM is led by Steve Hassell, formerly of the WIPM. In St Eustatius the DP won 3 seats and the St Eustatius Alliance won the remaining two.

Bonaire

BONAIRE, second largest of the five islands comprising the Netherlands Antilles, is 38 km long and 6½-11½ km wide and 288 km square. It lies 80 km N of Venezuela, 50 km E of Curaçao, 140 km E of Aruba, at 12° 5' N and 86°25' W, outside the hurricane belt. The S part of the crescent-shaped island is flat and arid, much of it given over to the production of salt. The N end of the island is more hilly, the highest point being Mount Brandaris, and is a national park. There is little agriculture and most of the island is covered in scrub and a variety of cacti, many of which reach a height of 6m. Despite its lack of natural resources, it is, however, known as 'Diver's Paradise', for its rich underwater life and is also valued by bird watchers. The windward coast is rough and windy, while the leeward coast is sheltered and calm.

HORIZONS

Klein Bonaire, a small (608 ha), flat, rocky and uninhabited islet one km off Bonaire's shores, is frequented by snorkellers and divers. It has sandy beaches but no natural shade and only a few shelters used by tour boats.

Bonaire is the least densely populated of the islands and the inhabitants, who number around 11,200 and are mostly of mixed Arawak, European and African descent, are a very friendly and hospitable people. The island is quiet, peaceful and very safe. As in Curaçao and Aruba, Dutch is the official language, Papiamento the colloquial tongue, and Spanish and English are both widely spoken.

THE ECONOMY

Bonaire has a fairly diversified economy with salt mining, oil trans-shipment, a textile factory, rice mill and radio communications industry. The Antilles International Salt Company has reactivated the long dormant salt industry, which benefits so greatly from the constant sunshine (with air temperatures averaging 27°C and water 26°C), scant rainfall (less than 560 mm a year), and refreshing trade winds.

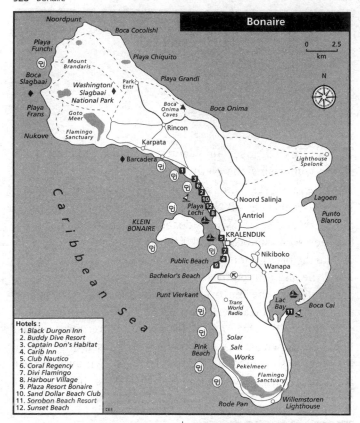

Bonaire

0   2.5
km

N

Hotels :
1. Black Durgon Inn
2. Buddy Dive Resort
3. Captain Don's Habitat
4. Carib Inn
5. Club Nautico
6. Coral Regency
7. Divi Flamingo
8. Harbour Village
9. Plaza Resort Bonaire
10. Sand Dollar Beach Club
11. Sorobon Beach Resort
12. Sunset Beach

However, for foreign exchange, the island is overwhelmingly dependent on tourism, even if it is highly specialized. In 1995, stayover tourist arrivals rose by 6.4% to 59,410 of which 46% came from North America and 34% from Europe. Daytrippers added another 3,953 to the total. The USA is the largest single market (44%), followed by the Netherlands (24%) and Venezuela (8%). The Venezuelan market has shrunk because of that country's economic crisis and limitations on foreign currency for travel, as well as stiff competition from Miami. Cruise ship passenger arrivals have risen sharply since the 1980s but fell back to 10,563 passengers in 1995 from 17,604 in 1993. Divers are the main category among stayover visitors (45% of the total), although their proportion of the total has fallen as the attractions of windsurfing and birdwatching have been publicized more widely. Accommodation for tourists is split fairly evenly between hotels and condominiums or villas, amounting to about 1,000 rooms and still growing. Financial assistance for the development of tourism has been provided by the EU, which has financed the expansion of the airport and development of other infrastructure.

FLORA AND FAUNA

The old salt pans of Pekelmeer, needed by the Salt Company, posed an ecological problem: Bonaire has one of the largest Caribbean flamingo colonies in the Western Hemisphere, and these birds build their conical mud nests in the salt pans. Pleas from wild-life conservationists convinced the company that it should set aside an area of 56 ha for a flamingo sanctuary, with access strictly prohibited. The birds, initially rather startled by the sudden activity, have settled into a peaceful coexistence, so peaceful in fact that they have actually doubled their output and are now laying two eggs a year instead of their previous one. There are said to be over 15,000 flamingoes on the island, and they can be seen wading in Goto Meer Bay in the NW, in the salt lake near Playa Grandi, and in Lac Bay on the SE coast of Bonaire, feeding on algae which give them their striking rose-pink colour. It is an impressive sight to witness the flamingoes rising from the water in the evening as they prepare to overnight in Venezuela.

There are also two smaller bird sanctuaries at the Solar Salt Works and Goto Meer. At Pos'i Mangel, in the National Park, thousands of birds gather in the late afternoon. Bronswinkel Well, also in the Park, is another good place to see hundreds of birds and giant cacti. The indigenous Bonaire Green Parrot can be seen in the Park and at Onima. About 190 species of birds have been found on Bonaire as well as the flamingoes. An annual Birdwatching Olympics and Nature Week is held in Sept, with prizes for those who spot the greatest number of species.

There are lots of iguanas and lizards of all shapes and sizes. The big blue lizards are endemic to Bonaire, while the Anolis, a tree lizard with a yellow dewlap, is related to the Windward Islands Anolis species rather than to the neighbouring Venezuelan species. The interior has scant vegetation but the enormous cacti provide perching places for yellow-winged parrots. The most common mammal you are likely to see is the goat, herds of which roam the island eating everything in sight except the cacti.

BEACHES AND WATERSPORTS

Bonaire is not noted for its beaches; the sand is usually full of coral and gritty, which is rather hard on the feet, and those on the leeward coast are narrow. Beaches in front of some hotels have been helped with extra sand. However, they do offer peace and quiet, and you will not get pestered by people trying to sell you things. Recommended are Sorobon (a private, nudist resort where non-guests pay US$10 for admission), Lac Bay which has an area of mangroves at the N end of the bay, and in the NE Playa Chiquito. Be careful at Playa Chiquito, or Chikito, there is a memorial plaque there for good reason. The surf is strong and it is dangerous to swim but it is pleasant for sunbathing. There were a few huts for shade but they are in a poor state of repair. Another reasonable, but shadeless beach is Pink Beach, S of Kralendijk, past the Salt Pier, the water is shallow and good for swimming but the strip of sand is narrow and gritty. In the Washington-Slagbaai National Park are two attractive bays: Playa Funchi, which is good for snorkelling, but has no sand and no facilities so the area is very smelly, and Boca Slagbaai, which is popular with tour boats for snorkelling and you can see flamingoes wading in the salina behind the beach. At the latter, there are clean toilets and showers in a restored 19th century house and salt barn (ask the attendant to open them for you) and drinks and snacks are available. A very pleasant break in a hot and sweaty tour round the National Park. Fishing, sailing, windsurfing and waterskiing are all popular as an alternative to diving, which is what most people come to Bonaire to enjoy.

You can charter a fishing boat through your hotel and arrange half or full day trips with tackle and food included. Bonaire has good bonefishing and also deep sea fishing. Two independent charter companies are Piscatur, run by Captain Chris Morkos, T 8774, F 4784, half day US$275 for 4 people, US$425 full day in 30-ft diesel boat, or US$125 half day for 2 people, US$225 full day in 15-ft skiff; and *Slamdunk*, a 30-ft Topaz, T 5111 Captain Rich at the Marina, same rates but for 6 people. Captain Freddy, T 5661, F 5662, has a boat for charter which can be equipped for fishing, or you can cruise to the Venezuelan Islands. Captain Bob, T 7070, F 7071, also does fishing charters, half or full day, with his boat *Its About Time*. Fishing boats with diving gear can be chartered from Club Nautico, Kaya Jan NE Craane 24, T 5800, F 5850/1. There is an annual Bonaire International Fishing Tournament, held at the end of March, which attracts participants from throughout the Americas.

The annual Bonaire Sailing Regatta is held in mid-October. This has grown into a world class event with races for seagoing yachts, catamarans, sunfishes, windsurfers and local fishing boats. The smaller craft compete in Kralendijk Bay, while the larger boats race round Bonaire and Klein Bonaire. Held over five days, the event attracts crowds and hotel reservations need to be made well in advance. For information call the Regatta office, T 5555, F 5576. There is also an annual Nautical Race in Nov for small boats. Speed races are held in Kralendijk Bay. The Marina at *Harbour Village* is the only facility of its kind in Bonaire. There are 60 slips for boats up to 110 ft with showers, laundry, fuel, waste disposal etc, and has a 120-ton syncrolift and supply shop for repairs.

Sailing trips with snorkelling and beach barbecue, often on Klein Bonaire, or sunset booze cruises, from US$25 pp plus 10% service, are offered on *Samur* (PO Box 287, T/F 5592), a 56-ft Siamese junk built in Bangkok in 1968, based at the *Sand Dollar Dive and Photo*, with pick up service from most resorts. Others include *Oscarina*, a 42-ft cutter, T 8290, 8819, and the *Bonaire Dream*, a glass bottom boat which sails out of Harbour Village Marina, tickets available in hotels, Bonaire Book Store, *La Sonrisa Soda Fountain*, Super Corner or T 8239, 4514, F 4536. Several charter yachts offer trips as far as the Venezuelan islands, eg *Sea Witch*, contact Capt Robert, T 5433, F 7678, PO Box 348, a dive master who carries dive gear on board and takes a maximum of four guests on his 56-ft ketch; *Woodwind* is a 37-ft trimaran offering sailing and snorkelling around Bonaire, T 8285; Bonsail Charters go wherever you want, T (5999) 607159 or F 5398.

Conditions are ideal for windsurfing with winds of 15-25 knots in Dec-Aug and 12-18 knots in Sept-November. On the leeward side offshore winds allow you to sail to Klein Bonaire. At Lac Bay on the windward side of the island where the water is calm and shallow, there is a constant onshore wind. The bay is about 3 miles long and 1½ miles wide but a coral reef just outside the bay breaks up the waves. However, the adventurous can get out of the bay at one end where long, high waves enable you to wave ride, jump or loop. Windsurfing Bonaire is based here, PO Box 301, T/F 5363, fax before 0830 for a free hotel pick up 0900 or 1300, instruction and board rental; windsurfing US$20 for 1 hr, US$50/day, lessons US$20, ocean kayaks US$10/hrs, US$30/day. Windsurfing rentals and instruction are also available at Great Adventures Bonaire at the *Harbour Village Beach Resort*, T 7500, along with kayak, sunfish, mini speed boats, water skiing, sea biscuit rides and water taxi service to Klein Bonaire. *Sunset Beach Resort*, T 5300, F 8593, offers small hobie cat and sunfish rentals, waterscooters, waterskiing, hydrosliding and paddle boats. Waterskiing also from Goodlife Watersport, T 4588. Many dive shops rent kayaks, quite a good way of getting to Klein Bonaire without a boatload of other people. Jibe City rents kayaks for a whole or half day, T 7363, F 5363.

DIVING AND MARINE LIFE

The least developed and least populated of the ABC islands, Bonaire has a special appeal to devotees of the sea, whose treasures are unsurpassed in the Caribbean. Surrounding the island, with submarine visibility up to 60m, are coral reefs harbouring over a thousand different species of marine creatures. Ranked as one of the three top dive spots in the world, and number one in the Caribbean (followed by Grand Cayman Island and Cozumel), Bonaire is a leader in the movement for preservation of underwater resources and the whole island is a protected marine park. Two areas have been designated marine reserves, with no diving allowed; along Playa Frans, N to Boca Slogbaai, and W of Karpata. Lac Bay may also become a protected area because of its mangroves and seagrass beds. Stringent laws passed in 1971 ban spearfishing and the removal of any marine life from Bonaire's waters. It is a serious offence to disturb the natural life of the coral reefs, and the local diving schools have set up permanent anchors in their dive spots to avoid doing any unwarranted damage. With about 600 dives a day, conservation is essential. You are requested not to touch the coral or other underwater life, such as sea horses; not to feed the fish, as it is not natural and encourages the more aggressive species; not to drop litter, particularly plastic which does not decompose and can be harmful to sea creatures, and not to kick up sand with your fins as it can choke and kill the coral. Advanced buoyancy courses are available free of charge and are highly recommended for divers to train you to keep horizontal along the reef and limit fin damage to coral. Several sea turtles can be seen around Bonaire but they are rare. If you see one, in the water or on a beach, report the sighting to the Sea Turtle

ClubBonaire, c/o Tom van Eijck (Project Manager), *Sunset Beach Hotel*, T 5300 or contact the Bonaire Marine Park, T 8444.

On the E side of the island there is a shelf and a drop-off about 12m from the shore down to a 30m coral shelf and then another drop down to the ocean floor. The sea is rather rough for most of the year although it sometimes calms down in Oct or November. Along the W side of the island there are numerous dive sites of varying depths with wrecks as well as reefs. The most frequently dived sites include, Calabas Reef, Pink Beach, Salt City, Angel City and the Town Pier. There are also several sites for boat dives off Klein Bonaire, just 1½ km from Kralendijk. The Bonaire Marine Park Guide is recommended and can be obtained from dive shops or from the environmental group, STINAPA.

Snorkelling is recommended at Nukove, Boca Slagbaai, Playa Funchi, Playa Benge, Windsock Steep and Klein Bonaire. Salt Pier, where the wooden support pilings give shelter to small fish, and the *Divi Flamingo Hotel* pier encrusted with coral, are also popular. Dive boats usually take snorkellers along when dive sites are close to shore, about US$12 for 2-hr trip with divers on one tank. A guided snorkel programme has been started, offering training and marine education with experienced guides.

Whether you dive or snorkel, you are certain to enjoy the underwater world of Bonaire. Most visitors are tempted to take at least the one-day 'resort' or crash diving course. This enables you to decide if you'd like to continue, but one day will not make a diver of anyone. The main schools are (Peter Hughes) Dive Bonaire (T 8285, F 8238, at the *Divi Flamingo Beach Resort*), Buddy Dive Resort (PO Box 231, T 5080, F 7080), Habitat Dive Center (T 8290, F 8240, PO Box 88), *Carib Inn* (PO Box 68, T 8819, F 5295), Dive Inn Bonaire (PO Box 362, T 8761, F 8513, at the *Sunset Beach Hotel*, *Sunset Ocean Front Apartments* and next to the *Sunset Inn*), Sand Dollar Dive and Photo at the *Sand Dollar Beach Club* (T 5252, F 8760, also has photo shop), Great Adventures Bonaire (PO Box 312, T 7500, F 7507) at the *Harbour Village Beach Resort*, with instruction in several languages, Bon Bini Divers (PO Box 380, T 5425, F 5680) at the *Coral Regency Resort* and Bonaire Scuba Centre (T 8978, F 8846, at the *Black Durgon Inn*). Blue Divers Diveshop has been rec, Swiss and Belgian owned, English, German, Dutch, French and Spanish spoken, good value accommodation available, excellent guided dives with Bonairian Franklin Winklaar, who has been diving the reef for over 20 years, helping the likes of Jacques Cousteau, next to *Leeward Inn*, Kaya Grandi 60, Kralendijk, T 6860, F 6865. Prices are competitive, ranging from US$25-50 for a 2-tank dive if you have your own equipment. Add a 10% service charge on most diving. All packages include tank, air, weights and belt; equipment rental varies, US$6-11 for a BC jacket, US$6-11 for a regulator, US$6-7 for mask, snorkel and fins. Camera and other equipment rental widely available (Jerry Schnabel and Susan Swygert run Photo Tours, T/F 8060/ 4089). Dive Inn and Carib Inn are among the cheapest. All dive operations are well equipped and well staffed with a good safety record. If booking a package deal check whether their week-long dive packages include nightly night dives, or only one a week. For less experienced divers it is worth choosing a dive boat which keeps staff on board while the leader is underwater, in case you get into difficulties. We have received reports that in the case of reasonably experienced divers, some dive masters do not always get into the water but stay on board. Shore diving is available nearly everywhere. Dive packages are available at most hotels including the following: *Captain Don's Habitat, Carib Inn, Coral Regency, Divi Flamingo, Harbour Village, Sand Dollar Beach Club, Sunset Beach Hotel, Sunset Inn, Sunset Oceanfront Apartments* and *Sunset Villas*.

There is a US$10 pp levy for maintenance of the marine park which has to be paid only once a year.

OTHER SPORTS

There are tennis courts at the *Divi Flamingo Beach Resort*, open 0800-2200, T 8285; the *Harbour Village Beach Resort*; *Sand Dollar Beach Club*, open 0900-2100, T 8738; and at *Sunset Beach Hotel*, open 0800-1030, 1530-2100, T 5300. There is also horse riding but little else in the way of land based sports. Kunuku Warahama has horses and playgrounds for the children as well as lots of other animals. Lunch and dinner also available, T 5558/7537. Walking and birdwatching are popular in the Washington/Slagbaai National Park, particularly climbing up Mount Brandaris. A bridge club, Ups and Downs, meets at the *Hotel Rochaline*, T 8286, welcomes guest players, enroll before 1400, play starts 1930.

KRALENDIJK

Kralendijk, meaning coral dike, the capital of Bonaire, is a small, sleepy town with colourful buildings one or two storeys high. It is often referred to locally as simply 'Playa', because of its historic position as the main landing place. About 1,700 people live here and it is just a few blocks long with some streets projecting inland. Most of the shops are in the small Harbourside Shopping Mall and on the main street, the name of which changes from J A Abraham Boulevard to Kaya Grandi to Breedestraat. Places to visit include the Museum (Department of Culture), Sabana 14, T 8868, open weekdays 0800-1200, 1300-1700, folklore, archaeology and a shell collection; the small Fort Oranje, the plaza called Wilhelminaplein, and the fish market built like a Greek temple.

EXCURSIONS

Hire a car if you do not want to go on an organized tour. The island can be toured

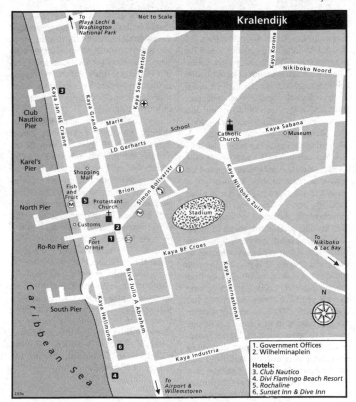

Kralendijk

To Playa Lechi & Washington National Park

Not to Scale

Kaya Korona

Nikiboko Noord

Kaya Soeur Bartola

Kaya Grandi

Kaya Jan NE Craane

Club Nautico Pier

Marie

School

Kaya Sabana

Catholic Church

○ Museum

LD Gerharts

Karel's Pier

Shopping Mall

Simon Bolivarstr

Brion

Kaya Nikiboko Zuid

North Pier

Fish and Fruit

Protestant Church

Stadium

Customs

Pol

Ro-Ro Pier

Fort Oranje

Kaya BF Croes

To Nikiboko & Lac Bay

C a r i b b e a n   S e a

South Pier

Blvd Julio A Abraham

Kaya Hellmund

Kaya Internashonal

N

Kaya Industria

To Airport & Willemstoren

1. Government Offices
2. Wilhelminaplein

Hotels:
3. Club Nautico
4. Divi Flamingo Beach Resort
5. Rochaline
6. Sunset Inn & Dive Inn

in a day if you start early but it is more pleasant to do a N tour on one day and a S tour another. Take food and drinks, there are rarely any available along the way, and aim to picnic somewhere you can swim to cool off. N of Kralendijk the road passes most of the hotels and planned developments, past the Water Distillation Plant along the 'scenic' road, which offers several descents to the sea and some excellent spots for snorkelling or diving along the rocky coastline. The first landmark is the radio station which has masses of aerials. Note that the road is one-way, do not turn round, but beware of pot holes and watch out for lizards sunbathing. At the National Parks Foundation building you can turn

right on a better road to **Rincon**, climbing to the top of the hill for a steep descent and a good view of Rincon and the Windward coast. Alternatively, continue along to the Bonaire Petroleum Company where the road turns inland to Goto Meer Bay, the best place to see flamingoes, on another road to Rincon, Bonaire's oldest village where the slaves' families lived. Past Rincon is a side road to the **Boca Onima** caves with their Arawak Indian inscriptions. Indian inscriptions in several caves around the island can still be seen, but they have not been decyphered.

The road leading N from Rincon takes you to **Washington/Slagbaai National Park**, which occupies the N portion of the island, about 6,075 ha, and contains more than 130 species of birds. The park is open to the public daily (entrance fee NAf 5, US$3, children up to 15 NAf 0.75) from 0800 to 1700 (no entry after 1500). There is a small museum of local historical items opposite the office and a room with geological explanations, bird pictures and a shell collection behind the office. Toilet at the entrance. Bring food and water. No hunting, fishing, 2-wheeled transport or camping is permitted. You can choose from a 34-km or a 24-km tour, the roads being marked by yellow or green arrows. You will get a route map when you pay to get in; a more detailed and attractively illustrated guidebook is available in English for NAf 10. The road is dirt, rough in parts, and the long route can be very hot and tiring unless you make several stops to swim and cool off. It is possible to drive round in an ordinary car but 4-wheel drive is preferable. Allow plenty of time as once you have chosen your route you have to stick to it. Even the short route takes a minimum of 2 hrs. Check your spare tyre before you start. Do not expect much variation in vegetation, the overall impression is of miles of scrub and cactus, broken only by rocks or salinjas. You can drive to Goto Meer on the longer route but you can get a better view from the observation point outside the Park. The return to Kralendijk is inland through the villages of **Noord Salinja** and **Antriol**. It is not well marked but you are unlikely to get lost for long.

The tour S passes the airport and Trans World Radio's towering 213m antenna which transmits 3 million watts, making it the hemisphere's most powerful radio station. Its shortwave broadcasts can be picked up in almost any part of the world. The coastal area S of Kralendijk is being heavily developed for tourism with construction of time share apartments, villas and hotels. The salt pier dominates the view along the coastal road and the salt pans are a stunning pink/purple colour. Further on are the snow-white salt piles and the three obelisks: blue, white, and orange, dating from 1838, with the tiny huts that sheltered the slaves who worked the saltpans. The roofs start at waist level and it is startling to think of men sharing one of these structures. Remember the flamingoes are easily frightened, so move quietly if near them.

At the S tip of the island is **Willemstoren**, Bonaire's lighthouse, which dates from 1837. Pass Sorobon Beach and the mangrove swamps to **Boca Cai** at landlocked **Lac Bay**, with its clear water excellent for underwater exploration. The extensive seagrass beds and surrounding mangroves are an important nursery for marine creatures; the Government plans to turn Lac into a protected area. What seem to be snow-capped hills from a distance are great piles of empty conch shells left by the local fishermen at Boca Cai. Near the Sorobon Resort is the Marcultura fish farming project (conch, lobster, shrimp etc), which you can tour Tues, Wed, Thur 1400-1500 with marine biologist, adults US$2, children under 12 US$1, T 8595 in advance. Take the road back to Kralendijk through the village of **Nikiboko**.

Information for travellers

● **Airlines**
ALM/KLM, T 8300 ext 220/1, after business hours, T 8500. Air Aruba, reservations, T 8300 ext 222, confirmations, T 7880, 7890. Servivensa, T 8361.

● **Banks**
Open 0830- 1200, 1400- 1600, Mon- Fri. Algemene Bank Nederland NV, Kaya Grandi No 2, T 8429; Maduro & Curiel's Bank (Bonaire) NV, T 5520, with a branch in Rincon, T 6266; Bank van de Nederlandse Antillen, T 8507; Banco de Caribe NV, T 8295.

● **Public holidays**
New Year's Day, Good Friday, Easter Monday, Queen's Birthday (30 April), Labour Day (1 May), Ascension Day, Bonaire Day (6 Sept), Christmas Day and Boxing Day.

BEFORE TRAVELLING

● **Documents**
See below under Curaçao Information for travellers.

● **Health**
The Hospital in Kralendijk has a decompression chamber, T 8900/8445. The emergency phone number for the hospital is T 110, and for Police, Fire and Ambulance T 114.

● **Religion**
Roman Catholic, San Bernardo Church, Kralendijk, T 8304, Our Lady of Coromoto, Antriol, T 4211, or San Ludovico Church, Rincon; United Protestant Church, T 8086; Evangelical Alliance Mission, T 6245; Jehovah's Witnesses, Antriol; New Apostolic Church, Nikiboko, T 8483; Seventh Day Adventist Church, T 4254.

GETTING THERE

AIR

If you fly with ALM you are entitled to a free return flight to Curaçao as part of your ticket. KLM flies from Amsterdam three times a week, of which one flight comes via Caracas. If you are a diver and it is specified on your airline ticket, KLM will allow you an extra 10 kg baggage allowance for diving equipment (regular allowance 20 kg tourist class, 30 kg business class) without incurring overweight charges. ALM flies from Aruba, Curaçao, Atlanta, Miami and several other places via Curaçao. Air Aruba flies from Aruba, Tampa, Baltimore, Miami and New York. Bonaire Airways fly from Aruba and Curaçao.

SEA

There is no regular ferry service from Venezuela but a coaster, *Don Andrés*, makes a weekly run from Muaco, La Vela. You have to contact the captains direct, try the *capitanía* or the maritime agency 2 blocks from the Plaza Bolívar. It is a long journey, heavy seas, not rec for the seasick or women.

● **Shopping**
Open 0800-1200 and 1400-1800, Mon- Sat, or until 2100 on Fri, and for a few hours on Sun if cruise ships are in port. Bonaire is not a major shopping centre, though some shops do stock high quality low duty goods. The Harbourside Shopping Mall contains small boutiques and a 1- hr photo processing shop, Kodalux. Photo Bonaire at *Divi Flamingo* is good for underwater photographic equipment to buy or hire. Photo Tours on Kaya Grandi 68, T 8060, also offers full underwater facilities. Local arts and crafts are largely shellwork, coral jewellery and fabrics. The state owned Fundashon Arte Industri Bonairano and the privately owned Caribbean Arts and Crafts shop are both in Kralendijk for souvenirs. In Kralendijk there is a supermarket on Kaya L D Gerharts, just past the Exito bakery, wellstocked, good. Uncle Buddy's Sand Dollar Grocery, open daily, is located in a small plaza in from of the *Sand Dollar Beach Club* along with *Lovers Ice Cream Parlour*. Near the *Divi Flamingo* a turning opposite leads to Joke's grocery and mini-market. Health food or snacks from Je-Mar Health shop, Kaya Grandi 5.

● **Voltage**
127 volts, 50 cycles.

ON DEPARTURE

● **Departure tax**
There is a departure tax of US$5.75 (NAf 10) on local flights and US$10 (NAf 18) on international flights.

ACCOMMODATION

● **Hotels**

Price guide

L1	over US$200	L2	US$151-200
L3	US$101-150	A1	US$81-100
A2	US$61-80	A3	US$46-60
B	US$31-45	C	US$21-30
D	US$12-20	E	US$7-11
F	US$4-6	G	up to US$3

High season rates (Dec 16 to 2 weeks after Easter) are roughly double low-season rates in the more expensive hotels; the cheaper ones tend to charge the same all year round. August is 'family month' with lots of good deals. Dive packages are available at most resorts. A 5% or US$4.50 per person per night government tax and 10-15% service charge must be added. All the hotels with on site dive shops, and some others besides, offer dive packages which give better value than the rack rates listed here.

On the leeward coast, S of Kralendijk are **A1** *Sunset Inn*, PO Box 333, T 8291/8448, F 4870/8865, only 7 rooms, some rooms with kitchenettes, bicycle rental, across the road from the sea, within easy walking distance of town, next to Dive Inn dive shop, use other *Sunset Resort* facilities, these include *Sunset Beach Hotel, Sunset Oceanfront Apartments, Sunset Inn, Sunset Villas, Sunset Hamlet Villas, Sunset Bel-Air Apartments* and *Sunset Diversion Apartments*, all with same T/F, in USA T 800-344-4439, 305-225-0572, F 305-225-0527; **L1-L2** *Divi Flamingo Beach Resort & Casino*, T 8285, F 8238, in USA 800-367-3484, F 919-419-2075, 105 units, standard rooms or more luxurious in the *Divi Club Flamingo*, is on a small artificial beach, snorkelling or diving just off the beach is excellent, Dive Bonaire and Photo Bonaire based here, tennis, pools, jacuzzi, dining is outdoors, some rooms in need of refurbishment, friendly staff but front office slow and inefficient, heavy tax and service charges, no food available after 2200 for late arrivals; next door is **A2** *Carib Inn*,

T 8819, F 5295, PO Box 68, one-bedroomed apartments and 2 bedrooms, a/c, cable TV, pool, dive shop. **L1-L2** *Plaza Resort Bonaire*, opened 1995 by Van der Valk group, previously known as The Point, 200 rooms, striving to be 5-star resort, J A Abraham Blvd, T 2500, F 2517; **L1-L2** *Port Bonaire Resort*, a condo-resort, villas and apartments, on waterfront, pool, not far to beaches, T 5636, F 3639, PO Box 269, in USA T 800-223-9815, F 212-251-1767.

Two cheaper hotels in Kralendijk are **A3** *Hotel Rochaline*, T 8286, F 8258, 25 rooms, functional, bar facing sea, restaurant, and **A3** *Leeward Inn*, T 5516, F 5517, 500m away at Kaya Grandi 60, 5 rooms, single, double, triple or suite, weekly rates cheaper, credit cards 5% extra, one room wheelchair accessible, *Harthouse Café* on site for all meals, clean, comfortable, very friendly, several recs. Also popular and often full is the **A3** lodge attached to *Blue Divers Diveshop* on Kaya Grandi, T 6860, F 6865, 4 rooms, common shower and kitchen, big garden, clean, cosy, rec for budget travellers/divers. The **A2** *Blue Iguana*, bed and breakfast, Kaya Prinses Marie 6, T/F 6855, 7 rooms, walking distance of seafront and shops.

Going N out of Kralendijk are **L1-L2** *Club Nautico Bonaire*, Kaya Jan NE Craane 24, T 5800, F 5850, short walk to town, 1-bedroom suites sleep 4, 2-bedroom penthouses sleep 6, fully equipped, balconies overlooking charter boats; **L1** *Harbour Village Beach Resort and Marina* on Playa Lechi, PO Box 312, T 7500, F 7507, 64 rooms or suites, a/c, cable TV, restaurants, bars, fitness centre, tennis, pool, spa, private beach, Great Adventures Bonaire dive shop, and non-motorized watersports, a growing, upmarket resort, look out for promotional packages, also watch out for extra charges such as breakfast, or incoming phone calls. **L3-A1** *Sunset Beach Hotel*, on Playa Lechi, T 8448, F 4870, part of *Sunset Resorts*, see above, 145 rooms and suites, a/c, cable TV, tennis, watersports, dive shop, good breakfast, ideal for divers; **L1-L3** *Sand Dollar Condominiums & Beach Club*, Kaya Gobernador N Debrot 79, T 8738, F 8760, T 1-800-288-4773, PO Box 262, 75 condominiums and 10 town houses, a/c, rocky shoreline, tennis, pool, sailing, sport fishing, Sand Dollar Dive and Photo, *Green Parrot* restaurant and grocery/delicatessen; **A1** *Buddy Beach and Dive Resort*, PO Box 231, T 5080, F 8647, 22 apartments all with sea views, a/c, kitchen, pool, Buddy Watersports Center; **L1-L2** *Coral Regency*, Kaya Gobernador N Debrot 91, PO Box

380, T 5580, F 5680, 31 1-2 bedrooms, suites, with kitchen, a/c, cable TV, pool, restaurant, Bon Bini Divers, more suites and entertainment complex planned; **L1-A1** *Captain Don's Habitat*, PO Box 88, T 8290, F 8240, in USA T 800-327 6709, F 305-371 2337, rooms, 11 cottages and 11 nice villas of differing standards with more under construction, well laid out seafront bar and restaurant, dive packages, family packages, special excursions for children during their family month every Aug, pool, dive shop with world's youngest snorkelling instructor, mountain bike rental; a little further along the coast is **L3-A2** *Black Durgon Inn/Pilot Fish Apartments*, Kaya Gobernador N Debrot 145, T 5736, F 8846, 8-room inn, 1-bedroom apartments, 2/3-bedroom villa, with view of Klein Bonaire, relaxing, non-commercial, a/c, cable TV, Bonaire Scuba Center dive shop; right by the radio masts is **A1-A2** *Bonaire Caribbean Club*, T 7901, F 7900, good view from *Hill Top Bar and Restaurant*, bicycles and snorkelling gear for rent, caves nearby, good walking.

On the windward coast are the **L1-L3** *Sorobon Beach Resort*, at Lac Bay, T 8080, F 5686, clothes optional, 23 chalets, snack bar, 6% charge for credit cards, and **L3-A1** *Lac Bay Resort*, T 8198, F 5198, in protected nature area, good seafood at *De Roode Pelikaan* restaurant. Also *Lac Bay Apartments*, T 8080, F 5363.

The Tourist Office has a more extensive list, including apartments and villas, of properties approved by Bonhata.

FOOD AND DRINK

International food at the major hotels varies on different nights of the week with barbecues or Indonesian nights, etc. Two good places to watch the fish are the **Green Parrot** at the *Sand Dollar Beach Club* and the **Chibi Chibi** at the *Divi Flamingo* (but do not feed them). Main courses in the upper- priced restaurants are about US$12- 20, but several restaurants do bar snacks if you want to economize. All food is imported, so even fruit and vegetables in the market are not cheap. Conch is rec, either fried or in a stew, as is goat stew. You may not want to try iguana soup, which may also be on the menu. If you want to eat lobster, check where the restaurant gets its supplies, some lobster fishermen are reported to be unauthorized and disapproved of by divers and conservationists.

● **Restaurants**
In Kralendijk, *Rendez-Vous*, Kaya L D Gerharts 3, T 8454, is rec, seafood specials, vegetarian choice, good vegetables, small and friendly, closed Sun; *Mona Lisa*, on Kaya Grandi, T 8718, closed Sun, bar and restaurant, interesting, imaginative food, Dutch chef enjoys discussing the menu, expect to pay NAf 25-35 for main course, friendly service, popular; *Mi Peron*, Kaya Caracas 1, a block from Roman Catholic Church, T 5199, many antiques, welcoming patio, daily specials, authentic *krijollo* restaurant, open 1200-1400, 1800-2200; *Otello Italian Restaurant and Bar*, Kaya Prinses Marie 4, T 4449, traditional Italian dishes from US$5-20; *Beefeater*, Kaya Grandi 12, T 8773/8081, open 1830- 2300, closed Sun, steak and seafood, pricey, small; *Raffles*, at the harbourside, T 8617, open 1830- 2230, tiny, smokey dining room, nice terrace, reasonable prices at lunch, closed Mon, Indonesian and international; *Zeezicht*, on the waterfront, does breakfast, lunch and dinner, sandwiches and omelettes as well as fish and some Indonesian, food all right but service criticized; a cheap place to eat is *Ankertje*, but view nothing special, overlooks the small industrial harbour; *Restaurant Lisboa*, in *Hotel Rochaline*, outdoor dining on waterfront, T 8286, grills and seafood, lobster; also some more modestly priced dishes; in the new shopping mall upstairs is *Jardin Tropical Restaurant*, open 1800-2200, closed Mon, T 5718, 5716, downstairs there is a pizza bar, *Cozzoli's Pizza*, for fast food; S of town, just past *Carib Inn* is *Richard's* waterfront dining, happy hour 1730-1830, dinner 1830- 2230, closed Mon, seafood specialities; *Den Laman Seafood Restaurant*, between the *Sunset Beach Hotel* and the *Sand Dollar Beach Club*, lots of fresh fish and lobster, 1800-2300, T 8955; *Toy's Grand Café*, on airport road opposite *Point Resort*, Indonesian, French or barbecue food, open from 1700, T 6666; *Twins Chicken Salad Bar*, in restored 19th century building on Kaya L D Gerharts, takeaway service available, lots of chicken dishes, lots of salads, open daily 1100-2400, T 4433; *Maiky Snack Kaminda*, New Amsterdam 30, an out-in-the-country spot to get home-made local food, soup, main dish and drink US$8.50, lunch from 1200 until the food runs out, get there early; *Sandwich Factory* in Kralendijk, T 7369, American-style deli.

There are a few good Chinese restaurants in town, the best of which is probably the

China Garden in an old restored mansion on Kaya Grandi, which is open for lunch and dinner, T 8480, closed Tues. *Mentor's*, about 1½ miles from *Sunset Beach*, is rec, cheap, large portions of Chinese food. *Bon Appetit*, Kaya BF Croes and Blvd Julio A Abraham, Chinese, good *nasi goreng*. *Borobudur*, Antriol village, Indonesian, eat in or takeaway. *Super Bon* vegetarian restaurant, open 0700-1800, closed Sat, good for snacks and juices, at Kaya Fraternan di Tilburg 2, T 8337. There are several snack bars in Kralendijk. *Josanana Snack*, Kaya Amsterdam 5, T 7869, takeaway food from 1900-2230 or later.

● **Water**

Comes from a desalinization plant and is safe to drink. Take water with you on excursions. Do not, however, wash in or drink water from outside taps. This is *sushi* (dirty) water, treated sufficiently for watering plants but nothing more.

GETTING AROUND

LAND TRANSPORT

● **Motoring**

The best way of getting about is to hire a car, scooter or mountain bike. Distances are not great but the heat is. Some hotels have a shuttle service to town. Hitching is fairly easy.

The speed limit in built-up areas is 33 kph, outside towns it is 60 kph unless otherwise marked. Many of the roads in Kralendijk and the N of the island are one-way.

There are filling stations at Kralendijk, Antriol and Rincon, open Mon-Sat 0700-2100. The Kralendijk station is also open Sun 0900-1530.

● **Car hire**

A B Car Rental at the airport, PO Box 339, T 8980 and in town, T 8667, also at *Divi Flamingo Beach Hotel*, T 8285 ext 32, run by the Toyota dealer, good cars, reliable. Dollar Rent A Car at Kaya Grandi No 86, Kralendijk, T 8888 and at airport T 5588, F 7788, new cars in excellent condition. Budget at Kaya L D Gerharts No 22, Kralendijk, T 8300 ext 225, also at *Divi Flamingo Beach Hotel*, T 8300 ext 234, at Shopping Gallery, Kaya Grandi, T 8460, Airport, T 8315, *Sunset Beach Hotel*, *Harbour Village Beach Resort*, and *Captain Don's Habitat*, F 8865/8118. Sunray Car Rental, at the airport, T 8980. Trupial Car Rental, Kaya Grandi No 96, T 8487. Camel Rent A Car, Kaya Betico Croes 28, T 5120, airport, T 5124, low rates for Suzuki cars, jeeps and vans. Avis, J A Abraham Blvd 4, Kralendijk, T 5795, F 5791. Daily rates, unlimited mileage start at US$30 for a minibus (dive car), US$33 for a Toyota Starlet, US$40 for a Suzuki jeep, not including tax and insurance. There are several other companies not listed here, plenty of choice. At the busiest times of the year, it is best to reserve a car in advance. 4-wheel drive vehicles are not easy to find, there are not many on the island, and it is best to order one in advance. Some companies prohibit the use of ordinary cars on unmade roads and in Washington/Slagbaai Park.

● **Motorcycles**

Small motorcycles can be rented from US$12 a day, contact Bonaire Motorcycle Rentals, Gobernador N Debrot 28, T 8488, or Happy Chappy Rentals at *Dive Inn*, Kaya C E B Hellmund 27, T 8761. Prices are high compared with car rental and there are several inconveniences: the tanks are small and filling stations are few and far between, and you are not allowed into Washington/Slagbaai National Park.

● **Bicycles**

Bicycles are available to rent from most hotels' front desks. Cycle Bonaire, T 7558, F 7690 at Kaya LD Gerharts 11 D, has TREK bicycles and offers rentals, sales, repairs and guided tours. The roads in the S are flat and in good condition but there is no shade and you would need lots of water and sun screen. In the N it is more hilly and the roads are not so good. For mountain bikers there are lots of unpaved trails and goat paths. Either way cycling is hot, hard work.

● **Bus**

There is no regular bus, but a so-called 'autobus' passes at certain places in town and takes you to the street or place you want to go for a few guilders.

● **Taxis**

There are taxis at the airport but they are difficult to find around the island. Taxis do not 'cruise' so you must telephone for one, T 8100. Drivers carry list of officially approved rates, including touring and waiting time, but be sure to agree a price beforehand. The short trip from the airport to the *Divi Flamingo Beach Resort* is US$8.50; airport to *Sunset Beach Hotel*, US$10.50; fares increase by 25% 2000-midnight and by 50% from midnight-0600. Taxis have TX on their licence plates.

COMMUNICATIONS

● **Postal services**
J A Abraham Blvd, Kralendijk, on the corner of Plaza Reina Wilhelmina opposite the ABN bank, open 0730- 1200, 1330- 1700 for stamps and postage, 1330- 1600 for money orders etc. Airmail to the USA and Canada is NAf1.75 for letters, NAf0.90 for postcards. There is also Express Mail and Federal Express Mail.

● **Telecommunications**
Direct dialling to the USA with a credit card is available at the airport and at Landsradio in town. The international code for Bonaire is 599-7, followed by a 4 digit local number.

MEDIA

● **Radio**
The news is broadcast in Dutch on Voz di Bonaire, FM 94.7 MHz, Mon-Sat on the hour 0700-1800. Transworld Radio broadcasts in English on 800 KHz MW daily 0700-0830, 2200-2400, news 0700 Mon-Fri, 0800 and 2200 daily, 2300 Sat and Sun; Caribbean weather forecast 0730 Mon-Fri, 0800 Sat and Sun. Radio Nederland, 6020 KHz at 0630, 6165 and 15315 KHz at 2030, 9590 and 11720 KHz at 2330. The Papiamento broadcast is on Ritmo FM, 97.1 FM.

ENTERTAINMENT

Nightlife is not well developed but there are a few places to go. Late night dancing takes place at the *E Wowo* and *Dynamite* discos and at the *Zeezicht Bar and Restaurant*. There is a casino at the *Divi Flamingo Beach Resort* (open 2000 except Sun). There is a modest cinema in Kralendijk.

TOURIST INFORMATION

● **Local tourist office**
Kaya Simón Bolívar 12, Kralendijk, T 8322/ 8649, F 8408. Their home page address is http:www.interknowledge.com/bonaire. The Bonaire Tourist Map shows all the dive and snorkelling sites around the island as well as the best bird watching places. The Official Roadmap with Dive Sites is available in some shops and adequate for most purposes. It gives a good street plan of Kralendijk, dive sites and points of interest on Bonaire and Klein Bonaire, but tends to indicate as 'beach' areas which are rocky cliffs.

● **Local travel agents**
Bonaire Tours, T 8778 or 8300 ext 212, F 8118, head office Kaya L D Gerharts 22 or at any Budget Rent A Car desk, 2- hrs N or S tour US$13, half or full day Washington Park tour, day trip to Curaçao. Bonaire Nature Tours for small groups, max 7 people, 0900-1800, led by Dutch biologist/dive instructor, tours can be tailor-made, T/F 7714. Taxis have fixed prices for sightseeing tours.

● **Tourist offices overseas**
In **Brazil**: Atomic Comunição E, Marketing S/C Ltda, R Marconi, 31-6 andar, CEP 01047, São Paulo, T 5511-231 2583, F 258 1013.

In **Canada**: RMR Group Inc, Taurus House, 512 Duplex Avenue, Toronto, Ontario, M4R 2E3, T (416) 484-4864, F (416) 485 8256.

In **Europe**: Interreps BV, Visseringlaan 24, 2288 ER Rijswijk, The Netherlands, T (31) 070-395 4444, F (31) 070-3368333.

In the **USA**: Adams Unlimited, 10 Rockefeller Plaza, Suite 900, New York, NY 10020, T (212) 956-5911, F 800-826-6247.

In **Venezuela**: Organización Ebor CA, Torre Capriles, Piso 2, Oficina 202, Plaza Venezuela, PO Box 52031, Sabana Grande, Caracas, T 782 3591, F 781 7445.

Bonhata, the Bonaire Hotel and Tourist Association, also promotes the island, T 5134, F 8240, PO Box 358.

ACKNOWLEDGEMENTS

The editors are most grateful to Larry Greenwood, Miami, for help with updating this chapter.

Curaçao

CURAÇAO, the largest of the five islands comprising the Netherlands Antilles, lies in the Caribbean Sea 60 km off the Venezuelan coast at a latitude of 12°N, outside the hurricane belt. It is 65 km long and 11 km at its widest, with an area of 448 square km. The landscape is barren, because of low rainfall (560 mm a year) which makes for sparse vegetation (consisting mostly of cactus thickets), and although it is not flat, the only significant hill is Mount Christoffel in the NW, which rises to a height of 375m. On a clear day you can see Aruba, Bonaire and Venezuela from the top. Deep bays indent the S coast, the largest of which, Schottegat, provides Willemstad with one of the finest harbours in the Caribbean. On the island cactus plants grow up to 6m high, and the characteristic wind-distorted divi divi trees reach 3m, with another 3m or so of branches jutting out away from the wind at right angles to the trunk.

HORIZONS

The population of 170,000 (1995 est) is truly cosmopolitan, and 79 nationalities are represented, of whom 16% were born outside the Netherlands Antilles.

THE ECONOMY

Curaçao has a more diversified economy than the other islands, yet even so, it suffered severe recession in the 1980s and unemployment is around 13% of the labour force. The major industry is the oil refinery dating back to 1917, now one of the largest in the world, to which the island's fortunes and prosperity are tied. Imports of crude oil and petroleum products make up two thirds of total imports, while exports of the same are 95% of total exports. That prosperity was placed under threat when Shell pulled out of the refinery in 1985, but the operation was saved when the island government purchased the plant, and leased it to Venezuela for US$11mn a year. Despite the need for a US$270mn reconstruction, principally to reduce pollution, the Venezuelan company, PDVSA, signed a 20-year lease agreement which came into effect in 1995, ending its previous system of short term operating leases. Bunkering has also become an important segment of the economy, and the terminal at Bullenbaai is one of the largest bunkering ports in the world. Besides oil, other exports include the famous Curaçao liqueur, made from the peel of the native orange. The island's extensive trade makes it a port of call for a great many shipping lines.

Coral reefs surrounding the island, constant sunshine, a mean temperature

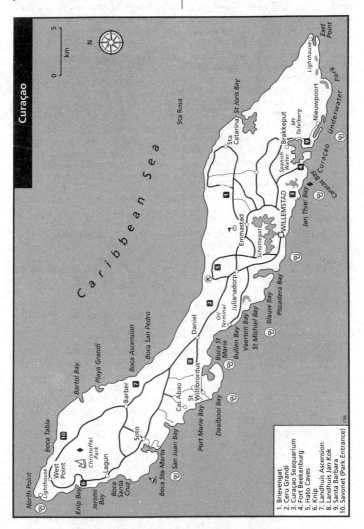

Curaçao

1. Brievengat
2. Ceru Grandi
3. Curaçao Seaquarium
4. Fort Beekenburg
5. Hato Caves
6. Knip
7. Landhuis Ascension
8. Landhuis Jan Kok
9. Santa Barbara
10. Savonet (Park Entrance)

of 27°C (81°F), and refreshing trade winds lure visitors the year round, making tourism the second industry. Curaçao used to be a destination for tourists from Venezuela, but a devaluation of the bolívar in 1983 caused numbers to drop by 70% in just one year and several hotels had to be temporarily taken over by the Government to protect employment. A restructuring of the industry has led to a change of emphasis towards attracting US and European tourists, as well as South Americans, and numbers have now increased. Stayover visitors in 1995 numbered 223,788 compared with 226,132 in 1994, while cruise ship passengers were 171,675, up from 160,516 the previous year, although the number of cruise ships calling declined from 256 to 237. Average hotel occupancy improved in 1995 to 73.5%, from 63.1% in 1994. The single largest market for visitors to Curaçao is Holland, with 30% of stayover arrivals, followed by the USA with 15% and Venezuela with 14%. Most rooms are in top grade hotels, with only a few in guest houses, but self-catering apartments, time share and condominiums are growing fast. There are about 2,000 hotel rooms, with another 2,500 planned to be built. Diving has been promoted and Curaçao now registers about 10,000 visiting divers a year. A dive improvement programme is being funded by the EC together with a beach improvement programme and a visitor information programme.

A third major foreign currency earner, the offshore financial sector, saw its operations severely curtailed in the 1980s. Once a centre for booking the issue of Eurobonds because of its favourable tax laws, the repeal of witholding tax in the USA in 1984 eliminated Curaçao's advantages and virtually wiped out the business. A second blow came with the cancellation by the USA, followed by similar action by the UK, of its double taxation treaty. These changes have led to greatly reduced income for the island's Government, although the offshore centre is actively seeking new areas of business, including captive insurance and mutual funds, in a highly competitive market. There are 61 banks, of which only 14 are licenced to carry out domestic business, the rest are offshore. After the crisis of the mid-1980s, assets in the offshore banks have risen steadily again.

DIVING AND MARINE LIFE

The waters around Curaçao contain a wide variety of colourful fish and plant life and several wrecks (*Superior Producer*, near the water distillation plant, and a tugboat in Caracas Bay) which have foundered on the coral reef just offshore. The reef surrounds the island and consists generally of a gently sloping terrace to a depth of about 10m, then a drop off and a reef slope with an angle of about 45°. The coral formations are spectacular in places and there are many huge sponges; one in Boca Sta Martha is so big it is known as 'the double bed'. There are lots of fish and you are likely to see barracuda, moray, eels, spiny lobsters, turtles, manta rays and maybe sharks. Underwater visibility averages 24m and water temperature varies between 24-27°C. There are lots of opportunities for successful underwater photography.

Scuba diving is becoming increasingly popular in Curaçao and many of the large resort hotels have dive shops on site. They have been encouraged by the establishment in 1983 of the Curaçao Underwater Park managed by the Netherlands Antilles National Parks Foundation (Stinapa), which stretches from the *Princess Beach Hotel* to East Point. The Park extends out from the shore to a depth of 60m and covers 600 ha of reef and 436 ha of inner bays. There is an underwater trail for snorkellers (accessible by boat) between the Seaquarium and Jan Thiel Bay.

Over 40 permanent mooring buoys for boats have been placed at dive sites along the S coast as part of Stinapa's programme for sustained utilization of the reef. A few of the sites can be dived from the shore (West Point, Blauwbaa, Port Marie, Daaibooi, Vaersen Bay, San Juan, Playa Kalki), but most of the coastal strip is private property and boat dives are necessary. The *Guide to the Curaçao Underwater Park*, by Jeffrey Sybesma & Tom van't Hof, published in 1989 by Stinapa and available in bookshops locally, describes the sites and discusses conservation. For independent divers and snorkellers without a boat there is the *Complete Guide to Landside Diving and Snorkelling Locations in Curaçao*, by Jeffrey Sybesma and Suzanne Koelega, including a map with the sites and roads to them. No harpoons or spear guns are allowed and make sure you do not damage or remove coral or any other sea creatures.

There are many dive operators, not all of which are mentioned here, and it is worth shopping around before booking a package deal. Most operators offer a single boat dive for around US$30-35, a 2-tank dive for US$55-60 and snorkelling trips including equipment for about US$15-20, but check when booking whether 10% service is included in the quoted price. Underwater Curaçao (T 618100, F 618200) at the *Lions Dive Hotel* next to the Seaquarium is one of the larger operations with 2 dive boats for 20 divers each and 2 scheduled dives a day. It has a large air station equipment rental, a retail shop and offers several courses. Princess Divers, a highly recommended Peter Hughes diving operation, T 658991, F 655756, has 2 new dive boats and offers snorkelling, boat dives, shore dives, PADI courses, photo equipment rental and services at the *Princess Beach Resort and Casino*. *Curaçao Caribbean Hotel* has the Seascape Diving Shop on site, with 3 dive boats, a glass bottom boat, sailing boats and jet skis, T 625000 ext 6031, F 625846. Coral Cliff Diving at Santa Martha Bay (PO Box 3782, T 642822, F 642237) has a deliberately sunk airplane in shallow water just

offshore for divers and also offers introductory or certification courses and package deals, also windsurfing US$10/hrs, with sunfish, hobiecats and pedalboats available, prices not including 10% service. Sami Scuba Centre Dive School Wederfoort has been in operation since 1966, very friendly, reputable, mostly shore dives, the drop starts 25m from dive centre; a 6-day package including air, weights and no tank limit, costs US$120, a PADI open water course is US$257, accommodation available, contact Eric and Yolanda Wederfoort, Marine Beach Club, St Michielsbaai, T 684414, F 692062.

The Seaquarium, SE of Willemstad, just beyond the *Lions Dive Hotel*, has a collection of undersea creatures and plants found around the island, which live in channelled sea water to keep them as close as possible to their natural environment. Some tanks are incorrectly marked, the inhabitants have obviously been moved. The Seaquarium was built in 1984, the lagoons and marina being excavated so as to leave the original coastline untouched and do minimal damage to the reef offshore. A new attraction is the shark and animal encounter programme, good for photography, US$27.50 for diving, US$16.50 snorkelling. Open 0830-2200, entrance US$12.50, children under 15 US$7, after 1600 US$3 and US$1.50 respectively, T 616666. There is a restaurant, snack bar and shops selling shells and coral in marked contrast to the conservation efforts of the Underwater Park administration. The Seaquarium can be reached by bus marked Dominguito from the Post Office at 35 mins past the hour (except for 1335), which passes the *Avila Beach Hotel*.

The *Seaworld Explorer* is a cruising underwater observatory, not a submarine, you sit in the hull and look out of the windows as the vessel moves along the wall. The boat leaves from the Seaquarium, 1630, one-hour trip, US$29, children US$19, T 604892.

BEACHES AND WATERSPORTS

There are several nice beaches on Curaçao. The NW coast is rugged and rough for swimming, but the W coast offers some sheltered bays and beaches with excellent swimming and snorkelling. Windsurfing, waterskiing, yachting and fishing are available at resorts. Many of the beaches are private and make a charge per car (amount depends on day of the week and popularity, US$3-6) but in return you usually get some changing facilities, toilets and refreshments. Public beaches are free but most have no facilities and some are rather dirty and smelly round the edges. Topless sunbathing is not recommended on public beaches but is tolerated on private beaches.

Heading S out of Willemstad is the small, artificial beach at the *Avila Beach Hotel*, where non-residents pay an entrance fee. The sand is very gritty at the water's edge and the sea is not calm enough to see much if you snorkel. You can get to the beach at Piscadera Bay near the *Curaçao Caribbean* hotel by catching one of their shuttle buses from beside the Rif Fort in Otrabanda. SE of Willemstad, by the *Princess Beach Hotel*, the *Lions Dive Hotel* and the Seaquarium (see above), is a 450m, man-made beach and marina with all watersports available. Entrance to the beach is US$1.50. It can be crowded and noisy from music and motorized watersports. Showers and toilets. Past the Seaquarium is a residential area and private beach on Jan Thiel Bay, good swimming and snorkelling, entrance free for tourists, changing facilities, drinks and snacks, closed Tues. Santa Barbara located at the mouth of Spanish Water Bay on the Mining Company property, is a favourite with locals and has changing rooms, toilets and snack bars, open 0800-1800. Entrance US$2.25 pp. You can take a bus from the Post Office, get off at the Mining Company gate and hitchhike down to the beach, or take a taxi, it is too far

to walk. Across the bay, which is one of the island's beauty spots, is the Curaçao Yacht Club, with a pleasant bar. There are four yacht clubs in Spanish Water.

Travelling NW from Willemstad heading towards Westpoint, there are lots of coves and beaches worth exploring. A left turn soon after leaving town will take you to Blauw Bay, good for snorkelling but a Curasol development is under construction and the beach is now closed, or to St Michiel's Bay, a fishing village and tanker clearing harbour (free). Daaibooibaai, S of St Willibrordus is a public beach and gets very crowded on a Sun. Further up the coast, Port Marie (private, charge per car) is sandy but there is no shade. Cas Abao beach is the best: pretty with good snorkelling and diving from shore in beautiful clear water, changing facilities, showers, shade huts, lounge chairs, US$3/car per day, US$5 at weekends and holidays, snacks and beverages. San Juan, a private beach with lots of coral is off to the left of the main Westpoint road down a poor track, entrance fee charged. Boca Sta Martha, where the *Coral Cliff Resort* is located, is quiet with nice sea, beach entrance US$4.50 for non-residents, no pets or food allowed on the beach, some shade provided. Lagun is a lovely secluded beach in a small cove with cliffs surrounding it and small fishing boats pulled up on the sand. It is safe for children and good for snorkelling, there are facilities and some shade from trees. Some buses pass only 50m from the beach. Jeremi, a public beach with no charge, is of the same design, slightly larger sandy beach with a steep drop to deep water and boats moored here, protected by the cliffs. Further up the coast, Knip is a more open, larger, sandy beach again with cliffs at either end. Many people used to rate this the best beach on the island but it has become littered and dirty. There are some facilities here and it is very popular at weekends when there is loud music and it gets crowded and noisy.

A charge per car is being considered even though it is a public beach. Playa Abau is big, sandy, with beautiful clear water, surrounded by cliffs, some shade provided, toilets, well organized, popular at weekends and busy. Nearing the W tip, Playa Forti has dark sand and good swimming. There is a restaurant on the cliff top overlooking the sea which gets very busy at weekend lunchtimes. The beach at Westpoint below the church is stoney and littered, the only shade comes from the poisonous manchineel trees, but there is so much litter under them you would not be tempted to sit there. Fishing boats tie up at the pier but bathers prefer to go to Playa Forti. Beyond Westpoint is Kalki beach which is good for snorkelling and diving as well as bathing. Westpoint is the end of the road, about 45 mins by car or 1 hr by bus from Otrabanda, US$0.85.

Many charter boats and diving operators go to Klein Curaçao, a small, uninhabited island off East Point which has sandy beaches and is good for snorkelling and scuba diving, a nice day trip with lunch provided. The most popular and respected charter boats are *Mermaid* and *Something Special*, both operated by Bart Schoonen, T 601530, F 616569, he also does sunset trips, deep sea fishing, private parties etc, his sunset trips from Spanish Waters past *Princess Beach* and *Avila* hotels into St Anna Harbour are particularly recommended, US$25 with music, wine, beer, soft drinks and snacks, very good and fun. *Waterworld* leaves from the Seaquarium Marina for snorkelling trips (US$20), sunset trips (US$30), Klein Curaçao day trips (US$20) and to Banda Abou (US$25) every Fri for barbecue on the beach; motor boat takes 100 passengers and departures sometimes depend on whether there is a cruise ship in port, T 656042, F 617600. There are also day sailing trips from Willemstad up the coast with barbecue lunches at, for example, Port Marie, for about US$55, and weekend sailing trips to Bonaire,

accommodation on board, for about US$225. One such sailing ship is the 120 ft *Insulinde*, T 601340.

The Curaçao International Sailing Regatta is held in January with competitions in three categories, short distance (windsurfers, hobie cats, sunfish etc), long distance (yachts race 112 km to Klein Curaçao and back) and open boat (trimarans, catamarans etc race 32 km to Spanish Water and back), all starting from the *Princess Beach Hotel*. For details, contact the Seaquarium, T 616666. The Sami Sail Regatta in April is organized by the fishing village of Boca St Michiel. The International Blue Marlin tournament is held in March. The Yacht Club is at Brakkeput Ariba, z/n, T 673038 or contact Mr B van Eerten, T 675275. Sail Curaçao has sailing courses, rentals and boat trips, also surfing lessons, T 676003. They also own *Vira Cocha* at the Seaquarium, which does snorkelling, picnic and sunset trips (US$20-25).

OTHER SPORTS

Rancho Alegre, T 681181, does horse riding for US$15/hr, including transport. Ashari's Ranch offers horses for hire by the hour inland, or 1½ hrs including a swim at the beach, open 1000-1900, Groot Piscadera Kaya A-23, T 690315, beginners as well as experienced riders, playground for children. There is bowling on the island, Curaçao Bowling Club, Chuchubiweg 10, T 379275, 6 lanes, US$11/hr, reservations advised. The Curaçao Golf and Squash Club at Wilhelminalaan, Emmastad, has a 10-hole sand golf course open 0800-1230, green fee US$15 for 18-hole round, and 2 squash courts, US$7, open 0800-1800, T 373590. Santa Catharina Sport and Country Club, T 677028/677030, F 677026, has 6 hard tennis courts, a swimming pool, bar and restaurant. The large hotels have tennis courts: the *Curaçao Caribbean*, *Holiday Beach*, *Sonesta* and the *Princess Beach* have a pro.

FESTIVALS

Curaçao, Aruba and Bonaire all hold the traditional pre-Lent carnival. On the Sunday a week before is the children's parade. Curaçao's main parade is on the Sunday at 1000 and takes 3 hrs to pass, starting at Otrabanda. The following Monday most shops are closed. On the Monday at 1500 there is a children's farewell parade and there is a Farewell Grand Parade on the Tuesday evening when the Rey Momo is burned.

Several music festivals are held throughout the year. You can hear *tumba* around carnival time. Contact the Curaçao Jazz Foundation, T 658043, for details of the May and November jazz festivals and the Festival Center, T 376343, for details of *salsa* (August) and *merengue* (May) festivals. For the Golden Artists Music Festival in October, T 655777.

WILLEMSTAD

Willemstad, capital of the Netherlands Antilles and of the island of Curaçao (population about 140,000), is full of charm and colour. The architecture is a joyous tropical adaptation of 17th-century Dutch, painted in storybook colours. Pastel shades of all colours are used for homes, shops and government buildings alike. Fanciful gables, arcades, and bulging columns evoke the spirit of the Dutch colonial burghers.

The earliest buildings in Willemstad were exact copies of Dutch buildings of the mid-17th century, high-rise and close together to save money and space. Not until the first quarter of the 18th century did the Dutch adapt their northern ways to the tropical climate and begin building galleries on to the façades of their houses, to give shade and more living space. The chromatic explosion is attributed to a Governor-General of the islands, the eccentric Vice-Admiral Albert Kikkert ('Froggie' to his friends), who blamed his headaches on the glare

of white houses and decreed in 1817 that pastel colours be used. Almost every point of interest in the city is in or within walking distance of the shopping centre in **Punda**, which covers about five blocks. Some of the streets here are only 5m wide, but attract many tourists with their myriad shops offering international goods at near duty-free prices. The numerous jewellery shops in Willemstad have some of the finest stones to be found anywhere. There is a red and white trolley train which takes 60 passengers around the streets of Punda several times a day.

The Floating Market, a picturesque string of visiting Venezuelan, Colombian and other island schooners, lines the small canal leading to the Waaigat, a small yacht basin. Fresh fish, tropical fruit, vegetables and a limited selection of handicrafts are sold with much haggling. Visit early in the morning.

In the circular, concrete, public market building nearby there are straw hats and bags, spices, butcheries, fruit and vegetables for sale, while in the old market building behind, local food is cooked over charcoal and sold to office workers at lunchtime.

Nearby on Hanchi Snoa, is one of the most important historical sites in the Caribbean, the **Mikvé Israel-Emanuel synagogue**, which dates back to 1732, making it the oldest in the Western Hemisphere. In the 1860s, several families broke away from the Mikvé Israel congregation to found a Sephardi Reform congregation which was housed in the Temple Emanuel (1867-1964) on the Wilhelminaplein. In 1964, however, they reunited to form the Mikvé Israel-Emanuel congregation, which is affiliated with both the Reconstructionist Foundation and the World Union for Progressive Judaism. Services are held Fri 1830 and Sat 1000. Normally open 0900-1145 and 1430-1700, free. The big brass chandeliers are believed to be 300 years older than their synagogue, originating in Spain and Portugal, their

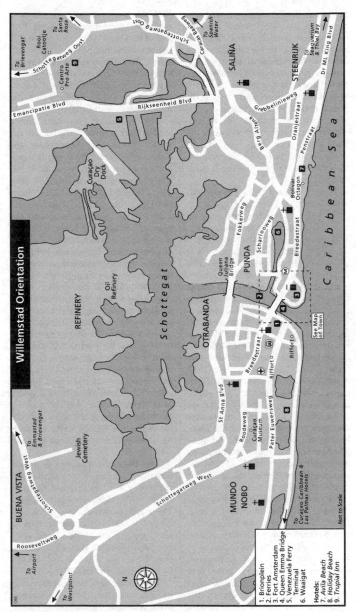

Willemstad Orientation

To Santa Rosa

Rooi Catootje

To Brievengat

Schottegatweg Oost

Centro Pro Arte

9

1500 Schottegatweg

Curaçaobaaiweg

To Spanish Water

SALIÑA

Emancipatie Blvd

Rijkseenheid Blvd

STEENRIJK

To Seaquarium & Thiel Bay

Dr ML King Blvd

Grebbelinieweg

Berg Altena

Oranjestraat

Penstraat

5

Curaçao Dry Dock

REFINERY

Oil Refinery

Schottegat

Fokkerweg

Queen Juliana Bridge

PUNDA

Bolivar

Octagon

7

Scharlooweg

Breedestraat

6

M

2

3

1

4

See Map of Town

C a r i b b e a n   S e a

OTRABANDA

Rifford

Rifford

Breedestraat

8

St Anna Blvd

Roodeweg

Curaçao Museum

Pater Euwensweg

To Emmastad & Brievengat

Jewish Cemetery

BUENA VISTA

Schottegatweg West

To Westpoint

To Airport

Rooseveltweg

Schottegatweg West

MUNDO NOBO

To Curaçao Caribbean & Las Palmas Hotels

Not to Scale

N

1. Brionplein
2. Ferries
3. Fort Amsterdam
4. Queen Emma Bridge
5. Venezuela Ferry Terminal
6. Waaigat

Hotels:
7. *Avila Beach*
8. *Holiday Beach*
9. *Trupial Inn*

candles are lit for Yom Kippur and special occasions. The names of the four mothers, Sara, Rebecca, Leah and Rachel are carved on the four pillars and there are furnishings of richly carved mahogany with silver ornamentation, blue stained glass windows and stark white walls. The traditional sand on the floor is sprinkled there daily, some say, to symbolize the wandering of the Israelites in the Egyptian desert during the Exodus. Others say it was meant to muffle the sound of the feet of those who had to worship secretly during the Inquisition period.

In the courtyard is the **Jewish Museum**, occupying two restored 18th century houses, which harbours an excellent permanent exhibition of religious objects, most of which have been donated by local Jewish families. There are scrolls, silver, books, bibles, furniture, clothing and household items, many 18th century pieces and family bequeathments. Two circumcision chairs are still in use. Outside are some tombstones and a ritual bath excavated during restoration work. The Museum is open Mon-Fri 0900-1145, 1430-1645, closed Jewish and public holidays, entrance US$2, children US$1, T 611633. A small shop sells souvenirs, the Synagogue Guide Book and *Our Snoa*, papiamento for Synagogue, produced for the 250th anniversary in 1982. *Sephardim: The Spirit That Has Withstood The Times*, by Piet Huisman (Huisman Editions, The Netherlands, 1986) is an interesting illustrated account of the Sephardic communities of the Caribbean and the Americas, setting them in their historical context. Available in the synagogue shop and bookshops in town. Unfortunately, for those who want deeper research of the Jewish families, the *History of the Jews of the Netherlands Antilles*, by Isaac S and Suzanne A Emmanuel, two volumes, is no longer in print. W of the city, on the Schottegatweg Nord, is one of the two Jewish cemeteries, Bet Chayim (or Beth Haim), consecrated in 1659 and still in use. There are more than 1,700 tombstones from the 17th and 18th centuries, with bas-relief sculpture and inscriptions, many still legible. It is a little out of the way but well worth a visit. It is also a fine example of what atmospheric pollution can do, as the tombstones have suffered from the fumes from the surrounding oil refinery.

The 18th century Protestant church, the **Fortkerk**, located at the back of the square behind **Fort Amsterdam**, the Governor's palace, still has a British cannonball embedded in its walls. It has recently been renovated, T 611139, open Mon-Fri 0900-1200, 1400-1700. Admission US$2/NAf3, children US$1, you get a guided tour of the church and the associated museum. It is not as large as the synagogue museum, but well laid out, with some interesting items, eg original church silver and reproductions of old maps and paintings of Curaçao. Note the clock in the ceiling of the church and make sure you are shown the still-functioning rain water cistern inside the church. It was once the main source of fresh water for the garrison.

Two forts, **Rif Fort** and **Water Fort** were built at the beginning of the 19th century to protect the harbour entrance and replace two older batteries. All that is left of Rif Fort is a guard house dating from about 1840 but you can walk on the walls and eat at the restaurants in the vaults. The Water Fort Arches have been converted to house shops, bars and restaurants.

The Philatelic Museum is on the corner of Keukenstraat and Kuiperstraat in a recently restored building which is the oldest in Punda (1693). There is a comprehensive permanent display of Dutch Caribbean stamps, plus temporary exhibitions. Open Mon-Fri, 0900-1700, Sat 1000-1500, admission US$2 or NAf3.50 for adults, US$1 for children, T 658010.

The Central Bank of the Netherlands Antilles owns and operates a **Numismatic Museum**, Breedestraat 1, Punda,

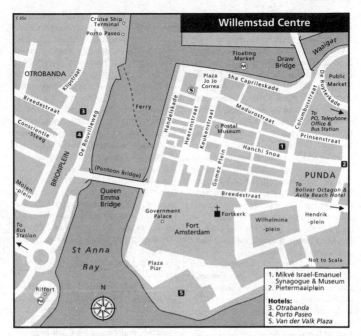

Willemstad Centre

1. Mikvé Israel-Emanuel
   Synagogue & Museum
2. Pietermaaiplein

Hotels:
3. Otrabanda
4. Porto Paseo
5. Van der Valk Plaza

Not to Scale

with a collection of coins and notes from the Netherlands Antilles and some from other countries, as well as a display of precious and semi-precious gemstones on loan from a local collector. Open Mon-Fri 0830-1130, 1330-1630, free admission, T 613600, F 615004.

The Octagon, Simón Bolívar's sisters' house where Simón Bolívar stayed during his exile in Curaçao in 1812, is near the *Avila Beach Hotel* reached down a small road off Penstraat just before you get to the hotel. The building is in need of some repair work and looks neglected although there is an attendant (make sure his dogs are chained). There is one octagonal room downstairs, with some manuscripts, pictures and books, and a similar one upstairs, with a bed and some furniture; not much to see unless you are a Bolívar aficionado. Closed lunchtimes.

The swinging **Queen Emma bridge** spans St Anna Bay, linking the two parts of the city, Punda and Otrabanda (the latter means 'the other side' in Papiamento, and people tend to refer to 'Punda' and 'Otrabanda' rather than 'Willemstad'). Built on sixteen great pontoons, it is swung aside some thirty times a day to let ships pass in and out of the harbour. The present bridge, the third on the site, was built in 1939. While the bridge is open, pedestrians are shuttled free by small ferry boats. The bridge is closed to vehicular traffic.

The new **Queen Juliana** fixed bridge vaults about 50m over the bay and connects Punda and Otrabanda by a 4-lane highway. Taxis will often offer to stop at the bridge so you can get a panoramic view and photo of Willemstad on one side and the oil refinery on the other. Although you can reach it on foot it is not open for pedestrians; the wind and the way it shakes will explain why.

Parts of **Otrabanda** are gradually being restored and there are many old houses here, both small, tucked away down alleys, and large mansions or town houses. The Belvedere, an Otrabanda landmark, was restored in 1992-93. Breedestraat is the main shopping street, the **Basilica Santa Ana**, founded in 1752 and made a Basilica in 1975 by Pope Paul VI, is just off here. The houses fronting on to the Pater Euwensweg, the highway heading W along the coast, once overlooked the Rifwater lagoon, now reclaimed land. Along St Anna Bay, past the ferry landing, is **Porto Paseo**, a restored area with bars and restaurants, popular on Fri evenings when there is music and dancing, or you can just sit and admire the view. The old hospital has been restored and is now the *Hotel and Casino Porto Paseo*.

On the outskirts of Otrabanda, on van Leeuwenhoekstraat, is the **Curaçao Museum**, founded in 1946 (housed in an old quarantine station built in 1853) with a small collection of artefacts of the Caiquetio Indian culture, as well as 19th and 20th century paintings, antique locally-made furniture, and other items from the colonial era. Labels are inadequate and the hand-out leaflets only partly make up for this. In the basement there is a children's museum of science, but it is limited and rather outdated, almost a museum piece in itself. On the roof is a 47-bell carillon, named The Four Royal Children after the four daughters of Queen Juliana of the Netherlands, which was brought from Holland and installed in 1951. Lots of explanatory leaflets are given out at the museum, with a suggested route map. The museum is open daily, except Sat, admission US$2.25, US$1.25 for children under 14 (open Mon-Fri 0900-1200 and 1400-1700, Sun 1000-1600, T 623873).

Another area within walking distance of Punda and worth exploring, is **Scharloo**, across the Wilhelmina bridge from the floating market. A former Jewish merchant housing area, now under renovation, there are many substantial properties with all the typical architectural attributes; note the green house with white trimmings known as the Wedding Cake House at Scharlooweg 77. Under a 5-10 year plan to restore the buildings, companies or government departments take them over for use as offices in many cases. Reading matter of architectural enthusiasts includes the expensive but magnificently illustrated *Scharloo - a nineteenth century quarter of Willemstad, Curaçao: historical architecture and its background*, by Pauline Pruneti-Winkel (Edizioni Poligrafico Fiorentino, Florence 1987), and a more general collection of essays with illustrations, *Building up the Future from the Past: Studies on the Architecture and Historic Monuments of the Dutch Caribbean*, edited by Henry E Coomans and others (De Walburg Pers, Zutphen, the Netherlands, 1990).

The **S E L Maduro Library** is at the **Landhuis Rooi Catootje**, the site, in 1954, of the Round Table Conferences which led to the Statuut between the Dutch Kingdom and its Caribbean territories. The library, in the beautifully restored landhuis, contains all manner of things Caribbean and the conference table still stands in the dining room. Open weekdays 0900-1200, T 375119. Take the Rond minibus from Punda and ask to be let off next to the chicken factory, a site better known to most drivers than the house itself.

EXCURSIONS

The restored country estate houses, or *landhuizen*, emerge here and there in the parched countryside. Not all of them are open to the public but it is worth visiting some of those that are. Set in 503 ha in the E part of the island is **Brievengat**. Its exact date of construction is unknown, but it is believed to date from the early 18th century. It was used in the 19th century to produce cattle, cochineal and aloe, but a hurricane in 1877 devastated the plantation and the house which were gradually abandoned. Shell later took over the property to extract water from the subsoil, but in 1954 when it was in a state of ruin Shell donated it to the Government who restored it to its former grandeur. The windows and the roof are typical of the local style but unusual are the arches extending the length of the house and the two towers at either side, which were once used to incarcerate slaves. Open daily 0915-1215, 1500-1800, entrance US$1.10, children half price, bar and snacks, live music on Wed and Fri and often on Sun, check beforehand, open house on Sun 1000-1500 with folklore show at 1700 on last Sun of the month, T 378344. Take the bus marked Punda-Hato from Punda at 15 mins past the hour and get off at the Sentro Deportivo Korsou, US$0.40.

Chobolobo, at Salinja, came into the Senior family in 1948 and Senior & Co make the Curaçao liqueur here, using a copper still dating from 1896 and the original Valencia orange known locally as Laraha. Open Mon-Fri 0800-1200, 1300-1700, visitors may taste the liqueur. The clear, orange, amber, red, green and blue are for cocktails and all taste the same; others are chocolate, coffee, rum raisin. Chobolobo is worth visiting, but if you resist the temptation to buy Senior & Co's products you will find them cheaper in the duty free lounge at Hato Airport. Entrance free, T 613526.

Near the Hato international airport are the **Hato Caves** which contain stalactites and stalagmites, a colony of long nose bats and pools among spectacular limestone formations. There are also some Caquetio rock drawings believed to be 1,500 yrs old. Guided tours every hour, the last one at 1600, open 1000-1800, closed Mon, T 680379, US$4.50.

Jan Kok is the oldest landhouse on the island, dating from 1654 and overlooking the salt flats where flamingoes gather. It is open for private tours by reservation only Mon-Fri, T 648087, open on Sun 1100-2000, when local food

and Dutch pancakes are served. Take the bus marked Lagun and Knip from the Riffort, Otrabanda, at half past the even hour in the morning or half past the odd hour in the afternoon, US$1. **Santa Martha**, built in 1700 and restored in 1979, is used as a day care centre for the physically and mentally handicapped but is open Mon-Thur, 0900-1200, 1300-1500, Fri 0900-1200, first Sun in the month 0900-1300, T 641559. **Ascension**, built in 1672 and restored in 1963, is used by Dutch marines stationed on the island and is only open to the public the first Sun of the month 1000-1400, with local music, handicrafts and snacks, T 641950. Take bus marked Westpunt from Otrabanda (see below). **Landhuis Kenepa** or **Knip**, near the beach of the same name, is a restored 17th century landhouse where there was a slave rebellion in 1795. It has a collection of antique furniture and an exhibition about the Kenepa people. Open Mon-Sun 0900-1600, US$2, children US$1, T 640244, F 640385. On the same bus route as Jan Kok.

The Christoffel Park covers an area of 1,860 ha in the W of the island, including Mount Christoffel at 375m, which was formerly 3 plantations. These plantations, Savonet, Zorgvlied and Zevenbergen, are the basis for a system of well-marked trails, blue (9km), green (7.5km or 12km) and yellow (11km), and there is a red walking trail up Mount Christoffel which takes about 3 hrs there and back. You can see a wide range of fauna and flora, including orchids, the indigenous *wayacá (lignum vitae)* plant, acacias, aloe, many cacti, calabash and the tiny Curaçao deer. The ruins of the Zorgvlied landhouse can be seen off the green route. The Savonet route takes you to the coast and along to Amerindian rock drawings, painted between 500 and 2,000 years ago in terracotta, black and white. In this area there are also two caves (take a strong torch), one of which is about 125m long and you have to crawl in before you can stand up (lots of bats and lots of guano on the ground) and walk to the 'white chamber'(stalactites and stalagmites) and the 'cathedral'. The 17th century **Savonet Plantation House** is at the entrance to the Park on the Westpoint road, but it is not open to the public. However, several outbuildings are used; there is a small museum with archaeological exhibits, open Mon-Sat 0800-1600, Sun 0600-1500, US$1.40, T 640363. The Park is also open from 0800 Mon-Sat, US$9 pp, admission to the mountain side closes at 1400 and to the ocean side at 1500, although you can stay in until later. On Sun the Park opens at 0600 and closes at 1500, no admittance after 1300 and 1400 for inland or sea routes. Guided tours are available, special walks at dawn or dusk are organized at random, check in the newspapers, evening walking tours to see the Curaçao deer, maximum 8 people, reservations essential, T 640363. Stinapa publishes an excellent *Excursion Guide to the Christoffel Park, Curaçao*, by Peer Reijns, 1984, which is available at the Park administration. A basic map of the trails is also provided. The bus Otrabanda- Westpunt passes the entrance to the Park.

Behind Spanish Water Bay on the S coast rises Mount Tafelberg, where phosphate mining used to take place.

Information for travellers

BEFORE TRAVELLING

● Documents

All visitors must have an onward ticket to a destination outside the Netherlands Antilles. US citizens do not need a passport; a birth certificate, alien registration card or naturalization papers are sufficient. Canadians must have a valid passport or birth certificate. Transit visitors and cruise ship visitors must have proof of identity for a 24-hr, or less, stay on the island. Immigration procedures at the airport are quick and easy.

● Health

The climate is healthy and non-malarial; epidemic incidence is slight. Rooms without air-conditioning or window and door screens may need mosquito nets during the wetter months of Nov and Dec and sometimes May and June, and, although some spraying is done in tourist areas, mosquitoes are a problem. Some anti-mosquito protection is rec if you are outdoors any evening. The 550-bed St Elisabeth Hospital is a well-equipped and modern hospital with good facilities including a coronary unit and a recompression chamber. For emergencies, T 624900 (hospital), 625822 (ambulance). The Sentro Mediko Santa Rosa, at Santa Rosaweg 329, is open 7 days a week, 0700-0000, laboratory on the premises, T 676666, 672300.

Warning Beware of a tree with small, poisonous green apples that borders some beaches. This is the manchineel (*manzanilla*) and its sap causes burns on exposed skin.

MONEY

● Currency

The currency is the guilder, divided into 100 cents. There are coins of 1, 2½, 5, 10, 25, 50 cents and 1 and 2½ guilders, and notes of 5, 10, 25, 50, 100, 250 and 500 guilders. Old and new coins are in circulation. The older ones are bigger, the newer $\frac{1}{2}$, 1 and $2\frac{1}{2}$ guilder coins are gold coloured.

● **Exchange**
The exchange rate is US$1=NAf1.77 for bank notes, NAf1.79 for cheques, although the rate of exchange offered by shops and hotels ranges from NAf1.75-1.80. Credit cards and US dollars are widely accepted.

GETTING THERE

AIR
Curaçao is very well served by airlines from Europe, the USA, Central and South America and the Caribbean, but the companies and their routes change frequently so check the latest flight guide.

From Europe: KLM flies direct from Amsterdam several times a week (some via Caracas) and has connecting flights to Guayaquil and Quito. TAP flies from Lisbon.

From North America: There are flights from New York, Tampa and Baltimore with Air Aruba, and from Miami with Air Aruba, American Airlines and ALM. ALM also flies from Atlanta, Georgia and Orlando, Florida. American Airlines flies from Baltimore and Nashville and Guyana Airways flies from New York (JFK).

From South America: Avianca flies from Barranquilla and Bogotá; Air Aruba flies from Bogotá and Medellín; ALM, Servivensa, fly from Caracas; ALM also flies from Valencia and Servivensa from Las Piedras and Maracaibo, Venezuela, while Bonaire Airways flies from Coro. ALM and Surinam Airways fly from Paramaribo and Guyana Airways from Georgetown.

From the Caribbean: Caribbean island destinations include Aruba (Air Aruba, ALM, Avia Air, Bonaire Airways), Bonaire (ALM, Bonaire Airways), Kingston (ALM), Port au Prince (ALM), Sint Maarten (ALM), Santo Domingo in the Dominican Republic (ALM and Aerotour Dominicana) and Port of Spain (ALM).

SEA
There is no longer a regular ferry from Venezuela, but it is possible for the adventurous and persistent to get a boat from Muaco at La Vela. You have to contact the captains direct as the practice of taking passengers is discouraged. Try Nelson García (T 522 533) of *Carmen Reynely* or Douglas Zavala (T 78268) of Trinidad II (neither speaks English). The *capitania* is not much help, try the maritime agency 2 blocks from Plaza Bolívar for help in contacting captains. The journey takes 9 hrs, head seas all the way, not for the seasick, not rec for women.

ON ARRIVAL

● **Airlines**
ALM (T 613033) has an office in Gomezplein in Punda where you can pay your departure tax and avoid the queues at Hato Airport. There is also an ALM office in the International Trade Centre and at the airport, T 338888, F 338300. ALM often has flights at rather unsociable hours, tends to lose luggage and is jokingly known in Dutch as 'Altijd Laat Maatschappij', the Always Late Company. KLM (T 686747/ 636646) and BWIA (T 687835/613033) offices are also at Gomezplein; Avianca, T 680122; Servivensa, T 680500; Air Portugal, T 686241; Air Aruba, T 683777/683659; American Airlines, T 695707. Pelican Air, T 628155, does helicopter tours of the island.

● **Banks**
ABN-AMRO Bank, McLaughlin's Bank, Maduro & Curiel Bank on Plaza Jojo Correa, T 611100, Banco di Caribe on Schottegatweg Oost, T 616588. Banking hours are 0800-1530 Mon to Fri. At the airport the bank is open 0800-2000 Mon-Sat, 0800-1600 Sun. ATMs at ABN-AMRO Bank and Maduro & Curiel Bank (Visa, Mastercard and Cirrus).

● **Official time**
Atlantic Standard Time, 4 hrs behind GMT, 1 ahead of EST.

● **Public holidays**
New Year's Day, Carnival Monday (Feb), Good Friday, Easter Monday, Queen's Birthday (30 April), Labour Day (1 May), Ascension Day, Flag Day (2 July), Christmas on 25 and 26 December.

● **Religion**
Curaçao has always had religious tolerance and as a result there are many faiths and denominations on the island. Details of services can be found in the official free guide, *Curaçao Holiday*, which lists Anglican, Catholic, Jewish, Protestant and other churches. Anglican Church, Leidenstraat, T 53251; Holy Family Church (Roman Catholic), Mgr Neiwindstraat, Otrabanda, T 62527; Methodist Church, Abr de Veerstraat 10, T 75834; Mikvé Israel – Emanuel Synagogue, Hanchi Snoa 29,

Punda, T 611067; Ebenezer Church of the United Protestant Congregation, Oranjestraat, T 53121; Christian Heritage Ministries (Evangelical), Polarisweg 27, Zeelandia, T 615663; Church of Christ, 40 Schottegatweg West, T 627628; Church of God Prophecy (Ecumenical), Caricauweg 35, T 75306.

● Security

There is a drugs problem in Willemstad and you are advised to be careful in Otrabanda at night and avoid the outer stretches of Pietermaai even by day (crack houses). If strangers stop you on the street asking 'alles goed?' (everything OK?) be assured they are not enquiring after your mood.

● Shopping

Open on Sun morning and lunchtimes if cruise ships are in port. Weekday opening is 0830-1200 and 1400-1800. The main tourist shopping is in Punda (see above) where you can pick up all sorts of bargains in fashion, china etc. Willemstad's jewellery shops are noted for the quality of their stones. Arawak Craft Products, Mattheywerf 1, Otrabanda, T 627249, F 628394, near cruise ship dock and ferry, tiles, reliefs of Dutch style houses and other ceramics, you can watch the potters and artists and even make your own, Arawak Art Gallery upstairs, open 0830-1700, on Sun also if cruise ship in dock.

Bookshops: Boekhandel Mensing in Punda has a limited selection of guide books and maps. Larger and more well stocked bookshops are out of the centre of Willemstad. Boekhandel Salas in the Foggerweg has good maps and guide book section as has Mensings' Caminada in the Schottegatweg and Van Dorp in the Promenade Shopping Centre. The public Library is a modern building in Scharloo, cross the bridge by the floating market, turn right along the water and it is on your left. The Reading Room has books in Dutch, English, Spanish, French and Papiamento, T 617055.

● Useful addresses

Police and fire: T 114 or 44444; Ambulance: 112, 625822, 89337 or 89266.

● Voltage

110/130 volts AC, 50 cycles.

ON DEPARTURE

● Departure tax

There is an airport tax of US$6 on departure to the Netherlands Antilles or US$12.50 to Aruba or other destinations. This must be paid at a separate kiosk after you check in. Alternatively it can be paid at the ALM office in Punda (see above, Airlines).

ACCOMMODATION

● Hotels

Price guide

L1	over US$200	L2	US$151-200
L3	US$101-150	A1	US$81-100
A2	US$61-80	A3	US$46-60
B	US$31-45	C	US$21-30
D	US$12-20	E	US$7-11
F	US$4-6	G	up to US$3

There is a 7% government tax and 10% (sometimes 12-15%) service charge to be added to any quoted room rate and many hotels add an extra US$3 per day energy surcharge. Many hotels have no hot water taps, only cold. This is because the water pipes in Curaçao are laid overground, the water in them being warmed by the sun during the day and cold at night. Time your shower accordingly.

In Willemstad, L3 Plaza Hotel and Casino in the Van der Valk chain, on Punda seafront, very central, huge tower dominates the skyline by the fortress walls, T 612500, F 618347, price per room inc service, tax, breakfast, bargain for a cheaper rate for several nights, popular with the Dutch, good food; L3 Otrabanda Hotel and Casino, opened Dec 1990 and still rather sterile, on Breedestraat just by the bridge in Otrabanda, excellent location, good for business travellers, standard rooms small but comfortable, single rooms available, suites are larger rooms with sofas, coffee shop and restaurant with good view of Punda and floating bridge, inc excellent buffet breakfast in coffee shop, pleasant service, pool planned, T 627400, F 627299, or reservations through International Travel & Resorts, New York, T 800-223-9815, F 212-251-1767, or in Holland, Holland International, T 70-395 7957, F 70-395 7747; also very central is L1-L3 Hotel and Casino Porto Paseo, de Rouvilleweg 47, room or 2-bedroom suite, inc breakfast, swimming pool, dive shop, in attractive restored old hospital, T 627878, F 627989; A3-B Pelikaan Hotel, Lange Straat 78, T 623555, F 626063, in the heart of Otrabanda, newly rebuilt, small, comfortable, clean, 40 rooms, a/c, restaurant; further W along the main road is the L2-L3 Holiday Beach, a concrete block on a manmade beach, but convenient and elegant inside, 10 mins walk to shops and restaurants, T 625400, F 624397/625409, 200 rooms in need of decoration, a/c, phone, TV, casino and banks of gaming machines, mediocre food at high prices, pool, tennis, dive shop on site, US$125 for 5 dive package, conference rooms, reservations through ITR. 15 mins walk E of the centre is the family-owned **L3-A1** *Avila Beach*, Penstraat 130, PO Box 791, T 614377, F 611493, built in 1811 as Governor's residence but most rooms in an old hospital wing, small and with no sea view, very popular, always full, cool reception area, service friendly but slow, no pool, lovely bar shaped like a ship's prow on the beach (rather gritty and painful on the feet at water's edge), great for evening cocktails, pleasant outdoor dining. A new extension has been built in an attractive colonial style, **L1-L2** *La Belle Alliance*, the other side of the pier (bar and restaurant, *Blues*) on another man-made beach, 40 hotel rooms, and some apartments, all rooms and suites with sea view, conference facilities and ballroom, tennis; **A1-A2** *Trupial Inn*, Groot Davelaarweg 5, T 378200, F 371545, in residential area, 74 rooms, a/c, newly decorated, nice, pool, restaurant, tennis, open air bar, entertainment, shuttle bus to downtown, suites available; **A3** *Hotel San Marco*, Columbusstraat 5, Punda, T 612988, F 616570, 89 rooms, completely renovated, a/c, TV, safe, clean, excellent value.

The Tourist Board main office at Pietermaai 19 has a list of guesthouses and apartments (not all of which it recommends) inc some cheap hotels such as **B-D** *Stelaris* close to the *Otrabanda*, looking out over to the floating market, seedy, T 625337, cheaper rooms with fan, no bath, others, a/c, with bath; **C** *Estoril*, Breedestraat 181, Otrabanda, T 625244; in Scharloo, **B-D** *Park*, on Frederikstraat 84, T 623112, bath and fan, not nice, noise from road, fleas, not clean enough, both *Estoril* and *Park* cater to 'short stay' visitors, not rec; **C** *Mira Punda*, Van de Brandhofstraat 12, near floating market, fan, cold water, clean, private bath, in restored mansion, bar downstairs has lots of local colour; **A3** *Bon Auberge*, Dutch owned, friendly, clean, conveniently located in Otrabanda close to shops and transport, Hoogstraat 63- 65, T 627902/627540, F 627579, 23 rooms, hot water, some have a/c, others fans, not all have bath, 4 apartments for US$200/week, rec. A rec small hotel is **B** *Buona Sera (Bonacera) Inn*, T 618286/658565, Pietermaai 104, on the road to the Bolívar museum, 16 rooms, sleep 1-4, a/c, private bathroom, recently built seaview restaurant and bar, plans to create small beach, family-run, friendly, English, Dutch, Spanish, French and Papiamento spoken. **A3** *Bramendie Apartments*, Bramendieweg 103, T 655 337, F 371 711, in Dominguito, 10 apartments with kitchenette, porch, TV, a/c, phone with deposit, car rental, good discount for long stay; **A3** *Douglas Apartments*, Saliña 174, PO Box 3220, T 614549, F 614467, a/c, cots available, towels and linen provided, kitchenettes, a/c, phone, fax facilities, on first floor of shopping gallery, bus stop outside; outside town, **A3** *Wayaca Apartments and Bungalows*, Gosieweg 153, T 375589, F 369797, a/c, TV, phone, supermarket, launderette, tennis, min 1 week, car rental can be included; houses also available usually on weekly basis or longer.

East of Willemstad on the Dr Martin Luther King Boulevard is the **L1-L3** *Princess Beach Resort and Casino*, a Crowne Plaza hotel, 600m from the Seaquarium on a narrow beach, T 367888, F 614131/617205, pools, restaurants, bars, shops, 341 rooms and suites make this the biggest resort on the island, popular, food good at all 3 restaurants, newly constructed conference centre, excellent Princess Divers on site, dive packages available, fitness centre with massage, good entertainment, impressive time share; next door is the **L3** *Lion's Dive*, attractive, not high rise, wooden balconies give it style but needs renovating, poor plumbing, 72 rooms, TV, small pool, unlimited use of Seaquarium, dive shop on site, dive packages available, fitness centre, windsurfing, 3 restaurants, nice atmosphere, friendly staff, helpful service, caters for hardcore diving fraternity, courtesy bus to town, T 618100, F 618200.

Heading W of Willemstad along the coast are **A3** *El Conde Hotel*, Roodeweg 75, near hospital, some rooms noisy, basic, 7 rooms, a/c, T/F 627611; **L1-L2** *Sonesta Beach Hotel and Casino*, 248 luxury rooms and suites, very comfortable, excellent service, 2 children under 12 sharing room free, this new, upmarket resort, built in Dutch colonial style is on a private beach and offers a freeform pool, whirlpools, tennis, watersports, casino, conference facilities and is next to the International Trade Centre, Piscadera Bay, PO Box 6003, T 368800, F 627502; 2 resorts overlook Piscadera Bay, one of which has been sold and temporarily closed; and **L1-L2** *Curaçao Caribbean*, 200 rooms and suites, upmarket facilities, but in need of redecoration, executive floor, a/c, casino, bar opening out on to terrace, good food, pleasant ambience, diving, watersports, tennis, T 625000, F 625846, in USA, T 1-800-344-1212; **L1-A1** *Seru Coral*, a new resort in the E part of the island, in the middle of nowhere but great restaurant, nice pool, nice studios, apartments and villas, 3 miles from beach, 18 from airport, 9 miles from town, Koral Partier 10, T 678499, F 678256; *Santa Catharina Sport & Country Club*, same ownership, T 677028/30, F 677026, tennis, fitness centre, football pitch, pool, restaurant, bar, with studios, suites and bungalows all with kitchenettes, phone, TV, terrace overlooking NE coast; 2 mins from the airport is **A2** *Holland*, 45 rooms, a/c, TV, phone, business services, restaurant, pool, car rental, T 688044, F 688114; **L3-A1** *Bulado Inn*, in Boca St Michiel fishing village, Red A'Weg, T695943, F 695487, family run, new, very nice but rather pricey, 17 a/c junior suites, all ocean view, restaurant, bar, pool, nicely landscaped, tennis, meeting rooms, car rental, parking, 10 mins walk from beach; **A3** *Landhuis Cas Abao*, dates from 1751 rebuilt 1993, stylish, rooms vary but have good views, secluded beach, min stay 4 days, no credit cards, beautiful area, restaurant closed in evenings and owners leave premises after 1900, long drive to find a decent evening meal, T 603525, F 649460; in the centre of the island, at Weg naar Westpunt Z/N, is the 17th century **A3-B** *Landhuis Daniel*, a small hotel, 4 rooms in the landhouse (best) with bathrooms, and 4 small cabin rooms by the pool, shared bathrooms, clean and simple, management changed 1996, check locally for quality now, T/F 648400, F 648900; **L1-A2** *Coral Cliff*, resort and casino on Santa Marta Bay, quiet beach, nice sea, some shade provided, entrance NAf8 for non- residents, sprawling, concrete block hotel, rather run down, rooms or suites, PO Box 3782, T 641610, F 641781, good sea view from restaurant on hill, dive shop on premises, excellent diving from beach, watersports, mini golf, horse riding arranged, free airport pickup, shuttle service to town; **A2-A3** *Bahia Inn*, near Lagun beach, small, basic, adequate, several beds in each room, PO Box 3501, T 684417, building work all along this coastal road; at Westpunt, **A3-B** *Jaanchie Christian's* is a popular restaurant with 4 rooms to let, a/c, bathroom, breakfast included, double beds, can fit extras in, usually full, phone for reservation, T 640126, 640354.

New hotel, villa or timeshare developments are springing up all over Curaçao. **L1** *Kadushi Cliff Resort*, at Westpoint is open although more building work is still being done, kitchenettes, pool, TV, scuba, T 640282; several huge resorts are planned around Knip beach, Lagun, Cas Abao, Piscadera, Parasasa, Cornelis Bay and Jan Thiel. Be prepared for construction work.

● **Camping**

Brakkeput, adjoining Spanish Waters, Arowakenweg 41A, PO Box 3291, T 674428, school parties catered for, sports fields, showers and toilets, tents available, US$1.25 pp overnight with min charge US$18.75, cheaper for youth organizations. Camping is allowed on some beaches, but there are no facilities and you have to bring your own fresh water supplies.

FOOD AND DRINK

● **Food**

Native food is filling and the meat dish is usually accompanied by several different forms of carbohydrate, one of which may be *funchi*, a corn meal bread in varying thickness but usually looking like a fat pancake (the same as *cou-cou* in the Eastern Caribbean). Goat stew (*stoba di kabritu*) is popular, slow cooked and mildly spicey (milder and tastier than Jamaican curry goat), rec. Soups (*sopi*) are very nourishing and can be a meal on their own, grilled fish or meat (*la paria*) is good although the fish may always be grouper, red snapper or conch (*karkó*), depending on the latest catch; meat, chicken, cheese or fish filled pastries (*pastechi*) are rather like the *empanadas* of South America or Cornish pasties.

While in the Netherlands Antilles, most visitors enjoy trying a *rijsttafel* (rice table), a sort of Asian *smørgasbørd* adopted from Indonesia, and delicious. Because *rijsttafel* consists of anywhere from 15 to 40 separate dishes, it is usually prepared for groups of diners, although some Curaçao restaurants will do a modified version of 10 or 15 dishes.

● **Restaurants**

10% service is added to the bill in restaurants but an extra 5% is appreciated. One of the most highly regarded restaurants in Willemstad is *The Wine Cellar* on Concordiastraat,

T 612178/674909, owned by chef Nico Cornelisie, a master rotisseur, in small old house, only 8 tables, chilly a/c, very good food but unexciting wine list, reservations rec, open for lunch Tues-Fri, dinner Tues-Sun; *Alouette*, in a restored house, Orionweg 12, T 618222, very popular, reservations rec, French-style food, low-calorie or vegetarian meals available, comparatively small menu but changed frequently, except for the goat cheese crêpe which is such a favourite it is a permanent fixture, excellent food and service, attractive decor, open 1200-1430, 1900-2200, later at weekends; *Larousse*, also in an old house on Penstraat 5, almost opp the *Avila Beach*, T 655418, French menu with local and imported North Sea fish, quiet, open 1800-2400, closed Mon; *Fort Nassau* has a spectacular location with a panoramic view from the 200-year old fort, American-style menu using local ingredients, open Mon-Fri 1200-1400, Mon-Sun 1830-2300, reservations T 613086; *De Taveerne*, in an octagonal mansion, Landhuis Groot Davelaar, T 370669, beef and seafood, à la carte menu, antique furnishings, closed Sun; *Bistro Le Clochard*, in the Rif Fort walls overlooking the harbour, French and Swiss cuisine, T 625666/625667, open Mon-Fri 1200-1400, 1830 onwards, Sat evenings only, open Sun in Dec-Mar; in the Waterfort Arches is *Seaview*, open air or indoors, bar and international restaurant, lunch 1200-1400, dinner 1800-2300 daily, T 616688; *Grill King*, also in the Waterfort Arches is friendly and has good international food, open 1200-1400, 1700-2300, later at weekends, T 616870. There are several restaurants in the Arches, nice variety, pleasant location, good for a meal or just drinks. Great fruit shakes at *Trax's*, a van at the Otrabanda side of the Queen Emma bridge. Some other moderately priced yet good restaurants include *Fort Waakzaamheid and Terrace Bistro Bon Bini*, T 623633, lovely sunset views from the terrace on top of the fort, which is on a hill above Otrabanda, closed Tues, open every other day from 1700, barbecue and salad bar from 1800, seafood, early bird special 1700-1900, 3 courses, US$14; *Tasca Restaurant Don Quijote*, Gosieweg 148, T 369835, Spanish, seafood and daily specials, good paella, takeaway, happy hour 1700-2000, open weekdays 1700-0100, closed Tues; *Green Mill*, Salinja Galleries, T 658821, lunches or dinners, happy hour Mon-Thur 1800-1900, Fri 1700-1830, menu with good variety;

Promenade Café-Restaurant at the Promenade Shopping Centre, T 376784/376 929; *Cactus Club* Tex Mex food, fun atmosphere, Van Staverenweg 6, T 371600, in the Mahaai area; *Hard Rock Society*, good, sandwiches, soups, salads, burgers or grills, rock music, outdoors under trees or indoors at the bar, open Mon-Thur 0930-0100, Fri and Sat 0930-0200, Sun 1530-0100, happy hour Thur-Fri 1730-1830, Sun 1700-1900, pool, darts and backgammon upstairs, Keuken Plein, Punda, T 656633.

For an Indonesian meal it is best to make up a party to get the maximum number of dishes but this is not essential. The *Indonesia*, Mercuriusstraat 13, wonderful Javanese food specializing in 16 or 25-dish rijstaffel, essential to book, often several days ahead, restaurant badly needed redecorating in 1994, T 612606/612999, open 1200-1400, 1800-2130 daily, dinner only on Sun; the *Garuda* at the *Curaçao Caribbean* is currently the best place for a rijstaffel, open air dining overlooking the sea, Indonesian owner uses old family recipes, nice atmosphere, good portions and prices, T 626519, open 1200-1400 daily except Sat, 1830-2200, closed Mon; *Surabaya* in the Waterfort Arches has good food but overpriced and no hot plates to keep it warm, vegetarian menu too, T 617388, open Tues-Fri 1200-1400, Tues-Sun 1800-2300.

The best place to try local food in Willemstad is the old market building beyond the round concrete market tower by the floating market, here many cooks offer huge portions of good, filling local food cooked in huge pots on charcoal fires, at reasonable prices, choose what you want to eat and sit down at the closest bench or one of the nearby tables having first ordered, takeaway available, very busy at lunchtimes, the best dishes often run out, make sure you have the right money available; the best restaurant for local food is *The Golden Star*, Socratesstraat 2, T 54795/54865, informal, friendly, plastic table cloths and permanent Christmas decorations, tacky but fun, TV showing American sport, home cooking, very filling, goat stew washed down by a couple of Amstels rec, popular with locals and tourists, open daily 1100-0100; outside town, *Martha Koosje* on the left on the Westpoint road, Colombian and local specialities particularly seafood, outdoor dining, family run, open 1500-2300, the bar is open until 0200, T 648235; further along the same road, opp the entrance to the Christoffel Park, is

Oasis, seafood and creole dishes but also offering chicken and ribs, open 1200-2400, weekends 1030-0300, dinner served until 2100, dancing afterwards, T 640085; *Playa Forti*, atop a cliff overlooking beach of same name, wonderful view, very popular lunchtime at weekends, Colombian and local dishes; further along the road in Westpoint is *Jaan-chie's*, another weekend lunchtime favourite with local families although no sea view, huge, filling portions, see the bananaquits eating sugar, parties catered for, takeaway service, bus stops outside for return to Willemstad, T 640126; near the airport excellent local food at Chez Susenne, Blomonteweg 1, Santa Maria, cosy atmosphere, very popular, T 688545.

A good fish restaurant is *Pisces*, at the end of Caracasbaaiweg, reservations rec, T 672181; *El Marinero*, moderately priced seafood dishes, lunch 1200-1500, dinner 1830-2330, Schottegatweg Noord 87B, T 379833; *Pirates Seafood Restaurant*, also reasonably priced and good food, open daily 1200-1500, 1830-2330, T 628500, located in *Caribbean Hotel*; *Buccaneer*, same owner as *El Marinero* and *Pirates*, opened a new open air restaurant in 1996 next to *Sonesta* and *Caribbean* hotels, great food, good prices; *Fisherman's Wharf*, Dr Martin Luther King Blvd, close to *Princess Beach*, T 657558, very good seafood, lunch and dinner; *Villa Elizabeth Shellfish House*, M L King Blvd, opp *Princess Beach Hotel*, open 1800-2300, closed Tues, very good food, lovely atmosphere, European and South American cooking, T 657565; italian food at *Baffo & Bretella*, in the Seaquarium, homemade pasta, seafood, open 1200-1400, 1900-2300, closed Tues, reservations required, T 618700; *Seaside Terrace*, little beachside restaurant near *Princess Beach Hotel*, more like a snack stand but great fresh lobster for US$20 and a US$6 barbecue on Sun with live entertainment, a few tables to watch sunset, open 1000-2200 daily; *La Pergola*, in the Waterfont Arches, also serves Italian food, fish, pizza, terrace or a/c dining, T 613482, open 1200-1400 Mon-Sat, 1830-2230 daily; Chinese food at *Ho Wah*, Saturnusstraat 93, T 615745; for drinks, snacks or cheap lunches, *Downtown Terrace*, also in Gomezplein, T 616722, you can hear the chimes from the Spritzer and Fuhrmann bells, great selection of Belgian beers. There is plenty of fast food to cater for most tastes, including pancake houses, and *Pizza Hut* at Pietermaiplein prides itself on

having won awards. *Denny's* is open 24 hrs, attached to side of *Holiday Beach Hotel*, good food at good prices, some local dishes, T 625232, takeaway available. Late night fast food, local fashion, can be found at truk'i pans, bread trucks which stay open until 0400-0500 and sell sandwiches filled with conch, goat stew, salt fish and other Antillean specialities.

● **Drink**

A selection of European, South American (mostly Chilean) and Californian wines is usually available in restaurants. Curaçao's gold-medal-winning Amstel beer, the only beer in the world brewed from desalinated sea water, is very good indeed and available throughout the Netherlands Antilles. Amstel brewery tours are held on Tues and Thur at 1000, T 612944, 616922 for information. Some Dutch and other European beers can also be found. Fresh milk is difficult to get hold of and you are nearly always given evaporated milk with your tea or coffee. Curaçao's tap water is excellent; also distilled from the sea.

GETTING AROUND

LAND TRANSPORT

● **Car hire**

There are about 4 car rental agencies at the airport, all the offices are together so it is easy to pick up price lists for comparison. One or 2 companies usually have desks in each of the major hotels. Look in local tourist literature or newspapers for news of special deals on offer, there is lots of choice. There have been problems with unsafe cars, inadequate insurance and licensing. Those listed here are considered reputable. Companies include Budget, Express Rent-a-Car, good selection, Europcar/National, Avis, Caribe Rentals, U Save Car Rental, Dollar Rent a Car, Star Rent a Car, Visa Car Rental. Prices start at about US$35 daily, unlimited mileage, including insurance, deposits from US$250; jeeps, minimokes, buggies, scooters and bikes also available. Foreign and international driving licences are accepted. Traffic moves on the right.

● **Buses**

There are collective taxis, called buses, and identified by an AC prefix on their licence plates. *Konvoois* are big buses which run to a schedule and serve outlying areas of Curaçao. There is a terminal at the Post Office in Punda and another near the Rif Fort in Otrabanda. To the airport get a bus marked Hato from Punda at 15 mins past the hour from 0615 to 2315, or from Otrabanda at 15 mins past the hour from 0615 to 2320, US$0.40, returning on the hour, usually full. Buses to Westpunt leave from Otrabanda on the odd hour, last bus 2300, US$1, return on the even hour. Buses to Dominguito (the Seaquarium) and Caracas Bay run from Punda at 35 mins past the hour but minibuses also do this route. A bus marked Schottegat runs from Punda via the Octagon Bolívar Museum, the *Trupial Inn Hotel*, the Curaçao Golf and Squash Club, the Jewish cemetery and the Curaçao Museum to Otrabanda every 2 hrs from 0620-2320 at 20 mins past the hour in either direction. The Lagun and Knip bus route leaves Otrabanda at half past the even hour in the mornings and on the odd hour in the afternoons via the Curaçao Museum, the University, Landhuis Jan Kok, Santa Cruz beach, Jeremi beach, Lagun Beach and Bahia beach, returning from Knip on the alternate hour. The standard city bus fare is US$0.50; *autobuses* (ie colectivos) charge US$1. For more information T 684733.

● **Taxis**

Taxis are easily identified by the signs on the roof and TX before the licence number. There are taxi stands at all hotels and at the airport, as well as in principal locations in Willemstad. It is not always possible to get a taxi to the airport early in the morning or late at night so if you are going to a night club arrange your taxi in advance (sometimes the driver will turn up a little early and join you on the dance floor). Fares from the airport to *Holiday Beach*, US$12, *Van der Valk Plaza* or *Avila Beach* US$15, *Lions Dive* US$18, *Coral Cliff* US$25, *Kadushi Cliffs* US$35. Airport displays taxi fares to main hotels. Try and pay in guilders as taxi drivers do not always have the right change for dollars. Taxi meters are to be installed. Fares for sightseeing trips should be established at beginning of trip, the usual price is US$20 for the first hour and US$5 for each subsequent 15 mins. Tipping is not strictly obligatory. The high price of taxis is a common complaint. Taxis do not always go looking for business and it can be difficult to hail one. Best to telephone from a hotel lobby or restaurant/bar, one will arrive in a couple of minutes (Dispatch T 616711, complaints T 615577, main office T 690747/ 690752), or go to a taxi stand and just get into an empty car, the driver will then turn up. Drivers do not always know the area

as well as they should, even restaurants can sometimes be tricky for them to find. The rear windows of many taxis do not work, which makes the car uncomfortable in the hot climate. Courtesy vans operated by the hotels can be more comfortable.

COMMUNICATIONS

● **Telecommunications**

All American Cables & Radio Inc, Keukenstraat; Kuyperstraat; Radio Holland NV, De Ruytergade 51; Sita, Curaçao Airport. Telephone rates abroad are published in the telephone book, but beware if phoning from a hotel, you can expect a huge mark up, check their rates before you call. To Europe, US$3.05 a minute, to the USA US$1.60, to Australia and Africa US$5.55, to the Netherlands Antilles US$0.55, Central America US$3.90, Venezuela US$1.10, Leeward and Windward Islands US$1.75.

ENTERTAINMENT

For 'night-owls', there are casinos. All the large hotels have them, with many gaming tables and rows and rows of fruit machines, open virtually all hours. There are many nightclubs and discothèques, several of which are in the Salinja area: *Façade* (Lindbergweg 32-34, T 614640, open 2200-0400 except Mon and Thur, happy hour on Fri from 1800) and *L'Aristocrat* (Lindbergweg, T 614353, open 0800-0200, Fri and Sat 2200-0400, closed Mon) are favoured by wealthy locals of all ages, you will not be let in wearing jeans or trainers and they have airport-style metal detectors at the door; *Infinity* is at Fort Nassau, open Fri and Sat, 2100-0200, T 613450; for all-night music and dancing, *The Tunnel, La Paix* and *De Fles* (the *Flask*) have been rec for salsa and merengue, you may be the only foreigner there, take local currency; *The Pub*, Salinja, T 612190, open daily from 2100, happy hour 2100-2200, noisy, favoured by Dutch marines and their girlfriends, a youngish crowd; in Otrabanda, *Rum Runners* is rec for cocktails and harbour view; the *Lion's Dive Hotel* has a trendy bar and Sun evening happy hour is rec. The Centro Pro Arte presents concerts, ballets and plays. While on the subject of entertainment, one of the most bizarre sights of Curaçao, not dealt with in the tourist brochures, is the government-operated red-light area, aptly named Campo Alegre. Close to the airport, it resembles a prison camp and is even guarded by a policeman.

TOURIST INFORMATION

● **Local tourist office**

The main office of the Curaçao Tourism Development Bureau is at Pietermaai 19, Willemstad, PO Box 3266, T 616000, F 612305. There is an information office on Breedestraat, E of Hendrikplein, and at the airport. The Curaçao Hotel and Tourism Association (CHATA) is at the International Trade Centre, Piscadera Bay, T 636260 and the airport, T 686789, offering helpful information, assistance in finding a hotel, brochures, maps, etc. There are also several Visitor Information Centres dotted round Willemstad and some booths sponsored by resort hotels, which have irregular hours. Members of Curaçao Hospitality Services look after the parking lots and are trained in first aid and how to give directions.

● **Tourist offices overseas**

Holland: Vasteland 82-84, 3011 BP Rotterdam, PO Box 23227, T (3110) 414 2639, F (3110) 4136834. **UK**: 421a Finchley Road, London NW3 6HJ, T 0171-431 4045, F 0171-431 7920. **Germany**: Arnulfstrasse 44, D-8000 Munich 2, T (49 89) 59 8490, F (49 89) 5232212. **Argentina**: Paraguay 880, 1st floor of 7 (1057), Buenos Aires, T (541) 311-5965/2488, F (541) 312-8849. **USA**: 475 Park Avenue South, Suite 2000, New York, NY10016, T (212) 683 7660, (1-800) 270-3350, F (212) 683-9337; 330 Biscayne Blvd, Suite 808, Miami, FL33132, T (305) 374-5811, F (305) 374-6741. **Venezuela**: Toore la Previsora, Local No 3, Planta Baja, Av las Acacias con Bolívar, Urb las Caobos, PO Box 63345, Caracas, T (602) 781-4622, F (602) 782 6582.

● **Local travel agents**

The best island tour available is with Casper Tours, T 653010, informative, fun, covers E to W, 0900-1600 inc lunch at *Jaanchie's* (see above) for US$30 (cruise ships' tours from US$15) in a/c, mini buses, English, Dutch and Spanish spoken. Daltino Tours (a good travel agency conveniently located at Breedestraat, downtown Punda) do island coach tours eg to the E US$10, to the W US$16, day trips to Aruba, US$175, to Bonaire US$135, to Caracas US$195, T 614888; Taber Tours (branch at airport) do an E tour including the Seaquarium and glass bottomed boat trip for US$27.50 adults, US$17.50 children under 12, a W tour is US$12, children US$6, to Aruba US$162, Bonaire US$140. Old City Tours do a walking tour of Otrabanda, 1715-1900, US$5.55 including a drink, T 613554.

● **Maps**

Curoil nv publishes a good road map with a satellite photo of the island with superimposed information, town street plans and an excellent index, available in Mensing and other bookshops.

● **Further reading**

Now ...Curaçao, free tourism publication, very good, interesting articles on Curaçao's history, culture and natural resources. *Curaçao Holiday* is a free guide, but not updated very often, the walking tour of Willemstad described in the brochure is recommended. For business travellers, *Business Curaçao* (monthly) is a useful source of information.

ACKNOWLEDGEMENTS

We are very grateful to Nan Elisa, formerly resident in Curaçao, for her help in updating this section.

Aruba

ARUBA, smallest and most W of the ABC group, lies 25 km N of Venezuela and 68 km W of Curaçao, at 12° 30'N, outside the hurricane belt. It is 31.5 km long, 10 km at its widest, with an area of 184 sq km. The average yearly temperature is 27.5°C, constantly cooled by NE trade winds, with the warmest months being Aug and Sept, the coolest Jan and February. Average annual rainfall is less than 510 mm, and the humidity averages 76%. Like Curaçao and Bonaire, Aruba has scant vegetation, its interior or *cunucu* is a dramatic landscape of scruffy bits of foliage, mostly cacti, the weird, wind-bent divi divi trees and tiny bright red flowers called *fioritas*, plus huge boulders, caves and lots of dust.

HORIZONS

Aruba is one of the very few Caribbean islands on which the Indian population was not exterminated although there are no full-blooded Indians now. The Aruban today is a descendant of the indigenous Arawak Indians, with a mixture of Spanish and Dutch blood from the early colonizers. There was no plantation farming in Aruba, so African slaves were never introduced. Instead, the Indians supervised the raising of cattle, horses, goats and sheep, and their delivery to the other Dutch islands. They were generally left alone and maintained regular contact with the mainland Indians. They lived mostly in the N at Ceru Cristal and then at Alto Vista, where in 1750 the first Catholic church was founded. The last Indians to speak an Indian language were buried in urns about 1800; later Indians lost their language and culture. When Lago Oil came to Aruba many workers from the British West Indies came to work in the refinery in San Nicolas, leading to Caribbean English becoming the colloquial tongue there instead of Papiamento. Of the total population today of about 72,100, including some 40 different nationalities, only about two-thirds were actually born on the island. The official language here, as in the other Netherlands Antilles, is Dutch, but Papiamento is the colloquial tongue. English and Spanish are widely spoken and the people are extremely welcoming. The crime rate is low and there are very few attacks on tourists.

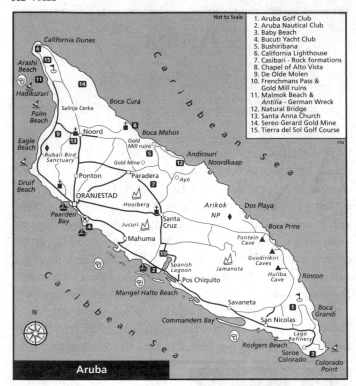

Not to Scale

1. Aruba Golf Club
2. Aruba Nautical Club
3. Baby Beach
4. Bucuti Yacht Club
5. Bushiribana
6. California Lighthouse
7. Casibari - Rock formations
8. Chapel of Alto Vista
9. De Olde Molen
10. Frenchmans Pass &
    Gold Mill ruins
11. Malmok Beach &
    Antilia - German Wreck
12. Natural Bridge
13. Santa Anna Church
14. Sereo Gerard Gold Mine
15. Tierra del Sol Golf Course

Aruba

THE ECONOMY

Gold was discovered in 1825, but the mine ceased to be economic in 1916. In 1929, black gold brought real prosperity to Aruba when Lago Oil and Transport Co, a subsidiary of Exxon, built a refinery at San Nicolas at the E end of the island. At that time it was the largest refinery in the world, employing over 8,000 people. In Mar 1985 Exxon closed the refinery, a serious shock for the Aruban economy, and one which the Government has striven to overcome. In 1989, Coastal Oil of Texas signed an agreement with the Government to reopen part of the refinery by 1991, with an initial capacity of 150,000 barrels a day, but despite plans to increase it, present capacity is only about 140,000 b/d.

Aruba has three ports. San Nicolas is used for the import and transshipment of crude oil and materials for the refinery and for the export of oil products. There are also two sea-berths at San Nicolas capable of handling the largest tankers in the world. Oranjestad is the commercial port of Aruba, and it is open for day and night navigation. In 1962 the port of Barcadera was built to facilitate shipment of products from Aruba's new industrial zone on the leeward coast.

The economic crisis of 1985 forced the Government to turn to the IMF for help. The Fund recommended that Aruba promote tourism and increase the number of hotel rooms by 50%. The Government decided, however, to triple hotel capacity to 6,000 rooms, which it was estimated would provide employment for 20% of the population. Hotel construction has expanded rapidly and marketing efforts have attracted investors and visitors from as far afield as Japan. By 1990 tourist accommodation in 15 major high rise and low rise hotels reached 3,326 rooms, with many more available in small hotels, guest houses and apartments. Nevertheless, by 1992 the

Aruba: fact file

Geographic
Land area	193 sq km

Demographic
Population (1995)	72,700
annual growth rate (1990-95)	2.9%
density	376.7 per sq km
Religious affiliation	
Roman Catholic	88%
Birth rate per 1,000 (1992)	18.1
	(world av 26.0)

Education and Health
Life expectancy at birth,	
male	71.1 years
female	77.1 years
Infant mortality rate	
per 1,000 live births (1989)	9.6
Physicians (1992)	1 per 936 persons
Hospital beds	1 per 234 persons
Literacy (over 15)	95%

Economic
GDP (1993 market prices)	
	US$1,200mn
GDP per capita	US$17,400
Public external debt (1990)	US$198mn
Tourism receipts (1993)	US$464mn
Radio	1 per 1.8 persons
Television	1 per 3.8 persons
Telephone	1 per 3.3 persons

Employment
Population economically active (1991)	
	31,100
% of labour force in	
agriculture, fishing	0.5
mining, manufacturing	
and public utilities	7.3
construction	10.4
trade, hotels and restaurants	35.4

Source Encyclopaedia Britannica

Government was facing a financial crisis because of state guarantees totalling NG516mn for three hotel projects which had run into financial difficulties and on which work had ceased: the 466-room *Beta Hotel* (NG170mn), the 376-room *Eagle Beach Hotel* (NG186mn) and the 411-room *Plantation Bay Hotel* (NG160mn). Although the Dutch government provided a loan for the hotels' completion in 1992, the Aruban government now faces heavy interest and principal repayments for 15 years to banks. These will be funded by unpopular higher excise duties, petrol prices and import duties. In mid-1993, the *Plantation Bay Hotel* was sold to the Marriott chain. In 1995 its opening raised the total to 6,626 rooms in hotels, employing 4,973 staff.

The economy is now overwhelmingly dependent on tourism for income, with some 580,000 stayover visitors a year. Over 56% of tourists come from the USA; the next largest country of origin is Venezuela. A further 250,000 passengers arrive on cruiseships.

Efforts are being made to diversify away from a single source of revenues into areas such as re-exporting through the free trade zone, and offshore finance. Aruba is still dependent on the Netherlands for budget support and the aim is to reduce the level of financial assistance. New legislation has been approved to encourage companies to register on the island by granting tax and other benefits. Regulations are generally flexible and unrestricting on offshore business, although efforts are being made to ensure an efficient level of supervision.

There is very little unemployment on Aruba and labour is imported for large projects such as the refinery and construction work. Turkish guest workers came to help get Coastal started and Philippinos work in the high rise hotels. The Government is encouraging skilled Arubans to return from Holland but is hampered by a housing shortage and a consequent boom in real estate prices.

FLORA AND FAUNA

About 170 species of birds can be found on Aruba, and about 50 species breed on the island but if you include the migratory birds which come in Nov-Jan the total rises to around 300 species. The most common birds are the trupiaal (with its bright orange colours), the chuchubi, the prikichi (a little parrot) and the barika geel (the little yellow-bellied bird you will find eating the sugar on the table in your hotel). An interesting site to see waterfowl is the Bubali Plassen, opposite the Olde Molen. Here you can often find cormorants, herons and fish eagle. Brown pelicans can be found along the S shore. As well as various kinds of lizards, Aruba has large iguanas. These animals are hunted to prepare a typical Arubian soup. Two kinds of snakes can be found on Aruba: the Santanero, a harmless little snake (however, be careful when you pick it up, because it defecates in your hand) and the not so harmless rattle snake. Aruba's rattle snake is a unique subspecies and does not use its rattle. Rattle snakes live in the triangular area between the Jamanota, Fontein and San Nicolas. The best place to go looking for rattle snakes, if you really want to, is the area S of the Jamanota mountain. In the unlikely event that you get a bite from a rattle snake, go immediately to the hospital. They have anti-serum.

BEACHES AND WATERSPORTS

Of the three ABC islands, Aruba stands out as having the best beaches, all of which are public and free. There are good, sandy beaches on both sides of the island although fewer on the E side which is rough and not so good for swimming. Travelling N along the W coast from Oranjestad an excellent road takes you to the main resort areas where nearly all the hotels are gathered. Druif beach starts at the *Tamarijn Aruba Beach Resort*, extending and widening along the coast to the sister hotel, the *Divi Aruba*, with good windsurfing. At the *Best Western Manchebo* there is a huge expanse of sand, often seen in advertisements; Caribasurf, *Manchebo Beach Resort*, T 23444, F 32446, windsurfing boards and instruction. N of here is Eagle Beach where the 'low rise' hotels are separated from the beach by the road, and then Palm Beach where the 'high rise' hotels front directly on to the beach. These three sandy beaches extend for several miles, the water is calm, clear and safe for children, although watch out for watersports and keep within markers where provided.

North of Palm Beach is an area of very shallow water with no hotels to break the wind, known as Fisherman's Huts, which is excellent for very fast windsurfing. Surfers from all over the world come here to enjoy their sport and professionals often come here for photo sessions. Although speeds are high and there is a strong offshore wind, surfing is quite safe and there are several rescue boats to get you back if the wind blows you to Panama. This beach is called Malmok (S end) or Arashi (N end) and there are many villas and guesthouses across the road which cater for windsurfers. Windsurfing Aruba is a sympathetic small firm by the Heineken flags at the huts which rents equipment and gives lessons to beginners and intermediates at reasonable prices, T 33472, F 34407. There are other operators of high quality with higher prices: Roger's Windsurf Place, L G Smith Blvd 472, T/F 21918, windsurf packages available, boards and accommodation; Sailboard Vacation, L G Smith Blvd 462, T 21072, boards of different brands for rent. For information about the Aruba Hi-Winds Pro/Am boardsailing competitions, contact the B T A Group at L G Smith Boulevard 62, T 35454, F 37266. They usually take place in June.

A residential area and the new golf course stretches up from Arashi to the lighthouse and the coast is indented with tiny rocky bays and sandy coves, the water is beautiful and good for snorkelling, while shallow and safe for children. It is also a fishing ground for the brown pelicans. At night they normally sleep in the shallow water close to the lighthouse. A little way after the lighthouse there is a very spectacular place where high waves smash against the rocks at a small inlet. There is a blow hole, where water sometimes spouts up more than 5m.

At the other end of the island is Seroe Colorado, known as 'the colony', which used to be a residential area for Exxon staff but is currently used as temporary housing. You have to enter the zone through a guard post, but there is no entrance fee and no hindrance. There are two W facing beaches here worth visiting. Rodgers Beach has a snack bar, showers, yachts and is protected by a reef but is in full view of the refinery. Baby Beach, on the other hand, is round the corner, out of sight of the refinery, in a lovely sandy bay, protected by the reef, nice swimming and snorkelling, very busy on Sun, with toilets but little shade. Sea Grape Grove and Boca Grandi, on the E coast of the S tip has good snorkelling and swimming, being protected by a reef, and is popular with tours who come to see the largest elkhorn coral. Experienced windsurfers come here to wave jump. The prison is near here, remarkable for the pleasant sea view from the cells. Other beaches on the E side of the island are Boca Prins, where there are sand dunes, and further N from there, reached by a poor road, is Dos Playa where there is good surf for body surfing. The landscape is hilly and barren because of serious overgrazing by herds of goats. Andicouri is also popular with surfers, note that you may not approach it through the coconut grove which is private property, there are signs to direct you the right way.

Virtually every type of watersport is available and most hotels provide extensive facilities. Activities which are not offered on site can be arranged through several tour agencies such as De Palm Watersports, T 24545, Pelican Tours and Watersports, T 32128/ 25374. Watersports companies are too numerous to mention in further detail, but you can hire jetskis, waterskis, wave runners, banana boats, snorkelling equipment and other toys. Parasailing can be done from the high-rise hotels. Glass bottomed boat trips from various locations are around US$20-25, but can be more for a sunset cruise. Several yachts and catamarans offer cruises along the coast with stops for snorkelling and swimming. A morning cruise often includes lunch (about US$40-50), an afternoon trip will be drinks only – and then there are the sunset booze cruises (about US$20-30). *Pelican I* is a 50-ft catamaran running along the W coast from Pelican pier; *Balia*, a 53-ft racing catamaran operated by Red Sail Sports, does all the usual cruises and is available for private charter at US$450 an hour, minimum 2 hrs; *Wave Dancer*, another catamaran, departs from *Holiday Inn* beach, T 25520; *Octopus* is a 40-ft trimaran, departing from *Holiday Inn* pier, is also available for private charter, snorkelling and sailing cruises, US$20-35, T 33081; *Tranquilo*, a yacht, can be contacted through Mike, its captain T 47533, or Pelican Tours T 31228. *Mi Dushi* is an old sailing ship which starts cruises from the *Tamarijn Beach Resort*, morning and lunch US$35, snorkelling and sunset US$24, sunset booze cruise US$20, pirate sails and beach party US$40, T 25842 or De Palm Tours.

Near Spanish Lagoon is the Aruba Nautical Club complex, with pier facilities offering safe, all-weather mooring for almost any size of yacht, plus gasoline, diesel fuel, electricity and water. For information, write to PO Box 161. A short sail downwind from there is the Bucuti Yacht Club with clubhouse and storm-proofed pier providing docking, electricity, water and other facilities. Write to PO Box 743. The Heineken Catamaran Regatta is held annually in November, with competitors from USA, Europe and Venezuela.

Over a dozen charter boats are available for half or whole day deep sea fishing. The Tourist Office has a list so you can contact the captain direct, or else go through De Palm Tours. Whole day trips including food and drinks range from US$350-480, depending on the number of people on board. Deep sea fishing tournaments are held in Oct and Nov at the Aruba Nautical Club and the Bucuti Yacht Club.

DIVING AND MARINE LIFE

Visibility in Aruban waters is about 30m in favourable conditions and snorkelling and scuba diving is very good, although not as spectacular as in the waters around Bonaire. A coral reef extends along the W side of the island from California reef in the N to Baby Beach reef in the S, with dives varying in depth from 5 to 45m. There are lots of dive sites suitable for beginners where you can see morays, grouper, eagle rays, manta rays and sting rays, as well as lobsters, parrot fish, angel fish and others. The coral is in good condition and varied. The other side of the island is only for experienced divers as there are strong currents and it is often rough. Organized boat trips regularly visit two wrecks worth exploring, although they can get a bit crowded. One is a German freighter, the *Antilia*, which was scuttled just after WW II was declared and is found in 20m of water off Malmok beach on the W coast. You can see quite a lot just snorkelling here as parts of the wreck stick up above the water. Snorkelling boat trips usually combine Malmok beach and the wreck. The other wreck is nearby in 10m of water, the *Pedernales*, a flat-bottomed oil tanker which was hit in a submarine attack in May 1941, while ferrying crude oil from Venezuela to Aruba. Only the central part of the tanker remains, the US military took away the two end pieces, welded them together and made a new ship which was used in the Normandy invasion. Be very careful not to touch

anything underwater; not all the dive masters bother to warn you of the dangers of fire coral and hydroids.

There are several scuba diving operations and prices start from about US$50 for a single tank dive. Snorkelling from a dive boat varies from US$10-22. *The Talk of the Town* has a beach bar and pool opposite the hotel and across the road, in full view of the airport runway; Aruba Aqua Sports on the premises operates a set schedule of daily dives, T 23380 ext 254. Aruba Pro Dive is on the beach at *Playa Linda*, T 25520, F 37723. S E A Scuba (PADI, NAUI, SSI) operates out of Seaport Market, T 34877, F 34875, quite good on safety checks, instruction available in German, 40-ft boat, also deep sea fishing charters. Red Sail Sports, L G Smith Blvd 83, PO Box 218, T 61603, F 66657, and at hotels, sailing, snorkelling, diving with certification courses, windsurfing, waterskiing, hobie cats etc, accommodation packages available, this is a large, reputable international operation and an expensive one. Mermaid Sport Divers, between *Manchebo* and *Bucuti Beach Resorts*, T 35546, not very professional, few safety checks, boat smells of diesel. Scuba Aruba has a retail operation in Seaport Village selling all watersports equipment, open Mon-Sat, 0900-1900, T 34142. Their dive operation is cheaper than most, at US$30 for one tank including equipment. They say the difference is in having a less plush boat.

The Atlantis Submarine has hourly dives 1000-1500 most days from the Seaport Village Marina. A catamaran takes you past the airport and the local garbage dump to where the submarine begins its 1-hr tour of the Barcadera reef to a depth of 50m, turning frequently so that both sides can see. Recommended for those who are interested in marine life but do not scuba dive, but not for anyone who is claustrophobic. The submarine takes 46 passengers and is nearly always full, particularly when a cruise ship is in port, so book beforehand,

US$58 adults, Arubans and children aged 4-12 US$29, no children under 4 allowed, T 36090. Lunchtime is quite a good time to go, it is not so full then; Thur is a bad day when a lot of cruise ships come in. Throwaway cameras with 400 ASA film, US$20, are available at the ticket office.

OTHER SPORTS

In 1995 the 18-hole, par 71, Tierra del Sol Golf Course opened near the lighthouse, designed to fit in with the natural landscape and with the sea on two sides. A community of homes and villas has also been designed to blend in with the surrounding vegetation with a full-service clubhouse, swimming pool, golf practice range and tennis and fitness complex. It took over 30 years to get the golf course built because of difficulties with the barren landscape and the lack of water. Many hotels are signing up for preferential rates for their guests, otherwise contact Tierra del Sol on T 37800, 67800, F 24970, 64970. There is a 9-hole golf course with oiled sand greens and goats near San Nicolas, golf clubs for rent US$6, green fee US$10 for 18 holes, US$7.50 for 9 holes, T 42006, Sat and Sun members only, open daily 0800-1700. At the *Holiday Inn* is an 18-hole mini-golf course. A mini golf course called Adventure Golf has been built opposite *La Cabana*, close to Bubali, in a nice garden.

There are tennis courts at most major hotels. Horseriding at Rancho El Paso, Washington 44, near Santa Ana Church, T 73310, Paso Fino horses, daily rides except Sun, 1 hr through countryside, US$15, or 2 hrs part beach, part *cunucu*, US$30. Rancho Daimiri also has Paso Fino horses and offers 2½-hr rides with snorkelling, daily at 0900 and 1500, a/c transport from your hotel included, T 60239. Rancho del Campo takes riders into the National Park, 2½ hrs, 0930 or 1530, US$45 including transport and snorkelling. The Eagle Bowling Palace at Pos Abou has 12 lanes, of which 6 are

for reservation, open 1000-0200, US$9 from 1000-1500, US$10.50 from 1500-0200, US$1.20 shoe rental; also 3 racquetball courts available. Wings Over Aruba, at the airport, T 37104, F 37124, has a pilot school, with sightseeing flights, aerial photography, aircraft rental; sightseeing in a seaplane US$130/30 mins, trial flying lesson US$120/90 mins. Sailcarts available at a special rink not on the beach, Aruba Sailcart N V, Bushiri 213, T 36005, open 0900-sunset, US$15/30 mins for a single cart, US$20/30 mins for a double cart. Drag races are held several times a year at the Palo Marga circuit near San Nicolas. Triathlons and marathons are held periodically, contact the Tourist Office for details.

FESTIVALS

The most important festival of the year is Carnival, held from the Sun two weeks preceding Lent, starting with Children's Carnival. There are colourful parades and competitions for best musician, best dancer, best costume etc. The culmination is the Grand Parade on the Sun preceding Lent. Other festive occasions during the year include New Year, when fireworks are let off at midnight and musicians and singers go round from house to house (and hotel to hotel); National Anthem and Flag Day on 18 March, when there are displays of national dancing and other folklore, and St John's Day on 24 June, which is another folklore day: 'Derramento di Gai'. For visitors who do not coincide their trip with one of the annual festivals, there is a weekly Bonbini show in the courtyard of the Fort Zoutman museum on Tues 1830-2030, US$3, music, singing and dancing, interesting but overenthusiastic MC, bartenders from hotels mix cocktails and special drinks. The programme is altered every week, so those on a 2-week holiday do not sit through the same thing twice. Local dance music, such as the fast, lively *tumba* is very influenced by Latin America. Arubans are fond of *merengue*. In June there is a well-attended and popular festival of jazz and Latin American music, with many famous musicians and bands playing. Contact the Aruba Tourism Authority, PO Box 1019, Oranjestad, T 23777, F 34702, for information on the programme and package tours available. Throughout the year there are several different music festivals. The International Theatre Festival takes place annually; for information contact CCA, Vondellaan 2, T 21758. There is also a Dance Festival in Oct, for information T 24581.

ORANJESTAD

Oranjestad, the capital of Aruba, population about 21,000, is a bustling little freeport town where 'duty-free' generally implies a discount rather than a bargain. The main shopping area is on Caya G F (Betico) Croes, formerly named Nassaustraat, and streets off it; also shops in the Port of Call Market Place, Seaport Village Mall, Harbour Town, The Galleries, Strada I and II and the Holland Aruba Mall. Many of the buildings in the colourful Antillean style are actually modern and do not date from colonial times as in Willemstad, Curaçao.

There is a small museum in the restored 17th century Fort Zoutman/Willem III Tower, Zoutmanstraat, T 26099, open Mon-Sat, 1000-1200, 1330-1630, entrance Afl 1. Named the **Museo Arubano**, it contains items showing the island's history and geology, with fossils, shells, tools, furniture and products. It is not particularly well laid out, the displays are unimaginative and old-fashioned but it is still worth going if only to see the building. The fort, next to the Parliament buildings, opposite the police station, dates from 1796 and marks the beginning of Oranjestad as a settlement. Built with four guns to protect commercial traffic, in 1810-1911 it sheltered the government offices. The tower was added around

1868 with the first public clock and a petrol lamp in the spire, which was first lit on King Willem III's birthday in 1869 and served as a lighthouse. The Fort was restored in 1974 and the tower in 1980-83. The **Archaeological Museum** on Zoutmanstraat 1, T 28979, is open Mon-Fri 0800-1200, 1330-1630. Small, but cleverly laid out in three parts, Preceramic, Ceramic (from 500 AD) and Historic (from 1500-1800 AD when the Indians used European tools). The two main sites excavated are Canashitu and Malmok and most objects come from these. The descriptions are in English and Papiamento, easy to read and educational. There are some interesting publications available in English. Recommended, the best museum in the ABCs. A numismatic museum, **Mario's Worldwide Coin Collection**, also known as the **Museo Numismatico**, Zuidstraat 7, not far from Fort Zoutman and the Central Bank of Aruba (where it is possible to buy specimen sets of Aruba's extremely attractive coins) has a large collection of coins from over 400 countries and coins from ancient Greece, Rome, Syria and Egypt. A bit cramped, but with a lot of fascinating material, the museum is run by the daughter of the collector, Mario Odor; donations welcomed. Open Mon-Fri, 0900-1200, 1400-1700. There is an extensive collection of shells at De Man's Shell Collection, Morgenster 18, T 24246 for an appointment. The Cas di Cultura, Vondellaan 2, has concerts, ballet, folklore shows and art exhibitions, T 21010. *Gasparito* Restaurant/Art Gallery has an exhibition of Aruban art for sale and display, Gasparito 3, T 37044, open 0900-2300 daily.

EXCURSIONS

The landscape is arid, mostly scrub and cactus with wind blown divi divi (watapana) trees and very dusty. Traditional

Aruban houses are often protected from evil spirits by 'hex' signs molded in cement around the doorways and are surrounded by cactus fences. Flashes of colour are provided by bougainvillea, oleanders, flamboyant, hibiscus and other tropical plants. You will need a couple of days to see everything on offer inland without rushing. The Esso Road Map marks all the sites worth seeing and it is best to hire a car (4 wheel drive if possible, but not essential) as you have to go on dirt roads to many of them and there is no public transport. Tour agencies do excursions, about US$20-28 for a half day tour of the island, see **Information for**

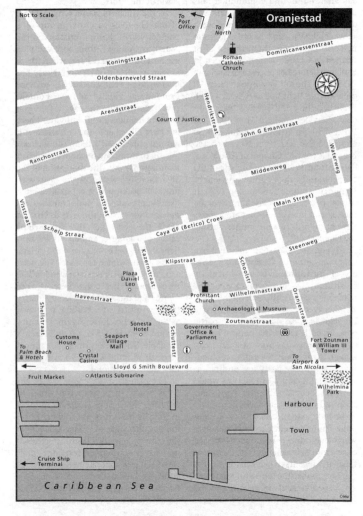

travellers.

The village of **Noord** is known for the **Santa Anna Church**, founded in 1766, rebuilt in 1831 and 1886, the present stone structure was erected in 1916 by Father Thomas V Sadelhoff, whose portrait is on the twelfth station of the Cross. It has heavily carved neo-Gothic oak altar, pulpit and communion rails made by the Dutchman, Hendrik van der Geld, which were the prize work shown at the Vatican Council exhibition in 1870. They were then housed in St Anthony's Church at Scheveningen in Holland, before being given to Aruba in 1928. The church is popular for weddings, being light and airy with a high vaulted ceiling and stained glass windows. Services are held Mon, Wed and Fri at 1830, Sat at 1900 and Sun at 0730 and 1800. Not far from Noord on the N coast is the tiny **Chapel of Alto Vista**, dating from 1952 but on the site of the chapel built by the Spanish missionary, Domingo Antonio Silvester in 1750. It is in a spectacular location overlooking the sea and is so small that stone pews have been built in semi circles outside the Chapel.

Also on the N coast are the ruins of a gold mine at **Seroe Gerard** and a refinery at **Bushiribana** in a particularly bleak and sparsely vegetated area. The machinery at the mill, right on the coast, was damaged by sea spray and moved to Frenchman's Pass in 1824. A partly paved road leads to the natural bridge where long ago the roof of a cave collapsed, leaving only the entrance standing. It is actually fairly low and not as spectacular as tourist brochures would have you believe. There is a souvenir shop and you can get snacks here.

Inland, extraordinary rock formations can be seen at **Casibari** and **Ayó**, where huge, diorite boulders have been carved into weird shapes by the wind. At Casibari steps have been made so that you can climb to the top, from where you get a good view of the island and the Haystack. There is a snack bar and souvenir shop. Ayó does not have steps, you have to clamber up, but a wall is being built up around the rocks to keep out the goats. There are some Indian inscriptions. Toilets, a snack bar and souvenir shop are planned. The 541-ft **Hooiberg**, or Haystack, has steps all the way up. Very safe, even with children, the view is worth the effort.

At the village of **Santa Cruz**, just SE of the Haystack, a cross on top of a boulder marks the first mission on the island. Travelling E from here you pass the **Arikok National Park**, where there are some well laid out trails for easy, but hot, walking. The road leads to Boca Prins (dune sliding) and the **Fontein** cave. Admission to the cave is free, you can hire helmets and flashlights. There is a large chamber at the entrance, with natural pillars, and a 100m tunnel leading off, halfway down which are Indian paintings. Despite the desolation of the area, there is a well near the caves with brackish water, which a Japanese man uses to cultivate vegetables for the Chinese restaurants on the island. Further along the coast are the **Guadirikiri** caves, two large chambers lit by sunlight, connected by passages and pillars, with a 100m tunnel, for which you need a torch. Bats live in this cave system. The road around the coast here is very bumpy and dusty, being used by quarry trucks. A third cave, **Huliba**, is known as the Tunnel of Love. Again, no entry fee but helmets (US$2.50) and torches available. The walk through the tunnel takes 20-30 mins with a 10-minute return walk overground.

The road then takes you to **San Nicolas** where there is a strong smell of oil. After the closure of the oil refinery in 1985, San Nicolas was a ghost town, but now that Coastal Oil has taken over the refinery, activity is beginning to pick up. Old wooden houses are being demolished and new concrete houses built instead. A landmark is *Charlie's Bar*, which has been in operation since 1941; a good place to stop for refreshment to see the souvenirs hanging everywhere.

Returning NW towards Oranjestad you pass through Savaneta, where the Dutch marines have a camp. Turn off to the left to *Brisas del Mar*, a good seafood restaurant open to the sea, very popular. At Pos Chiquito, a walkway leads through mangroves to *Isla di Oro*, a restaurant built like a ship where there is dancing at weekends and pedalos and watersports. A little further on a bay with shallow water and mangroves is ideal for snorkelling beginners. The view is not spectacular but you can see many colourful fish. **Spanish Lagoon**, once a pirates' hideout, is a seawater channel, at the mouth of which is the Aruba Nautical Club and the water desalination plant. At the other end is a bird sanctuary where parakeets breed and the ruins of the Balashi gold mill dating from 1899, where the machinery is better preserved than at Bushiribana. There is quicksand in the area around the bird sanctuary, so it is not advisable to walk there. Nearby is **Frenchman's Pass** where the French attacked the Indians in 1700. From here you can turn E again to drive up **Jamanota**, at 188m the highest elevation on the island.

Information for travellers

BEFORE TRAVELLING

● Documents

US and Canadian citizens only require proof of identity, such as birth certificate, certificate of naturalization or voter registration card. Other nationalities need a passport. A return or onward ticket and proof of adequate funds are also required. Dogs and cats are permitted entry if they have a valid rabies and health certificate. However, no pets are allowed from South or Central America. Check with your hotel to see if they are allowed to stay

● Customs

If flying out to the USA, you will clear US customs and immigration in Aruba, which saves you time at the other end (US Immigration, T 31316). There is no in-transit facility, so if you are passing through (eg making a connection to Bonaire or Curaçao) you have to collect your luggage, clear customs and immigration, then walk (no trolleys) down to the queue for departure tax exemption and clear immigration again on your way out.

● Climate

Aruba is out of the hurricane belt and the climate is dry. The hottest months are Aug-Oct and the coolest are Dec-Feb, but the temperature rarely goes over 90°F or below 80°F. A cooling trade wind can make the temperature deceptive. Average rainfall is 20 ins a year, falling in short showers during Oct-December.

● Health

All the major hotels have a doctor on call. There is a well-equipped, 280-bed hospital (Dr Horacio Oduber Hospital, L G Smith Blvd, T 74300) near the main hotel area with modern facilities and well-qualified surgeons and dentists. The emergency telephone number for the Ambulance and Fire Department is 115. Also for ambulance in Oranjestad, T 21234 and in San

Nicolas, T 45050. Drinking water is distilled from sea water and consequently is safe. The main health hazard for the visitor is over-exposure to the sun. Be very careful from 1100-1430, and use plenty of high factor suntan lotion.

MONEY

● **Currency**

Aruba has its own currency, the Aruban florin, not to be confused with the Antillean guilder, which is not accepted in shops and can only be exchanged at banks. The exchange rate is Afl1.77=US$1, but shops' exchange rate is Afl1.80. US dollars and credit cards are widely accepted, even on buses, and the Venezuelan bolívar is also used. ATMs dispense only Aruban currency.

GETTING THERE

AIR

From Europe: KLM has direct flights from Amsterdam and some via Caracas; some continue to Lima.

From North America: American Airlines and Air Aruba fly from New York (JFK and Newark); Air Aruba, American Airlines and ALM fly from Miami; ALM from Atlanta; American Airlines and Air Aruba from Baltimore, American Airlines connects with many US cities through San Juan, Puerto Rico, they also fly from Chicago, Orange County and with Air Aruba from Tampa, Florida.

From South America: Avianca, Aerorepública and SAM fly from Barranquilla, SAM and Air Aruba from Medellín and Avianca, SAM, Aerorepública, Servivensa and Air Aruba from Bogotá. Servivensa flies from Maracaibo and there are lots of flights from Caracas with Servivensa, ALM, Aserca and Air Aruba; from Las Piedras on the Paraguaná Peninsula with Servivensa and Avia Air, and from Valencia with Aeroservicios Carabobo (Aserca) and Servivensa. VASP flies from Brasilia via São Paulo and Manaus, Air Aruba has flights from São Paulo.

From the Caribbean: From San Juan with American Airlines, as well as frequent flights from Bonaire and Curaçao with ALM, Bonaire Airways, Avia Air and Air Aruba.

ON ARRIVAL

● **Airlines**

Airline offices for all airport lines T 24800;

American Airlines, T 22700; Air Aruba, T 36600, (also Vasp); ALM, T 38080; Avianca ISAM, T 26277; KLM, T 23546/7; Viasa, T 36526; Avensa/Servivensa, T 27779.

● **Banks**

Algemene Bank Nederland NV, Caya G F (Betico) Croes 89, T 21515, F 21856, also a branch on van Zeppen Feldstraat, San Nicolas and at the Port of Call shopping centre (close to the harbour where the cruise ships come in) on L G Smith Blvd. Aruba Bank NV, Caya G F (Betico) Croes 41, T 21550, F 29152, and at L G Smith Blvd 108, T 31318; Banco di Caribe NV, L G Smith Blvd 90-92, T 32168, F 34222; Caribbean Mercantile Bank NV, Caya G F (Betico) Croes 53, T 23118, F 24373; Interbank, Caya G F (Betico) Croes 38, T 31080, F 24058; First National Bank, Caya G F (Betico) Croes 67, T 33221, F 21756. American Express representative for refunds, exchange or replacement of cheques or cards is SEL Maduro & Sons, Rockefellerstraat 1, T 23888, open Mon-Fri 0800-1200, 1300-1700. Aruba Bank, Caribbean Mercantile Bank and Interbank are Visa/Mastercard representatives with cash advance.

● **Clothing**

Swim suits are not permitted in the shopping area. Most casinos require men to wear jackets and smart clothes are expected at expensive restaurants, otherwise casual summer clothes worn all year.

● **Embassies and consulates**

Brazil: E Pory Ierlandstraat 19, T 21994; **Chile**: H de Grootstraat 1, T 21085; **Costa Rica**: Savaneta 235-B, T 47193; **Denmark**: L G Smith Blvd 82, T 24622; **Dominican Republic**: J G Emanstraat 79, T 36928; **Germany**: Scopetstraat 13, T 21767; **Honduras**: Bilderdijkstraat 13, T 21187; **Italy**: Caya G F Betico Croes 7, T 22621; **Liberia**: Windstraat 20, T 21171; **Panama**: Weststraat 15, T 22908; **Peru**: Waterweg 3, T 25355; **Portugal**: Seroe Colorado 73, T 46178; **El Salvador**: H de Grootstraat 1, T 21085; **Spain**: Madurostraat 9, T 23163; **Sweden**: Havenstraat 33, T 21821; **Venezuela**: Adriane Lacle Blvd 8, T 21078.

● **Hours of business**

Banks are open 0800-1200, 1330-1600, Mon-Fri, although some banks remain open during lunch and until 1800 on Fri. Shops are open 0800-1830, Mon-Sat, although some shut for lunch. Some shops open on Sun or holidays when cruise ships are in port. Late night shopping at the Alhambra Bazaar 1700-2400.

● **Laundry**
Wash 'n Dry Laundromat, Turibana Plaza, Noord; Hop Long Laundromat, Grensweg 7, San Nicolas.

● **Official time**
Atlantic Standard Time, 4 hrs behind GMT, 1 ahead of EST.

● **Public holidays**
New Year's Day, Carnival Monday (beginning of Feb), Flag Day (18 Mar), Good Friday, Easter Monday, Queen's Birthday (30 April), Labour Day (1 May), Ascension Day (May), Christmas Day, Boxing Day.

● **Religion**
A wide range of churches is represented on Aruba, including Catholic, Jewish and Protestant. There are Methodists, Baha'i, Baptists, Church of Christ, Evangelical, Jehovah's Witnesses and 7th Day Adventists. Check at your hotel for the times of services and the language in which they are conducted.

● **Shopping**
A wide range of luxury items are imported from all over the world for resale to visitors at cut rate prices. Liquor rates are good, but prices for jewellery, silverware and crystal are only slightly lower than US or UK prices. There is no sales tax. There are also local handicrafts such as pottery and art work, try Artesanía Arubiano, on L G Smith Blvd 178, opposite *Tamarijn Hotel*, or ask the Institute of Culture, T 22185, or the Aruba Tourism Authority, T 23777, for more information.

Bookshops: Van Dorp in Caya G F (Betico) Croes is the main town centre bookshop. The light and airy Captains Log in the new Harbour Town development has a few books and reading material but is mostly souvenirs. Many bookshops in the hotels have some paperbacks.

● **Voltage**
110 volts, 60 cycles AC.

ON DEPARTURE

● **Departure tax**
Airport tax US$20, or Afl36.

ACCOMMODATION

● **Hotels**

Price guide			
L1	over US$200	**L2**	US$151-200
L3	US$101-150	**A1**	US$81-100
A2	US$61-80	**A3**	US$46-60
B	US$31-45	**C**	US$21-30
D	US$12-20	**E**	US$7-11
F	US$4-6	**G**	up to US$3

A cluster of glittering luxury hotels has sprung up along Druif Bay, and Eagle and Palm beaches; decent, cheap accommodation is now very difficult to find. High season winter rates (16 Dec to 15 April) quoted here are roughly double low season rates. A 5% government tax and 10-15% service charge must be added; some hotels also add a US$3-5/day energy surcharge.

Closest to the airport, but only a 10-15 mins walk into town, is the **L1-L3** *Best Western Talk of the Town*, L G Smith Blvd 2, T 23380, F 32446/33208, convenient for business travellers, 63 rooms and suites built round a pool, children under 18 sharing free, large rooms, most with kitchenette, oceanside rooms are cheaper than pool side as they overlook the road but a/c reduces traffic noise, beach club and watersports centre across the road, guests may use facilities at the other Best Western hotels. In Oranjestad on the waterfront is the **L1** *Sonesta*, L G Smith Blvd 82, T 36000, F 34389, deluxe highrise, 300 rooms and 25 suites, Seaport Village shops and Crystal casino on the premises, no beach at the hotel but guests may use a private island reached by motor launch from the hotel lobby which has watersports and all facilities, even a private honeymooners' beach, the only drawback being that the island is right at the end of the airport runway. A cheap hotel in town is **A3** *Central*, behind the main street, clean, basic, a/c, usually full of construction workers. Just outside town to the W in a rather unattractive industrial area immediately after the free zone, is the **L2** *Bushiri*, L G Smith Blvd 35, T 25216, F 26789, a 150-room hotel school and all-inclusive, often booked solid, reserve in advance, price pp, on man-made beach, gym, table tennis, lots of activities, good reputation for food.

The low-rise resort hotel development starts on Punta Brabo Beach, Druif Bay, all hotels are on the beach and offer swimming pools, tennis, watersports, shops, restaurants etc. **L1** *Tamarijn Aruba Beach Resort*, J E Irausquin Boulevard 41, T 24150, F 34002, all-inclusive, rates fluctuate monthly, highest at Christmas, watersports, land sports, all meals, snacks, drinks etc, rates fall the week before Christmas, resort is next to Alhambra Bazaar and Casino; **L1** *Divi Aruba Beach Resort*, next along the beach at J E Irausquin Blvd 45, T 23300, F 34002, rooms and suites, honeymoon and windsurfing packages available, tennis, pool. Next is the **L2** *Best Western Manchebo Beach Resort*, T 23444, F 32446/33667, 70 rooms with balcony or terrace, dive shop (Mermaid Divers, see above) and windsurfing on huge expanse of beach; under same management with shared facilities is the **L1-L2** *Bucuti Beach Resort*, same phone numbers, 63 rooms, some with kitchenette, some suites, balconies, sea view. **L1** *Casa del Mar*, T 27000, F 26557, 147 luxury 2-bedroom (timeshare) apartments on the beach and 1-bedroom suites not on the beach, children's playground, gamesroom, tennis, pool, minimarket, laundromats. **L1-L2** The *Aruba Beach Club*, same phone numbers, shared facilities, 131 rooms with kitchenette, for up to 4 people.

At Eagle Beach the road splits the hotels/timeshare from the beach, where it is prohibited to build. *La Cabana*, T 79000, F 75474, 801 studios and suites, racquetball, squash, fitness centre, waterslide, children's pool and playground, casino and condominiums, ecoconscious management, some recycling, avoiding plastic where possible. **L2-L3** *Amsterdam Manor*, T 71492, F 71463, 70 painted Dutch colonial style studios and apartments with sea view, kitchen, pool, bar and restaurant. **L1-L2** *Paradise Beach Villas*, T 34000, F 31662, 43 suites, family oriented, pool, tennis, racquetball, watersports. **L2-L3** *La Quinta*, T 74133, 45 suites and rooms with kitchenette, pools, tennis, racquetball, expanding.

After the sewage treatment plant and Pos Chiquito the road curves round Palm Beach where all the high rise luxury hotels are. All have at least one smart restaurant and another informal bar/restaurant, some have about 5, all have shops, swimming pools, watersports, tennis and other sports facilities on the premises and can arrange anything else. Hotels with 300 rooms have casinos. The first one is the former *Aruba Royal*, abandoned for some time but acquired in 1995 by Divi Hotels, who are to demolish the main tower, which was

intended to be a Ramada resort. It could reopen in 1996, but no details known as we went to press. **L1-L2** *Aruba Hilton and Casino*, T 64466/64470, F 68217, reopened Dec 1994 after extensive US$42mn renovation, 474 rooms, behind it is the restaurant *De Olde Molen*, an imported windmill around which a condominium resort **L1-L2** *The Mill Resort* has been built, T 67700, waterslide, racquetball. **L1-L2** *Aruba Palm Beach*, T 63900, F 61941, 172 rooms and suites, Olympic size swimming pool. The oldest hotel along here is the renewed and extended **L1-L2** *Radisson Aruba Caribbean*, T 66555, F 63260, 378 rooms and suites, not all with sea view, golf putting, usual luxury facilities. **L2-L3** *Americana Aruba*, T 64500, F 63191, 421 rooms and suites with sea view and balcony, Red Sails diving and watersports on site. The next hotel along is the new and glittering **L1** *Hyatt Regency Aruba*, T 61234, 360 rooms and suites, designed for a luxury holiday or for business meetings and incentive trips, built around a huge 3-level pool complex with waterfalls, slides and salt water lagoon, in beautiful gardens, health and fitness centre, Red Sail diving and watersports, very popular, great for children or business travellers, always full. **L1** *Playa Linda*, T 61000, F 65210, a timeshare resort of suites and efficiencies, health club, games room. **L1-L2** *Holiday Inn Aruba*, T 63600, F 65165, 602 rooms with balcony, refurbished and relandscaped 1993-94, pools, tennis, diving, casino, lots of other facilities.

In 1995 Marriott were due to open a 413-room hotel next to the *Holiday Inn*, lots of facilities and luxuries.

● **Apartments**

The Aruba Tourism Authority publishes a list of apartments and guesthouses. Weekly or monthly rates are more advantageous. If you arrive at a weekend the Tourist Office in town will be shut and you cannot get any help except at the airport. In residential Oranjestad, **A2** *Aruba Apartments*, George Madurostraat 7, T 24736; **B** *Aulga's Place*, Seroe Blanco 31, T 22717; **C** *Camari Guesthouse*, Hospitaalstraat 10, T 28026; **A2-A3** *Camacuri Apartments*, Fergusonstraat 46-B, T 26805. In the district of Noord, **A3-B** *Cactus Apartments*, Matadera 5, Noord, T 22903; **A3-B** *Coconut Inn*, Noord 31, T 66288, F 65433; **A2-A3** *Turibana Plaza Apartments*, Noord 124, T 67292, F 62658;

C *Montaña Apartments*, Montaña 6-A, Noord, T 74981; *Roger's (windsurf) Place*, windsurfing packages only, L G Smith Blvd 472, PO Box 461, Malmok, T 61918, F 69045; **A1** *Boardwalk Vacation*, Bakval 20, Noord, T/F 66654; *The Villas*, L G Smith Blvd 462, *The Boulevards*, L G Smith 486, and *The Edges Guesthouse*, L G Smith Blvd 458, all run by Sailboat Vacations Windsurf Villages, windsurfing packages only, T 62527, F 61870; **A2** *Vistalmar*, Bucutiweg 28, T 28579 daytime, T 47737 evenings, F 22200, 1-bedroom apartments with car run by Alby and Katy Yarzagaray, friendly, wooden jetty for swimming and sunbathing, near airport, laundry facilities. Mrs B de Blieck has some comfortable apartments **B-C** within walking distance of Oranjestad and also the beach, shopping mall and laundromat, Dutch owners, hospitable, a/c, clean, price depends on size of apartment, rec, Stadionweg 9, T 22560; also Mr and Mrs Kemp, **B** *A1 Apartments*, Pagaaistraat 5, T 28963, F 34447, fully-furnished a/c rooms with kitchenette, 10-15 mins walk from main shopping centre and public beach at *Bushiri Beach Hotel*.

● **Camping**

Permit needed from police station, on Arnold Schuttrstraat, Oranjestad, who will advise on locations. It can take 10 days to get a permit and you must have a local address (ie hotel room). The permit costs one Afl4 stamp and it appears you can camp anywhere.

FOOD AND DRINK

With few exceptions, meals on Aruba are expensive and generally of the beef-and-seafood variety, but you can get some excellent food. Service charge on food and drinks is 15% at the hotels but at other places varies from 10% to 15%. Most tourists are on MAP at the hotels, many of which have a choice of formal or informal restaurants. Good wine is often difficult to find and always check that you get what you ordered, the waiter may not know that there is a difference between French and Californian wines which bear the same name.

● **Restaurants**

For Aruban specialities, *Gasparito*, Gasparito 3, T 67044, Aruban and seafood, wins awards for cuisine, open daily except Wed 1700-2300, Art Gallery attached; *Mamas & Papas*, Dakota Shopping Centre, T 26537, open 1200-1400; *Mi Cushina*, Noord Cura Cabai 24, T 48335,

Aruban and seafood, open 1200-1400, 1800-2200, closed Thur, rec, on road to San Nicolas, about 1 mile from San Nicolas; *Brisas del Mar*, Savaneta 222A, T 47718, seafood specialities, right on the sea, cool and airy, rec, reasonable prices, open 1200-1430, 1830-2200; *La Nueva Marina Pirata*, seafood and Aruban dishes at Spanish Lagoon, T 47150, open 1800-2300, Sun 1200-2300, closed Tues, follow the main road to San Nicolas, turn right at *Drive Inn*. The hotels have some very good gourmet restaurants, but outside the hotels the best French restaurant is *Chez Mathilde*, Havenstraat 23, T 34968, open for lunch and dinner, expect to pay over US$25pp; *Boonoonoonoos*, Wilhelminastraat 18A, T 31888, open 1800-2300, has French and Caribbean specialities and the average price is around US$15; *Chalet Suisse*, J E Irausquin Blvd 246, T 75054, between low rise and high rise hotels, beef from New York, try the chocolate fondue, open Mon-Sat, 1800-2230, reservations advised. *Villa Germania*, Seaport Market Place, T 36161, German food for breakfast, lunch and dinner. For US prime steak and seafood, *Cattle Baron*, L G Smith Blvd 228, T 22977, open 1200-1500, 1800-2400; *Twinkle Bone's*, Turibana Plaza, Noord 124, open 1800-2300, prices around US$18. Several Argentine restaurants serving steak, seafood and Argentine specialities, *El Gaucho*, Wilhelminastraat 80, T 23677, open 1130-1430, 1800-2300; *Buenos Aires*, Noord 41, T 27913, open 1800-2300; and *La Cabana Argentina*, Oude Schoolstraat 84, T 27913, open 1800-2400. *The Buccaneer*, Gasparito 11 C, T 66172, decorated as a sunken pirate's ship with aquariums, seafood, open Mon-Sat from 1730, no reservations. *The Steamboat Buffet and Deli*, opposite the *Hyatt* has a good brunch buffet, 0600-1200, dinner buffet, 1800-2300, open 24hrs, no reservations, T 66700; *Qué Pasa?* is a good, cheap and intimate restaurant in the centre of Oranjestad.

Lots of Chinese restaurants, including the highly rec *Kowloon*, Emmastraat 11, T 24950, open 1100-2230, regional specialities; *Dragon Phoenix*, Havenstraat 31, T 21928, open 1100-2300; *Far East Restaurant*, Havenstraat 25, T 21349, good food, roast pork dish, rec; and *Astoria*, Crijnsenstraat 6, T 45132, open 0800-2100, indoor and outdoor dining, low prices; *Warung Djawa*, Wilhelminastraat 2, T 34888, serves Indonesian and Surinamese food, open Mon-Fri, 1130-1400 for weekday rijstafel buffet lunch, and Wed-Mon 1800-2300, all you can eat, many recs; *Surindo Snackbar*, Zoutmanstraat 3, T 32040, has Indonesian snacks, 0800-2200, closed Tues nights.

There are plenty of Italian restaurants to choose from, *Cosa Nostra*, is on Scheopstraat 20, T 33872, pizza, salads and other Italian dishes, open Mon-Fri 1200-0300, Sat 1700-0100; *La Paloma*, Noord 39, T 74611, open 1800-2400, Mon-Fri, closed Tues, Northern Italian and seafood; *Pizza Pub*, L G Smith Blvd 54, T T 29061, open daily around the clock, 24 hr delivery service. At the Alhambra Bazaar, *Roseland Buffet*, a good buffet meal for US$11, they also serve good pizzas (munchies) at a reasonable price. The *New York Deli*, Alhambra Bazaar, serves soup and oversized sandwiches, open 0800-0200; *Charlie's Bar*, Zeppenfeldtstraat 56, San Nicholas, T 45086, is also good for Aruban light meals, open 1200-2130, bar until 2200. *Café The Paddock* on L G Smith Blvd near *Wendy's* has outside seating, very good, great saté, inexpensive for Aruba. Amstel on draught and the *daghap* (dish of the day) for Afl 14.50; *The Silver Skate*, Caya G F Croes 42, is a *broodjeszaak* (sandwich shop) with imported Dutch cheese, chocolate milk, draught Amstel and bottled Grolsch beer, all at reasonable prices. *The Plaza* at the Harbour Town Shopping Centre has a nice terrace and you can get a good, reasonably priced meal there. The *Coca Plum* on Cay Betico Croes serves a good meal and refreshing fruit juices on a terrace. There is a wide array of fast food outlets, including *Burger King, Kentucky Fried Chicken, McDonalds, Wendy's, Taco Bell, Dunkin Donuts, Subway* and *Domino Pizza*. For night owls in need of food the white trucks (mobile restaurants) serve local food and snacks from 2100- 0500 at around US$5, located at Wilhelmina Park, the Post Office and the Courthouse.

GETTING AROUND

LAND TRANSPORT
● Motoring
Beware the local drivers, who are aggressive. Driving is on the right and all traffic, except bicycles, coming from the right should be given right of way, except at T junctions. Good maps are available at petrol stations, US$0.90.

● Car hire
You must have a valid foreign or international driver's licence and be at least 21 to rent a car.

Airways (T 21845/29112), Hertz (T 24545 24886), Avis (T 28787/25496), Budget (T 28600/25423), National (T 21967/25451), Dollar (T 22783/25651) and Thrifty (T 35300/35335) have offices in Oranjestad and at the airport. Many companies also have desks in the hotels. Prices begin at US$35 daily, US$215 weekly, with unlimited mileage. Often when you rent a 4WD vehicle (rec for getting to beaches like Dos Playa) you cannot take out all risks insurance. George Rental is the biggest 4WD rental company.

● Motorcycles
Motorcycles, mopeds, and bicycles can also be rented; a 50cc moped or scooter costs around US$30 a day, a 250cc motorcycle US$40, a Harley Davidson SP1100 US$90 and insurance is US$8-15 a day, depending on the size of engine. Melchor Cycle Rental has all sorts of motorbikes, T 23448, Tanki Leendert 170-A, driver's licence required, drivers must be 18 or over. Pablito's Bikes Rental, L G Smith Blvd 228, T 75010/78655/30623, at *La Quinta Beach Resort*, Eagle Beach, men's, ladies, children's bicycles, US$3/hrs, US$8 until 1700, US$12/24 hrs. The Tourist Office has a list of rental companies.

● Buses
The bus station is behind Parliament on Zoutmanstraat. Route 1 starts in San Nicolas and runs through Oranjestad via the hospital to Malmok, Mon-Sat, 0455-2255 hourly, returning from Malmok on the hour, journey time 55 mins. Route 2 also runs from San Nicolas on a slightly different route to Oranjestad and Palm Beach, more or less hourly, 0525-2200. Route 3 runs between Oranjestad and San Nicolas, 0550-2030 and Route 4 runs from Oranjestad through Noord to Palm Beach almost hourly on the half hour. There are also extra buses running between Oranjestad and the *Holiday Inn* (schedules available at the hotels and the Tourist Office). One-way fare is US$1. Otherwise there are 'jitney cars' which operate like colectivos; the fare is US$1.25. A jitney or bus from Oranjestad to San Nicolas will drop you at the airport.

● Taxis
Telephone the dispatcher at Alhambra Bazaar or Boulevard Centre, T 22116/21604. Drivers speak English, and individual tours can be arranged. Taxis do not have meters. Ask for flat rate tariffs. From the airport to Oranjestad is US$9, to the low rise hotels US$11 and to the high rise hotels US$12.

FERRIES

The harbour is 5 mins' walk from the town, there are a tourist information centre and some souvenir shops which open if a cruise ship is in. A fruit boat leaves once a week for Punto Fijo, Venezuela; check with Agencia Marítima La Confianza, Braziliëstraat 6 (T 23814), Oranjestad. There used to be a ferry to Venezuela, check with Rufo U Winterdaal, Eman Trading Co, LG Smith Blvd 108, Oranjestad (PO Box 384), T 21533/21156, F 22135, Telex: 5027.

COMMUNICATIONS

● Postal services
The Post Office at J E Irausquinplein is open 0730-1200, 1300-1630. Postal rates to the USA, Canada and the Netherlands are Afl 0.40, for letters, and Afl 0.60, for post cards. The local television station is Tele-Aruba, but US programmes are also received.

● Telecommunications
Modern telephone services with direct dialling are available. Aruba's country and area code is 2978. Hotels add a service charge on to international calls. The ITT office is on Boecoetiweg 33, T 21458. Phone and fax calls, telex, telegrams, electronic mailgram and mariphone calls at Servicio di Telecommunicacion di Aruba (Setar), at Palm Beach opp *Americana Hotel*, in Oranjestad just off the Plaza and next to the Post Office Building at Irausquinplein, Oranjestad.

ENTERTAINMENT

The major attraction is gambling and there are many casinos on the island. Hotels must have 300 rooms before they can build one; those that do usually start at 1000 and operate 2 shifts. Their open air bars close around that time. Arubans are allowed in to casinos only 4 times a month. Some casinos also offer dancing and live bands. The place to be for a disco night out is *Visage*, next to the *Pizza Pub* at L G Smith Blvd 54. Other discothèques include *Blue Wave* on Shellstraat, T 38856; *Chesterfield Nightclub*, Zeppenfeldstraat 57, San Nicolas, T 45109; and plenty of others in hotels or elsewhere.

TOURIST INFORMATION

● Local tourist offices
L G Smith Boulevard 172, Oranjestad, PO Box 1019, near the harbour, T 23777, F 34702. Also at airport (open daily until about 1900, helpful for accommodation) and cruise dock. Staff are friendly and efficient. The Aruba Hotel and Tourism Association, PO Box 542, Oranjestad, T 22607, 33188, F 24202.

● Tourist offices overseas
Canada: 86 Bloor Street West, Suite 204, Toronto, Ontario M5S 1M5, T (416) 975 1950, F (416) 975 1947, toll free 800-268 3042.
Colombia: Calle 100, No. 8A-49, Torre B, Edificio World Trade Center, Bogotá, T 226 9013, F 226 8929.
The Netherlands: Schimmelpennincklaan 1, 2517 JN, Den Haag, T (70) 3566220, F 3604877.
USA: 199 Fourteenth Street, N E, Suite 1506, Atlanta, GA 30309-3686, T (404) 892-7822, F (404) 873-2193; 2344 Salzedo Street, Miami, Florida 33134-5033, T (305) 567-2720, F (305) 567-2721; 1000 Harbor Blvd, Ground level, Weehawken, N J 07087, T (201) 330-0800, F 330-8757, toll free (800) TO ARUBA.
Venezuela: Centro Ciudad Comercial Tamanaco, Torre C, Piso 8, Oficina C-805, Chuao, Caracas, T 959 1256, F 959 6346.

● Local travel agents
Pelican Tours PO Box 1194, T 24739/31228, F 32655, lobby desks in many hotels, also at Pelican Pier, Palm Beach, between *Holiday Inn* and *Playa Linda*, sightseeing trips, cruises, watersports. De Palm Tours, L G Smith Blvd 142, PO Box 656, T 24400, F 23012, also with offices in many hotels, sightseeing tours of the island and excursions to nearby islands or Venezuela. Their Mar-Lab Biological Tour, US$25 includes a visit to Seroe Colorado, and snorkelling at Boca Grandi. Aruba Transfer Tours and Taxi, PO Box 723, L G Smith Blvd 82, T 22116. Julio Maduro, Corvalou Tours, T 21149, specializes in archaeological, geological, architectural, botanical and wildlife tours, a mine of information on anything to do with Aruba, strongly rec. For a combination 6-hr tour with lunch, US$35, call archaeologist E Boerstra, T 41513, or Julio Maduro, or Private Safaris educational tour, T 34869. There are lots of companies offering tours of the island by minibus with a swimming and snorkelling stop at Baby Beach, about US$30 pp.

Rounding up

ACKNOWLEDGEMENTS

We are very grateful to all travellers who have written to us over the last year. Lucy Briggs (Axbridge, UK); Erna Brummel and Theo Veninga (Utrecht, The Netherlands); Joanne Brydon (Gloucester, Canada); J Burk (Los Angeles, USA); Jean Burnett (London, UK); Nicholas R Camp (Bethel, Montserrat); Lynda Cheetham (Miami, Florida)); Peter Clark (Lower Hutt, New Zealand); Marie-Ann Coninsx (Brussels, Belgium); Christine Eickelmann (Bristol, UK); Miss M Ekuman (Reading, UK); Robert Euler (Waterloo, Canada); Bernard Fison (London, UK); Gilly Goddard (Kingsbridge, UK); Bill Graham (Reuilly, France); Ms Barbara Grant (Elizabeth, USA); Camden Griffin (Jensen Beach, USA); Beate Hammond (Vienna, Austria); Thomas Haynes (Chicago, USA); Alan Hickey (Paris); Peter Hoell (Eureka, USA); Dr GEL Holton (Northcote, Australia); Kim and Sue Russell; Marina Nabuyon-Ahels (Germany); Andrea Hudolin (Vienna, Austria); Bruno Hugi (Frankfurt, Germany); Volkmar E Janicke (Munich, Germany); Ian and Margaret Jefferies (Buntingford, UK); Christa Jeker (Oberdorf, Switzerland); Nicholas Jenkins and Siri Huntoon (Brooklyn, USA); Jan Jorgensen & Jette Lindstrom (Odense, Denmark); Robert Joy (New Milford, USA); Mikael Kirkenseaard (Copenhagen, Denmark); Thomas Loderach (Rio de Janeiro, Brazil) and Magda Herrera (Bern, Switzerland); Judith E Long (Sag Harbor, USA); Christa Lopuhaa and Nicolette van Heusden (Amsterdam and Rotterdam, The Netherlands); Gerald Lorin (Kourou, French Guyane); Avigdor Meroz (Rio de Janeiro, Brazil); Eileen Morris (Abbotsford, Canada); R V Naylor (St Annes-on-Sea, UK); Gunilla & Sture Nilsson (Kungsbacka, Sweden); Ger Jan Onrust (Curacao, Netherlands Antilles); Gary Palmer (Portsmouth, UK); Taeke and Suzanne van der Ploeg (Wormer, The Netherlands); George Poppelwell (St Helier, Jersey); Nayo Potter (San José, Marcala, Honduras); Scott A. Rasmussen (San Francisco, USA); Beate Reiser (Munich, Germany); Su Roper (Colby, Isle of Man); Felix Rutschmann (Zurich, Germany); Paul Saunders (Sherbourne, Canada); Günther Schäfer (Osaka, Japan); Paul Secker (Stockport, Cheshire); Nicholas Stott (Aberdeen, UK); Caroline Sullivan (Bristol, UK); Van Svoboda (Vancouver, Canada); Rodolfo Taccheo (Formentera, Spain); Sarah Turner (High Halstow, UK); Yves Tychon (Gonderange, Luxembourg); Brian and Margaret Wardlow (Sheffield, UK); and Marti Werner (Wintethur, Switzerland).

ADVERTISERS

Caribbean Festivals at a glance

	Page	Jan	Feb	Mar	Easter	April	May	June	July	Aug	Sept	Oct	Nov	Dec
Aruba	967	F	C	F				F,M,W					S,A	
Anguilla	525				R						C,R			
Antigua	480				R				C					
Bahamas	67							F	F		F			C
Barbados	770		F	W	F				C			M		R,S
Bonaire	927		C					F			F	R/F		
British Virgin Islands	446			R,W	F			W	F					
Carriacou	750		C		F					R				
Cayman Islands	196					C	F,A					R/F		
Cuba	142	F					F		C			F	M	
Curaçao	946		C		F				F			M		
Dominica	658		C										F	
Dominican Republic	337		C				A,W	M	F	M	M			F
Grenada	744	A,R,S	F		R			F		C,F		R		
Guadeloupe	593		C						F				F	
Guyana	862		F	F									F	
Guyane	895		C						F					
Haiti	300	F	C											
Isla de Margarita	900		C		F									
Jamaica	221					C				F,M		A		
Martinique	631	R/W	C	R		R	F	W	F,R				F	M
Montserrat	538				F	F					F			C
Nevis	502								C					
Puerto Rico	384			W		C	M	F,M	F		F,A	R		

Caribbean Festivals at a glance

	Page	Jan	Feb	Mar	Easter	April	May	June	July	Aug	Sept	Oct	Nov	Dec
Saba	556								C					F
Sint Maarten	563		R		C,F								F	
St Eustatius	578								C					
St Kitts	502													C
St Lucia	683		C,F			R,M	F,W			F		F	F	F
St Vincent	713							C		R				F
Bequia	720			R										
Union Island	725			S		F								
St-Barthélémy	620	C							F	F				
St-Martin	613		R,C						F					
Suriname	613			F									F	
Tobago	807		C,A	F				F	M	R		F		
Trinidad	807		C,F					F		F		F,M	F,M	
Turks & Caicos:														
Grand Turk	268											F		
Providenciales	277								A	C,R				
South Caicos	273					R								
North Caicos	268								F					
Middles Caicos	268									F				
USVI:														
St Thomas	426		W		C				W					
St John	433								C					
St Croix	438		F									M,R		F

Key: C = Carnival (in Feb normally means pre-Lenten); F = Festival; M = Music and arts festival; A = Angling tournament; R = Regatta; W = Windsurf races; S = other sports.

/ = two types of event combined;   , = two separate events fall within same month. Where an event begins in one month and ends in another, the month of commencement is given. See Festivals, watersports, Culture and National Holidays sections in text below for precise details.

Climatic Tables

The following table has been very kindly furnished by Mr RK Headland, the notes by Mark Wilson. Each weather station is given with its altitude in metres (m). Temperatures (Centigrade) are given as averages for each month; the first line is the maximum and the second the minimum. The third line is the average number of wet days encountered in each month.

	Jan	Feb	Mar	Apr	May	June	July	Aug	Sept	Oct	Nov	Dec
Havana	26	27	28	29	30	31	31	32	31	29	27	26
49m.	18	18	19	21	22	23	24	24	24	23	21	19
	6	4	4	4	7	10	9	10	11	11	7	6
Kingston	30	29	30	30	31	31	32	32	32	31	31	30
7m.	22	22	23	24	25	25	26	26	25	25	24	23
	3	2	3	3	5	6	3	6	6	12	5	3
Nassau	25	25	27	28	29	31	31	32	31	29	28	26
10m.	17	17	18	20	22	23	24	24	24	22	20	18
	6	5	5	6	9	12	14	14	15	13	9	6
Port-au-Prince	31	31	32	33	33	35	35	35	34	33	32	31
41m.	23	22	22	23	23	24	25	24	24	24	23	22
	3	5	7	11	13	8	7	11	12	12	7	3
Port of Spain	30	32	31	32	32	31	31	31	32	31	31	30
12m.	20	21	21	21	23	23	23	23	23	22	22	21
	11	8	2	8	9	19	23	17	16	13	17	16
San Juan, PR	27	27	27	28	29	29	29	29	30	30	28	27
14m.	21	21	22	22	23	24	24	24	24	24	23	22
	13	7	8	10	15	14	18	15	14	12	13	14
Santo Domingo	28	28	29	29	30	30	31	31	31	31	30	29
14m.	20	19	20	21	22	23	23	23	23	23	22	21
	7	6	5	7	11	12	11	11	11	11	10	8
Willemstad	28	29	29	30	30	31	31	31	32	31	30	29
23m.	24	23	23	24	25	26	25	26	26	26	24	24
	14	8	7	4	7	9	8	6	9	15	16

Use these tables with caution; variations within islands can be dramatic. On the mountainous islands, such as the Windwards, rainfall is generally about 3000 mm (120 inches) in the interior, but only 1500mm (60 inches) in coastal rain shadow areas. Rain falls in intense showers, so even on a wet day there may be plenty of sunshine too. In most of the Caribbean, the wet season is from June to November, but there is plenty of fine weather at this time of year, and it is quite likely to rain in the dry season too. June to November is also the hurricane season which has recently affected principally the northeastern islands.

Temperatures are generally very steady. Nights are much warmer than in (for example) a Mediterranean summer. It generally feels much cooler on the windward (east) coasts; and it actually *is* a lot cooler in the mountains, where temperatures may fall to around 16°C (60°F). At high altitudes, there may be an almost continuous cover of low cloud at certain times of year. The winter season (January to March) is generally dry and not too hot. A possible hazard at this time of year are cold fronts or 'northers', which can bring surprisingly cold winds and heavy rain to Jamaica and the northern Caribbean. Don't worry too much about the weather, the Caribbean's reputation is well deserved, and on most islands at most times of year, you can't go too far wrong.

Index

Maps

Map Symbols

Administration

International Border

State / Province Border

Cease Fire Line

Neighbouring country

Neighbouring state

State Capitals □

Other Towns ○

Roads and travel

Main Roads
(National Highways)

Other Roads

Jeepable Roads, Tracks

Railways with station

Water features

River *Paradise River*

Lakes, Reservoirs, Tanks

Seasonal Marshlands

Sand Banks, Beaches

Ocean

Waterfall

Ferry

Reefs

Dive sites

Boat anchorage

Windsurfing

Topographical features

Contours (approx),
Rock Outcrops

Mountains

Mountain Pass

Gorge

Escarpment

Palm trees

Deciduous/fir trees

Cities and towns

Built Up Areas

Main through routes
Main streets
Minor Streets
Pedestrianized Streets

One Way Street

National Parks, Gardens, Stadiums

Fortified Walls

Airport

Banks

Bus Stations (named in key)

Hospitals

Market

Police station

Post Office

Telegraphic Office

Tourist Office

Key Numbers

Bridges

Stupa

Mosque

Cathedral, church

Guided routes

National parks, trekking areas

National Parks and
Bird Sanctuaries

Hide

Camp site

Refuge

Motorable track

Walking track

Other symbols

Archaeological Sites

Places of Interest ○

Viewing point

Golf course

Footprint Handbooks

All of us at Footprint Handbooks hope you have enjoyed reading and travelling with this Handbook, one of the first published in the new Footprint series. Many of you will be familiar with us as Trade & Travel, a name that has served us well for years. For you and for those who have only just discovered the Handbooks, we thought it would be interesting to chronicle the story of our development from the early 1920's.

It all started 75 years ago in 1921, with the publication of the Anglo-South American Handbook. In 1924 the South American Handbook was created. This has been published each year for the last 73 years and is the longest running guidebook in the English language, immortalised by Graham Greene as "the best travel guide in existence".

One of the key strengths of the South American Handbook over the years, has been the extraordinary contact we have had with our readers through their hundreds of letters to us in Bath. From these letters we learnt that you wanted more Handbooks of the same quality to other parts of the world.

In 1989 my brother Patrick and I set about developing a series modelled on the South American Handbook. Our aim was to create the ultimate practical guidebook series for all travellers, providing expert knowledge of far flung places, explaining culture, places and people in a balanced, lively and clear way. The whole idea hinged, of course, on finding writers who were in tune with our thinking. Serendipity stepped in at exactly the right moment: we were able to bring together a talented group of people who know the countries we cover inside out and whose enthusiasm for travelling in them needed to be communicated.

The series started to grow. We felt that the time was right to look again at the identity that had brought us all this way. After much searching we commissioned London designers Newell & Sorrell to look at all the issues. Their solution was a new identity for the Handbooks representing the books in all their aspects, looking after all the good things already achieved and taking us into the new millennium.

The result is Footprint Handbooks: a new name and mark, simple yet assertive, bold, stylish and instantly recognisable. The images we use conjure up the essence of real travel and communicate the qualities of the Handbooks in a straightforward and evocative way.

And for us here in Bath, it has been an extraordinary exercise working through this dramatic change. Already the 'new us' fits like our favourite travelling clothes and we cannot wait to get more and more Footprint Handbooks onto the book shelves and out onto the road.

The Footprint list

Caribbean Islands Handbook
East Africa Handbook
Egypt Handbook
India Handbook
Indonesia Handbook
Malaysia & Singapore Handbook
**Mexico & Central America
  Handbook**
Pakistan Handbook
South Africa Handbook
South American Handbook
Sri Lanka Handbook
Tibet Handbook

New in Spring 1997
Andalucía Handbook
Brazil Handbook
Cambodia Handbook
Chile Handbook
Ecuador and Galápagos Handbook
Laos Handbook
Morocco Handbook
  with Mauritania
Myanmar (Burma) Handbook
Namibia Handbook
Peru Handbook
Thailand Handbook
Tunisia Handbook with Libya
Vietnam Handbook
Zimbabwe & Malawi Handbook
    with Botswana, Moçambique &
    Zambia

Mail Order

Footprint Handbooks are available worldwide in good bookstores. They can also be ordered directly from us in Bath (see below for address). Please contact us if you have difficulty finding a title.

Footprint T-shirt

The Footprint T-shirt is available in 100% cotton in various colours.

There are always more titles in the pipeline. For the most up-to-date information and to join our mailing list please contact us at:

Footprint Handbooks

6 Riverside Court
Lower Bristol Road
Bath BA2 3DZ, England
T +44(0)1225 469141
F +44(0)1225 469461
E Mail handbooks@footprint.compulink.co.uk

DATE DUE

MAY 1 6 199	DEC 1 2 2002				
DEC 1 9 1997	FEB 2 4 2004				
MAY 0 7 1998	OCT 2 6 2005				
JUN 2 9 1998					
MAY 1 5 2000	DEC 1 5 2006				
OCT 1 8 2000	DEC 1 5 2008				
MAY 7 2000					
MAR 2 0 2001					
FEB 1 9 2002					
OCT 2 4 2002					
DEC 1 6 2002					

**Original Adventures in
MEXICO, GUATEMALA
BELIZE, COSTA RICA**

On excellent 15 to 24-day journeys travel by train, plane, bus and riverboat through the mysterious lands of the Aztec and the Maya. We visit the great sites of Mexico City and the ancient complex of Monte Alban, the spectacular Sumidero Canyon and Indian San Cristobal. Plus the vast temple complexes of Palenque, Tikal, Uxmal and Chichen Itza. View the exotic wildlife and jungle sites of Belize and discover the tropical rainforest and towering volcanoes of Costa Rica. Come and see for yourself!

...and in South America too

Plus many other exciting 2-5-week journeys in Peru, Bolivia, Paraguay, Brazil, Argentina, Chile, Venezuela and Ecuador. Small groups. Over 170 original exploratory holidays In more than 90 countries around the world.

Get our 100-page brochure NOW!

Explore Worldwide (TTH)
UK: 1 Frederick Street, Aldershot, Hants GU11 1LQ.
☎ **01252 344161 Fax: 01252 343170**

Eire: ☎ Dublin 677 9479. **Australia:** ☎ Sydney 9956 7766, Perth 221 2300, Melbourne 9670 0125, Brisbane 3229 0599, Adelaide 231 6844,
New Zealand: ☎ Auckland 09524 5118. **USA:** ☎ Emeryville (510) 654 1879.
Canada: ☎ Edmonton (403) 439 0024, Calgary (403) 283 6115, Toronto (416) 922 7584, Vancouver (604) 734 1066.

GULF OF

MEXICO

Tampa
St. Petersburg
Tampa
Lakeland
U.S.A.
Ft. Myers
Lake
Okeechobee
West Palm Beach
Freeport
Grand
Bahama I.
Great Abaco I.
The Everglades
C. Romano
Fort
Lauderdale
Miami
C. Sable
New
Providence
Nassau
Eleuthera I.
BAHA
Cat I.

Key West   Florida Keys
Straits of Florida
Andros I.
Exuma Is.

Republic of Cancer
La Habana   Matanzas   Sagua la Grande
Marianao   Cárdenas
Pinar del Río   Güines   Santa Clara
Guane   Golfo de   Cienfuegos   Caibarién   Morón
Batabanó   Archo. de los   Sancti   Ciego de
Nueva Gerona   Canarreos   Trinidad   Spíritus   Ávila   Nuevitas
Isla de la Juventud   CUBA   Camagüey   Victoria de
las Tunas
Manzanillo   Bayamo   Holguín
Great   Santa   Turquino   Santiago
de Cuba

Gt. Exuma

Long I

C. San
Antonio
C. Catoche
I. Mujeres
Cozumel I.
Cancún
Puerto
Juárez

Progreso   Tizimín
Mérida   Yucatán

20°   Campeche

Yucatán   Channel

Little
Cayman
Grand
Cayman   Cayman Brac
Cayman Islands
(U.K.)
Georgetown

Montego Bay   St. Ann's Bay
Black River   Port
Antonio
JAMAICA   Kingston

MEXICO

Yucatán
Peninsula
Términos
Lagoon   Chetumal
Corozal   Chetumal
Bay
Ambergris Cay
Belmopan   Belize   Tumeffe Is.
BELIZE   Swan I.
Gulf of   (Honduras)
Honduras
Bay Is.

CARIBB

Punta Gorda   Pto.
GUATEMALA   Barrios   Tela   La Ceiba
Colhs   San Pedro Sula   C. Camarón
Quetzaltenango   Copán   Caratasca
Guatemala   HONDURAS   Mosquitia   Lagoon
Antigua   City   Comayagua   Tegucigalpa   C. Gracias á Dios
Escuintla   Santa Ana
San Jose   San Salvador   Pto. Cabezas
La Libertad   San Vicente
EL SALVADOR   NICARAGUA   Prinzapolca   I. de Providencia
G. of Fonseca   (Colombia)
Chinandega   Rama   Is. del Maíz
Corinto   Managua   Granada   Bluefields   (Nicaragua
& U.S.A.)
Jinotepe   Lake   I. de San Andrés
Rivas   Nicaragua   (Colombia)
C. Sta. Elena   S. Juan del Norte
Liberia   San Juan
Nicoya
Peninsula   Puerto
Puntarenas   Limón
Cartago
COSTA   Barranqui
Baranaa
C. Blanco   Chiriquí   Gulf of   San   Cartagena   Turbaco
Pta. S. Pedro   Lagoon   Colón   Miguelito   Is. de   Gulf of   Arjona
Pto. Quepos   PANAMA   San Blas   Darién   Carmeco
David   Balboa   Panamá   Sincelejo
Pto. Armuelles   City   Cereté
Pta. Burica   Santiago   Archo. de   El Real   Montería   Puerto Rey
Coiba I.   Azuero   las Perlas   Turbo
Peninsula   Gulf of
Panamá

PACIFIC

OCEAN

10°

90°   85°

©Collins-Longman